T0224026

Lecture Notes in Computer Science 9293

Commenced Publication in 1973
Founding and Former Series Editors:
Gerhard Goos, Juris Hartmanis, and Jan van Leeuwen

Editorial Board

More information about this series at http://www.springer.com/series/7410

Tim Güneysu · Helena Handschuh (Eds.)

Cryptographic Hardware and Embedded Systems – CHES 2015

17th International Workshop
Saint-Malo, France, September 13–16, 2015
Proceedings

Springer

Editors
Tim Güneysu
University of Bremen
Bremen
Germany

Helena Handschuh
Cryptography Research Inc.
San Francisco, CA
USA

ISSN 0302-9743   ISSN 1611-3349   (electronic)
Lecture Notes in Computer Science
ISBN 978-3-662-48323-7   ISBN 978-3-662-48324-4   (eBook)
DOI 10.1007/978-3-662-48324-4

Library of Congress Control Number: 2015947097

LNCS Sublibrary: SL4 – Security and Cryptology

Springer Heidelberg New York Dordrecht London

Printed on acid-free paper

Springer-Verlag GmbH Berlin Heidelberg is part of Springer Science+Business Media
(www.springer.com)

Preface

The 17th International Workshop on Cryptographic Hardware and Embedded Systems (CHES 2015) was held at the Palais du Grand Large, Saint-Malo, France, September 13–16, 2015. The workshop was sponsored by the *International Association for Cryptologic Research*.

CHES 2015 received 128 submissions from all over the world. Each paper was anonymously reviewed by at least 4 Program Committee members. Papers submitted by Program Committee members were reviewed by at least 5 other Program Committee members. An impressive total of more than 510 reviews were written by the Program Committee members as well as the 210 external reviewers that offered their help to them. This year CHES implemented a new paper submission policy whereby the submissions needed to closely match the final versions in length and format published by Springer. During the review process we received thoroughly positive feedback on this new policy mostly because it allowed the Program Committee members to better anticipate the shape and content of each submission as it would appear in the proceedings. Finally, the Program Committee selected 34 papers for publication in these proceedings.

The program was completed by an excellent invited talk by Matthew Green from Johns Hopkins University on *Secure Protocols in a Hostile World*. In addition several papers were nominated for Best Paper Award and the Program Committee voted to award the Best Paper Award to Patrick Haddad, Viktor Fischer, Florent Bernard, and Jean Nicolai for their work on *A Physical Approach for Stochastic Modeling of TERO-based TRNG*. The other two papers on the podium were *Multi-variate High-Order Attacks of Shuffled Tables Recomputation* by Nicolas Bruneau, Sylvain Guilley, Zakaria Najm, and Yannick Teglia, and *Assessment of Hiding the Higher-Order Leakages in Hardware, What are the Achievements versus Overheads?* by Amir Moradi and Alexander Wild. The authors of these articles were invited to submit an extended version to the *Journal of Cryptology*. In addition, two tutorials were given on the day preceding the workshop by Debdeep Mukhopadhyay and Sikhar Patranabis on *Fault Analysis of Cryptosystems – Attacks, Countermeasures, and Metrics* as well as by David Oswald and Timo Kasper on *RFID and NFC Security in Practice*. As a continued tradition, CHES 2015 also featured two poster sessions on the second and third day of the conference.

Among the numerous people that contributed to the success of CHES 2015, we would first of all like to thank all the authors who submitted their research papers to the conference. Without them, this conference would not exist. The selection of the 34 papers that were eventually presented at the workshop was a challenging and time-consuming task and we sincerely thank the 41 Program Committee members as well as their external reviewers for the hard work and endless hours spent reviewing, assessing, and discussing each of the 128 submissions. This year, for each submitted paper, the authors also received a summary of the discussions that were held in the

Program Committee together with the reviewer comments. This meant that authors could be provided with feedback about the impact of their rebuttals. We would also like to sincerely thank Carolyn Whitnall and Kimmo Järvinen for taking excellent care of all aspects of the poster sessions including collecting and reviewing poster submissions and coordinating the presentation with the authors and local organizers.

We are very much indebted to the General Chairs, Emmanuel Prouff, Guénaël Renault, and Matthieu Rivain, for organizing all aspects of the conference in such a wonderful location; we also extend our thanks to Tancrède Lepoint, the webmaster, for promptly putting online all relevant information for submitters, authors of accepted papers, and conference attendees alike, as well as the local organizers for putting together an entertaining CHES Challenge.

The submission process as well as the review process and the editing of the final proceedings was greatly simplified by the software written by Shai Halevi and we thank him for his kind and immediate support throughout the whole process. Last but not least, we are very grateful for the financial support received from our many generous sponsors, including our Platinum Sponsor Cryptography Research, Gold Sponsors Serma Technologies, Thales, la Région Bretagne, and Pôle D'Excellence Cyber, as well as Sponsors Bosch, Texas Instruments, NXP, Riscure, UL, Orange Labs, Oberthur Technologies, Microsemi, Scytl, Invia, Technicolor, CEA, Infineon, ChaoLogix, SecureIC, and Gemalto.

We hope that the research published in this volume proves valuable to the CHES community and that all attendees enjoyed the event as much as we have enjoyed preparing it over the last few months.

June 2015   Tim Güneysu
                                                          Helena Handschuh

CHES 2015

Workshop on Cryptographic Hardware and Embedded Systems 2015

Palais du Grand Large, Saint-Malo, France
September 13–16, 2015

Sponsored by the *International Association for Cryptologic Research*

General Chairs

Emmanuel Prouff	ANSSI, France
Guénaël Renault	UPMC, France
Matthieu Rivain	CryptoExperts, France

Program Chairs

Tim Güneysu	University of Bremen, Germany
Helena Handschuh	Cryptography Research, USA and KU Leuven, Belgium

Program Committee

Onur Aciiçmez	Samsung Research America, USA
Lejla Batina	Radboud University Nijmegen, The Netherlands
Dan J. Bernstein	University of Illinois at Chicago, USA and Technische Universiteit Eindhoven, The Netherlands
Guido Bertoni	STMicroelectronics, Italy
Doug Cheng	National Taiwan University, Taiwan
Jean-Sébastien Coron	University of Luxembourg, Luxembourg
Thomas Eisenbarth	Worcester Polytechnic Institute, USA
Junfeng Fan	Open Security Research and Neutron Security Inc., China
Wieland Fischer	Infineon Technologies, Germany
Pierre-Alain Fouque	Université Rennes 1 and Institut Universitaire de France, France
Kris Gaj	George Mason University, USA
Benedikt Gierlichs	KU Leuven, Belgium
Louis Goubin	University of Versailles, France
Naofumi Homma	Tohoku University, Japan
Michael Hutter	Cryptography Research, USA
Marc Joye	Technicolor, USA

Ilya Kizhvatov	Riscure, The Netherlands
François Koeune	Université Catholique de Louvain, Belgium
Kerstin Lemke-Rust	Bonn-Rhein-Sieg University of Applied Sciences, Germany
Roel Maes	Intrinsic-ID, The Netherlands
Marcel Medwed	NXP Semiconductors, Austria
Amir Moradi	Ruhr-Universität Bochum, Germany
Elke De Mulder	Cryptography Research, France
Christof Paar	Ruhr-Universität Bochum, Germany
Dan Page	University of Bristol, UK
Eric Peeters	Texas Instruments, USA
Axel Poschmann	NXP Semiconductors, Germany
Bart Preneel	KU Leuven, Belgium
Emmanuel Prouff	ANSSI, France
Francesco Regazzoni	ALaRI-USI, Switzerland
Matthieu Rivain	CryptoExperts, France
Matthew J.B. Robshaw	Impinj, USA
Ulrich Rührmair	Technical University Munich, Germany
Akashi Satoh	University of Electro-Communications, Japan
Patrick Schaumont	Virginia Tech, USA
Peter Schwabe	Radboud University Nijmegen, The Netherlands
Daisuke Suzuki	Mitsubishi Electric, Japan
Mehdi Tibouchi	NTT Secure Platform Laboratories, Japan
Assia Tria	CEA-TECH, France
Michael Tunstall	Cryptography Research, USA
Meng-Day (Mandel) Yu	Verayo, USA and KU Leuven, Belgium

Local Organizing Committee

Ryad Benadjila	ANSSI, France
Tancrède Lepoint	CryptoExperts, France
Emmanuel Prouff	ANSSI, France
Guénaël Renault	UPMC, France
Matthieu Rivain	CryptoExperts, France
Adrian Thillard	ANSSI, France

External Reviewers

Driss Aboulkassimi	Thomas Baignères	Georg Becker
Elena Andreeva	Josep Balasch	Sonia Belaïd
Samuel Antao	Valentina Banciu	Sebastien Bellon
Gilles Van Assche	Subhadeep Banik	Ryad Benadjila
Nuttapong Attrapadung	Guillaume Barbu	David Bernhard
Aydin Aysu	Ali Galip Bayrak	Alexandre Berzati
Steve Babbage	Andrew Becker	Scott Best

Luk Bettale
Shivam Bhasin
Begül Bilgin
Clive Bittlestone
Florian Boehl
Joppe Bos
Raphael Bost
Jakub Breier
Cees-Bart Breunesse
Julien Bringer
Dan Brown
Nicolas Bruneau
Samuel Burri
Martin Butkus
Eleonora Cagli
Yun-An Chang
Ricardo Chaves
Chienning Chen
Cong Chen
Ming-Shing Chen
Lukasz Chmielewski
Tom Chothia
Tung Chou
Jean-Michel Cioranesco
Ruan de Clercq
Christian Cornesse
Joan Daemen
Nicolas Debande
Jeroen Delvaux
William Diehl
Kurt Dietrich
Ning Ding
Christoph Dobraunig
Guerric Meurise
   de Dormale
Emmanuelle Dottax
Benedikt Driessen
Léo Ducas
Markus Dürmuth
Orr Dunkelman
François Durvaux
Jean-Max Dutertre
Baris Ege
Nadia El-Mrabet
Nicolas Estibals
Sebastian Faust

Claudio Favi
Martin Feldhofer
Ahmed Ferozpuri
Viktor Fischer
Jacques Fournier
Daisuke Fujimoto
Marc Fyrbiak
Jake Longo Galea
Jean-François Gallais
Berndt M. Gammel
Laurie Genelle
Nahid Farhady Ghalaty
Gilbert Goodwill
Chris Gori
Karin Greimel
Vincent Grosso
Sylvain Guilley
Benoît Gérard
Bilal Habib
Mike Hamburg
Neil Hanley
Karine Heydemann
Matthias Hiller
Takato Hirano
Ekawat Homsirikamol
Harald Homulle
Wei-Chih Hong
Gorka Irazoqui
Brian Jarvis
Anthony Journault
Philipp Jovanovic
Dina Kamel
Elif Bilge Kavun
Yutaka Kawai
Ronny Van Keer
Karim Khalfallah
Taechan Kim
Christian Kison
Philipp Koppe
Thomas Korak
Tim Kouzminov
Po-Chun Kuo
Sebastian Kutzner
Joyce Kwong
Tanja Lange
Martin Lauridsen

Andrew Leiserson
Wen-Ding Li
Yang Li
Tzu-Huan Lin
David Lubicz
Mark Marson
Albert Martinez
Luke Mather
Filippo Melzani
Andrea Miele
Shugo Mikami
Oliver Mischke
Julien Montmasson
Debdeep Mukhopadhyay
Yumiko Murakami
Yusuke Naito
Shoei Nashimoto
Giorgio Di Natale
Phuong Ha Nguyen
Ruben Niederhagen
Ventzislav Nikov
Yasuyuki Nogami
David Oswald
Pascal Paillier
Paolo Palmieri
Jing Pan
Louiza Papachristodoulou
Kostas Papagiannopoulos
Roel Peeters
Guilherme Perin
Peter Pessl
Duong Hieu Phan
Antonio de la Piedra
Christian Pilato
Roberta Piscitelli
Thomas Plos
Thomas Pöppelmann
Ilia Polian
Olivier Potin
Romain Poussier
Santos Merino del Pozo
Ling Ren
Oscar Reparaz
Sebastien Riou
Bruno Robisson
Thomas Roche

Contents

Side-Channel Attacks on Public Key Cryptography

Cipher Design and Cryptanalysis

True Random Number Generators and Entropy Estimations

Side-Channel Attacks in Practice

Lattice-Based Implementations

Processing Techniques
in Side-Channel Analysis

Robust Profiling for DPA-Style Attacks

Carolyn Whitnall[✉] and Elisabeth Oswald

Department of Computer Science, University of Bristol,
Merchant Venturers Building, Woodland Road, Bristol BS8 1UB, UK
{carolyn.whitnall,elisabeth.oswald}@bris.ac.uk

Abstract. Profiled side-channel attacks are understood to be powerful when applicable: in the best case when an adversary can comprehensively characterise the leakage, the resulting model leads to attacks requiring a minimal number of leakage traces for success. Such 'complete' leakage models are designed to capture the scale, location and shape of the profiling traces, so that any deviation between these and the attack traces potentially produces a mismatch which renders the model unfit for purpose. This severely limits the applicability of profiled attacks in practice and so poses an interesting research challenge: how can we design profiled distinguishers that can tolerate (some) differences between profiling and attack traces?

This submission is the first to tackle the problem head on: we propose distinguishers (utilising unsupervised machine learning methods, but also a 'down-to-earth' method combining mean traces and PCA) and evaluate their behaviour across an extensive set of distortions that we apply to representative trace data. Our results show that the profiled distinguishers are effective and robust to distortions to a surprising extent.

1 Introduction

1.1 Motivation

The aim of side-channel analysis is to discover—'learn'—information about the (secret) internal configuration of a cryptographic device from physical measurements (power consumption, electromagnetic radiation, run time, etc.) collected while the device is in operation. The discipline of machine learning is precisely concerned with computational algorithms which are able to 'learn' from data— discover patterns, arrive at meaningful generalisations, make predictions about previously unseen data instances, and so on. There is consequently a very natural overlap between the two fields, and increasing attention has been paid to the potential uses of machine learning techniques as tools for extracting information from side-channel measurements.

One pertinent problem when learning from data arises when the data is noisy and some characteristics change across data sets. Such changes are unfortunately to be expected in the context of side-channel attacks for at least two reasons. Firstly, an adversary is unlikely to have access to the precise target device during the learning phase and will be forced to make do with a duplicate device.

© International Association for Cryptologic Research 2015
T. Güneysu and H. Handschuh (Eds.): CHES 2015, LNCS 9293, pp. 3–21, 2015.
DOI: 10.1007/978-3-662-48324-4_1

Secondly, the measurement setup during the attack might not be the same as the lab setup used during the learning phase. We are hence interested, given the multitude of machine learning methods, which (if any), could be somewhat robust with regards to some practically meaningful disparities between the data sets used for profiling and the data set used during an attack.

1.2 Machine Learning for Profiling

The umbrella term 'machine learning' covers a variety of methods, which we categorise loosely as 'supervised' and 'unsupervised'. The former describes procedures which are provided (in a training phase) with a set of data instances and corresponding a priori known outputs (or 'labels'), and subsequently aim to generalise the relationship between the instances and the outputs in such a way as to reliably map new instances to their corresponding, otherwise unknown, outputs. The latter describes procedures which do not have access to any known outputs but seek to find patterns based on the inherent attributes of the instances relative to one another.

The earliest proposals that utilised some form of 'learned' characteristics from profiling data sets achieved this via Bayesian classification in a supervised manner: so called template DPA attacks utilise multivariate Gaussian distributions, which are built in a profiling phase [6] from traces with a known key. Recent strategies have incorporated more explicit machine learning tools such as support vector machines (SVM) [11,12,14] and random forests [14]. Theoretically, any supervised classification method could be chosen—with varying degrees of success as different algorithms are more or less suited to different underlying data structures. This is already a much-explored theme of recent research and we do not intend to extend it in this work.

We will focus rather on *unsupervised* techniques—in particular, unsupervised clustering algorithms. Clustering is the task of grouping objects (in this case, observed power consumption traces) in such a way that the objects inside any given group are *similar* to one another whilst objects in different groups are *dissimilar*. Unlike supervised classification, where new objects are assigned to an existing class based on knowledge of objects already within that class, a clustering algorithm aims to find a meaningful arrangement of objects with no a priori knowledge about the number or characteristics of the underlying classes.

1.3 Unsupervised Clustering in Conjunction with Partition-Based DPA

By applying an unsupervised clustering algorithm to leakage measurements with known sensitive values we thus learn a *meaningful partition* of the target values (a 'nominal power model' in the terminology of [25]). Our suggestion is to extract such a nominal power model in a profiling phase designed to be followed by a partition-based DPA attack [20] (mutual information (MI) [10], Kolmogorov-Smirnov (KS) [23], the variance ratio (VR) [20] and its multivariate extension in the context of Differential Cluster Analysis (DCA) [4], to name a few examples).

Such a strategy represents an interesting middle course between completely unprofiled attacks relying on difference-of-means or on 'typical' power models such as the Hamming weight (HW) (which in many cases—especially in attacks against hardware implementations—do not apply), and fully profiled attacks which comprehensively (and expensively) characterise entire multivariate distributions for leakage traces. A 'nominal' power model need not be perfect in order for a partition-based DPA to succeed; as long as it captures some (part of a) meaningful pattern then, provided there is enough data to estimate the distinguishing statistic sufficiently precisely, key recovery becomes feasible[1].

A key advantage of the suggested method is that it is potentially highly robust and portable: since no 'meaning' is ever attached to the cluster labels, there is less scope for their relevant interpretation to be disrupted by changes between the profiling and attack scenarios (e.g. measurement set-up, environmental conditions, device age, and imprecise location of interesting windows); all that is required for the power model to apply effectively to the attack measurements is that the arrangement of 'similarly leaking values' be preserved. This is *far* less stringent than requiring the characteristics and precise locations of conditional multivariate Gaussian distributions to be preserved, which is necessary in order to port Bayesian templates. The practical challenges of template attacks when the profiling and attack measurements are generated by distinct devices (or even just distinct acquisition campaigns) are the subject of considerable attention in the literature [8,18]; Choudhary et al. [7] find that the main difference is a DC offset, which may be compensated for to some extent by simply mean-centering the traces and/or via well-chosen compression techniques such as linear discriminant analysis or PCA. However, to our knowledge, none of the proposed methods are able to handle the type of *horizontal* misalignment or discrepancy between the profiling and attack measurements to which our (intentionally less precise) method is robust.

1.4   Our Contributions

Firstly, we present a general strategy to integrate (unsupervised) clustering into a DPA attack flow, which is independent of the particular clustering algorithm and partition-based distinguisher selected. This is important because the effectiveness of machine learning tasks is notoriously sensitive to the choice of algorithm; the 'best' choice depends on the form of the data and is generally not known *a priori*.

Secondly, we present a couple of example realisations (using K-means and agglomerative hierarchical clustering, with the univariate [20] and multivariate [4] variance ratio as DPA distinguisher) and show that they do indeed succeed against a hardware as well as a software implementation of AES. We also propose

---

[1] Note that, in the case that the target function is injective (e.g. the AES S-box), the 'trivial' nominal power model which treats each intermediate value as a distinct class *invariably* fails to distinguish between key hypotheses in *any* partition-based DPA (see [20,25]). Therefore, a meaningful non-trivial grouping is required.

an heuristic for extracting a *proportional* power model under identical profiling assumptions, for use in a subsequent correlation DPA. This approach outperforms the clustered profiling in the software setting (where the device leaks approximately the Hamming weight of the intermediates); naturally, clustered profiling maintains an advantage in the hardware setting (where the leakage of the device is a complex function).

Thirdly, we evaluate the distinguishers across a wide range of 'distortions' that we apply to our real world data. We find that the distinguishers remain effective in a wide range of scenarios where full templating is impossible (or in the best case very problematic), such as small profile samples, inaccuracy in identifying exact leakage points, and misalignment, varying measurement precision, and alternative pre-processing between the attack and profile samples.

1.5 Outline

The rest of the paper proceeds as follows. In Sect. 2.1 we overview DPA, with special attention to profiling and to the variance ratio as a DPA distinguisher; in Sect. 2.2 we overview unsupervised clustering in general, and K-means and hierarchical clustering in particular; in Sect. 2.3 we overview Principal Component Analysis. Then, in Sect. 3 we describe our general methodology for 'rough-and-ready' profiling and the subsequent attack phases. In Sect. 4 we present our experimental results, and we conclude in Sect. 5.

2 Preliminaries

2.1 Differential Power Analysis

We consider a 'standard DPA attack' scenario as defined in [16], and briefly explain the underlying idea as well as introduce the necessary terminology here. We assume that the power consumption $\mathbf{P} = \{P_1, ..., P_T\}$ of a cryptographic device (as measured at time points $\{1, ..., T\}$) depends, for at least some $\tau \subset \{1, ..., T\}$, on some internal value (or state) $F_{k^*}(X)$ which we call the *target*: a function $F_{k^*} : \mathcal{X} \to \mathcal{Z}$ of some part of the known plaintext—a random variable $X \overset{R}{\in} \mathcal{X}$—which is dependent on some part of the secret key $k^* \in \mathcal{K}$. Consequently, we have that $P_t = L_t \circ F_{k^*}(X) + \varepsilon_t, t \in \tau$, where $L_t : \mathcal{Z} \to \mathbb{R}$ describes the data-dependent leakage function at time t and ε_t comprises the remaining power consumption which can be modeled as independent random noise (this simplifying assumption is common in the literature—see, again, [16]). The attacker has N power measurements corresponding to encryptions of N known plaintexts $x_i \in \mathcal{X}$, $i = 1, ..., N$ and wishes to recover the secret key k^*. The attacker can accurately compute the internal values as they would be under each key hypothesis $\{F_k(x_i)\}_{i=1}^N$, $k \in \mathcal{K}$ and uses whatever information he possesses about the true leakage functions L_t to construct a prediction model (or models) $M_t : \mathcal{Z} \to \mathcal{M}_t$.

A distinguisher D is some function which can be applied to the measurements and the hypothesis-dependent predictions in order to quantify the correspondence between them, the intuition being that the predictions under a correct key guess should give more information about the true trace measurements than an incorrect guess. For a given such comparison statistic, D, the *theoretic* attack vector is $\mathbf{D} = \{D(L \circ F_{k^*}(X) + \varepsilon, M \circ F_k(X))\}_{k \in \mathcal{K}}$, and the *estimated* vector from a practical instantiation of the attack is $\hat{\mathbf{D}}_N = \{\hat{D}_N(L \circ F_{k^*}(\mathbf{x}) + \mathbf{e}, M \circ F_k(\mathbf{x}))\}_{k \in \mathcal{K}}$ (where $\mathbf{x} = \{x_i\}_{i=1}^N$ are the known inputs and $\mathbf{e} = \{e_i\}_{i=1}^N$ is the observed noise). Then the attack is *o-th order theoretically successful* if $\#\{k \in \mathcal{K} : \mathbf{D}[k^*] \leq \mathbf{D}[k]\} \leq o$ and *o-th order successful* if $\#\{k \in \mathcal{K} : \hat{\mathbf{D}}_N[k^*] \leq \hat{\mathbf{D}}_N[k]\} \leq o$.

Profiled DPA. A profiled DPA attack is one in which the adversary has access to (and control of) a device matching the one they intend to target. They can therefore, in a preliminary stage, build informed models for the secret-value-dependent form of the device leakage [6,12,19]. The measurements obtained from a target device can then be compared with these models (e.g. using Bayesian classification) to reveal the most likely secret values. The motivation behind our clustering-based profiled DPA attack is to use an unsupervised clustering algorithm to obtain a meaningful mapping from intermediate values to leakage classes in a profiling phase, which can be used in a subsequent attack phase to hypothetically map new traces to classes under each key guess, thus revealing the secret key as the one associated with the most demonstrably 'meaningful' arrangement. Of course, we do not expect such a method to be anywhere near as *efficient* as a detailed, multivariate Gaussian template in the key recovery phase of the attack, but it is precisely its lack of detail and specificity which enables it to remain *effective* in non-ideal attack scenarios.

The Variance Ratio as a DPA Distinguisher. Because clustered profiling outputs a 'nominal' power model—a labelling of distinct leakage classes where the labels themselves are arbitrary—the DPA phase of the attack must use a distinguishing statistic which is invariant to re-labelling of those classes (as per [25]). These coincide with the 'partition-based' distinguishers identified by Standaert et al. in [20], and include the MI [10], the KS two sample test statistic [23], and the variance ratio [20].

We choose to practically verify our strategy using the latter of these, because of its conceptual simplicity, its computational efficiency, its good performance in previous studies [20,24], and the fact that it very naturally extends to multivariate DCA attacks as shown by Batina et al. in [4]. The variance ratio ranks hypothesis-dependent cluster arrangements according to the proportion of the overall variance which is accounted for:

$$D_{\text{VR}}(k) = \frac{\sum\limits_{t \in \tau'} \text{var}(\{P_{t,i}\}_{i=1}^N)^2}{\frac{1}{N} \sum\limits_{m \in \mathcal{M}} n_m \sum\limits_{t \in \tau'} \text{var}(\{P_{t,i} | M \circ F_k(x_i) = m\})^2}, \tag{1}$$

where τ' is the attacker's best knowledge about τ (one hopes that $\tau' \cap \tau \neq \emptyset$), M is a nominal approximation (taking values in $\mathcal{M}$) for the leakage output by unsupervised cluster-based profiling, and $n_m = \#\{x_i | M \circ F_k(x_i) = m\}$, i.e. the number of observations in the trace set for which the predicted cluster label is m.[2]

2.2 Unsupervised Clustering

Clustering is the task of grouping objects together so that those inside any given group are *similar* to one another whilst those in different groups are *dissimilar*, without any *a priori* knowledge about the number or characteristics of the underlying classes (unlike supervised classification). All methods learn through an iterative process involving trial and error, and vary widely in application and effectiveness depending on the assumed cluster model (hierarchical, centroid-based, density- or distribution-based, graph-based, and so on) the chosen 'similarity' measure (e.g. the Euclidean distance between objects), the thresholds chosen for inclusion or exclusion, and the conjectured number of clusters.

K-means Clustering. K-means clustering aims to partition the N data objects into K clusters such that each object belongs to the cluster with the nearest mean. The mean vectors are called the cluster *centroids*. Whilst conceptually simple, the actual arrangement is computationally difficult to achieve (NP-hard, in fact). Fortunately, heuristic algorithms exist which converge quickly to *local* optima over a series of refining iterations.

Formally, if $\{\mathbf{x}_i\}_{i=1}^N$ is a set of (real-valued) d-dimensional observations, the objective of K-means is to partition the N observations into $K < N$ clusters $\mathbf{C} = \{C_1, C_2, \ldots, C_K\}$ so as to minimise the within-cluster sum of squares

$$\underset{\mathbf{C}}{\arg\min} \sum_{j=1}^{K} \sum_{\mathbf{x}_i \in C_j} ||\mathbf{x}_i - \mu_{\mathbf{j}}||^2.$$

'Lloyd's algorithm' is a popular heuristic solution:

1. Initialisation: Pick a set of K vectors to serve as the initial centroids (e.g. by choosing K observations at random from the dataset, by choosing K points uniformly at random from within the range of the dataset, or by computing the means of random clusters).
2. Assignment: Assign each observation to the "nearest" centroid, according to some appropriate distance metric (for example, the Euclidean, Manhattan or Hamming distance, or one minus the sample correlation between observations, depending on the type of data).
3. Update: If the assignments changed in step 2, calculate the means of the observations in the clusters and set these to be the new centroids; else, return.

---

[2] The variances in Eq. (1) are squared as per [4]; this makes the univariate VR slightly different to the original definition given in [20], but (importantly) consistent with the multivariate version.

For our experiments, we use the in-built Matlab command `kmeans`, which performs the above as a preliminary phase (which may or may not converge to a local minimum). It then treats the output as the starting point for an 'online' phase, in which points are reassigned *individually* (if doing so reduces the sum of distances), and the centroids recalculated after each reassignment (instead of in batch). This *will* converge to a local minimum, but it may not be a global minimum. Using several replicates with different random starting points can increase the likelihood of finding a solution which is a global minimum. We initialise the centroids by drawing K observations at random for each of 5 replicate runs, and we measure closeness according to the Euclidean distance.

Of course, since we are primarily interested in what can be achieved without prior information on the leakage, we suppose that the correct number of clusters K is unknown and must be discovered from the data as part of the machine learning task. We propose to search over different values of K and see which produces the 'best' clustering. Different notions of cluster quality exist; we choose to work with the *silhouette value*, defined for the ith object as $S_i = \frac{b_i - a_i}{\max(a_i, b_i)}$, where a_i is the average distance from the ith object to the other objects in the same cluster, and b_i is the minimum (over all clusters) average distance from the ith object to the objects in a different cluster. In our experiments, we select the number of clusters K to be the one producing the highest mean silhouette value.

Hierarchical Clustering. Hierarchical clustering arranges data objects into a multi-level tree of nested partitions. Clusters which are close on one level are joined at the next level, so that once objects are associated with each other they remain so at all higher levels of the tree. Strategies to achieve this can either be *agglomerative*, so that each observation starts in its own cluster, and clusters are merged as the tree is ascended, or they can be divisive, so that all observations start in one single cluster which is incrementally split as the tree is descended.

An agglomerative procedure proceeds as follows:

1. Compute pairwise 'dissimilarity' between objects: Typical notions of distance include Euclidean, Manhattan, Minkowski, Mahalanobis and Chebychev, but the algorithm is flexible to other dissimilarity measures which may or may not strictly satisfy the definition of a metric.
2. Initialise the clusters: We begin with N singleton clusters comprising the individual objects of the dataset.
3. While $K > 1$ (i.e., until all objects are collected together in a single cluster at the top of the tree):
   - Compute distance between clusters: Once there is more than one object in a cluster, there are different ways to do this, e.g., the shortest, furthest, or average distance between objects in two clusters.
   - Merge 'close' clusters in pairs.

4. Identify clusters: Partition objects according to the tree structure, either by computing the *inconsistency* associated with each link[3] and selecting those above a certain threshold, or by pruning the tree at the point corresponding to a fixed desired number of clusters.

Our experiments use the Matlab implementation of the above, with the Euclidean distance as the dissimilarity measure (step 1) and average cluster linking (step 3). For step 4, partitioning according to consistency thresholds should lead to the 'most natural' arrangement and number of clusters; because of the difficulty of *a priori* selecting the appropriate consistency threshold, we tested all values from 0.9 to 1.2 in increments of 0.02 and, as for the K-means clustering, choose the one producing the largest silhouette index.

2.3 Principal Component Analysis

Principal component analysis (PCA) is a popular method for dimensionality reduction. An $n \times m$ matrix is orthogonally transformed so that the m columns in the new matrix are linearly uncorrelated and sorted in decreasing order of variance. By construction, the columns are the eigenvectors of the covariance matrix, sorted according to the size (largest to smallest) of the corresponding eigenvalues $\lambda_1, \ldots, \lambda_m$. The first $q < m$ of these columns maximise (w.r.t. all other $n \times q$ transformations) the total variance preserved whilst minimising the mean squared reconstruction error $\sum_{i=q+1}^{m} \lambda_i$. The hope is that all of the 'important' information will be concentrated into a small number of components.

PCA has been proposed as a means of locating 'points of interest' for inclusion in Gaussian templates [2,17]. It has also been used to pre-process traces for more efficient non-profiled correlation DPA attacks [5]. Moreover, it is typically used in combination with unsupervised clustering algorithms to concentrate the relevant information into a lower dimensional data space so as to avoid the problem of sparseness, where *no* observations are 'close' (sometimes called the 'curse of dimensionality'). It is natural, then, for us to transform the trace data so as to work with high-ranked principal components only in the clustering phase. The precise number to retain is normally determined by (arbitrarily) setting a threshold for the proportion of total variance explained, but since our goal is to find the 'best' cluster arrangement we select the number of projected dimensions (up to 10) depending on the silhouette values attained in each case.

3   Methodology

The profiling strategy we suggest is independent of the specific choice of learning algorithm: it can operate with any clustering technique $\mathcal{C}$ which returns a mapping M from intermediate values of the algorithm $z \in \mathcal{Z}$ to a set of nominal

---

[3] Defined as the height of the individual link minus the mean height of all links at the same hierarchical level, all divided by the standard deviation of all the heights on that level.

cluster labels $m \in \mathcal{M}$. The success of the subsequent attack stage depends, of course, on the validity of the clusters discovered by the learning algorithm[4].

3.1   Our General Profiling Strategy

Let $\{\mathbf{t}_1, \ldots, \mathbf{t}_{\mathbf{N_p}}\}$ be a set of $1 \times T$ trace measurements taken from a profiling device sufficiently similar to the target. Let $\{z_i\}_{i=1}^{N_p}$ be a set of known intermediate values handled by the device during the interval spanned by the measurements. The strategy, in its most general form, is as follows:

1. Partition the data according to the intermediate values and compute the mean traces $\{\bar{\mathbf{t}}_z\}_{z \in \mathcal{Z}}$.
2. Obtain a mapping $M : \mathcal{Z} \longrightarrow \mathcal{M}$ by clustering the mean traces. Values in $\mathcal{Z}$ not represented in the profiling dataset are mapped to cluster $C+1$ where C is the total number of clusters identified by the chosen algorithm (essentially, an 'other' category).
3. Use M as the power model in 'partition-based' DPA.

3.2   Model Building and Distinguishers

In practice, there are many options open to the attacker in steps 2 and 3. It is notoriously difficult to a priori apply the most well-suited machine learning solution to any particular problem instance [26], and an exhaustive testing of all possible strategies is infeasible. Given the infeasibility to find 'optimal' strategies across scenarios, we provide some meaningful choices using the methods outlined in Sect. 2.2 with varying parameters. We suggest to first perform PCA on the mean traces[5] and then to experimentally obtain the best clusterings we can via each of the two algorithms. We vary the number of components retained as well as a) the specified number of clusters for the K-means algorithm, or b) the consistency threshold for the agglomerative hierarchical algorithm. In both cases the 'best' cluster arrangements are identified according to the silhouette index. This 'best' model is the one used for the DPA attack, which (for the purposes of verifying feasibility) we perform using the variance ratio for its conceptual and computational simplicity, and its natural multivariate extension DCA from [4]. For the univariate variant (denoted VR(M), where M is either the K-means acquired (M_{KM}) or the hierarchical clustering acquired (M_{HC}) power model) we compute Eq. (1) pointwise across the window and select the (key guess,time point) pair which produces the largest score (see Eq. (2) below); for the multivariate variant (DCA(M)) we compute Eq. (1) for the entire window in one go (see Eq. (3)).

---

[4] In particular, in the notation of Sect. 2.1, the extent to which $\{z' | M(z') = M(z)\} \approx \{z' | L(z') = L(z)\} \forall z \in \mathcal{Z}$—see [25].

[5] Note that this process involves centering around the global mean, thereby avoiding the DC offset problems highlighted by [7].

$$D_{\mathrm{VR}(M)}(k) = \max_{t \in \tau'} \left\{ \frac{\mathrm{var}(\{P_{t,i}\}_{i=1}^{N})^2}{\frac{1}{N} \sum_{m \subset \mathcal{M}} n_m \mathrm{var}(\{P_{t,i}|M \circ F_k(x_i) = m\})^2} \right\}, \qquad (2)$$

$$D_{\mathrm{DCA}(M)}(k) = \frac{\sum_{t \in \tau'} \mathrm{var}(\{P_{t,i}\}_{i=1}^{N})^2}{\frac{1}{N} \sum_{m \in \mathcal{M}} n_m \sum_{t \in \tau'} \mathrm{var}(\{P_{t,i}|M \circ F_k(x_i) = m\})^2}, \qquad (3)$$

where M is either the K-means acquired (M_{KM}) or the hierarchical clustering acquired (M_{HC}) power model.

We also (by way of comparison) introduce a counterpart heuristic to 'profile' for correlation DPA on a similar basis. Firstly (denoted M_{P1}), we use the projection of the mean traces along the first principal direction as the power model; secondly (denoted M_{P2}), we take all the projections accounting for 70 % of the variance in the mean traces, weight them by their contribution, and either add or subtract them from a running total depending on their positive or negative correlation with the first principal direction (thus allowing for the possibility that the relevant variation is contained in more than one component). Analogous to the nominal profiling, values in $\mathcal{Z}$ which are not represented in the sample are mapped to the global mean. We exploit these power models by computing the univariate correlation distinguishing vectors at each point in time in the attacked traces, and choosing the (key guess,time point) pair producing the highest score (see Eq. (4) below). Correlation DPA seems a fitting benchmark because of its known good performance, but we certainly do not make any claims about the optimality of our 'profiling' methods—they are merely heuristics to produce power models under the same restrictions as the clustering analyses.

$$D_{\mathrm{Corr}(M)}(k) = \max_{t \in \tau'} \left\{ \frac{\mathrm{cov}(\{P_{t,i}\}_{i=1}^{N}, M \circ F_k(\mathbf{x}))}{\sqrt{\mathrm{var}(\{P_{t,i}\}_{i=1}^{N})\mathrm{var}(M \circ F_k(\mathbf{x}))}} \right\}, \qquad (4)$$

where M is the proportional model acquired either from the first principal direction (M_{P1}) or by combining information from the directions accounting for 70 % of the variance (M_{P2}).

3.3   Experimentally Verifying 'Robustness'

Different measurement set-ups, pre-processing and device ageing introduce discrepancies between the profiling and attack samples. DC offset has been recognised as a significant obstacle to classical Gaussian templating which can be overcome by appropriate compression and normalisation [7]. Since our method naturally incorporates these steps, it is also robust to DC offset. However, it goes much further: it operates on the raw attack-stage traces, without requiring to know or apply the principal subspace projection derived and applied in the profiling stage, nor even the precise points or window of points for which the profiled models were built. Hence acquisitions from the target device need not be made at the same frequency, nor subjected to the same filtering or compression techniques, for the attack to be implemented. We test the effectiveness of our method against the following practically relevant scenarios[6]:

- The precise width and location of the window of points used to build the cluster-based power model is not known in the attack phase. We simulated this scenario by choosing non-matching windows. (See Sect. 4.3).
- The attack traces are measured at a different resolution to those from which the template is built. We achieved this by binning trace values with increasing coarseness. (See Sect. 4.4).
- The attack traces contain more measurement error. We achieved this by adding Gaussian noise in increasingly large proportion to the observed conditional noise. Note that this incorporates the scenario in which the traces are misaligned (possibly deliberately, via 'hiding in the time dimension' [15]). Assuming *some* proportion of the traces coincide for a given intermediate value, the signal will persist weakly, with the remaining (non-aligned) traces functioning as noise. (See Sect. 4.5).
- The attack traces have been differently pre-processed. We achieved this by taking a moving average of increasing window width. (See Sect. 4.6).
- The attack traces are imperfectly aligned, as though (for example) the dynamic power saving technique of [9] had been in operation, or a hiding countermeasure such as [27]. Whilst methods exist to improve alignment (see, e.g. [22]), none are known to remove the problem entirely. By ranging from small to greater distortions, we approximate cases in which alignment methods have been applied with varying success. We achieved this by inserting an increasing number of 'interpolated' values in random positions in each trace. (See Sect. 4.7).

4   Experimental Results

We test our strategies on leakages acquired from two unprotected implementations of AES—one software, running on an ARM microcontroller (10,000 traces total); one hardware, designed for an RFID-type system (5,000 traces total)[7]. In each case, we perform repeated experiments on random subsamples of the data, for increasing profiling and (disjoint) attack sample sizes with a fixed window width (20 for the software traces, 10 for the hardware, because of the

---

[6] All our data stems from *real devices*: one implementation of AES on an ARM7 processor, and one implementation of AES in dedicated hardware (an ASIC custombuilt for the TAMPRES project [1, 13]) using a 32-bit architecture but with a serial Sbox look-up. In order to create data sets with different characteristics we did however not change the measurement setups as this would have been a too cumbersome process. Instead we manipulated the original data sets and hence, strictly speaking, the distorted data was created by simulations.

[7] The different sample sizes reflect the fact that we sourced independently-generated datasets for our experiments rather than relying on acquisition set-ups over which we had full control.

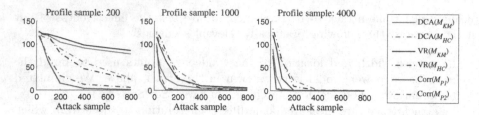

Fig. 1. Guessing entropy of partially profiled DPA attacks against an unprotected software implementation of AES. Window width: 20; reps: 500.

coarser granularity of the latter) around the (already identified) 'most interesting' point.[8] We then explore the robustness of the attacks to different window widths and to the various profiling/attack trace discrepancies detailed above.

4.1 'Straightforward' (Software) Scenario

Figure 1 shows the guessing entropies (average ranks of the correct subkey [21]) after attacks against the output of the first S-box in software as the sample sizes vary. Crucially, the clustering strategy can be seen to 'work'—that is, *all* the variants reduce uncertainty about the subkey. The K-means clustering (denoted '(M_{KM})' in the legend) appears to require a larger profiling sample to produce an effective power model than the hierarchical clustering (denoted '(M_{HC})'), but eventually outperforms the latter. The multivariate VR distinguisher (aka DCA [4]) outperforms the univariate one in the case of both clustered profiles. In this 'straightfoward' scenario (the leakage is known to correspond closely to the HW) our heuristics for acquiring proportional power models also prove effective so that both correlation attacks (denoted 'Corr(M_{P1})' and 'Corr(M_{P2})') outperform all those using clustered profiling, with slight advantage to the one relying only on the first principal direction (M_{P1}). These are even able to recover the subkey within 800 attack measurements from a profiling dataset of just 200.

4.2 'Problematic' (Hardware) Scenario

Hardware leakages are typically less 'easy' to exploit (e.g. in simple attacks using the HW power model; indeed, we tested and found such attacks to fail to recover the key even when provided with the full 5,000 measurements). The implementation that we target has two working 32-bit registers, with the byte substitutions in each column occurring in parallel with the MixColumns operation on the previous column. This makes it much harder to isolate a single contributory process in the overall leakage.

---

[8] Identified by using the (point-wise) conditional means as optimal power models in (point-wise) correlation DPA, and selecting the one giving the strongest margin of success.

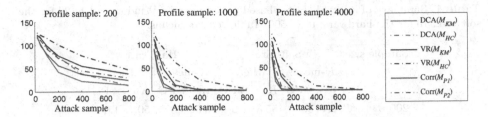

Fig. 2. Guessing entropy of partially profiled DPA attacks against an unprotected hardware implementation of AES. Window width: 10; reps: 500.

Preliminary investigations revealed considerable variation in the exploitability of the different S-boxes; we picked one (S-box 14) which was more amenable to attack in order to report interesting (but clearly not definitive) results (see Fig. 2). In this case, the K-means-based profiling coupled with the (multivariate) DCA distinguisher performs particularly strongly, even outperforming the best of the two correlation attacks (especially when only 200 traces are available for profiling).

We thus learn that there may be cases where 'cheap' rough-and-ready nominal profiling, with minimal prior knowledge, is a relatively effective option. However, our results are by no means conclusive: performance of machine learning methods is notoriously scenario-dependent [26], so that (e.g.) minor alterations in the chosen location or width of the trace window, as well as different algorithms or parameters, may produce wildly different outcomes. (We test for this in the next section). Moreover, we have not here strived towards a 'best' method for acquiring a proportional power model to act as a definitive benchmark. Nonetheless, we consider these experimental results to be an interesting insight into what is possible.

Table 1 summarises the parameters chosen by our cluster model selection rule. As the software profiling sample size increases, the number of clusters (on average) detected by K-means also increases, close to 9 (unsurprisingly—it is known to closely follow the HW leakage function). The mean is around 7 or 8 for all sample sizes in the case of the hardware leakage (where less is known a priori); around 5 principal components are retained in both cases. The hierarchical algorithm finds quite different (less concise) arrangements, almost always using only one principal component. However, it clearly captures *something* meaningful about the true arrangement of the target values, as the effective (though inefficient) attack phases confirm.

4.3   Discrepancy in Window Width and Location

Because (in our application) the k-means clustering method consistently outperforms the hierarchical method, and because the first of our heuristics for deriving a proportional power model outperforms the second, from here on, we present outcomes only of the attacks associated with those two power models.

Table 1. Summary of selected cluster-based power models. Window width: 20 for the software, 10 for the hardware; reps: 500. Table reports means.

Sample size	Software				Hardware			
	K-means		Hier.		K-means		Hier.	
	K	#PC	K	#PC	K	#PC	K	#PC
200	2.1	5.2	55.8	1.0	6.5	5.3	50.1	1.0
1000	4.3	5.3	93.6	1.0	7.9	5.2	92.6	1.0
4000	8.6	5.2	94.1	1.0	8.4	5.3	94.6	1.0

Table 2. Outcomes as the profiling and attack window widths vary. (100 repetitions; profiling sample of 4000, attack sample of 400).

Attack width ⟶			DCA(M_{KM})					VR(M_{KM})					Corr(M_{P1})				
			1	4	10	20	40	1	4	10	20	40	1	4	10	20	40
Software	Profile width	1	1	1	1	1	1	1	1	1	1	1	1	1	1	1	1
		4	1	1	1	1	1	1	1	1	1	1	1	1	1	1	1
		10	1	1	1	1	1	1	1	1	1	1	1	1	1	1	1
		20	1	1	1	1	1	1	1	1	1	1	1	1	1	1	1
		40	2	2	2	2	2	2	2	2	2	2	1	1	1	1	1

Attack width ⟶			DCA(M_{KM})					VR(M_{KM})					Corr(M_{P1})				
			1	4	10	20	40	1	4	10	20	40	1	4	10	20	40
Hardware	Profile width	1	1	1	1	85	132	1	1	1	1	1	1	1	1	1	1
		4	1	1	1	47	116	1	1	1	1	1	1	1	1	1	1
		10	1	1	1	60	113	1	1	1	1	1	1	1	1	1	1
		20	1	1	1	54	107	1	1	1	1	1	67	80	69	71	74
		40	1	1	1	68	119	1	1	1	1	1	126	118	109	118	123

Full results (additionally spanning a wider range of sample sizes) can be found in the supplementary material to this submission and will be made available online in the event of publication.

We now consider scenarios in which the trace window used to derive the power models varies, and in which it differs (in width and/or location) to the window selected for the attack.

The top half of Table 2 shows the guessing entropies attained by the attacks against the software traces for different trace window widths. We fixed the profiling sample size at 4000 and the attack sample size at 400 whilst varying both the profiling and attack window widths, keeping the known interesting point central. All of the attacks continue to successfully recover the key, with the exception of the cluster-based DCA and VR when the profiling sample size is as large as 40.

In the case of the hardware traces (bottom half of Table 2) the (multivariate) DCA attack is robust to wider profiling windows, but suffers substantially for the increase of the attack window. By contrast, profiling for the correlation-based attacks becomes less effective for a wider profiling window, but when a decent model *has* been estimated it remains effective as the attack window widens. The (univariate) VR attack is robust to either change.

Table 3. Outcomes when the attack sample window is misaligned with the profiling window. (100 repetitions; window width of 20 for the software implementation, 10 for the hardware; profiling sample of 4000).

Attack sample size →		Software						Hardware					
		DCA(M_{KM})		VR(M_{KM})		Corr(M_{P1})		DCA(M_{KM})		VR(M_{KM})		Corr(M_{P1})	
		50	400	50	400	50	400	50	400	50	400	50	400
Offset	$-\lfloor w/2\rfloor$	53	1	87	1	15	1	121	65	68	1	22	1
	$-\lfloor w/4\rfloor$	37	1	65	1	3	1	51	1	66	1	20	1
	0	34	1	72	1	1	1	15	1	65	1	21	1
	$\lfloor w/4\rfloor$	27	1	83	1	1	1	25	1	76	1	24	1
	$\lfloor w/2\rfloor$	74	4	109	1	22	1	66	1	113	3	90	1

Table 3 shows the results of varying the *location* of the attack window relative to the profiling window in attacks against both implementations, for fixed window widths of 20 and 10 for the software and hardware implementations respectively, and a fixed profiling sample size of 4000 (to ensure that the models themselves are well fitted). The cost of the offset is evident in small sample sizes for all of the tested attacks against the software traces; larger samples help to compensate for this.

The clustered and the correlation attacks appear fairly robust in the case of the hardware traces, with substantial degradation only occurring once the window is shifted by half its own width, suggesting that by that point most of the informative leakage is outside the window.

4.4 Discrepancy in Measurement Resolution

We next simulate discrepancy in measurement resolution, by discretising the attack sample measurements into fewer numbers of equally-sized bins. Table 4 shows the subsequent outcomes: with the exception of the (univariate) VR against the software traces, the effectiveness of the attacks is largely unchanged, although with some eventual increase in the number of traces required to achieve the same reduction in guessing entropy as the measurements reach their most granular.

4.5 Discrepancy in Measurement Error

Increased measurement error can be simulated simply by adding, to the raw traces, a (zero mean) Gaussian distributed random sample. The variance is chosen in increasing proportion to the (time point specific) conditional variance of the raw traces, computed via the residuals (the mean for all traces sharing the same intermediate value, subtracted from the raw measurement). For example (because of the additive properties of variance) to double the total conditional variance, one adds a sample with the same variance again; to triple it, one adds a sample with twice the variance, and so on.

Table 4. Outcomes when the attack acquisition is measured with less precision than the profiling sample. (100 repetitions; window width of 20 for the software implementation, 10 for the hardware).

Attack sample size →	Software						Hardware					
	DCA(M_{KM})		VR(M_{KM})		Corr(M_{P1})		DCA(M_{KM})		VR(M_{KM})		Corr(M_{P1})	
	50	400	50	400	50	400	50	400	50	400	50	400
Number of bins 256	30	1	86	1	5	1	16	1	68	1	23	1
128	28	1	83	1	5	1	16	1	66	1	21	1
64	38	1	81	1	9	1	17	1	62	1	29	1
32	68	1	107	1	29	1	20	1	65	1	32	1
16	70	1	135	133	26	1	33	1	71	1	55	1

Table 5. Outcomes when noise in the attack sample increases relative to the profiling sample. (100 repetitions; window width of 20 for the software implementation, 10 for the hardware)

Attack sample size →	Software						Hardware					
	DCA(M_{KM})		VR(M_{KM})		Corr(M_{P1})		DCA(M_{KM})		VR(M_{KM})		Corr(M_{P1})	
	50	400	50	400	50	400	50	400	50	400	50	400
Noise factor 1	31	1	93	1	9	1	22	1	86	1	29	1
2	71	1	103	1	33	1	56	1	107	1	65	1
4	100	3	118	8	78	1	71	1	100	14	80	2
8	124	14	115	38	103	1	116	7	123	50	95	9
16	115	52	133	107	129	14	112	40	113	85	114	67

Noise has the expected effect on all tested strategies (Table 5): they remain effective, but the number of traces required for equivalent success scales proportionally. This is by contrast with, for example, strategies using Gaussian templates with Bayesian likelihood key recovery, which suppose that the random as well as the deterministic parts of the profiled leakage distributions match those of the attack-stage measurements.

4.6 Discrepancy in Trace Pre-processing

It is straightforward to apply additional filtering to the attack traces; we do so by computing moving averages within a window of increasing width. Table 6 shows the outcomes as the smoothing window widens; they are very robust against the software implementation—smoothing over two observations actually appears to *aid* the attacks—and slightly less so against the hardware (as we would expect, since the latter completes in fewer clock cycles thereby giving rise to already shorter, more coarsely sampled traces). As before, the (generally more efficient) correlation variant is also robust to this particular discrepancy.

4.7 Non-fixed Sampling Frequency

Next we explore what happens to the attack outcomes when the traces are misaligned in some way which the attacker was unable to fully 'undo'—candidate

Table 6. Outcomes when the attack acquisition is smoothed via a moving average of increasing window width. (100 repetitions; window width of 20 for the software implementation, 10 for the hardware)

Attack sample size →	Software						Hardware					
	$DCA(M_{KM})$		$VR(M_{KM})$		$Corr(M_{P1})$		$DCA(M_{KM})$		$VR(M_{KM})$		$Corr(M_{P1})$	
	50	400	50	400	50	400	50	400	50	400	50	400
Smoothing window 1	43	1	96	1	16	1	19	1	62	1	19	1
2	44	1	75	1	5	1	24	1	59	1	17	1
4	51	1	104	1	5	1	74	1	100	4	79	1
8	77	1	106	1	16	1	111	32	121	54	100	17
16	115	5	123	3	53	1	112	82	118	94	113	64

Table 7. Outcomes when the attack traces are misaligned, as the proportion of sample points padded increases. (100 repetitions; window width of 20 for the software implementation, 10 for the hardware)

Attack sample size →	Software						Hardware					
	$DCA(M_{KM})$		$VR(M_{KM})$		$Corr(M_{P1})$		$DCA(M_{KM})$		$VR(M_{KM})$		$Corr(M_{P1})$	
	50	400	50	400	50	400	50	400	50	400	50	400
Insertions (prop.) 0.005	133	125	131	124	139	137	122	125	122	97	117	46
0.01	126	111	134	119	128	135	135	127	123	146	139	108
0.05	120	135	133	123	131	123	125	117	126	127	125	131
0.1	141	134	131	127	129	134	131	116	138	135	126	135
0.5	130	113	138	121	116	131	143	131	128	138	134	131

causal scenarios include the power saving strategy proposed in [9] and the related DPA hiding countermeasure in [27] (though successfully circumvented in [3]). We simulate this distortion in our (already filtered) trace dataset by 'padding' an increasing proportion of sample points with simply interpolated additional values[9] in random positions which vary by trace.

The attack outcomes are presented in Table 7. Under these conditions, all of the tested strategies fail; the correct key ranking does not improve, even as the number of traces increases.

5   Summary

We have shown that unsupervised clustering can recover nominal power models for use in effective 'partition-based' key recovery attacks, with minimal requirements in the profiling phase and a degree of flexibility in the attack phase, particularly when it comes to distorted attack traces. Via DCA they present a naturally multivariate methodology to exploit multiple trace points without requiring alignment, identical measurement set-up, or equivalent pre-processing between the profile and attack samples. We have also shown that proportional power models may also be recovered under the same assumptions, leading to

---

[9] Computed as the mean of the preceding and following measurements.

successful correlation DPA attacks which are generally more efficient and almost as robust as the 'partition-based' strategies. Neither are suitable for the task of *evaluation*, which requires considering 'worst case' attacks in ideal scenarios, but they do provide further insight into the capabilities of attackers with limited powers.

Avenues for further work include exploring whether other clustering algorithms are able to improve on the observed example results, and whether there exist attack strategies better able to deal with the particular distortion of misalignment within an acquisition.

Acknowledgements. The authors would like to thank Thomas Korak, Thomas Plos and Michael Hutter at TU Graz for supplying us with data from the TAMPRES project [1,13]. The authors have been supported by an EPSRC Leadership Fellowship EP/I005226/1.

References

1. TAMPRES: Tamper Resistant Sensor Nodes. http://www.tampres.eu, 2009–2013
2. Archambeau, C., Peeters, E., Standaert, F.-X., Quisquater, J.-J.: Template attacks in principal subspaces. In: Goubin, L., Matsui, M. (eds.) CHES 2006. LNCS, vol. 4249, pp. 1–14. Springer, Heidelberg (2006)
3. Baddam, K., Zwolinski, M.: Evaluation of dynamic voltage and frequency scaling as a differential power analysis countermeasure. In: 20th International Conference on VLSI Design, pp. 854–862. IEEE Computer Society (2007)
4. Batina, L., Gierlichs, B., Lemke-Rust, K.: Differential cluster analysis. In: Clavier, C., Gaj, K. (eds.) CHES 2009. LNCS, vol. 5747, pp. 112–127. Springer, Heidelberg (2009)
5. Batina, L., Hogenboom, J., van Woudenberg, J.G.J.: Getting more from PCA: first results of using principal component analysis for extensive power analysis. In: Dunkelman, O. (ed.) CT-RSA 2012. LNCS, vol. 7178, pp. 383–397. Springer, Heidelberg (2012)
6. Chari, S., Rao, J., Rohatgi, P.: Template attacks. In: Kaliski, B., Koç, Ç., Paar, C. (eds.) CHES 2002. LNCS, vol. 2523, pp. 51–62. Springer, Heidelberg (2003)
7. Choudary, O., Kuhn, M.G.: Template attacks on different devices. In: Prouff, E. (ed.) COSADE 2014. LNCS, vol. 8622, pp. 179–198. Springer, Heidelberg (2014)
8. Elaabid, M., Guilley, S.: Portability of templates. J. Crypt. Eng. **2**(1), 63–74 (2012)
9. Ernst, D., Kim, N.S., Das, S., Pant, S., Rao, R., Pham, T., Ziesler, C., Blaauw, D., Austin, T., Flautner, K., Mudge, T.: Razor: a low-power pipeline based on circuit-level timing speculation. In: Proceedings of the 36th Annual IEEE/ACM International Symposium on Microarchitecture, pp. 7–18 (2003)
10. Gierlichs, B., Batina, L., Tuyls, P., Preneel, B.: Mutual information analysis. In: Oswald, E., Rohatgi, P. (eds.) CHES 2008. LNCS, vol. 5154, pp. 426–442. Springer, Heidelberg (2008)
11. Heuser, A., Zohner, M.: Intelligent machine homicide. In: Schindler, W., Huss, S.A. (eds.) COSADE 2012. LNCS, vol. 7275, pp. 249–264. Springer, Heidelberg (2012)
12. Hospodar, G., Gierlichs, B., Mulder, E.D., Verbauwhede, I., Vandewalle, J.: Machine learning in side-channel analysis: a first study. J. Crypt. Eng. **1**(4), 293–302 (2011)

13. Korak, T., Plos, T., Hutter, M.: Attacking an AES-enabled NFC tag: implications from design to a real-world scenario. In: Schindler, W., Huss, S.A. (eds.) COSADE 2012. LNCS, vol. 7275, pp. 17–32. Springer, Heidelberg (2012)
14. Lerman, L., Bontempi, G., Markowitch, O.: Power analysis attack: an approach based on machine learning. IJACT **3**(2), 97–115 (2014)
15. Mangard, S., Oswald, E., Popp, T.: Power Analysis Attacks: Revealing the Secrets of Smart Cards. Springer, New York (2007)
16. Mangard, S., Oswald, E., Standaert, F.-X.: One for all - all for one: unifying standard DPA attacks. IET Inf. Secur. **5**(2), 100–110 (2011)
17. Rechberger, C., Oswald, E.: Practical Template Attacks. In: Lim, C.H., Yung, M. (eds.) WISA 2004. LNCS, vol. 3325, pp. 440–456. Springer, Heidelberg (2005)
18. Renauld, M., Standaert, F.-X., Veyrat-Charvillon, N., Kamel, D., Flandre, D.: A formal study of power variability issues and side-channel attacks for nanoscale devices. In: Paterson, K.G. (ed.) EUROCRYPT 2011. LNCS, vol. 6632, pp. 109–128. Springer, Heidelberg (2011)
19. Schindler, W., Lemke, K., Paar, C.: A stochastic model for differential side channel cryptanalysis. In: Rao, J.R., Sunar, B. (eds.) CHES 2005. LNCS, vol. 3659, pp. 30–46. Springer, Heidelberg (2005)
20. Standaert, F.-X., Gierlichs, B., Verbauwhede, I.: Partition vs. comparison side-channel distinguishers: an empirical evaluation of statistical tests for univariate side-channel attacks against two unprotected CMOS devices. In: Lee, P.J., Cheon, J.H. (eds.) ICISC 2008. LNCS, vol. 5461, pp. 253–267. Springer, Heidelberg (2009)
21. Standaert, F.-X., Malkin, T.G., Yung, M.: A unified framework for the analysis of side-channel key recovery attacks. In: Joux, A. (ed.) EUROCRYPT 2009. LNCS, vol. 5479, pp. 443–461. Springer, Heidelberg (2009)
22. van Woudenberg, J.G.J., Witteman, M.F., Bakker, B.: Improving differential power analysis by elastic alignment. In: Kiayias, A. (ed.) CT-RSA 2011. LNCS, vol. 6558, pp. 104–119. Springer, Heidelberg (2011)
23. Veyrat-Charvillon, N., Standaert, F.-X.: Mutual information analysis: how, when and why? In: Clavier, C., Gaj, K. (eds.) CHES 2009. LNCS, vol. 5747, pp. 429–443. Springer, Heidelberg (2009)
24. Whitnall, C., Oswald, E.: A fair evaluation framework for comparing side-channel distinguishers. J. Crypt. Eng. **1**(2), 145–160 (2011)
25. Whitnall, C., Oswald, E., Standaert, F.-X.: The myth of generic DPA...and the magic of learning. In: Benaloh, J. (ed.) CT-RSA 2014. LNCS, vol. 8366, pp. 183–205. Springer, Heidelberg (2014)
26. Wolpert, D.H., Macready, W.G.: No free lunch theorems for optimization. IEEE Trans. Evol. Comput. **1**(1), 67–82 (1997)
27. Yang, S., Wolf, W., Vijaykrishnan, N., Serpanos, D., Xie, Y.: Power attack resistant cryptosystem design: a dynamic voltage and frequency switching approach. In: Proceedings of Design, Automation and Test in Europe, vol. 3, pp. 64–69, March 2005. doi:10.1109/DATE.2005.241, ISSN:1530-1591

Less is More

Dimensionality Reduction from a Theoretical Perspective

Nicolas Bruneau[1,2(✉)], Sylvain Guilley[1,3], Annelie Heuser[1],
Damien Marion[1,3], and Olivier Rioul[1,4]

[1] Institut Mines-Télécom, Telecom ParisTech, Paris, France
{nicolas.bruneau,sylvain.guilley,annelie.heuser,damien.marion,
olivier.rioul}@telecom-paristech.fr
[2] AST Division, STMicroelectronics, Rousset, France
[3] Threat Analysis Business Line, Secure-IC S.A.S., Rennes, France
[4] Applied Mathematics Department, École Polytechnique, Palaiseau, France

Abstract. Reducing the dimensionality of the measurements is an
important problem in side-channel analysis. It allows to capture multi-
dimensional leakage as one single compressed sample, and therefore also
helps to reduce the computational complexity. The other side of the coin
with dimensionality reduction is that it may at the same time reduce the
efficiency of the attack, in terms of success probability.

In this paper, we carry out a mathematical analysis of dimensionality
reduction. We show that optimal attacks remain optimal after a first pass
of preprocessing, which takes the form of a linear projection of the samples. We then investigate the state-of-the-art dimensionality reduction
techniques, and find that asymptotically, the optimal strategy coincides
with the linear discriminant analysis.

1 Introduction

Side-channel analysis exploits leakages from devices. Embedded systems are targets of choice for such attacks. Typical leakages are captured by instruments
such as oscilloscopes, which sample power or electromagnetic traces. The resulting leaked information about sensitive variables is spread over time.

In practice, two different attack strategies coexist. On the one hand, the
various leaked samples can be considered individually—this is typical of *non-
profiled attacks* such as Correlation Power Analysis [4]. On the other hand, *profiled attacks* characterize the leakage in a preliminary phase. An efficient leakage
modelization should then involve a multi-dimensional probabilistic representation [6].

The large number of samples to feed into the model has always been a problematic issue for multi-dimensional side-channel analysis. One solution is to use
techniques to select *points of interest*. Most of them, such as sum-of-square differences (SOSD) and t-test (SOST) [14], are *ad hoc* in that they result from

---

Annelie Heuser is a Google European fellow in the field of privacy and is partially
founded by this fellowship.

T. Güneysu and H. Handschuh (Eds.): CHES 2015, LNCS 9293, pp. 22–41, 2015.
DOI: 10.1007/978-3-662-48324-4_2

a criterion which is independent from the attacker's key extraction objective. Recent criteria, such as leakage maximization by sensitive value [1], avoid this problem. Other formal criteria, related to *non-profiled* attacks, have also been proposed [18,23].

Therefore, there seems to be a converging effort, in both non-profiled and profiled attacks, to *reduce the dimensionality* of multi-dimensional measurements. This desirable property of dimensionality reduction achieves several goals simultaneously:

- it simplifies the side-channel problem (to a single multivariate pdf);
- it concentrates the information (to distinguish using fewer traces); and
- it improves computational speed.

It can be argued, however, that like every preprocessing technique, dimensionality reduction would lose information.

Contributions. In this paper, we tackle this problem of dimensionality reduction from a theoretical viewpoint. Provided that the attacker has full knowledge of the leakage model, we find that "less is more": the advantages of dimensionality reduction can come with no impact on the attack success probability, while improving computational speed.

We derive that the optimal dimensionality reduction process consists in a *linear combination* of samples, which we explicit as a projection on a specific one-dimensional space. For white noise, it turns out that the improved signal-to-noise ratio (SNR) *after* projection is simply the *sum* of the signal-to-noise ratios at the various samples *before* projection.

Finally, we show that the optimal dimensionality reduction technique asymptotically matches the linear discriminant analysis (LDA) preprocessing. We find that LDA generally outperforms principal component analysis (PCA) for which the SNR increases to a lesser extend than LDA, except in the case of white homoscedastic noise where PCA and LDA become equivalent.

We also validate in practice those results on the DPA CONTEST v2 traces [34].

Review of the State-of-the-Art. Dimensionality reduction is part and parcel of profiled attacks. The seminal paper on template attacks [6] is motivated by keeping covariance matrices involved in the training phase sufficiently well conditioned. Manual selection of *relevant leaking points* was discussed in [24] as *educated guesses*. Several automated techniques were proposed, such as sum-of-square differences (SOSD) and t-test (SOST) [14], and also wavelet transforms [11].

Several related metrics were proposed for *leakage detection*. The ANOVA (ANalysis Of VAriance) *F-test* is a ratio between the explained variance and the total variance—see e.g. [7,10] and [3] where it is named *Normalized Inter-Class Variance* (NICV). Also used for linear regression analysis, it is known as the *coefficient of determination*, denoted by the symbol "R^2". It is employed in the context of side-channel analysis in [33] as *multivariate regression analysis* in the presence of white noise, and in [29], where it is used as a distinguisher and as a linearity metric.

PCA has been used to compact traces in [2] and templates in [1]. The eigen-values of PCA can be viewed as a security metric [15] or even as a distin-guisher [30]. This technique is particularly attractive as it can be easily and accurately computed with no divisions involved. It is advocated in [21] that PCA aims at maximizing the inter-class variance, yet it is also important to take the intra-class variance into account. For this reason, LDA has been promoted as an improved alternative. Empirical comparisons were investigated in [26,31,32]. Unfortunately, despite some differences in terms of qualitative efficiency, there is no clear rationale to prefer one method over the other. In fact, it is unclear which of the intrinsic virtue of statistical tools, their implementation, or the dataset is actually responsible for the performance of dimensionality reduction.

Other works attempted to consider different *objective functions*. In [23], the correct key correlation is taken as the objective to be maximized. A similar goal is pursued in [16–19]. Still other dimensionality reduction techniques exist, such as quadratic discriminant analysis, but have not been studied in the side-channel literature. We mention that similar questions have also been raised in the presence of masking countermeasures [5,12,27].

Outline. The remainder of the paper is as follows. The optimal dimensionality reduction is derived theoretically in Sect. 2. Section 3 provides illustrative exam-ples. A comparison with state-of-the-art techniques such as PCA, and LDA [31] is given in Sect. 4. Practical validations on real traces are in Sect. 5. Section 6 concludes.

2   Theoretical Solution in the Presence of Gaussian Noise

2.1   Notations

We adopt a matrix notation. The different queries are indexed by $q = 1, \ldots, Q$, where Q is the number of traces. The different samples in a given trace are indexed by $d = 1, \ldots, D$. Any matrix containing D samples from Q queries is denoted by:

$$M^{D,Q} = (M_{d,q})_{d,q},$$

where $d = 1, \ldots, D$ is a row index and $q = 1, \ldots, Q$ is a column index. We also denote all dth samples for all traces as $(M_{d,q})_q = M_d^Q$, and all the samples for the qth trace as $(M_{d,q})_d = M_q^D$. Thus, M_d^Q is a row vector and M_q^D is a column vector. Two matrices noted side-by-side are implicitly multiplied.

The notation $(\cdot)^{\mathsf{T}}$ is for transpose. For instance, if $u = u^D$ is $D \times 1$ matrix, then $u^{\mathsf{T}} = (u^D)^{\mathsf{T}}$ is a $1 \times D$ matrix. The usual scalar product on $\mathbb{R}^D$ is denoted by $\langle u \mid v \rangle = u^{\mathsf{T}} v \in \mathbb{R}$. The associated 2-norm of u is $\|u\|_2 = \sqrt{\langle u \mid u \rangle}$.

Random variables will be denoted by capital letters. The probability density function of a random variable X, as a function of x, is denoted by $p_X(x)$ or simply $p(x)$ if the context is clear.

2.2 Model

For most devices, the leakage signal may be represented as a continuous curve as illustrated in Fig. 1. The practical acquisition is done through a temporal series of D "discrete samples" within one clock period.

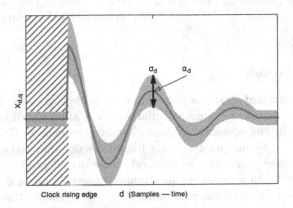

Fig. 1. Example of a modulated trace X_q^D

A sensitive variable that depends on the unknown secret key k^* is leaking through a leakage function ϕ. Typically, ϕ is the Hamming weight function, a sum of weighted bits, or its composition with a substitution box function. In order to further simplify the mathematical derivations, we assume that ϕ is centered. In deriving the optimal attack, it is assumed that the leakage model is perfectly known to the attacker. The model for a given key byte hypothesis k is given by

$$Y_q(k) = \phi(T_q \oplus k), \tag{1}$$

where the random variable T_q denotes a plain or cipher text byte, which is the same for all values of d. Without loss of generality we may assume that $Y_q(k)$ has normalized variance, i.e., $\mathrm{Var}(Y_q(k)) = \mathbb{E}(Y_q^2(k)) = 1$ for all values of q. The actual leakage can be written as

$$X_{d,q} = \alpha_d Y_q(k^*) + N_{d,q}, \tag{2}$$

where the weights α_d are not all zero, k^* is the (unknown) correct key, and $N_{d,q}$ is some random measurement noise. The α_d and noise distribution are assumed known to the attacker.

In matrix notation, we can summarize the equations for different values of d and q by a single matrix equation

$$X^{D,Q} = \alpha^D Y^Q(k^*) + N^{D,Q} \tag{3}$$

where α^D is a single column matrix and $Y^Q(k^*)$ is a single row matrix, whose product is a $D \times Q$ matrix.

We make the stationarity assumption that the noise distribution does not depend on the particular query, that is, the N_q^D are independent and identically distributed independently of the value of q. For a given q, however, the noise samples of N_q^D can very well be correlated. We assume that N_q^D follows a D-dimensional zero-mean Gaussian distribution $\mathcal{N}(0, \Sigma)$, where covariance matrix Σ is a symmetric positive definite $D \times D$ matrix. Therefore, there exists a matrix $\Sigma^{1/2}$, which is such that $\Sigma^{1/2}\Sigma^{1/2} = \Sigma$. We assume that the matrix Σ is known by the attacker.

2.3   Optimal Attack

We focus on the optimal attack as part of our scientific approach to the problem. It is always possible that for some peculiar reason a suboptimal attack actually performs better in the presence of dimensionality reduction. But by the *data processing theorem* [9] any preprocessing like dimensionality reduction can only decrease information about the secret, and, therefore, degrade performance of the *optimal* attack. As a result, it does make sense to minimize the impact of dimensionality reduction on the success rate for this optimal attack so as not to be biased by performance loss or gain due to other factors.

The optimal attack, also known as the template attack [6], consists in applying the *maximum likelihood* principle [20]. Having collected Q traces of dimensionality D in a matrix $x^{D,Q}$, where each trace x_q^D corresponds to a known plaintext t_q, the best key guess that maximizes the probability of success is given by

$$\mathcal{D}(x^{D,Q}, t^Q) = \arg \max_k \ p(x^{D,Q}|t^Q, k^* = k) \tag{4}$$

$$= \arg \max_k \ p_{N^{D,Q}}(x^{D,Q} - \alpha^D y^Q(k)) \tag{5}$$

$$= \arg \max_k \ \prod_{q=1}^{Q} p_{N^{q,D}}(x_q^D - \alpha^D y_q(k)) \tag{6}$$

where

$$p_{N^{q,D}}(z^D) = \frac{1}{\sqrt{(2\pi)^D|\det \Sigma|}} \exp\left(-\frac{1}{2}(z^D)^{\mathsf{T}}\Sigma^{-1}z^D\right). \tag{7}$$

We have used the independence of the queries in (6) and the assumption that at each query, the noise distribution is the same in (7).

Notice that, the optimal attack can as well be a *simple power attack* (if $Q = 1$) or a *differential power attack* (if $Q > 1$), using the terminology from [22]. Still, in the sequel, we focus on attacks which require many traces ($Q \gg 1$).

2.4   Optimal Dimensionality Reduction

We state our main result in the following Theorem 1:

Theorem 1. *The optimal attack on the multivariate traces $x^{D,Q}$ is equivalent to the optimal attack on the monovariate traces $\tilde{x}^Q$, obtained from $x^{D,Q}$ by the formula:*

$$\tilde{x}_q = \frac{\left(\alpha^D\right)^{\mathsf{T}} \Sigma^{-1} x_q^D}{\left(\alpha^D\right)^{\mathsf{T}} \Sigma^{-1} \alpha^D} \qquad (q = 1, \dots, Q). \tag{8}$$

Proof. By taking the logarithm of the expression to be maximized in Eqs. (4)–(7), the optimal distinguisher $\mathcal{D}(x^{D,Q}, t^Q)$ rewrites

$$\mathcal{D}(x^{D,Q}, t^Q) = \arg\min_k \sum_{q=1}^{Q} \left(x_q^D - \alpha^D y_q(k)\right)^{\mathsf{T}} \Sigma^{-1} \left(x_q^D - \alpha^D y_q(k)\right). \tag{9}$$

For each trace index q, the terms in the sum expand to

$$\underbrace{\left(x_q^D\right)^{\mathsf{T}} \Sigma^{-1} x_q^D}_{\text{cst. } C \text{ independent of } k} - 2(\alpha^D)^{\mathsf{T}} y_q(k) \Sigma^{-1} x_q^D + (y_q(k))^2 (\alpha^D)^{\mathsf{T}} \Sigma^{-1} \alpha^D$$

$$= C - 2y_q(k) \left[(\alpha^D)^{\mathsf{T}} \Sigma^{-1} x_q^D\right] + (y_q(k))^2 \left[(\alpha^D)^{\mathsf{T}} \Sigma^{-1} \alpha^D\right]$$

$$= \left[(\alpha^D)^{\mathsf{T}} \Sigma^{-1} \alpha^D\right] \left(y_q(k) - \frac{(\alpha^D)^{\mathsf{T}} \Sigma^{-1} x_q^D}{(\alpha^D)^{\mathsf{T}} \Sigma^{-1} \alpha^D}\right)^2 + C'.$$

The latter division is valid since Σ is positive definite and α^D is a nonzero vector. Therefore,

$$\mathcal{D}(x^{D,Q}, t^Q) = \arg\min_k \sum_{q=1}^{Q} \left(y_q(k) - \frac{(\alpha^D)^{\mathsf{T}} \Sigma^{-1} x_q^D}{(\alpha^D)^{\mathsf{T}} \Sigma^{-1} \alpha^D}\right)^2 \left[(\alpha^D)^{\mathsf{T}} \Sigma^{-1} \alpha^D\right]$$

$$= \arg\min_k \sum_{q=1}^{Q} \frac{\left(\tilde{x}_q - y_q(k)\right)^2}{\tilde{\sigma}^2}, \tag{10}$$

where

$$\begin{cases} \tilde{x}_q &= \dfrac{(\alpha^D)^{\mathsf{T}} \Sigma^{-1} x_q^D}{(\alpha^D)^{\mathsf{T}} \Sigma^{-1} \alpha^D}, \\[2mm] \tilde{\sigma} &= \left((\alpha^D)^{\mathsf{T}} \Sigma^{-1} \alpha^D\right)^{-1/2}. \end{cases} \tag{11}$$

We have shown that (9) and (10) are equivalent expressions for the same optimal distinguisher, computed either:

– on multivariate traces x_q^D, with a noise covariance matrix Σ, or:
– on monovariate (i.e., scalar) traces $\tilde{x}_q$, with scalar noise of variance $\tilde{\sigma}^2$. □

Theorem 1 shows that in fact, the optimal attack already integrates an optimal dimensionality reduction. The maximal success rate is not altered.

Definition 2 (Projection vector). *Let V^D be a column of D elements. We call the projection of an acquisition campaign $X^{D,Q}$ on V^D the new mono-sample traces $(V^D)^\mathsf{T} X^{D,Q}$. That is, every trace X_q^D $(1 \leq q \leq Q)$ of the initial campaign is summarized as one sample $(V^D)^\mathsf{T} X_q^D = \langle V^D \mid X_q^D \rangle$.*

Based on this definition, Theorem 1 can be interpreted as follows.

Corollary 3. *The optimal dimensionality reduction is made by a linear combination of the samples where each multivariate trace is projected on the vector $V^D = \frac{\Sigma^{-1}\alpha^D}{(\alpha^D)^\mathsf{T}\Sigma^{-1}\alpha^D}$, of size $D \times 1$.*

Proof. By Theorem 1,

$$\underbrace{\tilde{x}^Q}_{1 \times Q \text{ matrix}} = \underbrace{\frac{(\alpha^D)^\mathsf{T}\Sigma^{-1}}{(\alpha^D)^\mathsf{T}\Sigma^{-1}\alpha^D}}_{1 \times D \text{ matrix } (V^D)^\mathsf{T}} \underbrace{x^{D,Q}}_{D \times Q \text{ matrix}} . \qquad \square$$

In addition, after this projection, the leakage becomes scalar and can be characterized by a signal-to-noise ratio as shown in the following.

Corollary 4. *After optimal dimensionality reduction, the signal-noise-ratio is given by*

$$\frac{1}{\tilde{\sigma}^2} = (\alpha^D)^\mathsf{T}\Sigma^{-1}\alpha^D.$$

Proof. This is in line with Eq. (10). The random leakage $X^{D,Q}$ is protected onto V^D to yield $\tilde{X}_q = Y_q(k) + \tilde{N}$ $(q = 1,\ldots,Q)$ where $\tilde{N}$ is an additive white Gaussian noise (AWGN) distributed as $\mathcal{N}(0, ((\alpha^D)^\mathsf{T}\Sigma^{-1}\alpha^D)^{-1})$. Recall that the variance of the leakage model has been assumed normalized $= 1$. Therefore, the signal-to-noise ratio equals

$$\frac{\mathrm{Var}(Y_q(k))}{\mathrm{Var}(\tilde{N})} = \frac{1}{((\alpha^D)^\mathsf{T}\Sigma^{-1}\alpha^D)^{-1}} = (\alpha^D)^\mathsf{T}\Sigma^{-1}\alpha^D . \qquad \square$$

The SNR is an interesting metric on its own, because it quantifies how much the signal has been concentrated (its power increased) for a given noise level. Furthermore, the SNR directly relates to the success rate of optimal attacks [13].

2.5   Discussion

It is interesting to note that the optimal dimensionality reduction does not depend on the actual distribution of $Y^D(k)$, the deterministic part of the leakage model. This means that irrespective of the leakage function ϕ, the best dimensionality reduction depends only on signal weights α^D and on noise covariance Σ.

Similarly, the optimal dimensionality reduction does not depend on the *confusion coefficient* of the leakage model [13]: for identical weight and noise distribution, the optimal linear combination of leakages is the same whether an XOR or a substitution box operation is targeted.

3   Examples

3.1   White Noise

One interesting situation is when the noise samples are uncorrelated (see for instance [33] for an experimental setup). The covariance matrix Σ is diagonal:

$$\Sigma = \begin{pmatrix} \sigma_1^2 & 0 & \cdots & 0 \\ 0 & \sigma_2^2 & \cdots & 0 \\ \vdots & \vdots & \ddots & \vdots \\ 0 & 0 & \cdots & \sigma_D^2 \end{pmatrix}.$$

Proposition 5. *For white noise, the optimal dimensionality reduction takes the form:*

$$\tilde{x}_q = \frac{\displaystyle\sum_{d=1}^{D} \frac{\alpha_d}{\sigma_d^2} x_{d,q}}{\displaystyle\sum_{d=1}^{D} \frac{\alpha_d^2}{\sigma_d^2}} \qquad (q = 1, \ldots, Q) \tag{12}$$

Proof. Apply Theorem 1, where Σ^{-1} is diagonal with diagonal entries $1/\sigma_d^2$. $\square$

Let $\mathrm{SNR}_d = \alpha_d^2/\sigma_d^2$ be the initial signal-to-noise ratio at the dth sample *before* dimensionality reduction.

Proposition 6. *For white noise, the equivalent signal-to-noise ratio* after *optimal dimensionality reduction is given by the sum*

$$\widetilde{SNR} = \sum_{d=1}^{D} SNR_d. \tag{13}$$

Proof. By Corollary 4, $\widetilde{\mathrm{SNR}} = (\alpha^D)^{\mathsf{T}} \Sigma^{-1} \alpha^D = \sum_{d=1}^{D} \frac{\alpha_d^2}{\sigma_d^2} = \sum_{d=1}^{D} \mathrm{SNR}_d.$ $\square$

Thus, combining independent multidimensional samples within one trace increases the signal-to-noise as if those samples were captured in D independent traces. In this case having Q traces of D samples each is simply the same as having $Q \times D$ independent monovariate traces.

3.2   Correlated Autoregressive Noise

A more general situation is when the samples are correlated like an autoregressive process. More precisely, assume that all samples share the same noise distribution of variance σ^2, and that two consecutive noise samples have correlation factor equal to $\rho \in]-1, +1[$. The correlation factors ρ typically models an autoregressive low-pass filtering of the acquisition setup (see Sect. 5.2 for a real-world example). The noise covariance matrix takes the Toeplitz form:

$$\Sigma = \sigma^2 \begin{pmatrix} 1 & \rho & \rho^2 & \rho^3 & \cdots & \rho^{D-2} & \rho^{D-1} \\ \rho & 1 & \rho & \rho^2 & \cdots & \rho^{D-3} & \rho^{D-2} \\ \rho^2 & \rho & 1 & \rho & \cdots & \rho^{D-4} & \rho^{D-3} \\ \rho^3 & \rho^2 & \rho & 1 & \cdots & \rho^{D-5} & \rho^{D-4} \\ \vdots & \vdots & \vdots & \vdots & \ddots & \vdots & \vdots \\ \rho^{D-2} & \rho^{D-3} & \rho^{D-4} & \rho^{D-5} & \cdots & 1 & \rho \\ \rho^{D-1} & \rho^{D-2} & \rho^{D-3} & \rho^{D-4} & \cdots & \rho & 1 \end{pmatrix} = \left(\sigma^2 \rho^{|d-d'|} \right)_{1 \le d,d' \le D}.$$

We emphasize that $|\rho|$ is strictly smaller than one in keeping with the assumption that Σ be positive definite. When $\rho = 0$, the noise becomes white as in the preceding subsection.

Proposition 7. *For autoregressive noise, the optimal dimensionality reduction takes the form:*

$$\tilde{x}_q = \frac{1}{\sigma^2(1-\rho^2)}\left[(\alpha_1 - \rho\alpha_2)x_{q,1} + \sum_{d=2}^{D-1}((1+\rho^2)\alpha_d - \rho(\alpha_{d-1} + \alpha_{d+1}))x_{d,q}\right.$$
$$\left. + (\alpha_D - \rho\alpha_{D-1})x_{q,D}\right]. \quad (14)$$

Proof. It can easily be checked that Σ^{-1} is tridiagonal:

$$\Sigma^{-1} = \frac{1}{\sigma^2(1-\rho^2)} \begin{pmatrix} 1 & -\rho & 0 & 0 & \cdots & 0 & 0 \\ -\rho & 1+\rho^2 & -\rho & 0 & \cdots & 0 & 0 \\ 0 & -\rho & 1+\rho^2 & -\rho & \cdots & 0 & 0 \\ 0 & 0 & -\rho & 1+\rho^2 & \cdots & 0 & 0 \\ \vdots & \vdots & \vdots & \vdots & \ddots & \vdots & \vdots \\ 0 & 0 & 0 & 0 & \cdots & 1+\rho^2 & -\rho \\ 0 & 0 & 0 & 0 & \cdots & -\rho & 1 \end{pmatrix}.$$

Then apply Theorem 1:

$$\tilde{x}_q = \frac{1}{\sigma^2(1-\rho^2)} \begin{pmatrix} \alpha_1 & \alpha_2 & \cdots & \alpha_{D-1} & \alpha_D \end{pmatrix} \begin{pmatrix} 1 & -\rho & \cdots & 0 & 0 \\ -\rho & 1+\rho^2 & \cdots & 0 & 0 \\ \vdots & \vdots & \ddots & \vdots & \vdots \\ 0 & 0 & \cdots & 1+\rho^2 & -\rho \\ 0 & 0 & \cdots & -\rho & 1 \end{pmatrix} \begin{pmatrix} x_{q,1} \\ x_{q,2} \\ \vdots \\ x_{q,D-1} \\ x_{q,D} \end{pmatrix}$$

and expand.   □

Notice that in the optimal dimensionality reduction, each leakage sample $x_{d,q}$ is not only weighted by its corresponding α_d but also by its two neighbor weights $\alpha_{d\pm1}$, provided the latter exist.

Proposition 8. *For autoregressive noise, the equivalent signal-to-noise ratio after optimal dimensionality reduction is given by*

$$\widetilde{SNR} = \frac{1}{\sigma^2(1-\rho^2)}\left[\alpha_1^2 + (1+\rho^2)\sum_{d=2}^{D-1}\alpha_d^2 + \alpha_D^2 - 2\rho\sum_{d=1}^{D-1}\alpha_d\alpha_{d+1}\right]. \quad (15)$$

Proof. Apply Corollary 4:

$$\widetilde{SNR} = \tfrac{1}{\sigma^2(1-\rho^2)} \begin{pmatrix} \alpha_1 & \alpha_2 & \cdots & \alpha_{D-1} & \alpha_D \end{pmatrix} \begin{pmatrix} 1 & -\rho & \cdots & 0 & 0 \\ -\rho & 1+\rho^2 & \cdots & 0 & 0 \\ \vdots & \vdots & \ddots & \vdots & \vdots \\ 0 & 0 & \cdots & 1+\rho^2 & -\rho \\ 0 & 0 & \cdots & -\rho & 1 \end{pmatrix} \begin{pmatrix} \alpha_1 \\ \alpha_2 \\ \vdots \\ \alpha_{D-1} \\ \alpha_D \end{pmatrix}$$

and expand.   □

Corollary 9. *For equal weights* $\alpha_1 = \cdots = \alpha_D = \alpha$, *i.e., when initial signal-to-noise ratios* $SNR_1 = \cdots = SNR_D = SNR$ *are the same, one has*

$$\widetilde{SNR} = SNR \times \frac{D(1-\rho) + 2\rho}{1+\rho}. \tag{16}$$

Proof. Proposition 8 reduces to

$$\widetilde{SNR} = \frac{\alpha^2}{\sigma^2(1-\rho^2)} \left(2 + (D-2)(1+\rho^2) - 2\rho(D-1) \right)$$

$$= \frac{\alpha^2}{\sigma^2(1-\rho)(1+\rho)} \left((1-\rho)(D - \rho(D-2)) \right)$$

$$= \frac{\alpha^2}{\sigma^2} \frac{1}{1+\rho} (D - \rho(D-2)) = SNR \times \frac{D(1-\rho) + 2\rho}{1+\rho}. \qquad □$$

In other words, optimal dimensionality reduction has the effect of multiplying the monovariate SNR by the factor $\frac{D - \rho(D-2)}{1+\rho}$. This gain factor is of course equal to 1 for dimension $D = 1$, but becomes strictly greater than 1 for larger dimensions, since $\frac{D-\rho(D-2)}{1+\rho} > \frac{D-(D-2)}{2} = 1$ where we have used that $\rho > -1$ or $\frac{1}{1+\rho} > \frac{1}{2}$.

For very small values of correlation ρ, Taylor expansion about $\rho = 0$ gives $\frac{D-\rho(D-2)}{1+\rho} = D - 2(D-1)\rho + \mathcal{O}(\rho^2)$. The SNR gain is equal to the dimension D at first order, which is consistent with Proposition 6. In addition, that gain is never greater than D, since $\frac{D(1-\rho)+2\rho}{1+\rho} \le \frac{D(1-\rho)+2D\rho}{1+\rho} = D$. Therefore, when $SNR_1 = \ldots = SNR_D$, nonzero values of correlation ρ decrease the efficiency of dimensionality reduction, the most favorable situation being the case of white noise samples.

4   Comparison with PCA and LDA

When the attacker does not precisely know the model given by Eq. (2), the optimal dimensionality reduction cannot be applied directly. In this section, we analyse theoretically two well-known engineering solutions to reduce the dimensionality: PCA and LDA. Both techniques are based on eigen decompositions.

4.1   Principal Components Analysis (PCA)

Principal components analysis aims at identifying directions in the *centered* data set $M^{D,Q} = (M_{d,q})_{d,q}$ defined by

$$M_{d,q} = X_{d,q} - \frac{1}{Q} \sum_{q'=1}^{Q} X_{d,q'} \qquad (1 \leq q \leq Q, 1 \leq d \leq D). \qquad (17)$$

The directions of PCA are the eigenvectors of $M^{D,Q}(M^{D,Q})^{\mathsf{T}}$.

Proposition 10. *Asymptotically as* $Q \longrightarrow +\infty$,

$$\frac{1}{Q} M^{D,Q}(M^{D,Q})^{\mathsf{T}} \longrightarrow \alpha^D (\alpha^D)^{\mathsf{T}} + \Sigma. \qquad (18)$$

Proof. By the law of large numbers,

$$\frac{1}{Q} \sum_{q=1}^{Q} M_{d,q} M_{d',q} \longrightarrow \mathrm{Cov}(M_{d,q}, M_{d',q})$$

almost surely, where the covariance term can be computed as: $\mathrm{Cov}(M_{d,q}, M_{d',q}) = \mathrm{Cov}(\alpha_d Y_q + N_{d,q}, \alpha_{d'} Y_q + N_{d',q})$. When expanding this expression, cross terms disappear by independence of Y^Q and $N^{D,Q}$. There remains:

$$\mathrm{Cov}(M_{d,q}, M_{d',q}) = \alpha_d \alpha_{d'} + \Sigma_{d,d'}$$

where we have used the hypothesis that Y_q has unit variance. $\square$

The classical PCA has the drawback that $M^{D,Q}(M^{D,Q})^{\mathsf{T}}$ depends both on the *signal* and on the *noise*. *Inter-class PCA* has been introduced in [1]. The matrix $M^{D,Q}$ used in the PCA is traded for a more simple matrix $Z^{D,\#Y}$, where each column, indexed by y, is the centered column $\frac{1}{\sum_{\substack{1 \leq q \leq Q \\ Y_q = y}} 1} \sum_{\substack{1 \leq q \leq Q \\ Y_q = y}} X_q^D$. One advantage of this method is that it explicitly takes into account the sensitive variables Y.

It can be easily checked, that, asymptotically, each column Z_y^D tends to $\alpha^D y$ when $Q \longrightarrow +\infty$. Therefore, $Z^{D,\#Y}(Z^{D,\#Y})^{\mathsf{T}}$ tends to a $D \times D$ matrix proportional to $\alpha^D(\alpha^D)^{\mathsf{T}}$. Here, the noise has been averaged away in each class y, which is a second advantage. Therefore, in the sequel, we shall refer to the inter-class PCA of [1] simply as PCA.

We have the following spectral characterization of the asymptotic PCA:

Proposition 11. *Asymptotically, PCA has only one principal direction, namely the vector* α^D.

Proof. By Proposition 10, the PCA matrix tends asymptotically to $\alpha^D(\alpha^D)^\top$. This $D \times D$ matrix has rank one, because all its columns are multiple of α^D. Since

$$(\alpha^D(\alpha^D)^\top)\alpha^D = \alpha^D((\alpha^D)^\top\alpha^D) = \|\alpha^D\|_2^2 \times \alpha^D,$$

α^D is the eigenvector with corresponding nonzero eigenvalue $= \|\alpha^D\|_2^2$.   □

Notice that the uniqueness of the eigenvector for PCA holds in our model (2). However, Proposition 11 would not hold if e.g., the noise were correlated to the signal.

Remark 1. The classical PCA has the same eigenvector α^D if the noise is *isotropic*, i.e., white and of same variance in every dimension.

The paper [1] presents an optimization procedure to find the eigenelements.

Proposition 12. *The asymptotic signal-to-noise ratio after projection using PCA is equal to* $\dfrac{\|\alpha^D\|_2^4}{(\alpha^D)^\top\Sigma\alpha^D}$.

Proof. After projection on the (asymptotic) eigenvector α^D, the leakage becomes: $(\alpha^D)^\top\alpha^D Y_q(k^*) + (\alpha^D)^\top N_q^D$. The projected signal is $((\alpha^D)^\top\alpha^D)Y_q(k^*)$. The projected noise is $(\alpha^D)^\top N_q^D$, which remains centered. Its variance is equal to the expectation of its square:

$$\mathrm{Var}((\alpha^D)^\top N_q^D) = \mathbb{E}\left((\alpha^D)^\top N_q^D\right)^2 = \mathbb{E}\left((\alpha^D)^\top N_q^D(N_q^D)^\top\alpha^D\right)$$
$$= (\alpha^D)^\top \mathbb{E}\left(N_q^D(N_q^D)^\top\right)\alpha^D = (\alpha^D)^\top\Sigma\alpha^D.$$

Therefore,

$$\mathrm{SNR_{PCA}} = \frac{\mathrm{Var}(((\alpha^D)^\top\alpha^D)Y_q(k^*))}{\mathrm{Var}((\alpha^D)^\top N_q^D)} = \frac{\mathrm{Var}(\|\alpha^D\|_2^2 Y_q(k^*))}{(\alpha^D)^\top\Sigma\alpha^D} = \frac{\|\alpha^D\|_2^4}{(\alpha^D)^\top\Sigma\alpha^D}.$$ □

Example 13. For white noise (Sect. 3.1)

$$\mathrm{SNR_{PCA}} = \frac{\left(\sum_{d=1}^D \alpha_d^2\right)^2}{\sum_{d=1}^D \alpha_d^2\sigma_d^2}. \tag{19}$$

Example 14. For autoregressive noise (Sect. 3.2)

$$\mathrm{SNR_{PCA}} = \frac{\sum_{d=1}^D \alpha_d^2}{\sigma^2}\frac{1}{1 + \frac{2}{\sum_{d=1}^D \alpha_d^2}\sum_{d=1}^{D-1}\rho^d\sum_{d'=1}^{D-d}\alpha_{d'}\alpha_{d'+d}}. \tag{20}$$

We can now compare the performance of the asymptotic PCA to the optimal dimensionality reduction.

Theorem 15. *The SNR of the asymptotic PCA is smaller than the SNR of the optimal dimensionality reduction.*

Proof. By assumption the noise covariance matrix is symmetric positive definite, hence there exists a matrix $\Sigma^{1/2}$, which is such that $\Sigma^{1/2}\Sigma^{1/2} = \Sigma$. By Cauchy-Schwarz inequality,

$$\left(\langle \Sigma^{-1/2}\alpha^D \mid \Sigma^{1/2}\alpha^D\rangle\right)^2 \leq \left\|\Sigma^{-1/2}\alpha^D\right\|_2^2 \cdot \left\|\Sigma^{1/2}\alpha^D\right\|_2^2.$$

Therefore, $\text{SNR}_{\text{PCA}} = \frac{((\alpha^D)^\mathsf{T}\alpha^D)^2}{(\alpha^D)^\mathsf{T}\Sigma\alpha^D} \leq (\alpha^D)^\mathsf{T}\Sigma^{-1}\alpha^D = \widetilde{\text{SNR}}.$ □

Corollary 16. *The asymptotic PCA has the same SNR as the the optimal dimensionality reduction if and only if α^D is an eigenvector of Σ. In this case, both dimensionality reductions are equivalent.*

Proof. Equality holds in Theorem 15 if and only if there exists a nonzero real number λ such that $\Sigma^{1/2}\alpha^D = \lambda\Sigma^{-1/2}\alpha^D$, i.e., $\Sigma\alpha^D = \lambda\alpha^D$, i.e., α^D is an eigenvector of Σ.

In this case, the optimal protection is on the vector $\Sigma^{-1}\alpha^D = \frac{1}{\lambda}\alpha^D$, which is proportional to the projection vector belonging to the asymptotic PCA.   □

Remark 2. Assume white noise (Sect. 3.1) where all values σ_d^2 ($1 \leq d \leq D$) are different. Then, by Corollary 16, the asymptotic PCA is optimal only if $\alpha^D = (0, 0, \cdots, 0, 1, 0, \cdots, 0)$, which we may consider unrealistic since only one sample out of D would leak secret information.

In contrast, if $\sigma_1 = \cdots = \sigma_D = \sigma$, the covariance matrix has only one eigenvalue, namely $(1, 1, \cdots, 1)$, which has multiplicity D. Thus, for white homoscedastic noise, PCA is asymptotically optimal if and only if $\alpha_1 = \cdots \alpha_D = \alpha$, that is, the SNR is the same for each sample.

Still in the case of white noise, we can lower bound the SNR of the asymptotic PCA:

Lemma 17. *For white noise, the SNR of the asymptotic PCA is not less than the worst SNR among the samples, but can be strictly smaller than the higher SNR among the samples.*

Proof. We have

$$\sum_{d=1}^D \alpha_d^2\sigma_d^2 = \sum_{d=1}^D \frac{\sigma_d^2}{\alpha_d^2}\alpha_d^4 \leq \left(\max_{d=1}^D \frac{\sigma_d^2}{\alpha_d^2}\right)\sum_{d=1}^D \alpha_d^4.$$

Since $\left(\max_{d=1}^D \frac{\sigma_d^2}{\alpha_d^2}\right)^{-1} = \min_{d=1}^D \frac{\alpha_d^2}{\sigma_d^2} = \min_{d=1}^D \text{SNR}_d$, the expression of the SNR of the asymptotic PCA given by Eq. (19) is such that

$$\text{SNR}_{\text{PCA}} = \frac{\left(\sum_{d=1}^D \alpha_d^2\right)^2}{\sum_{d=1}^D \alpha_d^2\sigma_d^2} \geq \frac{\left(\sum_{d=1}^D \alpha_d^2\right)^2}{\sum_{d=1}^D \alpha_d^4}\min_{d=1}^D \text{SNR}_d \geq \min_{d=1}^D \text{SNR}_d \qquad (21)$$

where we have used Cauchy-Schwarz inequality $\sum_{d=1}^D \alpha_d^2\alpha_d^2 \leq \left(\sum_{d=1}^D \alpha_d^2\right)^2$.

Conversely, we can give an example for which $\mathrm{SNR_{PCA}} < \max_{d=1}^{D} \frac{\alpha_d^2}{\sigma_d^2}$. Take $D = 2$, $\alpha_1 = \alpha_2 = 1$, $\sigma_1 = 1$ and $\sigma_2 = 10$. Then $\mathrm{SNR_{PCA}} = 4/(1+10^2) = 4/101$, which is strictly smaller than $\alpha_1^2/\sigma_1^2 = 1$. □

4.2 Linear Discriminant Analysis (LDA)

LDA has been introduced in side-channel analysis in [31]. With respect to inter-class PCA, it computes the eigenvectors of the matrix $S_w^{-1} S_b$, where:

- S_w is the *within-class scatter matrix*, asymptotically equal to Σ, and
- S_b is the *between-class scatter matrix*, equal to $\alpha^D (\alpha^D)^{\mathsf{T}}$.

We have the following spectral characterization of the asymptotic LDA:

Proposition 18. *Asymptotically, LDA has only one principal direction, namely the vector $\Sigma^{-1}\alpha^D$.*

Proof. The matrix $S_w^{-1} S_b = \Sigma^{-1}\alpha^D (\alpha^D)^{\mathsf{T}}$ has rank one. Indeed, $\alpha^D (\alpha^D)^{\mathsf{T}}$ has rank one, and multiplying by an invertible matrix (namely Σ^{-1}) keeps the rank unchanged. Since

$$(\Sigma^{-1}\alpha^D (\alpha^D)^{\mathsf{T}})\Sigma^{-1}\alpha^D = \Sigma^{-1}\alpha^D ((\alpha^D)^{\mathsf{T}}\Sigma^{-1}\alpha^D) = \left((\alpha^D)^{\mathsf{T}}\Sigma^{-1}\alpha^D\right) \times \Sigma^{-1}\alpha^D,$$

$\Sigma^{-1}\alpha^D$ is the unique eigenvector with corresponding eigenvalue $(\alpha^D)^{\mathsf{T}}\Sigma^{-1}\alpha^D > 0$. This eigenvalue is equal to the SNR of the asymptotic LDA. □

By Corollary 4, the SNR of the asymptotic LDA is equal to the SNR of the optimal dimensionality reduction, denoted by $\widetilde{\mathrm{SNR}}$. In fact, we have the following.

Theorem 19. *The asymptotic LDA computes exactly the optimal dimensionality reduction.*

Proof. Compare Theorem 1 with Proposition 18: in both cases, the projection vector is collinear with $\Sigma^{-1}\alpha^D$. □

4.3 Numerical Comparison Between Asymptotic PCA and LDA

Numerical comparison between asymptotic PCA and LDA is given in Fig. 2(a) and (b), for $D = 6$ samples. The noise is chosen autoregressive, with $\sigma = 1$ and different values for ρ (Sect. 3.2). The vector α^D is chosen equal to $(1,1,1,1,1,1)^{\mathsf{T}}$ in Fig. 2(a) and to $\sqrt{6.0/6.4} \cdot (1.0, 1.1, 1.2, 1.3, 0.9, 0.5)^{\mathsf{T}}$ in Fig. 2(b), such that $\widetilde{\mathrm{SNR}} = 6$ when $\rho = 0$. The SNR of the asymptotic LDA is that of the optimal dimensionality reduction (cf. Corollary 4), and that of the asymptotic PCA can be found in Example 14. The first case (Fig. 2(a)) fits the situation depicted in Corollary 9. The asymptotic PCA and LDA are almost similar. Besides, when $\rho \to 1^-$, both SNRs tend to 1 (recall Eqs. (20) and (16)). But, when the SNR varies over the D samples (Fig. 2(b)), the asymptotic LDA can be significantly better than the asymptotic PCA. The sample-wise extremal SNRs ($\text{SNR}_d = \alpha_d^2/\sigma^2$) are also represented: the SNR of the PCA can be smaller than the largest SNR, namely $\max_{1 \leq d \leq D} \text{SNR}_d$, (recall Lemma 17), which is not the case of the SNR of the LDA. Actually, the SNR of LDA increases to infinity because $\widetilde{\text{SNR}} \approx 0.164/(1 - \rho)$ when $\rho \to 1^-$ (see Eq. (15)).

(a) Equal $\text{SNR}_d = 1$, $1 \leq d \leq D$ (b) Varying SNR_d, $1 \leq d \leq D$

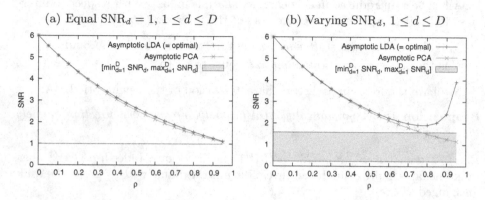

Fig. 2. Comparison of the SNR of asymptotic LDA (optimal) and of asymptotic PCA

5 Practical Validation

In this section, we investigate real traces. Experiments are carried out on the DPA CONTEST v2 [34] traces. One clock cycle lasts $D = 200$ samples. As traces are captured from a hardware implementation of an AES, we consider the Hamming distance leakage model (in accordance with most attacks reported on the analyzed device [8], namely a SASEBO-GII board with a Xilinx XC5VLX30 FPGA [28]). In the sequel, we focus on the Hamming distance between the byte 0 of the last round and that of the cipher text. That is, the function ϕ in Eq. (1) is a normalized Hamming weight; precisely, $\phi : z \in \mathbb{F}_2^n \mapsto \frac{2}{\sqrt{n}}\left(w_H(z) - \frac{n}{2}\right)$, where $n = 8$, because AES is a byte-oriented block cipher. In addition, we emphasize that our model (Eq. (2)) is indeed suitable to leakage dimensionality reduction within one clock period.

5.1 Precharacterization of the Model Parameters α^D and Σ

In order to characterize the model, we need to recover the column matrix α^D and the $D \times D$ covariance matrix Σ of the noise.

Proposition 20. *The parameters of the model* (2) *which minimize the fitting error are given by*

$$\hat{\alpha}^D = \frac{X^{D,Q}(Y^Q)^{\mathsf{T}}}{Y^Q(Y^Q)^{\mathsf{T}}}.$$

Proof. The goal (minimizing the fitting error) is similar to that of the optimal distinguisher, namely maximize the probability of $p_{N^{D,Q}}(X^{D,Q} - \alpha^D Y^Q)$ (Eq. (6)). But in the context of characterization, the correct key is known. Therefore, we wish to minimize in α^D and Σ the following objective function:

$$\text{objective}(\alpha^D, \Sigma) = \sum_{q=1}^{Q} \left\{ \left(x_q^D - \alpha^D y_q(k^*) \right)^\mathsf{T} \Sigma^{-1} \left(x_q^D - \alpha^D y_q(k^*) \right) \right\}, \quad (22)$$

which reminds of Eq. (9) (except that now, the key $k = k^*$ is known). We use the notation $(\hat{\alpha}^D, \hat{\Sigma}) = argmin_{(\alpha^D, \Sigma)} \text{objective}(\alpha^D, \Sigma)$.

We fix Σ and minimize only on α^D. The gradient of $\text{objective}(\alpha^D, \Sigma)$ w.r.t. $(\alpha^D)^\mathsf{T}$ writes:

$$\frac{\partial}{\partial (\alpha^D)^\mathsf{T}} \text{objective}(\alpha^D, \Sigma) = \sum_{q=1}^{Q} -2 y_q(k^*) \left(\Sigma^{-1} x_q^D - y_q(k^*) \Sigma^{-1} \alpha^D \right). \quad (23)$$

The objective function is extremal in $\hat{\alpha}^D$ if and only if its derivative is equal to zero at this point. Let Y^Q be an abbreviation for $Y^Q(k^*)$. This condition takes the form of a *normal equation*

$$\hat{\alpha}^D = \frac{\sum_{q=1}^{Q} y_q x_q^D}{\sum_{q=1}^{Q} y_q^2} = \frac{X^{D,Q}(Y^Q)^\mathsf{T}}{Y^Q(Y^Q)^\mathsf{T}}. \quad (24)$$

where the numerator is the inter-covariance matrix of $X^{D,Q}$ and Y^Q, and the denominator is the covariance matrix of Y^Q. □

Interestingly, the most likely value $\hat{\alpha}^D$ of α^D does not depend on the noise covariance matrix. As $N^{D,Q} = X^{D,Q} - \hat{\alpha}^D Y^Q$ has zero mean, the latter can be evaluated on its own as the well-known unbiased estimator of Σ:

$$\hat{\Sigma} = \frac{1}{Q-1} (X^{D,Q} - \hat{\alpha}^D Y^Q)(X^{D,Q} - \hat{\alpha}^D Y^Q)^\mathsf{T}. \quad (25)$$

By plugging Eq. (24) into Eq. (25), one obtains

$$\hat{\Sigma} = \frac{1}{Q-1} \left(X^{D,Q} - X^{D,Q} \frac{(Y^Q)^\mathsf{T} Y^Q}{Y^Q(Y^Q)^\mathsf{T}} \right) \left(X^{D,Q} - X^{D,Q} \frac{(Y^Q)^\mathsf{T} Y^Q}{Y^Q(Y^Q)^\mathsf{T}} \right)^\mathsf{T}$$

$$= \frac{1}{Q-1} X^{D,Q} \left(I^{Q,Q} - \frac{(Y^Q)^\mathsf{T} Y^Q}{Y^Q(Y^Q)^\mathsf{T}} \right)^2 (X^{D,Q})^\mathsf{T} \quad (26)$$

$$= \frac{1}{Q-1} X^{D,Q} \left(I^{Q,Q} - \frac{(Y^Q)^\mathsf{T} Y^Q}{Y^Q(Y^Q)^\mathsf{T}} \right) (X^{D,Q})^\mathsf{T} \quad (27)$$

$$= \frac{1}{Q-1} \left(X^{D,Q}(X^{D,Q})^\mathsf{T} - \frac{X^{D,Q}(Y^Q)^\mathsf{T} Y^Q (X^{D,Q})^\mathsf{T}}{Y^Q(Y^Q)^\mathsf{T}} \right).$$

In Eq. 26, $I^{Q,Q}$ denotes the $Q \times Q$ identity matrix, and we use in Eq. 27 the fact that the matrix $I^{Q,Q} - (Y^Q)^\mathsf{T} Y^Q / (Y^Q (Y^Q)^\mathsf{T})$ is idempotent, i.e., equal to its square.

Remark 3. We have the following remarkable identity:

$$X^{D,Q}(X^{D,Q})^\mathsf{T} = \hat{\alpha}^D (\hat{\alpha}^D)^\mathsf{T} Y^Q (Y^Q)^\mathsf{T} + (Q-1)\hat{\Sigma}.$$

This equation is the non-asymptotic version of Proposition 10.

5.2 Computation of SNRs on the AES Traces from DPA Contest v2 Last Round

The values $\hat{\alpha}^D$ and $\hat{\Sigma}$ are represented in Fig. 3. We obtain:

- $\max_{d=1}^D \hat{\alpha}_d^2 / \hat{\Sigma}_{d,d} = 1.69 \cdot 10^{-3}$ (no dimensionality reduction)
- $\mathrm{SNR_{PCA}} = \frac{((\hat{\alpha}^D)^\mathsf{T} \hat{\alpha}^D)^2}{(\hat{\alpha}^D)^\mathsf{T} \hat{\Sigma} \hat{\alpha}^D} = 1.36 \cdot 10^{-3}$ (PCA)
- $\mathrm{SNR_{LDA}} = (\hat{\alpha}^D)^\mathsf{T} \hat{\Sigma} \hat{\alpha}^D = 12.78 \cdot 10^{-3}$ (LDA).

Therefore, the LDA has the largest SNR: it is about seven times larger than the maximum sample-wise SNR. The PCA has, in this example, an SNR smaller than the maximum univariable SNR (see Lemma 17).

Interestingly, one can see in Fig. 3 that the noise is locally autoregressive, for instance between samples 107 and 117.

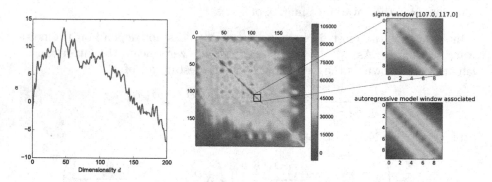

Fig. 3. Estimated $\hat{\alpha}^D$ (*left*) and $\hat{\Sigma}$ (*right*), for $Q = 10,000$ traces

6   Conclusions and Perspectives

Dimensionality reduction is common practice in side-channel analysis. This preprocessing technique has many virtues, such as an elegant multivariate description of the leakages, the concentration of information which reduces the required number of measurements to extract the key, and the increase of computational efficiency. Nonetheless, as any processing, dimensionality reduction can only reduce some information.

Using a mathematical approach, we have shown that dimensionality reduction is actually part of the optimal attack. This proves rigorously that dimensionality reduction can be achieved without loss in terms of attack success probability in extracting a secret key. As it turns out, the optimal dimensionality reduction consists in a linear projection of the trace samples.

We have also shown that the linear discriminant analysis asymptotically achieves the same projection, and hence becomes optimal as the number of traces increases. When the various samples are weakly correlated, we have found that PCA is nearly equivalent to the optimal dimensionality reduction and to LDA. Thus, in realistic contexts, state-of-the-art dimensionality reduction techniques are actually close to the optimal method.

Finally, we show how to estimate the model parameters (modulation vector α^D and noise covariance matrix Σ), and compute them on a real traces. An SNR gain factor of 7 can be obtained with respect to sample-wise SNR, which stresses the practical interest of dimensionality reduction.

As a perspective, we note that it should also be possible to obtain similar results when the noise is non-Gaussian (e.g., uniform). It is also desirable to compare dimensionality reduction based on linear projections to machine-learning techniques which are also multidimensional, such as SVM, random forests, K-means, etc.

Acknowledgements. The authors would like to thank François-Xavier Standaert for interesting discussions, and also gratefully acknowledge the constructive comments of the reviewers which helped improve the clarity of the paper.

References

1. Archambeau, C., Peeters, E., Standaert, F.-X., Quisquater, J.-J.: Template attacks in principal subspaces. In: Goubin, L., Matsui, M. (eds.) CHES 2006. LNCS, vol. 4249, pp. 1–14. Springer, Heidelberg (2006)
2. Batina, L., Hogenboom, J., van Woudenberg, J.G.J.: Getting more from PCA: first results of using principal component analysis for extensive power analysis. In: Dunkelman, O. (ed.) CT-RSA 2012. LNCS, vol. 7178, pp. 383–397. Springer, Heidelberg (2012)
3. Bhasin, S., Danger, J.-L., Guilley, S., Najm, Z.: Side-channel leakage and trace compression using normalized inter-class variance. In: Proceedings of the Third Workshop on Hardware and Architectural Support for Security and Privacy, HASP 2014, pp. 7:1–7:9. ACM, New York (2014)
4. Brier, E., Clavier, C., Olivier, F.: Correlation power analysis with a leakage model. In: Joye, M., Quisquater, J.-J. (eds.) CHES 2004. LNCS, vol. 3156, pp. 16–29. Springer, Heidelberg (2004)

5. Bruneau, N., Danger, J.-L., Guilley, S., Heuser, A., Teglia, Y.: Boosting higher-order correlation attacks by dimensionality reduction. In: Chakraborty, R.S., Matyas, V., Schaumont, P. (eds.) SPACE 2014. LNCS, vol. 8804, pp. 183–200. Springer, Heidelberg (2014)
6. Chari, S., Rao, J.R., Rohatgi, P.: Template attacks. In: Kaliski, B.S., Koç, K., Paar, C. (eds.) CHES 2002. LNCS, vol. 2523, pp. 13–28. Springer, Heidelberg (2002)
7. Choudary, O., Kuhn, M.G.: Efficient template attacks. In: Francillon, A., Rohatgi, P. (eds.) CARDIS 2013. LNCS, vol. 8419, pp. 253–270. Springer, Heidelberg (2014)
8. Clavier, C., Danger, J.-L., Duc, G., Elaabid, M.A., Gérard, B., Guilley, S., Heuser, A., Kasper, M., Li, Y., Lomné, V., Nakatsu, D., Ohta, K., Sakiyama, K., Sauvage, L., Schindler, W., Stöttinger, M., Veyrat-Charvillon, N., Walle, M., Wurcker, A.: Practical improvements of side-channel attacks on AES: feedback from the 2nd DPA contest. J. Cryptogr. Eng. **4**, 1–16 (2014)
9. Cover, T.M., Thomas, J.A.: Elements of Information Theory, 2nd edn. Wiley-Interscience, New York (2006). ISBN-10: ISBN-10: 0471241954, ISBN-13: 978-0471241959
10. Danger, J.-L., Debande, N., Guilley, S., Souissi, Y.: High-order timing attacks. In: Proceedings of the First Workshop on Cryptography and Security in Computing Systems, CS2 2014, pp. 7–12. ACM, New York (2014)
11. Debande, N., Souissi, Y., Elaabid, M.A., Guilley, S., Danger, J.-L.: Wavelet transform based pre-processing for side channel analysis. In: 45th Annual IEEE/ACM International Symposium on Microarchitecture, MICRO 2012, Workshops Proceedings, Vancouver, BC, Canada, 1–5 December 2012, pp. 32–38. IEEE Computer Society (2012)
12. Durvaux, F., Standaert, F.-X., Veyrat-Charvillon, N., Mairy, J.-B., Deville, Y.: Efficient selection of time samples for higher-order DPA with projection pursuits. In: Mangard, S., Poschmann, A.Y. (eds.) COSADE 2015. LNCS, vol. 9064, pp. 34–50. Springer, Heidelberg (2015). http://eprint.iacr.org/2014/412
13. Fei, Y., Luo, Q., Ding, A.A.: A statistical model for DPA with novel algorithmic confusion analysis. In: Prouff, E., Schaumont, P. (eds.) [25], pp. 233–250
14. Gierlichs, B., Lemke-Rust, K., Paar, C.: Templates vs. stochastic methods. In: Goubin, L., Matsui, M. (eds.) CHES 2006. LNCS, vol. 4249, pp. 15–29. Springer, Heidelberg (2006)
15. Guilley, S., Chaudhuri, S., Sauvage, L., Hoogvorst, P., Pacalet, R., Bertoni, G.M.: Security evaluation of WDDL and SecLib countermeasures against power attacks. IEEE Trans. Comput. **57**(11), 1482–1497 (2008)
16. Hajra, S., Mukhopadhyay, D.: Multivariate leakage model for improving non-profiling DPA on noisy power traces. In: Lin, D., Xu, S., Yung, M. (eds.) Inscrypt 2013. LNCS, vol. 8567, pp. 325–342. Springer, Heidelberg (2014)
17. Hajra, S., Mukhopadhyay, D.: SNR to success rate: reaching the limit of non-profiling DPA. Cryptology ePrint Archive, Report 2013/865 (2013). http://eprint.iacr.org/2013/865/
18. Hajra, S., Mukhopadhyay, D.: On the optimal pre-processing for non-profiling differential power analysis. In: Prouff, E. (ed.) COSADE 2014. LNCS, vol. 8622, pp. 161–178. Springer, Heidelberg (2014)
19. Hajra, S., Mukhopadhyay, D.: Reaching the limit of nonprofiling DPA. IEEE Trans. CAD Integr. Circ. Syst. **34**(6), 915–927 (2015)
20. Heuser, A., Rioul, O., Guilley, S.: Good is not good enough. In: Batina, L., Robshaw, M. (eds.) CHES 2014. LNCS, vol. 8731, pp. 55–74. Springer, Heidelberg (2014)

21. Karsmakers, P., Gierlichs, B., Pelckmans, K., De Cock, K., Suykens, J., Preneel, B., De Moor, B.: Side channel attacks on cryptographic devices as a classification problem. COSIC technical report (2009)
22. Kocher, P.C., Jaffe, J., Jun, B.: Differential power analysis. In: Wiener, M. (ed.) CRYPTO 1999. LNCS, vol. 1666, pp. 388–397. Springer, Heidelberg (1999)
23. Oswald, D., Paar, C.: Improving side-channel analysis with optimal linear transforms. In: Mangard, S. (ed.) CARDIS 2012. LNCS, vol. 7771, pp. 219–233. Springer, Heidelberg (2013)
24. Oswald, E., Mangard, S., Herbst, C., Tillich, S.: Practical second-order DPA attacks for masked smart card implementations of block ciphers. In: Pointcheval, D. (ed.) CT-RSA 2006. LNCS, vol. 3860, pp. 192–207. Springer, Heidelberg (2006)
25. Prouff, E., Schaumont, P. (eds.): CHES 2012. LNCS, vol. 7428. Springer, Heidelberg (2012)
26. Renauld, M., Standaert, F.-X., Veyrat-Charvillon, N., Kamel, D., Flandre, D.: A formal study of power variability issues and side-channel attacks for nanoscale devices. In: Paterson, K.G. (ed.) EUROCRYPT 2011. LNCS, vol. 6632, pp. 109–128. Springer, Heidelberg (2011)
27. Reparaz, O., Gierlichs, B., Verbauwhede, I.: Selecting time samples for multivariate DPA attacks. In: Prouff, E., Schaumont, P. (eds.) [25], pp. 155–174
28. Satoh, A.: Side-channel Attack Standard Evaluation Board, SASEBO-GII. Project of the AIST - RCIS (Research Center for Information Security). http://www.rcis.aist.go.jp/special/SASEBO/SASEBO-GII-en.html. Accessed 31 May 2015
29. Souissi, Y., Debande, N., Mekki, S., Guilley, S., Maalaoui, A., Danger, J.-L.: On the optimality of correlation power attack on embedded cryptographic systems. In: Askoxylakis, I., Pöhls, H.C., Posegga, J. (eds.) WISTP 2012. LNCS, vol. 7322, pp. 169–178. Springer, Heidelberg (2012)
30. Souissi, Y., Nassar, M., Guilley, S., Danger, J.-L., Flament, F.: First principal components analysis: a new side channel distinguisher. In: Rhee, K.-H., Nyang, D.H. (eds.) ICISC 2010. LNCS, vol. 6829, pp. 407–419. Springer, Heidelberg (2011)
31. Standaert, F.-X., Archambeau, C.: Using subspace-based template attacks to compare and combine power and electromagnetic information leakages. In: Oswald, E., Rohatgi, P. (eds.) CHES 2008. LNCS, vol. 5154, pp. 411–425. Springer, Heidelberg (2008)
32. Strobel, D., Oswald, D., Richter, B., Schellenberg, F., Paar, C.: Microcontrollers as (in)security devices for pervasive computing applications. Proc. IEEE 102(8), 1157–1173 (2014)
33. Sugawara, T., Homma, N., Aoki, T., Satoh, A.: Profiling attack using multivariate regression analysis. IEICE Electron. Express 7(15), 1139–1144 (2010)
34. TELECOM ParisTech. DPA Contest, 2nd edition. http://www.DPAcontest.org/v2/. Accessed 31 May 2015

Blind Source Separation from Single Measurements Using Singular Spectrum Analysis

Santos Merino Del Pozo[✉] and François-Xavier Standaert

ICTEAM/ELEN/Crypto Group, Université catholique de Louvain,
Louvain-la-Neuve, Belgium
{santos.merino,fstandae}@uclouvain.be

Abstract. Singular Spectrum Analysis (SSA) is a powerful data decomposition/recompose technique that can be used to reduce the noise in time series. Compared to existing solutions aiming at similar purposes, such as frequency-based filtering, it benefits from easier-to-exploit intuitions, applicability in contexts where low sampling rates make standard frequency analyses challenging, and the (theoretical) possibility to separate a signal source from a noisy source even if both run at the same frequency. In this paper, we first describe how to apply SSA in the context of side-channel analysis, and then validate its interest in three different scenarios. Namely, we consider unprotected software, masked software, and unprotected hardware block cipher implementations. Our experiments confirm significant noise reductions in all three cases, leading to success rates improved accordingly. They also put forward the stronger impact of SSA in more challenging scenarios, e.g. masked implementations (because the impact of noise increases exponentially with the number of shares in this case), or noisy hardware implementations (because of the established connection between the amount of noise and the attacks' success rate in this case). Since noise is a fundamental ingredient for most countermeasures against side-channel attacks, we conclude SSA can be an important element in the toolbox of evaluation laboratories, in order to efficiently preprocess their measurements in a black box manner.

1 Introduction

Successful side-channel attacks against embedded cryptographic implementations generally require a multidisciplinary combination of informal steps. First, good *measurements* of, e.g., the power consumption or electromagnetic radiation of the target devices must be obtained. Second, these measurements are usually sent to a *preprocessing* phase, in order to facilitate their cryptographic treatment. Third, some *modeling* is required to extract information from the leakages. Eventually, the information extracted is *exploited* and turned into, e.g., a key recovery. A look at the literature suggests a wide variety of tools for the last two (modeling and exploitation) steps. They typically include a plethora of (profiled and non-profiled) distinguishers, including but not limited to [4,9,17,39], exploited via

© International Association for Cryptologic Research 2015
T. Güneysu and H. Handschuh (Eds.): CHES 2015, LNCS 9293, pp. 42–59, 2015.
DOI: 10.1007/978-3-662-48324-4_3

simple divide-and-conquer approaches [24], or more elaborate strategies, e.g., collision-based [27] or algebraic [37]. By contrast, the measurement and pre-processing steps are in general less discussed, despite their importance from an engineering point-of-view. Indeed, while quite formal solutions now exist to guarantee that the modeling and exploitation of side-channel leakages are close to optimal [14], the evaluation of measurement setups and preprocessing methods is left with a comparative approach. Namely, we can tell whether one is better than another, but not guarantee that it is good. This situation creates strong incentive to study state-of-the-art methods in this respect, which this paper aims to do in the (limited but relevant) context of preprocessing methods.

State-of-the-Art. An informal classification of some popular preprocessing tools is given in Table 1, based on whether these tools aim at decreasing the noise, increasing the signal, include some feature selection or compress the output.

For example, averaging only aims at reducing the noise, and does some implicit feature selection by assuming that the useful part of the measurements is in their means (which is only relevant in the context of unprotected implementations, and would be useless in the context of masked implementations for which the information lies in higher-order moments of the leakage distribution [8]). Detecting Points-of-Interest (POIs) can be viewed as a kind of feature selection that compresses the measurements. Dimensionality reductions such as Principal Component Analysis (PCA) and Linear Discriminant Analysis (LDA), introduced to side-channel attacks in [1,40], and recently revisited in [2,7,10,11], project samples into subspaces that optimize the side-channel signal and Signal-to-Noise Ratio (SNR), respectively. Other "compressive" linear transforms (using other optimization criteria) include [15,30]. Eventually, filtering typically aims at selecting the frequency band in which side-channel attacks perform best.

Concretely, this latter solution (filtering) is especially interesting since it can be applied to single measurements (contrary to averaging), which makes it relevant to countermeasures such as masking or shuffling [20], and it does not compress the leakage traces, hence nothing prevents to combine it with dimensionality reduction afterwards. As a result, a variety of works have investigated the opportunities offered by filtering methods, or even tried to perform side-channel analysis directly in the frequency domain, including but not lim-

Table 1. Informal classification of some existing preprocessing methods.

	Noise reduction	Signal increase	Feature selection	Compressed output
averaging	✓	✗	implicit	✗
POI detection	✗	✗	✓	✓
filtering	✓	✗	✓	✗
PCA	✗	✓	✓	✓
LDA	✓	✓	✓	✓

ited to [12,16,22,25,26,43,44]. Very summarized, the common outcome of these works is that (*i*) filtering works best in contexts where the adversary/evaluator has some intuitions regarding the interesting frequency bands and (*ii*) frequency analysis generally benefits from acquisition devices with higher sampling rates.

Our Contribution. Starting from this state-of-the-art, our main contribution is to introduce Singular Spectrum Analysis (SSA) [19,45] to the field of side-channel analysis, as an efficient alternative to filtering. SSA is an emerging method in the field of time series analysis, that aims at decomposing the original series into the sum of a small number of independent and interpretable components, which has proved to be relevant to a wide range of applications (in physics and economics, typically), e.g. by allowing significant noise reductions. In this respect, we first note that despite some connection with frequency analysis (see, e.g. [3]), SSA is based on totally a different mathematical background, and is in fact closer to dimensionality reductions such as PCA and LDA. Indeed, it is based on a decomposition in independent components. Intuitively, it can therefore be viewed as a (heuristic) tool enabling blind source separation, such as Independent Component Analysis (ICA) [21], yet with the significant difference that it works based on single observations (whereas ICA requires at least N independent observations to recover the original series made of N sources). Concretely though, and when used for noise reduction purposes as we will consider next, SSA shares the goals of filtering, with two significant advantages. First, it allows easier intuitions in the selection of the components to be integrated in the signal reconstruction, because these components can be "rated" according to their eigenvalues, just as in PCA and LDA. Second, the signal decomposition and reconstruction can be successful even in situations where the sampling rate is low. So it provides actual solutions for the two previously mentioned limitations of the filtering preprocessing. Besides, it can theoretically succeed in contexts where filtering is unapplicable, e.g. when two independent sources (corresponding to some signal and noise) are observed at exactly the same frequency.

In order to confirm the relevance of this new tool, we apply it in three different scenarios: first an unprotected implementation of the AES in a microcontroller, second a masked implementation of the AES in the same microcontroller, third an unprotected FPGA implementation of PRESENT. In all three cases, we show that SSA allows very significant improvements of the traces SNR, which translates into concrete gains in the success rates of attacks exploiting this preprocessing. Our experiments further exhibit the increased interest of SSA in the context of masking (since the impact of noise on the success rate increases exponentially in the number of shares used when masking), and more noisy implementations such as our hardware one (for which the SNR is small enough for its impact on the attacks success rate to follow theoretical predictions such as [13]). Since noise is a fundamental ingredient in the analysis of most countermeasures against side-channel attacks, and in particular for masking [42] and shuffling [46], we conclude SSA can be an important tool in the analysis of the concrete security level of implementations protected by these means.

2   Background

Notations. In the rest of the paper, capital letters are used for random variables and small caps for their realizations. Vectors and matrices are denoted with bold notations, functions with sans serif fonts and sets with calligraphic ones.

2.1   Attacks

Preprocessing leakage traces aims to improve the efficiency of side-channel attacks, allowing for a reduction in their acquisition and computation time. In order to evaluate the efficiency of SSA in this context, raw and preprocessed power traces are compared using state-of-the-art attacks that are briefly summarized next. For this purpose, a cryptographic device performing the key addition $\oplus$ between an input x and the secret key k followed by a b-bit S-box S, i.e., $z = \mathsf{S}(x \oplus k)$, is considered. The leakage trace generated by the target device when performing this S-box computation with the attacker-supplied input $\{x_i\}_{i=1}^n$, where n is the number of queries performed by the adversary, is denoted as $l_{x,k}^i$. Whenever accessing the tth time sample of this trace, the notation $l_{x,k}^{i,t}$ will be used. Subscripts/superscripts will be omitted when not necessary.

Template Attack (TA). Introduced by Chari *et al.* [9] at CHES 2002 as a powerful attack against cryptographic implementations, TA essentially extracts secret information based on probabilistic leakage models (next denoted as $\hat{\mathsf{Pr}}_{\text{model}}$). For this purpose, the authors of [9] assume that leakages can be interpreted as the realizations of a random variable which generates samples according to a Gaussian distribution. In the context of this work, where the target intermediate value is a key addition, it holds that $\hat{\mathsf{Pr}}_{\text{model}}[l_{x,k}|x,k] \approx \hat{\mathsf{Pr}}_{\text{model}}[l_{x,k}|x \oplus k] \sim \mathcal{N}(\hat{\boldsymbol{\mu}}_{x,k}, \hat{\boldsymbol{\Sigma}}_{x,k}^2)$, with $\hat{\boldsymbol{\mu}}_{x,k}$ and $\hat{\boldsymbol{\Sigma}}_{x,k}^2$ the mean vector and covariance matrices corresponding to the target intermediate value $x \oplus k$. In case of *univariate attacks* (that are typically successful against unprotected implementations), the Gaussian templates are further simplified to the corresponding means and covariances, and can be exploited to compute key probabilities as follows:

$$\hat{\mathsf{Pr}}_{\text{model}}[k^*|x_i, l_{x,k}^{i,t}] = \frac{\mathcal{N}(l_{x,k}^{i,t}|\hat{\mu}_{x,k}, \hat{\sigma}_{x,k}^2)}{\sum_{k^* \in \mathcal{K}} \mathcal{N}(l_{x,k}^{i,t}|\hat{\mu}_{x,k^*}, \hat{\sigma}_{x,k^*}^2)},$$

where k^* is a key candidate. By contrast, cryptographic software implementations protected with a 1st-order masking scheme, where the masked intermediate value and the corresponding output mask are processed sequentially at t_1 and t_2, are vulnerable to *bivariate attacks*. In such a scenario, adversaries can launch a TA exploiting the two leaking samples by means of Gaussian mixtures:

$$\hat{\mathsf{Pr}}_{\text{model}}[k^*|x_i, l_{x,k}^{i,t_1}, l_{x,k}^{i,t_2}] = \frac{\sum_{q^* \in \mathcal{Q}} \mathcal{N}(l_{x,k}^{i,t_1}, l_{x,k}^{i,t_2}|\hat{\boldsymbol{\mu}}_{x,k,q^*}, \hat{\boldsymbol{\Sigma}}_{x,k,q^*}^2)}{\sum_{k^* \in \mathcal{K}} \sum_{q^* \in \mathcal{Q}} \mathcal{N}(l_{x,k}^{i,t_1}, l_{x,k}^{i,t_2}|\hat{\boldsymbol{\mu}}_{x,k^*,q^*}, \hat{\boldsymbol{\Sigma}}_{x,k^*,q^*}^2)},$$

where q^* is the guessed output mask. In order to recover the key, TA then estimates probabilities for each candidate k^*, e.g., in the unprotected case:

$$p_{k^*} = \prod_{i=1}^{n} \hat{\mathrm{Pr}}_{\mathrm{model}}[k^*|x_i, l_{x,k}^{i,t}].$$

Correlation Power Analysis (CPA). In order to distinguish the correct key guess among the others, CPA [4] classifies univariate leakages $l_{x,k}^{i,t}$ using Pearson's correlation coefficient and an a-priori chosen leakage model $m_{k^*}^i = \mathsf{M}(\mathsf{S}(x_i \oplus k^*))$:

$$\hat{\rho}_{k^*}^t = \frac{\hat{\mathsf{E}}_i[l_{x,k}^{i,t} \cdot m_{k^*}^i] - \hat{\mathsf{E}}_i[l_{x,k}^{i,t}] \cdot \hat{\mathsf{E}}_i[m_{k^*}^i]}{\sqrt{\hat{\mathsf{Var}}_i(l_{x,k}^{i,t}) \cdot \hat{\mathsf{Var}}_i(m_{k^*}^i)}},$$

where $\hat{\mathsf{E}}$ and $\hat{\mathsf{Var}}$ denote the sample versions of the mean and variance, respectively. Usually in practice, $\mathsf{M}(\cdot)$ corresponds to the Hamming weight (HW) or distance (HD) model when targeting software or hardware implementations, respectively. Finally, the best key candidate $\tilde{k}$ is taken such that:

$$\tilde{k} = \arg\max_{k^*} \hat{\rho}_{k^*}^t.$$

Moments-Correlating DPA (MC-DPA). In [28], Moradi and Standaert proposed a so-called Moments-Correlating Collision DPA (MCC-DPA) as a tweak of Correlation-Enhanced Power Analysis Collision Attack (CEPACA) [27], where the correlation of "moments with moments" is replaced by the correlation of "moments with samples", hence preserving the metric feature of Pearson's correlation coefficient. In order to perform a MCC-DPA attack, the dth-order (raw, central, standardized) moments are estimated "on-the-fly" from a vector of leakage traces $\mathbf{l}_{x_0,k_0}^{\mathrm{t}} = \{l_{x_0,k_0}^{i,t_1}\}_{i=1}^n$ corresponding to the target S-box computation at time t_1, i.e., $z_0 = \mathsf{S}(x_0 \oplus k_0)$. The leakage traces $\mathbf{l}_{x_1,k_1}^{\mathrm{t}} = \{l_{x_1,k_1}^{i,t_2}\}_{i=1}^n$ for the second S-box at time t_2, i.e., $z_1 = \mathsf{S}(x_1 \oplus k_1)$, are aligned with the 2^b moments $\hat{\mathbf{M}}_{x_0,k_0}^d$ and then correlated by permuting $\mathbf{l}_{x_1,k_1}^{\mathrm{t}}$ according to $\Delta = k_0 \oplus k_1$. Lastly, the best value of Δ is chosen such that (e.g., for the dth-order raw moments):

$$\tilde{\Delta} = \arg\max_{\Delta} \hat{\rho}(\hat{\mathbf{M}}_{x_0,k_0}^d, (\mathbf{l}_{x_1,k_1 \oplus \Delta}^{\mathrm{t}})^d).$$

The profiled extension of CEPACA, i.e., Moments-Correlating Profiled DPA (MCP-DPA), correlates the statistical moments corresponding to one single S-box. First, a profiling vector of leakage traces $\mathbf{l}_{x,k}^{\mathrm{p}} = \{l_{x,k}^{i,t_1}\}_{i=1}^{n_p}$ for the target intermediate value $z = \mathsf{S}(x \oplus k)$ is used to estimate the 2^b moments $\hat{\mathbf{M}}_{x,k}^d$ and then, a second vector of test traces $\mathbf{l}_{x,k}^{\mathrm{t}} = \{l_{x,k}^{i,t_1}\}_{i=1}^{n_t}$ is correlated with $\hat{\mathbf{M}}_{x,k}^d$ permuted according to the key guess k^*. The best key candidate is selected according to (again for the raw moments):

$$\tilde{k} = \arg\max_{k^*} \hat{\rho}(\hat{\mathbf{M}}_{x,k^*}^d, (\mathbf{l}_{x,k}^{\mathrm{t}})^d).$$

In this work MCP-DPA is extended to the bivariate setting in order to evaluate the software implementation of a 1st-order masking scheme. Experiments performed in this case will only consider MCP-DPA with 2nd-order moments, i.e., $d_1 = d_2 = 1$, hence the use of central mixed statistical moments:

$$\mathbf{CM}_{x,k^*}^{d_1,d_2} = \mathsf{E}\Big(\big(\mathsf{l}_{x,k^*}^{\mathsf{p},t_1} - \mathsf{E}(\mathsf{l}_{x,k^*}^{\mathsf{p},t_1})\big)^{d_1} \cdot \big(\mathsf{l}_{x,k^*}^{\mathsf{p},t_2} - \mathsf{E}(\mathsf{l}_{x,k^*}^{\mathsf{p},t_2})\big)^{d_2}\Big).$$

Analogously to its univariate counterpart, the best key candidate $\tilde{k}$ can then be chosen according to the following equation:

$$\tilde{k} = \arg\max_{k^*} \; \hat{\rho}\Big(\mathbf{CM}_{x,k^*}^{d_1,d_2}, \big(\mathsf{l}_{x,k}^{\mathsf{t},t_1} - \mathsf{E}(\mathsf{l}_{x,k}^{\mathsf{t},t_1})\big)^{d_1} \cdot \big(\mathsf{l}_{x,k}^{\mathsf{t},t_2} - \mathsf{E}(\mathsf{l}_{x,k}^{\mathsf{t},t_2})\big)^{d_2}\Big).$$

2.2   Evaluation Metrics

Security evaluations of cryptographic devices usually pursue two objectives [41]. Firstly, it is of interest to measure how much information is leaking from the target implementation, independently of the attacker, and secondly how easy this information can be exploited by an adversary. In the context of this work, both questions deserve attention since the aim of any preprocessing step is to maximize the information leakages in order to make attacks easier. We will therefore use the two types of metrics briefly introduced next.

Information Theoretic Metrics. Information theoretic (IT) metrics are intended to measure how much information is leaking from the device under test. The *Signal-to-Noise Ratio* (SNR) introduced by Mangard at CT-RSA 2004 [23] is a simple and intuitive solution for this purpose:

$$\text{SNR} = \frac{\hat{\mathsf{Var}}_{x,k}\big(\hat{\mathsf{E}}_i[l_{x,k}^i]\big)}{\hat{\mathsf{E}}_{x,k}\big[\hat{\mathsf{Var}}_i(l_{x,k}^i)\big]},$$

where $\hat{\mathsf{Var}}$ and $\hat{\mathsf{E}}$ respectively denote the sample variance and mean that are estimated from a set of test traces. In comparison with other IT metrics, such as the mutual information (MI) introduced in [41] that allows capturing any leakage PDF, the SNR is limited to 1st-order moments. However, when considering univariate Gaussian random variables, it has been shown that Pearson's correlation coefficient can be connected with the SNR [23] and the MI [24]:

$$\mathsf{MI}(X;Y) \approx -\frac{1}{2} \cdot \log_2\big(1 - \rho(X,Y)^2\big) = -\frac{1}{2} \cdot \log_2\left(1 - \left(\frac{1}{\sqrt{1 + \frac{1}{\text{SNR}}}}\right)^2\right).$$

Since our goal in the following is to quantify noise reduction by SSA, which applies independently on each trace (i.e. from single measurements), we are indeed in a context where the SNR brings all the necessary intuition, and we will limit our information theoretic analysis to this metric. (As will be detailed, this just requires taking advantage of mask knowledge in the protected case).

Security Metrics. We will evaluate the efficiency of our experimental attacks with the 1st-*order success rate* defined in [41], i.e., the probability that the correct secret key is the most likely key candidate provided by an attack. In practice, the success rate is widely used in the security evaluation of many cryptographic implementations because of its ease of use and understandability.

3   Singular Spectrum Analysis

SSA is a non-parametric technique used in time series analysis that was first presented in the eighteenth century [33], but only gained interest with the more recent publications by Broomhead and King [5,6] in the late twentieth century. So far, SSA has been successfully applied in many different areas, e.g., engineering and medicine, becoming a standard tool in some of them, e.g., meteorology and geophysics. In the following, its two main steps (i.e., *decomposition* and *reconstruction*) are introduced based on our previous notations. We additionally provide a couple of insights on how to take advantage of SSA in practice.

3.1   Decomposition

The first step of SSA is the decomposition of the original time series into a set of elementary matrices required during the reconstruction phase. This process is based on the *embedding* and *singular value decomposition* that we describe next.

Embedding. Given an N-time series $l = (l^1, l^2, \ldots, l^N)$ and the window length W such that $2 < W \leq N/2$, we define $D = N - W + 1$ delayed vectors:

$$\mathbf{l}_i = (l^i, l^{i+1}, \ldots, l^{i+W-1})^\top \text{ for } 1 \leq i \leq D,$$

and the trajectory matrix:

$$\mathbf{L} = (\mathbf{l}_1, \mathbf{l}_2, \ldots, \mathbf{l}_D) = \begin{pmatrix} l^1 & l^2 & \cdots & l^D \\ l^2 & l^3 & \cdots & l^{D+1} \\ \vdots & \vdots & \ddots & \vdots \\ l^W & l^{W+1} & \cdots & l^N \end{pmatrix},$$

which is a Hankel matrix, i.e., a matrix with constant skew diagonals. The window length W plays a key role in the performance and accuracy of SSA, hence the importance of choosing its optimal value. Too large or too small values can lead to decompositions where the components are mixed-up between them, making the reconstruction step difficult. In the context of noise reduction, conditions are relaxed allowing practitioners to consider other aspects, e.g., performance, while keeping the accuracy of the tool high. In this work, we will use the following rule-of-thumb:

$$W = \lfloor \log{(N)}^c \rfloor \text{ with } c \in [1.5, 3], \tag{1}$$

which has been shown near optimal for signal vs. noise separation [35].

Singular Value Decomposition. Given the trajectory matrix $\mathbf{L}$ from the previous step, its *singular value decomposition* (SVD) [18] is computed. First, the eigenvalues of $\mathbf{L}\mathbf{L}^\top$ in decreasing order of magnitude $\lambda_1 \geq \lambda_2 \geq \cdots \geq \lambda_d$, i.e., the so called *singular spectrum* which gives name to SSA, and the corresponding eigenvectors $\mathbf{u}_1, \mathbf{u}_2, \ldots, \mathbf{u}_d$ (with $d = W$ if none of the eigenvalues is zero) are obtained. The SVD decomposition of the trajectory matrix can be written as:

$$\mathbf{L} = \mathbf{L}_1 + \mathbf{L}_2 + \cdots + \mathbf{L}_d, \tag{2}$$

where the $W \times D$ elementary matrix $\mathbf{L}_i = \sqrt{\lambda_i}\mathbf{u}_i\mathbf{v}_i^\top$ and $\mathbf{v}_i = \mathbf{L}^\top\mathbf{u}_i/\sqrt{\lambda_i}$, for $1 \leq i \leq d$. Computing (2) is the most time-consuming step in SSA, however only the leading components are required during the reconstruction phase. In order to alleviate this complexity burden the *partial SVD* (PSVD), which only calculates a subset of the $\mathbf{L}_i$ matrices in (2), is considered in the remaining sections.

3.2 Reconstruction

After having obtained the SVD decomposition of the original time series in the previous phase, the reconstruction step aims for the extraction of its underlying components. It is based on the *diagonal averaging* and *grouping* described next.

Diagonal Averaging. If $\mathbf{X}$ is a $W \times D$ matrix with elements $x_{i,j}$ for $1 \leq i \leq W$ and $1 \leq j \leq D$, it can be immediately turned into the series $\tilde{\mathbf{x}} = \{\tilde{x}^t\}_{t=1}^N$ if and only if $\mathbf{X}$ is a Hankel matrix. In that case, each entry $\tilde{x}^t$ is equal to all elements $x_{i,j}$ along the anti-diagonal $i + j = t + 1$ of $\mathbf{X}$. However, if $\mathbf{X}$ does not have constant skew diagonals, an additional step is required. Namely, the averaging of the anti-diagonals $i + j = k + 1$ will transform $\mathbf{X}$ into the series $\tilde{\mathbf{x}} = \{\tilde{x}^t\}_{t=1}^N$ in a process which is also known as Hankelization [38]:

$$\tilde{x}^t = \begin{cases} \dfrac{1}{t}\displaystyle\sum_{m=1}^{t} x_{m,t-m+1} & \text{for } 1 \leq t < W^*, \\[2ex] \dfrac{1}{W^*}\displaystyle\sum_{m=1}^{W^*} x_{m,t-m+1} & \text{for } W^* \leq t \leq D^*, \\[2ex] \dfrac{1}{N-t+1}\displaystyle\sum_{m=t-D^*+1}^{N-D^*} x_{m,t-m+1} & \text{for } D^* < t \leq N, \end{cases}$$

where $W^* = \min(W, D)$ and $D^* = \max(W, D)$. Because matrices $\mathbf{L}_i$ in (2) are not Hankel matrices, by applying this procedure each matrix $\mathbf{L}_i$ in (2) is transformed into the ith (so-called) principal component $\mathbf{g}_i$ of length N.

Grouping. Under the assumption of weak separability [19], the original N-time series l can then be reconstructed by:

$$l = \mathbf{g}_1 + \mathbf{g}_2 + \cdots + \mathbf{g}_d.$$

At this stage, the set of indices $I = \{1, \ldots, d\}$ is partitioned into m disjoint subsets $I_1, \ldots, I_m$. Since in the context of this work, SSA aims for signal vs. noise decomposition, we are typically looking for a partitioning such that $m = 2$ and $I = \{I_{\text{signal}}, I_{\text{noise}}\}$. The analysis of the eigenvalues λ_i in the SVD step is the most common method for splitting I according to some criteria that depend on the application area. In our case, indices whose respective eigenvalues are small, usually producing a slowly decreasing sequence, are included in the group of noisy components. The remaining components can be exhaustively tested in order to find the combination bringing a better reconstruction of the noise-free signal. In the following, we will determine the best grouping based on the SNR. Summarizing, this section presented the main steps involved in SSA, that can be recalled with the following equation:

$$\overbrace{l \longrightarrow \mathbf{L}}^{\text{Embedding}} = \overbrace{\mathbf{L}_1 + \mathbf{L}_2 + \cdots + \mathbf{L}_d}^{\text{SVD}} = \overbrace{\mathbf{g}_1 + \mathbf{g}_2 + \cdots + \mathbf{g}_d}^{\text{Averaging}} = \overbrace{\sum_{i \in I_{\text{signal}}} \mathbf{g}_i + \sum_{i \in I_{\text{noise}}} \mathbf{g}_i}^{\text{Grouping}}.$$

Next, three different case studies will be presented, where raw and preprocessed traces are compared in terms of the corresponding attacks' performance. Additionally, decisions taken for the application of SSA such as the window length W and the grouping of components will be discussed in more details.

4   Practical Experiments

4.1   Measurement Setup

In order to evaluate the efficiency of SSA in the context of side-channel attacks, two different (software and hardware) platforms have been considered. A LeCroy HRO66Zi WaveRunner 12-bit oscilloscope with maximum 2GS/s sampling rate and a passive probe have been used to measure the voltage drop over a $1\,\Omega$ resistor in the VDD path of both targets. We tested various sampling rates (between $500\,\text{MS/s}$ to $2\,\text{GS/s}$) and consistently found similar experimental results.

Our first target device is an 8-bit Atmel ATMega644p microcontroller clocked at $20\,\text{MHz}$. We considered both an unprotected and a Boolean masked implementation on this platform. The 1st-order masking scheme implemented comes from [34]. Two (input and output) mask bytes m and q are considered for each plaintext byte. First, a masked S-box table such that $\mathsf{S}'(x \oplus k \oplus m) = \mathsf{S}(x \oplus k) \oplus q$ is precomputed in memory for every possible state byte $x \oplus k$. Afterwards, the AddRoundkey and MaskedSubBytes operations are performed. Note that in order to avoid possible 1st-order leakages, the device has been provided with the masked plaintext byte $x \oplus m$. We evaluated this scheme based on 128 000 profiling traces and 2 000 attack traces. In order to limit our storage requirements, only the last rounds of the precomputation and the subsequent operations have been recorded, together with the randomly chosen bytes used for masking.

Our second target device is the crypto FPGA embedded in a SAKURA-G board, namely a Xilinx Spartan-6 LX75 FPGA, driven at a frequency of 3 MHz. We evaluated an implementation of the PRESENT-80 block cipher based on the *Profile 1* in [32] on this platform. It corresponds to a serialized architecture without any countermeasure against side-channel attacks. Because of the higher noise, our evaluations of this second (more noisy) case were based on non-profiled attacks only. We used a total of 100 000 power traces acquired by using randomly generated plaintexts and keeping the secret key value constant for this purpose.

4.2 Unprotected and Masked AES in an Atmel Microcontroller

Because of place constraints, our focus in this section will be on the practical evaluation of SSA against the 1st-order Boolean masking scheme implemented on our Atmel chip. The application to the unprotected implementation essentially follows similar steps (and its results will be mentioned at the end of this section, for comparison purposes). Both profiled and non-profiled attacks are considered in this context. In particular, the SNR of our software implementation was (as expected) reasonably high, which allowed us to obtain accurate templates using the previously mentioned sets of 128 000 profiling traces and 2 000 attack traces. For illustration, an exemplary power trace is shown in Fig. 1(a).

In order to keep the efficiency of SSA high, the window length W has been taken accordingly to Eq. (1) by setting $c = 1.5$. Preprocessing the raw traces with $W = \lfloor \log(5\ 500)^{1.5} \rfloor = 25$ produces the singular spectrum shown in Fig. 1(b). When applied to the problem of signal vs. noise decomposition, such a singular spectrum generally allows for easy detection of interesting components by mere visual inspection. In this particular case, the first component dominates among the others, which usually indicates that it corresponds to low-frequency noise. For the other leading components, and following the heuristic approach used in the context of PCA and LDA, we tested a couple of re-constructions and concluded that most of the useful signal was lying in the second component. As can be seen in Fig. 1(c), the resulting preprocessed trace is very clean.

In order to reach a first intuition regarding the efficiency of SSA, and since it is the criteria used to choose the best grouping, the SNR of the preprocessed traces has been computed. Note that this is possible because the analysis is being conducted in a profiling setting, and thus the knowledge of the masks allows for the computation of the SNR as if the target was an unprotected implementation. Figure 2 shows a comparison of the SNR before and after preprocessing the traces with SSA. As it can be seen, gains are close to a factor of 2.5.

In general, higher SNRs should translate into more successful attacks. This has been practically verified by running bivariate attacks using raw and preprocessed traces. The results of a bivariate MCP-DPA and TA exploiting Gaussian mixtures over the number of attack traces, and the corresponding success rate curves, are depicted in Figs. 3 and 4, respectively. As mentioned earlier, the method applies similarly to unprotected devices (since the SSA transform is applied independently on every trace). For comparison purposes, we therefore add the success rate curves of an attack against the same masked implementation, but with all the

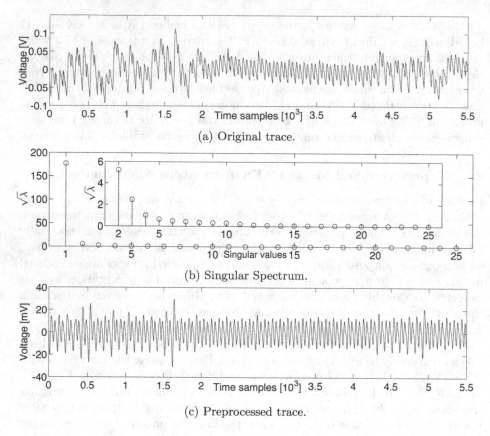

(a) Original trace.

(b) Singular Spectrum.

(c) Preprocessed trace.

Fig. 1. 1st-order masked implementation: power traces & singular spectrum.

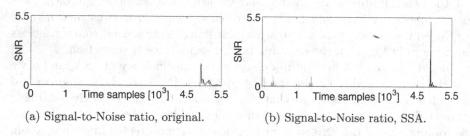

(a) Signal-to-Noise ratio, original.   (b) Signal-to-Noise ratio, SSA.

Fig. 2. 1st-order masked implementation, SNR.

masks set to zero (which is then equivalent to an unprotected implementation), in Appendix A, Fig. 9. Interestingly, one could expect that the factor 2.5 for the SNR gain translates into a gain in the measurement complexity of the attacks of 2.5 for the unprotected implementation, and 2.5^2 for the masked one. Yet, and despite significant, these gains are not that large. But this is easily explained by the too high SNRs of our case study. That is, and as carefully discussed in [13], these theoretical expectations are only verified for low enough SNRs (typically below 1/10).

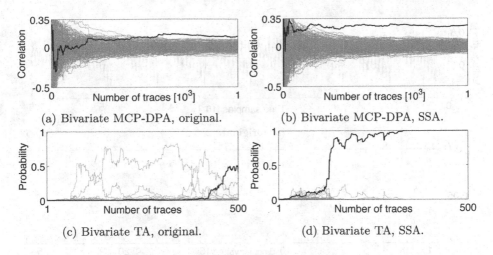

(a) Bivariate MCP-DPA, original.   (b) Bivariate MCP-DPA, SSA.

(c) Bivariate TA, original.   (d) Bivariate TA, SSA.

Fig. 3. 1st-order masked implementation, attack results.

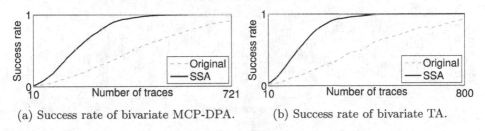

(a) Success rate of bivariate MCP-DPA.   (b) Success rate of bivariate TA.

Fig. 4. 1st-order masked implementation, success rate curves.

So based on these first experiments, we can already conclude that SSA is applicable to masking, without any particular intuition regarding the target implementation. And we move to the next section to investigate the relevant case of a more noisy hardware implementation.

4.3   Unprotected PRESENT in a Xilinx FPGA

In this second case study, we performed a very similar evaluation, with the minor difference that our attacks were all performed in a non-profiled attack setting. As previously mentioned, this choice was motivated by the more noisy leakage traces (so the more challenging profiling). Besides, it turned out that a Hamming distance leakage model anyway provided us with satisfying results.

We again start by illustrating a power trace of this implementation, covering 9 clock cycles which correspond to the computation of 9 S-boxes, in Fig. 5(a). The window length for SSA has been taken using $c = 1.5$ as in the previous case and thus, $W = \lfloor \log(6\,000)^{1.5} \rfloor = 25$. The singular spectrum in Fig. 5(b) is also interpreted as in the previous section. Hence, only the second component is used for signal reconstruction, leading to quite clean traces in Fig. 5(c).

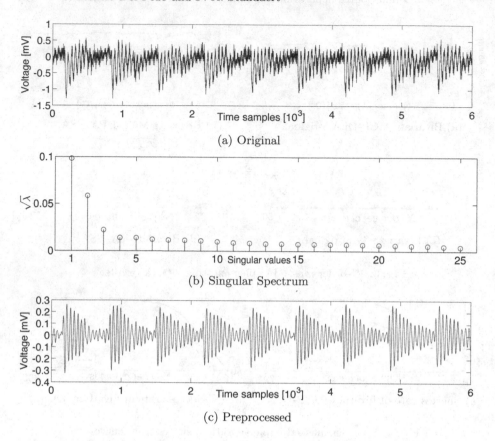

(a) Original

(b) Singular Spectrum

(c) Preprocessed

Fig. 5. Unprotected PRESENT implem., power traces & singular spectrum.

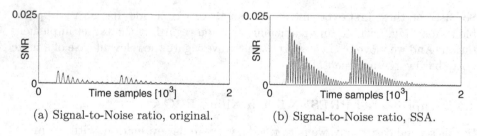

(a) Signal-to-Noise ratio, original.   (b) Signal-to-Noise ratio, SSA.

Fig. 6. Unprotected PRESENT implem., SNR.

Next, Fig. 6 depicts the SNR gains in this hardware context, which are now close to a factor of 4. Since this time the SNR values are indeed in the range of 1/10, it implies that we should observe gains of similar proportions in the attacks. This is indeed exhibited by the results of CPA using the Hamming distance between two consecutive S-box outputs, and MCC-DPA, that are shown in Fig. 7. The connection between the SNR gains and the attacks' measurement complexity is further confirmed by the success rate curves in Fig. 8 where a reduction by a factor close to 4 in the number of attack traces is achieved. So despite being in a non-profiled attack scenario, the reduction of the noise now quite accurately follows what is expected for standard DPA attacks.

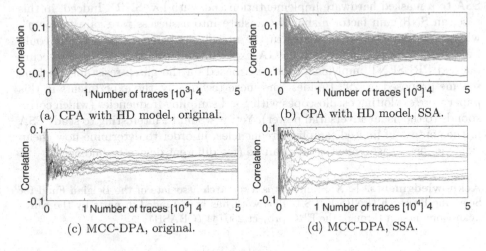

(a) CPA with HD model, original.　　　　(b) CPA with HD model, SSA.

(c) MCC-DPA, original.　　　　　　　　(d) MCC-DPA, SSA.

Fig. 7. Unprotected PRESENT implem., attack results.

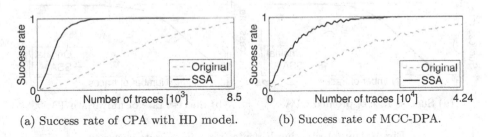

(a) Success rate of CPA with HD model.　　(b) Success rate of MCC-DPA.

Fig. 8. Unprotected PRESENT implem., success rate curves.

5　Conclusions

This work has introduced SSA in the context of side-channel attacks. Our different case studies have shown that, even when the amplitude of the signal is small and the noise level high, SNR gains up to a factor 4 are achieved by applying a signal vs. noise decomposition of individual power traces. Furthermore, it has also been verified that these SNR gains translate into successful attacks with reduced measurement complexity. Unlike some advanced signal processing techniques working in the frequency domain, the described technique is very easy to use. Practitioners just have to set a window length (which can take advantage of a standard rule-of-thumb), and then select their components by mere visual inspection of the singular spectrum (in view of the limited amount of components that usually represent the signal, this step can even take advantage of exhaustive testing). In view of these promising results, a natural open problem is to apply SSA to a masked hardware implementation (i.e. with low SNR). Indeed, in this case, an SNR gain factor g should translate into a success rate gain factor g^d, where d is the number of shares in the masking scheme. Such a result could be obtained by extending our FPGA experiments towards a 1st-order secure masked PRESENT implementation, e.g. based on the glitch-resistant masking scheme proposed in [29]. Besides, and more technically, the experiments in this paper were exploiting oscilloscopes with good sampling frequencies (which corresponds to the usual adversarial power). Yet, it would be interesting to study SSA in the context of limited sampling frequencies, in order to determine how cheap side-channel measurement setups can be (for different device technologies).

Acknowledgments. F.-X. Standaert is a research associate of the Belgian Fund for Scientific Research (FNRS-F.R.S.). This work has been funded in parts by the European Commission through the ERC project 280141 (CRASH).

A   Univariate Attacks

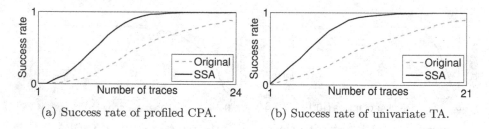

(a) Success rate of profiled CPA.   (b) Success rate of univariate TA.

Fig. 9. Unprotected implementation, success rate curves.

References

1. Archambeau, C., Peeters, E., Standaert, F.-X., Quisquater, J.-J.: Template attacks in principal subspaces. In: Goubin, L., Matsui, M. (eds.) CHES 2006. LNCS, vol. 4249, pp. 1–14. Springer, Heidelberg (2006)
2. Batina, L., Hogenboom, J., van Woudenberg, J.G.J.: Getting more from PCA: first results of using principal component analysis for extensive power analysis. In: Dunkelman, O. (ed.) CT-RSA 2012. LNCS, vol. 7178, pp. 383–397. Springer, Heidelberg (2012)

3. Bozzo, E., Carniel, R., Fasino, D.: Relationship between singular spectrum analysis and fourier analysis: theory and application to the monitoring of volcanic activity. Comput. Math. Appl. **60**(3), 812–820 (2010)
4. Brier, E., Clavier, C., Olivier, F.: Correlation power analysis with a leakage model. In: Joye, M., Quisquater, J.-J. (eds.) CHES 2004. LNCS, vol. 3156, pp. 16–29. Springer, Heidelberg (2004)
5. Broomhead, D.S., King, G.P.: Extracting qualitative dynamics from experimental data. Phys. D Nonlin. Phenom. **20**(2), 217–236 (1986)
6. Broomhead, D.S., King, G.P.: On the qualitative analysis of experimental dynamical systems. Nonlin. Phenom. Chaos **113**, 114 (1986)
7. Bruneau, N., Danger, J.-L., Guilley, S., Heuser, A., Teglia, Y.: Boosting higher-order correlation attacks by dimensionality reduction. In: Chakraborty, R.S., Matyas, V., Schaumont, P. (eds.) SPACE 2014. LNCS, vol. 8804, pp. 183–200. Springer, Heidelberg (2014)
8. Chari, S., Jutla, C.S., Rao, J.R., Rohatgi, P.: Towards sound approaches to counteract power-analysis attacks. In: Wiener, M. (ed.) CRYPTO 1999. LNCS, vol. 1666, p. 398. Springer, Heidelberg (1999)
9. Chari, S., Rao, J.R., Rohatgi, P.: Template attacks. In: Jr., B.S.K., Koç, Ç.K., Paar, C. (eds.) CHES 2002. LNCS, vol. 2523, pp. 13–28. Springer, Heidelberg (2002). http://dx.doi.org/10.1007/3-540-36400-5_3
10. Choudary, O., Kuhn, M.G.: Efficient template attacks. In: Francillon, A., Rohatgi, P. (eds.) CARDIS 2013. LNCS, vol. 8419, pp. 253–270. Springer, Heidelberg (2014)
11. Choudary, O., Kuhn, M.G.: Template attacks on different devices. In: Prouff, E. (ed.) COSADE 2014. LNCS, vol. 8622, pp. 179–198. Springer, Heidelberg (2014)
12. Dehbaoui, A., Lomne, V., Maurine, P., Torres, L., Robert, M.: Enhancing electromagnetic attacks using spectral coherence based cartography. In: Becker, J., Johann, M., Reis, R. (eds.) VLSI-SoC 2009. IFIP AICT, vol. 360, pp. 135–155. Springer, Heidelberg (2011)
13. Duc, A., Faust, S., Standaert, F.-X.: Making masking security proofs concrete. In: Oswald, E., Fischlin, M. (eds.) EUROCRYPT 2015. LNCS, vol. 9056, pp. 401–429. Springer, Heidelberg (2015)
14. Durvaux, F., Standaert, F.-X., Veyrat-Charvillon, N.: How to certify the leakage of a chip? In: Nguyen, P.Q., Oswald, E. (eds.) EUROCRYPT 2014. LNCS, vol. 8441, pp. 459–476. Springer, Heidelberg (2014)
15. Durvaux, F., Standaert, F.-X., Veyrat-Charvillon, N., Mairy, J., Deville, Y.: Efficient selection of time samples for higher-order DPA with projection pursuits. In: IACR Cryptology ePrint Archive 2014, 412 (2014). http://eprint.iacr.org/2014/412
16. Gebotys, C.H., Ho, S., Tiu, C.C.: EM analysis of rijndael and ECC on a wireless java-based PDA. In: Rao and Sunar [36], pp. 250–264. http://dx.doi.org/10.1007/11545262_19
17. Gierlichs, B., Batina, L., Tuyls, P., Preneel, B.: Mutual information analysis. In: Oswald and Rohatgi [31], pp. 426–442. http://dx.doi.org/10.1007/978-3-540-85053-3_27
18. Golub, G.H., Reinsch, C.: Singular value decomposition and least squares solutions. Numer. Math. **14**(5), 403–420 (1970). http://dx.doi.org/10.1007/BF02163027
19. Golyandina, N., Zhigljavsky, A.: Singular Spectrum Analysis for Time Series. Springer, Heidelberg (2013)
20. Herbst, C., Oswald, E., Mangard, S.: An AES smart card implementation resistant to power analysis attacks. In: Zhou, J., Yung, M., Bao, F. (eds.) ACNS 2006. LNCS, vol. 3989, pp. 239–252. Springer, Heidelberg (2006)

21. Hyvärinen, A., Karhunen, J., Oja, E.: Independent Component Analysis, vol. 46. Wiley, Chichester (2004)
22. Lu, Y., Boey, K., O'Neill, M., McCanny, J.V., Satoh, A.: Is the differential frequency-based attack effective against random delay insertion? In: Proceedings of the IEEE Workshop on Signal Processing Systems, SiPS 2009, 7–9 Oct 2009, Tampere, Finland, pp. 051–056, IEEE (2009). http://dx.doi.org/10.1109/SIPS.2009.5336291
23. Mangard, S.: Hardware countermeasures against DPA – a statistical analysis of their effectiveness. In: Okamoto, T. (ed.) CT-RSA 2004. LNCS, vol. 2964, pp. 222–235. Springer, Heidelberg (2004)
24. Mangard, S., Oswald, E., Standaert, F.-X.: One for all - all for one: unifying standard differential power analysis attacks. IET Inf. Secur. 5(2), 100–110 (2011). http://dx.doi.org/10.1049/iet-ifs.2010.0096
25. Meynard, O., Réal, D., Flament, F., Guilley, S., Homma, N., Danger, J.: Enhancement of simple electro-magnetic attacks by pre-characterization in frequency domain and demodulation techniques. In: Design, Automation and Test in Europe, DATE 2011, Grenoble, France, 14–18 March 2011, pp. 1004–1009, IEEE (2011). http://ieeexplore.ieee.org/xpls/abs_all.jsp?arnumber=5763163
26. Meynard, O., Réal, D., Guilley, S., Flament, F., Danger, J.-L., Valette, F.: Characterization of the electromagnetic side channel in frequency domain. In: Lai, X., Yung, M., Lin, D. (eds.) Inscrypt 2010. LNCS, vol. 6584, pp. 471–486. Springer, Heidelberg (2011)
27. Moradi, A., Mischke, O., Eisenbarth, T.: Correlation-enhanced power analysis collision attack. In: Mangard, S., Standaert, F.-X. (eds.) CHES 2010. LNCS, vol. 6225, pp. 125–139. Springer, Heidelberg (2010)
28. Moradi, A., Standaert, F.-X.: Moments-correlating DPA. In: IACR Cryptology ePrint Archive 2014, 409 (2014). http://eprint.iacr.org/2014/409
29. Nikova, S., Rijmen, V., Schläffer, M.: Secure hardware implementation of nonlinear functions in the presence of glitches. J. Cryptol. 24(2), 292–321 (2011). http://dx.doi.org/10.1007/s00145-010-9085-7
30. Oswald, D., Paar, C.: Improving side-channel analysis with optimal linear transforms. In: Mangard, S. (ed.) CARDIS 2012. LNCS, vol. 7771, pp. 219–233. Springer, Heidelberg (2013)
31. Oswald, E., Rohatgi, P. (eds.): CHES 2008. LNCS, vol. 5154. Springer, Heidelberg (2008)
32. Poschmann, A., Moradi, A., Khoo, K., Lim, C., Wang, H., Ling, S.: Side-channel resistant crypto for less than 2, 300 GE. J. Cryptol. 24(2), 322–345 (2011). http://dx.doi.org/10.1007/s00145-010-9086-6
33. de Prony, R.: Essai expérimental et analytique sur les lois de la dilatabilité des fluides élastiques et sur celles de la force expansive de la vapeur de l'eau et la vapeur de l'alkool, à différentes températures. J de lEcole Polytechnique (Paris) 1(2), 24–76 (1795)
34. Prouff, E., Rivain, M.: A generic method for secure SBox implementation. In: Kim, S., Yung, M., Lee, H.-W. (eds.) WISA 2007. LNCS, vol. 4867, pp. 227–244. Springer, Heidelberg (2008)
35. Rahman Khan, M.A., Poskitt, D.S.: Window length selection and signal-noise separation and reconstruction in singular spectrum analysis. Technical report (2011)
36. Rao, J.R., Sunar, B. (eds.): CHES 2005. LNCS, vol. 3659. Springer, Heidelberg (2005)

37. Renauld, M., Standaert, F.-X., Veyrat-Charvillon, N.: Algebraic side-channel attacks on the AES: why time also matters in DPA. In: Clavier, C., Gaj, K. (eds.) CHES 2009. LNCS, vol. 5747, pp. 97–111. Springer, Heidelberg (2009)
38. Salgado, D.R., Alonso, F.J.: Tool wear detection in turning operations using singular spectrum analysis. J. Mater. Proc. Technol. **171**(3), 451–458 (2006)
39. Schindler, W., Lemke, K., Paar, C.: A stochastic model for differential side channel cryptanalysis. In: Rao and Sunar [36], pp. 30–46. http://dx.doi.org/10.1007/11545262_3
40. Standaert, F.-X., Archambeau, C.: Using subspace-based template attacks to compare and combine power and electromagnetic information leakages. In: Oswald and Rohatgi [31], pp. 411–425. http://dx.doi.org/10.1007/978-3-540-85053-3_26
41. Standaert, F.-X., Malkin, T.G., Yung, M.: A unified framework for the analysis of side-channel key recovery attacks. In: Joux, A. (ed.) EURO-CRYPT 2009. LNCS, vol. 5479, pp. 443–461. Springer, Heidelberg (2009). http://dx.doi.org/10.1007/978-3-642-01001-9_26
42. Standaert, F.-X., Veyrat-Charvillon, N., Oswald, E., Gierlichs, B., Medwed, M., Kasper, M., Mangard, S.: The world is not enough: another look on second-order DPA. In: Abe, M. (ed.) ASIACRYPT 2010. LNCS, vol. 6477, pp. 112–129. Springer, Heidelberg (2010). http://dx.doi.org/10.1007/978-3-642-17373-8_7
43. Sugawara, T., Hayashi, Y., Homma, N., Mizuki, T., Aoki, T., Sone, H., Satoh, A.: Spectrum analysis on cryptographic modules to counteract side-channel attacks. EMC **9**, 21–24 (2009)
44. Tiran, S., Ordas, S., Teglia, Y., Agoyan, M., Maurine, P.: A model of the leakage in the frequency domain and its application to CPA and DPA. J. Crypt. Eng. **4**(3), 197–212 (2014). http://dx.doi.org/10.1007/s13389-014-0074-x
45. Vautard, R., Yiou, P., Ghil, M.: Singular-spectrum analysis: a toolkit for short, noisy chaotic signals. Phys. D Nonlin. Phenom. **58**(1), 95–126 (1992)
46. Veyrat-Charvillon, N., Medwed, M., Kerckhof, S., Standaert, F.-X.: Shuffling against side-channel attacks: a comprehensive study with cautionary note. In: Wang, X., Sako, K. (eds.) ASIACRYPT 2012. LNCS, vol. 7658, pp. 740–757. Springer, Heidelberg (2012). http://dx.doi.org/10.1007/978-3-642-34961-4_44

Cryptographic Hardware
Implementations

Highly Efficient $GF(2^8)$ Inversion Circuit Based on Redundant GF Arithmetic and Its Application to AES Design

Rei Ueno[1]($^{\boxtimes}$), Naofumi Homma[1], Yukihiro Sugawara[1], Yasuyuki Nogami[2], and Takafumi Aoki[1]

[1] Graduate School of Information Sciences, Tohoku University,
6-6-05 Aramaki Aza Aoba, Aoba-ku, Sendai-shi 980-8579, Japan
ueno@aoki.ecei.tohoku.ac.jp
[2] Graduate School of Natural Science and Technology, Okayama University,
Tsushima-naka, Kita-ward, Okayama-shi 700-8530, Japan

Abstract. This paper proposes a compact and efficient $GF(2^8)$ inversion circuit design based on a combination of non-redundant and redundant Galois Field (GF) arithmetic. The proposed design utilizes redundant GF representations, called Polynomial Ring Representation (PRR) and Redundantly Represented Basis (RRB), to implement $GF(2^8)$ inversion using a tower field $GF((2^4)^2)$. In addition to the redundant representations, we introduce a specific normal basis that makes it possible to map the former components for the 16th and 17th powers of input onto logic gates in an efficient manner. The latter components for $GF(2^4)$ inversion and $GF(2^4)$ multiplication are then implemented by PRR and RRB, respectively. The flexibility of the redundant representations provides efficient mappings from/to the $GF(2^8)$. This paper also evaluates the efficacy of the proposed circuit by means of gate counts and logic synthesis with a 65 nm CMOS standard cell library and comparisons with conventional circuits, including those with tower fields $GF(((2^2)^2)^2)$. Consequently, we show that the proposed circuit achieves approximately 40 % higher efficiency in terms of area-time product than the conventional best $GF(((2^2)^2)^2)$ circuit excluding isomorphic mappings. We also demonstrate that the proposed circuit achieves the best efficiency (i.e., area-time product) for an AES encryption S-Box circuit including isomorphic mappings.

Keywords: Compact hardware implementation · $GF(2^8)$ inversion · S-Box · AES

1 Introduction

The substitution function, sometimes defined as arithmetic functions over $GF(2^m)$, is one of the most important parts of the Substitution Permutation Network (SPN) and Feistel structures [6]. Inversion functions, in particular, play an essential role in modern ciphers. Many ISO/IEC standard ciphers, such as

© International Association for Cryptologic Research 2015
T. Güneysu and H. Handschuh (Eds.): CHES 2015, LNCS 9293, pp. 63–80, 2015.
DOI: 10.1007/978-3-662-48324-4_4

AES and Camellia, employ an inversion function over $GF(2^8)$ in substitution functions [1,9]. For example, SubBytes of AES consists of an inversion over $GF(2^8)$ (i.e., S-Box) and an affine transformation over $GF(2)$. The hardware performance of such ciphers heavily depends on the inversion circuits used. As a result of the explosive increase in resource-constrained devices in the context of Internet of Things (IoT) applications, there is currently substantial demand for lightweight implementation of inversion functions.

Many approaches to reducing the hardware cost of $GF(2^8)$ inversion circuits have been proposed. Among them, the tower field approach, which calculates a^{-1} $(= a^{254})$ $(a \in GF(2^8))$ using the equivalent tower field, is a promising approach for achieving the compact implementation. This technique converts the original field $GF(2^8)$ into a tower field, such as $GF(((2^2)^2)^2)$ and $GF((2^4)^2)$, in the middle of the inversion. Researchers have previously shown that the tower field approach is efficient because the subfields $GF((2^2)^2)$ and $GF(2^4)$ operations are designed more compactly than the original field operations. Satoh and Morioka [14] were the first to present a compact implementation of the AES S-Box by the tower field $GF(((2^2)^2)^2)$ represented by Polynomial Bases (PB). Canright [3] further reduced the gate count of the AES S-Box by using Normal Bases (NB) and optimizing the isomorphic mappings. Canright's implementation was the smallest for a long time. Nogami et al. [11] recently mixed polynomial and normal bases to achieve the most efficient implementation. They showed that the product of gate count and critical delay for the inversion circuit could be reduced by the Mixed Bases (MB). Some implementations using $GF((2^4)^2)$ have also been proposed by researchers such as Rudra et al. [13] and Jeon et al. [8], who presented PB-based $GF((2^4)^2)$ inversion circuit designs. These results suggest that such field representations have a significant impact on hardware performance.

The above bases (i.e., PB, NB, and MB) represent each element of $GF(2^m)$ using m bits in a non-redundant manner. However, there are two redundant representations, namely, Polynomial Ring Representation (PRR) and Redundantly Represented Basis (RRB), which use n $(> m)$ bits to represent each element of $GF(2^m)$. The modular polynomial of these redundant representations is given by an n-degree reducible polynomial, whereas that of non-redundant representations is given by an m-degree irreducible polynomial. This means that redundant representations provide a wider variety of polynomials that can be selected as a modular polynomial than non-redundant representations. Drolet [5] showed that the use of PRR makes it possible to select a binomial $x^n + 1$ as a modular polynomial, which can lead to the design of small-complexity arithmetic circuits. Wu et al. [16] and Nekado et al. [10] showed that RRB-based designs were useful for designing efficient inversion circuits.

This paper presents a technique in which non-redundant and redundant GF arithmetic are combined to achieve a compact and efficient $GF(2^8)$ inversion circuit design. The key idea underlying the proposed circuit is calculation of the inversion of the tower field $GF((2^4)^2)$ by the NB, PRR, and RRB combination. The former part for the 16th and 17th powers of the input is calculated by an NB with a symmetric property. This is followed by calculation of the latter parts for $GF(2^4)$ inversion and $GF(2^4)$ multiplication by PRR and RRB, respectively. The mapping from NB to PRR/RRB is efficiently implemented by the symmetric property of the NB. The efficacy of the proposed circuit is evaluated by means of gate counts and logic synthesis results using a TSMC 65 nm CMOS standard cell library. The proposed circuit is approximately 19 % higher efficiency (i.e., area-time product) excluding isomorphic mappings than any other conventional circuits, including those with the tower field $GF(((2^2)^2)^2)$. In addition, the flexibility of redundant representations in the proposed circuit enables it to have the best efficiency even including isomorphic mappings from/to $GF(2^8)$. To the best of our knowledge, the proposed circuit is the most efficient tower field arithmetic-based implementation for the AES encryption S-Box.

The remainder of this paper is organized as follows. Section 2 introduces preliminary and related work associated with the design of $GF(2^8)$ inversion circuits. The redundant GF representations introduced in the proposed circuit are also described. Section 3 presents the proposed $GF(2^8)$ inversion circuit. Section 4 evaluates the proposed circuit by comparing the results of gate count and logic synthesis with those from conventional circuits. Section 5 presents the AES S-Box design that incorporates the proposed inversion circuit and its isomorphic mappings. Finally, Sect. 6 presents concluding remarks.

2 Preliminaries and Related Works

2.1 Inversion Circuits by Tower Fields

This section briefly describes previous work on the design of $GF(2^8)$ inversion circuits based on tower field arithmetic. The inverse element of a non zero $a \in GF(2^8)$ is given by $a^{-1} = a^{254}$ because any non zero element of $GF(2^8)$ satisfies $a = a^{256}$. (The inverse element of zero is usually defined to be zero.) The basic idea underlying the tower field approach is reduction of hardware cost by exploiting smaller arithmetic operations over subfield $GF((2^2)^2)$ or $GF(2^4)$ instead of $GF(2^8)$. There is a one-to-one mapping (i.e., an isomorphism) between the elements of $GF(2^8)$ and those of the tower field. This GF inversion over a tower field is efficiently implemented in the Itoh-Tsujii Algorithm (ITA) [7].

Figure 1 illustrates a $GF(2^8)$ inversion circuit presented in [3], where the datapath is divided into upper and lower 4 bits and each component denotes an arithmetic circuit over subfield $GF((2^2)^2)$. Let $a \in GF(((2^2)^2)^2)$ be the input given by $h\alpha^{16} + l\alpha$ in an NB $\{\alpha^{16}, \alpha\}$, where h and l ($\in GF((2^2)^2)$) are respectively the upper and lower 4 bits of a, and α is a root of a second degree irreducible polynomial over $GF((2^2)^2)$ (i.e., a modular polynomial for extending $GF((2^2)^2)$ to $GF(((2^2)^2)^2)$). The inversion of a is calculated in the following three stages: (1) Calculation of the 16th and 17th powers, (2) Subfield inversion, and (3) Final multiplication. Note that the above $GF((2^2)^2)$ operators are replaced with the $GF(2^4)$ operators in the case of the tower field $GF((2^4)^2)$.

The performance of this inversion circuit depends on the tower field and its basis representation. Three of the best known circuit structures are based on the tower field of $GF(((2^2)^2)^2)$. Satoh and Morioka first designed this kind of

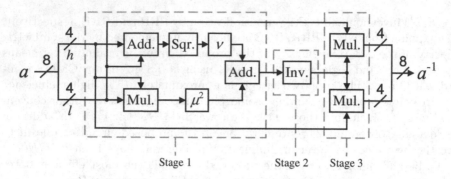

Fig. 1. Inversion circuit over $GF(((2^2)^2)^2)$ in [3].

$GF(((2^2)^2)^2)$ inversion circuit using PB [14]. Canright then designed a more compact circuit based on NB [3]. The hardware cost of inversion and exponentiation operations can be reduced by NB because the squaring operation is performed solely by wiring. Nogami et al. presented the possibility of MB, which employs both polynomial and normal bases for the input and output data, respectively [11]. Their method exhibited improved performance in the product of gate count and critical delay for the $GF(((2^2)^2)^2)$ inversion circuit and the AES S-Box, including isomorphic mappings. In addition to $GF(((2^2)^2)^2)$, it is possible to design efficient inversion circuits using another tower field of $GF((2^4)^2)$. Rudra et al. [13] and Jeon et al. [8] designed $GF((2^4)^2)$ inversion circuits based on PB with smaller critical delay than those of $GF(((2^2)^2)^2)$ inversion circuits.

2.2 Redundant Representations for Galois Fields

Polynomial Ring Representation (PRR). is a redundant representation of GF [5] An extension field $GF(2^m)$ based on a PB has a set of elements (i.e., polynomials) whose degrees are at most $m-1$ (i.e., m bits). Elements of an NB-based $GF(2^m)$ are also represented by m bits. On the other hand, an extension field $GF(2^m)$ based on PRR has a set of polynomials whose degrees are up to $n-1$ (i.e., n bits), where $n > m$ [5]. In other words, whereas a PB- or an NB-based $GF(2^m)$ is defined as an m-dimensional linear space over $GF(2)$, a PRR-based $GF(2^m)$ is defined as an m-dimensional subspace of an n-dimensional linear space. PRR is also equivalent to Cyclic Redundancy Code (CRC), a kind of error-correction code.

Let x and $H(x)$ be an indeterminate element and an irreducible polynomial over $GF(2)$, respectively. Let $G(x)$ be a polynomial of degree $n-m$, which is relatively prime to $H(x)$, and is satisfied with $G(0) \neq 0$. Let $P(x)$ be a polynomial (of degree n) given by the product of $G(x)$ and $H(x)$. A set of polynomials of degrees less than or equal to $n-1$, where each polynomial is divisible by $G(x)$, together with modulo $P(x)$ arithmetic is isomorphic to $GF(2^m)$. Note here that $n = m + \deg G(x)$. The representation of $GF(2^m)$ using such a residue ring

Table 1. Example of correspondence between PB- and PRR-based $GF(2^4)$.

PB where $\beta^4 + \beta^3 + \beta^2 + \beta + 1 = 0$		PRR where $P(x) = x^5 + 1$	
Polynomial	Binary vector form	Polynomial	Binary vector form
0	0000	0	00000
1	0001	$x^4 + x^3 + x^2 + x$	11110
$\beta^2 + \beta$	0110	$x^2 + x$	00110
$\beta^3 + \beta + 1$	1011	$x^4 + x^2$	10100
β^2	0100	$x^4 + x^3 + x + 1$	11011
$\beta^2 + \beta + 1$	0111	$x^4 + x^3$	11000
$\beta^3 + \beta^2 + 1$	1101	$x^4 + x$	10010
$\beta^3 + \beta^2 + \beta + 1$	1111	$x^3 + x^2 + x + 1$	01111
$\beta + 1$	0011	$x + 1$	00011
$\beta^3 + \beta$	1010	$x^3 + x$	01010
β	0010	$x^4 + x^3 + x^2 + 1$	11101
$\beta^3 + \beta^2$	1100	$x^3 + x^2$	01100
$\beta^3 + 1$	1001	$x^3 + 1$	01001
β^3	1000	$x^4 + x^2 + x + 1$	10111
$\beta^3 + \beta^2 + \beta$	1110	$x^4 + 1$	10001
$\beta^2 + 1$	0101	$x^2 + 1$	00101

is called PRR. A PRR can be constructed from any PB-based $GF(2^m)$. (See Appendix for a construction method and corresponding example).

Table 1 shows an example of elements for a PB-based $GF(2^4)$ and a constructed PRR-based $GF(2^4)$, where β and x are the indeterminate elements of PB and PRR, respectively. Note that whereas the PB-based $GF(2^4)$ represents elements by at most third degree polynomials (i.e., 4 bits), the PRR-based $GF(2^4)$ represents elements by up to the fourth degree polynomial (i.e., 5 bits). It is known that the performance of the GF circuit generally improves as the number of terms in the modular polynomial decreases [17]. Here, a binomial $x^n + 1$ is available for the modular polynomial of PPR-based $GF(2^m)$, whereas it is unavailable for GFs based on non-redundant representations. This is because the modular polynomial $P(x)$ is given by a reducible polynomial (i.e., $G(x) \times H(x)$). Thus, the performance of PRR-based GF arithmetic circuits can be better than those of PB- and NB-based arithmetic circuits. For example, we can use $x^{m+1} + 1$ for $P(x)$ if the m-th degree All One Polynomial (AOP) is irreducible according to the following formula over $GF(2)$:

$$x^{m+1} + 1 = (x + 1)(x^m + x^{m-1} + \cdots + 1), \qquad (1)$$

where the polynomial $x^m + x^{m-1} + \cdots + 1$ is called the m-th degree AOP.

The major advantages of using the binomial are as follows: (i) Parallel multiplication can be given as the discrete time Wiener-Hopf equation, and

(ii) Squaring and a part of constant multiplication are performed only by bitwise permutation (i.e., wiring). This suggests that the PRR-based design can be more efficient than conventional designs.

Redundantly Represented Basis (RRB). is another redundant representation of GF [10]. Each element is represented by a root of an m-th degree irreducible polynomial, similarly to PB and NB.

RRB is available when the m-th degree AOP is irreducible. Let β be a root of the AOP. The m elements (i.e., bases) $\beta^{m-1}, \beta^{m-2}, \ldots$, and β^0 are linearly independent and then compose a PB. In contrast, RRB employs a binomial $\beta^{m+1} - 1$ as the modular polynomial, which is satisfied with the following equation:

$$\beta^{m+1} - 1 = (\beta + 1)(\beta^m + \beta^{m-1} + \cdots + 1) = 0. \tag{2}$$

The set $\{\beta^m, \beta^{m-1}, \ldots, \beta^0\}$ is called RRB. Because the degree of the binomial is $m + 1$, each element is represented by a linear combination of $\beta^m, \beta^{m-1}, \ldots$ and β^0. Note that the elements of such an RRB-based $GF(2^m)$ are represented in a non-unique manner because $\beta^m, \beta^{m-1}, \ldots$ and β^0 are linearly dependent[1].

RRB-based $GF(2^m)$ squaring can be performed by bitwise permutation, as is the case with NB. This is because RRB is equivalent to an extended (Type-I) Optimal Normal Basis (ONB). We can derive RRB by adding a base $\{1\} (= \{\beta^0\})$ to ONB. This means that an efficient multiplication method for ONB, called the Cyclic Vector Multiplication Algorithm (CVMA) [12], is also available for RRB. Thus, we can design more compact and efficient multipliers by combining RRB and CVMA. As an example, let us consider a $GF(2^4)$ multiplier based on RRB. Let s and t ($\in GF(2^4)$) be the inputs and u ($\in GF(2^4)$) be the output. Let β be a root of the fourth degree AOP. In RRB, s is given by $s_4\beta^4 + s_3\beta^3 + \cdots + s_0$, where $s_0, s_1, \ldots$, and $s_4 \in GF(2)$. (t and u are also given in the same manner.) The multiplication is represented by

$$u = s \times t = u_4\beta^4 + u_3\beta^3 + u_2\beta^2 + u_1\beta + u_0, \tag{3}$$

where

$$u_0 = (s_1 + s_4)(t_1 + t_4) + (s_2 + s_3)(t_2 + t_3), \tag{4}$$

$$u_1 = (s_0 + s_1)(t_0 + t_1) + (s_2 + s_4)(t_2 + t_4), \tag{5}$$

$$u_2 = (s_0 + s_2)(t_0 + t_2) + (s_3 + s_4)(t_3 + t_4), \tag{6}$$

$$u_3 = (s_0 + s_3)(t_0 + t_3) + (s_1 + s_2)(t_1 + t_2), \tag{7}$$

$$u_4 = (s_0 + s_4)(t_0 + t_4) + (s_1 + s_3)(t_1 + t_3). \tag{8}$$

The critical delay of such an RRB-based multiplier is $T_A + 2T_X$, while those of multipliers based on non-redundant representations are $T_A + 3T_X$ [10]. The gate count of the RRB-based multiplier requires only 10 AND and 25 XOR gates [10], whereas that of a PRR-based multiplier requires 25 AND and 20 XOR gates [5]. Nekado et al. [10] designed a more efficient $GF((2^4)^2)$ inversion circuit based on RRB by utilizing the above advantage.

---

[1] The elements of PRR-based $GF(2^m)$ is represented uniquely—a typical difference between PRR and RRB.

3 Proposed $GF(2^8)$ Inversion Circuit

This section presents our proposed $GF(2^8)$ inversion circuit that takes full advantage of the above redundant GF arithmetic. The important ideas are to employ the tower field $GF((2^4)^2)$ inside the circuit and perform the subfield (i.e., $GF(2^4)$) operations using redundant GF arithmetic. We introduce PRR for the $GF(2^4)$ inversion because we can exploit a modular polynomial, $P(x) = x^5 + 1$, thanks to the irreducible fourth degree AOP. We also introduce RRB for the $GF(2^4)$ multiplication. In addition, we employ an NB for the input in order to exploit the Frobenius mapping feature, which performs the 16th power of input solely by wiring.

In accordance with ITA, our inversion circuit consists of three stages, as shown in Fig. 1. Here, we represent the inputs of Stages 1, 2, and 3 by NB, PRR, and RRB, respectively. In particular, we employ an NB that has a symmetric property, which makes it possible to convert the elements from NB to PRR without increasing the circuit delay.

Figure 2 shows a block diagram of our proposed circuit, where components H, L, and F respectively calculate $H_{i,j}, L_{i,j}$, and $F_{i',j'}$ described in the following. When input a is represented by $h\alpha^{16} + l\alpha$, components NBtoRRB convert h and l from NB to RRB solely by wiring. Note that H and L are shared with Stages 1 and 3. The stages in the proposed circuit are designed as follows:

1. Calculation of the 16th and 17th powers.

Stage 1 performs the 16th and 17th powers of input, where input a is given by NB, and outputs a^{16} and a^{17} are given by RRB and PRR, respectively. Let α be a root of a second degree irreducible polynomial over $GF(2^4)$. The irreducible polynomial is given by $\alpha^2 + \mu\alpha + \nu$, where μ and ν are the constants of $GF(2^4)$. When input a is represented by $a = h\alpha^{16} + l\alpha$ in an NB $\{\alpha^{16}, \alpha\}$, a^{16} and a^{17} are respectively given by

$$a^{16} = l\alpha^{16} + h\alpha, \qquad (9)$$
$$a^{17} = hl\mu^2 + (h + l)^2\nu. \qquad (10)$$

Equation (9) indicates that a^{16} is performed by twisting wires.

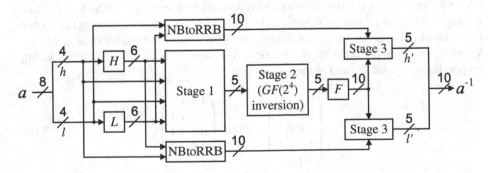

Fig. 2. Proposed inversion circuit.

The isomorphic mapping from NB to RRB does not require any additional gates because the NB (e.g., $\{\beta^4, \beta^3, \beta^2, \beta^1\}$) can be considered as a reduced version of RRB (e.g., $\{\beta^4, \beta^3, \beta^2, \beta^1, \beta^0\}$) with the same root of the 4th degree AOP. Conversely, the isomorphic mapping from NB to PRR requires some gates. However, the symmetric property of the NB used in our circuit provides a mapping that does not increase the circuit delay.

Let us now look at the isomorphic mapping from NB to PRR. Here, an isomorphic mapping is represented by $z' = \Gamma(z)$, where an element z in one GF representation is converted into an element z' in another GF representation. In the binary vector form, the output z' is obtained from the product of a conversion matrix γ and the transposed input (i.e., $z' = \gamma z^T$) when the conversion matrix γ represents the isomorphism Γ. The PRR-based $GF(2^4)$ is given with the modular polynomial $P(x) = x^5 + 1$ ($G(x) = x + 1$ and $H(x) = x^4 + x^3 + x^2 + x + 1$) and the conversion matrix from NB to PRR is as follows:

$$\phi = \begin{pmatrix} 1 & 1 & 1 & 1 \\ 0 & 1 & 1 & 1 \\ 1 & 0 & 1 & 1 \\ 1 & 1 & 0 & 1 \\ 1 & 1 & 1 & 0 \end{pmatrix}, \tag{11}$$

where the least significant bits are in the upper left corner. (See Appendix for an explanation of how to obtain the matrix.) Let d ($= d_4 x^4 + d_3 x^3 + \cdots + d_0$) be the output of Stage 1 (i.e., the 17th power of input in PRR), where $d_0, d_1, \ldots,$ and d_4 are the elements of $GF(2)$. The output is provided by applying the isomorphism Φ from NB to PRR to a^{17} (i.e., the product of the conversion matrix ϕ and the transposed vector form of a^{17}). However, the multiplication of ϕ and the output of Eq. (10) requires an additional circuit with $2T_X$ delay if the multiplication is performed explicitly. To avoid such additional circuit, we derive another output equation from Eq. (10) as follows:

$$\begin{aligned} d &= \Phi(hl\mu^2 + (h+l)^2 \nu) \\ &= \Phi(\mu^2(hl)) + \Phi(\nu((h+l)^2)) \\ &= \Phi'(hl) + \Phi''((h+l)^2), \end{aligned} \tag{12}$$

where Φ' and Φ'' are the linear functions obtained by merging Φ with the constant multiplications of μ^2 and ν, respectively. Note that constant multiplications over GF can also be given as linear functions represented by conversion matrices. When $\mu = \beta^4 + \beta$ and $\nu = \beta$, the resulting matrices ϕ' and ϕ'' representing respectively Φ' and Φ'' are given as

$$\phi' = \begin{pmatrix} 0 & 1 & 1 & 0 \\ 0 & 0 & 1 & 1 \\ 0 & 0 & 0 & 1 \\ 1 & 0 & 0 & 0 \\ 1 & 1 & 0 & 0 \end{pmatrix}, \quad \phi'' = \begin{pmatrix} 1 & 1 & 1 & 0 \\ 1 & 1 & 1 & 1 \\ 0 & 1 & 1 & 1 \\ 1 & 0 & 1 & 1 \\ 1 & 1 & 0 & 1 \end{pmatrix}, \tag{13}$$

where the least significant bits are in the upper left corners. The resulting elements of PRR are shown in Table 1.

To design the circuit defined by Eq. (12), we exploit an NB with the symmetric property that h and l are given by $h = h_4\beta^4 + h_3\beta^3 + h_2\beta^2 + h_1\beta$ and $l = l_4\beta^4 + l_3\beta^3 + l_2\beta^2 + l_1\beta$ with a common NB $\{\beta^4, \beta^3, \beta^2, \beta^1\}$, where $h_1, \ldots, h_4$ and $l_1, \ldots, l_4$ are the elements of $GF(2)$ [2]. As a result, the outputs $d_0, d_1, \ldots,$ and d_4 are given by

$$d_0 = (h_1l_2 + h_2l_1 + h_3l_4 + h_4l_3 + h_1l_1 + h_4l_4)$$
$$+(h_1 + l_1 + h_3 + l_3 + h_4 + l_4), \tag{14}$$

$$d_1 = (h_1l_2 + h_2l_1 + h_1l_3 + h_3l_1 + h_2l_2 + h_4l_4)$$
$$+(h_1 + l_1 + h_2 + l_2 + h_3 + l_3 + h_4 + l_4), \tag{15}$$

$$d_2 = (h_1l_3 + h_3l_1 + h_1l_4 + h_4l_1 + h_2l_3 + h_3l_2 + h_2l_2)$$
$$+(h_1 + l_1 + h_2 + l_2 + h_4 + l_4), \tag{16}$$

$$d_3 = (h_1l_4 + h_4l_1 + h_2l_3 + h_3l_2 + h_2l_4 + h_4l_2 + h_3l_3)$$
$$+(h_2 + l_2 + h_3 + l_3 + h_4 + l_4), \tag{17}$$

$$d_4 = (h_2l_4 + h_4l_2 + h_3l_4 + h_4l_3 + h_1l_1 + h_3l_3)$$
$$+(h_1 + l_1 + h_2 + l_2 + h_3 + l_3), \tag{18}$$

respectively. Here, the symmetric property enable us to factor Eqs. (14)–(18) as follows:

$$d_0 = H_{1,2} \vee L_{1,2} + H_{3,4} \vee L_{3,4} + h_2 \vee l_2 + h_3l_3, \tag{19}$$

$$d_1 = H_{1,2} \vee L_{1,2} + H_{1,3}L_{1,3} + h_3 \vee l_3 + h_4 \vee l_4, \tag{20}$$

$$d_2 = H_{1,3} \vee L_{1,3} + H_{1,4}L_{1,4} + H_{2,3} \vee L_{2,3} + h_4 \vee l_4, \tag{21}$$

$$d_3 = H_{1,4} \vee L_{1,4} + H_{2,3} \vee L_{2,3} + H_{2,4}L_{2,4} + h_1 \vee l_1, \tag{22}$$

$$d_4 = H_{2,4} \vee L_{2,4} + H_{3,4} \vee L_{3,4} + h_1 \vee l_1 + h_2l_2, \tag{23}$$

where $H_{i,j} = h_i + h_j$, $L_{i,j} = l_i + l_j$ $(1 \leq i < j \leq 4)$, and $\vee$ denotes the OR operator (i.e., $a \vee b = a + b + ab$). The component denoted by Stage 1 in Fig. 2 performs the computations corresponding to Eqs. (19)–(23). Therefore, the proposed Stage 1 is performed with only $T_A + 3T_X$ (or $T_O + 3T_X$) delay, whereas conventional $GF(((2^2)^2)^2)$ inversion implementations are performed with at least $6T_X$ delay, where T_A, T_O, and T_X denote the delays of the AND, OR, and XOR gates, respectively.

2. Subfield Inversion.

Stage 2 performs the inversion over the subfield $GF(2^4)$, where the input and output are given by PRR and RRB, respectively. We first describe the architecture of the PRR-based $GF(2^4)$ inversion, and then show the isomorphic mapping from PRR to RRB below.

---

[2] The notation of bases in the NB is frequently given by $(\beta^{2^3}, \beta^{2^2}, \beta^{2^1}, \beta^{2^0}) = (\beta^3, \beta^4, \beta^2, \beta^1)$. In this paper, we employ the notation $(\beta^4, \beta^3, \beta^2, \beta^1)$ to simplify the correspondence between the NB and PRR/RRB.

The inversion over $GF(2^4)$ is performed by the 14th power of the input. The input (i.e., the output of Stage 1) d $(= d_4x^4 + d_3x^3 + \cdots + d_0)$ is given as an element of the PRR-based $GF(2^4)$. The input is satisfied with the condition (called the linear recurrence relation) $d_0 + d_1 + d_2 + d_3 + d_4 = 0$ [3] because it is equivalent to the codeword of a CRC generated by $G(x)$ $(= x + 1)$, which makes it possible to perform the exponentiation by bitwise operations over the PRR-based $GF(2^4)$ in an efficient manner.

Let e $(= e_4x^4 + e_3x^3 + \cdots + e_0)$ be the inverse element of d in PRR, where $e_0, e_1, \ldots$, and e_4 are the elements of $GF(2)$. Using the linear recurrence relation, we can derive $e_0, e_1, \ldots$, and e_4 as follows:

$$e_0 = (d_1 \vee d_4)(d_2 \vee d_3), \tag{24}$$
$$e_1 = ((d_4 + 1)(d_1 + d_2)) \vee (d_0d_4(d_2 \vee d_3)), \tag{25}$$
$$e_2 = ((d_3 + 1)(d_2 + d_4)) \vee (d_0d_3(d_1 \vee d_4)), \tag{26}$$
$$e_3 = ((d_2 + 1)(d_1 + d_3)) \vee (d_0d_2(d_1 \vee d_4)), \tag{27}$$
$$e_4 = ((d_1 + 1)(d_3 + d_4)) \vee (d_0d_1(d_2 \vee d_3)). \tag{28}$$

According to Eqs. (24)–(28), the proposed Stage 2 requires $T_A + T_O + T_X$ delay, whereas the conventional structures [3,10,11,14] require at least $T_A + 3T_X$. Note that when the multiplicative unit element $E(x)$ $(= x^4 + x^3 + x^2 + x)$ is given as the input, the output becomes not $E(x)$ but 1. However, the output is acceptable in Stage 3 (i.e., $GF(2^4)$ multiplication) because both $E(x)$ and 1 are the idempotent elements in the residue ring modulo $P(x)$.

Let us now look at the PRR-to-RRB mapping. To provide it uniquely, we focus on the definition of PRR in [5], in which the mapping Ψ from PRR defined by x to another representation defined by β is isomorphism. Let f $(= f_4\beta^4 + f_3\beta^3 + \cdots + f_0)$ be the output of Stage 2 in RRB, where $f_0, f_1, \ldots$, and f_4 are the elements of $GF(2)$. The output can be given by

$$f = \Psi(e) = e_4\beta^4 + e_3\beta^3 + e_2\beta^2 + e_1\beta + e_0. \tag{29}$$

This means that the PRR-to-RRB mapping is performed without any additional circuit, assuming that $f_0 = e_0, \ldots$, and $f_4 = e_4$. As a result, the PRR-based design provides inversion and isomorphic mapping with fewer logic gates.

3. Final multiplication.

Stage 3 generates the final output using two $GF(2^4)$ multiplication operations, where both the inputs and output are given by RRB. As stated above, the RRB-based $GF(2^4)$ multiplier is known to be one of the most efficient multipliers [10].

Let h' $(= h'_4\beta^4 + h'_3\beta^3 + \cdots + h'_0)$ be the upper 5 bits of the final output a^{-1} in RRB, where $h'_0, h'_1, \ldots$, and h'_4 are the elements of $GF(2)$. Multiplying f and

---

[3] The linear recurrence relation is used for error detection in CRC. A polynomial is a codeword of a CRC iff the relation is satisfied.

l, we can calculate elements $h'_0, h'_1, \ldots$, and h'_4 as follows:

$$h'_0 = L_{1,4}F_{1,4} + L_{2,3}F_{2,3}, \tag{30}$$
$$h'_1 = l_1 F_{0,1} + L_{2,4}F_{2,4}, \tag{31}$$
$$h'_2 = l_2 F_{0,2} + L_{3,4}F_{3,4}, \tag{32}$$
$$h'_3 = l_3 F_{0,3} + L_{1,2}F_{1,2}, \tag{33}$$
$$h'_4 = l_4 F_{0,4} + L_{1,3}F_{1,3}, \tag{34}$$

where $F_{i',j'}$ denotes $f_{i'} + f_{j'}$ $(0 \leq i' < j' \leq 4)$. The lower five bits of a^{-1} (denoted by l') are also obtained in the same manner as in Eqs. (30)–(34). The component denoted by Stage 3 in Fig. 2 performs the computations corresponding to Eqs. (30)–(34). Note here that the calculations for $F_{i',j'}$ can be shared within Stage 3. As a result, the number of circuit components for the two multipliers in Stage 3 is reduced.

4 Performance Evaluation

Table 2 shows the circuit delay and gate count of the proposed inversion circuit, where $(g_0, g_1, g_2, g_3, g_4, g_5, g_6)$ in the Gate count column respectively indicate the number of AND, OR, XOR, XNOR, NOT, NAND and NOR gates, and Rep. indicates the GF representation(s) used in the circuit. For comparison, the table also shows those of the conventional inversion circuits. The critical delay paths of all the conventional ones were given by reference to [10]. On the other hand, the gate counts of the conventional ones were individually given because there was no single reference data covering all the conventional ones. The gate count of [3] was given from the original paper [3], that of [14] was given from a public source code by the authors [15], and those of [8], [10,13] were given by reference to [10]. The gate count of [11] was given from a straightforward structure designed by us according to [11] because there was no public data and source code.

The critical paths of Stages 1, 2, and 3 in the proposed circuit require $T_A + 3T_X$, $T_A + T_O + T_X$, and $T_A + 2T_X$ delay, respectively. As a result, the total delay of our inversion circuit is $3T_A + T_O + 6T_X$, which compared with the other inversion circuits, is the smallest. The gate count in this work is smaller or comparable to the conventional ones. In total, our circuit is more efficient than any other circuits because fewer XOR and XNOR gates are required compared to the other implementations.

To conduct a detailed evaluation, some of the above $GF(2^8)$ inversion circuits were synthesized using Synopsys Design Compiler with a TSMC 65 nm CMOS standard cell library. Table 3 shows the synthesis results, where Area indicates the circuit area estimated based on a two-way NAND equivalent gate size (i.e., gate equivalents (GE)), Time indicates the circuit delay under the worst-case conditions, and Area-Time product indicate the product of Area and Time. For the best performance comparison, an area optimization option (which maximizes the effort of minimizing the number of gates without flattening the description) was applied. Note that the results were consistent even when the following speed

Table 2. Critical delay and gate count of inversion circuits over tower fields.

	Field	Rep.	Gate count $(g_0, g_1, g_2, g_3, g_4, g_5, g_6)$	Critical delay path
Satoh et al. [14]	$GF(((2^2)^2)^2)$	PB	(30, 0, 96,0, 0, 6, 0)	$4T_A + 17T_X$
Canright [3]	$GF(((2^2)^2)^2)$	NB	(0, 0, 56, 0, 0, 34, 6)	$4T_A + 15T_X$
Nogami et al. [11]	$GF(((2^2)^2)^2)$	MB	(36, 0, 95, 0, 0, 0, 0)	$4T_A + 14T_X$
Rudra et al. [13]	$GF((2^4)^2)$	PB	(60, 0, 72, 0, 0, 0, 0)	$4T_A + 10T_X$
Jeon et al. [8]	$GF((2^4)^2)$	PB	(58, 2, 67, 0, 0, 0, 0)	$4T_A + 10T_X$
Nekado et al. [10]	$GF((2^4)^2)$	NB, RRB	(42, 0, 68, 2, 0, 0, 0)	$4T_A + 7T_X$
This work	$GF((2^4)^2)$	NB, PRR, RRB	(38, 16, 51, 0, 4, 0, 0)	$3T_A + T_O + 6T_X$

Table 3. Performance evaluation of inversion circuits over tower fields.

	Area [GE]	Time [ns]	Power [uW]	Area-time product
Satoh et al. [14]	280.67	3.02	95.27	847.62
Canright [3]	237.33	2.92	80.76	693.00
Nogami et al. [11]	388.67	3.67	148.88	1,426.42
Nekado et al. [10]	272.67	1.89	99.63	515.35
This work	229.67	1.81	74.14	415.70

optimization (which searches for the minimum timing without increasing the area obtained from the prior area optimization) options was applied. The conventional inversion circuits were also synthesized using the same option. The source codes of [3,14] were obtained from authors' websites [4,15], respectively. (Like them, we also applied gate-reduction techniques to our inversion circuit.) The source codes of [10,11] were described by us according to the structures given in the papers. Consequently, we confirmed that the proposed circuit achieves the smallest area of 229.67 GE and the smallest circuit delay of 1.81 ns. The area-time product of the proposed circuit is 19.3 % smaller than that of the conventional best circuit.

5   Application to AES S-Box

The proposed inversion circuit was efficiently applied to the AES S-Box design. The AES S-Box consists of a $GF(2^8)$ inversion and an affine transformation over $GF(2)$. Here, the $GF(2^8)$ is represented in a PB and the $GF(2^8)$ inversion is performed with an irreducible polynomial $x^8 + x^4 + x^3 + x + 1$. Therefore, an isomorphic mapping between $GF(2^8)$ and $GF((2^4)^2)$ is required if the inversion over $GF((2^4)^2)$ is applied. Figure 3 shows an overview of the AES S-Box with tower field arithmetic. The input (in the PB-based $GF(2^8)$) is initially mapped to the tower field by applying an isomorphic mapping Δ_f. After the inversion

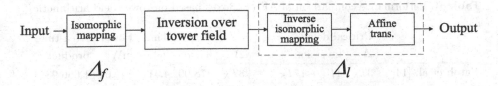

Fig. 3. Overview of AES S-Box based on tower field arithmetic.

operation over the tower field, the inverse mapping and affine transformation are finally performed in series. Here, we can merge the inverse mapping into the affine transformation because both of them are represented in the form of constant matrices over $GF(2)$. The merged mapping is denoted by Δ_l. This merging reduces the delay and gate counts.

The matrices for the mappings Δ_f and Δ_l have an impact on the performance of S-Box. When tower field $GF((2^4)^2)$ is used, the matrices are defined by the bases of $GF(2^4)$ and the modular polynomials for the extension of $GF(2^4)$ to $GF((2^4)^2)$. The efficiency of the two matrices for mappings Δ_f and Δ_l is determined by the largest Hamming weight in the columns. For example, if the largest Hamming weight in the columns is four, the critical path becomes $2T_X$ delay. If it is five, the critical path becomes $3T_X$ delay. Therefore, the matrices should be selected with a view to minimizing the largest Hamming weight in the columns.

In our design, we found efficient conversion matrices δ_f and δ_l respectively for Δ_f and Δ_l when the $GF(2^4)$ elements of Stage 1 are represented in an NB $\{\beta^4, \beta^3, \beta^2, \beta^1\}$ and the modular polynomial for the extension is given by $\alpha^2 + (\beta^4 + \beta)\alpha + \beta$. As an example, the matrices δ_f and δ_l are given by

$$
\delta_f = \begin{pmatrix} 0&1&0&1&1&1&0&0 \\ 1&0&1&0&0&0&1&1 \\ 1&0&0&1&0&0&0&1 \\ 0&0&0&0&0&1&0&0 \\ 0&1&1&0&1&1&0&0 \\ 1&0&1&0&1&0&0&0 \\ 1&1&1&0&0&0&0&1 \\ 0&0&1&1&0&0&0&1 \end{pmatrix}, \delta_l = \begin{pmatrix} 1&1&1&1&0&1&0&0&1&0 \\ 0&0&1&1&0&1&1&1&0&1 \\ 1&1&1&1&0&0&1&0&1&0 \\ 1&0&0&0&1&1&1&1&0&1 \\ 1&1&0&1&1&1&0&0&0&1 \\ 1&0&0&0&1&1&0&1&1&1 \\ 0&0&1&0&1&0&0&1&0&1 \\ 1&0&1&0&0&1&1&0&1&1 \end{pmatrix}, \tag{35}
$$

where the least significant bits are in the upper left corners. Here, the largest Hamming weight in the columns of δ_f is at most four while that of δ_l is at most six. This means that the former and latter mappings are implemented with delays of $2T_X$ and $3T_X$, respectively. Note that the matrix δ_l does not include the constant addition of affine transformation in S-Box. The addition does not lead to the increase of delay for our S-Box since the largest Hamming weight of in the columns is at most six.

Table 4 shows the critical delay of the proposed AES S-Box compared with the conventional implementations. Our circuit achieves $3T_A + T_O + 11T_X$ delay, which is smaller than the conventional S-Boxes with tower field arithmetic. The table also shows the synthesis results (area, delay time, and power) obtained

Table 4. Performance comparison of AES S-Boxes based on tower field arithmetic.

	Critical delay			Area	Time	Power	Area-time
	Δ_f	Inversion	Δ_l	[GE]	[ns]	[uW]	product
Satoh et al. [14]	$3T_X$	$4T_A + 17T_X$	$3T_X$	378.00	4.41	151.61	1,666.98
Canright [3]	$3T_X$	$4T_A + 15T_X$	$3T_X$	315.67	4.30	126.55	1,357.38
Nogami et al. [11]	$2T_X$	$4T_A + 14T_X$	$2T_X$	522.67	4.78	221.79	2,498.36
Rudra et al. [13]	$3T_X$	$4T_A + 10T_X$	$3T_X$	–	–	–	–
Jeon et al. [8]	$3T_X$	$4T_A + 10T_X$	$3T_X$	–	–	–	–
Nekado et al. [10]	$2T_X$	$4T_A + 7T_X$	$3T_X$	386.00	3.29	151.01	1,269.94
This work	$2T_X$	$3T_A + T_O + 6T_X$	$3T_X$	332.00	3.17	132.58	1,052.44

from the same tool and synthesis options as the above[4]. The source codes were given from the same methods as Table 3. Note here that Canright's design in [3] supports both encryption and decryption, and we have slightly changed it to support only encryption to allow a fair comparison to our design. As a result, the area-time product of our AES S-Box is more than 22.5 % better than Canright's S-Box, which had been the most efficient for a long time, and more than 17.1 % better than Nekado's latest S-Box.

A further evaluation with full AES implementations is being left for the future study. For example, our current design does not directly lead to the most efficient one if we should support both encryption and decryption. For such evaluation, another optimization (e.g. considering the overall architecture and conversion matrices specified for both encryption and decryption) should be discussed. On the other hand, the practical impact of the proposed method would be even more visible in that case.

Another discussion point when applying the proposed method to cryptographic cores is the well-known side channel issue. In particular, the resource sharing of Stages 1 and 3 would cause glitches during the computation. To apply our method to pipelining-based countermeasures for reducing glitch problems, we need to decompose shared resources, which results in the increase of 12 XOR gates in total. Note however that such increase would also happen in other works (e.g., [3,10]) using the similar optimization. In contrast, our method is more suitable for multiplexing-based countermeasures, such as WDDL, due to the high efficiency. A further and comprehensive study on the side-channel security is definitely one of the important future topics for our method.

---

[4] According to [2], a logic minimization method can further reduce the total gates of [3]. However, the same minimization can also be applied to other circuits including ours. Therefore, we did not apply the minimization in this paper.

6   Conclusion

This paper proposed a new $GF(2^8)$ inversion circuit that utilizes a combination of non-redundant and redundant GF arithmetic. The proposed circuit, which is based on tower field arithmetic, was designed by utilizing PRR and RRB for the subfield inversion and multiplication, respectively. The flexibility of such redundant representations can provide efficient isomorphic mappings from/to $GF(2^8)$. The efficiency of our proposed inversion circuit and its AES encryption S-Box was evaluated by gate count and logic synthesis results with a 65 nm CMOS standard cell library. As a result, we confirmed that the proposed inversion circuit is approximately 38 % faster than the conventional best $GF(((2^2)^2)^2)$ circuit without any area overhead. Further, even including isomorphic mappings to AES GF, the proposed circuit exhibited the best efficiency compared with existing inversion circuits based on tower field arithmetic.

Redundant GF representations, such as PRR and RRB, provide high flexibility for GF arithmetic circuit design. It is definitely possible to obtain efficient circuit structures using them because the search space of isomorphic mappings increases as a result of their flexibility. In addition, a combination of non-redundant and redundant GF representations has the potential to further improve GF circuits, as shown in this paper. On the other hand, our AES S-Box design is optimized only for the encryption. If an AES design should support both encryption and decryption, our current design does not directly lead to the most efficient one. In that case, another specific optimization for the overall architecture and conversion matrices for both encryption and decryption should be considered. An isomorphic mapping optimization method for other applications still remains as future work. Further research is being conducted to expand the application of our design methodology. Other block ciphers and error-correction circuits, including GF inversion circuits, are possible applications. It is also worth considering efficient implementation of countermeasures against side-channel attacks by redundant GF arithmetic.

Acknowledgments. We are deeply grateful to Dr. Amir Moradi for his insightful and valuable advices. This work has been supported by JSPS KAKENHI Grant No. 25240006. We also appreciate their support.

Appendix: Construction Method of PRR and Its Example

Construction of an isomorphic mapping from a PB-based $GF(2^m)$ to a PRR-based $GF(2^m)$ is accomplished as follows. We first define the multiplicative unit element of PRR for the construction. Let $U(x)$ and $V(x)$ be polynomials that satisfy

$$U(x)G(x) + V(x)H(x) = 1. \tag{36}$$

$H(x)$ is an irreducible polynomial of the PB-based $GF(2^m)$ and $G(x)$ is a polynomial of degree $n - m$, which is relatively prime to $H(x)$. Such $U(x)$ and $V(x)$ are always found since $G(x)$ and $H(x)$ are relatively prime. We can easily derive them using the extended Euclidean algorithm. The multiplicative unit element $E(x)$, which is an idempotent of the PRR-based $GF(2^m)$, is given by $U(x)G(x)$. This is explained by multiplying Eq. (36) and $U(x)G(x)$ as follows:

$$\{U(x)G(x)\}^2 + U(x)G(x)V(x)H(x) = U(x)G(x). \tag{37}$$

Therefore,

$$\{E(x)\}^2 \equiv E(x) \bmod P(x), \tag{38}$$

where $P(x) = G(x)H(x)$. Note that $V(x)H(x)$ is not included in the PRR-based $GF(2^m)$ because $V(x)H(x)$ is indivisible by $G(x)$.

With the above relations, we obtain the relational expression between the indeterminate elements of PB and PRR. Let β be a root of $H(x)$ (i.e., $H(\beta) = 0$). The multiplication of Eq. (36) and x is given as follows:

$$xU(x)G(x) + xV(x)H(x) = x. \tag{39}$$

Assuming that we substitute β for x in Eq. (39), both LHS and RHS become β. This means that β is mapped to/from $x \times E(x)$. We also obtain the corresponding relational expressions between β^i and $x^i \times E(x)$ for an integer i ($0 \leq i \leq m - 1$). As a result, we can construct the isomorphic mapping using the relational expressions. Let $C_i(x)$ be an element of the PRR-based $GF(2^m)$ corresponding to β^i. $C_i(x)$ is then given by

$$C_i(x) \equiv x^i \times E(x) \bmod P(x). \tag{40}$$

Note that $C_0(x), C_1(x), \ldots,$ and $C_{m-1}(x)$ are linearly independent in the polynomial ring over $GF(2)$ because $\{\beta^{m-1}, \beta^{m-2}, \ldots, \beta^0\}$ composes a PB of $GF(2^m)$. Therefore, the conversion matrix $\phi_{PB \to PRR}$ for the isomorphic mapping from PB- to PRR-based $GF(2^m)$ is given by

$$\phi_{PB \to PRR} = \left(\mathbf{c}_0^T \ \mathbf{c}_1^T \ \ldots \ \mathbf{c}_{m-1}^T \right), \tag{41}$$

where $\mathbf{c}_i^T$ denotes the transposed binary vector form of $C_i(x)$. The least significant bits are in the upper left corner.

As an example of PRR, we present the construction of a PRR-based $GF(2^4)$. Here, the modular polynomial $P(x)$ is given by $x^5 + 1$ and its factors $G(x)$ and $H(x)$ are given by

$$G(x) = x + 1, \tag{42}$$
$$H(x) = x^4 + x^3 + x^2 + x + 1. \tag{43}$$

We first compute the multiplicative unit element $E(x)$, which is derived from $G(x)$ and $H(x)$ by using the extended Euclidean algorithm as follows:

$$(x^3 + x) \times G(x) + 1 \times H(x) = 1. \tag{44}$$

Therefore, $E(x) = (x^3 + x) \times G(x) = x^4 + x^3 + x^2 + x$. $C_0(x), C_1(x), C_2(x)$ and $C_3(x)$ are then obtained as follows:

$$C_0(x) = x^4 + x^3 + x^2 + x, \tag{45}$$
$$C_1(x) = x^4 + x^3 + x^2 + 1, \tag{46}$$
$$C_2(x) = x^4 + x^3 + x + 1, \tag{47}$$
$$C_3(x) = x^4 + x^2 + x + 1, \tag{48}$$

which correspond to $\beta^0, \beta^1, \beta^2$ and β^3, respectively. Thus, a conversion matrix $\phi_{PB \to PRR}$ from the PB-based $GF(2^4)$ with $H(\beta)$ to a PRR-based $GF(2^4)$ with $P(x)$ is given by

$$\phi_{PB \to PRR} = \begin{pmatrix} 0 & 1 & 1 & 1 \\ 1 & 0 & 1 & 1 \\ 1 & 1 & 0 & 1 \\ 1 & 1 & 1 & 0 \\ 1 & 1 & 1 & 1 \end{pmatrix}, \tag{49}$$

where the least significant bits are in the upper left corner. The conversion matrix ϕ_{NB} from the NB-based $GF(2^4)$ with $H(\beta)$ to the PRR-based $GF(2^4)$ is also constructed by using the NB $\{\beta^4, \beta^3, \beta^2, \beta^1\}$. $\phi_{NB \to PRR}$ is given by

$$\phi_{NB \to PRR} = \begin{pmatrix} 1 & 1 & 1 & 1 \\ 0 & 1 & 1 & 1 \\ 1 & 0 & 1 & 1 \\ 1 & 1 & 0 & 1 \\ 1 & 1 & 1 & 0 \end{pmatrix}, \tag{50}$$

where the least significant bits are in the upper left corner.

References

1. Aoki, K., Ichikawa, T., Kanda, M., Matsui, M., Moriai, S., Nakajima, J., Tokita, T.: Specification of *Camallia* – an 128-bit Block Cipher. http://info.isl.ntt.co.jp/crypt/eng/camellia/dl/01espec.pdf, Sep 2001
2. Boyer, J., Matthews, M., Peralta, T.: Logic minimization techniques with applications to cryptology. J. Crypt. **26**(2), 280–312 (2013)
3. Canright, D.: A very compact S-Box for AES. In: Rao, J.R., Sunar, B. (eds.) CHES 2005. LNCS, vol. 3659, pp. 441–455. Springer, Heidelberg (2005)
4. Canright, D.: http://faculty.nps.edu/drcanrig/, May 2015
5. Drolet, G.: A new representation of elements of finite fields $GF(2^m)$ yielding small complexity arithmetic circuits. IEEE Trans. Comput. **47**(9), 938–946 (1997)
6. Hirotomo, M., Mohri, M., Morii, M.: Generalized polynomial ring representation over $GF(2^m)$ and its application. IEICE denshijouhoutsushingakkaironbunshi A. **J89-A**(10), 790–800 (2006). (Japanese edition)
7. Itoh, T., Tsujii, S.: A fast algorithm for computing multiplicative inverses in. $GF(2^m)$ using normal bases. Inf. Comput. **78**, 171–177 (1988)

8. Jeon, Y., Kim, Y., Lee, D.: A compact memory-free architecture for the AES algorithm using resource sharing methods. J. Circ. Syst. Comput. **19**(5), 1109–1130 (2010)

9. National Institute of Standards and Technology (NIST): Advanced Encryption Standard (AES) FIPS Publication 197. http://csrc.nist.gov/publications/fips/fips197/fips-197.pdf, Nov 2001

10. Nekado, K., Nogami, Y., Iokibe, K.: Very short critical path implementation of AES with direct logic gates. In: Hanaoka, G., Yamauchi, T. (eds.) IWSEC 2012. LNCS, vol. 7631, pp. 51–68. Springer, Heidelberg (2012)

11. Nogami, Y., Nekado, K., Toyota, T., Hongo, N., Morikawa, Y.: Mixed bases for efficient inversion in $\mathbb{F}_{((2^2)^2)^2}$ and conversion matrices of subbytes of AES. In: Mangard, S., Standaert, F.-X. (eds.) CHES 2010. LNCS, vol. 6225, pp. 234–247. Springer, Heidelberg (2010)

12. Nogami, Y., Saito, A., Morikawa, Y.: Finite extension field with modulus of all-one polynomial field and representation of its elements of for fast arithmetnic operations. IEICE Trans. Fundam. Electron. Commun. Comput. Sci. **E86–A**(9), 2376–2387 (2003)

13. Rudra, A., Dubey, P.K., Jutla, C.S., Kumar, V., Rao, J.R., Rohatgi, P.: Efficient Rijndael encryption implementation with composite field arithmetic. In: Koç, Ç.K., Naccache, D., Paar, C. (eds.) CHES 2001. LNCS, vol. 2162, pp. 171–184. Springer, Heidelberg (2001)

14. Satoh, A., Morioka, S., Takano, K., Munetoh, S.: A compact Rijndael hardware architecture with S-Box optimization. In: Boyd, C. (ed.) ASIACRYPT 2001. LNCS, vol. 2248, pp. 239–254. Springer, Heidelberg (2001)

15. Tohoku University: Cryptographic Hardware Project. http://www.aoki.ecei.tohoku.ac.jp/crypto/., May 2015

16. Wu, H., Hasan, M.A., Blake, I.F.: Highly regular architectures for finite field computation using redundant basis. In: Koç, Ç.K., Paar, C. (eds.) CHES 1999. LNCS, vol. 1717, pp. 269–279. Springer, Heidelberg (1999)

17. Wu, H.: Low complexity Bit-parallel finite field arithmetic using polynomial basis. In: Koç, Ç.K., Paar, C. (eds.) CHES 1999. LNCS, vol. 1717, pp. 280–291. Springer, Heidelberg (1999)

NaCl's Crypto_box in Hardware

Michael Hutter[1]($\boxtimes$), Jürgen Schilling[2], Peter Schwabe[3]($\boxtimes$),
and Wolfgang Wieser[2]

[1] Rambus Cryptography Research Division, 425 Market Street, 11th Floor,
San Francisco, CA 94105, USA
michael.hutter@cryptography.com
[2] Graz University of Technology, IAIK, Inffeldgasse 16a, 8010 Graz, Austria
j.schilling@student.tugraz.at, w.wies3r@gmail.com
[3] Radboud University, Digital Security Group,
PO Box 9010, 6500 Nijmegen, The Netherlands
peter@cryptojedi.org

Abstract. This paper presents a low-resource hardware implementation of the widely used crypto_box function of the Networking and Cryptography library (NaCl). It supports the X25519 Diffie-Hellman key exchange using Curve25519, the Salsa20 stream cipher, and the Poly1305 message authenticator. Our targeted application is a secure communication between devices in the Internet of Things (IoT) and Internet servers. Such devices are highly resource-constrained and require carefully optimized hardware implementations. We propose the first solution that enables 128-bit-secure public-key authenticated encryption on passively-powered IoT devices like WISP nodes. From a cryptographic point of view we thus make a first step to turn these devices into fully-fledged participants of Internet communication. Our crypto processor needs a silicon area of 14.6 kGEs and less than 40 μW of power at 1 MHz for a 130 nm low-leakage CMOS process technology.

Keywords: Internet of things · ASIC · Salsa20 · Poly1305 · Curve25519

1 Introduction

We need to empower computers with their own means of gathering information, so they can see, hear and smell the world for themselves, in all its random glory. RFID and sensor technology enable computers to observe, identify and understand the world—without the limitations of human-entered data. —Kevin Ashton, June 2009 [2]

This work was done while Michael Hutter was with Graz University of Technology. This work was supported by the Austrian Science Fund (FWF) under the grant number TRP251-N23 and by the Netherlands Organisation for Scientific Research (NWO) through Veni 2013 project 13114 Permanent ID of this document: 34306665f6a71562852503d8aa28f0f9. Date: June 16, 2015.

T. Güneysu and H. Handschuh (Eds.): CHES 2015, LNCS 9293, pp. 81–101, 2015.
DOI: 10.1007/978-3-662-48324-4_5

In 1999, Ashton coined the term of the "Internet of Things" (IoT) for a network of sensors that communicate data over the Internet and thus give computers a way of sensing the world. Since then, various technological advances have brought us closer to turning this vision into reality and large companies are working on implementing these technologies on large scale. For example, Hewlett Packard's "Central Nervous System for the Earth (CeNSE)" project aims at implementing "a highly intelligent network of billions of nanoscale sensors designed to feel, taste, smell, see, and hear what is going on in the world" [10].

A representative platform for implementing sensors is called Wireless Identification and Sensing Platform (WISP), first proposed by Sample, Yeager, Powledge and Smith in [31]. WISP nodes are passively powered, wireless computing and sensing devices that communicate data to an ultra-high-frequency (UHF) RFID reader.

Most applications of this Internet of Things are safety-critical, security-critical, or involve processing private data. For example, HP lists as applications of CeNSE "roads, buildings, bridges, and other infrastructures; machines such as those used in airplanes and manufacturing plants; and organizations that work on health and safety issues, such as the contamination of food and water, disease control, and patient monitoring". Communicating such sensitive data over the Internet obviously raises security concerns. From a cryptographic point of view, the ideal solution is to communicate all data end-to-end authenticated and encrypted between a WISP node and the server processing the data. Key management for secret-key cryptography does not scale well, so authentication of billions of sensor nodes distributed over the whole planet calls for public-key cryptography.

For the communication of servers and large client computers such as desktop computers, laptops, and smartphones there exist various cryptographic libraries and frameworks that set up such end-to-end public-key authenticated encryption. However the question remains whether at least one of these frameworks is compatible with the highly restricted computational capabilities of WISP nodes.

This paper answers this question positively. More specifically, we present a carefully optimized hardware architecture of the basic primitives of the open Networking and Cryptography library (NaCl) [8]. In particular, we ported the crypto_box primitive into hardware including the X25519 elliptic-curve Diffie-Hellman key exchange [4], the Salsa20 stream cipher [5], and the Poly1305 secret-key one-time authenticator [3]. Our design is able to run a 128-bit-secure public-key authenticated encryption at the following hardware performance: Our smallest design of all primitives requires 14.6 kGEs of silicon area and is able to establish a secure Internet connection within 1.7 seconds when clocked at 4 MHz. Our fastest design needs 18 kGEs and performs public-key authenticated encryption within about 400 ms. Our crypto-processor can be used and integrated into WISPs and related low-resource sensor nodes. Optimizations of other mandatory system components such as random-number generation, analog front-end and protocol handling for RF communication, or non-volatile memory are not covered in this paper and need further investigation.

The application described above defines the optimization goals we aimed at in both choices of primitives and implementation as follows:

Low power, not low energy. WISPs harvest the power that is emitted by an RF-signal-emitting reader device. The maximal power available to the core is usually only a few tens of microwatts per megahertz. As the device is not battery-powered, energy consumption is a minor concern.

Compatibility with Internet crypto. We want our solution to be easy to integrate with existing crypto used for Internet communication. A somewhat heavy-weight choice would be SSL/TLS with a suitable selection of primitives [22]. We instead decided to go with the approach taken by NaCl, which is easier to integrate and very efficient in software. This paper shows that it can also be very efficient in hardware.

No need for signatures. There are two main differences between public-key authentication as used by NaCl's `crypto_box` and cryptographic signatures. One difference is that the authenticating parties have to be online at the same time to establish a key via static Diffie-Hellman, which prohibits a delegation of trust to offline parties. In this setting, we assume that the WISP node knows that the public key of the server is authentic which is a reasonable assumption in the IoT scenario where WISPs transmit sensed data to a specific (trusted) server in the Internet. Furthermore, the service of non-repudiation is not essentially necessary in this context, we can therefore avoid the overheads of implementing digital signatures.

Small and fast public-key authenticated encryption. The aim of the proposed design is not to optimize a single primitive, but to obtain small area and reasonable speed for a *combination of primitives* for public-key authenticated encryption. For example, a standalone hardware implementation of AES (or even a lightweight cipher such as PRESENT [9]) would be much smaller than a standalone implementation of Salsa20. Similarly, AES-GCM would be more efficient than Salsa20+Poly1305 for secret-key authenticated encryption. However, the public-key part needs arithmetic on big integers, which we compose of arithmetic on 32-bit integers. This approach gives us all the building blocks we need for Salsa20 and Poly1305 almost for free in terms of silicon area.

We believe that it is possible to achieve even smaller area if we resorted to a binary elliptic curve for Diffie-Hellman and combined this with, for example, AES-GCM. Obviously it is possible to obtain even better efficiency when reducing the security to, for example, 80 bits. However, the central contribution of this paper is to show that we can achieve 128-bit secure public-key authenticated encryption with a conservative choice of primitives on low-resource WISP nodes having a very small footprint in terms of area and power.

Nonce generation. NaCl's `crypto_box` receives as one input a public nonce. This paper does not discuss how this nonce is generated; for a discussion of how nonces are integrated into higher-level protocols, see [8, Sec. 2].

Related Work. The cryptographic primitives used in NaCl for the `crypto_box` public-key authenticated encryption have been designed for high software performance. Consequently, the primitives have so far mainly been implemented in software. Most of this software is included in the eBACS SUPERCOP benchmarking framework [7]. There also exist optimized implementations for embedded microcontrollers (e.g., AVRs, MSP430, or ARM Cortex M) which are not supported by SUPERCOP. Examples are given in [11,17,19,27]

The focus on software implementations does not mean that there exist no implementations in hardware. In particular for the Salsa20 stream cipher there exist various hardware implementations with different optimization targets. For example, there are FPGA implementations [12,24,34] and also ASIC designs [13, 16,38]. The only hardware implementation of Curve25519 that we are aware of is the throughput-optimized FPGA implementation by Sasdrich and Güneysu, which achieves a throughput of more than $32,000$ scalar multiplications per second on a Xilinx Zynq 7020 FPGA [32]. Besides Curve25519 however there exist a broad range of other elliptic-curve implementations over $\mathbb{F}_p$. Most of them perform scalar multiplication on Weierstrass curves and target various FPGA platforms. Typical examples—that have a similar security level as Curve25519—are given in [1,14,15,25,26,28,30,35].

We are not aware of any hardware implementations of Poly1305.

Notation. In [4], Bernstein introduced a high-security high-performance elliptic-curve Diffie-Hellman key-exchange scheme called Curve25519. The name originally referred to the complete scheme, but was later also used to refer to the specific elliptic curve used in this scheme. To eliminate possible confusion, Bernstein recently suggested to use the term *X25519* for the "recommended Montgomery-X-coordinate DH function" and the term *Curve25519* for the underlying elliptic curve. We adopt this new terminology in this paper.

Availability of Results. We will make all results described in this paper available online. In particular we will place the HDL implementation described in this paper into the public domain to maximize reusability of our results[1]. The entire implementation avoids all patents that the authors are aware of.

Roadmap. The paper is organized as follows. In Sect. 2, we will give a short introduction into NaCl and its underlying cryptographic primitives. Section 3 presents our processor and describes the hardware architecture and all its implemented components. In Sect. 4, we describe the machine-code implementation including X25519, Salsa20, and Poly1305. Finally, results are given in Sect. 5.

2   Preliminaries – The Crypto_box Function

The Networking and Cryptography library (short: NaCl), developed by Bernstein, Lange, and Schwabe, advertises a "simple high-level API" [8]. The core functionality of this API is the crypto_box function, which offers public-key authenticated encryption. It computes an authenticated ciphertext from a message, a nonce, the

---

[1] The source code is available at http://mhutter.org/research/vlsi/#naclhw and at http://cryptojedi.org/crypto/#naclhw.

sender's private key, and the receiver's public key. The receiver feeds this authenticated ciphertext together with the nonce, his private key, and the sender's public key into the `crypto_box_open` function to verify the authentication tag and recover the message.

In principle, NaCl supports different independent implementations of this function with different underlying primitives. However, the default construction used in NaCl (and targeted in previous NaCl optimization papers) is a construction based on the X25519 elliptic-curve Diffie-Hellman (ECDH) key exchange, the XSalsa20 stream cipher, and the Poly1305 secret-key one-time authenticator. We briefly review these three primitives in the following subsections.

Curve25519 and the X25519 Function. In 2006, Bernstein proposed the X25519 ECDH scheme [4]. The scheme is based on arithmetic on the Montgomery curve "Curve25519" with equation $E : y^2 = x^3 + 486662x^2 + x$ defined over the field $\mathbb{F}_{2^{255}-19}$. This curve was chosen for high security and high performance. For details about the security properties see [4, Sec. 3].

X25519 secret keys are byte arrays of length 32. Inside X25519, such a byte array is interpreted as a little-endian-encoded 256-bit integer. Before this integer is used as a scalar in elliptic-curve scalar multiplication, the most significant bit is set to 0, the second-most significant bit is set to 1, and the three least significant bits are set to 0. X25519 public keys are also byte arrays of length 32, and encode the x-coordinate of a point on Curve25519.

X25519 uses the fast x-coordinate-only differential-addition chain proposed by Montgomery in [29] to compute a shared secret kP from a secret key k and a public key P. Key-pair generation uses the same computation with a fixed basepoint. The computation involves 255 "ladder steps" and one final inversion in $\mathbb{F}_{2^{255}-19}$. Each ladder step involves 5 multiplications, 4 squarings, one multiplication by the constant $(486662 + 2)/4$, and some additions and subtractions in $\mathbb{F}_{2^{255}-19}$. The final inversion can be computed as exponentiation with $\mathbb{F}_{2^{255}-21}$. An efficient addition chain for this exponentiation proposed in [4] takes 254 squarings and 11 multiplications.

The XSalsa20 Stream Cipher. The Salsa20 stream cipher is an eSTREAM finalist designed by Bernstein [5] and performes 20 rounds on an internal state. The XSalsa20 stream cipher was introduced by Bernstein in [6]. It uses the same core as Salsa20, but supports a 192-bit nonce instead of the Salsa20 64-bit nonce. This is achieved by a fast nonce-setup, called HSalsa20, followed by Salsa20 keystream generation. This combination is denoted as XSalsa20. For details see [6, Sec. 2].

The computations inside HSalsa20 and Salsa20 are very similar, in particular they both use the same 20-round transformation on blocks of 64 bytes. A block is treated as a 4×4-matrix of 32-bit words. Each of the 20 rounds consists of 16 add-rotate-xor sequences, such as

```
s4 = x0 + x12
x4 ^= (s4 >>> 25)
```

The main difference between HSalsa20 and Salsa20 is that they use a different final-ization computation to produce a 64-byte output block in the case of Salsa20 and a 32-byte output block in the case of HSalsa20.

Poly1305 Secret-Key Authentication. The Poly1305 authenticator was intro-duced by Bernstein in [3]. The security of this authenticator requires that a key is used only once; inside crypto_box this is ensured by prepending a 32-byte zero-block in front of the message and then using the XSalsa20 encryption of this zero block as authentication key. The computations in Poly1305 are based on arithmetic in the finite field $\mathbb{F}_{2^{130}-5}$. The authentication tag is computed by processing the input in 16-byte blocks. For each block, Poly1305 treats the block as an element of $\mathbb{F}_{2^{130}-5}$, adds this element into a state, and multiplies the state by a secret value $r \in \mathbb{F}_{2^{130}-5}$, which is essentially the first half of the 32-byte secret key with some bits set to zero. After the whole message has been processed, the authentication tag is computed as addition of the state with the second half of the 32-byte secret key.

3   A Crypto_box Specific Instruction-Set Processor

Implementing public-key authenticated encryption in hardware is a challenging task and requires many different design decisions. Since we aim for a very efficient architecture in terms of low-resource requirements, we decided to implement an Application Specific Instruction Set Processor (ASIP). In contrast to microproces-sors, ASIPs are usually less flexible because there might be no compiler support for the custom processor. The machine code needs to be implemented "by-hand" or by self-written compilers that support the optimized instruction set. On the other hand, ASIPs can benefit in terms of efficiency, i.e., higher speeds and lower area and power requirements. Basically, the main features of our design can be summarized as follows:

Resource efficiency. Our processor was designed with resource efficiency in mind. This means that we aimed for a low-area architecture that re-uses resources as much as possible. Our hardware components such as the imple-mented hardware multiplier have been chosen to require only a low number of logic gates while providing appropriate speeds.

Platform independency. Our design does not make use of any technology-specific components. It is therefore flexible in the sense that it can be synthe-sized on different CMOS-process technologies and FPGAs.

Security. All implemented cryptographic primitives share a security level of 128 bits. Furthermore, we avoided to use any secret branch conditions in our imple-mentation and guarantee that all operations run in constant time. We therefore offer a baseline implementation that can be used to compare with related work and that can be extended in future to integrate hiding and masking counter-measures that offer protections against DPA and correlation-collision attacks etc.

Compatibility with the NaCl API. We are fully compatible to the existing software NaCl interface which offers easy integration of the processor in existing infrastructures and applications.

Support of efficient primitives. Our processor supports a set of high-level primitives (that originally have been designed to achieve high speeds) to offer a range of demanded cryptographic services. We support the following functions:

1. Establishing secure session keys using the X25519 Diffie-Hellman key exchange [4] by running `crypto_dh_curve25519`.
2. Data encryption and decryption using XSalsa20 [5,6].
3. Message authentication using Poly1305 [3].
4. Public-key authenticated encryption by executing the `crypto_box` function. The server can then verify the message authenticity by calling `crypto_box_open` of the NaCl API.
5. Verification and decryption of NaCl authenticated ciphertexts for secure transmission of control messages.

3.1 Hardware Implementation Overview

Our design mainly consists of a memory unit, a controller, and a `crypto_box`-specific Arithmetic Logic Unit (ALU). The ASIP can be accessed through a 32-bit interface.

Memory is one of the most critical components in efficient hardware designs. Especially in implementations of public-key cryptography, it often takes up to 80 % of the entire circuit area and also consumes a significant amount of power. We therefore decided to implement a memory with very generic elements, which can be efficiently replaced by highly optimized platform-dependent memory technologies. For volatile memory, we decided to implement a random-access memory (RAM) instead of a register file. Our design thus supports efficient RAM macros for specific CMOS process technologies. We also stored all constants regularly in a read-only memory (ROM) table. This allows a better optimization by the hardware synthesizer and also enables the use of more efficient ROM macros.

We decided to implement a 32-bit single-port RAM. Single-port memories have the advantage that they are usually smaller in size compared to multi-port memories. This fact makes them attractive for implementations running in resource-constrained environments. Essentially, there are two main reasons for their smaller footprint: (1) each memory cell is basically composed of 6 transistors while 8 transistors are usually required for dual-port memories; and (2) the additional address logic and read/write drivers of multiple ports cause an additional increase in required resources. For example, Faraday Technology Corporation offers a synchronous dual-port register-file RAM (with $32 \times 64 = 2048$ bits) that requires $0.035\,\text{mm}^2$ while a synchronous single-port register-file RAM of the same company requires only $0.023\,\text{mm}^2$ on a low-leakage 130 nm CMOS-process technology. Generally, one-port memories are about 1.4 to 1.7 times smaller than dual-port memories.

The main drawback of single-port RAMs however is *throughput*. While dual-port memories can simultaneously read and/or write two words at different addresses, single-port memories can access only one address per clock cycle. This is the reason that most of (not only high-speed but also resource-constrained) ECC implementations use dual-port memories to keep the arithmetic unit busy in each clock cycle. In particular, multi-precision multiplication (which is often the efficiency bottleneck of those implementations) requires that many partial products are calculated, each needing two operands in each clock cycle.

Optimized Single-Port Memory Arithmetic. We address the issue of low memory throughput and apply a method that allows us to keep the arithmetic unit busy despite the low throughput of single-port memories. More specifically, we use product-scanning-based multiplication but process two columns in parallel. In each clock cycle, two operands from two columns are chosen while one operand is kept in a 32-bit register and re-used in the next cycle. This allows to perform one 32×32-bit multiplication in each cycle.

Selective Memory-Bank Access. Both RAM and ROM are logically divided into a set of memory banks with a data width of 256 bits each. The RAM is composed of 9 memory banks: 1×256 bits are needed for storing the x-coordinate of the (fixed or random) base point, 1×256 bits are needed to store the private key of the X25519 Diffie-Hellman key exchange, and 7×256 bits are required for scalar multiplication. The ROM is composed of 6 memory banks, which contain constants for modular reductions in $\mathbb{F}_{2^{255}-19}$ for Curve25519 and $\mathbb{F}_{2^{130}-5}$ for Poly1305, 2 logic masks, the curve parameter $a24$, and σ for XSalsa20.

We restricted access to the memory from the I/O interface and only allow read/write to RAM banks with index 0 and 1. All other memory banks are not accessible from outside.

Secret-Key-Dependent Memory-Bank Switching. Curve25519 uses the Montgomery powering ladder [20,29] as scalar-multiplication method. In each ladder-step iteration, two curve-point coordinates need to be swapped depending on a secret scalar bit. To avoid secret-key dependent branch conditions, we implemented an additional memory logic that conditionally swaps the addresses of two memory banks depending on a single bit in constant time. This avoids a secret-key dependent branch condition in software and makes a swap-function implementation unnecessary.

3.2   The Controller

The controller is composed of two program ROMs, a program-counter, an instruction decoder, a dedicated multiplication controller, and a flattened memory-management unit including address decoding and page-table control.

We decided to implement two distinct program ROMs: one that contains the program code for Curve25519 and one that mainly contains the code for XSalsa20 and Poly1305. During implementation, it has been shown that both program ROMs have nearly the same code size (the ROM for Curve25519 is slightly smaller in size so that we padded the remaining bytes with zero to obtain equally sized

ROMs). Splitting the ROMs has the advantage that (1) the critical path is reduced due to smaller tables, (2) the area is reduced since modern hardware synthesizers can apply better optimizations, and (3) splitting allows to effectively "isolate" one ROM to reduce power consumption while the other ROM is active.

The Special-Purpose Instruction Set. We implemented 46 instructions, out of which 26 instructions are general-purpose instructions and 20 are special instructions tailored for efficient NaCl crypto_box computations. From these 46 instructions, there are 6 program-flow instructions that for example allow the use of subroutine calls to reduce code size. Almost all instructions directly load operands from or store to memory, which improves performance and avoids the need of (costly) CPU registers.

Crypto_box-Optimized Memory Paging. We further applied the following optimization in order to reduce the memory-instruction width and necessary opcode size, respectively. By analyzing our crypto_box implementation, we identified that in most cases only access to a limited amount of memory banks is necessary (especially in subroutines). This is why we decided to implement a lightweight memory-management unit that makes use of a *memory-paging technique* in order to reduce the length of the total opcode. Thus, we reserve only 2 bits for memory-page addressing. A page consists of 4 non-contiguous memory banks that are pre-determined and statically stored in a page-address table in ROM. During execution, only 1 page can be concurrently active and instructions can access only the 4 memory banks of this page. A memory page can be selected using the Memory Page Select (MPS) instruction, for subroutines we implemented the dedicated Memory Page Increment (MPI) and Memory Page Decrement (MPD) instruction that both increment/decrement the page index.

By applying these enhancements, only 9 bits of opcode are needed for all instructions. From these 9 bits, up to 5 bits are used for memory addressing purposes: two bits are needed to select one memory-bank from the active page and three bits are needed to select a single 32-bit word from the virtual 256-bit memory bank.

Single-Level Subroutines and Parameter Passing. Our memory-paging technique also enables easy address-parameter passing to subroutines. By simply selecting different pages, subroutines can operate on different memory banks without additional lines of code and without additional registers to store the parameters. To enable single-level subroutines, we integrated an 11-bit register that holds the return address. An additional multiplexer is used to update the program counter after returning from the subroutine. To efficiently address the subroutines in the program ROM, we implemented an address decoder using a ROM lookup-table.

Improving Speed by Operand Prefetching. In order to increase the speed of our ASIP design, we apply *operand prefetching*. This allows that instructions can already preset the address of an operand that is needed in the subsequent instruction. Since loading from RAM generally requires two cycles, this improves performance by simply "prefetching" an operand during execution of the previous instruction.

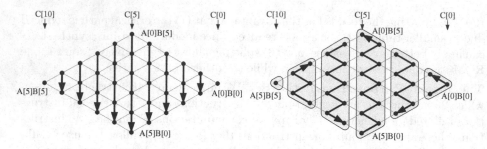

Fig. 1. Column-wise product-scanning multiplication (left) and 2-column parallel product-scanning multiplication (right).

To store prefetched operands, we integrated a dedicated 32-bit *prefetch buffer*. This buffer is located right at the input of the Arithmetic Logic Unit (ALU). The ALU can then either load the prefetched operand from the buffer or it can directly load constants from ROM within a single clock cycle.

2-Column Product-Scanning Hardware Multiplier Control. The performance of Curve25519 and Poly1305 largely depends on the performance of big-integer multiplication. We build this big-integer multiplication from 32×32-bit multiplications, but instead of implementing it in software, we integrated a dedicated controller that is used to provide fast multiplication based on product-scanning multiplication. Instead of processing all partial products column-wise (which is often done by executing a multiply-accumulate instruction on many platforms), we process two columns in parallel. The controller chooses operands from one and the other column alternately, therefore "hopping" between the columns as shown in Fig. 1. The figure shows an $A \times B = 6 \times 6$-word multiplication as an example, where all word multiplications $A[i] \times B[i]$ with index $i \in [0, 5]$ are represented as black dots and the processing is indicated with an arrow. The processing starts from right to left and the result C is the sum of all partial-product columns.

For three consecutive word multiplications, two operands are always the same because of the parallel processing of the two columns. This allows to *buffer* one operand in a 32-bit register while another operand can be prefetched from memory. The ALU is therefore busy in each clock cycle.

3.3   The Arithmetic Logic Unit

The ALU consists of a digit-serial multiplier, a rotation unit, a carry-handling logic, a prefetch buffer, and an accumulator register.

The core element of the ALU is a *digit-serial multiplier*. This type of multiplier processes several bits (so-called digits) in parallel in contrast to bit-serial multipliers which process one operand bit-by-bit only. They are therefore significantly faster while requiring less resources than single-cycle array multipliers (in terms of both area and power). We pay for these advantages with a longer critical path delay[2] that limits the maximum frequency of our design to a few MHz. For our targeted application range, this is not a problem.

We made our multiplier flexible such that the digit size can be configured before synthesis (parameter $w \in \{2, 4, 8, 12, 16\}$ defines parallelism). By changing this parameter we can trade higher speed for smaller area. The main components of our multiplier are a set of adders that are connected in series and that are shifted by one bit each. The output of the multiplier is then fed to an optimized *multi-operation logic* (MOL) that is able to perform both arithmetic as well as logic operations. Configured as an adder, it can be used to add the partial products of the digit-serial multiplier to the accumulator register. Besides this, it can be also configured to subtract operands (e.g., for modular reduction) or to perform an AND, OR, or XOR operation.

`Crypto_box`-Dedicated Rotating. To keep the area requirements low, we decided to implement a `crypto_box` dedicated rotation logic that is able to rotate the accumulator register by several fixed offsets that are required for implementing the `crypto_box` function. Also for the digit-serial multiplication, the accumulator register can be rotated by w bits to the right and it can be rotated back to further *multiply-and-accumulate* partial products without the need of additional registers to buffer the intermediate results (or to store or load them from memory). For Salsa20 it is necessary to rotate the accumulator by 7, 9, 13, and 18 bits to the right. To speed up the reduction in Poly1305, we also support rotation by 2 and 30 bits to the right.

For ECC scalar multiplication, one might expect an accumulator size of 67 bits: 2×32 bits for holding the words of the multiplication results, and 3 bits for storing carries. However, as we process two columns in parallel, it is necessary to extend the size of the accumulator by 32 bits to store the intermediate result. The accumulator has thus a size of 99 bits in total.

For efficient carry handling, we implemented a dedicated register that stores the carry bit. This is especially necessary for modular reduction where the prime modulus (loaded from ROM) is either added or subtracted depending on the carry/borrow of the underlying operation. To achieve constant runtime, we also load the prime modulus from ROM and perform an addition or subtraction operation in the case of already reduced results. In this case, however, we deactivate the addition/subtraction logic so that the unmodified number will be written back to memory (which equals to adding/subtracting zero).

4   Machine-Code Implementations

In this section, we summarize the implementation of Curve25519, XSalsa20, and Poly1305 using our special-purpose instruction set. In total, our implementation needs 9×256 bits of memory, i.e., 9 memory banks (further denoted by R0,..., R8). Only two memory banks are user-accessible to load and store input/output data, the remaining banks are read/write protected.

---

[2] Our multiplier is part of the critical path and constitutes 40–53 % of the total delay.

Table 1. The supported ASIP command set

Command	Hex	Description
DH-1	0x00	X25519 Diffie-Hellman key exchange: computes public key
DH-2	0x01	X25519 Diffie-Hellman key exchange: computes session key
INIT	0x02	HSalsa20: computes extended session key
FIRST	0x03	XSalsa20: computes first cipher block
UPDATE	0x04	XSalsa20: computes next cipher block
FINALIZE	0x05	Poly1305: computes authentication tag
DECRYPT	0x06	XSalsa20/Poly1305: decrypts and authenticates a single block

The general communication flow works as follows. Data can be sent via the 32-bit I/O interface. The input data (e.g., the plaintext) can be stored in either R0 or R1. After that, a `crypto_box` operation can be started by sending one out of five supported commands listed in Table 1. In particular, we implemented a *busy-wait polling* mechanism to sample the status of the `crypto_box`-operation processing. If the busy flag is set, the device still performs operations; data (e.g., the ciphertext) can be accessed from R0 or R1 after the busy flag is cleared.

4.1   The X25519 Key Exchange

The first step in X25519 is to generate a public key. This can be done by our ASIP as follows. First, the private key needs to be written to R0 and the base point of Curve25519 to R1. Second, by sending the DH-1 command, the public key is calculated which can be retrieved from R1 after busy-wait polling.

In the second step, the secret-key is established by exchanging the public-keys. For this purpose, the public-key of the opponent is written to R1, R0 still holds the private key of the device and remains the same. After sending the DH-2 command, a session-key is established and stored in the (read-protected) memory-bank R6.

Initialization. Our implementation of X25519 starts with an initialization phase were all memory banks are initialized. Some of the memory banks are initialized to zero or one; others are initialized to the x-coordinate of the point. In DH-1 this is the fixed base P, in DH-2 it is the public-key received from the communication partner. Additionally, it is necessary to apply masking operations to the 32-byte secret key (see Sect. 2). In total, the initialization for X25519 needs 77 instructions and 77 cycles.

Curve25519 Differential Addition-and-Doubling. We implemented the Montgomery powering ladder to perform scalar multiplication. Since Curve25519 is a curve in Montgomery form, it allows to perform efficient x-coordinate-only operations. To keep the memory-requirements as low as possible, we efficiently re-ordered the Montgomery formula [29] and provide an explicit formula requiring $5M + 4S + 8add + 1M_{a24}$ while needing only 6 working registers (plus the register

Listing 1. Differential addition-and-doubling on x-coord-only Montgomery curves using $5M + 4S + 8\text{add} + 1M_a$ and $6 + \{x_D\}$ registers and $a24 = (a + 2)/4$.

Require: $X_1, X_2, Z_1, Z_2, x_D, a24$
Ensure: X_1, X_2, Z_1, Z_2

1:
1. $R_1 \leftarrow X_2 + Z_2$	7. $Z_2 \leftarrow Z_2 \times Z_2$	13. $X_1 \leftarrow Z_2 \times X_1$
2. $X_2 \leftarrow X_2 - Z_2$	8. $X_1 \leftarrow X_1 \times X_1$	14. $Z_2 \leftarrow R_1 - X_2$
3. $Z_2 \leftarrow X_1 + Z_1$	9. $R_2 \leftarrow Z_2 - X_1$	15. $Z_2 \leftarrow Z_2 \times Z_2$
4. $X_1 \leftarrow X_1 - Z_1$	10. $Z_1 \leftarrow R_2 \times a24$	16. $Z_2 \leftarrow Z_2 \times x_D$
5. $R_1 \leftarrow R_1 \times X_1$	11. $Z_1 \leftarrow Z_1 + X_1$	17. $X_2 \leftarrow R_1 + X_2$
6. $X_2 \leftarrow X_2 \times Z_2$	12. $Z_1 \leftarrow R_2 \times Z_1$	18. $X_2 \leftarrow X_2 \times X_2$

2: **return** (X_1, Z_1, X_2, Z_2)

---

to store the base point x_D). One variable $a24 = (a + 2)/4$ is stored as a constant. The formula is shown in Listing 1.

Modular-Arithmetic Subroutines. To reduce code size, we implemented the modular arithmetic for addition, subtraction, and multiplication in subroutines. These subroutines are called by the main program. Furthermore, each subroutine can be called with different memory-page selection indices, which allows the subroutine to operate on different memory banks. Note that these subroutine implementations are responsible for the major part of the program ROM.

Modular reduction has been implemented efficiently by exploiting the underlying pseudo-Mersenne prime field form of $2^{255} - 19$. Fast reduction can be applied by basically shift and add operations. Shifting is done by multiplications with a constant. We applied an iterative modular reduction method, meaning that we first perform the arithmetic operation and reduce the result afterwards (to lower complexity). For modular reduction after a 256-bit addition/subtraction, we stored the carry/borrow bit using custom instructions named STC, STI, and STX. Then, we add/subtract the constant 38 from the result depending on the carry/borrow bit; otherwise zero is added/subtracted to provide constant runtime. For modular reduction after a 256-bit multiplication, the higher 256 bits of the result are multiplied with 38 and added to the lower 256 bits. This can efficiently be done using the special-purpose MULADD and MULACC instructions.

We implemented modular inversion based on Fermat's little theorem. It requires 11 multiplications and 254 squarings for a 256-bit modular inversion and runs in constant time. Squarings can be faster than multiplication, but we decided to re-use the multiplication routine to avoid additional code size for modular squaring. In our implementation, the same multiplication instruction is consecutively called up to 99 times. It is worth to note that we also evaluated if a dedicated loop instruction would further reduce the area requirements. However, it turns out that the required repeating logic would take more area than the synthesizer is able to optimize in look-up tables so we decided to keep the repetition of several multiplication instructions in ROM.

4.2 A Streaming API for Crypto_box

We decided to implement a streaming API that allows efficient authenticated encryption on WISPs. Basically, our implementation is able to encrypt and authenticate arbitrarily long data. However, due to the limited resources that we have available, we decided to work on 64-byte chunks only. It is therefore necessary to stream the data from external (non-volatile) memory (where WISPs usually store sensed data) and to perform encryptions in a streaming mode. The data authentication tag is calculated in parallel and can be retrieved after the encryption of the last data block. The format of the crypto_box output *starts* with the authentication tag, so our streaming API requires the reader to re-arrange data. This is no problem for a reader with reasonably large memory; it is impossible in the small memory of our ASIP if we want to support messages that are longer than 64 bytes. In addition to that, we provide a method to decrypt and authenticate one block of data which leads to a plaintext data payload of 32 bytes. These 32 bytes can for example be used to submit commands or status data to the WISP device (e.g., an Internet server requests sensitive data from the WISP or confirms the receipt of authenticated encrypted data).

The streaming API supports four commands: INIT, FIRST, UPDATE, and FINALIZE (listed in Table 1). We describe these commands now in a more detail:

Initialization. The INIT command initializes the internal state for authenticated encryption. The state for HSalsa20 has 512 bits and therefore requires two memory banks. It is initialized with a 192-bit nonce that needs to be stored into R0 before calling INIT. Additionally, the state is initialized with the XSalsa20 constant σ, which is loaded from ROM, a dedicated block counter value that is incremented after each processed block, and the session key that is stored in R6 after calling DH-2. The INIT process runs in constant time and needs to be executed only once after DH-2 invocation.

Keystream Update. The FIRST and UPDATE commands are used to update the internal state of the keystream. The ciphertext is calculated by performing block encryption. In addition, also the state of the Poly1305 authentication tag is updated after encryption. Note that FIRST needs to be executed only for the first 64-byte plaintext, after that, UDPATE must be called. Before calling these commands, a 64-byte plaintext block needs to be stored in R0 and R1. This plaintext block is then encrypted by applying the Salsa20 function on the internal state. At the end of Salsa20, the inital state has to be added to the internal state to obtain the final keystream. To save memory, we do not copy this at the beginning but calculate it on-the-fly. All needed data is already stored in RAM and ROM and therefore the execution time is not increased. The ciphertext is generated by XORing the internal state with the plaintext. Finally, the calculation of the authentication tag starts using Poly1305.

The special treatment for the first 64-byte block is necessary because this block is used as initialization state for Poly1305. As described in Sect. 2, this block consists of 32 bytes of zero and 32 bytes of plaintext stored in R0 and R1. When FIRST is called, the plaintext is encrypted using Salsa20 and the encryption result of the

first 32 zero-bytes is used to obtain the key for Poly1305. Note that during the
FIRST process, the first 32 bytes of the ciphertext are zero. These zeros need to be
replaced by the Poly1305 message authentication tag after the stream encryption.

After every 16 bytes of the ciphertext, Poly1305 is called to update the authentication tag. During the FIRST process, Poly1305 is executed twice, because R1
contains only 32 bytes of valid ciphertext. During the UPDATE process, Poly1305
is executed 4 times because the ciphertext is stored in both R0 and R1. Note that
the preliminary authentication tag is stored in an internal memory bank and is
updated after each UPDATE invocation. The main difference between UPDATE and
FIRST is that during an update R0 holds a valid plaintext and therefore needs to
be replaced with the appropriate ciphertext. Furthermore, the keys for Poly1305
are already generated.

Message-Authentication Tag. By sending the FINALIZE command, the final
message authentication tag is calculated. The 16-byte tag is moved to the user-
accessible memory-bank R0 where all other remaining bytes are set to zero.

The command flow for authenticated stream-encryption is given as follows:

1. Write a 192-bit nonce into the memory bank R0 and start the streaming operation by sending the INIT command.
2. Busy-wait polling until processor is ready.
3. Set the first 32 bytes of R0 to zero (this is the place holder for the zero-padded
   16-byte message-authentication tag); send also the first 32 bytes of the plaintext to R1 and start the operation by sending the FIRST command.
4. Busy-wait polling until processor is ready; read back the 64 bytes of ciphertext
   from R0 and R1.
5. Write 64 bytes of the plaintext into R0 and R1 and continue authenticated
   encryption by sending the UPDATE command.
6. Busy-wait polling; read back the 64 bytes of ciphertext from R0 and R1.
7. Repeat Steps 5 to 6 until the whole plaintext is processed.
8. Send the FINALIZE command to generate the message-authentication tag.
9. Busy-wait polling until processor is ready; read back 32 bytes from R0 that
   contains the zero-padded 16-byte authentication tag.
10. Overwrite the first 32 bytes of the ciphertext (which have been previously set
    to zero) with the 32 bytes obtained in Step 9.

Decryption. The DECRYPTION command is used to decrypt and authenticate a
64-byte block of data. This block contains the zero-padded 16-byte authentication tag written into R0 and the 32-byte ciphertext written into R1. In a first step,
the authentication tag of the ciphertext in R1 is calculated using Poly1305. This
new tag is then subtracted from R0. If both tags match, the whole memory bank
R0 will be zero and the ciphertext can be considered authentic. If the tags do not
match, R0 will be different from zero. Finally, the ciphertext in R1 is decrypted
using XSalsa20 as also done during the execution of FIRST except of the fact that
only one memory bank needs to be processed to obtain the 32-byte plaintext stored
in R1. Authenticated decryption is done as follows:

1. Write the 16-byte authentication tag into the memory bank R0 and set all other bytes to zero; store the corresponding 32-byte ciphertext into R1 and start the decryption operation by sending the DECRYPT command.
2. Busy-wait polling until processor is ready; read back the 32-byte plaintext from R1 and check if R0 is zero.

5   Implementation Results

We implemented our design in VHDL and used Cadence Encounter®RTL Compiler (v08.10-s238_1, 64-bit) for synthesis. For the following evaluation, we used the UMC 130 nm 1.2V/3.3V 1P8M LL logic CMOS process. For this process, one gate equivalent (GE) corresponds to the area of a two-input NAND gate of size 5.12 μm^2. All designs have been synthesized for a target frequency of 1 MHz. Furthermore, all area results are post-synthesis results (to make a fair comparison with related work) but note that the area requirements change during back-end design where the overhead for placement and routing (clock distribution, wire interconnections, etc.) is included. For power evaluations, we considered these overheads by simulating after place and route using First Encounter (v08.10-s273_1, 64bit) with NanoRoute (v08.10-s155).

Table 2 shows the results of our design for several multiplier configurations. We provide results for a digit size $w = 2, 4, 8, 12, 16$ to report numbers for a trade-off between speed and area. In terms of speed, most speed-up is observed for the X25519 key exchange. Depending on w, both Diffie-Hellman operations DH-1 and DH-2 require between 811 170 and 3 455 394 clock cycles. Note that DH-2 needs an additional amount of 34 cycles compared to DH-1 because it requires an inversion of the word order of the session key. Authenticated encryption using XSalsa20 and Poly1305 requires 6 641 cycles for initialization, the streaming update function needs between 7 443 and 9 291 cycles per 64-byte data block, and preparing the authentication tag needs only 62 cycles. Decryption of control messages can be performed in between 7 271 to 9 085 cycles.

In terms of area, our smallest design (using a 2-bit parallel digit-serial multiplier) requires 14.6 kGEs; the largest design needs 18 kGEs. The area of the controller is nearly the same independent of the size of the multiplier. The two program ROMs for Curve25519 and XSalsa20/Poly1305 have different lengths: 1 088 Lines of Code (LOC) are needed for Curve25519 and 1 625 LOCs are needed for XSalsa20/Poly1305. The ALU, in contrast, gets larger the more bits are processed in parallel. ROM for constants needs about 310 GEs and the 32-bit I/O interface needs 157 GEs. A closer look at the controller and datapath components shows that the major parts are due to the program ROM (31–50 %), the multiplier (9–31 %), the rotation unit (9–11 %), the multi-operation logic (4–5 %), the accumulator (4–5%), and the prefetch buffer (2–6 %).

Our smallest design needs around 40 μW of power at 1 MHz while the fastest design needs about 70 μW. Half of the power is spent for the RAM, the remaining power is consumed by the program ROM (15–26 %), the accumulator (8–24 %), the digit-serial multiplier (7–18 %), and the rotation logic (8 %).

Table 2. Performance of our `crypto_box` implementation for different multiplier digit-sizes w. We report numbers for X25519 key exchange (`DH-1` and `DH-2`) and authenticated encryption using XSalsa20 and Poly1305

w	Speed [Cycles][a]					Area [GEs][b]			
	`DH-1`	`DH-2`	`FIRST`	`UPDATE`	`DECRYPT`	Ctrl+ALU	ROM	Total incl. RAM	
								std-cells	macro
2	3 455 394	3 455 428	8 117	9 291	9 085	10 555	307	29 319	14 648
4	1 957 282	1 957 316	7 705	8 465	8 049	10 761	308	29 526	14 855
8	1 151 906	1 151 940	7 685	8 427	7 513	11 484	311	30 252	15 581
12	971 682	971 716	7 557	8 171	7 385	11 794	313	30 564	15 893
16	811 170	811 184	7 443	7 943	7 271	13 869	311	32 637	17 966

[a] `INIT` takes 6 641 cycles and `FINALIZE` needs 62 cycles for all digit sizes w.
[b] Total area is given for a 2 304-bit standard-cell based RAM design (18.3 kGEs) as well as an optimized synchronous one-port register file RAM with the FSC0L_D_SY memory technology from Faraday Technologies (needing 3 629 GEs).

We also had a closer look at the critical path of our design to evaluate the maximum supported frequency. The path starts at the instruction buffer in the controller, goes through the ROM in the memory unit and takes its way through the digit-serial multiplier in the ALU, and finally ends in RAM. Depending on the width of the multiplier, the duration of the critical-path delay is between 53.4 and 82.6 nano seconds. Thereof, the largest delay (64–75%) is caused by the adder structure of the digit-serial multiplier. The maximum frequency of our design is therefore 12–18 MHz (depending on configuration). This is fast enough for our targeted applications which are typically clocked with only a few MHz.

Further Area/Speed Trade-Offs. Further optimizations are possible, e.g., the entire 256-bit finite-field multiplication can be implemented as program code without needing a dedicated multiply control. For example, we implemented the multiplication as a classical product-scanning multiplication using 209 additional instructions. For the 130-bit multiplication in Poly1305, 83 additional instructions are necessary. As a result, we reduced the area requirements to 13.2 kGEs (including the RAM macro) for a 32-bit multiplier digit size of $w = 2$. The number of clock cycles for `DH-1` is however increased by 10.3 % to 3.852 million cycles. The cycle count for `FIRST` is increased by 12.3 % to 9 257 cycles and the `UPDATE` command takes 19.7 % longer, i.e., 11 571 cycles.

Comparison with Related Work. Table 3 lists different ASIC implementations of ECC that have similar field sizes (192–256 bits). While most related work focuses on efficient scalar multiplication on different types of curves, it shows that our design competes well even though more cryptographic services are offered. In fact, our processor supports a high-security stream cipher, a message authenticator, and a Diffie-Hellman key exchange using Curve25519. The required resources for those services, e.g., storage for the public key during key agreement is included in our numbers. Having these services available, our design is able to perform 128-bit public-key authenticated encryption using the given primitives while most related

Table 3. Comparison of ASIC implementations of ECC with similar field sizes

	Features of the (Co-)processor	Size [bits]	Time [Cycles]	Area [GEs][a] std-cells	macro	Area·Time std-cells	macro
Wolkerstorfer [37]	Weierstraß $\mathbb{F}_p/\mathbb{F}_{2^m}$	256	1 175 451	37 200[b]	n.a.	43.73	n.a.
Lai et al. [21]	Weierstraß $\mathbb{F}_p/\mathbb{F}_{2^m}$	256	252 067	197 028	n.a.	49.66	n.a.
Satoh et al. [33]	Weierstraß $\mathbb{F}_p/\mathbb{F}_{2^m}$	256	880 000	55 647	n.a.	48.97	n.a.
Liu et al. [23]	Twisted Edwards $\mathbb{F}_p = 2^{207} - 5131$	207	182 653	n.a.[c]	n.a.	n.a.	n.a.
Hutter et al. [18]	NIST P192, AES, SHA1	192	753 393	n.a.	21 502	n.a.	16.20
Wenger [36]	NIST P256	256	3 367 000	n.a.	27 244	n.a.	91.73
Ours (smallest)	Curve25519,	255	3 455 394	29 319	14 648	101.31	50.61
Ours (fastest)	Salsa20, Poly1305		811 170	32 637	17 966	26.47	14.57

[a]Area numbers include memory in either standard-cell based RAM technology or optimized RAM macro blocks. We list both for a fair comparison.
[b]Wolkerstorfer reported 31 kGEs for his core but this excludes the storage for the private key (scalar) and public key (X and Y coordinates). For a more fair comparison we included 6.2 kGE required for this memory.
[c]Authors reported 5 821 GEs for the size of their ALU. Memory is not included.

work targets authentication services only. In terms of Salsa20, we can compare our work with the smallest implementation reported so far which is due to Henzen, Carbognani, Felber, and Fichtner [16]. Their Salsa20 implementation needs 9.97 kGEs. For Poly1305 there are no previous hardware implementations to compare with.

When looking at the area-time-power (ATP) product, our design outperforms related work by more than a factor of 3. Wolkerstorfer reports a power consumption of more than $500\,\mu W$ for a frequency of 1 MHz on a 192-bit curve using a 350 nm CMOS cell library. This corresponds to more than $130\,\mu W$ on 130 nm CMOS and with a 256-bit curve (ATP: > 5.68, standard-cell RAM). Hutter et al. report 1.6 mW on a 350 nm CMOS yielding an even larger ATP. Lai reported $578\,\mu W$ for a 160-bit curve (ATP: 28.70, standard-cell RAM). Wenger's design, which is based on an 8-bit AVR clone, needs $76\,\mu W$ (ATP: 6.97, RAM macros). Our fastest design needs $70\,\mu W$, which yields an ATP product of only 1.02 with RAM macros and 1.85 with standard-cell RAM.

Acknowledgements. We would like to thank Christof Paar for his valuable suggestions throughout preparing the final version of this paper.

References

1. Ananyi, K., Alrimeih, H., Rakhmatov, D.: Flexible hardware processor for elliptic curve cryptography over NIST prime fields. IEEE Trans. Very Large Scale Integr. (VLSI) **17**(8), 1099–1112 (2009). 4
2. Ashton, K.: That 'internet of things' thing. RFID J. **22**, 97–114 (2009). http://www.rfidjournal.com/articles/view?4986. 1

3. Bernstein, D.J.: The Poly1305-AES message-authentication code. In: Gilbert, H., Handschuh, H. (eds.) FSE 2005. LNCS, vol. 3557, pp. 32–49. Springer, Heidelberg (2005). http://cr.yp.to/papers.html#poly1305. 2, 6, 7

4. Bernstein, D.J.: Curve25519: new Diffie-Hellman speed records. In: Yung, M., Dodis, Y., Kiayias, A., Malkin, T. (eds.) PKC 2006. LNCS, vol. 3958, pp. 207–228. Springer, Heidelberg (2006). http://cr.yp.to/papers.html#curve25519. 2, 4, 5, 7

5. Bernstein, D.J.: The Salsa20 family of stream ciphers. In: Robshaw, M., Billet, O. (eds.) New Stream Cipher Designs. LNCS, vol. 4986, pp. 84–97. Springer, Heidelberg (2008). http://cr.yp.to/papers.html#salsafamily. 2, 5, 7

6. Bernstein, D.J.: Extending the Salsa20 nonce. In Workshop record of Symmetric Key Encryption Workshop 2011 (2011). http://cr.yp.to/papers.html#xsalsa. 5, 7

7. Bernstein, D.J., Lange, T.: eBACS: ECRYPT benchmarking of cryptographic systems. http://bench.cr.yp.to. Accessed 28 Sep 2014. 4

8. Bernstein, D.J., Lange, T., Schwabe, P.: The security impact of a new cryptographic library. In: Hevia, A., Neven, G. (eds.) LatinCrypt 2012. LNCS, vol. 7533, pp. 159–176. Springer, Heidelberg (2012). http://cryptojedi.org/papers/#coolnacl. 2, 3, 4

9. Bogdanov, A.A., Knudsen, L.R., Leander, G., Paar, C., Poschmann, A., Robshaw, M., Seurin, Y., Vikkelsoe, C.: PRESENT: an ultra-lightweight block cipher. In: Paillier, P., Verbauwhede, I. (eds.) CHES 2007. LNCS, vol. 4727, pp. 450–466. Springer, Heidelberg (2007). https://www.emsec.rub.de/research/publications/present-ultra-lightweight-block-cipher/. 3

10. Hewlett-Packard Development Company. CeNSE. http://www8.hp.com/us/en/hp-information/environment/cense.html. Accessed 25 Sep 2014. 2

11. Düll, M., Haase, B., Hinterwälder, G., Hutter, M., Paar, C., Sánchez, A.H., Schwabe, P.: High-speed Curve25519 on 8-bit, 16-bit, and 32-bit microcontrollers. Des. Codes Cryptograph. **17**, 1–22 (2015). http://dx.doi.org/10.1007/s10623-015-0087-1. 4

12. Gaj, K., Southern, G., Bachimanchi, R.: Comparison of hardware performance of selected Phase II eSTREAM candidates. In: State of the Art of Stream Ciphers Workshop - SASC 2007 (2007). http://www.ecrypt.eu.org/stream/papersdir/2007/027.pdf. 4

13. Good, T., Benaissa, M.: Hardware results for selected stream cipher candidates. In: Workshop on The State of the Art of Stream Ciphers - SASC 2007, pp. 191–204. ECRYPT (2007). http://www.ecrypt.eu.org/stream/papersdir/2007/023.pdf. 4

14. Guillermin, N.: A high speed coprocessor for elliptic curve scalar multiplications over $\mathbb{F}_p$. In: Mangard, S., Standaert, F.-X. (eds.) CHES 2010. LNCS, vol. 6225, pp. 48–64. Springer, Heidelberg (2010). http://dx.doi.org/10.1007/978-3-642-15031-9_4. 4

15. Güneysu, T., Paar, C.: Ultra High Performance ECC over NIST Primes on Commercial FPGAs. In: Oswald, E., Rohatgi, P. (eds.) CHES 2008. LNCS, vol. 5154, pp. 62–78. Springer, Heidelberg (2008). http://iacr.org/archive/ches2008/51540064/51540064.pdf. 4

16. Henzen, L., Carbognani, F., Felber, N., Fichtner, W.: VLSI hardware evaluation of the stream ciphers Salsa20 and ChaCha and the compression function Rumba. In: International Conference on Signals, Circuits and Systems - SCS 2008, pp. 1–5. IEEE (2008). 4, 18

17. Hinterwälder, G., Moradi, A., Hutter, M., Schwabe, P., Paar, C.: Full-Size high-security ECC implementation on MSP430 microcontrollers. In: Aranha, D.F., Menezes, A. (eds.) LATINCRYPT 2014. LNCS, vol. 8895, pp. 31–47. Springer, Heidelberg (2015). http://www.emsec.rub.de/research/publications/Curve25519MSPLatin2014/. 4

18. Hutter, M., Feldhofer, M., Wolkerstorfer, J.: A cryptographic processor for low-resource devices: canning ECDSA and AES like sardines. In: Ardagna, C.A., Zhou, J. (eds.) WISTP 2011. LNCS, vol. 6633, pp. 144–159. Springer, Heidelberg (2011). http://mhutter.org/papers/Hutter2011ACryptographicProcessor.pdf. 18

19. Hutter, M., Schwabe, P.: NaCl on 8-bit AVR microcontrollers. In: Youssef, A., Nitaj, A., Hassanien, A.E. (eds.) AFRICACRYPT 2013. LNCS, vol. 7918, pp. 156–172. Springer, Heidelberg (2013). http://cryptojedi.org/papers/#avrnacl. 4

20. Joye, M., Yen, S.-M.: The Montgomery powering ladder. In: Kaliski, B.S., Koç, Ç.K., Paar, C. (eds.) CHES 2002. LNCS, vol. 2523, pp. 291–302. Springer, Heidelberg (2003). http://cr.yp.to/bib/2003/joye-ladder.pdf. 8

21. Lai, J.-Y., Huang, C.-T.: A highly efficient cipher processor for dual-field elliptic curve cryptography. IEEE Trans. Circ. Syst II Express Briefs 56(5), 394–398 (2009). 18

22. Langley, A., Chang, W.-T.: ChaCha20 and Poly1305 based cipher suites for TLS: Internet draft. https://tools.ietf.org/html/draft-agl-tls-chacha20poly1305-04. Accessed 1 Feb 2015. 3

23. Liu, Z., Wang, H., Großschädl, J., Hu, Z., Verbauwhede, I.: VLSI implementation of double-base scalar multiplication on a twisted edwards curve with an efficiently computable endomorphism. Cryptology ePrint Archive: Report 2015/421 (2015). http://eprint.iacr.org/2015/421.pdf. 18

24. Alpha Technology (INT) LTD. Implementation and analysis of Scrypt algorithm in FPGA (proof of concept). Technical report, Alpha Technology, Manchester, England (2013). https://alpha-t.net/wp-content/uploads/2013/11/Alpha-Technology-Scrypt-Analysis-on-FPGA-proof-of-concept.pdf

25. Ma, Y., Liu, Z., Pan, W., Jing, J.: A high-speed elliptic curve cryptographic processor for generic curves over GF(p). In: Lange, T., Lauter, K., Lisoněk, P. (eds.) SAC 2013. LNCS, vol. 8282, pp. 421–437. Springer, Heidelberg (2014). http://www.iacr.org/archive/ches2010/62250046/62250046.pdf. 4

26. McIvor, C.J., McLoone, M., McCanny, J.V.: Hardware elliptic curve cryptographic processor over GF(p). IEEE Trans. Circ. Syst. 53(9), 1946–1957 (2006). 4

27. Meiser, G., Eisenbarth, T., Lemke-Rust, K., Paar, C.: Efficient implementation of eSTREAM ciphers on 8-bit AVR microcontrollers. In: International Symposium on Industrial Embedded Systems - SIES 2008, pp. 58–66 (2008). 4

28. Mentens, N.: Secure and efficient coprocessor design for cryptographic applications on FPGAs. PhD thesis, Katholieke Universiteit Leuven, Leuven-Heverlee, Belgium (2007). 4

29. Montgomery, P.L.: Speeding the Pollard and elliptic curve methods of factorization. Math. Comput. 48(177), 243–264 (1987). http://www.ams.org/journals/mcom/1987-48-177/S0025-5718-1987-0866113-7/S0025-5718-1987-0866113-7.pdf. 5, 8, 13

30. Sakiyama, K., De Mulder, E., Preneel, B., Verbauwhede, I.: A parallel processing hardware architecture for elliptic curve cryptosystems. In: IEEE International Conference on Acoustics, Speech and Signal Processing - ICASSP 2006, vol. 3, pp. 904–907. IEEE (2006). http://www.cosic.esat.kuleuven.be/publications/article-714.pdf. 4

31. Sample, A.P., Yeager, D.J., Powledge, P.S., Smith, J.R.: Design of a passively-powered, programmable sensing platform for UHF RFID systems. In: 2007 IEEE International Conference on RFID, pp. 149–156. IEEE (2007). https://sensor.cs.washington.edu/pubs/WISP-IEEE-RFID07-PostConf.pdf. 2

32. Sasdrich, P., Güneysu, T.: Efficient elliptic-curve cryptography using Curve25519 on reconfigurable devices. In: Goehringer, D., Santambrogio, M.D., Cardoso, J.M.P., Bertels, K. (eds.) ARC 2014. LNCS, vol. 8405, pp. 25–36. Springer, Heidelberg (2014). https://www.ei.rub.de/media/sh/veroeffentlichungen/2014/03/25/paperarc14 curve25519.pdf. 4

33. Satoh, A., Takano, K.: A scalable dual-field elliptic curve cryptographic processor. IEEE Trans. Comput. **52**(4), 449–460 (2003). 18

34. Sugier, J.: Low-cost hardware implementations of Salsa20 stream cipher in programmable devices. J. Pol. Saf. Reliab. Assoc. 4(1), 121–128 (2013). http://jpsra.am.gdynia.pl/upload/SSARS2013PDF/VOL1/SSARS2013-Sugier.pdf. 4

35. Varchola, M., Güneysu, T., Mischke, O.: MicroECC: a lightweight reconfigurable elliptic curve crypto-processor. In: 2011 International Conference on Reconfigurable Computing and FPGAs, pp. 204–210 (2011). 4

36. Wenger, E.: A lightweight ATmega-based application-specific instruction-set processor for elliptic curve cryptography. In: Avoine, G., Kara, O. (eds.) LightSec 2013. LNCS, vol. 8162, pp. 1–15. Springer, Heidelberg (2013). https://online.tugraz.at/tug_online/voe_main2.getvolltext?pCurrPk=70640. 18

37. Wolkerstorfer, J.: Is elliptic-curve cryptography suitable for small devices? In: Oswald, E. (ed.) Workshop on RFID and Lightweight Crypto - RFIDsec 2005 (2005). 18

38. Yan, J., Heys, H.M.: Hardware implementation of the Salsa20 and Phelix stream ciphers. In: Canadian Conference on Electrical and Computer Engineering - CCECE 2007, pp. 1125–1128. IEEE (2007). http://www.engr.mun.ca/~howard/PAPERS/ccece07_yan.pdf. 4

Lightweight Coprocessor for Koblitz Curves: 283-Bit ECC Including Scalar Conversion with only 4300 Gates

Sujoy Sinha Roy[✉], Kimmo Järvinen, and Ingrid Verbauwhede

KU Leuven ESAT/COSIC and iMinds, Kasteelpark Arenberg 10 bus 2452,
3001 Leuven-Heverlee, Belgium
{sujoy.sinharoy,kimmo.jarvinen,ingrid.verbauwhede}@esat.kuleuven.be

Abstract. We propose a lightweight coprocessor for 16-bit microcontrollers that implements high security elliptic curve cryptography. It uses a 283-bit Koblitz curve and offers 140-bit security. Koblitz curves offer fast point multiplications if the scalars are given as specific τ-adic expansions, which results in a need for conversions between integers and τ-adic expansions. We propose the first lightweight variant of the conversion algorithm and, by using it, introduce the first lightweight implementation of Koblitz curves that includes the scalar conversion. We also include countermeasures against side-channel attacks making the coprocessor the first lightweight coprocessor for Koblitz curves that includes a set of countermeasures against timing attacks, SPA, DPA and safe-error fault attacks. When the coprocessor is synthesized for 130 nm CMOS, it has an area of only 4,323 GE. When clocked at 16 MHz, it computes one 283-bit point multiplication in 98 ms with a power consumption of 97.70 μW, thus, consuming 9.56 μJ of energy.

Keywords: Elliptic curve cryptography · Koblitz curves · Lightweight implementation · Side-channel resistance

1 Introduction

Elliptic curve cryptography (ECC) is one of the prime candidates for bringing public-key cryptography to applications with strict constraints on implementation resources such as power, energy, circuit area, memory, etc. Lightweight applications that require strong public-key cryptography include, e.g., wireless sensor network nodes, RFID tags, medical implants, and smart cards. Such applications will have a central role in actualizing concepts such as the Internet of Things and, hence, providing strong cryptography with low resources has been an extremely active research field in the recent years. As a result of this research line, we have several proposals for efficient lightweight implementations of ECC. These proposals focus predominately on 163-bit elliptic curves which provide medium security level of about 80 bits [4–6,15,24,26,34,42,43]. We provide a coprocessor architecture that implements ECC using a high security 283-bit Koblitz curve and includes countermeasures against side-channel attacks.

© International Association for Cryptologic Research 2015
T. Güneysu and H. Handschuh (Eds.): CHES 2015, LNCS 9293, pp. 102–122, 2015.
DOI: 10.1007/978-3-662-48324-4_6

Koblitz curves [23] are a special class of elliptic curves which enable very efficient point multiplications and, therefore, they are an attractive alternative also for lightweight implementations. However, these efficiency gains can be exploited only by representing scalars as specific τ-adic expansions. Most cryptosystems require the scalar also as an integer (see, e.g., ECDSA [31]). Therefore, cryptosystems utilizing Koblitz curves need both the integer and τ-adic representations of the scalar, which results in a need for conversions between the two domains. This is not a major problem in applications which have sufficient resources because fast methods for on-the-fly scalar conversion are available [8,37]. Consequently, very fast ECC implementations using Koblitz curves have been presented for both software [39] and hardware [18]. For lightweight implementations, however, the extra overhead introduced by these conversions has so far prevented efforts to use Koblitz curves in lightweight implementations. A recent paper [4] showed that Koblitz curves result in a very efficient lightweight implementation if τ-adic expansions are already available but the fact that the conversion is not included seriously limits possible applications of the implementation. An alternative approach was provided in a very recent paper [20] which provides a solution that delegates conversions from the lightweight implementation to a powerful server. However, this solution is not suitable for applications where both communicating parties are lightweight implementations and it also requires minor modifications to the cryptosystems which may hinder its use in some applications. Computing conversions directly in the lightweight implementation would be a better option in many cases and, hence, we focus on that alternative in this paper. All previous hardware implementations of the conversions [1,7,8,19,36] are targeted on high speed which makes them unsuitable for lightweight implementations.

To the best of our knowledge, we present the following novel contributions:

- We present the first lightweight implementation of high security ECC by using a 283-bit Koblitz curve offering roughly 140 bits of security. By high security, we mean security levels exceeding 128 bits (e.g., AES-128). Because security of a cryptosystem utilizing multiple cryptographic algorithms is determined by its weakest algorithm, our implementation is the first lightweight implementation of ECC that can be combined, e.g., with AES-128 without reducing the security level of the entire system.
- We present the first complete lightweight implementation of Koblitz curves that also includes on-the-fly scalar conversion. We achieve this by presenting a lightweight variant of the conversion algorithm from [8] which is optimized for word-serial computations. As mentioned above, the first implementation introduced in [4] does not include the conversion which limits the possible applications of the implementation. All conversion algorithms and architectures available in the literature focus on the speed of the conversion.
- The first lightweight implementation of Koblitz curves [4] does not include any countermeasures against side-channel attacks. We present the first lightweight implementation of Koblitz curves with countermeasures against side-channel attacks such as simple power analysis (SPA), differential power analysis (DPA), timing attacks, and safe-error fault attacks.

The paper is structured as follows. In Sect. 2, we provide a brief background on ECC and Koblitz curves. Then in Sects. 3 and 4, we describe our scalar conversion and point multiplication techniques. Our lightweight coprocessor architecture is presented in Sect. 5. We provide synthesis results in 130 nm CMOS and comparisons to other works in Sect. 6. We end with conclusions in Sect. 7.

2   Preliminaries

The use of elliptic curves for cryptography was independently proposed by Victor Miller [29] and Neal Koblitz [22] in the mid-1980 s. Points that satisfy the equation of an elliptic curve form an additive Abelian group E together with a special point $\mathcal{O}$, which is the zero element of the group. Elliptic curves over finite fields $\mathbb{F}_q$ are used in cryptography and we focus on elliptic curves over binary fields $\mathbb{F}_{2^m}$ (finite fields over characteristic two) with polynomial basis. Let $P_1, P_2 \in E$. The group operation $P_1 + P_2$ is called point addition when $P_1 \neq \pm P_2$ and point doubling when $P_1 = P_2$. The fundamental operation of ECC is the elliptic curve point multiplication $Q = kP$, where $k \in \mathbb{Z}$ and $Q, P \in E$.

Point multiplication is computed with a series of point additions and point doublings. The basic approach to compute point multiplications is to use the double-and-add algorithm (also called the binary algorithm) which iterates over the bits of k one at a time and computes a point doubling for every bit and a point addition if the bit is one. Each point operation involves several operations in the underlying finite field. Projective coordinates are typically used for representing points as (X, Y, Z) in order to reduce the number of inversions in $\mathbb{F}_{2^m}$. We use the López-Dahab coordinates [27] and specifically the point addition formulae from [2]. Another option that we considered was to use the λ-coordinates [33] which offer slightly faster point additions. In our case, however, the cost of obtaining the λ-coordinate representation, which includes an inversion in $\mathbb{F}_{2^m}$, overweighs the cheaper point additions.

Koblitz curves introduced by Koblitz in [23] are a special class of elliptic curves defined by the following equation:

$$y^2 + xy = x^3 + ax^2 + 1 \tag{1}$$

with $x, y \in \mathbb{F}_{2^m}$ and $a \in \{0, 1\}$. Koblitz curves offer efficient point multiplications because they allow trading computationally expensive point doublings to cheap Frobenius endomorphisms. Many standards use Koblitz curves including NIST FIPS 186-4 [31] which describes the (Elliptic Curve) Digital Signature Standard (ECDSA) and defines five Koblitz curves NIST K-163, K-233, K-283, K-409, and K-571 over the finite fields $\mathbb{F}_{2^{163}}$, $\mathbb{F}_{2^{233}}$, $\mathbb{F}_{2^{283}}$, $\mathbb{F}_{2^{409}}$, and $\mathbb{F}_{2^{571}}$, respectively.

The Frobenius endomorphism for a point $P = (x, y)$ is given by $\phi(P) = (x^2, y^2)$ and, for Koblitz curves, it holds that $\phi(P) \in E$ for all $P \in E$. It can be also shown that $\phi^2(P) - \mu\phi(P) + 2P = \mathcal{O}$ for all $P \in E$, where $\mu = (-1)^{1-a}$ [23]. Consequently, the Frobenius endomorphism can be seen as a multiplication by the complex number $\tau = (\mu + \sqrt{-7})/2$ [23].

Representing the scalar k as a τ-adic expansion $t = \sum_{i=0}^{\ell-1} t_i \tau^i$ allows computing point multiplications with a Frobenius-and-add algorithm, which is similar to the double-and-add algorithm except that point doublings are replaced by Frobenius endomorphisms. Depending on the application, a τ-adic expansion can be found by converting an integer into a τ-adic expansion [8,23,28,37] and/or by finding a random τ-adic expansion directly [23,25]. In the latter case, a conversion in the other direction is typically required because most cryptosystems (e.g., ECDSA [31]) require the scalar as an integer, too. Conversions in either direction can be expensive [8] but once the τ-adic expansion is obtained, the point multiplication is significantly faster, which typically makes Koblitz curves more efficient than other standardized elliptic curves. So far, no efficient lightweight implementations of these conversions exist ruling Koblitz curves out of the domain of lightweight cryptography.

Because the negative of a point is given simply as $-P = (x, x+y)$, the cost of point subtraction is practically equal to the cost of point addition and significant performance improvements can be obtained by using signed-bit representations for the scalar. In that case, a point addition is computed if $t_i = +1$ and a point subtraction is computed if $t_i = -1$. The most widely used signed-bit representation for Koblitz curves is the τ-adic nonadjacent form (τNAF) introduced by Solinas in [37] and it has an average density of $1/3$ for nonzero coefficients. Solinas also presented the window τNAF (w-τNAF) that allows even lower densities of $1/(w+1)$ by utilizing precomputations to support an increased set of possible values for coefficients: $t_i \in \{\pm1, \pm3, \pm5, \ldots, \pm(2^{w-1} - 1)\}$.

Both τNAF and w-τNAF have the serious downside that they are vulnerable against side-channel attacks because the pattern of point operations depends on the key bits. The basic approach for obtaining resistance against side-channel attacks for ECC is to use Montgomery's ladder [30] which employs a constant pattern of point operations. Unfortunately, Montgomery's ladder is not a viable choice for Koblitz curves because then all benefits of cheap Frobenius endomorphisms are lost. Certain options (e.g., by using dummy operations) have been proposed in [14]. In this paper, we reuse the idea of using a zero-free τ-adic representation [32,41], that contains only nonzero digits, i.e., $t_i \in \{-1, +1\}$. When this representation is scanned with windows of size $w \geq 2$, the resulting point multiplication algorithm is both efficient and secure against many side-channel attacks because it employs a constant pattern of operations [32,41].

3 Koblitz Curve Scalar Conversion

The zero-free representation for an integer scalar k is found so that k is first reduced to $\rho = b_0 + b_1\tau \equiv k \pmod{\tau^m - 1}$ and the zero-free representation t is generated from the reduced scalar ρ [32,37,41]. The overhead of these conversions is specifically important for lightweight implementations. Another important aspect is resistance against side-channel attacks. In the following, we describe our lightweight and side-channel resistant scalar conversion algorithms. Only SPA countermeasures are required because only one conversion is required per

---

Input: Integer scalar k
Output: Reduced scalar $\rho = b_0 + b_1\tau \equiv k \pmod{\tau^m - 1}$
1 $(a_0, a_1) \leftarrow (1, 0)$, $(b_0, b_1) \leftarrow (0, 0)$, $(d_0, d_1) \leftarrow (k, 0)$
2 **for** $i = 0$ **to** $m - 1$ **do**
3      $u \leftarrow d_0[0]$; /* The lsb of d_0, the remainder before division by τ */
4      $d_0 \leftarrow d_0 - u$
5      $(b_0, b_1) \leftarrow (b_0 + u \cdot a_0, b_1 + u \cdot a_1)$
6      $(d_0, d_1) \leftarrow (d_1 - d_0/2, -d_0/2)$;   /* Division of (d_0, d_1) by τ */
7      $(a_0, a_1) \leftarrow (-2a_1, a_0 - a_1)$
8 $\rho = (b_0, b_1) \leftarrow (b_0 + d_0, b_1 + d_1)$

Algorithm 1. Scalar reduction algorithm from [8]

k. The scalar k is typically a nonce but even if it is used multiple times, t can be computed only once and stored.

3.1 Scalar Reduction

We choose the scalar reduction technique called lazy reduction (described as Algorithm 1) from [8]. The algorithm reduces an integer scalar by repeatedly dividing it by τ for m times. This division can be implemented with shifts, additions, and subtractions. This makes the scalar reduction algorithm [8] attractive for lightweight implementations. However, the only known hardware implementations of this algorithm [8] and its speed-optimized versions [1,36] use full-precision integer arithmetic and parallelism to minimize cycle count. Hence the reported architectures consume large areas and are thus not suitable for lightweight implementations. We observe that the original lazy reduction algorithm [8] can also be implemented in a word-serial fashion to reduce area requirements but such a change in the design decision increases cycle count. To reduce the number of cycles, we optimize the computational steps of Algorithm 1. Further, we investigate side-channel vulnerability of the algorithm and propose lightweight countermeasures against SPA.

Computational Optimization. In lines 6 and 7 of Algorithm 1, computations of d_1 and a_0 require subtractions from zero. In a word-serial architecture with only one adder/subtracter circuit, they consume nearly 33 % of the cycles of the scalar reduction. We use the iterative property of Algorithm 1 and eliminate these two subtractions by replacing lines 6 and 7 with the following ones:

$$(d_0, d_1) \leftarrow (d_0/2 - d_1, d_0/2)$$
$$(a_0, a_1) \leftarrow (2a_1, a_1 - a_0) \tag{2}$$

However with this modification, (a_0, a_1) and (d_0, d_1) have a wrong sign after every odd number of iterations of the for-loop in Algorithm 1. It may appear that this wrong sign could affect correctness of (b_0, b_1) in line 5. Since the remainder u (in line 3) is generated from d_0 instead of the correct value $-d_0$, a wrong sign is also assigned to u. Hence, the multiplications $u \cdot a_0$ and $u \cdot a_1$ in line 5 are always correct, and the computation of (b_0, b_1) remains unaffected of the wrong signs.

After completion of the for-loop, the sign of (d_0, d_1) is wrong as m is an odd integer for secure fields. Hence, the correct value of the reduced scalar should be computed as $\rho \leftarrow (b_0 - d_0, b_1 - d_1)$.

Protection Against SPA. In line 5 of Algorithm 1, computation of new (b_0, b_1) depends on the remainder bit (u) generated from d_0 which is initialized to k. Multi-precision additions are performed when $u = 1$; whereas no addition is required when u is zero. A side-channel attacker can detect this conditional computation and can use, e.g., the techniques from [8] to reconstruct the secret key from the remainder bits that are generated during the scalar reduction.

One way to protect the scalar reduction from SPA is to perform dummy additions $(b'_0, b'_1) \leftarrow (b_0 + a_0, b_1 + a_1)$ whenever $u = 0$. However, such countermeasures based on dummy operations require more memory and are vulnerable to fault attacks [11]. We propose a countermeasure inspired by the zero-free τ-adic representations from [32,41]. A zero-free representation is obtained by generating the remainders u from $d = d_0 + d_1\tau$ using a map $\Psi(d) \rightarrow u \in \{1, -1\}$ such that $d - u$ is divisible by τ, but additionally not divisible by τ^2 (see Sect. 3.2). We observe that during the scalar reduction (which is basically a division by τ), we can generate the remainder bits u as either 1 or -1 throughout the entire for-loop in Algorithm 1. Because $u \neq 0$, new (b_0, b_1) is always computed in the for-loop and protection against SPA is achieved without dummy operations. The following equation generates u by observing the second lsb of d_0 and lsb of d_1.

$$
\begin{aligned}
&\text{Case 1: If } d_0[1] = 0 \text{ and } d_1[0] = 0, \text{ then } u \leftarrow -1 \\
&\text{Case 2: If } d_0[1] = 1 \text{ and } d_1[0] = 0, \text{ then } u \leftarrow 1 \\
&\text{Case 3: If } d_0[1] = 0 \text{ and } d_1[0] = 1, \text{ then } u \leftarrow 1 \\
&\text{Case 4: If } d_0[1] = 1 \text{ and } d_1[0] = 1, \text{ then } u \leftarrow -1
\end{aligned}
\tag{3}
$$

The above equation takes an odd d_0 and computes u such that the new d_0 after division of $d - u$ by τ is also an odd integer.

Algorithm 2 shows our computationally efficient SPA-resistant scalar reduction algorithm. All operations are performed in a word-serial fashion. Since the remainder generation in (3) requires the input d_0 to be an odd integer, the lsb of d_0 is always set to 1 (in line 3) when the input scalar k is an even integer. In this case, the algorithm computes the reduced scalar of $k + 1$ instead of k and after the completion of the reduction, the reduced scalar should be decremented by one. Algorithm 2 uses a one-bit register e to implement this requirement. The final subtraction in line 10 uses e as a borrow to the adder/subtracter circuit. In the next section, we show that the subtraction $d_0 - u$ in line 6 also leaks information about u and propose a countermeasure that prevents this.

Input: Integer scalar k
Output: Reduced scalar $\rho = b_0 + b_1\tau \equiv k \pmod{\tau^m - 1}$
1 $(a_0, a_1) \leftarrow (1, 0)$, $(b_0, b_1) \leftarrow (0, 0)$, $(d_0, d_1) \leftarrow (k, 0)$
2 $e \leftarrow \neg d_0[0]$;   /* Set to 1 when d_0 is even */
3 $d_0[0] \leftarrow 1$
4 **for** $i = 0$ **to** $m - 1$ **do**
5      $u \leftarrow \Psi(d_0 + d_1\tau)$;   /* Remainder $u \in \{1, -1\}$, computed using (3) */
6      $d_0 \leftarrow d_0 - u$
7      $(b_0, b_1) \leftarrow (b_0 + u \cdot a_0, b_1 + u \cdot a_1)$
8      $(d_0, d_1) \leftarrow (d_0/2 - d_1, d_0/2)$;   /* Saves one subtraction */
9      $(a_0, a_1) \leftarrow (2a_1, a_1 - a_0)$;   /* Saves one subtraction */
10 $\rho = (b_0, b_1) \leftarrow (b_0 - d_0 - e, b_1 - d_1)$; /* Subtraction instead of addition */

Algorithm 2. SPA-resistant scalar reduction

Input: Reduced scalar $\rho = b_0 + b_1\tau$ with b_0 odd
Output: Zero-free τ-adic bits $(t_{\ell-1}, \cdots t_0)$
1 $i \leftarrow 0$
2 **while** $|b_0| \neq 1$ or $b_1 \neq 0$ **do**
3      $u \leftarrow \Psi(b_0 + b_1\tau)$;   /* Computed using (3) */
4      $b_0 \leftarrow b_0 - u$
5      $(b_0, b_1) \leftarrow (b_1 - b_0/2, -b_0/2)$
6      $t_i \leftarrow u$
7      $i \leftarrow i + 1$
8 $t_i \leftarrow b_0$

Algorithm 3. Computation of zero-free τ-adic representation [32]

3.2 Computation of τ-adic Representation

For side-channel attack resistant point multiplication, we use the zero-free τ-adic representation proposed in [32,41] and described in Algorithm 3. In this paper, we add the following improvements to the algorithm.

Computational Optimization. Computation of b_1 in line 5 of Algorithm 3 requires subtraction from zero. Similar to Sect. 3.1 this subtraction can be avoided by computing $(b_0, b_1) \leftarrow (b_0/2 - b_1, b_0/2)$. With this modification, the sign of (b_0, b_1) will be wrong after an odd number of iterations. In order to correct this, the sign of t_i should be flipped for odd i (by multiplying it with $(-1)^i$).

Protection Against SPA. Though point multiplications with zero-free representations are resistant against SPA [32], the generation of τ-adic bits (Algorithm 3) is vulnerable to SPA. In line 3 of Algorithm 3, a remainder u is computed as per the four different cases described in (3) and then subtracted from b_0 in line 4. We use the following observations to detect the side-channel vulnerability in this subtraction and to propose a countermeasure against SPA.

1. For Case 1, 2 and 3 in (3), the subtractions of u are equivalent to flipping two (or one) least significant bits of b_0. Hence, actual subtractions are not computed in these cases.
2. For Case 4, subtraction of u from b_0 (i.e. computation of $b_0 + 1$) involves carry propagation. Hence, an actual multi-precision subtraction is computed in this case.
3. If any iteration of the while-loop in Algorithm 3 meets Case 4, then the new value of b_1 will be even. Hence, the while-loop will meet either Case 1 or Case 2 in the next iteration.

Based on the differences in computation, a side-channel attacker using SPA can distinguish Case 4 from the other three cases. Hence, the attacker can reveal around 25 % of the bits of a zero-free representation. Moreover, the attacker knows that the following τ-adic bits are biased towards 1 instead of -1 with a probability of $1/3$.

We propose a very low-cost countermeasure that skips this special addition $b_0 + 1$ for Case 4 by merging it with the computation of new (b_0, b_1) in Algorithm 3. In line 5, we compute a new b_0 as:

$$b_0 \leftarrow \left(\frac{b_0 + 1}{2} - b_1\right) = \left(\frac{b_0 - 1}{2} - \{b_1', 0\}\right). \tag{4}$$

Since b_1 is an odd number for Case 4, we can represent it as $\{b_1', 1\}$ and subtract the least significant bit 1 from $(b_0 + 1)/2$ to get $(b_0 - 1)/2$. Since b_0 is always odd, the computation of $(b_0 - 1)/2$ is just a left-shift of b_0.

The computation of $b_1 \leftarrow (b_0 + 1)/2$ in line 5 of Algorithm 3 involves a carry propagation and thus an actual addition becomes necessary. We solve this problem by computing $b_1 \leftarrow (b_0 - 1)/2$ instead of the correct value $b_1 \leftarrow (b_0 + 1)/2$ and remembering the difference (i.e., 1) in a flag register h. Correctness of the τ-adic representation can be maintained by considering this difference in the future computations that use this wrong value of b_1. Now as per observation 3, the next iteration of the while-loop meets either Case 1 or 2. We adjust the previous difference by computing the new b_0 as follows:

$$b_0 \leftarrow \left(\frac{b_0}{2} - (b_1 + h)\right) = \left(\frac{b_0}{2} - b_1 - 1\right). \tag{5}$$

In a hardware architecture, this equation can be computed by setting the borrow input of the adder/subtracter circuit to 1 during the subtraction.

In (6), we show our new map $\Psi'(\cdot)$ that computes a remainder u and a new value h' of the difference flag following the above procedure. We consider $b_1[0] \oplus h$ (instead of $b_1[0]$ as in (3)) because a wrong b_1 is computed in Case 4 and the difference is kept in h.

Case 1: If $b_0[1] = 0$ and $b_1[0] \oplus h = 0$, then $u \leftarrow -1$ and $h' \leftarrow 0$
Case 2: If $b_0[1] = 1$ and $b_1[0] \oplus h = 0$, then $u \leftarrow 1$ and $h' \leftarrow 0$
Case 3: If $b_0[1] = 0$ and $b_1[0] \oplus h = 1$, then $u \leftarrow 1$ and $h' \leftarrow 0$ $\qquad$ (6)
Case 4: If $b_0[1] = 1$ and $b_1[0] \oplus h = 1$, then $u \leftarrow -1$ and $h' \leftarrow 1$

Input: Reduced scalar $\rho = b_0 + b_1\tau$
Output: τ-adic bits $(t_{ell-1}, \cdots t_0)$ and flag f
1   $f \leftarrow$ assign_flag$(b_0[0], b_1[0])$
2   $(b_0[0], b_1[0]) \leftarrow$ bitflip$(b_0[0], b_1[0], f)$;   /* Initial adjustment */
3   $i \leftarrow 0$
4   $h \leftarrow 0$
5   **while** $i < m$ **or** $|b_0| \neq 1$ **or** $b_1 \neq 0$ **do**
6 | $(u, h') \leftarrow \Psi'(b_0 + b_1\tau)$;   /* Computed using (6) */
7 | $b_0[1] \leftarrow \neg b_0[1]$;   /* Second LSB is set to 1 when Case 1 occurs */
8 | $(b_0, b_1) \leftarrow (\frac{b_0}{2} - b_1 - h, \frac{b_0}{2})$
9 | $t_i \leftarrow (-1)^i \cdot u$
10 | $h \leftarrow h'$
11 | $i \leftarrow i + 1$
12 $t_i \leftarrow (-1)^i \cdot b_0$

Algorithm 4. SPA-resistant generation of a zero-free τ-adic representation

The same technique is also applied to protect the subtraction $d_0 - u$ in the scalar reduction in Algorithm 2.

Protection Against Timing Attack. The terminal condition of the while-loop in Algorithm 3 is dependent on the input scalar. Thus by observing the timing of the computation, an attacker is able to know the higher order bits of a short τ-adic representation. This allows the attacker to narrow down the search domain. We observe that we can continue the generation of zero-free τ-adic bits even when the terminal condition in Algorithm 3 is reached. In this case, the redundant part of the τ-adic representation is equivalent to the value of b_0 when the terminal condition was reached for the first time; hence the result of the point multiplication remains correct. For example, starting from $(b_0, b_1) = (1, 0)$, the algorithm generates an intermediate zero-free representation $-\tau - 1$ and again reaches the terminal condition $(b_0, b_1) = (-1, 0)$. The redundant representation $-\tau^2 - \tau - 1$ is equivalent to 1. If we continue, then the next terminal condition is again reached after generating another two bits. In this paper we generate zero-free τ-adic representations that have lengths always larger than or equal to m of the field $\mathbb{F}_{2^m}$. To implement this feature, we added the terminal condition $i < m$ to the while-loop.

In Algorithm 4, we describe an algorithm for generating zero-free representations that applies the proposed computational optimizations and countermeasures against SPA and timing attacks. The while-loops of both Algorithms 3 and 4 require b_0 to be an odd integer. When the input ρ has an even b_0, then an adjustment is made by adding one to b_0 and adding (subtracting) one to (from) b_1 when b_1 is even (odd). This adjustment is recorded in a flag f in the following way: if b_0 is odd, then $f = 0$; otherwise $f = 1$ or $f = 2$ depending on whether b_1 is even or odd, respectively. In the end of a point multiplication, this flag is checked and $(\tau + 1)P$ or $(-\tau + 1)P$ is subtracted from the point multiplication result if $f = 1$ or $f = 2$, respectively. This compensates the initial addition of $(\tau + 1)$ or $(-\tau + 1)$ to the reduced scalar ρ described in line 2 of Algorithm 4.

Input: An integer k, the base point $P = (x, y)$, a random element $r \in \mathbb{F}_{2^m}$
Output: The result point $Q = kP$
1 $(t, f) \leftarrow$ Convert(k) ;   /* Alg. 2 and 4 */
2 $P_{+1} \leftarrow \phi(P) + P$
3 $P_{-1} \leftarrow \phi(P) - P$
4 **if** ℓ *is odd* **then** $Q = (X, Y) \leftarrow t_{\ell-1} P; \ i \leftarrow \ell - 3$
5 **else** $Q = (X, Y) \leftarrow t_{\ell-1} P_{t_{\ell-2} t_{\ell-1}}; \ i \leftarrow \ell - 4$
6 $Q = (X, Y, Z) \leftarrow (Xr, Yr^2, r)$
7 **while** $i \geq 0$ **do**
8 $\quad \mid \quad Q \leftarrow \phi^2(Q)$
9 $\quad \mid \quad Q \leftarrow Q + t_{i+1} P_{t_i t_{i+1}}$
10 $\quad \mid \quad i \leftarrow i - 2$
11 **if** $f = 1$ **then** $Q \leftarrow Q + P_{-1}$
12 **else if** $f = 2$ **then** $Q \leftarrow Q - P_{+1}$
13 $Q = (X, Y) \leftarrow (X/Z, Y/Z^2)$
14 **return** Q

Algorithm 5. Zero-free point multiplication with side-channel counter-measures

4 Point Multiplication

We base the point multiplication algorithm on the use of the zero-free representation discussed in Sect. 3. We give our modification of the point multiplication algorithm of [32,41] with window size $w = 2$ in Algorithm 5. The algorithm includes countermeasures against SPA, DPA, and timing attacks as well as inherent resistance against safe-error fault attacks. Implementation details of each operation used by Algorithm 5 are given in Appendix A. Below, we give a high-level description.

Line 1 computes the zero-free representation t given an integer k using Algorithms 2 and 4. It outputs a zero-free expansion of length ℓ with $t_i \in \{-1, +1\}$ represented as an ℓ-bit vector and a flag f. Lines 2 and 3 perform the precomputations by computing $P_{+1} = \phi(P) + P$ and $P_{-1} = \phi(P) - P$. Lines 4 and 5 initialize the accumulator point Q depending on the length of the zero-free expansion. If the length is odd, then Q is set to $\pm P$ depending on the msb $t_{\ell-1}$. If the length is even, then Q is initialized with $\pm\phi(P) \pm P$ by using the precomputed points depending on the values of the two msb's $t_{\ell-1}$ and $t_{\ell-2}$. Line 6 randomizes Q by using a random element $r \in \mathbb{F}_{2^m}$ as suggested by Coron [9]. This randomization offers protection against DPA and attacks that calculate hypotheses about the values of Q based on its known initial value (e.g., the doubling attack [12]).

Lines 7 to 10 iterate the main loop of the algorithm by observing two bits of the zero-free expansion on each iteration. Each iteration begins in line 8 by computing two Frobenius endomorphisms. Line 9 either adds or subtracts $P_{+1} = (x_{+1}, y_{+1})$ or $P_{-1} = (x_{-1}, y_{-1})$ to or from Q depending on the values of t_i and t_{i+1} processed by the iteration. It is implemented by using the equations from [2] which compute a point addition in mixed affine and López-Dahab [27] coordinates. Point addition and subtraction are carried out with the exactly same pattern of operations (see Appendix A). Lines 11 and 12 correct the adjustments that ensure that b_0 is odd before starting the generation of the zero-free representation (see Sect. 3.2). Line 13 retrieves the affine point of the result point Q.

The pattern of operations in Algorithm 5 is almost constant. The side-channel properties of the conversion (line 1) were discussed in Sect. 3. The precomputation (lines 2 and 3) is fixed and operates only on the base point, which is typically public. The initialization of Q (lines 4 and 5) can be carried out with a constant pattern of operations with the help of dummy operations. The randomization of Q protects from differential power analysis (DPA) and comparative side-channel attacks (e.g., the doubling attack [12]). The main loop operates with a fixed pattern of operations on a randomized Q offering protecting against SPA and DPA. Lines 11 and 12 depend on t (and, thus, k) but they leak at most one bit to an adversary who can determine whether they were computed or not. This leakage can be prevented with a dummy operation. Although the algorithm includes dummy operations, it offers good protection also against safe-error fault attacks. The reason is that the main loop does not involve any dummy operations and, hence, even an attacker, who is able to distinguish dummy operations, learns only few bits of information (at most, the lsb and the msb and whether the length is odd or even). Hence, fault attacks that aim to reveal secret information by distinguishing dummy operations are not a viable attack strategy.

5   Architecture

In this section, we describe the hardware architecture (Fig. 1) of our ECC coprocessor for 16-bit microcontrollers such as TI MSP430F241x or MSP430F261x [40]. Such families of low-power microcontrollers have at least 4 KB of RAM and can run at 16 MHz clock. We connect our coprocessor to the microcontroller using a memory-mapped interface [35] following the drop-in concept from [42] where the coprocessor is placed on the bus between the microcontroller and the RAM and memory access is controlled with multiplexers. The coprocessor consists of the following components: an arithmetic and logic unit (ALU), an address generation unit, a shared memory and a control unit composed of hierarchical finite state machines (FSMs).

The Arithmetic and Logic Unit (ECC-ALU) has a 16-bit data path and is used for both integer and binary field computations. The ECC-ALU is interfaced with the memory block using an input register pair (R_1, R_2) and an output multiplexer. The central part of the ECC-ALU consists of a 16-bit integer adder/subtracter circuit, a 16-bit binary multiplier and two binary adders. A small *Reduction-ROM* contains several constants that are used during modular reductions and multiplications by constants. The accumulator register pair (CU, CL) stores the intermediate or final results of any arithmetic operation.

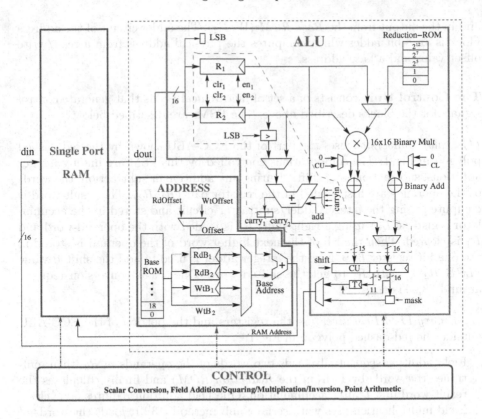

Fig. 1. Hardware architecture of the ECC coprocessor

Finally, the output multiplexer is used to store the contents of the registers CL, T and a masked version of CL in the memory block, which sets the msb's of the most significant word of an element to zero.

The Memory Block is a single-port RAM which is shared by the ECC coprocessor and the 16-bit microcontroller. Each 283-bit element of $\mathbb{F}_{2^{283}}$ requires 18 16-bit words totaling 288 bits. The coprocessor requires storage for 14 elements of $\mathbb{F}_{2^{283}}$ (see Appendix A), which gives 4032 bits of RAM (252 16-bit words). Some of these variables are reused for different purposes during the conversion.

The Address Unit generates address signals for the memory block. A small *Base-ROM* is used to keep the base addresses for storing different field elements in the memory. During any integer operation or binary field operation, the two address registers RdB_1 and RdB_2 in the address unit are loaded with the base addresses of the input operands. Similarly the base addresses for writing intermediate or final results in the memory block are provided in the register WtB_1

and in the output from the *Base-ROM* (WtB_2). The adder circuit of the address block is an 8-bit adder which computes the physical address from a read/write offset value and a base address.

The Control Unit consists of a set of hierarchical FSMs that generate control signals for the blocks described above. The FSMs are described below.

(1) Scalar Conversion uses the part of the ECC-ALU shown by the red dashed polygon in Fig. 1. The computations controlled by this FSM are mainly integer additions, subtractions and shifts. During any addition or subtraction, the words of the operands are first loaded in the register pair (R_1, R_2). The result-word is computed using the integer adder/subtracter circuit and stored in the accumulator register CL. During a right-shift, R_2 is loaded with the operand-word and R_1 is cleared. Then the lsb of the next higher word of the operand is stored in the one-bit register LSB. Now the integer adder is used to add the shifted value $\{LSB, R_2/2\}$ with R_1 to get the shifted word. One scalar conversion requires around 78,000 cycles.

(2) Binary Field Primitives use the registers and the portion of the ECC-ALU outside the red-dashed polygon in Fig. 1.

- Field addition sequentially loads two words of the operands in R_2, then multiplies the words by 1 (from the *Reduction-ROM*) and finally calculates the result-word in CL after accumulation. One field addition requires 60 cycles.
- Field multiplication uses word-serial comb method [13]. It loads the words of the operands in R_1 and R_2, then multiplies the words and finally accumulates. After the completion of the comb multiplication, a modular reduction is performed requiring mainly left-shifts and additions. The left-shifts are performed by multiplying the words with the values from the *Reduction-ROM*. One field multiplication requires 829 cycles.
- Field squaring computes the square of an element of $\mathbb{F}_{2^{283}}$ in linear time by squaring its words. The FSM first loads a word in both R_1 and R_2 and then squares the word by using the binary multiplier. After squaring the words, the FSM performs a modular reduction. The modular reduction is shared with the field multiplication FSM. One field squaring requires 200 cycles.
- Field inversion uses the Itoh-Tsujii algorithm [17] and performs field multiplications and squarings following an addition chain $(1, 2, 4, 8, 16, 17, 34, 35, 70, 140, 141, 282)$ for $\mathbb{F}_{2^{283}}$. One inversion requires 65,241 cycles.

(3) Point Operations and Point Multiplication are implemented by combining an FSM with a hardwired program ROM. The program ROM includes subprograms for all operations of Algorithm 5 and the address of the ROM is controlled by the FSM in order to execute Algorithm 5 (see Appendix A for details).

Algorithm 5 is executed so that the microcontroller initializes the addresses reserved for the accumulator point Q with the base point (x, y) and the random element r by writing $(X, Y, Z) \leftarrow (x, y, r)$. The scalar k is written into the

RAM before the microcontroller issues a start point multiplication command. When this command is received, the reduction part of the conversion is executed followed by the computation of the msb(s) of the zero-free expansion. After this, the precomputations are performed by using (x, y) and the results are stored into the RAM. The initialization of Q is performed by writing either P_{+1} or P_{-1} in (X, Y) if the length of the expansion is even; otherwise, a dummy write is performed. Similarly, the sign of Q is changed if $t_{\ell-1} = -1$ and a dummy operation is computed otherwise. The main loop first executes two Frobenius endomorphisms and, then, issues an instruction that computes the next two bits of the zero-free expansion. By using these bits, either a point addition or a point subtraction is computed with P_{+1} or P_{-1}. One iteration of the main loop takes 9537 clock cycles. In the end, the affine coordinates of the result point are retrieved and they become available for the microcontroller in the addresses for the X and Y coordinates of Q.

6   Results and Comparisons

We described the architecture of Sect. 5 by using mixed Verilog and VHDL and simulated it with ModelSim SE 6.6d. We synthesized the code with Synopsys Design Compiler D-2010.03-SP4 using the regular compile for UMC 130 nm CMOS with voltage of 1.2 V by using Faraday FSC0L low-leakage standard cell libraries. The area given by the synthesis is 4,323 GE including everything in Fig. 1 except the single-port RAM. Computing one point multiplication requires in total 1,566,000 clock cycles including the scalar conversion. The power consumption at 16 MHz is 97.70 μW which gives an energy consumption of approximately 9.56 μJ per point multiplication. Table 1 summarizes our synthesis results together with several other lightweight ECC implementations from the literature.

Among all lightweight ECC processors available in the literature, the processor from [4] is the closest counterpart to our implementation because it is so far the only one that uses Koblitz curves. Even it has many differences with our architecture which make fair comparison difficult. The most obvious difference is that the processor from [4] is designed for a less secure Koblitz curve NIST K-163. Also the architecture of [4] differs from ours in many fundamental ways: they use a finite field over normal basis instead of polynomial basis, they use a bit-serial multiplier that requires all bits of both operands to be present during the entire multiplication instead of a word-serial architecture that we use, they store all variables in registers embedded into the processor architecture instead of an external RAM, and they also do not provide support for scalar conversions or any countermeasures against side-channel attacks. They also provide implementation results on 65 nm CMOS. Our architecture is significantly more scalable for different Koblitz curves because, besides control logic and RAM requirements, other parts remain almost the same, whereas the entire multiplier needs to be changed for [4]. It is also hard to see how scalar conversions or side-channel countermeasures could be integrated into the architecture of [4] without significant increases on both area and latency.

Table 1. Comparison to other lightweight coprocessors for ECC. The top part consists of relevant implementations from the literature. We also provide estimates for other parameter sets in order to ease comparisons to existing works.

Work	Curve	Conv	RAM	Tech. (nm)	Freq. (MHz)	Area (GE)	Latency (cycles)	Latency (ms)	Power (μW^a)
[5], 2006	B-163	n/a	no	130	0.500	9,926	95,159	190.32	<60
[6], 2008	B-163	n/a	yes	220	0.847	12,876	–	95	93
[15], 2008	B-163	n/a	yes	180	0.106	13,250	296,299	2,792	80.85
[24], 2006	B-163	n/a	yes	350	13.560	16,207	376,864	27.90	n/a
[26], 2008	B-163	n/a	yes	130	1.130	12,506	275,816	244.08	32.42
[43], 2011	B-163	n/a	yes	130	0.100	8,958	286,000	2,860	32.34
[42], 2013	B-163	n/a	no	130	1.000	4,114	467,370	467.37	66.1
[34], 2014	P-160	n/a	yes	130	1.000	12,448[b]	139,930	139.93	42.42
[4], 2014	K-163	no	yes[c]	65	13.560	11,571	106,700	7.87	5.7
Our, est	B-163	yes	no	130	16.000	≈3,773	≈485,000	≈30.31	≈6.11
Our, est	K-163	yes	no	130	16.000	≈4,323	≈420,900	≈26.30	≈6.11
Our, est	B-283	yes	no	130	16.000	≈3,773	≈1,934,000	≈120.89	≈6.11
Our, est	K-283	yes	yes[d]	130	16.000	10,204	1,566,000	97.89	>6.11
Our	K-283	yes	no	130	16.000	4,323	1,566,000	97.89	6.11

[a] Normalized to 1 MHz.
[b] Contains everything required for ECDSA including a Keccak module.
[c] All variables are stored in registers inside the processor.
[d] The 256 × 16-bit RAM is estimated to have an area of 5794 GE because the size of a single-port 256 × 8-bit RAM has an area of 2897 GE [42].

Table 1 includes also implementations that use the binary curve B-163 and the prime curve P-160 from [31]. The area of our coprocessor is on the level of the smallest coprocessors available in the literature. Hence, the effect of selecting a 283-bit elliptic curve instead of a less secure curve is negligible in terms of area. The price to pay for higher security comes in the form of memory requirements and computation latency. The amount of memory is not a major issue because our processor shares the memory with the microcontroller which typically has a large memory (e.g. TI MSP430F241x and MSP430F261x have at least 4 KB RAM [40]). Also the computation time is on the same level with other published implementations because our coprocessor is designed to run on the relatively high clock frequency of the microcontroller which is 16 MHz.

In this work our main focus was to investigate feasibility of lightweight implementations of Koblitz curves for applications demanding high security. To enable a somewhat fair comparison with the existing lightweight implementations over $\mathbb{F}_{2^{163}}$, Table 1 provides estimates (see Appendix B) for area and cycles of ECC coprocessors that follow the design decisions presented in this paper and perform point multiplications on curves B-163 or K-163. Our estimates show that our coprocessors for both B-163 and K-163 require more cycles in comparison to [43] which also uses a 16-bit ALU. The reason behind this is that [43] uses a dual-port RAM, whereas our implementation uses a single-port RAM (as it works as a coprocessor of MSP430). Moreover [43] has a dedicated squarer circuit to minimize cycle requirement for squaring.

Table 1 provides estimates for cycle and area of a modified version of the coprocessor that performs point multiplications using the Montgomery's ladder on the NIST curve B-283. The estimated cycle count is calculated from the cycle counts of the field operations described in Sect. 5. From the estimated value, we see that a point multiplication on B-283 requires nearly 23.5 % more time. However, the coprocessor for B-283 is smaller by around 550 GE as no scalar conversion is needed.

Although application-specific integrated circuits are the primary targets for our coprocessor, it may be useful also for FPGA-based implementations whenever small ECC designs are needed. Hence, we compiled our coprocessor also for Xilinx Spartan-6 XC6SLX4-2TQG144 FPGA by using Xilinx ISE 13.4 Design Suite. After place & route, it requires only 209 slices (634 LUTs and 309 registers) and runs on clock frequencies up to 106.598 MHz.

Our coprocessor significantly improves speed, both classical and side-channel security, memory footprint, and energy consumption compared to leading lightweight software [3,10,16,21,38]. For example, [10] reports a highly optimized Assembly implementation running on a 32-bit Cortex-M0+ processor clocked at 48 MHz that computes a point multiplication on a less secure Koblitz curve K-233 without strong side-channel countermeasures. It computes a point multiplication in 59.18 ms (177.54 ms at 16 MHz) and consumes 34.16 μJ of energy.

7   Conclusions

In this paper we showed that implementing point multiplication on a high security 283-bit Koblitz curve is feasible with extremely low resources making it possible for various lightweight applications. We also showed that Koblitz curves can be used in such applications even when the cryptosystem requires scalar conversions. Beside these contributions, we improved the scalar conversion by applying several optimizations and countermeasures against side-channel attacks. Finally, we designed a very lightweight architecture in only 4.3 kGE that can be used as a coprocessor for commercial 16-bit microcontrollers. Hence, we showed that Koblitz curves are feasible also for lightweight ECC even with on-the-fly scalar conversions and strong countermeasures against side-channel attacks.

Acknowlegments. S. Sinha Roy was supported by the Erasmus Mundus PhD Scholarship and K. Järvinen was funded by FWO Pegasus Marie Curie Fellowship. This work was supported by the Research Council KU Leuven: TENSE (GOA/11/007), by iMinds, by the Flemish Government, FWO G.0550.12N, G.00130.13N and FWO G.0876.14N, and by the Hercules Foundation AKUL/11/19. We thank Bohan Yang for his help with ASIC synthesis and simulations.

A   Implementation of Operations Used by Algorithm 5

The operations required by Algorithm 5 are implemented by combining an FSM and a program ROM. The program ROM includes subprograms for all operations of Algorithm 5 and the FSM sets the address of the ROM to the first instruction of the subprogram according the phase of the algorithm and t_{i+1}, t_i.

Table 2 shows the contents of the program ROM. The operations required by Algorithm 5 are in this ROM as follows:

- Line 0 obtains the next bits of the zero-free representation.
- Lines 1–23 perform the precomputation that computes $(x_{+1}, y_{+1}) = \phi(P) + P$ and $(x_{-1}, y_{-1}) = \phi(P) - P$.
- Line 24 computes the negative of Q during the initialization and Line 25 is the corresponding dummy operation.
- Lines 26–28 randomize the projective coordinates of Q by using the random $r \in \mathbb{F}_{2^{283}}$ which is stored in Z.
- Lines 29–34 compute two Frobenius endomorphisms for Q.
- Lines 35–37 set $(x_p, y_p) \leftarrow (x_{+1}, y_{+1}) = \phi(P) + P$ and compute the y-coordinate of its negative to y_m.

Table 2. The program ROM includes instructions for the following operations

0 Convert(k)	20 $y_{-1} \leftarrow y_{-1} \times T_1$	40 $y_m \leftarrow x_{+1} + y_{-1}$	60 $T_2 \leftarrow x_p \times Z$
1 $x_{+1} \leftarrow X^2$	21 $y_{-1} \leftarrow y_{-1} + x_{-1}$	41 $x_p \leftarrow x_{+1}$	61 $T_2 \leftarrow T_2 + X$
2 $y_{+1} \leftarrow Y^2$	22 $y_{-1} \leftarrow y_{-1} + Y$	42 $y_m \leftarrow y_{+1}$	62 $Y \leftarrow Y + Z$
3 $x_{+1} \leftarrow X + x_{+1}$	23 $y_{-1} \leftarrow y_{-1} + X$	43 $y_p \leftarrow x_{+1} + y_{+1}$	63 $Y \leftarrow Y \times T_2$
4 $x_{-1} \leftarrow x_{+1}^{-1}$	24 $Y \leftarrow X + Y$	44 $x_p \leftarrow x_{-1}$	64 $T_1 \leftarrow Z^2$
5 $T_1 \leftarrow Y + y_{+1}$	25 $T_1 \leftarrow X + Y$	45 $y_m \leftarrow y_{-1}$	65 $T_1 \leftarrow T_1 \times y_m$
6 $y_{-1} \leftarrow T_1 \times x_{-1}$	26 $X \leftarrow X \times Z$	46 $y_p \leftarrow x_{-1} + y_{-1}$	66 $Y \leftarrow Y + T_1$
7 $T_1 \leftarrow y_{-1}^2$	27 $T_1 \leftarrow Z^2$	47 $T_1 \leftarrow Z^2$	67 $x_{+1} \leftarrow Z$
8 $T_1 \leftarrow T_1 + y_{-1}$	28 $Y \leftarrow Y \times T_1$	48 $T_1 \leftarrow T_1 \times y_p$	68 $x_{-1} \leftarrow x_{+1}^{-1}$
9 $x_{+1} \leftarrow T_1 + x_{+1}$	29 $Y \leftarrow Y^2$	49 $T_1 \leftarrow T_1 + Y$	69 $X \leftarrow X \times x_{-1}$
10 $T_1 \leftarrow x_{+1} + X$	30 $Y \leftarrow Y^2$	50 $T_2 \leftarrow Z \times x_p$	70 $x_{-1} \leftarrow x_{-1}^2$
11 $y_{+1} \leftarrow T_1 + y_{-1}$	31 $X \leftarrow X^2$	51 $T_2 \leftarrow T_2 + X$	71 $Y \leftarrow Y \times x_{-1}$
12 $y_{+1} \leftarrow y_{+1} + x_{+1}$	32 $X \leftarrow X^2$	52 $X \leftarrow T_2^2$	72 $X \leftarrow x_{+1}$
13 $y_{+1} \leftarrow y_{+1} + Y$	33 $Z \leftarrow Z^2$	53 $X \leftarrow X + T_1$	73 $Y \leftarrow y_{+1}$
14 $x_{-1} \leftarrow x_{-1} \times X$	34 $Z \leftarrow Z^2$	54 $T_2 \leftarrow T_2 \times Z$	74 $X \leftarrow x_{-1}$
15 $y_{-1} \leftarrow y_{-1} + x_{-1}$	35 $x_p \leftarrow x_{+1}$	55 $X \leftarrow X \times T_2$	75 $Y \leftarrow y_{-1}$
16 $T_1 \leftarrow x_{-1}^2$	36 $y_p \leftarrow y_{+1}$	56 $Y \leftarrow T_1 \times T_2$	76 $T_1 \leftarrow x_{+1}$
17 $x_{-1} \leftarrow x_{-1} + T_1$	37 $y_m \leftarrow x_{+1} + y_{+1}$	57 $T_1 \leftarrow T_1^2$	77 $T_2 \leftarrow y_{+1}$
18 $x_{-1} \leftarrow x_{-1} + x_{+1}$	38 $x_p \leftarrow x_{-1}$	58 $X \leftarrow X + T_1$	
19 $T_1 \leftarrow x_{-1} + X$	39 $y_p \leftarrow y_{-1}$	59 $Z \leftarrow T_2^2$	

- Lines 38–40 set $(x_p, y_p) \leftarrow (x_{-1}, y_{-1}) = \phi(P) - P$ and compute the y-coordinate of its negative to y_m.
- Lines 41–43 compute $(x_p, y_p) \leftarrow -(x_{+1}, y_{+1}) = -\phi(P) - P$ and set the y-coordinate of its negative to y_m.
- Lines 44–46 compute $(x_p, y_p) \leftarrow -(x_{-1}, y_{-1}) = -\phi(P) + P$ and set the y-coordinate of its negative to y_m.
- Lines 47–66 compute the point addition $(X, Y, Z) \leftarrow (X, Y, Z) + (x_p, y_p)$ in López-Dahab coordinates using the equations from [2].
- Lines 67–71 recover the affine coordinates of Q by computing $(X, Y) \leftarrow (X/Z, Y/Z^2)$.
- Lines 72–73 and lines 74–75 initialize Q with (x_{+1}, y_{+1}) and (x_{-1}, y_{-1}), respectively, and lines 76–77 perform a dummy operation for these operations.

Point addition and point subtraction are computed with exactly the same sequence of operations. This is achieved by introducing an initialization which sets the values of three internal variables x_p, y_p, and y_m according to Table 3 (these are in lines 35–46 in Table 2). This always requires two copy instructions followed by an addition. After this initialization, both point addition and point subtraction are computed with a common sequence of operations which adds the point (x_p, y_p) to Q. The element x_m is the y coordinate of the negative of (x_p, y_p) and it is also used during the point addition.

Table 3. Initialization of point addition and point subtraction

t_{i+1}, t_i	1st	2nd	3rd
$+1, +1$	$x_p \leftarrow x_{+1}$	$y_p \leftarrow y_{+1}$	$y_m \leftarrow x_{+1} + y_{+1}$
$+1, -1$	$x_p \leftarrow x_{-1}$	$y_p \leftarrow y_{-1}$	$y_m \leftarrow x_{-1} + y_{-1}$
$-1, +1$	$x_p \leftarrow x_{-1}$	$y_m \leftarrow y_{-1}$	$y_p \leftarrow x_{-1} + y_{-1}$
$-1, -1$	$x_p \leftarrow x_{+1}$	$y_m \leftarrow y_{+1}$	$y_p \leftarrow x_{+1} + y_{+1}$

B   Estimates for B-163 and K-163

Our estimated cycle count for scalar multiplication over $\mathbb{F}_{2^{163}}$ is based on the following facts:

1. A field element in $\mathbb{F}_{2^{163}}$ requires 11 16-bit words, and hence, is smaller by a factor of 0.61 than a field element in $\mathbb{F}_{2^{283}}$. Since field addition and squaring have linear complexity, we estimate that the cycle counts for these operations scale down by a factor of around 0.61 and become 37 and 122 respectively. In a similarly way we estimate that field multiplication (which has quadratic complexity) scales down to 309 cycles. A field inversion operation following an addition chain $(1, 2, 4, 5, 10, 20, 40, 81, 162)$ requires nearly 22,700 cycles.

2. The for-loop in the scalar reduction operation (Algorithm 2) executes 163 times in $\mathbb{F}_{2^{163}}$ and performs linear operations such as additions/subtractions and shifting. Moreover the length of τ-adic representation of a scalar reduces to 163 (thus reducing by a factor of 0.57 in comparison to $\mathbb{F}_{2^{283}}$). So, we estimate that the cycle count for scalar conversion scales down by a factor of 0.57×0.61 and requires nearly 27,000 cycles.

3. One Frobenius-and-add operation over $\mathbb{F}_{2^{283}}$ in Algorithm 5 spends total 9,537 cycles among which 6,632 cycles are spent in eight quadratic-time field multiplications, and the rest 2,905 cycles are spent in linear-time operations. After scaling down, the cycle count for one Frobenius-and-add operation over $\mathbb{F}_{2^{163}}$ can be estimated to be around 4,250. The point multiplication loop iterates nearly 82 times for a τ-adic representation of length 164. Hence the number of cycles spent in this loop can be estimated to be around 348,500.

4. The precomputation and the final conversion steps are mainly dominated by the cost of field inversions. Hence the cycle counts can be estimated to be around 45,400.

As per the above estimates we see that a point multiplication using K-163 requires nearly 420,900 cycles. Similarly, we estimate that Montgomery's ladder for B-163 requires nearly 485,000 cycles.

References

1. Adikari, J., Dimitrov, V., Järvinen, K.: A fast hardware architecture for integer to τNAF conversion for Koblitz curves. IEEE Trans. Comput. **61**(5), 732–737 (2012)
2. Al-Daoud, E., Mahmod, R., Rushdan, M., Kilicman, A.: A new addition formula for elliptic curves over $GF(2^n)$. IEEE Trans. Comput. **51**(8), 972–975 (2002)
3. Aranha, D.F., Dahab, R., López, J., Oliveira, L.B.: Efficient implementation of elliptic curve cryptography in wireless sensors. Adv. Math. Commun. **4**(2), 169–187 (2010)
4. Azarderakhsh, R., Järvinen, K.U., Mozaffari-Kermani, M.: Efficient algorithm and architecture for elliptic curve cryptography for extremely constrained secure applications. IEEE Trans. Circ. Syst. I–Regul. Pap. **61**(4), 1144–1155 (2014)
5. Batina, L., Mentens, N., Sakiyama, K., Preneel, B., Verbauwhede, I.: Low-cost elliptic curve cryptography for wireless sensor networks. In: Buttyán, L., Gligor, V.D., Westhoff, D. (eds.) ESAS 2006. LNCS, vol. 4357, pp. 6–17. Springer, Heidelberg (2006)
6. Bock, H., Braun, M., Dichtl, M., Hess, E., Heyszl, J., Kargl, W., Koroschetz, H., Meyer, B., Seuschek, H.: A milestone towards RFID products offering asymmetric authentication based on elliptic curve cryptography. In: Proceedings of the 4th Workshop on RFID Security – RFIDSec 2008 (2008)
7. Brumley, B.B., Järvinen, K.U.: Koblitz curves and integer equivalents of frobenius expansions. In: Adams, C., Miri, A., Wiener, M. (eds.) SAC 2007. LNCS, vol. 4876, pp. 126–137. Springer, Heidelberg (2007)
8. Brumley, B.B., Järvinen, K.U.: Conversion algorithms and implementations for Koblitz curve cryptography. IEEE Trans. Comput. **59**(1), 81–92 (2010)
9. Coron, J.-S.: Resistance against differential power analysis for elliptic curve cryptosystems. In: Koç, Ç.K., Paar, C. (eds.) CHES 1999. LNCS, vol. 1717, pp. 292–302. Springer, Heidelberg (1999)

10. De Clercq, R., Uhsadel, L., Van Herrewege, A., Verbauwhede, I.: Ultra low-power implementation of ECC on the ARM Cortex-M0+. In: Design Automation Conference – DAC 2014, pp. 1–6. ACM (2014)

11. Fan, J., Verbauwhede, I.: An updated survey on secure ECC implementations: attacks, countermeasures and cost. In: Naccache, D. (ed.) Cryphtography and Security: From Theory to Applications. LNCS, vol. 6805, pp. 265–282. Springer, Heidelberg (2012)

12. Fouque, P.-A., Valette, F.: The doubling attack – why upwards is better than downwards. In: Walter, C.D., Koç, Ç.K., Paar, C. (eds.) CHES 2003. LNCS, vol. 2779, pp. 269–280. Springer, Heidelberg (2003)

13. Hankerson, D., Menezes, A.J., Vanstone, S.: Guide to Elliptic Curve Cryptography. Springer-Verlag New York, Inc., Secaucus (2003)

14. Hasan, M.A.: Power analysis attacks and algorithmic approaches to their countermeasures for Koblitz curve cryptosystems. IEEE Trans. Comput. **50**(10), 1071–1083 (2001)

15. Hein, D., Wolkerstorfer, J., Felber, N.: ECC is ready for RFID – a proof in silicon. In: Avanzi, R.M., Keliher, L., Sica, F. (eds.) SAC 2008. LNCS, vol. 5381, pp. 401–413. Springer, Heidelberg (2009)

16. Hinterwälder, G., Moradi, A., Hutter, M., Schwabe, P., Paar, C.: Full-size high-security ECC implementation on MSP430 microcontrollers. In: Aranha, D.F., Menezes, A. (eds.) LATINCRYPT 2014. LNCS, vol. 8895, pp. 31–47. Springer, Heidelberg (2015)

17. Itoh, T., Tsujii, S.: A fast algorithm for computing multiplicative inverses in $GF(2^m)$ using normal bases. Inf. Comput. **78**(3), 171–177 (1988)

18. Järvinen, K.: Optimized FPGA-based elliptic curve cryptography processor for high-speed applications. Integr. VLSI J. **44**(4), 270–279 (2011)

19. Järvinen, K., Forsten, J., Skyttä, J.: Efficient circuitry for computing τ-adic non-adjacent form. In: Proceedings of the 13th IEEE International Conference on Electronics, Circuits and Systems – ICECS 2006, pp. 232–235. IEEE (2006)

20. Järvinen, K., Verbauwhede, I.: How to use Koblitz curves on small devices? In: Joye, M., Moradi, A. (eds.) CARDIS 2014. LNCS, vol. 8968, pp. 154–170. Springer, Heidelberg (2015)

21. Kargl, A., Pyka, S., Seuschek, H.: Fast arithmetic on ATmega128 for elliptic curve cryptography. Cryptology ePrint Archive, Report 2008/442 (2008)

22. Koblitz, N.: Elliptic curve cryptosystems. Math. Comput. **48**(177), 203–209 (1987)

23. Koblitz, N.: CM-curves with good cryptographic properties. In: Feigenbaum, J. (ed.) CRYPTO 1991. LNCS, vol. 576, pp. 279–287. Springer, Heidelberg (1992)

24. Kumar, S., Paar, C.: Are standards compliant elliptic curve cryptosystems feasible on RFID? In: Handouts of the Workshop on RFID Security – RFIDSec 2006 (2006)

25. Lange, T.: Koblitz curve cryptosystems. Finite Fields Appl. **11**, 200–229 (2005)

26. Lee, Y.K., Sakiyama, K., Batina, L., Verbauwhede, I.: Elliptic-curve-based security processor for RFID. IEEE Trans. Comput. **57**(11), 1514–1527 (2008)

27. López, J., Dahab, R.: Improved algorithms for elliptic curve arithmetic in $GF(2^n)$. In: Tavares, S., Meijer, H. (eds.) SAC 1998. LNCS, vol. 1556, pp. 201–212. Springer, Heidelberg (1999)

28. Meier, W., Staffelbach, O.: Efficient multiplication on certain nonsupersingular elliptic curves. In: Brickell, E.F. (ed.) CRYPTO 1992. LNCS, vol. 740, pp. 333–344. Springer, Heidelberg (1993)

29. Miller, V.S.: Use of elliptic curves in cryptography. In: Williams, H.C. (ed.) CRYPTO 1985. LNCS, vol. 218, pp. 417–426. Springer, Heidelberg (1986)

30. Montgomery, P.L.: Speeding the Pollard and elliptic curve methods of factorization. Math. Comput. **48**, 243–264 (1987)
31. National Institute of Standards and Technology (NIST): Digital signature standard (DSS). Federal Information Processing Standard, FIPS PUB 186–4, July 2013
32. Okeya, K., Takagi, T., Vuillaume, C.: Efficient representations on Koblitz curves with resistance to side channel attacks. In: Boyd, C., González Nieto, J.M. (eds.) ACISP 2005. LNCS, vol. 3574, pp. 218–229. Springer, Heidelberg (2005)
33. Oliveira, T., López, J., Aranha, D.F., Rodríguez-Henríquez, F.: Lambda coordinates for binary elliptic curves. In: Bertoni, G., Coron, J.-S. (eds.) CHES 2013. LNCS, vol. 8086, pp. 311–330. Springer, Heidelberg (2013)
34. Pessl, P., Hutter, M.: Curved tags — a low-resource ECDSA implementation tailored for RFID. In: Sadeghi, A.-R., Saxena, N. (eds.) RFIDSec 2014. LNCS, vol. 8651, pp. 156–172. Springer, Heidelberg (2014)
35. Schaumont, P.R.: A Practical Introduction to Hardware/Software Codesign, 2nd edn. Springer, US (2013)
36. Sinha Roy, S., Fan, J., Verbauwhede, I.: Accelerating scalar conversion for Koblitz curve cryptoprocessors on hardware platforms. IEEE Trans. Very Large Scale Integr. (VLSI) Syst. **23**(5), 810–818 (2015)
37. Solinas, J.A.: Efficient arithmetic on Koblitz curves. Des. Codes Crypt. **19**(2–3), 195–249 (2000)
38. Szczechowiak, P., Oliveira, L.B., Scott, M., Collier, M., Dahab, R.: NanoECC: testing the limits of elliptic curve cryptography in sensor networks. In: Verdone, R. (ed.) EWSN 2008. LNCS, vol. 4913, pp. 305–320. Springer, Heidelberg (2008)
39. Taverne, J., Faz-Hernández, A., Aranha, D.F., Rodríguez-Henríquez, F., Hankerson, D., López, J.: Speeding scalar multiplication over binary elliptic curves using the new carry-less multiplication instruction. J. Cryptographic Eng. **1**(3), 187–199 (2011)
40. Texas Instruments: MSP430F261x and MSP430F241x, Jun 2007, Rev Nov 2012. http://www.ti.com/lit/ds/symlink/msp430f2618.pdf. Accessed 4 June 2015
41. Vuillaume, C., Okeya, K., Takagi, T.: Defeating simple power analysis on Koblitz curves. IEICE Trans. Fundam. Electron. Commun. Comput. Sci. **E89–A**(5), 1362–1369 (2006)
42. Wenger, E.: Hardware architectures for MSP430-based wireless sensor nodes performing elliptic curve cryptography. In: Jacobson, M., Locasto, M., Mohassel, P., Safavi-Naini, R. (eds.) ACNS 2013. LNCS, vol. 7954, pp. 290–306. Springer, Heidelberg (2013)
43. Wenger, E., Hutter, M.: A hardware processor supporting elliptic curve cryptography for less than 9 kGEs. In: Prouff, E. (ed.) CARDIS 2011. LNCS, vol. 7079, pp. 182–198. Springer, Heidelberg (2011)

Single Base Modular Multiplication for Efficient Hardware RNS Implementations of ECC

Karim Bigou and Arnaud Tisserand[(✉)]

CNRS, IRISA, INRIA Centre Rennes - Bretagne Atlantique and University Rennes 1,
6 rue Kerampont, CS 80518, 22305 Lannion Cedex, France
{karim.bigou,arnaud.tisserand}@irisa.fr

Abstract. The paper describes a new RNS modular multiplication algorithm for efficient implementations of ECC over $\mathbb{F}_P$. Thanks to the proposition of RNS-friendly Mersenne-like primes, the proposed RNS algorithm requires 2 times less moduli than the state-of-art ones, leading to 4 times less precomputations and about 2 times less operations. FPGA implementations of our algorithm are presented, with area reduced up to 46 %, for a time overhead less than 10 %.

Keywords: Residue number system, Modular multiplication algorithm, Base extension, ECC, Hardware implementation, FPGA

1 Introduction

Over the last decade, the *residue number system* (RNS) has been increasingly proposed to speed up arithmetic computations on large numbers in asymmetric cryptography. This representation allows to quickly perform addition, subtraction and multiplication thanks to a high degree of internal parallelism (see state-of-art in Sect. 3). This nice property has been used for implementing fast cryptographic primitives in both software and hardware systems. For some years, RNS is becoming a popular representation in implementations of *elliptic curve cryptography* (ECC) over $\mathbb{F}_P$ [8,11,14,31]. RNS is also proposed to implement other asymmetric cryptosystems: *RSA* (*e.g.* [4,15,21,23]), *pairings* (*e.g.* [10,32]) and very recently *lattice based cryptography* (*e.g.* [5]). In this paper, we only deal with hardware implementations of ECC.

RNS is a *non positional* number system without an implicit weight associated to each digit like in the standard representation. Then comparison, sign determination, division and modular reduction operations are very costly in RNS. The *modular multiplication*, one of the most important arithmetic operation in asymmetric cryptography, is significantly more costly than a simple multiplication. Thus, many algorithms and optimizations have been proposed for RNS modular multiplication, see [1,2,9,12,14,18,24,26,27].

In RNS, a number is represented by its *residues* (or remainders) modulo a set of *moduli* called the *base*. The base *bit width* denotes the sum of the bit sizes of all moduli. For representing $\mathbb{F}_P$ elements, the RNS base should be large

© International Association for Cryptologic Research 2015
T. Güneysu and H. Handschuh (Eds.): CHES 2015, LNCS 9293, pp. 123–140, 2015.
DOI: 10.1007/978-3-662-48324-4_7

enough: the bit width of the base must be greater than the bit width of the field elements. For instance, [14] uses 8 moduli of 33 bits for $\mathbb{F}_P$ of 256 bits.

Up to now, every RNS modular multiplication algorithm from the literature requires to double the bit width of the base for representing the full product before modular reduction. This is not the case in the standard representation where efficient algorithms allow to merge internal operations of the product and reduction only using intermediate values on the field bit width plus a few additional guard bits. Another current weak point of RNS is the lack of efficient modular reduction algorithm for specific characteristics such as (pseudo-)Mersenne primes ($P = 2^\ell - 1$ or $2^\ell - c$ with $c < 2^{\ell/2}$ for some ℓ) in the standard binary system.

In this paper, we propose a new RNS modular multiplication algorithm which only requires a *single base bit width* instead of a double one. Our algorithm uses field characteristics P specifically selected for very efficient computations in RNS. As far as we know, this new algorithm is the first one which performs an RNS modular multiplication without intermediate values larger than the field bit width (plus a few guard bits). It requires up to 2 times less operations and 4 times less pre-computations than state-of-art algorithms. In ECC standards, the field characteristics have been selected for fast computations in the standard binary representation (*e.g.* $P_{521} = 2^{521} - 1$ in NIST standard [22]). In this work, we propose a new direction to select parameters for very efficient RNS implementations of ECC. We expect scalar multiplications in RNS to be up to 2 times faster for a similar area, or twice smaller for the same computation time (other trade-offs are also possible).

The outline of the paper is as follows. Sections 2 and 3 introduce notations and state-of-art, respectively. The new modular multiplication algorithm is presented in Sect. 4. The theoretical cost of our algorithm is analyzed in Sect. 5. Section 6 presents and comments some FPGA implementation results. Section 7 provides an estimation of the impact of our proposition on complete ECC scalar multiplications in RNS. Finally, Sect. 8 concludes the paper.

2   Notations and Definitions

- Capital letters, *e.g.* X, are $\mathbb{F}_P$ elements or large integers
- $|X|_P$ is $X \bmod P$ and P is an ℓ-bit prime
- $n = \lceil \ell/w \rceil$, *i.e.* the *minimal number of moduli* to represent an ℓ-bit value
- The RNS *base* $\mathcal{B}_a = (m_{a,1}, \ldots, m_{a,n_a})$ composed of n_a *moduli* where all $m_{a,i}$ are *pairwise coprimes* of the form $m_{a,i} = 2^w - h_{a,i}$ and $h_{a,i} < 2^{\lfloor w/2 \rfloor}$
- $\overrightarrow{(X)_a}$ is X in the RNS base $\mathcal{B}_a$, abridged $\overrightarrow{X_a}$ when no confusion is possible, and is defined by:

$$\overrightarrow{(X)_a} = (x_{a,1}, \ldots, x_{a,n_a}) \qquad \text{where} \qquad x_{a,i} = |X|_{m_{a,i}} \tag{1}$$

- $M_a = \prod_{i=1}^{n_a} m_{a,i}, \quad M_{a,i} = \frac{M_a}{m_{a,i}}, \quad \overrightarrow{T_a} = (|M_{a,1}|_{m_{a,1}}, \ldots, |M_{a,n_a}|_{m_{a,n_a}})$
- Similar definitions and notations stand for $\mathcal{B}_b$, an RNS base coprime to $\mathcal{B}_a$

- EMM is a w-bit *elementary modular multiplication* (e.g. $|x_i \cdot y_i|_m$)
- EMW is a w-bit *elementary memory word* (for storage)
- $\overrightarrow{(X)}_{a|b}$ is X in the RNS base $\mathcal{B}_{a|b} = (m_{a,1}, \ldots, m_{a,n_a}, m_{b,1}, \ldots, m_{b,n_b})$ *i.e.* the concatenation of $\mathcal{B}_a$ and $\mathcal{B}_b$
- MSBs are the most significant bits of a value
- MM denotes the state-of-art RNS modular multiplication

3   State of Art

RNS was proposed independently in [13, 29] for signal processing applications in the 50s. RNS is a representation where large numbers are split into *small independent* chunks. The RNS *base* $\mathcal{B}$ is the *set of moduli* $(m_1, \ldots, m_n)$ where all m_i are (small) pairwise coprimes. The representation of the integer X in RNS is $\overrightarrow{X}$, the set of residues $x_i = X \bmod m_i$, $\forall m_i \in \mathcal{B}$. In ECC applications, field elements of hundreds bits are usually split into 16 to 64-bit chunks. Addition/subtraction and multiplication of 2 integers are fast operations in RNS:

$$\overrightarrow{X} \diamond \overrightarrow{Y} = \left(|x_1 \diamond y_1|_{m_1}, \ldots, |x_n \diamond y_n|_{m_n} \right) \quad \forall \diamond \in \{+, -, \times\},$$

where the internal computations are performed *independently* over the *channels* (the i-th channel computes $|x_i \diamond y_i|_{m_i}$). There is *no carry propagation* between the channels. This leads to efficient *parallel* implementations [8, 11, 14]. This property was also used to *randomize* the computations over the channels (in time or space) as a protection against some side-channel attacks [6, 15, 23]. Another RNS advantage is its *flexibility*: the required number of moduli n and the number of physically implemented channels can be different. A physical channel can support several moduli and store the corresponding pre-computations. For instance, [21] presents an RSA implementation over 1024 to 4096 bits.

Conversion from standard representation to RNS is straightforward, one computes all residues of X modulo m_i. To convert back, one must use the *Chinese remainder theorem* (CRT). The CRT states that any integer X can be represented by its residues $x_i = |X|_{m_i}$, if $X < M$ (the product of all moduli) and all moduli are pairwise coprimes. The conversion uses the CRT relation:

$$X = |X|_M = \left| \sum_{i=1}^{n} |x_i \cdot M_i^{-1}|_{m_i} \times M_i \right|_M. \tag{2}$$

As one can observe, the result of the CRT is reduced modulo M, *i.e.* all integers greater than M will be automatically reduced modulo M by the CRT relation. In addition to $\{+, -, \times\}$ operations, some divisions can be performed in parallel in RNS. Exact division by a constant c coprime with M can be computed by multiplying each residue x_i by the inverse $|c^{-1}|_{m_i}$ for each channel.

3.1 Base Extension

All fast algorithms for RNS modular multiplication in state-of-art use the *base extension* (BE) introduced in [30]. It converts $\overrightarrow{X_a}$ in base $\mathcal{B}_a$ into $\overrightarrow{X_b}$ in base $\mathcal{B}_b$. After a BE, X is represented in the concatenation of the two bases $\mathcal{B}_a$ and $\mathcal{B}_b$ denoted $\mathcal{B}_{a|b}$. There are mainly two types of BE algorithms: those based on the CRT relation (Eq. 2) [18,25,28], and those using an intermediate representation called *mixed radix system* (MRS) [3,7,30]. In hardware, the most efficient BE implementations in state-of-art use the CRT based solution [12,14]. Our proposed modular multiplication algorithm can be used with both types of BE algorithm. In this paper, we focus on the CRT based solution since it has less data dependencies and leads to faster hardware implementations.

The state-of-art BE at Algorithm 1 from [18] computes an approximation of Eq. 2 and directly reduces it modulo each $m_{b,i}$ of the new base $\mathcal{B}_b$. One can rewrite Eq. 2 by $X = \sum_{i=1}^{n_a} \left(\left| x_{a,i} \cdot M_{a,i}^{-1} \right|_{m_{a,i}} M_{a,i} \right) - q\, M_a$ in base $\mathcal{B}_a$, where q is the quotient of the sum part by M_a. Then one has:

$$q = \left\lfloor \sum_{i=1}^{n_a} \frac{\left| x_{a,i} \cdot M_{a,i}^{-1} \right|_{m_{a,i}}}{m_{a,i}} \right\rfloor = \left\lfloor \sum_{i=1}^{n_a} \frac{\xi_{a,i}}{m_{a,i}} \right\rfloor. \tag{3}$$

In order to get the value of q, the reference [18] proposed to approximate the value of $\frac{\xi_{a,i}}{m_{a,i}}$ by using $\frac{\mathrm{trunc}(\xi_{a,i})}{2^w}$ (*i.e.* a few MSBs of $\xi_{a,i}$). In Algorithm 1, this approximation is corrected using a selected parameter σ_0. If X is small enough, then the approximation is the exact value. Otherwise it returns either $\overrightarrow{X_b}$ or $\overrightarrow{(X + M_a)_b}$, and this is easily managed in MM algorithms (see details in [18]).

Algorithm 1. Base extension (BE) from [18].

Input: $\overrightarrow{X_a}$, $\mathcal{B}_a$, $\mathcal{B}_b$, σ_0 (*fixed as a global parameter*)

Precomp.: $\overrightarrow{\left(T_a^{-1}\right)_a}$, $\overrightarrow{\left(T_a\right)_b}$, $\overrightarrow{\left(-M_a\right)_b}$

Output: $\overrightarrow{X_b}$

1 $\overrightarrow{\xi_a} = \overrightarrow{X_a} \times \overrightarrow{\left(T_a^{-1}\right)_a}$, $\overrightarrow{X_b} = \overrightarrow{0_b}$, $\sigma = \sigma_0$

2 **for** $i = 1, \ldots, n_a$ **do**

3 $\quad$ $\sigma = \sigma + \mathrm{trunc}(\xi_{a,i})$

4 $\quad$ $q = \lfloor \sigma \rfloor$ $\qquad\qquad\qquad\qquad$ /*q = 0 or 1 */

5 $\quad$ $\sigma = \sigma - q$

6 $\quad$ **for** $j = 1, \ldots, n_b$ **do**

7 $\quad\quad$ $x_{b,j} = \left| x_{b,j} + \xi_{a,i} \cdot M_{a,i} + q \cdot (-M_a) \right|_{m_{b,j}}$

8 **return** $\overrightarrow{X_b}$

BE algorithms are far more expensive than a simple RNS multiplication. For instance, in Algorithm 1, the CRT relation is computed on each channel of the second base. This BE costs $(n_a\, n_b + n_a)$ EMMs. In the usual case $n_a = n_b = n$, the BE cost is $n^2 + n$ against n EMMs for a simple multiplication.

3.2   RNS Montgomery Modular Multiplication

As far as we know, the best state-of-art RNS modular multiplication has been proposed in [26] (presented Algorithm 2). It is an adaptation for RNS of the Montgomery modular multiplication [20], originally in radix-2. Various optimizations have been proposed in [12,14] (factorization of some products by constants).

Algorithm 2. RNS Montgomery Reduction from [26].

Input: $(\overrightarrow{X_a}, \overrightarrow{X_b})$, $(\overrightarrow{Y_a}, \overrightarrow{Y_b})$

Precomp.: $(\overrightarrow{P_a}, \overrightarrow{P_b})$, $\overrightarrow{(-P^{-1})_a}$, $\overrightarrow{(M_a^{-1})_b}$

Output: $\overrightarrow{S} = \left| XY|M^{-1}|_P \right|_P + \delta \overrightarrow{P}$ in $\mathcal{B}_a$ and $\mathcal{B}_b$ with $\delta \in \{0,1,2\}$

1 $\overrightarrow{U_a} \leftarrow \overrightarrow{X_a} \times \overrightarrow{Y_a}$, $\overrightarrow{U_b} \leftarrow \overrightarrow{X_b} \times \overrightarrow{Y_b}$

2 $\overrightarrow{Q_a} \leftarrow \overrightarrow{U_a} \times \overrightarrow{(-P^{-1})_a}$

3 $\overrightarrow{Q_b} \leftarrow \mathrm{BE}\left(\overrightarrow{Q_a}, \mathcal{B}_a, \mathcal{B}_b\right)$

4 $\overrightarrow{R_b} \leftarrow \overrightarrow{U_b} + \overrightarrow{Q_b} \times \overrightarrow{P_b}$

5 $\overrightarrow{S_h} \leftarrow \overrightarrow{R_h} \times \overrightarrow{(M_a^{-1})_h}$

6 $\overrightarrow{S_a} \leftarrow \mathrm{BE}\left(\overrightarrow{S_b}, \mathcal{B}_b, \mathcal{B}_a\right)$

7 **return** $(\overrightarrow{S_a}, \overrightarrow{S_b})$

The first step of Algorithm 2 computes XY on $\mathcal{B}_a$ and $\mathcal{B}_b$. This full product requires a total bit width of $2nw$ bits. Then, we need to perform a multiplication modulo M_a and an exact division by M_a, which is analogous to modular reduction and division by 2^r in the classic Montgomery multiplication. However, modular reduction by M_a is only easy in $\mathcal{B}_a$ (thanks to Eq. (2)) and the exact division by M_a is only easy in $\mathcal{B}_b$ (which is coprime with $\mathcal{B}_a$). Then 2 BEs are required at lines 3 and 6. The result is given in the 2 bases, and is less than $3P$ (with BE from [18]). Using optimizations from [12] and [14], the MM costs $2\,n_a\,n_b + 2n_a + 2n_b$ EMMs (or when $n_a = n_b = n$ one has $2\,n^2 + 4\,n$).

4   Proposed RNS Modular Multiplication Algorithm

Our proposed RNS modular multiplication algorithm, called *single base modular multiplication* (SBMM) relies on two main ideas. First, instead of working on intermediate values represented on two "full" n-moduli RNS bases, it works with only two *half-bases* $\mathcal{B}_a$ and $\mathcal{B}_b$ of $n_a = n_b = n/2$ moduli. It reduces the leading term of the computation cost from n^2 to $\frac{n^2}{4}$ EMMs for a BE. Second, we select the field characteristic $P = M_a^2 - 2$ in order to use these half-bases efficiently, and reduce the computation cost of the RNS modular multiplication from $2n^2$ to n^2 EMMs. This type of P can be seen as analogous to Mersenne primes ($2^\ell - 1$) for the binary representation.

4.1 Decomposition of the Operands

In order to decompose the operands, we use a similar method than the one presented in [9]. Algorithm 3 decomposes the integer X represented by $\overrightarrow{X_{a|b}}$ on the concatenation of both half-bases. The Split function returns $\overrightarrow{(K_x)_{a|b}}$ and $\overrightarrow{(R_x)_{a|b}}$ such that $\overrightarrow{X_{a|b}} = \overrightarrow{(K_x)_{a|b}} \times \overrightarrow{(M_a)_{a|b}} + \overrightarrow{(R_x)_{a|b}}$, i.e. the quotient and the remainder of X by M_a. Using $P = M_a^2 - 2$, we have $M_a = \left\lceil \sqrt{P} \right\rceil$ and Split divides X of nw bits into the two integers K_x and R_x of $\frac{n}{2}w$ bits.

Algorithm 3. Proposed decomposition algorithm (Split).

Input: $\overrightarrow{X_{a|b}}$

Precomp.: $\overrightarrow{\left(M_a^{-1}\right)_b}$

Output: $\overrightarrow{(K_x)_{a|b}}$, $\overrightarrow{(R_x)_{a|b}}$ with $\overrightarrow{X_{a|b}} = \overrightarrow{(K_x)_{a|b}} \times \overrightarrow{(M_a)_{a|b}} + \overrightarrow{(R_x)_{a|b}}$

1 $\overrightarrow{(R_x)_b} \leftarrow \text{BE}\left(\overrightarrow{(R_x)_a}, \mathcal{B}_a, \mathcal{B}_b\right)$

2 $\overrightarrow{(K_x)_b} \leftarrow \left(\overrightarrow{X_b} - \overrightarrow{(R_x)_b}\right) \times \overrightarrow{\left(M_a^{-1}\right)_b}$

3 **if** $\overrightarrow{(K_x)_b} = \overrightarrow{-1}$ **then**

4     $\overrightarrow{(K_x)_b} \leftarrow \overrightarrow{0}$

5     $\overrightarrow{(R_x)_b} \leftarrow \overrightarrow{(R_x)_b} - \overrightarrow{(M_a)_b}$

6 $\overrightarrow{(K_x)_a} \leftarrow \text{BE}\left(\overrightarrow{(K_x)_b}, \mathcal{B}_b, \mathcal{B}_a\right)$

7 **return** $\overrightarrow{(K_x)_{a|b}}$, $\overrightarrow{(R_x)_{a|b}}$

At line 1 of Algorithm 3, a BE computes $R_x = |X|_{M_a}$ in $\mathcal{B}_b$ (thanks to CRT). Then, line 2 computes the quotient K_x of the decomposition by dividing by M_a (in base $\mathcal{B}_b$). Finally K_x is converted from $\mathcal{B}_b$ to $\mathcal{B}_a$ and the algorithm returns (K_x, R_x) in both bases.

Lines 3 to 5 in Algorithm 3 are required due to the approximation in the BE algorithm from [18] for efficient hardware implementation. As seen in Sect. 3.1, $\overrightarrow{(R_x)_b}$ is either R_x or $R_x + M_a$ in base $\mathcal{B}_b$. If an approximation error occurs, actually $(K'_x, R'_x) = (K_x - 1, R_x + M_a)$ is computed. It still satisfies $X = K'_x M_a + R'_x$, and adds one bit to R_x (i.e., $R'_x < 2M_a$). Line 3 checks $K_x = -1$ in base $\mathcal{B}_b$ since this case is not compatible with BE from [18]. This test can be easily performed in $\mathcal{B}_b$, but ambiguity remains for $K_x = -1$ and $K_x = M_b - 1$. To avoid this ambiguity, we select $M_b > M_a$, then $(M_b - 1)M_a \geq M_a^2 > P$ and it ensures $K_x < M_b - 1$. Then lines 4–5 set $K_x = 0$ and subtract M_a to R_x.

Random $\mathbb{F}_P$ elements have a probability $2^{-\ell/2}$ to be less than M_a (i.e. less than $\sqrt{P}$). On the minimum field size in standards [22] $\ell = 160$ bits, the probability to perform the correction at lines 4–5 is 2^{-80}. Then, the implementation of this test can be highly optimized with a very low probability of pipeline stall.

The theoretical cost of Algorithm 3 is analyzed in Sect. 5. Algorithm Split mainly costs 2 "small" BEs between half bases i.e. $\frac{n^2}{2}$ EMMs.

4.2   Proposed RNS Modular Multiplication SBMM

Our SBMM algorithm is presented at Algorithm 4. We decompose $X \in \mathbb{F}_P$ into the pair (K_x, R_x) directly from $\overrightarrow{X}$ using Split. To recover X from (K_x, R_x), it is sufficient to compute $K_x M_a + R_x$ in both half bases $\mathcal{B}_a$ and $\mathcal{B}_b$. The product X by Y decomposed as (K_x, R_x) and (K_y, R_y) gives:

$$
\begin{aligned}
XY &\equiv (K_x M_a + R_x) \cdot (K_y M_a + R_y) \mod P \\
&\equiv K_x K_y M_a^2 + (K_x R_y + K_y R_x) M_a + R_x R_y \mod P \\
&\equiv 2 K_x K_y + R_x R_y + (K_x R_y + K_y R_x) M_a \mod P \\
&\equiv 2 K_x K_y + R_x R_y + (K_x K_y + R_x R_y - (K_x - R_x)(K_y - R_y)) M_a \mod P \\
&\equiv U + V M_a \mod P .
\end{aligned}
$$

The first line of the previous equation is the definition of the (K_x, R_x) decomposition. The next line uses $M_a^2 = 2 \mod P$. Then we reduce the number of multiplications thanks to the Karatsuba-Ofman trick [17]. Finally we define $U = (2K_x K_y + R_x R_y)$ and $V = (K_x R_y + K_y R_x)$. By definition K_x, K_y, R_x and R_y are less than M_a, thus $U, V < 3M_a^2$. The values U and V must be representable in the base $\mathcal{B}_{a|b}$, so we need at least $3M_a^2 < M_a M_b$.

However $U + V M_a$ is too large for $\mathcal{B}_{a|b}$, thus Split is used a second time. It gives the decompositions (K_u, R_u) and (K_v, R_v) then:

$$
\begin{aligned}
XY &\equiv U + V M_a \mod P \\
&\equiv K_u M_a + R_u + K_v M_a^2 + R_v M_a \mod P \\
&\equiv (K_u + R_v) M_a + R_u + 2 K_v \mod P \\
&\equiv K_z M_a + R_z \mod P.
\end{aligned}
$$

Algorithm 4. Proposed Single Base Modular Multiplication (SBMM).

Parameters: $\mathcal{B}_a$ such that $M_a^2 = P + 2$ and $\mathcal{B}_b$ such that $M_b > 6M_a$

Input: $\overrightarrow{(K_x)_{a|b}}$, $\overrightarrow{(R_x)_{a|b}}$, $\overrightarrow{(K_y)_{a|b}}$, $\overrightarrow{(R_y)_{a|b}}$ with $K_x, R_x, K_y, R_y < M_a$

Output: $\overrightarrow{(K_z)_{a|b}}$, $\overrightarrow{(R_z)_{a|b}}$ with $K_z < 5M_a$ and $R_z < 6M_a$

1 $\overrightarrow{U_{a|b}} \leftarrow 2K_x K_y + R_x R_y$

2 $\overrightarrow{V_{a|b}} \leftarrow K_x R_y + R_x K_y$

3 $\left(\overrightarrow{(K_u)_{a|b}}, \overrightarrow{(R_u)_{a|b}} \right) \leftarrow \text{Split}(\overrightarrow{U_{a|b}})$

4 $\left(\overrightarrow{(K_v)_{a|b}}, \overrightarrow{(R_v)_{a|b}} \right) \leftarrow \text{Split}(\overrightarrow{V_{a|b}})$

5 **return** $\left(\overrightarrow{(K_u + R_v)_{a|b}}, \overrightarrow{(2 \cdot K_v + R_u)_{a|b}} \right)$

Using the property $M_a^2 \equiv 2 \mod P$, we can compute K_z and R_z which is the decomposition of $XY \mod P$. From $U < 3M_a^2$ and $V < 2M_a^2$, one can see that $K_z < 4M_a$ and $R_z < 5M_a$. The decomposition of the $Z = XY \mod P$ is $K_z M_a + R_z < 5P$ (*i.e.*, this is equivalent to have $Z \in [0, 5P[$).

Our proposition is similar to the use of Mersenne primes in the binary system where the modular reduction is performed by the sum of "high" and "low" parts of the operand. In our case, K_x behaves as the "high" part and R_x as the "low" part. In our algorithm, the split dominates the total cost. In the standard binary system, the multiplication part is costly while the split is free (constant shifts). The complete method is described in Algorithm 4 where U, V are computed at lines 1–2, decompositions at lines 3–4 and finally K_z, R_z are returned at line 5.

Using the approximated BE from [18], we have $K_z < 5M_a$ and $R_z < 6M_a$. Then we choose $M_b > 6M_a$ in Algorithm 4 (instead of $M_b > 5M_a$).

In Algorithm 4, the two decompositions using Split dominates the total cost which is equivalent to only one classical BE. Then our algorithm requires about half operations compared to the state-of-art one (see details in Sect. 5).

Our algorithm has been tested over millions of random modular multiplications, for $\ell = 160, 192, 256, 384$ and 512 bits.

4.3   Selecting $P = M_a^2 - 2$ for RNS Efficient Implementations

We choose to use specific forms of the characteristic in order to significantly speed up computations. For instance, $K_x K_y M_a^2 \bmod P$ becomes $2K_x K_y \bmod P$ using $P = M_a^2 - 2$. We also tried specific forms such as $P = M_a^2 - c$ and $P = dM_a^2 - c$ where c and d are small integers. The constraint for selection is that P must be prime. For instance, using $c = 0$ or 1 and $d = 1$, P is never prime (in those cases P is a multiple of M_a or $M_a + 1$). The specific form of the characteristic $P = M_a^2 - 2$ seems to be the best solution at the implementation level.

We wrote a Maple program to find P with the fixed parameters n and w. We randomly choose odd moduli of the form $m_{a,i} = 2^w - h_{a,i}$ with $h_{a,i} < 2^{\lfloor w/2 \rfloor}$. Each new $m_{a,i}$ must be coprime with the previously chosen ones. In practice, this step is very fast and easy as soon as w is large enough (i.e. $w \geq 16$ bits for ECC sizes). Using several M_a candidates from the previous step, we can check the primality of $P = M_a^2 + 2$ using a probabilistic test in a first time. This gives us very quickly a large set of P candidates. For the final selection in a real full cryptographic implementation, a deterministic primality test must be used. As an example for $\ell = 512$ bits, it took us $15\,\mathrm{s}$ to generate $10,000$ different couples (P, M_a) of candidates on a simple laptop ($2.2\,\mathrm{GHz}$ core I7 processor with $4\,\mathrm{GB}$ RAM). For selecting the second base, M_b just needs to be coprime with M_a and verifies $M_b > 6M_a$. As far as we know, there is not specific theoretical attack on ECC over $\mathbb{F}_P$ based on the form of the prime characteristic. In the current state-of-art, the theoretical security of ECC is directly related to the working subgroup of points of the curve, and in particular its order. This is why in the NIST standards [22] are chosen very specific P (Mersenne and pseudo-Mersenne primes). We propose to have the same approach for our RNS-friendly primes.

4.4   Controlling the Size of SBMM Outputs

Our SBMM at Algorithm 4 returns values on a slightly wider domain than the one of its inputs (i.e., $K_x, K_y, R_x, R_y < M_a$ lead to $K_z < 5M_a$ and $R_z <$

$6M_a$). In case of successive SBMM calls, one has to manage intermediate values with increasing sizes. For instance, computing $|X^8|_P$ (*i.e.* 3 squares), one gets $K_{X^8} < 30374M_a$ and $R_{X^8} < 42946M_a$. Then the architecture parameters must be selected to support this expansion. In practice, the bit width of the RNS base must be large enough for the worst case of intermediate value. This can be done by selecting an adequate $\mathcal{B}_b$. As the number of modular multiplications in ECC is very important, we must find a way to compress some intermediate values.

A first way to limit this expansion is to compute $|X \cdot 1|_P$ using SBMM. Then, the decomposition of 1 is just $(0, 1)$ then $U = R_x$, $V = K_x$, and the compressed outputs are $K_z, R_z < 3M_a$. This a simple but not very efficient solution.

Algorithm 5. Proposed compression of a pair (K, R) (Compress).

Input: $\overrightarrow{K_{a|b|m_\gamma}}$ and $\overrightarrow{R_{a|b|m_\gamma}}$ with $K, R < (m_\gamma - 1)M_a$

Precomp.: $\left|M_a^{-1}\right|_{m_\gamma}$

Output: $\overrightarrow{(K_c)_{a|b|m_\gamma}}$, $\overrightarrow{(R_c)_{a|b|m_\gamma}}$ with $K_c < 3M_a$ and $R_c < 3M_a$

1 $|R_k|_{m_\gamma} \leftarrow \text{BE}\left(\overrightarrow{K_a}, \mathcal{B}_a, m_\gamma\right)$ /* $\overrightarrow{(R_k)_a} = \overrightarrow{K_a}$ */

2 $K_k \leftarrow \left|(K - R_k)M_a^{-1}\right|_{m_\gamma}$

3 $\overrightarrow{(R_k)_b} \leftarrow \overrightarrow{K_b} - (K_k)_b \times (M_a)_b$

4 $|R_r|_{m_\gamma} \leftarrow \text{BE}\left(\overrightarrow{R_a}, \mathcal{B}_a, m_\gamma\right)$ /* $\overrightarrow{(R_r)_a} = \overrightarrow{R_a}$ */

5 $K_r \leftarrow \left|(R - R_r)M_a^{-1}\right|_{m_\gamma}$

6 $\overrightarrow{(R_r)_b} \leftarrow \overrightarrow{R_b} - (K_r)_b \times (M_a)_b$

7 **return** $\overrightarrow{(K_r + R_k)_{a|b|m_\gamma}}$, $\overrightarrow{(R_r + 2K_k)_{a|b|m_\gamma}}$

A faster method involving extra hardware is proposed in Algorithm 5 (named Compress). It requires a dedicated small extra modulo m_γ, typically $m_\gamma = 2^6$, and the inputs are assumed such that $K, R < (m_\gamma - 1)M_a$. To compress a pair (K, R), one converts $R_k = |K|_{M_a}$ from $\mathcal{B}_a$ to m_γ thanks to a BE at line 1 (this BE on only one moduli just requires n_a operations modulo m_γ). One can now computes $K_k = \left\lceil \frac{K}{M_a} \right\rceil$ modulo m_γ. Since K_k is less than $m_\gamma - 1$ and is less than all moduli, it can be directly used in $\mathcal{B}_a$ and $\mathcal{B}_b$. This enables to compute R_k in $\mathcal{B}_b$ at line 3 without a BE. Now (K_k, R_k) is such that $K = K_k M_a + R_k$, in $\mathcal{B}_{a|b|m_\gamma}$. Lines 4–6 perform the same computations to get (K_r, R_r). Finally, one can use the property $M_a^2 = 2 \bmod P$ because (K, R) is the decomposition of $X \in \mathbb{F}_P$, then we have:

$$\begin{aligned} X &\equiv K M_a + R \bmod P \\ &\equiv K_k M_a^2 + R_k M_a + K_r M_a + R_r \bmod P \\ &\equiv (R_k + K_r)M_a + 2K_k + R_r \bmod P \\ &\equiv K_c M_a + R_c \bmod P. \end{aligned}$$

Using approximated BE from [18], we have $K_c < 2M_a + m_\gamma < 3M_a$ and $R_c < 2M_a + 2m_\gamma < 3M_a$ (using an exact BE, one gets $K_c < 2M_a$ and $R_c < 2M_a$). Using SBMM on inputs in the domain $K < 3M_a$ and $R < 3M_a$ gives outputs $K_z < 29M_a$ and $R_z < 38M_a$, so it is sufficient to choose $m_\gamma = 2^6$ to compress the outputs back in the domain $[0, 3M_a[$. The main parts of the Compress algorithm can be performed in parallel, on a channel dedicated to m_γ. The cost of Algorithm 5 is evaluated in Sect. 5 and examples of applications are presented in Sect. 7.

5   Theoretical Cost Analysis

As usually done in state-of-art references, we evaluate the cost of our algorithms (Split Algorithm 3, SBMM Algorithm 4 and Compress Algorithm 5) by counting the number of EMMs while modular additions and other very cheap operations are neglected. Below, we use the case $n_a = n_b = n/2$ since it is the most interesting one.

First, Split at Algorithm 3 is mainly made of 2 BEs. The multiplication by the constant $\overrightarrow{(M_a^{-1})_b}$ at line 2 can be combined with the one by the constant $\overrightarrow{T_a^{-1}}$ at line 1 in BE Algorithm 1, this saves $n/2$ EMMs. The test at line 3 is neglected because the probability to perform lines 4–5 is very low and they do not contain any EMM. Then Split costs 2 BEs on 2 half bit width bases or $\frac{n^2}{2} + n$ EMMs.

In SBMM in Algorithm 4, we need $3n$ EMMs at lines 1, 2 and 5. Multiplication by 2 is performed using an addition. To compute the 4 products $K_x K_y$, $R_x R_y$, $K_x R_y$ and $K_y R_x$ on $\mathcal{B}_{a|b}$, we use the Karatsuba-Ofman's trick [17], it costs $3n$ EMMs. The 2 Splits at lines 3–4 cost $2\left(\frac{n^2}{2} + n\right)$ EMMs. Finally, our SBMM algorithm leads to $n^2 + 5n$ EMMs, against $2n^2 + 4n$ for the state-of-art algorithm from [12].

Compress in Algorithm 5 performs 2 BEs from $\mathcal{B}_a$ to m_γ, which costs $n/2$ EMMs on $\mathcal{B}_a$ and $n/2$ very cheap multiplications modulo m_γ, typically on 6 bits (this type of small multiplications modulo m_γ is denoted GMM). Lines 2 and 5 require two more GMMs. Finally, 2 RNS multiplications on $\mathcal{B}_b$ are required at lines 3 and 6 for a cost of $2(n/2)$ EMMs. Thus Compress costs $2n$ EMMs and $(n+2)$ GMMs.

Table 1 sums up the required precomputations for SBMM (including Split and its BE) and Compress. Globally, our proposition requires 4 times less EMWs than the state-of-art algorithm. Dividing by 2 the bit widths in a quadratic cost leads to the 1/4 factor. Table 2 compares the different costs analyzed in this section for state-of-art algorithm and our algorithm.

6   Hardware Implementation

6.1   Proposed Architecture

Our SBMM architecture, depicted in Fig. 1, uses the Cox-Rower architecture from [18] (similarly to state-of-art implementations). A Rower unit is dedicated

Table 1. Precomputations details for SBMM and Compress in EMWs (* denotes modulo m_γ values).

SBMM		Compress
$\overrightarrow{(T_a^{-1})_a} : n/2$	$\overrightarrow{(-M_a)_b} : n/2$	$\overrightarrow{(-M_a \times T_b^{-1})_b} : n/2$
$\overrightarrow{\left(\dfrac{-1}{m_{a,i}M_{b,j}}\right)_b} : n^2/4$	$\overrightarrow{(T_b^{-1})_b} : n/2$	$|M_{a,i}|_{m_\gamma} : n/2^*$
$\overrightarrow{\left(\dfrac{M_{b,j}}{M_a}\right)_b} : n/2$	$\overrightarrow{(-M_b)_a} : n/2$	$|-M_a|_{m_\gamma} : 1^*$
$\overrightarrow{(T_{b,i})_a} : n^2/4$	$\overrightarrow{(T_b)_b} : n/2$	$|M_a^{-1}|_{m_\gamma} : 1^*$

Table 2. Cost summary for main operations and precomputations for our solution and the state-of-art one.

Algorithms	MM [12]	SBMM	SBMM + Compress
Operations (EMM)	$2n^2 + 4n$	$n^2 + 5n$	$(n^2 + 7n)$ EMM $+ (n+2)$ GMM
Precomputations (EMW)	$2n^2 + 10n$	$\frac{n^2}{2} + 3n$	$\frac{n^2}{2} + 4n + 2$

to each channel for computations modulo $m_{a,i}$ and $m_{b,i}$. The Cox is a small unit required to compute fast BEs. Our architecture implements $n/2$ Rowers based on the ones presented in [14]. A small 6-bit Rower is implemented to compute on the m_γ channel. This small additional channel has 2 different roles. First, for computations over $\mathcal{B}_b$, it adds the extra modulo m_γ for $\mathcal{B}_b$ and enables $M_b > 6M_a$. Second, it is used to compute modulo m_γ in Compress from Sect. 4.4. In Fig. 1, the white circles are control signals (clock and reset are not represented). The small squares (in red) are just wire selections to extract the 6 MSBs of a w-bit word. The bottom right rectangle (in blue) between the extra Rower and the multiplexer just pads $w - 6$ zeros to the MSBs.

Our Rowers are implemented in a 6-stage pipeline as the one proposed in [14]. Then we designed our extra Rower for computations modulo m_γ on 6 stages to simplify synchronizations. We select $m_\gamma = 2^6$ and all other moduli as odd values to make this unit very small and simple.

Our architecture, depicted in Fig. 1, is close to the state-of-art one presented in [14]. The 2 differences are the number of Rowers and the presence of an extra 6-bit channel. We only have $n/2$ Rowers in our architecture instead of n in the state-of-art one. The control in both architectures is similar. We choose to only implement $n/2$ Rowers to reduce the silicon area in this paper. In the future, we will implement another version with more Rowers to speed up computations. Our SBMM algorithm allows to use n Rowers (instead of $n/2$ in the current version) and really leads up to 2 times faster computations while the state-of-art algorithm do not lead to a doubled speed when using $2n$ moduli (due to dependencies). In our algorithm, the 2 independent Splits and the other operations over $\mathcal{B}_{a|b}$ can be performed in parallel over n Rowers.

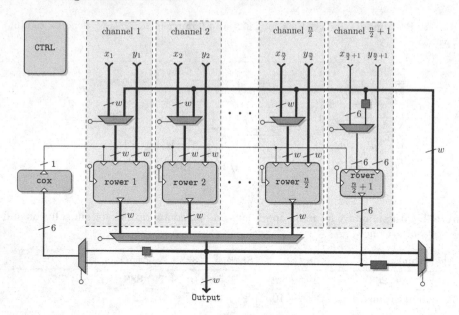

Fig. 1. Proposed architecture for our SBMM algorithm with an extra 6-bit channel (Color figure online).

Both architectures have been validated using numerous VHDL simulations for several sets of parameters (see Table 3).

6.2   Implementation Results on Various FPGAs

We have completely implemented, optimized and validated both the state-of-art algorithm from [12] and our SBMM algorithm on various FPGAs. The results are given for 3 FPGA families: two low cost Spartan 6 (XC6SLX45 denoted S6 or XC6SLX100 denoted S6* when the LX45 is too small), a high performance Virtex 5 (XC5VLX220 denoted V5) and a recent mid-range technology Kintex 7 (XC7K70T denoted K7) all with average speed grade. We used ISE 14.6 tools with medium efforts. Below, we report results for a single MM and a single SBMM without Compress. Currently, Compress control is not yet implemented, we will add it and evaluate complete ECC scalar multiplication algorithms and architectures in the future.

The selected parameters are given in Table 3. In order to compute a MM over ℓ bits using the state-of-art algorithm, one needs an RNS base with a bit

Table 3. Selected (n, w) parameters couples for the 3 evaluated field sizes ℓ.

Algorithms	$\ell = 192$	$\ell = 384$	$\ell = 512$
MM	$(12, 17)$	$(12, 33)$	$(16, 33)$
SBMM	$(12, 16)$	$(12, 32)$	$(16, 32)$

Table 4. FPGA implementation results of state-of-art MM and SBMM algorithms **with** DSP blocks and BRAMs.

Algorithm	FPGA	ℓ	Slices(FF/LUT)	DSP/BRAM	#cycles	Freq.(MHz)	Time(ns)
MM	S6	192	1733(2780/5149)	36/0	50	140	357
MM	S6	384	3668(6267/11748)	58/0	50	71	704
MM	S6	512	5457(8617/18366)	58/0	58	70	828
SBMM	S6	192	1214(1908/3674)	18/0	58	154	376
SBMM	S6	384	2213(3887/6709)	41/0	58	78	743
SBMM	S6	512	2912(5074/8746)	56/0	66	76	868
MM	V5	192	1941(2957/6053)	26/0	50	184	271
MM	V5	384	3304(5692/10455)	84/12	50	118	423
MM	V5	512	6180(7557/15240)	112/16	58	116	500
SBMM	V5	192	1447(1973/4682)	15/0	58	196	295
SBMM	V5	384	2256(3818/8415)	42/6	58	124	467
SBMM	V5	512	3400(4960/10877)	57/8	66	123	536
MM	K7	192	1732(2759/5075)	36/0	50	260	192
MM	K7	384	3278(5884/9841)	84/0	50	171	292
MM	K7	512	4186(7814/13021)	112/0	58	170	341
SBMM	K7	192	999(1867/3599)	18/0	58	272	213
SBMM	K7	384	2111(3889/6691)	41/0	58	179	324
SBMM	K7	512	3104(5076/8757)	56/0	66	176	375

width slightly larger than ℓ bits. In state-of-art architectures, the fastest ones are obtained for moduli with 1 additional bit (instead of an additional w-bit channel).

Both architectures have been implemented with and without DSP blocks. The corresponding results are reported in Tables 4 and 5 respectively. Parameter n impacts the clock cycles count while w impacts the clock period (frequency).

These results are graphically compared in Figs. 2 and 3 for area and computation time, respectively. Our SBMM algorithm leads to 26 to 46 % area reduction (in slices) for up to 10 % computation time increase. When using DSP blocks,

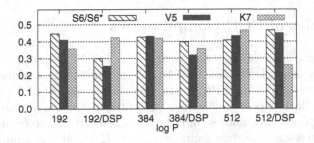

Fig. 2. Summary of obtained area reductions (in number of slices).

Table 5. FPGA implementation results of state-of-art MM and SBMM algorithms **without** DSP blocks and BRAMs.

Algorithm	FPGA	ℓ	Slices(FF/LUT)	#cycles	Freq.(MHz)	Time(ns)
MM	S6	192	3238(4288/10525)	50	114	438
MM	S6*	384	7968(8868/27323)	50	70	714
MM	S6*	512	10381(11750/35751)	58	45	1288
SBMM	S6	192	1793(2539/6085)	58	142	408
SBMM	S6*	384	4577(5302/15160)	58	91	637
SBMM	S6*	512	6163(6875/20147)	66	90	733
MM	V5	192	3358(3991/11136)	50	126	396
MM	V5	384	8675(7624/29719)	50	109	458
MM	V5	512	11401(10109/39257)	58	106	547
SBMM	V5	192	1980(2444/6888)	58	147	394
SBMM	V5	384	4942(4696/16672)	58	125	464
SBMM	V5	512	6466(6186/22411)	66	122	540
MM	K7	192	3109(4060/10568)	50	200	250
MM	K7	384	7241(7631/27377)	50	140	357
MM	K7	512	9202(10102/35696)	58	132	439
SBMM	K7	192	1999(2494/6368)	58	231	251
SBMM	K7	384	4208(4649/15137)	58	162	358
SBMM	K7	512	4922(6146/19269)	66	152	434

the reduction of the number of slices is in the range 26–46 % and the number of DSP blocks is divided by 2. Without DSP blocks, SBMM leads to 40–46 % area reduction w.r.t. state-of-art MM (except for $\ell = 192$ on K7).

Using DSP blocks (bottom of Fig. 3) the computation time required for SBMM is very close to the state-of-art one (overhead from 4 % to 10 %). Without DSP blocks (top of Fig. 3), our solution is as fast as the state-of-art or slightly faster. For the widest fields on the low-cost FPGA Spartan 6 devices, the MM area is so large that it brings down the frequency.

7   Examples of ECC Computations

We evaluate the gain of our SBMM method for full ECC scalar multiplication example. This example is used in [14] and [8] the two best state-of-art RNS implementations of ECC on FPGA with a protection against SPA (simple power analysis [19]). Both papers use formulas presented in Table 6, originally proposed in [3], with (X, Z) coordinates and the Montgomery ladder from [16]. These formulas use the *lazy reduction* from [3]: $(AB + CD) \bmod P$ is computed instead of $(AB) \bmod P$ and $(CD) \bmod P$, separately.

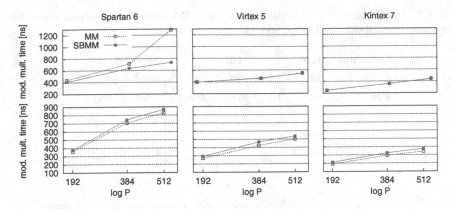

Fig. 3. Time for a single modular multiplication with SBMM and MM, with (bottom) and without (top) DSP blocks activated

Table 6. Formulas for Weierstrass form ($y^2 = x^3 + ax + b$), RNS optimizations from [3], (X, Z) coordinates and Montgomery ladder from [16].

Point operation	$\mathbf{P_1} + \mathbf{P_2}$ (ADD)	$2\,\mathbf{P_1}$ (DBL)
Formulas	$A = Z_1 X_2 + Z_2 X_1$	$E = Z_1^2$
	$B = 2X_1 X_2$	$F = 2X_1 Z_1$
	$C = 2Z_1 Z_2$	$G = X_1^2$
	$D = aA + bC$	$H = -4bE$
	$Z_3 = A^2 - BC$	$I = aE$
	$X_3 = BA + CD + 2X_G Z_3$	$X_3 = FH + (G - I)^2$
		$Z_3 = 2F(G + I) - EH$

Figure 4 describes a computation flow example for formulas of Table 6. It shows that each intermediate value can be compressed in parallel with a new SBMM call, except for Z_3 and I. In these cases, one has two choices: wait for the compression function or add few bits to m_γ to be able to compress more bits. To compress the result of 2 successive multiplications, m_γ must be at least 2^{10}. Moreover, 2 additional bits are required due to the lazy reduction. For this example, we consider $m_\gamma = 2^{12}$.

Point addition (ADD) from Table 6 requires 6 modular reductions and 11 multiplications (5 without reduction). Multiplications by 2 are performed using additions. Point doubling (DBL) requires 7 modular reductions and 9 multiplications. Each multiplication without reduction costs $2n$ EMMs using the state-of-art algorithm and $3n$ EMMs using SBMM (to compute U and V). ADD requires 3 compressions for D, Z_3 and X_3, and DBL requires 4 compressions for H, I, X_3 and Z_3, since m_γ is defined to support compression after 2 successive multiplications. The total costs for ADD and DBL are reported in Table 7 for both algorithms.

Table 7. Operation costs (in EMMs) for MM and SBMM algorithms, various curve-level operations, formulas from Table 6 and Montgomery ladder (ML).

Algorithms	ADD	DBL	ADD+DBL (ML)
MM	$12n^2 + 34n$	$14n^2 + 32n$	$26n^2 + 66n$
SBMM	$6n^2 + 51n$	$7n^2 + 49n$	$13n^2 + 100n$

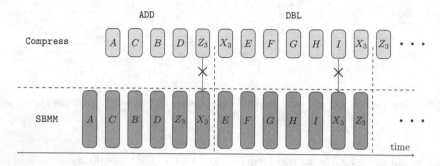

Fig. 4. Example of execution flow using SBMM and Compress in parallel using formulas of Table 6.

The reduction in the number of EMMs for various practical values of n (from [14] and [8]) is: 25 % for $n = 8$, 33 % for $n = 12$, 37 % for $n = 16$, 41 % for $n = 24$ and 43 % for $n = 32$. In case we deal with the pessimistic cost assumption GMM = EMM, the reduction lies in the range 23–42 % (instead of 25–43 %).

8   Conclusion

In this paper, we proposed a new method to efficiently compute modular multiplication in RNS for ECC computations over $\mathbb{F}_P$. This method relies on the selection of pseudo-Mersenne like primes as field characteristic for $\mathbb{F}_P$. These specific primes lead to very efficient RNS modular multiplication with only one single RNS base instead of two for state-of-art algorithms. Our new algorithm theoretically costs about 2 times less operations and 4 times less precomputations than the state-of-art RNS modular multiplication. Our FPGA implementations leads up to 46 % of area reduction for a time overhead less than 10 %.

In the future, we plan to implement a complete ECC accelerator in RNS with this new technique and we expect important improvements at the protocol level. In this paper, we designed an operator with reduced area but without speed improvement. We will design other versions with a non reduced area but significant speed up (or other trade-offs).

Acknowledgment. We thank the anonymous reviewers for their valuable comments. This work has been supported in part by the PAVOIS project (ANR 12 BS02 002 01).

References

1. Bajard, J.-C., Didier, L.-S., Kornerup, P.: An RNS montgomery modular multiplication algorithm. IEEE Trans. Comput. **47**(7), 766–776 (1998)
2. Bajard, J.-C., Didier, L.-S., Kornerup, P.: Modular multiplication and base extensions in residue number systems. In: Proceedings 15th Symposium on Computer Arithmetic (ARITH), pp. 59–65, IEEE, April 2001
3. Bajard, J.-C., Duquesne, S., Ercegovac, M.D.: Combining leak-resistant arithmetic for elliptic curves defined over Fp and RNS representation. Technical report 311, IACR Cryptology ePrint Archive, May 2010
4. Bajard, J.-C., Eynard, J., Gandino, F.: Fault detection in RNS montgomery modular multiplication. In: Proceedings 21th Symposium on Computer Arithmetic (ARITH), pp. 119–126, IEEE, April 2013
5. Bajard, J.-C., Eynard, J., Merkiche, N., Plantard, T.: Babaï round-off CVP method in RNS: application to lattice based cryptographic protocols. In: Proceedings 14th International Symposium on Integrated Circuits (ISIC), pp. 440–443, IEEE, December 2014
6. Bajard, J.-C., Imbert, L., Liardet, P.-Y., Teglia, Y.: Leak resistant arithmetic. In: Joye, M., Quisquater, J.-J. (eds.) CHES 2004. LNCS, vol. 3156, pp. 62–75. Springer, Heidelberg (2004)
7. Bajard, J.-C., Kaihara, M., Plantard, T.: Selected RNS bases for modular multiplication. In: Proceedings 19th Symposium on Computer Arithmetic (ARITH), pp. 25–32, IEEE, June 2009
8. Bajard, J.-C., Merkiche, N.: Double level montgomery cox-rower architecture, new bounds. In: Joye, M., Moradi, A. (eds.) CARDIS 2014. LNCS, vol. 8968, pp. 139–153. Springer, Heidelberg (2015)
9. Bigou, K., Tisserand, A.: RNS modular multiplication through reduced base extensions. In: Proceedings 25th IEEE International Conference on Application-specific Systems, Architectures and Processors (ASAP), pp. 57–62, IEEE, June 2014
10. Cheung, R.C.C., Duquesne, S., Fan, J., Guillermin, N., Verbauwhede, I., Yao, G.X.: FPGA implementation of pairings using residue number system and lazy reduction. In: Preneel, B., Takagi, T. (eds.) CHES 2011. LNCS, vol. 6917, pp. 421–441. Springer, Heidelberg (2011)
11. Esmaeildoust, M., Schinianakis, D., Javashi, H., Stouraitis, T., Navi, K.: Efficient RNS implementation of elliptic curve point multiplication over GF(p). IEEE Trans. Very Large Scale Integr. (VLSI) Syst. **21**(8), 1545–1549 (2013)
12. Gandino, F., Lamberti, F., Paravati, G., Bajard, J.-C., Montuschi, P.: An algorithmic and architectural study on Montgomery exponentiation in RNS. IEEE Trans. Comput. **61**(8), 1071–1083 (2012)
13. Garner, H.L.: The residue number system. IRE Trans. Electron. Comput. **EC–8**(2), 140–147 (1959)
14. Guillermin, N.: A high speed coprocessor for elliptic curve scalar multiplications over $\mathbb{F}_p$. In: Mangard, S., Standaert, F.-X. (eds.) CHES 2010. LNCS, vol. 6225, pp. 48–64. Springer, Heidelberg (2010)
15. Guillermin, N.: A coprocessor for secure and high speed modular arithmetic. Technical report 354, Cryptology ePrint Archive (2011)
16. Joye, M., Yen, S.-M.: The Montgomery powering ladder. In: Kaliski, B.S., Koç, K., Paar, C. (eds.) CHES 2002. LNCS, vol. 2523, pp. 291–302. Springer, Heidelberg (2002)

17. Karatsuba, A., Ofman, Y.: Multiplication of multi-digit numbers on automata. Doklady Akad. Nauk SSSR, **145**(2), 293–294 (1962). Translation in Soviet. Physics-Doklady **44**(7), 595–596 (1963)

18. Kawamura, S., Koike, M., Sano, F., Shimbo, A.: Cox-Rower architecture for fast parallel Montgomery multiplication. In: Preneel, B. (ed.) EUROCRYPT 2000. LNCS, vol. 1807, pp. 523–538. Springer, Heidelberg (2000)

19. Mangard, S., Oswald, E., Popp, T.: Power Analysis Attacks: Revealing the Secrets of Smart Cards. Springer, New York (2007)

20. Montgomery, P.L.: Modular multiplication without trial division. Math. Comput. **44**(170), 519–521 (1985)

21. Nozaki, H., Motoyama, M., Shimbo, A., Kawamura, S.: Implementation of RSA algorithm based on RNS Montgomery multiplication. In: Koç, K., Naccache, D., Paar, C. (eds.) CHES 2001. LNCS, vol. 2162, pp. 364–376. Springer, Heidelberg (2001)

22. National Institute of Standards and Technology (NIST). FIPS 186–2, digital signature standard (DSS) (2000)

23. Perin, G., Imbert, L., Torres, L., Maurine, P.: Electromagnetic analysis on RSA algorithm based on RNS. In: Proceedings 16th Euromicro Conference on Digital System Design (DSD), pp. 345–352, IEEE, Sept 2013

24. Phillips, B.J., Kong, Y., Lim, Z.: Highly parallel modular multiplication in the residue number system using sum of residues reduction. Appl. Algebra Eng. Commun. Comput. **21**(3), 249–255 (2010)

25. Posch, K.C., Posch, R.: Base extension using a convolution sum in residue number systems. Computing **50**(2), 93–104 (1993)

26. Posch, K.C., Posch, R.: Modulo reduction in residue number systems. IEEE Trans. Parallel Distrib. Syst. **6**(5), 449–454 (1995)

27. Schinianakis, D., Stouraitis, T.: An RNS Barrett modular multiplication architecture. In: Proceedings IEEE International Symposium on Circuits and Systems (ISCAS), pp. 2229–2232, June 2014

28. Shenoy, A.P., Kumaresan, R.: Fast base extension using a redundant modulus in RNS. IEEE Trans. Comput. **38**(2), 292–297 (1989)

29. Svoboda, A., Valach, M.: Operátorové obvody (operator circuits in czech). Stroje na Zpracování Informací (Information Processing Machines) **3**, 247–296 (1955)

30. Szabo, N.S., Tanaka, R.I.: Residue Arithmetic and its Applications to Computer Technology. McGraw-Hill, New York (1967)

31. Szerwinski, R., Güneysu, T.: Exploiting the power of GPUs for asymmetric cryptography. In: Oswald, E., Rohatgi, P. (eds.) CHES 2008. LNCS, vol. 5154, pp. 79–99. Springer, Heidelberg (2008)

32. Yao, G.X., Fan, J., Cheung, R.C.C., Verbauwhede, I.: Faster pairing coprocessor architecture. In: Abdalla, M., Lange, T. (eds.) Pairing 2012. LNCS, vol. 7708, pp. 160–176. Springer, Heidelberg (2013)

Homomorphic Encryption in Hardware

Accelerating Homomorphic Evaluation on Reconfigurable Hardware

Thomas Pöppelmann[1(✉)], Michael Naehrig[2],
Andrew Putnam[2], and Adrian Macias[3]

[1] Horst Görtz Institute for IT-Security, Ruhr-University Bochum, Bochum, Germany
thomas.poeppelmann@rub.de
[2] Microsoft Research, Redmond, WA, USA
{mnaehrig,anputnam}@microsoft.com
[3] Altera Corporation, San Diego, CA, USA
amacias@altera.com

Abstract. Homomorphic encryption allows computation on encrypted data and makes it possible to securely outsource computational tasks to untrusted environments. However, all proposed schemes are quite inefficient and homomorphic evaluation of ciphertexts usually takes several seconds on high-end CPUs, even for evaluating simple functions. In this work we investigate the potential of FPGAs for speeding up those evaluation operations. We propose an architecture to accelerate schemes based on the ring learning with errors (RLWE) problem and specifically implemented the somewhat homomorphic encryption scheme YASHE, which was proposed by Bos, Lauter, Loftus, and Naehrig in 2013. Due to the large size of ciphertexts and evaluation keys, on-chip storage of all data is not possible and external memory is required. For efficient utilization of the external memory we propose an efficient double-buffered memory access scheme and a polynomial multiplier based on the number theoretic transform (NTT). For the parameter set ($n = 16384, \lceil \log_2 q \rceil = 512$) capable of evaluating 9 levels of multiplications, we can perform a homomorphic addition in $0.94\,\mathrm{ms}$ and a homomorphic multiplication in $48.67\,\mathrm{ms}$.

Keywords: Homomorphic encryption · Ring learning with errors · FPGA · Reconfigurable computing

1 Introduction

A homomorphic encryption scheme enables a third party to perform meaningful computation on encrypted data and a prime example for an application is the outsourcing of a computational task into an untrusted cloud environment (see, e.g., [5,12,13,28]). Such schemes come in different flavors, the most versatile being a fully homomorphic encryption (FHE) scheme, which allows an

T. Pöppelmann—This work was mainly carried out when the author was an intern in the Cryptography Research group at Microsoft Research, Redmond.

© International Association for Cryptologic Research 2015
T. Güneysu and H. Handschuh (Eds.): CHES 2015, LNCS 9293, pp. 143–163, 2015.
DOI: 10.1007/978-3-662-48324-4_8

unlimited number of operations. The first FHE scheme was proposed by Gentry in 2009 [23] and led to many new schemes optimized for better efficiency or security (e.g., [6,8,16,24,26,30,39]). FHE schemes usually consist of a so-called somewhat or leveled homomorphic scheme with limited functionality together with a procedure to bootstrap its capabilities to an arbitrary number of operations. The somewhat homomorphic encryption (SHE) schemes are usually a lot more efficient than their corresponding FHE counterparts because bootstrapping imposes a significant overhead. Examples of SHE schemes are the BGV [8] and LTV [30] schemes and the subsequent YASHE [4] scheme, which are relatively straightforward and conceptually simple as they mainly require polynomial multiplication and (bit level) manipulation of polynomial coefficients for evaluation of ciphertexts (i.e., mul, add). But even limited SHE schemes are still slow and especially for relatively complex computations, evaluation operations can take several hours, even on high-end CPUs [25,29]. A natural question concerning FHE and SHE is whether reconfigurable hardware can be used to accelerate the computation. However, as ciphertexts and keys are large and require several megabytes or even gigabytes of storage for meaningful parameter sets, the internal memory of FPGAs is quickly exhausted, and required data transfers between host and FPGA might degrade the achievable performance.

These may be reasons that previous work mainly focuses on using GPUs [19,40,41] and ASICs [21,44], and that FPGA implementations either work only with small parameters and on-chip memory [11] or explicitly do not take into account the complexity of transferring data between an FPGA and a host [9,35]. For our implementation we use the Catapult data center acceleration platform [34], which provides a Stratix V FPGA on a PCB with two 4 GB memory modules inserted into the expansion slot of a cloud server. This fits nicely into the obvious scenario in which homomorphic evaluation operations are carried out on encrypted data stored in the cloud. Since future data centers might be equipped with such accelerators, it makes sense to consider the Catapult architecture as a natural platform for evaluating functions with homomorphic encryption.

Our Contribution. To our knowledge, we provide the first fully functional FPGA implementation of the homomorphic evaluation operations of an RLWE-based SHE scheme. Our main contribution is an efficient architecture for performing number theoretic transforms, which is used to implement the SHE scheme YASHE. Compared to previous FPGA implementations of integer-based FHE schemes (e.g., [9]) we especially take into account the complexity of using off-chip memory. Thus we propose and evaluate the usage of the cached-NTT [2,3] for bandwidth-efficient computations of products of large polynomials in $\mathbb{Z}_q[X]/(X^n+1)$ and the YASHE specific parts of the KeySwitch and Mult algorithms. The main computational burden is handled by a large integer multiplier built out of DSP blocks and modular reduction using Solinas primes. An implementation of the parameter set ($n = 16384$, $\lceil \log_2 q \rceil = 512$) that can handle computations on the encrypted data of multiplicative depth up to $L = 9$ levels (for $t = 1024$) roughly matches the performance of a software implementation of the parameter set ($n = 4096$, $\lceil \log_2 q \rceil = 128$) supporting just one level [29]. With only 48.67 ms for a homomorphic multiplication (instead of several seconds in software) we provide evidence that hardware-accelerated somewhat homomorphic cryptography can be made practical for certain application scenarios.

2 Background

2.1 Somewhat Homomorphic Scheme YASHE

The homomorphic encryption scheme YASHE [4] is based on the multi-key FHE scheme from [30] and the modified, provably-secure version of NTRU in [38]. In [4], two versions of YASHE are presented. We use the more efficient variant.

The system parameters are fixed as follows: a positive integer $m = 2^k$ that determines the ring $R = \mathbb{Z}[X]/(X^n + 1)$ and its dimension $n = \varphi(m) = m/2$, two moduli q and t with $1 < t < q$, discrete probability distributions $\chi_{\text{key}}, \chi_{\text{err}}$ on R, and an integer base $w > 1$. We view R to be the ring of polynomials with integer coefficients taken modulo the m-th cyclotomic polynomial $X^n + 1$. Let $R_q = R/qR \cong \mathbb{Z}_q[X]/(X^n + 1)$ be defined by reducing the elements in R modulo q, similarly we define R_t. A polynomial $\mathbf{a} \in R_q$ can be decomposed using base w as $\mathbf{a} = \sum_{i=0}^{\ell_{w,q}-1} \mathbf{a}_i w^i$, where the $\mathbf{a}_i \in R$ have coefficients in $(-w/2, w/2]$. The scheme YASHE makes use of the functions $\mathsf{Dec}_{w,q}(\mathbf{a}) = ([\mathbf{a}_i]_w)_{i=0}^{\ell_{w,q}-1}$ and $\mathsf{Pow}_{w,q}(\mathbf{a}) = ([\mathbf{a}w^i]_q)_{i=0}^{\ell_{w,q}-1}$, where $\ell_{w,q} = \lfloor \log_w(q) \rfloor + 1$. Both functions take a polynomial and map it to a vector of polynomials in $R^{\ell_{w,q}}$. They satisfy the scalar product property $\langle \mathsf{Dec}_{w,q}(\mathbf{a}), \mathsf{Pow}_{w,q}(\mathbf{b}) \rangle = \mathbf{ab} \pmod{q}$.

YASHE consists of the following algorithms. Note that homomorphic multiplication Mult consists of two parts, the rounded multiplication RMult and the key switching step KeySwitch.

$\mathsf{KeyGen}(d, q, t, \chi_{\text{key}}, \chi_{\text{err}}, w)$: Sample $\mathbf{f}' \leftarrow \chi_{\text{key}}$ until $\mathbf{f} = [t\mathbf{f}' + 1]_q$ is invertible modulo q. Compute the inverse $\mathbf{f}^{-1} \in R$ of $\mathbf{f}$ modulo q, sample $\mathbf{g} \leftarrow \chi_{\text{key}}$ and set $\mathbf{h} = [t\mathbf{g}\mathbf{f}^{-1}]_q$. Sample $\mathbf{e}, \mathbf{s} \leftarrow \chi_{\text{err}}^{\ell_{w,q}}$, compute $\boldsymbol{\gamma} = [\mathsf{Pow}_{w,q}(\mathbf{f}) + \mathbf{e} + \mathbf{h} \cdot \mathbf{s}]_q \in R^{\ell_{w,q}}$ and output $(\mathsf{pk}, \mathsf{sk}, \mathsf{evk}) = (\mathbf{h}, \mathbf{f}, \boldsymbol{\gamma})$.

$\mathsf{Encrypt}(\mathbf{h}, \mathbf{m})$: For a message $\mathbf{m} \in R/tR$, sample $\mathbf{s}, \mathbf{e} \leftarrow \chi_{\text{err}}$, scale $[\mathbf{m}]_t$ by the value $\lfloor q/t \rfloor$, and output $\mathbf{c} = \left[\lfloor \frac{q}{t} \rfloor [\mathbf{m}]_t + \mathbf{e} + \mathbf{h}\mathbf{s} \right]_q \in R$.

$\mathsf{Decrypt}(\mathbf{f}, \mathbf{c})$: Compute $[\mathbf{f}\mathbf{c}]_q$ modulo q, scale it down by t/q over the rational numbers, round it and reduce it modulo t, i.e. output $\mathbf{m} = \left[\left\lfloor \frac{t}{q} [\mathbf{f}\mathbf{c}]_q \right\rceil \right]_t \in R$.

$\mathsf{Add}(\mathbf{c}_1, \mathbf{c}_2)$: Add the two ciphertexts modulo q, i.e. output $\mathbf{c}_{\text{add}} = [\mathbf{c}_1 + \mathbf{c}_2]_q$.

$\mathsf{RMult}(\mathbf{c}_1, \mathbf{c}_2)$: Compute $\mathbf{c}_1 \mathbf{c}_2$ without reduction modulo q over the integers, scale by t/q, round the result and reduce modulo q to output $\tilde{\mathbf{c}}_{\text{mult}} = \left[\left\lfloor \frac{t}{q} \mathbf{c}_1 \mathbf{c}_2 \right\rceil \right]_q$.

$\mathsf{KeySwitch}(\tilde{\mathbf{c}}_{\text{mult}}, \mathsf{evk})$: Compute the w-decomposition vector of $\tilde{\mathbf{c}}_{\text{mult}}$ and output the scalar product with evk modulo q: $\mathbf{c}_{\text{mult}} = [\langle \mathsf{Dec}_{w,q}(\tilde{\mathbf{c}}_{\text{mult}}), \mathsf{evk} \rangle]_q$.

Table 1. YASHE parameter sets and supported number of multiplicative levels for different plaintext moduli t, using discrete Gaussian error parameter $s = 8$.

Set	n	q	q'	$\ell_{w,q}$	Levels			
					$t = 2^{20}$	$t = 2^{10}$	$t = 2^5$	$t = 2$
I	4096	$2^{124} - 2^{64} + 1$	$2^{262} - 2^{56} + 1$	2	0	1	1	1
II	16384	$2^{512} - 2^{32} + 1$	$2^{1040} - 2^{32} + 1$	8	6	9	11	14

Mult($\mathbf{c}_1, \mathbf{c}_2$, evk): First apply RMult to $\mathbf{c}_1$ and $\mathbf{c}_2$ and then KeySwitch to the result. Output the ciphertext $\mathbf{c}_{\text{mult}} = \text{KeySwitch}(\text{RMult}(\mathbf{c}_1, \mathbf{c}_2), \text{evk})$.

In Table 1, we provide the implemented parameter sets and their number of supported multiplicative levels determined by the worst case bounds given in [4]. The plaintext modulus in our implementation is $t = 1024$ for both parameter sets. Since changing t is relatively easy, we also give the number of multiplicative levels for various other choices to illustrate the dependence on t and possible trade-offs. According to the analysis in [29], moduli stay below the maximal bound to achieve 80 bits of security against the distinguishing attack with advantage 2^{-80} as discussed there. The error distribution χ_{err} is the n-dimensional discrete Gaussian with parameter $s = 8$ and the key distribution samples polynomials with uniform random coefficients in $\{-1, 0, 1\}$. Note that one ciphertext requires $n\lceil \log_2(q) \rceil$ bits (1 MiB for Set II) and the evaluation key is $(\ell_{w,q})n\lceil \log_2(q) \rceil$ bits large (8 MiB for parameter Set II).

2.2 Number Theoretic Transform

Polynomial multiplication can be performed with $\mathcal{O}(n \log n)$ operations in $\mathbb{Z}_q$ using the number theoretic transform (NTT), which is basically an FFT defined over a finite field or ring. Given a primitive n-th root of unity ω the forward transformation $\text{NTT}_q(\mathbf{a})$ of a length-n sequence $(\mathbf{a}[0], .., \mathbf{a}[n-1])$ with elements in $\mathbb{Z}_q$ is defined as $\mathbf{A}[i] = \sum_{j=0}^{n-1} \mathbf{a}[j]\omega^{ij} \bmod q$ and the inverse transformation $\text{INTT}_q(\mathbf{A})$ as $\mathbf{a}[i] = n^{-1}\sum_{j=0}^{n-1} \mathbf{A}[j]\omega^{-ij} \bmod q$ for $i = 0, 1, ..., n-1$ (see [18,31,45] for more information on the NTT). For efficient multiplication of polynomials in $R_q = \mathbb{Z}_q[X]/(X^n + 1)$, one can use the negative wrapped convolution, which removes the need for zero padding of input polynomials. Let ω be a primitive n-th root of unity in $\mathbb{Z}_q$ and $\psi^2 = \omega$. For two polynomials $\mathbf{a} = \mathbf{a}[0] + \mathbf{a}[1]X + \cdots + \mathbf{a}[n-1]X^{n-1}$ and $\mathbf{b} = \mathbf{b}[0] + \mathbf{b}[1]X + \cdots + \mathbf{b}[n-1]X^{n-1}$ of degree at most $n-1$ with elements in $\mathbb{Z}_q$, we define $\mathbf{d} = \mathbf{d}[0] + \cdots + \mathbf{d}[n-1]X^{n-1}$ as the negative wrapped convolution of $\mathbf{a}$ and $\mathbf{b}$ so that $\mathbf{d} = \mathbf{a} * \mathbf{b} \bmod (X^n + 1)$. We further define the representation $\hat{\mathbf{y}} = \mathbf{y}[0] + \psi\mathbf{y}[1]X + \cdots + \psi^{n-1}\mathbf{y}[n-1]X^{n-1}$ and use it as $\hat{\mathbf{a}}, \hat{\mathbf{b}}$ and $\hat{\mathbf{d}}$. In this case it holds that $\hat{\mathbf{d}} = \text{INTT}_q(\text{NTT}_q(\hat{\mathbf{a}}) \circ \text{NTT}_q(\hat{\mathbf{b}}))$, where $\circ$ means coefficient-wise multiplication [18,45].

Various algorithms that implement the FFT efficiently and which are directly applicable for the NTT are reviewed in [14]. A popular choice is a radix-2, in-place, decimation-in-time (DIT) [15] or decimation-in-frequency (DIF) [22] algorithm that requires roughly $\frac{n}{2}\log_2(n)$ multiplications in $\mathbb{Z}_q$ (see [1,33,36] for implementation results). Note that in the FFT context precomputed powers of the primitive root of unity ω are often referred to as *twiddle factors*.

The primes q and q' we use in our implementation are Solinas primes of the form $q = 2^y - 2^z + 1$, $y > z$ such that $q \equiv 1 \pmod{2n}$. In order to find a primitive $2n$-th root of unity $\psi \in \mathbb{Z}_q$ that is needed in the NTT transforms as mentioned above, we simply chose random non-zero elements in $a \in \mathbb{Z}_q$, until $a^{(q-1)/2n} \neq 1$ and $a^{(q-1)/2} = -1$ and then set $\psi = a^{(q-1)/2n}$.

2.3 Cached-FFT

The general idea of the cached-FFT algorithm [2,3], as visualized in Fig. 1, is to divide the FFT computation into epochs (E) after which an out-of-place reordering step becomes necessary. In an epoch itself the data is split into groups (G) consisting of $C = n/G$ coefficients and computations require only access to members of a group but do not interfere with or require values from other groups. The required computation on a group is just a standard Cooley-Tukey, radix-2, in-place, DIT FFT/NTT [14,15], denoted as C-NTT and the number of stages or passes (recursive divisions into sub-problems) of the C-NTT is $P = \log_2(n/G)$. Thus one C-NTT on a group requires $\frac{Pn}{2G}$ multiplications in $\mathbb{Z}_q$. As a consequence, during the computation of an NTT/FFT on a group, this group can be stored in a small cache or local memory that supports fast access to coefficients.

For the actual details of the implementation of address generation we refer to the description in [2,3]. However, referring to the $E = 2$ case displayed in Fig. 1, it is easy to see that, with a hardware implementation in mind, it is necessary to read $2n$ coefficients from the main memory and to write $2n$ coefficients back to the main memory to compute the FFT. However, only two of these reads/writes are non-consecutive (i.e., the reordering) while two read/writes are in order.

2.4 Catapult Architecture/Target Hardware

Because a primary application of homomorphic encryption is use in untrusted clouds, we chose to implement YASHE using a previously proposed FPGA-based datacenter accelerator infrastructure called Catapult [34]. Catapult augments a conventional server with an FPGA card attached via PCIe that features a medium size Stratix V GS D5 (5GSMD5) FPGA, two 4 GB DDR3-1333 SO-DIMM (small outline dual inline memory module) memory modules, and a private inter-FPGA 2-D torus network. In the original work, Catapult was used to accelerate parts of the Bing search engine, and a prototype consisting of 1,632 servers was deployed. The two DRAM controllers on the board can be used either independently or combined in a unified interface. When used independently the DIMM modules are clocked with 667 MHz. The Catapult shell [34, Sect. 3.2.] provides a simple interface to access the DRAM and to communicate with the host server. It uses roughly 23 % of the available device resources, depending on the used functionality like DRAM, PCIe, or 2-D torus network. Application logic is implemented as a role.

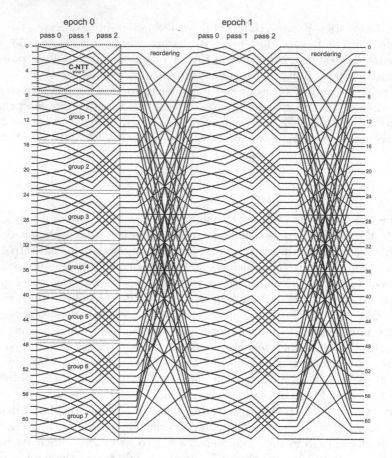

Fig. 1. Dataflow diagram of a 64-point cached-FFT split into two epochs with eight coefficients in each group/cache parameterized as ($n = 64$, $E = 2$, $G = 8$, $P = 3$, $C = 8$). This figure is based on [3, Fig. 3].

For our design, we restrict the accelerator to only a single FPGA card per server. Spanning multiple FPGAs is a promising avenue for improving performance, but is left for future work. Note also that none of the work presented here is exclusive to Catapult and that any FPGA board with two DRAM channels, a sufficiently large FPGA, and fast connection to a host server will suffice. However, Catapult is specifically designed for datacenter workloads, so it presents realistic constraints on cost, area, and power for our accelerator.

3   High Level Description

The goal of our implementation is to accelerate the (cloud) server-based evaluation operations Mult and Add of YASHE (and polynomial multiplication in general) without interaction with the host server using the Catapult infrastructure. Key generation, encryption, and decryption are assumed to be performed on a client and are not in the scope of this work. However, we would like to note that except for a Gaussian sampler, most components required for key generation, encryption, and decryption are already present in our design.

Our main building block is a scalable NTT-based polynomial multiplier that supports the two moduli q and q'. The computation of the NTT is by far the most expensive operation and necessary for the polynomial multiplications in RMult and KeySwitch, which are called during a Mult operation. Other computations like polynomial addition or pointwise multiplication are realized using the hardware building blocks from the NTT multiplier. The modulus $q' > nq^2$ is used to compute

$$\mathbf{c}_1\mathbf{c}_2 = \mathrm{INTT}_{q'}(\mathrm{NTT}_{q'}(\mathbf{c}_1)\circ\mathrm{NTT}_{q'}(\mathbf{c}_2))$$

in RMult exactly without modular reduction as each coefficient of $\mathbf{c}_1$ and $\mathbf{c}_2$ is smaller than q and thus each coefficient of the result is guaranteed to be smaller than nq^2. Reductions modulo q are required for the computation of the scalar product $\mathbf{c}_{\mathrm{mult}} = [\langle\mathsf{Dec}_{w,q}(\tilde{\mathbf{c}}_{\mathrm{mult}}),\mathsf{evk}\rangle]_q$ in KeySwitch and the polynomial addition in Add. A naive implementation of KeySwitch would require $\ell_{w,q}$ polynomial multiplications and $\ell_{w,q} - 1$ polynomial additions. By using the NTT and its linearity we just compute

$$\mathsf{KeySwitch}\,(\tilde{\mathbf{c}}_{\mathrm{mult}}, \overline{\mathsf{evk}}) = \mathrm{INTT}_q\left(\sum_{i=0}^{\ell_{w,q}-1} \mathrm{NTT}_q\left([(\mathbf{c}_{\mathrm{mult}})_i]_w\right) \circ \overline{\mathsf{evk}}_i\right) \qquad (1)$$

and store the evaluation keys evk_i in NTT form as $\overline{\mathsf{evk}}_i = \mathrm{NTT}_q(\mathsf{evk}_i)$ for $i \in [0, \ell_{w,q} - 1]$ (similar to [19, Algorithm 2]). To deal with the limited internal memory when computing the NTT we use the aforementioned cached-FFT algorithm [2,3]. This enables us to exploit the memory hierarchy on Catapult where we have access to fast but small FPGA-internal memory ($\approx$4.9 MiB) and large but slow external DRAM (two times 4 GB). We also incorporate some of the optimizations to the NTT proposed in [36]. By merging the multiplication by powers of ψ into the twiddle factors of the main NTT computation we not only save n multiplications but also eliminate expensive read and write operations. To optimally utilize the burst read/write capabilities of the DRAM[1] we have designed our core in a way that we balance non-continuous reorderings and continuous reads or writes. While we only implemented two main parameter sets, our approach is scalable and could be extended to even larger parameter sets and is also generally applicable as we basically implement polynomial multiplication, which is common in most RLWE-based homomorphic encryption schemes.

The general architecture of our `HomomorphicCore` design is shown in Fig. 2. We have divided our implementation into a memory management unit (`NTTMemMgr`) and an NTT computation unit (`NttCore`). The `NTTMemMgr` component loads or stored groups while `NttCore` is responsible for the computation of the C-NTT on the cache. Both components have access to the memories

---

[1] The throughput of the DRAM is drastically increased if large continuous areas of the memory are read at once using the so called *burst mode*.

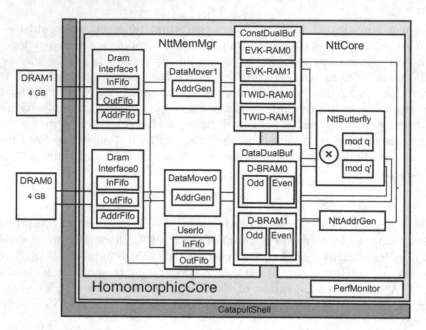

Fig. 2. Block diagram of our HomomorphicCore core used to implement YASHE. The design is controlled by a host server using the `CatapultShell` and has access to two 4 GB DDR3-1333 DRAMs.

`ConstDualBuf` and `DataDualBuf`. The `DataDualBuf` buffer contains a configurable number of groups of a polynomial and the `ConstDualBuf` buffer contains the constants (e.g., twiddle factors or evaluation keys) that correspond to the groups in `DataDualBuf`. To the `NttCore` it does not matter which subset of the cached-NTT has to be computed as this is only determined by the loaded data and twiddle factors. This makes the design simpler and also easier to test. To support moduli q and q' we implemented two butterfly units that share one large integer multiplier. Both buffers are double-buffered so that the `NttCore` component can compute on one subset of the data while the `NTTMemMgr` component can load or store a new subset from or into the other buffer. Ciphertexts, NTT constants, and keys are held in one of the two DRAMs (`Dram0` or `Dram1`) and are provided to the core from the outside over the `UserIo` and `CatapultShell` components. The `CatapultShell` component implements a simple PCI Express (PCIe) interface that allows the host server to issue commands (e.g., Add, or Mult) and to transfer data. Evaluated ciphertexts are also stored in the DRAM and can be read by the host after a computation is finished.

4   Hardware Architecture

In this section we describe our hardware architecture with an emphasis on the memory bandwidth-friendly cached-NTT polynomial multiplier.

4.1   Implementation of the Cached-NTT and Memory Addressing

A crucial aspect when implementing the cached-NTT is efficient access to the main memory (i.e., DRAM) and the use of burst transfers. In this section we describe how data is transferred between the main memory (Dram0 and Dram1) and the cache memory (DataDualBuf and ConstDualBuf) and how these transfers are optimized.

General Idea. The cached-FFT has been designed for systems with a small cache that supports fast access to coefficients during the computation of a C-NTT on a group. For our core we do not have a transparent cache, like on a CPU, but implement the fast directly addressable internal on-chip memories DataDualBuf and ConstDualBuf using BRAMs. As we know exactly which values are required at which time, we explicitly load a group into the internal memory before and write it back after a C-NTT computation. The necessary reordering (see Fig. 1) is either performed before or after a computation on a group and done when reading from or writing data into the DRAM. As the DRAM is large enough, plenty of memory is available for temporary storage, but one epoch has to be computed completely and the reordering has to be finished before the next epoch can be computed. In general, it would be sufficient to just store one group consisting of $C = n/G$ coefficients in each buffer of DataDualBuf. However, we allow the storage and computation on K groups/caches (configurable as generic during synthesis) in D-BRAM0 and D-BRAM1 at the same time (when computing modulo q). One reason is that for relatively small groups we can then avoid frequent waiting for the pipeline to clear after a C-NTT has been computed. Additionally, storing of multiple groups allows more efficient usage of burst reads and writes.

For efficiency (due to less memory transfers) and simplicity we restrict our implementation to a cached-NTT with two epochs[2]. We thus support only dimensions $n = 2^{2n'}$ for $n' \in \mathbb{N}$. For Set I we use ($n = 4096, E = 2, G = 64, P = 6$) and for Set II ($n = 16384, E = 2, G = 128, P = 7$).

Supported Commands. To simplify the implementation of homomorphic evaluation algorithms (see Sect. 5) and to abstract away implementation details we support a specific set of instructions to store or load groups or constants and to compute the C-NTT on such stored groups. A complete set of available commands is provided in Table 2. These commands could also be used to implement other homomorphic schemes and they can be directly used to realize polynomial multiplication in $\mathbb{Z}_q[X]/(X^n + 1)$ and $\mathbb{Z}_{q'}[X]/(X^n + 1)$.

Each command consists of a name, which is mapped to an opcode, and zero, one, or two parameters that define the source or destination of data to be transferred or the buffer on which a computation should be performed. A command either blocks Dram0, Dram1, or NttCore and commands can be executed in parallel, in case no resource conflict happens. Memory transfer and computation

---

[2] With only one epoch the cached-NTT becomes the standard Cooley-Tukey NTT and the cache contains all n coefficients.

commands do not interfere due to the dual-buffering. Additionally, commands can be configured for specific situations. For commands operating on Dram0 or Dram1 the configuration describes how a storage operation should be performed. Supported modes are a continuous burst transfer ([burst]), or bit-reversal of coefficients ([bitrev]), and/or cached-NTT reordering ([ro]) during a write or read operation. The [q] and [q'] configuration determines whether transfers operate on polynomials modulo q or polynomials modulo q'. When a homomorphic operation has to be performed the top-level state machine also has to provide the base address of the inputs and the base address of the result memory block. Each command also supports a specific maximum burst transfer size.

The commands itself are described in Table 2. As an example, the load-group[burst](t,x) command loads groups x to $x+K-1$ from the DRAM at base-address of t into a buffer using the DRAM's fast burst mode. The store-group[ro, bitrev](t,x) command stores the groups x to $x+K-1$ in the DRAM at base-address of t but performs the reordering of the cached-NTT and also a bit-reversal. A command used to load constants is the load-twiddles[fwd,q](x,y) command that loads the twiddle factors required to compute groups x to $x+K-1$ in epoch y using burst mode. While the previous commands can be used to implement general polynomial multiplication, we also provide the YASHE specific load-group-expand, load-chunks, and store-chunks commands. The reason is that the KeySwitch algorithm requires the expansion of one polynomial into $\ell_{w,q}$ polynomials (from now on also referred to as *chunks*). For efficiency reasons, the computations are thus performed in parallel on all decomposed polynomials and the larger amount of data to be transferred is handled by the previously mentioned commands. The width of the data ports of DataDualBuf and ConstDualBuf is $\frac{q'}{2}$ bits so that we can either store one coefficient modulo q in one position or half of a coefficient modulo q'. As a consequence, the minimal size of D-BRAM0 and D-BRAM1 is $\frac{\lceil \log_2 q' \rceil \cdot K \cdot n \cdot \ell_{w,q}}{2G}$ bits.

Usage of Burst Transfers. A significant advantage of storing multiple groups is that this allows the usage of the DRAM's burst mode. In case memory is written or read continuously ([burst]) it is straightforward to see that $K \cdot C$ coefficients can be handled in one burst transfer. But also when performing the cached-NTT reordering ([ro]) the simultaneous reordering of multiple groups allows better utilization of burst operations[3]. By iterating over the groups and then over the addresses we can write K coefficients using burst mode and thus reduce memory transfer times significantly. Note that the non-continuous access to memory in D-BRAM0 or D-BRAM1 does not introduce a performance bottleneck as the memory is implemented using BRAMs that do not cause a performance penalty when being accessed non-continuously.

---

[3] In the following we only discuss the case of writing coefficients from the FPGA (BRAM) into the external memory (DRAM) in reordered or reordered and bit-reversed fashion. However, the same ideas can be also applied for loading from the DRAM and writing into the BRAM on the FPGA.

Table 2. Commands that are used to implement YASHE with `HomomorphicCore`. Depending on the configuration of each memory transfer command, different burst widths can be realized.

Command	Param. p_1	Param. p_2	Resource	Configuration
load-group-expand	DRAM address	group	Dram0	[burst]
Loads groups p_2 to $p_2 + K - 1$ using p_1 as base address, performs the decomposition $\mathrm{Dec}_{w,q}(\bar{c}_{\mathrm{mult}}) = ([(\bar{c}_{\mathrm{mult}})_i]_w)_{i=0}^{\ell_{w,q}-1}$ into $\ell_{w,q}$ polynomials, and stores the decomposed polynomials in the `DataDualBuf` buffer.				
store-chunks	DRAM address	group	Dram0	[burst,q], [burst,q']
Saves groups p_2 to $p_2 + K - 1$ of all $\ell_{w,q}$ decomposed polynomials ([q]) or spitted coefficients modulo q' ([q']) stored in `DataDualBuf` at base address p_1.				
load-chunks	DRAM address	group	Dram0	[burst,q'], [ro,q'] [ro,bitrev,q'], [ro,q]
Equivalent to store-chunks.				
store-group	DRAM address	group	Dram0	[burst], [ro,bitrev], [ro]
Saves groups p_2 to $p_2 + K - 1$ of the polynomial stored in `DataDualBuf` at base address p_1.				
load-group	DRAM address	group	Dram0	[burst], [bitrev]
Equivalent to store-group.				
load-twiddles	group G	epoch E	Dram1	[(fwd|inv),q], [(fwd|inv),q']
Loads the precomputed forward or inverse twiddle factors for modulus q or q' for groups p_1 to $p_1 + K$ and epoch $E = p_2$ into `ConstDualBuf` using burst read.				
load-psis	group G	-	Dram1	[q], [q']
Loads the powers of ψ^{-1} for groups p_1 to $p_1 + K - 1$ and moduli q or modulus q' from DRAM using burst read and saves them in `ConstDualBuf`.				
load-evks	DRAM address	group	Dram1	-
Loads the $\ell_{w,q}$ different evaluation key parts for groups p_2 to $p_2 + K - 1$ stored at base address p_1 into `ConstDualBuf` using burst read.				
ntt-on-buffer	chunk	-	NttCore	[q], [q']
Computes the C-NTT on chunk p_1 stored in `DataDualBuf` using either modulus q or modulus q' and requiring $\frac{Pn}{2G}$ multiply accumulate (MAC) operations.				
mul-psi	chunk	-	NttCore	[(q|q'),round]]
Multiplies chunk p_1 stored in `DataDualBuf` by powers of ψ^{-1} stored in `ConstDualBuf`. If configured with [round] the YASHE rounding operation is performed after the NTT.				
mul-evk	chunk	-	NttCore	[q]
Multiplies chunk p_1 in `DataDualBuf` by the evaluation keys stored in `ConstDualBuf`.				
accumulate	chunk	-	NttCore	-
Adds chunks p_1 to chunk 0 stored in `DataDualBuf`.				
mul-point-wise	-	-	NttCore	[q], [q']
Performs point-wise multiplication.				

Another improvement is achieved by the combination of the bit-reversal with the reordering procedure of the cached-NTT ([ro,bitrev]) in which case it is possible to write a whole group ($C = n/G$ coefficients) using burst mode. As a consequence, it is even preferable to compute the reordering together with the bit-reversal instead of only the reordering, as the size of the burst write is even larger in this case for relevant parameters (i.e., n/G instead of G).

4.2   Computation of the C-NTT on the Cache

The C-NTT is computed on each group in the cache (see the dotted box in Fig. 1) and requires arithmetic operations that dominate the area costs of our implementation. Each C-NTT on a group requires $\frac{Pn}{2G}$ multiplications in $\mathbb{Z}_q$ (or $\mathbb{Z}_{q'}$) and the whole cached-NTT requires $EG\frac{Pn}{2G} = \frac{n\log_2(n)}{2}$ multiplications in $\mathbb{Z}_q$ (or $\mathbb{Z}_{q'}$). The address generation in NttCore, which implements the C-NTT, is independent of the group or epoch that is processed. This allows a simple data-path and also testability independently of the memory transfer commands. To saturate the pipelined butterfly unit of the NTT, two reads and two writes are required per cycle and we use the well-known fact that the buffer can be split into two memories, one for even and one for odd addresses (see [32]). While this approach might lead to wasted space in block memories if small polynomials do not fill a whole block RAM, as in [33] and optimized in [1,36], it is not a concern for the large parameter sets we are dealing with. The only input to the NTT, besides the actual polynomial coefficients, that depend on the current group or epoch are the constants like twiddle factors, powers of ψ^{-1}, or the evaluation key evk. We decided to store each constant in a continuous memory region and load them into the TWID-RAM or EVK-RAM buffers depending on the current group or epoch. While it would also be possible to compute the twiddle factors on-the-fly (as in [36]) this approach would require an additional expensive $q' \times q'$ multiplier and modulo unit. Additionally, we do not exploit redundancies in twiddle factors or other tricks so that we are able to load constants using the fast burst mode. The only important observation is that when $E = 2$ the same set of twiddle factors is used for the computation of all groups of the first epoch of the NTT.

For best performance of the NTT_q our architecture requires a pipelined NTT butterfly that is able to compute a $\log_2(q) \times \log_2(q)$ multiplication, modular reduction, and two accumulations per cycle. For the butterfly of the $\mathrm{NTT}_{q'}$, execution in one clock cycle is not necessary as the maximum data width of the ConstDualBuf and DataDualBuf components is $\frac{q'}{2}$. Thus, at least two cycles are needed to load a coefficient from the buffer in which one coefficient modulo q' is split into chunk 0 and chunk 1.

To instantiate the multiplier we used a traditional RTL design that uses four pipelined 72×72-bit multipliers generated using the Altera MegaWizard to instantiate a 144×144-bit multiplier. The instantiation of four 144×144-bit multipliers yields a 288×288-bit multiplier and finally a pipelined 576×576-bit multiplier. For modular reduction we restrict the moduli q and q' to Solinas primes [37] of the form $2^y - 2^z + 1$ for $y, z \in \mathbb{Z}$ and $y > z$. A modular reduction circuit can then be configured by providing the input bit width and the values y and z as generics/parameters. The implementation only requires a few shifts and few additions/subtractions to perform a modular reduction.

5   Configuration of Our Core for YASHE

For our prototype we have implemented YASHE's homomorphic evaluation operations Add and Mult using the architecture described in Sect. 4. As space is limited we only cover the RMult and KeySwitch functions in detail, which are essential for the implementation of Mult. All homomorphic evaluation operations use the hardware architecture described in Sect. 4 and the commands provided in Table 2. The commands are executed by a large state machine implemented in HomomorphicCore, which is also responsible for interaction with the Catapult shell and host PC.

5.1 Implementation of RMult

For RMult, a standard integer polynomial multiplication in $\mathbb{Z}_{q'}[X]/(X^n + 1)$ is required after which the result is rounded and reduced modulo q. Selecting $q' > nq^2$ guarantees that the product $c_1 c_2$ of two polynomials $c_1, c_2 \in \mathbb{Z}_q[X]/(X^n+1)$ is computed over the integers and not being reduced before it is rounded. Instead of using a single routine for RMult, the host server can make separate calls to a single forward transformation $\bar{c}_i = \mathsf{RMultFwd}(c_i)$ so that polynomials to be multiplied with multiple other polynomials have to be transformed only once into the NTT domain. The $\tilde{c}_{\mathrm{mult}} = \mathsf{RMultInv}(\bar{c}_1, \bar{c}_2)$ routine then takes two transformed polynomials $\bar{c}_1, \bar{c}_2$ as input and computes the product by performing point-wise multiplication, the inverse NTT, and rounding of the result. While we give up some efficiency (e.g., merging of forward transformation and point-wise multiplication) by this approach, it seems beneficial to provide this additional flexibility when computing homomorphic circuits.

The (simplified) sequence of executed commands for RMultFwd is provided in Algorithm 1, but for the actual implementation load/store operations and NTT computations are executed in parallel to make use of the double-buffer capability of the DataDualBuf and ConstDualBuf components. In step 5 of RMultFwd the input polynomial is expected to be saved in bitreversed order already. This is either ensured by the user when the polynomial is initially transferred to the device or by our implementation in the last step of KeySwitch. The only execution of a reordering load operation is performed in step 11 and all other loads or stores use the burst mode. Thus the second reordering is delayed till the pointwise multiplication in RMultInv which is given in Algorithm 2. In RMultInv the first block of operations (steps 3 to 7) is responsible for the pointwise multiplication. Note that the Add operation of YASHE is basically this loop but mul-point-wise is exchanged by a command for addition in $\mathbb{Z}_q$. The first NTT-related load is performed in step 11 in which the final reordering of the forward transform together with the bitreversal step is performed. The final rounding operation $\left[\left[\frac{t}{q} t_2\right]\right]_q$ is included into the mul-psi$[q', \mathrm{round}]$ command. After that the result $\tilde{c}_{\mathrm{mult}}$ is in $\mathbb{Z}_q[X]/(X^n+1)$. Note that it is not possible to merge the multiplication by powers of ψ^{-1} into the NTT twiddle factors for the inverse transformation [36] as we use the Cooley-Tukey butterfly. The multiplication by powers of ψ^{-1} is performed by the mul-psi command and the constants are loaded into the memory space reserved for the evaluation key during the forward transformation by load-psis. The multiplication by the scalar n^{-1} is merged into the ψ^{-1} values.

Algorithm 1. Forward transformation of an input polynomial in RMult

```
1:  function RMultFwd(c_i)
2:      //Epoch 0
3:      load-twiddles[fwd,q'](0,0)
4:      forall groups x ∈ 0 ... G/K − 1:
5:          load-group[burst](c_i, Kx)
6:          ntt-on-buffer[q'](0)
7:          store-chunks[burst,q'](t,
    Kx)
8:      //Epoch 1
9:      forall groups x ∈ 0 ... G/K − 1:
10:         load-twiddles[fwd,q'](Kx,1)
11:         load-chunks[ro,q'](t, Kx)
12:         ntt-on-buffer[q'](0)
13:         store-chunks[burst,q'](c̄_i,
    Kx)
14:     return c̄_i
15: end function
```

Algorithm 2. Pointwise multiplication and inv. transformation in RMult

```
1:  function RMultInv(c̄_1, c̄_2)
2:      //Pointwise multiplication
3:      forall groups x ∈ 0 ... G/K − 1:
4:          load-chunks[burst,q'](c_1,
    Kx)
5:          load-chunks[burst,q'](c_2,
    Kx)
6:          mul-point-wise[q']()
7:          store-chunks[burst,q'](t_1,
    Kx)
8:      //Epoch 0
9:      load-twiddles[inv,q'](0,0)
10:     forall groups x ∈ 0 ... G/K − 1:
11:         load-
    chunks[ro,bitrev,q'](t_1, Kx)
12:         ntt-on-buffer[q'](0)
13:         store-chunks[burst,q'](t_2,
    Kx)
14:     //Epoch 1
15:     forall groups x ∈ 0 ... G/K − 1:
16:         load-twiddles[inv,q'](Kx,1)
17:         load-psis[q'](Kx)
18:         load-chunks[ro,q'](t_2, Kx)
19:         ntt-on-buffer[q'](0)
20:         mul-psi[q', round](0)
21:         store-
    group[ro,bitrev](c̃_mult, Kx)
22:     return c̃_mult
23: end function
```

5.2   Implementation of KeySwitch

The control-flow used to implement KeySwitch based on the commands introduced in Sect. 4 and Eq. 1 is given in Algorithm 3. For the forward transformation (step 2 to step 19) the coefficients of the input polynomial $\tilde{c}_{mult}$ can be loaded using the burst mode as they have already been stored in bitreversed representation in RMultInv. The decomposition $\text{Dec}_{w,q}(\tilde{c}_{mult}) = ([(\tilde{c}_{mult})_i]_w)_{i=0}^{\ell_{w,q}-1}$ is performed on-the-fly inside the FPGA using the load-group-expand[burst] command. The NTT is then performed on all $\ell_{w,q}$ decomposed polynomials in the buffer. As the twiddle factors are the same for each polynomial we only have to load and store K sets of twiddle factors into the ConstDualBuf component (each set containing $P \cdot \ell_{w,q}/2$ coefficients). During the NTT computation on all polynomials the results are accumulated (step 18) and then stored (step 19). The relatively slow reordering operation load-chunks[ro, q] is performed at the beginning of the second epoch and not after the first epoch as the accumulation and multiplication with the evaluation keys takes additional time so that we can balance the time required for memory transfers and computation. As the forward transformed polynomials are already stored in the correct order, we just have to perform a burst read at the beginning of the inverse transformation in step 24. Additionally, the computation is much less involved as we only have to compute one INTT_q and not $\ell_{w,q}$ computations of NTT_q caused by the decomposition.

Algorithm 3. Key switching in YASHE

1: **function** KeySwitch ($\tilde{c}_{mult}$, $\tilde{evk}$)
2:      //Fwd. transform and accumulation:
3:      load-twiddles[fwd,q]$(0, 0)$
4:      //Epoch 0
5:      **forall** groups $x \in 0 \ldots G/K - 1$:
6:          load-group-expand[burst]$(\tilde{c}_{mult}, Kx)$
7:          **forall** chunks $y \in 0 \ldots \ell_{w,q} - 1$:
8:              ntt-on-buffer[q](y)
9:          store-chunks[burst,q]$(\mathbf{t}_1, Kx)$
10:     //Epoch 1
11:     **forall** groups $x \in 0 \ldots G/K - 1$:
12:         load-twiddles[fwd,q]$(Kx, 1)$
13:         load evk($\tilde{evk}, Kx$)
14:         load-chunks[ro, q]$(\mathbf{t}_1, Kx)$
15:         **forall** chunks $y \in 0 \ldots \ell_{w,q}$:
16:             ntt-on-buffer[q](y)
17:             mul-evk[q](y)
18:             accumulate(y)
19:         store-group[ro, bitrev]$(\mathbf{t}_2, Kx)$
20:     //Inverse transform:
21:     load-twiddles[inv,q]$(0, 0)$
22:     //Epoch 0
23:     **forall** groups $x \in 0 \ldots G/K - 1$:
24:         load-group[burst]$(\mathbf{t}_2, Kx)$
25:         ntt-on-buffer[q](0)
26:         store-group[ro]$(\mathbf{t}_1, Kx)$
27:     //Epoch 1
28:     **forall** groups $x \in 0 \ldots G/K - 1$:
29:         load-twiddles[inv,q]$(Kx, 1)$
30:         load-psis[q](Kx)
31:         load-group[burst]$(\mathbf{t}_1, Kx)$
32:         ntt-on-buffer[q](0)
33:         mul-psi[q](0)
34:         store-group[ro, bitrev]$(\mathbf{c}_{mult}, Kx)$
35:     **return** $\mathbf{c}_{mult}$
36: **end function**

---

6   Results and Comparison

In this section we provide post place-and-route (post-PAR) results and performance measurements of our implementation on the Catapult board [34] equipped with an Altera Stratix V (5GSND5H) FPGA and two 4 GB DRAMs.

6.1   Resource Consumption and Performance

The resource consumption of our implementation is reported in Table 3. Achieving a high clock frequency for parameter Set II is challenging. One reason seems to be that, due to our design choices, we have to deal with extremely large structures like several thousand bit wide adders and a large integer multiplier. Such structures are tedious to manually optimize and it is hard to determine an optimal pipeline length. Another reason is that the design is congested and that placement and fitting have to satisfy strict constraints imposed by the PCIe and DRAM controllers in the Catapult shell. Still, switching to larger devices to reduce congestion would also increase costs.

Table 3. Resource consumption of our implementation (including communication).

Implementation	ALM	FF	DSP	BRAM Bits	MHz
Set I ($n=4096, K=8$)	69,058 (40%)	144,747	144 (9%)	8,031,568 (19%)	100
Set II ($n=16384, K=4$)	141,090 (82%)	391,773	577 (36%)	17,626,400 (43%)	66

Table 4. Cycle counts and runtimes for the different evaluation algorithms of YASHE measured on the Catapult board.

Implementation		Mult	Add	KeySwitch	RMult	RMultFwd	RMultInv
Set I ($n=4096$) 100 MHz ($K=8$)	cycles	675,326	19,057	478,911	196,415	160,693	157,525
	time	6.75 ms	0.19 ms	4.79 ms	1.96 ms	1.61 ms	1.58 ms
Set II ($n=16384$) 66 MHz ($K=4$)	cycles	3,212,506	61,775	1,372,519	1,839,987	587,664	664,659
	time	48.67 ms	0.94 ms	20.80 ms	27.88 ms	8.90 ms	10.07 ms

Cycle counts for evaluation operations are given in Table 4 and are obtained using the `PerfMonitor` component that logs cycle counts and transfers them to the host server over PCIe, if requested. The usual approach of obtaining cycle counts from simulation is not possible as we are using an external DRAM without a cycle accurate simulation model. Note that the Mult operation requires to execute RMult and KeySwitch. Also note that the runtime does not simply scale for higher clock frequencies as the DDR memory interface is running in its own clock domain and thus the memory bandwidth is not significantly increased by higher clock frequencies of the `HomomorphicCore` component.

A good indicator for the efficiency of our memory addressing is the saturation of the $\log(q) \times \log(q)$ modular multiplier. One NTT requires $\frac{n}{2}\log_2(n)$ multiply-accumulate (MAC) operations so that KeySwitch takes at least $C_{KS}(\ell_{w,q}, n) = (\ell_{w,q}+1)(\frac{n}{2}\log_2(n) + n)$ cycles assuming one clock cycle per MAC ($\ell_{w,q}$ forward and one inverse NTT, see Eq. 1). For parameter Set II we get $C_{KS}(8,16384) = 1,179,648$ as lower bound on the number of cycles for KeySwitch which is close to the measured 1,372,519 cycles. For RMult approx. $C_{RM}(n) = 3(4\frac{n}{2}\log_2 n) + 2(4n)$ cycles are required (three transformations, pointwise and ψ^{-1} multiplication; four cycles per MAC) and the saturation of the MAC unit is $\frac{C_{RM}(16384)}{1,839,987} = 0.82$.

6.2 Comparison with Previous Work

Cao et al. [9] describe an implementation of the integer-based FHE scheme in [16] on a Virtex-7 FPGA (XC7VX980T) but explicitly do not take into account the bottleneck that may be caused by accessing off-chip memory. Their implementation achieves a speed up factor of 11.25 compared to a software implementation but for large parameter sets, which might promise some performance gains, the design does not fit on current FPGAs. An FPGA implementation of an integer multiplier for the Gentry-Halevi [24] FHE scheme is proposed in [43]. The architecture requires about 462,983 ALUs, and 720 DSPs on a Stratix-V

(55GSMD8N3F45I4) and allows 768K-bit multiplications. It is reported to be about two times faster than a similar implementation on an NVIDA C2050 GPU. Another 768K-bit multiplication architecture is proposed by Wang et al. in [44] targeting ASICs and FPGAs. An outline of an implementation of a homomorphic encryption scheme is given in [17] using Matlab/Simulink and the Mathwork HDL coder. The used tools limit the available basic multiplier width to 128 bits and the design requires multiple FPGAs to deal with long vectors.

An ASIC implementation of a million-bit multiplier for integer-based FHE schemes is presented by Doröz et al. in [21]. The computation of the product of two 1,179,648-bit integers takes 5.16 million clock cycles. Synthesis results for a chip using the TSMC 90 nm cell library show a maximum clock frequency of 666 MHz and thus a runtime of 7.74 ms for this operation, equivalent to that of a software implementation. This shows, similar to our result, that the biggest challenges in the implementation of homomorphic cryptography in hardware are the large ciphertext sizes that do not fit into block RAMs (our case) or caches instantiated with the standard library (Doröz et al. [21]).

Wang et al. [42] present the first GPU implementation of an FHE scheme and provide results for the Gentry-Halevi [24] scheme on an NVIDIA C2050 GPU. The results were subsequently improved in [40]. A GPU implementation of the leveled FHE scheme by Brakerski et al. [8] is given in [41]. In [19] Dai et al. provide an implementation of the DHS [20] FHE scheme that is based on the scheme in [30]. For the parameters ($n = 16384, \log_2(q) = 575$), they require 0.063 s for multiplication and 0.89 s for relinearization (key switching) on a 2.5 GHz Xeon E5-2609 equipped with an NVIDIA GeForce GTX 690.

A software library that implements the Brakerski-Gentry-Vaikuntanathan (BGV) [7,8] scheme is described in [27]. In [29], a software implementation of YASHE is reported which for the parameter set ($n = 4096, q = 2^{127} - 1, w = 2^{32}$) executes Add in 0.7 ms, RMult in 18 ms, and KeySwitch in 31 ms on an Intel Core i7-2600 running at 3.4 GHz. So our hardware implementation can evaluate Mult on a parameter set supporting 9 levels in 48.67 ms while the software requires 49 ms for parameters supporting only 1 multiplicative level.

Roy et al. [35] proposed an implementation of YASHE with $n = 2^{15}$ and a modulus of $\log_2(q) = 1228$ bits. They use a much larger next generation FPGA (Virtex-7 XC7V1140T) from a different vendor so that a comparison with our work is naturally hard - especially regarding the economical benefits of using FPGAs. We see the biggest contribution of the work by Roy et al. in their efficient implementation of independent processors that use the CRT to decompose polynomials. This approach avoids large integer multipliers and simplifies routing and performance tuning. When we designed our core, the added complexity and the need to lift polynomials from CRT to natural representations in hardware appeared to be too expensive. However, the authors of [35] do not consider the costs of moving data between external memory and the FPGA but just assume unlimited memory bandwidth. This naturally simplifies the design and placement but does not appear to be a realistic assumption. In our work a considerable amount of time was spent to implement efficient memory transfers and to optimize the algorithms in this regard. However, we see our work and the work of Roy et al. as a first step towards an efficient accelerator.

7   Future Work

While implementing the scheme we encountered several challenges that might also be a good start for future work. A big issue was verification and simulation time due to the large problem sizes. Different design or simulation approaches are probably needed for larger parameter sets. Another area of future work is the design of a more efficient and easier to synthesize large-integer modular multiplier and further design space exploration and implementation of larger parameter sets. Additionally, it might also make sense to investigate the applicability of the Chinese remainder theorem (CRT) in combination with the cached-NTT.

References

1. Aysu, A., Patterson, C., Schaumont, P.: Low-cost and area-efficient FPGA implementations of lattice-based cryptography. In: 2013 IEEE International Symposium on Hardware-Oriented Security and Trust, HOST 2013, Austin, TX, USA, 2–3 June 2013, pp. 81–86. IEEE Computer Society (2013). 5, 12
2. Baas, B.M.: An approach to low-power, high performance, fast fourier transform processor design. Ph.D. thesis, Stanford University, Stanford, CA, USA (1999). 2, 5, 7
3. Baas, B.M.: A generalized cached-FFT algorithm. In: 2005 IEEE International Conference on Acoustics, Speech, and Signal Processing, ICASSP 2005, Philadelphia, Pennsylvania, USA, 18–23 March 2005, pp. 89–92. IEEE (2005). 2, 5, 6, 7
4. Bos, J.W., Lauter, K., Loftus, J., Naehrig, M.: Improved security for a ring-based fully homomorphic encryption scheme. In: Stam, M. (ed.) IMACC 2013. LNCS, vol. 8308, pp. 45–64. Springer, Heidelberg (2013). 2, 3, 4
5. Bos, J.W., Lauter, K.E., Naehrig, M.: Private predictive analysis on encrypted medical data. J. Biomed. Inform. 50, 234–243 (2014). 1
6. Brakerski, Z.: Fully homomorphic encryption without modulus switching from classical GapSVP. In: Safavi-Naini, R., Canetti, R. (eds.) CRYPTO 2012. LNCS, vol. 7417, pp. 868–886. Springer, Heidelberg (2012). 2
7. Brakerski, Z., Gentry, C., Vaikuntanathan, V.: Fully homomorphic encryption without bootstrapping. IACR Cryptology ePrint Archive, 2011:277 (2011). 18
8. Brakerski, Z., Gentry, C., Vaikuntanathan, V.: (Leveled) fully homomorphic encryption without bootstrapping. In: Goldwasser, S. (ed.) Innovations in Theoretical Computer Science 2012, Cambridge, MA, USA, 8–10 January 2012, pp. 309–325. ACM (2012). 2, 18
9. Cao, X., Moore, C., O'Neill, M., Hanley, N., O'Sullivan, E.: High-speed fully homomorphic encryption over the integers. In: Böhme, R., Brenner, M., Moore, T., Smith, M. (eds.) FC 2014 Workshops. LNCS, vol. 8438, pp. 169–180. Springer, Heidelberg (2014). Extended version: [10]. 2, 17, 19
10. Cao, X., Moore, C., O'Neill, M., O'Sullivan, E., Hanley, N.: Accelerating fully homomorphic encryption over the integers with super-size hardware multiplier and modular reduction. IACR Cryptology ePrint Archive, 2013:616 (2013). Conference version of [9]. 19

11. Chen, D.D., Mentens, N., Vercauteren, F., Sinha Roy, S., Cheung, R.C.C., Pao, D., Verbauwhede, I.: High-speed polynomial multiplication architecture for Ring-LWE and SHE cryptosystems. IACR Cryptology ePrint Archive, 2014:646 (2014). 2
12. Cheon, J.H., Kim, M., Kim, M.: Search-and-compute on encrypted data. Cryptology ePrint Archive, Report 2014/812 (2014). http://eprint.iacr.org/2014/812. 1
13. Cheon, J.H., Kim, M., Lauter, K.: Homomorphic computation of edit distance. Cryptology ePrint Archive, Report 2015/132 (2015). http://eprint.iacr.org/2015/132. 1
14. Chu, E., George, A.: Inside the FFT Black Box Serial and Parallel Fast Fourier Transform Algorithms. CRC Press, Boca Raton (2000). 4, 5
15. Cooley, J.W., Tukey, J.W.: An algorithm for the machine calculation of complex Fourier series. Math. Comput. **19**, 297–301 (1965). 5
16. Coron, J.-S., Mandal, A., Naccache, D., Tibouchi, M.: Fully homomorphic encryption over the integers with shorter public keys. In: Rogaway, P. (ed.) CRYPTO 2011. LNCS, vol. 6841, pp. 487–504. Springer, Heidelberg (2011). 2, 17
17. Cousins, D., Rohloff, K., Peikert, C., Schantz, R.E.: An update on SIPHER (scalable implementation of primitives for homomorphic encryption) - FPGA implementation using simulink. In: IEEE Conference on High Performance Extreme Computing, HPEC 2012, Waltham, MA, USA, 10–12 September 2012, pp. 1–5. IEEE (2012). 17
18. Crandall, R., Pomerance, C.: Prime Numbers: A Computational Perspective. Springer, New York (2001). 4
19. Dai, W., Doröz, Y., Sunar, B.: Accelerating NTRU based homomorphic encryption using GPUs. IACR Cryptology ePrint Archive, 2014:389 (2014). To appear in IEEE Transaction on Computers. 2, 7, 18
20. Doröz, Y., Yin, H., Sunar, B.: Homomorphic AES evaluation using NTRU. IACR Cryptology ePrint Archive, 2014:39 (2014). 18
21. Doröz, Y., Öztürk, E., Sunar, B.: Evaluating the hardware performance of a million-bit multiplier. In: 2013 Euromicro Conference on Digital System Design, DSD 2013, Los Alamitos, CA, USA, 4–6 September 2013, pp. 955–962. IEEE Computer Society (2013). 2, 17
22. Gentleman, W.M., Sande, G.: Fast fourier transforms: for fun and profit. In: American Federation of Information Processing Societies: Proceedings of the AFIPS 1966 Fall Joint Computer Conference, 7–10 November 1966, San Francisco, California, USA. AFIPS Conference Proceedings, vol. 29, pp. 563–578. AFIPS/ACM/Spartan Books, Washington D.C. (1966). 5
23. Gentry, C.: Fully homomorphic encryption using ideal lattices. In: Mitzenmacher, M. (ed.) Proceedings of the 41st Annual ACM Symposium on Theory of Computing, STOC 2009, Bethesda, MD, USA, May 31 - June 2, 2009, pp. 169–178. ACM (2009). 2
24. Gentry, C., Halevi, S.: Implementing Gentry's fully-homomorphic encryption scheme. In: Paterson, K.G. (ed.) EUROCRYPT 2011. LNCS, vol. 6632, pp. 129–148. Springer, Heidelberg (2011). 2, 17, 18
25. Gentry, C., Halevi, S., Smart, N.P.: Homomorphic evaluation of the AES circuit. In: Safavi-Naini, R., Canetti, R. (eds.) CRYPTO 2012. LNCS, vol. 7417, pp. 850–867. Springer, Heidelberg (2012). 2
26. Gentry, C., Sahai, A., Waters, B.: Homomorphic encryption from learning with errors: conceptually-simpler, asymptotically-faster, attribute-based. In: Canetti, R., Garay, J.A. (eds.) CRYPTO 2013, Part I. LNCS, vol. 8042, pp. 75–92. Springer, Heidelberg (2013). 2

27. Halevi, S., Shoup, V.: Algorithms in HElib. In: Garay, J.A., Gennaro, R. (eds.) CRYPTO 2014, Part I. LNCS, vol. 8616, pp. 554–571. Springer, Heidelberg (2014). https://shaih.github.io/HElib/. 18

28. Lauter, K.E., Naehrig, M., Vaikuntanathan, V.: Can homomorphic encryption be practical? In: Cachin, C., Ristenpart, T. (eds.) Proceedings of the 3rd ACM Cloud Computing Security Workshop, CCSW 2011, Chicago, IL, USA, 21 October 2011, pp. 113–124. ACM (2011). 1

29. Lepoint, T., Naehrig, M.: A comparison of the homomorphic encryption schemes FV and YASHE. In: Pointcheval, D., Vergnaud, D. (eds.) AFRICACRYPT. LNCS, vol. 8469, pp. 318–335. Springer, Heidelberg (2014). 2, 3, 4, 18

30. López-Alt, A., Tromer, E., Vaikuntanathan, V.: On-the-fly multiparty computation on the cloud via multikey fully homomorphic encryption. In: Karloff, H.J., Pitassi, T. (eds.) Proceedings of the 44th Symposium on Theory of Computing Conference, STOC 2012, New York, NY, USA, 19–22 May 2012, pp. 1219–1234. ACM (2012). 2, 3, 18

31. Nussbaumer, H.J.: Fast Fourier Transform and Convolution Algorithms. Springer Series in Information Sciences, vol. 2. Springer, Berlin (1982). 4

32. Pease, M.C.: An adaptation of the fast Fourier transform for parallel processing. J. ACM 15(2), 252–264 (1968). 12

33. Pöppelmann, T., Güneysu, T.: Towards efficient arithmetic for lattice-based cryptography on reconfigurable hardware. In: Hevia, A., Neven, G. (eds.) LatinCrypt 2012. LNCS, vol. 7533, pp. 139–158. Springer, Heidelberg (2012). 5, 12

34. Putnam, A., Caulfield, A.M., Chung, E.S., Chiou, D., Constantinides, K., Demme, J., Esmaeilzadeh, H., Fowers, J., Gopal, G.P., Gray, J., Haselman, M., Hauck, S., Heil, S., Hormati, A., Kim, J.-Y., Lanka, S., Larus, J.R., Peterson, E., Pope, S., Smith, A., Thong, J., Xiao, P.Y., Burger, D.: A reconfigurable fabric for accelerating large-scale datacenter services. In: ACM/IEEE 41st International Symposium on Computer Architecture, ISCA 2014, Minneapolis, MN, USA, 14–18 June 2014, pp. 13–24. IEEE Computer Society (2014). 2, 5, 16

35. Sinha Roy, S., Järvinen, K., Vercauteren, F., Dimitrov, V.S., Verbauwhede, I.: Modular hardware architecture for somewhat homomorphic function evaluation. IACR Cryptology ePrint Archive, 2015:337 (2015). To appear in Güneysu, T., Handschuh, H. (eds.) CHES 2015. LNCS, vol. 9293, pp, xx–yy. Springer, Heidelberg (2015). 2, 18

36. Roy, S.S., Vercauteren, F., Mentens, N., Chen, D.D., Verbauwhede, I.: Compact ring-LWE cryptoprocessor. In: Batina, L., Robshaw, M. (eds.) CHES 2014. LNCS, vol. 8731, pp. 371–391. Springer, Heidelberg (2014). 5, 7, 12, 14

37. Solinas, J.A.: Generalized Mersenne numbers. Technical Report MCORR 99–39, Faculty of Mathematics, University of Waterloo (1999). 13

38. Stehlé, D., Steinfeld, R.: Making NTRU as secure as worst-case problems over ideal lattices. In: Paterson, Kenneth G. (ed.) EUROCRYPT 2011. LNCS, vol. 6632, pp. 27–47. Springer, Heidelberg (2011). 3

39. van Dijk, M., Gentry, C., Halevi, S., Vaikuntanathan, V.: Fully homomorphic encryption over the integers. In: Gilbert, H. (ed.) EUROCRYPT 2010. LNCS, vol. 6110, pp. 24–43. Springer, Heidelberg (2010). 2

40. Wang, W., Hu, Y., Chen, L., Huang, X., Sunar, B.: Exploring the feasibility of fully homomorphic encryption. IEEE Trans. Comput. 64(3), 698–706 (2015). 2, 18

41. Wang, W., Chen, Z., Huang, X.: Accelerating leveled fully homomorphic encryption using GPU. In: IEEE International Symposium on Circuits and Systemss, ISCAS 2014, Melbourne, Victoria, Australia, 1–5 June 2014, pp. 2800–2803. IEEE (2014). 2, 18

42. Wang, W., Hu, Y., Chen, L., Huang, X., Sunar, B.: Accelerating fully homomorphic encryption using GPU. In: IEEE Conference on High Performance Extreme Computing, HPEC 2012, Waltham, MA, USA, 10–12 September 2012, pp. 1–5. IEEE (2012). 18
43. Wang, W., Huang, X.: FPGA implementation of a large-number multiplier for fully homomorphic encryption. In: 2013 IEEE International Symposium on Circuits and Systems (ISCAS2013), Beijing, China, 19–23 May 2013, pp. 2589–2592. IEEE (2013). 17
44. Wang, W., Huang, X., Emmart, N., Weems, C.C.: VLSI design of a large-number multiplier for fully homomorphic encryption. IEEE Trans. VLSI Syst. **22**(9), 1879–1887 (2014). 2, 17
45. Winkler, F.: Polynomial Algorithms in Computer Algebra. Texts and Monographs in Symbolic Computation, 1st edn. Springer, Wien (1996). 4

Modular Hardware Architecture for Somewhat Homomorphic Function Evaluation

Sujoy Sinha Roy[1]([✉]), Kimmo Järvinen[1], Frederik Vercauteren[1],
Vassil Dimitrov[2], and Ingrid Verbauwhede[1]

[1] KU Leuven ESAT/COSIC and iMinds, Kasteelpark Arenberg 10, Bus 2452, 3001
Leuven-Heverlee, Belgium
{Sujoy.SinhaRoy,Kimmo.Jarvinen,Frederik.Vercauteren,
Ingrid.Verbauwhede}@esat.kuleuven.be
[2] The University of Calgary, Canada and Computer Modelling Group, Ltd.,
2500 University Dr. NW, Calgary, AB T2N 1N4, Canada
vdvsd103@gmail.com

Abstract. We present a hardware architecture for all building blocks
required in polynomial ring based fully homomorphic schemes and use it
to instantiate the somewhat homomorphic encryption scheme YASHE.
Our implementation is the first FPGA implementation that is designed
for evaluating functions on homomorphically encrypted data (up to a certain multiplicative depth) and we illustrate this capability by evaluating
the SIMON-64/128 block cipher in the encrypted domain. Our implementation provides a fast polynomial operations unit using CRT and NTT
for multiplication combined with an optimized memory access scheme;
a fast Barrett like polynomial reduction method; an efficient divide and
round unit required in the multiplication of ciphertexts and an efficient
CRT unit. These building blocks are integrated in an instruction-set
coprocessor to execute YASHE, which can be controlled by a computer
for evaluating arbitrary functions (up to the multiplicative depth 44 and
128-bit security level). Our architecture was compiled for a single Virtex-
7 XC7V1140T FPGA, where it consumes 23 % of registers, 50 % of LUTs,
53 % of DSP slices, and 38 % of BlockRAM memory. The implementation
evaluates SIMON-64/128 in approximately 157.7 s (at 143 MHz) and it
processes 2048 ciphertexts at once giving a relative time of only 77 ms per
block. This is 26.6 times faster than the leading software implementation
on a 4-core Intel Core-i7 processor running at 3.4 GHz.

Keywords: Fully homomorphic encryption · YASHE · FPGA · NTT ·
CRT

1 Introduction

The concept of fully homomorphic encryption (FHE) was introduced by Rivest,
Adleman, and Dertouzos [34] already in 1978 and allows evaluating arbitrary functions on encrypted data. Constructing FHE schemes proved to be

© International Association for Cryptologic Research 2015
T. Güneysu and H. Handschuh (Eds.): CHES 2015, LNCS 9293, pp. 164–184, 2015.
DOI: 10.1007/978-3-662-48324-4_9

a difficult problem that remained unsolved until 2009 when Gentry [22] proposed the first FHE scheme by using ideal lattices. Despite its groundbreaking nature, Gentry's proposal did not provide a practical solution because of its low performance. Since then, many researchers have followed the blueprints set out by Gentry's proposal with an objective to improve the performance of FHE [6,7,14,17,20,24,25,32]. Most schemes are either based on (ring) learning with errors ((R)LWE) or N-th degree truncated polynomial ring (NTRU) and thus manipulate elements in modular polynomial rings, or on the approximate greatest common divisor (GCD) problem which manipulates very large integers. In this paper, we focus on the former category. Although major advances have been made, we are still lacking FHE schemes with performance levels that would allow large-scale practical use. Software implementations still require minutes or hours to evaluate even rather simple functions. For instance, evaluating the lightweight block cipher SIMON-64/128 [4] requires 4193 s (an hour and 10 min) on a 4-core Intel Core-i7 processor [29]. Note that homomorphic evaluation of a block cipher decryption is required to reduce the network communication to the data size following the proposal in [32]: data is encrypted with a block cipher by the user and then the server decrypts the ciphertext by evaluating the block cipher homomorphically by using a homomorhic encryption of the key. If FHE could achieve performance levels that would permit large-scale practical use, it would have a drastic effect on cloud computing: users could outsource computations to the cloud without the need to trust service providers and their mechanisms for protecting users' data from outsiders.

Application-specific integrated circuits (ASIC) and field-programmable gate arrays (FPGA) have been successfully used for accelerating performance-critical computations in cryptology (see, e.g., [28]). Hence, it is somewhat surprising that, so far, mainly standard software implementations of FHE have been published, because hardware acceleration could bring FHE significantly closer to practical feasibility. Only few publications have reported results on (hardware) acceleration of FHE and most are dealing with manipulation of very large integers. Wang et al. [38] implemented primitives for the Gentry-Halevi (GH) FHE scheme [23] using Graphics Processing Unit (GPU) and observed speedups up to 7.68. They focused particularly on the multi-million-bit modular multiplication by using Strassen multiplication and Barrett reduction. Wang and Huang [39,40] later showed that this multiplication can be further accelerated by a factor of approximately two together with significant reductions in power consumption by using FPGA and ASIC. Doröz et al. [18] presented a million-bit multiplier for the GH scheme on ASIC. They reported that the performance remains roughly the same as on Intel Xeon CPU, but with a significantly smaller area than the CPU. Moore et al. [31] studied the use of hardwired multipliers inside FPGAs for accelerating large integer multiplication. The same researchers later presented the first implementation of the full FHE encryption in [10]. They reported a speedup factor of 44 compared to a corresponding software implementation. Cousins et al. [15,16] drafted an architecture of an FPGA accelerator for FHE using Simulink extension to Matlab but they did not provide any implementation results for their architecture. To conclude, only few works are available on hardware acceleration of FHE schemes. So far, no results are available on hardware acceleration of function evaluation on homomorphically encrypted data, although this is the most crucial part of FHE schemes in application scenarios.

We present the first efficient FPGA implementation of the building blocks required in modular polynomial ring based fully homomorphic schemes such as those built on RLWE [8] or NTRU [30]. These building blocks are sufficiently generic to allow implementation of such FHE schemes, and to illustrate this, we integrate these building blocks into a coprocessor architecture that can evaluate functions encrypted with the FHE scheme called Yet Another Somewhat Homomorphic Encryption (YASHE) [6]. To the best of our knowledge, it is the first FPGA implementation that supports function evaluation of homomorphically encrypted data. We use several standard optimization techniques such as the Chinese remainder theorem (CRT) representation, the number theoretic transformation (NTT) and fast modular polynomial reduction, but introduce several optimizations specific for the FPGA platform such as a specific memory access scheme for the NTT. We compile the architecture for Xilinx Virtex-7 XC7V1140T FPGA. We show that a single FPGA achieves speedups up to factor 26.6 in executing SIMON-64/128 compared to a corresponding software implementation running on a 4-core Intel Core i7 processor from [29].

The paper is structured as follows. Section 2 describes the mathematical objects underlying FHE and recaps the YASHE scheme. Section 3 contains a high level description of known optimization techniques to speed-up computations in modular polynomial rings and describes how we represent polynomials using CRT in order to parallelize computations. We present our hardware architecture for the primitives of YASHE in Sect. 4. We provide implementation results on a Xilinx Virtex-7 FPGA and compare them to existing software results in Sect. 5. We end with conclusions and future work in Sect. 6.

2   System Setup

2.1   Modular Polynomial Rings

The FHE schemes based on RLWE [8] or NTRU [30] compute in modular polynomial rings of the form $R = \mathbb{Z}[x]/(f(x))$ where $f(x)$ is a monic irreducible polynomial of degree n. A very popular choice is to take $f(x) = x^n + 1$ with $n = 2^k$, since this is compatible with a $2n$-degree NTT and reduction modulo $f(x)$ comes for free due to the NTT. However, we put no restriction on $f(x)$, which allows us to deal with any cyclotomic polynomial $\Phi_d(x)$ and thus to utilize single instruction multiple data (SIMD) operations [36,37].

For an integer q, we denote by $R_q = R/qR$, i.e. the polynomial ring where the coefficients are reduced modulo q. The plaintext space in FHE schemes typically will be R_2, and if one wants to utilize SIMD operations the polynomial $f(x)$ should be chosen such that $f(x) \bmod 2$ splits into many different irreducible factors, each factor corresponding to "one slot" in the SIMD representation. It is easy to see that this excludes the most popular choice $x^n + 1$ with $n = 2^k$, since it results in only one irreducible factor modulo 2. In most polynomial ring based FHE schemes, a ciphertext consists of one or two elements in R_q. However, not all operations take place in the ring R_q; sometimes (see below for an illustration with YASHE) one is required to temporarily work in R itself before mapping down into R_q again using (typically) a divide and round operation.

2.2 YASHE

The YASHE scheme was introduced by Bos et al. in [6] in 2013. The scheme works in the ring $R = \mathbb{Z}[x]/(f(x))$, with $f(x) = \Phi_d(x)$ the d-th cyclotomic polynomial. The plaintext space is chosen as R_t for some small t (typically $t = 2$) and a ciphertext consists of only one element in the ring R_q for a large integer q. The main security parameters of the scheme are the degree of $f(x)$ and the size of q. We note that q is not required to be a prime and can be chosen as a product of small primes to speed-up computations (see Sect. 3). To define the YASHE scheme we also require two probability distributions defined on R, namely χ_{key} and χ_{err}. In practice one often takes χ_{err} to be a discrete Gaussian distribution, whereas χ_{key} can be simply sampling each coefficient from a narrow set like $\{-1, 0, 1\}$. Given an element $a \in R_q$ and a base w, we can write a in base w by splicing each of its coefficients, i.e. write $a = \sum_{i=0}^{u} a_i w^i$ with each $a_i \in R$ and coefficients in $(-w/2, w/2]$ and $u = \lfloor \log_w(q) \rfloor$. Decomposing an element $a \in R_q$ into its base w components $(a_i)_{i=0}^{u}$ is denoted by $\mathsf{WordDecomp}_{w,q}(a)$. For an element $a \in R_q$, we define $\mathsf{PowersOf}_{w,q}(a) = (aw^i)_{i=0}^{u}$, the vector that consists of the element a scaled by the different powers of w. Both operations can be used to provide an alternative description of multiplication in R_q, namely:

$$\langle \mathsf{WordDecomp}_{w,q}(a), \mathsf{PowersOf}_{w,q}(b) \rangle = a \cdot b \bmod q.$$

The advantage of the above expression is that the first vector contains small elements, which limits error expansion in the homomorphic multiplication.

An FHE scheme is an augemented encryption scheme that defines two additional operations on ciphertexts, YASHE.Add and YASHE.Mult that result in a ciphertext encrypting the sum (respectively the product) of the underlying plaintexts. The YASHE scheme is then defined as follows (full details can be found in the original paper [6]).

- YASHE.ParamsGen(λ): For security parameter λ, choose a polynomial $\Phi_d(x)$, moduli q and t and distributions χ_{err} and χ_{key} attaining security level λ. Also choose base w and return the system parameters $(\Phi_d(x), q, t, \chi_{err}, \chi_{key}, w)$.
- YASHE.KeyGen($\Phi_d(x), q, t, \chi_{err}, \chi_{key}, w$): Sample $f', g \leftarrow \chi_{key}$ and set $f = (tf' + 1) \in R_q$. If f is not invertible in R_q choose a new f'. Define $h = tgf^{-1} \in R_q$. Sample two vectors $\mathbf{e}, \mathbf{s}$ of $u+1$ elements from χ_{err} and compute $\gamma = \mathsf{PowersOf}_{w,q}(f) + \mathbf{e} + h\mathbf{s} \in R_q^{u+1}$ and output $(pk, sk, evk) = (h, f, \gamma)$.
- YASHE.Encrypt(h, m): To encrypt a message $m \in R_t$ sample $s, e \leftarrow \chi_{err}$ and output the ciphertext $c = \Delta \cdot m + e + sh \in R_q$ with $\Delta = \lfloor q/t \rfloor$.
- YASHE.Decrypt(f, c): Recover m as $m = \lfloor \frac{t}{q} \cdot [f \cdot c]_q \rceil \in R_t$ with $[\cdot]_q$ reduction in the interval $(-q/2, q/2]$.

Input: Polynomial $a(x) \in \mathbb{Z}_q[\mathbf{x}]$ of degree $N-1$ and N-th primitive root $\omega_N \in \mathbb{Z}_q$ of unity
Output: Polynomial $A(x) \in \mathbb{Z}_q[\mathbf{x}] = \text{NTT}(a)$
1 **begin**
2 $\quad A \leftarrow BitReverse(a)$;
3 $\quad$ **for** $m = 2$ *to* N *by* $m = 2m$ **do**
4 $\quad\quad \omega_m \leftarrow \omega_N^{N/m}$;
5 $\quad\quad \omega \leftarrow 1$;
6 $\quad\quad$ **for** $j = 0$ *to* $m/2 - 1$ **do**
7 $\quad\quad\quad$ **for** $k = 0$ *to* $N - 1$ *by* m **do**
8 $\quad\quad\quad\quad t \leftarrow \omega \cdot A[k + j + m/2]$;
9 $\quad\quad\quad\quad u \leftarrow A[k + j]$;
10 $\quad\quad\quad\quad A[k + j] \leftarrow u + t$;
11 $\quad\quad\quad\quad A[k + j + m/2] \leftarrow u - t$;
12 $\quad\quad\quad \omega \leftarrow \omega \cdot \omega_m$;

Algorithm 1. Iterative NTT [13]

- YASHE.Add(c_1, c_2): Return $c_1 + c_2 \in R_q$.
- YASHE.KeySwitch(c, evk): Return $\langle \text{WordDecomp}_{w,q}(c), evk \rangle \in R_q$
- YASHE.Mult(c_1, c_2, evk): Return $c = $ YASHE.KeySwitch(c', evk) with $c' = \lfloor \frac{t}{q} c_1 c_2 \rceil \in R_q$.

YASHE Paramater Set: We use the parameter set Set-III from [29] that supports homomorphic evaluations of SIMON-64/128; in particular $d = 65535$ (and thus the degree of $f(x)$ is $32768 = 2^{15}$), $\log_2(q) = 1228$ and χ_{err} a discrete Gaussian distribution with parameter $\sigma = 8$. The paper [29] claims that this set has security level 128-bits, but this is an underestimate due to a small error in the security derivation. We chose SIMON because it has a smaller multiplicative depth (e.g. AES), and because it offers direct comparability to the existing software implementation [29].

3   High Level Optimizations

To efficiently implement YASHE we have to analyze the two main operations in detail, namely homomorphic addition and homomorphic multiplication. Homomorphic addition is easy to deal with since this simply corresponds to polynomial addition in R_q. Homomorphic multiplication is much more involved and is the main focus of this paper. As can be seen from the definition of YASHE.Mult in Sect. 2.2, to multiply two ciphertexts c_1 and c_2 one first needs to compute $c_1 \cdot c_2$ over the integers, then scale by t/q and round, before mapping back into the ring R_q. The fact that one first has to compute the result over the integers (to allow for the scaling and rounding) has a major influence on how elements of R_q are represented and on how the multiplication has to be computed.

First we will consider polynomial multiplication in R_q where the modulus $f(x)$ is an arbitrary polynomial of degree n. Since each element in R_q therefore can be represented as a polynomial of degree $n - 1$, the resulting product will have degree $2n - 2$. As such we choose the smallest $N = 2^k > 2n - 2$, and compute the product of the two polynomials in the ring $\mathbb{Z}_q[x]/(x^N - 1)$ by using the N-fold NTT (see Algorithm 1). The NTT requires the N-th roots of unity to exist in $\mathbb{Z}_q$, so we either choose q a prime with $q \equiv 1 \bmod N$ or q a product of small primes q_i with each $q_i \equiv 1 \bmod N$. It is the latter choice that will be used throughout this paper.

The product of two elements $a, b \in R_q$ is then computed in two steps: firstly, the product modulo $x^N - 1$ (note that there will be no reduction, since the degree of the product is small enough) is computed using two NTT's, N pointwise multiplications modulo q and then finally, one inverse NTT. To recover the result in R_q, we need a reduction modulo $f(x)$. For general $f(x)$ this reduction does not come for free (unlike the choice $f(x) = x^n + 1$) and for the parameters used in the YASHE scheme the polynomial $f(x)$ is in fact quite dense (although almost all coefficients are ± 1). We have to consider general $f(x)$ because the most obvious choice $f(x) = x^n + 1$ does not allow SIMD operations, since $f(x) \bmod 2$ has only one irreducible factor. The polynomial $\Phi_d(x)$ from the YASHE parameter set splits modulo 2 in 2048 different irreducible polynomials, which implies that we can work on 2048 bits in parallel using the SIMD method first outlined in [36].

To speed-up the reduction modulo $f(x)$ we rely on a polynomial version of Barrett reduction [21], where one precomputes the inverse of $x^n f(1/x)$ modulo x^n. The quotient and remainder can then be recovered at the cost of two polynomial multiplications.

Note that the multiplication of c_1 and c_2 in YASHE.Mult is performed over integers. To get the benefit of NTT based polynomial multiplication, we perform this multiplication in a ring R_Q where Q is a sufficiently large modulus of size $\sim 2 \log q$ such that the coefficients of the result polynomial are in $\mathbb{Z}$.

CRT Representation of Polynomials: In the cryptosystems based on the RLWE problem, computations are performed on the polynomials of a ring R_q. The reported FPGA-based architectures [3,33,35] of such cryptosystems use BRAM slices to store the polynomials and use arithmetic components made up of DSP multipliers and LUTs. The biggest challenge while designing a homomorphic processor is the complexity of computation. During a homomorphic operation, computations are performed on polynomials of degree 2^{15} or 2^{16} and coefficients of size $\sim$1,200 or $\sim$2,500 bits. If we use a bit-parallel coefficient multiplier, then a $2,500 \times 2,500$-bit multiplier will not only result in an enormous area, but will also result in a very low operating frequency. On the other side, a word-serial multiplier is too slow for homomorphic computations.

To tackle the problem of long integer arithmetic, we take inspiration from the application of the CRT in the RSA cryptosystems. We choose the moduli q and Q as products of many small prime moduli q_i, such that $q = \prod_0^{l-1} q_i$ and $Q = \prod_0^{L-1} q_i$, where $l < L$. We map any long integer operation modulo q or Q into small computations moduli q_i, and apply CRT whenever a reverse mapping is required. We use the term *small residue* to represent coefficients modulo q_i and the term *large residue* to represent coefficients modulo q or Q.

Parallel Processing: Beside making the long integer operations easy, such small-residue representation of the coefficients have a tremendous effect on the computation time. Since the computations in the small-residue representations are independent of each other, we can exploit this parallelism and speedup the computations using several parallel cores.

The size of the moduli q_i is an important design decision and depends on the underlying platform. We use the largest Xilinx Virtex-7 FPGA *XC7VX1140T* to implement our homomorphic processor and tune the design decisions accordingly. The FPGA has 3,360 25×18-bit DSP multipliers [1]. One could implement a slightly larger multiplier by combining DSP multipliers with LUTs. For the set of moduli, we choose in total 84 primes (hence $l = 41$ and $L = 84$) of size 30 bits, (the primes from 1008795649 onwards) satisfying $q_i \equiv 1 \mod N$. The reasons for selecting only 30-bit of primes are: 1) there are sufficiently many primes of size 30-bit to compose 1,228-bit q and 2,517-bit Q, 2) the data-paths for performing computations modulo q_i become symmetric, and 3) the basic computation blocks, such as adders and multipliers of size 30-bit can be implemented efficiently using the available DSP slices and a few LUTs.

4   Architecture

We propose an architecture (Fig. 1) to perform the operations in the YASHE scheme. The central part of the architecture is an FPGA based accelerator that works as a coprocessor of a computer and executes the computationally intensive operations. We call this coprocessor the *HE-coprocessor*. The HE-coprocessor

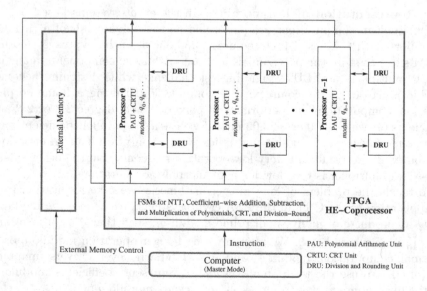

Fig. 1. Overview of the HE architecture

supports the following operations: NTT of a polynomial, coefficient wise addition/subtraction/multiplication of two polynomials, computation of the residues using the CRT, computation of the coefficients modulo Q from the residues, and the scaling of the coefficients. The external memory in this architecture is implemented using high-speed RAMs and is used to store the polynomials during a homomorphic computation. The computer in Fig. 1 works in master-mode and instructs the HE-coprocessor and the controller of the external memory. Since the execution of the homomorphic scheme is controlled by a software program in the computer, a level of flexibility to implement other homomorphic schemes based on a similar set of elementary operations is offered.

The HE-coprocessor comprises of three main components: the polynomial arithmetic unit (PAU), the CRT unit (CRTU), and the division and rounding unit (DRU). We do not implement the discrete Gaussian sampling in the HE-coprocessor as sampling is required only during an encryption, which is a less frequent operation. Since the samples from a narrow discrete Gaussian distribution can be generated very efficiently using lookup tables in software [11], we use the master-computer (Fig. 1) for this purpose.

4.1 Polynomial Arithmetic Unit

To exploit the parallelism provided by the small-residue representation of the polynomials, the PAU has h parallel processors to perform computations on h residue polynomials simultaneously. We call this *horizontal parallelism*. Since the targeted FPGA does not provide sufficient resources to process all the small-residue polynomials in parallel, we design the processors in a generic way such that a processor can be time-shared by a group of $\lceil L/h \rceil$ prime moduli. To add an additional degree of acceleration, we add v parallel cores in each processor. We call this *vertical parallelism*. The cores in a processor are connected to a group of BRAMs through a switching matrix.

Optimization in the Routing: During an NTT computation (Algorithm 1), coefficients are fetched from the memory and then butterfly operations are performed on the coefficients. Let us assume that a residue polynomial of $N = 2^{16}$ coefficients is stored in b BRAMs and then processed using v butterfly cores. If v is a divisor of b, then we can split the NTT computation in equal parts among the v parallel butterfly cores. However there are two main technical issues related to the memory access that would affect the performance of the NTT computation. The first one is: all the parallel cores read and write simultaneously in the memory blocks. Since a simple dual port BRAM has one port for reading and one port for writing, it can support only one read and write in a clock cycle. Hence a memory block can be read (or written) by one butterfly core in a cycle and thus address generation by the parallel butterfly cores should be free from conflicts. The second issue is related to the routing complexity. Since a residue polynomial is stored in many BRAMs, access of data from a BRAM that is very far from a butterfly core will result in a very long routing distance. Now in Algorithm 1 we see that the maximum difference between the indexes of the two coefficients is $N/2$. In the FPGA, fetching data from memory locations at a relative distance of 2^{15} will result in a long routing, and thus could drastically reduce the frequency.

To address these two technical challenges, we have developed a memory access scheme by analysing the address generation during different iterations of the loops in the NTT (Algorithm 1) We segment the set of b BRAMs into b/v groups. The read ports of a group are accessed by only one butterfly core. This *dedicated read* prevents any sort of conflict during the memory read operations. Moreover, in the FPGA the group of BRAMs can be placed close to the corresponding butterfly core and thus the routing complexity can be reduced.

We describe the proposed memory access scheme during an execution of the NTT by parallel cores in Algorithm 2. The module *butterfly-core* performs butterfly operations on two coeffecent pairs following the optimization technique in [35]. In the algorithm the v parallel butterfly cores of a processor are indexed by c where $c \in [0, v-1]$. During the m-th loop of a NTT, the twiddle factor in the c-th core is initialized to a constant value $\omega_{m,c}$. In the hardware, these constants are stored in a ROM. The counter $I_{twiddle}$ denotes the interval between two consecutive calculations of the twiddle factors. Whenever the number of butterfly operations ($N_{butterfly}$) becomes a multiple of $I_{twiddle}$, a new twiddle factor is computed. The c-th butterfly core reads the c−th group of BRAMs $MEMORY_c$ using two addresses $address_1$ and $address_2$. The addresses are computed from the counters: *base*, *increment*, and *offset*, that represent the starting memory address, the increment value, and the difference between $address_1$ and $address_2$ respectively. A butterfly core outputs the two addresses and the four coefficients $s_{1,c}, s_{2,c}, s_{3,c}, s_{4,c}$. These output signals from the parallel butterfly cores are collected by a set of parallel modules *memory-write* that are responsible for writing the groups of BRAMs. The input coefficients that will be read by the adjacent butterfly core in the next iteration of the m-th loop, are selected for the writing operation in $MEMORY_c$ by the c-th memory-write module. The top module *Parallel-NTT* instantiates v butterfly cores and memory write blocks. These instances run in parallel and exchange signals.

Internal Architecture of the PAU: In Fig. 2 we show the internal architecture of the vertical cores that we use inside the horizontal processors in Fig. 1. We follow the pipelined RLWE encryption architecture presented in Fig. 2 of [35] and design our cores to support additional computations required in the YASHE scheme. We design the cores in a more generic way such that a single core can perform computations with respect to several moduli.

The input register bank in Fig. 2 contains registers to store data from the BRAMs and data from the CRTUs. In addition, the register bank also contains shift registers to delay the input coefficients in a pipeline during a NTT computation (see [35] for more details). The register bank has several ports to provide data to several other components present in the core. We use the common name $D_{regbank}$ to represent all data-outputs from the register bank. The small ROM block in Fig. 2 contains the twiddle factors and the value of N^{-1} to support the computation of NTT and INTT. Though the figure shows only one such

```
/* This module computes butterfly operations                                    */
1  module butterfly-core(input c; output m, address₁, address₂, s₁,c, s₂,c, s₃,c, s₄,c)
2  begin
3      (I_twiddle, offset) ← (N/2, 1)
4      for m = 0 to log N − 1 do
5          ω_m ← 2^m-th primitiveroot(1)
6          N_butterfly ← 0          /* Counts the number of butterfly operation in a m-loop */
7          ω ← ω_{m,c}              /* Initialization to a power of ω_m for a core-index c */
8          for base = 0 to base < offset do
9              increment ← 0
10                 while base + offset + increment < N/2v do
11                     (address₁, address₂) ← (base + increment, base + offset + increment)
12                     (t₁, u₁) ← MEMORY_c[address₁]          /* Read from c-th group of RAMs */
13                     (t₂, u₂) ← MEMORY_c[address₂]
14                     if m < log N − 1 then
15                         (t₁, t₂) ← (ω · t₁, ω · t₂)
16                         (s₁,c, s₂,c, s₃,c, s₄,c) ← (u₁ + t₁, u₁ − t₁, u₂ + t₂, u₂ − t₂)
17                         N_butterfly ← N_butterfly + 2
18                         increment = increment + 2 · offset
19                         if N_butterfly ≡ I_twiddle then  ω ← ω · ω_m^{v/2}
20                     else
21                         t₁ ← ω · t₁; ω ← ω · ω_m^{v/2}
22                         t₂ ← ω · t₂; ω ← ω · ω_m^{v/2}
23                         (s₁,c, s₂,c, s₃,c, s₄,c) ← (u₁ + l₁, u₁ − t₁, u₂ + t₂, u₂ − t₂)
24                         N_butterfly ← N_butterfly + 2
25                         increment = increment + 2 · offset
26             I_twiddle ← I_twiddle/2
27             if offset < v/2 then  offset ← 2 · offset

/* This module writes the coefficients computed by two butterfly-cores          */
28  module memory-write(input c, m, address₁, address₂, s₁,₀, ··· s₄,v−1)
29  begin
30      if 2^m < v/2 then gap ← 2^m
31      else gap ← v/2          /* This represents the index gap between the two cores */
32      if c < v/2 then
33          MEMORY_c[address₁] ← (s₂,c, s₁,c)
34          MEMORY_c[address₂] ← (s₂,c+gap, s₁,c+gap)
35      else
36          MEMORY_c[address₁] ← (s₄,c, s₃,c)
37          MEMORY_c[address₂] ← (s₄,c+gap, s₃,c+gap)

/* This is the top module that executes butterfly-core in parallel              */
38  module Parallel-NTT()
39  begin
40      butterfly-core bc₀(0, m, address₁, address₂, s₁,₀, s₂,₀, s₃,₀, s₄,₀)
41      memory-write mw₀(0, m, address₁, address₂, s₁,₀, ··· s₄,v−1)
42      ···
43      butterfly-core bc_{v−1}(v − 1, m, address₁, address₂, s₁,v−1, s₂,v−1, s₃,v−1, s₄,v−1)
44      memory-write mw_{v−1}(v − 1, m, address₁, address₂, s₁,₀, ··· s₄,v−1)
```

Algorithm 2. Routing Efficient Parallel NTT using v cores

ROM block, there are actually $\lceil \frac{L}{h} \rceil$ such ROM blocks, since a core is shared by $\lceil \frac{L}{h} \rceil$ primes. The integer multiplier (shown as a circle in Fig. 2) is a 30×30-bit multiplier. We maintain a balance between area and speed by combining two DSP multipliers and additional LUT based small multipliers to form this multiplier. After an integer multiplication, the result is reduced using the Barrett reduction circuit shown in Fig. 2. We use the Barrett reduction technique due to two reasons. The first reason is that the primes used in this implementation are not of pseudo-Mersenne type which support fast modular reduction technique [26]. The second reason is that the cores are shared by several prime moduli, and hence, a generic reduction circuit is more preferable than several dedicated reduction circuits. The Barrett reduction circuit is bit parallel to process the outputs from the bit-parallel multiplier in a flow. The reduction consists of three 31×31-bit multipliers and additional adders and subtractors. The multipliers are implemented by combining two DSP multipliers with additional LUTs. Thus in total, the Barrett reduction block consumes six DSP multipliers. Beside performing the modular reduction operations, the multipliers present in the Barrett reduction circuit can be reused to perform 30×59-bit multiplications during the CRT computations. The adder/subtracter and the subtracter circuits after the Barrett reduction block in Fig. 2 are used to compute the butterfly operations during a NTT computation and to perform coefficient-wise additions and subtractions of polynomials. Finally, the results of a computation are stored in the output register bank and then the registers are written back in the memory. To achieve high operating frequency, we follow the pipelining technique from [35] and put pipeline registers in the data paths of the computation circuits. In Fig. 2, the pipeline registers are shown as magenta colored lines.

4.2 CRT Unit

We accelerate polynomial arithmetic by representing the polynomials of R_q as smaller residue polynomials moduli q_j, $j \in [0, l-1]$. However, this representation also has the following overhead:

– The multiplication of the input polynomials c_1 and c_2 in YASHE.Mult is performed in the larger ring R_Q (see Sect. 2.2). Since c_1 and c_2 are in R_q, we need to first lift the polynomials from R_q to R_Q. This lifting operation essentially computes the residue polynomials moduli q_j, $j \in [l, L-1]$ from the residue polynomials moduli q_i, $i \in [0, l-1]$ by applying the CRT. We call this operation the *small-CRT*.

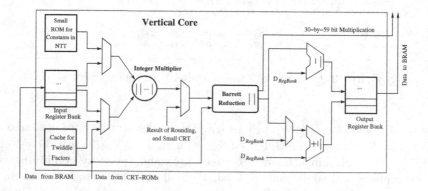

Fig. 2. Architecture for the vertical cores

– After the multiplication of c_1 and c_2, the result is a set of residue polynomials moduli q_j, $j \in [0, L-1]$. The scaling operation in YASHE.Mult requires the coefficients of the result in the form of modulo Q. Hence, we apply the CRT to get back the coefficients modulo Q from the small residue polynomials moduli q_j, $j \in [0, L-1]$. We call this operation the *large-CRT*.

Architecture for the Small-CRT Unit: In the case of CRT, we solve a set of congruences $[a]_{q_i}$ where $i \in [0, l-1]$, and compute a simultaneous solution $[a]_q$, using the following equation:

$$[a]_q = [\sum [a]_{q_i} \cdot (\frac{q}{q_i}) \cdot [(\frac{q}{q_i})^{-1}]_{q_i}]_q \tag{1}$$

When the moduli are fixed, the computation cost is reduced by storing the fixed values $b_i = (\frac{q}{q_i}) \cdot [(\frac{q}{q_i})^{-1}]_{q_i}$ in a table. Still, the computation of $[a]_q$ involves long multiplications as the b_i values are around $\log_2(q)$ bits long. In the case of small-CRT, we actually do not need to compute the solution $[a]_q$, but a solution $[a]_{q_j}$ where q_j is a small 30-bit prime moduli and $j \in [l, L-1]$. We can avoid long multiplications if we compute the solution in the following way:

$$[a]_{q_j} = [\sum [a]_{q_i} \cdot b_i]_{q_j} = [\sum [a]_{q_i} \cdot [b_i]_{q_j}]_{q_j} \tag{2}$$

In the above equation, the constant values $[b_i]_{q_j}$ are 30-bit integers, and hence we need only 30-bit multiplications for all the l residues to accumulate the results. Finally, the result is reduced modulo q_j to get $[a]_{q_j}$. We show our architecture for the small-CRT computations in the left half of Fig. 3. The red boxes represent the vertical cores present in a processor of our HE-coprocessor. During a small-CRT, the modular multiplier and some registers that are present inside a core are reused. The figure shows how the residue polynomials are stored in the BRAM. Here $[a]_{q_i}[k]$ represents the kth coefficient of a residue polynomial $[a]_{q_i}$. The Small-CRT ROM is a BRAM that contains the constants required during a small-CRT computation. The result of a modular multiplication $[[a]_{q_i}[k] \cdot [b_i]_{q_j}]_{q_j}$ is accumulated in a register acc_c, where c represents the core-index. In the end of the accumulation process, the final result is reduced with respect to the modulus q_j using the Barrett reduction circuit present in the modular multiplier.

Architecture for the Large-CRT Unit: In this case, we compute simultaneous solution with respect to the large modulus Q. Hence, this CRT is more costly than the small-CRT. Our large-CRT architecture is shown in the right half of Fig. 3. The constant values b_i are stored in a ROM and then multiplied word-serially with the coefficients from the BRAMs. We set the word size of the ROMs to 59 bits in order to reuse the 31×59-bit multipliers of the Barrett reduction circuits (Fig. 2) for the 30-by-59 bit multiplications. The computation is distributed among the vertical cores of a processor. In our HE-coprocessor, there are 16 vertical cores in a processor. These cores are divided into two groups: Core-0 to Core-7 form the first group, whereas Core-8 to Core-15 form the second group. Each group computes one large-CRT in parallel. Since there are 84

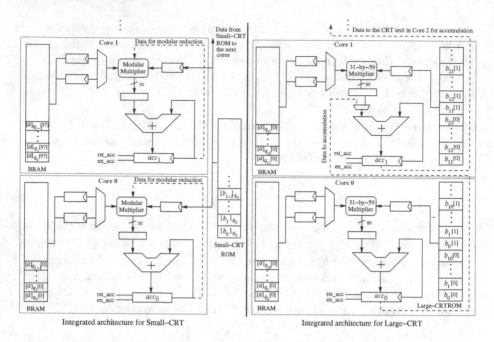

Fig. 3. Architecture for the Small and Large CRT. The computation blocks are aligned along a horizontal processor. Exchange of data between the cores occur during a Large-CRT computation.

b_i constants (Eq. 1), each core in a group computes multiplications with a maximum of 11 b_i constants. The results of the multiplications are accumulated in the accumulation registers. After that, the partially accumulated results are then added together as follows: the register acc_0 is added with acc_1 and the result is stored in acc_1. Then acc_1 is added with acc_2 and finally acc_2 is added with acc_3. In parallel, acc_7 down to acc_4 are added together and the result is stored in acc_4. Finally acc_4 is added with acc_3 and the result is stored in acc_3. This final result is then stored in a small distributed RAM (not shown in the figure) which is read by the DRU. Similar computations are performed in the group consisting of Core-8 to Core-15.

4.3   Division and Rounding Unit

The DRU computes $\lfloor tc/q \rceil$ where $t = 2$, c is a coefficient from the Large-CRTU, and $\lfloor \cdot \rceil$ denotes rounding towards the nearest integer. The division is carried out by precomputing the reciprocal $r = 2/q$ and then computing $r \times c$. The DRU outputs 59-bit words that can be directly reduced modulo the 30-bit q_i using the existing Barrett reduction circuitries in the PAU that operate on inputs of size $< q_i^2$. The word size of the DRU was selected to be 118 bits (2×59) as a compromise between area and latency.

To round a division of two k-bit integers correctly to k-bits, the quotient must be computed correctly to $2k + 1$ bits [27, Theorem 5.2]. In our case, the

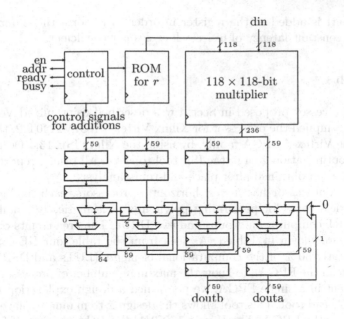

Fig. 4. The Division and Rounding Unit (DRU)

computation of $\lfloor tc/q \rceil$ requires a division of a k_1-bit dividend by a k_2-bit divisor. The precision that we will need in this case to guarantee correct rounding, based on the above, is $k_1 + k_2 + 1$ bits. The divisor q is a 1228-bit constant integer and the dividend c is an at most 2492-bit integer[1], which gives a bound of 3721 bits. Hence, the reciprocal r is computed up to a precision of 32 118-bit words, of which 22 words are nonzero.

Figure 4 shows the architecture of the DRU. The multiplication $r \times c$ is computed by using a 118×118-bit multiplier that computes $22^2 = 484$ partial multiplications. This multiplier performs a 118-bit Karatsuba multiplication by using three 59×59-bit multipliers generated with the Xilinx IP Core tool (which supports only up to 64-bit multipliers). The 59-bit multipliers each require 16 DSP blocks giving the total number of 48 DSP blocks. In order to achieve a high clock frequency, the 118-bit multiplier utilizes a 23-stage pipeline, of which 18 stages are in the 59-bit multipliers (the optimal number according to the tool).

The partial products from the 118-bit multiplier are accumulated into a 241-bit ($2 \times 118 + 5$) register using the Comba algorithm [12]. These additions are computed in a 4-stage pipeline with three 59-bit adders and one 64-bit adder, which are all implemented with LUTs. Whenever all partial products of an output word have been computed, the register is shifted to the right by 118 bits and the overflowing bits are given at the output of the DRU. Once the computation proceeds to the first word after the fractional point, then the msb of the

---

[1] The dividend c is a sum of 2^{16} integers, each in $[0, (q-1)^2]$ (2455-bit integers). Further growth by 14 bits is introduced by the polynomial modular reduction and 7 bits by the large-CRT computation.

fractional part is added to the register in order to perform the rounding. The DRU has a constant latency of 687 clock cycles per coefficient.

5 Results

The HE-coprocessor proposed in Sect. 4 was described using mixed Verilog and VHDL. We compiled the processor for Xilinx Virtex-7 XC7V1140T-2, the largest device of the Virtex-7 FPGA family, by using the Xilinx ISE 13.4 Design Suite. We set the optimization goal in the ISE tool to *speed*. All results reported in the section have been obtained after place-and-route analysis.

The HE-coprocessor has $h = 8$ horizontal processors, each having $v = 16$ parallel vertical cores for performing polynomial arithmetic, 16 small-CRTUs, two large-CRT computation groups and two DRUs. The area counts of our HE-coprocessor are shown in Table 1. As seen from the table, our HE-coprocessor consumes nearly 50 % of the computational elements (LUTs and DSP multipliers) available in the FPGA. To know the maximum number of processors that we can implement in a single FPGA, we performed a design exploration using the Xilinx PlanAhead tool. This tool allows the designer to manually place different components in the FPGA. The Virtex-7 XCV1140 FPGA consists of four super large logic regions (SLRs). From the design exploration we have found that we can put two processors in one SLR. If we put three processors in one SLR (occupies around 70 % of the SLR-area), then the Xilinx tool reports congestion of routing channels and the place-and-route analysis fails. From this design exploration we conclude that we can implement two processors per SLR, and hence eight processors in one Virtex-7 XCV1140 FPGA.

Table 2 gives the latencies of different operations supported by our HE-coprocessor. The operating frequency of our HE-coprocessor is 143 MHz after place-and-route analysis. NTT and INTT computations are performed on polynomials of $N = 2^{16}$ coefficients. To save memory requirement, we compute the twiddle factors on the fly at the cost of N integer multiplications. One NTT computation using $v = 16$ cores requires $(N + \frac{N}{2} \log_2(N))/16$, i.e. 36,864 multiplications. However the computation of the twiddle factors in the pipelined data path of the PAU (Fig. 2) has data dependencies and thus causes bubbles in the pipeline. Following [35], we use a small register-file that stores four consecutive twiddle factors, and reduce the cycles spent in the pipeline bubbles to around 10,000. In the case of an INTT computation, the additional cycles are spent

Table 1. The area results on Xilinx Virtex-7 XCV1140TFLG1930-2 FPGA

Resource	Used	Avail.	Percentage
Slice registers	339,086	1,424,000	23 %
Slice LUTs	360,353	712,000	50 %
BlockRAM	640 BRAM36, 152 BRAM18	1,880	38 %
DSP48	1,792	3,360	53 %

Table 2. Latencies and timings at 143 MHz after place-and-route

Operation	Clocks	Time	Rel. time[†]
NTT	47,795	0.334 ms	0.163 μs
INTT	51,909	0.363 ms	0.177 μs
Poly-add/sub/mult	4,096	0.029 ms	0.014 μs
Small-CRT	118,784	0.831 ms	0.405 μs
Large-CRT	2,752,512	19.248 ms	9.398 μs
Divide-and-round	2,813,952	19.678 ms	9.559 μs
YASHE.Add*	24,576	0.172 ms	0.083 μs
YASHE.Mult*	16,019,635	112.025 ms	54.699 μs
SIMON-32/64*	8,202,053,120	57.357 s	28.006 ms
SIMON-64/128*	22,555,646,080	157.731 s	77.017 ms

[†] Time per slot in SIMD operations (in total 2048 slots)
* Excluding interfacing with the computer and the external memory

during scaling operation by N^{-1}. Cycle count per coefficient for the small-CRT is 58. It is computed for $2^{15} = 32,768$ coefficient using 16 vertical cores and accumulators and, hence, the total cost is 118,784 cycles. Similarly, the costs of large-CRT and the division-and-rounding are 672 and 687 cycles per coefficient respectively. However, the cycles spent for the large-CRT operations are not a part of the actual cost, as the large-CRT operation runs in parallel with the division-and-rounding operations during a homomorphic multiplication. The division-and-rounding operations are computed 2^{16} times using 16 DRUs (two from each horizontal processor) at the cost of 2,813,952 cycles.

Table 2 includes estimates for the latencies of YASHE.Add and YASHE.Mult as well as the evaluations of SIMON-32/64 and SIMON-64/128. The YASHE.Mult computes small-CRT, polynomial multiplication, scaling and YASHE.KeySwitch operations. The cycle count for YASHE.Mult is derived as follows. First the input polynomials c_1 and c_2 are lifted from R_q to R_Q using two small-CRTs; then a polynomial multiplication (including Barrett polynomial reduction) is performed using 4 NTTs, 3 INTTs, 3 Poly-mul and 1 Poly-sub. Since there are 84 moduli, we compute these operations in 11 batches using $h = 8$ processors. After the polynomial multiplication, a scaling operation by t/q is performed to compute c'. The YASHE.KeySwitch operation, which is $\langle \mathsf{WordDecomp}_{w,q}(c'), evk \rangle$, uses NTT of the fixed evk (22 polynomials) and decomposes c' into 22 polynomials. First 22 NTTs and then 22 coefficient-wise multiplications, followed by 21 coefficient-wise additions are performed. Finally one INTT is computed and the result is reduced using Barrett reduction (2 NTTs, 2 INTTs, 2 coefficient-wise multiplications, and 1 coefficient-wise subtraction). All these computations are performed in six batches. Estimates for SIMON consider only YASHE.Mult, which dominate the costs of function evaluations. SIMON-32/64 and SIMON-64/128 require 512 (32 rounds with 16 ANDs) and 1,408 (44 rounds with 32 ANDs) YASHE.Mult, respectively. In addition to the latencies and timings for a single execution of the operations, we also provide the relative timings which represent the timings per slot (in total 2048 slots).

Lepoint and Naehrig [29] presented C++ implementations for homomorphic evaluations of SIMON-32/64 and SIMON 64/128 with YASHE running on a 4-core Intel Core i7-2600 at 3.4 GHz. They reported computation times of 1029 s (17.2 min) and 4193 s (69.9 min) for SIMON-32/64 and SIMON-64/128 using all 4 cores, respectively. The implementations included 1800 and 2048 slots and, hence, the relative times per slot were 0.57 s and 2.04 s, respectively. With one core, they achieved 16500 s (275 min) for SIMON-64/128. The homomorphic evaluation of SIMON-64/128 on our FPGA implementation takes 157.7 s (2.6 min) and it also allows 2048 slots giving a relative time of only 77 ms per slot. Hence, our single FPGA implementation offers a speedup of up to 26.6 (or 104.6) times compared to the 4-core (or 1-core) software implementation.

6   Conclusions and Future Work

We showed that modern high-end FPGAs (such as Virtex-7) have sufficient logic, hardwired multipliers, and internal memory resources for efficient computation of primitives required for evaluating functions on FHE encrypted data. Despite this, memory requirements and the speed of memory access is critical. Only ciphertexts that are currently being processed fit into the internal memory of the FPGA and other ciphertexts must be stored in external memory. Interface with the external memory may become a bottleneck unless it is done with special care. Sufficiently fast memory access can be achieved by using high bandwidth memory and/or parallel memory chips. Many FPGAs include dedicated transceivers for fast interfacing that could be used for fast data access in FHE computations. Moreover, most of the memory access can be performed in parallel with computation using a ping-pong scheme of two sets of BRAMs in the FPGA. The FPGA and the master-computer operate on these two sets alternatively between two consecutive instructions: when the FPGA operates on the first set, the master-computer operates on the second, and vice versa.

We presented a single-FPGA design of homomorphic evaluation with YASHE. An obvious way to improve the performance would be to use a multi-FPGA design (a cluster). We see four parallelization approaches. The first and simplest option is to instantiate parallel FPGAs so that each of them computes different homomorphic evaluations independently of each other. This approach improves throughput, but the latency of an individual evaluation remains the same. The second approach is to divide independent homomorphic operations inside a single homomorphic evaluation to parallel FPGAs. Thanks to the numerous independent computations included, e.g., in homomorphic evaluations of block ciphers, this approach is likely to improve both throughput and latency. While this is conceptually a simple approach, it may still face difficulties because data needs to be transferred between multiple FPGAs. The third option is to divide different parts of a homomorphic multiplication to different FPGAs and perform them in a pipelined fashion in order to increase throughput. The fourth option is to mix the other three options and it may lead to good tradeoffs that avoid the disadvantages of the other options. The techniques represented in this paper can be extrapolated to support these options.

The SIMD approach achieves high throughput, but it has been argued that low latency can be more important in practice [29]. The leading software implementation [29] requires as much as 200 s for a single slot evaluation of SIMON-32/64 with YASHE. Our FPGA-based implementation achieves smaller latencies even for SIMON-64/128 with an implementation that allows 2048 slots. Reducing the number of slots to one would allow more efficient parameters (see Sect. 2). We plan to investigate such schemes in the future.

We evaluated the performance of our architecture for YASHE by providing performance values for SIMON in order to provide straightforward comparisons to the leading software implementation from [29]. However, SIMON is not necessarily an optimal cipher for FHE purposes. For instance, the low-latency Prince cipher [5] may lead to better performance [19]. FHE-friendly symmetric encryption that is designed to minimize the multiplicative size and depth can offer significant improvements over SIMON (and Prince) [2,9]. Our architecture is able to evaluate arbitrary functions (up to a certain multiplicative depth) and, hence, these options will be studied in the future. Performance can be further increased by tuning the parameters of the architecture for these specific functions. Such changes can be easily done because our architecture is highly flexible.

We presented the first FPGA implementation for function evaluation on homomorphically encrypted data. Although it already achieves competitive performance compared to leading software implementations, we see several ways to optimize the architecture and these issues will be explored further in the future. For instance, we can increase throughput of NTT by precomputing certain values. We used Barrett reduction for the primes but choosing 'nice' primes and optimizing reduction circuitries by hand could offer speedups. However, in that case the performance would be bounded by the worst prime and finding suitably many 'nice' primes may be challenging. The architecture uses simple data-flow and pipelining in order to keep high clock frequency, but it results in pipeline bubbles that increase the latencies of operations. A more elaborated data-flow could allow removing the pipeline bubbles and reducing the latencies. More research is required also in balancing the pipelines so that even higher clock frequencies can be achieved for the architecture. The architecture utilizes parallelism on various levels and degrees of parallelism in different parts of the architecture should be fine-tuned to achieve optimal resource utilization and performance. Our source code is highly flexible and significant parts of it were generated with scripts. This allows us to perform parameter space explorations that will enable us to find more optimal parameters for the architecture.

Acknowlegments. S. Sinha Roy was supported by Erasmus Mundus PhD Scholarship, K. Järvinen was funded by FWO Pegasus Marie Curie Fellowship and V. Dimitrov was supported by NSERC. This work was supported by the Research Council KU Leuven: TENSE (GOA/11/007), by iMinds, by the Flemish Government,

FWO G.0550.12N, G.00130.13N and FWO G.0876.14N, by the Hercules Foundation AKUL/11/19, by the European Commission through the ICT programme under contract FP7-ICT-2013-10-SEP-210076296 PRACTICE, and by H2020-ICT-644209 HEAT. We thank Nele Mentens, Jochen Vandorpe, and Jo Vliegen for their help with the Xilinx PlanAhead tool.

References

1. Xilinx 7 Series FPGAs Overview, DS180 (v1.16.1), 17 December 2014. http://www. xilinx.com/support/documentation/data_sheets/ds180_7Series_Overview.pdf
2. Albrecht, M.R., Rechberger, C., Schneider, T., Tiessen, T., Zohner, M.: Ciphers for MPC and FHE. In: Oswald, E., Fischlin, M. (eds.) EUROCRYPT 2015. LNCS, vol. 9056, pp. 430–454. Springer, Heidelberg (2015)
3. Aysu, A., Patterson, C., Schaumont, P.: Low-cost and area-efficient FPGA Implementations of lattice-based cryptography. In: HOST, pp. 81–86. IEEE (2013)
4. Beaulieu, R., Shors, D., Smith, J., Treatman-Clark, S., Weeks, B., Wingers, L.: The SIMON and SPECK families of lightweight block ciphers. Cryptology ePrint Archive, Report 2013/404 (2013). http://eprint.iacr.org/
5. Borghoff, J., Canteaut, A., Güneysu, T., Kavun, E.B., Knezevic, M., Knudsen, L.R., Leander, G., Nikov, V., Paar, C., Rechberger, C., Rombouts, P., Thomsen, S.S., Yalçın, T.: PRINCE – a low-latency block cipher for pervasive computing applications. In: Wang, X., Sako, K. (eds.) ASIACRYPT 2012. LNCS, vol. 7658, pp. 208–225. Springer, Heidelberg (2012)
6. Bos, J.W., Lauter, K., Loftus, J., Naehrig, M.: Improved security for a ring-based fully homomorphic encryption scheme. In: Stam, M. (ed.) IMACC 2013. LNCS, vol. 8308, pp. 45–64. Springer, Heidelberg (2013)
7. Brakerski, Z.: Fully homomorphic encryption without modulus switching from classical GapSVP. In: Safavi-Naini, R., Canetti, R. (eds.) CRYPTO 2012. LNCS, vol. 7417, pp. 868–886. Springer, Heidelberg (2012)
8. Brakerski, Z., Vaikuntanathan, V.: Fully homomorphic encryption from ring-LWE and security for key dependent messages. In: Rogaway, P. (ed.) CRYPTO 2011. LNCS, vol. 6841, pp. 505–524. Springer, Heidelberg (2011)
9. Canteaut, A., Carpov, S., Fontaine, C., Lepoint, T., Naya-Plasencia, M., Paillier, P., Sirdey, R.: How to compress homomorphic ciphertexts. Cryptology ePrint Archive, Report 2015/113 (2015). http://eprint.iacr.org/
10. Cao, X., Moore, C., O'Neill, M., Hanley, N., O'Sullivan, E.: High-speed fully homomorphic encryption over the integers. In: Böhme, R., Brenner, M., Moore, T., Smith, M. (eds.) FC 2014 Workshops. LNCS, vol. 8438, pp. 169–180. Springer, Heidelberg (2014)
11. de Clercq, R., Sinha Roy, S., Vercauteren, F., Verbauwhede, I.: Efficient software implementation of ring-LWE encryption. Cryptology ePrint Archive, Report 2014/725 (2014). http://eprint.iacr.org/
12. Comba, P.G.: Exponentiation cryptosystems on the IBM PC. IBM Syst. J. **29**(4), 526–538 (1990)
13. Cormen, T., Leiserson, C., Rivest, R.: Introduction to Algorithms. http://staff. ustc.edu.cn/csli/graduate/algorithms/book6/toc.htm
14. Coron, J.-S., Lepoint, T., Tibouchi, M.: Scale-invariant fully homomorphic encryption over the integers. In: Krawczyk, H. (ed.) PKC 2014. LNCS, vol. 8383, pp. 311–328. Springer, Heidelberg (2014)

15. Cousins, D.B., Rohloff, K., Peikert, C., Schantz, R.: SIPHER: scalable implementation of primitives for homomorphic encryption – FPGA implementation using Simulink. In: Proceedings of the 15th Annual Workshop on High Performance Embedded Computing (HPEC 2011) (2011)
16. Cousins, D.B., Rohloff, K., Peikert, C., Schantz, R.: An update on SIPHER (scalable implementation of primitives for homomorphic encryption) – FPGA implementation using Simulink. In: Proceedings of the 2012 IEEE High Performance Extreme Computing Conference (HPEC 2012), pp. 1–5 (2012)
17. van Dijk, M., Gentry, C., Halevi, S., Vaikuntanathan, V.: Fully homomorphic encryption over the integers. In: Gilbert, H. (ed.) EUROCRYPT 2010. LNCS, vol. 6110, pp. 24–43. Springer, Heidelberg (2010)
18. Doröz, Y., Öztürk, E., Sunar, B.: Evaluating the hardware performance of a million-bit multiplier. In: Proceedings of the 16th Euromicro Conference on Digital System Design (DSD 2013), pp. 955–962 (2013)
19. Doröz, Y., Shahverdi, A., Eisenbarth, T., Sunar, B.: Toward practical homomorphic evaluation of block ciphers using prince. In: Böhme, R., Brenner, M., Moore, T., Smith, M. (eds.) FC 2014 Workshops. LNCS, vol. 8438, pp. 208–220. Springer, Heidelberg (2014)
20. Fan, J., Vercauteren, F.: Somewhat practical fully homomorphic encryption. Cryptology ePrint Archive, Report 2012/144 (2012). http://eprint.iacr.org/
21. von zur Gathen, J., Gerhard, J.: Modern Computer Algebra. Cambridge University Press, New York (1999)
22. Gentry, C.: Fully homomorphic encryption using ideal lattices. In: Proceedings of the 41st ACM Symposium on Theory of Computing (STOC 2009), pp. 169–178 (2009)
23. Gentry, C., Halevi, S.: Implementing Gentry's fully-homomorphic encryption scheme. In: Paterson, K.G. (ed.) EUROCRYPT 2011. LNCS, vol. 6632, pp. 129–148. Springer, Heidelberg (2011)
24. Gentry, C., Halevi, S., Smart, N.P.: Homomorphic evaluation of the AES circuit. In: Safavi-Naini, R., Canetti, R. (eds.) CRYPTO 2012. LNCS, vol. 7417, pp. 850–867. Springer, Heidelberg (2012)
25. Gentry, C., Sahai, A., Waters, B.: Homomorphic encryption from learning with errors: conceptually-simpler, asymptotically-faster, attribute-based. In: Canetti, R., Garay, J.A. (eds.) CRYPTO 2013, Part I. LNCS, vol. 8042, pp. 75–92. Springer, Heidelberg (2013)
26. Hankerson, D., Menezes, A.J., Vanstone, S.: Guide to Elliptic Curve Cryptography. Springer-Verlag New York Inc., Secaucus (2003)
27. Karp, A.H., Markstein, P.: High-precision division and square root. ACM Trans. Math. Softw. 23(4), 561–589 (1997)
28. Koç, C.K. (ed.): Cryptographic Engineering 1st. Springer Publishing Company (2008)
29. Lepoint, T., Naehrig, M.: A comparison of the homomorphic encryption schemes FV and YASHE. In: Pointcheval, D., Vergnaud, D. (eds.) AFRICACRYPT. LNCS, vol. 8469, pp. 318–335. Springer, Heidelberg (2014)
30. López-Alt, A., Tromer, E., Vaikuntanathan, V.: On-the-fly multiparty computation on the cloud via multikey fully homomorphic encryption. In: Proceedings of the Forty-fourth Annual ACM Symposium on Theory of Computing, pp. 1219–1234. ACM, New York, NY, USA (2012)

31. Moore, C., Hanley, N., McAllister, J., O'Neill, M., O'Sullivan, E., Cao, X.: Targeting FPGA DSP slices for a large integer multiplier for integer based FHE. In: Adams, A.A., Brenner, M., Smith, M. (eds.) FC 2013. LNCS, vol. 7862, pp. 226–237. Springer, Heidelberg (2013)
32. Naehrig, M., Lauter, K., Vaikuntanathan, V.: Can homomorphic encryption be practical? In: Proceedings of the 3rd ACM Workshop on Cloud Computing Security Workshop (CCSW 2011), pp. 113–124. ACM (2011)
33. Pöppelmann, T., Güneysu, T.: Towards practical lattice-based public-key encryption on reconfigurable hardware. In: Lange, T., Lauter, K., Lisoněk, P. (eds.) SAC 2013. LNCS, vol. 8282, pp. 68–86. Springer, Heidelberg (2014)
34. Rivest, R.L., Adleman, L., Dertouzos, M.L.: On data banks and privacy homomorphisms. Found. Secure Comput. 4(11), 169–180 (1978)
35. Sinha Roy, S., Vercauteren, F., Mentens, N., Chen, D.D., Verbauwhede, I.: Compact ring-LWE cryptoprocessor. In: Batina, L., Robshaw, M. (eds.) CHES 2014. LNCS, vol. 8731, pp. 371–391. Springer, Heidelberg (2014)
36. Smart, N.P., Vercauteren, F.: Fully homomorphic encryption with relatively small key and ciphertext sizes. In: Nguyen, P.Q., Pointcheval, D. (eds.) PKC 2010. LNCS, vol. 6056, pp. 420–443. Springer, Heidelberg (2010)
37. Smart, N., Vercauteren, F.: Fully homomorphic SIMD operations. Des. Codes Cryptogr. 71(1), 57–81 (2014)
38. Wang, W., Hu, Y., Chen, L., Huang, X., Sunar, B.: Accelerating fully homomorphic encryption using GPU. In: IEEE Conference on High Performance Extreme Computing (HPEC 2012), pp. 1–5 (2012)
39. Wang, W., Huang, X.: FPGA implementation of a large-number multiplier for fully homomorphic encryption. In: IEEE International Symposium on Circuits and Systems (ISCAS 2013), pp. 2589–2592 (2013)
40. Wang, W., Huang, X.: VLSI design of a large-number multiplier for fully homomorphic encryption. IEEE Trans. Very Large Scale Integr. (VLSI) Syst. 22(9), 1879–1887 (2014)

Accelerating LTV Based Homomorphic Encryption in Reconfigurable Hardware

Yarkın Doröz[1]([⊠]), Erdinç Öztürk[2], Erkay Savaş[3], and Berk Sunar[1]

[1] Worcester Polytechnic Institute, Worcester, USA
{ydoroz,sunar}@wpi.edu
[2] Istanbul Commerce University, Istanbul, Turkey
eozturk@ticaret.edu.tr
[3] Sabanci University, Istanbul, Turkey
erkays@sabanciuniv.edu

Abstract. After being introduced in 2009, the first fully homomorphic encryption (FHE) scheme has created significant excitement in academia and industry. Despite rapid advances in the last 6 years, FHE schemes are still not ready for deployment due to an efficiency bottleneck. Here we introduce a custom hardware accelerator optimized for a class of reconfigurable logic to bring LTV based somewhat homomorphic encryption (SWHE) schemes one step closer to deployment in real-life applications. The accelerator we present is connected via a fast PCIe interface to a CPU platform to provide homomorphic evaluation services to any application that needs to support blinded computations. Specifically we introduce a number theoretical transform based multiplier architecture capable of efficiently handling very large polynomials. When synthesized for the Xilinx Virtex 7 family the presented architecture can compute the product of large polynomials in under 6.25 msec making it the fastest multiplier design of its kind currently available in the literature and is more than 102 times faster than a software implementation. Using this multiplier we can compute a relinearization operation in 526 msec. When used as an accelerator, for instance, to evaluate the AES block cipher, we estimate a per block homomorphic evaluation performance of 442 msec yielding performance gains of 28.5 and 17 times over similar CPU and GPU implementations, respectively.

Keywords: Somewhat homomorphic encryption · NTT multiplication · FPGA

1 Introduction

Fully homomorphic encryption (FHE) is a promising new technology that enables efficient blinded computations on semi-trusted servers. The introduction of the first plausible FHE construction by Gentry in 2009 [19, 20], fueled the race to develop more efficient schemes. More specifically, lattice-based [21, 22, 32], integer-based [10, 11, 15] and learning-with-errors (LWE) or (ring) learning with

© International Association for Cryptologic Research 2015
T. Güneysu and H. Handschuh (Eds.): CHES 2015, LNCS 9293, pp. 185–204, 2015.
DOI: 10.1007/978-3-662-48324-4_10

errors ((R)LWE) based encryption [6,23,24] schemes were introduced in just a few years. Despite the rapid progression of new FHE optimization techniques such as ones developed to render expensive bootstrapping evaluations obsolete [5] and ones for more effective parallel processing through *batching* of multiple data bits into a ciphertext [4,9,33], FHE is still far from being ready for use in real-life applications. For instance, an implementation by Gentry et al. [25] homomorphically evaluates the AES circuit in about 36 hours resulting in an amortized per block evaluation time of 5 minutes. Another NTRU based proposal by Doröz et al. [16] manages to evaluate AES roughly an order of magnitude faster than [25]. Still it does not come close to what is acceptable in practice. The main difficulty in developing efficient FHE schemes is to overcome the massive parameter sizes necessary to retain security while allowing evaluation of deep circuits.

Clearly the gap between what is currently achievable on a CPU and what is practical is too far to consider software only solutions. This led researchers to investigate the use of alternative platforms such as graphic processing units (GPUs), reconfigurable logic such as FPGAs, and even further domain specific ASIC designs to accelerate homomorphic evaluations. Using Nvidia GPUs, for instance, Wang et al. [35] managed to accelerate the earlier implementation of the recryption primitive of Gentry and Halevi [23] by roughly an order of magnitude. The GPU library is capable to evaluate AES under 8 seconds. On the hardware side, Cousins et al. report the first reconfigurable logic implementations in [12,13], in which Matlab Simulink was used to design the FHE primitives. This was followed by further investigation in this direction [7,29,36,37]. Specifically, in [36], Wang et al. present an optimized version of their result [37], which achieves speed–up factors of 174, 7.6 and 13.5 for encryption, decryption and the recryption operations on an NVIDIA GTX 690, respectively, when compared to results of the implementation of Gentry and Halevi's FHE scheme [22] that runs on an Intel Core i7 3770 K machine. Cao et al. [7] proposed a number theoretical transform (NTT)-based large integer multiplier combined with Barrett reduction to alleviate the multiplication and modular reduction bottlenecks required in many FHE schemes. The encryption step in the proposed integer based FHE schemes by Coron et al. [10,11] were designed and implemented on a Xilinx Virtex-7 FPGA. The synthesis results show speed up factors of over 40 over existing software implementations of this encryption step [7]. A more recent work by Dai et al. [14] reports GPU acceleration for NTRU based FHE evaluating Prince and AES block ciphers, with 2.57 times and 7.6 times speedup values, respectively, over an Intel Xeon software implementation. Finally, in [17] and later in [18] Doröz et al. present an architecture for ASIC that implements a full set of FHE primitives including bootstrapping.

In Table 1, we present an overview of previous FHE implementations on various platforms. Clearly, since the platforms vary greatly according to available memory, clock speed, area/price of the hardware a side-by-side comparison is not possible and therefore this information is only meant to give an idea of what is achievable on various platforms. As evident from Table 1, significant gains are possible by developing custom tailored designs for FPGA and ASIC platforms.

Table 1. Overview of specialized FHE Implementations. GH-FHE: Gentry & Halevi's FHE scheme; CMNT-FHE: Coron et al.'s FHE schemes [10,11,22]; NTRU based FHE, e.g. [27,34]

DESIGN	SCHEME	PLATFORM	PERFORMANCE
CPU			
AES [25]	BGV-FHE	2.0 GHz Intel Xeon	5 min / AES block
AES [16]	NTRU-FHE	2.9 GHz Intel Xeon	55 sec / AES block
Full FHE [31]	NTRU-FHE	2.1 GHz Intel Xeon	275 sec / per bootst.
GPU			
NTT mul / reduction [35]	GH-FHE	NVIDIA C250 GPU	0.765 ms
NTT mul [35]	GH-FHE	NVIDIA GTX 690	0.583 ms
AES [14]	NTRU-FHE	NVIDIA GTX 690	7 sec / AES block
FPGA			
NTT transform [37]	GH-FHE	Stratix V FPGA	0.125 ms
NTT modmul / enc. [7]	CMNT-FHE	Xilinx Virtex7 FPGA	13 msec / enc.
ASIC			
NTT modmul [17]	GH-FHE	90 nm TSMC	2.09 sec
Full FHE [18]	GH-FHE	90 nm TSMC	3.1 sec / recrypt

Much of the development so far has focused on the Gentry-Halevi FHE [22], which intrinsically works with very large integers (million bit range). Therefore, a good number of works focused on developing FFT/NTT based large integer multipliers [17,18,35,35]. Currently, the only full-fledged (with bootstrapping) FHE hardware implementation is the one reported by Doröz et al. [18], which also implements the Gentry-Halevi FHE. At this time, there is a lack of hardware implementations of the more recently proposed FHE schemes, i.e. Coron et al.'s FHE schemes [10,11], BGV-style FHE schemes [5], [22] and NTRU based FHE, e.g. [27,34]. We, therefore, focus on providing hardware acceleration support for one particular family of FHE's: NTRU-based FHE schemes, where arithmetic with very large polynomials (both in degree and coefficient size) is crucial for performance.

Our Contribution. In this work, we present an FPGA architecture to accelerate NTRU based FHE schemes. Our architecture may be considered as a proof-of-concept implementation of an external FHE accelerator that will speed up homomorphic evaluations taking place on a CPU. Specifically, the architecture we present manages to evaluate a full large degree, e.g. 2^{15}, polynomial multiplication efficiently by utilizing a number theoretical transform (NTT) based approach. Using this FPGA core we can evaluate polynomial multiplication 28 times faster than on a similar CPU and 17 times faster than a similar GPU implementations. Furthermore, by facilitating efficient exchange using a PCI Express connection, we evaluate the overhead incurred in a sustained homomorphic computations of deep circuits. For instance, also taking into account the cycles lost in data transfer our hardware can evaluate a full 10 round AES circuit in under 440 msec per block.

2 Background

In this section we briefly outline the primitives of the LTV-based fully homomorphic encryption scheme, and later discuss the arithmetic operations that will be necessary in its hardware realization.

2.1 LTV-Based Fully Homomorphic Encryption

While the arithmetic and homomorphic properties of NTRU have been long known by the research community, a full-fledged fully homomorphic version was proposed only very recently in 2012 by López-Alt, Tromer and Vaikuntanathan (LTV) [27]. The LTV scheme is based on a variant of NTRU introduced earlier by Stehlé and Steinfeld [34]. The LTV scheme uses a new operation called relinearization as well as existing techniques such as modulus switching for noise control. While the LTV scheme can support homomorphic evaluation in a multi-key setting where each participant is issued their own keys, here we focus only on the single user case for brevity.

The primitives of the LTV scheme operate on polynomials in $R_q = \mathbb{Z}_q[x]/\langle x^N + 1 \rangle$, i.e. with degree N, where the coefficients are processed using a prime modulus q. In the scheme an error distribution function χ – a truncated discrete Gaussian distribution – is used to sample random, small B-bounded polynomials. The scheme consists of four primitive functions:

KeyGen. We select decreasing sequence of primes $q_0 > q_1 > \cdots > q_d$ for each level. We sample $g^{(i)}$ and $u^{(i)}$ from χ, compute secret keys $f^{(i)} = 2u^{(i)} + 1$ and public keys $h^{(i)} = 2g^{(i)}(f^{(i)})^{-1}$ for each level. Later we create evaluation keys for each level: $\zeta_\tau^{(i)}(x) = h^{(i)} s_\tau^{(i)} + 2e_\tau^{(i)} + 2^\tau (f^{(i-1)})^2$, where $\{s_\tau^{(i)}, e_\tau^{(i)}\} \in \chi$ and $\tau = [0, \lfloor \log q_i \rfloor]$.

Encrypt. To encrypt a bit b for the ith level we compute: $c^{(i)} = h^{(i)} s + 2e + b$ where $\{s, e\} \in \chi$.

Decrypt. In order to compute the decryption of a value for specific level i we compute: $m = c^{(i)} f^{(i)} \pmod 2$.

Evaluate. The multiplication and addition of ciphertexts correspond to XOR and AND operations, respectively. The multiplication operation creates a significant noise, which is handled with using relinearization and modulus switching. The relinearization computes $\tilde{c}^{(i)}(x) = \sum_\tau \zeta_\tau^{(i)}(x) \tilde{c}_\tau^{(i-1)}(x)$, where $\tilde{c}_\tau^{(i-1)}(x)$ are 1-bounded polynomials that are equal to $\tilde{c}^{(i-1)}(x) = \sum_\tau 2^\tau \tilde{c}_\tau^{(i-1)}(x)$. In case of modulus switching, we do the computation $\tilde{c}^{(i)}(x) = \lfloor \frac{q_i}{q_{i-1}} \tilde{c}^{(i)}(x) \rceil_2$ to cut the noise level by $\log (q_i / q_{i-1})$ bits. The operation $\lfloor \cdot \rceil_2$ is matching the parity bits.

2.2   Arithmetic Operations

To implement the costly large polynomial multiplication and relinearization operations we follow the strategy of Dai et al. [14]. For instance, in the case of polynomial multiplication we first convert the input polynomials using the Chinese Remainder Theorem (CRT) into a series of polynomials of the same degree, but with much smaller word-sized coefficients. Then, pairwise product of these polynomials is computed efficiently using Number Theoretical Transform (NTT)-based multiplier as explained in subsequent sections. Finally, the resulting polynomial is recovered from the partial products by the application of the inverse CRT (ICRT) operation. For relinearization we follow a similar route; however, we do not compute the ICRT until the final relinearization result is obtained in the residue space.

CRT Conversion. As an initial optimization we convert all operand polynomials with large coefficients into many polynomials with small coefficients by a direct application of the Chinese Remainder Theorem (CRT) on the coefficients of the polynomials: $\mathsf{CRT} : \mathsf{A}_j \longrightarrow \{\mathsf{A}_j \bmod p_0, \mathsf{A}_j \bmod p_1, \cdots, \mathsf{A}_j \bmod p_{l-1}\}$, where p_i's are selected small primes, l is the number of these small primes, and A_j is a coefficient of the original polynomial. Through CRT conversion we obtain a set of polynomials $\{A^{(0)}(x), A^{(1)}(x), \cdots, A^{(l-1)}(x)\}$ where $A^{(i)}(x) \in R_{p_i} = \mathbb{Z}_{p_i}[x]/\varPhi(x)$. These small coefficient polynomials provide us with the advantage of performing arithmetic operations on polynomials in a faster and efficient manner. Any arithmetic operation is performed between the reduced polynomials with the same superscripts, e.g. the product of $A(x) \cdot B(x)$ is going to be $\{A^{(0)}(x) \cdot B^{(0)}(x), A^{(1)}(x) \cdot B^{(1)}(x), \cdots, A^{(l-1)}(x) \cdot B^{(l-1)}\}$. A side benefit of using the CRT is that it allows us to accommodate the change in the coefficient size during the levels of evaluation, thereby yielding more flexibility. When the circuit evaluation level increases, since q_i gets smaller, we can simply decrease the number of primes l. Therefore, both multiplication and relinearization become faster as we proceed through the levels of evaluation. After the operations are completed, a coefficient of the resulting polynomial, $\mathsf{C}(x)$ is computed by the Inverse CRT (ICRT):

$$\mathsf{ICRT}(\mathsf{C}_j) = \sum_{i=0}^{l-1} \left(\frac{q}{p_i}\right) \cdot \left(\left(\frac{q}{p_i}\right)^{-1} \cdot C_j^{(i)} \bmod p_i\right) \bmod q,$$

where $q = \prod_{i=0}^{i=l-1} p_i$. Note that we will drop the superscript notation used for the reduced polynomials by the CRT for clarity of writing since we will deal with mostly the reduced polynomials henceforth in this paper.

Polynomial Multiplication. The fundamental operation in the LTV scheme, during which the majority of execution time is spent, is the multiplication of two polynomials of very large degrees. More specifically, we need to multiply two polynomials, $A(x)$ and $B(x)$ over the ring of polynomials $\mathbb{Z}_p[x]/(\varPhi(x))$, where

p is an odd integer and degree of $\Phi(x)$ is $N = 2^n$. Namely, we have $A(x) = \sum_{i=0}^{N-1} A_i x^i$ and $B(x) = \sum_{i=0}^{N-1} B_i x^i$. The classical multiplication techniques such as the schoolbook algorithm have quadratic complexity in the asymptotic case, namely $\mathcal{O}(N^2)$. In general, the polynomial multiplication requires about N^2 multiplications and additions and subtractions of similar numbers in $\mathbb{Z}_p$. Other classical techniques such as Karatsuba algorithm [26] can be utilized to reduce the complexity of the polynomial multiplication to $\mathcal{O}(N^{\log_2 3})$. Nevertheless, the classical polynomial multiplication techniques do not yield feasible solutions for SWHE implementations, where we would need to perform billions of arithmetic operations in $\mathbb{Z}_p$ since N is a large number. The number theoretic transform (NTT)-based multiplication achieves a quasi-linear complexity for polynomial multiplication, which is especially beneficial for large values of N.

The NTT can essentially be considered as a Discrete Fourier Transform defined over the ring of polynomials $\mathbb{Z}_p[x]/(\Phi(x))$. Simply speaking, the forward NTT takes a polynomial $A(x)$ of degree $N-1$ over $\mathbb{Z}_p[x]/(\Phi(x))$ and yields another polynomial of the form $\mathcal{A}(x) = \sum_{i=0}^{N-1} \mathcal{A}_i x^i$. The coefficients $\mathcal{A}_i \in \mathbb{Z}_p$ are defined as $\mathcal{A}_i = \sum_{j=0}^{N-1} A_j \cdot w^{ij} \bmod p$, where $w \in \mathbb{Z}_p$ is referred as the twiddle factor. For the twiddle factor we have $w^N = \bmod p$ and $\forall i < N$ $w^i \neq 1 \bmod p$. The inverse transform can be computed in a similar manner $A_i = N^{-1} \cdot \sum_{j=0}^{N-1} \mathcal{A}_j \cdot w^{-ij} \bmod p$. Once the NTT is applied to two polynomials, $A(x)$ and $B(x)$, their multiplication can be performed using coefficient-wise multiplication over $\mathcal{A}_i$ and $\mathcal{B}_i$ in $\mathbb{Z}_p$; namely we compute $\mathcal{A}_i \times \mathcal{B}_i \bmod p$ for $i = 0, 1, \ldots N - 1$. Then, the inverse NTT (INTT) is used to retrieve the resulting polynomial $C(x) = INTT(NTT(A(x) \odot NTT(B(x)))$, where the symbol $\odot$ denotes the coefficient-wise multiplication of $\mathcal{A}(x)$ and $\mathcal{B}(x)$ in $\mathbb{Z}_p$. Note that the polynomial multiplication yields a polynomial $C(x)$ of degree $2N - 1$. Therefore, before applying the forward NTT, $A(x)$ and $B(x)$ should be padded with N zeros to have exactly $2N$ coefficients. Consequently, for the twiddle factor we should have $w^{2N} = 1 \bmod p$ and $\forall i < 2N$ $w^i \neq 1 \bmod p$.

Cooley–Tukey algorithm [8], described in Algorithm 1, is a very efficient method of computing forward and inverse NTT. The permutation in Step 2 of Algorithm 1 is implemented by simply reversing the indexes of the coefficients of A_i. The new position of the coefficient A_i where $i = (i_n, i_{n-1}, \ldots, i_1, i_0)$ is determined by reversing the bits of i, namely $(i_0, i_1, \ldots, i_{n-1}, i_n)$. For example, the new position of A_{12} when $N = 16$ is 3. The inverse NTT can also be computed with Algorithm 1, using the inverse of the twiddle factor, i.e. $w^{-1} \bmod p$. Therefore, we can use the same circuit for both forward and inverse NTT. Note that the NTT-based multiplication technique returns a polynomial of degree $2N - 1$, which should be reduced to a polynomial of degree $N - 1$ by diving it by $\Phi(x)$ and keeping the remainder of the division operation. When the reduction polynomial $\Phi(x)$ is of a special form such as $x^N + 1$, the NTT is known as Fermat Theoretic Transform (FTT) [1] and the polynomial reduction can be performed easily as described in [30] and [2]. However, for efficient SWHE implementation, we need to use reduction polynomials of general form.

Algorithm 1. Iterative Version of Number Theoretic Transformation

input : $A(x) = A_0 + A_1x + \ldots + A_{N-1}x^{N-1}$, $N = 2^n$, and w

output: $\mathcal{A}(x) = \mathcal{A}_0 + \mathcal{A}_1x + \ldots + \mathcal{A}_{N-1}x^{N-1}$

1 for $i = N$ **to** $2N - 1$ **do**
$\quad |\quad A_i = 0$;
end

2 $(\mathcal{A}_0, \mathcal{A}_1, \ldots, \mathcal{A}_{2N-1}) \leftarrow \text{Permutation}(A_0, A_1, \ldots, A_{2N-1})$;

3 for $M = 2$ **to** $2N$ **do**

4 $\quad$ **for** $j = 0$ **to** $2N - 1$ **do**

5 $\quad\quad$ **for** $i = 0$ **to** $\dfrac{M}{2} - 1$ **do**

6 $\quad\quad\quad x \leftarrow i \times \dfrac{2N}{M}$;

7 $\quad\quad\quad \mathcal{I} \leftarrow j + i$;

8 $\quad\quad\quad \mathcal{J} \leftarrow j + i + \dfrac{M}{2}$;

9 $\quad\quad\quad \mathcal{A}[\mathcal{I}] \leftarrow \mathcal{A}[\mathcal{I}] + w^{x \bmod 2N} \times \mathcal{A}[\mathcal{J}] \bmod p$;

10 $\quad\quad\quad \mathcal{A}[\mathcal{J}] \leftarrow \mathcal{A}[\mathcal{I}] - w^{x \bmod 2N} \times \mathcal{A}[\mathcal{J}] \bmod p$;

$\quad\quad\quad i \leftarrow i + 1$;
$\quad\quad$ **end**
$\quad\quad j \leftarrow j + M$;
$\quad$ **end**
$\quad M \leftarrow M \times 2$;
end

Relinearization. Relinearization takes a ciphertext and set of evaluation keys $(EK_{i,j})$ as inputs, where $i \in [0, l-1]$ and $j \in [0, \lceil \log(q)/r \rceil - 1]$, l is the number of small prime numbers and r is the level index. Algorithm 2 describes relinearization as implemented in this work. We pre-compute the CRT and NTT of the evaluations keys (since they are fixed) and in the computations we perform the multiplications and additions in the NTT domain. The result is evaluated by taking l INTT and one ICRT at the end. An r-bit windowed relinearization involves $\lceil \log(q)/r \rceil$ polynomial multiplications and additions, which are performed again in the NTT domain. Since operand coefficients are kept in residue form, before relinearization we need to compute the inverse CRT of $\tilde{c}_\tau$.

3 Architecture Overview

3.1 Software/Hardware Interface

The performance of the NTRU based FHE scheme heavily depends on the speed of the large degree polynomial multiplication and relinearization operations. Since the relinearization operation is reduced to the computation of many polynomial multiplications, a fast large degree polynomial multiplication is the key to

---

Algorithm 2. Relinearization with r bit windows

input : Polynomial c with $(n, \log(q))$
output: Polynomial d with $(2n, \log(nq\log(q)))$

1   $\{\tilde{C}_\tau\} = \mathsf{NTT}(\{\tilde{c}_\tau\})$;
   for $i = 0$ **to** $l - 1$ **do**
2   load $EK_{i,0}, EK_{i,1}, \cdots, EK_{i,\lceil\log(q)/r\rceil-1}$;
3      $\{D_i\} = \{\sum_{\tau=0}^{\lceil\log(q)/r\rceil-1} \tilde{C}_\tau \cdot EK_{i,\tau}\}$;
   end
4   $\{d_i\} = \mathsf{INTT}(\{D_i\})$;
5   $d = \mathsf{ICRT}(\{d_i\})$;

---

achieve a high performance in the NTRU-FHE scheme. The complexity of NTT-based polynomial multiplication operation is quasi-linear $O(N \log N \log \log N)$, and the security levels require the degree of the polynomials to be $N = 2^{15}$ for applications such as LTV-AES in [16]. Having a large degree N increases the computation requirements significantly, therefore a standalone software implementation on a general-purpose computing platform fails to provide a sufficient performance level for polynomial multiplications. The NTT-based polynomial multiplication algorithm is highly suitable for parallelization, which can lead to performance boost when implemented in hardware. On the other hand, the overall scheme is a complex design demanding prohibitively huge memory requirements (e.g., in LTV-AES [16] key requirements exceed 64-GB of memory). Therefore, a standalone architecture for SWHE fully implemented in hardware is not feasible to meet the requirements of the scheme.

In order to cope with the performance issues we designed the core NTT-based polynomial multiplication in hardware, where the polynomials have relatively small coefficients (i.e., 32-bit integers) to use it in more complicated polynomial multiplications and relinearization evaluations. The designed hardware is implemented in an FPGA device, which is connected to a PC with a high speed interface, e.g. PCI Express (PCIe). The PC handles simple and non-costly computations such as memory transactions, polynomial additions and etc. In case of a large polynomial multiplication or NTT conversion (in case of relinearization), the PC using the CRT technique, computes an array of polynomials whose coefficients are 32-bit integers from the input polynomials of much larger coefficients. The array of polynomials with small coefficients are sent in chucks to the FPGA via the high-speed PCIe bus. The FPGA computes the desired operation: polynomial multiplications or only NTT conversion. Later, the PC receives the resulting polynomials from the FPGA and if necessary, i.e. before modulus switching or relinearization, evaluates the inverse-CRT to compute the result.

3.2   PCIe Interface

The PCIe is a serial bus standard used for high speed communication between devices which in our case are PC and the FPGA board. As the target FPGA board, we use Virtex-7 FPGA VC709 Connectivity Kit and can operate at 8 GT/s, per lane, per direction with each board having 8 lanes. The system is capable of sending the data packets in bursts. This allows us to achieve real time data transaction rate close to the given theoretical transaction rate as the packet sizes become larger.

3.3   Arithmetic Core Units

In order to achieve multiplication of two polynomials of degree 2^{15}, we first designed hardware implementations for basic arithmetic building blocks to perform operations on the polynomial coefficients such as modular addition, modular subtraction and modular multiplication. We base our design on an architecture to perform modular arithmetic operations for 32-bit numbers.

32-Bit Modular Addition/Subtraction. The modular addition circuit, takes one clock cycle to perform one modular addition operation where operands A, B and the modulus p are all 32-bit integers and $A, B < p$. Since the largest value of $A+B$ can be at most $2p-2$, at most one final subtraction of the modulus p from $A + B$ will be sufficient to achieve full modular reduction after addition operation. Similarly the subtraction unit is optimized to take one clock cycle to finish one modular subtraction operation on a target device.

Integer Multiplication. The target FPGA device features many DSP units that are capable of performing very fast multiply and accumulate operations. Since these DSP units are highly optimized, it is particularly beneficial to utilize them in our core modular multiplier design. A DSP unit takes three inputs A, B and C, which are 18 bits, 25 bits and 48 bits, respectively. A and B are multiplicand inputs, and C is the accumulate input. The output is a 48-bit integer, which can be defined as $D = A \times B + C$. Therefore, we can accumulate the results of many 18×25–bit multiplications without overflow. Since our operands are 32 bits in length, first we need to perform a full multiplication operation of 32–bit numbers. The operand lengths of the DSP units dictate that we need to perform four 16×16–bit multiplication operations to achieve a 32–bit multiplication operation. Utilizing four separate DSP slices, we could perform a 32–bit multiplication with 1 clock cycle throughput. However, this brings additional complexity to the hardware and because of the overall structure of the polynomial multiplication algorithm, 1–cycle throughput is not crucial for our design. Therefore, we decided to utilize a single DSP unit and perform the four required 16×16–bit multiplication operations to achieve a 32–bit multiplication operation on the same DSP unit. This results in a 4–cycle throughput. In our design, we use Barrett's algorithm [3] for modular reduction, which requires 33×33–bit multiplication operations. Therefore, we use DSP slices to perform 17×17–bit integer multiplications at a time, instead of 16×16–bit multiplications, where both operations have exactly the same complexity. To minimize critical path delays, we utilize the optional registers for the multiplicand inputs and the accumulate output ports of the DSP unit. These registers increase the latency of a single 33×33-bit multiplication to 6 clock cycles. On the other hand, the throughput is still four clock cycles, which allows the multiplier unit to start a new multiplication every four clock cycles.

32-Bit Modular Multiplication. We use Barrett's modular reduction algorithm [3] to perform modular multiplication operations. The Montgomery reduction algorithm [28], which is a plausible alternative to the Barrett reduction, can also be used for modular multiplication of 32-bit integers. Indeed, integer multiplications during the Montgomery reduction are slightly less complicated and can result in area efficiency. On the other hand, using the Montgomery reduction would not change the throughput, which is four clock cycles for a single modular multiplication in our design. Furthermore, the Montgomery arithmetic requires transformations to and from the residue domain, which can lead to complications in the design. Therefore, we prefer using the Barrett's algorithm in our implementation to alleviate the mentioned complications in the design.

4 $2^{15} \times 2^{15}$ Polynomial Multiplier

We implemented a $2^{15} \times 2^{15}$ polynomial multiplier, with 32–bit coefficients. Throughout the paper, we will use the term $32K$ to denote the $2^{15} \times 2^{15}$ polynomial multiplier. We do not utilize any special modulus, to achieve a generic and robust polynomial multiplier as we use Barrett's reduction algorithm for coefficient arithmetic. Instead of the classical schoolbook method for polynomial multiplication, we utilized the NTT–based multiplication algorithm, as explained in Sect. 2.2 and described in Algorithm 3. It should be noted that step 5 of Algorithm 3 is implemented by coefficient–wise 32–bit modular multiplications.

Algorithm 3. NTT–based $32K$ polynomial multiplication

    input : $A(x) = A_0 + A_1 x + \cdots + A_{32767} x^{32767}$,
              $B(x) = B_0 + B_1 x + \cdots + B_{32767} x^{32767}$, p
    output: $C(x) = A(x) \times B(x)$

1 $NTT_A(x) \leftarrow$ NTT of polynomial $A(x)$;
2 $NTT_B(x) \leftarrow$ NTT of polynomial $B(x)$;
3 $NTT_C(x) \leftarrow$ Inner products of polynomials $NTT_A(x)$ and $NTT_B(x)$;
4 $T(x) \leftarrow$ Inverse NTT of polynomial $NTT_C(x)$;
5 $C(x) \leftarrow T(x) \times (32768^{-1} \bmod p)$;

4.1   NTT Operation

NTT Algorithm. We apply the NTT operation on a polynomial $A(x)$ of degree $32K - 1$ over $\mathbb{Z}_p[x]/(\varPhi(x))$. Since the result of the NTT–based multiplication will be of degree $64\,K$, we need to zero–pad the polynomial $A(x)$ to make it also a polynomial of degree $64\,K$ as follows $A(x) = \sum_{j=0}^{32K-1} A_j \cdot x^j + \sum_{j=32K}^{64K-1} 0 \cdot x^j$. When we apply the NTT transform on $A(x)$, the resulting polynomial is $\mathcal{A}(x) = \sum_{i=0}^{64K-1} \mathcal{A}_i \cdot x^i$, where the coefficients $\mathcal{A}_i \in \mathbb{Z}_p$ are defined as $\mathcal{A}_i = \sum_{j=0}^{64K-1} A_j \cdot w^{ij} \bmod p$, and $w \in \mathbb{Z}_p$ is referred as the twiddle factor. Since the size of the NTT operation is actually $64\,K$, we need to choose a twiddle factor w which satisfies the property $w^{64K} \equiv 1 \bmod p$ and $\forall i < 64\,K\ w^i \neq 1 \bmod p$. As we are utilizing generic modular multipliers, no special form of w is required to achieve more efficient multiplications.

To achieve fast NTT operations, we utilize the Cooley–Tukey approach, as explained in Sect. 2.2. Cooley–Tukey approach works by splitting up the NTT–transform into two parts, performing the NTT operation on the smaller parts, and performing a final reconstruction to combine the results of the two half–size NTT transform results into a full–sized NTT operation. For the coefficients of NTT, we have $\mathcal{A}_i = \sum_{j=0}^{32K-1} A_{2j} \cdot w^{i(2j)} \bmod p + w^i \sum_{j=0}^{32K-1} A_{2j+1} \cdot w^{i(2j)} \bmod p$ and denote this expression as $\mathcal{A}_i = E_i + w^i O_i$, where E_i and O_i represent the ith coefficients of the $32\,K$ NTT operation on the even and odd coefficients of the polynomial $A(x)$, respectively. It is important to note that if the twiddle factor of the $64\,K$ NTT operation is w, the twiddle factor of the smaller $32\,K$ operation will be w^2. Because of the periodicity of the NTT operation, we know that $E_{i+32K} = E_i$ and $O_{i+32K} = O_i$. Therefore, we have $\mathcal{A}_i = E_i + w^i O_i$ for $0 \leq i < 32K$ and $\mathcal{A}_i = E_{i-32K} + w^i O_{i-32K}$ for $32K \leq i < 64K$. For the twiddle factor, it holds that $w^{i+32K} = w^i \cdot w^{32K} = -w^i$. Consequently, we can achieve a full $64K$ NTT operation with two small $32\,K$ NTT operations utilizing the following reconstruction operation

$$
\begin{aligned}
\mathcal{A}_i &= E_i + w^i O_i, \\
\mathcal{A}_{i+32K} &= E_i - w^i O_i.
\end{aligned}
\tag{1}
$$

The reconstruction operation is performed iteratively over very large number of coefficients. An 8×8 NTT circuit is illustrated in Fig. 1. Note that, in a full $64\,K$ NTT circuit, the twiddle factor w^{16484} is used in 8×8 NTT circuits.

Coefficient Multiplication and Accumulation. Since our target FPGA has multiple number of DSP units and Block RAMs, we are able to parallelize the multiplication and accumulation operations at each level of the iterative NTT operation. We can utilize $3 \cdot K$ DSP units to achieve K modular multiplications in parallel, with a 4–cycle throughput, where K is a design parameter that depends on the number of available DSP units in the target architecture. In our design, K is chosen as a power of 2.

To be able to feed the DSP units with correct polynomial coefficients during multiplication cycles, we utilize K separate Block RAMs (BRAM)) to store the polynomial coefficients. The algorithm used to access the polynomial coefficients in parallel is described in Algorithm 4. The algorithm takes the BRAM content (i.e., the coefficients of $A(x)$), the degree $N = 2^n$, the current level m, and the

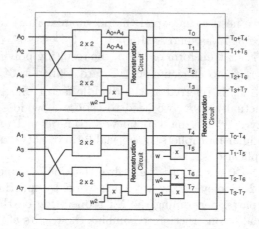

Fig. 1. Construction of the 8×8 NTT circuit iteratively.

number of modular multipliers $K = 2^\kappa$ as input, and generates the indexes in a parallel manner. Every four clock cycles, we try to feed modular multipliers the number of coefficients which is as close to K as possible. Ideally, it is desirable to perform exactly K modular multiplications in parallel, which is not possible due to the access pattern to the powers of w. Algorithm 4, on the other hand, achieves a good utilization of modular multiplication units.

For level m, we use the $2^m \times 2^m$ NTT circuit. The coefficients are arranged in $2^m \times 2^m$ blocks. For example when $K = 256$, for the first level of the NTT operation, where $m = 2$, we need to multiply every $4th$ coefficient of the polynomial with $w_2 = w^{16384}$. Since the coefficients are perfectly dispersed, we can read 256 coefficients to feed the 256 multipliers in four clock cycles. This is perfect as the throughput of our multipliers are also four cycles. When the multiplication operations are complete, with an offset of 19 cycles (four clock cycles are for the warm up of the pipeline whereas 15 clock cycles are the tail cycles necessary in a pipelined design to finish the last operation), the results are written back to the same address of the RAM block as the one the coefficients are read from. Since we are utilizing dual port RAM structures, and we guarantee different read and write addresses on each block, collisions never occur with this organization.

We provide formulae for the number of multiplications in each level and an estimate of the number of clock cycles needed for their computation in our architecture. Suppose $N = 2^n$ and $K = 2^\kappa$ ($n > \kappa$) are the number of coefficients in our polynomial and the number of modulo multipliers in our target device, respectively. The coefficients are stored in block RAMS (BRAMs), with a word size of 32 bits and an address length of 10 bits (1024 coefficients per BRAM). For ideal case, the number of modular multipliers should be 4 times the number of BRAMS required to store a single polynomial. The formula for the number of multiplications for the level $m > 1$ can be given as $\mathcal{M} = 2^{n+1-m} \cdot (2^{m-1} - 1)$. Also, using $K = 2^\kappa$ multipliers, the number of clock cycles to compute all multiplications in a given level $1 < m \leq n + 1$ can be formulated as

---

Algorithm 4. Parallel access to polynomial coefficients

> **input** : $A(x) = A_0 + A_1 x + \ldots + A_{2N-1} x^{2N-1}$, n, m, and $\kappa < n$
> **output**: $B_i[j]$

1 $mCnt \leftarrow 2^{m-1} - 1$;   /* number of multiplications in a block */
2 $bSize \leftarrow 2^m$;   /* size of a block */
3 $BRAMCnt \leftarrow 2^{\kappa-2}$;   /* number of BRAMs */
4 **if** $bSize \leq 2^{\kappa-2}$ **then**

   for $t = 0$ **to** 1024 **do**

       for $i = 0$ **to** $BRAMCnt$ **do in parallel**

           for $j = i + bSize - mCnt$ **to** $i + bSize$ **do**

               for $k = 0$ **to** 3 **do**

5   Access $BRAM_j[t + 2k]$;

6   Access $BRAM_j[t + 2k + 1]$;

                   $k \leftarrow k + 1$;

               end

               $j \leftarrow j + 1$;

           end

           $i \leftarrow i + bSize$;

       end

       $t \leftarrow t + 8$;

   end

end

7 **else**

   for $i = 0$ **to** $BRAMCnt$ **do in parallel**

       for $j = 0$ **to** 1024 **do**

           for $k = 2^{m-\kappa+1}$ **to** $2^{m-\kappa+2}$ **do**

8   Access $BRAM_i[k + j]$;

               $k \leftarrow k + 1$;

           end

           $j \leftarrow j + 2^{m-\kappa+2}$;

       end

       $i \leftarrow i + 1$;

   end

end

$$CC_m = \begin{cases} 4 + 4 \cdot \left\lfloor \dfrac{\mathcal{M}}{\alpha \cdot \lfloor K/\alpha \rfloor} \right\rfloor + 15 & \kappa \geq m \\[3mm] 4 + 4 \cdot \left(\dfrac{\beta}{K} + 1 \right) \cdot 2^{n+1-m} + 15 & \kappa < m, \end{cases}$$

where $\alpha = 2^{\kappa-m} \cdot (2^{m-1} - 1)$ and $\beta = 2^{m-1} - 2^{\kappa}$. In the formula, the first (4) and the last terms (15) account for the warm up and the tail cycles.

As mentioned before, the modulo multipliers are not always fully utilized during the NTT computation. For example when $K = 2^8$ and $N = 2^{15}$, for $m = 2$, we have to read every 4th coefficient from the BRAMs. Because the coefficients are perfectly dispersed throughout the 64 BRAMS, we can only read $16 \cdot 2 = 32$ coefficients every clock cycle, which yields a number of 128 concurrent multiplications every four clock cycles. Consequently, we can finish all the modular multiplications in the first level in $4 + 128 \cdot 4 + 15 = 531$ clock cycles. Since we can use half the modular multipliers, we achieve half utilization in the first level. However, when $m = 3$, we have to read every 6th, 7th and 8th out of every 8 coefficients. We can read $24 \cdot 2 = 48$ coefficients every clock cycle from the BRAMs. This means we can only utilize 192 out of 25 modular multipliers since the irregularity of the access to the polynomial coefficients. This, naturally, results in a slightly low utilization. However, since we can read 2 coefficients from each BRAM every clock cycle, we are at almost perfect utilization, resulting in $4 + 128 \cdot 4 + 15 = 531$ clock cycles for this and the rest of the stages.

Since the operands of the both operations are accessed in a regular manner, the number of clock cycles spent on modular additions and subtractions are calculated as $\frac{2^{n+1} \cdot (n+1)}{2^{\tau}}$, when there are 2^{τ} modular adders and 2^{τ} subtractors.

Reconstruction. Once we are done with the multiplications, we utilize 64 modular adders and 64 modular subtractors to realize the addition and subtraction operations as shown in Eq. 1.

4.2 Inner Multiplication

Inner multiplication of two 64 K polynomials is trivial for our hardware design. We can load 256 coefficients from each polynomial every 4 cycles and feed the multipliers, without increasing the 4–cycle throughput. For a 64 K polynomial inner multiplication we spend $1024 + 15 = 1039$ clock cycles.

4.3 Inverse NTT

The Inverse NTT operation is identical to the NTT operation, except that instead of the twiddle factor w, we use the twiddle factor $w_i = w^{-1} \bmod p$. The precomputed twiddle factors of the inverse NTT are stored in the same block RAMs as the forward NTT twiddle factors, with an address offset. Therefore, the same control block can be utilized with a simple address change for the w coefficients for the inverse NTT operation.

4.4 Final Scaling

Final scaling is similar to the inner multiplication phase. We load each coefficient of the resulting polynomial, and multiply them with the precomputed scaling factor. Similar to the inner multiplication phase, we can load 256 coefficients from the resulting polynomial in 4 cycles cycle and feed the multipliers, without increasing the 4–cycle throughput. For a 64 K polynomial final scaling operation, we spend 1039 clock cycles.

Table 2. Virtex-7 XC7VX690T device utilization of the multiplier

	Total	Used	Used (%)
Slice LUTs	433,200	219,192	50.59
Slice registers	866,400	90,789	10.47
RAMB36E1	1470	193	13.12
DSP48E1	3600	768	21.33

5   Implementation Results

We developed the architecture described in the previous section into Verilog modules and synthesized it using Xilinx Vivado tool for the Virtex 7 XC7VX690T FPGA family. The synthesis results are summarized in Table 2. We synthesized the design and achieved an operating frequency of 250 MHz for multiplication of polynomials of degree $n = 32,768$ with a small word size of $\log p = 32$ bit. The FPGA multiplier is used to process each component of the CRT representation of our large coefficient ciphertexts with $\log q = 1271$ bits. In fact we keep all ciphertexts in CRT representation and only compute the polynomial form when absolutely necessary, e.g. for parity correction during modulus switching and before relinearization. We assume any data sent from the PC through the PCIe interface to the FPGA is stored in onboard BRAM units.

CRT Computation Cost. To facilitate efficient computation of multiplication and relinearization operations we use a series of equal sized prime numbers to construct a CRT conversion. In fact, we chose the primes p_is such that $q = \prod_{i=0}^{l} p_i$. During the levels of homomorphic evaluation, this representation allows us to easily switch modulus by simply dropping the last p_i following by a parity correction. Also, since we have an RNS representation on the coefficients we no longer need to reduce by q. This also eliminates the need to consider any overflow conditions. Thus, $l = \log(q)/31 = 41$. We efficiently compute the CRT residue in software on the CPU for each polynomial coefficient as follows:

- Precompute and store $t_k = 2^{64 \cdot k} \pmod{p_i}$ where $k \in [0, \lceil \log(q/64) - 1 \rceil]$.
- Given a coefficient of c, we divide it into 64-bit blocks as $c = \{\ldots, w_k, \ldots, w_0\}$.
- We compute the CRT result by evaluating $\sum t_k \cdot w_k \pmod{p_i}$ iteratively.

The CRT computation cost for 41 primes p_i per ciphertext polynomial is in the order of 89 msec on the CPU. The CRT inverse is similarly computed (with the addition of a word carry) before each modulus switching operation at essentially the same cost. Note that this high latency is a significant contributor of our choice to keep the operands in the CRT representation.

Communication Cost. The PCIe bus is only used for transactions of input/output values, NTT constants and transport of evaluation keys to the FPGA board. With 8 lanes each capable of supporting 8 Gbit/sec transport speed the PCIe is capable to transmit a 5 MB ciphertext in about 0.65 msec.

Note that the NTT parameters used during multiplication also need to be transported since we do not have enough room in the BRAM components to keep them permanently. We have two cases to consider:

- Multiplication: We transport two polynomials of 5 MB each along with the NTT parameters of 5 MB and receive a polynomial of 10 MB, which costs about 3.25 msec per multiplication.
- Relinearization: We need to transport the ciphertext we want to relinearize, the NTT parameters and a set of $\log(q)/16 \approx 80$ evaluation keys (ciphertexts), where a window size of 16-bit is used, resulting in a 52 msec delay.

Multiplication Cost. We compute the product of two polynomials with coefficients of size $\log(p) = 32$ bits using 256 modular multipliers in 12720 cycles, which translates to 152 μsec. This figure is comprised of two NTT and one inverse NTT operations and one inner product computation. The addition of I/O transactions will increase the timing by 79 μsec. Using the multiplication time, the latency of large polynomial multiplication may be broken down as follows:

- Cost of small coefficient polynomial multiplications $41.152 \, \mu$sec $= 6.25$ msec.
- The PCIe transaction of the two input polynomials, the NTT coefficients and the double sized output polynomial is 3.25 msec.

Thus, the total latency for large polynomial multiplication in the CRT representation is computed in 9.51 msec.

Polynomial Modular Reduction. Since all operations are computed in a polynomial ring with a characteristic polynomial as modulus without any special structure, we use Barrett's reduction technique to perform the reductions. Note that precomputing the constant polynomial $x^{2N}/\Phi(x)$ (truncated division) in the CRT representation we do not need to compute any CRT or inverse CRT operations during modular reduction. Thus we can compute the reduction using two product operations in about 19 msec.

Modulus Switching. We realize the modulus switching operation by dropping the last CRT coefficient followed by parity correction. To compute the parity of the cut polynomial we need to compute an inverse CRT operation. The following parity matching and correction step takes negligible time. Note that the parities are single bit and therefore we do not need to compute another CRT operation. Therefore, modulus switching can be realized using one inverse CRT computation in 89 msec.

Relinearization Cost. To realinearize a ciphertext polynomial

- We need to convert the ciphertext polynomial coefficients into integer representation using one inverse CRT operation, which takes 89 msec.
- The evaluation keys are kept in NTT representation, therefore we only need to compute two NTT operations for one operand and the result. For $l = 41$ primes and $\log(q)/16 \approx 80$ products the NTT operations take 331 msec.

Table 3. Primitive operation timings including I/O transactions.

	Timings (msec)		Timings (msec)
CRT	**89**	**Modulus switch**	**89**
Multiplication	**9.51**	**Relinearization**	**526**
NTT conversions	6.25	CRT conversions	89
PCIe cost	3.26	NTT conversions	331
Modular reduction	**19**	PCIe cost	52

- We need to transport the ciphertext, the NTT parameters and 80 evaluation keys (ciphertexts) resulting in a 52 msec delay.
- The summation of the partial products takes negligible time compared to the multiplications and the PCIe communication cost.

Then, the total relinearization operation takes 526 msec. With the current implementation, the actual NTT computations still dominate over the other sources of latency such as PCIe communication latency and the CRT computations. However, if the design is further optimized, e.g. by increasing the number of processing units on the FPGA or by building custom support for CRT operations on the FPGA, then the PCIe communication overhead will become more dominant. The timing results are summarized in Table 3.

6   Comparison

To understand the improvement gained by adding custom hardware support in leveled homomorphic evaluation of a deep circuit, we *estimate* the homomorphic evaluation time for the AES circuit and compare it with a similar software implementation by Doröz et al. [16].

Homomorphic AES evaluation. Using the NTRU primitives we implemented the depth 40 AES circuit following the approach in [16]. The tower field based AES SBox evaluation is completed using 18 Relinearization operations and thus 2,880 Relinearizations are needed for the full AES. The AES circuit evaluation requires 5760 modular multiplications. During the evaluation we also compute 6080 modulus switching operations. This results in a total AES evaluation time of 15 min. Note that during the homomorphic evaluation with each new level the operands shrink linearly with the levels thereby increasing the speed. We conservatively account for this effect by dividing the evaluation time by half. With 2048 message slots, the amortized AES evaluation time becomes 439 msec.

We have also modified Doröz et al.'s homomorphic AES evaluation code to compute relinearization with 16-bits windows (originally single bit). This simple optimization dramatically reduces the evaluation key size and speeds up the relinearization. The results are given in Table 4. We also included the GPU optimized implementation by Dai et al. [14] on an NVIDIA GeForce GTX 680. With

Table 4. Comparison of multiplication, relinearization times and AES estimate

	Mul (msec)	Speedup	Relin (sec)	Speedup	AES (sec)	Speedup
CPU [16]	970	1×	103	1×	55	1×
GPU [14]	340	2.8×	8.97	11.5×	7.3	7.5×
CPU (16-bit)	970	1×	6.5	16×	12.6	4.4×
FPGA (ours)	**9.5**	**102×**	**0.53**	**195×**	**0.44**	**125×**

custom hardware assistance we obtain a significant speedups in both multiplication and relinearization operations. The estimated AES block evaluation is also improved significantly where some of the efficiency is lost to the PC to FPGA communication and CRT computation latencies.

7 Conclusions

We presented a custom hardware design to address the performance bottleneck in leveled SWHE evaluations. Given the large parameters used in such systems we design a large NTT based multiplier capable of multiplying very large degree polynomials. With the implementation of a CRT representation on the coefficients we managed to build a custom core capable of supporting polynomial multiplications with very large degree and very large coefficient polynomials. The design is highly optimized using numerous techniques to speedup the NTT computations, and to reduce the burden on the PC/FPGA interface. The resulting architecture dramatically improves the modular multiplication and relinearization speeds of the LTV SWHE scheme over comparable software implementations. To demonstrate the effectiveness of the accelerator, we estimated the AES evaluation performance and determined a speedup of about 28 times.

Acknowledgments. Funding for this research was in part provided by the US National Science Foundation CNS Award #1319130.

References

1. Agarwal, R.C., Burrus, C.S.: Fast convolution using fermat number transforms with applications to digital filtering. IEEE Trans. Acoust. Speech Signal Process. **22**(2), 87–97 (1974)
2. Aysu, A., Patterson, C., Schaumont, P.: Low-cost and area-efficient fpga implementations of lattice-based cryptography. In: HOST, pp. 81–86. IEEE (2013)
3. Barrett, P.: Implementing the rivest shamir and adleman public key encryption algorithm on a standard digital signal processor. In: Odlyzko, A.M. (ed.) CRYPTO 1986. LNCS, vol. 263, pp. 311–323. Springer, Heidelberg (1987)
4. Brakerski, Z., Gentry, C., Halevi, S.: Packed ciphertexts in LWE-based homomorphic encryption. IACR Cryptology ePrint Archive 2012/565 (2012)

5. Brakerski, Z., Gentry, C., Vaikuntanathan, V.: Fully homomorphic encryption without bootstrapping. Electron. Colloquium Comput. Complex. (ECCC) **18**, 111 (2011)
6. Brakerski, Z., Vaikuntanathan, V.: Efficient fully homomorphic encryption from (standard) LWE. In: FOCS, pp. 97–106 (2011)
7. Cao, X., Moore, C., O'Neill, M., O'Sullivan, E., Hanley, N.: Accelerating fully homomorphic encryption over the integers with super-size hardware multiplier and modular reduction. IACR Cryptology ePrint Archive 2013/616 (2013)
8. Cooley, J.W., Tukey, J.W.: An algorithm for the machine calculation of complex fourier series. Math. comput. **19**(90), 297–301 (1965)
9. Coron, J.S., Lepoint, T., Tibouchi, M.: Batch fully homomorphic encryption over the integers. IACR Cryptology ePrint Archive 2013/36 (2013)
10. Coron, J.-S., Mandal, A., Naccache, D., Tibouchi, M.: Fully homomorphic encryption over the integers with shorter public keys. In: Rogaway, P. (ed.) CRYPTO 2011. LNCS, vol. 6841, pp. 487–504. Springer, Heidelberg (2011)
11. Coron, J.-S., Naccache, D., Tibouchi, M.: Public key compression and modulus switching for fully homomorphic encryption over the integers. In: Pointcheval, D., Johansson, T. (eds.) EUROCRYPT 2012. LNCS, vol. 7237, pp. 446–464. Springer, Heidelberg (2012)
12. Cousins, D., Rohloff, K., Schantz, R., Peikert, C.: SIPHER: Scalable implementation of primitives for homomorphic encrytion. Internet Source, September 2011
13. Cousins, D., Rohloff, K., Peikert, C., Schantz, R.E.: An update on SIPHER (scalable implementation of primitives for homomorphic encRyption) - FPGA implementation using simulink. In: HPEC, pp. 1–5 (2012)
14. Dai, W., Doröz, Y., Sunar, B.: Accelerating NTRU based homomorphic encryption using GPUs. In: HPEC (2014)
15. van Dijk, M., Gentry, C., Halevi, S., Vaikuntanathan, V.: Fully homomorphic encryption over the integers. In: Gilbert, H. (ed.) EUROCRYPT 2010. LNCS, vol. 6110, pp. 24–43. Springer, Heidelberg (2010)
16. Doröz, Y., Hu, Y., Sunar, B.: Homomorphic AES evaluation using NTRU. IACR ePrint Archive (2014), https://eprint.iacr.org/2014/039.pdf
17. Doröz, Y., Öztürk, E., Sunar, B.: Evaluating the hardware performance of a million-bit multiplier. In: 2013 16th Euromicro Conference on Digital System Design (DSD) (2013)
18. Doröz, Y., Öztürk, E., Sunar, B.: Accelerating fully homomorphic encryption in hardware. IEEE Trans. Comput. **64**(6), 1509–1521 (2015)
19. Gentry, C.: A Fully homomorphic encryption scheme. Ph.D. thesis, Stanford University (2009)
20. Gentry, C.: Fully homomorphic encryption using ideal lattices. In: STOC, pp. 169–178 (2009)
21. Gentry, C., Halevi, S.: Fully homomorphic encryption without squashing using depth-3 arithmetic circuits. IACR Cryptology ePrint Archive 2011/279 (2011)
22. Gentry, C., Halevi, S.: Implementing gentry's fully-homomorphic encryption scheme. In: Paterson, K.G. (ed.) EUROCRYPT 2011. LNCS, vol. 6632, pp. 129–148. Springer, Heidelberg (2011)
23. Gentry, C., Halevi, S., Smart, N.P.: Better bootstrapping in fully homomorphic encryption. IACR Cryptology ePrint Archive 2011/680 2011 (2011)
24. Gentry, C., Halevi, S., Smart, N.P.: Fully homomorphic encryption with polylog overhead. IACR Cryptology ePrint Archive Report 2011/566 (2011). http://eprint. iacr.org/

25. Gentry, C., Halevi, S., Smart, N.P.: Homomorphic evaluation of the AES circuit. IACR Cryptology ePrint Archive 2012 (2012)
26. Karatsuba, A., Ofman, Y.: Multiplication of many-digital numbers by automatic computers. Doklady Akad. Nauk SSSR **145**(293–294), 85 (1962)
27. López-Alt, A., Tromer, E., Vaikuntanathan, V.: On-the-fly multiparty computation on the cloud via multikey fully homomorphic encryption. In: STOC (2012)
28. Montgomery, P.L.: Modular multiplication without trial division. Math. Comput. **44**(170), 519–521 (1985)
29. Moore, C., Hanley, N., McAllister, J., O'Neill, M., O'Sullivan, E., Cao, X.: Targeting FPGA DSP slices for a large integer multiplier for integer based FHE. In: Adams, A.A., Brenner, M., Smith, M. (eds.) FC 2013. LNCS, vol. 7862, pp. 226–237. Springer, Heidelberg (2013)
30. Pöppelmann, T., Güneysu, T.: Towards efficient arithmetic for lattice-based cryptography on reconfigurable hardware. In: Hevia, A., Neven, G. (eds.) LatinCrypt 2012. LNCS, vol. 7533, pp. 139–158. Springer, Heidelberg (2012)
31. Rohloff, K., Cousins, D.B.: A scalable implementation of fully homomorphic encryption built on NTRU. In: Böhme, R., Brenner, M., Moore, T., Smith, M. (eds.) FC 2014 Workshops. LNCS, vol. 8438, pp. 221–234. Springer, Heidelberg (2014)
32. Smart, N.P., Vercauteren, F.: Fully homomorphic encryption with relatively small key and ciphertext sizes. In: Nguyen, P.Q., Pointcheval, D. (eds.) PKC 2010. LNCS, vol. 6056, pp. 420–443. Springer, Heidelberg (2010)
33. Smart, N.P., Vercauteren, F.: Fully homomorphic SIMD operations. IACR Cryptology ePrint Archive 2011/133 (2011)
34. Stehlé, D., Steinfeld, R.: Making NTRU as secure as worst-case problems over ideal lattices. In: Paterson, K.G. (ed.) Advances in Cryptology – EUROCRYPT 2011. LNCS, vol. 6632, pp. 27–47. Springer, Heidelberg (2011)
35. Wang, W., Hu, Y., Chen, L., Huang, X., Sunar, B.: Accelerating fully homomorphic encryption using GPU. In: HPEC, pp. 1–5 (2012)
36. Wang, W., Hu, Y., Chen, L., Huang, X., Sunar, B.: Exploring the feasibility of fully homomorphic encryption. IEEE Trans. Comput. **99**, 1 (2013). (PrePrints)
37. Wang, W., Huang, X.: FPGA implementation of a large-number multiplier for fully homomorphic encryption. In: ISCAS, pp. 2589–2592 (2013)

Side-Channel Attacks on Public Key Cryptography

Stealing Keys from PCs Using a Radio: Cheap Electromagnetic Attacks on Windowed Exponentiation

Daniel Genkin[1,2], Lev Pachmanov[2], Itamar Pipman[2], and Eran Tromer[2]([✉])

[1] Technion, Haifa, Israel
danielg3@cs.technion.ac.il
[2] Tel Aviv University, Tel Aviv, Israel
{levp,itamarpi,tromer}@tau.ac.il

Abstract. We present new side-channel attacks on RSA and ElGamal implementations that use sliding-window or fixed-window (m-ary) modular exponentiation. The attacks extract decryption keys using a very low measurement bandwidth (a frequency band of less than 100 kHz around a carrier under 2 MHz) even when attacking multi-GHz CPUs.

We demonstrate the attacks' feasibility by extracting keys from GnuPG (unmodified ElGamal and non-blinded RSA), within seconds, using a nonintrusive measurement of electromagnetic emanations from laptop computers. The measurement equipment is cheap and compact, uses readily-available components (a Software Defined Radio USB dongle or a consumer-grade radio receiver), and can operate untethered while concealed, e.g., inside pita bread.

The attacks use a few non-adaptive chosen ciphertexts, crafted so that whenever the decryption routine encounters particular bit patterns in the secret key, intermediate values occur with a special structure that causes observable fluctuations in the electromagnetic field. Through suitable signal processing and cryptanalysis, the bit patterns and eventually the whole secret key are recovered.

Keywords: Side channel · Electromagnetic analysis · RSA · ElGamal

1 Introduction

1.1 Overview

Even when a cryptographic scheme is mathematically secure and sound, its implementations may be vulnerable to side-channel attacks that exploit physical emanations. Such emanations can leak information about secret values inside the computation and have been exploited by attacks on many cryptographic implementations (see [8,25,27] for surveys). Most research on physical side-channel attacks has focused on small devices such as smartcards, FPGAs and other simple embedded hardware. On general-purpose PCs (laptop and desktop computers, servers, etc.), software-based side-channel attacks on PCs (e.g.,

© International Association for Cryptologic Research 2015
T. Güneysu and H. Handschuh (Eds.): CHES 2015, LNCS 9293, pp. 207–228, 2015.
DOI: 10.1007/978-3-662-48324-4_11

exploiting timing and CPU cache contention) have been extensively studied. But physical side channels in PCs received less academic attention, and involve several difficulties:

1. **Complexity.** As opposed to small devices, which often contain a single main chip and some auxiliary components, PCs are highly complex systems containing multiple large chips, numerous electric components, asynchronous mechanisms, and a complicated software stack.
2. **Acquisition Bandwidth.** Typical side-channel approaches require the analog leakage signals to be acquired at a bandwidth greater than the device's clockrate. For the case of PCs running a GHz-scale CPU, recording such high-bandwidth signals requires expensive, cumbersome, and delicate-to-operate lab equipment, and a lot of storage and processing power.
3. **Signal Integrity.** Multi-GHz bandwidths are also hard to acquire with high fidelity, especially non-intrusively, since such high frequencies are usually filtered close to their source using cheap and compact components and are often subject to rapid attenuation, reflections, and so forth. Quantization noise is also a concern, due to limited ADC dynamic range at such frequencies (typically under 8 bits, as opposed to 16 or more bits at low frequencies).
4. **Attack Scenario.** Traditional side-channel attacks often require that the attacker have undeterred access to the target device. These scenarios often make sense for devices such as smartcards, which are easily pilfered or even handed out to potential attackers (e.g., cable-TV subscription cards). Yet when attacking other people's PCs, the physical access is often limited to brief, nonintrusive access that can go unobserved.

Physical side-channel attacks on PCs have been reported only at a low bandwidth leakage (less than a MHz). Emanations of interest have been shown at the USB port [30] and through the power outlet [12]. Recently, low-bandwidth physical side-channel *key-extraction* attacks on PCs were demonstrated [20,21], utilizing various physical channels. These last two works presented two different low-bandwidth attacks, with different equipment and attack time requirements:

- **Fast, Non-adaptive MF Attack.** A non-adaptive chosen-ciphertext attack exploiting signals circa 2 MHz (Medium Frequency band), obtained during several decryptions of a single ciphertext. While both ElGamal and RSA keys can be extracted using this attack in just a few seconds of measurements, the attack used expensive low-noise lab-grade signal acquisition hardware.
- **Slow, Adaptive VLF/LF Attack.** Adaptive chosen-ciphertext attack exploiting signals of about 15–40 kHz (Very Low / Low Frequency bands) obtained during several decryptions of every ciphertext. Extraction of 4096-bit RSA keys takes approximately one hour, using common equipment such as a sound card or a smartphone.

This leaves a practicality gap: the attacks require either expensive lab-grade equipment (in the non-adaptive case), or thousands of adaptively-chosen ciphertexts decrypted over an hour (in the adaptive case). See Table 1 for a comparison.

Table 1. Comparison of physical key extraction attacks on PCs. #ciphertexts counts the number of distinct ciphertexts; measurements may be repeated to handle noise.

Scheme	Algorithm	Ciphertext choice	Number of Ciphertexts	Time	Frequency	Equipment	Ref.
RSA	Square and multiply	Adaptive	$\frac{key\ bits}{4}$	1 hour	50 kHz	Common	[21]
RSA, ElGamal	Square and always multiply	Non-adaptive	1	seconds	2 MHz	Lab-grade	[20]
RSA ElGamal	Sliding/fixed window	Non-adaptive	16 8	seconds	2 MHz, 100 kHz bandwidth	Common	This work

Another limitation of [20, 21] is that they target the square-and-multiply algorithm. These attacks do not work for sliding-window or fixed-window exponentiation, used in most RSA and ElGamal implementations nowadays.

1.2 Our Contribution

In this work we make progress on all fronts outlined above. We present and experimentally demonstrate a new physical side-channel key-extraction attack, which is the first to achieve the following:

1. **Windowed Exponentiation on PCs.** The attack is effective against RSA and ElGamal implementations that use sliding-window or fixed-window (m-ary) exponentiation, as in most cryptographic libraries, and running on PCs.

Moreover, the attack *concurrently* achieves all of the following properties (each of which was achieved by some prior work on PCs, but never in combination with the other properties, and not for sliding-window exponentiation):

2. **Speed.** This attack uses as few as 8 (non-adaptively) chosen ciphertexts and is able to extract the secret key in just several seconds of measurements.
3. **Low Frequency and Bandwidth.** The attack measures signals at a frequency of merely 2 MHz, and moreover at a low bandwidth (less than 100 kHz around the carrier). This makes signal acquisition robust and inexpensive.
4. **Small, Cheap and Readily-Available Setup.** Our attack can be mounted using simple and readily available equipment, such as a cheap Software Defined Radio USB dongle attached to a loop of cable and controlled by a laptop or a small SoC board (see Figs. 8(a) and 7). Alternatively, in some cases all that is required is a common, consumer-grade radio, with its audio output recorded by a phone (see Fig. 8(b)). In both cases, we avoid the expensive equipment used in prior attacks, such as low-noise amplifiers, high-speed digitizers, sensitive ultrasound microphones, and professional EM probes.

Approach. Our attack utilizes the fact that, in the sliding-window or fixed-window exponentiation, the values inside the table of ciphertext powers can be partially predicted. Using a suitable ciphertext, we cause the value at a specific table entry to have a certain structure. This structure, coupled with a subtle control flow difference deep inside GnuPG's multiplication code, causes a difference in the leakage whenever a multiplication by this structured value occurs. Such a ciphertext is crafted separately for each table index. During its decryption, we nonintrusively measure the EM leakage, focusing on a narrowband frequency-modulated signal around 1.5–2 MHz. After filtering, demodulation, distortion compensation and averaging, a clean aggregate trace is produced for that table index, revealing all the locations inside the secret exponent where the specific table entry is selected by the bit pattern in the window. We then recover the key by combining the (misaligned but partially-overlapping) aggregate traces.

1.3 Vulnerable Software and Hardware

Similarly to [20,21], this work targets commodity laptop computers. We have tested numerous laptops of various models and makes. In this paper our examples use Lenovo 3000 N200 laptops, which exhibit a particularly clear signal.

GnuPG. We focused on GnuPG 1.4.18 [3], which is the latest version at the time of writing this paper. We compiled GnuPG using the MinGW GCC 4.6.2 [5] and ran it on Windows XP.[1] GnuPG 2.1 (developed in parallel to GnuPG 1.x), as well as its underlying cryptographic library, libgcrypt (version 1.6.2), utilize very similar cryptographic codes and thus may also be vulnerable to our attack.

Following past attacks [20,21], GnuPG uses ciphertext randomization for RSA (but not for ElGamal; see Sect. 4). To test our attack on RSA with sliding-window exponentiation, we disabled that countermeasure, making GnuPG decrypt the ciphertext directly. The ElGamal attack applies to unmodified GnuPG.

Current Status. We worked with the authors of GnuPG to suggest several countermeasures and verify their effectiveness (see CVE-2014-3591 [29]). GnuPG 1.4.19 and Libgcrypt 1.6.3, resilient to these attacks, were released concurrently with the public announcement of the results presented in this paper.

Chosen Ciphertext Injection. GnuPG is often invoked to decrypt external inputs, from numerous frontends, via emails, files, chat and web pages. The list of GnuPG frontends [4] contains dozens of such applications, each of them can be potentially exploited for our attack. Concretely, as observed in [20,21], Enigmail [17], a plugin for the Mozilla Thunderbird e-mail client, automatically decrypts incoming emails, passing them to GnuPG. Thus, it is possible to inject ciphertexts into GnuPG by sending them as a PGP/MIME-encoded e-mail [16].

1.4 Related Work

Side-channel attacks have been demonstrated on numerous cryptographic implementations, via various channels (see [8,25,27] and the references within).

---

[1] Similar effects where observed on other version of Windows as well as on Linux.

EM Side Channel. The electromagnetic (EM) side channel has been exploited for attacking smartcards and other small devices (e.g., [7,19,33]). On PCs, [39] observed EM leakage (but did not show cryptanalytic applications), and [20] demonstrated EM attacks on a side-channel protected PC implementation of the square-and-multiply exponentiation of RSA and ElGamal.

Attacks on Sliding Window Exponentiation. While most attacks on public key schemes focus on variants of the square-and-multiply algorithm, several focus on attacking sliding window exponentiation on small devices (sampling much faster than the target's clockrate). These either exploit high-bandwidth operand-dependent leakage of the multiplication routine [13,23,24,35] or utilize the fact that it is possible to distinguish between squarings and multiplications [6,18].

Neither of the above approaches fits our case. The first approach requires very high-bandwidth leakage the acquisition of which, even for small and slow embedded devices, requires expensive lab equipment. Non-intrusive acquisition of such signals for the PC class of devices (running multi-GHz CPUs) is especially difficult. The second approach is blocked by a countermeasure to the attack of [37]: GnuPG uses the same code for squaring and multiplications (and the resulting EM leakage indeed appears indistinguishable at low bandwidth).

Side-channel Attacks on PCs. Physical side-channel attacks of PCs were demonstrated by observing leakage through the USB port [30] or through the power outlet [12]. Key extraction attacks have been presented on PCs, utilizing timing differences [10] and cache access patterns [9,31,32]. Recently, low-bandwidth key-extraction attacks that utilize physical channels such as sound [21] and chassis potential [20] were demonstrated on GnuPG running on PCs.

Cache Attacks in GnuPG. Yarom and Falkner [37] presented an L3 cache attack on the square-and-multiply algorithm, achieving key extraction by directly observing the sequence of squarings and multiplications performed. In a concurrent work, Yarom et al. presented [38] an attack on sliding-window exponentiation by observing the access patterns to the table of ciphertext powers.

2 Cryptanalysis

2.1 GnuPG's Sliding-Window Exponentiation Routine

GnuPG uses an internal mathematical library called MPI (based on GMP [2]) in order to perform the big-integer operations occurring in ElGamal and RSA. In recent versions, exponentiation is performed using a sliding-window algorithm. MPI stores big integers as arrays of *limbs* (32-bit words, in our case). Algorithm 1 is a pseudocode of the exponentiation routine. The function SIZE_IN_LIMBS(x) returns the number of limbs in the t-bit number x, namely $\lceil t/32 \rceil$.

Consider lines 8–12. For a fixed value of w, these compute a table indexed by $1, 3, 5, \ldots, 2^w - 1$, mapping each odd w-bit integer u to the group element g^u. We will show how to exploit this table to create exponent-dependent leakage during the main loop of Algorithm 1, leading to full key extraction.

Algorithm 1. GnuPG's modular exponentiation (simplified).

```
 1: procedure MOD_EXP(g, d, p)                              ▷ return g^d mod p
 2:     if SIZE_IN_LIMBS(d) > 16 then                ▷ compute w, the window size
 3:         w ← 5
 4:     else if SIZE_IN_LIMBS(d) > 8 then
 5:         w ← 4
        . . .
 6:     else
 7:         w ← 1
 8:     g_0 ← 1, g_1 ← g, g_2 ← g^2
 9:     for i ← 1 to 2^{w-1} - 1 do              ▷ precompute table of small powers of g
10:         g_{2i+1} ← g_{2i-1} · g_2
11:         if SIZE_IN_LIMBS(g_{2i+1}) > SIZE_IN_LIMBS(p) then
12:             g_{2i+1} ← g_{2i+1} mod p
13:     a ← 1, j ← 0
14:     while d ≠ 0 do                          ▷ main loop for computing g^d mod p
15:         j ← j + COUNT_LEADING_ZEROS(d)
16:         d ← SHIFT_LEFT(d, j)                          ▷ shift d to the left j bits
17:         for i ← 1 to j + w do
18:             a ← a · a mod p                    ▷ using multiplication, not squaring
19:         t ← d_1 ··· d_w
20:         j ← COUNT_TRAILING_ZEROS(t)
21:         u ← SHIFT_RIGHT(t, j)                          ▷ shift t to the right j bits
22:         a ← a · g_u mod p
23:         d ← SHIFT_LEFT(d, w)                           ▷ shift d to the left w bits
24:     for i ← 1 to j do
25:         a ← a · a mod p                        ▷ using multiplication, not squaring
26:     return a
```

2.2 ElGamal Attack Algorithm

We start by describing the attack algorithm on GnuPG's ElGamal implementation, which uses sliding-window exponentiation. At the end of the section we discuss the fixed-window version.

Let *SM-sequence* denote the sequence of squaring and multiplications performed in lines 18, 22 and 25 of Algorithm 1. Note that this sequence depends only on the exponent d. If an attacker were to learn the SM-sequence, and moreover obtain for each multiplication in line 22 the corresponding table index u used to index into the table, then the exponent could be recovered.

Revealing the Locations of a Table Index. We now discuss how, for any given table index u, the attacker can learn the locations where multiplications by g_u, as performed by line 22, occur inside the SM-sequence. In what follows, for any given table index u, we shall refer to such locations as SM-locations. For 3072-bit ElGamal, GnuPG chooses a secret exponent of about 400 bits. Thus $w = 4$, so the table indices are odd 4-bit integers. Given an odd 4-bit integer

u, the attacker chooses the ciphertext so that multiplications by g_u produce different side-channel leakage compared to multiplications by $g_{u'}$ for all $u' \neq u$.

First, the attacker selects a number $y \in \mathbb{Z}_p^*$ containing many zero limbs and computes its u-th root, i.e., x, such that $x^u \equiv y \pmod{p}$. It is likely that for all other odd 4-bit integer $u' \neq u$, there are few zero limbs in $x^{u'} \bmod p$ (otherwise, the attacker selects a different y and retries). Finally, the attacker requests the decryption of (x, δ) for some arbitrary value δ and measures the side channel leakage produced during the computation of MOD_EXP(x, d, p).

Distinguishing Between Multiplications. The above process of selecting x given an odd 4-bit integer u allows an attacker to distinguish multiplications by g_u from multiplications by $g_{u'}$ for all $u' \neq u$, during the main loop of MOD_EXP(x, d, p). Indeed, by the code of Algorithm 1 we have that $g_u = x^u \bmod p = y$, which contains many zero limbs. Conversely, for any $u' \neq u$, $g_{u'} = x^{u'} \bmod p$ which contains few (if any) zero limbs. The number of zero limbs in the second operand of the multiplication can be detected via side channels, as observed by [20,21]. Thus, it is possible to distinguish the multiplications by g_u in line 22 of Algorithm 1 from multiplications by $g_{u'}$ where $u' \neq u$.

Distinguishing Between Squarings and Multiplications. GnuPG implements the squaring in lines 18 and 25 using the same multiplication code used for line 22 (this is a countermeasure to the attack of [37]). In the case of squaring, the argument a supplied to the multiplication routine is an intermediate value which is unlikely to contain any zero limbs. Thus, the squaring operations will produce similar leakage to that produced by multiplications by $g_{u'}$ for some $u' \neq u$. Thus the attacker can still determine the SM-locations of g_u.

Key Extraction. Applying this method across all ciphertexts, the attacker learns the SM-locations of multiplications by g_u performed in line 22 for all possible u. Since u is an odd 4-bit number, only 8 possible values of u exist. Any remaining locations must correspond to a squaring operation performed by lines 18 or 25. At this point, the attacker has learned the entire SM-sequence performed by Algorithm 1 and obtained the corresponding value of u for each multiplication performed by line 22, allowing him to recover the secret exponent.

Attacking the Fixed-Window Method. The fixed-window (m-ary) exponentiation method (see [28, Algorithm 14.109]) avoids the key-dependent shifting of the window, thus reducing side-channel leakage. The exponent is split into contiguous, fixed-size m-bit words. Each word is handled in turn by performing m squaring operations and a single multiplication by an appropriate value selected from a precomputed table using the current word as the table index.

In attacking fixed-window ElGamal, each table index u may be targeted similarly as in the sliding window case by having the attacker select a number $y \in \mathbb{Z}_p^*$ containing many zero limbs and compute the u-th root of y, x, such that $x^u \equiv y$. Like in the sliding window case, for any other m-bit word $u' \neq u$, it is likely that $x^{u'} \bmod p$ will contain few (if any) zero limbs. The remainder of the attack—leakage analysis and key extraction—is the same as for sliding window.

2.3   RSA Attack Algorithm

Unlike ElGamal, the security of RSA already breaks down if the top half of the bits of any of the secret exponents (d_p, d_q) is leaked [15]. We now adapt the ElGamal attack presented in Sect. 2.2 to RSA, first for GnuPG's sliding window implementation, and then for the fixed window version.

Revealing the Location of Table Indices. For 4096-bit RSA since GnuPG's RSA uses the CRT, the exponents d_p and d_q 2048 bits long; hence, $w = 5$. Given an odd 5-bit table index u, the attacker wishes to learn the SM-locations of multiplications by g_u performed during the modular exponentiation routine. Unlike for ElGamal, the attacker does not know p and cannot select a number y with many zero limbs and compute x such that $x^u \equiv y \pmod{p}$. Neither can he compute u-th roots modulo N to compute $x^u \equiv y \pmod{N}$, as this would contradict the security of RSA with public exponent u.

Approximating the Location of Table Indices. However, locating the precise locations is not, in fact, necessary. Instead, we relax the requirements so that, given a 5-bit odd integer u, the attacker learns all the SM-locations of multiplication by $g_{u'}$ for some $u' \leq u$. To this end, the attacker no longer relies on solving modular equations over composite-order groups, but rather on the fact that, during the table computation phase inside GnuPG's exponentiation routine, as soon as the number of limbs of some table value g_u exceeds the number of limbs in the prime p, the table value g_u is reduced modulo p (see line 11 of Algorithm 1). Thus, given a 5-bit odd integer u, the attacker requests the decryption of a number t such that t contains many zero limbs and that $t^u \leq 2^{2048} < t^{u+1}$. The two above requirements are instantiated by computing the largest integer k such that $k \cdot u \leq 2048$ and requesting the decryption of 2^k. Finally, the side-channel leakage produced during the computation of $\mathrm{MOD\_EXP}(2^k, d_p, p)$ is recorded.

Distinguishing Between Multiplication. Fix an odd 5-bit integer u and let k be the largest integer such that $\left(2^k\right)^u \leq 2^{2048}$. The SM-sequence resulting from the computation of $\mathrm{MOD\_EXP}(2^k, d_p, p)$ contains three types of multiplication operations, creating two types of side-channel leakage.

1. **Multiplication by $g_{u'}$ where $u' \leq u$.** In this case $\left(2^k\right)^{u'} \leq \left(2^k\right)^u \leq 2^{2048}$ and therefore $g_{u'} = 2^{k \cdot u'} \bmod p$ does not undergo a reduction modulo p. Thus $g_{u'} = 2^{k \cdot u'}$, which is a number containing many zero limbs.
2. **Multiplication by $g_{u'}$ where $u' > u$.** In this case $2^{2048} < \left(2^k\right)^{u'}$ and therefore $g_{u'} = 2^{k \cdot u'} \bmod p$ undergoes a reduction modulo p, making it a random-looking number that will contain very few (if any) zero limbs.
3. **Multiplication Resulting from Squaring Operations.** As mentioned in Sect. 2.2, GnuPG implements the squaring in lines 18 and 25 using the same multiplication code used for line 22. In the case of squaring, the argument a supplied to the multiplication routine is a random-looking intermediate value. Thus, the squaring operations will produce similar leakage to case 2 above.

Next, as in the attack presented in Sect. 2.2, since the leakage produced by GnuPG's multiplication routine depends on the number of zero limbs in its second operand, it is possible to distinguish between multiplications by $g_{u'}$ where $u' \leq u$ (case 1 above) and all other multiplications (cases 2 and 3 above). Thus, the attacker learns the SM-locations of all multiplications by $g_{u'}$ where $u' \leq u$.

Key Extraction. Applying the above for every table index u (since u is an odd 5-bit integer, only 16 possible values of u exist). The attacker deduces the SM-locations of all multiplication performed by line 22. Moreover, for each multiplication, by finding the lowest u such that the leakage of the multiplication corresponds to case 1 above, the the index of its second operand is also deduced.

The attacker has now learned the sequence of table indices (i.e., odd 5-bit values) that occur as the sliding window moves down the secret exponent d_p. To recover the secret exponent, the attacker need only discover the amounts by which the window slides between these values (due to runs of zero bits in d_p). This sliding is realized by the loops in lines 18 and 25 of Algorithm 1, and can thus be deduced from the SM-locations of the squaring operations in lines 18 and 25. These SM-locations are simply the remaining SM-locations after accounting for those of the multiplications in line 22, already identified above. The attacker has now learned the position and value of all bits in d_p.

Attacking the Fixed-Window Method. As for ElGamal case, this attack can also be applied to the fixed-window (m-ary) exponentiation case. This is done by modifying the attack above to approximate the location of all m-bit table indexes (as opposed to only odd m-bit indexes). The remainder of the attack—leakage analysis and key extraction—is the same as for the sliding window case.

3   Experimental Results

3.1   SDR Experimental Setup

Our first setup uses Software Defined Radio to study EM emanations from laptop computers at frequencies of 1.5–2 MHz, as detailed below (see also Fig. 1(a)).

Probe. As a magnetic probe, we constructed a simple shielded loop antenna using a coaxial cable, wound into 3 turns of 15 cm diameter, and with suitable conductor soldering and center shield gap [34]. The placement of the EM probe relative to the laptop influences the measured signal. We measured the EM emanations close to the CPU's voltage regular, located on the laptop's motherboard, yet without case intrusion. The voltage regulator is typically located in the rear left corner, and placing the probe there usually yields the best signal.

Receiver. We recorded the signal using a FUNcube Dongle Pro+ [1] SDR receiver. The FUNcube Pro+ is an inexpensive (GBP 125) USB dongle that contains a software-adjustable mixer and a 192 Ksample/sec ADC.

Amplification. In order to extend the attack range, we added a 50 dB gain stage using a pair of inexpensive amplifiers (Mini-Circuits ZFL-500LN+ and ZFL-1000LN+ in series, USD 175 total) between the loop antenna and the SDR receiver. We also added a low-pass filter before the amplifiers. See Fig. 1(b).

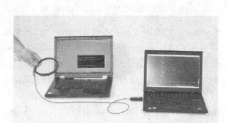
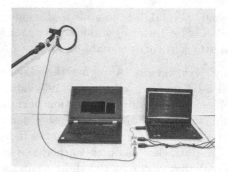

(a) A loop antenna (handheld) attacking a target laptop (left). The antenna is connected to an SDR receiver dongle attached to the attacker's computer (right).

(b) The loop antenna is held 50cm above the target, and is connected to a low-pass filter, followed by a pair of amplifiers, leading to the SDR receiver dongle and the attacker's computer.

Fig. 1. The SDR-based setup attacking a Lenovo 3000 N200 target.

Attack Range. Using our loop antenna and SDR receiver we achieved key extraction from a range of about 20 cm(Figs. 1(a) and 8(a)). Using a cheap mini-circuits amplifiers we extended the attack range to half a meter (Fig. 1b).

3.2   Signal Analysis

Exponent-Dependent Leakage. Confirming the dependence of leakage on exponents, Fig. 2 shows how ElGamal decryptions using different exponents can be distinguishable by their EM leakage. The same holds for RSA.

Fig. 2. EM measurement (0.5 sec, 1.49–1.57 MHz) of four GnuPG ElGamal decryptions executed on a Lenovo 3000 N200 laptop. The exponent is overridden to be the 3072-bit number obtained by repeating the bit pattern written to the right. In all cases, the modulus p is the same and the ciphertext c is set to be such that $c^{15} \equiv 2^{3071} \pmod{p}$. Note the subtly different side lobes around the 1527 kHz carrier.

Demodulation. As can be seen in Fig. 2, when using periodic exponents the leakage signal takes the form of a central peak surrounded by distinguishable side

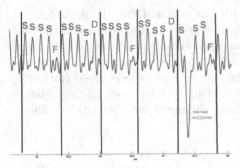

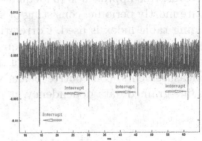

(a) A segment of the demodulated trace. Squaring is marked by S, and multiplication by the used table index u (here, 0xD or 0xF). When u = 0xF, dips occur. Algorithm 1 main-loop iterations are marked by vertical lines.

(b) Demodulation of the signal obtained during the entire decryption. The interrupts, occurring every 15 ms, are marked by arrows.

Fig. 3. Frequency demodulation of the first leakage signal from Fig. 2. The exponent is overridden to be the 3072-bit number obtained by repeating the bit pattern 0xFD, and the ciphertext c is set to be such that $c^{15} \equiv 2^{3071} \pmod{p}$.

lobes. This is a strong indication that the secret bit exponents are modulated by the carrier. As in [20], the carrier signal turned out to be frequency modulated.

Different targets produce such FM-modulated signals at different, and often multiple, frequencies. In each experiment, we chose one such carrier and applied a band-pass filter around it. We then sampled the signal using our SDR, and performed digital signal demodulation. After additional digital filtering, we received a demodulated trace as shown in Fig. 3(a).

Signal Distortions. In principle, a single demodulated trace is needed per chosen ciphertext. However, the signals obtained with our setup (especially those recorded from afar) have insufficient signal-to-noise ratio for key extraction.

Moreover, there are various distortions in the signal, making key extraction difficult. The signals are corrupted every 15 msec, by the timer interrupt on the target laptop. Each interrupt corrupts the trace for a duration of several bits, and may also create a time shift relative to other traces (see Figs. 3(b) and 4). Also, traces exhibit a gradual drift, increasing the duration between two adjacent peaks (relative to other traces), making signal alignment even more problematic.

The attack of [20], targeting square-and-always-multiply exponentiation, overcame interrupts and time drift using the fact that every given stage in the decryption appears in non-corrupted form in most of the traces. They broke the signal down into several time segments and aligned them using correlation, thereby resolving shift issues. Since, in their case, the baseband signal reflected a sequence of random-looking key bits, correlation proved sufficient aligning trace segments.

However, this approach is inadequate for our attack. Here, the demodulated traces are mostly periodic, consisting of similar peaks that change when the corresponding table index is used. Correlating such signals produces an ambiguity as to the actual shift compensation required for proper alignment. The problem is exacerbated by the low bandwidth of the attack: had we performed clockrate-scale measurements, consecutive peaks would likely have been distinguishable due to fine-grained data dependency, making alignment via correlation viable.

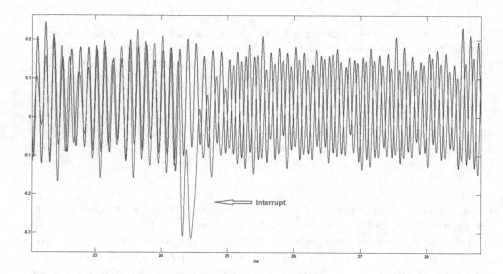

Fig. 4. FM demodulation of an EM measurement during two ElGamal decryptions of the same ciphertext and key. The red signal is shifted relative to the blue signal (Color figure online).

Aligning the Signals. As a first attempt to align the signals and correct distortions, we applied the "Elastic Alignment" [36] algorithm to the demodulated traces; however, for our signals the results were very unreliable. For more robust key extraction, we used a more problem-specific algorithm.

Initial Synchronization. We first aligned all traces belonging to decryptions of the same ciphertext. We used the fact that the computations performed just prior to the exponentiation produced a consistent pattern at the start of each trace. Correlation was used to align this pattern in all traces relative to a reference trace, chosen randomly from the trace set. Next, we independently compared each trace to the reference trace, correcting distortions as follows.

Handling Interrupts. In order to align the signals despite the interrupt-induced shifts, a search for interrupts was performed across both the current and reference trace, from beginning to end. Interrupts are easily detected, as they cause large frequency fluctuations. Whenever an interrupt was encountered, the delay it induced was estimated by correlating a short segment immediately following the interrupt in both signals. The samples corresponding to the interrupt were then removed from the interrupted signal, to locally restore alignment. This process was repeated until the signals were fully aligned. Note that the delay created by the interrupts was usually shorter than the peaks in the demodulated trace, so there was no ambiguity in the correlation and resulting delay estimate.

Handling Drifts. The slow drifts were handled by adding another step to the above process. Between each pair of interrupts, we performed a periodic comparison (by direct correlation) and compensated for the drift by removing samples from the appropriate signal. In order to avoid ambiguity, the comparisons were made frequently so that the drift never created a delay longer than half a peak.

Aggregating Aligned Traces. The foregoing process outputs fully-aligned traces that still contain occasional interrupts (since the interrupt duration is usually several peaks long but creates a delay of no more than one peak, the compensation process does not completely remove the interrupt). In order to obtain a clean *aggregate trace*, the signals were combined via a mean-median filter. At each time point, the samples from different traces were sorted, and the highest and lowest several values discarded. The remaining values were averaged, resulting in an interrupt free trace. Finally, even after we combined several aligned traces, the peak amplitudes across each aggregate trace varied greatly. To facilitate peak detection, the peak amplitudes were equalized by extracting the signal envelope, followed by low-pass filtering and smoothing. See Fig. 5(a).

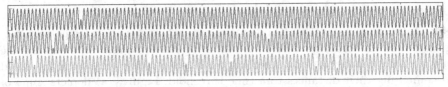

(a) After peak amplitudes equalization (the horizontal axis is given in miliseconds)

(b) After peak detection (the horizontal axis is the peak/dip number and the vertical axis is "high" for peaks and "low" for dips)

Fig. 5. Aggregate traces for table indices 1,3,5 obtained during our ElGamal attack.

3.3   ElGamal Key Extraction

When attacking ElGamal, we first iterated over the 8 table indices, and for each measured and aggregated multiple traces of decryptions of that ciphertext. This resulted in 8 aggregate traces, which were further processed as follows.

Peak Detection. For each aggregate trace corresponding to a table index u, we derived a vector of binary values representing the peaks and dips in this trace. This was done by first detecting all local maxima exceeding some threshold amplitude. The binary vector then contains a bit for every consecutive pair of peaks, set to 1 if the peaks are close (below some time threshold), and set to 0 if they are further apart, meaning there is a dip between them; see Fig. 5(b).

Revealing the ElGamal SM-sequence. Observing that dips occur during multiplication by operands having many zero limbs, coupled with the analysis of Sect. 2.2, we expect the 0 value to appear in this vector only at points corresponding to times when multiplication by g_u is performed.

Across all ciphertexts, these binary vectors allow the attacker to deduce the exact SM-sequence and, moreover, to obtain, for each multiplication performed by line 22 of Algorithm 1, the corresponding value of the table index u. As explained in Sect. 2.2, the key is then easily deduced.

Overall Attack Performance. Applying our attack to a randomly-generated 3072-bit ElGamal key by measuring the EM emanations from a Lenovo 3000 N200 laptop, we extracted all but the first three bits of the secret exponent. For each chosen ciphertext, we used traces obtained from 40 decryption operations, each taking about 0.1 sec. We thus measured a total of $8 \cdot 40 = 320$ decryptions.

3.4 RSA Key Extraction

Analogously to the above, when attacking RSA following Sect. 2.3, we obtained 16 aggregate traces, one for each table index and its chosen ciphertext.

Peak Detection. As in the ElGamal case, for each aggregate trace corresponding to a table index u, we derived a vector of binary values representing the peaks and dips in this trace by detecting peaks above some amplitude threshold and comparing their distances to a time threshold. Figure 6(a) depicts some of the aggregated traces obtained during the RSA attack presented in Sect. 2.3. As predicted in Sect. 2.3, any dip first appearing in some trace corresponding to some table index u also appears in traces corresponding to table indices $u' > u$.

However, note that in each subsequent trace the length of each dip gets progressively shorter and harder to observe. This is because the larger the value $u' - u$ is, the shorter the value stored in the u-th table index during the decryption of the ciphertext targeting the u'-th table index (and in particular this value contains less zero limbs). Eventually, the dips become so short as to be indistinguishable from the regular distance between two peaks (with no dip in between), making the dip impossible to observe. Thus, the extracted vectors inevitably contain missing dips, requiring corrections as described next.

Inter-Window Dip Aggregation. In order to recover the undetected dips, we had to align all the aggregate vectors (corresponding to different table indices). Luckily, even though the dips get progressively shorter, in adjacent vectors there are many common dips to allow for alignment. Thus, the following iterative process was performed for every two adjacent vectors: First, the current vector

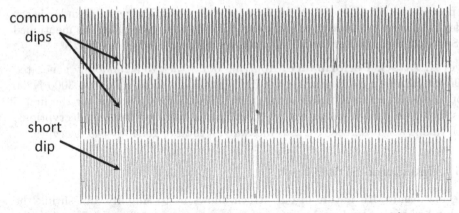

(a) Before peak detection (the horizontal axis is given in miliseconds)

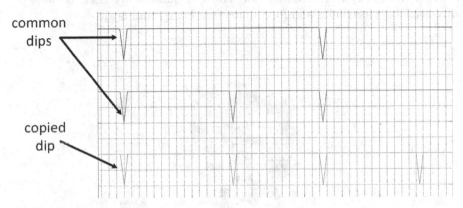

(b) After peak detection (the horizontal axis is the peak/dip number and the vertical axis is "high" for peaks and "low" for dips)

Fig. 6. Aggregate traces for table indices 3,5,7 obtained during our RSA attack.

was aligned to the previous one. Next, going from left to right, all missing dips were copied from the previous vector to the current one, as follows: going over the vectors from start to end, as soon as a dip was located in the previous vector that was missing from the current vector, it was copied to the current vector, shifting all other vector elements one coordinate to the right. See Fig. 6(b).

Revealing the RSA SM-sequence. Note that each multiplication corresponds to a dip in one of the vectors obtained in the previous stage. Thus, since in the above aggregation process dips are propagated across adjacent vectors, the last vector contains all the SM-locations, where each multiplication is marked with a dip and each squaring is marked with a peak. In order to recover the key, it remains for the attacker to learn the table index corresponding to every multiplication in the SM-sequence. Since each vector contains all the dips of all previous vectors, for each multiplication, the corresponding table index is the index of the vector where the dip appeared for the first time. Thus, as mentioned in Sect. 2.3, the attacker has all the data required to recover the key.

Overall Attack Performance. Applying our attack to a randomly generated 4096-bit RSA key by measuring the EM emanations from a Lenovo 3000 N200 laptop, we extracted the most-signicant 1250-bits for d_p except for the first 5 bits. For each chosen ciphertext, we used traces obtained from 40 decryptions, each taking about 0.2 sec. We thus measured a total of $16 \cdot 40 = 640$ decryptions.

3.5   Untethered SDR Attack

The low bandwidth nature of our attack allows us to simplify and shrink the analog and analog-to-digital portion of the setup, compared to prior works. Our prototype, the Portable Instrument for Trace Acquisition (PITA), is built of readily-available electronics and food items (see Figs. 7 and 8(a)).

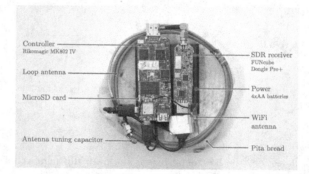

Fig. 7. Portable Instrument for Trace Acquisition (PITA), a compact untethered measurement device for low-bandwidth electromagnetic key-extraction attacks.

Functionality. The PITA can be operated in two modes. In *online mode*, it connects to a nearby station via WiFi and provides real-time streaming of the digitized signal. The live stream helps optimize probe placement and allows adaptive recalibration of the carrier frequency and SDR gain adjustments (see Fig. 8(a)). In *autonomous mode*, the PITA is configured to continuously measure the electromagnetic field around a designated carrier frequency; it records the digitized signal into an internal microSD card for later retrieval, by physical access or via WiFi. In both cases, signal analysis is done offline, on a workstation.

Hardware. The PITA uses an unshielded loop antenna made of copper wire, wound into 3 turns of diameter 13 cm, with a tuning capacitor chosen to maximize sensitivity at 1.7 MHz (see Fig. 7). These are connected to an SDR receiver

(a) Portable Instrument for Trace Acqui-   (b) Experimental setup using a con-
sition (PITA), measuring the target and   sumer AM radio receiver, placed near the
streaming the filtered signal over WiFi.   target and recorded by a smartphone.

Fig. 8. Two of our experimental setups for key extraction.

dongle. We controlled the SDR using a small embedded computer, the Riko-
magic MK802 IV. This is an inexpensive (USD 68) Android TV dongle supporting USB host mode, WiFi and flash storage. We replaced the operating system
with Linux in order to run our software, which operates the SDR receiver via
USB and communicates via WiFi. Power was provided by 4 AA batteries.

Overall Attack Performance. Applying our attack to a randomly generated
3072-bit ElGamal key, we extracted all the bits of the secret exponent, except
the most significant bit and the three least significant bits, from a Lenovo 3000
N200 laptop. As before, we used a total of 320 decryptions, taking 0.1 sec each.

3.6 Consumer-Radio Attack

Despite its low cost and compact size, assembly of the PITA still requires the
purchase of an SDR device. We now show how to improvise a side-channel attack
setup for extracting ElGamal keys, using common household items.

As discussed, the leakage signal is *frequency* modulated (FM) around a carrier circa 1.7 MHz. While the signal processing can be performed in software, we
could not find any household item able to digitize external signals at such frequencies. Since the bandwidth of the demodulated signal is only a few kHz, an
alternative approach is to perform demodulation in hardware and then digitize
the result. While most household radios can demodulate FM, the frequencies
used in commercial FM broadcasting are 88–108 MHz. Even when using lab-
grade equipment, we did not observe key-dependent leakage within the commercial FM band. Despite this, we managed to use a plain consumer-grade radio
receiver to acquire the desired signal, as described below, replacing the magnetic
probe and SDR. After appropriate tuning, all that remained was to record the
radio's headphone jack output, and digitally process the signal. See Fig. 8(b).

Demodulation Principle. Most consumer radios are able to receive amplitude modulated (AM) broadcasts in addition to FM. AM radio broadcasts typically use parts of the Medium Wave band (0.5–1.7 MHz), in which our signal of interest resides. AM signals are routed through a different analog path than the FM signals, so the radio's FM demodulator cannot be used in these ranges. It *is* possible, however, to use the AM analog chain to perform unconventional FM demodulation. The AM path consists of an antenna, a tuning filter, and an AM demodulation block. In normal operation, the filter is set so that its center frequency exactly matches that of the incoming signal. An FM signal would pass through the tuning filter unchanged, but be completely suppressed by the AM block since its amplitude is essentially constant. But by setting the center frequency of the tuning filter to a few kHz away from the FM carrier, the slope of the filter effectively acts as an FM to AM converter, transforming the frequency changes of the signal into changes in amplitude. The AM demodulation block then extracts and amplifies these amplitude changes. See Fig. 9.

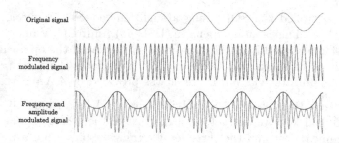

Fig. 9. FM to AM conversion using the AM tuning filter slope. The top signal is some periodic baseband signal. The middle signal is an FM modulation of the top signal. The bottom signal is obtained by filtering the FM-modulated signal through a slightly skewed bandpass filter; the resulting signal is both AM and FM modulated. The baseband signal can be reconstructed by extracting the envelope of the resulting signal. (For visual clarity, we compensate for the filter's time delay and attenuation).

Experimental Setup. This setup requires an AM radio receiver and an audio recorder (such as a smartphone microphone input or a computer's audio input). We used a plain hand-held radio receiver ("Road Master" brand) and recorded its headphone output by connecting it to the microphone input of an HTC EVO 4G phone, sampling at 48 Ksample/sec, through an adapter cable (see Fig. 8(b)). The radio replaced the magnetic probe, SDR and digital demodulation.

Further Digital Signal Processing. The radio's headphone jack produced a signal at 8 kHz, which is similar to the frequency of the peaks Fig. 4. After low-pass filtering at 16 kHz, traces similar to Figs. 3(a) and 4 were obtained. We then applied the remainder of the signal processing algorithms from Sect. 3.2.

Overall Attack Performance. Applying our attack to a randomly generated 3072-bit ElGamal key by measuring the EM emanations from a Lenovo 3000

N200 laptop, we extracted all but the first bit of the secret exponent. For each chosen ciphertext, we used traces obtained from 40 decryption operations, each taking about 0.1 sec. Similar results were obtained by directly connecting the radio's output to a computer's audio input, recording at 48 Ksample/sec.

4   Discussion

We presented and experimentally demonstrated new side-channel attacks on cryptographic implementations using sliding-window and fixed-window exponentiation. Our techniques simultaneously achieve low analog bandwidth and high attack speed, and the measurement setup is compact, cheap and unintrusive.

The attack does not rely on detecting movement of the sliding window, but detects the key-dependent use of specific table entries "poisoned" by a chosen ciphertext. Thus, the attack is applicable to exponentiation algorithms that have a fixed schedule of squarings and multiplications, such as the fixed-window method. Likewise, it is oblivious to cache-attack mitigations that fix or randomize the table access patterns.

Future Work. In order to achieve key extraction, our attack requires traces obtained during 40 decryption operation for each chosen ciphertext. We leave the task of reducing the total number of required traces as an open problem.

Next, while public key encryption schemes were proven to vulnerable to physical low-bandwidth chosen-ciphertext key-extraction attacks on PCs, attacks on other public key primitives (such as digital signatures), as well as non-chosen ciphertext attacks were not yet demonstrated for the case of PCs.

Finally, physical key extraction attacks on symmetric key primitives were also never demonstrated for the PCs. Presumably since the frequencies of the externally-available leakage is too low given the high execution speed of such primitives. We leave the task of attacking such primitives as an open problem.

Software Countermeasures. Our attack chooses ciphertexts that target specific table indices. For a targeted table index, the attacker learns the locations of the index in the sequence of squarings and multiplications. Since the sequence of squarings and multiplications only depends on the secret exponent, the attacker is able to reconstruct the secret exponent after recovering the location of all table indices in the sequence of squarings and multiplications.

One class of countermeasures is an *exponent randomization*, which alters the sequence of squarings and multiplications between invocations of the modular exponentiation. One such method is *multiplicative exponent randomization*, adding a random multiple of $p - 1$ to the secret exponent (see [26]). Unfortunately, in the case of GnuPG's ElGamal implementation this incurs significant slowdown, since the secret exponent is selected to be short (about 400 bits), but adding a multiple of $p - 1$ increases it to over 3072-bits, incurring a slowdown of $\times 3072/400 \approx 7$. A cheaper exponent randomization alternative is *additive exponent randomization*, in which the exponent is additively divided into two shares (see [11,14] and a related patent [22]). In GnuPG's ElGamal, this requires two exponentiations with 400 bit exponents, incurring a $\times 2$ slowdown.

Another countermeasure that generally blocks chosen ciphertext attacks is *ciphertext randomization (blinding)*, which randomizes the base of the exponentiation. For RSA decryption, this is a common countermeasure with low overhead: instead of decrypting a ciphertext c by directly computing c^d mod n, one generates a random r, computes r^e (which is cheap since the encryption exponent e is small, typically 65537), decrypts $r^e \cdot c$ and divides by r to obtain c^d. Current versions of GnuPG already do this for RSA, preventing Sect. 2.3's attack.

For ElGamal, ciphertext randomization is more expensive. Instead of computing $\gamma^{-x} \cdot \delta$ mod p directly, one generates a random r and computes $y_1 = r^x$ mod p, $y_2 = (\gamma \cdot r)^{-x}$ mod p and finally $y_1 \cdot y_2 \cdot \delta$ mod p. For GnuPG's ElGamal, this requires two exponentiations with 400-bit exponents, plus an inversion, incurring again a $\times 2$ slowdown. A new version of GnuPG, implementing this countermeasure, was released concurrently with the public announcement of our results.

Acknowledgments. We thank Werner Koch, lead developer of GnuPG, for the prompt response to our disclosure and the productive collaboration in adding suitable countermeasures. We thank Sharon Kessler for editorial advice.

This work was sponsored by the Check Point Institute for Information Security; by European Union's Tenth Framework Programme (FP10/2010-2016) under grant agreement no. 259426 ERC-CaC, by the Leona M. and Harry B. Helmsley Charitable Trust; by the Israeli Ministry of Science and Technology; by the Israeli Centers of Research Excellence I-CORE program (center 4/11); and by NATO's Public Diplomacy Division in the Framework of "Science for Peace".

References

1. FUNcube Dongle. http://www.funcubedongle.com
2. GNU multiple precision arithmetic library. http://gmplib.org/
3. GNU Privacy Guard. https://www.gnupg.org
4. GnuPG Frontends. https://www.gnupg.org/related_software/frontends.html
5. Minimalist GNU for Windows. http://www.mingw.org
6. SPA/SEMA vulnerabilities of popular RSA-CRT sliding window implementations. Presented During Workshop on Cryptographic Hardware and Embedded Systems (CHES) 2012 Rump Session (2012). https://www.cosic.esat.kuleuven.be/ches2012/ches_rump/rs5.pdf
7. Agrawal, D., Archambeault, B., Rao, J.R., Rohatgi, P.: The EM side—channel(s). In: Kalisk, B.S., Koç, Ç.K., Paar, C. (eds.) CHES 2002. LNCS, vol. 2523, pp. 29–45. Springer, Heidelberg (2002)
8. Anderson, R.J.: Security Engineering - A Guide to Building Dependable Distributed Systems, 2nd edn. Wiley, New York (2008)
9. Bernstein, D.J.: Cache-timing attacks on AES (2005). http://cr.yp.to/papers.html#cachetiming
10. Brumley, D., Boneh, D.: Remote timing attacks are practical. Comput. Netw. **48**(5), 701–716 (2005)
11. Chari, S., Jutla, C.S., Rao, J.R., Rohatgi, P.: Towards sound approaches to counteract power-analysis attacks. In: Wiener, M. (ed.) CRYPTO 1999. LNCS, vol. 1666, pp. 398–412. Springer, Heidelberg (1999)

12. Clark, S.S., Mustafa, H., Ransford, B., Sorber, J., Fu, K., Xu, W.: Current events: identifying webpages by tapping the electrical outlet. In: Crampton, J., Jajodia, S., Mayes, K. (eds.) ESORICS 2013. LNCS, vol. 8134, pp. 700–717. Springer, Heidelberg (2013)
13. Clavier, C., Feix, B., Gagnerot, G., Roussellet, M., Verneuil, V.: Horizontal correlation analysis on exponentiation. In: Soriano, M., Qing, S., López, J. (eds.) ICICS 2010. LNCS, vol. 6476, pp. 46–61. Springer, Heidelberg (2010)
14. Clavier, C., Joye, M.: Universal exponentiation algorithm. In: Koç, Ç.K., Naccache, D., Paar, C. (eds.) CHES 2001. LNCS, vol. 2162, pp. 300–308. Springer, Heidelberg (2001)
15. Coppersmith, D.: Small solutions to polynomial equations, and low exponent RSA vulnerabilities. J. Cryptol. 10(4), 233–260 (1997)
16. Elkins, M., Torto, D.D., Levien, R., Roessler, T.: MIME security with OpenPGP. RFC 3156 (2001). http://www.ietf.org/rfc/rfc3156.txt
17. Enigmail Project, T.: Enigmail: A simple interface for OpenPGP email security. https://www.enigmail.net
18. Fouque, P.-A., Kunz-Jacques, S., Martinet, G., Muller, F., Valette, F.: Power attack on small RSA public exponent. In: Goubin, L., Matsui, M. (eds.) CHES 2006. LNCS, vol. 4249, pp. 339–353. Springer, Heidelberg (2006)
19. Gandolfi, K., Mourtel, C., Olivier, F.: Electromagnetic analysis: concrete results. In: Koç, Ç.K., Naccache, D., Paar, C. (eds.) CHES 2001. LNCS, vol. 2162, pp. 251–261. Springer, Heidelberg (2001)
20. Genkin, D., Pipman, I., Tromer, E.: Get your hands off my laptop: physical side-channel key-extraction attacks on PCs. In: Batina, L., Robshaw, M. (eds.) CHES 2014. LNCS, vol. 8731, pp. 242–260. Springer, Heidelberg (2014)
21. Genkin, D., Shamir, A., Tromer, E.: RSA key extraction via low-bandwidth acoustic cryptanalysis. In: Garay, J.A., Gennaro, R. (eds.) CRYPTO 2014, Part I. LNCS, vol. 8616, pp. 444–461. Springer, Heidelberg (2014)
22. Goubin, L.: Method for protecting an electronic system with modular exponentiation-based cryptography against attacks by physical analysis, US Patent 6,973,190 (2005)
23. Heyszl, J., Ibing, A., Mangard, S., De Santis, F., Sigl, G.: Clustering algorithms for non-profiled single-execution attacks on exponentiations. In: Francillon, A., Rohatgi, P. (eds.) CARDIS 2013. LNCS, vol. 8419, pp. 79–93. Springer, Heidelberg (2014)
24. Homma, N., Miyamoto, A., Aoki, T., Satoh, A., Shamir, A.: Collision-based power analysis of modular exponentiation using chosen-message pairs. In: Oswald, E., Rohatgi, P. (eds.) CHES 2008. LNCS, vol. 5154, pp. 15–29. Springer, Heidelberg (2008)
25. Kocher, P., Jaffe, J., Jun, B., Rohatgi, P.: Introduction to differential power analysis. J. Cryptograph. Eng. 1(1), 5–27 (2011)
26. Kocher, P.C.: Timing attacks on implementations of Diffie-Hellman, RSA, DSS, and other systems. In: Koblitz, N. (ed.) CRYPTO 1996. LNCS, vol. 1109, pp. 104–113. Springer, Heidelberg (1996)
27. Mangard, S., Oswald, E., Popp, T.: Power Analysis Attacks: Revealing the Secrets of Smart Cards. Springer, New york (2007)
28. Menezes, A.J., Vanstone, S.A., Oorschot, P.C.V.: Handbook of Applied Cryptography, 1st edn. CRC Press Inc., Boca Raton (1996)
29. MITRE: Common vulnerabilities and exposures list, entry CVE-2014-3591 (2014). http://cve.mitre.org/cgi-bin/cvename.cgi?name=CVE-2014-3591

30. Oren, Y., Shamir, A.: How not to protect PCs from power analysis. Presented During CRYPTO 2006 Rump Session (2006). http://iss.oy.ne.ro/HowNotToProtectPCsFromPowerAnalysis
31. Osvik, D.A., Shamir, A., Tromer, E.: Cache attacks and countermeasures: the case of AES. In: Pointcheval, D. (ed.) CT-RSA 2006. LNCS, vol. 3860, pp. 1–20. Springer, Heidelberg (2006)
32. Percival, C.: Cache missing for fun and profit. Presented at BSDCan (2005). http://www.daemonology.net/hyperthreading-considered-harmful
33. Quisquater, J.-J., Samyde, D.: ElectroMagnetic analysis (EMA): measures and counter-measures for smart cards. In: Attali, S., Jensen, T. (eds.) E-smart 2001. LNCS, vol. 2140, pp. 200–210. Springer, Heidelberg (2001)
34. Smith, D.: Signal and noise measurement techniques using magnetic field probes. In: IEEE International Symposium on Electromagnetic Compatibility (EMC 1999), vol. 1, pp. 559–563. IEEE (1999)
35. Walter, C.D.: Sliding windows succumbs to big mac attack. In: Koç, Ç.K., Naccache, D., Paar, C. (eds.) CHES 2001. LNCS, vol. 2162, pp. 286–299. Springer, Heidelberg (2001)
36. van Woudenberg, J.G.J., Witteman, M.F., Bakker, B.: Improving differential power analysis by elastic alignment. In: Kiayias, A. (ed.) CT-RSA 2011. LNCS, vol. 6558, pp. 104–119. Springer, Heidelberg (2011)
37. Yarom, Y., Falkner, K.: FLUSH+RELOAD: a high resolution, low noise, L3 cache side-channel attack. In: USENIX Security Symposium 2014, pp. 719–732. USENIX Association (2014)
38. Yarom, Y., Liu, F., Ge, Q., Heiser, G., Lee, R.B.: Last-level cache side-channel attacks are practical. In: IEEE Symposium on Security and Privacy (S&P). IEEE (2015)
39. Zajic, A., Prvulovic, M.: Experimental demonstration of electromagnetic information leakage from modern processor-memory systems. IEEE Trans. Electromagn. Compat. (EMC) 56(4), 885–893 (2014)

Exclusive Exponent Blinding May Not Suffice to Prevent Timing Attacks on RSA

Werner Schindler$^{(\boxtimes)}$

Bundesamt für Sicherheit in der Informationstechnik (BSI),
Godesberger Allee 185–189, 53175 Bonn, Germany
Werner.Schindler@bsi.bund.de

Abstract. The references [1,3,9] treat timing attacks on RSA with CRT and Montgomery's multiplication algorithm in unprotected implementations. It has been widely believed that exponent blinding would prevent any timing attack on RSA. At cost of significantly more timing measurements this paper extends the before-mentioned attacks to RSA with CRT when Montgomery's multiplication algorithm and exponent blinding are applied. Simulation experiments are conducted, which confirm the theoretical results. Effective countermeasures exist. In particular, the attack efficiency is higher than in the previous version [12] while large parts of both papers coincide.

Keywords: Timing attack · RSA · CRT · Exponent blinding · Montgomery's multiplication algorithm

1   Introduction

In 1996 Paul Kocher introduced timing analysis [6]. In particular, [6] presents a timing attack on an unprotected RSA implementation, which does not apply the Chinese Remainder Theorem (CRT). Reference [9] introduced a new timing attack on RSA implementations, which apply CRT and Montgomery's multiplication algorithm [8]. This attack was extended to OpenSSL (RSA, CRT, sliding window exponentiation algorithm, Montgomery's multiplication algorithm) [3], and later optimized [1]. Also [5,9–11] consider timing attacks on RSA implementations that apply Montgomery's multiplication algorithm. All these attacks target unprotected RSA implementations.

Besides presenting the first timing attack on RSA (without CRT) [6] proposes various countermeasures ([6], Section 10), including exponent blinding where a random multiple of Euler's ϕ function of the modulus is added to the secret exponent. Since then (exclusive) exponent blinding has widely been assumed to be effective to prevent (any type of) timing attacks on RSA, at least no successful timing attacks against exponent blinding have been known. The present paper extends the timing attack from [9] to RSA implementations, which apply exponent blinding, proving that exclusive exponent blinding (without additional countermeasures) does not always prevent timing attacks on RSA.

© International Association for Cryptologic Research 2015
T. Güneysu and H. Handschuh (Eds.): CHES 2015, LNCS 9293, pp. 229–248, 2015.
DOI: 10.1007/978-3-662-48324-4_12

However, the presence of exponent blinding increases the number of timing measurements enormously.

In Sect. 2 the targeted implementation is described (RSA with CRT, square & multiply, Montgomery's multiplication algorithm, exponent blinding), assumptions are formulated and justified. Section 3 contains the theoretical foundations of our attack while in Sect. 4 the attack is specified and experimental results are given. Moreover, the attack is adjusted to table-based exponentiation algorithms, and effective countermeasures are proposed.

In this paper the attack efficiency is higher than in [12]. For several proofs in Sect. 3 and an parameter estimation process we refer to [12]. Apart from that and from editorial improvements both papers essentially coincide in large parts.

2   Modular Exponentiation with Montgomery's Multiplication Algorithm

In this section we describe the targeted RSA implementation. More precisely, we begin with the modular arithmetic, and finally we specify the modular exponentiation algorithm. Moreover, two assumptions are formulated and analysed, which will be applied later.

Montgomery's multiplication algorithm (MM) [8] fits perfectly to the hardware architecture of a computer, smart card or microcontroller since modulo operations and divisions only have to be carried out for moduli and divisors, which are powers of 2.

Definition 1. *For a positive integer $M > 1$ we set $Z_M := \{0, 1, \ldots, M - 1\}$. We write $a \equiv b \bmod M$ if $(a - b)$ is a multiple of M. The term $b(\bmod M)$ denotes the unique element in Z_M, which is congruent to b modulo M.*

For an odd modulus M the integer $R := 2^t > M$ is called Montgomery's constant, and $R^{-1} \in Z_M$ denotes its multiplicative inverse modulo M. Moreover, $M^* \in Z_R$ satisfies the integer equation $RR^{-1} - MM^* = 1$.

On input (a, b) Montgomery's algorithm returns $\mathrm{MM}(a, b; M) := abR^{-1}(\bmod M)$. This value is computed with a multiprecision version of Montgomery's multiplication algorithm, which is adjusted to the particular device. More precisely, let ws denote the word size for the arithmetic operations (typically, $ws = 8, 16, 32, 64$), which divides the exponent t of R. Further, $r = 2^{ws}$, so that in particular $R = r^v$ with $v = t/ws$ (numerical example: $(ws, t, v) = (16, 1024, 64)$). In Algorithm 1 a, b and s are expressed in the r-adic representation. That is, $a = (a_{v-1}, \ldots, a_0)_r$, $b = (b_{v-1}, \ldots, b_0)_r$ and $s = (s_{v-1}, \ldots, s_0)_r$. Finally, $m^* = M^* \pmod{r}$. In particular, $MM^* = RR^{-1} - 1 \equiv -1 \bmod R$ and thus $m^* \equiv -M^{-1} \bmod r$.

After Step 3 $s \equiv abR^{-1} \bmod M$ and $s \in [0, 2M)$. The instruction $s := s - M$ in Step 4, called 'extra reduction' (ER), is carried out iff $s \in [M, 2M)$. This conditional integer subtraction is responsible for timing differences. Whether an ER is necessary does not depend on the chosen multiprecision variant but only on the quadruple (a, b, M, R) [9], Remark 1. This allows to consider the case

---

Algorithm 1. Montgomery's multiplication algorithm (MM), multiprecision variant

---

1. Input: $a, b \in Z_M$
2. $s := 0$
3. For $i = 0$ to $v - 1$ do {

    $u := (s + a_i b_0) m^* (\mathrm{mod}\, r)$

    $s := (s + a_i b + uM)/r$

    }
4. If $(s \geq M)$ then $s := s - M$ [= extra reduction (ER)]
5. return s $(= abR^{-1}(\mathrm{mod}\, M) = \mathrm{MM}(a, b; M))$

$ws = t$ (i.e. $v = 1$) when analyzing the stochastic behaviour of the ERs in modular exponentiations.

Algorithm 2 combines Montgomery's multiplication algorithm with the square & multiply exponentiation algorithm.

Algorithm 2. Square & multiply with Montgomery's algorithm (s&m, MM)

```
Computes   y ↦ y^d(mod M) for   d = (d_{w-1}, ..., 0)_2
   temp := y_R := MM(y, R^2(mod M); M)      (Pre-multiplication)
   for i=w-1 down to 0 do {
      temp := MM(temp, temp; M)
      if (d_i=1) then temp := MM(temp, y_R; M)
      }
   MM(temp, 1; M)                               (Post-multiplication)
   return temp   ( = y^d(mod M) )
```

As usual, $n = p_1 p_2$ and R denotes the Montgomery constant while $\mathrm{MM}(a, b; n) := abR^{-1}(\mathrm{mod}\, n)$ stands for the Montgomery multiplication of a and b. The computation of $v = y^d(\mathrm{mod}\, n)$ is performed in several steps:

Assumption 1. For fixed modulus M and fixed Montgomery constant R

$$\mathrm{Time}\,(\mathrm{MM}(a, b; M)) \in \{c, c + c_{\mathrm{ER}}\} \quad \text{for all } a, b \in Z_M, \tag{1}$$

which means that an MM operation costs time c if no ER is needed, and c_{ER} equals the time for an ER. (The values c and c_{ER} depend on the concrete device.)

Remark 1. [Justification of Assumption 1]
(i) Since the divisions and the modular reductions in Step 3 of Algorithm 1 can be realized by shifts and masking operations the calculations within the for-loop are essentially integer additions and integer multiplications or parts thereof, respectively. For fixed M and R the time per iteration of the for-loop should be constant. Since usually $\log_2(M) \approx \log_2(R)$ for known input attacks the leading words a_{v-1} and b_{v-1} are the factor always non-zero, at least if $ws \geq 16$, and thus may expect that (1) is fulfilled.

Algorithm 3. RSA, CRT, s&m, MM, exponent blinding

1. (a) Set $y_1 := y(\mathrm{mod}\,p_1)$ and $d_1 := d(\mathrm{mod}\,(p_1 - 1))$
   (b) (Exponent blinding) Generate a random number $r_1 \in \{0, 1, \ldots, 2^{eb} - 1\}$ and compute the blinded exponent $d_{1,b} := d_1 + r_1 \phi(p_1) = d_1 + r_1(p_1 - 1)$.
   (c) Compute $v_1 := y_1^{d_{1,b}}(\mathrm{mod}\,p_1)$ with Algorithm 2 ($M = p_1$).
2. (a) Set $y_2 := y(\mathrm{mod}\,p_2)$ and $d_2 := d(\mathrm{mod}\,(p_2 - 1))$
   (b) (Exponent blinding) Generate a random number $r_2 \in \{0, 1, \ldots, 2^{eb} - 1\}$ and compute the blinded exponent $d_{2,b} := d_2 + r_2 \phi(p_2) = d_2 + r_2(p_2 - 1)$.
   (c) Compute $v_2 := y_2^{d_{2,b}}(\mathrm{mod}\,p_2)$ with Algorithm 2 ($M = p_2$).
3. (Recombination) Compute $v := y^d(\mathrm{mod}\,n)$ from (v_1, v_2), e.g. with Garner's algorithm: $v := v_1 + p_1\left(p_1^{-1}(\mathrm{mod}\,p_2) \cdot (v_2 - v_1)(\mathrm{mod}\,p_2)\right)(\mathrm{mod}\,n)$

(ii) Our timing attack is an adapted chosen input attack, for which in the course of the attack in many Montgomery multiplications one factor has one or more leading zero words. For smart cards and microcontrollers one might assume that this feature may not violate Assumption 1 since optimizations of rare events (within the normal use of the device) seem to be unlikely.

(iii) On a PC cryptographic software might process small operands (i.e., those with leading zero-words) in Step 3 of Algorithm 1 differently, e.g. because different integer multiplication algorithm is applied (e.g., OpenSSL: normal multiplication vs. Karatsuba multiplication [1,3]). Such effects, however, may complicate our attack but should not prevent it [1,3].

Assumption 2. Assumption 1 holds for the modular multiplications $(\mathrm{mod}\,p_1)$ and $(\mathrm{mod}\,p_2)$ with identical time constants c and c_{ER}. The attacker knows the values c and c_{ER}.

Remark 2. (i) Usually, the r-adic representations of p_1 and p_2 comprise the same number of words, i.e. $\lceil \log_2(p_1)/ws \rceil = \lceil \log_2(p_2)/ws \rceil$, and R is identical in both cases. With regard to Remark 1 this justifies the first claim of Assumption 2. (If the number of words should be different we may expect unequal triplets $(R_1, c_1, c_{ER,1})$ and $(R_2, c_2, c_{ER,2})$, which would complicate the attack.)
(ii) In the best case (from the attacker's point of view) the attacker either knows c and c_{ER} or is able to determine them precisely with a simulation tool. Otherwise, he may estimate both values, see [12], Subsect. 4.4.

3   Theoretical Background of Our Attack

This section contains the theoretical foundations of our attack. The main results are the mean value and the variance of the execution time of Algorithm 3 (Subsects. 3.1 and 3.2) and the distinguisher, which allows to decide whether a given interval contains / does not contain a multiple of p_1 or p_2. (Subsect. 3.3).

3.1   Exponentiation $(\bmod \mathrm{p}_i)$

In Subsect. 3.1 we consider the stochastic timing behaviour of the exponentiations modulo p_1 and modulo p_2. More precisely, we focus on the for-loop in Algorithm 2 when applied by Step i(c) of Algorithm 3 with $M = p_i$ for $i = 1, 2$. By Step i(b) of Algorithm 3 the blinding factor r_i is a randomly selected eb-bit number, i.e. $r_i \in \{0, \ldots, 2^{eb} - 1\}$ for $i = 1, 2$. We interpret the measured execution times as realizations of random variables.

Definition 2. *Random variables are denoted by capital letters, and realizations (i.e., values taken on) of these random variables are denoted with the corresponding small letter. The abbreviation 'iid' stands for 'independent and identically distributed'. For a random variable Y the terms $E(Y)$, $E(Y^2)$ and $\mathrm{Var}(Y)$ denote its expectation (mean), its second moment and its variance, respectively. The term $Y \sim N(\mu, \sigma_2)$ means that the random variable N is normally distributed with mean μ and variance σ^2. The cumulative distribution of the standard normal distribution $N(0, 1)$ is given by $\Phi(x) := (2\pi)^{-1/2} \int_{-\infty}^{x} e^{-t^2/2} \, dt$.*

The distinguisher and the attack in Sect. 4 consider input values of the form $y = uR^{-1} (\bmod n)$. A simple calculation shows that the pre-multiplication step in Algorithm 2 transforms the input value y into $y_{R,i} := u (\bmod \mathrm{p}_i)$ ([9], Sect. 3, after formula (5)). Consequently, we interpret the execution time of the for-loop in Algorithm 2 as a realization of a random variable $Z_i(u)$. With this notation

$$Z_i(u) := (Q_i + M_i)c + X_i \, c_{\mathrm{ER}} \tag{2}$$

expresses the random computation time for the exponentiation $(\bmod \mathrm{p}_i)$ in terms of the random variables Q_i, M_i and X_i. The random variables Q_i and M_i denote the random number of squarings and multiplications within the for loop in Step i(c) while X_i quantifies the number of extra reductions (ERs) in these squarings and multiplications $(i = 1, 2)$. Unfortunately, the random variables Q_i, M_i and X_i are not independent.

The main goal of this subsection is to calculate $E(Z_i(u))$ and $\mathrm{Var}(Z_i(u))$. By definition

$$E\left(Z_i^v(u)\right) = \sum_{q_j} \sum_{m_k} \sum_{x_r} P(Q_i = q_i, M_i = m_k, X_i = x_r) \left((q_i + m_k)c + x_r \, c_{\mathrm{ER}}\right) =$$

$$\sum_{q_j} P(Q_i = q_j) \sum_{m_k} P(M_i = m_k \mid Q_i = q_j) \sum_{x_r} P(X_i = x_r \mid Q_i = q_j, M_i = m_k) \times$$

$$\times \quad \left((q_i + m_k)c + x_r \, c_{\mathrm{ER}}\right)^v . \tag{3}$$

Clearly, $x_r \in \{0, \ldots, q_j + m_k\}$, $m_k \in \{0, \ldots, q_j\}$ and $q_j \in \{k - 1, \ldots, k + eb - 1\}$. Lemma 1 collects several facts, which will be needed in the following. Recall that $p_i < R$.

Lemma 1. *As in Sect. 2 the term y_i stands for $y (\bmod p_i)$.*
(i) For $y := uR^{-1} (\bmod n)$ the MM-transformed basis for the exponentiation $(\bmod p_i)$ equals $u_i' := u (\bmod p_i)$.

(ii) If $d_{i,b}$ is a k_i'-bit integer the computation of $y_i^{d_{i,b}} \pmod{p_i}$ needs $q_i := k_i' - 1$ squarings and $m_i := \operatorname{ham}(d_{i,b}) - 1$ multiplications where $\operatorname{ham}(\cdot)$ denotes the Hamming weight of its argument.

(iii) The (conditional) random variable $(X_i \mid Q_i = q_i, M_i = m_i) c_{ER}$ quantifies the overall random execution time for all extra reductions if $Q_i = q_i$ and $M_i = m_i$. Let

$$p_{i*} := \frac{p_i}{3R}, \quad p_{i(u')} := \frac{u_i'}{2p_i}, \quad \operatorname{cov}_{i,\mathrm{MS}(u_i')} := 2p_{i(u')}^3 p_{i*} - p_{i(u')}p_{i*}, \qquad (4)$$

$$\operatorname{cov}_{i,\mathrm{SM}(u_i')} := \frac{9}{5} p_{i(u')} p_{i*}^2 - p_{i(u')}p_{i*}, \quad \operatorname{cov}_{i,\mathrm{SS}} := \frac{27}{7} p_{i*}^4 - p_{i*}^2. \qquad (5)$$

The random variable $(X_i \mid Q_i = q_i, M_i = m_i)$ is normally distributed with expectation

$$E(X_i \mid Q_i = q_i, M_i = m_i) = q_i p_{i*} + m_i p_{i(u')} \qquad \text{and variance} \qquad (6)$$

$$\operatorname{Var}(X_i \mid Q_i = q_i, M_i = m_i) = q_i p_{i*}(1 - p_{i*}) + m_i p_{i(u')}(1 - p_{i(u')}) +$$
$$2m_i \operatorname{cov}_{i,\mathrm{SM}(u_i')} + 2(m_i - 1)\operatorname{cov}_{i,\mathrm{MS}(u_i')} + 2(q_i - m_i)\operatorname{cov}_{i,\mathrm{SS}} \qquad (7)$$

(iv) The random variable $(M_i \mid Q_i = q_i)$ quantifies the random number of multiplications if $Q_i = q_i$. It is approximately $N(q_i/2, q_i/4)$-distributed. In particular, $E(M_i^2 \mid Q_i = q_i) = \frac{1}{4}(q_i + q_i^2)$.

Proof. see [12], proof of Lemma 1.

Theorem 1. *Combining the previous results we obtain*

$$E\left(Z_i(u)\right) = E(Q_i)\left(\frac{3}{2}c + \left(p_{i*} + \frac{1}{2}p_{i(u')}\right)c_{ER}\right) \qquad (8)$$

and

$$\operatorname{Var}\left(Z_i(u)\right) = \operatorname{Var}(Q_i)\left(\frac{3}{2}c + (p_{i*} + \frac{1}{2}p_{i(u')})c_{ER}\right)^2$$

$$+ E(Q_i)\Big(\frac{1}{4}c^2 + \frac{1}{2}p_{i(u')}c\,c_{ER} + (p_{i*}(1 - p_{i*}) + \frac{1}{2}p_{i(u')}(1 - p_{i(u')})$$

$$+ 2p_{i(u')}^3 p_{i*} + \frac{9}{5}p_{i(u')}p_{i*}^2 - 2p_{i(u')}p_{i*} + \frac{27}{7}p_{i*}^4 - p_{i*}^2 + \frac{1}{4}p_{i(u')})c_{ER}^2\Big)$$

$$- 2(2p_{i(u')}^3 p_{i*} - 2p_{i(u')}p_{i*})c_{ER}^2. \qquad (9)$$

Proof. see [12], proof of Theorem 1.

Lemma 2 provides explicit expressions for $E(Q_i)$ and $\operatorname{Var}(Q_i)$, which may be substituted into (8) and (9). Note that $p_i < 2^k \le R$.

Lemma 2. *Let p_i be a k-bit number, and let $\gamma_i := p_i/2^k$.*
(i) Unless eb is artificially small approximately

$$E(Q_i) = (k - 1) + eb - \frac{1}{\gamma_i} \qquad (10)$$

$$\operatorname{Var}(Q_i) = \frac{3}{\gamma_i} - \frac{1}{\gamma_i^2} \qquad (11)$$

Table 1. Expectation and variance for several sets of parameters $(R, eb, p_i/R, c_{ER}/c)$

				$\frac{u'}{p_i} = 0.0$		$\frac{u'}{p_i} = 0.5$		$\frac{u'}{p_i} = 1.0$	
$\log_2(R)$	eb	$\frac{p_i}{R}$	c_{ER}	$E(Z_i(u))$	$\mathrm{Var}(Z_i(u))$	$E(Z_i(u))$	$\mathrm{Var}(Z_i(u))$	$E(Z_i(u))$	$\mathrm{Var}(Z_i(u))$
512	64	0.75	$0.03\,c$	$864.8\,c$	$148.5\,c^2$	$866.4\,c$	$150.2\,c^2$	$868.0\,c$	$151.9\,c^2$
512	64	0.80	$0.03\,c$	$865.2\,c$	$148.5\,c^2$	$866.9\,c$	$150.3\,c^2$	$868.7\,c$	$152.0\,c^2$
512	64	0.85	$0.03\,c$	$865.6\,c$	$148.4\,c^2$	$867.4\,c$	$150.3\,c^2$	$869.3\,c$	$152.2\,c^2$
512	64	0.75	$0.05\,c$	$867.7\,c$	$148.7\,c^2$	$870.4\,c$	$151.5\,c^2$	$873.0\,c$	$154.3\,c^2$
512	64	0.80	$0.05\,c$	$868.3\,c$	$148.7\,c^2$	$871.1\,c$	$151.6\,c^2$	$874.0\,c$	$154.6\,c^2$
512	64	0.85	$0.05\,c$	$868.9\,c$	$148.6\,c^2$	$871.9\,c$	$151.7\,c^2$	$875.0\,c$	$154.9\,c^2$
1024	64	0.75	$0.03\,c$	$1636.6\,c$	$276.6\,c^2$	$1639.7\,c$	$279.7\,c^2$	$1642.8\,c$	$282.8\,c^2$
1024	64	0.80	$0.03\,c$	$1637.3\,c$	$276.6\,c^2$	$1640.6\,c$	$279.9\,c^2$	$1643.8\,c$	$283.2\,c^2$
1024	64	0.85	$0.03\,c$	$1638.0\,c$	$276.5\,c^2$	$1641.4\,c$	$280.0\,c^2$	$1644.9\,c$	$283.5\,c^2$
1024	64	0.75	$0.05\,c$	$1642.1\,c$	$276.9\,c^2$	$1647.2\,c$	$282.1\,c^2$	$1652.3\,c$	$287.4\,c^2$
1024	64	0.80	$0.05\,c$	$1643.1\,c$	$276.8\,c^2$	$1648.5\,c$	$282.4\,c^2$	$1654.0\,c$	$288.0\,c^2$
1024	64	0.85	$0.05\,c$	$1644.1\,c$	$276.8\,c^2$	$1649.9\,c$	$282.7\,c^2$	$1655.7\,c$	$288.6\,c^2$

(ii) In particular, $E(Q_i)$ is monotonously increasing in γ_i and assumes values in $(k-1+eb-2, k-1+eb-1)$. The variance $\mathrm{Var}(Q_i)$ assumes values in $(2, 2.25]$. The maximum value 2.25 is taken on for $\gamma_i = 2/3$. If $2^k = R$ (typical case) then $\gamma_i = 3p_{i*}$.

Proof. see [12], proof of Lemma 2.

Remark 3. (i) Setting $\mathrm{Var}(Q_i) = 0$ and $E(Q_i) = k - 1$ Theorem 1 provides the formulae for non-blinded implementations.
(ii) Numerical experiments verify that (11) approximates $\mathrm{Var}(Q_i)$ very well.

Table 1 evaluates the terms (8), (9), (10) and (11) for exemplary parameter sets.

3.2 Further Arithmetic Operations and Noise

The random variables $Z_1(u)$ and $Z_2(u)$ quantify the random timing behaviour of the for-loop in Algorithm 2 when called in Step 1(c) and Step 2(c) of Algorithm 3, respectively. However, the computation of $(uR^{-1}(\mathrm{mod}\,n))^d(\mathrm{mod}\,n)$ requires several further steps: Step 1(a) and Step 2(a) (reduction modulo p_i), Step 1(b) and Step 2(b) (exponent blinding), Step 1(c) and Step 2(c) (here: pre-multiplication and post-multiplication of Algorithm 2), Step 3 (recombination), time for input and output etc. In analogy to Subsect. 3.1 we view the required overall execution time for these before-mentioned steps as a realization of a random variable $Z_3(u)$.

It seems reasonable to assume that the time for input and output of data, for recombination and blinding as well as the reduction $(\mathrm{mod}\,p_i)$ in Step 1(a) and Step 2(a) of Algorithm 3 do not (or at most weakly) depend on u. The postprocessing step in Algorithm 2 never needs an ER. (By [13], Theorem 1, in Algorithm 1, after Step 3 we have $s \le M + \mathrm{temp} \cdot r^{-v} < M + 1$, and thus $s \le M$. If $s = M$ then $\mathrm{temp} = 0$ after the extra reduction, which can only happen if u is a multiple of $M = p_i$ but then $y_R \equiv uR^{-1}R \equiv 0\,\mathrm{mod}\,p_i$, and Algorithm 2 does not need any extra reduction at all.) In the pre-multiplication in Algorithm 2 an ER may occur or not. Altogether, we may assume

$$E(Z_3(u)) \approx \bar{z}_3 \qquad \text{for all } u \in Z_n \quad \text{and} \tag{12}$$

$$\text{Var}(Z_3(u)) \ll \text{Var}(Z_1(u)), \text{Var}(Z_2(u)) \tag{13}$$

Assumption 3. In the following we assume $E(Z_3(u)) = \bar{z}_3$ for all u and interpret the centered random variable $Z_3(u) - \bar{z}_3$ as part of the noise, which is captured by the random variable N_e. If $\text{Var}(N_e) = \sigma_N^2 > 0$ we assume $N_e \sim N(\mu_N, \sigma_N^2)$ while $\sigma_N^2 = 0$ means 'no noise' and $N_e = \bar{z}_3$ with probability 1.

Remark 4. (Justification of Assumption 3) The part of Assumption 3, which concerns $Z(u)$, follows from the preceding arguments. Measurement errors are usually assumed to be Gaussian distributed, and if the noise comprises of several contributions (of comparable size) the Central Limit Theorem may be used as an additional argument for the assumption of Gaussian noise. However, the core of our attack is a distinguisher, which separates two probability distributions with different mean values. As long as the noise is assumed to be data-independent the distinguisher should work for arbitrary noise distributions (maybe the number of timing measurements varies).

3.3   The Distinguisher

Now we derive a distinguisher, which will be the core of our attack (to be developed in Sect. 4). With regard to the preceding the overall random execution time for input u is described by the random variable

$$Z(u) = Z_1(u) + Z_2(u) + \bar{z}_3 + N_e. \tag{14}$$

In the following we assume

$$0 < u_1 < u_2 < n \qquad \text{and } u_2 - u_1 \ll p_1, p_2. \tag{15}$$

Theorem 1 implies

$$E\left(Z(u_2) - Z(u_1)\right) = E\left(Z_1(u_2) - Z_1(u_1)\right) + E\left(Z_2(u_2) - Z_2(u_1)\right) \tag{16}$$

$$= \frac{1}{2} \sum_{i=1}^{2} E(Q_i) \left(p_{i(u'_{(2)})} - p_{i(u'_{(1)})} \right) c_{\text{ER}} \quad \text{with } u'_{(j)} = u_j (\text{mod } p_i)$$

As in [9] we distinguish between three cases:

Case A: The interval $\{u_1 + 1, \ldots, u_2\}$ does not contain a multiple of p_1 or p_2.
Case B: The interval $\{u_1 + 1, \ldots, u_2\}$ contains a multiple of p_s but not of p_{3-s}.
Case C: The interval $\{u_1 + 1, \ldots, u_2\}$ contains a multiple of p_1 and p_2.

Let's have a closer look at (16). By (4)

$$p_{i(u'_{(2)})} - p_{i(u'_{(1)})} \begin{cases} = \frac{u_2 - u_1}{2R} c_{\text{ER}} \approx 0 & \text{Case A, Case B (for } i \neq s) \\ \approx -\frac{p_i}{2R} c_{\text{ER}} & \text{Case B (for } i = s \text{), Case C} \end{cases} \tag{17}$$

Further,

$$E(Q_i) = k_i + eb - 1 - \gamma_i^{-1} = 2^{\lceil \log_2(p_i) \rceil} + eb - 1 - \frac{2^{k_i}}{p_i}$$

$$= \log_2(R) + (\lceil \log_2(p_i) \rceil - \log_2(R)) + eb - 1 - \frac{R}{p_i} \cdot \frac{2^{k_i}}{R} \tag{18}$$

where $\lceil x \rceil$ denotes the smallest integer $\geq x$. At the beginning of our attack we have no concrete information on the size of the primes p_1 and p_2, and thus we use the rough approximation

$$p_1, p_2 \approx \sqrt{n} \quad \text{and set } \beta := \frac{\sqrt{n}}{R}. \tag{19}$$

With approximation (19) formula (18) simplifies to

$$E(Q_i) \approx \log_2(R) + eb - 1 - \beta^{-1} \quad \text{if } \sqrt{0.5} < \beta < 1, \text{ and similarly} \tag{20}$$
$$\text{Var}(Q_i) \approx 3\beta^{-1} - \beta^{-2} \quad \text{if } \sqrt{0.5} < \beta < 1 \tag{21}$$

since $k_i = \lceil \log_2(p_i) \rceil = \log_2(R)$ then. Finally (17) and (20) imply

$$E\left(Z(u_2) - Z(u_1)\right) \approx \begin{cases} 0 & \text{in Case A} \\ -\frac{1}{4}\left((\log_2(R) + eb - 1)\beta - 1\right)c_{\text{ER}} & \text{in Case B} \\ -\frac{1}{2}\left((\log_2(R) + eb - 1)\beta - 1\right)c_{\text{ER}} & \text{in Case C} \end{cases} \tag{22}$$

In the following we focus on the case $\sqrt{0.5} < \beta < 1$, which is the most relevant case since then $0.5R^2 < n < R^2$, i.e. n is a $2\log_2(R)$ bit modulus and, consequently, p_1 and p_2 are $\log_2(R)$-bit numbers. We point out that the case $\beta < \sqrt{0.5}$ can be treated analogously. In (20) and (21) the parameter β_i^{-1} then should be better replaced by $\beta_i^{-1} 2^{\lceil \log_2(p_i) \rceil - \log_2(R)}$. However, the 'correction factor' may not be unambiguous, which might lead to some inaccuracy in the formulae, finally implying a slight loss of attack efficiency.

From (14) we obtain

$$\text{Var}\left(Z(u_2) - Z(u_1)\right) = \sum_{j=1}^{2}\left(\sum_{i=1}^{2} \text{Var}\left(Z_i(u_j)\right) + \text{Var}(N_{c,j})\right) \tag{23}$$

For given $R, eb, c, c_{\text{ER}}, u$ the variance $\text{Var}(Z_i(u))$ is nearly independent of p_i/R and increases somewhat when the ratio u/p_i increases (see Table 1). Since the true values p_1/R and p_2/R are unknown during the attack we approximate (23) by

$$\text{Var}\left(Z(u_2) - Z(u_1)\right) \approx 4\text{var}_{\beta;max} + 2\sigma_N^2 \tag{24}$$

Here 'var$_{\beta;max}$' suggestively stands for the term (9) with βR in place of p_i and u', i.e. we replace the probabilities p_{i*} and $p_{i(u')}$ by $\beta/3$ and $\beta/2$, respectively. We point out that variance (23) has no direct influence on the decision strategy of our attack but determines the required sample size. Usually, (24) should overestimate (23) somewhat. Moreover, decision errors can be detected and corrected (cf. Section 4, 'confirmed intervals'). So we should be on the safe side anyway. For fixed p_i the mean $E(Z_i(u))$ increases monotonically in u/p_i (see (8)). In fact, our attack exploits these differences.

On basis of execution times for input values (bases) $y = u_i R^{-1} (\text{mod } n)$ ($i = 1, 2$) the attacker has to decide for hundreds of intervals $\{u_1 + 1, \ldots, u_2\}$ whether they contain p_1 or p_2. By (22) the value

$$\text{decbound} := -\frac{1}{8}((\log_2(\text{R}) + \text{eb} - 1)\beta - 1)\, c_{\text{ER}} \tag{25}$$

is a natural decision boundary. In fact, for given $u_1 < u_2$ and $y_i :=$ $(u_i R^{-1}(\text{mod}\, n))$ this suggests the following decision rule:

Decide for Case A iff $(\text{Time}(y_2^d(\text{mod}\, n)) - \text{Time}(y_1^d(\text{mod}\, n)) > \text{decbound})$,

and for (Case B or Case C) else. $\tag{26}$

(Note that we do not need to distinguish between Case B and Case C.) Here $\text{Time}(y_i^d(\text{mod}\, n))$ denotes the execution time for input value y_i, which of course depends on the blinding factors for the modular exponentiation $(\text{mod}\, p_1)$ and $(\text{mod}\, p_2)$. However, since the variance $\text{Var}(Z(u_2) - Z(u_1))$ is too large for reliable decisions we consider N iid random variables $Z_{[1]}(u), \ldots, Z_{[N]}(u)$ in place of $Z(u)$, which are distributed as $Z(u)$ (corresponding to N exponentiations with input value $y = uR^{-1}(\text{mod}\, n)$). Unlike for decision strategy (26) we evaluate the average timing difference from N pairs of timing measurements (see Sect. 4). For N_τ the inequality

$$\sqrt{\text{Var}\left(\frac{1}{N_\tau}\sum_{j=1}^{N_\tau}\left(Z_{[j]}(u_2) - Z_{[j]}(u_1)\right)\right)} \approx \sqrt{\frac{4\text{var}_{\beta;max} + 2\sigma_N^2}{N_\tau}}$$

$$\leq \frac{|\text{decbound} - 0|}{\tau} \quad \text{implies}$$

$$N_\tau \geq \frac{\tau^2(4\text{var}_{\beta;max} + 2\sigma_N^2)}{|\text{decbound}|^2} = \frac{64\tau^2(4\text{var}_{\beta;max} + 2\sigma_N^2)}{\left((\log_2(R) + eb - 1)\beta - 1\right)^2 c_{\text{ER}}^2}. \tag{27}$$

Applying the above decision strategy (26) to $N \geq N_\tau$ pairs of timing differences the Central Limit Theorem then implies

$$\text{Prob}(\text{wrong decision}) \leq \Phi(-\tau). \tag{28}$$

Table 2 evaluates (27) for several parameter sets with $\sigma_N^2 = 0$. If $\sigma_N^2 = \alpha \cdot (2\text{var}_{\beta;max})$ the sample size N_τ increases by factor $(1 + \alpha)$.

At the end of Phase 1 our attack algorithm from Sect. 4 has found u_1 and u_2 with $p_i \in \{u_1 + 1, \ldots, u_2\}$ for $i = 1$ or $i = 2$. Thus in Phase 2 we may replace β by the more precise estimate $\beta_{(2)} := (u_1 + u_2)/(2R)$, which may be substituted into the formulae (20) to (27). In particular, we obtain a new decision boundary

$$decbound_{\text{II}} := -\frac{1}{8}((\log_2(R) + eb - 1)\beta_{(2)} - 1)\, c_{\text{ER}}, \tag{29}$$

which should be 'better' centered between the mean values $E(Z(u_2) - E(u_1))$ for Case A and for Case B than decbound.

Table 2. Exemplary sample sizes N_τ for several parameter sets for $\sigma_N^2 = 0$ (no noise). Note that $\Phi(-2.5) = 0.0062$ and $\Phi(-2.7) = 0.0035$. Larger τ reduces the error probability for each decision but increases the sample size N_τ.

$\log_2(R)$	eb	c_{ER}	$\beta = \frac{\sqrt{n}}{R}$	$N_{2.5}$	$N_{2.7}$	$\beta = \frac{\sqrt{n}}{R}$	$N_{2.5}$	$N_{2.7}$
512	64	$0.03\,c$	0.75	1458	1701	0.85	1137	1326
512	64	$0.05\,c$	0.75	533	622	0.85	417	486
1024	64	$0.03\,c$	0.75	758	885	0.85	592	690
1024	64	$0.05\,c$	0.75	277	324	0.85	217	253

4 The Attack

In this section we describe and analyse the attack algorithm. Two improvements increase its efficiency compared to [12]. We provide experimental results and adjust our attack to table-based exponentiation algorithms. Effective countermeasures are proposed. Amazingly, the attack algorithm and its underlying ideas are rather similar to the attack on unprotected implementations.

4.1 The Attack Algorithm

To simplify notation we introduce the abbreviation

$$\mathrm{MeanTime}(u, N) := \frac{1}{N} \sum_{j=1}^{N} \mathrm{Time}(y_j^d (\mathrm{mod}\, n)) \quad \text{with } y_j := uR^{-1}(\mathrm{mod}\, n) \quad (30)$$

That is, $\mathrm{MeanTime}(u, N)$ denotes the average time of N modular exponentiations $y^d(\mathrm{mod}\, n)$ with basis $y = uR^{-1}(\mathrm{mod}\, n)$. The sample size N is selected with regard to the results from Subsect. 3.3. In our simulation experiments we used $N_{2.5}$. The attack falls into three phases. The goal of Phase 1 is to find an interval $\{u_1 + 1, \ldots, u_2\}$, which contains p_1 or p_2. In Phase 2 this interval is successively bisected into two halves where that halve is maintained, which is assumed to contain p_i. Phase 2 ends when the attacker knows the upper half plus few bits of the binary representation of p_i, and in Phase 3 the prime p_i is computed with Coppersmith's algorithm, which transfers the search for p_i into a lattice problem [4]. With regard to Phase 3 one should take care that in Phase 1 and Phase 2 indeed p_1 or p_2 are targeted and not just an integer multiple thereof. If the most relevant case where $p_i > 0.5R$ (definitely fulfilled if $\beta = \sqrt{n}/R > \sqrt{0.5}$) the interval $[\beta R, R]$ contains p_1 or p_2 but no multiple. The following attack may require a pre-step in which the timing parameters c and c_{ER} are estimated (see Remark 1).

The Attack.

Phase 1
    Select an integer u somewhat smaller than βR, set (e.g.) $\Delta := 2^{-6}R$

$u_1 := u, u_2 := u_1 + \Delta$
while $(\text{MeanTime}(u_2, N) - \text{MeanTime}(u_1, N) > \text{decbound})$ do*{
    $u_1 := u_2, u_2 := u_2 + \Delta$
}

Phase 2

while $(\log_2(u_2 - u_1) > 0.5 \log_2(R) - 10)$ do {
    $u_3 := \lfloor (u_1 + u_2)/2 \rfloor$
    if$(\text{MeanTime}(u_2, N) - \text{MeanTime}(u_3, N) > \text{decbound}_{\text{II}})$ then $u_2 := u_3^*$
    else $u_1 := u_3^{**}$}

Phase 3

Apply Coppersmiths algorithm to determine p_i
* The attacker believes that Case A is correct
** The attacker believes that Case B or Case C is correct

After Phase 2 the upper $\approx 0.5 \log_2(p_i) + 10$ bits of u_1 and u_2 coincide, which yields $\approx 0.5 \log_2(p_i) + 10$ bits of p_i. That is, $p_i = \widetilde{p}_i + x_0$ with known $\widetilde{p}_i$ and unknown x_0 and $\log_2(x_0) \approx 0.5 \log_2(R) - 10$. The division $n/\widetilde{p}_i$ yields an analogous decomposition $p_{3-i} = \widetilde{p}_{3-i} + y_0$. Altogether, we obtain a bivariate polynomial equation

$$f(x, y) := (\widetilde{p}_i + x)(\widetilde{p}_{3-i} + y) - n = p_1 p_2 - n = 0, \tag{31}$$

for which (x_0, y_0) is a 'small' solution. Reference [4] transfers the problem into a shortest vector problem, which can be solved with the LLL algorithm. This requires that $\log_2(x_0), \log_2(y_0) < 0.25 \log_2(n)$. In Phase 2 we determine ≈ 10 bits more than the upper halve of the bits of p_i to speed up the execution time of the LLL algorithm. We did not solve the lattice problem in our experiments. We counted an attack successful if after Phase 2 p_1 or p_2 was contained in the final interval $\{u_1 + 1, \ldots, u_2\}$.

Of course, if after the end of Phase 2 $\{u_1 + 1, \ldots, u_2\}$ does not contain p_1 or p_2 in Phase 3 the modulus n cannot be factored and thus the attack fails. This means that all decisions until the end of Phase 2 must be correct. For 1024 bit primes, for instance, the algorithm requires about 550 individual decisions. Fortunately, it is very easy to check whether an intermediate interval $\{u_1 + 1, \ldots, u_2\}$ indeed contains a prime (cf. [9], Sect. 5).

Confirmed Intervals. (i) Assume that after Phase 1 or during Phase 2 the attack algorithm has determined an interval $\{u_1 + 1, \ldots, u_2\}$. To check whether this interval indeed contains p_1 or p_2 one may perform $2N$ new timing measurements, compute $\text{MeanTime}(u_2, N) - \text{MeanTime}(u_1, N)$ and apply the above decision rule. If the time difference is $< decbound_{\text{II}}$ we are convinced that $\{u_1 + 1, \ldots, u_2\}$ contains p_1 or p_2, and we call $\{u_1 + 1, \ldots, u_2\}$ a 'confirmed interval'. If not, we repeat the test with $2N$ new timing measurements: in case of '$< decbound_{\text{II}}$' we believe that the first test result has been false, and $\{u_1 + 1, \ldots, u_2\}$ is the new confirmed interval. If again '$> decbound_{\text{II}}$' we believe that an earlier decision was wrong and restart the attack at the preceding confirmed interval. Confirmed intervals should be established after con decisions. The value con

should be selected with regard to the probability for a wrong individual decision. The first confirmed interval should be established at the end of Phase 1.

(ii) Of course, an erroneously confirmed interval will let the attack fail. This probability can be reduced e.g. by applying a 'majority of three' decision rule where the 'original' interval $\{u_1+1, \ldots, u_2\}$ (determined by our attack algorithm) unlike in (i) does not count. Alternatively, the algorithm might jump back to the last but one confirmed interval if the preceding confirmed interval turns out to be wrong with high probability.

Improvements Compared to [12]. Compared to [12] the attack algorithm features two improvements: First of all, it aims at the larger prime, which increases the difference $E(Z(u_2)) - E(Z(u_1))$ for Case B and Case C, and in Phase 2 it applies the readjusted decision boundary (29) in place of (25). A comparision between the simulation results in Table 3 with those in Table 3 in [12] shows that these improvements reduce the average number of timing measurements significantly. Additional options to further increase the attack efficiency might be to optimize the selection of con in dependence of τ and to apply sequential analysis as in [1].

Remark 5. [Scaling] We assume $eb \ll \log_2(R)$ (typical case).

(i) By (25), (29) and (9) doubling the length of the prime factors p_1 and p_2 roughly doubles decbound, decbound$_{II}$ and var$_{\beta;max}$. If $\sigma_N^2 \approx 0$ by (27) N_τ decreases to approximately 50 %. On the other hand, the attack needs about twice as many individual decisions. This points to the surprising fact that the overall number of timing measurements per attack is to a large extent independent of the modulus length if $\sigma_N^2 \approx 0$.

(ii) Similarly, halving c_{ER} halves decbound and decbound$_{II}$ but leaves var$_{\beta;max}$ nearly unchanged. If $\sigma_N^2 \approx 0$ by (27) the attack then requires about 4 times as many timing measurements. The decision boundaries depend linearly on c_{ER} (25). For realistic ratios c_{ER}/c in (9) the $E(Q_i)(\ldots)$-term, and within the bracket the first summand dominates. Consequently, (27) implies that the number of timing measurements increases roughly like $(c_{ER}/c)^{-2}$.

Remark 6. As its predecessors in [1,3,9] our attack and its variants for table-based exponentiation algorithms (Subsect. 4.3) are adaptive chosen input attacks. We point out that our attack would also work for input values $(u+x)R^{-1}(\mathrm{mod}\,n)$ with $|x| \ll n^{1/4}$ in place of the input values $uR^{-1}(\mathrm{mod}\,n)$. This property allows to meet possible minor restrictions on the input values (e.g. some set bits), which might be demanded by the targeted RSA application.

4.2 Experimental Results

In this subsection we present experimental results. As already mentioned in Sect. 2 it only depends on the quadruple (a, b, M, R) but not on any features of the implementation whether $\mathrm{MM}(a, b; M)$ requires an extra reduction. This property allows to simulate the modular exponentiations $y^d(\mathrm{mod}\,n)$ and to count the number of extra reductions, which finally corresponds to an attack under perfect timing measurements and with $E(Z_3(u)) = \bar{z}_3$, $\mathrm{Var}(Z_3(u)) = 0$, i.e. $Z_3(u) \equiv z_3$ for all $0 < u < n$, which is an idealization of (12) and (13). Consequently, also in the absence of noise in real-life experiments the number of timing measurements thus should be somewhat larger than for our simulation experiments. The impact of noise was quantified in Subsect. 3.3.

In our experiments we selected the primes p_1 and p_2 pseudorandomly. The table entry $p_i/R = 0.75$, for instance, means that p_i has been selected pseudorandomly in the interval $[0.75 - 0.025, 0.75 + 0.025]R$. The secret exponent d was computed according to the public exponent $e = 2^{16} + 1$. Table 3 provides experimental results for several sets of parameters. In our experiments we assumed $\sigma_N^2 = 0$. We calculated N_τ with formula (27) (in Phase 2 with decbound$_\mathrm{II}$), which also allows to extrapolate the number of timing measurements for any noise level. Table 3 confirms the considerations from Remark 5. Several experiments with $p_1/R \approx p_2/R$ were conducted, which verify that the attack becomes the more efficient the larger these ratios are. The reason is that $|\mathrm{decbound}|$ and $|\mathrm{decbound}_\mathrm{II}|$ depend almost linearly on β while $\mathrm{var}_{\beta;max}$ remains essentially unchanged. To save computation time many experiments were conducted for 512-bit primes and ratio $c_\mathrm{ER}/c \approx 0.05$, which may seem to be relatively large for real-world applications. Remark 5 allows the extrapolation of the simulation results to smaller ratios c_ER/c and to other modulus lengths.

The number of timing measurements, which are required for a successful attack, has non-negligible variance. The reason is that if an error has been detected the algorithm steps back to the preceding confirmed interval. We established confirmed intervals after the end of Phase 1, after the end of Phase 2 and regularly after $con = 40$ decisions. For fixed value con a larger τ increases the success rate of the attack but also the number of timing measurements per individual decision.

4.3   Table-Based Exponentiation Algorithms

The timing attack against unprotected implementations can be adjusted to table-based exponentiation algorithms [1,3,9]. This is also possible in case of exponent blinding.

We first consider the fixed-window exponentiation ([7], 14.82), which is combined with Montgomery's exponentiation algorithm. The window size is $b > 1$. In Step i(c) of Algorithm 3 (exponentiation modulo p_i) for basis $y = uR^{-1}(\mathrm{mod}\,p_i)$ the following precomputations are carried out:

$$y_{0,i} = R(\mathrm{mod}\,p_i), y_{1,i} = \mathrm{MM}(y, R^2(\mathrm{mod}\,p_i), p_i) = u(\mathrm{mod}\,p_i), \quad \text{and}$$

$$y_{j,i} := \mathrm{MM}(y_{j-1,i}, y_{1,i}, p_i) \quad \text{for } j = 2, \dots, 2^b - 1. \tag{32}$$

The exponentiation modulo p_i requires $(2^b - 3) + (\log_2(R) + ebr)/(b2^b)$ Montgomery multiplications by $y_{1,i}$ in average (table initialization + exponentiation phase; the computation of $y_{2,i}$ is actually a squaring operation). The attack tries to exploit these Montgomery multiplications modulo p_1 or p_2, respectively.

Table 3. Simulated attack: experimental results. The average numbers of exponentiations (rounded to thousands) refer to the successful attacks. As explained above the primes have been selected pseudorandomly within small intervals around the values in the fourth and fifth column.

$\log_2(R)$	eb	c_{ER}	$\frac{p_1}{R}$	$\frac{p_2}{R}$	τ	success rate	av.#exponentiations
512	64	$0.02\,c$	0.75	0.85	2.5	24/25	$830,000$
512	64	$0.025\,c$	0.75	0.85	2.5	24/25	$541,000$
512	64	$0.03\,c$	0.75	0.85	2.5	24/25	$395,000$
512	64	$0.05\,c$	0.75	0.85	2.5	25/25	$140,000$
512	64	$0.05\,c$	0.70	0.70	2.5	24/25	$203,000$
512	64	$0.05\,c$	0.80	0.80	2.5	24/25	$141,000$
512	64	$0.05\,c$	0.85	0.85	2.5	25/25	$140,000$
512	64	$0.05\,c$	0.90	0.90	2.5	23/25	$127,000$
768	64	$0.03\,c$	0.75	0.85	2.5	23/25	$382,000$
768	64	$0.05\,c$	0.75	0.85	2.5	23/25	$139,000$
1024	64	$0.025\,c$	0.75	0.85	2.5	24/25	$590,000$
1024	64	$0.03\,c$	0.75	0.85	2.5	24/25	$410,000$
1024	64	$0.05\,c$	0.75	0.85	2.5	24/25	$152,000$

Compared to the s&m exponentiation algorithm the attack efficiency decreases significantly since the percentage of 'useful' operations (here: the multiplications by y_1) shrinks tremendously. The Montgomery multiplications by $y_{1,i}$ are responsible for the mean timing difference between Case A and (Case B or Case C). In analogy to (25) for $\sqrt{0.5} < \beta < 1$ we conclude

$$decbound_b = -\frac{1}{2}\left(\frac{E(Q)}{b2^b} + 2^b - 3\right)\frac{\sqrt{n}}{2R}\,c_{\mathrm{ER}} \tag{33}$$

$$= -\frac{1}{4}\left(\frac{(\log_2(R) + eb - 1)\beta - 1}{b2^b} + (2^b - 3)\beta\right)c_{\mathrm{ER}}.$$

The computation of $\mathrm{Var}_b(Z_i(u))$ may be organized as in the s&m case. We do not carry out these lengthy calculations in the following but derive an approximation (34), which suffices for our purposes. We yet give some advice how to organize an exact calculation. First of all, the table initialisation modulo p_i costs an additional squaring. In average, there are $E(Q)/b2^b + 2^b - 3$ multiplications by $y_{i,1}$ (responsible for exploitable timing differences), $E(Q)/b2^b$ multiplications by $y_{i,0}$ (do not need extra reductions) and altogether $(2^b - 2)E(Q)/b2^b$ multiplications by some $y_{i,j}$ with $j > 1$. When computing the second moment additionally to the s&m case the covarianc $\mathrm{cov}_{i,\mathrm{MM}(u_i')}$ $(2^b - 4$ times, table initialization) occur. The term $\mathrm{cov}_{i,\mathrm{MM}(u_i')}$ is defined and calculated analogously to $\mathrm{cov}_{i,\mathrm{SM}(u_i')}, \mathrm{cov}_{i,\mathrm{MS}(u_i')}$ and $\mathrm{cov}_{i,\mathrm{SS}}$.

To assess the efficiency of our timing attack on b-bit fixed window exponentiation we estimate the ratio of the variances $\mathrm{Var}_b(Z_i(u))$ and $\mathrm{Var}(Z_i(u))$ (s&m case). Therefore, we simply count the number of Montgomery operations in both cases (neglecting the different ratios between squarings and multiplications). This gives the rough estimate

$$\frac{\text{Var}_b(Z_i(u))}{\text{Var}(Z_i(u))} \approx \frac{E(Q) + E(Q)/b + 2^b}{E(Q) + 0.5E(Q)} = \frac{2(b+1)}{3b} + \frac{2^{b+1}}{3E(Q)} =: f_1(b). \tag{34}$$

Finally, we obtain a pendant to (27)

$$N_{\tau,b} \geq \frac{\tau^2(4\text{var}_{\beta;max_b} + 2\sigma_N^2)}{|\text{decbound}_b|^2} \approx \frac{\tau^2(4\text{var}_{\beta;max}f_1(b) + 2\sigma_N^2)}{|\text{decbound}|^2 f_2^2(b)} \tag{35}$$

with $f_2(b) := |\text{decbound}_b/\text{decbound}|$. In particular, if $\sigma_N^2 \approx 0$ then

$$N_{\tau,b} \approx N_\tau \frac{f_1(b)}{f_2^2(b)}. \tag{36}$$

Remark 7. In analogy to (29) after Phase 1 decbound$_b$ may be adjusted to decbound$_{b,\text{II}}$. Replacing decbound$_b$ and decbound by decbound$_{b,\text{II}}$ and decbound$_\text{II}$ should not significantly change $f_2(b)$ and $N_{\tau,b}$. The sliding window exponentiation below allows analogous considerations.

For b-bit sliding window exponentiation the table initialization the comprises the following operations:

$$y_{1,i} = \text{MM}(y, R^2(\text{mod } p_i), p_i), y_{2,i} := \text{MM}(y_{1,i}, y_{1,i}, p_i) \quad \text{and}$$
$$y_{2j+1,i} := \text{MM}(y_{2j-1,i}, y_{2,i}, p_i) \quad \text{for } j = 1, \ldots, 2^{b-1} - 1. \tag{37}$$

In the exponentiation phase the exponent bits are scanned from the left to the right. In the following we derive an estimate for the number of multiplications by the table entries within an exponentiation (mod p_i). Assume that the last window either 'ended' at exponent bit $d_{i,b;j}$ or already at $d_{i,b;j+t'}$, followed by exponent bits $d_{i,b;j+t'-1} = \cdots = d_{i,b;j} = 0$. Let $d_{i,b;j-t}$ denote the next bit that equals 1. We may assume that t is geometrically distributed with parameter $1/2$. The next window 'ends' with exponent bit $d_{i,b;j-t}$ iff $d_{i,b;j-t-1} = \cdots = d_{i,b;j-t-(b-1)} = 0$. In this case table entry $y_{1,i}$ is applied, and this multiplication is followed by $(b-1)$ squarings that correspond to the exponent bits $d_{i,b;j-t-1}, \ldots, d_{i,b;j-t-(b-1)}$. Alternatively, the next window might end with exponent bit $d_{i,b;j-t-2}$ (resp. with exponent bit $d_{i,b;j-t-3}, \ldots, d_{i,b;j-t-(b-1)}$) iff $d_{i,b;j-t-2} = 1$, $d_{i,b;j-t-3} = \cdots = d_{i,b;j-t-(b-1)} = 0$ (resp. iff $d_{i,b;j-t-3} = 1$, $d_{i,b;j-t-4} = \cdots = d_{i,b;j-t-(b-1)} = 0, \ldots$, iff $d_{i,b;j-t-(b-1)} = 1$). Of course, if the window ends before exponent bit $d_{i,b;j-t-(b-1)}$ it is followed by some squarings. Altogether, the exponent bits $d_{i,b;j-1}, \ldots, d_{i,b;j-t-(b-1)}$ need one multiplication by some table entry. Neglecting boundary effects one concludes that sliding window exponentiation requires one multiplication by a table entry per

$$\sum_{s=1}^{\infty} s2^{-s} + (b-1) = 2 + b - 1 = b + 1 \tag{38}$$

exponent bits in average. This gives the pendant to (34):

$$\frac{\text{Var}_{b,sw}(Z_i(u))}{\text{Var}(Z_i(u))} \approx \frac{\left(1 + \frac{1}{b+1}\right) E(Q) + 2^{b-1} + 1}{E(Q) + 0.5E(Q)}$$

$$= \frac{2(b+2)}{3(b+1)} + \frac{2^b + 2}{3E(Q)} =: f_{1,sw}(b). \qquad (39)$$

where the subscript 'sw' stands for 'sliding window'. Since there is a bijection between the table entries and the $(b-1)$ exponent bits $(d_{i,b;j-t-1} \cdots, d_{i,b;j-t-b+1})$ all table entries are equally likely. For many parameter sets $(\log_2(R) + eb, b)$ the table entry $y_{1,i}$ occurs less often than $y_{2,i}$, which is carried out $2^{b-1} - 1$ times within the table initialization. (Numerical example: For $(\log_2(R) + eb, b) = (1024 + 64, 5)$ in average $E(Q)/(16(5+1)) \approx 11.3 < 15$ multiplications with table entry $y_{1,i}$ occur.) Then, as in [1] our attack then focuses on the Montgomery multiplications by $y_{2,i}$. In particular, we then obtain the decision boundary

$$decbound_{b,sw} = -\frac{1}{2}\left(2^{b-1} - 1\right)\frac{\sqrt{n}}{2R}c_{\text{ER}} = -\frac{1}{4}\left(2^{b-1} - 1\right)\beta\, c_{\text{ER}} \qquad (40)$$

(Of course, if $2^{-(b-1)}E(Q_i)/(b+1) > 2^{b-1} - 1$ then in (40) the term $(2^{b-1} - 1)$ should be replaced by $2^{-(b-1)}E(Q_i)/(b+1)$, and the attack should focus on the multiplications by table value $y_{i,1}$.) Setting

$$f_{2,sw}(b) := |decbound_{b,sw}|/decbound| \qquad (41)$$

we obtain an analogous formula to (36):

$$N_{\tau,b,sw} \approx N_\tau \frac{f_{1,sw}(b)}{f_{2,sw}^2(b)}. \qquad (42)$$

Example 1. $\log_2(R) = 1024$ (i.e., 2048-bit RSA), $eb = 64$, $\beta = 0.8$, and $\sigma_N^2 \approx 0$.
(i) $[b = 6]$ For fixed window exponentiation $N_{\tau,b} \approx 59N_\tau$, i.e. the overall attack costs ≈ 59 times the number of timing measurements for s&m. For sliding window exponentiation we obtain $N_{\tau,b,sw} \approx 240N_\tau$. We applied formula (21) to estimate $E(Q_i)$.
(ii) $[b = 5]$ $N_{\tau,b} \approx 189N_\tau$, $N_{\tau,b,sw} \approx 1032N_\tau$.
(iii) $[b = 4]$ $N_{\tau,b} \approx 277N_\tau$, $N_{\tau,b,sw} \approx 322N_\tau$.
(iv) $[b = 3]$ $N_{\tau,b} \approx 104N_\tau$, $N_{\tau,b,sw} \approx 54N_\tau$.
(v) $[b = 2]$ $N_{\tau,b} \approx 16N_\tau$, $N_{\tau,b,sw} \approx 8N_\tau$.
Note: For $b = 2, 3, 4$ the timing attack on sliding window exponentiation aims at the multiplications by $y_{i,1}$, for $b = 5, 6$ on the multiplications by $y_{2,i}$ during the table initialization. For $b = 4, 5, 6$ the attack on fixed window exponentiation is more efficient than the attack on sliding window exponentiation while for $b = 2, 3$ the converse is true.

It is hardly possible to define a clear-cut lower bound for the number of timing measurements from which on the attack should be viewed impractical. The maximum number of available timing measurements clearly depends on the concrete attack scenario. Cryptographic software on PCs and servers usually applies a large table size b, and the timing measurements are often to some degree noisy. Example 1 shows that for large window size b and realistic ratios c_{ER}/c the attack requires a gigantic number of timing measurements, all the more in the presence of non-negligible noise. Example 1 provides these numbers relative to the square & multiply case. The absolute numbers of timing measurements depend on the ratios c_{ER}/c and p_i/R and on the level of noise (cf. Remark 5(ii), Subsects. 4.2 and 3.3).

4.4 Countermeasures

The most solid countermeasure is to avoid extra reductions entirely. In fact, one may resign on the extra reductions within modular exponentiation if $R > 4p_i$ ([13], Theorem 3 and Theorem 6). This solution (resigning on extra reductions) was selected for OpenSSL as response on the instruction cache attack described in [2]. We point out that the present attack could also be prevented by combining exponent blinding with base blinding ([6], Sect. 10), for example, which in particular would also prevent the attack from [2]. However, the first option is clearly preferable as it prevents any type of timing attack.

5 Conclusion

It has widely been assumed that exclusive exponent blinding would prevent timing attacks. This paper shows that this assumption is not generally true (although exponent blinding reduces the efficiency of our timing attack significantly). In the presence of little or moderate noise our attack is a practical threat against square & multiply exponentiation and should be considered (see also Remark 6). Our attack can also be applied to fixed window exponentiation and to sliding window exponentiation. However, for large window size b the attack requires a very large number of timing measurements. The attack may be practically infeasible then, in particular for small ratios c_{ER}/c or in the presence of non-negligible noise. Fortunately, effective countermeasures exist.

References

1. Acıiçmez, O., Schindler, W., Koç, Ç.K.: Improving brumley and boneh timing attack on unprotected SSL implementations. In: Meadows, C., Syverson, P. (eds.) 12th ACM Conference on Computer and Communications Security – CCS 2005, pp. 139–146. ACM Press, New York (2005)
2. Acıiçmez, O., Schindler, W.: A vulnerability in RSA implementations due to instruction cache analysis and its demonstration on openSSL. In: Malkin, T. (ed.) CT-RSA 2008. LNCS, vol. 4964, pp. 256–273. Springer, Heidelberg (2008)

3. Brumley, D., Boneh, D.: Remote timing attacks are practical. In: Proceedings of the 12th Usenix Security Symposium (2003)
4. Coppersmith, D.: Small solutions to polynomial equations, and low exponent RSA vulnerabilities. J. Cryptology **10**, 233–260 (1997)
5. Dhem, J.-F., Koeune, F., Leroux, P.-A., Mestré, P.-A., Quisquater, J.-J., Willems, J.-L.: A practical implementation of the timing attack. In: Quisquater, J.-J., Schneier, B. (eds.) Smart Card - Research and Applications, LNCS, pp. 175–191. Springer, Berlin (2000)
6. Kocher, P.C.: Timing attacks on implementations of diffie-hellman, RSA, DSS, and other systems. In: Koblitz, N. (ed.) CRYPTO 1996. LNCS, vol. 1109, pp. 104–113. Springer, Heidelberg (1996)
7. Menezes, A.J., van Oorschot, P.C., Vanstone, S.C.: Handbook of Applied Cryptography. CRC Press, Boca Raton (1997)
8. Montgomery, P.L.: Modular multiplication without trial division. Math. Comp. **44**, 519–521 (1985)
9. Schindler, W.: A timing attack against RSA with the chinese remainder theorem. In: Paar, C., Koç, Ç.K. (eds.) CHES 2000. LNCS, vol. 1965, pp. 110–125. Springer, Heidelberg (2000)
10. Schindler, W., Koeune, F., Quisquater, J.-J.: Improving divide and conquer attacks against cryptosystems by better error detection / correction strategies. In: Honary, B. (ed.) Cryptography and Coding 2001. LNCS, vol. 2260, pp. 245–267. Springer, Heidelberg (2001)
11. Schindler, W.: Optimized timing attacks against public key cryptosystems. Statist. Decisions **20**, 191–210 (2002)
12. Schindler, W.: Exponent blinding may not prevent timing attacks on RSA. Cryptology ePrint Archive, Report 2014/869, Version 20141022:205703 (2014). https:// eprint.iacr.org/2014/869
13. Walter, C.D.: Precise bounds for montgomery modular multiplication and some potentially insecure RSA moduli. In: Preneel, B. (ed.) CT-RSA 2002. LNCS, vol. 2271, pp. 30–39. Springer, Heidelberg (2002)

Who Watches the Watchmen?: Utilizing Performance Monitors for Compromising Keys of RSA on Intel Platforms

Sarani Bhattacharya$^{(\boxtimes)}$ and Debdeep Mukhopadhyay

Department of Computer Science and Engineering,
Indian Institute of Technology Kharagpur, Kharagpur 721302, India
{sarani.bhattacharya,debdeep}@cse.iitkgp.ernet.in

Abstract. Asymmetric-key cryptographic algorithms when implemented on systems with branch predictors, are subjected to side-channel attacks exploiting the deterministic branch predictor behavior due to their key-dependent input sequences. We show that branch predictors can also leak information through the hardware performance monitors which are accessible by an adversary at the user-privilege level. This paper presents an iterative attack which target the key-bits of 1024 bit RSA, where in offline phase, the system's underlying branch predictor is approximated by a theoretical predictor in literature. Subsimulations are performed to classify the message-space into distinct partitions based on the event branch misprediction and the target key bit value. In online phase, we ascertain the secret key bit using branch mispredictions obtained from the hardware performance monitors which reflect the behavior of the underlying predictor hardware. We theoretically prove that the probability of success is equivalent to the accurate modelling of the theoretical predictor to the underlying system predictor. Experimentations reveal that the success-rate increases with message-count and reaches such a significant value so as to consider side-channel from the performance counters as a real threat to RSA-like ciphers due to the underlying branch predictors and needs to be considered for developing secured-systems.

Keywords: Branch misprediction · HPC · Public-key cipher · Side-channel

1 Introduction

Micro-architectural features leave footprints in the processor which is often captured by side-channels. Side-channel attacks allow malicious user to gain access to sensitive data of the system under attack by monitoring power consumption, timing, or electro-magnetic radiation of the microprocessor. In recent microprocessors, various architectural components are incorporated in the system to improve the system performance and these are emerging as new sources of side-channel leakage.

© International Association for Cryptologic Research 2015
T. Güneysu and H. Handschuh (Eds.): CHES 2015, LNCS 9293, pp. 248–266, 2015.
DOI: 10.1007/978-3-662-48324-4_13

In the pioneering work in [7] it was first shown that the time to process different inputs can be used as a side-channel information to find the exponent bits of the secret keys for RSA, Diffie-Hellman, DSS etc. In [1], the penalty for mispredicted branches in number of clock cycles is observed as side-channel to identify the data dependent operations of the public-key cryptosystem. On a standard RSA implementation, four different types of attacks were performed exploiting the Branch Prediction Unit (BPU) by using both synchronous and asynchronous techniques. Using timing as the side-channel in [1], the misprediction information is modeled to identify the secret key. While in the synchronous and asynchronous attacks the Branch Target Buffer (BTB) is modified by the attacker to surface the attack.

Hardware performance counters (HPCs) are a set of special-purpose registers to store the counts of hardware-related activities within the microprocessor. These counters contain rich source of information of the internal activities of the processor and hence can find usage for both attacks and their countermeasures. In [11,12], these HPCs are exploited as side-channels for time based cache attacks. HPC L1 and L2 D-cache miss counters have been exploited as side-channels in [12] for performing timing based cache attacks on symmetric-key algorithms, like AES. While the paper shows that the HPCs can be used as potential source of leakage, the attacks were sensitive to noise introduced through loops, branches and also compiler optimizations to retain the tables. In this paper, we show that asymmetric ciphers like RSA, which does not have tables and have several branches and due to the underlying algorithm and the internal multipliers used, can be successfully attacked by monitoring the event branch miss through HPCs.

In this attack, we target the branch-predictors which were previously shown to lead to attacks using timing as side-channel [1]. Several research work has been developed to thwart these attacks by fuzzying the timestamp counters, adding noise etc. However, we show that powerful side-channels may still exist through the HPCs which monitor the branch misses at the user-privilege. Interestingly, we show through real experiments that though the underlying branch predictors are unknown, the attacker can approximate them by theoretical models which correlate well with the actual statistics of branch misses. Using these approximations, one can launch an attack and successfully recover a full 1024-bits key of RSA algorithm implemented with key bit dependent conditional operations. The modular exponentiation of RSA has been implemented using both naïve square and multiply and Montgomery ladder, while the underlying multiplication and squaring has been implemented using Montgomery's method. The attack iteratively recovers the key bits and has two distinct phases:

- An offline phase, during which the system branch predictor is approximated by a theoretical model (namely, two-bit, two-level adaptive predictor) and is used to classify the message space into distinct partitions based on the event of branch misprediction and assuming the value of the ith key bit.
- In the online phase, we perform the actual attack to ascertain the ith key bit using the branch mispredictions obtained from the values of the performance

monitors which provides us with the real information of the branch miss due to the actual predictor hardware in the architecture.

We provide a theoretical proof to justify that the probability of success is equivalent to how closely the theoretical predictor models the underlying system predictor hardware to guess the ith bit correctly. It is also noted that success probability increases with number of messages and reaches a significant value to consider the side-channels due to performance counters a real threat to RSA-like ciphers exploiting the underlying branch predictors. What makes this result more relevant is the fact that protections which fuzz the timing channels are not sufficient to thwart these attacks, and presents performance counters as a distinct side-channel which needs to be considered for developing secured systems.

In the later part of this paper, we extend our attack to the RSA-OAEP randomized padding procedure where we target the decryption phase of the implementation and the branch miss side-channel information of the entire decoding procedure can be successfully exploited to reveal the secret exponent.

The organization of the paper is as follows:- The following Sect. 2 provides a brief idea on modular exponentiation algorithms and some well-known predictor algorithms. In Sect. 3 we demonstrate the vulnerability due to the event "branch-misses" as side-channel. The attack algorithm is described in Sect. 4 with the detailed analysis on the retrieval of secret key bits in two phases. A formal analysis on the success of the algorithm is presented in Sect. 5. Section 6 provides the experimental validation for the attack strategy. A brief discussion on the future prospects of the work and some probable countermeasures are provided in Sect. 7 and final section concludes the work we present here.

2   Preliminaries

In this section, we provide a background on some key-concepts, which include some implementation algorithms for public-key ciphers and some well-known branch predictors which have been subjected to attack.

2.1   Exponentiation Algorithms and Underlying Multiplication Primitive

In RSA-like asymmetric-key cryptographic algorithms, inputs(M) are encrypted and decrypted by performing modular exponentiation with modulus N on public or private keys represented as n bit binary string. While during encryption the exponent(e) is public, the target for attackers is the exponentiation carried out while decryption, where the secret key(d) is used as the exponent. The most popular algorithm to implement modular exponentiation is the square and multiply algorithm. The square and multiply algorithm as described in Algorithm 1, performs squaring at each step, while there is a conditional multiplication operation which is performed only if the exponent bits are set. This algorithm performs unbalanced instruction execution conditioned on the exponent bits. Due to this

---

Algorithm 1. Binary version of Square & Multiply Exponentiation

```
begin
    S ← M ;
    for i from 1 to n − 1 do
        S ← S * S mod N ;
        if d_i = 1 then
        |   S ← S * M mod N ;
        end
    end
    return S ;
end
```

Algorithm 2. Montgomery Ladder Algorithm

```
begin
    R_0 ← 1
    R_1 ← M
    for i from 0 to n − 1 do
        if d_i = 0 then
            R_1 ← (R_0 * R_1)  mod N
            R_0 ← (R_0 * R_0)  mod N
        end
        else if d_i = 1 then
            R_0 ← (R_0 * R_1)  mod N
            R_1 ← (R_1 * R_1)  mod N
        end
    end
    return R_0
end
```

---

extra computation step (which is being conditioned on the secret exponent bit), simple power attacks (SPA) and timing attacks exploit this conditional instruction execution and eventually retrieves the secret exponent.

A naïve modification to protect the side-channel leakage of square and multiply exponentiation algorithm is to have a balanced instruction execution and is proposed in the Montgomery ladder Algorithm [6] explained in Algorithm 2. This algorithm performs the entire exponentiation by alternatively modifying the values of two dummy variables depending on the exponent bits. Algorithm 2 has both "if" and "else" statements, and everytime one of the two possible sets of instructions are getting executed. Unlike the square and multiply, here the number of squarings and multiplications executed will always be constant and equal to the length of the key which inhibits simple power and timing attack.

A highly efficient algorithm for performing modular squaring and modular multiplication operation (in these modular exponentiation algorithms) is the Montgomery Multiplication Algorithm [9], since it avoids the time consuming integer division operation. Montgomery Multiplication as in Algorithm 3 computes modular multiplication of form $a * b \pmod{N}$. If the RSA modulus N is a k-bit number then a variable R is assumed to be 2^k. Montgomery Multiplication calculates $Z = A * B * R^{-1} \pmod{N}$ where $A = a * R \pmod{N}$, $B = b * R \pmod{N}$ and $R^{-1} * R = 1 \pmod{N}$. There is an extra reduction step at the 4th line of the Algorithm 3 which is particularly of interest to the attackers. The conditional execution of the reduction statement depend on the inputs, thus can be exploited in modular exponentiation scenario to surface a timing attack.

In situations when both public key exponent e and input m are small then the modular exponentiation can be reverted efficiently and the encryption fails to fulfill the criteria for asymmetric key ciphers. RSA being a deterministic algorithm

---

Algorithm 3. Montgomery Multiplication Algorithm

```
begin
    S ← A * B ;
    S ← (S + (S * N⁻¹ mod R) * N)/R ;
    if S > N then
    |   S ← S − N ;
    end
    return S ;
end
```

---

is not semantically secure and an intelligent adversary can launch known cipher-text attacks on this cipher. This effectively leads to message padding schemes which encodes messages first then allows encryption on these encoded messages. In the next subsection a brief overview of randomized message padding procedure is provided.

2.2 RSA-OAEP Randomized Padding Scheme

RSA encryption along with PKCS#1 v1.5 encoding was shown to be insecure in [3] as it reveals information regarding the plaintexts by examining the cipher-text in polynomial time. To overcome this security problems of the chosen cipher-text attacks, OAEP encoding scheme was introduced to detect any manipulation while decrypting the ciphertext and outputs an error message if any tampering with the ciphertext is performed.

In RSA-OAEP randomized padding procedure, the public key encryption (as in modular exponentiation) is performed on the encoded message (which we refer to as the plaintext) instead of the original message (though in the previously stated algorithms the plaintext is same as the message). The decryption and decoding procedure in RSA-OAEP is reverse to the encryption process and is illustrated in Fig. 1. The input ciphertext is decrypted with the secret key to reveal the plaintext. The plaintext while decoded as in Fig. 1 refuses to output any message if the specifications of the decrypted ciphertext string is not met. The criteria are illustrated in diagonal boxes in the Fig. 1 and if violated, the decoding process outputs "error message". The detailed specifications to the Mask Generation Function (MGF), hash function, selection of parameter and seed generation are provided in [10]. The existing side-channel attacks against this scheme exploits fault and timing analysis on three checking conditions separately to identify the ciphertexts (which can be decoded to messages successfully) in Chosen-ciphertext attacks.

This paper evaluates the security of implementations of public-key ciphers on standard processors using branch misses from the hardware performance counters (HPCs). The leakage is caused due to the presence of branch predictors in the modern architecture. Some of the very popular branch predictor algorithms are explained in the next subsection.

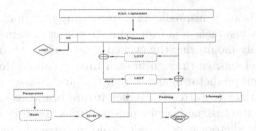

Fig. 1. Decryption in RSA-OAEP procedure [8]

2.3 Dynamic Branch Predictor

The 2-bit dynamic branch predictor state machine is one of the various predictor algorithms that is most oftenly used in practice [5]. This is a deterministic algorithm predicting next branch to be *taken* or *not taken* depending on the history of previously taken branches. In a 2-bit prediction scheme the predictor must miss twice before the prediction changes. But conditional branches that occurs in a regular recurring pattern are not predicted well by this bimodal predictor.

In such cases a two-level adaptive predictor [13] works better as the predictor remembers the last k occurrences of a branch instruction and uses a s-bit prediction function (such as a s-bit predictor) for each of the 2^k history of patterns. The first level of the two level adaptive predictor uses a *branch history register*, which is a shift register storing the history of the last k branches. The branch history register indices to a second level called *pattern history table*, which can hold 2^k entries, each of s bits. When a conditional branch B is getting predicted, content of the k bit history register is the address to pattern history table.

In the next section we will provide a brief motivation for considering branch misses from performance counters as side-channel to attack public-key ciphers.

3 Modelling Branch Miss as Side-Channel from HPC

3.1 Using Event Branch-Misses as Side-Channel

In this work, hardware performance counters (HPCs) are exploited to monitor side-channel information of the **number of branch misses** on the **square and multiply** exponentiation algorithm which uses Montgomery multiplication algorithm as subroutine for the operations like squaring and multiplication. As observed in Algorithm 1, the code while in execution can proceed in any of two paths, since the multiplication operation is performed only if the particular exponent bit is set. In addition to this, the Montgomery multiplication subroutine used for the squaring and multiplication operation also has an extra conditional reduction statement which gets executed when the intermediate input exceeds the modulus N. Thus, there exists a side-channel information via the hardware performance event **"branch-misses"**. Though timing side-channel can also be used to monitor the misprediction delays due to branch misses but when we wish to exploit only the branch mispredictions, measuring the time of a misprediction delay (of an event when measured from a multitasking system) is less significant compared to actually monitoring the event branch misses through HPCs.

The side-channel leakage through branch miss is caused due to the presence of underlying branch predictor in architecture. Branch misses rely on the ability of the branch predictor to correctly predict future branches to be taken. If the prediction is false, the instruction pipeline is flushed leading to a branch miss. Thus the branch predictors play a major role in correctly predicting the next target instruction and reducing the misprediction penalty.

The performance counters leak information of branch misses while exponentiation operation is performed on the secret exponent bits for the public-key ciphers. The profiling of the HPCs can be done using performance monitoring tools and is considered as a side-channel source since it provides a simple user interface to different hardware event counts.

3.2   Strong Correlation Between Two-Bit Predictor and System Branch Predictor

State machine of the 2-bit dynamic predictor as explained in Sect. 2.3 has been extensively used as an underlying predictor in the older versions of the Intel family of microprocessors [4]. But the actual predictor structure in architecture (inbuilt in the recent processors) is not disclosed by the processor manufacturers. In order to monitor the information of branch misses from the HPCs, we aim to exploit a strong correlation of branch misses from the actual inbuilt predictor and some of the well-known predictor algorithms. In order to approximate the branch mispredictions from system's underlying predictor algorithm, we first made an installation of Perf tool on Linux OS Ubuntu 12.04.1 LTS to monitor the event "branch-misses", which indicates number of branch mispredictions suffered by an executable. The following **command can be executed at the user privilege**.

$ perf stat -e branch-misses executable-name

With the aim of approximating the underlying system predictor with the well known 2-bit dynamic predictor, branch misses for performing exponentiation are observed on 10000 separate random keystream, each of 1024 bits on Intel i5 platform. An observation on the number of branch misses simulated from the 2-bit dynamic predictor and the corresponding branch misses as obtained through performance counter values is illustrated in Fig. 2. Two sets of information are correlated in the following manner

- Each of these 1024 bit random key is simulated on 2-bit dynamic predictor and the number of branch misses are observed for each of them.
- The number of branch misses are also observed from the performance monitoring tool over the square and multiply exponentiation algorithm for each of the random keystreams. The branch miss information for a particular key is averaged after exponentiations over 1000 inputs to reduce noise.

– The number of branch misses obtained from performance counters is found to
be increasing as the total number of predicted branch misses on a key-stream
increases as in Fig. 2.

The absolute values of branch misses obtained from HPCs as plotted in Fig. 2
are much larger than the theoretically simulated values of the 2-bit predictor
algorithm. It may appear to the observer to be counter-intuitive since the actual
branch predictors in hardware are much sophisticated compared to the primitive
2-bit dynamic predictor. But the rationale behind this may be explained as that
the HPCs report branch miss statistics for the entire execution of the executable
and thus are affected by the environmental running processes as well.

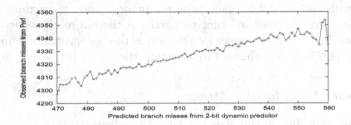

Fig. 2. Variation of branch-misses from performance counters with increase in branch
miss from 2-bit predictor algorithm

A direct correlation is observed in Fig. 2 for the branch misses from performance counters and branch misses from the simulated 2-bit dynamic predictor
over a sample of exponent bitstream. This confirms our assumption of 2-bit
dynamic predictor being an approximation to the underlying system branch
predictor and in our work, we modelled this strong effect of the bimodal predictor to exploit the side-channel leakage of branch misses from the performance
counters. As a further extension, we also perform the attack by approximating
the branch predictor by a two level adaptive predictor, where the second level is
a dynamic 2-bit predictor model itself. We later show that the accuracy of our
attack improves with the correlation between the actual and the model assumed,
which is quite high as also supported by our experiments.

4   Attack Algorithm Featuring Performance Counters Monitoring Branch Misses

In the attack algorithm, we claim to identify the secret bit by utilizing the behavior of the well known predictor algorithms as an approximation to underlying
system branch predictor, to simulate the mispredictions for initial known secret
exponent bits over each input ciphertexts. Later we perform an analysis phase
based on branch misprediction information from actual HPCs to reveal secret
bits. The attack is an adaptation of direct timing attack demonstrated in [1],

where the paper talks about observing a separation in timing between distinct input sets, the sets being separated by a hypothetical predictor algorithm. The hypothetical attack scenario presented in [1] cannot be implemented on real systems until and unless the adversary gets to know the actual structure of the branch predictor architecture of the target system. None of the leading processor manufacturers publish their architectural details since this puts their intellectual property at risk, making the whole idea of proposed attack unrealistic. In this present work, we extend the attack algorithm and the novelty of the work lies in the fact that the adversary, inspite of having no knowledge of the underlying architecture, can actually target real systems and reveal secret exponent bits, exploiting the branch miss as side-channel from HPCs. In order to target real systems, we perform the subsimulations on some well-known predictors like 2-bit dynamic predictor and two-level adaptive predictor as they approximate the real predictor to a great extent in order to partition the entire ciphertext set into smaller ones. In the latter phase, we perform actual experiments using branch misses from HPCs as side-channel to ascertain the secret bit.

4.1 Threat Model for the Attack

The basic assumptions of the attack is that the adversary targets the modular exponentiation while RSA decryption is taking place. The attacker knows the first i bits of the private key and he wants to determine next unknown bit d_i of the key $(d_0, d_1, \cdots, d_i, \cdots, d_{n-1})$. The attack algorithm runs in two phases, where in the offline phase for an input m, the attacker can only simulate for the partially known bits and the assumed target bit. In this phase, the subsimulations for each input is fed to a predictor model to generate mispredictions and based on this event misprediction, the entire ciphertext set is partitioned. The adversary neither has an access to the HPCs nor any access to do a partial computation on the target machine. Whereas in the online phase, the adversary can only observe branch misses over entire secret key for various input ciphertexts. In this phase, the attacker is not allowed to perform any subsimulation on the secret key.

In the next subsection, we present an iterative attack algorithm in two phases where the following analysis can be performed to identify individual secret key bits one after another.

4.2 Offline Phase

In this phase, the adversary partitions a sample input set M by simulating the branch mispredictions for the conditional reduction of Montgomery multiplication at the $(i + 1)^{th}$ squaring step of Square and multiply algorithm. For any input $m \in M$, the attacker can simulate the execution of the exponentiation algorithm for the initial i bits (that are already known) and can generate a trace of branches as $(t_{m,1}, t_{m,2}, \cdots, t_{m,i})$ following steps of Algorithm 1, 3. Here $t_{m,i}$ is simulated as either a taken or not taken branch depending whether the conditional reduction branch statement at the ith squaring operation is being executed. As we already have the knowledge of bits $(d_0, d_1, \cdots, d_{i-1})$, the trace of branches can be simulated by the attacker as $(t_{m,1}, t_{m,2}, \cdots, t_{m,i})$.

At this stage, the adversary assumes both $d_i = 0$ and 1, and separately does the following analysis in the offline phase. Under the assumption of d_i having value j, where $j \in \{0, 1\}$, appropriate value of $t^j_{m,i+1}$ is simulated. This situation is illustrated in Fig. 3. The $(i+1)^{th}$ squaring (being executed by Montgomery multiplication subroutine), the execution of an extra reduction step at line 4 (of Montgomery Multiplication as in Algorithm 3) is purely dependent on the sample input m as well as value of unknown d_i.

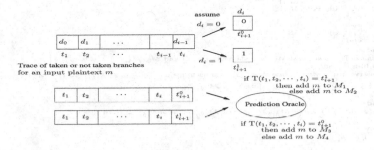

Fig. 3. Partitioning randomly generated Ciphertexts set based on simulated Branch miss Modelling

For the simulated branch history traces for a random ciphertext m, a misprediction occurs at $(i+1)^{th}$ squaring only if the theoretically predicted branch for $(t_{m,1}, t_{m,2}, \cdots, t_{m,i})$ observes a mismatch with the $t^j_{m,i+1}$-th branch execution. Let the theoretical predictor be T and $(i+1)^{th}$ bit predicted by it be $p_{m,i+1} = T(t_{m,1}, t_{m,2}, \cdots, t_{m,i})$. The partitioning of the ciphertext set is performed based on this **simulated misprediction**. The algorithm for partitioning is explained step by step in Algorithm 4 and is also illustrated in Fig. 3.

So the attacker can create 4 different sets due to a misprediction event during the Montgomery Multiplication (MM) at $(i+1)^{th}$ squaring:

1. $M_1 = \{m | m$ does not cause a miss during MM of $(i+1)^{th}$ squaring if $d_i = 1\}$
2. $M_2 = \{m | m$ causes a misprediction during MM of $(i+1)^{th}$ squaring if $d_i = 1\}$
3. $M_3 = \{m | m$ does not cause a miss during MM of $(i+1)^{th}$ squaring if $d_i = 0\}$
4. $M_4 = \{m | m$ causes a misprediction during MM of $(i+1)^{th}$ squaring if $d_i = 0\}$

But there may exist a situation for a ciphertext m, such that $m \in M_2$ and $m \in M_4$, which may suffer a misprediction when d_i is assumed to be 0 as well as 1. Thus these ciphertexts may add to the noise while actually determining the secret bit, as in this case, the event misprediction does not signify whether $d_i = 0$ or 1. Likewise for the sets M_1 and M_3. Hence we ensure that there must be no common ciphertexts in sets (M_1, M_3) and (M_2, M_4) and the sets should be disjoint. The 4 sets of ciphertexts are generated by the attacker in offline phase.

Algorithm 4. Adversary Attack Algorithm

```
Input: (d_0, d_1, ···, d_{i-1}), M
Output: Probable next bit nb_i
begin
    Offline Phase;
    for ∀m ∈ M do
        Generate taken/ not-taken trace for input m as t_{m,1}, t_{m,2}, ···, t_{m,i} ;
        Assume d_i = 0, generate t^0_{m,i+1} ;
        Similarly, assume d_i = 1, generate t^1_{m,i+1} ;
        p_{m,i+1} = T(t_{m,1}, t_{m,2}, ···, t_{m,i}) ;
        if p_{m,i+1} = t^1_{m,i+1} then
        |   Add m to M_1 ;
        end
        else
        |   Add m to M_2 ;
        end
        if p_{m,i+1} = t^0_{m,i+1} then
        |   Add m to M_3 ;
        end
        else
        |   Add m to M_4 ;
        end
    end
    Remove Duplicate Ciphertexts in the sets M_1, M_3 and M_2, M_4;
    Online Phase;
    Observe distribution of branch misses from performance counters as M_{M_1}, M_{M_2}, M_{M_3}, M_{M_4} ;
    if (avg(M_{M_2}) > avg(M_{M_1})) and (avg(M_{M_4}) < avg(M_{M_3})) then
    |   nb_i = 1 ;
    end
    if (avg(M_{M_4}) > avg(M_{M_3})) and (avg(M_{M_2}) < avg(M_{M_1})) then
    |   nb_i = 0 ;
    end
    return nb_i ;
end
```

The Offline phase for the Montgomery Ladder algorithm differs to some extent from subsimulation and misprediction computation of square and multiply. In the Montgomery Ladder Algorithm 2, both the squaring and multiplication operations are conditioned on the exponent bits and in addition to this, there are two sets of squaring and multiplication operations that are getting executed in Algorithm 2. For a input ciphertext m, when exponent bit is 0 then lines 6, 7 are executed otherwise lines 8, 9 are getting executed. If we target to observe misprediction for the conditional reductions of the squaring statement, then unlike the square and multiply algorithm, the subsimulation generates two traces for taken and not taken branches (two traces correspond to squarings at line 7 and 9 respectively) for the partially known key. Similar to the previous strategy in order to identify the secret bit d_i, we assume the target bit d_i to be both 0 and 1 and separate ciphertext into 4 sets. When we assume $d_i = 0$, then mispredictions are simulated over the trace corresponding to line 7 and alternatively for line 9 when $d_i = 1$. The partitioning of ciphertexts as well as the Online phase are exactly same as explained for the square and multiply algorithm.

4.3   Online Phase

In the Online phase, branch misses from the HPCs are monitored for execution of cipher over the entire secret key for each ciphertexts in all of the 4 sets while the RSA decryption is taking place. Let the branch mispredictions observed $\forall m \in M$ from the HPCs for decryption of the cipher, forms a distribution of branch misses and we denote such distribution as $\mathcal{M}$. Branch misses for exponentiation are monitored on each ciphertexts for these 4 separate sets M_1, M_2, M_3, M_4 for the entire secret key and results in 4 distinct distributions $\mathcal{M}_{M_1}$, and so on.

Since the ith bit of the exponent can either be 0 or 1 and cannot be both at the same time, intuitively from these two pair of sets - (M_1, M_2) and (M_3, M_4), one of the pair corresponding to the correct assumption of d_i will show a consistent positive difference in the observed branch misses while in the other pair, the differences will be zero or negative. This is due to the fact, if the classification is correct, then expected mispredictions of one set (which stores the ciphertexts causing a misprediction) should be greater than the other set. If the guess is wrong, the classification being random does not exhibit this statistics.

The probable next bit is decided following the Algorithm 4.

- If$(avg(\mathcal{M}_{M_2}) > avg(\mathcal{M}_{M_1}))$ and $(avg(\mathcal{M}_{M_4}) < avg(\mathcal{M}_{M_3}))$, then the next bit $(nb_i) = 1$
- Otherwise, if $(avg(\mathcal{M}_{M_4}) > avg(\mathcal{M}_{M_3}))$ and $(avg(\mathcal{M}_{M_2}) < avg(\mathcal{M}_{M_1}))$ then, next bit $(nb_i) = 0$

5 Formally Modelling the Success

In this section we claim that the success of correctly identifying the actual key bits can be alternatively stated as, how closely the theoretical dynamic 2-bit predictor follows the real predictor which is inbuilt in the processor.

In the Offline phase of the attack algorithm, for an assumption of the secret bit the set of ciphertexts M was separated in two disjoint sets based on the criteria whether they suffer from a simulated misprediction at the conditional reduction statement of $(i + 1)^{th}$ squaring step. Essentially in the offline phase,

$Pr[m_1 \in M_1] = Pr[p_{m_1,i+1} = t^1_{m_1,i+1}]$

$Pr[m_2 \in M_2] = Pr[p_{m_2,i+1} \neq t^1_{m_2,i+1}]$ (assuming $d_i = 1$)

and, $Pr[m_3 \in M_3] = Pr[p_{m_3,i+1} = t^0_{m_3,i+1}]$

$Pr[m_4 \in M_4] = Pr[p_{m_4,i+1} \neq t^0_{m_4,i+1}]$ (assuming $d_i = 0$)

Also, since we remove duplicate elements from (M_1, M_3) and (M_2, M_4) in the Offline Phase, for any input m, if $m \in M_1$ then $m \notin M_3$, thus $m \in M_4$. Alternatively, we can say, $\forall m \in M$, $t^0_{m,i+1} \neq t^1_{m,i+1}$.

While in the Online Phase, let nb_i be the bit which the attacker concludes to be the next secret bit by monitoring branch misses from HPCs for the corresponding plaintext sets following the attack algorithm. Let the expectation of the distribution of branch misses $(\mathcal{M}_M, \forall m \in M)$ be $\overline{\mathcal{M}_M}$. Thus we can decide the next bit defining the following probabilities, for $\forall m_i \in M_i, i \in 1, 2, 3, 4$ as:

$Pr[nb_i = 0] = Pr[(\overline{\mathcal{M}_{M_4}} - \overline{\mathcal{M}_{M_3}}) > 0 \wedge (\overline{\mathcal{M}_{M_2}} - \overline{\mathcal{M}_{M_1}}) < 0]$

$Pr[nb_i = 1] = Pr[(\overline{\mathcal{M}_{M_2}} - \overline{\mathcal{M}_{M_1}}) > 0 \wedge (\overline{\mathcal{M}_{M_4}} - \overline{\mathcal{M}_{M_3}}) < 0]$. These **observed mispredictions** are actually affected by the deterministic algorithm of underlying real predictor of the system. Let us assume that the real predictor inbuilt in the system be R and $(i + 1)^{th}$ bit predicted by the real predictor for the known trace is $r_{m,i+1}$ for input m. Let the $i + 1^{th}$ branch instruction has trace $B_{m,i+1}$ for unknown bit d_i. If $d_i = 0$, then $B_{m,i+1} = t^0_{m,i+1}$, otherwise if $d_i = 1$,

$B_{m,i+1} = t^1_{m,i+1}$. Thus we can rewrite the previous equation as

$$\Pr[nb_i = 0] = \Pr[(\overline{\mathcal{M}_{M_4}} - \overline{\mathcal{M}_{M_3}}) > 0 \wedge (\overline{\mathcal{M}_{M_2}} - \overline{\mathcal{M}_{M_1}}) < 0]$$
$$= \Pr[(r_{m_4,i+1} \neq B_{m_4,i+1}) \wedge (r_{m_3,i+1} = B_{m_3,i+1}) \wedge (r_{m_2,i+1} = B_{m_2,i+1}) \wedge (r_{m_1,i+1} \neq B_{m_1,i+1})]$$

Similarly,

$$\Pr[nb_i = 1] = \Pr[(\overline{\mathcal{M}_{M_2}} - \overline{\mathcal{M}_{M_1}}) > 0 \wedge (\overline{\mathcal{M}_{M_4}} - \overline{\mathcal{M}_{M_3}}) < 0]$$
$$= \Pr[(r_{m_2,i+1} \neq B_{m_2,i+1}) \wedge (r_{m_1,i+1} = B_{m_1,i+1}) \wedge (r_{m_4,i+1} = B_{m_4,i+1}) \wedge (r_{m_3,i+1} \neq B_{m_3,i+1})]$$

Since an attacker is unaware of the underlying predictor model, the correctness of separation relies on the criteria that how closely the theoretical predictor approximates the real one. Thus the extent of correct partitioning of the random ciphertext set relies on the efficiency of the theoretical predictor model. We define the event *Success* as true if the maximum difference in branch misses is observed from HPCs over input sets for the correct assumption. In other words,

- If difference in average branch miss $(\overline{\mathcal{M}_{M_4}} - \overline{\mathcal{M}_{M_3}}) > 0$, $(\overline{\mathcal{M}_{M_2}} - \overline{\mathcal{M}_{M_1}}) < 0$ and the secret bit is actually 0.
- If difference in branch miss $(\overline{\mathcal{M}_{M_2}} - \overline{\mathcal{M}_{M_1}}) > 0$, $(\overline{\mathcal{M}_{M_4}} - \overline{\mathcal{M}_{M_3}}) < 0$ and the secret bit is actually 1. Thus,

$$\Pr(\text{Success}) = \Pr[nb_i = d_i] = \Pr[nb_i = 0 \wedge d_i = 0] + \Pr[nb_i = 1 \wedge d_i = 1]$$
$$= \Pr[nb_i = 0 \mid d_i = 0] \cdot \Pr[d_i = 0] + \Pr[nb_i = 1 \mid d_i = 1] \cdot \Pr[d_i = 1]$$

If $d_i = 0$, we replace $B_{m,i+1} = t^0_{m,i+1}$ in Eq. 1 as,

$$\Pr[nb_i = 0 \mid d_i = 0] = \Pr[(r_{m_4,i+1} \neq t^0_{m_4,i+1}) \wedge (r_{m_3,i+1} = t^0_{m_3,i+1}) \wedge (r_{m_2,i+1}$$
$$= t^0_{m_2,i+1}) \wedge (r_{m_1,i+1} \neq t^0_{m_1,i+1})]$$
$$= \Pr[(r_{m_4,i+1} \neq t^0_{m_4,i+1}) \wedge (r_{m_3,i+1} = t^0_{m_3,i+1})$$
$$\wedge (r_{m_2,i+1} \neq t^1_{m_2,i+1}) \wedge (r_{m_1,i+1} = t^1_{m_1,i+1})]$$
$$\text{(since } t^0_{m_2,i+1} \neq t^1_{m_2,i+1} \text{ and } t^1_{m_1,i+1} \neq t^0_{m_1,i+1})$$

Substituting the events from Offline Phase,

$$\Pr[nb_i = 0 \mid d_i = 0] = \Pr[(r_{m_4,i+1} = p_{m_4,i+1}) \wedge (r_{m_3,i+1} = p_{m_3,i+1}) \wedge (r_{m_2,i+1}$$
$$= p_{m_2,i+1}) \wedge (r_{m_1,i+1} = p_{m_1,i+1})]$$
$$= \Pr[(r_{m,i+1} = p_{m,i+1})]$$

Similar calculations reveal,

$$\Pr[nb_i = 1 \mid d_i = 1] = \Pr[(r_{m,i+1} = p_{m,i+1})]$$

Thus, combining equations we get,

$$\Pr(\text{Success}) = \Pr[r_{m,i+1} = p_{m,i+1}] \cdot [\Pr(d_i = 0) + \Pr(d_i = 1)]$$
$$= \Pr[r_{m,i+1} = p_{m,i+1}]$$

Thus we conclude from this that the probability of success is equal to the probability that the theoretical predictor closely models the real predictor.

6 Experimental Validation for the Online Phase of the Attack

In this section we present the validation of previous discussion through experiments. The experiments are performed on RSA algorithm, the exponents being 1024 bits. The experiments are performed on various Intel processors like Intel Core-2 Duo E7400, Intel Core i3 M350 and Intel Core i5-3470. We illustrate our results by varying following parameters:

- Branch misses from performance counters are captured from the statistic reported by the Perf tool for executables running Square and Multiply algorithm and Montgomery Ladder algorithm using Montgomery multiplication subroutine for performing squaring and multiplications.
- The exponentiations are computed for random inputs of 64 bits that are randomly chosen.
- The performance counter measurements are observed over say L number of inputs. In between every iteration, we perform dummy exponentiation with randomly generated key-bits to flush the effect of the previous iterations from the predictor.
- The entire process is repeated for I number of iterations.

The offline phase of the attack separates a big pool of random inputs M into sets M_1, M_2, M_3 and M_4 based on mispredictions being simulated and results are furnished using 2-bit prediction as well as two-level adaptive predictor.

6.1 Experiments on Square and Multiply and Montgomery Ladder Algorithm

Initially the attack is performed on the square and multiply exponentiation implementation targeting the conditional reduction of the $(i+1)^{th}$ squaring step. Figure 4 shows the correct and incorrect separations for all 4 sets (separated by simulations over two-level adaptive predictor) for the randomly chosen 548th bit location of the target key-stream. Figure 4(a) plots average branch misses observed from performance counters for each elements in set M_1 and M_2 (each set having $L = 1000$ elements) and the experiment is repeated over $I = 1000$ iterations in order to check the consistency of the output. It is evident from the figure that in most of the iterations the average branch miss for set M_2 is more than the branch misses for set M_1(as expected). On the contrary, Fig. 4(b) plots average branch misses observed from performance counters for each elements in set M_3 and M_4. But we observe an incorrect separation as in most of this case, ciphertexts in set M_4 is having lesser branch misses than in set M_3 which is incorrect since theoretically it should be the reverse. Thus from this two figures, the correct exponent can be easily identified showing correct difference in branch misses.

The offline phase for Montgomery Ladder implementation slightly differs from the square and multiply algorithm as appears in Sect. 4.2. The separation of inputs are performed based on two separate subsimulated traces, and the misprediction is simulated selecting one of them depending on the assumption of the secret bit. The online phase of the attack is carried out similar to the previous

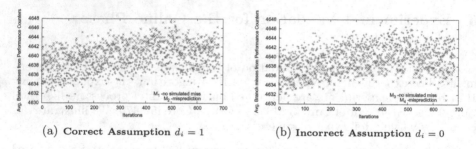

(a) **Correct Assumption** $d_i = 1$ (b) **Incorrect Assumption** $d_i = 0$

Fig. 4. Branch misses from HPCs on square and multiply correctly identifies secret bit $d_i = 1$, ciphertext set partitioned by simulated misses of two-level adaptive predictor

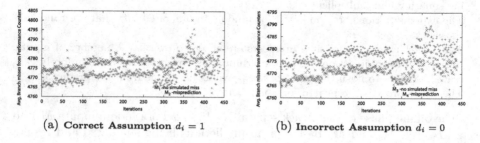

(a) **Correct Assumption** $d_i = 1$ (b) **Incorrect Assumption** $d_i = 0$

Fig. 5. Branch misses from HPCs on Montgomery Ladder correctly identifies secret bit $d_i = 1$, ciphertext set partitioned by simulated misses of two-level adaptive predictor

experiment having L = 1000 and I = 1000. Figure 5(a) and (b) shows the correct and incorrect assumptions of the target location for all the 4 ciphertext sets (separated by simulations over two-level adaptive predictor), which illustrates that it can identify the target secret bit correctly. In the following subsection, timing is used as side-channel instead of branch miss in the same experimental scenario but unlike branch miss, timing information fails to reveal the secret bit.

6.2   Comparing Timing as Side-Channel to Branch Misses from HPC

Timing side-channel as compared to branch misses will require significantly larger number of random inputs so that the adversary can identify next bit correctly. To establish our claim, similar experiments as previous has been experimented with parameters $L = 1000$ and $I = 1000$ and the execution time of the exponentiations over the entire secret key is monitored. Figure 6(a) and (b) illustrates that there is no clear demarcation so as to identify the secret bit. The timing side-channel has to be observed on significantly huge number of inputs to observe the accuracy that the adversary is able to observe using branch misses from HPCs. Thus we conclude that branch misses from HPCs can be viewed as stronger side-channel while exploiting the vulnerabilities of public-key ciphers.

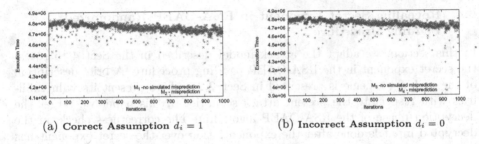

(a) Correct Assumption $d_i = 1$ (b) Incorrect Assumption $d_i = 0$

Fig. 6. No identification of secret bit is possible using timing as side-channel with $L = 1000$ and $I = 1000$

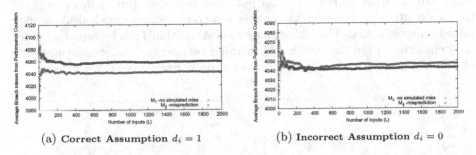

(a) Correct Assumption $d_i = 1$ (b) Incorrect Assumption $d_i = 0$

Fig. 7. Variation in the separation of branch misses for correct secret bit $= 1$ showing positive difference for M_1 and M_2 with the increase in number of ciphertexts(L), I = 100

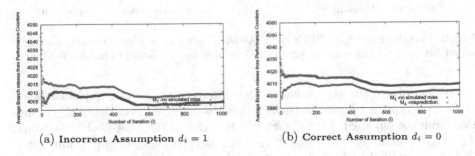

(a) Incorrect Assumption $d_i = 1$ (b) Correct Assumption $d_i = 0$

Fig. 8. Variation in the separation of branch misses for correct secret bit $= 0$ showing positive difference for M_3, M_4 with the increase in number of iteration(I), L = 1000

6.3   Variation of Parameters Such as Number of Inputs (L) and Iteration (I)

Figures 7 and 8 shows the variation of the differences in branch misses for the 4 ciphertext sets respectively. In these experiments the ciphertext sets are separated by simulation from the 2-bit dynamic predictor. Thus, from the experimental results as illustrated in Figs. 7 and 8, we can conclude that the identification of secret bit requires reasonably smaller number of inputs(L) (compared to timing side-channel) and the results are consistent across several iterations(I).

6.4   Revealing Secret Exponent in RSA-OAEP Randomized Padding Procedure

In this section, we adapt the attack model described in the Sect. 4 to reveal the secret exponent in the RSA-OAEP padding procedure. A brief description of the padding scheme is presented in Sect. 2.2 and we present its vulnerabilities with respect to the present attack scenario. In this paper we target the decryption phase of the RSA-OAEP algorithm. The correctness check on the decrypted input is done after the exponentiation over the secret exponent has been performed. The entire decryption and decoding is operated over a set of randomly generated ciphertexts which may not output valid messages (as they might fail to satisfy all criteria to output valid message). But in this process of the exponentiation operation, the unknown secret exponent gets leaked through branch mispredictions. The offline phase as in Algorithm 4 can be constructed for each ciphertext from the randomly generated set and the online measurements of branch misses over the separate sets eventually reveals the correct guess.

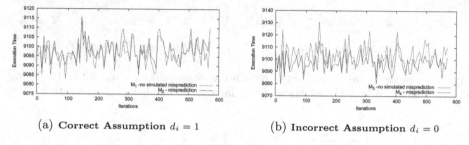

(a) **Correct Assumption** $d_i = 1$ (b) **Incorrect Assumption** $d_i = 0$

Fig. 9. Branch misses from HPCs on RSA-OAEP implementation, correctly identifies secret bit $d_i = 1$, ciphertext set partitioned by simulated misses of bimodal predictor

We performed the experiments with a Montgomery Ladder implementation of RSA decryption followed by the $RSA\_padding\_check\_PKCS1\_OAEP()$ function from the OpenSSL 1.0.0 library which performs the RSA-OAEP decoding. The experimental results for the RSA-OAEP decryption procedure is illustrated in Fig. 9(a) and (b) which clearly shows that for the actual secret bit there is a correct separation while incorrect separation can be observed for the wrong guess. Thus it be stated that, even though Randomized message padding encryptions make ciphers semantically secure, it cannot guarantee security against this attack as the side-channel leakage through branch miss event can be intelligently exploited to reveal the individual key bits one after another, while the exponentiation operation is being performed on the secret exponent for each randomly generated ciphertexts.

7   Discussions

Branching and conditional statements has been first targeted by side-channel cryptanalysts exploiting timing as side-channel. There has been several countermeasures like fuzzying timestamp counters, constant time implementations which have been proposed in literature to thwart the attacks from timing variations. But in most of these countermeasures, threat exists through HPCs as side-channel since the sequence of conditional statements that are being executed remains dependent on the key bits. In the present work though we have illustrated the attacks on RSA-like asymmetric key ciphers but this work can be extended to standard Double and Add Algorithm which is used to implement Elliptic Curve Scalar Multiplication. This forms the basis of the future scope of the study. We propose some of the feasible algorithmic countermeasures which are capable to thwart the present attack:

- Our attack targets the conditional reduction statement of Montgomery Multiplication (MM) and identifies secret key bits on observing branch miss distribution over separate ciphertext sets. If input to MM algorithm is masked such that 2 random numbers are generated at runtime and inputs are modified as $(a_r = a + r_1)$ and $(b_r = b + r_2)$, the branch predictor observes conditional branches which depend on r_1, r_2. However the final product is $a * b$ as effect of r_1, r_2 can be nullified by adding correction terms. This masking strategy will prevent the adversary from simulating branch miss, since r_1, r_2 are randomly generated at run time.
- There are other implementations of RSA, like CRT-RSA, which can be more resistant against the proposed attacks, since the adversary cannot perform the necessary subsimulations without knowing the prime factors of the RSA modulus.

However in context to such implementations, the performance counters can still pose a threatening side-channel, if stronger attack models are considered. For example, if the adversary is capable of introducing a transient bit fault in the secret exponent, and observes the differences in the values of the performance counters, leakages due to the branch predictor still occurs [2].

All these experiments, show that HPCs form a threatening side-channel for the existing implementations of RSA-like public key ciphers and any such implementation which has branching statements conditioned on secret key bits are vulnerable to attacks exploiting branch misprediction information from HPCs. This side-channel should also be considered along with other well-known side-channels like timing, power, and faults. The information provided by the Performance Counters should be possibly computed to provide the user means to access the performance, without providing a mechanism to extract secret information.

8   Conclusion

This paper shows that HPCs, which are used as performance monitors (watchmen) in modern computer systems can be utilized to retrieve the secret keys by reasonably modelled adversaries. The attack that we illustrate exploit the characteristics of branch predictor and show formally that the leakage of the key increases with the ability of the attacker to model the predictor more accurately. The experimental results clearly present the correct identification of the secret bits of 1024 bit RSA running on real life Intel platforms. We follow by a claim that branch misses from HPCs are indeed more significant side-channel compared to timing. For future work these experiments should be widened to model secure predictors which will inherently prevent information leakage.

References

1. Acıiçmez, O., Koç, Ç.K., Seifert, J.-P.: Predicting secret keys via branch prediction. In: Abe, M. (ed.) CT-RSA 2007. LNCS, vol. 4377, pp. 225–242. Springer, Heidelberg (2006)
2. Bhattacharya, S., Mukhopadhyay, D.: Fault attack revealing secret keys of exponentiation algorithms from branch prediction misses. IACR Cryptology ePrint Archive 2014, 790 (2014). http://eprint.iacr.org/2014/790
3. Bleichenbacher, D.: Chosen ciphertext attacks against protocols based on the RSA encryption standard PKCS #1. In: Krawczyk, H. (ed.) CRYPTO 1998. LNCS, vol. 1462, pp. 1–12. Springer, Heidelberg (1998)
4. Fog, A.: The Microarchitecture of Intel and AMD CPU's, An Optimization Guide for Assembly Programmers and Compiler Makers (2009)
5. Hennessy, J.L., Patterson, D.A.: Computer Architecture: A Quantitative Approach, 4th edn. Morgan Kaufmann, Boston (2006)
6. Joye, M., Yen, S.-M.: The montgomery powering ladder. In: Kaliski Jr., B.S., Koç, Ç.K., Paar, C. (eds.) CHES 2002. LNCS, vol. 2523, pp. 291–302. Springer, Heidelberg (2002)
7. Kocher, P.C.: Timing attacks on implementations of Diffie-Hellman, RSA, DSS, and other systems. In: Koblitz, N. (ed.) CRYPTO 1996. LNCS, vol. 1109, pp. 104–113. Springer, Heidelberg (1996)
8. Manger, J.: A chosen ciphertext attack on RSA optimal asymmetric encryption padding (OAEP) as standardized in PKCS #1 v2.0. In: Kilian, J. (ed.) CRYPTO 2001. LNCS, vol. 2139, pp. 230–238. Springer, Heidelberg (2001)
9. Montgomery, P.L.: Modular multiplication without trial division. Math. Comput. 44(170), 519–521 (1985)
10. RSA Laboratories, R.S.I.: Rsaes-oaep encryption scheme (2000)
11. Tiri, K., Acıiçmez, O., Neve, M., Andersen, F.: An analytical model for time-driven cache attacks. In: Biryukov, A. (ed.) FSE 2007. LNCS, vol. 4593, pp. 399–413. Springer, Heidelberg (2007)
12. Uhsadel, L., Georges, A., Verbauwhede, I.: Exploiting hardware performance counters. In: Breveglieri, L., Gueron, S., Koren, I., Naccache, D., Seifert, J.P. (eds.) FDTC, pp. 59–67. IEEE Computer Society (2008)
13. Yeh, T.Y., Patt, Y.N.: Two-level adaptive training branch prediction. In: MICRO, pp. 51–61 (1991)

Cipher Design and Cryptanalysis

Improved Cryptanalysis of the DECT Standard Cipher

Iwen Coisel$^{(\boxtimes)}$ and Ignacio Sanchez

Institute for the Protection and the Security of the Citizen (IPSC),
Joint Research Centre (JRC), European Commission, Digital Citizen Security Unit,
Via Enrico Fermi 2749, 21027 Ispra, VA, Italy
{iwen.coisel,ignacio.sanchez}@jrc.ec.europa.eu

Abstract. The DECT Standard Cipher (DSC) is a 64-bit key stream cipher used in the Digital Enhanced Cordless Telecommunications (DECT) standard to protect the confidentiality of the communications. In this paper we present an improved cryptanalysis approach which is more effective than the Nohl-Tews-Weinmann (NTW) attack and requires four times less plaintext material. Under the best conditions, our known plaintext attack requires only 3 min of communication compared to 10 min for the NTW attack. Our approach is able to quickly recover the secret key with a success rate of more than 50 % by analysing 2^{13} keystreams and performing an exhaustive search over 2^{31} keys. Additionally, the attack was successfully conducted against real intercepted DECT traffic where the plaintext was only 90 % accurate. To the best of our knowledge, the approach we present in this paper is the most effective cryptanalysis published so far against the DSC cipher.

Keywords: DECT · Privacy · Security · Cryptanalysis · Stream cipher

1 Introduction

The Digital Enhanced Cordless Telecommunications standard (DECT) is an ETSI standard used in cordless telephony, widely deployed worldwide both in residential and enterprise environments[1]. In traditional residential scenarios, the DECT base station is directly connected to the analogue telephone line and provides telephony and a battery recharge point for one or more wireless handsets. This is the scenario that is typically found today, where the DECT cordless phones have replaced a significant number of classic wired phones.

In enterprise environments DECT cordless phones are often integrated into the corporate Unified Communication Systems. These systems integrate several types of voice and data communications, such as VoIP and Videoconferencing,

---

I. Coisel and I. Sanchez—These authors have contributed equally and are presented in alphabetical order.

[1] The number of DECT devices sold reaches 820 million with a proliferation of 100 million new devices per year.

© International Association for Cryptologic Research 2015
T. Güneysu and H. Handschuh (Eds.): CHES 2015, LNCS 9293, pp. 269–286, 2015.
DOI: 10.1007/978-3-662-48324-4_14

which have recently become available in the consumer market. Nowadays it is common to find low-cost DECT cordless phones able to handle both land-line and VoIP communications. Despite the massive adoption of mobile telephony, the DECT standard has reinforced its position as one of the main wireless communication protocols in Smart Home ecosystems.

When encryption is not used, the DECT voice communications are vulnerable to remote eavesdropping attacks, as demonstrated by Lucks et al. [3] employing special purpose hardware. More recently, Sanchez et al. [7] demonstrated that eavesdropping of non-encrypted DECT voice communications can be effectively performed using widely available low cost Software Defined Radios (SDR). To mitigate these vulnerabilities and to protect the confidentiality of the communications, the DECT standard foresees the usage of a proprietary stream cipher, the DECT Standard Cipher (DSC). Currently, the privacy of the personal voice communications of hundreds of millions of citizens depends on the security of the DSC encryption algorithm.

Although the details of the DSC algorithm were never made openly available in the public standard[2], Nohl et al. [6] reverse engineered it from a hardware implementation and published the details of the algorithm along with a reference software implementation.

The literature detailing the security of the DSC encryption algorithm is quite limited, especially when compared to other encryption algorithms such as A5/1 used in mobile telephony. In [5] McHardy et al. demonstrated an active replay attack against DSC, and they were able to decrypt a recorded call by interactively recovering the keystreams used to encrypt it. Nohl et al. [6] proposed the first (and only) cryptanalysis method, the Nohl-Tews-Weinmann (NTW) attack, capable of recovering the DSC key after analysing large quantities of encrypted traffic. Their work constitutes the foundation of the present paper.

In [1], Coisel and Sanchez have presented an attack aiming at retrieving the long term key of the DECT device. While this attack is efficient (approx. 2^{10} operations), it requires that a key establishment protocol happens between the handset and the base station. Such protocol typically never takes place in a residential environment as the devices are paired in advance by the manufacturers.

In this paper we present an improved cryptanalysis of the DSC encryption algorithm that is faster than the NTW attack and requires substantially less plaintext material to be effective, making its usage viable in practical scenarios.

The paper is structured as follows. In Sect. 2 we review in detail the DSC stream cipher and its functions. In Sect. 3 we describe the Nohl-Tews-Weinmann attack and its results. In Sect. 4 we introduce our attack against DSC, and in Sect. 5 we describe the working implementation. In Sect. 6 we present and analyse the results obtained by our approach, and we compare with the results obtained by the Nohl-Tews-Weinmann method. Finally, in Sect. 7 we present the conclusions and we outline future research lines on the topic.

---

[2] The internal detail and reference implementation of the DSC algorithm is only available under non-disclosure agreements.

2 The DECT Standard Cipher

The DECT Standard Cipher (DSC) is a proprietary stream cipher designed as part of the DECT ETSI standard [2]. Although the DSC details were never made public in the DECT standard, Nohl et al. [6] presented a reference software implementation that they obtained through a reverse engineering procedure.

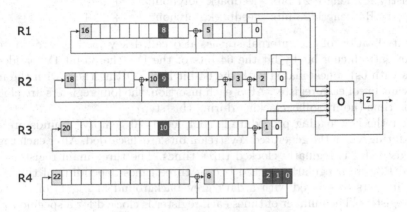

Fig. 1. DSC stream cipher

Concisely, the DSC is a 64-bit key stream cipher based on 4 irregularly clocked linear feedback shift registers (LFSRs) $R_1, \ldots, R_4$ in Galois configuration and a non-linear output combiner O with memory z. The three first registers are used to produce the keystream, i.e. the symmetric key used in the One-Time Pad algorithm to encrypt the plaintext. The fourth LFSR register is used, in combination with the others, to control the clocking of the three main registers. As will be described in detail later on, the DSC is initialized with a 35 bits long Initialization Vector and a 64-bit key, respectively denoted IV and KEY.

Each pair of IV and KEY is used to produce 720 bits of keystream that are split in two KeyStream Segments (KSS) of 360 bits each. The first KSS is used to encrypt the DECT frames sent by the base station (Fixed Part), and the second to encrypt the frames sent by the phone (Portable Part). In each case, the first 40 bits are used to encrypt the C-Channel data (that contains control data), whilst the rest of the bits are used to encrypt the B-Field (digitally encoded voice). More details can be found in the DECT ETSI standard [2]. The DSC cipher is depicted in Fig. 1 and formally described in the following subsections.

2.1 The DSC Internal Configuration

The internal status of the DSC stream cipher is composed of 81 bits spread amongst the 4 LFSRs and the memory bit of the output combiner. The three first registers, R1, R2 and R3, are used to provide input to the output combiner, as will be described in detail in Sect. 2.2. The last register, R4, is used exclusively to control the irregular clocking of the other registers after each round of the DSC. The four LFSR, depicted in Fig. 1, are formally described below together with their respective feedback polynomials.

- Registry R1: length 17 bits - feedback polynom: $x^{17} + x^6 + 1$
- Registry R2: length 19 bits - feedback polynom: $x^{19} + x^{11} + x^4 + x^3 + 1$
- Registry R3: length 21 bits - feedback polynom: $x^{21} + x + 1$
- Registry R4: length 23 bits - feedback polynom: $x^{23} + x^9 + 1$

The initialization of the internal status, also called key loading procedure, is done by introducing bit by bit the 64 bits of the IV (the 35-bit IV padded to 64 bits with 0s) concatenated with the 64-bit key, XORing them with the most significant bit of each register. After each insertion, the four registers are clocked a single time (no irregular clocking during this step).

After the key loading procedure is completed, 40 "empty" rounds are executed during which the generated keystream bits are discarded. After each round, the register R4 is regularly clocked three times. The three main registers, R1, R2 and R3, are irregularly clocked two or three times depending of the values of specific bits (displayed with a dark grey background in Fig. 1) of the three other registers. The number of times each register is clocked for a specific round, denoted irr_cl_i, is defined as follows, where $x_{i,j}$ denotes the j-th less significant bit, starting from 0, of the register i.

$$irr\_cl_1 = 2 + (x_{4,0} \oplus x_{2,9} \oplus x_{3,10})$$
$$irr\_cl_2 = 2 + (x_{4,1} \oplus x_{1,8} \oplus x_{3,10})$$
$$irr\_cl_3 = 2 + (x_{4,2} \oplus x_{1,8} \oplus x_{2,9})$$

Once the initialization procedure is completed, the round 0 of the DSC starts and produces the first bit of the keystream, denoted z_0. More generally, the keystream bit z_i is output at the end of the round i. All the keystream bits are generated by the output combiner as detailed in the next subsection.

2.2   The Output Combiner

The output combiner O is a non-linear function, more precisely a cubic function. It takes as inputs the two least significant bits of the three main registers, R1, R2 and R3, and the bit from the memory slot corresponding to the previous bit of the keystream. From now on, these 6 bits, taken from the three main registers, constitute what is called in the following the *status* of the DSC, and it is obviously dependent on the round number as well as the key and the IV.

Every round, the output combiner generates a bit that is stored in the memory slot, denoted z in Fig. 1. The bit previously stored in the memory slot will be output as a keystream bit, provided the initial 40 rounds were already completed. The new bit stored in the memory slot will be used as part of the input of the output combiner in the next round.

The output combiner is defined as follows, where $S = (x_{1,0}, x_{1,1}, x_{2,0}, x_{2,1}, x_{3,0}, x_{3,1})$ is the status of the DSC for the current round.

$$O(S, z) = x_{1,1}x_{1,0}z \oplus x_{2,0}x_{1,1}x_{1,0} \oplus x_{1,1}z \oplus x_{2,1}x_{1,0}z \oplus x_{2,1}$$
$$\oplus x_{2,1}x_{2,0}x_{1,0} \oplus x_{3,0}z \oplus x_{3,0}x_{1,0}z \oplus x_{3,1} \oplus x_{3,1}z$$
$$\oplus x_{3,0}x_{2,0}x_{1,0} \oplus x_{1,1}x_{1,0} \oplus x_{2,0}x_{1,1} \oplus x_{3,1}x_{1,0}$$

The main purpose of the function is to break the linearity of the three main registers. Over the 128 possible combination of inputs (64 possible statuses plus 2 possible values of the memory slot), half of them output 0 whilst the others output 1. At first sight the function seems to be balanced.

Any modification of a given status would modify in average the output bit in 50 % of the cases. However the output bit remains the same in 56.25% of the cases when only the bits of a single register are modified. When bits of at least two registers are modified, the outputs are again balanced. Furthermore, we have noticed that the probability that the output bit remains the same is dependent on the input. We will not elaborate further on this last fact since we do not use it in our attack yet it is an interesting line of research that may potentially improve the success rate of the attack.

2.3 Notations Used in the Rest of the Paper

In order to facilitate the readability of the paper, we introduce some notations that will be used in the following sections.

$S_{sc}(\text{KEY}, \text{IV})$, for $sc = (c_1, c_2, c_3)$, is the status of the DSC, initialized with KEY and IV, when the 3 main registers are respectively clocked c_1, c_2, and c_3 times. $S_l(\text{KEY}, \text{IV})$, is the status of the DSC, initialized with KEY and IV, that has been used to produce the bit output at the end of the round l. When it does not bring confusion, we do not mention KEY and IV.

tc_i denotes an hypothesis about the real clock of the register i, while $c_{i,l}$ denotes the real clock of the register i at the round l.

We abusively call the couple (IV, KS), composed by a keystream KS and the associated initial vector IV, a sample of plaintext (or wlog plaintext), as the "real" plaintext can be recovered from the ciphertext and the keystream. $\mathscr{P} = \{(IV, KS)\}$ denotes the set of available samples of plaintext.

We also extend the XOR operator and define the XOR operation of two statuses where the bits of the statuses are mutually XORed together.

3   The Nohl-Tews-Weinmann Attack

The Nohl-Tews-Weinmann (NTW) attack is a known-plaintext attack which, given a set of plaintext $\mathscr{P}$, is able to recover the 64-bit DSC key faster than an exhaustive search over the 2^{64} possible keys.

The first phase of the attack determines a certain amount of affine linear equations that specify relations about the key bits. In a second phase, the remaining bits of the key are brute-forced in order to obtain the 64-bit key.

Due to the linearity of the 4 DSC registers, each bit of each register, for a given number of clocks, can be defined as a linear combination of the bits of the key and the bits of the initial vector. Guessing correctly a bit $x_{i,j}$ for a given clock determines a linear equation. The goal of the attack is to guess correctly the status of the DSC and the corresponding clocks (c_1, c_2, c_3) in order to obtain a sufficiently large number of equations. Once n independent equations have been derived, the 64-bit key can be recovered following an exhaustive search over the remaining 2^{64-n} values.

3.1 Guessing Correctly a Status

In this section, we describe how the NTW attack manages to retrieve the status of the DSC. In order to do so, first we must explain how the clocks c_i of the three main registers can be guessed for a given round. This part of the attack takes advantage of the linearity of the DSC stream cipher, or more precisely, the fact that the following equality holds for any triplet of clocks $sc = (c_1, c_2, c_3)$.

$$S_{sc}(\text{KEY}, \text{IV}) = S_{sc}(\text{KEY}, 0) \oplus S_{sc}(0, \text{IV})$$

Assuming that a register is clocked twice with a probability of 50 %, the clock c_i for the round l is distributed according to a shifted binomial distribution with mode $2.5l + 100$. Based on the distribution, the most probable triplet(s) of clocks can be selected. As an example, the most probable triplets for the first round are those where each clock is either 102 or 103. The equality $S_{sc}(\text{KEY}, \text{IV}) = S_l(\text{KEY}, \text{IV})$ obviously holds if the registers are clocked accordingly to the values in sc at the end of the round l. The generated status and the bits of the keystream also always verify the equation $O(S_{sc}(\text{KEY}, \text{IV}), z_{l-1}) = z_l$. Such equation is denoted $eqn(sc, l)$ in the rest of the paper.

Both the key and $S_{sc}(\text{KEY}, \text{IV})$ are unknown. However, the IVs and the bits of the keystream are known (as it is a known-plaintext attack). Therefore it is possible to evaluate this equation with the 64 possible statuses. The correct status will necessarily belong to the subset S of the 32 candidate statuses that verify this particular equation. Using the corresponding IV, $\tilde{s} = S_{sc}(0, \text{IV})$ can be computed. As a conclusion, if sc is the correct triplet of clocks, then $S_{sc}(\text{KEY}, 0)$ is in the subset $\tilde{S} = \{\tilde{s} \oplus s^*; \forall\, s^* \in S\}$.

On the contrary, if the triplet sc is not the triplet of clocks of the round l, the correct status still has a probability of 50 % to be in this set according to Nohl et al. [6]. Consequently, the correct status has more than 50 % of chance to be in this set, whilst this probability is 50 % for all the other statuses.

This experiment can be seen as a Bernoulli trial where a success is the presence of the status is in the list of candidates. If repeated sufficiently, the most frequent status should therefore be the one of $S_{sc}(\text{KEY}, 0)$ due to this bias.

3.2 Determination of More Equations

If the evaluated equation $eqn(sc, l)$ is properly selected, then the previous step has successfully determined 6 equations for the DSC key, one for each bit of the status. However, the reduction of the key space would still be insufficient, as the brute-force of the remaining 58 bits of the key would require too much computational time. In order to determine more equations for the DSC key, the NTW attack extends this principle for each possible combination of clocks in a large range (35 in their article) considering several bits of the keystream (19 in their article). For each triplet of clock, a frequency table is generated to store the "score" of each potential candidate status.

Once all the samples have been processed, the value of a bit of a given register for a given clock is estimated according to all the frequency tables where this bit is involved in. By doing so, 108 bits are defined leading to 108 equations. A subset of these equations is selected according to a certain rank (see [6] for more details) and the solvability of the obtained system. When enough equations have been selected (around 30) the remaining bits are brute-forced.

3.3   Results of the Nohl-Tews-Weinmann Attack

Nohl et al. have conducted their known-plaintext attack against both the C-Channel and the B-Field considering the availability of different quantities of plaintext. They consider the probability that the system of equations defined is valid regarding the correct key. Their experiments consider different sizes for the system, from 10 to 40 equations. For comparison purposes, we summarise in Table 1 the most relevant results for the C-Channel and the B-Field respectively for different quantities of available plaintext. Full details about the results obtained by the NTW attack can be found in the original article [6].

Table 1. Success rate of the C-Channel and B-Field attack

Number of plaintext	C-Channel			B-Field		
	8192	16384	32768	16384	32768	65536
10 equations	2 %	30 %	96 %	2 %	30 %	92 %
20 equations	0 %	2 %	78 %	0 %	2 %	65 %
30 equations	0 %	1 %	48 %	0 %	0 %	28 %
40 equations	0 %	0 %	11 %	0 %	0 %	4 %

To reach a probability of success of 50 % against the C-Channel in order to define 30 equations the attack requires at least 32,768 plaintexts. Against the B-Field, this attack reaches a probability of success of 28 % for 30 equations with approximately 65,536 different samples of plaintext. Slightly better results can be found in the paper of Weiner et al. [8] following an optimisation based on a new key ranking procedure. As an example, the success probability for 32,768 available keystreams and 22 equations goes from 71 % to 90 %.

4   A Theoretical Model of an Improved Cryptanalysis

Instead of considering separately each bit of the internal status of the DSC as is done in the NTW attack, our attack processes directly the entire status for a given range of clocks. By doing so, all the irrelevant candidates (due to the equality of some bits and the feedback of the registers) are discarded in a first step. Furthermore, the underlying theoretical model used to give score to the potential candidate has been refined, leading to more accurate results. Before entering into details we summarise below the full process of our attack.

The first stage of the attack aims to retrieve the 6-bit statuses of the DSC for each triplet of clocks of a given range of length len_c. As the statuses of two consecutive clocks share three bits, the final targeted status is $3(len_c+1)$-bit long. A frequency table containing all these possible combinations, called candidates, is generated to store their *score*. All the equations $eqn(sc, l)$ relevant for this range of clocks are evaluated for each possible candidate. The candidates that verify a given equation increase their score by a value, called weight, specific to this particular equation. The weight of an equation is computed according to the probability that the correct status belongs to the specific subset of candidates that satisfy this equation for a random pair of IV and keystream.

Once all the plaintext samples are processed, all the candidates are ordered according to the score they have obtained. $3(len_c + 1)$ linear equations linking together the bits of the DSC key can be derived from a candidate. Starting with the first candidate the remaining bits of the key ($64 - 3(len_c + 1)$ bits) are then brute-forced in the last step of the attack.

4.1   Computation of the Weights

In a preliminary phase, the weight of each possible equation $eqn(sc, l)$ for the selected range of clocks, is calculated. Only the equations with non-null weights will be evaluated during the attack. This preliminary step is also achieved in the NTW attack. However, we have noticed experimentally that their values were not accurate. Based on this observation, we have refined the theoretical model that includes the non-homogeneous behaviour of the output combiner.

The weight of an equation is based on the probability that the output combiner outputs the same keystream bit when it takes as input either $S_{(tc_1,tc_2,tc_3)}$ or S_l. As a reminder, the equation $eqn((tc_1, tc_2, tc_3), l)$ is said verified if:

$$O(S_l, z_{l-1}) = O\big(S_{(tc_1,tc_2,tc_3)}, z_{l-1}\big).$$

Obviously, if the registers are respectively clocked tc_1, tc_2, and tc_3 times in the round l, then this equation is verified with a 100% probability and the correct status will necessarily be in the subset of candidates. In the following, we assume that the probability that a register clocks twice is 50% as the one that it clocks three times. We assume that the clocking decision of each register is independent from the other registers. The probability that a single register i

is clocked exactly tc_i times after the round l is:

$$Pr[c_{i,l} = tc_i] = \binom{40 + l}{tc_i - (80 + 2l)} 2^{-(40+l)}.$$

The probability, denoted p_1, that the three main registers are respectively clocked tc_1, tc_2, and tc_3 times after the round l, is defined as follows. For the sake of clarity we omit (tc_1, tc_2, tc_3) and l in the notation of the probabilities.

$$p_1 = \prod_{i=1}^{3} Pr[c_{i,l} = tc_i].$$

When at least one clock differs from the targeted one, as stated in the article [6], we could expect that the correct status is in the subset of candidates with a probability of 50 %. However, due to the particular behaviour of the output combiner previously described in Sect. 2.2, the probability that the equation remains verified is not exactly 50 % when the clocks differ. Indeed, if two targeted clocks are correct the equation is verified with a probability of 56.25 %. The global probability of success can therefore be refined. For clarity we introduce two intermediate probabilities, the probability p_2 that only one register is not clocked the targeted number of times and the probability p_3 that at least two registers are not clocked the targeted number of times.

$$p_2 = \sum_{i=1}^{3} (1 - Pr[c_{i,l} = tc_i]) \prod_{\substack{j \neq i; \\ j=1}}^{3} Pr[c_{j,l} = tc_j]$$

$$p_3 = \sum_{i=1}^{3} \left[Pr[c_{i,l} = tc_i] \prod_{\substack{j \neq i; \\ j=1}}^{3} (1 - Pr[c_{j,l} = tc_j]) \right] + \prod_{k-1}^{3} (1 - Pr[c_{k,l} = tc_k])$$

The probability that a given equation is verified can now be expressed.

$$Pr[eqn(sc, l)] = p_1 + 0.5625 * p_2 + 0.5 * p_3$$

As an example, the equation $((102, 102, 102), 1)$ corresponding to the production of the keystream bit z_1, is verified in 50.338 % of the cases. Following the approach of [4], the weight w_{eqn} associated to an equation is computed as the logarithmic likelihood of the probability, namely

$$w(eqn(sc, l)) = log\left(\frac{Pr[eqn]}{1 - Pr[eqn]}\right).$$

The weight of all possible equations according to a given range of clocks and a given range of keystream bits are precomputed using these results.

4.2   Determination of the Best Candidates

The precomputed weights are now used in the first step of the attack to guess the most probable statuses of $S_{sc}(\text{KEY}, 0)$ for the largest possible range of clocks $\mathcal{R}$ and a given set of bits of the keystream $\mathcal{K}$. $\mathscr{T}$ denotes the table that contains the $2^{3(len_c+1)}$ possible combinations of bits for the given range of clocks. The score of each candidate is equal to the addition of all the weights of the equations verified by this particular candidate.

For all triplet of clocks $sc \in \mathcal{R}^3$ and all rounds $l \in \mathcal{K}$, the equations $eqn(sc, l)$ are evaluated for all the possible candidates in $\mathscr{T}$. As a reminder, the statuses that verify a given equation are those potentially corresponding to $\tilde{s} = S_{sc}(\text{KEY}, IV)$. The "IV part" of the status can be removed thanks to the DSC linearity, as $s^* = S_{sc}(0, IV)$ can be computed. Therefore, the candidates that shall receive the weight of an equation are $s = \tilde{s} \oplus s^*$. As in the NTW attack, the more plaintexts are used, the higher the chances are that the correct status belongs to the subset of the ones with the bigger scores.

4.3   Exhaustive Search Among the Remaining Bits

A system of $3(len_c + 1)$ linear equations to the key with 64 unknowns can be defined from each candidate in the table $\mathscr{T}$. The key is a solution of the system defined by the correct candidate. To ease the brute-force step the Gaussian reduction of the system is used. All the obtained equations are independent if the length of the range of clock is below 17 (size of the smaller register). Thus $3(len_c + 1)$ bits of the key are determined by these equations while the remaining ones need to be brute-forced.

In order to carry out the last step, we have developed a CPU SIMD-based implementation that loads the equations derived in the cryptanalysis step and performs the exhaustive search over the remaining bits of the key. For each possible combination of keybits to be explored it retrieves the remaining bits of the candidate key using the linear relations. Then the implementation compares the generated keystream with a portion of known keystream at least longer than the number of keybits to be explored. Our implementation evaluates 500 million keys/sec in a Core i7 (AVX) workstation.

5   Improved Implementation of the Cryptanalysis

The attack described in the previous section may retrieve the searched key with a relatively good probability of success, whilst requiring a considerable amount of computing time to define enough linear relations among the key bits. In this section we present a success/time trade-off to hasten considerably the execution time whilst maintaining a good success rate.

5.1   Efficiency Consideration

The parameter that ultimately influences the efficiency of the attack is the length len_c of the clock range. Increasing it speeds the final brute-force step, but also increases the number of equations n_{eq} to be evaluated as well as the size of the candidate table $\mathcal{T}$, that are both cubic function in len_c, as formally defined below.

$$n_{eq} = len_c^3 . len_k$$
$$|\mathcal{T}| = 2^{3(len_c+1)}$$

The evaluation of the equations for all the candidates of $\mathcal{T}$ is a process that can be highly parallelised due to the independency of the actions. Consequently, a HPC may be able to achieve this step in a few hours for a length of 7. However, this length only allows the determination of 20 bits of the key. According to the implementation of [8], the brute-force of the remaining bits would take around 30 hours on a modern GPU.

To reduce the workload, we could split the range of clocks in sub-ranges and apply our attack to them. Combining the best candidates of each frequency table allows the determination of the same amount of status bits as in the initial range while reducing the computing time required. Unfortunately, this technique also reduces the probability of success due to the loss of contribution from the equations related to clocks that overlap these sub-ranges. Adding some redundancies in the definition of the sub-ranges can be a compromise between computing time required to carry out the attack and probability of success. The small gain in the probability of success is not really relevant compared to the loss of efficiency experienced following this approach. Indeed, more sub-ranges would be required to obtain the same amount of linear equations.

5.2   A Time-Accuracy Trade-Off

Our trade-off use several sub-ranges of reasonable length (typically 3 or 4 clocks each) without any redundancies on which we apply the attack previously defined in Sect. 4. A frequency table is generated for each of these sub-ranges. Then a joint table of the two first sub-ranges is created and populated with the cartesian product of the N_T most promising candidates from each sub-tables. The score associated to these new candidates is initially set to the sum of the two scores taken from the original candidate tables. The attack described in Sect. 4.2 is reapplied to this new subset considering the equations that use clocks overlapping amongst these two sub-ranges. Note that the equations already processed in the prior stage are not evaluated a second time. The most N_R promising candidates from the merged frequency table are again extracted and combined with the next sub-range and so on until all the sub-ranges have been processed.

The numbers N_T and N_R of the most promising candidates to be taken from the table of candidates is a critical parameter as it allows to hasten the experiment to the detriment of the success probability. A small value decreases the number of candidates that will be evaluated against the equations for a wider range of clocks. At the same time, it reduces the chances that the correct candidate belongs to the reduced list and thus that the attack is successful.

Indeed, if the algorithm fails to capture the right status in a reduced list of a sub-range, it is certain that it will not be present in the final joint table.

To find out the most convenient threshold for the selection of the most promising candidates, we have experimentally determined the probability that the correct candidate was in the reduced list. We have conducted these experiments for different quantity of available plaintexts, for several sub-ranges against both the C-Channel and the B-Field. Figures 2a and 2b present the probabilities that the correct candidate is in the top N_T of the corresponding sub-ranges for respectively 16384 and 32768 available plaintexts when attacking the B-Field.

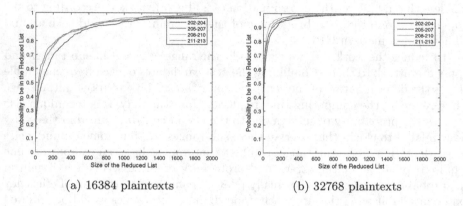

(a) 16384 plaintexts   (b) 32768 plaintexts

Fig. 2. Probability that the correct candidate is in the top N_T for several sub-ranges while attacking the B-Field.

As it can be observed in these figures, the increase of available plaintexts increases the chances that the correct candidate is in the reduced table. However, it should be kept in mind that it also increases the time required for the evaluation of all equations. As a consequence, the size of the reduced table should be selected taking into consideration the quantity of available plaintext, the desired probability of success and the available time to conduct the attack. An interesting fact is that even if the right candidate was not in a good position in one or more tables during the experiments we conduct (see Sect. 6 for more details on these experiments), it can be the first one in the final one, due to the fact the wider the range, the more equations will contribute to the determination of the most probable candidate.

5.3   Selection of the Relevant Equations

Following the approach described in the previous subsection, we divide the full range in four sub-ranges of three clocks each. For each sub-range we only consider the keystream bits for which the associated equations have a relevant weight for this range of clocks. Indeed, the impact of a certain keystream bit on a given sub-range is directly dependent on the shifted binomial distribution of the clocks.

As an example, the first bit of the keystream has much more impact on the range [102, 104] than on the range [111, 113] as the distribution of the clocks is centred in 102.5. Therefore, by evaluating in every sub-range only the relevant set of equations we optimise the performance of the attack.

For a given set of clocks and a given bit of keystream, the bias of the corresponding equation is the difference between the probability that such equation is verified and the expected probability of 50 %. Given a range of clocks and a keystream bit, the associated accumulated bias is the sum of the bias of each possible equation from the given range of clocks for the specific bit of the keystream. Figure 3 represents graphically the computed accumulated bias for different keystream bits sub-ranges of clocks. Based on these results, we have selected the list of pertinent equations to be evaluated in each sub-range.

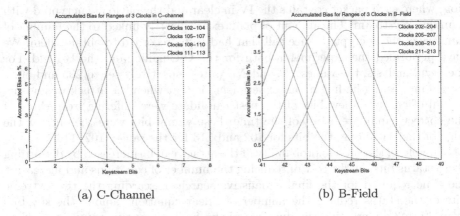

(a) C-Channel   (b) B-Field

Fig. 3. Accumulated bias for sub-ranges of 3 clocks

It can be observed in Fig. 3 that the accumulated bias for a given keystream bit decreases proportionally to the position of the bit considered. For example, the accumulated bias of the bit 41 (first bit of the keystream related to the B-Field) is almost half compared to the first bit of the keystream. This is a direct result of the irregular clocking and the increasing uncertainty about the specific combination of clocks that generated that bit. Therefore, the probability that an equation related to this bit gets verified, decreases as well. That is the reason why more plaintext samples are required to successfully attack the B-Field data compared to the C-Channel one, as it will be described in the next section.

6   Experimental Results of Our Attack

In order to test experimentally the cryptanalysis attack we have described, we have conducted several experiments, both with simulated and actual data, aimed at validating and benchmarking our attack. Both the attacks against the C-Channel and the B-Field have been considered, using the ranges of clocks [102, 113] and [202, 213] respectively.

For all the experiments, we have followed the approach described in the previous section where the full range is divided in four sub-ranges of three clocks each and the first 9 bits of keystream are used for the attack.

6.1 Results Based on Simulated Data

In this subsection we present the results obtained in our experiments using simulated data. In our experiments we have generated a total of 200 random DSC keys and for each one we have created several sets of plaintext samples (IV and keystream) of different sizes. For each of the 200 keys, the first IV of the first sample was generated randomly and the subsequent IVs incrementally, mimicking the behaviour of actual DECT devices.

Each set of plaintext represents a recording of an encrypted DECT conversation, where each packet contains the IV in clear and the payload encrypted with a unique keystream. The amount of plaintext is directly linked to the number of minutes of the encrypted voice call that had to be recorded to obtain them. We have performed the experiments both for the C-Channel and the B-Field. For the cryptanalysis, the values N_T and N_R were respectively set to 200 and 50.

An interesting finding in our experiments is that when the attack was unsuccessful often only a few bits of the best candidate were differing from those of the correct candidate. Most of the time these wrong bits were the ones at the edge of the range (e.g. the bits for 102 and 113 for the range [102, 113]).

Therefore, the success probability of the attack can be increased by discarding these status bits, at the cost of reducing the number of equations and increasing the time required for the final exhaustive search. Discarding the two extreme bits of the status reduces the number of linear equations among the key bits from 39 to 33, increasing the duration of the final exhaustive search step. Nevertheless, the exhaustive search would still be conducted in seconds while this choice will sensibly increase the success probability, potentially outputting the correct candidate even if it was previously discarded in a preliminary sub-list.

Table 2 displays the percentage of time the correct status was output in first position by our attack so that they can be compared on a fair basis with the results of the NTW attack [6]. These results are slightly better (up to 10 % additional keys retrieved) when the brute-force step evaluates the other possible statuses output by the final step. For example, while the success probability is about 69 % when extracting 39 equations attacking the B-Field with 32 K plaintexts, it reaches 76 % by considering the final output list. Considering 33 equations, our attack guesses the correct candidate with a probability slightly higher than 50 % when using around 8192 plaintexts from the C-Channel. In this case, the final exhaustive search step is able to retrieve the correct key with a probability of $1 - 2^{-64} \approx 100\%$ in around 5 seconds using our CPU SIMD-based implementation with an Core i7 (AVX) workstation. To reach a more or less equivalent success rate, the NTW cryptanalysis attack requires at least four times more plaintext material. The success probability can be raised to more than 70 % using only 21 equations at the price of a longer but still reasonable exhaustive search of less than 5 hours.

Table 2. Success rate of the C-Channel and B-Field attack for the respective range [102, 113] and [202, 213]

Number of plaintext	C-Channel			B-Field		
	4096	8192	16384	8192	16384	32768
9 equations	35%	85%	98%	19%	69%	94%
21 equations	16%	73%	97%	10%	57%	90%
33 equations	6%	**55%**	95%	3%	**36%**	82%
39 equations	2%	33%	84%	1%	21%	66%

Although at a first sight it seems much more interesting to attack the C-Channel rather than the B-Field, based on the number of requested plaintext, it shall be noted that only a limited amount of DECT packets per second (around 5) are typically sent over the C-Channel, in comparison with the 100 that are sent per second in the B-Field. Consequently, 20 times more plaintext is produced in the B-Field which makes the attack over the B-Field more realistic in terms of minimum call duration required to conduct the attack.

To illustrate this we present some values regarding the communication time. To reach a 50% chance to retrieve the key using C-Channel plaintext, 20 min of conversation have to be recorded whilst the NTW attack requires around 1 hour and 50 min to reach the same success rate. Considering a B-Field attack, we achieve a success rate of 30% using just 180 seconds of communication when the NTW attack needs more than ten minute for the same result.

6.2   Results Based on Real Data

In order to validate our findings with actual data, we have performed a set of experiments applying our cryptanalysis to break actual DECT encrypted calls. For that purpose we have used several DECT cordless phones, from several manufacturers, that we have previously verified and found to be encrypted following the approach described by Sanchez et al. [7].

The attacks we have performed were focused on B-Field data. Since our attack, like the NTW one, is a known-plaintext attack, the attacker requires knowledge about the first 9 bits of keystream. The approach followed for the experiments was to use the silence transmitted by the call in order to obtain the plaintext, assuming it would be encoded as all ones by the G726 codec. However, during our experiments, we have noticed that often the sound transmitted was not perfect silence leading to less than 100% accurate prediction of the plaintext.

In a first round, we validated our attack assuming 100% accuracy in the prediction of the plaintext. In order to do so, we followed the approach described by Coisel and Sanchez in [1] to obtain the long-term key shared by the base station and the handset. With this knowledge the session key derived at the beginning of the communication can be retrieved and thus the communication can be decrypted leading to a full knowledge of the plaintext.

This step is by no means required to conduct the cryptanalysis attack described in this paper and it was performed with the sole purpose of helping us to debug the process and work with a perfect accurate prediction of the plaintext. A more realistic scenario where the complete recovery of the plaintext material is not possible is presented in the experiments described in the next section.

Our first attempts to recover key were performed by analysing 5 min DECT encrypted calls (corresponding to 32 K samples) from several handsets of different brands. In our first attempts, our tests had a success rate of over sixty-six percent. When analysing calls over 10 min, our tests were all successful.

6.3 Partially-Known Plaintext Attack

As said in the previous section, in practice an attacker would encounter many difficulties predicting the 9 bits of keystream required to conduct the attack against the B-Field. We have found out that depending on the background and equipment noise, the accuracy of the recovered keystream, under the assumption that the plaintext was pure silence, ranges from 85 % to 95 %.

When one of the keystream bits used in an equation is wrong, the probability that the correct status belongs to the candidate list drops to 50 %. We could consider that in this case, the vote cast by that equation is randomly distributed among the possible status candidates. This fact reduces the overall probability that the candidate belongs to the reduced list of a sub-ranges.

To verify this statement, we have experimentally determined the probability that the correct candidate is included in the reduced list of the sub-range [202, 204], for several degrees of inaccuracy in the prediction of the keystream. Figure 4 displays the results of the experiment. The loss of accuracy can be compensated by increasing the size of the reduced list at the price of the overall efficiency. Analysing more plaintext can as well compensate the loss of accuracy. To measure the decrease of the success probability we have benchmarked our attack using simulated data against the B-Field assuming the knowledge of 32,768 and 64,536 plaintexts for several degrees of accuracy. The results presented in Table 3 are the success probabilities to retrieve the session key among the final output list of candidates.

We have applied the attack on the real capture we made for different parameters to validate that our attack works in practice even if the plaintext is only partially known. The plaintext used in the attack represents mostly silence and is accurate at approximately 90 %. All our attempts using 65 K plaintexts whilst defining 39 linear relations amongst the key bits were successful. The success rate of the tests we have conducted using 32 K plaintexts are in agreement with the results of Table 3.

We have made an interesting discovery analysing decrypted data coming from our practical experiments intercepting DECT communications. The distribution of the zeros, bits differing from pure silence, is not uniform over the 9 bits of the keystream. We have noticed unexpected patterns in groups of 4 bits, probably derived from the way the G726 encodes the voice. This fact opens the door to an

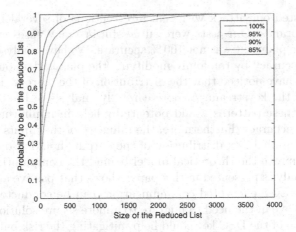

Fig. 4. Probability that the correct candidate belongs to the reduced list

Table 3. Success rate of the B-Field attack for the range [202,213]

Accuracy of plaintext	32768 plaintexts				65536 plaintexts			
	100%	95%	90%	85%	100%	95%	90%	85%
9 equations	96%	92%	71%	55%	100%	100%	100%	92%
21 equations	91%	78%	57%	37%	100%	100%	96%	81%
33 equations	85%	65%	42%	21%	99%	98%	87%	70%
39 equations	81%	56%	28%	11%	99%	94%	85%	63%

optimisation of our cryptanalysis attack for these scenarios where the accuracy in the recovery of the keystream is not 100%. Indeed, given the fact that some keystream bits are more likely to be ones than others, the weight of the equations can be adjusted on the basis of the probability that the keystream bit is guessed correctly. This improvement would reduce the impact of the loss of accuracy and will be explored in future research.

7   Conclusions and Future Developments

In this paper we have presented an improved cryptanalysis attack against the DECT Standard Cipher, leveraging over the clock guessing approach introduced by the NTW attack. In comparison, our approach offers better accuracy and requires substantially less amount of keystream material.

One of the limitations of the former NTW attack was precisely the difficulty to obtain enough keystreams. To reach a 50% success probability whilst defining 30 linear equations, the NTW attack requires 1 hour and 50 min of communication in the case of the C-Channel and more than 15 min in the case of the B-Field. Our attack retrieves the key with better success probabilities requiring over twenty-five percent less plaintext, respectively analysing a 27 min call for the C-Channel or 3 min one for the B-Field.

We have tested our attack with real interceptions of several DECT phones from different brands. Our tests were successful in many cases even when the prediction of the plaintext was not 100 % accurate. We have analysed the impact of this loss of accuracy by randomly modifying the plaintext in our simulation.

However we have noticed that the distribution of the "errors" is not uniform over the bits of the keystream. A more carefully analysis of the origin and the distribution of these patterns would potentially help in minimising the impact form the loss of accuracy. Furthermore, the influence of the inputs to the output combiner in the probability distribution of the output should also be considered to refine and improve the theoretical model behind the computation of weights.

The cryptanalysis presented in this paper shows that passive attacks against the privacy of DECT encrypted communications can be conducted in practice. We strongly believe in the need to migrate to a more secure solution. A continuous renegotiation of the DSC key could help mitigating the risk but, on the basis of our results, it should be done at least every 30 seconds so that an attacker would not be able to retrieve enough plaintext material to launch an effective attack. However, a definitive solution will only arrive with the effective deployment of DECT devices using the new DSC2 algorithm recently included in the standard, which up until now has shown no similar weaknesses.

References

1. Coisel, I., Sanchez, I.: Practical interception of DECT encrypted voice communication in unified communications environments. In: IEEE Joint Intelligence and Security Informatics Conference, JISIC 2014, pp. 115–122. IEEE (2014)
2. ETSI: ETSI DECT Official Website (2013). http://www.etsi.org/technologies-clusters/technologies/dect/
3. Lucks, S., Schuler, A., Tews, E., Weinmann, R.-P., Wenzel, M.: Attacks on the DECT authentication mechanisms. In: Fischlin, M. (ed.) CT-RSA 2009. LNCS, vol. 5473, pp. 48–65. Springer, Heidelberg (2009)
4. Maximov, A., Johansson, T., Babbage, S.: An improved correlation attack on A5/1. In: Handschuh, H., Hasan, M.A. (eds.) SAC 2004. LNCS, vol. 3357, pp. 1–18. Springer, Heidelberg (2004)
5. McHardy, P., Schuler, A., Tews, E.: Interactive decryption of DECT phone calls. In: Proceedings of the fourth ACM Conference on Wireless Network Security, pp. 71–78. ACM (2011)
6. Nohl, K., Tews, E., Weinmann, R.-P.: Cryptanalysis of the DECT standard cipher. In: Hong, S., Iwata, T. (eds.) FSE 2010. LNCS, vol. 6147, pp. 1–18. Springer, Heidelberg (2010)
7. Sanchez, I., Baldini, G., Shaw, D., Giuliani, R.: Experimental Passive Eavesdropping of Digital enhanced cordless telecommunication voice communications through low-cost software defined radios. Secur. Commun. Netw. 8(3), 403–417 (2014)
8. Weiner, M., Tews, E., Heinz, B., Heyszl, J.: FPGA implementation of an improved attack against the DECT standard cipher. In: Proceedings of the 13th International Conference on Information Security and Cryptology, ICISC 2010, pp. 177–188. Springer-Verlag (2011)

Practical Key Recovery for Discrete-Logarithm Based Authentication Schemes from Random Nonce Bits

Aurélie Bauer[1](✉) and Damien Vergnaud[2]

[1] Agence Nationale de la Sécurité des Systèmes d'Information,
51 Boulevard de la Tour-Maubourg, 75700 Paris 07 SP, France
aurelie.bauer@ssi.gouv.fr
[2] École Normale Supérieure – C.N.R.S. – I.N.R.I.A.,
45, rue d'Ulm, 75230 Paris Cedex 05, France

Abstract. We propose statistical cryptanalysis of discrete-logarithm based authentication schemes such as Schnorr identification scheme or Girault-Poupard-Stern identification and signature schemes. We consider two scenarios where an adversary is given some information on the nonces used during the signature generation process or during some identification sessions. In the first scenario, we assume that some bits of the nonces are known exactly by the adversary, while no information is provided about the other bits. We show, for instance, that the GPS scheme with 128-bit security can be broken using only 710 signatures assuming that the adversary knows (on average) one bit per nonce. In the second scenario, we assume that all bits of the nonces are obtained from the correct ones by independent bit flipping with some small probability. A detailed heuristic analysis is provided, supported by extensive experiments.

Keywords: Schnorr identification · Girault-Poupard-Stern identification · Girault-Poupard-Stern signatures · Statistical cryptanalysis

1 Introduction

Since the introduction of the ElGamal signature scheme [6], many works have been devoted to design digital signatures and identification schemes, based on the *discrete logarithm problem* in a finite cyclic group $\mathbb{G}$ of order q (*e.g.* [14]). After Schnorr's proof of knowledge for discrete logarithms in groups of known prime order [22] (that can be used as an interactive identification scheme or be converted into a digital signature scheme using the Fiat-Shamir paradigm [8]), many other signature schemes have been designed, including the standard DSA [17]. Another variant, proposed by Girault [9] and further analysed by Poupard and Stern [10,21] – called GPS – allows to use groups of unknown order.

All these signature and identification schemes perform randomized authentication: they use a *nonce* (or *ephemeral key*) r in $\{0, 1, \ldots, q-1\}$ for each message (or identification session) and compute g^r with g some generator of $\mathbb{G}$. These

© International Association for Cryptologic Research 2015
T. Güneysu and H. Handschuh (Eds.): CHES 2015, LNCS 9293, pp. 287–306, 2015.
DOI: 10.1007/978-3-662-48324-4_15

random nonces can be generated using either a (true) random number generator or a pseudo-random one. Obviously extreme care is required in sampling such nonces since a predictable (or reused) output of the (pseudo)random generator may lead to a total break of the scheme. As an example, Bellare, Goldwasser and Micciancio mounted [2] a polynomial time key-recovery attack against the DSA signature scheme when the random nonces are generated using a (truncated) linear congruential generator. In [5], Bleichenbacher found a bias in the original DSA pseudorandom number generator specification, that could reveal the signer's private key and this attack was made practical recently [16].

Using *side-channel attacks*, partial information can be obtained on the nonce r from the run of the algorithm that computes g^r. In [15], Kuwakado and Tanaka proposed a polynomial-time algorithm that recovers the signer's private key given only two signatures with nonces smaller than $\sqrt{q}$ or where half of the nonces' bits are known to the adversary. Nguyen and Shparlinski [18] presented a polynomial-time algorithm that recovers the secret key of the signer when a few consecutive bits of the nonces are known for several signatures. Their algorithm runs in polynomial time when approximately $\sqrt{\log q}$ bits are known for a number of signatures in $O(\log q)$. Note that in practice, side-channel attacks will not generally reveal consecutive bits of the nonces used. Moreover, if countermeasures are used, only noisy information on the secrets may leak through power consumption (or other side-channel attacks) and an adversary may obtain partial information on the nonces (but not with perfect certainty).

In [11], it was reported that memory persistence times can be increased with simple cooling techniques and that an attacker with physical access to a machine may be able to recover some random part of cryptographic key information. Motivated by this work, Heninger and Shacham presented in [13] a new method for recovering RSA private keys given a fraction of private data (see also [20]). Their method succeeds with good probability in quadratic time if a fraction of at least 0.27 of the private key bits are known with certainty. In [12], Henecka, May and Meurer addressed the situation where no RSA private key bits are known with certainty but where a candidate for each secret key bit is known to the adversary in such a way that most bits are correct but some of them (unknown to the adversary) are flipped (in a symmetric way). In [19], Paterson, Polychroniadou and Sibborn brought a coding-theoretic viewpoint to bear on this problem. In particular, they highlighted the fact that the papers [12,13] considered the problem of error-correcting noisy RSA private keys in the binary erasure channel and the binary symmetric channel (respectively). This coding-theoretic viewpoint enabled them to design a new algorithm in another channel model more relevant for the so-called "cold-boot attacks" from [11] and to derive bounds on the performance of the proposed algorithms.

Contributions of the Paper. We propose attacks on discrete-logarithm based authentication schemes where an adversary has some information on the nonces used in the signature generation or in some identification sessions. This information may come from the use of a biased (pseudo)random generator, a side-channel attack or a cold-boot attack. Using the coding-theoretic viewpoint from [19], we consider the following two scenarios:

– *erasure correction scenario:* we assume that some bits of the nonces are known exactly by the adversary, while no information at all is known about the other bits. This is defined in terms of a parameter δ representing the fraction of erasures. In standard coding terminology, this corresponds to an erasure model for errors, and an erasure channel.

– *error correction scenario:* we assume that all bits of the nonces are obtained from the correct ones by independent bit flipping with probability defined by a parameter also denoted δ. In coding-theoretic terms, this corresponds to a (memoryless) binary symmetric channel with crossover probability δ.

Our attacks apply to discrete-logarithm based authentication schemes where the "authentication relation" holds over the integers (instead of modulo the group order q). In particular, they can be applied readily to the GPS identification and the GPS signature schemes. However, they can also be mounted against Schnorr identification protocol if the adversary is first allowed to interact with the prover in a "dishonest" way before trying to impersonate her. In this *active attack model* [4,7], which is the standard *de facto* security notion, an adversary can simply choose small challenges in the identification session in order to obtain an authentication relation that holds over the integers (after a small brute force search of the size of the chosen challenge).

In the erasure correction scenario, we provide an algorithm that, given t signatures or identification sessions (with $t \geq 2$) and partial information on the corresponding nonces with a fraction of erasures $\delta \simeq \ln(2)/t$, recovers the corresponding secret key in (heuristic) quadratic time. The algorithm recovers the nonces bit-by-bit, starting from the least significant bit to the most significant one, by growing a search tree and pruning it to remove partial solutions which do not match the known key bits. The algorithm is similar to the one proposed in [13] but works for any $t \geq 2$ and requires a more complex analysis. We implemented it and performed extensive experiments; in particular, we attack a 128-bit security level instantiation of GPS signature scheme that uses 512-bit nonces [10,21] with $\delta \simeq 1/512$ (*i.e.* with on average only one nonce bit known for each signature). Our analysis guarantees that the private key can be recovered given only 710 signatures and a very naïve implementation actually gives the secret key in a few minutes. In the error correction scenario, we provide an algorithm that, given t signatures or identification sessions (with $t \geq 2$) and partial information on the corresponding nonces with a fraction of errors $\delta \simeq 1/2 - \sqrt{\ln(2)/2t}$, recovers the corresponding secret key in (heuristic) quadratic time. We implemented our algorithm and performed extensive experiments using it. The attack analysis is simpler and follows closely the one presented in [12].

2   Preliminaries

Schnorr Identification. Let $\mathbb{G} = \langle g \rangle$ be a group of (known) prime order q and P and V denote a prover and a verifier. By engaging in the protocol, P proves to V that she knows the discrete logarithm x of a public group element $y = g^x$. The protocol has three simple moves:

Commitment. P selects a random $r \in \{0, 1, \ldots, q-1\}$ and sends $k = g^r$ to V.
Challenge. V picks a random $c \in \{0, 1, \ldots, q-1\}$ and sends c to P.
Response. P computes and sends $s = r + cx \bmod q$ to V.

Eventually, V checks that $g^s \cdot y^{-c} = k$ and recognizes that P knows x if the equality holds. Schnorr's scheme is one of the most important ingredients in the design of cryptographic protocols and proofs of knowledge. It readily gives rise to an identification scheme where P proves her knowledge of the discrete logarithm of her public key.

The strongest form of attack against an identification scheme is an *active attack*, where the adversary (that wants to impersonate P) interacts with P, posing as V, but not necessarily following V's protocol. Since active attacks are quite feasible in practice, this model has become the standard *de facto* security notion for identification scheme. In [4], Bellare and Palacio proved that Schnorr identification scheme is secure against active attacks assuming the *one-more discrete logarithm assumption* in $\mathbb{G}$ (see [3]).

GPS Identification and Signature Scheme. The GPS schemes were proposed by Girault in [9] and further analysed by Poupard and Stern [10, 21]. The schemes are similar to Schnorr's but allow to use groups of unknown order. Given a group $\mathbb{G} = \langle g \rangle$ generated by g, of (possibly) unknown order and three parameters $R, S, C \in \mathbb{N}$, the protocol has three simple moves to prove the knowledge of $x \in \{0, \ldots, S\}$ such that $y = g^x$:

Commitment. P selects a random $r \in \{0, 1, \ldots, R\}$ and sends $k = g^r$ to V.
Challenge. V picks a random $c \in \{0, 1, \ldots, C\}$ and sends c to P.
Response. P computes and sends $s = r + cx$ to V.

Eventually, V checks that $g^s = ky^c$ and recognizes that P knows x if the equality holds and $s \in \{0, 1, \ldots, R + CS\}$. GPS signature scheme is derived from the identification scheme using the Fiat-Shamir heuristic [8]: to sign a message $m \in \{0, 1\}^*$, the signer selects a random $r \in \{0, 1, \ldots, R\}$, computes $k = g^r$, computes $c = \mathcal{H}(m, k)$ where $\mathcal{H} : \{0, 1\}^* \longrightarrow \{0, 1, \ldots, C\}$ is a cryptographic hash function and outputs the pair (s, c) where $s = r + cx$ as the signature of the message m. The security of the signature scheme against existential forgeries under chosen message attacks was proven (when $\mathcal{H}$ is modelled as a random oracle) in [10] under the assumption that computing discrete logarithms in $\mathbb{G}$ with exponents in $\{0, 1, \ldots, S\}$ is hard. For a k-bit security level, the analysis requires to use $S \simeq 2^{2k}$, $C \simeq 2^k$ and $R \simeq 2^{4k}$.

Authentication Relation. In the following, we call the authentication relation of a discrete-logarithm based authentication scheme, the relation used in the **Response** phase of the three-move identification scheme (or in the signature generation protocol). Our attacks apply to all discrete-logarithm based authentication scheme for which this authentication relation holds over the integers. This is obviously the case for GPS identification and signature schemes. However, our attack also applies to Schnorr identification if one considers an adversary allowed to mount an active attack and that has access to partial information on the nonce bits used in the different identification sessions. Such an adversary posing as V can indeed pick small challenges c (e.g. always $c = 1$). Since we have $s = r + cx \bmod q$ in Schnorr identification scheme, we obtain $s = r + cx + \alpha q$, where $\alpha \in \mathbb{Z}_-$ and $|\alpha| \leq c$. By performing an exhaustive search on the small set of values for α (e.g. $\alpha \in \{-1, 0\}$ when $c = 1$), the adversary obtains an authentication relation that holds over the integers.

Note that for all these discrete-logarithm based schemes, the knowledge of the random values generated during the signature process/identification session provides precious information on the signer's secret key. In particular, if an adversary is given access to a valid signature/identification transcript $\sigma = (s, c)$ (possibly for some message m), and to the nonce r such that $g^s = g^r y^c$ then he can retrieve the value of the signer's secret key x in polynomial time. Therefore, in the following, we will focus on attacks that aim to recover a complete nonce from partial information on nonces used in several signatures/identification sessions.

3   Erasure Correction Scenario

In this section, we focus on the *erasure correction scenario* described in the introduction where part of the bits of the random value r generated during the signature process are revealed to the attacker. To be more precise, we denote the binary decomposition of r as $r_0 + r_1 2^1 + \cdots + r_{n-1} 2^{n-1}$ and we introduce a parameter δ, with $0 \leq \delta \leq 1$, to define the probability that, at a given position $i \in \{0, \ldots, n-1\}$, the bit r_i is known to the adversary (and probability $(1 - \delta)$ that bit r_i is unknown).

Assuming that t signatures have been processed, we determine a lower-bound on δ allowing the attacker to fully recover the secret key x in (heuristic) polynomial time. We focus on the particular case of the GPS signature scheme, but as explained previously any other signature or identification scheme using authentication relations defined over the integers can be attacked similarly. In the following we first focus on the simple case of two signatures, and then generalize the study for a higher number of signatures.

3.1   The Attack Knowing Two Signatures

We assume that the adversary is given access to two valid signatures $\sigma_1 = (s_1, c_1)$ and $\sigma_2 = (s_2, c_2)$, respectively related to the messages m_1 and m_2. According to the description of the GPS scheme, provided in Sect. 2, the following relations hold:

$$s_1 = r_1 + c_1 x \text{ and } s_2 = r_2 + c_2 x \tag{1}$$

where r_1 and r_2 are nonces generated during the signature process and $c_i = \mathcal{H}(m_i, g^{r_i})$ (for $i \in \{1, 2\}$). Eliminating the unknown x in (1), we get:

$$C = r_1 c_2 - r_2 c_1 \tag{2}$$

where $C = s_1 c_2 - s_2 c_1$. Our algorithm will construct all pairs $(\vartheta_1, \vartheta_2)$ that satisfy (2) and match the known partial information on (r_1, r_2) - in the sequel we denote as $\mathcal{L}$ the list of such elements - and eventually, select, among them, the one that verifies the relations (1).

General Idea. Following [13], our method to construct the set $\mathcal{L}$ consists in performing an exhaustive search on all pairs $(\vartheta_1, \vartheta_2)$ satisfying Eq. (2), guessing each of their bits from the least significant one to the most significant, and detecting invalid candidates during the process. Given a pair $(\vartheta_1, \vartheta_2)$ for which the relation (2) holds, if we denote $\vartheta_\alpha^{(i)} = \vartheta_{\alpha,0} + 2\vartheta_{\alpha,1} + \ldots + \vartheta_{\alpha,i} 2^i$ where $\vartheta_\alpha^{(i)} = \vartheta_\alpha \bmod 2^{i+1}$ and $\vartheta_{\alpha,j} \in \{0,1\}$ for $\alpha \in \{1,2\}$ and $j \in \{0, \ldots, i\}$, we get:

$$
\begin{cases}
C = \vartheta_{1,0}\, c_2 - \vartheta_{2,0}\, c_1 \quad \bmod 2 \\
C = (\vartheta_{1,0} + 2\vartheta_{1,1})c_2 - (\vartheta_{2,0} + 2\vartheta_{2,1})c_1 \quad \bmod 2^2 \\
\quad \vdots \\
C = (\sum_{i=0}^{n-1} \vartheta_{1,i}\, 2^i)c_2 - (\sum_{i=0}^{n-1} \vartheta_{2,i}\, 2^i)c_1 \quad \bmod 2^n
\end{cases}
\tag{3}
$$

Thus one can verify, at each step of the bit generations of $\vartheta_{1,i}$ and $\vartheta_{2,i}$, for i from 0 to $(n-1)$, whether the equation modulo 2^{i+1} of System (3) holds for the pair. If not, the corresponding bit-values for $(\vartheta_{1,i}, \vartheta_{2,i})$ are not kept as valid ones in the sequel of the bit-generations of $(\vartheta_{1,j}, \vartheta_{2,j})$ for j going from $(i+1)$ to $(n-1)$. This technique allows to reduce the size of the list $\mathcal{L}$ containing all final potential candidates $(\vartheta_1, \vartheta_2)$. In the following, we show that, in fact, this method leads to a polynomial time algorithm.

Description of the Technique. Let us now explain how to construct the list $\mathcal{L}$. In the analysis that follows, we use the notation $\mathcal{L}^{(k)}$ to refer to the state of list $\mathcal{L}$ at step k of the algorithm. Such a list will be defined as containing elements $(\vartheta_1, \vartheta_2)$ that are reduced modulo 2^{k+1}.

The basic principle of the algorithm can be sum up that way: the list $\mathcal{L}^{(0)}$ is first initialized with all pairs of bits $(\vartheta_{1,0}, \vartheta_{2,0})$ that satisfy Eq. 1 of System (3) modulo 2 and that coincide with the bit-values preliminary known by the adversary on r_1 and r_2. All pairs $(\vartheta_{1,0}, \vartheta_{2,0})$ in $\mathcal{L}^{(0)}$ are then lifted to construct values modulo 2^2. To do so, one has to generate all possible values for pairs of bits $(\vartheta_{1,1}, \vartheta_{2,1})$ (which again coincide with the bits known by the adversary on $r_{1,1}$ and $r_{2,1}$) and to construct $\vartheta_1^{(1)}$ and $\vartheta_2^{(1)}$ respectively as $\vartheta_{1,0} + 2\vartheta_{1,1}$ and $\vartheta_{2,0} + 2\vartheta_{2,1}$. From now the obtained values $(\vartheta_1^{(1)}, \vartheta_2^{(1)})$ are checked to determine whether they satisfy Eq. 2 of System (3) modulo 2^2. In case of an invalid answer, the corresponding bit-values for $(\vartheta_{1,1}, \vartheta_{2,1})$ are evicted and all remaining valid pairs $(\vartheta_1^{(1)}, \vartheta_2^{(1)})$ are put in $\mathcal{L}^{(1)}$. The process then continues from a bit-position i to the following one, taking all pairs $(\vartheta_1^{(i)}, \vartheta_2^{(i)})$ belonging to $\mathcal{L}^{(i)}$ at step i, lifting them by generating all possible bit-pairs $(\vartheta_{1,i+1}, \vartheta_{2,i+1})$ that coincide with the known bits on $r_{1,i+1}$ and $r_{2,i+1}$ and by creating new values $\vartheta_1^{(i+1)} = \vartheta_1^{(i)} + 2^{i+1}\vartheta_{1,i+1}$ and $\vartheta_2^{(i+1)} = \vartheta_2^{(i)} + 2^{i+1}\vartheta_{2,i+1}$, and checking whether Equation

$(i+2)$ of System (3) is satisfied modulo 2^{i+2}. Again, invalid solutions are evicted and the remaining pairs constitute the set $\mathcal{L}^{(i+1)}$. The algorithm finally stops when i equals n. A description of the whole process is provided in Algorithm 1.

Algorithm 1. Generic Attack on Two Signatures

Require: c_1, c_2, C and δ : partial bit information on r_1 and r_2
Ensure: $\mathcal{L}$ a list of pairs $(\vartheta_1, \vartheta_2)$ possible candidates for (r_1, r_2)
1: $\mathcal{L}^{(0)} = \{\}$
2:
    ——/* *Initialisation - Case i = 0* */——
3:   Generate all bit pairs for $(\vartheta_{1,0}, \vartheta_{2,0})$: $\mathcal{E} = (0,0), (1,0), (0,1), (1,1)$
4:   **for each** element $(\vartheta_{1,0}, \vartheta_{2,0}) \in \mathcal{E}$ **do**
5:      **if** $(\vartheta_{1,0}, \vartheta_{2,0})$ coincides with knowledge of $(r_{1,0}, r_{2,0})$ **then**
6:         **if** $(\vartheta_{1,0}, \vartheta_{2,0})$ satisfies Equation (1) of System (3) modulo 2 **then**
7:            Add element $(\vartheta_{1,0}, \vartheta_{2,0})$ to $\mathcal{L}^{(0)}$
8:
    ——/* *Main loop for i from 1 to n − 1* */——
9:   **for** i from 1 to $n - 1$ **do**
10:    $\mathcal{L}^{(i)} = \{\}$
11:    Generate all bit pairs for $(\vartheta_{1,i}, \vartheta_{2,i})$: $\mathcal{E} = (0,0), (0,1), (1,0), (1,1)$
12:    **for each** element $(\vartheta_{1,i}, \vartheta_{2,i}) \in \mathcal{E}$ **do**
13:      **if** $(\vartheta_{1,i}, \vartheta_{2,i})$ coincides with knowledge of $(r_{1,i}, r_{2,i})$ **then**
14:         **for each** element $(\vartheta_1^{(i-1)}, \vartheta_2^{(i-1)}) \in \mathcal{L}^{(i-1)}$ **do**
15:            Lift $\vartheta_1^{(i)} = \vartheta_1^{(i-1)} + 2^i\,\vartheta_{1,i}$ and Lift $\vartheta_2^{(i)} = \vartheta_2^{(i-1)} + 2^i\,\vartheta_{2,i}$
16:            **if** $(\vartheta_1^{(i)}, \vartheta_2^{(i)})$ satisfies Equation $(i + 1)$ of System (3) modulo 2^{i+1} **then**
17:               Add $(\vartheta_1^{(i)}, \vartheta_2^{(i)})$ to $\mathcal{L}^{(i)}$
18: **return** $\mathcal{L}^{(n-1)}$

Complexity Analysis. Estimating the overall complexity of Algorithm 1 can be reduced to the cost of constructing the list $\mathcal{L}^{(n-1)}$. Since this list has been built recursively from the previous ones $\mathcal{L}^{(n-2)}, \mathcal{L}^{(n-3)}, \ldots, \mathcal{L}^{(0)}$, we have to evaluate the expected cardinal of all $\mathcal{L}^{(i)}$ for i going from 0 to $(n - 1)$ (denoted $\mathcal{N}^{(i)}$).

Let us first count the number of elements belonging to $\mathcal{L}^{(0)}$. By definition, this list contains all bit pairs $(\vartheta_{1,0}, \vartheta_{2,0})$ coinciding with the (possible) knowledge of $(r_{1,0}, r_{2,0})$ and satisfying Eq. (1) of System (3). In fact, the number of solutions to that equation strongly relies on the parity of both c_1 and c_2. Indeed, two even values would give four pairs of solutions (in the general case) opposed to only two for odd values c_1 and c_2. For this reason, we have to split the analysis that follows in two scenarios, depending on the 2-adic valuation[1] of both c_1 and c_2. In the sequel, we denote as ℓ_1 (resp. ℓ_2) the 2-adic valuation of c_1 (resp. c_2).

- **First analysis when $\ell_1 = \ell_2$**

Before coming back to the evaluation of the cardinality of the list $\mathcal{L}^{(0)}$, let us first see how the relation $\ell_1 = \ell_2$ impacts the shape of the equations belonging to System (3). When ℓ_1 and ℓ_2 are equal, Eq. (2) can be simplified by dividing both sides of the equality by 2^{ℓ_1}. Indeed as this can be done for c_1 and c_2, this

---

[1] We remind that the 2-adic valuation of a number c denotes the largest power of 2 dividing c.

is obviously also the case for C. Thus, the shape of the relation does not change and the new obtained constants $c_1/2^{\ell_1}$ and $c_2/2^{\ell_1}$ are odd. In the following, for the sake of simplicity (and as this does not change the analysis, at the cost of renaming the variables), we still work with Eq. (2) (and thus with System (3)) but assuming that the constants c_1 and c_2 are odd.

From now on, one can easily describe the elements that belong to $\mathcal{L}^{(0)}$ as bit-values of the form $(\vartheta_{1,0}, \vartheta_{2,0})$ satisfying $C = \vartheta_{1,0} + \vartheta_{2,0} \mod 2$, and such that $(\vartheta_{1,0}, \vartheta_{2,0})$ coincide with possible knowledge of $(r_{1,0}, r_{2,0})$. This description allows to evaluate $\mathcal{N}^{(0)}$, see Lemma 1 (a proof can be found in the full version of the paper [1]).

Lemma 1. *We have $\mathcal{N}^{(0)} = \delta^2 - 2\delta + 2$.*

We now have to find, for a fixed i between 1 and $(n-1)$, an expression of $\mathcal{N}^{(i)}$ in function of $\mathcal{N}^{(i-1)}$. By definition $\mathcal{L}^{(i)}$ can be described as the set of elements $(\vartheta_1^{(i)}, \vartheta_2^{(i)})$ defined as $\vartheta_1^{(i)} = \vartheta_1^{(i-1)} + 2^i \vartheta_{1,i}$ and $\vartheta_2^{(i)} = \vartheta_2^{(i-1)} + 2^i \vartheta_{2,i}$ with $(\vartheta_1^{(i-1)}, \vartheta_2^{(i-1)}) \in \mathcal{L}^{(i-1)}$, $(\vartheta_{1,i}, \vartheta_{2,i}) \in \{0,1\}^2$ and satisfying Equation $(i+1)$ of System (3), namely:

$$C = (\vartheta_1^{(i-1)} + 2^i \vartheta_{1,i})c_2 - (\vartheta_2^{(i-1)} + 2^i \vartheta_{2,i})c_1 \mod 2^{i+1} \tag{4}$$

Moreover, the pairs $(\vartheta_{1,i}, \vartheta_{2,i})$ should coincide with possible information on $(r_{1,i}, r_{2,i})$. Knowing that $(\vartheta_1^{(i-1)}, \vartheta_2^{(i-1)})$ belong to $\mathcal{L}^{(i-1)}$, the relation $C = \vartheta_1^{(i-1)} c_2 - \vartheta_2^{(i-1)} c_1 \mod 2^i$ necessarily holds. As a consequence, there exists an integer $k \in \mathbb{Z}$ such that $C = \vartheta_1^{(i-1)} c_2 - \vartheta_2^{(i-1)} c_1 + k2^i$. Putting this relation into Eq. (4) and simplifying the whole expression allows to reach the following new condition:

$$k = \vartheta_{1,i} + \vartheta_{2,i} \mod 2 \tag{5}$$

The choice of $(\vartheta_{1,i}, \vartheta_{2,i})$ solutions to (5) and coinciding with possible information on $(r_{1,i}, r_{2,i})$, strongly depends on whether $(\vartheta_1^{(i-1)}, \vartheta_2^{(i-1)})$ equals $(r_1^{(i-1)}, r_2^{(i-1)})$ or not. Indeed, if these values are equal, namely $(\vartheta_1^{(i-1)}, \vartheta_2^{(i-1)})$ is the beginning of the *right* solution, then when $r_{1,i}$ and $r_{2,i}$ are known, Eq. (5) necessarily holds (obviously as this is the searched solution). In that case, one will choose $(\vartheta_{1,i}, \vartheta_{2,i}) = (r_{1,i}, r_{2,i})$. To the contrary, when $(\vartheta_1^{(i-1)}, \vartheta_2^{(i-1)}) \neq (r_1^{(i-1)}, r_2^{(i-1)})$, a value is fixed for k and the knowledge of $(r_{1,i}, r_{2,i})$ does not necessarily make Eq. (5) be satisfied. In that case, the choice $(r_{1,i}, r_{2,i})$ will not be maintained. As we cannot determine whether Eq. (5) would be satisfied or not, we introduce a new parameter $\gamma \in [0,1]$, which is only defined when $(\vartheta_1^{(i-1)}, \vartheta_2^{(i-1)}) \neq (r_1^{(i-1)}, r_2^{(i-1)})$, corresponding to the probability that Eq. (5) holds. A detailed discussion on the value of γ is given in Sect. 3.3 (see also the full version of the paper [1]).

We can finally express the number of elements belonging to $\mathcal{L}^{(i)}$ in function of those of $\mathcal{L}^{(i-1)}$, as claimed by the following lemma.

Lemma 2. *Under our heuristic, we have $\mathcal{N}^{(i)} = \mathcal{N}^{(i-1)}(\gamma\delta^2 - 2\delta + 2) + \delta^2(1-\gamma)$.*

A proof of this lemma can be found in the full version of the paper, see [1]. Combining Lemmas 1 and 2, we obtain:

$$\mathcal{N}^{(n-1)} = \mathcal{N}^{(n-2)}(\gamma\delta^2 - 2\delta + 2) + \delta^2(1 - \gamma)$$

$$\vdots$$

$$= (\gamma\delta^2 - 2\delta + 2)^{n-1}(\delta^2 - 2\delta + 2) + \frac{\delta^2(1-\gamma)}{2\delta - \gamma\delta^2 - 1}(1 - (\gamma\delta^2 - 2\delta + 2)^{n-1})$$

The goal of the adversary being to construct the set $\mathcal{L}^{(n-1)}$ in polynomial time, this attack will only be made practical if the quantity $(\gamma\delta^2 - 2\delta + 2)$ is strictly smaller than 1. In that case, the cardinality of the list $\mathcal{L}^{(n-1)}$ will not grow too fast when n tends toward infinity. Since γ is unknown, we have to evaluate it in order to reach some necessary condition on δ. Setting γ to $1/2$ seems to be a reasonable choice, see Sect. 3.3. We finally reach the condition $\frac{1}{2}\delta^2 - 2\delta + 2 < 1$, which is satisfied for $\delta > 2 - \sqrt{2} \simeq 0.59$. By taking this value as a lower bound on δ, we are able to determine the expected size of the set $\mathcal{L}^{(n-1)}$, namely $(3 - 2\sqrt{2})n + 1$. Knowing that n refers to the bit-size of the random values generated during the signature process, we thus obtain a polynomial time complexity for our attack.

Theorem 1 (Two Signatures and $\ell_1 = \ell_2$). *An adversary able to learn a proportion of $\delta = (2 - \sqrt{2})$ bits of the random nonces used during the generation of two known signatures can (heuristically) break the scheme in polynomial time. In that case, the expected space required for performing the attack is $(3 - 2\sqrt{2})n^2 + 1 \simeq 0.17n^2 + 1$.*

• *Second analysis when $\ell_1 \neq \ell_2$*

The study is a bit more tedious here, but the analysis can be adapted to prove Theorem 2. The entire proof is provided in the full version of the paper [1].

Theorem 2 (Two Signatures and $\ell_1 < \ell_2$). *An adversary, able to learn a proportion of $\delta = (2 - \sqrt{2})$ bits of the random nonces used during the generation of two known signatures, can (heuristically) break the scheme in polynomial time. In that case, the expected space required for performing the attack is $(\sqrt{2}-1)n^2 + 1 \simeq 0.41n^2 + 1$.*

When comparing Theorems 1 and 2, one notices that the lower bound on δ is the same for both cases "$\ell_1 = \ell_2$" and "$\ell_1 < \ell_2$". However the space required to construct the sets $\mathcal{L}^{(i)}$ is higher when $\ell_1 \neq \ell_2$ than in the other case. This actually impacts the efficiency of the attack since the number of constructed solutions is larger.

3.2   The Attack Knowing t Signatures

Let us now consider the case of an adversary that is given access to t signatures $\sigma_1, \ldots, \sigma_t$ corresponding to known messages $m_1, \ldots, m_t$. We denote $\sigma_i = (s_i, c_i)$ the signatures and r_i the nonces used in their generation (s.t. $c_i = \mathcal{H}(m_i, g^{r_i})$)

for i in $\{1, \ldots, t\}$. We denote $r_{i,j}$ the j-th bit of r_i for each j in $\{1, \ldots, n\}$ and i in $\{1, \ldots, t\}$. We have $s_i = r_i + c_i \cdot x$ for $i \in \{1, \ldots, t\}$ and we obtain:

$$
\begin{cases}
C_{1,2} = r_1 c_2 - r_2 c_1 \\
\quad \vdots \\
C_{1,t} = r_1 c_t - r_t c_1
\end{cases}
\tag{6}
$$

where $C_{1,j} = s_1 c_j - s_j c_1$ for $j \in \{2, \ldots, t\}$. As above, our algorithm retrieves the nonces $r_1, \ldots, r_t$ by collecting all tuples $(\vartheta_1, \ldots, \vartheta_t)$ satisfying System (6) and coinciding with possible knowledge on the bits $r_{i,j}$. As previously, $\mathcal{L}$ denotes the set containing such elements[2]. The complexity of the attack can thus be reduced to the cost of constructing $\mathcal{L}$.

General Idea. As for the "two-signature case", a way to retrieve $(r_1, \ldots, r_t)$ would consist in performing an exhaustive search on all bit-values $r_{i,j}$, for i going from 1 to t and j from 0 to $(n-1)$, using some possible additional information on the bits $r_{i,j}$, and to detect the invalid candidates during the process. The technique consists in generating all tuples $(\vartheta_1^{(k)}, \ldots, \vartheta_t^{(k)})$ satisfying System (6) modulo 2^{k+1} and to select among them, the one that can be lifted to solutions modulo 2^{k+2}. Of course, these operations should be consistent with the possible knowledge on some bits of the r_i's. In this algorithm, parameter k will vary from 0 to $(n-1)$. At the end of the procedure, the set $\mathcal{L}^{(n-1)}$ containing all elements $(\vartheta_1^{(n-1)}, \ldots, \vartheta_t^{(n-1)})$ satisfying System (6) modulo 2^n and coinciding with known information on the bits $r_{i,j}$, is in fact the desired one: $\mathcal{L}$. A precise description of the whole method is provided in Algorithm 2.

Complexity Analysis. Let us now determine the number of elements belonging to $\mathcal{L}$ by evaluating the expected cardinal of all $\mathcal{L}^{(i)}$ for i going from 0 to $(n-1)$ (denoted $\mathcal{N}^{(i)}$). We start with $\mathcal{L}^{(0)}$ which, by definition, contains all tuples $(\vartheta_{1,0}, \ldots, \vartheta_{t,0})$ in $\{0,1\}^t$ coinciding with possible knowledge on bits $(r_{1,0} \ldots, r_{t,0})$ and verifying System (6) modulo 2. One notices that the number of such solutions strongly depends on the 2-adic valuations of $c_1, \ldots, c_t$. For this reason, and similarly to the "two signatures case", we split the analysis in two configurations depending on whether the 2-adic valuations of $c_1, \ldots, c_t$ are all equal or not. In the rest of the paper, we denote as ℓ_i the 2-adic valuation of c_i (for $i \in \{1, \ldots, t\}$).

• **First analysis with $\ell_1 = \ell_2 = \cdots = \ell_t$**

When the 2-adic valuations are all equal, System (6) can be simplified by dividing each equation by 2^{ℓ_1}. One thus reaches a new system involving simpler equations,

---

[2] Obviously once $(r_1, \ldots, r_t)$ has been retrieved, the signers' secret key x can easily be recovered. Theoretically only one of the r_i's is really necessary to retrieve x, but we see in the following that recovering one such element requires in fact to retrieve all r_is simultaneously.

Algorithm 2. Generic Attack on t Signatures

Require: $(c_1, \ldots, c_t)$, $(C_{1,1}, \ldots, C_{1,t})$, δ and partial bit information on $(r_1, \ldots, r_t)$
Ensure: $\mathcal{L}$ a list of tuples $(\vartheta_1, \ldots, \vartheta_t)$ possible candidates for $(r_1, \ldots, r_t)$
1: $\mathcal{L}^{(0)} = \{\}$
2:
    —/* Initialisation - Case $k = 0$ */—
3: Generate all bit tuples for $(\vartheta_{1,0}, \ldots, \vartheta_{t,0})$, say $\mathcal{E} = \{0, 1\}^t$
4: **for** each element $(\vartheta_{1,0}, \ldots, \vartheta_{t,0}) \in \mathcal{E}$ **do**
5:     **if** $(\vartheta_{1,0}, \ldots, \vartheta_{t,0})$ coincides with knowledge of $(r_{1,0}, \ldots, r_{t,0})$ **then**
6:         **if** $(\vartheta_{1,0}, \ldots, \vartheta_{t,0})$ satisfies System (6) modulo 2 **then**
7:             Add element $(\vartheta_{1,0}, \ldots, \vartheta_{t,0})$ to $\mathcal{L}^{(0)}$
8:
    —/* Main loop for k from 1 to $n-1$ */—
9: **for** k from 1 to $n-1$ **do**
10:    $\mathcal{L}^{(k)} = \{\}$
11:    Generate all bit tuples for $(\vartheta_{1,k}, \ldots, \vartheta_{t,k})$, say $\mathcal{E} = \{0, 1\}^t$
12:    **for** each element $(\vartheta_{1,k}, \ldots, \vartheta_{t,k}) \in \mathcal{E}$ **do**
13:       **if** $(\vartheta_{1,k}, \ldots, \vartheta_{t,k})$ coincides with knowledge of $(r_{1,k}, \ldots, r_{t,k})$ **then**
14:          **for** each element $(\vartheta_1^{(k-1)}, \ldots, \vartheta_t^{(k-1)}) \in \mathcal{L}^{(k-1)}$ **do**
15:             Lift $\vartheta_1^{(k)} = \vartheta_1^{(k-1)} + 2^k \vartheta_{1,k}$

16:             $\vdots$
17:             Lift $\vartheta_t^{(k)} = \vartheta_t^{(k-1)} + 2^k \vartheta_{t,k}$
18:          **if** $(\vartheta_1^{(k)}, \ldots, \vartheta_t^{(k)})$ satisfies System (6) modulo 2^{k+1} **then**
19:             Add $(\vartheta_1^{(k)}, \ldots, \vartheta_t^{(k)})$ to $\mathcal{L}^{(k)}$
20: **return** $\mathcal{L}^{(n-1)}$

say $C'_{1,j} = r_1 d_j - r_j d_1$ where $C'_{1,j} = C_{1,j}/2^{\ell_1}$ is known to the attacker. To simplify the analysis that follows - and since it does not change anything but renaming the variables - we assume that we keep working with System (6) but using odd values c_i. Now if we come back to our analysis on the set $\mathcal{L}^{(0)}$, namely considering System (6) modulo 2, we reach the following new system:

$$
\begin{cases}
C_{1,2} = \vartheta_{1,0} + \vartheta_{2,0} & \mod 2 \\
\vdots & \vdots \\
C_{1,t} = \vartheta_{1,0} + \vartheta_{t,0} & \mod 2
\end{cases}
\tag{7}
$$

It now becomes easy to count the number of elements belonging to $\mathcal{L}^{(0)}$. Indeed, either none of the $r_{i,0}$ is known by the adversary, and in that case there are two possible values for $\vartheta_{1,0}$, say 0 or 1 and each of them fixes the rest for $\vartheta_{2,0}, \ldots, \vartheta_{t,0}$. In the second configuration, when there is at least one of the $r_{i,0}$ which is known by the attacker (say $r_{1,0}$ for instance[3]), the value $\vartheta_{1,0}$ is fixed to $r_{1,0}$ and thus the other values $\vartheta_{2,0}, \ldots, \vartheta_{t,0}$ are fixed too (see System (7)). As a consequence, there is unique solution for the uple $(\vartheta_{1,0}, \ldots, \vartheta_{t,0})$. The construction of the whole set $\mathcal{L}^{(0)}$ is summed up in Algorithm 2a, which can be seen as an adaptation of the initialisation phase of Algorithm 2 when all ℓ_i are equal (process to a replacement of lines 3–7 of Algorithm 2 by Algorithm 2a).

The expected cardinal $\mathcal{N}^{(0)}$ of the list $\mathcal{L}^{(0)}$ can thus be expressed easily:

– when none of the $r_{i,0}$'s is known, which holds with probability $(1 - \delta)^t$, there are two candidates for $(\vartheta_{1,0}, \ldots, \vartheta_{1,t})$.

---

[3] One can easily reorder the random values r_i to make such an assumption true.

Algorithm 2a. Init. phase of Algorithm 2 when $\ell_1 = \ldots = \ell_t$ (lines 3–7)

> **if** (None of the $r_{i,0}$'s is known) **then**
>   Add $\{(0, C_{1,2} \mod 2, \ldots, C_{1,t} \mod 2), (1, C_{1,2} + 1 \mod 2, \ldots, C_{1,t} + 1 \mod 2)\}$ to $\mathcal{L}^{(0)}$
> **else**
>   /*At least one of the $r_{i,0}$'s is known, say for instance $r_{1,0}$*/
>   Add $(r_{1,0}, C_{1,2} + r_{1,0} \mod 2, \ldots, C_{1,t} + r_{1,0} \mod 2)$ to $\mathcal{L}^{(0)}$

- when at least one of the $r_{i,0}$ is known, what happens with probability $1 - (1 - \delta)^t$, there is a unique solution for $(\vartheta_{1,0}, \ldots, r_{t,0})$.

One can thus reach $\mathcal{N}^{(0)} = 2(1 - \delta)^t + 1 - (1 - \delta)^t = 1 + (1 - \delta)^t$. We will now determine by induction the expected size $\mathcal{N}^{(k)}$ from $\mathcal{N}^{(k-1)}$ for $k \in \{1, \ldots, n-1\}$, knowing that it contains all elements of the form $(\vartheta_1^{(k)}, \ldots, \vartheta_t^{(k)})$ coinciding with possible knowledge on $(r_{1,k}, \ldots, r_{t,k})$ and satisfying:

$$\begin{cases} C_{1,2} = (\vartheta_{1,0} + \cdots + \vartheta_{1,k} \, 2^k) \cdot c_2 + (\vartheta_{2,0} + \cdots + \vartheta_{2,k} \, 2^k) \cdot c_1 \mod 2^{k+1} \\ \vdots \qquad\qquad\qquad\qquad\qquad \vdots \\ C_{1,t} = (\vartheta_{1,0} + \cdots + \vartheta_{1,k} \, 2^k) \cdot c_t + (\vartheta_{t,0} + \cdots + \vartheta_{t,k} \, 2^k) \cdot c_1 \mod 2^{k+1} \end{cases} \tag{8}$$

Putting such expressions inside System (8) finally leads to the following new relations:

$$k_j = \vartheta_{1,k} + \vartheta_{j,k} \mod 2 \text{ for } j \in \{1, \ldots, t\} \tag{9}$$

Now it is easier to determine the number of solutions $(\vartheta_{1,k}, \ldots, \vartheta_{t,k})$ that will be chosen to lift elements $(\vartheta_1^{(k-1)}, \ldots, \vartheta_t^{(k-1)})$ from $\mathcal{L}^{(k-1)}$ to $\mathcal{L}^{(k)}$. Nevertheless one should be careful during this analysis, since it strongly depends on whether the chosen element $(\vartheta_1^{(k-1)}, \ldots, \vartheta_t^{(k-1)})$ equals $(r_1^{(k-1)}, \ldots, r_t^{(k-1)})$ or not. Indeed when this condition is not satisfied, the choice of an element $(\vartheta_1^{(k-1)}, \ldots, \vartheta_t^{(k-1)})$ fixes all integers $k_1, \ldots, k_t$ implying some possible *invalid* restrictions on the values $\vartheta_{1,k}, \ldots, \vartheta_{t,k}$. As a consequence, when some of the $r_{i,k}$'s are known (precisely more than two), the corresponding equalities in (9) are not necessarily satisfied. Since we do not know in advance when it happens, we assume each equation in (9) holds *independently* with some fixed probability $\gamma \in [0, 1]$ during the whole run of our algorithm[4]. In the other case, namely when the $r_{i,k}$'s are unknown or when the element $(\vartheta_1^{(k-1)}, \ldots, \vartheta_t^{(k-1)})$ corresponds to the *right* solution, the lifting process behaves as usual, see the "two signatures case". Taking all these considerations into account, one can finally determine the size of the set $\mathcal{L}^{(k)}$, see Algorithm 2b for a precise description (this algorithm can be seen as an adaptation of the main loop of Algorithm 2, lines 10 –19).

From now on, we are able to deduce the size $\mathcal{N}^{(k)}$ of the set $\mathcal{L}^{(k)}$, knowing that:

- when the adversary does not know any of the $r_{i,k}$, what holds with probability $(1 - \delta)^t$, there are $2\mathcal{N}^{(k-1)}$ solutions;
- when exactly one of the $r_{i,k}$ is known, which happens with probability $t\delta(1 - \delta)^{t-1}$, there are $\mathcal{N}^{(k-1)}$ solutions;

---

[4] We remind that γ is only defined when $(\vartheta_1^{(k-1)}, \ldots, \vartheta_t^{(k-1)}) \neq (r_1^{(k-1)}, \ldots, r_t^{(k-1)})$.

– in the other case, this number depends on the element $(\vartheta_1^{(k-1)}, \ldots, \vartheta_t^{(k-1)})$. When this element is equal to $(r_1^{(k-1)}, \ldots, r_t^{(k-1)})$ (this is the *right candidate*), there is a unique solution. In the other case, there are $\gamma(\mathcal{N}^{(k-1)} - 1)$ solutions when exactly two $r_{i,k}$ are known, what holds with probability $\binom{t}{2}\delta^2(1-\delta)^{(t-2)}$; there are $\gamma^2(\mathcal{N}^{(k-1)} - 1)$ solutions when exactly three $r_{i,k}$ are known, which holds with probability $\binom{t}{3}\delta^3(1-\delta)^{(t-3)}$; and so on; there are $\gamma^{t-1}(\mathcal{N}^{(k-1)} - 1)$ solutions when all the $r_{i,k}$ are known, what happens with probability $\binom{t}{t}\delta^t$.

Algorithm 2b. Main loop of Algorithm 2 when $\ell_1 = \cdots = \ell_t$ (lines $10 - 19$)

$\mathcal{L}^{(k)} = \{\}$
if none of $r_{1,k}, \ldots, r_{t,k}$ is known **then**
  for each element $(\vartheta_1^{(k-1)}, \ldots, \vartheta_t^{(k-1)}) \in \mathcal{L}^{(k-1)}$ **do**
    for each element $\vartheta_{1,k}$ in $\mathcal{E} - \{0, 1\}$ **do**
      Construct $\vartheta_1^{(k)} = \vartheta_1^{(k-1)} + 2 \cdot \vartheta_{1,k}$
      for each index j in $\{2, \ldots, t\}$ **do**
        Compute k_j such that $k_j \cdot 2^k = C_{1,j} - \vartheta_1^{(k-1)} 2^{k-1} c_j - \vartheta_j^{(k-1)} 2^{k-1} c_1$
        Compute $\vartheta_{j,k} = \vartheta_{1,k} + k_j \mod 2$; construct $\vartheta_j^{(k)} = \vartheta_j^{(k-1)} + 2\vartheta_{j,k} \mod 2^{k+1}$
      Add element $(\vartheta_1^{(k)}, \ldots, \vartheta_t^{(k)})$ in $\mathcal{L}^{(k)}$
else if there exists a unique i such that $r_{i,k}$ is known /*say for instance $r_{1,k}$*/ **then**
  for each element $(\vartheta_1^{(k-1)}, \ldots, \vartheta_t^{(k-1)}) \in \mathcal{L}^{(k-1)}$ **do**
    Construct $\vartheta_1^{(k)} = \vartheta_1^{(k-1)} + 2 \cdot \vartheta_{1,k}$
    for each index j in $\{2, \ldots, t\}$ **do**
      Compute k_j such that $k_j \cdot 2^k = C_{1,j} - \vartheta_1^{(k-1)} 2^{k-1} c_j - \vartheta_j^{(k-1)} 2^{k-1} c_1$
      Compute $\vartheta_{j,k} = \vartheta_{1,k} + k_j \mod 2$; construct $\vartheta_j^{(k)} = \vartheta_j^{(k-1)} + 2\vartheta_{j,k} \mod 2^{k+1}$
    Add element $(\vartheta_1^{(k)}, \ldots, \vartheta_t^{(k)})$ in $\mathcal{L}^{(k)}$
else
  /*two or more $r_{i,k}$ are known, assume $r_{1,k}$ is concerned*/
  for each element $(\vartheta_1^{(k-1)}, \ldots, \vartheta_t^{(k-1)}) \in \mathcal{L}^{(k-1)}$ **do**
    for each index j in $\{1, \ldots, t\}$ **do**
      Compute k_j such that $k_j \cdot 2^k = C_{1,j} - \vartheta_1^{(k-1)} 2^{k-1} c_j - \vartheta_j^{(k-1)} 2^{k-1} c_1$
    Set $\vartheta_{1,k} = r_{1,k}$
    for each index j in $\{2, \ldots, t\}$ **do**
      Compute $\vartheta_{j,k} = \vartheta_{1,k} + k_j \mod 2$
    if $(\vartheta_{1,k}, \ldots, \vartheta_{t,k})$ coincide with possible knowledge on $(r_{1,k}, \ldots, r_{t,k})$ **then**
      for each index j in $\{1, \ldots, t\}$ **do**
        Compute $\vartheta_j^{(k)} = \vartheta_j^{(k-1)} + 2 \cdot \vartheta_{j,k} \mod 2^{k+1}$
      Add element $(\vartheta_1^{(k)}, \ldots, \vartheta_t^{(k)})$ to $\mathcal{L}^{(k)}$

By combining all these results, we obtain the following formula for $\mathcal{N}^{(k)}$:

$$2(1 - \delta)^t \mathcal{N}^{(k-1)} + (1 - (1 - \delta)^t) + \frac{1}{\gamma}(\mathcal{N}^{(k-1)} - 1) \sum_{i=1,\ldots,t} \binom{t}{i}(\gamma\delta)^i(1 - \delta)^{t-i}$$

Evaluating the quantity inside the summation leads to the following relation:

$$\mathcal{N}^{(k)} = \mathcal{N}^{(k-1)}\left(\frac{1}{\gamma}(\gamma\delta + 1 - \delta)^t + (2 - \frac{1}{\gamma})(1 - \delta)^t\right) + 1 - \frac{1}{\gamma}(\gamma\delta + 1 - \delta)^t + \left(\frac{1}{\gamma} - 1\right)(1 - \delta)^t$$

Denoting as $\mathcal{A}(\gamma, \delta)$ the quantity $\frac{1}{\gamma}(\gamma\delta + 1 - \delta)^t + (2 - \frac{1}{\gamma})(1 - \delta)^t$ and using the formula obtained for $\mathcal{N}^{(0)}$, we reach:

$$\mathcal{N}^{(n-1)} = (1 + (1 - \delta)^t)\mathcal{A}(\gamma, \delta)^{n-1}$$
$$+ \left(1 - \tfrac{1}{\gamma}(\gamma\delta + 1 - \delta)^t + (\tfrac{1}{\gamma} - 1)(1 - \delta)^t\right) \sum_{i=0...n-2} \mathcal{A}(\gamma, \delta)^i$$

The goal of the adversary being to construct the set $\mathcal{L}^{(n-1)}$ in polynomial time, this attack will only be made practical if the quantity $\mathcal{A}(\gamma, \delta)$ is strictly smaller than 1. In that case, the size of the list $\mathcal{L}^{(n-1)}$ will not grow too fast when n tends toward infinity. Setting γ to $1/2$ (see Sect. 3.3 for experimental results on that point) leads to the condition $2(1 - \frac{\delta}{2})^t < 1$, which is satisfied for $\delta > 2 - 2^{1-1/t}$. By taking this value as a lower bound on δ, we are able to determine the expected maximum size of the set $\mathcal{L}^{(n-1)}$, namely $(2^{1-\frac{1}{t}} - 1)^t n + 1$.

Theorem 3 (t Signatures and $\ell_1 = \cdots = \ell_t$). *An adversary able to learn a proportion of $\delta = 2 - 2^{1-1/t}$ bits of the random nonces used in the generation of t known signatures can (heuristically) break the scheme in polynomial time. In that case, the expected space required for performing the attack is $(2^{1-\frac{1}{t}} - 1)^t n^2 + 1$.*

• *Second analysis when some of the ℓ_i's are different*

The analysis is more tedious here but can still be adapted to the case when some of the ℓ_i's are different, see Theorem 4 below (the proof is provided in the full version of the paper [1]).

Theorem 4 (t Signatures with ℓ_i Different). *An adversary able to learn a proportion of $\delta = 2 - 2^{1-1/t}$ bits of the random nonces used in the generation of t known signatures can (heuristically) break the scheme in polynomial time. In that case, the expected space required for performing the attack[5] is $(2^{1-\frac{1}{t}} - 1)^e n^2 + 1$.*

Remark 1. Using the coding viewpoint from [19], one can obtain limits on the performance of any algorithm for selecting candidate nonces in the erasure correction scenario. Their argument is based on the converse to Shannon's noisy-channel coding theorem[6]. The underlying code is made of the 2^n words on tn bits obtain by the naive algorithm without pruning (*i.e.* with code rate $1/t$) so simple variants of our algorithm cannot be efficient for $\delta < 1/t$ and our algorithm is optimal up to the multiplicative constant $\ln(2)$.

3.3   Experimental Results

To confirm the validity of the attack and of our heuristic, extensive experiments have been performed for various values of t and δ. For each pair (t, δ), the attack

---

[5] Here, the index e is defined such that $\ell_1 = \ell_2 = \cdots = \ell_e < \ell_{e+1} \leq \cdots \leq \ell_t$.

[6] This theorem states that no combination of code and decoding procedure can jointly achieve arbitrarily reliable decoding when the code rate exceeds the capacity of the channel.

has been launched and its complexity has been measured by counting the sum of the cardinality of the sets $\mathcal{L}^{(i)}$ for i in $\{0, \ldots, n\}$. The obtained results are analysed below.

With 32 and 64 Signatures. We performed experiments using 32 and 64 signatures (using a security parameter κ equal to 128). Since the experiments were time-consuming, we performed 1000 experiments for each pair (t, δ). The results for $t = 32$ are provided on Fig. 1, for values of δ varying from 0.04 to 0.06 and the ones for $t = 64$ are illustrated on Fig. 2, for values of δ between 0.02 and 0.04 (namely from 2 % to 4 %). These experiments show that it works better in practice than what was predicted. Indeed, the bounds below which the attack begins to become unpractical are approximately 0.04 for $t = 32$ signatures and 0.02 for $t = 64$. These values are better than the ones reached by the theoretical analysis, say $2 - 2^{1-1/32} \simeq 0.043$ and $2 - 2^{1-1/64} \simeq 0.022$.

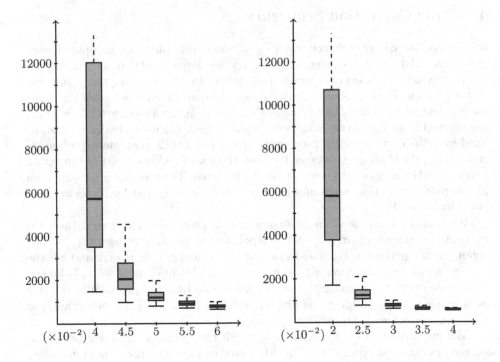

Fig. 1. Total number of constructed $(\vartheta_1, \ldots, \vartheta_{32})$ in function of δ ($t = 32$ and $\kappa = 128$).

Fig. 2. Total number of constructed $(\vartheta_1, \ldots, \vartheta_{64})$ in function of δ ($t = 64$ and $\kappa = 128$).

With 710 Signatures. We finally considered the case where the adversary knows (on average) only one bit per nonce r_i (*i.e.* $\delta = 1/512$). For a security parameter κ equals to 128, our theoretical analysis claims that an attacker will be able to break the scheme knowing 710 signatures. In this case, our attack succeeded in a few minutes (using a very naive implementation) with a total size of generated elements equal to 2437. To go further, we also tried to launch the attack for a smaller number of signatures, but still keeping $\delta = 1/512$. The cases $t = 650$ and $t = 600$ were also successful. The time required for the last case was approximately a few hours and the total sum of elements was 53770 (again using a very naive implementation).

Impact of γ. The formula obtained in Sects. 3.1 and 3.2 strongly depend on the value of the parameter γ. In our theoretical analysis, we decided to take $\gamma = 1/2$. In practice, several tests have been launched to determine whether this assumption is correct. In every experiments we performed, the observed value for γ was very near from $1/2$, what confirms our initial assumption.

4   Error Correction Scenario

In the *erasure correction scenario* (see previous sections), we compared each nonce candidate with its given fragmentary version in order to determine the nonce uniquely with overwhelming probability. In this section, the *error correction scenario*, we proceed similarly: we assume an adversary obtain some error-prone nonces in a discrete-logarithm based authentication scheme which are derived from the actual nonces by flipping each bit individually with some fixed probability $\delta \in [0, 1/2)$. Intuitively, if δ is below $1/2$, then among all nonce candidates, the Hamming distance between the least significant bits of the actual nonces and the nonces with noise should be minimal. The analysis is simpler than in the previous section and relies on the technique proposed by Henecka, May and Meurer in [12].

We consider the case of an adversary that is given access to t signatures (or authentication sessions) $\sigma_1, \ldots, \sigma_t$ corresponding to known messages $m_1, \ldots, m_t$. Again, each signature σ_i is defined as a pair (s_i, c_i) where $s_i = r_i + c_i x$ and x is the signers' secret key. Moreover we assume that each bit of each nonce r_i is known with some error: to formalize this model we denote by δ the probability that for each nonce r_i, its j-th bit $r_{i,j}$ is flipped (for j in $\{1, \ldots, n\}$). By definition, the bit $r_{i,j}$ is correct with probability $(1 - \delta)$.

Making the quantity x disappear from all the expressions, one reaches the simple system of equations (6). The adversary can retrieve the nonces $r_1, \ldots, r_t$ by collecting all tuples $(\vartheta_1, \ldots, \vartheta_t)$ satisfying System (6) and minimizing the Hamming distance with the bits $r_{i,j}$. The algorithm performs a clever exhaustive search, consisting in generating all tuples $(\vartheta_1^{(k)}, \ldots, \vartheta_t^{(k)})$ satisfying System (6) modulo 2^{k+1} and then selecting among them, those that can be lifted to solutions modulo 2^{k+2}. These operations should minimize the distance with the knowledge on some bits of the r_i's.

Contrary to the erasure correction scenario, one cannot easily prune partial solutions that do not coincide with the known secret key bits. Indeed this process may discard the correct solution, since this solution does not fully agree with the noisy nonce material. Thus, in this scenario, we do no longer compare bit by bit but we compare larger blocks of bits. More precisely, we grow subtrees of depth T (for some parameter T) for each t-tuple of nonce candidate. We will see that this results in 2^T new candidates which we all compare with our noisy nonce material. If the Hamming distance with this material in these T bits is above some threshold parameter d we keep the candidate, otherwise we discard it. The only difficulty here consists in estimating these parameters T and d:

- the parameter T cannot be chosen too large since in each iteration the search tree grows by a factor 2^T;
- the parameter T has to be sufficiently large in order to guarantee that the actual t-tuple of nonces has a small Hamming distance with the noisy nonce material (in each block of successive T bits) but incorrect t-tuples of nonces are separable by the threshold parameter d;
- the threshold parameter d has to be large enough to guarantee that with probability close to 1 the actual t-tuple of nonces will never be discarded during the execution of the algorithm;
- the parameter d cannot be chosen too large since otherwise we obtain too many faulty t-tuples candidates for the next iteration.

• **First analysis with $\ell_1 = \ell_2 = \cdots = \ell_t$**

As above, one can assume we are using odd values c_i. We have to determine the size $\mathcal{N}^{(k)}$ of the sets $\mathcal{L}^{(k)}$. For $k = 0$, since none of the $r_{i,0}$ is known for sure by the adversary, there are two possible values for the bit $\vartheta_{1,0}$ and each of them fixes the other bits $\vartheta_{2,0}, \ldots, \vartheta_{t,0}$ (using System (7)). Therefore, we obtain $\mathcal{N}^{(0)} = 2$. Similarly, using System (9), one can see that if there is no pruning at the depth k then $\mathcal{N}^{(k)}$ is simply equal to $2\mathcal{N}^{(k-1)}$.

• **Second analysis when some of the ℓ_i's are different**

In this case, we can still show that $\mathcal{N}^{(0)} = 2$ and that we have, before pruning[7], $\mathcal{N}^{(T-1)} = 2^T$ at iteration T (see [1] for a complete proof of this result).

We now consider the pruning phase. Let us define a random variable X_c for the number of matching bits between the actual t-tuple of nonces and the noisy nonce material in a block of T consecutive bits. Clearly X_c is the binomial distribution with parameters tT and probability $(1 - \delta)$: $\Pr[X_c = m] = \binom{tT}{m}(1 - \delta)^m \delta^{tT-m}$ for m in $\{0, \ldots, tT\}$.

Considering an incorrect partial solution for the t-tuple of nonces, we denote X_b for the number of matching bits between the expansion of this incorrect solution by T bits and the noisy nonce material in the corresponding block of T consecutive bits. We make use of the following heuristic assumption.

Heuristic 1. *Every solution generated by applying the expansion phase to an incorrect partial solution is an ensemble of T randomly chosen bit slices.*

---

[7] In particular, in both cases, one gets before pruning $\mathcal{N}^{(T-1)} = 2^T$ at iteration T (instead of $\mathcal{N}^{(T-1)} = 2^{tT}$ for a naive approach).

Therefore every expansion of an incorrect candidate in the expansion phase results in tT uniformly random bits. We verified the validity of this heuristic experimentally. Under this assumption, we obtain $\Pr[X_b = m] = \binom{tT}{m}(2)^{-tT}$ for $m \in \{0, \ldots, tT\}$.

Henecka, May and Meurer proved in [12, Main Theorem 7] that these conditions are sufficient to insure the existence of an expansion parameter T and a threshold parameter d such that the two distributions are sufficiently separated and the growing factor 2^T in the expansion phase is polynomial.

Theorem 5 ([12]). *Under the previous heuristic, for every $\epsilon > 0$, the following holds: let $n, t \geq 2$ be two integers, let $T = \left\lceil \frac{\ln(n)}{t\epsilon^2} \right\rceil, \gamma = \sqrt{(1 + 1/T)\frac{\ln(2)}{2t}}$, and $d = tT\left(\frac{1}{2} + \gamma\right)$. An adversary able to learn (in the error correction scenario) the individual bits of random nonces of t known signatures of length n with probability $\delta < \frac{1}{2} - \gamma - \epsilon$ can recover the nonces (and therefore the secret key) in expected time $O(n^{2+\ln(2)/t\epsilon^2})$ with success probability at least $1 - (m\epsilon^2/\ln(n) + 1/n)$.*

Remark 2. The following table gives the limit crossover probability δ (*i.e.* with $\epsilon \longrightarrow 0$ and $T \longrightarrow +\infty$) in the error correction scenario depending on the number of signatures/identification sessions available t known to the adversary:

t	2	3	4	5	6	7	8	9	t
δ	0.084	0.160	0.205	0.237	0.260	0.277	0.292	0.303	$1/2 - \sqrt{\ln(2)/2t}$
δ^*	0.110	0.174	0.214	0.243	0.264	0.281	0.295	0.306	$H_2^{-1}(1 - 1/t)$

The value δ^* corresponds to the optimal value of δ one can derive from the converse to Shannon's noisy-channel coding theorem as in Remark 1 using the fact that the channel capacity of (memoryless) binary symmetric channel with crossover probability δ is $1 - H_2(\delta)$ where $H_2(\delta) = -\delta \log_2(\delta) - (1 - \delta)\log_2(1 - \delta)$ is the entropy function. For a 128-bit security level, with nonces of binary length 512, each signature provides only one bit of information for $\delta \simeq 1/2 - 10^{-4}$ and one needs in theory around $70 \cdot 10^6$ signatures in order to recover the secret key.

5   Conclusion

In this paper, we proposed attacks on discrete-logarithm based authentication schemes where an adversary has some information on the nonces used during the signature generation process or during some identification sessions, in the *erasure correction scenario* and the *error correction scenario*. The following table sums up the limit crossover probability δ in the two scenarios depending on the number N_r of signatures/identification sessions known to the adversary:

N_r	2	3	4	5	6	7	t
δ (erasure correction)	0.586	0.413	0.318	0.259	0.218	0.188	$\simeq \ln(2)/t$
δ (error correction)	0.084	0.160	0.205	0.237	0.260	0.277	$1/2 - \sqrt{\ln(2)/2t}$

Our methods can be generalized to the Z-channel considered in [19].

Acknowledgments. The authors are supported in part by the French ANR JCJC ROMAnTIC project (ANR-12-JS02-0004).

References

1. Bauer, A., Vergnaud, D.: Practical key recovery for discrete-logarithm based authentication schemes from random nonce bits. Full version of the paper, Cryptology ePrint Archive (2015)
2. Bellare, M., Goldwasser, S., Micciancio, D.: "Pseudo-random" number generation within cryptographic algorithms: the DSS case. In: Kaliski Jr., B.S. (ed.) CRYPTO 1997. LNCS, vol. 1294, pp. 277–291. Springer, Heidelberg (1997)
3. Bellare, M., Namprempre, C., Pointcheval, D., Semanko, M.: The one-more-RSA-inversion problems and the security of Chaum's blind signature scheme. J. Cryptol. **16**(3), 185–215 (2003)
4. Bellare, M., Palacio, A.: GQ and Schnorr identification schemes: proofs of security against impersonation under active and concurrent attacks. In: Yung, M. (ed.) CRYPTO 2002. LNCS, vol. 2442, pp. 162–177. Springer, Heidelberg (2002)
5. Bleichenbacher, D.: On the generation of one-time keys in dl signature schemes. Presentation at IEEE P1363 Working Group meeting, November 2000. Unpublished
6. El Gamal, T.: A public key cryptosystem and a signature scheme based on discrete logarithms. In: Blakely, G.R., Chaum, D. (eds.) CRYPTO 1984. LNCS, vol. 196, pp. 10–18. Springer, Heidelberg (1985)
7. Feige, U., Fiat, A., Shamir, A.: Zero-knowledge proofs of identity. J. Cryptol. **1**(2), 77–94 (1988)
8. Fiat, A., Shamir, A.: How to prove yourself: practical solutions to identification and signature problems. In: Odlyzko, A.M. (ed.) CRYPTO 1986. LNCS, vol. 263, pp. 186–194. Springer, Heidelberg (1987)
9. Girault, M.: Self-certified public keys. In: Davies, D.W. (ed.) EUROCRYPT 1991. LNCS, vol. 547, pp. 490–497. Springer, Heidelberg (1991)
10. Girault, M., Poupard, G., Stern, J.: On the fly authentication and signature schemes based on groups of unknown order. J. Cryptol. **19**(4), 463–487 (2006)
11. Halderman, J.A., Schoen, S.D., Heninger, N., Clarkson, W., Paul, W., Calandrino, J.A., Feldman, A.J., Appelbaum, J., Felten,E.W.: Lest we remember: cold boot attacks on encryption keys. In: van Oorschot, P.C. (ed.) Proceedings of the 17th USENIX Security Symposium, July 28–August 1, 2008, San Jose, CA, USA, pp. 45–60. USENIX Association (2008)
12. Henecka, W., May, A., Meurer, A.: Correcting errors in RSA private keys. In: Rabin, T. (ed.) CRYPTO 2010. LNCS, vol. 6223, pp. 351–369. Springer, Heidelberg (2010)
13. Heninger, N., Shacham, H.: Reconstructing RSA private keys from random key bits. In: Halevi, S. (ed.) CRYPTO 2009. LNCS, vol. 5677, pp. 1–17. Springer, Heidelberg (2009)

14. Horster, P., Petersen, H., Michels, M.: Meta-El-Gamal signature schemes. In: ACM CCS 1994: 2nd Conference on Computer and Communications Security, pp. 96–107. ACM Press (1994)

15. Kuwakado, H., Tanaka, H.: On the security of the elgamal-type signature scheme with small parameters. IEICE Trans. **82–A**(1), 93–97 (1999)

16. De Mulder, E., Hutter, M., Marson, M.E., Pearson, P.: Using Bleichenbacher's solution to the hidden number problem to attack nonce leaks in 384-bit ECDSA. In: Bertoni, G., Coron, J.-S. (eds.) CHES 2013. LNCS, vol. 8086, pp. 435–452. Springer, Heidelberg (2013)

17. FIPS PUB 186–2: Digital Signature Standard (DSS). National Institute for Standards and Technology, Gaithersburg, MD, USA (2000)

18. Nguyen, P.Q., Shparlinski, I.: The insecurity of the digital signature algorithm with partially known nonces. J. Cryptol. **15**(3), 151–176 (2002)

19. Paterson, K.G., Polychroniadou, A., Sibborn, D.L.: A coding-theoretic approach to recovering noisy RSA keys. In: Wang, X., Sako, K. (eds.) ASIACRYPT 2012. LNCS, vol. 7658, pp. 386–403. Springer, Heidelberg (2012)

20. Percival, C.: Cache missing for fun and profit. In: Proceedings of BSDCan 2005

21. Poupard, G., Stern, J.: On the fly signatures based on factoring. In: ACM CCS 1999: 6th Conference on Computer and Communications Security, pp. 37–45. ACM Press, November 1999

22. Schnorr, C.-P.: Efficient signature generation by smart cards. J. Cryptol. **4**(3), 161–174 (1991)

The Simeck Family of Lightweight Block Ciphers

Gangqiang Yang$^{(\boxtimes)}$, Bo Zhu, Valentin Suder,
Mark D. Aagaard, and Guang Gong

Department of Electrical and Computer Engineering,
University of Waterloo, Waterloo, ON N2L 3G1, Canada
{g37yang,bo.zhu,vsuder,maagaard,ggong}@uwaterloo.ca

Abstract. Two lightweight block cipher families, SIMON and SPECK, have been proposed by researchers from the NSA recently. In this paper, we introduce Simeck, a new family of lightweight block ciphers that combines the good design components from both SIMON and SPECK, in order to devise even more compact and efficient block ciphers. For Simeck32/64, we can achieve 505 GEs (before the Place and Route phase) and 549 GEs (after the Place and Route phase), with the power consumption of 0.417 μW in CMOS 130 nm ASIC, and 454 GEs (before the Place and Route phase) and 488 GEs (after the Place and Route phase), with the power consumption of 1.292 μW in CMOS 65 nm ASIC. Furthermore, all of the instances of Simeck are smaller than the ones of hardware-optimized cipher SIMON in terms of area and power consumption in both CMOS 130 nm and CMOS 65 nm techniques. In addition, we also give the security evaluation of Simeck with respect to many traditional cryptanalysis methods, including differential attacks, linear attacks, impossible differential attacks, meet-in-the-middle attacks, and slide attacks. Overall, all of the instances of Simeck can satisfy the area, power, and throughput requirements in passive RFID tags.

Keywords: Lightweight · Block cipher · ASICs · Passive RFID

1 Introduction

In recent years, low-end embedded devices have been deployed in an increasing number and used in various applications, such as D.Radio Frequency Identification (RFID) tags and wireless sensor networks (WSNs). Providing security solutions to these widely used devices has attracted a lot of attention from cryptography researchers. These kinds of devices have very limited power consumption, constrained memory and computing capability, and thus applying traditional security solutions, such as TLS and IPsec, in these contexts is often impractical. Hence, lightweight cryptography has been developed in order to provide compact algorithms and protocols that fit in resource-constrained environments.

Numerous lightweight ciphers have appeared. Among them are a large number of block ciphers such as TEA [31], XTEA [26], PRESENT [9], KATAN and KTANTAN [11], LED [16], EPCBC [33], KLEIN [15], LBlock [32], Piccolo [29],

© International Association for Cryptologic Research 2015
T. Güneysu and H. Handschuh (Eds.): CHES 2015, LNCS 9293, pp. 307–329, 2015.
DOI: 10.1007/978-3-662-48324-4_16

Twine [30], and the more recent SIMON and SPECK [3]. There exist also some lightweight stream ciphers such as Trivium [12], Grain [17] and WG [25], which provide suitable security and small implementations for resource-constrained devices.

The recently proposed lightweight block ciphers, SIMON and SPECK [3], have led to papers concerning their security [1,7,10]. This is partially due to the fact that these ciphers are recognized to be the smallest block ciphers in each of the block/key size categories when used in resource-constrained environments. SIMON is optimized for hardware implementation, while SPECK is optimized for software. Inspired by the designs of SIMON and SPECK, we combine their good components in order to get a new design of block cipher family, called Simeck. We use a slightly modified version of SIMON's round function, and reuse it in the key schedule like SPECK does. Moreover, we take the benefits of using Linear Feedback Shift Register (LFSR) based constants in the key schedule in order to further reduce hardware implementation footprints. The new family of lightweight block ciphers Simeck aims to have comparable security levels but more efficient hardware implementations.

Based on the aforementioned motivations, we have the detailed design goals as follows.

Hardware. First, we want to minimize the area and power consumption of the Application Specific Integrated Circuit (ASIC) implementations. We also want to allow a range of options in the area, throughput, and power consumption. Finally, we want to keep the maximum operating frequency as high as possible.

Applications. Take the application of passive RFID tags for example, Simeck should satisfy the following requirements in order to be used in practice: (1) The area of Simeck should be less than 2000 GEs [2,18]. (2) The power consumption of Simeck should be very small. (3) The typical passive RFID tag's operating frequency is 2 MHz and the data rate is 64 Kbps [14,34], and thus the throughput is $64K/2M \approx 1/32$. Therefore, if the tag's operating frequency is 100 KHz (for benchmarking purpose), the throughput of Simeck should at least be $100 K \cdot 1/32$ bps ≈ 3.1 Kbps.

Security. Although SIMON and SPECK were designed with small, simple round functions, they are iterated a sufficient number of times in order to resist traditional attacks. We follow the same strategy with Simeck, and due to its similarity with SIMON, we benefit from its analysis carried so far.

In this paper, we offer a wide range of options between area, throughput, and power consumption for the implementations of Simeck. All the Simeck's family members can meet our security, hardware, and applications design goals. We compare our results to the previous constructions with comparable block sizes and key sizes as given in Table 1. Table 1 gives our smallest area results for all the instances of Simeck from before and after the Place and Route (P&R) in CMOS 130 nm and CMOS 65 nm ASICs. In addition, the corresponding throughput and power consumption after the Place and Route are also provided. In particular, Table 1 presents our hardware implementation results of SIMON which cost less

Table 1. Comparison of Hardware Implementations of Lightweight Block Ciphers

Size	Algorithm	Tech (nm)	Area		Throughput	Power	Source
			Before P&R (GEs)	After P&R (GEs)	@100KHz (Kbps)	@ 100KHz (μW)	
32/64	SIMON	130	523	-	5.6	-	[3]
	SPECK		580	-	4.2	-	[3]
	SIMON		**517**	**562**	5.6	0.421	**here**
	Simeck		**505**	**549**	5.6	0.417	**here**
	SIMON	65	**466**	**501**	5.6	1.311	**here**
	Simeck		**454**	**488**	5.6	1.292	**here**
48/96	SIMON	130	739	-	5.0	-	[3]
	SPECK		794	-	4.0	-	[3]
	SIMON		**733**	**796**	5.0	0.579	**here**
	Simeck		**715**	**778**	5.0	0.576	**here**
	SIMON	65	**661**	**711**	5.0	1.812	**here**
	Simeck		**645**	**693**	5.0	1.805	**here**
	EPCBC	180	1008	-	12.1	-	[33]
64/128	SIMON	130	958	-	4.2	-	[3]
	SPECK		966	-	3.4	-	[3]
	SIMON		**944**	**1026**	4.2	0.762	**here**
	Simeck		**924**	**1005**	4.2	0.754	**here**
	SIMON	65	**845**	**908**	4.2	2.336	**here**
	Simeck		**828**	**891**	4.2	2.304	**here**
	LED	180	1265	-	3.4	-	[16]
	PRESENT		1339	-	12.1	-	[33]

area than the original results in [3]. Moreover, the hardware implementations of our Simeck block cipher family are even smaller than our implementations of SIMON in terms of area and power consumption.

More specifically in Table 1, we can achieve a small area of 505 GEs before the Place and Route with a throughput of 5.6 Kbps and 0.417 μW power consumption for Simeck32/64 in CMOS 130 nm ASIC. With a fair comparison (before the Place and Route) in CMOS 130 nm, Simeck32/64 can achieve 2.3 % smaller than our implementations of SIMON32/64, and 3.4 % smaller than the original implementations of SIMON32/64. Correspondingly, we can get an even smaller area of 454 GEs before the Place and Route and 1.292 μW power consumption in CMOS 65 nm ASIC. In this case, Simeck32/64 is 2.6 % smaller than our implementations of SIMON32/64.

Similarly, Simeck48/96, 64/128 are 2.5 %, 2.1 %, respectively, smaller than our implementations of SIMON48/96, 64/128, and they are 3.3 %, 3.5 %, respectively, smaller than the original implementations of SIMON48/96, 64/128 in CMOS 130 nm. Correspondingly in CMOS 65 nm, Simeck48/96, 64/128 are 2.4 %, 2.0 %, respectively, smaller than our implementations of SIMON48/96,

64/128. Moreover, with only a little extra area (GEs) and power consumption, we can increase Simeck's throughput a lot.

This paper is organized as follows. In Sect. 2, we describe the specifications and design rationales of the Simeck family. Section 3 first presents our metrics and design flow in CMOS 130 nm and CMOS 65 nm ASICs. Then, we give two different hardware architectures of Simeck in order to make a trade-off between area, throughput, and power consumption. Later, the hardware evaluations in CMOS 130 nm and CMOS 65 nm are given with a thorough analysis. In Sect. 4, we compare our results of Simeck and SIMON with the results in [3]. Before concluding this paper, we provide a security analysis of our new block ciphers in Sect. 5.

2   Design Specifications and Rationales

In this section, we give the specifications, as well as design rationales, of our block cipher family Simeck. We use the following notations throughout the rest of the paper.

$x \lll c$ denotes the cyclic shift of x to the left by c bits.
$x \odot y$ is the bitwise AND of x and y.
$x \oplus y$ is the exclusive-or (XOR) of x and y.

2.1   Specifications of Simeck

Our lightweight block cipher family Simeck is denoted Simeck$2n/mn$, where n is the word size and n is required to be 16, 24 or 32; while $2n$ is the block size and mn is the key size. More specifically, our Simeck family includes Simeck32/64, Simeck48/96, and Simeck64/128. For example, Simeck32/64 refers to perform encryptions or decryptions on 32-bit message blocks using a 64-bit key. These three size choices of the ciphers aim to fit different applications of embedded systems including RFID systems, and these sizes are also contained in the specifications of SIMON and SPECK families of block ciphers.

Simeck is designed to be extremely small in hardware footprints and to be compact in software implementations as well. The round function and the key schedule algorithm follow the Feistel structure. A plaintext to be encrypted is first divided into two words l_0 and r_0, where l_0 contains the most significant n bits, and r_0 consists of the least significant n bits. Then these two words are processed by the Simeck round function for certain number of rounds, and finally the two output words l_T and r_T are concatenated to form a complete ciphertext, where T denotes the total number of rounds.

Round Function. We define the round function (of the i-th round) as the following function,

$$R_{k_i}(l_i,\ r_i) = (r_i \oplus f(l_i) \oplus k_i,\ l_i),$$

where l_i and r_i are the two words for the internal state of Simeck, k_i is the round key, and the function f is defined as

$$f(x) = (x \odot (x \lll 5)) \oplus (x \lll 1).$$

Fig. 1 illustrates the operations of the round function R_{k_i}.

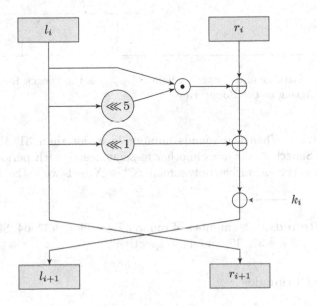

Fig. 1. The Round Function of Simeck

Key Schedule/Expansion. To generate the round key k_i from a given master key K, the master key K is first segmented into four words and loaded as the initial states (t_2, t_1, t_0, k_0) of the feedback shift registers shown in Fig. 2. The least significant n bits of K are loaded into k_0; while the most significant n bits are put into t_2. To update the registers and generate round keys, we reuse the round function with a round constant $C \oplus (z_j)_i$ acting as the round key, i.e. $R_{C \oplus (z_j)_i}$. The updating operation can be expressed as

$$\begin{cases} k_{i+1} = t_i, \\ t_{i+3} = k_i \oplus f(t_i) \oplus C \oplus (z_j)_i, \end{cases}$$

where $0 \le i \le T - 1$. The value k_i is used as the round key of the i-th round.

The value of the constant C is defined by $C = 2^n - 4$, where n is the word size. $(z_j)_i$ denotes the i-th bit of the sequence z_j. Simeck32/64 and Simeck48/96 use the same sequence z_0, i.e. $j = 0$, which is an m-sequence with period 31 and can be generated by the primitive polynomial $X^5 + X^2 + 1$ with the initial

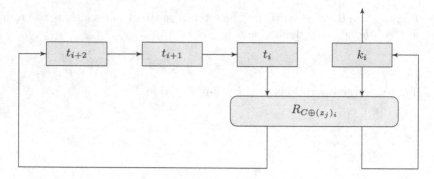

Fig. 2. The Key Expansion of Simeck, where $R_{C \oplus (z_j)_i}$ is the Simeck Round Function with $C \oplus (z_j)_i$ Acting as the Round Key

state $(1, 1, 1, 1, 1)$. When the rounds number is larger than 31, the sequence repeats itself. Simeck64/128 uses another m-sequence z_1 with period 63, which is generated by the primitive polynomial $X^6 + X + 1$ with the initial state $(1, 1, 1, 1, 1, 1)$.

Number of Rounds. The number of rounds T for Simeck32/64, Simeck48/96, and Simeck64/128 are 32, 36, and 44, respectively.

2.2 Design Rationales

In Simeck, we use a slightly simplified version of the round function of SIMON. The round function of SIMON can be expressed as

$$R'_{k_i}(l_i, \ r_i) = (((l_i \lll 1) \odot (l_i \lll 8)) \oplus (l_i \lll 2) \oplus r_i \oplus k_i, \ l_i),$$

where l_i and r_i are the input words, and k_i is the round key. The operations of the round function only contain bitwise AND, XOR and cyclic shifts, and they are very efficient for hardware implementations. In particular, for Simeck, we change these shift numbers from $(1, 8, 2)$ to $(0, 5, 1)$. We choose our shift numbers in order to realize an acceptable trade-off between hardware performance and security. These modifications will improve the efficiency of hardware implementations, but will have comparable security strengths against certain attacks. More discussions will be given in the following sections.

For the key expansion/schedule algorithm of Simeck, we learn the idea of re-using the round function to update the round-key registers from the design of SPECK.

Concerning the number of rounds for Simeck, we choose the same numbers as the corresponding block ciphers in the SIMON family, in order to have comparable security levels and fair hardware implementation evaluations.

To defeat certain self-similarity attacks such as slide attacks and rotational attacks, we add the round constants C and $(z_j)_i$ into the key expansion process.

The constant $C = 2^n - 4$ is also used in the key expansion of SIMON. The polynomials for the two m-sequences z_0 and z_1 are chosen to have minimum numbers of components, such that their hardware implementations will have small footprints.

3   Hardware Implementations

We discuss the hardware implementations of the Simeck family of block ciphers in this section.

3.1   Metrics and Design Flow

We use the Synopsys Design Compiler Version D-2010.03-SP4 to synthesize the RTL of the designs into netlist based on the STMicroelectronics CMOS 65 nm CORE65LPLVT_1.20V and IBM CMOS 130 nm CMR8SF-LPVT Process SAGE v2.0 standard cell libraries with both having a typical 1.2 V voltage, and 25°C temperature. Cadence SoC Encounter v09.12-s159_1 is used to finish the Place and Route phase in order to generate the layout of the designs. We use Mentor Graphics ModelSim SE 10.1a to conduct functional simulation of the designs and perform timing simulation by using the timing delay information generated from SoC Encounter as well. The areas of the designs after the logic synthesis are provided for comparisons with previous ciphers, and a more accurate area after the Place and Route is also provided for using the ciphers in practical cases. The densities used for the Place and Route phase for CMOS 130 nm and 65 nm are 0.92 and 0.93 respectively, in order to make a trade-off between area and maximum operating frequency when the densities are high enough. As usual, the area is measured in gate equivalents (GEs), and one GE is equivalent to the physical area required for the two-input one-output NAND gate with the lowest driving strength of the corresponding technology.

We use SoC Encounter v09.12-s159_1 to generate the accurate power consumption based on the activity information generated from the timing simulation with a frequency of 100 KHz, and a duration time of 0.1s. We do so because the 100 KHz clock frequency is widely used for benchmarking purpose in resource-constrained applications and 0.1 s is long enough to provide an accurate activity information for all the signals.

Moreover, the critical path is obtained after the Place and Route phase, which would be more accurate than the estimated value obtained from logic synthesis. Hence, the maximum clock frequency which can be operated for a specific design is obtained.

In fact, during the analysis of the previous results [3,11,24,27,28], the ASIC results for various implementations differ not only in the basic gate technology but also in the types of flip-flops used. In order to be fair to compare our results with the previous ones, we provide the areas of some basic gates in our specific libraries and the library used in [3] by the researchers from the NSA for SIMON in Table 2. In addition, all the areas of basic gates provided here are the smallest

Table 2. The Areas of Basic Gates in the Libraries

	IBM 130 nm-8RF (NSA [3])	IBM 130 nm-CMR8SF -LPLVT	ST CMOS 65 nm
NAND	1	1	1
AND	1.25	1.25	1.25
OR	1.25	1.25	1.5
NOT	0.75	0.75	0.75
XOR	2	2	2.25
XNOR	2	2	2.25
2-1 MUX	2.25	2.25	2
DFF	4.25	4.25	3.75
1-bit full adder	5.75	5.75	4.5
Scan FF	6.25	5.5	4.75

ones in the library. We observe that our IBM 130 nm library is almost the same as the IBM 130 nm library used by the researchers from the NSA [3] except the scan flip-flops in terms of the areas of the basic gates.

3.2 Two Different Hardware Architectures for Simeck

In this section, we target low-area implementations of Simeck and make a trade-off between area and throughput. Meanwhile, we still keep a very high operating frequency. We give two architectures for the implementations: one is parallel architecture, and another one is fully serialized architecture. Moreover, we provide a block diagram of the top-level I/O interface between the cipher and the outside environment in order to provide a benchmark for the future implementations and comparisons with other ciphers.

Parallel Architecture. The parallel architecture processes one round of the message in one clock cycle, and one round of the key schedule at the same clock cycle, as shown in Fig. 3. This architecture provides a very high throughput while keeping a compact design. The round function in Fig. 3(a) includes three parts: $2n$ flip-flops, a n-bit width 2-to-1 multiplexer, a combinational circuit (dashed box) to compute the feedback data for the multiplexer. Inside the $2n$ flip-flops, n flip-flops are for the message b, and the other n ones are for the message a. The multiplexer is used to select the initial plaintext or the feedback data from the combinational circuit for the message b. The combinational circuit includes one n-bit AND gate, three n-bit XOR gates, and two shift modules (cyclic shift to the left by 5 bits and 1 bit). The shift modules cost no extra hardware resources, because they can be done by rewiring the corresponding signals. When the cipher runs, the n-bit data from the message block b shifts to message block a, and simultaneously, the message block b loads a new n-bit data from the multiplexer

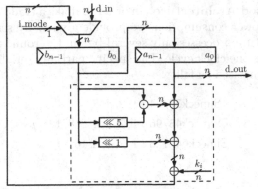

(a) Parallel Datapath for the Round Function

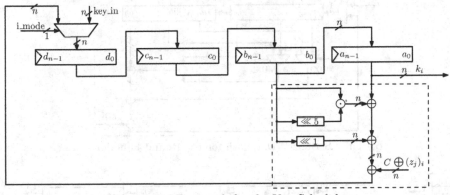

(b) Parallel Datapath for the Key Schedule

Fig. 3. Parallel Architecture for Simeck

until the cipher stops. The round key k_i in the combinational circuit for every round comes from the key schedule function, which generates a key for every rounds until the cipher outputs the ciphertext.

Different from the round function architecture, the key schedule in Fig. 3(b) has four n-bit key blocks and one input to the combinational circuit (dashed box) is different. This n-bit input to the key schedule is a combination of an $(n-1)$-bit constant and a 1-bit signal generated from the control circuit.

All the flip-flops in the round function and key schedule are standard flip-flops without chip-enable in our architecture. In addition, there are only two n-bit width 2-to-1 multiplexers in total in our architecture to select the initial data or feedback data, where one is for the round function, and the other is for the key schedule. Moreover, the latency for generating a ciphertext using our parallel architecture is $T + 4$, where T is the total number of rounds.

Partially Serialized Architecture. In order to make a trade-off between area, throughput, and power consumption, we provide a partially serialized architecture. This architecture processes only several bits in the round function and the key schedule during one clock cycle. The specific partially serialized size (par_sz) of Simeck are summarized as follows:

$$Simeck32/64 : 1, 2, 4, 8,$$
$$Simeck48/96 : 1, 2, 3, 4, 6, 8, 12,$$
$$Simeck64/128 : 1, 2, 4, 8, 16.$$

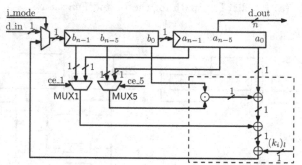

(a) Fully Serialized Datapath for the Round Function

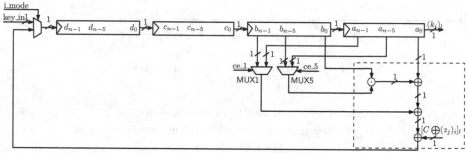

(b) Fully Serialized Datapath for the Key Schedule

Fig. 4. Fully Serialized Architecture for Simeck

Besides the round counter (i in Figs. 3 and 4) in the control circuit, there is another counter to control the rounds of the specific serialized size in the partially serialized architecture. The range of this serialized counter (l in Fig. 4) is between 0 and n/par_sz - 1. In total, the latency for generating a ciphertext is $(n/par\_sz) \cdot (T + 4)$, where T is the total number of rounds.

A fully serialized architecture is shown in Fig. 4. In this architecture, the multiplexer (MUX), and combinational circuit (dashed box) are all 1-bit width, which save a lot of area. Compared to the parallel architecture, there are two

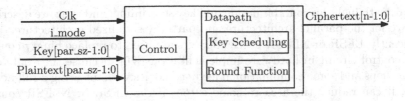

Fig. 5. The Top-level I/O Interface between the Cipher and the Outside Environment

more multiplexers. They are used to select the cyclic shift inputs. The MUX1 is used for the left shift by 1 bit, and MUX5 is used for left shift by 5 bits. The MUX1 selects b_{n-1} as input when the serialized counter equals 0, and chooses a_{n-1} when the serialized counter is larger than 0. Similarly, the MUX5 selects b_{n-5} when the serialized counter is smaller than or equal to 4, and chooses a_{n-5} when the serialized counter is larger than 4.

The partially serialized architecture with par_sz larger than 1 is similar to the fully serialized architecture, where the multiplexer and combinational circuit are par_sz-bit width and the selection signals for the multiplexers (MUXes selection circuitry) are different for various values of par_sz.

The Top-Level I/O Interface for Different Architectures. As discussed in Sect. 3.1, the area of the chip depends on not only the area of the basic gates, but also the adopted types of flip-flops. We provide a top-level I/O interface between the cipher and the outside environment as shown in Fig. 5. We do not have a Finite State Machine (FSM) to control the circuit with the purpose of reducing the entire area as much as possible. In our top-level architecture, the cipher is always running and it is controlled by the outside signal i_mode. Therefore, we only have two modes in our architecture: loading phase and running phase. The cipher goes into loading phase when i_mode equals 0, and it loads the initial data from the inputs Key and Plaintext. Later on, the cipher begins running phase when i_mode equals 1. The user obtains the Ciphertext at the end of the running phase. Then, i_mode returns back to 0, another Plaintext encryption begins. As our architecture never stops, all the flip-flops in the datapath are standard flip-flops without chip-enable signals. This property makes our design ever smaller in terms of area. This architecture presents a benchmark ASIC implementation of Simeck and can be used to fairly compare with the hardware results of other ciphers.

It is worth mentioning that the parallel architecture can be viewed as a special case of the partially serialized case when par_sz equals n. However, the two cases have different architectures as depicted in Figs. 3 and 4.

Our top-level architecture includes two parts: the control circuit and the datapath. The control circuit for the parallel architecture is used to provide the key constant from the LFSR as described in Sect. 2. However, an extra serialized counter in the control circuit is needed for the partially serialized architecture.

The datapath includes round function and key scheduling, and they are described as above for the parallel architecture and partially serialized architecture.

Recently, LFSR or NLFSR based counters are used to replace binary counter in the control circuit in hardware implementations [20], because they only contain flip-flops and some combinational feedback logics without using a full-adder. Hence, it can reduce the area to some extent if the LFSR or NLFSR counter does not incur extra area in the datapath. However, the serialized counter in our partially serialized architecture is used in two aspects: one is used to count the serialized rounds in the control circuit and another one is used to select the two multiplexers (MUX1 and MUX5) in the datapath. After a theoretical and practical analysis of the effects of the LFSR or NLFSR counter in our partially serialized architecture, we discovered that the total area using binary serialized counter is the smallest one because the LFSR or NLFSR counter results in more additional area in the datapath (i.e., the area of the multiplexers selection circuitry) than the area saved by replacing the binary counter with LFSR or NLFSR counter in the control circuit. Therefore, the binary serialized counter is used for our partially serialized architecture.

3.3   Hardware Evaluations of Simeck

We use three different compilation techniques in the Design Compiler to perform hardware optimizations: simple compile, compile ultra and compile ultra with clock gating. The simple compile option can provide us the hierarchical architectures of the design, and the areas of specific sub-modules. The compile ultra option can make deeper optimizations in a way of optimizing the entire module together, thereby reducing the area and power consumption significantly [11,20]. The clock gating technique can further reduce the area and power consumption [11]. However, we use all standard flip-flops without chip-enable signals for the parallel architecture. Only the LFSR generating the key constant in the control circuit uses the flip-flops with chip-enable signals, which costs 5, 6, and 6 flip-flops for Simeck32/64, Simeck48/96, and Simeck64/128 respectively. Therefore, the clock gating optimization affects only a little of our results in terms of area and power consumption. The ASIC implementation results of Simeck and SIMON in CMOS 130 nm are shown in Tables 3 and 4, and the corresponding results of Simeck and SIMON in CMOS 65 nm are shown in Tables 7 and 8. It is worth noting that these results are obtained without using scan registers.

We provide the best area results before and after the Place and Route phase using compile ultra or compile ultra plus clock gating. These results can be used for comparing with other ciphers or for practical purpose. The maximum frequency corresponding with the best optimization technique is given and it is calculated by using the critical path. The calculated throughput is based on the latency in our architectures and it is the same as SIMON. The difference of the total power consumption among the three different optimizations is marginal. Therefore, we only provide a total power consumption using compile ultra at 100 KHz, which is typical for benchmarking purpose. Since the operating frequency is too small, the static power consumption dominates the total power consumption.

Table 3. Our Implementation Results of Simeck32/64, 48/96, 64/128 in 130 nm

Simeck	Partial serial	CMOS 130 nm				
		Area (GEs)		Max frequency (MHz)	Throughput @100 KHz (Kbps)	Total power @100 KHz (μW)
		Before P&R	After P&R			
Simeck32/64	1-bit	505[a]	549[a]	292	5.6	0.417
	2-bit	510[b]	555[b]	288	11.1	0.431
	4-bit	533[b]	579[b]	312	22.2	0.463
	8-bit	591[b]	642[b]	289	44.4	0.523
	16-bit	695[a]	756[a]	526	88.9	0.606
Simeck48/96	1-bit	715[b]	778[b]	299	5.0	0.576
	2-bit	722[b]	785[b]	294	10.0	0.593
	3-bit	731[b]	794[b]	268	15.0	0.611
	4-bit	748[b]	813[h]	284	20.0	0.628
	6-bit	770[b]	837[b]	287	30.0	0.651
	8-bit	801[b]	871[b]	284	40.0	0.688
	12-bit	858[b]	933[b]	283	60.0	0.742
	24-bit	1027[a]	1117[a]	512	120.0	0.875
Simeck64/128	1-bit	924[a]	1005[a]	288	4.2	0.754
	2-bit	933[b]	1015[b]	303	8.3	0.778
	4-bit	958[b]	1041[b]	271	16.7	0.803
	8-bit	1013[b]	1101[b]	280	33.3	0.834
	16-bit	1132[b]	1231[b]	301	66.7	0.977
	32-bit	1365[a]	1484[a]	512	133.3	1.162

[a] Area obtained by using compile ultra only.
[b] Area obtained by using compile ultra and clock gating.

However, the static power consumption is larger in CMOS 65 nm than in CMOS 130 nm, which is the reason why the total power consumption is larger in CMOS 65 nm as shown in Tables 7 and 8.

Besides having a very small area, our another observation is that most part of the area for all the architectures are built of the sequential logics, especially for the fully serialized architecture. Take Simeck32/64 for example. 86 %, 85 %, 82 %, 76 %, and 70 % of the entire area are sequential logics for the cases that par_sz equals 1, 2, 4, 8, and 16 respectively. From the data provided, we can obtain that the fully serialized architecture is built of about 90 % sequential logics. Similar conclusions can be obtained for Simeck48/96 and Simeck64/128.

We provide a range of options between the area, throughput, and power consumption in our ASIC implementations. Taking Simeck32/64 in CMOS 130 nm for illustration, we can achieve a throughput of 5.6 Kbps at the area cost of 505 GEs (before the Place and Route) and 549 GEs (after the Place and Route)

Table 4. Our Implementation Results of SIMON32/64, 48/96, 64/128 in 130 nm

SIMON	Partial serial	CMOS 130 nm					
		Area (GEs)			Max frequency (MHz)	Throughput @100 KHz (Kbps)	Total power @100 KHz (μW)
		Before P&R	After P&R	NSA before P&R			
SIMON32/64	1-bit	517[b]	562[b]	523	331	5.6	0.421
	2-bit	532[a]	578[a]	535	306	11.1	0.439
	4-bit	563[b]	612[b]	566	283	22.2	0.479
	8-bit	623[a]	677[a]	627	367	44.4	0.540
	16-bit	715[a]	778[a]	722	456	88.9	0.645
SIMON48/96	1-bit	733[b]	796[b]	739	258	5.0	0.579
	2-bit	745[b]	810[b]	750	289	10.0	0.601
	3-bit	756[b]	822[b]	763	291	15.0	0.615
	4-bit	778[b]	846[b]	781	287	20.0	0.642
	6-bit	800[b]	869[b]	804	289	30.0	0.670
	8-bit	833[b]	905[b]	839	238	40.0	0.706
	12-bit	895[b]	973[b]	898	307	60.0	0.777
	24-bit	1055[a]	1147[a]	1062	467	120.0	0.929
SIMON64/128	1-bit	944[b]	1026[b]	958	225	4.2	0.762
	2-bit	955[b]	1038[b]	968	244	8.3	0.780
	4-bit	988[b]	1074[b]	1000	290	16.7	0.818
	8-bit	1043[b]	1134[b]	1057	296	33.3	0.866
	16-bit	1174[b]	1276[b]	1185	293	66.7	1.024
	32-bit	1403[a]	1524[a]	1417	465	133.3	1.239

[a] Area obtained by using compile ultra only.
[b] Area obtained by using compile ultra and clock gating.

with the power consumption of 0.417 μW. However, a two-fold throughput (11.1 Kbps) can be obtained with only 5 and 6 extra GEs (before and after the Place and Route respectively), and 0.014 μW extra power consumption. With more extra area and power consumption, we can get even higher throughput.

4   Result Comparisons Between **Simeck** and SIMON

We compare our area results before the Place and Route of Simeck and SIMON in CMOS 130 nm with the SIMON results of the NSA researchers [3]. This is because the NSA researchers only provide the area results before the Place and Route. The comparison is shown in Fig. 6. We can observe that our SIMON results are all smaller than that of NSA's results, and our Simeck results are even smaller than SIMON for all the cases shown in Fig. 6.

From the theoretical point of view, Simeck is designed to have a smaller area due to the following considerations: the simplified key schedule, the simplified LFSR to generate the key constant, and the decreased shift numbers in the

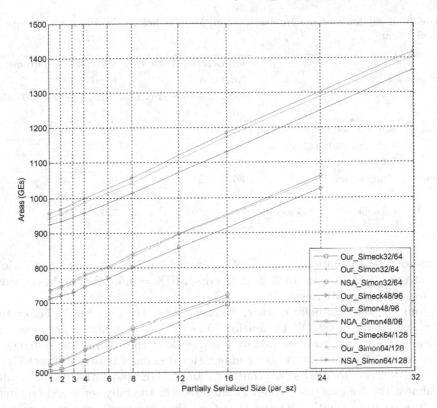

Fig. 6. Comparisons of Areas (before the Place and Route) between the Implementation Results of the NSA Researchers' and Ours in CMOS 130 nm

round function. It is worth noting that the decreased shift numbers do not affect any area in the parallel architecture, and it only affect the area in the partially serialized architecture.

The construction of the combinational circuit in the key schedule of SIMON32/64, 48/96, 64/128 and Simeck32/64, 48/96, 64/128 in the parallel architecture are shown as follows:

SIMON	$(2n+1)$ XOR $+ (n-1)$ XNOR
Simeck	$(n+1)$ XOR $+ (n-1)$ XNOR $+ n$ AND

In general, one XOR gate is larger than one AND gate. Therefore, the key schedule of SIMON is larger than that of Simeck. The LFSRs used to generate the key constants for SIMON32/64 and SIMON48/96 are defined by the primitive polynomial $X^5 + X^4 + X^2 + X + 1$, and the LFSR for SIMON64/128 is defined by $X^5 + X^3 + X^2 + X + 1$. They are all 2 XOR gates (4 GEs) bigger than the ones used in corresponding Simeck, as described in Sect. 2. The decreased shift numbers of the round function and key schedule reduce 1 MUX for the

Table 5. Breakdown of the Implementation Results before the Place and Route in CMOS 130 nm

Components		Simeck32/64 (130 nm)		Simon32/64 (130 nm)	
		Parallel (GEs)	Fully serialized (GEs)	Parallel (GEs)	Fully serialized (GEs)
Control		31	71	35	75
Datapath	Round_combinational circuit	112	7	112	7
	Key_combinational circuit	80	5	96	8
	Sequential + MUXes	474	434	474	443
Totals	Compile simple	697	517	717	533
	Compile ultra	695	505	717	520
	Compile ultra + clock gating	695	506	715	517

inputs to the combinational circuits of the round function and the key schedule respectively (2 MUXes in total, $2 \cdot 2.25$ GEs/MUX $= 4.5$ GEs), and also some logics to select the MUXes.

From the practical point of view, we break down the area results before the Place and Route in CMOS 130 nm for Simeck32/64, and Simon32/64 in our implementations, as shown in Table 5. For parallel architectures, the differences of the control circuits and the key combinational circuits between Simeck32/64 and Simon32/64 are 4 GEs (key constant) and 16 GEs respectively. The results are almost the same as the theoretical analysis. For the fully serialized architecture, the control circuit is reduced by 4 GEs (key constant), the key combinational circuit (dashed box in Fig. 4) is reduced by 3 GEs, and the 2 MUXes plus the MUXes selection circuitry are reduced by 9 GEs for Simeck32/64 (i.e., a total saving of 16 GEs), compared to that of Simon32/64. Therefore, the practical results match the theoretical analysis. Simeck is smaller than Simon for both parallel architecture and partially serialized architecture.

The main area cost for Simon comes from the registers storing the message block and the key. In order to design a smaller cipher than Simon, we can reduce the areas of only the round function, key schedule, key constant, and multiplexers. For fully serialized architecture of Simon32/64 (see Table 5), the combined area of these blocks is 34.5 GEs ($7 + 8 + 6 + 6 \cdot 2.25$/MUX), which accounts for only about 6.4 % (34.5/533) of the total area. Simeck32/64 reduces this by 16 GEs, a saving of more than 46 %. This reduction leads to 2.3 % smaller total area in comparison to our implementations of Simon32/64 in CMOS 130 nm, and 3.4 % smaller in comparison to the original Simon32/64 results (see Table 1). Similarly, the fully serialized architectures of Simeck48/96, 64/128 are 2.5 %, 2.1 %, respectively, smaller than our implementations of Simon48/96, 64/128 and they are 3.3 % and 3.5 %, respectively, smaller than the original implementation results of Simon48/96, 64/128 in CMOS 130 nm (see Table 1). For the parallel architectures of Simon, these blocks consume a larger fraction (about 29 %) of the total area (see Table 5). Simeck32/64, 48/96, 64/128 achieve the saving of 3.7 %, 3.3 %, and 3.7 % respectively, compared to the original results of SIMON32/64, 48/96, 64/128 (see Tables 3 and 4). The choice of the values of the shift numbers plays a significant role in the area reduction of the partially serialized architecture. Because the parallel architecture does not contain the MUXes for the inputs to the combinational circuit (dashed box), the total area reduction is only slightly greater than the fully serialized architecture.

From Tables 3 and 4, we can also observe that the power consumption of Simeck is smaller than SIMON for all the cases in CMOS 130 nm using the same optimizations. This is easy to understand because the area of Simeck is smaller than SIMON. This conclusion also holds for CMOS 65 nm in Tables 7 and 8.

In summary, Simeck is smaller than SIMON in terms of area and power consumption in both CMOS 130 nm and CMOS 65 nm techniques.

5 Security Analysis

In this section, we give the security analysis of the Simeck family of block ciphers. Due to its similitude with SIMON and SPECK, most of the next analysis follow from the best known attacks against the SIMON and SPECK families of block ciphers. As we show in the following, the security level of Simeck is comparable to those of SIMON, which is reasonable to be used in practice. Indeed, the number of rounds chosen for Simeck is sufficiently high with respect to the best known attacks on reduced versions. Moreover, it is worth noticing that the ARX (Addition-Rotation-XOR) design of Simeck borrowed from SPECK, using the round function as key-schedule, did not lead to a weakness so far. In a recent paper [22], Kölbl et al. study the influence of the shifts in SIMON-like ciphers. They provide some set of parameters that are optimal with respect to differential and linear properties, and diffusion. Our parameters seem comparable to theirs because we take also into account hardware efficiency and other types of cryptanalysis (e.g., impossible differential cryptanalysis).

Differential/Linear Attacks [6,23]. Since the differential and linear behaviors of SIMON and Simeck are very closely related, it makes sense to use the best known differential and linear attacks of SIMON to evaluate the security of Simeck against these attacks. This is why we have essentially followed the procedure of [7] to evaluate the security of Simeck against differential cryptanalysis. It is then possible to perform an attack on 19 rounds of Simeck32/64 with the time and data complexity 2^{34} and $2^{31.5}$ respectively. It is also possible to attack 20 rounds out of 36 of Simeck48/96 with the time and data complexity 2^{75} and 2^{46} as well as an attack of 26 rounds out of 44 of Simeck64/128 with the time and data complexity 2^{121} and 2^{63}.

For the best cryptanalytic result using linear attacks against SIMON, we refer to [1]. Because of the similar structure of Simeck, we verified that those results are also conform with respect to Simeck. For Simeck32/64, we can cover 12 rounds with the data complexity 2^{31}. For Simeck48/96, we can cover 15 rounds with the data complexity 2^{43}. Finally, it is possible to perform a linear cryptanalysis of Simeck64/128 up to 19 rounds with 2^{123} known plaintexts. All these attacks have a success probability of 0.997.

Table 6. Comparison of Impossible Differential Attacks against SIMON and Simeck

Algorithm	#Rounds	Data	Time	Memory
SIMON32/64 [10]	19	2^{32}	$2^{62.56}$	2^{44}
SIMON48/96 [10]	21	2^{48}	$2^{94.73}$	2^{70}
SIMON64/128 [10]	22	2^{64}	$2^{126.56}$	2^{75}
Simeck32/64	20	2^{32}	$2^{62.6}$	2^{56}
Simeck48/96	24	2^{48}	$2^{94.7}$	2^{74}
Simeck64/128	25	2^{64}	$2^{126.6}$	2^{79}

Table 7. Our Implementation Results of Simeck32/64, 48/96, 64/128 in 65 nm

Simeck	Partial Serial	CMOS 65nm				
		Area (GEs)		Max frequency (MHz)	Throughput @100 KHz (Kbps)	Total power @100 KHz (μW)
		Before P&R	After P&R			
Simeck32/64	1-bit	454^a	488^a	1754	5.6	1.292
	2-bit	465^b	500^b	1428	11.1	1.311
	4-bit	494^b	531^b	1388	22.2	1.376
	8-bit	550^a	592^a	1250	44.4	1.512
	16-bit	644^a	692^a	1428	88.9	1.716
Simeck48/96	1-bit	645^b	693^b	1562	5.0	1.805
	2-bit	656^b	706^b	1538	10.0	1.825
	3-bit	663^b	712^b	1282	15.0	1.857
	4-bit	686^b	738^b	1333	20.0	1.886
	6-bit	701^b	753^b	1282	30.0	1.919
	8-bit	732^b	787^b	1388	40.0	2.009
	12-bit	794^a	854^a	1219	60.0	2.212
	24-bit	951^a	1022^a	2325	120.0	2.44
Simeck64/128	1-bit	828^a	891^a	1369	4.2	2.304
	2-bit	838^b	901^b	1408	8.3	2.325
	4-bit	869^b	935^b	1098	16.7	2.372
	8-bit	918^b	987^b	1190	33.3	2.492
	16-bit	1042^a	1121^a	1086	66.7	2.869
	32-bit	1263^a	1358^a	1282	133.3	3.316

[a] Area obtained by using compile ultra only.
[b] Area obtained by using compile ultra and clock gating.

Since the best known differential and linear trails found on Simeck, and SIMON, only cover a reduced number of rounds, we believe that the full-round Simeck (any version) is sufficiently secure against differential and linear cryptanalysis.

Table 8. Our Implementation Results of SIMON32/64, 48/96, 64/128 in 65 nm

SIMON	Partial Serial	CMOS 65 nm				
		Area (GEs)		Max frequency (MHz)	Throughput @100 KHz (Kbps)	Total power @100 KHz (μW)
		Before P&R	After P&R			
SIMON32/64	1-bit	466[a]	501[a]	1428	5.6	1.311
	2-bit	476[a]	512[a]	1562	11.1	1.331
	4-bit	506[a]	544[a]	1408	22.2	1.381
	8-bit	570[a]	613[a]	1075	44.4	1.585
	16-bit	666[a]	716[a]	2222	88.9	1.751
SIMON48/96	1-bit	661[b]	711[b]	1204	5.0	1.812
	2-bit	670[b]	720[b]	1136	10.0	1.889
	3-bit	682[b]	733[b]	1086	15.0	1.86
	4-bit	699[b]	752[b]	1041	20.0	1.915
	6-bit	724[b]	779[b]	1369	30.0	1.962
	8-bit	757[b]	814[b]	1282	40.0	2.122
	12-bit	819[a]	881[a]	1176	60.0	2.305
	24-bit	982[a]	1056[a]	2222	120.0	2.542
SIMON64/128	1-bit	845[b]	908[b]	1282	4.2	2.336
	2-bit	858[b]	922[b]	1265	8.3	2.366
	4-bit	887[b]	954[b]	1250	16.7	2.423
	8-bit	944[b]	1015[b]	1265	33.3	2.577
	16-bit	1076[a]	1156[a]	1176	66.7	3.068
	32-bit	1305[a]	1403[a]	1694	133.3	3.398

[a] Area obtained by using compile ultra only.
[b] Area obtained by using compile ultra and clock gating.

Impossible Differential Attacks [4]. Impossible differential attacks against Simeck cover few more rounds (depending on the version) than for SIMON as it can be seen in Table 6. This is due to the fact that the diffusion of one bit difference is one round slower for Simeck than for SIMON. Nevertheless, this does not damage the overall security of the Simeck family, since the full versions have more rounds.

Algebraic Degree [21]. We computed that after 5 rounds, the algebraic degree of Simeck (any version) is 13, as the one of SIMON. It is sufficient to ensure that after few more rounds, no attack can exploit properties of the algebraic degree, such as algebraic attack or higher-order differential attack.

Meet-in-the-Middle Attacks [13]. Because of the key schedule algorithm of Simeck, many key bits of the master key are processed quickly in the round function of Simeck. This should ensure a good resistance of Simeck against Meet-in-the-Middle (MITM) attacks. Moreover, until now SIMON has not shown to be a good candidate for MITM attacks. As the round function of Simeck is very similar as the one of SIMON, we believe that Simeck will also be resistant against MITM attacks.

Slide Attacks and Rotational Attacks [8,19]. The round constant addition and the key schedule design prevent any efficient slide or rotational attacks.

Related-key Differential Attacks [5]. Although SIMON and SPECK have been extensively studied in the past years, no concrete attacks in the related-key setting have been shown. Like SPECK, Simeck reuses its round function in the key schedule part. It is reasonable to think that Simeck has also good cryptographic properties in the related key model.

6   Concluding Remarks

In this paper, we have presented Simeck, a new family of lightweight block ciphers. Simeck is very suitable for resource-constrained devices, such as passive RFID tags and wireless sensor networks. We have provided an extensive exploration for different hardware architectures in order to make a balance between area, throughput, and power consumption for SIMON and Simeck in both CMOS 130 nm and CMOS 65 nm techniques. We have shown that it is possible to design a smaller cipher than SIMON in terms of area and power consumption. Moreover, we have improved the hardware implementations of SIMON given in the original paper. In addition, the similarities between SIMON/SPECK and Simeck allow us to have an idea of the actual security offered by Simeck. Even if the round function of Simeck is quite simple, this round function is iterated a sufficient number of time to provide an adequate security against most known attacks. In conclusion, all of the instances in the Simeck family can meet the area, power consumption, and throughput requirements in the passive RFID tags and they are promising candidates for resource-constrained devices.

We have learnt and understood many techniques about designing hardware-oriented ciphers during the process of completing the design of Simeck. It is interesting to see if we can devise a block cipher with even smaller hardware footprints than Simeck. It also interests us whether we can design, from the theoretical point of view, a smallest block cipher with the minimum number of components. This should be very useful for cryptography researchers to get deep insights into designing and analyzing ciphers.

Acknowledgments. The authors would like to thank the anonymous reviewers for their helpful and constructive comments that greatly contributed to improving the final version of the paper. This work is supported by NSERC Discovery Grants, Strategic Project Grant, and Canadian Microelectronics Corporation.

Appendix A ASIC Implementation Results of Simon and Simeck in CMOS 65 nm

Tables 7 and 8 give our results of Simeck and SIMON in CMOS 65 nm.

Appendix B Test Vectors

Here we list some test vectors for the Simeck family of block ciphers, in the same format as the ones in [3].
Simeck32/64

Key: 1918 1110 0908 0100
Plaintext: 6565 6877
Ciphertext: 770d 2c76

Simeck48/96

Key: 1a1918 121110 0a0908 020100
Plaintext: 726963 20646e
Ciphertext: f3cf25 e33b36

Simeck64/128

Key: 1b1a1918 13121110 0b0a0908 03020100
Plaintext: 656b696c 20646e75
Ciphertext: 45ce6902 5f7ab7ed

References

1. Alizadeh, J., Alkhzaimi, H.A., Aref, M.R., Bagheri, N., Gauravaram, P., Kumar, A., Lauridsen, M.M., Sanadhya, S.K.: Cryptanalysis of SIMON variants with connections. In: Sadeghi, A.-R., Saxena, N. (eds.) RFIDSec 2014. LNCS, vol. 8651, pp. 90–107. Springer, Heidelberg (2014)
2. Armknecht, F., Hamann, M., Mikhalev, V.: Lightweight authentication protocols on ultra-constrained RFIDs - myths and facts. In: Sadeghi, A.-R., Saxena, N. (eds.) RFIDSec 2014. LNCS, vol. 8651, pp. 1–18. Springer, Heidelberg (2014)
3. Beaulieu, R., Shors, D., Smith, J., Treatman-Clark, S., Weeks, B., Wingers, L.: The SIMON and SPECK Families of Lightweight Block Ciphers. Cryptology ePrint Archive, Report 2013/404 (2013). http://eprint.iacr.org/
4. Biham, E., Biryukov, A., Shamir, A.: Cryptanalysis of skipjack reduced to 31 rounds using impossible differentials. J. Cryptology 18(4), 291–311 (2005)
5. Biham, E., Dunkelman, O., Keller, N.: A unified approach to related-key attacks. In: Nyberg, K. (ed.) FSE 2008. LNCS, vol. 5086, pp. 73–96. Springer, Heidelberg (2008)
6. Biham, E., Shamir, A.: Differential cryptanalysis of DES-like cryptosystems. J. Cryptology 4(1), 3–72 (1991)
7. Biryukov, A., Roy, A., Velichkov, V.: Differential analysis of block ciphers SIMON and SPECK. In: Cid, C., Rechberger, C. (eds.) FSE 2014. LNCS, vol. 8540, pp. 546–570. Springer, Heidelberg (2015)
8. Biryukov, A., Wagner, D.: Slide attacks. In: Knudsen, L.R. (ed.) FSE 1999. LNCS, vol. 1636, p. 245. Springer, Heidelberg (1999)
9. Bogdanov, A.A., Knudsen, L.R., Leander, G., Paar, C., Poschmann, A., Robshaw, M., Seurin, Y., Vikkelsoe, C.: PRESENT: an ultra-lightweight block cipher. In: Paillier, P., Verbauwhede, I. (eds.) CHES 2007. LNCS, vol. 4727, pp. 450–466. Springer, Heidelberg (2007)

10. Boura, C., Naya-Plasencia, M., Suder, V.: Scrutinizing and improving impossible differential attacks: applications to CLEFIA, camellia, LBlock and simon. In: Proceedings of Advances in Cryptology - ASIACRYPT 2014-20th International Conference on the Theory and Application of Cryptology and Information Security, Part I, pp. 179–199. Kaoshiung, Taiwan, R.O.C, December 7–11 (2014)
11. De Cannière, C., Dunkelman, O., Knežević, M.: KATAN and KTANTAN — a family of small and efficient hardware-oriented block ciphers. In: Clavier, C., Gaj, K. (eds.) CHES 2009. LNCS, vol. 5747, pp. 272–288. Springer, Heidelberg (2009)
12. De Cannière, C., Preneel, B.: Trivium specifications. eSTREAM, ECRYPT Stream Cipher Project, Report 2005/030 (2005)
13. Diffie, W., Hellman, M.E.: Exhaustive cryptanalysis of the NBS data encryption standard. Computer 10(6), 74–84 (1977)
14. EPCglobal. EPC Class 1 Generation 2 Standard (2013). http://www.gs1.org/sites/default/files/docs/uhfc1g2/uhfc1g2_2_0_0_standard_20131101.pdf
15. Gong, Z., Nikova, S., Law, Y.W.: KLEIN: a new family of lightweight block ciphers. In: Juels, A., Paar, C. (eds.) RFIDSec 2011. LNCS, vol. 7055, pp. 1–18. Springer, Heidelberg (2012)
16. Guo, J., Peyrin, T., Poschmann, A., Robshaw, M.: The LED block cipher. In: Preneel, B., Takagi, T. (eds.) CHES 2011. LNCS, vol. 6917, pp. 326–341. Springer, Heidelberg (2011)
17. Hell, M., Johansson, T., Meier, W.: Grain: a stream cipher for constrained environments. Int. J. Wireless and Mobile Comput. 2(1), 86–93 (2007)
18. Juels, A., Weis, S.A.: Authenticating pervasive devices with human protocols. In: Shoup, V. (ed.) CRYPTO 2005. LNCS, vol. 3621, pp. 293–308. Springer, Heidelberg (2005)
19. Khovratovich, D., Nikolić, I.: Rotational cryptanalysis of ARX. In: Hong, S., Iwata, T. (eds.) FSE 2010. LNCS, vol. 6147, pp. 333–346. Springer, Heidelberg (2010)
20. Knudsen, L., Leander, G., Poschmann, A., Robshaw, M.J.B.: PRINTcipher: a block cipher for IC-printing. In: Mangard, S., Standaert, F.-X. (eds.) CHES 2010. LNCS, vol. 6225, pp. 16–32. Springer, Heidelberg (2010)
21. Knudsen, L.R.: Truncated and higher order differentials. In: Preneel, B. (ed.) FSE 1994. LNCS, vol. 1008, pp. 196–211. Springer, Heidelberg (1995)
22. Kölbl, S., Leander, G., Tiessen, T.: Observations on the simon block cipher family. In: CRYPTO 2015, LNCS. Springer, Heidelberg (2015)
23. Matsui, M.: Linear cryptanalysis method for DES cipher. In: Helleseth, T. (ed.) EUROCRYPT 1993. LNCS, vol. 765, pp. 386–397. Springer, Heidelberg (1994)
24. Moradi, A., Poschmann, A., Ling, S., Paar, C., Wang, H.: Pushing the Limits: a very compact and a threshold implementation of AES. In: Advances in Cryptology - EUROCRYPT 2011, pp. 69–88. Springer, (2011)
25. Nawaz, Y., Gong, G.: WG: a family of stream ciphers with designed randomness properties. Inf. Sci. 178(7), 1903–1916 (2008)
26. Needham, R.M., Wheeler, D.J.: TEA Extensions, Technical Report, University of Cambridge, October 1997
27. Plos, T., Dobraunig, C., Hofinger, M., Oprisnik, A., Wiesmeier, C., Wiesmeier, J.: Compact hardware implementations of the block ciphers mCrypton, NOEKEON, and SEA. In: Galbraith, S., Nandi, M. (eds.) INDOCRYPT 2012. LNCS, vol. 7668, pp. 358–377. Springer, Heidelberg (2012)
28. Rolfes, C., Poschmann, A., Leander, G., Paar, C.: Ultra-lightweight implementations for smart devices – security for 1000 gate equivalents. In: Grimaud, G., Standaert, F.-X. (eds.) CARDIS 2008. LNCS, vol. 5189, pp. 89–103. Springer, Heidelberg (2008)

29. Shibutani, K., Isobe, T., Hiwatari, H., Mitsuda, A., Akishita, T., Shirai, T.: Piccolo: an ultra-lightweight block cipher. In: Preneel, B., Takagi, T. (eds.) CHES 2011. LNCS, vol. 6917, pp. 342–357. Springer, Heidelberg (2011)
30. Suzaki, T., Minematsu, K., Morioka, S., Kobayashi, E.: Twine: a lightweight, versatile block cipher. In: ECRYPT Workshop on Lightweight Cryptography, pp. 146–169 (2011)
31. Wheeler, D.J., Needham, R.M.: TEA: a tiny encryption algorithm. In: Proceedings of Fast Software Encryption: Second International Workshop. Leuven, pp. 363–366. Belgium, 14–16 December 1994
32. Wu, W., Zhang, L.: LBlock: a lightweight block cipher. In: Lopez, J., Tsudik, G. (eds.) ACNS 2011. LNCS, vol. 6715, pp. 327–344. Springer, Heidelberg (2011)
33. Yap, H., Khoo, K., Poschmann, A., Henricksen, M.: EPCBC - a block cipher suitable for electronic product code encryption. In: Lin, D., Tsudik, G., Wang, X. (eds.) CANS 2011. LNCS, vol. 7092, pp. 76–97. Springer, Heidelberg (2011)
34. Yeager, D.J., Sample, A.P., Smith, J.R., Smith, J.R.: WISP: a passively powered UHF RFID tag with sensing and computation. In: RFID Handbook: Applications, Technology, Security, and Privacy, pp. 261–278 (2008)

TriviA: A Fast and Secure Authenticated Encryption Scheme

Avik Chakraborti[1]([✉]), Anupam Chattopadhyay[2], Muhammad Hassan[3], and Mridul Nandi[1]

[1] Indian Statistical Institute, Kolkata, India
{avikchkrbrti,mridul.nandi}@gmail.com
[2] School of Computer Engineering, NTU, Singapore, Singapore
anupam@ntu.edu.sg
[3] RWTH Aachen University, Aachen, Germany
muhammad.hassan@rwth-aachen.de

Abstract. In this paper, we propose a new hardware friendly authenticated encryption (AE) scheme TriviA based on (i) a stream cipher for generating keys for the ciphertext and the tag, and (ii) a pairwise independent hash to compute the tag. *We have adopted one of the ISO-standardized stream ciphers for lightweight cryptography, namely Trivium, to obtain our underlying stream cipher.* This new stream cipher has a state that is a little larger than the state of Trivium to accommodate a 128-bit secret key and IV. *Our pairwise independent hash is also an adaptation of the EHC* or "Encode-Hash-Combine" hash, that requires the optimum number of field multiplications and hence requires small hardware footprint. We have implemented the design in synthesizable RTL. Pre-layout synthesis, using 65 nm standard cell technology under typical operating conditions, reveals that TriviA is able to achieve a high throughput of 91.2 Gbps for an area of 24.4 KGE. We prove that our construction has at least 128-bit security for privacy and 124-bit security of authenticity under the assumption that the underlying stream cipher produces a pseudorandom bit stream.

Keywords: Trivium · Stream cipher · Authenticated encryption · Pairwise independent · EHC · TriviA

1 Introduction

The emergence of Internet-of-Things (IoT) has made security an extremely important design goal. A huge number of embedded devices are online and this online presence opens myriads of possibilities to a third party intruder to alter the communication between two devices. Hence, a critical information transfer requires a secure channel. Symmetric-key encryption provides privacy by securing the channel, whereas message authentication codes (MACs) are used to provide integrity and authenticity assurances. Using an appropriate, efficient combination of symmetric key encryption and MAC, also called authenticated

© International Association for Cryptologic Research 2015
T. Güneysu and H. Handschuh (Eds.): CHES 2015, LNCS 9293, pp. 330–353, 2015.
DOI: 10.1007/978-3-662-48324-4_17

encryption [10, 25], one can achieve both privacy and authenticity. An interest in new efficient and secure solutions of authenticated encryption is manifested in the recently launched competition called CAESAR [3].

Authenticated encryption can be achieved using either a stream cipher or a block cipher or both. The general opinion seems to be that stream ciphers can be designed to offer high throughput/area ratios, a desired performance metric for embedded devices. Trivium [16], Grain [23], Mickey [9] etc. are prominent examples of implementation-friendly stream ciphers from the eSTREAM project [4]. Trivium has been specified as an International Standard under ISO/IEC 29192-3 for the lightweight cryptography category [5].

AUTHENTICATED ENCRYPTION BASED ON STREAM CIPHER. A method of using stream cipher for the construction of authenticated encryption scheme is described by Bernstein [12]. The authenticated encryption scheme HELIX [19] and later PHELIX [34] are designed based on a stream cipher. Both were later attacked [30, 35]. Grain has been modified to Grain-128 [24] to support an integrated authentication mechanism. To the best of our knowledge, in the ETSI specification [1], combining the stream cipher SNOW-3G [2] with polynomial hash, and later by Sarkar [32], a study on constructions of authenticated encryptions using stream cipher and ΔU hash have been made. Integrating universal hash with other cryptographic primitives has also been studied by Bernstein [11].

Our Contribution. In this paper, we propose a new stream cipher TriviA-SC which is a modification of Trivium [16], a well-studied and efficient (both in terms of software and hardware) stream cipher. Moreover, our new stream cipher has a key and a initial value of 128 bits. We introduce non-linearity in the output stream which helps to resist some known approaches of finding the key for Trivium. We also study a Δ-Universal hash EHC [31], parametrized by a parameter d, which requires a minimum number of field multiplications and can be implemented with small hardware footprint. In the paper by Nandi [31], the ΔU property (a close variant of pair-wise independent property) of EHC is shown for $d \leq 4$. Here we extend their result and show that the same hash function is a ΔU hash for $d = 5$. This choice of d helps us to make a higher security claim.

Finally, we describe an efficient integration of these primitives to construct a new authenticated encryption scheme-TriviA constructed as a variant of the stream cipher based modes described by Sarkar [32]. We would like to point out that EHC requires a variable key to incorporate variable length messages and the security of it relies on the assumption that all the keys are chosen independently. However, in an authenticated encryption mode, we have to leak the key through ciphertext and the independence assumption is no longer true. We show that TriviA achieves 128-bit security for privacy and 124-bit security for authenticity, assuming that Trivia-SC produces pseudorandom bit stream.

We also report the hardware performance of TriviA on both FPGA and ASIC platforms and make a comparative study with other authenticated encryption schemes implemented in a similar platform. We have observed that, TriviA is very efficient in terms of throughput, cycles per byte and area-efficiency. For area-efficiency metric TriviA is at least 3.8 times better than the closest candidate Ascon from our list.

2 Preliminaries

Notation. We represent a tuple $(X_a, \cdots, X_b)$ by $X[a \cdots b]$, when the X_i's are bit strings, we also identify the tuple as the concatenation $X_a \| \cdots \| X_b$. For a set S, let $S^+ = \cup_{i=1}^{\infty} S^i$, $S^{\leq n} = \cup_{i=1}^{n} S^i$ and $S^* = S^+ \cup \{\lambda\}$ where λ is the empty string. The usual choice of S is $\{0,1\}$. For $\forall x = x_1 \ldots x_n \in \{0,1\}^*$, denote n by $|x|$. The string with one followed by n zeroes is denoted by 10^n. Let the number of n-bit blocks in a Boolean string x be denoted by $\ell_x^n = |x|/n$.

Finite Field. Let $\mathbb{F}_{2^n}$ denote the finite field over $\{0,1\}^n$, for a positive integer n. In this paper, we consider the primitive polynomials [18,28] $p_{32}(x) = x^{32} + x^{22} + x^2 + x + 1$ and $p_{64}(x) = x^{64} + x^4 + x^3 + x + 1$ to describe $\mathbb{F}_{2^{32}}$ and $\mathbb{F}_{2^{64}}$ respectively. Denote the corresponding primitive elements by α and β which are binary representations of 2. The field addition or bit-wise addition is denoted as "xor" $\oplus$. Note that multiplication by powers of α, β are much simpler than multiplication between two arbitrary elements. For example, multiplication between an arbitrary element $a := (a_0, \ldots, a_{31}) \in \{0,1\}^{32}$ and α is $a \cdot \alpha = (b_0, \ldots, b_{31})$ where $b_0 = a_{31}$, $b_1 = a_0 \oplus a_{31}$, $b_2 = a_1 \oplus a_{31}$, $b_{22} = a_{21} \oplus a_{31}$ and for all other i, $b_i = a_{i-1}$. Similarly, we express the multiplication of other powers of primitive elements by some linear combinations of the bits a_i's. This representation is useful when we implement power of α and β multipliers in hardware.

2.1 Authenticated Encryption and Its Security Definitions

An authenticated encryption F_K is an integrated scheme that provides both privacy of a plaintext $M \in \{0,1\}^*$ and authenticity or data integrity of the plaintext M as well as the associate data $D \in \{0,1\}^*$. Thus, on the input of a public variable nonce N (it can be considered as an arbitrary number distinct for every encryption), associate data $D \in \{0,1\}^*$ and a plaintext $M \in \{0,1\}^*$, F_K produces a tagged-ciphertext (C, T) where $|C| = |M|$ and $|T| = t$ (tag-size, usually 128). Its inverse or decryption algorithm F_K^{-1} returns $\perp$ for all those (N, D, C, T) for which no such M exists, otherwise it returns M for which (C, T) is the tagged-ciphertext.

Privacy. A distinguishing advantage of A against two oracles $\mathcal{O}_1$ and $\mathcal{O}_2$ is defined as $\Delta_A(\mathcal{O}_1; \mathcal{O}_2) = |\Pr[A^{\mathcal{O}_1} = 1] - \Pr[A^{\mathcal{O}_2} = 1]|$. Given a nonce-respecting adversary A (nonces for every encryption are distinct) we define the **privacy** or **PRF-advantage of A against** F as $\mathbf{Adv}_F^{\mathrm{prf}}(A) := \Delta_A(F_K; \$)$ where $\$$ returns a random string of appropriate size. The PRF-advantage of F is defined as

$$\mathbf{Adv}_F^{\mathrm{prf}}(q, \sigma, t) = \max_A \mathbf{Adv}_F^{\mathrm{prf}}(A),$$

where the maximum is taken over all adversaries running in time t and making q queries with total bit-size of all responses at most σ.

Authenticity. We say that an adversary A **forges** an authenticated encryption F if A outputs a fresh (not obtained before through an F-query) (N, D, C, T) where $F_K^{-1}(N, D, C, T) \neq \perp$. In general, a forger can make q_f forging attempts where N can repeat. We denote the forging advantages as

$$\mathbf{Adv}_F^{\mathrm{auth}}(A) := \Pr[A^F \text{ forges}], \quad \mathbf{Adv}_F^{\mathrm{auth}}(q, q_f, \sigma, t) = \max_A \mathbf{Adv}_F^{\mathrm{auth}}(A),$$

where the maximum is taken over all adversaries running in time t making q queries and q_f forging attempts with total bit-size of all responses at most σ.

2.2 Examples of Universal Hash Functions

A keyed hash function $h(K; \cdot)$ over D is called an ϵ-ΔU (universal) hash function if for all δ, the δ-differential probability

$$\Pr[h(K; x) - h(K; x') = \delta] \leq \epsilon \text{ for all } x \neq x' \in D .$$

In this paper, we conventionally assume the hash keys are uniformly chosen from the key-space. A hash function h is called ϵ-**universal** (or ϵ-U) if the 0-differential probability (or *collision probability*) is at most ϵ for all $x \neq x'$. We call h ϵ-**balanced** if for all a, b, $\Pr[h(K; a) = b] \leq \epsilon$.

Examples. The Multi-linear hash $\mathsf{ML}(k_1; x_1) := k_1 \cdot x_1$ and Pseudo-dot-product (or PDP) hash $\mathsf{PDP}(k; x) := (x_1 \oplus k_1) \cdot (x_2 \oplus k_2)$, with $k = k_1 \| k_2$ and $x = x_1 \| x_2$ are two popular examples of 2^{-32}-ΔU hash where $x_1, x_2, k_1, k_2 \in \mathbb{F}_{2^{32}}$ and $k, x \in \mathbb{F}_{2^{64}}$. One can check that the ΔU property of a hash using independent keys is closed under summation. This is a useful technique to define a hash for larger domain, e.g. we can add the individual PDP values corresponding to the message and key blocks to obtain a ΔU hash $\bigoplus_{i=1}^m (k_{2i-1} \oplus x_{2i-1}) \cdot (k_{2i} \oplus x_{2i})$ for $x = (x_1, \cdots, x_{2m})$ and $k = (k_1, \cdots k_{2m})$.

3 EHC Hash

This section describes a Δ-Universal hash EHC or *Encode-Hash-Combine* hash, which is constructed using an error correcting code ECCode_d of distance d. We first describe a Vandermonde matrix of size $d \times \ell$, denoted $V_\gamma^{(d)}$, γ as a primitive element of $\mathbb{F}_{2^n}$ is defined below. For $n = 32$ and 64 the matrices are denoted by $V_\alpha^{(d)}$ and $V_\beta^{(d)}$ respectively.

$$V_\gamma^{(d)} = \begin{pmatrix} 1 & \cdots & 1 & 1 & 1 \\ \gamma^{\ell-1} & \cdots & \gamma^2 & \gamma & 1 \\ \gamma^{2(\ell-1)} & \cdots & \gamma^4 & \gamma^2 & 1 \\ \vdots & \cdots & \vdots & \vdots & \vdots \\ \gamma^{(\ell-1)(d-1)} & \cdots & \gamma^{2(d-1)} & \gamma^{d-1} & 1 \end{pmatrix}.$$

We have observed that, whenever $1, \gamma, \ldots, \gamma^{\ell-1}$ are distinct, any $s \leq d$ columns of V are linearly independent. We next describe the VMult algorithm for *multiplying* $V_\alpha^{(d)}$ *to a vector* $h = (h_1, \ldots, h_\ell) \in \mathbb{F}_{32}^\ell$ *in an online manner using Horner's rule without requiring* **any additional memory**.

Algorithm VMult$_{\alpha,d}$

Input: $x := (x_1, x_2, \ldots, x_\ell) \in \mathbb{F}_{2^{32}}^\ell$

Output: $y := (y_1, y_2, \ldots, y_d) \in \mathbb{F}_{2^{32}}^d$ such that $y = V_\alpha^{(d)} \cdot x$

---

1 $y_1 = \cdots = y_d = 0^{32}$
2 for $i = 1$ to ℓ
3   for $j = 1$ to d: $y_j \leftarrow \alpha^{j-1} \cdot y_j \oplus x_i$;   * VHorner module *\
4 **return** $(y_1, \ldots y_d)$;

Algorithm 1: VMult$_{\alpha,d}$ multiplies an ℓ-dimensional column vector $x = (x_1, \ldots, x_\ell)$ by a Vandermonde matrix $V_\alpha^{(d)}$ to output a d-dimensional vector $y := V_\alpha^{(d)} \cdot x$. Similarly we define VMult$_{\beta,d}$ for 64-bit field elements. Note that, α and β are the primitive elements of $\mathbb{F}_{2^{32}}$ and $\mathbb{F}_{2^{64}}$, respectively described in Sect. 2. When we implement this algorithm in hardware we only need to implement VHorner.

3.1   ECCode

We next describe the efficient instantiation of an error correcting code ECCode$_d$ with systematic form over $\{0,1\}^{64}$.

$$\mathsf{ECCode}_d(x_1, \ldots, x_\ell) = (x_1, \ldots, x_\ell, x_{\ell+1}, \ldots, x_{\ell+d-1}), \tag{1}$$

where $(x_{\ell+1}, \ldots, x_{\ell+d-1}) = \mathsf{VMult}_{\beta,(d-1)}(x_1, \ldots, x_\ell)$.

Example 1. Let $(x_1, x_2, x_3) \in (\{0,1\}^{64})^3$ be the input to ECCode$_4$. The output is $\mathsf{ECCode}_4(x_1, x_2, x_3) = (x_1, x_2, x_3, x_4, x_5, x_6)$ where, $x_4 = x_1 + x_2 + x_3$, $x_5 = \beta^2 x_1 + \beta x_2 + x_3$ and $x_6 = \beta^4 x_1 + \beta^2 x_2 + x_3$.

In [31], it has been shown that for $d = 4$, the above code has minimum distance 4. We next extend their result for $d = 5$ and show that it has minimum distance 5 for all $\ell \leq 2^{30}$. The result is described in Proposition 1 below.

Proposition 1. *ECCode$_5$ has minimum distance 5 over $\{0,1\}^{64\ell}$ for any fixed $\ell \leq 2^{30}$.*

Proof. ECCode$_5$ is a linear code with systematic form in which the expansion is determined by the matrix $V := V_\beta$. So it suffices to show that V_β is an MDS matrix, i.e., all square submatrices are non-singular. Clearly, any square submatrix of size 1 or 4 is a Vandermonde matrix and hence non-singular. Each of the submatrices of size 2 can be converted to a Vandermonde matrix by elementary column operations (multiplying the columns with non-zero constants).

We now consider the submatrices of size 3. If we consider the submatrices corresponding to the $1^{st}, 2^{nd}$ and the 3rd row or the $2^{nd}, 3^{rd}$ and the 4th row, then these submatrices can be transformed to a Vandermonde matrix by elementary column operations (by non-zero constant multiplications). If we consider the submatrices corresponding to the $1^{st}, 2^{nd}$ and the 4th row or the $1^{st}, 3^{rd}$ and the 4th row then the matrices have the form

$$\begin{pmatrix} 1 & 1 & 1 \\ \beta^i & \beta^j & \beta^k \\ \beta^{3i} & \beta^{3j} & \beta^{3k} \end{pmatrix} \text{ or } \begin{pmatrix} 1 & 1 & 1 \\ \beta^{2i} & \beta^{2j} & \beta^{2k} \\ \beta^{3i} & \beta^{3j} & \beta^{3k} \end{pmatrix}.$$

One can check that the submatrix corresponding to the $1^{st}, 2^{nd}$ and the 4th row is non-singular if and only if $1 + \beta^{(i-j)} + \beta^{(k-j)} \neq 0$, by computing the determinant. We have experimentally verified that the above condition holds for all $i < j < k \leq 2^{30}$. This completes the proof. $\qquad\qquad\square$

3.2 EHC Hash

EHC hash [31] is a 2^{-128}-ΔU hash which requires fewer multiplications than the Toeplitz hash [26] to process a message block. For a fixed length $\ell \leq 2^{30}$, the definition of $\mathsf{EHC}^{(d,\ell)}$ is given in the Algorithm 2 for all $d \leq 5$. PDP hash used in this construction is described in Sect. 2.

Algorithm $\mathsf{EHC}^{(d,\ell)}$
Input: $(k_1, \ldots, k_{\ell+d-1}) \in \{0,1\}^{64(\ell+d-1)}, x \in \{0,1\}^{64\ell}$

---

1   $(x_1, \ldots, x_{\ell+d-1}) \leftarrow \mathsf{ECCode}_d(x)$;
2   for $i = 1$ to $\ell + d - 1$: $g_i = \mathsf{PDP}(k_i, x_i)$;
3   return $\mathsf{VMult}_{\alpha, d}(g_1, g_2, \ldots, g_{\ell+d-1})$;

Algorithm 2: $\mathsf{EHC}^{(d,\ell)}$ [32] hash for a fixed length message.

The variable length hash $\mathsf{EHC}^{(d)}$ defined over all messages of sizes 64ℓ, $1 \leq \ell \leq 2^{30}$, is computed as follows:

$$\mathsf{EHC}^{(d)}((K, (V_1, V_2)); x) = \mathsf{EHC}^{(d,\ell)}(K; x) \oplus b_1 \cdot V_1 \oplus b_2 \cdot V_2,$$

where $x \in s^{64\ell}$, $K \in \{0,1\}^{64(\ell+d-1)}, V_1, V_2 \in \{0,1\}^{32d}$ and $(b_1, b_2) \in \{0,1\}^2$ is the binary representation of $\ell \mod 4$.

Example 1 (continued). We have already seen how $\mathsf{ECCode}_4(x_1, x_2, x_3) = (x_1, x_2, x_3, x_4, x_5, x_6)$ has been defined. Let $k = (k_1, \ldots, k_6) \in (\{0,1\}^{64})^6$ be the corresponding key. For $1 \leq i \leq 6$, denote, $x_i = x_{i1}\|x_{i2}$ and $k_i = k_{i1}\|k_{i2}$ with $x_{i1}, x_{i2}, k_{i1}, k_{i2} \in \{0,1\}^{32}$. For $1 \leq i \leq 6$, denote $g_i = \mathsf{PDP}(x_i, k_i) = (x_{i1} + k_{i1})(x_{i2} + k_{i2})$. Thus, $\mathsf{EHC}^{(4,3)}(k; x_1, x_2, x_3) = (o_1, o_2, o_3, o_4)$, where,

- $o_1 = g_1 + \ldots + g_5 + g_6$, $o_2 = \alpha^5 g_1 + \ldots + \alpha g_5 + g_6$,
- $o_3 = \alpha^{10} g_1 + \ldots + \alpha^2 g_5 + g_6$ $o_4 = \alpha^{15} g_1 + \ldots + \alpha^3 g_5 + g_6$

3.3 Discussions

ECCode_4 and ECCode_5 are MDS codes for $\ell \leq 2^{32}$ and $\ell \leq 2^{30}$ respectively (see [31] and Proposition 1). To incorporate arbitrary length messages, we define ECCode_d^* as follows. It first parses $x \in \mathbb{F}_{2^{64}}^+$ as $(X_1, \ldots, X_m)$ such that all X_i's, possibly excluding the last one, are 2^{30}-block elements. We call these X_i's **chunk**. The last one is possibly an incomplete chunk. Next, apply ECCode_d to all of these chunks individually. More formally,

$$\mathsf{ECCode}_d^*(x) = (\mathsf{ECCode}_d(X_1), \ldots, \mathsf{ECCode}_d(X_{m-1}), \mathsf{ECCode}_d(X_m)). \qquad (2)$$

Table 1. # 32-bit field multiplications needed for EHC-Hash, Toeplitz-Hash and Poly-Hash (with $d = 4$) to process a 64ℓ-bit message, $\ell \leq 2^{30}$. In case of Poly-Hash we need to apply 40-bit field multiplications for a 160-bit hash.

Tag size	d	# Multiplications EHC Hash	# Multiplications Toeplitz-PDP Hash	# Multiplications Poly-Hash
128	4	$\ell + 3$	4ℓ	4.5ℓ
160	5	$\ell + 4$	5ℓ	$4.5\,\ell$ [40]

We next extend the definition of $\mathsf{EHC}^{(d,\ell)}$, denoted as $\mathsf{xEHC}^{(d,\ell)}$, which works the same as $\mathsf{EHC}^{(d,\ell)}$ except it runs ECCode_d^* instead of ECCode_d (line 1 of Algorithm 2), i.e., the first step is executed as $(x_1, \ldots, x_{\ell+d-1}) \leftarrow \mathsf{ECCode}_d^*(x)$.

Comparison with $\mathsf{EHC}^{(d)}$ for Arbitrary Length and Other Hashes. We have chosen EHC hash as it requires much less multiplications than others (see Table 1). We have modified the processing of EHC for variable length messages. EHC uses a fixed length dependent key to deal with variable length messages, and the key needs to be stored, but we generate all the keys in run-time through the stream cipher so we do not need to store it. To achieve authenticity, one needs to apply a pairwise independent hash. By adding a length dependent key to the output of a Universal hash we can construct a Δ-Universal hash. Construction of a pairwise independent hash can be achieved by masking one more independent key to the output of a Δ-Universal hash. However, as we generate keys on the fly, our hash becomes pairwise independent and this further saves more storage. We provide a detailed discussion of hardware implementation in Sect. 6.

4   TriviA Authenticated Encryption

We first propose a stream cipher TriviA-SC[1] which has a similar design as the popular stream cipher Trivium [16]. Trivium is well studied and efficient both in terms of hardware and software. It uses an 80-bit secret key, an 80-bit nonce and a 288-bit internal state and provides 80-bit security. We aim to provide higher security while maintaining the simplicity and without increasing the state size much. In particular, we have made the following modifications:

1. We keep the size of state S to be 384 bits and increase the size of key K and nonce N to 128 bits.
2. We introduce a non-linear effect in the key stream computation.

Algorithm 3 describes all the basic modules used for the stream cipher TriviA-SC (see Fig. 1). A proper integration of these modules need to be defined to obtain a stream cipher or an authenticated encryption. For example, when we want to use it in stream cipher mode, we first run $\mathsf{Load}(K, IV)$ for an initial value IV, then Update for some reasonable rounds (to make the state random) and finally, both KeyExt and Update to obtain the key stream. However, in case

---

[1] Our authenticated encryption TriviA (a shorthand notation for Trivium-Authenticated Encryption) is based on the stream cipher TriviA-SC.

of authenticated encryption we additionally need to process the associate data and need to produce a tag.

Modules of TriviA-SC: The state $S := (S_1, S_2, \ldots, S_{384}) \in \{0, 1\}^{384}$ is represented by $A = (S_1, \ldots, S_{132})$, $B = (S_{133}, \ldots, S_{237})$ and $C = (S_{238}, \ldots, S_{384})$.

Load (K, N) / * **Key and IV Loading** * /
1    $A = K \| 1^4$, $B = 1^{105}$, $C = N \| 1^{19}$;

Update(S) / * **Update a Single Round** * /
2    $t_1 \leftarrow A_{66} \oplus A_{132} \oplus (A_{130} \wedge A_{131}) \oplus B_{96}$;
3    $t_2 \leftarrow B_{69} \oplus B_{105} \oplus (B_{103} \wedge B_{104}) \oplus C_{120}$;
4    $t_3 \leftarrow C_{66} \oplus C_{147} \oplus (C_{145} \wedge C_{146}) \oplus A_{75}$;
5    $(A_1, A_2, A_3, \ldots, A_{132}) \leftarrow (t_3, A_1, A_2, \ldots, A_{131})$;
6    $(B_1, B_2, B_3, \ldots, B_{105}) \leftarrow (t_1, B_1, B_2, \ldots, B_{104})$;
7    $(C_1, C_2, C_3, \ldots, C_{147}) \leftarrow (t_2, C_1, C_2, \ldots, C_{146})$;

Algorithm 3: Modules of TriviA-SC.

Trivia-SC is also parallelizable up to 64 bits, i.e., the stream cipher can produce upto 64 output bits at a single clock cycle (see KeyExt64). Similarly, the 64 round updates of Trivia-SC can also be computed in a single clock cycle (see Update64). KeyExt64 and Update64 are described in Algorithm 4.

KeyExt64 / * **Extract 64 Bit Key Stream** * /
1   Output $t = A_{[3\ldots66]} \oplus A_{[69\ldots132]} \oplus B_{[42\ldots105]} \oplus C_{[3\ldots66]} \oplus C_{[84\ldots147]}$
$\oplus A_{[39\ldots102]} \wedge B_{[3\ldots66]}$;

Update64 / * **Update 64 Rounds** * /
2    $t_1 \leftarrow A_{[3\ldots66]} \oplus A_{[69\ldots132]} \oplus (A_{[67\ldots130]} \wedge A_{[68\ldots131]}) \oplus B_{[33\ldots96]}$;
3    $t_2 \leftarrow B_{[6\ldots69]} \oplus B_{[42\ldots105]} \oplus (B_{[40\ldots103]} \wedge B_{[41\ldots104]}) \oplus C_{[57\ldots120]}$;
4    $t_3 \leftarrow C_{[3\ldots66]} \oplus C_{[84\ldots147]} \oplus (C_{[82\ldots145]} \wedge C_{[83\ldots146]}) \oplus A_{[12\ldots75]}$;
5    $(A_1, A_2, A_3, \ldots, A_{132}) \leftarrow (t_3, A_1, A_2, \ldots, A_{68})$;
6    $(B_1, B_2, B_3, \ldots, B_{105}) \leftarrow (t_1, B_1, B_2, \ldots, B_{41})$;
7    $(C_1, C_2, C_3, \ldots, C_{147}) \leftarrow (t_2, C_1, C_2, \ldots, A_{83})$;

Algorithm 4: 64-bit modules of Trivia-SC. Here $\wedge$ denotes "bitwise-and" of two 64-bit variables.

4.1   Specification of TriviA

Algorithm 5 describes our authenticated encryption algorithm TriviA.

Sarkar [32] has proposed several generic methods of combining ΔU hash and a stream cipher SC_K. Formally, a stream cipher supporting an n-bit initial value IV is a keyed function $SC_K : \{0, 1\}^n \times \mathbb{N} \to \{0, 1\}^+$ such that $SC_K(N; \ell) \in \{0, 1\}^\ell$. Whenever understood, we skip ℓ as an input for the sake of notational simplicity. We mention a scheme close to our design paradigm and state its security guarantee (in a revised and simplified form appropriate to our notation). **Theorem** [32] *Suppose H_τ is an ϵ-ΔU n-bit hash function and SC_K is a stream cipher. Let* AE *be an authenticated encryption scheme defined as*

$$\mathsf{AE}_{K,\tau}(N, D, M) = (C := M \oplus Z, \quad T := H_\tau(M) \oplus R),$$

where $(R, Z) = SC_K(H_\tau(N, A), |M| + n)$. Then, we have

Algorithm TriviA

Input: $(K, (N, D, M)) \in \{0,1\}^{128} \times (\{0,1\}^{128} \times \{0,1\}^* \times \{0,1\}^*)$, $\ell_M, \ell_D \leq 2^{30}$.

1   **Processing N :** Load(K, N),   Update64 18 times;
2   **Processing D :** $(z, SK) \leftarrow$ KeyGen$(\ell_D + 4)$;
3        $T' = \text{EHC}^{(5, \ell_D)}(SK ; \overline{D}) \oplus (z_{\ell_D+2} \| z_{\ell_D+3} \| z_{\ell_D+4}[1..32])$;
4        $S[1..160] = S[1..160] \oplus T'$, Update64 18 times;
5   **Processing M :** $(z, SK) \leftarrow$ KeyGen$(\ell_M + 3)$;
6   if 64 divides $|M|$ then $V = z_{\ell_M} \| z_{\ell_M+2}$;
7   else $V = z_{\ell_M+1} \| z_{\ell_M+3}$;
8        $C = M \oplus z$, $T = \text{EHC}^{(4, \ell_M)}(SK ; \overline{M}) \oplus V$;
9   return (C, T) ;

Module KeyGen(ℓ):
10   for $i = 1$ to ℓ: $z_i = $ KeyExt64, $SK_i = A[1..64]$, Update64 ;
11   return $(z_1 \| \cdots z_\ell, SK_1 \| \cdots SK_\ell)$;

Algorithm 5: TriviA Authenticated Encryption Scheme: Given a binary string x, we define $\overline{x} := x \| 10^d$ where d is the smallest non-negative number such that $|x| + d + 1$ is a multiple of 64 and we write $\ell_x = |\overline{x}|/64$. The nonce N is chosen unique for each encryption. Here $C = M \oplus z$ means that we xor M with the first $|M|$ bits of z.

1. $\mathbf{Adv}_{AE}^{prf}(q, \sigma, t) \leq \mathbf{Adv}_{SC}^{prf}(q, \sigma, t') + q^2\epsilon$ and
2. $\mathbf{Adv}_{AE}^{auth}(q, q_f, \sigma, t) \leq \mathbf{Adv}_{SC}^{prf}(q+1, \sigma, t') + (1+q^2)\epsilon$.

Where $t' \approx t + t_H$ and t_H is the total time required for hashing all queries.
HOW OUR CONSTRUCTION DIFFERS FROM $\text{AE}_{K,\tau}$. The above construction requires two keys K and τ. In our construction, we generate the key τ from the stream cipher and hence we require only one key K. As the stream cipher generates run time output bit stream, we can apply those universal hash functions requiring variable length keys, which are more efficient than those hash functions based on a single small key. For example, Poly-Hash [14,15,33] is not as hardware efficient as EHC and provides a weaker security bound.

4.2   Discussions

Authenticated Encryption for Larger Message/Associate Data. We can further extend TriviA for computing the intermediate data and the tag for arbitrary length message and associated data. The extended algorithm of TriviA for handling larger messages is functionally almost the same as TriviA, except that it uses $\text{xEHC}^{(d,\ell)}$ to compute the intermediate data (line 3 of Algorithm 5) and the tag, and the KeyGen algorithm will generate keystream according to the length of the codeword computed by ECCode_d^*. The algorithm also selects the part of the key z that appears in the same clock cycles with the message blocks so that we do not need to hold the key. This part of z is xored with the message to produce the ciphertext as before.

Nonce Misuse Scenario. We generalize the EHC hash to incorporate 160 bits hash for processing associate data. This would allow some room for repetition of

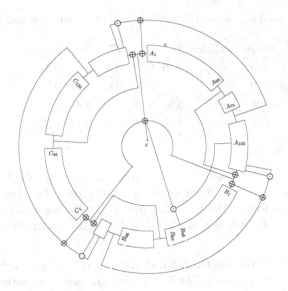

Fig. 1. TriviA-SC Stream cipher

the nonce (but no repetition of nonce, associated data pair) without degrading the security (see the privacy and authenticity bound for TriviA in Sect. 5).

5   Security Analysis

5.1   Security Against Known Attacks

Cube-Attack and Polynomial Density: The Cube Attack [17] is the best known algebraic attack on reduced round versions of Trivium [16]. Note that the output bits from the stream cipher can be described by a polynomial over the key and the nonce bits. The cube attack tries to analyze the polynomial $P(k_1, \cdots, k_n; iv_1, \cdots, iv_p)$ corresponding to the first output bit, where $k_1, \cdots, k_n$ are the secret key bits and $iv_1, \cdots, iv_p$ are the public nonce bits. Given a subset $S = \{iv_{v_1}, \cdots, iv_{v_k}\}$ of the set of all public nonce bits, P can be written as $P = iv_{v_1} \cdots iv_{v_k} P_S + P_R$, where no monomial of P_R is divisible by $iv_{v_1} \cdots iv_{v_k}$. P_S is called the *superpoly* yielded by S and $iv_{v_1} \cdots iv_{v_k}$ is called the *maxterm* if P_S is linear. The TriviA-SC with the recommended 1152-rounds initialization has no maxterm of size less than or equal to 29. Moreover, for the 896 and 832-round initialization version we have not found any maxterm of size 29 or less. But for the 768-round initialization version we have found some linear superpoly with cube size 20. This justifies our recommendation of the 1152-round initialization for TriviA-SC. We have also applied the Moebious Transform technique described by Fouque et al. [20] to estimate the polynomial density of the output boolean function. We restrict polynomial to 30 IV variables and the density of the monomials of degree less than 30 in the restricted polynomial has been calculated. The result is given in Table 2. For a random Boolean

Table 2. Monomial densities of TriviA-SC with 1152, 960, 896 and 832 rounds.

Monomial size	25	26	27	28	29
1152	0.49	0.49	0.5	0.52	0.4
960	0.5	0.5	0.5	0.51	0.36
896	0.5	0.49	0.5	0.47	0.5
832	0.43	0.36	0.29	0.14	0.03

function, we expect 50% density. The statistical tests on TriviA-SC have been performed by observing the output bit stream using the NIST Test Suite [6] and no weaknesses were found. We have also performed the same tests on a version of TriviA-SC where the key is a random 384-bit string and no weaknesses were found.

Resistance Against Guess-then-Find Attack [27]: The attack by Maximov et al. [27] works in two phases. The first phase guesses some internal state and makes linear approximations of some of the nonlinear state updation. This would help to produce a set of linear equations (and also several second degree equations) on the unguessed state bits using the output stream. In the second phase we simply solve all state bits provided we have sufficient number of equations. This idea is applicable for both reduced round versions of Trivium and Trivia-SC.

One possible approach of the first phase for the Trivium is an exhaustive guess on one-third of the state (96 bits with the indices that are a multiple of 3 stored in a set $\tau_0^{(t)}$ out of 288 bits). As the output bits are linear in the state bits, it is sufficient to guess 72 state bits and the remaining 32 state bits can be recovered easily. This actually happens, as indices of the bits in the output polynomial are multiple of 3 and the lifetime of a state bit in the internal state is at least 66 rounds before it is mixed with other bits. Using the guesses, we can obtain $n_1 = 100$ linear equations and $n_2 = 61$, 2-degree equations on the remaining state bits by observing the output stream. So the complexity for the second phase, denoted c, would be costly as we do not have sufficient linear equations.

There is an optimized version of the first phase which further makes linear approximation of the nonlinear terms in the state update functions to construct several other linear equations on the state bits in $\tau_0^{(t)}$. The complexity of the first phase for this version of the attack is $2^{83.5}$ and it forms $n_1 = 192$ linear equations. Thus, the complexity in the second phase would be small.

Unlike Trivium, TriviA-SC has a nonlinear function in the output stream so to obtain $n_1 = r$ linear equations one has to approximate r nonlinear equations ("AND" gate). In fact, as long as $r \leq 96$, the indices involved in these linear approximations are completely disjoint. Thus, the probability that all of these linear approximations hold is $(3/4)^r$. Now if we follow a similar approach mentioned above, we first make a guess of one-third of the internal state (128 bits out of 384). However, one can simply guess 106 state bits and the remaining 22 bits can be recovered from the output stream. As the output is nonlinear, we have to make a linear approximation for 22 round outputs. So the complexity of the first phase would be about $2^{128-22} \times (4/3)^{22}$. Now if we want to obtain $n_1 = 32$ linear equations for the second phase (which is in fact much less than sufficient linear equations to recover all unguessed state bits), the total complexity for the first phase becomes $2^{106} \times (4/3)^{22} \times (4/3)^{32} > 2^{128}$. So we can not perform the above guess-then-find attack strategy in our stream cipher.

5.2   Privacy of TriviA

An adversary is called nonce-respecting if it makes encryption queries with all distinct nonce. A relaxed nonce-respecting adversary makes queries such that the pairs (N, D) are distinct over all q encryption queries. In the following two theorems we assume that Trivia-SC generates a pseudorandom bit stream.

Theorem 1. *Let A be a relaxed nonce-respecting adversary which makes at most q encryption queries. Moreover we assume that A can make at most 2^{32} queries with a same nonce. Then, $\mathbf{Adv}^{\mathrm{priv}}_{\mathsf{TriviA}}(A) \leq \frac{q}{2^{129}}$.*

Proof. Let A makes q queries $(N_1, D_1, M_1), \ldots, (N_q, D_q, M_q)$ such that (N_i, D_i)'s are distinct and let Z_i and (C_i, T_i) be the respective key stream (including the state bit extraction) and final responses. Moreover let T'_i denote the intermediate tag obtained from the associated data which are inserted in the state after processing associated data. Let $\mathcal{N} = \{N : \exists i \ N = N_i\}$ denote the set of all distinct nonces. We denote $m = |\mathcal{N}|$. For each $N \in \mathcal{N}$, we write $\mathcal{I}_N = \{j : N_j = N\}$ and $|\mathcal{I}_N| = q_N$. Note that, $q_N \leq 2^{32}$ for all nonces N and $\sum_{N \in \mathcal{N}} q_N = q$. By our assumption on the stream cipher output, the key stream Z_i's would be independently distributed whenever we have distinct nonces. Thus, we define an event coll: there exists $i \neq j$ such that $N_i = N_j$ and $T'_i = T'_j$. If the coll event does not hold, then by using the ideal assumption of the stream cipher, all key streams Z_i's (even with same nonce) are independent and uniformly distributed. As (C_i, T_i)'s are injective functions of the key-stream Z_i, the distribution of (C_i, T_i)'s are independent and uniform. So the privacy advantage is bounded by the probability of the event coll. In Proposition 2 below, we show that the collision probability is bounded above by $\frac{q}{2^{129}}$ and hence the result follows.   □

Proposition 2. $Pr[\mathsf{coll}] \leq \frac{q}{2^{129}}$.

Proof. Fix a nonce $N \in \mathcal{N}$. The probability that there exists $i \neq j$ with $N_i = N_j = N$ such that $T'_i = T'_j$ is bounded by $\binom{q_N}{2} \times 2^{-160}$. This actually holds as this collision implies that $\mathsf{EHC}^5(D_i) = \mathsf{EHC}^5(D_j)$ and EHC^5 is a 2^{-160}-ΔU hash (the underlying code ECCode_5 is MDS as shown in Proposition 1). Summing up the probability for all choices of nonce N, we have

$$Pr[\mathsf{coll}] = \sum_{N \in \mathcal{N}} q_N^2 / 2^{161} \leq 2^{32} \sum_{N \in \mathcal{N}} q_N / 2^{160} = q/2^{129}.$$

5.3   Authenticity of TriviA

Now we show the authenticity of TriviA.

Theorem 2. *Let A be a relaxed nonce-respecting adversary which makes at most q queries such that nonce can repeat up to 2^{32} times. In addition, A is making at most q_f forging attempt. If the stream cipher Trivia-SC is perfectly secure then*

$$\mathbf{Adv}_{TriviA}^{\text{auth}}(A) \leq \frac{q}{2^{129}} + \frac{q_f}{2^{124}}.$$

Proof. Let the q queries be (D_i, N_i, M_i) and the corresponding responses be (C_i, T_i) with intermediate tags T_i', $1 \leq i \leq q$. We also denote the key stream for the ith query be Z_i. By applying the privacy bound, which is $q/2^{129}$, we may assume that all the q key streams $Z_1, \ldots, Z_q$ are uniformly and randomly distributed. We consider two cases depending on a forging attempt (N^*, D^*, C^*, T^*).

Case A. The adversary makes a forging attempt (N^*, D^*, C^*, T^*) with a fresh (N^*, D^*). In this case, let $\mathcal{I} = \{i : N_i = N^*\}$. By the restriction, $|\mathcal{I}| \leq 2^{32}$. Note that for all $j \notin \mathcal{I}$, the Z_j's are independent from Z^* the key-stream for the forging attempt. For all $i \in \mathcal{I}$, the Z_i's also would be independent from Z^* provide that the intermediate tag T_i''s do not collide with the intermediate tag T^* for the forging attempt. This can happen with probability at most $2^{32}/2^{160} = 2^{-128}$. Whenever Z^* behaves like a random string, the forging probability will be 2^{-128} (as the tag size is 128). So the total forging probability, in this case, will be at most $2^{-128} + 2^{-128} = 2^{-127}$.

Case B. Suppose the adversary makes a forging attempt with $(N^*, D^*) = (N_i, D_i)$ for some i. Note that one of the key-streams Z_i and Z^* would be a prefix of the other (depending on the length of the ciphertext). Note that for all other Z_j's, $j \neq i$ would be independent of Z^* and so we can ignore the responses of the other queries. So the forging probability is the same as

$$p := \Pr[(N_i, D_i, C^*, T^*) \text{ is valid } | (C_i, T_i) \text{ is response of } (N_i, D_i, M_i)]. \quad (3)$$

Claim $p \leq 2^{-124}$.

We postpone the proof of the claim. Assuming this claim, any forging attempt is successful with probability at most 2^{-124} (as the Case-A has lower success probability). Since A makes at most q_f attempts and adding the privacy advantage the forging probability would be bounded by $\frac{q}{2^{129}} + \frac{q_f}{2^{124}}$. This completes the proof.

Proof of the Claim. Let M^* be the message corresponding to C^*. We prove it by considering different cases based on $\ell := \ell_{M_i}$ and $\ell^* := \ell_{M^*}$. For simplicity, we assume that both M_i and M^* are complete block messages. The proof for incomplete message blocks is similar. We also write Z into a pair (SK, z) where SK denotes the state key and z denotes the output stream. Note that, the z-values can be leaked through the ciphertext and some of the z-values may be also used to compute the tag. We mainly need to handle different cases depending on how the z-values are leaked.

Case 1: $\ell^* = \ell$ In this case, the conditional forging event can simply be written as $\mathsf{EHC}^{4,\ell}(SK; M_i) \oplus \mathsf{EHC}^{4,\ell}(SK^*; M^*) = \delta := T_i \oplus T^*$. As, $\ell^* = \ell$, thus $SK = SK^*$. By using the known fact that EHC is a 2^{-128}-ΔU hash [31] we have $p \leq 2^{-128}$.

For the case 2 and 3, we denote, $\mathsf{EHC}^{4,\ell}(z; M_i) = (H_1, H_2)$ and similarly $\mathsf{EHC}^{4,\ell^*}(z^*; M^*) = (H_1^*, H_2^*)$ where H_i and H_i^*s are 64-bit strings. We similarly parse T and T^* as (T_1, T_2) and (T_1^*, T_2^*).

Case 2: $\ell^* = \ell+1$ In this case, all of the variable keys z are distinct and are not leaked through the ciphertext C_i. So the forging probability is equivalently written as

$$p = \Pr[H_1^* \oplus z_{\ell+1} = T_1^*, H_2^* \oplus z_{\ell+3} = T_2^* \mid H_1 \oplus z_\ell = T_1, H_2 \oplus z_{\ell+2} = T_2].$$

Thus, by using the entropy of $z_\ell, z_{\ell+1}, z_{\ell+2}$ and $z_{\ell+3}$, we get the bound.

Case 3: $\ell^* > \ell+1$ Except the case $\ell^* = \ell+2$, this case is same as before as all variable keys z are distinct and are not leaked through the ciphertext C_i. When $\ell^* = \ell+2$ we have three variable keys $z_\ell, z_{\ell+2}$ and $z_{\ell+4}$ which are masked to define the tags. So the forging probability is equivalently written as

$$p = \Pr[H_1^* \oplus z_{\ell+2} = T_1^*, H_2^* \oplus z_{\ell+4} = T_2^* \mid H_1 \oplus z_\ell = T_1, H_2 \oplus z_{\ell+2} = T_2].$$

The independence of the z values implies,

$$p = \Pr[H_2^* \oplus z_{\ell+4} = T_2^*] \times \Pr[H_1^* \oplus H_2 = T_1^* \oplus T_2 := \delta]$$

$$= 2^{-64} \times \Pr[H_1^* \oplus H_2 = T_1^* \oplus T_2 := \delta].$$

Now the effect of the state keys $SK_{\ell+4}, SK_{\ell+5}$ is not present in H_1^* but they influence H_2. By using 2^{-31}-balancedness of the pseudo-dot-product hash, we conclude that $\Pr[H_1^* \oplus H_2 := \delta] \leq 2^{62}$ and so $p \leq 2^{-126}$.

Case 4: $\ell^* < \ell-2$ In this case, the variable keys are different for both computations. Since one set of variable keys are leaked through the ciphertext and the other has full entropy we use the fact that EHC is 2^{-124}-balanced. Using this one can show that $p \leq 2^{-124}$.

Case 5: $\ell^* = \ell-1$ Again, all four variable keys are distinct and one of them is leaked. So we can apply the argument (using balancedness of one 64-bit equation) to show that $p \leq 2^{-126}$.

Case 6: $\ell^* = \ell-2$ Again, by simplifying the forging event with the notation described in case 3 we have

$$p = \Pr[H_1^* = z_{\ell-2} \oplus T_1^*, H_2^* \oplus z_\ell = T_2^* \mid H_1 \oplus z_\ell = T_1, H_2 \oplus z_{\ell+2} = T_2].$$

Here note that, unlike in case 2, the value of $z_{\ell-2}$ is leaked in the ciphertext. The above probability is the same as $\Pr[H_1^* = c_1, H_2^* \oplus H_1 = c_2]$ for some 64-bit constants c_1 and c_2. Based on the balanced property of H_1^* (based on the state key $SK_1, \ldots, SK_{\ell+1}$) and the balanced property of H_1 (based on the state key $SK_{\ell+2}, SK_{\ell+3}$) we can conclude that $p \leq 2^{-124}$.

Thus, we prove that $p \leq 2^{-124}$ which concludes the proof of the claim.   □

6 Hardware Implementation of TriviA-Ck

6.1 Cycles per Byte (cpb) Analysis

The TriviA design targets high speed implementation and requires 47 clock cycles to authenticate and encrypt one message block of 64 bits. 18 cycles are required for the initialization phase where the state register is updated in every cycle along with Z, the associated data AD is loaded and processed in 1 cycle, and during the checksum phase instead of loading the block, the checksum computed in an earlier stage is used as the input. The overall computation requires 4 cycles and an additional cycle is required to update the tag and the state register during AD processing. For message (msg) encryption, again, the same number of cycles are required but AD is replaced by msg. The rest of the process is the same with one minor difference, now the checksum is calculated only 3 times instead of 4 before the tag update. Analytically, the cycle count is represented below

$$cycle\ count = (init\_count * 2) + \frac{adlen}{8} + \frac{msglen}{8} + 4 + 1 + 3 + 1, \quad (4)$$

where $init\_count$ is 18 in TriviA, $adlen$ and $msglen$ are in bytes instead of bits. The corresponding cpb can be calculated using the following formula

$$cpb = \frac{cycle\ count}{msglen}. \quad (5)$$

Pipelining: So far, our analysis is done based on a design without any pipeline. Pipelining is a well-known technique to improve the throughput for a digital design. A three-stage pipelined design is employed for TriviA, which is explained later in this section. Pipelining affects latency adversely. In our case, the cycle count to authenticate and encrypt one message block of 64 bits increases to 49. Two additional clock cycles are required to flush the pipeline registers. The rest of the data processing flow remains the same. Similarly the cycle count for a pipelined design can be represented in the following manner.

$$cycle\ count = (init\_count * 2) + \frac{adlen}{8} + \frac{msglen}{8} + 9 + (pipe\_stages - 1), \quad (6)$$

where $pipe\_stages$ is equal to 3 in our case. As the number of $pipe\_stages$ increases, the corresponding cycle count will increase accordingly. The cpb can be calculated using Eq. (5).

6.2 Hardware Architectures

We have implemented two different architectures of TriviA: a base implementation without any pipelining, and a three-stage pipelined implementation. The implementation is performed in a modular manner, which offers excellent scalability. Due to the similarity in the operations for processing AD, and msg, the same hardware modules are used to process both kinds of data. A single bit switch is used to distinguish between the type of input data. The TriviA architecture consists of the following modules:

1. *State Registers*: The state registers are used to store the intermediate states after each iteration. The state registers are used for 384-bit State_Update, 256-bit Z register, 64-bit *block*, 160-bit *tag*, and 256-bit *checksum*.
2. State_Update: The State_Update module is nothing but a combination of Updated64, KeyExt64 which are used to update the current state of the stream cipher and generate key-stream. This module is used in each iteration during initialization, encryption, and finalization. It takes 128-bit key, 128-bit nonce (which is further divided into two 64-bit parts, namely pub and param) and a 384-bit state register as inputs and updates the stream cipher state.
3. Field Multiplication: The Field multiplication module takes two 32 bit inputs, calculates the pseudo dot product on the input, and produces a 32-bit output.
4. VHorner32: This module is used for Horner's multiplication for the 32-bit Vandermonde Matrix Multiplication (i.e. in the computation of VMult$_{\alpha,5}$). It takes two inputs, a 32-bit value from the field multiplication, and 160-bit tag value. It processes the input to generate a new tag of 160-bits. During the processing of AD, it processes all the 160-bits of the tag to give the output, whereas, for the message processing, only 128 bits are used.
5. VHorner64: This module is used for Horner's multiplication for the 64-bit Vandermonde Matrix Multiplication while computing the checksum for the error correcting code. It takes an input block of 64-bits, and the current checksum value of 256 bits as input. It generates a 256-bit checksum value as output. This modules executes its operations on 256 bits of the checksum when working on AD, otherwise it uses only 192 bits.

Base Implementation: We start with a base implementation of TriviA that exploits the parallelism inherent in the algorithm and processes 64 bits in each cycle, as shown in Fig. 2. The critical path is shown using a dotted line. Prior to initialization, the state register is loaded with Key, param, pub and 1 in the remaining bits on reset. Once the state registers are initialized, the initialization process starts where *state_register* is updated in each cycle with State_Update operation. After the initialization process, 8 bytes of AD are fetched to the *block* register, which feeds the Field Multiplication module after performing an *exclusive OR* between the 64-bit block and the 64-bit *state_register*. In parallel, an exclusive OR is also performed between the 64-bit block and the 64-bit Z to produce the *ciphertext*. The Field Multiplication module is followed by the VHorner32 module which generates the new tag. The Field Multiplication module

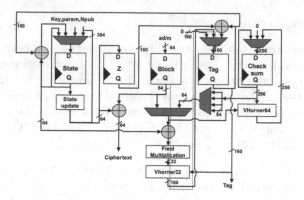

Fig. 2. TriviA basic hardware implementation

has 64 many 2×1 32-bit MUXes in series. The VHorner32 block diagram can be seen in Fig. 3.

The checksum is updated in the VHorner64 module which is also executed in parallel. When the AD is finished, the checksum is calculated hence we require a 4×1 64-bit MUX which fetches 64 bits of the checksum at a time to update the tag. Since the checksum is calculated at the end, we can share resources using a 2×1 64-bit MUX. The first input of the MUX comes from the $block$ register, while the second input comes in chunks of 64 bits from the checksum. All these operations are parallel, hence one round can be executed in a single cycle. At the end, after processing the checksum, the tag and the $state\_register$ are updated in single cycle. We require a 4×1 MUX at the input of $state\_register$ and a 3×1 MUX at the input of the tag register. The $state\_register$ takes input from four sources, initialization values on reset, State_Update after each cycle, the result of an exclusive OR between the $state\_register$ and the tag, and a feedback path. Similarly, tag takes values from three sources, initialization on reset, output of VHorner32, and Z exclusive ORed with tag.

The control of the complete design is implemented using a finite state machine (FSM), not shown in the schematic for the sake of simplicity. The FSM consists of 6 states, starting with an idle state followed by initialization. After initialization, FSM enters the processing state and stays there until all the data has been processed. Then it jumps to checksum processing, followed by tag update, and pipeline flush. A 3-bit register is required to store the state of the FSM.

The combinational logic can be easily reduced for lowering the area further by first, sharing computing resources and second, performing computation on smaller bit-widths. Consequently, the throughput will decrease leading to an area-delay trade-off.

Pipelined Implementation: After analyzing the basic implementation, we identified the critical path, and split that to achieve higher operating frequency. All the operations are unit operations except for the tag generation. Tag

generation requires two operations in series, which are using multiple MUXes in series. This long chain of MUXes reduces the clock speed of the whole design, hence other modules which can operate at higher frequencies are also limited by this. We break the critical path and insert a pipeline register after the Field Multiplication module. To balance the design, we also insert a pipeline register after the Z register. Using the pipelined architecture, as shown in Fig. 4, we could achieve higher throughput for TriviA.

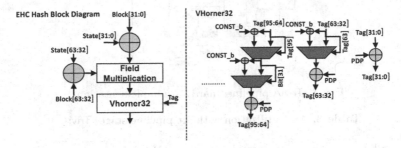

Fig. 3. EHC block diagram

Enc/Dec Implementation: Due to the similar structure of encryption and decryption algorithms, a combined hardware can also be designed with a small increase in area, while getting the same throughput. The encryption or decryption mode is selected using a *mode_select* signal. When the *mode_select* is set to *0*, the hardware operates in encryption mode, whereas when *mode_select* is set to *1*, the hardware operates in decryption mode.

6.3 Performance Results and Comparison

TriviA Results. The architectures of TriviA are described in Verilog HDL and synthesis is done with the Synopsys Design Compiler J-2014.09 using Faraday standard cell libraries in topographical mode. We used UMC 65 nm logic SP/RVT Low-K process technology node for synthesis. The implementation is performed till gate-level synthesis hence, the reported results are pre-layout. The area results are reported in terms of equivalent NAND gates. The area for the base implementation of TriviA was 23.6 KGE at a frequency of 1150 MHz, with 7.2 KGE required for sequential logic and 16.4 KGE required for combinational logic. The corresponding throughput turns out to be 73.9 Gbps, and the area-efficiency (throughput/area) is 3.13 Mbps/GE. The area utilization is shown in Table 3 where each module and its respective area is shown. The registers for *Tag*, *block*, and *checksum* are instantiated in the top-module, hence their distribution is not listed in the table.

The synthesis for pipelined implementation was performed under similar operating conditions, tools, and libraries. The design was successfully synthesized at 1425 MHz for an area of 24.4 KGE, with 7.7 KGE in sequential and

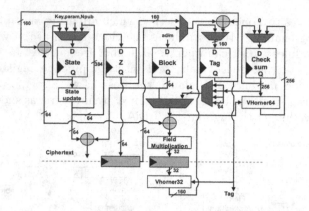

Fig. 4. TriviA pipelined hardware implementation

Table 3. Area utilization without pipeline stage, TriviA

Module	Base implementation		Pipelined implementation	
	Area (GE)	%	Area (GE)	%
Field multiplication	6275	26.0	6890	28.0
Update state	7214	30.0	7208	29.5
FSM	1260	5.3	1296	5.3
VHorner32	675	2.8	387	1.5
VHorner64	573	2.4	576	2.4

16.7 KGE in combinational logic. The design successfully achieved a throughput of 91.2 Gbps with an area-efficiency of 3.73 Mbps/GE. The module-wise break-down of area is shown in Table 3. The registers for *Tag*, *block*, *checksum*, and pipeline registers are instantiated in the top-module, hence their distribution is also not listed in the table.

For performance measures, different message lengths were considered to calculate cycles per byte, taking associated data length as a small value of 8 bytes. When the message length is 8 bytes, the overhead of initialization is very large in both the cases, base implementation and pipelined implementation, giving a high cycles per byte count. As we increase the message length, the overhead becomes smaller resulting in 0.12 cycle per byte for a very long message. This is shown in the Table 4. Hence, as we increase the message length the cycles per byte of both designs converge. Note that, if we assume that the associated data is of the same length as the message, then the cycle per byte doubles. For example, if both the *message* and *AD* are of 8192 bytes then 0.25 cycles per byte are required.

Comparison: The results for algorithms marked with a (*) in Table 5 have been scaled assuming a 2× improvement of achievable maximum clock frequency for

Table 4. TriviA performance (in clocks per byte or cpb)

Algorithm	Message length (Bytes)										
	8	16	32	64	128	256	512	1024	2048	8192	16384
TriviA-pipelined	6.12	3.12	1.62	0.87	0.50	0.31	0.21	0.17	0.14	0.13	0.12

Table 5. Benchmarking TriviA in ASIC

AE schemes		ASIC implementation			Cycles/Byte (cpb)
		Area (KGE)	Throughput (Gbps)	Efficiency (Mbps/GE)	
TriviA base		23.6	73.9	3.13	0.12
TriviA pipelined		24.4	91.2	3.73	0.12
Scream, iScream [22]		17.29	5.19	0.30	-
NORX* [8]		62	28.2	0.45	-
Ascon* [21]		7.95	7.77	0.98	0.75
AEGIS [13,36]	AO1	20.55	1.35	0.07	6.67
	AO2	60.88	37.44	0.61	0.33
	TO1	88.91	53.55	0.60	0.20
	TO2	172.72	121.07	0.70	0.07

every two generations of CMOS technology node, thus roughly following Moore's law [29]. Admittedly, this is a very rough comparison, without considering the effects of physical synthesis, diversity of cells in different technology libraries and synthesis constraints. The unavailability of the RTL code and the synthesis details in the presented papers makes the task even harder. Nevertheless, the performance gap is at least an order of magnitude in the area-efficiency, hence unlikely to close.

To the best of our knowledge, not all CAESAR candidates have hardware implementations in ASIC so far, and there is no other hardware implementation of TriviA as well, so, the comparison done with the known results listed in Table 5 shows that, the TriviA has a better throughput, cycles per byte and area-efficiency. Particularly, for the area-efficiency, the TriviA is at least 3.8 times better compared to the closest entry Ascon. We will offer the hardware implementation to the CAESAR candidates and also request corresponding RTL for a fair evaluation in similar technology settings.

Besides CAESAR candidates, it is also interesting to benchmark TriviA against state-of-the-art authenticated encryption engines that are commercially available. We take one particular example from [7], which provides high-speed authenticated encryption hardware based on AES-CCM mode. Based on the data provided at [7], for 130 nm CMOS technology, AES-CCM achieves > 800 Mbps at < $19K$ gates. Even with an optimistic technology scaling, this is still

Table 6. Benchmarking TriviA in FPGA

Xilinx FPGA Platform	AES-CCM [7]			TriviA-Base			TriviA-Pipelined
	# Slices	Gbps	Area-Efficiency (Mbps/Slice)	# Slices	Gbps	Area-Efficiency (Mbps/Slice)	Area-Efficiency (Mbps/Slice)
Spartan-6 -3	272	> 0.57	2.09	815	7.6	9.3	11.29
Virtex-5 -3	343	> 0.78	2.27	637	11.7	18.3	20.3
Virtex-6 -3	295	> 0.87	2.95	725	16	22	25
Kintex-7 -3	296	> 1	3.38	714	16.89	23.65	24.31
Virtex-7 -3	296	> 1	3.38	714	16.89	23.65	24.31

one order of magnitude inferior compared to the performance achieved with the TriviA.

More detailed results are provided at [7] for different FPGA platforms. There, the performance results reported are for AES-CCM cores which require 128-bit key, and 48 cycles to generate output cipher text. In order to benchmark, we performed pre-layout logic synthesis done for TriviA under typical conditions using Xilinx ISE 14.7. The results are collectively reported in Table 6. It can be noted that the area occupied for TriviA is generally larger compared to [7], since the computation in TriviA is done in parallel, processing 64 bits in 1 cycle. In comparison, [7] requires 48 cycles. When comparing the area-efficiency figures, it is clear that TriviA is much superior by showing at least $5.4 \times$ improvement for TriviA pipelined implementation compared to AES-CCM implementation of [7].

7   Conclusion

This paper introduces a hardware efficient authenticated encryption scheme TriviA. The structure of TriviA is simple and achieves high provable security. Our proposal uses a stream cipher and a pairwise independent hash function. We have constructed a stream cipher TriviA-SC, which is a variant of a well known stream cipher Trivium [16]. Trivium is well studied and very efficient in both hardware and software. We have also used a hardware efficient Δ-Universal hash function EHC, which requires minimum number of field multiplications to process a message. We have integrated these two primitives in an efficient way, such that the resultant construction is highly efficient in both hardware and software as well as it provides high security of 128-bits for privacy and 124-bits for authenticity. This work provides the details of the hardware implementation of TriviA and hardware comparison between TriviA and some of the CAESAR candidates. We have observed that, TriviA is very hardware efficient in terms of throughput, cycles per byte and area-efficiency. More specifically the area-efficiency of TriviA is at least 3.8 times better than the closest CAESAR candidate Ascon.

Acknowledgement. Avik Chakraborti and Mridul Nandi are supported by the Centre of Excellence in Cryptology and R.C. Bose Centre for Cryptology and Security, Indian Statistical Institute, Kolkata. We would like to thank Bart Preneel for his detailed comments and suggestions on our paper. We would also like to thank the anonymous reviewers for their useful comments on our paper.

References

1. ETSI/SAGE Specification: Specification of the 3GPP confidentiality and integrity ALgorithms UEA2 and UIA2. Document 5: Design and Evaluation Report, Version 1.1 (2006). Citations in this document: §1
2. ETSI/SAGE Specification: Specification of the 3GPP confidentiality and integrity ALgorithms UEA2 and UIA2. Document 2: SNOW 3G Specification (2006). Citations in this document: §1
3. CAESAR: Competition for authenticated encryption: security, applicability, and robustness. http://competitions.cr.yp.to/caesar.html (2014). Citations in this document: §1
4. eSTREAM: The ECRYPT stream cipher project. http://www.ecrypt.eu.org/stream. Citations in this document: §1
5. International Organization for Standardization, ISO/IEC 29192-3:2012: Information technology - security techniques - lightweight cryptography - Part 3: Stream ciphers. http://www.iso.org/iso/iso_catalogue/catalogue_tc/catalogue_detail.htm?csnumber=56426 (2102). Citations in this document: §1
6. National Institute of Standards and Technology: A statistical test suite for random and pseudorandom number generators for cryptographic applications. http://csrc.nist.gov/groups/ST/toolkit/rng/documentation_software.html (2010). Citations in this document: §5.1
7. Helion Technology, AES-CCM core. http://www.heliontech.com/aes_ccm.htm. Citations in this document: §6.3, §6.3, §6.3, §6.3, §6.3, §6.3, §6
8. Aumasson, J.-P., Jovanovic, P., Neves, S.: NORX: parallel and scalable AEAD. In: Kutyłowski, M., Vaidya, J. (eds.) ICAIS 2014, Part II. LNCS, vol. 8713, pp. 19–36. Springer, Heidelberg (2014). https://eprint.iacr.org/2015/034.pdf. Citations in this document: §5
9. Babbage, S., Dodd, M.: The eSTREAM finalists, pp. 191–209 (2008). Citations in this document: §1
10. Bellare, M., Namprempre, C.: Authenticated encryption: relations among notions and analysis of the generic composition paradigm. In: Okamoto, T. (ed.) ASIACRYPT 2000. LNCS, vol. 1976, pp. 531–545. Springer, Heidelberg (2000)
11. Bernstein, D.J.: The Poly1305-AES message-authentication code. In: Gilbert, H., Handschuh, H. (eds.) FSE 2005. LNCS, vol. 3557, pp. 32–49. Springer, Heidelberg (2005). Citations in this document: §1
12. Bernstein, D.J.: Cycle counts for authenticated encryption. In: Workshop Record of SASC 2007: The State of the Art of Stream Ciphers (2007). Citations in this document: §1
13. Bhattacharjee, D., Chattopadhyay, A.: Efficient hardware accelerator for AEGIS-128 authenticated encryption. In: Lin, D., Yung, M., Zhou, J. (eds.) Inscrypt 2014. LNCS, vol. 8957, pp. 385–402. Springer, Switzerland (2014)
14. Bierbrauer, J., Johansson, T., Kabatianskii, G.A., Smeets, B.J.M.: On families of hash functions via geometric codes and concatenation. In: Stinson, D.R. (ed.) CRYPTO 1993. LNCS, vol. 773, pp. 331–342. Springer, Heidelberg (1994)
15. den Boer, B.: A simple and key-economical unconditional authentication scheme. J. Comput. Secur. 2, 65–72 (1993)

16. De Cannière, Christophe, Preneel, Bart: TRIVIUM. In: Robshaw, Matthew, Billet, Olivier (eds.) New Stream Cipher Designs. LNCS, vol. 4986, pp. 244–266. Springer, Heidelberg (2008). Citations in this document: §1, §1, §4, §5.1, §7
17. Dinur, I., Shamir, A.: Cube attacks on tweakable black box polynomials. In: Joux, A. (ed.) EUROCRYPT 2009. LNCS, vol. 5479, pp. 278–299. Springer, Heidelberg (2009)
18. Fan, X., Gong, G.: Specification of the stream cipher WG-16 based confidentiality and integrity algorithms (2013). http://cacr.uwaterloo.ca/techreports/2013/cacr2013-06.pdf
19. Ferguson, N., Whiting, D., Schneier, B., Kelsey, J., Lucks, S., Kohno, T.: Helix: fast encryption and authentication in a single cryptographic primitive. In: Johansson, T. (ed.) FSE 2003. LNCS, vol. 2887, pp. 330–346. Springer, Heidelberg (2003)
20. Fouque, P.-A., Vannet, T.: Improving key recovery to 784 and 799 rounds of trivium using optimized cube attacks. In: Moriai, S. (ed.) FSE 2013. LNCS, vol. 8424, pp. 502–517. Springer, Heidelberg (2014)
21. GroSS, H., Wenger, E., Dobraunig, C., Ehrenhofer, C.: Suit up! Made-to-Measure hardware implementations of ASCON. https://eprint.iacr.org/2015/034.pdf (2014). Citations in this document: §5
22. Grosso, V., Leurent, G., Standaert, F., Varici, K., Durvaux, F., Gaspar, L., Kerckhof, S.: SCREAM and iSCREAM side-channel resistant authenticated encryption with masking. URL: http://competitions.cr.yp.to/round1/screamv1.pdf (2014). Citations in this document: §5
23. Hell, M., Johansson, T., Meier, W.: Grain: a stream cipher for constrained environments. Int. J. Wirel. Mob. Comput. Spec. Issue Towar. Ubiquit. Wirel. Commun. Integr. 3G/WLAN Netw. 2(4), 86–93 (2007). Citations in this document: §1
24. Hell, M., Johansson, T., Maximov, A., Meier, W.: A stream cipher proposal: grain-128. In: International Symposium on Information Theory-ISIT, IEEE (2006). Citations in this document: §1
25. Jutla, C.: Encryption modes with almost free message integrity. J. Cryptol. 21, 547–578 (2008)
26. Mansour, Y., Nissan, N., Tiwari, P.: The computational complexity of universal hashing. In: Twenty Second Annual ACM Symposium on Theory of Computing, pp. 235–243 (1990). Citations in this document: §3.2
27. Maximov, A., Biryukov, A.: Two trivial attacks on TRIVIUM. In: Adams, C., Miri, A., Wiener, M. (eds.) SAC 2007. LNCS, vol. 4876, pp. 36–55. Springer, Heidelberg (2007). Citations in this document: §5.1, §5.1
28. Moon, T.K.: Error Control Coding: Mathematical Methods and Algorithms. Wiley, Hoboken (2005)
29. Moore, G.E.: Cramming more components onto integrated circuits. http://download.intel.com/museum/Moores_Law/Articles-Press_Releases/Gordon_Moore_1965_Article.pdf (1965). Accessed 07 Jun 2015. Citations in this document: §6.3
30. Muller, F.: Differential attacks against the Helix stream cipher. In: Roy, B., Meier, W. (eds.) FSE 2004. LNCS, vol. 3017, pp. 94–108. Springer, Heidelberg (2004)
31. Nandi, M.: On the minimum number of multiplications necessary for universal hash functions. In: Cid, C., Rechberger, C. (eds.) FSE 2014. LNCS, vol. 8540, pp. 489–507. Springer, Heidelberg (2015). Citations in this document: §1, §1, §3.1, §3.2, §2, §3.3, §5.3
32. Sarkar, P.: Modes of operations for encryption and authentication using stream ciphers supporting an initialisation vector. Crypt. Commun. 6(3), 189–231 (2014). Citations in this document: §1, §1, §4.1, §4.1

33. Taylor, R.: Near optimal unconditionally secure authentication. In: De Santis, A. (ed.) EUROCRYPT 1994. LNCS, vol. 950, pp. 244–253. Springer, Heidelberg (1995)
34. Whiting, D., Schneier, B., Lucks, S., Muller, F.: Phelix: fast encryption and authentication in a single cryptographic primitive. http://www.ecrypt.eu.org/stream/ (2004). Citations in this document: §1
35. Wu, H., Preneel, B.: Differential-linear attacks against the stream cipher phelix. In: Biryukov, A. (ed.) FSE 2007. LNCS, vol. 4593, pp. 87–100. Springer, Heidelberg (2007)
36. Wu, H., Preneel, B.: AEGIS: a fast authenticated encryption algorithm. In: Lange, T., Lauter, K., Lisoněk, P. (eds.) SAC 2013. LNCS, vol. 8282, pp. 185–202. Springer, Heidelberg (2014)

True Random Number Generators and Entropy Estimations

A Physical Approach for Stochastic Modeling of TERO-Based TRNG

Patrick Haddad[1,2]([✉]), Viktor Fischer[1], Florent Bernard[1], and Jean Nicolai[2]

[1] Laboratoire Hubert Curien, Université Jean Monnet,
Member of Université de Lyon, 42000 Saint-etienne, France
{patrick.haddad,fischer,florent.bernard}@univ-st-etienne.fr
[2] STMicroelectronics, Advanced System Technology, 13790 Rousset, France
jean.nicolai@st.com

Abstract. Security in random number generation for cryptography is closely related to the entropy rate at the generator output. This rate has to be evaluated using an appropriate stochastic model. The stochastic model proposed in this paper is dedicated to the transition effect ring oscillator (TERO) based true random number generator (TRNG) proposed by Varchola and Drutarovsky in 2010. The advantage and originality of this model is that it is derived from a physical model based on a detailed study and on the precise electrical description of the noisy physical phenomena that contribute to the generation of random numbers. We compare the proposed electrical description with data generated in a 28 nm CMOS ASIC implementation. Our experimental results are in very good agreement with those obtained with both the physical model of TERO's noisy behavior and with the stochastic model of the TERO TRNG, which we also confirmed using the AIS 31 test suites.

Keywords: Hardware random number generators · Transition effect ring oscillator · Stochastic models · Entropy · Statistical tests

1 Introduction

Random number generation is a critical issue in most cryptographic applications. Random numbers are used as confidential keys, but also as initialization vectors, challenges, nonces, and random masks in side channel attack countermeasures. A security flaw in random number generation has a direct impact on the security of the whole cryptographic system. Contrary to generators used in Monte Carlo simulations and telecommunications, those designed for cryptography must generate unpredictable random numbers – having perfect statistical properties is necessary but not sufficient.

There are two main categories of random number generators: deterministic random number generators (DRNG) and true random number generators (TRNG), which can be physical (P-TRNG) or non-physical (NP-TRNG). While deterministic generators are based on algorithmic processes and are thus not

© International Association for Cryptologic Research 2015
T. Güneysu and H. Handschuh (Eds.): CHES 2015, LNCS 9293, pp. 357–372, 2015.
DOI: 10.1007/978-3-662-48324-4_18

truly random, TRNGs exploit an unpredictable process, such as analog phenomena in electronic devices, to produce a random binary sequence or a sequence of random numbers. The unpredictability of DRNGs is guaranteed computationally and that of TRNGs is guaranteed physically. A good knowledge of the underlying physical process in TRNG that ensures its randomness and hence its unpredictability is therefore necessary.

The statistical quality of TRNGs and DRNGs is usually evaluated using statistical test suites such as the one first proposed by George Marsaglia [6] and extended by the NIST [8]. The goal of these suites is to detect statistical weaknesses such as non-uniformity or the appearance of patterns in a generated random sequence of only limited size. In no case can these tests guarantee the unpredictability of the random binary sequence.

As summarized by Fischer in 2012 [3], the best way to ensure unpredictability is to carefully estimate the entropy rate at the generator output. The estimation of entropy must be based on a carefully constructed model of the random number generation process. In a P-TRNG, this model consists of a mathematical description of a link between the variations in the exploited unpredictable analog phenomena and the variations in the random binary sequence.

The entropy estimation based on an underlying stochastic model is mandatory in the security certification process, specifically at high levels of security [5]. Stochastic models are reasonably easy to construct, but it is sometimes difficult or even impossible to check all the underlying physical assumptions. A physical model could serve as a basis for validation of these assumptions, but it is much more difficult to construct and a detailed knowledge of contributing physical phenomena is necessary.

Some stochastic models are generic and can be adapted to several generators [4], but many TRNGs require their own specific stochastic models. Unfortunately, only a few existing generators have corresponding stochastic models, e.g. [1,2,10]. One of the interesting generators recently proposed by Varchola and Drutarovsky [11] uses a so-called transient effect ring oscillator (TERO) as a source of randomness. Although the generator produces good statistical results, a corresponding stochastic model has not yet been proposed and the generic model proposed in [4] is clearly not suitable in this case.

Our Contributions: (1) We propose and validate a novel physical TERO model including electric noises that serve as sources of randomness. (2) From the physical model, we derive a TERO stochastic model. (3) From the TERO model, we propose and validate a stochastic model of a complete TERO-based TRNG and illustrate the use of this model to estimate the entropy rate in conjunction with the output bit rate.

Organization of the Paper: In Sect. 2, we describe the structure of the TERO and its use in a P-TRNG. The physical (electrical) and derived stochastic model of the TERO are detailed in Sect. 3. The stochastic model of the complete TERO-based TRNG is presented in Sect. 4. We conclude the paper by a discussion concerning the relationship between the entropy rate and the output bit rate that can be set up using the proposed stochastic model.

2   The TERO Based RNG – Background

The TERO is an electronic circuit that oscillates temporarily. It is composed of an even number of inverters and a couple of gates that restart temporary oscillations (e.g. two NAND or two XOR gates). A typical TERO configuration is presented in the left panel of Fig. 1: it is composed of two NAND gates and two inverter branches. The TERO can be seen as an RS latch with two inputs featuring the same voltage V_{ctr} and two different outputs V_{out1} and V_{out2}.

Following the rising edge of the V_{ctr} input, the outputs V_{out1} and V_{out2} start to oscillate. The oscillations have a constant mean frequency, but their duty cycle varies over time: it changes monotonously and after a certain number of oscillations, it reaches the rate of either 0 % or 100 %. At this point, outputs V_{out1} and V_{out2} stop oscillating and remain stable at two opposite logic values. The right panel of Fig. 1 presents traces of the V_{ctr} input and V_{out1} output signal captured from oscilloscope. As can be observed, the output signal V_{out1} starts to oscillate following the rising edge of the V_{ctr} control signal.

The three zooms presented in this panel show the changing duty cycle: immediately after the rising edge of the V_{ctr} signal, it is close to 50 %, then decreases until it reaches 0 %. Consequently, signal V_{out1} stabilizes at logic level 0. Of course, signal V_{out2} behaves in the opposite way as far as the duty cycle is concerned and stabilizes at logic level 1.

The number of oscillations before the outputs stabilize is not constant but varies because it is impacted by the electronic noises that disturb the normal behavior of transistors in the TERO structure.

The P-TRNG based on the TERO structure (TERO TRNG) is depicted in Fig. 2. The TERO circuitry is followed by an n-bit counter that counts the rising edges of the temporary oscillations. The counter output shows realizations of the random variable, i.e. the number of oscillations in successive control periods. The random binary sequence is usually obtained by successively concatenating the least significant bits of the counter, i.e. only one T flip-flop is needed in the counter.

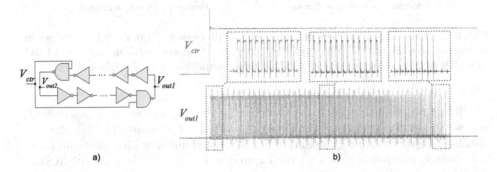

Fig. 1. Circuit diagram of a typical TERO structure and its input/output waveforms obtained experimentally

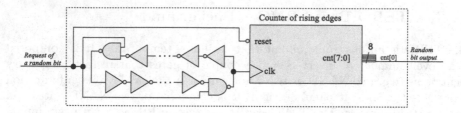

Fig. 2. True random number generator based on the TERO structure

To evaluate the physical parameters of the TERO TRNG, we implemented the generator in a CMOS BULK ASIC using the ST Microelectronics 28 nm technology. In our configurations, one of the two outputs of the TERO structure was connected to an 8-bit asynchronous counter. Figure 3 shows the distribution of the 8 million counter values obtained from the ASIC device for two different TERO topologies: in the first one, there was a relative difference between the two TERO branches of 24 % (left panel) and in the second one a relative difference 31 % (right panel). The differences between the TERO branches were obtained using a digital configurable delay chain.

It can be seen that in both cases the number of oscillations varied around a mean value according to a statistical law, which apparently is not a normal law. This is especially visible in the right panel of the figure. One of our objectives was to determine this law and its origin.

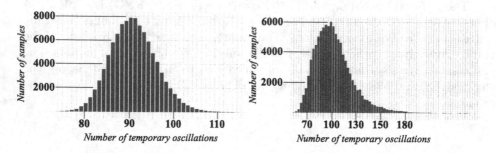

Fig. 3. Distribution of numbers of temporary oscillations for two TERO topologies in technology ST 28 nm: with the relative difference in delay between the two TERO branches of 24 % (left panel) and with the relative difference 31 % (right panel)

Before proceeding with the construction of the physical and stochastic models, we tested the statistical quality of generated bit streams. The bit streams obtained by successive concatenation of the least significant bits constituted the raw binary streams, which were then tested using the AIS31 protocol [KS11]. The data not only successfully passed all the tests of the Procedure B, but also those of the Procedure A aimed at testing the post-processed signals. This means that the generator is suitable for certification according to AIS31 for PTG1 and PTG2 levels even without post-processing.

As explained above, successful evaluation of the output of the generator using statistical tests is a necessary but not sufficient condition to ensure the unpredictability of the generated numbers. The only way to guarantee such a property is to show the link between variations in the distribution of the raw random binary sequence and the physical phenomena that are considered as random, unpredictable, and non-manipulable. Statistical modeling of underlying analog and digital processes should make it possible to quantify the uncertainty included in the generated random sequence by estimating the entropy rate in this sequence.

3   Physical and Stochastic Model of TERO

In this section, we discuss the main processes that transform noisy electric currents into random binary sequences and explain how these phenomena are interlinked.

3.1   Modeling the Number of Temporary Oscillations

Our study is based on an existing physical model of RS latches published by Reyneri *et al.* in [7]. We complete their noise free model by taking electric noises into account. For the sake of readability, the original model of the noise free inverter is presented in Appendix A.

Modeling a Noisy Inverter. Noisy behavior at transistor level is modeled by noisy currents that are added to the ideal noise-free current flowing between the source and the drain. As can be seen in Fig. 4(a) for a CMOS inverter, these noisy currents can be represented by two sources of current n_N and n_P, which are connected in parallel to output transistors and which are active only during inverter (gate) switching.

The inverter's noisy output V_{out} can be seen as a sum of two signals – $f(t)$ and $n(t)$:

- $f(t)$ represents an ideal component of the output signal, which contributes to the charge and discharge of the C_L capacitor by noise-free switching currents between the source and drain of output transistors MN and MP.
- $n(t)$ corresponds to the noisy component of the output signal, i.e. it contributes to the charge and discharge of the C_L by the noisy signals n_N and n_P.

Let t_0 be the last moment at which V_{out} is equal to V_{CC}. Since the noisy currents exist only during gate switching, $n(t_0) = 0$. It is therefore clear that:

$$n(t) = n(t) - n(t_0) = \frac{1}{C_L} \int_{t_0}^{t} [n_N(u) + n_P(u)] du$$

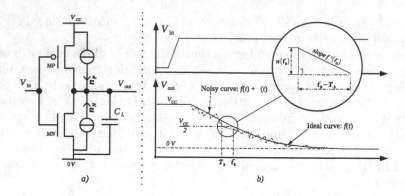

Fig. 4. Model of a noisy inverter and its response to a step function

In the following, we assume that n_N and n_P are Gaussian random variables. This assumption is reasonable, because the noise currents can be considered as sums of random variables associated with independent quantum processes in the transistors. Consequently, $n(t)$ can be represented as a stationary Gaussian random process[1].

Let us now analyze modifications in length of the pulse transmitted over one inverter as explained in Appendix A, but now in the presence of noisy currents. Let us consider that at $t = t_\downarrow$, signal V_{in} goes down from V_{CC} to 0, and we denote t_a the time, at which the signal V_{out} at the output of the inverter reaches $\frac{V_{CC}}{2}$. Similarly, at $t = t_\uparrow$, signal V_{in} goes up from 0 to V_{CC} and t_b corresponds to the time at which V_{out} is equal to $\frac{V_{CC}}{2}$. Finally, at $t = t_{end}$ signal V_{in} goes back to 0, ending one cycle. We denote $t_c = t_{end} - t_\downarrow$ the time that V_{in} needs to complete one cycle. For the sake of simplicity, we will denote p_{in} the length of one pulse at signal V_{in} and p_{out} the corresponding pulse at the output of an open chain of inverters.

Proofs of the following lemma and propositions are given in Appendix B.

Lemma 1. *Let T_a (resp. T_b) be the random variable representing the time at which the signal V_{out} reaches $\frac{V_{CC}}{2}$ after a falling edge (resp. rising edge) on V_{in}. Let $\overline{t_a}$ (resp. $\overline{t_b}$) denote the ideal time at which V_{out} should reach $\frac{V_{CC}}{2}$ in noise-free conditions. Let P_{out} be the random variable representing the length of a pulse at signal V_{out} corresponding to a pulse of length p_{in} at signal V_{in}. Then, with previous definitions of signals $f(t)$ and $n(t)$, we have:*

1. $T_a \sim \mathcal{N}\left(\overline{t_a}, \frac{\sigma^2}{f'(\overline{t_a})}\right)$ and $T_b \sim \mathcal{N}\left(\overline{t_b}, \frac{\sigma^2}{f'(\overline{t_b})}\right)$

---

[1] This may be not true at the device startup, but this assumption is reasonable after some time t_0. For each $t \geq t_0$, we assume that $n(t)$ follows a normal distribution with mean 0 and variance σ^2, denoted $n(t) \sim \mathcal{N}(0, \sigma^2)$ in the following.

2. If T_a and T_b are independent,

$$P_{out} \sim \mathcal{N}(\mu_{out}, \sigma_{out}^2) \text{ with } \begin{cases} \mu_{out} = \frac{t_c}{2} + \left(p_{in} - \frac{t_c}{2}\right)(1 + H_d) \\ \sigma_{out}^2 = \sigma^2 \left(\frac{1}{f'(t_a)} + \frac{1}{f'(t_b)}\right) \end{cases}$$

where H_d is the constant introduced in Appendix A.

Shortening of the Pulse While it Traverses a Delay Chain. Let us now consider an open chain of N inverters discussed in the previous section, where N is a non-zero positive integer. Let V_{in} be the input signal of the first inverter and V_{out_N} the output signal of the Nth inverter. P_{out_N} is the length of a pulse at V_{out_N} corresponding to a pulse p_{in} at signal V_{in}. The random behavior of P_{out_N} is given in Proposition 1.

Proposition 1. *If the noise source in the inverter is independent from the noise sources in other inverters, then*

$$P_{out_N} \sim \mathcal{N}(\mu_{out_N}, \sigma_{out_N}^2) \text{ with } \begin{cases} \mu_{out_N} = \frac{t_c}{2} + \left(p_{in} - \frac{t_c}{2}\right)(1 + H_d)^N \\ \sigma_{out_N}^2 = \sigma_{out}^2 \left(\frac{(1+H_d)^{2N}-1}{(1+H_d)^2-1}\right) \end{cases}$$

Modeling Temporary Oscillations in the TERO Structure. Let us now consider two chains of inverters, as discussed in the previous section. Let $\{K_j\}_{j=1...2M}$ represent the set of inverters in the first chain and $\{L_j\}_{j=1...2M}$ those in the second chain. We denote NK and NL the two NAND gates with outputs V_K and V_L. They are connected to chains $\{K_j\}_j$ and $\{L_j\}_j$ (as depicted in Fig. 5(a)) and complete a TERO. If V_{ctr} is equal to V_{CC}, NL (resp. NK) can be seen as the L_{2M+1}^{th} (resp. K_{2M+1}^{th}) inverter of the chain $L := \{L_j\}_{j=1...2M+1}$ (resp. $K := \{K_j\}_{j=1...2M+1}$) generating the mean delay τ_1 (resp. τ_2). Theoretically, τ_1 and τ_2 are identical, since both branches have the same topology. In practice, because of imperfections in the manufacturing process, their values differ slightly. Without any loss of generality, we can assume that $\tau_1 > \tau_2$.

At $t = 0$, let signal V_{ctr} go up from 0 to V_{CC}. As shown in Fig. 5(b), this rising edge forces the outputs of NAND gates NK and NL to fall from V_{CC} to 0. The falling edge created at V_K (resp. at V_L) propagates over K (resp. L). This creates a pulse of mean length τ_1 (resp. τ_2) at V_L (resp. V_K).

The two rising edges created on V_L and V_K start to propagate over elements L and K. After a mean delay τ_2 (resp. τ_1), they cause signal V_L (resp. V_K) to fall from V_{CC} to 0. The generated signals behave in the same way as the signals traversing set $\{I_j\}$ in the previous section with a cycle of length $t_c = \tau_1 + \tau_2$.

Proposition 2. *Let PL_0 (resp. PK_0) be the length of the pulse observed at signal V_L (resp. V_K) and PL_S (resp. PK_S) be the pulse length, once it has crossed S times over both sets K and L.*

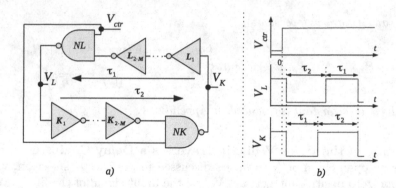

Fig. 5. Initial behavior of the TERO structure

If $PL_0 \sim \mathcal{N}(\tau_2, \sigma^2_{out_{2M+1}})$ and $PK_0 \sim \mathcal{N}(\tau_1, \sigma^2_{out_{2M+1}})$ and if the noise sources in all the inverters are independent, then

$$PL_S \sim \mathcal{N}(\mu_{L_S}, \sigma^2_{L_S}) \text{ with } \begin{cases} \mu_{L_S} = \frac{\tau_1 + \tau_2}{2} + \frac{\tau_2 - \tau_1}{2}R^S \\ \sigma^2_{L_S} = \sigma^2_{out}\dfrac{R^{2S+1} - 1}{(1 + H_d)^2 - 1} \end{cases}$$

$$PK_S \sim \mathcal{N}(\mu_{K_S}, \sigma^2_{K_S}) \text{ with } \begin{cases} \mu_{K_S} = \frac{\tau_1 + \tau_2}{2} + \frac{\tau_1 - \tau_2}{2}R^S \\ \sigma^2_{K_S} = \sigma^2_{out}\dfrac{R^{2S+1} - 1}{(1 + H_d)^2 - 1} \end{cases}$$

where $R = (1 + H_d)^{4M+2}$.

According to Proposition 2, $\mu_{L_S} + \mu_{K_S} = \tau_1 + \tau_2$. So the mean values of the duty cycles of signals V_K and V_L are always complementary. Since by definition, PL_S represents the length of the pulses observed at signal V_L and because of our assumption that $\tau_1 > \tau_2$, oscillations disappear when $PL_S = 0$. Consequently, the number of oscillations N_{OSC} corresponds to the last value of S for which PL_S is positive:

$$N_{OSC} = \max\{S|PL_S > 0\}. \tag{1}$$

Let q be a positive integer different from zero. From Eq. (1) it follows that if N_{OSC} is greater than q, then PL_q is positive and different from zero, too. Using this fact, we can derive the probability that N_{OSC} is greater than q from Proposition 2:

$$Pr\{N_{OSC} > q\} = Pr\{PL_q > 0\}. \tag{2}$$

Then

$$Pr\{N_{OSC} > q\} = \frac{1}{\sqrt{2\pi}\sigma_{L_S}} \int_{[\frac{\tau_1 - \tau_2}{2}]R^q - \frac{\tau_1 + \tau_2}{2}}^{+\infty} e^{-\frac{u^2}{2\sigma^2_{L_S}}} \, du, \tag{3}$$

or equivalently

$$Pr\{N_{OSC} > q\} = \frac{1}{2}\left[1 - erf\left(\frac{[\tau_1 - \tau_2]R^q - \tau_1 - \tau_2}{2\sqrt{2}\sigma_{out}\sqrt{\frac{R^{2q+1} - 1}{(1 + H_d)^2 - 1}}}\right)\right]. \tag{4}$$

Finally, from Eq. (4) we get the probability that N_{OSC} is smaller or equal to q:

$$Pr\{N_{OSC} \leq q\} = 1 - Pr\{N_{OSC} > q\} = \frac{1}{2}\left[1 - erf\left(K\frac{1 - R^{q-q_0}}{\sqrt{R^{2q+1} - 1}}\right)\right], \quad (5)$$

where K and q_0 are equal to:

$$K = \frac{\sqrt{R^2 - 1}}{2\sqrt{2}\sigma_r}, \quad (6)$$

$$q_0 = -\frac{\log(\Delta_r)}{\log(R)}, \quad (7)$$

and where

$$\sigma_r = \sigma_{out}\sqrt{\frac{R^2 - 1}{(1 + H_d)^2 - 1}}/(\tau_1 + \tau_2) = \sigma_{out4M+2}/(\tau_1 + \tau_2),$$

$$\Delta_r = (\tau_1 - \tau_2)/(\tau_1 + \tau_2).$$

Using Eq. (5), the probability p_q that N_{OSC} is equal to q can be estimated by

$$p_q = Pr\{N_{OSC} \leq q\} - Pr\{N_{OSC} \leq q-1\},$$

$$p_q = \frac{1}{2}\left[erf\left(K\frac{1 - R^{q-q_0-1}}{\sqrt{R^{2q} - 1}}\right) - erf\left(K\frac{1 - R^{q-q_0}}{\sqrt{R^{2q+2} - 1}}\right)\right]. \quad (8)$$

Equation (8) is very important, because it can be used to model the distribution of the number of temporary oscillations. Its main advantage is that the parameters of the model (R, σ_r and Δ_r) are easy to quantify (see Sect. 3.2). Parameter R is the ratio of the geometric series, σ_r is the relative jitter and Δ_r is the relative difference between TERO branches. The proposed model, as we will see later, can serve as a basis for the TERO TRNG stochastic model.

3.2   Experimental Validation of the TERO Stochastic Model

We validated the TERO model using the two TERO topologies presented in Sect. 2. We evaluated the appropriateness of the model using 65536 realizations $\{A_k\}_{k=1...65536}$ of the TERO temporary oscillations. The model parameters R, Δ_r, and σ_r were computed from acquired data by determining K and q_0 from Eqs. (6) and (7) as follows.

First, an approximation of the distribution of temporary oscillations N_{OSC} is obtained experimentally, the distribution $Pr\{N_{OSC} \leq q\}$ can be thus computed. Then, according to Eq. (5), the function

$$Y(q) = erf^{-1}\left(1 - 2Pr\{N_{OSC} \leq q\}\right) = K\frac{1 - R^{q-q_0}}{\sqrt{R^{2q+2} - 1}} \quad (9)$$

is obtained from the distribution $Pr\{N_{OSC} \leq q\}$. It is then possible to find the value of q_0 such that $Pr\{N_{OSC} \leq q\} = 1/2$. Finally, the value of R is determined. Knowing that $R \sim 1$ and $R > 1$, we are searching in a loop for $R > 1$ in a neighborhood of 1 the value R_{loop}, such that the ratio $Y(q)/Z(q)$ is constant (i.e. independent from q). This constant represents the value of K. As mentioned above, $Y(q)$ is obtained experimentally and $Z(q)$ is derived from Eq. (9) as follows:

$$Z(q) = \frac{1 - R_{loop}^{q-q_0}}{\sqrt{R_{loop}^{2q+2} - 1}} \tag{10}$$

The results are presented in Fig. 6. The distribution depicted in the left panel was obtained using parameter values: $R = 1.0153$; $\Delta_r = 0.2394$; $\sigma_r = 0.00174$ and the distribution shown in the right panel was modeled with parameters: $R = 1.013$; $\Delta_r = 0.310$; $\sigma_r = 0.0059$.

Next, we compared the model from Eq. (5) with the distribution of the experimental data $\{A_k\}$ obtained with the two hardware configurations using the χ^2 goodness-of-fit test. For the distribution presented in the left panel of Fig. 6, the counter values varied between 74 and 110, which corresponded to 38 degrees of freedom and the χ^2 test statistic was $T = 40.35$. At 38 degrees of freedom and a significance level $\alpha = 0.05$, for a good fit, the χ^2 test statistic T should be below 53.384, i.e. $Pr\{T < 53.384\} = 0.95$. Similarly, for the distribution presented in the right panel featuring 76 degrees of freedom, the χ^2 test statistic was equal to $T = 33.97$. At 76 degrees of freedom, for the same significance level, the threshold of the χ^2 test statistic is 97.351, i.e. $Pr\{T < 97.351\} = 0.95$.

In these two cases, but also in all the other experiments the χ^2 test statistic value T was below the threshold corresponding to the level of significance $\alpha = 0.05$. We can thus conclude that the model presented in Sect. 3.1 is suitable for the characterization of the probability distribution of the number of TERO oscillations N_{OSC}.

Just out of curiosity, we compared the two distributions with the distribution of the normal law. The χ^2 test statistics were $T = 149.3$ and $T > 2 \cdot 10^6$,

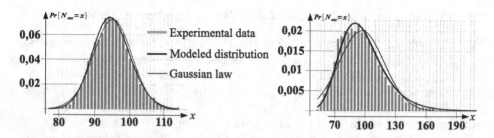

Fig. 6. Experimental validation of the model for two TERO topologies in technology ST 28 nm: with the relative difference in delay between the two TERO branches of 24 % (left panel) and with the relative difference 31 % (right panel)

respectively. In both cases, and especially in the second, the test statistic was clearly outside the required interval.

In the next section, we will use our model to estimate entropy at the TERO TRNG output.

4 Stochastic Model of the Complete TERO-Based TRNG

Let H_{osc} be the entropy contained in the sequence of number of oscillations N_{osc}. Since realizations of N_{osc} are assumed to be independent (the generator is restarted periodically and it is thus memory-less), this entropy is related to p_q from Eq. (8) as follows:

$$H_{N_{osc}} = -\sum_{q \in \mathbb{N}} p_q \log_2(p_q)$$

We computed the value of $H_{N_{osc}}$ for the two distributions depicted in Fig. 6. The distribution shown in the left panel had the entropy rate per sample (per byte) $H_{N_{osc}} = 4.47$ and that in the right panel had the entropy rate $H_{N_{osc}} = 6.32$.

Let p_b be the probability that the least significant bit of N_{osc} is equal to 1. This probability is related to p_q from Eq. (8) as follows:

$$p_b = \sum_{k=0}^{k=+\infty} p_{2k+1}. \tag{11}$$

For each realization, we select the least significant bit of N_{osc} to form a vector $(b_{n-1} \ldots b_0)_2$. This vector can be interpreted as a number $B_n \in \{0, \ldots, 2^n - 1\}$. As the TRNG is restarted after each acquisition of N_{osc}, bits $(b_k)_{k=0 \ldots n-1}$ are independent. Thus, for each n-bit integer $X_n = (x_{n-1} \ldots x_1 x_0)_2$

$$p_{X_n} = Pr(B_n = X_n) = \prod_{j=0}^{n-1} [1 - p_b]^{1-x_j} [p_b]^{x_j}.$$

If the random process associated with B_n is stationary, the entropy per bit at the generator output is equal to [9]:

$$H = \lim_{n \to +\infty} \frac{H_n}{n},$$

where

$$H_n = -\sum_{X_n \in \{0, \ldots, 2^n - 1\}} p_{X_n} \log_2(p_{X_n}).$$

Since jitter realizations are assumed to be independent, realizations of N_{osc} and b_k are assumed to be independent, too. Consequently, we consider that the generator does not have a memory and the generated random bits don't contain any short- or long-term dependencies.

Because realizations of b_k are considered to be independent, the entropy per bit at the generator output derived from our model can be simplified as follows:

$$H = -p_b \log_2(p_b) - (1 - p_b) \log_2(1 - p_b).$$

We computed the entropy rate per bit for the two TERO topologies discussed in Sect. 3.2. In both cases, the entropy rate was higher than 0.9999, meaning that the entropy per bit exceeded the value required by AIS 31. This was in perfect agreement with our experiments – results of the tests AIS 31 presented in Sect. 2.

5 Discussion

As we have seen above, the distribution of counter values is very well character-ized by the model parameters R, σ_r, and Δ_r and the entropy of the generated sequence depends on this distribution. Using the model, we can now observe the impact of the TERO design on the distribution of random numbers and hence on entropy.

First, entropy is determined by relative jitter, i.e. by parameter σ_r. Since designers cannot directly alter the sources of thermal noise, they can only change the relative jitter by reducing the delay of the two TERO branches. This corresponds to increasing the frequency of oscillations.

Another important model parameter that determines entropy rate is the relative difference between the two TERO branches, i.e. parameter Δ_r. With smaller relative differences, TERO accumulates more jitter because it oscillates longer. As we have seen in our example, the entropy rate per generated output byte was over 4.4 and 6.3, respectively. This means that if designers use only one bit per generated byte (the counter output), they would be discarding a high percentage of usable random data. Of course, some post-processing can be used to profit from as much entropy as possible, but it would require additional silicon area, especially if a sophisticated algorithm is used (which would be probably the case in order to maintain a maximum entropy rate). Another much more practical solution would be to unbalance the two TERO branches to the extent that the entropy rate per generated byte would be slightly higher than 1 and then to use only one bit per generated number. Because of the difference in delays in the two branches, the TERO would oscillate a shorter time and the output bit rate would consequently be higher. Since the entropy rate per generated number would be higher than one, each generated bit (the least significant bit of the counter) would have enough entropy and post-processing would not be necessary.

6 Conclusion

In this paper, we analyzed the processes that transform the noisy currents in the TERO circuitry into a random bit stream of the TERO based TRNG. First, we performed a detailed analysis of electric processes inside the TERO structure and, based on this analysis, we proposed the physical model of the TERO. We checked the model in two specific TERO topologies implemented in an ST 28 nm ASIC technology.

Next, based on this model, we proposed a stochastic model of a complete TERO based TRNG. We showed that the proposed stochastic model can be successfully used to estimate the entropy rate. The entropy estimations are in perfect agreement with the results of the AIS 31 test suites.

We also showed that the proposed TRNG stochastic model can be used not only to estimate the entropy rate at the output of the generator, but also for entropy management, by setting sufficient entropy rate while maintaining the maximum output bit rate.

Acknowledgments. This work has received fundings from the European ENIAC Joint Undertaking (JU) in the framework of the project TOISE (Trusted Computing for European Embedded Systems) and from the European Union's Horizon 2020 research and innovation programme in the framework of the project HECTOR (Hardware Enabled Crypto and Randomness) under grant agreement No 644052. The authors wish to thank Mr. Nicolas Bruneau, Mr. Michel Agoyan and Mr. Yannick Teglia for their help and availability in numerous discussions.

Appendix

A. Modeling an Ideal Noise-Free Inverter

We assume that TERO is built using ideal noise-free CMOS inverters as presented in Fig. 7(a). We note V_{in} and V_{out} the input and output signal of such an inverter, respectively. The noise-free model is based on the physical model of an inverter with a variable slope published by Reyneri et al. in [7]. As presented in Fig. 7(b), the model proposed in [7] divides the inverter into three entities:

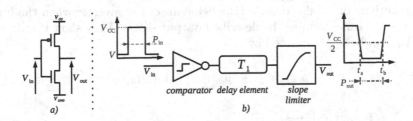

Fig. 7. Ideal noise-free CMOS inverter

- A comparator, which outputs V_{CC} if the input voltage V_{in} is smaller than $V_{CC}/2$ otherwise it outputs 0.

– A delay line, which delays comparator output signal by a static delay T_1.
– A slope limiter, which follows the delay line and generates the output signal V_{out}.

As depicted in Fig. 8, the model responds to a rising edge of the input signal by generating a signal that decreases linearly with the slope $-K_0$ until the output voltage reaches the value $(1-K_0) \cdot V_{CC}$² after which the output decreases exponentially until it reaches the final value V_{out}.

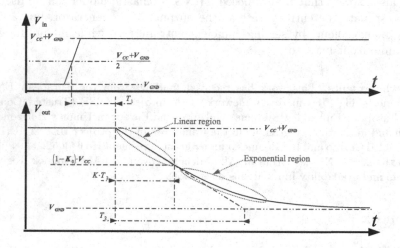

Fig. 8. Response of an ideal noise-free inverter to a step function

First, let us consider that at $t = 0$, signal V_{in} goes down from V_{CC} to 0 and $\overline{t_a}$ is the time at which the output signal V_{out} is equal to $\frac{V_{CC}}{2}$. At time $t = p_{in}$, signal V_{in} goes up from 0 to V_{CC} and at $\overline{t_b}$ output V_{out} is equal to $\frac{V_{CC}}{2}$. Finally, at $t = t_c$, V_{in} goes back to V_{GND}. Consequently, the length of the positive pulse at output V_{out} is equal to $p_{out} = \overline{t_b} - \overline{t_a}$.

The authors of [7] also describe the behavior of the inverter when the input signal has the same form as the described output signal. They show that in this case P_{out} can be approximated by:

$$p_{out} = \frac{t_c}{2} + \left[p_{in} - \frac{t_c}{2} \right] [1 + H_d] \tag{12}$$

where $H_d = 2e^{\left(\frac{K_0 \cdot T_2 - \frac{t_c}{2}}{(1-K_0) \cdot T_2} \right)}$.

B. Proofs

In this section, we give proofs of Lemma 1, Proposition 1 and Proposition 2.

---

² Where K_0 is a positive real number smaller than 1.

Proof of Lemma 1. *In a neighborhood of $\overline{t_a}$, $f(t)$ can be approximated by its tangent line at time $\overline{t_a}$, giving the relation $T_a - \overline{t_a} = \frac{n(\overline{t_a})}{f'(\overline{t_a})}$. Since $n(\overline{t_a}) \sim \mathcal{N}(0, \sigma^2)$, $T_a \sim \mathcal{N}\left(\overline{t_a}, \frac{\sigma^2}{f'(\overline{t_a})^2}\right)$. The same holds for T_b in a neighborhood of $\overline{t_b}$, because $n(t)$ is stationnary. By its definition, $P_{out} = T_b - T_a$. If T_a and T_b are independent, P_{out} follows a normal distribution with mean $\mu_{out} = \overline{t_b} - \overline{t_a} = \frac{t_c}{2} + \left[p_{in} - \frac{t_c}{2}\right][1 + H_d]$ from Appendix A and variance $\sigma_{out}^2 = \sigma_{T_b}^2 + \sigma_{T_a}^2 = \sigma^2 \left(\frac{1}{f'(\overline{t_a})^2} + \frac{1}{f'(\overline{t_b})^2}\right)$.*

Proof of Proposition 1 *(by recurrence on N). Lemma 1 gives expression of μ_{out_N} and $\sigma_{out_N}^2$ for $N = 1$. Let $\{I_j\}_{j=1...N+1}$ be a set of inverters and let V_N be the signal between the two last inverters. Logically, output of inverter I_N becomes input of inverter I_{N+1}. Let V_{in} be the input signal of the first inverter I_1 and V_{out} is the output signal of last inverter I_{N+1} in the chain. p_{in} is the length of a pulse at I_1. Let P_N be the length of the corresponding pulse appearing at signal V_N and P_{N+1} be the length of the pulse at V_{N+1}. By assumption of reccurence,*

$$P_N \sim \mathcal{N}(\mu_{out_N}, \sigma_{out_N}^2) \text{ with } \begin{cases} \mu_{out_N} = \frac{t_c}{2} + \left(p_{in} - \frac{t_c}{2}\right)(1 + H_d)^N \\ \sigma_{out_N}^2 = \sigma_{out}^2 \left(\frac{(1+H_d)^{2N}-1}{(1+H_d)^2-1}\right) \end{cases}$$

According to Lemma 1, $P_{N+1} \sim \mathcal{N}(\mu_{out}, \sigma_{out}^2)$ with $\mu_{out} = \frac{t_c}{2} + \left(p_n - \frac{t_c}{2}\right)(1 + H_d)$ where p_n is a realization of P_N. Assuming independence of noise sources in the chain, we have $\mu_{out_{N+1}} = \frac{t_c}{2} + \left(\mu_{out_N} - \frac{t_c}{2}\right)(1 + H_d)$ and $\sigma_{out_{N+1}}^2 = \sigma_{out_N}^2 (1 + H_d)^2 + \sigma_{out}^2$ giving

$$\mu_{out_{N+1}} = \frac{t_c}{2} + \left(\frac{t_c}{2} + (p_{in} - \frac{t_c}{2})(1+H_d)^N - \frac{t_c}{2}\right)(1 + H_d) = \frac{t_c}{2} + \left(p_{in} - \frac{t_c}{2}\right)(1+H_d)^{N+1}$$

and $\sigma_{out_{N+1}}^2 = \sigma_{out}^2 \left(\frac{(1+H_d)^{2N}-1}{(1+H_d)^2-1}\right)(1 + H_d)^2 + \sigma_{out}^2 =$

$$\sigma_{out}^2 \left(\frac{(1+H_d)^{2N+2}-(1+H_d)^2}{(1+H_d)^2-1} + 1\right) = \sigma_{out}^2 \left(\frac{(1+H_d)^{2N+2}-1}{(1+H_d)^2-1}\right).$$

The statement in Proposition 1 is true for $N + 1$. By recurrence over N, Proposition 1 is true for any N.

Proof of Proposition 2. *We propose the proof for PL_S (the same is valid for PK_S by replacing τ_1 with τ_2).*
Assuming that there is a pulse pl_{S-1} at V_L, the corresponding pulse PL_S at V_L after crossing the branches K and L (equivalent to a single chain of $4M + 2$ inverters) is given as follows (according to Proposition 1 with $N = 4M + 2$):

$$PL_S \sim \mathcal{N}\left(\frac{t_c}{2} + \left(pl_{S-1} - \frac{t_c}{2}\right)R, \underbrace{\sigma_{out}^2 \left(\frac{R^2 - 1}{(1 + H_d)^2 - 1}\right)}_{\sigma_{out_{4M+2}}^2}\right),$$

where $R = (1 + H_d)^{4M+2}$ and $t_c = \tau_1 + \tau_2$.

Thus, assuming independence of noise sources in chains K and L, we have two relations of reccurence on $\mu_{L_S} = \frac{\tau_1 + \tau_2}{2} + \left(\mu_{L_{S-1}} - \frac{\tau_1 + \tau_2}{2}\right) R$ and on $\sigma_{L_S}^2 = \sigma_{out_{4M+2}}^2 + \sigma_{L_{S-1}}^2 R^2$.

It is easy to show that $\forall S \geq 1$,

$$\mu_{L_S} = \frac{\tau_1 + \tau_2}{2} + (\mu_{L_0} - \frac{\tau_1 + \tau_2}{2})R^S = \frac{\tau_1 + \tau_2}{2} + \frac{\tau_1 - \tau_1}{2}R^S,$$
$$\sigma_{L_S}^2 = R^{2S}\sigma_{L_0}^2 + \sigma_{out_{4M+2}}^2 \sum_{i=0}^{S-1}(R^2)^i = R^{2S}\sigma_{out_{2M+1}}^2 + \sigma_{out_{4M+2}}^2 \frac{R^{2S}-1}{R^2-1}.$$

According to Proposition 1,

$$\sigma_{out_{2M+1}}^2 = \sigma_{out}^2 \frac{(1+H_d)^{4M+2}-1}{(1+H_d)^2-1} = \sigma_{out}^2 \frac{R-1}{(1+H_d)^2-1} \text{ and } \sigma_{out_{4M+2}} =$$
$$\sigma_{out}^2 \frac{((1+H_d)^{4M+2})^2-1}{(1+H_d)^2-1} = \sigma_{out}^2 \frac{R^2-1}{(1+H_d)^2-1},$$
therefore $\sigma_{L_S}^2 = \sigma_{out}^2 \frac{R^{2S+1}-1}{(1+H_d)^2-1}$.

References

1. Baudet, M., Lubicz, D., Micolod, J., Tassiaux, A.: On the security of oscillator-based random number generators. J. Cryptology **24**(2), 398–425 (2011)
2. Bernard, F., Fischer, V., Valtchanov, B.: Mathematical model of physical RNGs based on coherent sampling. Tatra Mountains Math. Publ. **45**(1), 1–14 (2010)
3. Fischer, V.: A closer look at security in random number generators design. In: Schindler, W., Huss, S.A. (eds.) COSADE 2012. LNCS, vol. 7275, pp. 167–182. Springer, Heidelberg (2012)
4. Killmann, W., Schindler, W.: A design for a physical RNG with robust entropy estimators. In: Oswald, E., Rohatgi, P. (eds.) CHES 2008. LNCS, vol. 5154, pp. 146–163. Springer, Heidelberg (2008)
5. Killmann, W., Schindler, W.: A proposal for: Functionality classes for random number generators (2011). https://www.bsi.bund.de
6. Marsaglia, G.: DIEHARD: Battery of Tests of Randomness (1996). http://stat.fsu.edu/pub/diehard/
7. Reyneri, L.M., Del Corso, D., Sacco, B.: Oscillatory metastability in homogeneous and inhomogeneous flip-flops. IEEE J. Solid State Circ. **25**(1), 254–264 (1990)
8. Rukhin, A., Soto, J., Nechvatal, J., Smid, M., Barker, E., Leigh, S., Levenson, M., Vangel, M., Banks, D., Heckert, A., Dray, J., Vo, S.: A Statistical Test Suite for Random and Pseudorandom Number Generators for Cryptographic Applications - NIST SP 800-22, rev. 1a (2010)
9. Shannon, C.: A mathematical theory of communication. Bell Syst. Technical J. **27**, 379–423, 623–656 (1948)
10. Sunar, B., Martin, W.J., Stinson, D.R.: A provably secure true random number generator with built-in tolerance to active attacks. IEEE Trans. Comput. **56**, 109–119 (2007)
11. Varchola, M., Drutarovsky, M.: New high entropy element for FPGA based true random number generators. In: Mangard, S., Standaert, F.-X. (eds.) CHES 2010. LNCS, vol. 6225, pp. 351–365. Springer, Heidelberg (2010)

Predictive Models for Min-entropy Estimation

John Kelsey[1]([⊠]), Kerry A. McKay[1], and Meltem Sönmez Turan[1,2]

[1] National Institute of Standards and Technology, Gaithersburg, MD, USA
john.kelsey@nist.gov
[2] Dakota Consulting Inc., Silver Spring, MD, USA

Abstract. Random numbers are essential for cryptography. In most real-world systems, these values come from a cryptographic pseudorandom number generator (PRNG), which in turn is seeded by an entropy source. The security of the entire cryptographic system then relies on the accuracy of the claimed amount of entropy provided by the source. If the entropy source provides less unpredictability than is expected, the security of the cryptographic mechanisms is undermined, as in [5,7,10]. For this reason, correctly estimating the amount of entropy available from a source is critical.

In this paper, we develop a set of tools for estimating entropy, based on mechanisms that attempt to predict the next sample in a sequence based on all previous samples. These mechanisms are called *predictors*. We develop a framework for using predictors to estimate entropy, and test them experimentally against both simulated and real noise sources. For comparison, we subject the entropy estimates defined in the August 2012 draft of NIST Special Publication 800-90B [4] to the same tests, and compare their performance.

Keywords: Entropy estimation · Min-entropy · Random number generation

1   Introduction

Random numbers are essential for generating cryptographic information, such as secret keys, nonces, random paddings, salts etc. Typically, these values are generated by a cryptographic pseudorandom number generator (PRNG). A good cryptographic PRNG is capable of generating outputs which can stand in for truly random numbers for cryptographic applications. However, PRNGs are deterministic algorithms; their security ultimately depends on a truly unpredictable seed.

The seed comes from an *entropy source*. To be useful, the entropy source's unpredictability must also be quantified – we need to know how many bits need to be drawn from the entropy source to produce a good seed. The unpredictability of the outputs of an entropy source is measured in terms of *entropy*. There are a number of different measures of entropy, such as Shannon entropy, Rényi entropy, and min-entropy. For seeding a cryptographic PRNG, the relevant measure is min-entropy, which corresponds to the difficulty of guessing or predicting

© International Association for Cryptologic Research 2015
T. Güneysu and H. Handschuh (Eds.): CHES 2015, LNCS 9293, pp. 373–392, 2015.
DOI: 10.1007/978-3-662-48324-4_19

the most-likely output of the entropy source. Correctly determining how much entropy is present in a sequence of outputs is critical–researchers have shown examples of deployed systems whose PRNG seeds were not sufficiently unpredictable, and as a result, cryptographic keys were compromised [5,7,10]. Estimating the amount of entropy that an entropy source provides is necessary to ensure that randomly generated numbers are sufficiently difficult to guess. However, entropy estimation is a very challenging problem when the distribution of the outputs is unknown and common assumptions (e.g. outputs are independent and identically distributed (i.i.d.)) cannot be made.

There are various approaches to entropy estimation. Plug-in estimators, also called maximum-likelihood estimators, apply the entropy function on empirical distributions (e.g., see [2,15]). Methods based on compression algorithms (e.g., see [11,20]) use match length or frequency counting to approximate entropy. Hagerty and Draper provided a set of entropic statistics and bounds on the entropy in [9]. Lauradoux et al. [12] provided an entropy estimator for non-binary sources with an unknown probability distribution that converges towards Shannon entropy.

Draft NIST Special Publication (SP) 800-90B [4] discusses procedures for evaluating how much entropy per sample can be obtained from an entropy source. It also provides a suite of five entropy estimators for sequences that do not satisfy the i.i.d. assumption. Each estimator takes a sequence of minimally-processed samples from the underlying unpredictable process in the entropy source, and uses them to derive an entropy estimate. The entropy assessment of the source is the minimum of the estimates obtained from the five estimators. This estimate is intended to be used for entropy sources that undergo validation testing in order to comply with Federal Information Processing Standard 140-2 [14].

It is important to note that good entropy estimation requires knowledge of the underlying nondeterministic process being used by the entropy source; statistical tests such as those referenced above and in this paper can only serve as a sanity check on that kind of estimate. Indeed, many of the experiments described in the remainder of this paper are based on using a non-cryptographic PRNG with a short seed to convincingly simulate an entropy source with some set of properties, in order to test the entropy estimators.

1.1   Entropy and Predictability

Shannon first investigated the relationship between the entropy and predictability of a sequence in 1951 [18], using the ability of humans to predict the next character in the text to estimate the entropy per character. In fact, predictability is exactly what we are interested in when considering the performance of an entropy source. An inadequate source of entropy allows the attacker to predict the PRNG's seed, and thus to predict all future pseduorandom numbers produced by the PRNG. More recently, in [1], there is a discussion of a method called a predictor, but details on how it works is missing.

1.2   Our Contributions

In this paper, we develop an alternative approach to estimating min-entropy, based on the ability of any of several models to successfully predict a source's outputs. These models are called *predictors*. Each predictor is an algorithm that attempts to predict each element in a sequence of samples, and updates its internal state based on the samples seen so far. A predictor that successfully predicts $\frac{1}{2}$ of the samples from a source demonstrates that the sequence elements can be predicted with probability at least $\frac{1}{2}$–at worst, an attacker could use the same algorithm to predict the sequence as is used by the predictor, but he might manage to find a better algorithm. That translates to a min-entropy of the source of at most 1 bit/sample, because $-\log_2(\frac{1}{2}) = 1$.

Our contributions include:

1. We introduce the use of *predictors* to estimate min-entropy of a noise source.
2. We describe a framework for using predictors for entropy estimation, including:
   (a) Entropy estimates from both global and local performance.
   (b) The use of ensemble predictors to combine similar predictors together.
   (c) The strategy of taking the minimum of all predictors' estimates.
3. We define a starting set of predictors which perform well in experiments, and which may be used directly for entropy estimation.
4. We describe a set of experiments to compare the performance of our predictors against that of the non-i.i.d. entropy estimators in the draft SP 800-90B [4], on two different kinds of data:
   (a) Data from simulated sources, whose correct entropy/sample is known.
   (b) Data from real-world hardware RNGs, whose correct entropy/sample is not known.
5. In both cases, our predictors performed very well, giving more accurate estimates than the 90B estimates where the correct entropy/sample was known, and comparable or lower estimates for the real-world sources.

1.3   Guide to the Rest of the Paper

The remainder of the paper is organized as follows. Section 2 provides fundamental definitions about entropy. Section 3 describes the entropy estimation using predictors, and Sect. 4 gives descriptions of several simple predictors. Section 5 provides experimental results, and the last section concludes the study with some future directions.

2   Preliminaries

Entropy sources, as defined in [4], are composed of three components; *noise sources* that extract randomness from physical phenomena, *health tests* that aim to ensure that entropy sources operate as expected, and (optional) *conditioning functions* that improve the statistical quality of the noise source outputs.

The conditioning function is deterministic, hence does not increase the entropy of the outputs of the noise source. In this study, we are concerned only with the noise source outputs, and estimating the entropy/sample present in them. Also, in this study, we assume that the samples obtained from a noise source consist of fixed-length bitstrings, which can be considered either as symbols in an alphabet, or as integers.

Let X be a discrete random variable taking values from the finite set $A = \{x_1, x_2, \ldots, x_k\}$, with $p_i = Pr(X = x_i), \forall x \in A$. The *min-entropy* of X is defined as $-\log_2(\max\{p_1, \ldots, p_k\})$.

If X has min-entropy h, then the probability of observing any particular value is no greater than 2^{-h}. The maximum possible value for min-entropy of an i.i.d random variable with k distinct values is $\log_2(k)$, which is attained when the random variable has a uniform probability distribution, i.e., $p_1 = p_2 = \ldots = p_k = \frac{1}{k}$.

A stochastic process $\{X_n\}_{n \in \mathbb{N}}$ that takes values from a finite set A is called a *first-order Markov chain*, if

$$Pr(X_{n+1} = i_{n+1} | X_n = i_n, X_{n-1} = i_{n-1}, \ldots, X_0 = i_0) = Pr(X_{n+1} = i_{n+1} | X_n = i_n),$$

for all $n \in \mathbb{N}$ and all $i_0, i_1, \ldots, i_n, i_{n+1} \in A$. The initial probabilities of the chain are $p_i = Pr(X_0 = i)$, whereas the transition probabilities p_{ij} are $Pr(X_{n+1} = j | X_n = i)$. In a d-th order Markov Model, the transition probabilities satisfy

$$Pr(X_{n+1} = i_{n+1} | X_n = i_n, \ldots, X_1 = i_1) = Pr(X_{n+1} = i_{n+1} | X_n = i_n, \ldots, X_1 = i_{n-d}).$$

The min-entropy of a Markov chain of length L is defined as

$$H = -\log_2\big(\max_{i_1, \ldots, i_L} p_{i_1} \prod_{j=1}^{L} p_{i_j i_{j+1}}\big).$$

The entropy per sample can be approximated by dividing H by L.

3   Entropy Estimation Using Predictors

A *predictor* contains a model that is updated as samples are processed sequentially. For each sample, the model offers a prediction, obtains the sample, and then updates its internal state, based on the observed sample value in order to improve its future predictions. The general strategy of the predictors is summarized in Fig. 1. It is important to note that predictors do not follow "traditional" supervised learning methods of training and evaluation. In particular, traditional methodologies contain disjoint *training* and *testing* sets. The training set is used to construct the model, possibly performing many passes over the data, and the testing data is used to evaluate the model but not update it. Predictors, on the other hand, use all observations to update the model. In other words, all observations are part of the training set. This allows the predictor to continually update its model, and remain in the training phase indefinitely. All observations are also part of the testing set, because a predictor is evaluated based on all predictions that were made since its initialization.

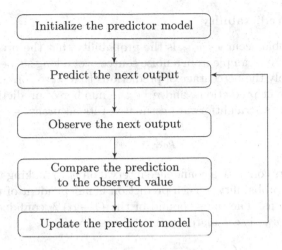

Fig. 1. General strategy of predictors

3.1 Predictor Performance and Entropy Bounds

There are two ways to broadly measure the performance of a predictor. The first one, which we call *global predictability*, considers the number of accurate predictions over a long period, whereas the second measure, called *local predictability*, considers the length of the longest run of correct predictions.

A predictive model that can predict each sample value with probability greater than a random guess, on average, will give the attacker a better than expected chance to guess a PRNG seed each time one is generated. A predictive model that usually gives a much lower probability of success, but which occasionally gives a lengthy run of correct predictions in a row, gives the attacker a chance at guessing a specific PRNG seed very cheaply.

A predictor's performance can be expressed as a probability, and it provides a *lower bound* on the best performance an attacker could get predicting the source's outputs–an attacker will never do *worse* than the predictor (he could just reuse it directly), but he may do *better*. That lower bound on the probability of making a correct prediction gives an *upper bound* on the entropy/sample of the source–the more predictable a source is, the less entropy it has. This relationship is easy to see in the formula for min-entropy: If p^* is the probability of predicting the next sample using the best possible predictor, then $H = -\log_2(p^*)$ is the min-entropy of the next sample. As p^* gets closer to one, H gets closer to 0; as p^* gets closer to 0, H gets bigger.

Our predictors estimate entropy by first estimating the probability of successful prediction (both globally and locally) with a 95 % upper bound, and then computing the min-entropy that would correspond to that success probability. The 95 % upper bound ensures somewhat conservative estimates, and also matches the way entropy estimates are calculated by the estimators in 90B.

3.2   Global Predictability

A predictor's global accuracy p_{acc} is the probability that the predictor will correctly predict a given sample from a noise source over a long sequence of samples. Accuracy is simply the percentage of predictions that were correct. Let c denote the count of correct predictions, and n be the number of predictions made. For a given predictor, a straightforward estimate of its accuracy is

$$\hat{p}_{acc} = \frac{c}{n}. \tag{1}$$

Our predictors compute a confidence interval on $\hat{p}_{acc}$, making the assumption that the success probability of each prediction is independent of the correctness of other predictions. The upper bound of the $(1 - \alpha)\%$ confidence interval on $\hat{p}_{acc}$, denoted as $\tilde{p}_{acc}$ is calculated as;.

$$\tilde{p}_{acc} = \begin{cases} 1 - \left(\frac{\alpha}{2}\right)^{\frac{1}{n}}, & \text{if } \hat{p}_{acc} = 0, \\ 1, & \text{if } \hat{p}_{acc} = 1, \\ \hat{p}_{acc} + t_\alpha \sqrt{\frac{\hat{p}_{acc}(1-\hat{p}_{acc})}{n-1}}, & \text{otherwise,} \end{cases} \tag{2}$$

where t_α refers to the upper $\alpha/2$ tail of Student's t-distribution with n-1 degrees of freedom[1]. Note that if $\hat{p}_{acc}$ is 1 or 0, computing a confidence interval using the Student's t-distribution is not valid. In these cases, confidence intervals are calculated using the binomial distribution.

The global min-entropy estimate for this predictor, $\hat{H}_{acc}$, is derived from $\tilde{p}_{acc}$ using

$$\hat{H}_{global} = -\log_2(\tilde{p}_{acc}). \tag{3}$$

3.3   Local Predictability

A second method to measure the performance of a predictor uses the length of the longest run of correct predictions. This estimate is valuable mainly when the source falls into a state of very predictable outputs for a short time. Should this happen, the estimated min-entropy per sample will be lower.

This entropy estimate can be obtained using statistical tools used to analyze recurrent events. Let r be one greater than the longest run of correct predictions (e.g., if the longest run has length 3, then $r = 4$). Then the probability that there is no run of length r, is calculated as

$$\alpha = \frac{1 - px}{(r+1-rx)q} \cdot \frac{1}{x^{n+1}}, \tag{4}$$

where $q = 1 - p$, n is the number of predictions and x is the real positive root of the polynomial $1 - x + qp^r x^{r+1} = 0$ [6]. The root x can be efficiently approximated using the recurrence relation $x_{i+1} = 1 + qp^r x_i^{r+1}$, as it converges on the root. In

---

[1] t_α can be approximated by the $1 - \frac{1}{2}\alpha$ percentile of a standard normal distribution, when $n \geq 30$.

our experiments, ten iterations appear to be sufficient to converge on the right answer. Note that there may be two real positive roots, one of which is $\frac{1}{p}$. This root is generally considered extraneous, and the recurrence relation will converge on it if and only if it is the only positive root. To find the min-entropy estimate, denoted as $\hat{H}_{local}$, using local predictability, first perform a binary search to solve for p, then the apply following equation

$$\hat{H}_{local} = -\log_2 p. \tag{5}$$

3.4   Deriving a Final Estimate

The final entropy estimate for a predictor is the minimum of the global and the local entropy estimates, i.e.,

$$\hat{H} = \min(\hat{H}_{global}, \hat{H}_{local}). \tag{6}$$

Entropy Estimation Using Multiple Predictors. In order to estimate the entropy of a given entropy source, we first select a set of predictors where each predictor is designed to successfully predict samples from sources with a certain kind of behavior. Then, we generate a long output sequence from the source, and evaluate the accuracy of each predictor, which provides an entropy estimate. After obtaining the estimates from the predictors, the final entropy estimate of the source is taken as the minimum of all the estimates.

If there is some predictable kind of behavior in the source, but no predictor is applied that can detect that behavior, then the entropy estimate will be overly generous. Because of this, it is important that a set of predictors that use different approaches be applied, and the lowest entropy estimate is taken as the final entropy estimate. By taking the minimum of all the predictors' estimates, we can guarantee that the predictor that was most effective at predicting the source's outputs determines the entropy estimate.

3.5   Underestimates and Overestimates

Predictors work in four steps:

1. Assume a probability model for the source.
2. Estimate the model's parameters from the input sequence on the fly.
3. Use these parameters to try to predict the still-unseen values in the input sequence.
4. Estimate the min-entropy of the source from the performance of these predictions.

This last step means that models that are a bad fit for the source can give big *overestimates*, but not big *underestimates* in entropy. A model that's a bad fit for the source will lead to inaccurate predictions (by definition), and thus will lead to a too-high estimate of the source's entropy. This distinguishes predictors from other entropy estimation mechanisms, such as those of [4], which give consistent, large underestimates for some source distributions.

Predictors can still give underestimates for the source's entropy, but these are based on successful predictions of the samples from the source. For example, a predictor which should be able to predict $\frac{1}{2}$ of the samples on average can have a run of unusually successful performance by chance, leading to an underestimate of entropy. Also, our predictors estimate a 95 % upper bound on the success probability of the predictor from its performance, which also leads to underestimates on average. However, both of these effects are easy to bound, and for reasonable numbers of samples, they are small; by contrast, several of the 90B estimators are subject to huge systematic underestimates of entropy.

This means that the strategy of applying a large set of very different predictors to the sequence of noise source samples, and taking the minimum estimate, is workable. If five predictors whose underlying models are very bad fits for the noise source are used alongside one predictor whose underlying model fits the source's behavior well, the predictor that fits well will determine the entropy estimate–predictors that are a bad fit will never give large systematic underestimates. Further, this means that it's reasonable to include many different predictors–adding one more predictor seldom does any harm, and occasionally will make the entropy estimate much more accurate.

4   A Concrete Set of Predictors for Entropy Estimation

In this section, we present a set of predictors for categorical and numerical data that are designed to characterize the behaviors of the noise sources. Entropy sources, defined in SP 800-90B [4], produce discrete values from a fixed alphabet, represented as bitstrings. Therefore, we consider predictors as a solution to a classification problem, rather than a regression problem. However, we can still build predictors for numerical data (samples whose integer values are meaningful as integers), as well.

Predictors can be constructed using existing methods from online and stream classification, but do not need to be complex. Classifiers are often designed to be domain specific. However, for noise sources where few assumptions about the underlying probability distribution can be made, it may be difficult to construct sophisticated learners.

4.1   Ensemble Predictors

Many of the predictors described below are *ensemble predictors*. An ensemble predictor is constructed using two or more subpredictors. At each point in the sequence of samples being processed, the ensemble predictor keeps track of which subpredictor has made the most correct predictions so far–that subpredictor's current prediction is used as the ensemble predictor's current prediction. Note that the ensemble predictor's final entropy estimate is based on the success of its own predictions. It is possible in principle for one of the subpredictors to have a higher final probability of successful prediction than the ensemble predictor.

Our ensemble predictors combine many similar subpredictors with slightly different model parameters–they allow us to construct a single predictor that in effect has many different choices for those model parameters at once, and which will choose the best set of parameters based on the data. A major benefit of using an ensemble predictor is that, for many sources, a collection of very similar predictors differing only in a few parameter choices would give very similar predictions. If we simply applied all these closely-related predictors directly and then took the minimum, we would introduce a systematic underestimate when all the closely-related predictors got similar results. By combining the similar predictors into a single ensemble predictor, we avoid this issue–adding more predictors with different parameters to the ensemble predictor will not introduce a bias toward underestimates.

4.2   Categorical Data Predictors

Here, we describe several predictors that assume that the samples represent categorical data, i.e., all samples have no numerical meaning or ordering, and serve as labels only.

Most Common in Window (MCW) maintains a sliding window of the most recently observed w samples, where w is a parameter which can be varied in different instances of the predictor. Its prediction is the most common value that has occurred in that window. If there is a tie for most common value in the window the window, the value that has occurred most recently is used. We expect the MCW predictor to perform well in cases where there is a clear most-common value, but that value varies over time. For example, a source whose most common value slowly changes due to environmental changes, such as operating temperature, might be approximated well by this predictor. In our experiments, this predictor is used inside the ensemble predictor *MultiMCW*.

Single Lag Predictor remembers the most recent N values seen, and predicts the one that appeared N samples back in the sequence, where N is a parameter to the predictor. We expect the single lag predictor to perform well on sources with strong periodic behavior, if N is close to the period. In our experiments, this predictor is used inside the *Lag* ensemble predictor.

Markov Model with Counting (MMC) remembers every N-sample string that has been seen so far, and keeps counts for each value that followed each N-sample string. N is a parameter for this predictor. We expect the MMC predictor to perform well on data from any process that can be accurately modeled by an Nth-order Markov model. In our experiments, this predictor is used inside the *MultiMMC* ensemble predictor.

LZ78Y keeps track of all observed strings of samples up to a maximum length of 32 until its dictionary reaches maximum size. For each such string, it keeps track of the most common value that immediately followed the string. (Note that even after the dictionary reaches maximum size, the counts continue to be updated.) Whenever the most recently seen samples match an entry in its dictionary, the predictor finds the longest such match, and predicts that the next sample will be the value that most often has followed this string so far. This predictor is based loosely on the LZ78 family of compression algorithms [17]. We expect the LZ78Y predictor to perform well the sort of data that would be efficiently compressed by LZ78-like compression algorithms. The LZ78Y predictor is used directly in our experiments.

Ensemble Predictors for Categorical Data. We make use of three ensemble predictors based on categorical data. Each of the three predictors contains many very similar subpredictors, keeps track of which subpredictor has performed the best on the sequence so far, and uses that as the source of its predictions. This minimizes the error in estimates introduced by having many distinct predictors with very similar performance – the ensemble predictor's performance is measured on its predictions, not on the performance of the predictions of any one of its subpredictors.

Multi Most Common in Window Predictor (MultiMCW) contains several MCW subpredictors, each of which maintains a window of the most recently observed w samples, and predicts the value that has appeared most often in that w-sample window. This ensemble predictor is parameterized by the window sizes of its subpredictors w, where $w \in \{63, 255, 1023, 4095\}$ for our experiments. We expect MultiMCW to perform well in cases where the most common value changes over time, but not too quickly. The wide range of window sizes is intended to give the predictor a good chance of tracking well with many different rates of change of the most common value.

Lag Predictor contains d subpredictors, one for each lag $i \in \{1, \ldots, d\}$, for a maximum depth d. This ensemble predictor is parameterized by d. We expect Lag to perform well on sources that exhibit periodic behavior, where the period is somewhere between 1 and d.

Multi Markov Model with Counting Predictor (MultiMMC) contains multiple MMC predictors. D is a parameter to the ensemble predictor, and specifies the number of MMC subpredictors, where each MMC sub predictor is parameterized by $N \in \{1, \ldots, D\}$. We expect MultiMMC to perform well on sources which can be modeled reasonably well by a Markov model of depth $\{1, \ldots, D\}$.

4.3   Numerical Predictors

We now describe predictors that assume that the samples are numerical–that is, that the integer values of the samples have some numerical meaning. Numerical models generally represent continuous data, whereas outputs of the entropy sources are discrete. This raises an issue that did not exist for categorical predictors: the outputs from a numerical model may not exist in the output alphabet of the source. Because of this discrepancy in data types, the numerical predictors are constructed from two parts:

1. A numerical model and numerical prediction function, and
2. A *grid* that remembers all values seen so far and rounds all predictions to the nearest value that has been seen so far.

Moving Average (MA) Predictors compute the average of the last w values seen, where w is a parameter to the predictor. Note that the MA predictor always rounds its prediction to the nearest integer value it has seen so far in the sequence–on a binary sequence, an average of 0.7 leads to a prediction of a 1. We expect MA to be most successful when there is some periodic component to the source's behavior with period close to w. In our experiments, MA is used inside the *MultiMA* ensemble predictor.

First Difference (D1) Equation Predictor constructs a difference equation on the two most recent sample values, and uses it to predict the next value. For example, if the difference between the previous value x_{t-1} and the one before that x_{t-2} was δ, then the predictor computes $x_{t-1} + \delta$, and then uses the output value seen so far that is closest to that value as the prediction. We expect D1 to be most successful when the source's behavior can be well-described by a first-order difference equation.

Ensemble Methods for Numerical Data. Our single ensemble predictor for numerical data works in the same way as the ensemble predictors for categorical data work–it keeps track of which subpredictor has made the most correct predictions, and uses that one to make the next prediction of its own. Once again, the entropy estimate that results is based on the success of the ensemble predictor's predictions, not necessarily that of its most successful subpredictor.

MultiMA Predictor contains multiple MA predictors, and is parameterized by the window sizes $w \in \{16, 32, 64, 128, 256, 512, 1024\}$ in our experiments.

5   Results

To determine whether simple predictive models were effective for the purpose of min-entropy estimation, we have applied the predictors presented above to simulated and real-world[2] data. We have also compared our results to the entropy estimators presented in SP 800-90B [4]. Our predictors in these experiments

---

[2] Any mention of commercial products or organizations is for informational purposes only; it is not intended to imply recommendation or endorsement by the National Institute of Standards and Technology nor is it intended to imply that the products identified are necessarily the best available for the purpose.

compute an $\alpha = 0.05$ upper-bound on the estimated probability from which a min-entropy estimate is computed. This matches the approach and value of α used in the 90B estimates.

5.1   NIST Entropy Estimation Suite

Draft NIST SP 800-90B [4] includes five estimators, which were originally specified in [8,9]. These estimators are suitable for sources that do not necessarily satisfy the i.i.d. assumption.

– *Collision test* computes entropy based on the mean time for a repeated sample value.
– *Partial collection test* computes entropy based on the number of distinct sample values observed in segments of the outputs.
– *Markov test* estimates entropy by modeling the noise source outputs as a first-order Markov model.
– *Compression test* computes entropy based on how much the noise source outputs can be compressed.
– *Frequency test* computes entropy based on the number of occurrences of the most-likely value.

We refer to the estimators as the 90B estimators.

5.2   Simulated Data

Datasets of simulated sequences were produced using the following distribution families:

– *Discrete Uniform Distribution:* This is an i.i.d. source in which the samples are equally-likely.
– *Discrete Near-Uniform Distribution:* This is an i.i.d source where all samples but one are equally-likely; the remaining sample has a higher probability than the rest.
– *Normal Distribution Rounded to Integers:* This is an i.i.d. source where samples are drawn from a normal distribution and rounded to integer values.
– *Time-varying Normal Distribution Rounded to Integers:* This is a non-i.i.d. source where samples are drawn from a normal distribution and rounded to integer values, but the mean of the distribution moves along a sine curve to simulate a time-varying signal.
– *Markov Model:* This is a non-i.i.d. source where samples are generated using a kth-order Markov model.

Eighty simulated sources were created in each of the classes listed above. A sequence of 100 000 samples was generated from each simulated source, and estimates for min-entropy were obtained from the predictors and 90B estimators for each sequence. For each source, the correct min-entropy was derived from the known probability distribution.

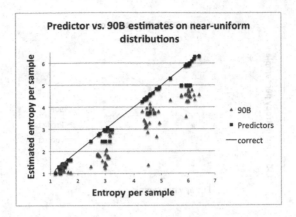

Fig. 2. Comparison of the lowest predictor entropy estimate, the lowest 90B entropy estimate, and the true entropy from 80 simulated sources with near-uniform distributions.

Figure 2 shows the results of the lowest estimate given by the 90B estimators[3] and the lowest estimate given by the predictors presented in this work, applied to simulated sources with near-uniform distributions. Near-uniform distributions are particularly interesting because the majority of the 90B estimators try to fit the data to a distribution in that family. Thus, one would expect the 9ss0B estimators to work quite well. However, the plot shows that this is not always the case – there are several points where the 90B methods give massive underestimates.

Figure 3 shows results for the simulated sources with normal distributions. For this class of simulated source, the 90B estimators are prone to large underestimates. In most cases, the minimum estimate is the result of the partial collection estimator, although the compression and collision estimates are quite low as well. The results of the partial collection and collision estimates are highly dependent on the segment size, and it is unclear whether the current strategy for selecting the segment size is optimal. The compression estimator, based on Maurer's universal statistic [13], does not contain the corrective factor $c(L, K)$ that is used to reduce the standard deviation to account for dependencies between variables, and this is likely a factor in the low estimates.

Figure 4 shows that none of the 90B or predictor estimates were overestimates for the uniform sources, which is to be expected. Overall, underestimates given by the predictors were smaller than those given by the 90B estimators.

Figures 5 and 6 show that predictors did give a number of overestimates when applied to the Markov and time-varying normal sources, particularly as the true min-entropy increases. This suggests that the predictors, with the parameters used in these experiments, were unable to accurately model these sources. The 90B estimators gave both significant overestimates and underestimates for the

---

[3] The implementation of the SP 800-90B estimators is slightly modified by removing the restriction that the output space is $[0, ..., 2^b - 1]$, where b is the maximum number of bits required to represent output values.

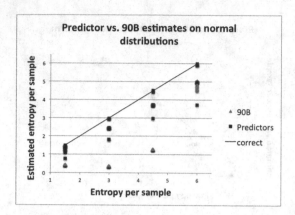

Fig. 3. Comparison of the lowest predictor entropy estimate, the lowest 90B entropy estimate, and the true entropy from 80 simulated sources with normal distributions.

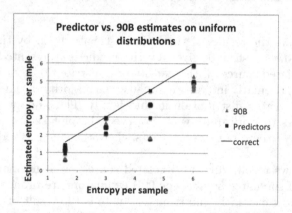

Fig. 4. Comparison of lowest predictor entropy estimate, lowest 90B entropy estimate, and the true entropy from 80 simulated sources with uniform distributions.

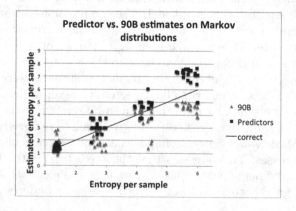

Fig. 5. Comparison of lowest predictor entropy estimate, lowest 90B entropy estimate, and the true entropy from 80 simulated sources with Markov distributions.

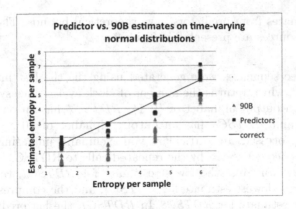

Fig. 6. Comparison of lowest predictor entropy estimate, lowest 90B entropy estimate, and the true entropy from 80 simulated sources with time-varying normal distributions.

Markov sources, and tended towards large underestimates for the time-varying normal sources.

While it can be useful to look at the trends, it is often more informative to compare the errors. Table 1 shows the mean squared error (MSE) of the lowest 90B estimate and the lowest predictor estimate over 80 sequences from each class of simulated sources. For all five classes, the MSE was lower for the predictors than it was for the 90B estimators. This suggests that the predictors are better estimators; however, the MSE does not tell the entire story. Because of the nature of the problem, underestimates are preferred to overestimates, and MSE does not capture the sign of the error. To capture this, the mean percentage error (MPE) is provided in Table 1 as well.

The MPE values show that the average errors from the 90B and predictor estimates have the same sign, except in the case of the Markov sources.

5.3   Real-World Data

Results were also obtained using random number generators deployed in the real world. The true entropy per sample for these sources is unknown, so no error can be computed for the estimators. However, the estimates from the predictors presented here can still be compared to the 90B estimates, based on the knowledge

Table 1. Error measures for the lowest 90B and predictor estimates by simulated source class.

Simulated data class	90B MSE	Predictor MSE	90B MPE	Predictor MPE
Uniform	2.4196	0.5031	37.9762	17.4796
Near-uniform	1.4136	0.1544	26.6566	6.4899
Normal	4.9680	0.4686	62.6330	14.1492
Time-varying normal	3.0706	0.2564	54.1453	3.1706
Markov	0.9973	0.8294	6.4339	-11.7939

that underestimates from predictors have theoretical bounds. The estimates of the real world sources are presented in Table 2.

RDTSC. Three sequences were generated using the the last bit returned by calls to RDTSC, which returns the number of clock cycles since system startup. *RDTSC1* has an output alphabet of $\{0, 1\}$, *RDTSC4* has an output alphabet of $\{0, \ldots, 15\}$, and *RDTSC8* has an output alphabet of $\{0, \ldots, 255\}$. These sequences are processed. In particular, Von Neumann unbiasing was applied to the raw sequence generated by the repeated calls to RDTSC.

The lag predictor gives the lowest estimate for *RDTSC1*, the MultiMMC predictor gives the lowest estimate for *RDTSC4*, and the compression estimate gives the lowest estimate for *RDTSC8*. In *RDTSC1*, the lag predictor provides an estimate 0.205 below that of the 90B collision estimate, suggesting that there was periodicity that the 90B estimators were unable to detect. The predictors did not achieve significant gains over uninformed guessing when applied to *RDTSC8*, with the LZ78Y estimator performing particularly poorly on this sequence.

RANDOM.ORG. [16] is a service that provides random numbers based on atmospheric noise. It allows the user to specify the minimum and maximum values that are output. The sequence used here consisted of bytes.

The predictors did not achieve significant gains over uninformed guessing when applied to this sequence, with the LZ78Y estimator performing particularly poorly on this sequence. One would expect that this is because of the cryptographic processing; the entropy estimates should be close to eight bits of entropy per sample. However, the 90B estimates are between 5.1830 and 5.6662. Although we cannot prove it, we suspect that this discrepancy comes from the inaccuracy of the estimators, rather than a weakness of the source.

Ubld.it. The final two real-world sequences in this paper come from a TrueRNG device by Ubld.it [19]. The *Ubld.it1* sequence contained bits, and the *Ubld.it8* is the byte interpretation of the *Ubld.it1* bit sequence.

The difference between the lowest 90B and predictor estimates for the *Ubld.it1* sequence was only 0.0071, which is not a significant difference. The results for *Ubld.it8* are similar to those of the *RANDOM.ORG* and *RDTSC8* datasets – the predictors did not achieve significant gains over uninformed guessing, and the LZ78Y estimator gave an impossibly high result.

Across Datasets. It is also informative to look at results across the real-world datasets, particularly when looking at bytes. For byte sequences, the 90B estimates are between five and six bits of entropy per sample, with the collision and compression estimators providing the lowest estimates. The LZ78Y predictor, on the other hand, provided impossible results of over 11 bits of entropy per sample. This indicates that the models constructed by the LZ78Y predictor are not good fits for these bytes sequences.

Table 2. Entropy estimates for real world sources. The lowest entropy estimate for each source is shown in bold font.

Estimator	RDTSC1	RDTSC4	RDTSC8	RANDOM.ORG	Ubld.it1	Ubld.it8
Collision	0.9125	3.8052	5.3240	**5.1830**	0.9447	**5.2771**
Compression	0.9178	3.6601	**5.3134**	5.1926	0.9285	5.5081
Frequency	0.9952	3.9577	5.8666	5.6662	0.8068	5.8660
Markov	0.9983	3.9582	5.7858	5.3829	0.8291	5.7229
Partial collection	0.9258	3.7505	5.3574	5.5250	0.9407	5.8238
D1	0.9616	3.9986	7.9619	7.9126	0.8734	7.9489
Lag	**0.7075**	3.9883	7.9546	7.9237	**0.7997**	7.9862
LZ78Y	0.9079	3.9989	11.9615	11.5924	**0.7997**	11.8375
MultiMA	0.9079	3.6458	7.9594	7.8508	0.8073	7.9441
MultiMCW	0.9079	3.9888	7.9381	7.9744	0.8072	7.9544
MultiMMC	0.9079	**3.6457**	7.9663	7.9237	0.8072	7.9880

5.4   General Discussion

It is interesting that in both the simulated and real-world datasets, the 90B estimators seem prone to greater underestimation as the sequence sample size goes from bits to bytes. There are two limiting factors as sample sizes increase. First, the near-uniform distribution only contains two probability levels (p and q, where $p > q$), and any source distribution with more than two levels seems to cause p to increase, and therefore, the entropy decreases. Second, the Markov estimate "maps down" the sequence so that only six bits are used to construct the first-order model. Therefore, estimates from the set of 90B estimators are capped at six bits of entropy per sample.

6   Conclusions

In this work, we attempted to estimate the min-entropy of entropy sources using predictive models, and show that even simplistic learners are capable of estimating entropy. We have also compared results from our simplistic learners with those of the entropy estimation suite provided in [4].

Barak and Halevi [3] criticize the approach of estimating the entropy from the point of an attacker, by just testing the outputs. We agree that the entropy estimation of a noise source should be done by analyzing the physical properties of the source, constructing a model of its behavior, and using that to determine how much unpredictability is expected from the source. However, there are still a number of places where external tests of entropy estimates are very useful:

For the Designer: The best efforts of the designer to understand the behavior of his noise source may not be fully successful. An independent test of the unpredictability of the source can help the designer recognize these errors.

For an Evaluator: A testing lab or independent evaluator trying to decide how much entropy per sample a source provides will have limited time and expertise to understand and verify the designer's analysis of his design. Entropy tests are very useful as a way for the evaluator to double-check the claims of the designer.

For the User: A developer making use of one or more noise sources can sensibly use an entropy estimation tool to verify any assumptions made by the designer.

Predictors are well-suited to providing a sanity-check on the entropy estimation done by the designer of a source based on some kind of deeper analysis, because they give an upper-bound estimate, which is very unlikely to be much below the correct entropy per sample. If the designer's model indicates that a source gives h bits of entropy per sample, and a predictor consistently estimates that it has much less than h bits/sample, this is strong evidence that the designer's estimate is wrong. Additionally, a designer who has a good model for his noise source can turn it into a predictor, and get an entropy estimate based on that model in a straightforward way. He can then evaluate the entropy of his source based on the minimum of these simple, general-purpose predictors and his own more carefully tailored one.

6.1   Future Work

This work shows the usefulness of a number of simple, generic predictors for entropy estimation. The predictor framework is very closely related to the classification problem in machine learning. While the predictors presented in this work are simple, more sophisticated learning techniques may be used to construct more complex predictors. In future work, we will adapt mainstream classification algorithms and data stream mining algorithms to fit the predictor framework, and examine their effectiveness as generic predictors. Also, in future work, we hope to adapt the predictor framework for real-time health testing of noise sources.

Our hope is that this work inspires additional research in two different directions:

1. We hope that experts on the physical properties of specific noise sources will use the predictor framework to design better predictors that capture the behavior of those sources more precisely than our generic predictors.
2. We hope that experts from the machine learning community will bring more sophisticated machine-learning tools to bear on the practical problem of the entropy estimation of noise sources.

Acknowledgments. We would like to thank Stefan Lucks for his suggestion to a performance metric that considered runs of correct predictions. We would also like to thank Tim Hall for his implementations of the entropy estimates in [9], and John Deneker, Tim Hall, and Sonu Sankur for providing samples from real-world noise sources for testing.

References

1. Cryptography Research Inc.: Evaluation of VIA C3 Nehemiah random number generator. Technical report. http://www.cryptography.com/public/pdf/VIA_rng.pdf. Accessed 27 Feb 2003

2. Antos, A., Kontoyiannis, I.: Convergence properties of functional estimates for discrete distributions. Random Struct. Algorithm. **19**(3–4), 163–193 (2001). http://dx.doi.org/10.1002/rsa.10019

3. Barak, B., Halevi, S.: A model and architecture for pseudo-random generation with applications to /dev/random. In: Proceedings of the 12th ACM Conference on Computer and Communications Security, CCS 2005, pp. 203–212. ACM, New York, NY, USA (2005). http://doi.acm.org/10.1145/1102120.1102148

4. Barker, E., Kelsey, J.: NIST draft special publication 800–90 B: recommendation for the entropy sources used for random bit generation, August 2012. http://csrc.nist.gov/publications/drafts/800-90/draft-sp800-90b.pdf

5. Dorrendorf, L., Gutterman, Z., Pinkas, B.: Cryptanalysis of the random number generator of the windows operating system. ACM Trans. Inf. Syst. Secur. **13**(1), 10:1–10:32 (2009)

6. Feller, W.: An Introduction to Probability Theory and its Applications, vol. One, Chap. 13. Wiley, New York (1950)

7. Gutterman, Z., Pinkas, B., Reinman, T.: Analysis of the linux random number generator. In: Proceedings of the 2006 IEEE Symposium on Security and Privacy, SP 2006, pp. 371–385. IEEE Computer Society, Washington, DC, USA (2006). http://dx.doi.org/10.1109/SP.2006.5

8. Hagerty, P.: Presentation of non-iid tests. In: NIST Random Bit Generation Workshop (2012). http://csrc.nist.gov/groups/ST/rbg_workshop_2012/hagerty.pdf

9. Hagerty, P., Draper, T.: Entropy bounds and statistical tests. In: NIST Random Bit Generation Workshop (2012). http://csrc.nist.gov/groups/ST/rbg_workshop_2012/hagerty_entropy_paper.pdf

10. Heninger, N., Durumeric, Z., Wustrow, E., Halderman, J.A.: Mining your Ps and Qs: detection of widespread weak keys in network devices. In: Proceedings of the 21st USENIX Security Symposium, Aug 2012

11. Kontoyiannis, I., Algoet, P., Suhov, Y.M., Wyner, A.: Nonparametric entropy estimation for stationary processes and random fields, with applications to English text. IEEE Trans. Inform. Theor. **44**, 1319–1327 (1998)

12. Lauradoux, C., Ponge, J., Roeck, A.: Online entropy estimation for non-binary sources and applications on iPhone. Research report RR-7663, INRIA, Jun 2011. https://hal.inria.fr/inria-00604857

13. Maurer, U.M.: A universal statistical test for random bit generators. J. Cryptol. **5**(2), 89–105 (1992). http://dx.doi.org/10.1007/BF00193563

14. FIPS PUB 140-2, Security requirements for cryptographic modules. U.S. Department of Commerce/National Institute of Standards and Technology (2002)

15. Paninski, L.: Estimation of entropy and mutual information. Neural Comput. **15**(6), 1191–1253 (2003). http://dx.doi.org/10.1162/089976603321780272

16. RANDOM.ORG: https://www.random.org/

17. Sayood, K.: Introduction to Data Compression, Third edn, Chap. 5. Morgan Kaufmann, San Francisco (2006)

18. Shannon, C.: Prediction and entropy of printed english. Bell Syst. Tech. J. **30**, 50–64 (1951). https://archive.org/details/bstj30-1-50
19. ubld.it: TrueRNG. http://ubld.it/products/truerng-hardware-random-number-generator/
20. Wyner, A.D., Ziv, J.: Some asymptotic properties of the entropy of a stationary ergodic data source with applications to data compression. IEEE Trans. Inf. Theor. **35**(6), 1250–1258 (1989)

Side-Channel Analysis and Fault Injection Attacks

Improved Side-Channel Analysis of Finite-Field Multiplication

Sonia Belaïd[1]([✉]), Jean-Sébastien Coron[2], Pierre-Alain Fouque[3],
Benoît Gérard[4], Jean-Gabriel Kammerer[5], and Emmanuel Prouff[6]

[1] École Normale Supérieure and Thales Communications and Security,
Gennevilliers, France
sonia.belaid@live.fr
[2] University of Luxembourg, Walferdange, Luxembourg
[3] Université de Rennes 1 and IRISA, Rennes, France
[4] DGA/MI and IRISA, Rennes, France
[5] DGA/MI and IRMAR, Rennes, France
[6] ANSSI, Paris, France

Abstract. A side-channel analysis of multiplication in $GF(2^{128})$ has
recently been published by Belaïd, Fouque and Gérard at Asiacrypt 2014,
with an application to AES-GCM. Using the least significant bit of the
Hamming weight of the multiplication result, the authors have shown
how to recover the secret multiplier efficiently. However such least significant bit is very sensitive to noise measurement; this implies that,
without averaging, their attack can only work for high signal-to-noise
ratios ($SNR > 128$). In this paper we describe a new side-channel attack
against the multiplication in $GF(2^{128})$ that uses the most significant bits
of the Hamming weight. We show that much higher values of noise can
be then tolerated. For instance with an SNR equal to 8, the key can
be recovered using 2^{20} consumption traces with time and memory complexities respectively equal to $2^{51.68}$ and 2^{36}. We moreover show that
the new method can be extended to attack the fresh re-keying countermeasure proposed by Medwed, Standaert, Großschädl and Regazzoni at
Africacrypt 2010.

Keywords: Side-channel analysis · Galois Field Multiplication · LPN
problem

1 Introduction

Side-Channel Attacks. The cornerstone of side-channel analysis (SCA for
short) is that information about some key-dependent variable x leaks through
e.g. the power consumption or the electromagnetic information of the device
manipulating x. A side-channel attack classically follows a *divide-and-conquer*
approach and the secret is recovered by exhaustively testing the likelihood of
every possible value for every secret piece. This *modus operandi* implicitly assumes
that x depends on a short portion of the secret (for example only 8 bits if x

© International Association for Cryptologic Research 2015
T. Güneysu and H. Handschuh (Eds.): CHES 2015, LNCS 9293, pp. 395–415, 2015.
DOI: 10.1007/978-3-662-48324-4_20

corresponds to the output of the AES sbox). It is particularly suited to the context of software implementations where the processing is sequentially split into operations on data whose size depends on the device architecture (*e.g.* 8 bit or even 32 bit for smart cards).

Side-Channel Analysis of Finite-Field Multiplication. At Asiacrypt 2014 [BFG14], Belaïd, Fouque and Gérard consider an attack scenario dedicated to hardware implementations where many operations are performed simultaneously. Following previous works as [MSGR10, MSJ12], they assume that when performing a multiplication $\mathbf{a} \cdot \mathbf{k}$ over $GF(2^n)$ for some known $\mathbf{a}$, only the Hamming weight of the result $\mathbf{a} \cdot \mathbf{k} \in GF(2^n)$ is leaking, with some noise; the goal is to recover the secret multiplier $\mathbf{k}$. Formally, after denoting by $\mathcal{N}(0, \sigma)$ the Gaussian distribution with null mean and standard deviation σ and by HW the Hamming weight over $GF(2^n)$, for a given basis of $GF(2^n)$, the SCA then amounts to solve the following problem:

Definition 1 (Hidden Multiplier Problem). *Let* $\mathbf{k} \leftarrow GF(2^n)$. *Let* $\ell \in \mathbb{N}$. *Given a sequence* $(\mathbf{a}_i, \mathcal{L}_i)_{1 \leq i \leq \ell}$ *where* $\mathbf{a}_i \leftarrow GF(2^n)$ *and* $\mathcal{L}_i = HW(\mathbf{a}_i \cdot \mathbf{k}) + \varepsilon_i$ *where* $\varepsilon_i \leftarrow \mathcal{N}(0, \sigma)$, *recover* $\mathbf{k}$.

The Belaïd-Fouque-Gérard Attack and the LPN Problem. As noted in [BFG14], for $\sigma = 0$ (no noise) the above problem is easy to solve. Namely the least significant bit of the Hamming weight of x is the xor of the bits of x. Hence for known $\mathbf{a}_i$ the least significant bit of $HW(\mathbf{a}_i \cdot \mathbf{k})$ is a linear function of the bits of the secret $\mathbf{k}$. Therefore every Hamming weight gives a linear equation over the n bits of $\mathbf{k}$ and, if the system of equations has rank n (which happens with good probability), the secret $\mathbf{k}$ can be recovered by solving a linear system. However such least significant bit is very sensitive to the observation noise ε_i. Even for relatively high signal-to-noise ratios (*i.e.*, low σ), this induces a significant error probability for the linear equations. This is all the more damageable that a device is never exactly leaking the Hamming weight of manipulated data, and a modeling (aka epistemic) error therefore adds to the observation noise. The problem of solving a system of noisy linear equations over $GF(2)$ is known as the Learning Parity with Noise (LPN) problem. New algorithms for solving LPN have recently been proposed [GJL14, BTV15]. The previous best method to solve the LPN problem was the Fouque-Levieil algorithm from [LF06], which is a variant of the algorithm BKW proposed by Blum, Kalai and Wasserman in [BKW00]. According to [BFG14] the Fouque-Levieil algorithm can solve the LPN for $n = 128$ bits with error probability $p = 0.31$ (corresponding to SNR $= 128$) with 2^{48} acquisitions and 2^{50} complexity (it becomes 2^{334} when SNR $= 8$). Therefore the Belaïd-Fouque-Gérard (BFG for short) algorithm for solving the Hidden Multiplier Problem is quite efficient for relatively high signal-to-noise ratios (SNR > 128); however it becomes prohibitively inefficient for smaller values (*e.g.*, larger values of σ).

Our New Attack. In this paper we describe a new algorithm for solving the Hidden Multiplier Problem, in which we use several most significant bits of the Hamming weight instead of the single least significant bit; we show that much smaller values of SNR can then be tolerated (SNR $\simeq 8$), which increases the practicability of the attack. Our technique works as follows. We only keep the observations with small Hamming weight or high Hamming weight. Namely if $\mathsf{HW}(\mathbf{a}_i \cdot \mathbf{k})$ is close to 0, this means that most of the bits of $\mathbf{a}_i \cdot \mathbf{k}$ are equal to 0. This can be written as a system of n equations over the bits of $\mathbf{k}$, all equal to 0, where some of the equations are erroneous. Similarly if the Hamming weight is close to n, we can assume that all n equations are equal to 1, and we obtain again a set of n noisy equations. Hence in both cases we obtain an instance of the LPN problem. For example, if we only keep observations with Hamming weight less than $n/4$ or greater than $3n/4$, we obtain a set of noisy equations with error probability less than $1/4$.

To solve the LPN problem we will use BKW style algorithms [BKW00]. The main drawback of these algorithms is the huge samples requirement that makes them unpractical for side-channel attacks. In this paper we use some improvements to reduce the query complexity using Shamir-Schroeppel [SS79] or the variant proposed by Howgrave-Graham and Joux in [HGJ10]. We also take advantage of secret-error switching lemma [Kir11, ACPS09] to further reduce the time complexity.

Since our attack is based on filtering for abnormally low or high Hamming weights, it is much less sensitive to noise in Hamming weight measurement than the BFG attack, which relies on the least significant bit of the Hamming weight. Namely even for small SNR (*i.e.*, close to 8), our filtering remains essentially correct, whereas the information from the least significant bit of the Hamming weight is buried in noise and becomes useless. However, for high SNR, our attack requires a larger amount of observations. Therefore in the latter contexts, the BFG attack stays better.

We also describe an attack when the messages $\mathbf{a}_i$ can be chosen. In that case, the attack becomes much more efficient. We also attack a fresh re-keying scheme proposed in [MSGR10] to defeat side-channel cryptanalysis. Whereas the latter scheme is not vulnerable to the technique used in [BFG14], we demonstrate that our attack enables to recover the secret key very efficiently.

Organization of the Paper. In Sect. 2, we recall the field multiplication for the AES-GCM, the leakage model, the LPN problem and the BKW algorithm. Then, we present our new attack in Sect. 3 and the new algorithmic techniques to reduce the number of queries. In Sect. 4 we describe a new chosen message attack and in Sect. 5 our attack on the fresh re-keying scheme. Finally, in Sect. 6 we present the result of our practical experiments.

2   Preliminaries

2.1   Galois Field Multiplication

For any positive integer n, the finite field of 2^n elements is denoted by $\mathsf{GF}(2^n)$ and the n-dimensional vector space over $\mathsf{GF}(2)$ is denoted by $\mathsf{GF}(2)^n$. Choosing a basis of $GF(2^n)$ over $GF(2)$ enables to represent elements of $GF(2^n)$ as elements of $GF(2)^n$ and *vice versa*. In the following, we assume that the same basis is always used to represent elements of $GF(2^n)$ over $GF(2)$.

This paper analyses the multiplication in the field $GF(2^n)$, with a particular focus on $n = 128$, with the representation $GF(2)[x]/(x^{128} + x^7 + x^2 + x + 1)$ which is used in the AES-GCM protocol. If $\mathbf{a} = (a_0, a_1, \cdots, a_{127})$ and $\mathbf{k} = (k_0, k_1, \cdots, k_{127})$ are two elements of $GF(2^{128})$ viewed as 128-bit vectors, the multiplication $\mathbf{a} \cdot \mathbf{k}$ can be represented by a matrix/vector product in the following way:

$$
\begin{pmatrix}
a_0 & a_{127} & \cdots & a_1 \oplus a_{127} \oplus a_{126} \\
a_1 & a_0 \oplus a_{127} & \cdots & a_2 \oplus a_{123} \oplus a_1 \oplus a_{127} \oplus a_{122} \\
\vdots & \vdots & \ddots & \vdots \\
a_{127} & a_{126} & \cdots & a_0 \oplus a_{127} \oplus a_{126} \oplus a_{121}
\end{pmatrix}
\cdot
\begin{pmatrix}
k_0 \\ k_1 \\ \vdots \\ k_{127}
\end{pmatrix}
=
\begin{pmatrix}
z_0 \\ z_1 \\ \vdots \\ z_{127}
\end{pmatrix}, \quad (1)
$$

where the product $\cdot$ is processed over $GF(2)$.

2.2   Probabilities

In this paper we shall use an upper-case letter, *e.g.* X, to denote a random variable, while the lower-case letter, x, shall denote a value taken by X. The probability of an event ev is denoted by $\Pr(ev)$. The *mean* and the *variance* of a random variable X are respectively denoted by $\mathbb{E}(X)$ and $\mathrm{Var}(X)$ (the *standard deviation* of X is the square root of the variance). A *continuous* random variable X with mean μ and variance σ^2 is said to follow a *normal* (Gaussian) distribution, denoted by $X \sim \mathcal{N}(\mu, \sigma)$, if, $\forall\, x \in \mathbb{R}$, $\Pr[X \leqslant x] = \int_{-\infty}^{x} \phi_{\mu,\sigma}(x)$ where $\phi_{\mu,\sigma}$ is the normal *probability distribution function* (pdf) defined by

$$
\phi_{\mu,\sigma}(x) = \frac{1}{\sigma\sqrt{2\pi}} e^{-\frac{(x-\mu)^2}{2\sigma^2}}.
$$

The other distributions used in this paper are the *uniform distribution* over $GF(2)^n$, denoted by $\mathcal{U}(GF(2)^n)$, and the Bernoulli distribution $\mathsf{Ber}(p)$ over $GF(2)$, with $\Pr[X = 1] = p$, for some $p \in [0,1]$. We shall also use the Binomial distribution which is defined over $\{0, \ldots, n\}$ by $\Pr[X = j] = \binom{n}{j} p^j (1-p)^{n-j}$ and is denoted by $\mathsf{B}(n, p)$.

2.3   Leakage Model

A common assumption is to consider that a processing on an embedded device leaks a noisy observation of the Hamming weight of the manipulated values. Namely, for such manipulated value $\mathbf{z} \in GF(2)^n$, it is assumed that the adversary obtains the following observation $\mathcal{L}(\mathbf{z})$:

$$
\mathcal{L}(\mathbf{z}) = \mathsf{HW}(\mathbf{z}) + \varepsilon, \quad (2)
$$

with an independent noise ε satisfying $\varepsilon \sim \mathcal{N}(0, \sigma)$. In practice, each bit of $\mathbf{z}$ can leak differently. Instead of the Hamming weight, the deterministic part of the observation can hence be modeled as a multivariate polynomial in the bits of $\mathbf{z}$, where the coefficients are taken in $\mathbb{R}$, see [SLP05, RKSF11, DDP13]. For most of current microprocessor architectures, the latter polynomial is well approximated by a linear combination of the bits of $\mathbf{z}$, leading to generalize (2) with $\mathcal{L}(\mathbf{z}) = \sum_{i=0}^{n-1} \beta_i z_i + \varepsilon$. For simplicity, we will describe our attack under the noisy Hamming Weight leakage model given by (2) but in Sect. 6, we will show that it also works for such generic leakage model.

In the rest of the paper, the level of noise in the observations is quantified with the *signal-to-noise ratio* (SNR for short), that we define as the ratio between the signal variance and the noise variance. This value, which equals $n/(4\sigma^2)$ under Assumption (2), is a useful notion to compare different contexts where the variances of both the signal and the noise are different (*e.g.* with different devices).

As in [BFG14], the main purpose of our attack is to show that the key $\mathbf{k}$ can be recovered with only the observations $\mathcal{L}(\mathbf{k} \cdot \mathbf{a_i})$ for many known $\mathbf{a_i}$'s. Thus, we assume that the attacker has no access to the internal leakage of the field multiplication $\mathbf{k} \cdot \mathbf{a_i}$ and that the n-bit results are stored in n-bit registers, which is the worst case to attack.

2.4 Learning Parities with Noise

As briefly explained in the introduction the problem of recovering a secret $\mathbf{k}$ from noisy observations of $\mathsf{HW}(\mathbf{a} \cdot \mathbf{k})$ relates to the well known LPN problem.

Definition 2 (Learning Parity with Noise (LPN) Problem). *Let* $\mathbf{k} \in \mathsf{GF}(2)^n$ *and* $p \in (0, 1/2)$. *Given a family of* ν *values* $(\mathbf{a_i})_{0 \leqslant i < \nu}$ *in* $\mathsf{GF}(2)^n$ *and the family of corresponding observations* $(b_i = \langle \mathbf{a_i}, \mathbf{k} \rangle + e_i)_{0 \leqslant i < \nu}$, *where* $\langle \cdot, \cdot \rangle$ *denotes the scalar product* $\in \mathsf{GF}(2)^n$ *and where the* $\mathbf{a_i}$ *are drawn uniformly in* $\mathsf{GF}(2^n)$ *and the* e_i *are generated according to Bernoulli's distribution* $\mathsf{Ber}(p)$ *with parameter* p, *recover* $\mathbf{k}$.

We denote by $\mathsf{LPN}(n, \nu, p)$ an instance of the LPN problem with parameters (n, ν, p). In this paper, the noisy equations $\langle \mathbf{a_i}, \mathbf{k} \rangle + e_i$ will come from the noisy observations of a device performing field (or ring) multiplications in the form $\mathbf{z} = \mathbf{a} \cdot \mathbf{k}$ in $\mathsf{GF}(2^n)$.

2.5 The BKW Algorithm and Its Variants

Blum *et al.* described in [BKW00] a subexponential algorithm for solving the LPN problem: it performs a clever Gaussian elimination using a small number of linear combinations, which reduces the dimension of the problem. Then, Levieil and Fouque proposed a practical improvement in [LF06] for the second phase of the algorithm and Kirchner [Kir11] proposed to switch secret and error [ACPS09] to further improve the method. Later Arora and Ge [AG11] proposed an algebraic approach for specifically structured noise. Recently Guo *et al.* proposed to use error-correcting codes [GJL14].

The BKW Algorithm. Given as input $b_i = \langle \mathbf{a}_i, \mathbf{k} \rangle + e_i$ for known $\mathbf{a}_i$'s, the goal of the BKW algorithm is to find linear combinations of the $\mathbf{a}_i$'s with ℓ terms such that:

$$\mathbf{a}_{i_1} \oplus \cdots \oplus \mathbf{a}_{i_\ell} = \mathbf{u}_j, \tag{3}$$

where $(\mathbf{u}_j)_{1 \le j < n}$ is the canonical basis, that is $\mathbf{u}_j$ has its jth coordinate equal to 1 and the other coordinates are 0. Then one gets:

$$\langle \mathbf{u}_j, \mathbf{k} \rangle = k_j = \bigoplus_{r=1}^{\ell} b_{i_r} \oplus \bigoplus_{r=1}^{\ell} e_{i_r}.$$

It is not difficult to evaluate the new bias of the linear combination of equations using the Piling-Up lemma. Letting $\delta = 1 - 2p$, for ℓ variables $e_1, \dots, e_\ell$ such that $\Pr[e_i = 1] = p = (1 - \delta)/2$, we have $\Pr[e_1 \oplus \cdots \oplus e_\ell = 0] = \frac{1+\delta^\ell}{2}$. This shows that if we sum ℓ error terms e_i with $\Pr[e_i = 1] = (1 - \delta)/2$, the resulting error term e is such that $\Pr[e = 1] = (1 - \delta')/2$ with $\delta' = \delta^\ell$. If ℓ is not too large, then the bias of the error term $\bigoplus_{r=1}^{\ell} e_{i_r}$ is also not too large and with enough such equations and a majority vote one can recover the jth coordinate of $\mathbf{k}$.

Finding linear combinations. To find linear combinations satisfying (3), we first split the $\mathbf{a}_i$'s into a blocks of b bits, where $n = a \cdot b$ (*e.g.* for $n = 128$ we can take $a = 8$ and $b = 16$). Initially we have ν vectors $\mathbf{a}_i$. Consider the rightmost b bits of each $\mathbf{a}_i$, and sort the $\mathbf{a}_i$'s into 2^b classes according to this value. We xor all elements of each class with a single one element of it, and we discard this element. Hence we get at least $\nu - 2^b$ new vectors $\mathbf{a}_i^{(1)}$, whose rightmost b bits are zero; these $\mathbf{a}_i^{(1)}$ are the xor of 2 initial vectors $\mathbf{a}_i$. One can then proceed recursively. For the next block of b bits we get at least $\nu - 2 \cdot 2^b$ vectors $\mathbf{a}_i^{(2)}$ whose rightmost $2b$ bits are zero; they are the xor of 4 initial vectors $\mathbf{a}_i$. Stopping at the last-but-one block, we get at least $\nu - (a-1) \cdot 2^b$ vectors, for which only the first b-bit block is possibly non-zero, and which are the xor of 2^{a-1} initial vectors $\mathbf{a}_i$. Among these $\nu - (a-1) \cdot 2^b$ vectors, we select the ones equal to the basis vectors $\mathbf{u}_j$ and we perform a majority vote. With the xor of $\ell = 2^{a-1}$ vectors, the bias is $(1 - 2p)^{2^{a-1}}$. Therefore for the majority vote we need roughly $c/(1-2p)^{2^{a-1}}$ such vectors, for some logarithmic factor c [BKW00]. A variant of BKW algorithm is described by Levieil and Fouque in [LF06]: it finds linear combinations similarly, however at the end, it uses a Walsh Transform to recover the last b bits of $\mathbf{k}$ at once.

3   Our New Attack

In this section, we describe our new side-channel attack on the result of the multiplication in $\mathsf{GF}(2^n)$, which benefits from being weakly impacted by the observation noise. As in [BFG14], we aim at recovering the n-bit secret key $\mathbf{k}$ from a sequence of t queries $(\mathbf{a}_i, \mathsf{HW}(\mathbf{k} \cdot \mathbf{a}_i) + \varepsilon_i)_{0 \le i < t}$ where the $\mathbf{a}_i$ are drawn uniformly in $\mathsf{GF}(2^n)$ and the ε_i are drawn from the Gaussian distribution $\mathcal{N}(0, \sigma)$.

3.1 Overview

The cornerstone of the attack is to filter the collected measurements to keep only the lowest and the highest Hamming weights. Then we assume that for each low (resp. high) Hamming weight, the multiplication result is exactly n bits of zeros (resp. ones). As a consequence, each filtered observation of $\mathbf{z}_i = \mathbf{a}_i \cdot \mathbf{k}$ gives n equations each with some error probability p. In our context, the equations correspond to the row-by-column scalar products in (1) and the binary error associated to the ith equation is denoted by e_i, with $\Pr[e_i = 1] = p$. Therefore given t messages and corresponding measurements, we get an instance of the $\mathsf{LPN}(n, n \cdot t, p)$ problem that we can solve using techniques described in Sect. 3.3. To correctly scale the latter techniques, we need to know the error probability p with good precision. In the next section we show how to compute p from the filtering threshold and the measurement noise σ in (2).

3.2 Filtering

We describe here how we filter the lowest and highest leakage and we compute the error probabilities of our final set of equations. In order to catch the extreme Hamming weight values of the multiplication results, we choose a threshold real value λ and we filter all the observations below $n/2 - \lambda s$ and above $n/2 + \lambda s$, with $s = \sqrt{n}/2$ the standard deviation of the leakage deterministic part (here the Hamming weight). In the first case, we assume that all the bits of the multiplication result are zeros and in the second case we assume that they are all set to one. In both cases, we get n linear equations on the key bits, each having the same error probability p.

We first compute the proportion of filtered acquisitions before focusing on the error probability p. Let $\mathbf{z} = \mathbf{a} \cdot \mathbf{k}$ be the result of a finite field multiplication; since $\mathbf{z} \sim \mathcal{U}(\mathsf{GF}(2)^n)$, we deduce $\mathsf{HW}(\mathbf{z}) \sim \mathsf{B}(n, 1/2)$. Moreover since $\mathcal{L}(\mathbf{z}) = \mathsf{HW}(\mathbf{z}) + \varepsilon$, with $\varepsilon \sim \mathcal{N}(0, \sigma)$, we obtain that the pdf h of $\mathcal{L}(\mathbf{z})$ is defined over $\mathbb{R}$ by:

$$h(x) = 2^{-n} \sum_{y=0}^{n} \binom{n}{y} \phi_{y,\sigma}(x).$$

Since our filtering rejects the observations with leakage $\mathcal{L}(\mathbf{z})$ between $n/2 - \lambda s$ and $n/2 + \lambda s$ for some parameter λ, the proportion of filtered acquisition $F(\lambda)$ is then:

$$\forall \lambda \in \mathbb{R}, \quad F(\lambda) = 1 - 2^{-n} \sum_{y=0}^{n} \binom{n}{y} \int_{n/2-\lambda s}^{n/2+\lambda s} \phi_{y,\sigma}(t) dt. \tag{4}$$

After filtering, our attack consists in assuming that the n bits of $\mathbf{z}$ are all zeros if $\mathcal{L}(\mathbf{z}) < n/2 - \lambda s$, and are all ones if $\mathcal{L}(\mathbf{z}) > n/2 + \lambda s$. Therefore in the first case out of the n equations, $\mathsf{HW}(\mathbf{z})$ equations are erroneous, whereas in the second case $n - \mathsf{HW}(\mathbf{z})$ equations are erroneous. In the first case, this corresponds to an error probability $\mathsf{HW}(\mathbf{z})/n$, while in the second case this corresponds to an error probability $1 - \mathsf{HW}(\mathbf{z})/n$. On average over filtered observations, we obtain an error probability:

$$p(\lambda) = \frac{1}{F(\lambda)} \sum_{y=0}^{n} \frac{\binom{n}{y}}{2^n} \left(\frac{y}{n} \int_{-\infty}^{n/2-\lambda s} \phi_{y,\sigma}(t)dt + \left(1 - \frac{y}{n}\right) \int_{n/2+\lambda s}^{+\infty} \phi_{y,\sigma}(t)dt \right).$$

This error probability $p(\lambda)$ (or p for short) is a crucial parameter as it gives the error probability in the LPN problem. Our goal is to minimize p in order to minimize the complexity of solving the LPN problem. This can be done by increasing the filtering threshold λ; however a larger λ implies that a larger number of observations must be obtained initially. Therefore a tradeoff must be found between the error probability p in the LPN problem and the proportion $F(\lambda)$ of filtered observations.

The main advantage of our attack is that this error probability p is quite insensitive to the noise σ in the observations, as illustrated in Table 1. For $n = 128$ and for various values of σ, we provide the corresponding filtering threshold λ that leads to a filtering probability $F(\lambda)$, expressed with $\log_2 1/F(\lambda)$; we then give the corresponding error probability p. For example, for SNR = 128, with $\lambda = 6.00$ we get a filtering probability $F(\lambda) = 2^{-30}$, which means that on average 2^{30} observations are required to get $n = 128$ equations for the LPN problem; in that case the error probability for the LPN problem is $p = 0.23$. We see that this error probability does not grow too fast as SNR decreases, as we get $p = 0.25$ for SNR = 8 and $p = 0.34$ for SNR = 0.5.

Study in the General Case. For completeness, we exhibit hereafter the expressions of the probabilities $F(\lambda)$ and $p(\lambda)$ when the leakage satisfies (2) for another function than $\mathsf{HW}(\cdot)$. If we relax the Hamming weight assumption but still assume that the noise is independent, additive and Gaussian, we get the following natural generalization of (2):

$$\mathcal{L}(\mathbf{z}) = \varphi(\mathbf{z}) + \varepsilon,$$

where $\varphi(\mathbf{z}) \doteq \mathbb{E}\left(\mathcal{L}(Z) \mid Z = \mathbf{z}\right)$ and $\varepsilon \sim \mathcal{N}(0, \sigma)$. This leads to the following generalization of (4):

$$\forall \lambda \in \mathbb{R}, \quad F(\lambda) = 1 - \sum_{y \in \mathrm{Im}(\varphi)} \mathbb{P}\left(\varphi(Z) = y\right) \int_{-\lambda s}^{\lambda s} \phi_{y,\sigma}(t + \mu)dt,$$

Table 1. Error probability p and λ w.r.t. the filtering proportion $F(\lambda)$ and the SNR

$\log_2(1/F(\lambda))$	30	25	20	15	10	5	30	25	20	15	10	5
	SNR = 128, $\sigma = 0.5$						SNR = 2, $\sigma = 4$					
λ	6.00	5.46	4.85	4.15	3.29	2.16	7.42	6.73	5.97	5.09	4.03	2.64
p	0.23	0.25	0.28	0.31	0.34	0.39	0.28	0.30	0.32	0.34	0.37	0.41
	SNR = 8, $\sigma = 2$						SNR = 0.5, $\sigma = 8$					
λ	6.37	5.79	5.14	4.39	3.48	2.28	10.57	9.58	8.48	7.21	5.71	3.73
p	0.25	0.27	0.29	0.32	0.35	0.40	0.34	0.36	0.37	0.39	0.41	0.44

where μ and s respectively denote the mean and the standard deviation of $\varphi(Z)$. Analogously, we get:

$$p(\lambda) = \frac{1}{F(\lambda)} \sum_{y=0}^{n} \frac{\binom{n}{y}}{2^n} \left(\frac{y}{n} \int_{-\infty}^{\lambda s} g_y(t + \mu) dt + \left(1 - \frac{y}{n}\right) \int_{\lambda s}^{+\infty} g_y(t + \mu) dt \right),$$

where for every y, the pdf $g_{\mathcal{L}|HW(Z)=y}$ is defined by:

$$g_y(\ell) = \binom{n}{y}^{-1} \sum_{z \in HW^{-1}(y)} \phi_{\varphi(\mathbf{z}),\sigma}(\ell).$$

In the case $\varphi = HW$ (*i.e.*, when the device leaks perfectly in the Hamming weight model), it can be checked that g_y is simply the pdf of $\mathcal{N}(HW(y), \sigma)$, otherwise it is a Gaussian mixture. In Sect. 6, we will approximate it by a Gaussian pdf with mean $\mathbb{E}\left(\mathcal{L}(Z) \mid HW(Z) = y\right)$ and standard deviation $\sqrt{\mathrm{Var}(\mathcal{L}(Z) \mid HW(Z) = y)}$.

3.3 Solving the LPN Problem

Numerous algorithms for solving LPN are known in the literature; a good survey is given by Pietrzak in [Pie12]. They generally require a huge number of LPN equations. However in our context, these equations come from side-channel acquisitions and thus remain in a rather scarce number. A well-known result of Lyubashevsky reduces the sample complexity, but its limitations on the noise render it inapplicable to our problem [Lyu05]. In this section we summarize the ideas we set-up for solving the LPN problem with a reduced number of samples and under reasonable levels of noise.

We take the point of view of an attacker: she has a limited quantity of side-channel information, thus a limited number of initial LPN samples. She also has a limited computing power and (most importantly) memory. She has two goals: firstly she wants to make sure that the attack will indeed be feasible in theory (this depends on the final number of reduced equations), thus she must compute it as exactly as possible (she cannot afford to miss one bit of complexity in the computations). Secondly, she has reasonable but limited resources and wants to make the attack as efficient as possible.

Algorithm Sketch. The main parameter of the algorithm is the initial bias: it determines the number of linear combinations steps we will be able to do before the final bias explodes. We fix it to 3 reductions (8 linear combinations). We look for small-weight linear combinations of initial equations that have their MSB cancelled. There's not enough initial LPN equations to use BKW or LF1 (*cf* Sect. 2.5) algorithms directly (they do not remove enough bits per iteration).

We thus first (rather artificially) square the number ν of LPN samples: for all elements $\mathbf{a}_i$ in the initial set, with error probability p (bias $\delta = 1 - 2p$), we build the set $(\mathbf{a}_{i,j})_{i \neq j} \doteq (\mathbf{a}_i \oplus \mathbf{a}_j)_{i,j}$. We then can do only 2 reductions. However, on the one hand, BKW-like algorithms will still not find enough reduced equations.

On the other hand, exhaustively looking for reduced equations among all linear combinations of at most 4 (corresponding to 2 reductions) amplified equations would not be very efficient. Consequently, we apply two steps of a generalized birthday paradox-like algorithm [Wag02].

Then assume that we obtain w-bits reduced equations. Once enough equations are found (this depends on the final bias of the equations, which is δ^8), we can directly apply a Walsh-Hadamard transform (WHT) to recover the w LSB of the secret if the attacker memory is greater than 2^w w-bits words. If we can only obtain equations reduced to $w' > w$ bits, we can simply guess the $w' - w$ bits of the secret and do a WHT on the last w bits. In this case, the search space can be reduced using the error/secret switching idea at the very beginning of the algorithm.

The algorithm steps as well as its time and space complexities are analyzed in details in [BCF+15]. From a practical perspective, the optimal choice depends on several parameters: number of traces, filtering ratio, level of noise, available memory, computing power. Several trade-offs are thus available to the attacker. The most obvious one is to trade side-channel measurements against computing needs. Using more traces either makes it possible to reduce the bias of the selected equations, or increases their number, reducing the reduction time (birthday paradox phase). In a nutshell, the more traces are available, the better. Given a fixed number of traces (order of magnitude 2^{20} to 2^{24}), the attacker fixes the filtering threshold λ. Increasing λ improves the bias of the selected equations. Thus less reduced equations are required for the WHT to correctly find w bits of the secret. Nonetheless, increasing λ also reduces the number of initial equations and thus makes the birthday paradox part of the algorithm slower. Concerning the reduction phase, it is well known that balancing the two phases of the generalized birthday paradox is the best way to reduce its complexity. Finally doubling the memory makes it possible recover one bit more with the WHT, while slightly more than doubling its time complexity: we fill the table with equations that are 1 bit less reduced, halving the time needed by the birthday paradox phase.

3.4   Comparison with State-of-the Art Attacks

Compared to [BFG14], our new attack performs better except in one scenario when SNR $= 128$ and the number of available queries is very limited by the context. Indeed, for SNR $= 128$ the attack in [BFG14] requires only 128 observations to get 128 equations with error probability 0.31 whereas our attack requires 2^{15} observations to achieve the same error probability. In the other contexts (*i.e.*, for higher levels of noise) the attack in [BFG14] faces strong limitations. Concretely, recovering the secret key becomes very hard if the inputs are not chosen. On the contrary, since our attack benefits from being quite insensitive to noise, it stays successful even for higher noise levels.

4   Extension to Chosen Inputs

In this section, we present a key-recovery technique which can be applied when the attacker is able to control the public multiplication operands $\mathbf{a}_i$. It is based on comparing the leakage for related inputs.

4.1   Comparing Leaks

In the so-called *chosen message model*, the attacker chooses ν messages $(\mathbf{a}_i)_{0 \leqslant i < \nu}$ in $\mathsf{GF}(2^n)$ and gets the corresponding leakages $\mathcal{L}(\mathbf{k} \cdot \mathbf{a}_i)$ as defined by Equation (2).

From the underlying associative property of the field $\mathsf{GF}(2^n)$, we remark[1] that the relation $(2 \cdot \mathbf{a}_i) \cdot \mathbf{k} = 2 \cdot (\mathbf{a}_i \cdot \mathbf{k})$ stands for every query $\mathbf{a}_i$. If the most significant bit of $\mathbf{a}_i \cdot \mathbf{k}$ is zero, then the latter relation implies that the bits of $\mathbf{a}_i \cdot k$ are simply shifted when computing $2 \cdot (\mathbf{a}_i \cdot \mathbf{k})$ which results in $\mathsf{HW}((2 \cdot \mathbf{a}_i) \cdot \mathbf{k}) = \mathsf{HW}(\mathbf{a}_i \cdot \mathbf{k})$. However, if the most significant bit of $\mathbf{a}_i \cdot \mathbf{k}$ is one, then the bits are also shifted but the result is summed with the constant value 23, which corresponds to the decimal representation of the binary coefficients of the non-leading monomials of the polynomial $x^{128} + x^7 + x^2 + x + 1$ involved in the representation of the field $\mathsf{GF}(2^{128})$ in AES-GCM. In this case, the Hamming weight values $\mathsf{HW}((2 \cdot \mathbf{a}_i) \cdot \mathbf{k})$ and $\mathsf{HW}(\mathbf{a}_i \cdot \mathbf{k})$ are necessarily different. Indeed, the bits are shifted, the less significant bit is set to one and the bits of $(\mathbf{a}_i \cdot \mathbf{k})$ at positions 0, 1 and 6 are flipped. Thus, the absolute value of the difference between both Hamming Weight values is equal to 3 with probability $1/4$ or to 1 with probability $3/4$.

Without noise, we can perfectly distinguish whether both Hamming weight values are equal or not, and thus get knowledge of the most significant bit of $\mathbf{a}_i \cdot \mathbf{k}$. Repeating the experiment for every power of two until 2^{128} (*i.e.*, with 128 queries) gives us the knowledge of every bit of the multiplication result and thus the recovery of $\mathbf{k}$. With noise, the recovery is no longer straightforward. To decide whether the noisy Hamming weights are equal or different, we fix a threshold τ depending on the SNR. Namely, if the distance $|\mathcal{L}((2 \cdot \mathbf{a}_i) \cdot \mathbf{k}) - \mathcal{L}(\mathbf{a}_i \cdot \mathbf{k})|$ is greater than τs where s is the signal standard deviation (here the standard deviation of $\mathsf{HW}(Z)$, say $\sqrt{n}/2$), then we decide that $\mathsf{HW}((2 \cdot \mathbf{a}_i) \cdot \mathbf{k}) \neq \mathsf{HW}(\mathbf{a}_i \cdot \mathbf{k})$ and thus that the most significant bit of $(\mathbf{a}_i \cdot \mathbf{k})$ equals one. The type I error probability p_{I} associated to this decision (*i.e.*, the probability of deciding that the Hamming weights are different while they are equal) satisfies:

$$p_{\mathrm{I}} = \mathbb{P}\left[|\mathcal{L}((2 \cdot \mathbf{a}_i) \cdot \mathbf{k}) - \mathcal{L}(\mathbf{a}_i \cdot \mathbf{k})| > \tau s \mid \mathsf{HW}((2 \cdot \mathbf{a}_i) \cdot \mathbf{k}) = \mathsf{HW}(\mathbf{a}_i \cdot \mathbf{k})\right]$$

$$= \mathbb{P}\left[|\varepsilon_{i+1} - \varepsilon_i| > \tau s\right] = 1 - \int_{-\tau s}^{\tau s} \phi_{\sigma\sqrt{2}}(u) du,$$

where we recall that, according to (2), the variable ε_i (resp. ε_{i+1}) corresponds to the noise in the ith (resp. $(i+1)$th) observation $\mathcal{L}(\mathbf{a}_i \cdot \mathbf{k})$ (resp. $\mathcal{L}(\mathbf{a}_{i+1} \cdot \mathbf{k}) = \mathcal{L}((2 \cdot \mathbf{a}_i) \cdot \mathbf{k})$).

---

[1] We can simply choose $\mathbf{a}_i$ equal to 1.

Similarly, the type II error probability p_{II} (of deciding that the Hamming weight values are equal when they are different) satisfies:

$$p_{II} = \frac{3}{8}\left(\int_{-\tau s-1}^{\tau s-1}\phi_{\sigma\sqrt{2}}(u)du + \int_{-\tau s+1}^{\tau s+1}\phi_{\sigma\sqrt{2}}(u)du\right)$$
$$+ \frac{1}{8}\left(\int_{-\tau s-3}^{\tau s-3}\phi_{\sigma\sqrt{2}}(u)du + \int_{-\tau s+3}^{\tau s+3}\phi_{\sigma\sqrt{2}}(u)du\right).$$

Since, the key bits are all assumed to be balanced between one and zero, the probability of error p for each key bit is equal to $\frac{1}{2}(p_I + p_{II})$. Table 2 gives the thresholds τ which minimizes the error probability for different values of standard deviations.[2]

Table 2. Optimal threshold and probability of deciding correctly w.r.t. the SNR

SNR (σ)	128 (0.5)	8 (2.0)	2 (4.0)	0.5 (8.0)
τ	0.094	0.171	0.301	0.536
p	0.003	0.27	0.39	0.46

Comparing to Table 1, the error probabilities in Table 2 are much more advantageous and only 129 queries are required. If the number of queries is not limiting, the traces can be averaged to decrease the noise and thus improve the success rate. Another improvement is to correlate not only two consecutive powers of 2 but also non-consecutive ones (e.g., 2^j and 2^{j+2}). Without noise, we do not get more information but in presence of noise we can improve the probability of deciding correctly.

4.2 Key Recovery

With the method described above, we only get 128 different linear equations in the key bits. Thus, we cannot use an LPN solving algorithm to recover the secret key in presence of errors. However, since we can average the measurements, we can significantly reduce the level of noise and remove the errors almost completely. For instance, with an SNR of 128 (which can also be achieved from an SNR of 2 and 64 repetitions), we get an average of $128 \times 0.003 = 0.384$ errors. Solving the system without error is straightforward when we use the powers of two since we directly have the key bits. Thus, inverting all the second members of the equations one-by-one to remove a single error leads to a global complexity of 2^7 key verifications. This complexity is easily achievable and remains reasonable to recover a 128-bit key.

5 Adaptation to Fresh Re-Keying

The core idea of the fresh re-keying countermeasure originally proposed in [MSGR10] for block cipher algorithm is to create a new *session* key from a

---

[2] Note that we did not consider so far the bias induced by the recovery of the less significant bits (whose values have been altered by previous squarings) since it is very negligible in practice.

public *nonce* for each new processing of the encryption algorithm. It guaranties that the secret (master) key is never used directly. To allow for the decryption of the ciphertext, the latter one is sent together with the nonce. For soundness, the fresh re-keying must satisfy two properties. First, it must be easy to protect against side-channel attacks. Secondly, it must have a good *diffusion* so that each bit of the new session key depends on a large number of bits of the master key, rendering attacks based on key-hypotheses testing inefficient. To satisfy the first property, [MSGR10] proposes to base the re-keying on linear functions. Efficient techniques are indeed known to secure the latter functions against SCA (*e.g.* higher-order masking has linear complexity for linear functions [ISW03, CGP+12]). To additionally satisfy the second property, [MSGR10] proposes to define the linear functions from *circulant* matrices deduced from the random nonce.

Let $\mathbf{k} \in \mathsf{GF}(2^8)^n$ denote the master key which must be protected and let $\mathbf{a} \in \mathsf{GF}(2^8)^n$ denote the nonce (generated at random). The square matrix whose lines correspond to all the rotations of the byte-coordinates of $\mathbf{a}$ (*e.g.* the ith row corresponds to the vector $\mathbf{a}$ right-rotated i times) is denoted by $\mathsf{circ}(a_0, \cdots, a_{n-1})$. It satisfies:

$$\mathsf{circ}(a_0, \cdots, a_{n-1}) = \begin{pmatrix} a_0 & a_{n-1} & a_{n-2} & \cdots & a_1 \\ a_1 & a_0 & a_{n-1} & \cdots & a_2 \\ \vdots & \vdots & \vdots & \ddots & \vdots \\ a_{n-1} & a_{n-2} & a_{n-3} & \cdots & a_0 \end{pmatrix},$$

and the session key $\mathbf{k}'$ is deduced from $(\mathbf{k}, \mathbf{a})$ as follows:

$$\mathbf{k}' = \mathsf{circ}(a_0, \cdots, a_{n-1}) \cdot \mathbf{k}, \tag{5}$$

where $\cdot$ denotes the scalar product in $\mathsf{GF}(2^8)^n$. After denoting the multiplication on $\mathsf{GF}(2^8)$ by $\otimes$, Equation (5) implies in particular that the ith byte of $\mathbf{k}'$ satisfies:

$$k'_i = \sum_{j=0}^{n-1} a_{i+j \bmod n} \otimes k_j.$$

It may be checked that the attack described in Sect. 3.1 applies against the multiplication specified by (5) similarly as for the multiplication in (1). Indeed, the matrix-vector product defined in (5) over $\mathsf{GF}(2^8)$ can be rewritten over $\mathsf{GF}(2)$ expressing each bit of $\mathbf{k}'$ as a linear combination of the bits of $\mathbf{k}$ with coefficients being themselves linear combinations of the bits of $\mathbf{a} \in \mathsf{GF}(2)^{128}$. Eventually, exactly like in previous section, for ν filtered messages the attack leads to an instance of the $\mathsf{LPN}(128, 128\nu, p)$ problem.[3] Actually, looking further in the fresh re-keying protocol, we can improve the attack by taking advantage of the context in which the fresh re-keying is used.

---

[3] As observed by the authors of [BFG14], the attack in [BFG14] does not apply to the multiplication specified by (5), essentially because of the circulant property of the matrix.

Until now, we have assumed that the multiplication output was stored in a 128-bit register, which essentially corresponds to an hardware implementation and is the worst case from the attacker point of view. If we switch to a software implementation e.g. running on a w-bit architecture, then the attacker can now target the manipulation of w-bit sub-parts of the refresh key $\mathbf{k}'$ which puts him in a more favourable context. By moreover assuming that $\mathbf{k}'$ is used as a secret parameter of a block cipher like AES (as proposed in [MSGR10]), then the attacker can exploit information leakage when the byte-coordinates of $\mathbf{k}'$ are manipulated separately. Observing the manipulation of each of the sixteen 8-bit chunks separately gives, for a same filtering ratio, a much lower error probability on the equations that what was achieved in the previous (hardware) context. This can be explained by the fact that exhibiting extreme Hamming weights is obviously much more easier on 8 bits than on 128 bits. For instance, filtering one observation over 2^{10} (i.e., $F(\lambda) = 2^{-10}$) with a SNR equal to 2 results in an error probability of $p = 0.28$ for $n = 128$ and $p = 0.065$ for $n = 8$, that is more than four times less. Table 3 gives the error probability p according to the proportion of filtered acquisitions $F(\lambda)$ for SNR equal to 128, 8, 2 and then 0.5 (as in Table 1) and $n = 8$.

Table 3. Error probability p according to the proportion of filtered acquisitions $F(\lambda)$.

$\log_2(1/F(\lambda))$	10	5	4	3	2	1	10	5	4	3	2	1
	SNR $= 128, \sigma = 0.125$						SNR $= 2, \sigma = 1$					
λ	2.93	2.15	2.02	1.47	1.33	0.71	3.88	2.62	2.28	1.89	1.42	0.83
p	$2.8 \cdot 10^{-19}$	0.09	0.11	0.17	0.21	0.28	$6.5 \cdot 10^{-2}$	0.16	0.19	0.22	0.26	0.32
	SNR $= 8, \sigma = 0.5$						SNR $= 0.5, \sigma = 2$					
λ	3.25	2.26	1.97	1.63	1.24	0.74	5.66	3.73	3.22	2.66	1.99	1.17
p	$5.9 \cdot 10^{-3}$	0.10	0.14	0.18	0.23	0.29	0.17	0.25	0.28	0.30	0.33	0.37

This confirms on different parameters that with much fewer observations, we have smaller error probabilities. Therefore, even for $F(\lambda) = 0.5$ (i.e., we only filter one observation over two), the system can be solved to recover the 128-bit key. Furthermore, it is worth noting that this new attack on an AES using a one-time key allows to recover the master key without observing any leakage in the fresh re-keying algorithm.

By using this trick which consists in observing the leakage of 8-bit session keys in the first round of the AES, we can also mount an attack towards the outlines of the approach proposed in [BFG14] against the AES-GCM multiplication. Since in this case only the first matrix row is involved in the computation, the coefficients of the key bits are different and each observation gives a useful linear equation. Plus, since we observe the leakage on 8-bit data, the noise impacts on the less significant bit of Hamming weight is reduced, which improves the system solving. However, the resulting attack remains much less efficient than our new attack, even in the number of required observations.

6 Practical Experiments

We showed in previous sections how to mount efficient side-channel attacks on finite-field multiplication over 128-bit data in different scenarios according to the attacker capabilities. In order to verify the truthfullness of our leakage assumptions, we have mounted few of these attacks in practice and made some simulations. In particular, we implemented the AES-GCM and the fresh re-keying protocol on an ATMega328p and measured the leakage using the ChipWhisperer kit [OC14]. We also obtained the 100,000 traces of AES-GCM multiplication from [BFG14] corresponding to EM radiations of an FPGA implementation on the Virtex 5 of a SASEBO board.

We first illustrate the leakage behavior we obtained on the ATMega328p. Then we present experimental confirmations that the attack on AES-GCM with known inputs can actually be mounted. Afterwards, we show how efficient is the attack on fresh re-keying when the attacker can exploit 8-bit leakages of the first round of AES. Eventually, the reader may find in the extended version of this paper [BCF+15] an experiment corresponding to the chosen-message attack presented in Section 4 for a 128-bit multiplication implemented on the ATMega328p.

6.1   ATMega328p Leakage Behaviour

Since we are in software on an 8-bit implementation, we simulate a 128-bit leakage by summing the intermediate leakage on 8-bit parts of the result[4]. We randomly generated $100,000$ vectors $\mathbf{a} \in \mathsf{GF}(2)^{128}$ and, for a fixed key $\mathbf{k}$, we measured the leakage during the processing of $\mathbf{z} = \mathbf{a} \cdot \mathbf{k}$ as specified in AES-GCM (see (1)). Each measurement was composed of $4,992$ points among which we detected 16 points of interest by following a T-test approach as *e.g.* described in [GJJR11]. We afterwards verified that these points corresponded to the manipulation of the byte-coordinates $\mathbf{z}[i]$ of $\mathbf{z}$ after the multiplication processing.

For each $i \in [1..16]$, we denote by $g_{\mathrm{Id},i}$ the function $z \mapsto \mathbb{E}\left(\mathcal{L}(\mathbf{z}[i]) \mid \mathbf{z}[i] = z\right)$ and by $g_{\mathrm{HW},i}$ the function $y \mapsto \mathbb{E}\left(\mathcal{L}(\mathbf{z}[i]) \mid \mathsf{HW}(\mathbf{z}[i]) = y\right)$ (the first function corresponds to the mean of the leakage $\mathcal{L}(\mathbf{z}[i])$ knowing $\mathbf{z}[i] = z \in \mathsf{GF}(2)^8$ and the second function corresponds to the mean of the leakage $\mathcal{L}(\mathbf{z}[i])$ knowing $\mathsf{HW}(\mathbf{z}[i]) = y \in [0..8]$). In the top of Fig. 1, we plot for each $i \in [1..16]$ the distribution of our estimations of the values of $g_{\mathrm{Id},i}()$ (left-hand figure) and the distribution of the values of $g_{\mathrm{HW},i}()$. First, it may be observed that all the byte-coordinates, except the first one, leak quite similarly. The average mean and standard deviation of the functions $g_{\mathrm{ID},i}$ are -0.0301 and 0.0051 respectively. They are -0.0291 and 0.0092 for the functions $g_{\mathrm{HW},i}$. While the left-hand figure shows that the distributions of values differ from normal distributions, the right-hand figure exhibits a strong dependency between them and the distribution of the Hamming weight values of $\mathbf{z}[i]$. This shows that our implementation is a good target for our attack which requires that the deterministic part of the leakage monotonously depends on the Hamming weight of the manipulated data.

---

[4] Our purpose was to test the practical soundness of our theoretical analyses; we hence chose to artificially build a 128-bit leakage. The application of our attack to 8-bit chunks is the purpose of Sect. 6.3 where it is shown that this situation is much more favourable to the attacker.

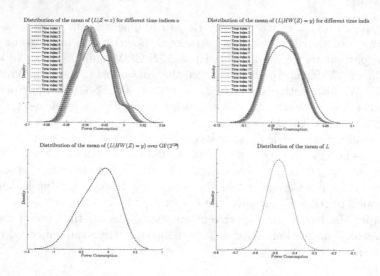

Fig. 1. Behaviour of the leakage w.r.t. the manipulated data Z

Eventually, we plot in the bottom-left figure an estimate (with kernel methods) of the distribution of the values $\mathbb{E}\left(\mathcal{L}(\mathbf{z})\right) \mid \mathsf{HW}(\mathbf{z}) = y$ when y ranges in $[0..128]$ and $\mathcal{L}(\mathbf{z}) \doteq \sum_{i=1}^{16} \mathcal{L}(\mathbf{z}[i])$. Once again, the distribution is a not a perfect binomial one, but the figure shows that the deterministic part of the leakage monotonously depends on the Hamming weight of the manipulated data. The mean and the standard deviation of the plotted distribution are -0.1781 and $0,2392$ respectively. For completeness, we also plot in the bottom-right of Fig. 1 the distribution of the leakage values (after combining the 16 point of interest): the distribution looks very close to a Gaussian one.

6.2 Attacks on AES-GCM with Known Inputs

The aforementioned attack of AES-GCM with known inputs was almost completely performed for 96-bit keys (simulations for more leakage traces) and partially performed for 128-bit keys (the error probabilities were confirmed in practice).

Experiments on Filtering.

ATMega328p (128-bit). In this context, the leakage $\mathcal{L}(\mathbf{z})$ is built by summing the sixteen leakages $\mathcal{L}(\mathbf{z}[i])$, with $i \in [1..16]$. Theoretically, summing the sixteen intermediate Hamming weight values gives us exactly the Hamming weight value of the multiplication result. And summing the sixteen noise of standard deviation σ_8 results in a Gaussian noise of standard deviation $\sigma_{128} = 4 \cdot \sigma_8$. In practice, we get an SNR of 8.21 on the 128-bit simulated leakage. In Table 4 we provide the experimental bounds λ_{exp} and error probabilities p_{exp} corresponding to few levels

Table 4. Experimental and theoretical parameters corresponding to filtering proportion $F(\lambda)$ on the ATmega for 128-bit AES-GCM.

$\log_2(1/F(\lambda))$	SNR $= 8.21, \sigma = 0.0206$						
	14	12	10	8	6	4	2
λ_{exp}	4.37	3.96	3.49	3.05	2.54	1.97	1.22
p_{exp}	0.383	0.386	0.393	0.407	0.420	0.434	0.452
λ_{the}	4.27	3.90	3.51	3.08	2.59	2.00	1.24
p_{the}	0.381	0.390	0.399	0.409	0.421	0.435	0.453

of filtering. We also indicate the theoretical estimates λ_{the} and p_{the} obtained by applying Formulas (3.2) and (3.2) to the template we obtained using the same set of traces. As it can be observed, the theoretical estimates are very close to the ones obtained experimentally (which validates our theoretical analysis, even for non Hamming weight model)[5].

Virtex 5 (128-bit). We additionally performed filtering on the traces from [BFG14] obtained from an FPGA implementation of GCM. Hereafter we provide theoretical (p_{the}) and experimental (p_{exp}) error probabilities for different values of the filtering parameter λ (Table 5). It must be noticed that experimental results correspond to expectations. The largest deviation (for $\lambda = 3.847$) is due to the fact that only 20 traces were kept after filtering[6].

Table 5. Error probabilities obtained from real traces.

λ	0.906	1.270	1.645	2.022	2.409	2.794	3.165	3.847
p_{the}	0.442	0.431	0.419	0.407	0.395	0.382	0.369	0.357
p_{exp}	0.441	0.430	0.418	0.405	0.392	0.379	0.370	0.361

ATMega328p (96-bit). As in the 128-bit case, the 96-bit leakage is simulated by summing the twelve intermediate 8-bit leakage of the multiplication result. Table 6 gives the bounds q and the error probabilities p corresponding to some levels of filtering[7].

---

[5] It must be noticed that a SNR equal to 8.21 in our experiments (with a noise standard deviation 0.0206) corresponds to a noise with standard deviation $\sigma = \sqrt{32/8.21} = 1.97$ in the theoretical Hamming weight model over 128-bit data.

[6] It must be noticed that, surprisingly, we also obtained an SNR equal to 8.21 in FPGA experiments but corresponding to a noise standard deviation of 7.11.

[7] An SNR equal to 8.7073 in our experiments (with a noise standard deviation 0.0173) corresponds to a noise with standard deviation $\sqrt{24/8.7073} = 1.66$ in the theoretical Hamming weight model over 96-bit data.

Table 6. Experimental and theoretical parameters corresponding to filtering proportion $F(\lambda)$ on the ATmega for 96-bit AES-GCM

SNR = 8.7073, σ = 0.0173						
$\log_2(1/F(\lambda))$	12	10	8	6	4	2
$\lambda_{\exp}$	4.27	3.80	3.29	2.76	2.14	1.31
$p_{\exp}$	0.377	0.387	0.402	0.414	0.429	0.449

LPN Experiments.

Attack on Simulated Traces (96-bit). We successfully performed our new attack on AES-GCM for a block-size reduced to 96 bits. We generated a 96-bit key **k**, then generated 2^{20} uniform random $\mathbf{a}_i$. We simulated a leakage corresponding to the one obtained on the ATMega328p (*i.e.*, with the same statistics) and chose λ equal to 3.80 (filtering with probability 2^{-10}, error probability 0.387). This kept 916 relations, the less noisy one having weight 25 (error rate 0.260). We used this relation for secret/error switch. All in all, we got 87840 $\approx 2^{16,42}$ LPN equations. After 6 hours of parallelized generalized birthday computation (32 cores, 200 GB of RAM), we got $\approx 2^{39}$ equations reduced down to 36 bits. After a 36-bit Walsh transform ($\approx$ 2000 seconds, same machine), we recovered the 36 least significant bits of the error that we converted in 36 bits of the secret. This heavy computation corresponds to the most complex part of the attack and validates its success. We can afterwards find the remaining bits by iterating the attack with the knowledge of the recovered bits. This is a matter of minutes: it corresponds to an attack on a 60-bit key, which is much less expensive than the 96-bit case.

Expected Attack Complexities (128-bit). We provide here theoretical complexities for the key-recovery attack on 128-bit secret key. Experiments have been performed on 96-bit secrets and presented in the previous paragraph which confirm the accuracy of our theoretical estimates. We can see in Fig. 2 the evolution of the time complexity as a function of the memory available for the attack. Plots are provided for three different data complexities. We notice that the time/memory trade-off is only exploitable up to one point. This is due to the fact that when lots of memory is available, one may perform a larger Walsh-Hadamard transform to obtain more reduced equations. At some point, the time complexity of this transform will be predominant compared to the birthday paradox step and thus there will be no gain in increasing the Walsh size. A relevant time/memory trade-off for 2^{20} acquisitions is a time complexity of $2^{51.68}$ for 2^{36} bytes in memory (servers with such amount of memory can be bought easily).

6.3 Attack on Fresh Re-Keying

We detail here the attack that aims at recovering the master key from the leakages corresponding to the first round of the AES when the secret key is generated

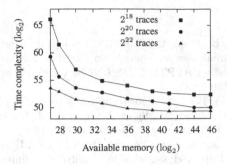

Fig. 2. Estimated complexities of the 128-bit attack (SNR = 8.21).

by the fresh re-keying primitive described in Sect. 5. We present the known-input version of the attack, the chosen-input attack is described in [BCF+15].

Leakage Acquisition. We randomly generated 15,000 vectors $\mathbf{a} \in \mathsf{GF}(2)^{128}$ and 15,000 vectors $\mathbf{b} \in \mathsf{GF}(2)^8$. We then measured the 8-bit leakage during the processing of $\mathsf{Sbox}(\mathbf{z}[0] \oplus \mathbf{b})$ with $\mathbf{z}[0]$ the first byte of the multiplication between $\mathbf{a}$ and $\mathbf{k}$.

Filtering. We filtered the extreme consumption measurements in order to exhibit the extreme Hamming weight values. Table 7 gives the empirical error probabilities according to the proportion of filtering on the 15,000 observations. As explained in Sect. 5, the error probabilities are naturally much lower than for a 128-bit leakage.

Table 7. Error probability p according to the proportion of filtered acquisitions $F(\lambda)$ on the ATMega328p for the fresh re-keying with known inputs

$\log_2(1/F(\lambda))$	9	8	7	6	5	4	3	2	1
SNR = 8.6921, $\sigma = 0.0165$									
λ		0.555	0.514	0.473	0.432	0.391	0.349	0.288	0.226	0.123
p		0.0	0.013	0.056	0.089	0.11	0.15	0.18	0.22	0.29

Key Recovery. With a sufficient (but still reasonable) filtering, we can directly recover the key by inverting the linear system of equations. For instance, in our experiments, filtering one observation over 2^9 gives $33 \times 8 = 264$ linear equations on the bits of $\mathbf{k}$ without a single error. Thus, inverting the system directly gives us the correct key.

References

[ACPS09] Applebaum, B., Cash, D., Peikert, C., Sahai, A.: Fast cryptographic primitives and circular-secure encryption based on hard learning problems. In: Halevi, S. (ed.) CRYPTO 2009. LNCS, vol. 5677, pp. 595–618. Springer, Heidelberg (2009)

[AG11] Arora, S., Ge, R.: New algorithms for learning in presence of errors. In: Aceto, L., Henzinger, M., Sgall, J. (eds.) ICALP 2011, Part I. LNCS, vol. 6755, pp. 403–415. Springer, Heidelberg (2011)

[BCF+15] Belaïd, S., Coron, J.-S., Fouque, P.-A., Gérard, B., Kammerer, J.-G., Prouff, E.: Improved side-channel analysis of finite-field multiplication. Cryptology ePrint Archive, Report 2015/542, (2015). http://eprint.iacr.org/

[BFG14] Belaïd, S., Fouque, P.-A., Gérard, B.: Side-Channel analysis of multiplications in GF(2128). In: Sarkar, P., Iwata, T. (eds.) ASIACRYPT 2014, Part II. LNCS, vol. 8874, pp. 306–325. Springer, Heidelberg (2014)

[BKW00] Blum, A., Kalai, A., Wasserman, H.: Noise-tolerant learning, the parity problem, and the statistical query model. In: 32nd ACM STOC, pp. 435–440. ACM Press, May 2000

[BTV15] Bogos, S., Tramer, F., Vaudenay, S.: On solving LPN using BKW and variants. Cryptology ePrint Archive, Report 2015/049, (2015). http://eprint.iacr.org/2015/049

[CGP+12] Carlet, C., Goubin, L., Prouff, E., Quisquater, M., Rivain, M.: Higher-Order masking schemes for S-boxes. In: Canteaut, A. (ed.) FSE 2012. LNCS, vol. 7549, pp. 366–384. Springer, Heidelberg (2012)

[CJRT05] Chekuri, C., Jansen, Rolim, K., J.D.P., Trevisan, L. (eds.) Approximation, randomization and combinatorial optimization, algorithms and techniques. In: 8th International Workshop on Approximation Algorithms for Combinatorial Optimization Problems, APPROX 2005 and 9th International Workshop on Randomization and Computation, RANDOM 2005, Berkeley, CA, USA, August 22–24, 2005, Proceedings, vol. 3624 of Lecture Notes in Computer Science. Springer, Heidelberg (2005)

[DDP13] Dabosville, G., Doget, J., Prouff, E.: A new second-order side channel attack based on linear regression. IEEE Trans. Comput. **62**(8), 1629–1640 (2013)

[GJJR11] Goodwill, G., Jun, B., Jaffe, J., Rohatgi, P.: A testing methodology for side-channel resistance validation. In: Workshop NIAT (2011)

[GJL14] Guo, Q., Johansson, T., Löndahl, C.: Solving LPN using covering codes. In: Sarkar, P., Iwata, T. (eds.) ASIACRYPT 2014. LNCS, vol. 8873, pp. 1–20. Springer, Heidelberg (2014)

[HGJ10] Howgrave-Graham, N., Joux, A.: New generic algorithms for hard knapsacks. In: Gilbert, H. (ed.) EUROCRYPT 2010. LNCS, vol. 6110, pp. 235–256. Springer, Heidelberg (2010)

[ISW03] Ishai, Y., Sahai, A., Wagner, D.: Private circuits: securing hardware against probing attacks. In: Boneh, D. (ed.) CRYPTO 2003. LNCS, vol. 2729, pp. 463–481. Springer, Heidelberg (2003)

[Kir11] Kirchner, P.: Improved generalized birthday attack. Cryptology ePrint Archive, Report 2011/377, (2011). http://eprint.iacr.org/2011/377

[LF06] Levieil, É., Fouque, P.-A.: An improved LPN algorithm. In: De Prisco, R., Yung, M. (eds.) SCN 2006. LNCS, vol. 4116, pp. 348–359. Springer, Heidelberg (2006)

[Lyu05] Lyubashevsky, V.: The parity problem in the presence of noise, decoding random linear codes, and the subset sum problem. In: Chekuri et al. (eds.) [CJRT05], pp. 378–389 (2005)

[MSGR10] Medwed, M., Standaert, F.-X., Großschädl, J., Regazzoni, F.: Fresh rekeying: security against side-channel and fault attacks for low-cost devices. In: Bernstein, D.J., Lange, T. (eds.) AFRICACRYPT 2010. LNCS, vol. 6055, pp. 279–296. Springer, Heidelberg (2010)

[MSJ12] Medwed, M., Standaert, F.-X., Joux, A.: Towards super-exponential side-channel security with efficient leakage-resilient PRFs. In: Prouff, E., Schaumont, P. (eds.) CHES 2012. LNCS, vol. 7428, pp. 193–212. Springer, Heidelberg (2012)

[OC14] O'Flynn, C., Chen, Z.: Chipwhisperer: an open-source platform for hardware embedded security research. Cryptology ePrint Archive, Report 2014/204 (2014). http://eprint.iacr.org/

[Pie12] Pietrzak, K.: Cryptography from learning parity with noise. In: Bieliková, M., Friedrich, G., Gottlob, G., Katzenbeisser, S., Turán, G. (eds.) SOFSEM 2012. LNCS, vol. 7147, pp. 99–114. Springer, Heidelberg (2012)

[RKSF11] Renauld, M., Kamel, D., Standaert, F.-X., Flandre, D.: Information theoretic and security analysis of a 65-nanometer DDSLL AES S-Box. In: Preneel, B., Takagi, T. (eds.) CHES 2011. LNCS, vol. 6917, pp. 223–239. Springer, Heidelberg (2011)

[SLP05] Schindler, W., Lemke, K., Paar, C.: A Stochastic Model for Differential Side Channel Cryptanalysis. In: Rao, J.R., Sunar, B. (eds.) CHES 2005. LNCS, vol. 3659, pp. 30–46. Springer, Heidelberg (2005)

[SS79] Schrocppel, R., Shamir, A.: A T $s^2 = o(2^n)$ time/space tradeoff for certain np-complete problems. In: 20th Annual Symposium on Foundations of Computer Science, pp. 328–336. IEEE Computer Society, San Juan, Puerto Rico, 29–31 October (1979)

[Wag02] Wagner, D.: A generalized birthday problem. In: Yung, M. (ed.) CRYPTO 2002. LNCS, vol. 2442, pp. 288–303. Springer, Heidelberg (2002)

Evaluation and Improvement
of Generic-Emulating DPA Attacks

Weijia Wang[1]([✉]), Yu Yu[1]([✉]), Junrong Liu[1,2], Zheng Guo[1,2],
François-Xavier Standaert[3]([✉]), Dawu Gu[1], Sen Xu[1], and Rong Fu[4]

[1] School of Electronic Information and Electrical Engineering,
Shanghai Jiao Tong University, Shanghai, China
{aawwjaa,yyuu,liujr,guozheng,dwgu,xusen0328}@sjtu.edu.cn
[2] Shanghai Viewsource Information Science and Technology Co., Ltd,
Shanghai, China
[3] ICTEAM/ELEN/Crypto Group, Université catholique de Louvain,
Louvain-la-Neuve, Belgium
fstandae@uclouvain.be
[4] Institute for Interdisciplinary Information Sciences,
Tsinghua University, Beijing, China

Abstract. At CT-RSA 2014, Whitnall, Oswald and Standaert gave the impossibility result that no generic DPA strategies (i.e., without any *a priori* knowledge about the leakage characteristics) can recover secret information from a physical device by considering an injective target function (e.g., AES and PRESENT S-boxes), and as a remedy, they proposed a slightly relaxed strategy "generic-emulating DPAs" free from the non-injectivity constraint. However, as we show in this paper, the only generic-emulating DPA proposed in their work, namely the SLR-based DPA, suffers from two drawbacks: unstable outcomes in the high-noise regime (i.e., for a small number of traces) and poor performance especially on real smart cards (compared with traditional DPAs with a specific power model). In order to solve these problems, we introduce two new generic-emulating distinguishers, based on lasso and ridge regression strategies respectively, with more stable and better performances than the SLR-based one. Further, we introduce the cross-validation technique that improves the generic-emulating DPAs in general and might be of independent interest. Finally, we compare the performances of all aforementioned generic-emulating distinguishers (both with and without cross-validation) in simulated leakages functions of different degrees, and on an AES ASIC implementation. Our experimental results show that our generic-emulating distinguishers are stable and some of them behave even better than (resp., almost the same as) the best Difference-of-Means distinguishers in simulated leakages (resp., on a real implementation), and thus make themselves good alternatives to traditional DPAs.

1 Introduction

Since the introduction of differential power analysis (DPA) by Kocher et al. [9], the CHES community has been focusing on efficient key recovery techniques

© International Association for Cryptologic Research 2015
T. Güneysu and H. Handschuh (Eds.): CHES 2015, LNCS 9293, pp. 416–432, 2015.
DOI: 10.1007/978-3-662-48324-4_21

by exploiting the physical information (typically the power consumption) captured from the implementation of a (leaking) cryptographic device, resulting in a rich body of literature on power analysis (see, e.g., [1,2,4,7,11,13,15] for an incomplete list). In this paper, we mainly consider non-profiled[1] power analysis techniques. We mention that some non-profiled attacks such as correlation power analysis (CPA) [2] and differential cluster analysis (DCA) [1] make some reasonable device-specific assumption about the power models. However, with the development of chip industry towards smaller technologies, the impact of power variability is becoming more and more significant, which makes common power models (e.g., Hamming weight, bit leakage) much less respected in practice (especially when reaching nanoscale devices) [10].

More recently, various non-profiled strategies such as mutual information analysis (MIA) using an identity power model [7], Kolmogorov-Smirnov (KS) method [13], Cramér-von Mises test method [13], linear regression[2] (LR)-based method [11] and copulas methods [14] were proposed. All these attacks enable to work in a context where no *a priori* knowledge is assumed about the power model, and DPAs of this form were termed as "generic DPAs" in [16]. The authors of [16] showed an impossibility result that all generic DPAs fail to work when applied to an injective target function. Fortunately, they observed that a slight relaxation of the generic condition (with the incorporation of some minimal "non-device-specific intuition") allows to bypass the impossibility result, for which they coined the name "generic-emulating DPAs". They further exemplified this by relaxing LR-based DPA (as a generic DPA) to stepwise linear regression (SLR)-based DPA (as a generic-emulating DPA) and demonstrated its effectiveness for injective target functions in simulation-based experiments.

However, despite the effectiveness on injective target functions, SLR-based DPA suffer from two drawbacks. First, it tends to be unstable for a small number of traces, reflecting a high variance of the outcomes (and thus lower success rates), which is illustrated in Sect. 5.1. Second, there is still a performance gap between SLR-based DPA and traditional one (e.g., CPA or DPA with the bit model), especially on real smart cards (which were not analyzed in [16]). In this paper, we address the above issues and make the following contributions.

First, we introduce in Sect. 3 two alternative generic-emulating distinguishers named lasso-based and ridge-based ones. We show that the new distinguishers enjoy a more stable and better performance than SLR-based ones (see Fig. 4). Intuitively, our improvement benefits from the fact that our distinguishers use a more continuous way to shrink the parameters than SLR-based ones (see Sect. 5.1 for a discussion).

---

[1] In contrast, a profiled power analysis (such as template attacks [4] and stochastic attacks [15]) takes advantage of an offline learning phase to gain additional information about an identical device (using a known key), which is not always practical.

[2] Unless otherwise specified, an LR-based distinguisher refers to one that uses a full basis of polynomial terms to construct the power model, and we often omit the term "with a full basis" for succinctness. We refer to Sect. 2.3 for a formal definition.

Second, we exploit in Sect. 4 a technique from statistical learning called 'cross-validation' that might be of independent interest (used in the context of profiled DPA in [5]), and show in Sect. 5 that it can be combined with generic-emulating DPAs to improve the performance in general.

Finally, for a comprehensive comparison, we illustrate in Sect. 5 the performances of SLR-based DPA, ridge-based DPA and lasso-based DPA in various settings, e.g., with and without cross-validation, against leakage function of different degrees and on a real smart card. Some of our attacks outperform the best Difference-of-means (DoM) attack[3] in simulation-based experiments and achieve almost the same performance as best DoM attack on real smart cards. Therefore, our results improve the work of [16] and can be considered as taking one concrete step forward towards making generic-emulating DPA practical.

2   Background

2.1   Differential Power Analysis

Following the 'divide-and-conquer' strategy, a DPA attack breaks down a secret key into a number of subkeys of small length and recovers them independently. Let X be a vector of some (partial) plaintext in consideration, i.e., $X = (X_i)_{i \in \{1,...,N\}}$, where N is the number of measurements and X_i corresponds to the (partial) plaintext of i-th measurement. Let k be a hypothesis subkey, let $F_k : \mathbb{F}_2^m \to \mathbb{F}_2^m$ be a target function, where m is the bit length of X_i, and thus the intermediate value $Z_{i,k} = F_k(X_i)$ is called a target and $Z_k = F_k(X) = (Z_{i,k})_{i \in \{1,...,N\}}$ is the target vector obtained by applying F_k to X component-wise.

Let $L : \mathbb{F}_2^m \to \mathbb{R}$ be the leakage function and let T be a vector of power consumptions. We have $T_i = L \circ Z_{i,k^*} + \varepsilon$ and $T = L \circ Z_{k^*} + \varepsilon$, where $\circ$ denotes function composition, k^* is the correct subkey key and ε denotes probabilistic noise. A trace t_i is the combination of power consumption T_i and plaintext X_i, i.e., $t_i = (T_i, X_i)$. Let the function $M : \mathbb{F}_2^m \to \mathbb{R}$ be the power model that approximates the leakage function L, namely, $T \approx M \circ F_{k^*}(X)$, where the noise information is also included in the power model.

In this paper, we assume that $F_k(\cdot)$ is an injective function (e.g., the AES S-Box). With the above definitions and notation, we can describe DPA as follows:

1. Make a subkey guess k and compute the corresponding target value $F_k(X_i)$.
2. Estimate the power consumptions of $F_k(X)$ with the power model $M(\cdot)$, i.e., $M(F_k(X))$.
3. Compute the correlation between the hypothetical $M(F_k(X))$ and the real trace T. The correlation should be highest upon correct key guess (which can be decided after repeating the above for all possible subkey guesses).

---

[3] Difference-of-means attack is a form of DPA that exploits the leakage of a single bit. It is generally seen as the 'best' attack strategy without a *prior* knowledge about the power model. The best DoM attack refers to the DoM attack in the best scenario, i.e., assuming additional knowledge about which target bit to exploit to achieve the highest correlation (among all possible target bits).

2.2   Generic DPA and its limitations

The generic DPA is defined in [16] with the definitions below:

Definition 1 (Generic Power Model). *The generic power model associated with key hypothesis k is the nominal mapping to the equivalence classes induced by the key-hypothesised target function $F_k(\cdot)$.*

Definition 2 (Generic   Compatibility). *A   distinguisher   is   generic-compatible if it is built from a statistic with operate on a nominal scale measurements.*

Definition 3 (Generic DPA). *A generic DPA strategy performs a standard univariate DPA attack using the generic power model paired with a generic-compatible distinguisher.*

Unfortunately, as shown in [16], no efficient generic DPA strategy is able to distinguish the correct subkey k^* from an incorrect hypothetical value k give that F_{k^*} and F_k are both injective. We refer to [16] for the details and proofs.

2.3   From LR-based DPA to Generic-Emulating DPA

As stated in [16] and [3], any leakage function L on input $z \in \mathbb{F}_2^m$ can be represented in the form of $L(z) = \sum_{u \in \mathbb{F}_2^m} \alpha_u z^u$ with coefficients $\alpha_u \in \mathbb{R}$, where $z = Z_{i,k^*}$, z^u denotes monomial $\prod_{j=1}^{m} z_j^{u_j}$, and z_j (resp., u_j) refers to the jth bit of z (resp., u). Therefore, for each subkey hypothesis k, we use a full basis of polynomial terms to construct the power model: $M_k(Z_{i,k}) = \alpha_0 + \sum_{u \subset \mathbb{U}} \alpha_u Z_{i,k}^u$, where $\mathbb{U} = \mathbb{F}_2^m \setminus \{0\}$. The degree of the power model is the highest degree of the non-zero terms in polynomial $M_k(Z_{i,k})$. We denote $\boldsymbol{\alpha} = (\alpha_u)_{u \in \mathbb{U}}$ as the vector of coefficients, which is estimated from $\boldsymbol{U}_k = (Z_{i,k}^u)_{i \in \{1,2,...,N\}, u \in \mathbb{U}}$ and T using ordinary least squares, i.e., $\boldsymbol{\alpha} = (\boldsymbol{U}_k^\mathsf{T} \boldsymbol{U}_k)^{-1} \boldsymbol{U}_k^\mathsf{T} T$, where $(Z_{i,k}^u)_{i \in \{1,2,...,N\}, u \in \mathbb{U}}$ is a matrix with (i,u) being row and column indices respectively, and $\boldsymbol{U}_k^\mathsf{T}$ is the transposition of $\boldsymbol{U}_k$. Finally, the goodness-of-fit (denoted as R^2), as a measurement of similarity between $M_k(Z_k)$ and the real power consumption T, can be computed for each M_k which separates the correct key hypothesis from incorrect ones[4]. This method, called Linear Regression-based DPA (LR-based DPA) with a full basis, falls into a special form of generic DPA, and thus it doesn't distinguish correct sub-keys from incorrect ones on injective target functions (see [16]).

To address the issue, generic-emulating DPA additionally exploits the characteristics of power models in practice (by losing a bit of generality) and it makes *a priori* constrain on $\boldsymbol{\alpha}$. As observed in [16], the coefficient vector $\boldsymbol{\alpha}$ is typically sparse for a realistic power model (under correct sub-key). Therefore, SLR-based DPA, as a generic-emulating DPA, starts from a power model with a full basis

---

[4] We use Pearson's coefficient to measure the goodness-of-fit in this paper, i.e., $R^2 = \rho(T, M_k(Z_k))$, where ρ is the Pearson's coefficient.

$U = \mathbb{F}_2^m \setminus \{0\}$ and excludes some 'insignificant' terms while keeping all the 'significant' ones in the basis. Then, it measures the goodness-of-fit R^2 to separate the correct sub-key from incorrect ones. Formally,

$$\hat{\alpha}^{SLR} \stackrel{\text{def}}{=} \underset{\alpha}{\text{argmin}} \sum_{i=1}^{N} (T_i - M_k(Z_{i,k}))^2,$$

$$\text{subject to} \sum_{u \in U} |\text{sign}(\alpha_u)| \leq s, \tag{1}$$

where the absolute value of signum function $|\text{sign}(\alpha_u)| = 0$ if $\alpha_u = 0$, and otherwise (i.e., $\alpha_u \neq 0$) $|\text{sign}(\alpha_u)| = 1$.

It should be noted that Eq. (1) and the description of SLR-based DPA in [16] are equivalent. The former one follows the definition of stepwise regression in [6], and the latter one more focuses on the algorithmic aspects of SLR-based DPA, and the parameter s come from the p-values in [16].

However, as we will show in Sect. 5.1, SLR-based DPA suffers from two drawbacks: (1) it is not stable for small number of traces; (2) in comparison with traditional DPA, SLR-based DPA has poor performance especially on real implementations. In next sections, we present two alternative generic-emulating distinguishers with more stable and improved performances, as well as a strategy called 'cross-validation' that might be of independent interest.

3   Alternative Generic-Emulating Distinguishers

In this section, we present two new generic-emulating distinguishers: the ridge-based and lasso-based distinguishers. For consistency with [16], we use the same power model as SLR-based DPA, i.e., $M_k(Z_{i,k}) = \alpha_0 + \sum_{u \in U} \alpha_u Z_{i,k}^u$. It should be noted that (in our terminology) generic-emulating DPAs and generic-emulating distinguishers are not exactly the same, the latter one output the coefficients while the former output key k^* (as its best guess) and the corresponding R^2.

3.1   Ridge-Based Distinguisher

Ridge-based distinguisher shrinks coefficients α_u by explicitly imposing an overall constraint on their size [8]:

$$\hat{\alpha}^{ridge} \stackrel{\text{def}}{=} \underset{\alpha}{\text{argmin}} \sum_{i=1}^{N} \left(T_i - M_k(Z_{i,k}) \right)^2,$$

$$\text{subject to} \sum_{u \in U} \alpha_u^2 \leq s. \tag{2}$$

An equivalent formulation to the above is

$$\hat{\alpha}^{ridge} = \underset{\alpha}{\text{argmin}} \left(\sum_{i=1}^{N} (T_i - M_k(Z_{i,k}))^2 + \lambda \sum_{u \in U} \alpha_u^2 \right), \tag{3}$$

whose optimal solution is given by:

$$\hat{\alpha}^{ridge} = (U_k^\mathsf{T} U_k + \lambda I)^{-1} U_k^\mathsf{T} T, \tag{4}$$

where matrix I is the $|\mathbb{U}| \times |\mathbb{U}|$ identity matrix, $|\mathbb{U}|$ denotes the cardinality of $\mathbb{U}$ and U_k is defined in Sect. 2.3.

How the Coefficients Shrink in the Ridge-Based Distinguisher?. As described in Sect. 3.1, the ridge-based distinguisher enforces a general constraint $\sum_{u \in \mathbb{U}} \alpha_u^2 < s$ on the coefficients of M_k, but it is not clear how each individual coefficient α_u shrinks (e.g., which coefficient shrinks more than the others). We show an interesting connection between the degree of a term $Z_{i,k}^u$ in M_k (i.e., the Hamming Weight of u) and the amount of shrinkage of its coefficient α_u.

First, we use a technical tool from "principal component analysis" (see, e.g., [8]). Informally, the principal components of U_k are a set of linearly independent vectors obtained by applying an orthogonal transformation to U_k, i.e., $P = U_k V$, where the columns of matrix P are called the principal components, and the columns of matrix V are called directions of the (respective) principal components. An interesting property is that columns of P, denoted by $P_1, \ldots, P_{2^m-1}$, have descending variances (i.e., P_1 has the greatest variance). Among the columns of V, the first one, denoted V_1 (the direction of P_1), has the maximal correlation to coefficient vector α. We refer to [8] for further discussions and proofs.

Then, we further study the correlation between V_1 and α, both seen as a vector of $2^m - 1$ components indexed by u. Figures 1 and 2 depict the direction of the first principle component V_1 and the degrees of terms in U_k respectively, and they represent a high similarity (albeit in a converse manner). Quantitatively, the Pearson's coefficient between V_1 and the corresponding vector of degrees is -0.9704, which is a nearly perfect negative correlation.

Finally, given that V_1 is positively correlated to $\alpha = (\alpha_u)_{u \in \mathbb{U}}$ while negatively correlated to their term degrees, we establish the connection that α_u is conversely proportional to the Hamming weight of u. In other words, the more Hamming weight that u has, the less α_u contributes to the power model. Therefore, ridge-based distinguisher is consistent with low-degree power models (e.g., the Hamming weight and bit models) in practice.

3.2 Lasso-Based Distinguisher

The lasso-based distinguisher is similar to the ridge-based one excepted for a different constraint on the parameters [8]:

$$\hat{\alpha}^{lasso} \stackrel{\text{def}}{=} \underset{\alpha}{\arg\min} \sum_{i=1}^{N} \left(T_i - M_k(Z_{i,k}) \right)^2, \tag{5}$$

$$\text{subject to} \sum_{u \in \mathbb{U}} |\alpha_u| \leq s. \tag{6}$$

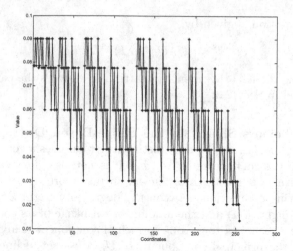

Fig. 1. An illustration of V_1 (the direction of the first principal component of $\boldsymbol{U}_k$).

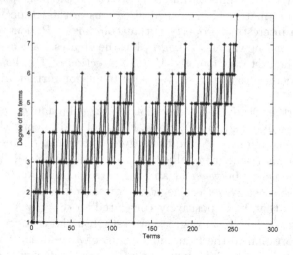

Fig. 2. An illustration of the degrees of the terms in $\boldsymbol{U}_k$.

A subtle but important difference between lasso-based and ridge-based regressions is their ways of shrinking the coefficients. By choosing a sufficiently small s, lasso-based distinguisher will have some of its coefficients exactly stuck to zero and in contrast, the ridge-based distinguisher will only shrink the coefficients (with the amounts of shrinkage conversely proportional to the degrees of terms). Thus, we can consider the lasso-based distinguisher as a tool inbetween SLR-based and ridge-based distinguishers.

Finding the optimal solution for lasso-based distinguishers is essentially a quadratic programming problem. Fortunately, there are known efficient algorithms and we use the "Least Angle Regression" algorithm for this purpose [6] (see Appendix A for full details).

4   Generic-Emulating DPAs with Cross-Validation

In this section, we combine generic-emulating DPA with the K-fold[5] cross-validation technique from statistical learning. We mention that cross-validation was already used for evaluation of side-channel security in the profiled setting [5]. Algorithm 1 shows how to combine generic-emulating DPA with cross-validation.

Algorithm 1. Generic-emulating DPA with cross-validation

Require: traces $t_i = \{T_i, x_i\}$ where $i \in \{1, ..., N\}$; the number of parts K ; target function $F_k(\cdot)$;
Ensure: $\hat{k}$ as the best guess for the subkey;
1: **for** $i = 1$; $i <= N$; $i{+}{+}$ **do**
2:    $\mathcal{S}_{x_i} = t_i$
3: **end for**
4: **for** $i = 1$; $i <= K$; $i{+}{+}$ **do**
5:    $\mathcal{C}_i = \{\mathcal{S}_{K*(i-1)+1}, ..., \mathcal{S}_{K*i}\}$
6: **end for**
7: **for all** k such that $k \in F_n^2$ **do**
8:    **for** $i = 1$; $i <= K$; $i{+}{+}$ **do**
9:       Compute the α using the traces in $\mathcal{C}_j$, where $j \in \{1...K\} \setminus \{i\}$
10:       Calculate the goodness-of-fit R_i^2 from $\mathcal{C}_i$
11:    **end for**
12:    $R_k^2 = (\sum_{i=1}^{K} R_i^2)/K$
13: **end for**
14: $\hat{k} = \mathrm{argmax}_k R_k^2$

As sketched in Fig. 3, the algorithm follows the steps below:

First, we classify the traces into 2^m sets based on the values of the corresponding input, denoted as $\mathcal{S}_{\{0...2^m-1\}}$. Otherwise said, all traces in each set correspond to the same value of input (partial plaintext).

Then, we split $\mathcal{S}_{\{1...2^m\}}$ into K parts $\mathcal{C}_{\{1...K\}}$ of roughly equal size. For each part $\mathcal{C}_i$, we compute the coefficients α_i using the rest $K-1$ parts from the trace set, and calculate the goodness-of-fit R_i^2 using the traces in $\mathcal{C}_i$. We then get the average goodness-of-fit $R_k^2 = (\sum_{i=1}^{K} R_i^2)/K$ for the hypothetical subkey k in consideration. Finally, we return the subkey candidate with the highest averaged goodness-of-fit.

For example, let the target function be an AES S-box, let $K = 8$ and use the ridge regression-based distinguisher, and thus the traces are classified into $\mathcal{C}_{\{1...8\}}$, where $\mathcal{C}_1 = \{S_1, ..., S_{32}\}$, $\mathcal{C}_2 = \{S_{33}, ..., S_{64}\}$, ..., $\mathcal{C}_8 =$

---

[5] We shall not confuse K with k, where K is a parameter as in the "K-fold cross-validation" and k is a subkey hypothesis.

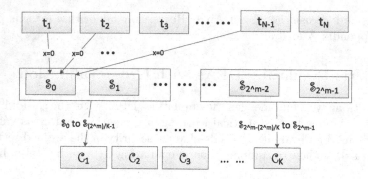

Fig. 3. Generic emulating DPA attack with cross-validation. The traces are divided into 2^m sets $\mathcal{S}_{\{0\ldots2^m-1\}}$, which are in turn categorized into K parts $\mathcal{C}_{\{1\ldots K\}}$ to mount cross-validation.

$\{\mathcal{S}_{225}, \ldots, \mathcal{S}_{256}\}$. For part $\mathcal{C}_1$, we first compute its coefficients $\boldsymbol{\alpha}$ using the traces from sets $\mathcal{S}_{33}, \mathcal{S}_{34}, \ldots, \mathcal{S}_{256}$, and then calculate the goodness-of-fit R^2 using sets $\mathcal{S}_1, \mathcal{S}_2 \ldots \mathcal{S}_{32}$, where k is a key hypothesis.

For a leakage function $L : \mathbb{F}_2^m \to \mathbb{R}$ with input space of size 2^m, the cross-validation technique can determine the coefficients $\boldsymbol{\alpha}$ from traces on only a portion of (rather than the whole) input space. As we will show in Sect. 5.1, the 'Non-Device-Specific' nature of cross-validation allows to relax the LR-based DPA from a generic DPA (with a full basis) to a generic-emulating one by learning the leakage function from a subset of the input space.

5   Experimental Results

In this section, we give experimental results based on both simulation-based environments and real smart cards. In the simulation-based experiments, we first show that SLR-based DPA tends to be unstable for small number of traces. Then, we give a comprehensive comparison between the performance of SLR-based DPA, ridge-based DPA and lasso-based DPA in various settings, e.g., with and without cross-validation, against power models of different degrees and on a real smart card. In particular, some of these attacks beat the best DoM attack (see Footnote 3) in simulation-based experiments and achieve almost the same performance as best DoM attack on real smart cards. This improves the work of [16], where the SLR-based DPA doesn't outperform best DoM attack in simulation-based experiments (and real implementations are not considered in [16]).

In both scenarios, we target the AES-128's first S-box of the first round with an 8-bit subkey (recall that AES-128's first round key is the same as its encryption key). Following [16], we do the following trace pre-processing to facilitate the evaluation: we average the traces based on their the input (an 8-bit plaintext) and use the resulting 256 mean power traces to mount the attack. Since the running time of generic-emulating DPA increases as the number of traces grows, it may become unbearable when we have hundreds of thousands of traces Therefore, it is reasonable to use a few mean power traces instead of a huge number of traces in both simulation-based and real attacks.

The parameters from different distinguishers, e.g., λ, s, and K from ridge-based, lasso-based distinguishers and cross-validation respectively, can also affect the success rate of the attacks. We will directly use the best values for these parameters, $\lambda = 800$, $s = 2$, $K = 7$, which were decided through searching over the space (up to some accuracy) in favor of best success rate. It should be though that the same parameters can be used in the various experimental settings (i.e., the variety of settings doesn't seem to affect the choice of the best parameters significantly).

5.1   Simulation-Based Experiments

SLR-based Distinguishers are Not Stable. By definition, the SLR-based distinguisher keeps only a subset of the terms from the basis. As a result, some 'insignificant' terms that still have some (although not much) contributions to the power model are discarded and it leads to instability of the results especially when the number of traces used in the attacks is small. Rephrased using the terminology of statistical learning, such a subset selection often leads to high variance of the outcomes due to the discretization process (see a discussion in [8]). In this context, the actual coefficients (corresponding to the correct key k^*) of the power model tend to be more evenly distributed since the noise is included in the power model, and the outcome of the SLR-based DPA (R^2 of the correct subkey) will be varying (dependent on which subset of the basis is selected) and thus leads to an unstable outcome with low success rate. In contrast, the ridge-based (and lasso-based) distinguishers only shrink the coefficients of the 'insignificant' terms rather than simply discarding them. In general, the shrinking techniques are continuous and do not suffer much from high variability [8], which makes these distinguishers good alternatives to the SLR-based one.

We use simulated-based experiments to illustrate the above issue. In the case of a fixed leakage function of degree 8 with SNR $= 0.1$, we use both SLR-based and ridge-based distinguishers to approximate the 255 coefficients of the power model with different trace sets and compute the corresponding variance (of the approximated coefficients). We then repeat this with different set sizes, which are depicted in Fig. 4. The variance of outcomes increases with the noise level[6] (i.e., the decrease of the number of traces), and for the same number of traces the ridge-based distinguisher has a much lower variance of its outcomes than the SLR-based one, and thus has a more stable performance.

---

[6] By "noise level" we refer to the overall amount of noise by combining all traces rather that the SNR of the measurement environment. In general, increasing the number of traces reduces the noise level, which can be seen by averaging the traces.

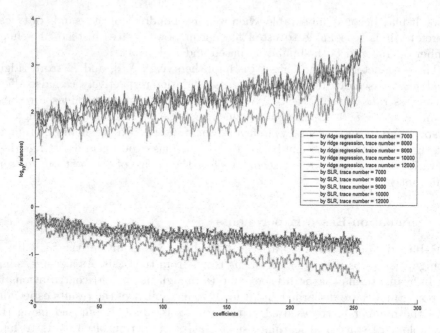

Fig. 4. Variances estimated of the estimated coefficients, for the ridge-based and SLR-based distinguishers, using different numbers of traces.

A Comparison of Various Attacks with Simulation-Based Experiments. Fig. 5 illustrates the (1st order[7]) success rates of all aforementioned DPAs on leakage functions of different degrees, in which we repeat each experiments 100 times (each time with a different random leakage function) to compute the success rates. In addition, we include the best DoM attack and known model DPA as baselines, where the former (resp., latter) is considered as the best traditional DPA attacks without any (resp., full) *a priori* knowledge about the power model. We have the following observations.

First, ridge-based DPA with cross-validation and lasso-based DPA have are among the best attacks in all settings (in particular they outperform the best DoM attacks, and are only less powerful than known power-model DPA). We attribute this to the intuition that generic-emulating DPAs are better suited for power models of moderate and high degrees than traditional DPA. Second, the new generic-emulating DPAs perform better than SLR-based one, which is consistent with the discussion in Sect. 5.1. Third and interestingly, cross-validation improves the performance of ridge-based DPA while it does not

---

[7] We shall not confuse the t-th order success rate with high order DPA. The t-th order success rate is a generalization of the ordinary success rate [12]. That is, the attack is considered as successful as long as the correct key is ranked among top t in the key candidate list produced by the distinguisher. Note that for t-th order success rate there remains a guessing entropy of $\log_2 t$.

Table 1. The running times for various attacks, where C-V stands for cross-validation.

SLR-based DPA	5.644 s
SLR-based DPA with C-V	26.011 s
Ridge-based DPA	4.290 s
Ridge-based DPA with C-V	16.930 s
Lasso-based DPA	3.308 s
Lasso-based DPA with C-V	3.140 s
Best DoM attack	0.363 s

(and may even worsen) SLR-based and lasso-based DPAs. (It also makes the LR-based DPA work even for injective target function). This fits the intuition that cross-validation cannot be a universal performance enhancer in a non-profiled setting (since its standard use is to avoid overfitting models in the profiled setting). However, experiments show that despite heuristic, its application in a non-profiled setting can be useful.

Finally, in order to fully exemplify the power of generic-emulating DPA, we also perform the attacks against some artificial leakage function, in which all low degree terms are discarded. More specifically, we consider the leakage function $L(z) = \sum_{u \in \mathcal{U}} \alpha_u z^u, \forall z \in \mathbb{F}_2^m$, where u is from $\mathbb{F}_2^m$ but excludes those whose Hamming weight is less than or equal to p. We simulate the traces for $p = 4, m = 8$ and show the success rates in Fig. 6. We can see that in this case, the best DoM attack behaves poorly and meanwhile the generic-emulating DPAs are not affected. Admittedly, this leakage case may be unrealistic, but it serves as a good example that generic-emulating DPAs can deal with a wider range of leakage function.

Table 1 below tabulates the running times of all attacks mentioned above (we use 256 averaged single-point traces so this running times also hold for the experiments on smart cards in the next section). We note that SLR-based and lasso-based distinguishers have the longest and shortest running time respectively. In general, cross-validation increases the running time for most (e.g., SLR-based and ridge-based) distinguishers except for the lasso-based one. This is due to that cross-validation actually only operates on a subset of the traces and thus makes the effective input length of the Least Angle Regression algorithm (used by the lasso-based distinguisher) shorter.

5.2 Experiments on Smart Cards

We carry out experiments on an AES microscale ASIC implementation, and measure the power consumptions using a LeCroy waverunner 610Zi digital oscilloscope at a sampling rate of 250 MHz.

The lefthand of Fig. 7 gives the success rates for all attacks discussed above on the real smart card. The experiment shows that cross-validation significantly improves the performance of generic-emulating DPAs on real smart cards.

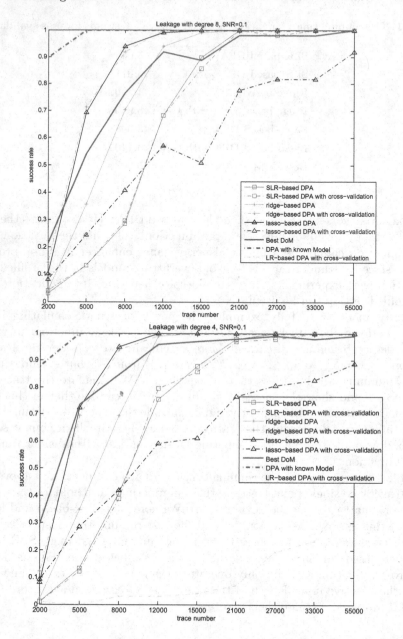

Fig. 5. The success rates of different attacks for different leakages and SNR = 0.1.

In addition, ridge-based DPA with cross-validation is the one with the closest performance to the best DoM DPA. Finally, unlike the simulation based case, the DPAs without cross-validation perform poorly and mostly do not work, and thus we conclude that cross-validation is a useful tool for generic-emulating DPAs

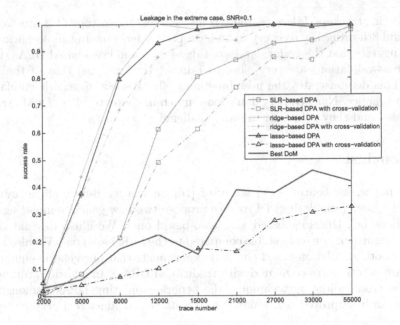

Fig. 6. The success rates of various attacks for an 'artificial' power model.

against real smart cards. As in the previous section, the exact reasons of this behavior are hard to explain due to their heuristic nature, but we can reasonably assume that it is mostly the less regular behavior of real measurements that make cross-validation more useful in this context.

The righthand of Fig. 7 gives the 8th-order success rates for all DPA attacks. This is for a better alignment with the DoM attack. That is, the best DoM attack assumes the knowledge of which target bit (out of 8 candidates) gives the highest correlation, but in practice there is a guessing entropy of $\log_2 8 = 3$ bits

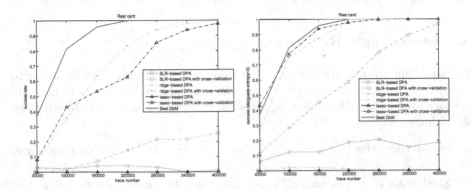

Fig. 7. The success rates of various attacks on a real AES ASIC implementation.

for realistic attackers. Likewise, there is also a guessing entropy of 3 bits from a successful 8th-order key recovery to an ideal (1st-order) one. In this scenario, the result suggests that the performances of ridge-based and lasso-based DPAs (both with cross-validation) are very close to (almost the same as) that of the best DoM. This demonstrates the usefulness and effectiveness of generic-emulating DPA in practice. Namely, they don't loose much in contexts where DoM attacks work best, and they gain a lot in more challenging scenarios.

6   Conclusion

In this paper, we continue the study of [16] on the feasibility, efficiency and limits of generic(-emulating) DPAs. We propose two new generic-emulating distinguishers, i.e., the ridge-based and lasso-based ones. We illustrate that these new distinguishers are more stable compared to the SLR-based one. We also show through both simulation-based and real experiments that our generic-emulating DPAs are practical (as compared with traditional DPAs). In addition, combined with the cross-validation technique, the generic-emulating DPAs demonstrate a significantly improved performance in our attacks against real cryptographic devices.

Acknowledgments. This research work was supported in parts by the National Basic Research Program of China (Grant 2013CB338004) and the European Commission through the ERC project 280141 (CRASH). Yu Yu was supported by the National Natural Science Foundation of China Grant (Nos. 61472249, 61103221). Zheng Guo was supported by the National Natural Science Foundation of China Grant (No. 61402286). F.-X. Standaert is a research associate of the Belgian Fund for Scientific Research (FNRS-F.R.S.). Dawu Gu was supported by the National Natural Science Foundation of China Grant (No. 61472250), the Doctoral Fund of Ministry of Education of China (No. 20120073110094), the Innovation Program by Shanghai Municipal Science and Technology Commission (No. 14511100300), and Special Fund Task for Enterprise Innovation Cooperation from Shanghai Municipal Commission of Economy and Informatization (No. CXY-2013-35).

A   Least Angle Regression

The algorithm to solve the lasso problem using least angle regression is similar to the SLR in [16]. But instead of including coefficients at each step, the coefficients are increased in their joint least squares direction (see below). We describe the algorithm as follows:

1. Standardize the terms $Z_k^u, \forall u \in \mathbb{U}$ to have zero mean and unit variance, where $Z_k^u = (Z_{i,k}^u)_{i \in \{1,2,\dots,N\}}$.
2. Start with $\dot{T} = T - mean(T)$, an empty set $\mathbb{A}$ and $\alpha_u = 0$ for all $u \in \mathbb{U}$ where $mean(T)$ is the mean of T.
3. Find u satisfying $u = \text{argmax}_u |(Z_k^u)^\mathsf{T} \dot{T}|$, and add u to set $\mathbb{A}$.

4. Increase all the coefficients α_j, in their joint least squares direction, i.e., the direction is: $((\boldsymbol{Z}_k^{\mathbb{A}})^{\mathsf{T}}\boldsymbol{Z}_k^{\mathbb{A}})^{-1}(\boldsymbol{Z}_k^{\mathbb{A}})^{\mathsf{T}}T$, where matrix $\boldsymbol{Z}_k^{\mathbb{A}} = (Z_{i,k}^u)_{i\in\{1,\dots,N\},u\in\mathbb{A}}$, where $j \in \mathbb{A}$, and take residuals $\dot{T} = T - \sum_{u\in\mathbb{A}} Z_k^u\alpha_u$ along the way until another $\bar{u}$ reaches $\mathrm{argmax}_{\bar{u}}|(Z_k^{\bar{u}})^{\mathsf{T}}\dot{T}|$. In the above process, whenever any coefficients α_l for $l \in \mathbb{A}$ reaches zero, remove l from $\mathbb{A}$. Add $\bar{u}$ to set $\mathbb{A}$.
5. Repeat items 3 and 4 until $\forall u : (Z_k^u)^{\mathsf{T}}\dot{T} = 0$ is satisfied.

References

1. Batina, L., Gierlichs, B., Lemke-Rust, K.: Differential cluster analysis. In: Clavier, C., Gaj, K. (eds.) CHES 2009. LNCS, vol. 5747, pp. 112–127. Springer, Heidelberg (2009)
2. Brier, E., Clavier, C., Olivier, F.: Correlation power analysis with a leakage model. In: Joye, M., Quisquater, J.-J. (eds.) CHES 2004. LNCS, vol. 3156, pp. 16–29. Springer, Heidelberg (2004)
3. Carlet, C.: Boolean functions for cryptography and error correcting codes. Boolean Model. Meth. Math. Comput. Sci. Eng. **2**, 257–397 (2010)
4. Chari, S., Rao, J.R., Rohatgi, P.: Template attacks. In: 4th International Workshop Cryptographic Hardware and Embedded Systems - CHES 2002, Redwood Shores, CA, USA, 13–15 August 2002, pp. 13–28, Revised Papers (2002)
5. Durvaux, F., Standaert, F.-X., Veyrat-Charvillon, N.: How to certify the leakage of a chip? In: Nguyen, P.Q., Oswald, E. (eds.) EUROCRYPT 2014. LNCS, vol. 8441, pp. 459–476. Springer, Heidelberg (2014)
6. Efron, B., Hastie, T., Johnstone, I., Tibshirani, R., et al.: Least angle regression. Ann. Stat. **32**(2), 407–499 (2004)
7. Gierlichs, B., Batina, L., Tuyls, P., Preneel, B.: Mutual information analysis. In: Oswald, E., Rohatgi, P. (eds.) CHES 2008. LNCS, vol. 5154, pp. 426–442. Springer, Heidelberg (2008)
8. Hastie, T., Tibshirani, R., Friedman, J.: The Elements of Statistical Learning: Data Mining, Inference, and Prediction, vol. 1, Second edn. Springer, New York (2009)
9. Kocher, P.C., Jaffe, J., Jun, B.: Differential power analysis. In: Wiener, M. (ed.) CRYPTO 1999. LNCS, vol. 1666, pp. 388–397. Springer, Heidelberg (1999)
10. Renauld, M., Standaert, F.-X., Veyrat-Charvillon, N., Kamel, D., Flandre, D.: A formal study of power variability issues and side-channel attacks for nanoscale devices. In: Paterson, K.G. (ed.) EUROCRYPT 2011. LNCS, vol. 6632, pp. 109–128. Springer, Heidelberg (2011)
11. Schindler, W., Lemke, K., Paar, C.: A stochastic model for differential side channel cryptanalysis. In: Rao, J.R., Sunar, B. (eds.) CHES 2005. LNCS, vol. 3659, pp. 30–46. Springer, Heidelberg (2005)
12. Standaert, F.-X., Malkin, T.G., Yung, M.: A unified framework for the analysis of side-channel key recovery attacks. In: Joux, A. (ed.) EUROCRYPT 2009. LNCS, vol. 5479, pp. 443–461. Springer, Heidelberg (2009)
13. Veyrat-Charvillon, N., Standaert, F.-X.: Mutual information analysis: how, when and why? In: Clavier, C., Gaj, K. (eds.) CHES 2009. LNCS, vol. 5747, pp. 429–443. Springer, Heidelberg (2009)
14. Veyrat-Charvillon, N., Standaert, F.-X.: Generic side-channel distinguishers: improvements and limitations. In: Rogaway, P. (ed.) CRYPTO 2011. LNCS, vol. 6841, pp. 354–372. Springer, Heidelberg (2011)

15. Whitnall, C., Oswald, E., Mather, L.: An exploration of the Kolmogorov-Smirnov test as a competitor to mutual information analysis. In: Prouff, E. (ed.) CARDIS 2011. LNCS, vol. 7079, pp. 234–251. Springer, Heidelberg (2011)
16. Whitnall, C., Oswald, E., Standaert, F.-X.: The myth of generic DPA..and the magic of learning. In: Benaloh, J. (ed.) CT-RSA 2014. LNCS, vol. 8366, pp. 183–205. Springer, Heidelberg (2014)

Transient-Steady Effect Attack on Block Ciphers

Yanting Ren[1,2], An Wang[1,2](✉), and Liji Wu[1,2](✉)

[1] Tsinghua National Laboratory for Information Science and Technology (TNList),
Beijing, China
[2] Institute of Microelectronics, Tsinghua University, Beijing, China
ryt10@mails.tsinghua.edu.cn
{wanganl,lijiwu}@mail.tsinghua.edu.cn

Abstract. A new Transient-Steady Effect attack on block ciphers called TSE attack is presented in this paper. The concept of transient-steady effect denotes the phenomenon that the output of a combinational circuit keeps a temporal value for a while before it finally switches to the correct value. Unlike most existing fault attacks, our attack does not need a large amount of encryptions to build a statistical model. By injecting a clock glitch to capture the temporal value caused by transient-steady effect, attackers can obtain the information of key from faulty outputs directly. This work shows that AES implementations, which have transient-steady property, are vulnerable to our attack. Experiments are successfully conducted on two kinds of unmasked S-boxes and one kind of masked S-box implemented in serial with FPGA board. After a moderate pre-computation, we need only 1 encryption to recover a key byte of the unmasked S-boxes, and 20 encryptions to recover a key byte of the masked S-box. Furthermore, we investigate the key recover method for parallel unmasked implementation, and discuss a possible attack scenario which may deem WDDL-AES insecure.

1 Introduction

Side-channel attacks have drawn much attention since being proposed by Kocher et al. [1]. Up to now, many attack methods have been introduced to analyze side-channel information leaked by cryptographic devices, such as correlation power analysis [2,3], template [4], collision [5,6], mutual information [7] and fault attack. Differential Fault Analysis (DFA) [8] is one of the most well-known *fault attacks*. In DFA attack, the ciphertext with fault injected during executing is called a faulty output. The key is recovered from correct outputs and corresponding faulty outputs based on a fault model.

In CHES 2010, Li et al. [9] proposed the Fault Sensitivity Analysis (FSA) based on the fact that the critical paths of some Advanced Encryption Standard (AES) S-box combinational circuits are data dependent. However, a large number of encryptions is needed in an FSA attack. The adversary has to encrypt every plaintext for many times and shorten the glitch cycle gradually, in order to obtain the critical frequency (the fault sensitivity) at which faulty outputs

© International Association for Cryptologic Research 2015
T. Güneysu and H. Handschuh (Eds.): CHES 2015, LNCS 9293, pp. 433–450, 2015.
DOI: 10.1007/978-3-662-48324-4_22

begin to appear. In 2011, Moradi et al. extended FSA to masked AES implementation by combining it with collision attack [10]. Their attack is carried out at a fixed glitch frequency, but it still requires a lot of encryptions to extract the distribution of faulty ciphertexts. In addition, as correlation-based methods, both of these attacks need to enumerate the values of the plaintext, which increase the total number of encryptions. In 2012, Li et al. presented the Clockwise Collision Fault Sensitivity Analysis (CC-FSA) attack on unmasked AES [11]. They pointed out: in an iterative AES implementation, if inputs of two consecutive cycles are identical, the setup time of the second cycle is extremely short, because there are almost no toggles in the combinational circuit. Soon after that, Wang et al. proposed an improved clockwise collision attack called Fault Rate Analysis (FRA) and broke a masked serial AES S-box implementation [12]. The two methods are carried out at fixed glitch frequency, but they both suffer from the inefficiency of detecting clockwise collisions, and need a large number of encryptions.

Our Contribution. In this paper, we propose a new fault attack based on Transient-Steady Effect (TSE attack). Transient-steady effect denotes the phenomenon that the output of a gate turns to a temporal value and keeps steady for a while before it switches to the final steady state. We analyze the circuits of several AES S-box implementations and find out that the path of the key is usually much shorter than other signals. Therefore, soon after the rising edge of the clock, the output turns to a value that is computed from the key in current clock cycle and other data in the last cycle. By injecting a clock glitch, we can capture the temporal value as a faulty output to recover the key. We propose several fault models based on the transient-steady effect and verify TSE attack on both unmasked and masked AES S-boxes. Our attack has the following features:

- In comparison to the existing works, TSE attack needs less encryptions in the attack stage. We only need to sweep the frequency of clock glitch for one time in the pre-computation stage. Then the attack stage can be conducted at a fixed frequency. Furthermore, the key can be recovered directly from faulty outputs, so we do not need a large amount of encryptions to build a statistical model.
- TSE attack is verified to be effective to a masked implementation of AES based on tower field. Other masking techniques with obvious transient-steady effect may also be insecure under this attack.
- TSE attack can break the protection strategy that changes the plaintext for every encryption, because correct outputs are not necessary.

Organization. We organize the rest part of this paper as follows. Related preliminaries are introduced in Sect. 2. The basic idea and attack scenarios are detailed in Sect. 3. We present experimental results and efficiency comparison in Sect. 4. Then we discuss about the application of our attack on parallel AES implementation and WDDL-AES in Sect. 5. Conclusions are given in Sect. 6.

2 Preliminaries

2.1 AES S-box and Masking

AES is a widely used symmetric cryptographic algorithm, which is composed of 10 rounds, and each round includes 16 S-boxes. When the area or the power consumption is limited, serial implementation of the algorithm is preferred. For example, a circuit with 4 S-boxes can accomplish one round in 4 cycles, and each S-box is reused for 4 times [13,14]. Many low-power and low-area S-boxes have been proposed. For example, Morioka et al. gave a low-power approach [15], and Canright proposed a low-area approach based on tower-field [16].

Masking is a regular countermeasure against power analysis. Mask values randomize sensitive intermediate values and minimize the dependency between data and power consumption. S-box is the only nonlinear operation in AES algorithm, and many masking schemes have been proposed for it, such as the approach based on tower-field [17].

As shown in Fig. 1, a standard masked S-box has one masked output and three inputs: the masked value x_m, the input mask m and the output mask w. We do not show the output mask as an output of S-box in Fig. 1, but it is also recorded for the next round.

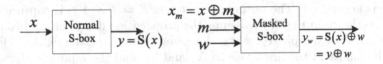

Fig. 1. Unmasked S-box (left) and masked S-box (right)

2.2 Fault-Based Clockwise Collision Analysis

CC-FSA attack was presented by Li et al. in 2012 [11]. The attack is based on the fact that if the inputs of a circuit do not change in two consecutive clock cycles, there will be almost no toggles in the second cycle. It is called a clockwise collision, and the setup time of the second clock cycle will be extremely short. They let the target circuit work normally in the first cycle, and insert a clock glitch to create a very short second cycle. If the output is correct, a clockwise collision will be detected.

3 Transient-Steady Effect Attack

In most standard logic designs, the lengths of data paths in combinational circuits are usually different. If we focus on a gate, we can see that after the rising edge of the clock, the inputs of the gate do not necessarily arrive simultaneously. For example, we can assume the path delay of signal a is shorter than that of signal b.

Hence, after the switch of a and before the arrival of b, the output turns to a transient illegal value. When the difference of the propagation delay between the two signals is large enough, the output stays at the illegal value for a while before all the propagations are done correctly. This is called the transient-steady effect. Related works have proved that transient-steady effect can lead to a data-dependent power consumption and leak the secret information *indirectly* [18–22]. However, in this paper we show that the temporal value caused by transient-steady effect can be captured and used to retrieve secret information *directly*.

Based on the transient-steady effect, we propose the TSE attack: We let the target circuit compute normally in the first cycle, and inject a clock glitch to create a very short second cycle. The normal output of the first clock cycle is computed from the short-path data and the long-path data in the first cycle. The faulty output of the second cycle is computed from the short-path data in the second cycle and the long-path data in the *first* cycle. By combining the outputs of the two consecutive clock cycles, we can recover information of the short-path data.

3.1 Basic Idea

Without loss of generality, we first look at a combinational circuit which computes the output with two inputs, e.g. X and Y. Their propagation delays are denoted as t_X and t_Y. The output, denoted as $Z = f(X, Y)$, is captured by a register. As shown in Fig. 2, we assume the propagation delays of the two inputs are different, for example, $t_Y \gg t_X$. Focusing on two specific clock cycles, we denote the inputs in the first cycle as X_1 and Y_1, and the inputs in the second cycle as X_2 and Y_2. After the rising edge of the second clock, the effects of X_2 and Y_2 begin to propagate along the two data paths, like two ripples with different speeds. After a period of time t ($t_Y > t > t_X$), X_2 has impacted all the gates in the circuit, but the ripple of Y_2 has not arrived at the output, so the output Z turns to a value of $f(X_2, Y_1)$. We assume the difference of path delays, denoted as $d = t_Y - t_X$, is large enough. Hence, the temporal value $f(X_2, Y_1)$ keeps steady at the output for a while. As presented in Fig. 3, if a glitch is injected to make the length of the second cycle within the range from t_X to t_Y, the temporal value can be stored in RegZ.

3.2 Attack Scenario on Unmasked S-box

First, we analyze the unmasked S-box. As mentioned in Sect. 2.1, we consider the serial implementation, where the inputs of different S-boxes are fed to the

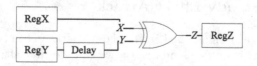

Fig. 2. An example of circuit with different propagation delays

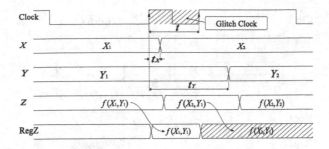

Fig. 3. The sequence diagram with clock glitch

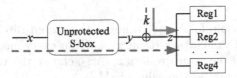

Fig. 4. The data path of unmasked S-box in the final AES round (Color figure online)

same combinational circuit in consecutive clock cycles. We assume the circuit executes the S-box operations of the final AES round consecutively. As in Fig. 4, there are two data paths in the circuit: The longer data path is marked with dashed red arrow, and its delay is denoted as t_y. The shorter one is marked with solid green arrow, and its delay is denoted as t_k.

As shown in Fig. 5, the output of first cycle $z_1 = S(x_1) \oplus k_1$ is stored in register Reg1 at the rising edge of the second cycle. After the duration time of t_k, k_2 propagates through the exclusive-or gate and the output switches to a temporal value $\tilde{z}_2 = S(x_1) \oplus k_2$. The temporal value stays for the duration time of $t_y - t_k$. If we inject a clock glitch after the first clock cycle, and make sure the length of the glitch cycle satisfies $t_y > t_g > t_k$, $\tilde{z}_2$ can be stored in Reg2. With z_1 and $\tilde{z}_2$, we can compute

$$
\begin{aligned}
z_1 \oplus \tilde{z}_2 &= S(x_1) \oplus k_1 \oplus S(x_1) \oplus k_2 \\
&= k_1 \oplus k_2 \\
&= \Delta k_{1,2} .
\end{aligned}
\tag{1}
$$

Since the data paths' delays are unknown to us, we conduct the TSE attack practically in the following steps:

- **Step 1**: Sweep the frequency of clock glitch, i.e. change the length of the clock glitch cycle gradually. At each frequency point, do encryptions with fixed x_1 and random x_2 for N_{pre} times and make a record for the faulty outputs.
- **Step 2**: Find out the range of glitch frequency in which the faulty outputs keep stable. According to the analysis above, with fixed x_1, the faulty output $\tilde{z}_2 = S(x_1) \oplus k_2$ should be a constant value independent of x_2.
- **Step 3**: Choose a proper glitch frequency in the range detected in Step 2.

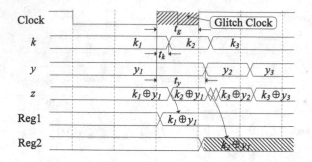

Fig. 5. Sequence diagram of unmasked S-box with clock glitch

- **Step 4**: Do encryptions for N_{attack} times at the chosen glitch frequency, record z_1, $\tilde{z}_2$, and compute the attack result $z_1 \oplus \tilde{z}_2$ for every encryption.
- **Step 5**: Among all the attack results $z_1 \oplus \tilde{z}_2$, choose the value which has the highest occurrence rate as the value of $\Delta k_{1,2}$.
- **Step 6**: Repeat Step 4 to 5 for other clock cycles to recover $\Delta k_{2,3}$, $\Delta k_{3,4}$, etc.

We call Step 1 to Step 3 as the pre-computation stage, which only needs to be done one time for a target circuit. Step 4 to 6, called the attack stage, can be done at a fixed frequency.

Note that there is no specific requirement on the unmasked S-box's structure, as long as the shortest data path delay of the S-box is sufficiently long.

3.3   Attack Scenario on Masked S-box

Masked S-box has three inputs: the masked value $x_m = x \oplus m$, the input mask m and the output mask w. The output is masked with w: $y_w = y \oplus w = S(x) \oplus w$. Since w is used to mask the output of S-box, its data path is usually shorter than x_m and m [12]. Here we focus on the masked S-box based on tower field [17]. As shown in Fig. 6, the data path of x_m and m, which is marked with dashed red arrow, is much longer than those of others. Similar to the unmasked S-boxes, the normal output of the first clock is captured in Reg1:

$$z_1 = y_{w_1} \oplus k_1 \oplus w_1$$
$$= S(x_1) \oplus w_1 \oplus k_1 \oplus w_1$$
$$= S(x_1) \oplus k_1 .$$

Here y_{w_1} represents the masked S-box output of the first clock cycle. We inject a glitch after the first clock cycle. If the length of the glitch cycle is shorter than the delay of x_m and m, and longer than that of w and k, the temporal output $\tilde{z}_2$ can be captured in Reg2:

$$\tilde{z}_2 = \tilde{y}_{w_2} \oplus k_2 \oplus w_2$$
$$= S(x_1) \oplus w_2 \oplus k_2 \oplus w_2$$
$$= S(x_1) \oplus k_2 .$$

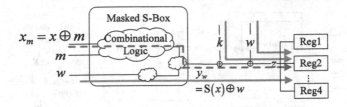

Fig. 6. Data path of masked S-box in the final AES round (Color figure online)

By combining z_1 and $\tilde{z}_2$, we have the result similar to unmasked S-box:

$$
\begin{aligned}
z_1 \oplus \tilde{z}_2 &= S(x_1) \oplus k_1 \oplus S(x_1) \oplus k_2 \\
&= k_1 \oplus k_2 \\
&= \Delta k_{1,2} \, .
\end{aligned}
\tag{2}
$$

Note that the attack described in this section is only applicable if the final unmasking is done within the same clock cycle as the final key addition.

4 Experiments and Efficiency

We verify the proposed TSE attack on two unmasked S-boxes [15,16] and one masked S-box [17] which are implemented on DE2-115 FPGA board with Altera Cyclone IV EP4CE115. We use a RIGOL DG4102 function generator as the input clock. The circuit diagram of attack on masked S-box is shown in Fig. 7, and the setup for unmasked S-box is similar. A PLL is employed in the glitch generator to create clock for the control module and the circuit under attack. The PLL outputs two clock signals. The low frequency signal is used as the normal clock, and high frequency signal is used as the clock glitch. A clock multiplexer is used to switch between the normal and clock glitch. The outputs of two consecutive clock cycles, z_1 and $\tilde{z}_2$, are stored in the registers Reg1 and Reg2 respectively, and the attack result $z_1 \oplus \tilde{z}_2$ is stored in RAM. As presented in Sect. 3, if no fault is injected, the attack result should be $S(x_1) \oplus k_1 \oplus S(x_2) \oplus k_2$. If the attack succeeds, it should be $k_1 \oplus k_2$.

4.1 Experiment on Unmasked S-box A

The S-box we attack in this section is presented in [15], We set the key bytes as $k_1 = 0xE2$ and $k_2 = 0x19$. If the attack succeeds, the result stored in RAM should be $\Delta k_{1,2} = 0xFB$.

Following the steps of TSE attack detailed in Sect. 3.2, we first do the pre-computation stage for S-box A: We choose 80 frequency points from 64 MHz to 480 MHz to sweep the glitch frequency. At every frequency point, the experiment is conducted as follows: We fix the value of x_1 as 0x31, and enumerate the value of x_2. For each x_2, we encrypt it for 256 times. Therefore, at each frequency point, 65536 attack results are stored. As shown in Fig. 8, we count the occurrence rates

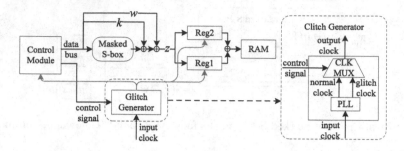

Fig. 7. Experimental circuit diagram of masked S-box

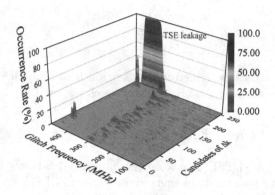

Fig. 8. Results of sweeping glitch frequency for S-box A

for all the possible values of $\Delta k_{1,2}$ at every frequency point. Within the range from 360 MHz to 430 MHz, the occurrence rate of the correct value of $\Delta k_{1,2}$ rises up to nearly 100 %. Obviously, the range is suitable for the TSE attack.

We also verify that the proper frequency range is valid for all the possible inputs of the S-box. The 256 occurrence rate curves of correct $\Delta k_{1,2}$ corresponding to all the 256 values of x_2 are plotted in Fig. 9. Even though the critical timing delay of the S-box depends on the Hamming weight of the inputs [9], we can conclude from Fig. 9 that there is a proper frequency range, i.e. from 360 MHz to 430 MHz, for all the possible inputs.

At the attack stage, TSE attack can be done at any glitch frequency within the range from 360 MHz to 430 MHz. However, to illustrate the result more clearly, we conduct attacks on all the frequency points, and the success rate of attack is in Fig. 10. Increasing the number of encryptions used for each attack, i.e. N_{attack}, can slightly widen the range of proper frequency. Even with only 1 encryption, our attack can achieve a success rate of nearly 100 %.

4.2 Experiment on Unmasked S-box B

We carry out experiments on a very compact unmasked S-box [16] in the same way of Sect. 4.1. The results are shown in Figs. 11, 12, and 13.

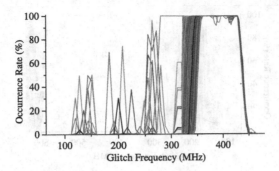

Fig. 9. The 256 occurrence rate curves of correct $\Delta k_{1,2}$ corresponding to 256 values of x_2 for S-box A.

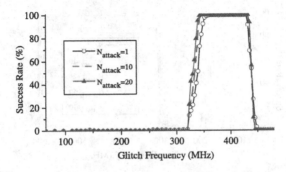

Fig. 10. Success rate *vs.* frequency with different N_{attack} for S-box A

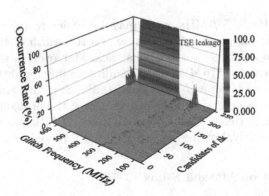

Fig. 11. Results of sweeping glitch frequency for S-box B

As shown in Fig. 11, the range of proper glitch frequency is from 320 MHz to 580 MHz. From Fig. 12, we can see that inputs of the S-box have little effect on the frequency range.

As shown in Fig. 13, a small peak appears at about 176 MHz when 50 or more encryptions are used. The frequency of the peak is much lower than the

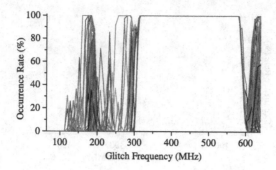

Fig. 12. The 256 occurrence rate curves of correct $\Delta k_{1,2}$ corresponding to 256 values of x_2 for S-box B.

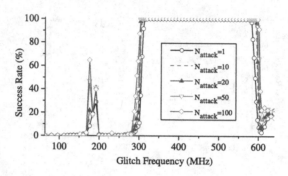

Fig. 13. Success rate *vs.* frequency with different N_{attack} for S-box B

range from 320 MHz to 580 MHz, so it may be easier to inject glitch at this frequency. However, the peak is very narrow, so the width of the glitch has to be very accurate to mount a success TSE attack. Moreover, as shown in Fig. 11, there are several peaks at 176 MHz corresponding to different attack results, for example, 0xFB (correct value of $\Delta k_{1,2}$) and 0xF3. Since we always choose the value which has the largest occurrence rate as $\Delta k_{1,2}$, the probability of choosing 0xF3 is also very high. Hence, by injecting glitch at 176 MHz, we may not be able to recover $\Delta k_{1,2}$ directly, but the key space can still be reduced significantly.

4.3   Experiment on Masked S-box C

S-box C is the masked version of S-box B [17]. We set the inputs of S-box as $x_1 = $ 0x9D, $x_2 = $ 0xE6, and the key bytes as $k_1 = $ 0x3F and $k_2 = $ 0x58. With no fault injected, the attack result should be $S(x_1) \oplus k_1 \oplus S(x_2) \oplus k_2 = $ 0xB7. If the attack succeeds, the result should be $\Delta k_{1,2} = $ 0x67.

We choose 72 frequency points between 50 MHz to 200 MHz for frequency sweeping. At each frequency point, we encrypt the plaintext with random masks m and w for 65536 times. As shown in Fig. 14, when the glitch frequency is lower than 75MHz, the occurrence rate of value 0xB7 is 100 %, namely no fault occurs.

When the glitch frequency gets higher, there is only one peak higher than 60 %, which corresponds to the value of $\Delta k_{1,2} = $ 0x67. The feasible frequency range for this S-box is from 145 MHz to 150 MHz.

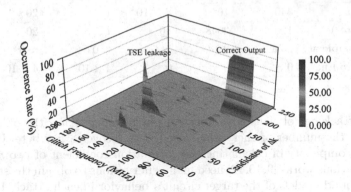

Fig. 14. Results of sweeping glitch frequency for S-box C

The results of the attack stage are shown in Fig. 15. With only one encryption for each attack, the success rate of TSE attack reaches to 90 % at the frequency of 150 MHz. With more encryptions, the range of proper glitch frequency is widened obviously. With more than 20 encryptions, our attack can have a success rate higher than 90 % within the frequency range from 142 MHz to 152 MHz.

It is worth noting that the proper glitch frequency for attacking the masked S-box is much lower than unmasked S-box. That is because, as a countermeasure against side-channel attacks, masking usually results in a longer data path delay for x_m and m, which turns out to be vulnerable to our attack.

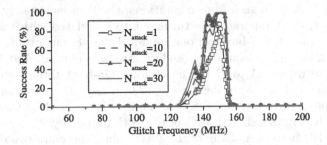

Fig. 15. Success rate *vs.* frequency with different N_{attack} for S-box C

4.4   Efficiency Comparison

We compare TSE attack with related fault based attacks on AES S-box in Table 1. The comparison is based on the effort to disclose 8-bit information of the

Table 1. Comparison with three fault based attacks

Method	FSA [9]	CTC [10]	FRA [12]	TSE Attack	TSE Attack
Target S-box	Unmasked	Masked	Masked	Unmasked	Masked
Num of Enc	840	10^6	8×10^4	1	20
Space (bytes)	120	2048	80	1	20
Offline Complexity	$256C_{\rho 7}$	$256C_{\rho 256}$	$1C_{div}$	≈ 0	≈ 0
Num of Pre-Enc	0	0	0	4×10^4	4×10^4

key. Our attack has obvious advantages in the memory space, the offline complexity and the number of encryptions needed to recover a key byte. Here C_{ρ_n} means the complexity of calculating the correlation coefficient of two n-sample vectors. Previous works [9,10,12] need many encryptions to obtain the statistical data or to build models of the target circuit's behavior in each attack. However, our attack puts most workload into the pre-computation stage, i.e. sweeps the glitch frequency for only one time to find a proper frequency range. Then, in the attack stage, it is feasible and efficient to obtain key-related information from the faulty output directly.

The last row in Table 1 denotes the number of encryptions needed in precomputation stage, the data in this row is estimated. Experienced attackers usually do not need so many encryptions.

5   Further Discussion

5.1   Key Recovery for Parallel AES Implementation

In some AES implementations, 16 S-boxes are implemented in parallel to achieve high throughput [23]. In such implementations, the transient-steady effect still exists. However, the temporal value turns out to be related with two adjacent rounds, rather than two S-boxes in one round. To apply our attack to parallel AES implementations, we focus on a standard structure of unmasked AES shown in Fig. 16. Here we use A to D to denote four 128-bit intermediate states in different stages, and use K to denote the 128-bit key. The index of rounds is denoted by the superscript, and the byte number is denoted by the subscript. For example, K_4^{10} means the 4th byte of the 10th round key.

As in Fig. 16, at the beginning of the 10th round, there are two data paths: the delay of the key is shorter than that of the red dashed path. Consequently, if we shorten the 10th clock cycle to a proper length, we can capture the temporal value $B^9 \oplus K^{10}$ as the faulty ciphertext $\tilde{D}^{10}$, before the intermediate value B^9 is contaminated. Without fault, the output of the circuit is the correct ciphertext $D^{10} = B^{10} \oplus K^{10}$. It is worth noting that both the correct output and faulty output are needed to attack a parallel implementation with TSE attack, which is different from the situation in serial implementation.

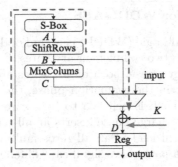

Fig. 16. Standard structure of parallel AES implementation (Color figure online)

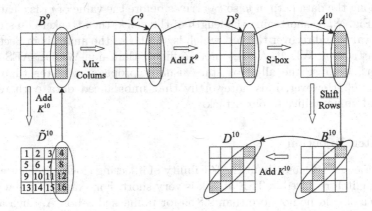

Fig. 17. Key recovery of parallel AES implementation

As shown in Fig. 17, we can deduce equations of K^9 and K^{10} as follows once we have D^{10} and $\tilde{D}^{10}$:

$$\begin{cases} \tilde{D}^{10} \oplus K^{10} = B^9 \\ \text{MixCol}\left(B^9\right) = C^9 \\ C^9 \oplus K^9 = D^9 \\ \text{Sbox}\left(D^9\right) = A^{10} = B^{10} \\ B^{10} \oplus K^{10} = D^{10} \end{cases} \tag{3}$$

$$\Rightarrow \text{Sbox}\left(\text{MixCol}\left(\tilde{D}^{10} \oplus K^{10}\right) \oplus K^9\right) \oplus K^{10} = D^{10} \,.$$

According to AES key schedule, K^9 can be expressed by K^{10}, so K^{10} is the only variable in (3). Solving the equation system in (3) is similar to breaking one round AES by algebraic attack, which can be solved by MiniSAT tool.

However, TSE attack on parallel implementation is feasible only if the round-key is precomputed and stored in registers. Otherwise, the data path of key schedule is comparable to that of S-box.

5.2   Attack Scenario for WDDL-AES

Wave Dynamic Differential Logic (WDDL) is a kind of dual-rail precharge logic. Every signal of WDDL has two complementary wires. Every clock cycle consists of two phases: in precharge phase, both of the wires are precharged to a fixed value, for example, (0, 0); in the evaluation phase, the values of two wires are either (1, 0) or (0, 1). WDDL is believed to be secure against setup violation faults [24]. Because the precharge phase inserts an all-zeros state in every clock, shortening a clock cycle will lead to an all-zeros faulty ciphertext. However, if the delays of different data paths have significant difference, the circuit may not be perfectly secure any more.

Considering a WDDL-AES implementation with the same structure in Fig. 4, we assume that after the rising edge of the clock, the all-zeros state propagates slow enough along the data path of y, so k_2 arrives before the value of y_1 is cleared. As shown in Fig. 18, by shortening the length of the clock, the attacker can store the temporal value and recover the key, which is similar to the analysis in Sect. 3.2.

TSE attack on WDDL-AES is more difficult than non-WDDL AES implementations, because the all-zeros state usually propagates faster than other states [25, 26]. However, it is noteworthy that unbalanced data path remains a potential vulnerability to our attack.

5.3   Glitch Injection

In this section, we discuss about the feasibility of injecting clock glitch externally. The clock glitch required in TSE attack is very short. For example, the width of clock glitch should be no more than 2.8 ns for unmasked S-box A. Such a short glitch may be filtered out when injected externally, even though it is reported in many literatures that the glitch width can be smaller than 3 ns [27, 28].

A straightforward way to bypass the obstacle is to do a semi-invasive attack: cut the clock line and connect it to a external glitch signal. Another option is to slow down the target circuit, so that TSE attack can be carried out with wider glitch.

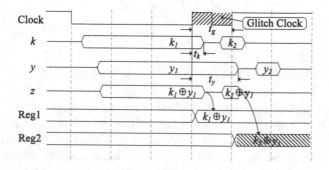

Fig. 18. Sequence diagram of WDDL-AES with clock glitch. The all-zeros state is denoted by Z (high impedance) state.

Fig. 19. Glitch injection experiment with reduced supply voltage

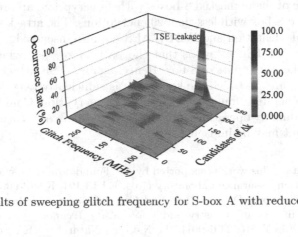

Fig. 20. Results of sweeping glitch frequency for S-box A with reduced supply voltage

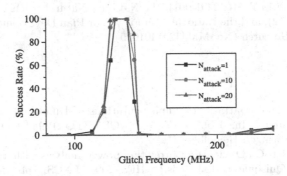

Fig. 21. Success rate *vs.* frequency with different N_{attack} for S-box A with reduced supply voltage

Under some conditions, the attacker can increase the delay of the target circuits. For example, by reducing the supply voltage, the propagation delay can be increased [29]. We reduce the supply voltage of FPGA chip from 1.5 V to

1.08V and rerun the experiments in Sect. 4.1. As shown in Fig. 19, we cut the power supply of Cyclone IV EP4CE115 and connect it to a DC power supply. The attack results are shown in Figs. 20 and 21. By reducing the voltage to 1.08 V, the feasible glitch frequencies go down to the range from 125 MHz to 136 MHz, which is about 1/3 of the frequency range with normal voltage.

6   Conclusions

In this paper, we propose a new TSE attack based on the transient-steady effect. By injecting glitch in clock signal, the transient-steady value can be captured to recover the key of AES. We conduct experiments on two kinds of unmasked S-boxes and one kind of masked S-box, and all the S-boxes are implemented in serial with an FPGA board. Experimental results show that TSE attack can recover a key byte of the unmasked S-boxes with 1 encryption, and recover a key byte of the masked S-box with less than 20 encryptions. The attack scenarios on parallel AES implementation and WDDL-AES are also discussed.

The foundation of TSE attack is that the path of key is obviously shorter than other data, i.e. the inputs of S-box. Hence, against TSE attack, we recommend the architectures in which the key's path is sufficiently long, for example, the roundkey is generated simultaneously with the encryption. Countermeasures such as inserting dummy operations into the key's path are also feasible options, but the throughput may be impacted.

Acknowledgments. This work is supported by the Foundation of Science and Technology on Information Assurance Laboratory (Nos. KJ-13-101, KJ-14-006), the Major Program Core of Electronic Devices, High-End General Chips, and Basis of Software Products of the Ministry of Industry and Information Technology of China (Nos. 2014ZX01032205, 2014ZX01032401-001), the National Natural Science Foundation of China (No. 61402252), and the National 12th Five-Year Plan Development Foundation for Cryptological Research (No. MMJJ201401009).

References

1. Kocher, P.C.: Timing attacks on implementations of Diffie-Hellman, RSA, DSS, and other systems. In: Koblitz, N. (ed.) CRYPTO 1996. LNCS, vol. 1109, pp. 104–113. Springer, Heidelberg (1996)
2. Brier, E., Clavier, C., Olivier, F.: Correlation power analysis with a leakage model. In: Joye, M., Quisquater, J.-J. (eds.) CHES 2004. LNCS, vol. 3156, pp. 16–29. Springer, Heidelberg (2004)
3. Oswald, E., Mangard, S., Herbst, C., Tillich, S.: Practical second-order DPA attacks for masked smart card implementations of block ciphers. In: Pointcheval, D. (ed.) CT-RSA 2006. LNCS, vol. 3860, pp. 192–207. Springer, Heidelberg (2006)
4. Chari, S., Rao, J.R., Paar, C.: Template attacks. In: Kaliski Jr., B.S., Koç, Ç.K., Paar, C. (eds.) CHES 2002. LNCS, vol. 2523, pp. 13–28. Springer, Heidelberg (2003)

5. Schramm, K., Wollinger, T., Paar, C.: A new class of collision attacks and its application to DES. In: Johansson, T. (ed.) FSE 2003. LNCS, vol. 2887, pp. 206–222. Springer, Heidelberg (2003)

6. Clavier, C., Feix, B., Gagnerot, G., Roussellet, M., Verneuil, V.: Improved collision-correlation power analysis on first order protected AES. In: Preneel, B., Takagi, T. (eds.) CHES 2011. LNCS, vol. 6917, pp. 49–62. Springer, Heidelberg (2011)

7. Gierlichs, B., Batina, L., Tuyls, P., Preneel, B.: Mutual information analysis. In: Oswald, E., Rohatgi, P. (eds.) CHES 2008. LNCS, vol. 5154, pp. 426–442. Springer, Heidelberg (2008)

8. Biham, E., Shamir, A.: Differential fault analysis of secret key cryptosystems. In: Kaliski Jr., B.S. (ed.) CRYPTO 1997. LNCS, vol. 1294, pp. 513–525. Springer, Heidelberg (1997)

9. Li, Y., Sakiyama, K., Gomisawa, S., Fukunaga, T., Takahashi, J., Ohta, K.: Fault sensitivity analysis. In: Mangard, S., Standaert, F.-X. (eds.) CHES 2010. LNCS, vol. 6225, pp. 320–334. Springer, Heidelberg (2010)

10. Moradi, A., Mischke, O., Paar, C., Li, Y., Ohta, K., Sakiyama, K.: On the power of fault sensitivity analysis and collision side-channel attacks in a combined setting. In: Preneel, B., Takagi, T. (eds.) CHES 2011. LNCS, vol. 6917, pp. 292–311. Springer, Heidelberg (2011)

11. Li, Y., Ohta, K., Sakiyama, K.: An extension of fault sensitivity analysis based on clockwise collision. In: Kutyłowski, M., Yung, M. (eds.) Inscrypt 2012. LNCS, vol. 7763, pp. 46–59. Springer, Heidelberg (2013)

12. Wang, A., Chen, M., Wang, Z., Wang, X.: Fault rate analysis: breaking masked AES hardware implementations efficiently. IEEE Trans. Circ. Syst. II **60**(8), 517–521 (2013)

13. Mangard, S., Aigner, M., Dominikus, S.: A highly regular and scalable AES hardware architecture. IEEE Trans. Comput. **52**(4), 483–491 (2003). IEEE

14. Feldhofer, M., Wolkerstorfer, J., Rijmen, V.: AES implementation on a grain of sand. IEE Proc. Inf. Secur. **152**(1), 13–20 (2005)

15. Morioka, S., Satoh, A.: An optimized S-box circuit architecture for low power AES design. In: Kaliski Jr., B.S., Koç, Ç.K., Paar, C. (eds.) CHES 2002. LNCS, vol. 2523, pp. 172–186. Springer, Heidelberg (2003)

16. Canright, D.: A very compact S-box for AES. In: Rao, J.R., Sunar, B. (eds.) CHES 2005. LNCS, vol. 3659, pp. 441–455. Springer, Heidelberg (2005)

17. Canright, D., Batina, L.: A very compact "Perfectly Masked" S-box for AES. In: Bellovin, S.M., Gennaro, R., Keromytis, A.D., Yung, M. (eds.) ACNS 2008. LNCS, vol. 5037, pp. 446–459. Springer, Heidelberg (2008)

18. Mangard, S., Popp, T., Gammel, B.M.: Side-channel leakage of masked CMOS gates. In: Menezes, A. (ed.) CT-RSA 2005. LNCS, vol. 3376, pp. 351–365. Springer, Heidelberg (2005)

19. Mangard, S., Pramstaller, N., Oswald, E.: Successfully attacking masked AES hardware implementations. In: Rao, J.R., Sunar, B. (eds.) CHES 2005. LNCS, vol. 3659, pp. 157–171. Springer, Heidelberg (2005)

20. Suzuki, D., Saeki, M., Ichikawa, T.: Random switching logic: a countermeasure against DPA based on transition probability. Cryptology ePrint Archive, Report 2004/346 (2004). http://eprint.iacr.org/2004/346

21. Suzuki, D., Saeki, M., Ichikawa, T.: DPA leakage models for CMOS logic circuits. In: Rao, J.R., Sunar, B. (eds.) CHES 2005. LNCS, vol. 3659, pp. 366–382. Springer, Heidelberg (2005)

22. Mangard, S., Schramm, K.: Pinpointing the side-channel leakage of masked AES hardware implementations. In: Goubin, L., Matsui, M. (eds.) CHES 2006. LNCS, vol. 4249, pp. 76–90. Springer, Heidelberg (2006)
23. Satoh, A., Morioka, S., Takano, K., Munetoh, S.: A compact rijndael hardware architecture with s-box optimization. In: Boyd, C. (ed.) ASIACRYPT 2001. LNCS, vol. 2248, pp. 239–254. Springer, Heidelberg (2001)
24. Guilley, S., Graba, T., Selmane, N., Bhasin, S., Danger, J.-L.: WDDL is protected against setup time violation attacks. In: FDTC, pp. 73–83. IEEE Computer Society, Los Alamitos (2009)
25. Moradi, A., Immler, V.: Early propagation and imbalanced routing, how to diminish in FPGAs. In: Batina, L., Robshaw, M. (eds.) CHES 2014. LNCS, vol. 8731, pp. 598–615. Springer, Heidelberg (2014)
26. Tiri, K., Akmal, M., Verbauwhede, I.: A dynamic and differential CMOS logic with signal independent power consumption to withstand differential power analysis on smart cards. In: ESSCIRC 2002, 403–406 (2002)
27. Takahashi, J., Fukunaga, T., Gomisawa, S., Li, Y., Sakiyama, K., Ohta, K.: Fault injection and key retrieval experiments on an evaluation board. In: Joye, M., Tunstall, M. (eds.) Fault Analysis in Cryptography, pp. 313–331. Springer, Heidelberg (2012)
28. Agoyan, M., Dutertre, J.-M., Naccache, D., Robisson, B., Tria, A.: When clocks fail: on critical paths and clock faults. In: Gollmann, D., Lanet, J.-L., Iguchi-Cartigny, J. (eds.) CARDIS 2010. LNCS, vol. 6035, pp. 182–193. Springer, Heidelberg (2010)
29. Guilley, S., Danger, J.L.: Global faults on cryptographic circuits. In: Joye, M., Tunstall, M. (eds.) Fault Analysis in Cryptography, pp. 295–311. Springer, Heidelberg (2012)

Higher-Order Side-Channel Attacks

Assessment of Hiding the Higher-Order Leakages in Hardware

What Are the Achievements Versus Overheads?

Amir Moradi(✉) and Alexander Wild

Horst Görtz Institute for IT-Security, Ruhr-Universität Bochum, Bochum, Germany
{Amir.Moradi,Alexander.Wild}@rub.de

Abstract. Higher-order side-channel attacks are becoming amongst the major interests of academia as well as industry sector. It is indeed being motivated by the development of countermeasures which can prevent the leakages up to certain orders. As a concrete example, threshold implementation (TI) as an efficient way to realize Boolean masking in hardware is able to avoid first-order leakages. Trivially, the attacks conducted at second (and higher) orders can exploit the corresponding leakages hence devastating the provided security. Hence, the extension of TI to higher orders was being expected which has been presented at ASIACRYPT 2014. Following its underlying univariate settings it can provide security at higher orders, and its area and time overheads naturally increase with the desired security order.

In this work we look at the feasibility of higher-order attacks on first-order TI from another perspective. Instead of increasing the order of resistance by employing higher-order TIs, we realize the first-order TI designs following the principles of a power-equalization technique dedicated to FPGA platforms, that naturally leads to hardening higher-order attacks. We show that although the first-order TI designs, which are additionally equipped by the power-equalization methodology, have significant area overhead, they can maintain the same throughput and more importantly can avoid the higher-order leakages to be practically exploitable by up to 1 billion traces.

1 Introduction

Side-channel attacks are a major threat to the security of modern embedded devices. If no particular attention is paid, the exploitation of physical leakages such as the power consumption and the electromagnetic radiation of a cryptographic implementation can lead to successful key recoveries, e.g., [2,16,27, 44,58]. As a consequence, the topic has been followed by a vast literature on potential solutions to defeat such attacks.

The countermeasures against side-channel attacks range from ad hoc to formal, and are defined to be applied at various abstraction levels. For instance, time randomizations (based on random delay insertion [14] or shuffling [54]) are frequently-used low-overhead heuristic-based approaches (mainly) for software-based applications. These *hiding* schemes are not limited to only those which

T. Güneysu and H. Handschuh (Eds.): CHES 2015, LNCS 9293, pp. 453–474, 2015.
DOI: 10.1007/978-3-662-48324-4_23

randomize the computations in time, but covers the approaches that add noise resources [18,24] as well as those aiming to equalize the power consumption [51,53]. The time randomizations can be overcome by preprocessing the leakage traces (e.g., combing [24]), and the effect of the noise additions can be mitigated by increasing the number of traces [24]. In contrast, the power-equalization techniques usually fail due to wrong assumptions (e.g., ignoring early propagation [50]) or overestimating the ability of the tools (e.g., balanced dual-rail routing [52]). Apart from [29,53], dual-rail precharge logic styles, which have been initially designed for ASIC-based applications (e.g., [13,40,41,51]), cannot be easily integrated into the FPGAs. Instead, other approaches like [3,19–21,23,36,47,57] have particularly been developed with respect to the resources available in certain FPGAs. However, each of such techniques suffers from a flaw that prevents them to be considered as a potential solution (see [56] for details of each flaw). Further, a design methodology which combines a dual-rail logic style and duplication in FPGAs [57] has also been shown to be flawed [55]. As an alternative, the technique presented in [56] (so-called GliFreD) seems to avoid the known pitfalls. It has been designed particularly for Xilinx FPGAs, and aims at avoiding early propagation, preventing the glitches, and relaxing the necessity of a dual-rail routing tool. It seems that GliFreD can satisfy its goals toward equalizing the power consumption, but an ideally-equal situation cannot still be achieved due to the process variation violating the balance between the cloned routes.

On the other hand, probably the most investigated and best understood protection against side-channel attacks is *masking* [12,15,46]. The underlying principle of masking is to represent any sensitive variable in the implementation by d shares in such a way that the computations are performed only on these shares. Assuming that the leakage of the shares are independent of each other, a successful key-recovery attack needs to observe – at least – the dth-order statistical moment of the leakage distributions, where the corresponding complexity increases exponentially with d.

However, the independence of leakages associated to the shares is an assumption which is usually violated in hardware applications. As an example, the masked AES Sbox designs [11,39], where the glitches are ignored, failed in practice to satisfy the desired security level, i.e., first-order resistance [25,32]. Instead, based on Boolean masking and multiparty computation, threshold implementations (TI) [37,38] can ensure first-order resistance in the presence of glitches. Indeed, not only its underlying principles are sound and realistic but also practical investigations confirmed its effectiveness [4,33]. Trivially, higher-order attacks are feasible on TI designs [4,26], which motivated the work presented in [5] where the concept of higher-order TI is demonstrated that extends its definitions to any order. Regardless of its significant overhead (e.g., requiring at least $d = 5$ for a second-order security) the note given in [45] and later practically confirmed in [49] made clear that the definitions of the higher-order TI stand valid only in univariate scenarios.

Our Contribution. Indeed, it is known to the community that hiding techniques (in particular power-equalizing approaches) are not *solely* capable to prevent key-recovery attacks. It is always suggested that such techniques should be combined with other countermeasures, but the benefit of such a combination has never truly been examined for a hardware platform. More precisely, exploiting higher-order leakages becomes extremely hard in practice when the leakage traces are sufficiently noisy [43]. Along the same lines, power-equalization schemes are also expected to reduce the signal (versus the noise) and have the same effect. To the best of our knowledge, the only work which tried to proceed toward this goal is [30], where a flawed masking scheme [11] has been implemented in a glitch-free setting. No particular attention has been payed on equalizing the power hence not a concrete hiding technique.

Our contribution in this work is to examine the benefit of combining two sound hardware-based countermeasures. More precisely, we aim at considering a provably (first-order) secure masking scheme (TI) and realize it under the principles of a proper power-equalizing technique (GliFreD). We pursue an investigation of our combined construction compared with:

- the same masking design (first-order TI) without employing any hiding technique, and
- the second-order TI of the same design excluding any power-equalization scheme.

Such comparisons with respect to the data complexity of leakage detection as well as time and area overheads of the designs allows us to have an overview on the tradeoff between the gains and overheads of different countermeasures as well as their combination.

Since the design overheads are application specific, we consider two design methodologies: first, a fully serialized architecture for lightweight applications with KATAN-32 cipher and second, a parallelized architecture for high-speed applications with PRESENT cipher. Amongst our achievements in this work – including a second-order TI of PRESENT – we can refer to the designs we developed with a combination of GliFreD and the first-order TI (of both KATAN-32 and PRESENT) which showed to be secure by up to 1 billion power traces measured from a Spartan-6 FPGA platform.

2 GliFreD

Dual-rail Precharge Logic (DPL) schemes are popular side-channel countermeasures for hardware circuits and assigned to the group of hiding techniques. Each DPL scheme places two contrary working (*true* and *false*) circuits on a device to *ideally* decorrelate the power consumption from the processed data. In common, DPL schemes have to deal with some implementation challenges. The three major challenges that the FPGA-based DPL designers face are: early propagation, glitches and different wire capacitance of coupled signals. GliFreD is a DPL scheme exclusively designed for FPGAs, and is amongst the few schemes which address all these three problems [56].

To overcome the aforementioned problems GliFreD defines the following design methodology. Each Look-Up Table (LUT) instance is connected to two global control signals: CLK and active; the later one toggles with half of the other one's frequency. These control signals determine whether the LUTs reside in precharge or in evaluation phase. Hence, the regulated LUT transitions overcome the definition of early evaluation [50]. To prevent the propagation of the LUT output transition, a register is connected to each LUT output. However, a single register stage in a DPL circuit contradicts the requirement of a constant gate and register transition per clock cycle [28] as inconstant and data-dependent transitions would result in data-dependent leakage. Therefore, the GliFreD principles require to place an even number of register stages between each two LUTs connected in the circuit. Consequently, GliFreD forms a pipeline architecture which prevents glitches by halting the propagation of a signal after each LUT. Figure 1(a) shows the timing diagram of a GliFreD circuit.

Similar to many DPL schemes, GliFreD also needs to place a dual of the circuit. Copying the routing structure is currently the best known way in FPGAs to keep the wire capacitances of the *false* circuit as equivalent as those of the *true* circuit. Hence, to perform the circuit dualization, i.e., placing the *false* circuit, a second horizontally-moved instance of the *true* circuit is placed on the FPGA. The copy process is performed on netlist level to pass on the routing information to the *false* circuit.

GliFreD allows an arbitrary LUT configuration; since both control signals CLK and active should be connected to each LUT, the function f each LUT can realize is limited to a 4-to-1 look-up table. The output of each LUT can be seen as $O = \text{active} \cdot \overline{\text{CLK}} \cdot f(I_2, \ldots, I_5)$[1], while the corresponding dual function (of the *false* circuit) becomes $\overline{O} = \text{active} \cdot \overline{\text{CLK}} \cdot \overline{f(\overline{I_2}, \ldots, \overline{I_5})}$. Figure 1 shows the GliFreD pendant of an exemplary function

$$y = x_0 + x_0 x_3 + x_2 x_3 + x_3 x_4 + x_3 x_6 + x_0 x_7 + x_2 x_7, \tag{1}$$

whose standard implementation is shown in Fig. 1(b).

Since the output of each LUT is buffered by a register, the critical path in a GliFreD circuit is minimized allowing to run the circuit at high frequencies. To this end the delay between the CLK and active signals should be kept minimum (see Fig. 1(a)), that can be achieved by forcing active signal to be routed through the clock trees. The GliFreD design methodology offers the ability to transfer a design into a fully-pipelined architecture, hence achieving a high throughput in combination with a high clock frequency. In general, large combinatorial circuits cause glitches which propagate through the whole circuit. Since GliFreD prevents those glitches, it may also reduce the power consumption. In small combinatorial circuits this benefit is faded and dominated by the increased amount of resources the GliFreD circuit utilizes. Nevertheless, GliFreD is a resource-costly solution. The LUT overhead (at most 8) required to form a GliFreD circuit strongly depends on the original design structure. Compared to the LUT utilization GliFreD causes

---

[1] I_0 and I_1 are reserved for CLK and active.

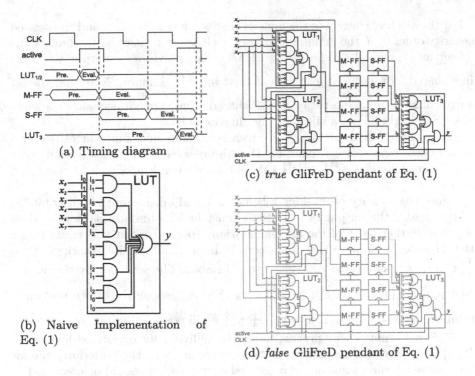

(a) Timing diagram

(b) Naive Implementation of Eq. (1)

(c) *true* GliFreD pendant of Eq. (1)

(d) *false* GliFreD pendant of Eq. (1)

Fig. 1. An exemplary function implemented in a standard 6-to-1 LUT architecture and its GliFreD representation including the timing diagram

a massive register overhead and hence an increased latency. The register overhead cannot be trivially estimated and depends on the LUT depth, width and the amount of registers in the original design.

3   Case Studies

Before giving the details of our case studies, we briefly restate the concept behind threshold implementation.

3.1   Threshold Implementation

As stated before, the masking scheme which we consider in this work is threshold implementation (TI) introduced and extended in [4,5,37,38]. Let us denote an intermediate value of a cipher by x made of s single-bit signals $\langle x_1, \ldots, x_s \rangle$. The underlying concept of TI is to use Boolean masking to represent x in a shared form $(x^1, \ldots, x^n)$, where $x = \bigoplus x^i$ and each x^i similarly denotes a vector of s single-bit signals $\langle x_1^i, \ldots, x_s^i \rangle$. A linear function $l(.)$ can be trivially applied over the shares of x as $l(x) = \bigoplus l(x^i)$. However, the realization of non-linear functions, e.g., an Sbox, over Boolean masked data is challenging. Following the concept of

TI, if the algebraic degree of the underlying Sbox is denoted by t and the desired security order by d, the minimum number of shares to realize the Sbox under the TI settings is $n = td + 1$. Further, such a TI Sbox provides the output $\boldsymbol{y} = S(\boldsymbol{x})$ in a shared form $(\boldsymbol{y}^1, \ldots, \boldsymbol{y}^m)$ with at least $m = \binom{n}{t}$ shares. Note that the bit length of $\boldsymbol{x}$ and $\boldsymbol{y}$ (respectively of their shared forms) are not necessary the same since $S(.)$ might be not a bijection, e.g., in case of DES.

Each output share $\boldsymbol{y}^{j \in \{1, \ldots, m\}}$ is given by a component function $f^j(.)$ over a subset of the input shares. To achieve the dth-order security, any d selection of the component functions $f^{j \in \{1, \ldots, m\}}(.)$ should be independent of at least one input share.

Since the security of masking schemes is based on the uniform distribution of the masks, the output of a TI Sbox must be also uniform as it is used as input in further parts of the implementation. To express the *uniformity* under the TI concept suppose that for a certain input $\mathbf{x}$ all possible sharings $\mathcal{X} = \left\{ (\boldsymbol{x}^1, \ldots, \boldsymbol{x}^n) | \mathbf{x} = \bigoplus \boldsymbol{x}^i \right\}$ are given to a TI Sbox. The set made by the output shares, i.e., $\left\{ (f^1(.), \ldots, f^m(.)) | (\boldsymbol{x}^1, \ldots, \boldsymbol{x}^n) \in \mathcal{X} \right\}$, should be drawn uniformly from the set $\mathcal{Y} = \left\{ (\boldsymbol{y}^1, \ldots, \boldsymbol{y}^m) | \mathbf{y} = \bigoplus \boldsymbol{y}^i \right\}$ as all possible sharings of $\mathbf{y} = S(\mathbf{x})$.

This uniformity check process should be individually performed for $\forall\, \mathbf{x} \in \{0,1\}^s$. We should note that for $d > 1$ where $m > n$ the uniformity cannot be achieved. Hence, some of the registered output shares should be combined to reduce the number of output shares to n. Afterward the uniformity can be examined. For more detailed information we refer to the original articles [5, 38].

3.2   KATAN-32

As stated in Sect. 2, the overhead and performance of a GliFreD circuit depends on the nature of the underlying application. If the target design is made of small combinatorial circuits, the overhead of the resulting GliFreD circuit is minimal. Therefore, KATAN [10] which benefits from a serialized architecture with very small combinatorial logics is a suitable candidate for our investigations. Further, both first- and second-order uniform TI representation of its non-linear functions are given in [5], allowing us to develop the design with minimal efforts.

The architecture of our designs are based on those given in [5]. Figure 2(a) shows an overview of such a serialized architecture considering KATAN-32 encryption engine with 32-bit plaintext and 80-bit symmetric key. The plaintext and key are serially loaded into the registers, and after 254 clock cycles the ciphertext can be taken from the state register[2]. The first-order TI of KATAN-32 with 3 shares (the minimum settings) needs the state (shift) registers to be tripled. Similar to that of [5], we do not represent the key (and the corresponding shift register) in a shared form. The XOR operations are easily repeated for each share, and the non-linear functions which are limited to the AND/XOR module (involved in function

---

[2] For more detailed information on the construction of functions f_a and f_b in Fig. 2(a) see [5, 10].

f_a and f_b of Fig. 2(a)) need to be realized under the concept of the first-order TI. An AND/XOR function receives a 3-bit input (a, b, c) and gives a single-bit output y as

$$y = a + bc.$$

Following the concept of *direct sharing* [6] the component functions (given in [5]) which realize a uniform first-order TI can be derived as

$$f^{i,j}(\langle a^i, b^i, c^i \rangle, \langle a^j, b^j, c^j \rangle) = a^j + b^j c^j + b^i c^j + b^j c^i, \qquad (2)$$

where each output share is made by an instance of such a component function as

$$y^1 = f^{1,2}(.,.), \qquad y^2 = f^{2,3}(.,.), \qquad y^3 = f^{3,1}(.,.).$$

The same procedure is followed to realize the second-order TI of KATAN-32. First, the minimum number of shares is increased to 5, and all state registers and linear functions need to be repeated accordingly. Further, a second-order TI representation of AND/XOR module (given in [5]) can be derived from Eq. (2) and the following component function

$$g^{i,j}(\langle a^i, b^i, c^i \rangle, \langle a^j, b^j, c^j \rangle) = b^i c^j + b^j c^i. \qquad (3)$$

In such a case, the output shares are made as

$$y^1 = f^{1,2}(.,.), \quad y^2 = f^{1,3}(.,.), \quad y^3 = f^{1,4}(.,.), \quad y^4 = f^{5,1}(.,.), \quad y^5 = f^{2,5}(.,.),$$

and

$$y^6 = g^{2,3}(.,.), \quad y^7 = g^{2,4}(.,.), \quad y^8 = g^{3,4}(.,.), \quad y^9 = g^{3,5}(.,.), \quad y^{10} = g^{4,5}(.,.).$$

As mentioned before, in a second-order case the output shares should be combined after being registered in order to reduce the number of shares back to 5. In this case, the reduction is done as

$$z^{i \in \{1,...,4\}} = y^i, \qquad z^5 = y^5 + y^6 + y^7 + y^8 + y^9 + y^{10},$$

thereby achieving a uniform second-order TI of the AND/XOR module [5]. For more clarification the formula for all the component functions are given in the extended version of this article [35].

3.3 PRESENT

As the second target we selected the PRESENT cipher [9] to be implemented in a round-based fashion. As Fig. 2(b) shows, 16 instances of the Sbox in addition to the PLayer operate in parallel to compute one cipher round. The reason for choosing such a target is to have an application for GliFreD with large combinatorial circuit compared to that of KATAN. Also, due to a possibility to decompose the PRESENT Sbox – as we express below – we are able to develop its uniform first- and second-order TI representations. We should note that we have not

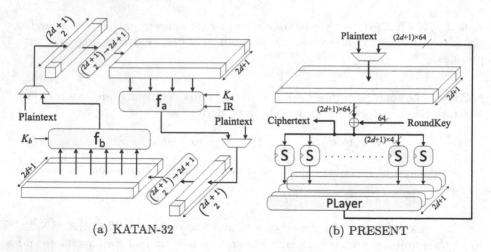

(a) KATAN-32   (b) PRESENT

Fig. 2. Architecture of the case studies, first ($d = 1$) and second ($d = 2$) order TI

selected the AES as a target because its first-order TI (in [4, 33]) can only be realized by remasking (requiring multiple fresh mask bits per clock cycle) and furthermore there is not yet a clear roadmap how to realize its second-order TI.

Similar to the case of KATAN, the first-order (respectively second-order) TI of the targeted PRESENT architecture employs a 3-share (respectively 5-share) Boolean masking. The PLayer (realized by routing in the round-based architecture) is repeated on each share, and the key XOR is applied on only one share as the 80-bit key is not represented in a shared form. Clearly the remaining part is the TI representation of the PRESENT Sbox. Previously Poschmann et al. [42] have shown a decomposition and a uniform first-order TI of such an Sbox. However, below we represent another decomposition allowing us to develop its both first- and second-order uniform TI representations.

The PRESENT Sbox $S(\boldsymbol{x}) = \boldsymbol{y}$ is a cubic bijection (i.e., with algebraic degree $t = 3$) leading to minimum $n = 4$ and $n = 7$ shares in the first- and second-order TI settings respectively. Therefore, it is preferable to decompose the Sbox into two (at most) quadratic bijections F and G, in such a way that $S(\boldsymbol{x}) = F(G(\boldsymbol{x}))$ (i.e., $S = F \circ G$). If so, each F and G can be shared with $n = 3$ and $n = 5$ (for first- and second-order TI). According to the classifications given in [7], the PRESENT Sbox belongs to the cubic class $\mathcal{C}_{266}$. It means that there exist affine transformations A and B, where $S(\boldsymbol{x}) = B(\mathcal{C}_{266}(A(\boldsymbol{x})))$. In other words, S and $\mathcal{C}_{266}$ are affine equivalent. To find the affine functions the algorithm given in [8] can be used; indeed there exist 4 such two affine functions. Also, as stated in [7] $\mathcal{C}_{266}$ can be decomposed into two quadratic bijections. One of the possibilities is $\mathcal{Q}_{294} \times \mathcal{Q}_{299}$. It means that there exist three affine functions A_1, A_2, A_3, where $\mathcal{C}_{266} = A_3 \circ \mathcal{Q}_{299} \circ A_2 \circ \mathcal{Q}_{294} \circ A_1$. Since $\mathcal{C}_{266}$ and S are affine equivalent, there exist also three affine functions to decompose the PRESENT Sbox as

$$S(x) = A_3\Bigg(\mathcal{Q}_{299}\bigg(A_2\Big(\mathcal{Q}_{294}(A_1(x)) \Big) \bigg) \Bigg). \tag{4}$$

We have found $229{,}376$ such 3-tuple affine bijections, and we have selected one of the most simplest solutions with respect to the number of terms in their Algebraic Normal Form (ANF) directly affecting the size of the corresponding circuit.

The next step is to provide the uniform first-order TI of the quadratic bijections $\mathcal{Q}_{294}$ and $\mathcal{Q}_{299}$ which can be easily achieved by direct sharing [7]. For $\mathcal{Q}_{294}$:0123456789BAEFDC we can write

$$e = a + bd, \qquad f = b + cd, \qquad g = c, \qquad h = d, \tag{5}$$

with $\langle a, b, c, d\rangle$ the 4-bit input, $\langle e, f, g, h\rangle$ the 4-bit output, and a and e the least significant bits. The component functions of the first-order TI of $\mathcal{Q}_{294}$ can be derived by $f_{\mathcal{Q}_{294}}^{i,j}(\langle a^i, b^i, c^i, d^i\rangle, \langle a^j, b^j, c^j, d^j\rangle) = \langle e, f, g, h\rangle$ as

$$e = a^i + b^i d^i + d^i b^j + b^i d^j \qquad g = c^i$$
$$f = b^i + c^i d^i + d^i c^j + c^i d^j \qquad h = d^i \tag{6}$$

The three 4-bit output shares provided by $f_{\mathcal{Q}_{294}}^{2,3}(.,.)$, $f_{\mathcal{Q}_{294}}^{3,1}(.,.)$ and $f_{\mathcal{Q}_{294}}^{1,2}(.,.)$ make a uniform first-order TI of $\mathcal{Q}_{294}$.

Following the same principle for $\mathcal{Q}_{299}$:012345678ACEB9FD as

$$e = a + ad + cd, \qquad f = b + ad + bc + cd, \qquad g = c + bd + cd, \qquad h = d, \tag{7}$$

we can define the component function $f_{\mathcal{Q}_{299}}^{i,j}(\langle a^i, b^i, c^i, d^i\rangle, \langle a^j, b^j, c^j, d^j\rangle) = \langle e, f, g, h\rangle$ as

$$e = a^i + (a^i d^i + d^i a^j + a^i d^j) + (c^i d^i + d^i c^j + c^i d^j)$$
$$f = b^i + (a^i d^i + d^i a^j + a^i d^j) + (b^i d^i + d^i b^j + b^i d^j) + (c^i d^i + d^i c^j + c^i d^j)$$
$$g = c^i + (b^i d^i + d^i b^j + b^i d^j) + (c^i d^i + d^i c^j + c^i d^j)$$
$$h = d^i. \tag{8}$$

Similarly, three 4-bit output shares provided by $f_{\mathcal{Q}_{299}}^{2,3}(.,.)$, $f_{\mathcal{Q}_{299}}^{3,1}(.,.)$ and $f_{\mathcal{Q}_{299}}^{1,2}(.,.)$ make a uniform first-order TI of $\mathcal{Q}_{299}$.

Since the affine transformations A_1, A_2, A_3 do not change the uniformity and should be applied on each 4-bit share separately, the decomposition in Eq. (4) provides a 3-share uniform first-order TI of the PRESENT Sbox. It should be noted that registers are required to be placed between the component functions of $\mathcal{Q}_{294}$ and $\mathcal{Q}_{299}$ to avoid the propagation of the glitches (see Fig. 3). Note that the affine function A_2 can be freely placed before or after the intermediate register.

For the second-order TI representations in addition to the above expressed component functions, we define $g_{\mathcal{Q}_{294}}^{i,j}(\langle a^i, b^i, c^i, d^i\rangle, \langle a^j, b^j, c^j, d^j\rangle) = \langle e, f, g, h\rangle$ as

$$e = d^i b^j + b^i d^j \qquad g = 0$$
$$f = d^i c^j + c^i d^j \qquad h = 0. \tag{9}$$

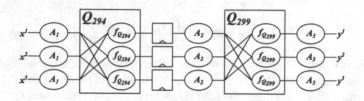

Fig. 3. A first-order TI of the PRESENT Sbox: $S(x) = y$

The 4-bit output shares $y^{i \in \{1,\dots,10\}}$ are provided by

$$y^1 = f^{2,3}_{\mathcal{Q}_{294}}(.,.), \quad y^2 = f^{3,4}_{\mathcal{Q}_{294}}(.,.), \quad y^3 = f^{4,5}_{\mathcal{Q}_{294}}(.,.), \quad y^4 = f^{5,1}_{\mathcal{Q}_{294}}(.,.),$$
$$y^5 = f^{1,2}_{\mathcal{Q}_{294}}(.,.), \quad y^6 = g^{2,4}_{\mathcal{Q}_{294}}(.,.), \quad y^7 = g^{3,5}_{\mathcal{Q}_{294}}(.,.), \quad y^8 = g^{1,4}_{\mathcal{Q}_{294}}(.,.),$$
$$y^9 = g^{2,5}_{\mathcal{Q}_{294}}(.,.), \quad y^{10} = g^{1,3}_{\mathcal{Q}_{294}}(.,.). \tag{10}$$

After a clock cycle, when $y^{i \in \{1,\dots,10\}}$ are stores in dedicate registers, the output shares should be combined as

$$z^{i \in \{1,\dots,5\}} = y^i + y^{i+5}, \tag{11}$$

which provides the uniform second-order TI of $\mathcal{Q}_{294}$.

The same procedure is valid in case of $\mathcal{Q}_{299}$ considering the component function $g^{i,j}_{\mathcal{Q}_{299}}(\langle a^i, b^i, c^i, d^i \rangle, \langle a^j, b^j, c^j, d^j \rangle) = \langle e, f, g, h \rangle$ as

$$e = d^i a^j + d^i c^j + a^i d^j + c^i d^j$$
$$f = d^i a^j + d^i b^j + d^i c^j + a^i d^j + b^i d^j + c^i d^j$$
$$g = d^i b^j + d^i c^j + b^i d^j + c^i d^j$$
$$h = 0. \tag{12}$$

By changing the indices from $\mathcal{Q}_{294}$ to $\mathcal{Q}_{299}$ in Eq. (10) and later applying the reduction in Eq. (11), a uniform second-order TI of $\mathcal{Q}_{299}$ is achieved. Hence by means of these component functions in addition to the affine transformations, we can realize a uniform second-order TI of the PRESENT Sbox. Figure 4 shows the graphical view of such a construction, and all the required formulas are given in the extended version of this article [35]. Note that the registers after the affine function A_2 can instead be place before A_2 right after the reduction from 10 to 5 shares.

3.4   Implementation

Based on the specifications given above and considering a Spartan-6 FPGA (indeed the XC6SLX75 of SAKURA-G [1]) we implemented six designs. The first three ones are different profiles of KATAN-32, and the next three designs realize the encryption of PRESENT with a round-based architecture. For each of the targeted cipher we implemented

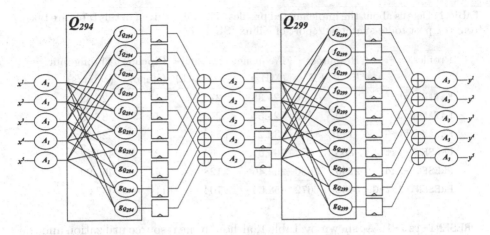

Fig. 4. A second-order TI of the PRESENT Sbox: $S(x) = y$

- the first-order TI, i.e., KATAN-1st and PRESENT-1st profiles,
- the second-order TI, i.e., KATAN-2nd and PRESENT-2nd profiles, and
- the first-order TI with GliFreD, i.e., KATAN-1st-G and PRESENT-1st-G profiles.

Although we did not consider any constraints on placement and routing of the four non-GliFreD profiles, following the principles of GliFreD the corresponding profiles have been realized by first defining an area on the target FPGA, where the component of the *true* part of the GliFreD circuit should be placed. After finishing the placement and routing, the corresponding dual circuit, i.e., the *false* part of the GliFreD circuit, has been cloned and dualized by means of the RapidSmith tool [22]. As a reference, the circuits shown in Fig. 1 are the normal and GliFreD realizations of the least significant bit e of Eq. (8).

Due to its serialized ring architecture, the KATAN-1st-G profile does not form a pipeline. The most important difference between such a profile and its original one (KATAN-1st) is on the one hand the number of required clock cycles to finish an encryption (i.e., latency) which is doubled and on the other hand the raised achievable clock frequency due to the minimal LUT depth. The max LUT depth in GliFreD circuits is 1, hence a very short critical path. However, the PRESENT-1st-G profile is implemented in a fully-pipelined way, so that the round-based architecture is able to hold 11 different cipher states. Hence, after $32 \times 11 \times 2 = 704$ clock cycles, 11 encryptions with the same key are performed. The pipelined architecture naturally increases the register utilization of the components but provides a much higher throughput.

Table 1 compares the overhead and performance of different design profiles. It indeed gives an overview on the disadvantage (area and time overheads) as well as the advantage (throughput) of employing GliFreD with respect to two different design architectures, i.e., a fully-serialized one which is register oriented (KATAN-1st-G) and a round-based one which is combinatorial oriented

Table 1. Details about the implemented profiles. The values given in this table are taken from the post route synthesis report of Xilinx ISE 14.7.

Profile	Resources		Frequency	Latency	Pipeline	Throughput
	LUT	FF	(MHz)	(#clock)	(stage)	(Mbit/s)
KATAN-1st	34	96	225.38	273	1	26.42
KATAN-2nd	65	180	321.54	273	1	37.69
KATAN-1st-G	114	548	438.21	546	1	25.68
PRESENT-1st	808	384	206.61	64	2	413.22
PRESENT-2nd	2245	1680	203.46	128	4	406.92
PRESENT-1st-G	5442	12672	458.09	704	11	458.09

(PRESENT-1st-G). As shown by Table 1, although the resource utilization and the latency of the GliFreD profiles are drastically increased, the throughput is still kept comparable with the original design profiles. Such achievements are mainly due to the naturally-minimized critical paths in the GliFreD designs allowing a high clock frequency.

4 Empirical Results

In addition to the performance and overhead figures given in Sect. 3.4, we practically examined the ability of each of our six developed designs to avoid side-channel leakages.

Setup. The experimental platform is a SAKURA-G [1] equipped with a Xilinx Spartan-6 FPGA. The side-channel leakages have been measured by collecting power consumption traces of the underlying FPGA by means of a Teledyne LeCroy HRO 66Zi digital oscilloscope at a sampling frequency of 500 MS/s and a limited bandwidth of 20 MHz. Due to the low peak-to-peak amplitude of the signals we also made use of the amplifier embedded on the SAKURA board. For all six design profiles, the target FPGA operated at a frequency of 24 MHz during the collection of the power traces. Our intuition on the measured power traces from our platform is that the traces are heavily filtered by the measurement setup including the shunt resistor, chip packaging, printed circuit board (PCB), and probes. Measuring the power traces with high bandwidth (> 20 MHz) leads to higher electrical noise. We have examined this behavior and observed leakages easier when the bandwidth is limited. Note that this intuition does not hold true in case of EM measurements.

It is noteworthy that such a frequency of operation has intentionally been taken in order to : i) cover the full power trace length in the measurements as the KATAN profiles need 254 clock cycles after data being loaded (respectively 508 for KATAN-1st-G), and ii) cause the power peaks of adjacent clock cycles slightly overlap each other. The later has been considered with respect to the note given in [45] that the second-order TI can still be vulnerable to a second-order bivariate attack. Recalling the techniques introduced in [31], employing certain amplifiers or running the device at a high clock frequency leads to converting multivariate leakages to univariate. It has been shown in [49] that a second-order TI design actually can exhibit a univariate second-order leakage if the measurement setup is employed by certain components, e.g., DC blockers and/or amplifiers. Hence, operating the device at 24 MHz allows us to easily cover the long traces in the measurements and provide particular situations, where second-order TI profiles may demonstrate second-order leakage.

Evaluation. As the evaluation metric we employed the leakage assessment methodology of [17,48] which is based on the Student's t-test. The reason for such a choice is twofold. First, the t-test can examine the existence of detectable leakages without performing any key-recovery attack, which significantly eases the evaluation process particularly where higher-order leakages using millions of traces should be examined. Moreover, the efficiency of the state-of-the-art

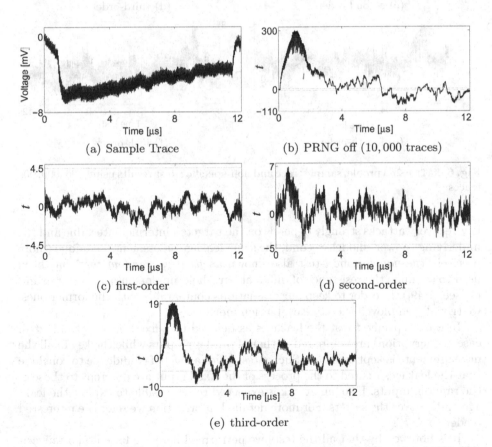

(a) Sample Trace

(b) PRNG off (10, 000 traces)

(c) first-order

(d) second-order

(e) third-order

Fig. 5. KATAN-1st profile, sample trace and non-specific t-test results using 1, 000, 000 traces

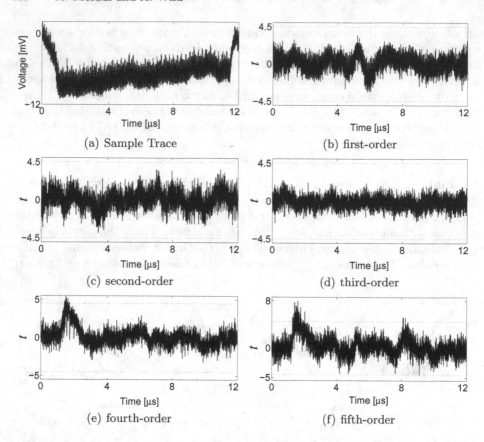

(a) Sample Trace   (b) first-order

(c) second-order   (d) third-order

(e) fourth-order   (f) fifth-order

Fig. 6. KATAN-2nd profile, sample trace and non-specific t-test results using $100,000,000$ traces

key-recovery attacks strongly depends on the targeted intermediate value and the underlying (power) model. Second, the same leakage assessment technique (more precisely the non-specific t-test also known as *fixed vs. random* test) has been used to examine the resistance of different threshold implementations (for example see [5,49]). In order to keep our evaluations comparable with the former ones, we trivially employed the same evaluation method.

In a non-specific t-test the leakages associated to a fixed input (plaintext in case of encryption) are compared to that of random inputs while the key in all the measurements is kept constant. Such a test gives a level of confidence to conclude that the leakages related to the process of the fixed input are different to those of the random inputs. If so, an attack is expected to be feasible to exploit the leakage and recover the secrets. For more detailed information we refer the interested reader to [5,17].

It is noteworthy that all the tests we performed here are based on a univariate scenario. In other words, we did not run any combination function on different sample points of each collected power trace. Further, we followed the same principle

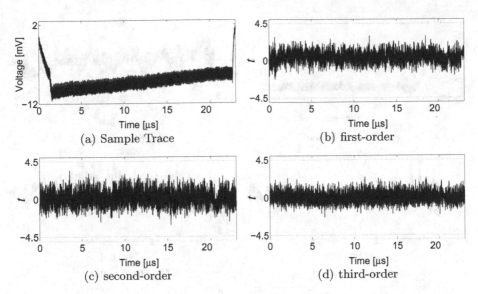

Fig. 7. `KATAN-1st-G` profile, sample trace and non-specific t-test results using $1,000,000,000$ traces

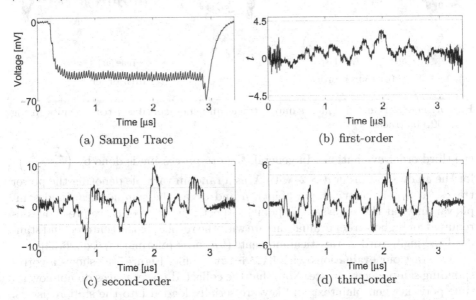

Fig. 8. `PRESENT-1st` profile, sample trace and non-specific t-test results using $10,000,000$ traces

explained in [5, 48] to conduct the tests at higher orders. It means that we made the power traces mean-free squared (at each sample point independently), i.e., $(X - \mu)^2$ for the second-order evaluations, and standardized cubed, i.e., $\left(\dfrac{X - \mu}{\sigma}\right)^3$ for

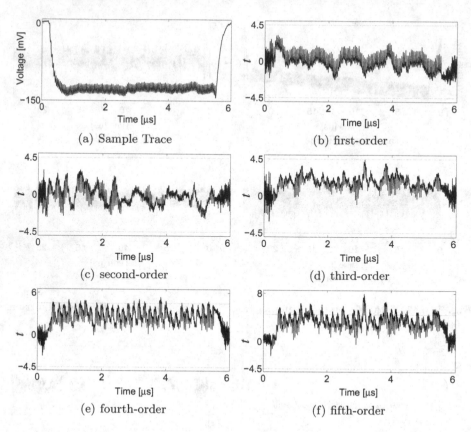

Fig. 9. PRESENT-2nd profile, sample trace and non-specific t-test results using $300,000,000$ traces

the third-order evaluations. In general, the pre-processing is done by $\left(\dfrac{X - \mu}{\sigma}\right)^d$ for the analyses at order $d > 2$, with X as a random variable denoting the power traces (at a particular sample point), μ and σ^2 as the sample mean and sample variance (at the same sample point) respectively. Indeed, these pre-processes required for higher-order evaluations are with the respect to the centered and standardized higher-order statistical moments (for more information see [26, 34]).

We start our evaluations with KATAN-1st profile. Figure 5(a) shows a corresponding sample power trace. Note that the collected power traces do not cover a time period, when plaintext and key are serially loaded into the shift registers. In order to have an overview about the quality of the measurement setup and verify the employed evaluation metric, for the first analysis we turned the PRNG off thereby forcing all masks to zero, used for sharing the plaintexts. As shown by Fig. 5(b), the first-order t-test shows clear detectable leakages using a few $10,000$ traces. By keeping the PRNG active and conducting the same non-specific t-tests up to third-order using $1,000,000$ traces we observed the curves shown by Fig. 5, which indeed confirm the first-order resistance and vulnerability at the second and third orders, as expected.

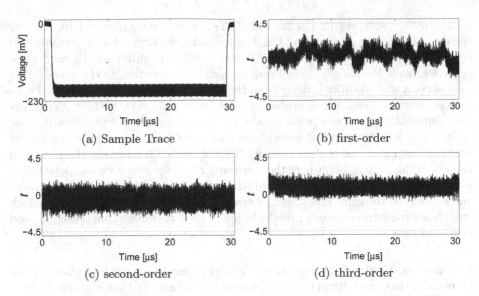

(a) Sample Trace

(b) first-order

(c) second-order

(d) third-order

Fig. 10. PRESENT-1st-G profile, sample trace and non-specific t-test results using $1,000,000,000$ traces

For the KATAN-2nd profile we had to collect much more traces to be able to observe the higher-order leakages. It is due to the high order of sharing, i.e., at least 5 shares (see Sect. 3.1) in case of a second-order TI. In fact, we observed the fourth- and fifth-order leakages using approximately $100,000,000$ traces, as shown in Fig. 6. However, in order to examine the issue reported in [45] (by operating the target at 24 MHz) we continued the collection of the traces up to $500,000,000$, but we have not observed any second-order leakage while the fourth- and fifth-order leakages became detectable – expectedly – with higher confidence. We should here refer to the issue addressed in [45] and the detectable second-order leakage reported in [49]. Based on the explanations of [45] a second-order bivariate leakage should be detectable, but such a bivariate leakage is not necessarily detectable from the consecutive clock cycles, that can additively be combined by means of an amplifier or running the device at a high clock frequency [31]. In case of the application of [49] apparently the consecutive clock cycles exhibit such a bivariate leakage, but it is not hold true for the serialized KATAN architecture. Further, compared to our design profiles the constructions in [49] make use of a kind of remasking which is a different methodology to ensure the uniformity.

Following the same scenario we performed the evaluations on the KATAN-1st-G profile and collected $1,000,000,000$ traces to perform the same t-tests at up to third order. The corresponding results which are depicted in Fig. 8 indeed confirm the effectiveness of the underlying hiding technique to significantly harden the higher-order attacks. The result of this profile can be compared to that of the KATAN-1st profile (Fig. 5), where $1,000,000$ traces are adequate to observe the second- and third-order leakages.

The same leakage assessment technique has been conducted on the three profiles of the round-based PRESENT architecture, and the corresponding results are shown in Figs. 8, 9 and 10. For the PRESENT-1st profile we required $10,000,000$ trace to observe the second- and third-order leakages. Respectively $300,000,000$ traces were necessary for the PRESENT-2nd profile to exhibit fourth- and fifth-order leakages. We should again bring the reader's attention to the infeasibility to observe a second-order leakage from the PRESENT-2nd profile. We indeed continued our evaluations on this profile by measuring $1,000,000,000$ traces as well as with different fixed inputs (with respect to the non-specific t-tests), but in none of the tests we observed a detectable second-order leakage. As an example, we give the results of one of such tests with $1,000,000,000$ traces in the extended version of this article [35], where the third-order leakage also becomes detectable. Finally, similar to the KATAN GliFreD design we collected $1,000,000,000$ traces and conducted the same non-specific t-tests on the PRESENT-1st-G profile, which still shows robustness to avoid the leakages to be detectable at first, second, and third orders.

Discussion. Comparing the presented practical results, at the first glance it can be noticed that the GliFreD profiles consume more energy than the other corresponding profiles. They also increase the number of required clock cycles (latency) particularly in case of the PRESENT design as its combinatorial circuit has a longer depth compared to the KATAN design. However, their achievement, i.e., hiding the higher-order leakages to make the higher-order attacks *practically* infeasible, is confirmed. Hence, it can be concluded that the combination of such a power-equalization technique and a proper masking scheme (i.e., first-order TI) gives a high level of confidence to argue the practical infeasibility of the key-recovery attacks.

Our comparisons are limited to the second-order TI of KATAN and PRESENT, which can be extended to higher-order TI designs. However, by increasing the desired order of security the number of shares and the required internal PRNGs respectively increase (e.g., at least 7 and 9 shares for third- and fourth-order TI). Note that the numbers given in Table 1 exclude the area required for the PRNGs.

Nonetheless, due to the local separation of false and true parts in GliFreD circuits, the resistance of our proposed method against higher-order EM attacks is still an open question and should be addressed in the future. Further, GliFreD is exclusively designed for FPGAs and uses the fixed LUT structure to realize Boolean functions of a circuit. Transforming this logic style naively to ASIC may not lead to the expected results especially with respect to the area overhead. The idea of combining TI with DPL styles can be adopted for ASICs by employing one of the logic styles designed for ASICs in addition to a customized router.

References

1. Side-channel AttacK User Reference Architecture. http://satoh.cs.uec.ac.jp/SAKURA/index.html
2. Balasch, J., Gierlichs, B., Verdult, R., Batina, L., Verbauwhede, I.: Power analysis of Atmel CryptoMemory – recovering keys from secure EEPROMs. In: Dunkelman, O. (ed.) CT-RSA 2012. LNCS, vol. 7178, pp. 19–34. Springer, Heidelberg (2012)

3. Bhasin, S., Guilley, S., Flament, F., Selmane, N., Danger, J.: Countering early evaluation: an approach towards robust dual-rail precharge logic. In: Workshop on Embedded Systems Security - WESS 2010, p. 6. ACM (2010)

4. Bilgin, B., Gierlichs, B., Nikova, S., Nikov, V., Rijmen, V.: A more efficient AES threshold implementation. In: Pointcheval, D., Vergnaud, D. (eds.) AFRICACRYPT. LNCS, vol. 8469, pp. 267–284. Springer, Heidelberg (2014)

5. Bilgin, B., Gierlichs, B., Nikova, S., Nikov, V., Rijmen, V.: Higher-order threshold implementations. In: Sarkar, P., Iwata, T. (eds.) ASIACRYPT 2014, Part II. LNCS, vol. 8874, pp. 326–343. Springer, Heidelberg (2014)

6. Bilgin, B., Nikova, S., Nikov, V., Rijmen, V., Stütz, G.: Threshold implementations of all 3 × 3 and 4 × 4 S-boxes. In: Prouff, E., Schaumont, P. (eds.) CHES 2012. LNCS, vol. 7428, pp. 76–91. Springer, Heidelberg (2012)

7. Bilgin, B., Nikova, S., Nikov, V., Rijmen, V., Tokareva, N., Vitkup, V.: Threshold implementations of small S-boxes. Cryptograph. Commun. $7(1)$, 3–33 (2015)

8. Biryukov, A., Cannière, C.D., Braeken, A., Preneel, B.: A Toolbox for Cryptanalysis: Linear and Affine Equivalence Algorithms. In: Biham, E. (ed.) EUROCRYPT 2003. LNCS, vol. 2656, pp. 33–50. Springer, Heidelberg (2003)

9. Bogdanov, A.A., Knudsen, L.R., Leander, G., Paar, C., Poschmann, A., Robshaw, M., Seurin, Y., Vikkelsoe, C.: PRESENT: an ultra-lightweight block cipher. In: Paillier, P., Verbauwhede, I. (eds.) CHES 2007. LNCS, vol. 4727, pp. 450–466. Springer, Heidelberg (2007)

10. De Cannière, C., Dunkelman, O., Knežević, M.: KATAN and KTANTAN — A Family of Small and Efficient Hardware-Oriented Block Ciphers. In: Clavier, C., Gaj, K. (eds.) CHES 2009. LNCS, vol. 5747, pp. 272–288. Springer, Heidelberg (2009)

11. Canright, D., Batina, L.: A very compact "perfectly masked" S-box for AES. In: Bellovin, S.M., Gennaro, R., Keromytis, A.D., Yung, M. (eds.) ACNS 2008. LNCS, vol. 5037, pp. 446–459. Springer, Heidelberg (2008)

12. Chari, S., Jutla, C.S., Rao, J.R., Rohatgi, P.: Towards sound approaches to counteract power-analysis attacks. In: Wiener, M. (ed.) CRYPTO 1999. LNCS, vol. 1666, pp. 398–412. Springer, Heidelberg (1999)

13. Chen, Z., Zhou, Y.: Dual-rail random switching logic: a countermeasure to reduce side channel leakage. In: Goubin, L., Matsui, M. (eds.) CHES 2006. LNCS, vol. 4249, pp. 242–254. Springer, Heidelberg (2006)

14. Coron, J.-S., Kizhvatov, I.: An efficient method for random delay generation in embedded software. In: Clavier, C., Gaj, K. (eds.) CHES 2009. LNCS, vol. 5747, pp. 156–170. Springer, Heidelberg (2009)

15. Duc, A., Dziembowski, S., Faust, S.: Unifying leakage models: from probing attacks to noisy leakage. In: Nguyen, P.Q., Oswald, E. (eds.) EUROCRYPT 2014. LNCS, vol. 8441, pp. 423–440. Springer, Heidelberg (2014)

16. Eisenbarth, T., Kasper, T., Moradi, A., Paar, C., Salmasizadeh, M., Shalmani, M.T.M.: On the power of power analysis in the real world: a complete break of the KEELOQ code hopping scheme. In: Wagner, D. (ed.) CRYPTO 2008. LNCS, vol. 5157, pp. 203–220. Springer, Heidelberg (2008)

17. Goodwill, G., Jun, B., Jaffe, J., Rohatgi, P.: A testing methodology for side channel resistance validation. In: NIST Non-invasive Attack Testing Workshop (2011). http://csrc.nist.gov/news_events/non-invasive-attack-testing-workshop/papers/08_Goodwill.pdf

18. Güneysu, T., Moradi, A.: Generic side-channel countermeasures for reconfigurable devices. In: Preneel, B., Takagi, T. (eds.) CHES 2011. LNCS, vol. 6917, pp. 33–48. Springer, Heidelberg (2011)

19. He, W., de la Torre, E., Riesgo, T.: A Precharge-absorbed DPL logic for reducing early propagation effects on FPGA implementations. In: Reconfigurable Computing and FPGAs - ReConFig 2011, pp. 217–222. IEEE Computer Society (2011)
20. He, W., Otero, A., de la Torre, E., Riesgo. T.: Automatic generation of identical routing pairs for FPGA implemented DPL logic. In: Reconfigurable Computing and FPGAs - ReConFig 2012, pp. 1–6. IEEE Computer Society (2012)
21. Kaps, J., Velegalati, R.: DPA resistant AES on FPGA using partial DDL. In: Field-Programmable Custom Computing Machines - FCCM 2010, pp. 273–280. IEEE Computer Society (2010)
22. Lavin, C., Padilla, M., Lamprecht, J., Lundrigan, P., Nelson, B., Hutchings, B., Wirthlin, M.: RapidSmith - a library for low-level manipulation of partially placed-and-routed FPGA designs. Technical report, Brigham Young University, September 2012
23. Lomné, V., Maurine, P., Torres, L., Robert, M., Soares, R., Calazans, N.: Evaluation on FPGA of triple rail logic robustness against DPA and DEMA. In: Design, Automation and Test in Europe - DATE 2009, pp. 634–639. IEEE Computer Society (2009)
24. Mangard, S., Oswald, E., Popp, T.: Power Analysis Attacks: Revealing the Secrets of Smart Cards. Springer, Heidelberg (2007)
25. Mangard, S., Pramstaller, N., Oswald, E.: Successfully attacking masked AES hardware implementations. In: Rao, J.R., Sunar, B. (eds.) CHES 2005. LNCS, vol. 3659, pp. 157–171. Springer, Heidelberg (2005)
26. Moradi, A.: Statistical tools flavor side-channel collision attacks. In: Pointcheval, D., Johansson, T. (eds.) EUROCRYPT 2012. LNCS, vol. 7237, pp. 428–445. Springer, Heidelberg (2012)
27. Moradi, A., Barenghi, A., Kasper, T., Paar, C.: On the vulnerability of FPGA bitstream encryption against power analysis attacks: extracting keys from xilinx Virtex-II FPGAs. In: ACM Conference on Computer and Communications Security - CCS 2011, pp. 111–124. ACM (2011)
28. Moradi, A., Eisenbarth, T., Poschmann, A., Paar, C.: Power analysis of single-rail storage elements as used in MDPL. In: Lee, D., Hong, S. (eds.) ICISC 2009. LNCS, vol. 5984, pp. 146–160. Springer, Heidelberg (2010)
29. Moradi, A., Immler, V.: Early propagation and imbalanced routing, how to diminish in FPGAs. In: Batina, L., Robshaw, M. (eds.) CHES 2014. LNCS, vol. 8731, pp. 598–615. Springer, Heidelberg (2014)
30. Moradi, A., Mischke, O.: Glitch-free implementation of masking in modern FPGAs. In: Hardware-Oriented Security and Trust - HOST 2012, pp. 89–95. IEEE (2012)
31. Moradi, A., Mischke, O.: On the simplicity of converting leakages from multivariate to univariate. In: Bertoni, G., Coron, J.-S. (eds.) CHES 2013. LNCS, vol. 8086, pp. 1–20. Springer, Heidelberg (2013)
32. Moradi, A., Mischke, O., Eisenbarth, T.: Correlation-enhanced power analysis collision attack. In: Mangard, S., Standaert, F.-X. (eds.) CHES 2010. LNCS, vol. 6225, pp. 125–139. Springer, Heidelberg (2010)
33. Moradi, A., Poschmann, A., Ling, S., Paar, C., Wang, H.: Pushing the limits: a very compact and a threshold implementation of AES. In: Paterson, K.G. (ed.) EUROCRYPT 2011. LNCS, vol. 6632, pp. 69–88. Springer, Heidelberg (2011)
34. Moradi, A., Standaert, F.-X.: Moments-correlating DPA. Cryptology ePrint Archive, Report 2014/409 (2014). http://eprint.iacr.org/
35. Moradi, A., Wild, A.: Assessment of hiding the higher-order leakages in hardware - what are the achievements versus overheads? Cryptology ePrint Archive (2015). http://eprint.iacr.org/

36. Nassar, M., Bhasin, S., Danger, J., Duc, G., Guilley, S.: BCDL: a high speed balanced DPL for FPGA with global precharge and no early evaluation. In: Design, Automation and Test in Europe - DATE 2010, pp. 849–854. IEEE Computer Society (2010)

37. Nikova, S., Rijmen, V., Schläffer, M.: Secure hardware implementation of non-linear functions in the presence of glitches. In: Lee, P.J., Cheon, J.H. (eds.) ICISC 2008. LNCS, vol. 5461, pp. 218–234. Springer, Heidelberg (2009)

38. Nikova, S., Rijmen, V., Schläffer, M.: Secure hardware implementation of nonlinear functions in the presence of glitches. J. Cryptol. 24(2), 292–321 (2011)

39. Oswald, E., Mangard, S., Pramstaller, N., Rijmen, V.: A side-channel analysis resistant description of the AES S-box. In: Gilbert, H., Handschuh, H. (eds.) FSE 2005. LNCS, vol. 3557, pp. 413–423. Springer, Heidelberg (2005)

40. Popp, T., Kirschbaum, M., Zefferer, T., Mangard, S.: Evaluation of the masked logic style MDPL on a prototype chip. In: Paillier, P., Verbauwhede, I. (eds.) CHES 2007. LNCS, vol. 4727, pp. 81–94. Springer, Heidelberg (2007)

41. Popp, T., Mangard, S.: Masked dual-rail pre-charge logic: DPA-resistance without routing constraints. In: Rao, J.R., Sunar, B. (eds.) CHES 2005. LNCS, vol. 3659, pp. 172–186. Springer, Heidelberg (2005)

42. Poschmann, A., Moradi, A., Khoo, K., Lim, C., Wang, H., Ling, S.: Side-channel resistant crypto for less than 2, 300 GE. J. Cryptol. 24(2), 322–345 (2011)

43. Prouff, E., Rivain, M., Bevan, R.: Statistical analysis of second order differential power analysis. IEEE Trans. Comput. 58(6), 799–811 (2009)

44. Rao, J.R., Rohatgi, P., Scherzer, H., Tinguely, S.: Partitioning attacks: or how to rapidly clone some GSM cards. In: IEEE Symposium on Security and Privacy, pp. 31–41. IEEE Computer Society (2002)

45. Reparaz, O.: A note on the security of higher-order threshold implementations. Cryptology ePrint Archive, Report 2015/001 (2015). http://eprint.iacr.org/

46. Rivain, M., Prouff, E.: Provably secure higher-order masking of AES. In: Mangard, S., Standaert, F.-X. (eds.) CHES 2010. LNCS, vol. 6225, pp. 413–427. Springer, Heidelberg (2010)

47. Sauvage, L., Nassar, M. Guilley, S., Flament, F., Danger, J., Mathieu, Y.: DPL on Stratix II FPGA: what to expect? In: Reconfigurable Computing and FPGAs - ReConFig 2009, pp. 243–248. IEEE Computer Society (2009)

48. Schneider, T., Moradi, A.: Leakage assessment methodology - a clear roadmap for side-channel evaluations. In: Güneysu, T., Handschuh, H. (eds.) CHES 2015. LNCS, vol. 9293, pp. xx–yy. Springer, Heidelberg (2015)

49. Schneider, T., Moradi, A., Güneysu, T.: Arithmetic addition over boolean masking - towards first- and second-order resistance in hardware. In: Malkin, T., Kolesnikov, V., Lewko, A.B., Polychronakis, M. (eds.) ACNS 2015. LNCS, vol. 9092, pp. 517–536. Springer, Heidelberg (2015)

50. Suzuki, D., Saeki, M.: Security evaluation of DPA countermeasures using dual-rail pre-charge logic style. In: Goubin, L., Matsui, M. (eds.) CHES 2006. LNCS, vol. 4249, pp. 255–269. Springer, Heidelberg (2006)

51. Tiri, K., Akmal, M., Verbauwhede, I.: A dynamic and differential CMOS logic with signal independent power consumption to withstand differential power analysis on smart cards. ESSCIRC 2002, 403–406 (2002)

52. Tiri, K., Hwang, D., Hodjat, A., Lai, B.-C., Yang, S., Schaumont, P., Verbauwhede, I.: Prototype IC with WDDL and differential routing – DPA resistance assessment. In: Rao, J.R., Sunar, B. (eds.) CHES 2005. LNCS, vol. 3659, pp. 354–365. Springer, Heidelberg (2005)

53. Tiri, K., Verbauwhede, I.: A logic level design methodology for a secure DPA resistant ASIC or FPGA implementation. In Design, Automation and Test in Europe - DATE 2004, pp. 246–251. IEEE Computer Society (2004)
54. Veyrat-Charvillon, N., Medwed, M., Kerckhof, S., Standaert, F.-X.: Shuffling against side-channel attacks: a comprehensive study with cautionary note. In: Wang, X., Sako, K. (eds.) ASIACRYPT 2012. LNCS, vol. 7658, pp. 740–757. Springer, Heidelberg (2012)
55. Wild, A., Moradi, A., Güneysu, T.: Evaluating the duplication of dual-rail precharge logics on FPGAs. In: Mangard, S., Poschmann, A.Y. (eds.) COSADE 2015. LNCS, vol. 9064, pp. 81–94. Springer, Heidelberg (2015)
56. Wild, A., Moradi, A., Güneysu, T.: GliFreD: glitch-free duplication - towards power-equalized circuits on FPGAs. Cryptology ePrint Archive, Report 2015/124 (2015). http://eprint.iacr.org/
57. Yu, P., Schaumont, P.: Secure FPGA circuits using controlled placement and routing. In: Hardware/Software Codesign and System Synthesis - CODES+ISSS 2007, pp. 45–50 (2007)
58. Zhou, Y., Yu, Y., Standaert, F.-X., Quisquater, J.-J.: On the need of physical security for small embedded devices: a case study with COMP128-1 implementations in SIM cards. In: Sadeghi, A.-R. (ed.) FC 2013. LNCS, vol. 7859, pp. 230–238. Springer, Heidelberg (2013)

Multi-variate High-Order Attacks of Shuffled Tables Recomputation

Nicolas Bruneau[1,2]($\boxtimes$), Sylvain Guilley[1,3], Zakaria Najm[1], and Yannick Teglia[2]

[1] TELECOM-ParisTech, Crypto Group, Paris, France
nicolas.bruneau@telecom-paristech.fr
http://www.telecom-paristech.fr/en/eng/home.html,
http://www.comelec.enst.fr/recherche/sen.en
[2] STMicroelectronics, AST Division, Rousset, France
http://www.st.com/
[3] Secure-IC S.A.S., Rennes, France
http://www.Secure-IC.com/

Abstract. Masking schemes based on tables recomputation are classical countermeasures against high-order side-channel attacks. Still, they are known to be attackable at order d in the case the masking involves d shares. In this work, we mathematically show that an attack of order strictly greater than d can be more successful than an attack at order d. To do so, we leverage the idea presented by Tunstall, Whitnall and Oswald at FSE 2013: we exhibit attacks which exploit the multiple leakages linked to one mask during the recomputation of tables. Specifically, regarding first-order table recomputation, improved by a shuffled execution, we show that there is a window of opportunity, in terms of noise variance, where a novel highly multivariate third-order attack is more efficient than a classical bivariate second-order attack. Moreover, we show on the example of the high-order secure table computation presented by Coron at EUROCRYPT 2014 that the window of opportunity enlarges linearly with the security order d.

Keywords: Shuffled table recomputation · Highly multivariate high-order attacks · Signal-to-noise ratio

1 Introduction

For several years now Side-Channel Attacks (SCA [13]) have been a threat against cryptographic algorithms in embedded systems. To protect cryptographic implementations against these attacks several countermeasures and protection techniques have been developed. Data masking schemes [12] are widely used since their security can be formally grounded.

The rationale of masking schemes goes as follows: each sensitive variable is randomly splitted in d shares (using $d - 1$ masks), in such a way that any tuple of $d - 1$ shares manipulated during the masked algorithm is independent from any sensitive variable. Masking schemes are the target of higher-order SCA

© International Association for Cryptologic Research 2015
T. Güneysu and H. Handschuh (Eds.): CHES 2015, LNCS 9293, pp. 475–494, 2015.
DOI: 10.1007/978-3-662-48324-4_24

[5,16,20,25]. A dth-order attack combines the leakages of d shares. A particular difficulty in the implementation of masking schemes is to compute non-linear parts of the algorithm, such as for example the S-Box of AES (a function from n bits to n bits). To solve this difficulty different methods have been proposed which can be classified in three categories [14].

- Algebraic methods [2,21]. The outputs of the S-Box will be computed using the algebraic representation of the S-box.
- Global Look-up Table [19,23] method. A table is precomputed off-line for each possible input and output masks.
- Table recomputation methods which precompute a masked S-Box stored in a table [1,5,15]; such tables can be recomputed only once per encryption to reach first-order security. More recently, Coron presented at EUROCRYPT 2014 [7] a table recomputation scheme secure against dth-order attacks. Since this countermeasure aims at high-order security ($d > 1$), it requires one table recomputation at each S-Box call.

These methods provide security against Differential Power Analysis [13] (DPA) or Higher-Order DPA (HODPA). Still, whatever the protection order, there is *at least one* leakage associated to each share: in practice, shares (typically masks) can leak *more than once*. For example attacks exploiting the multiplicity of leakages of the same mask during the table recomputation have been presented by Pan et al. in [18] and more recently by Tunstall et al. in [24]. Such attacks consist in guessing the mask in a first order horizontal Correlation Power Analysis [3] (CPA) and then conducting a first-order vertical CPA knowing the mask. Variants consist in using a machine learning technique to extract the mask [9]. Globally, we refer to these attacks as Horizontal-Vertical attacks (HV attacks).

Shuffling the table recomputation makes the HV attacks more difficult. Still shuffling can be bypassed if the random permutation is generated from a seed with low entropy, since both the mask and the shuffling seed can be guessed [24].

Our Contributions. Our first contribution is to describe a new HODPA tailored to target the table recomputation despite a highly entropic masking (unexploitable by exhaustive search). More precisely, we propose an innovative combination function, which has the specificity to be highly multivariate. We relate the combination function of HODPA attacks to their expected signal-to-noise ratio, which allows for a straightforward comparison the attacks based on their success rate. In particular, we compare the success rates of our highly multivariate HODPA (exploiting leakages in the table recomputation as well as in the masked algorithm, where the secret key is used) and of a state-of-the-art HODPA (exploiting only the leakages within the masked algorithm). Our analysis reveals that there is a window of opportunity, when the noise variance is smaller than a threshold, where our new HODPA is more successful than a straightforward HODPA, despite it is of higher-order.

For instance in this paper we attack a first-order masking scheme based on table recomputation with a $(2^{n+1} + 1)$-variate third-order attack more efficiently than with a classical bivariate second-order attack. In this case HV attacks could not be applied. This is the first time that a non minimal order attack is proved better (in terms of success rate) than the attack of minimal order. Actually, this non intuitive result arises from a relevant selection of leaking samples — this question is seldom addressed in the side-channel literature. We generalize our attack to a higher-order masking scheme based on tables recomputation (Coron, EUROCRYPT 2014), and prove that it remains better than a classical attack, with a window of opportunity that actually grows linearly with the masking order d.

Outline of the Paper. The rest of the paper is organized as follows. Sect. 2 introduce the notations used in this article. Sect. 3 provides a reminder on table recomputation algorithms and on the way to defeat and protect this algorithm using random permutations. In Sect. 4 we propose a new attack against the "protected" implementation of the table recomputation, prove theoretically the soundness of the attack and validate these results by simulation. In Sect. 5 we apply this attack on a higher-order masking scheme. Sect. 6 extends our results to the case where the leakage function is affine. Finally in Sect. 7 we validate our results on real traces.

2   Preliminary and Notations

In this article capital letters (e.g., U) denote random variables and lowercase letters denote their realizations (e.g., u).

Let $k^\star$ be the secret key of the cryptographic algorithm. T denotes the input or the ciphertext. We suppose that the computations are done on n-bit words which means that these words can be seen as elements of $\mathbb{F}_2^n$. As a consequence both $k^\star$ and T are expected to be elements of $\mathbb{F}_2^n$. Moreover as we study protected implementations of cryptographic algorithms these algorithms also take as input a set of uniform independent random variables (not known by an attacker). Let denote by $\mathcal{R}$ this set.

Let g be a mapping which maps the input data to a *sensitive variable*. A *sensitive variable* is an internal variable proceeded by the cryptographic algorithm which depends on a subset of the inputs not known by the attacker (e.g. the secret key but also the secret random value). A measured leakage could be defined by:

$$X = \Psi\left(g\left(k^\star, T, \mathcal{R}\right)\right) + N, \tag{1}$$

where $\Psi : \mathbb{F}_2^n \to \mathbb{R}$ denotes the leakage function. This leakage function is a specific characteristic of the target device. The leakage function could be for example the Hamming Weight (denoted by HW in this article). The random variable N denotes an independent additive noise. In order to conduct a dth-order attack an attacker should combine the leakages of d shares. To combine these leakages an attacker will use a *combination function* [5,16,17]. The degree of this combination function must be at least d for the attack to succeed.

The *combination function* will then be applied both on the measured leakages and on the model (this is the optimal HODPA). As a consequence, an HODPA is completely defined by the *combination function* used.

In the rest of the paper the SNR is given by the following definition:

Definition 1 (Signal to Noise Ratio). *The Signal to Noise Ratio of a leakage denoted by a random variable L depending on informative part denoted I is given by:*

$$\text{SNR}\,[L, I] = \frac{Var\,[\mathbb{E}\,[L|I]]}{\mathbb{E}\,[Var\,[L|I]]}. \tag{2}$$

An attack is said *sound* when it allows to recover the key $k^\star$ with success probability which tends to one when the number of measurements tends to the infinity.

3   Masking Scheme with Table Recomputation

3.1   Algorithm

In this article we consider Boolean masking schemes. In particular, we focus on schemes based on table recomputation where the masked S-Box is stored in a table and recomputed each time.

This algorithm begins by a key addition phase where one word of the plaintext t, one word the key k and a random mask word m, are Xored together.

Then, these values are passed through a non linear part stored in a table. The output of this operation could be masked by a different mask m'. Some linear operations could be done after the non linear part. Of course, in the whole algorithm, all the data are masked (exclusive-ored) with a random mask, to ensure the protection against first order attacks.

Masking the linear parts is straightforward but passing through the non linear one is less obvious. To realize this operation the table is recomputed. For all the elements of $\mathbb{F}_2^n$ the input mask is removed and then the output is masked by the output mask. In this step the key is never manipulated so all the leakages concern the mask. It can also be noticed that a new table S' of size $2^n \times n$ bits, is required for this step.

3.2   Classical Attacks

As the other masking schemes, masking schemes based on table recomputation can be defeated without the leakage of the table recomputation. Indeed an attacker can use:

- Second order attacks [5,16] such as second-order CPA (2O-CPA). It can be noticed that for such attacks, the adversary can also exploit the leakage of the mask during the table recomputation.
- Collisions attacks. If several S-Boxes are masked by the same mask the Collisions attacks may be practicable [6].

However these attacks do not take into account all the leakages due to table recomputation stage. An approach to exploit these leakages is to combine all of them with a leakage depending on the key. This method has been presented in [24] where an "horizontal" attack is performed on the table recomputation to recover the mask.

In such "horizontal" attacks two different steps can be targeted:

- An attacker could try to recover the output masks. In this case he should first recover the address in the table. In this case it is not necessary to recover the input mask but only the address value.
- An attacker could also try to recover the input masks.

The second step consists in a vertical attack which recover the key. In this second step the mask is now a known value. It can be noticed that the exact knowledge of the mask is not required to recover the key. Indeed if the probability to recover the mask is higher than $\frac{1}{2^n}$ then a first order attack is possible.

Recently, the optimal distinguisher in the case of masking has been studied in [4]: it is applied to the precomputation phase of masked table without shuffling in Sect. 5. This attack can be extended to the case of shuffled table recomputation but would require an enumeration of all shuffles, which is computationally unfeasible.

3.3   Classical Countermeasure

The strategy to protect the table recomputation against HV attacks and the distinguisher presented in [4] is to shuffle the recomputation, i.e. do the recomputation in a random order Algorithm 1.

Different methods to randomize the order are presented in [24]. One of the methods presented is based on a random permutation on a subset of $\mathbb{F}_2^n$.

If the random permutation over $\mathbb{F}_2^n$ is randomly drawn from a set of permutation $S \subset S_{2^n}$, where $card(S) \ll card(S_{2^n})$, it is still possible to take advantage of the table recomputation. Indeed as it is shown in [24] attacks could be built by including all the possible permutations in the key hypothesis. If the permutation is drawn over all S_{2^n} the number of added hypothesis is $2^n!$ which can be too much for attacks.

By generating permutation, such as defined in [24] or any pseudo random permutation generator (RC4 key scheduler...), a designer could protect table recomputation against HV attacks. Indeed using for example five or six bytes of entropy as seed for the permutation generator could be enough to prevent an attacker to guess all the possible permutations.

4   Totally Random Permutation and Attack

In this section we present a new attack against shuffled table recomputation. The success of this attack will not be impacted by the entropy used to generate the shuffle. As a consequence this attack will succeed when the HV attacks will failed

---

Algorithm 1. Shuffled Table recomputation

output: Mask SubBytes
1 $m \leftarrow_{\mathcal{R}} \mathbb{F}_2^n$, $m' \leftarrow_{\mathcal{R}} \mathbb{F}_2^n$ // Draw of random input and output masks ;
2 $\varphi \leftarrow_{\mathcal{R}} \mathbb{F}_2^n \to \mathbb{F}_2^n$ // Draw of random permutation of $\mathbb{F}_2^n$;
3 **for** $\varphi(\omega) \in \{\varphi(0), \varphi(1), \ldots, \varphi(2^n - 1)\}$ **do** // S-Box masking
4      $z \leftarrow \varphi(\omega) \oplus m$ // Masked input ;
5      $z' \leftarrow S[\varphi(\omega)] \oplus m'$ // Masked output ;
6      $S'[z] = z'$ // Creating the masked S-Box entry ;
7 **end**
8 **return** S'

---

because of the quantity of entropy used to generate the shuffle. We then express the condition where this attack will outperform the state of the art second order attack.

4.1 Defeating the Countermeasure

As the permutation φ is completely random, the value of the current index in the loop for (line 3 to line 7) is unknown. But it can be noticed that this current index is manipulated twice at each step of the loop (line 4, line 5):

$$z \leftarrow \varphi(\omega) \oplus m, \tag{3}$$
$$z' \leftarrow S[\varphi(\omega)] \oplus m'. \tag{4}$$

It can be noticed that [20] if U is a random variable uniformly drawn over $\mathbb{F}_2^n$ and $m \in \mathbb{F}_2^n$ then:

$$\mathbb{E}\left[(\mathrm{HW}[U] - \mathbb{E}\left[\mathrm{HW}[U]\right]) \times (\mathrm{HW}[U \oplus m] - \mathbb{E}\left[\mathrm{HW}[U \oplus m]\right])\right] = -\frac{\mathrm{HW}[m]}{2} + \frac{n}{4}. \tag{5}$$

As a consequence, it may be possible for an attacker to exploit the leakage depending on the two (3, 4) manipulations of the current random index in the loop. Indeed, at each of the 2^n steps of the loop of the table recomputation, the leakage of the $\varphi(\omega)$ in Eqs. 3 and 4 which plays the role of U in Eq. 5 will be combined (by a centered product) to recover a variable depending on the mask. Then these 2^n variables will be combined together (by a sum) before being combined (again by a centered product) with a leakage depending on the key. This gives us a rough idea of the attack, also illustrated in Fig. 1.

An attacker could want to perform the attack on the output of the S-Box. But depending on the implementation of the masking scheme the output masks can be different for each value of the S-Box (see for example the masking scheme of Coron [7]). To avoid loss of generality we focus our study on the S-Box input mask of the recomputation. Indeed by design of the table recomputation masking scheme, the input mask is the same for each value of the S-Box: the attacker can thus exploit it multiple times. Moreover an attacker can still take advantage of

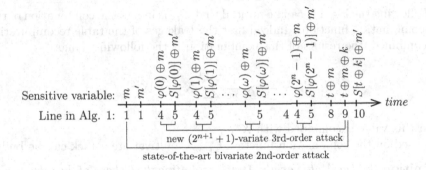

Fig. 1. State-of-the-art attack and new attack investigated in this article

the confusion of the S-Box [11] to better discriminate the various key candidates. Indeed he can target the input the of SubBytes operation of the last round.

4.2 Multivariate Attacks Against Table Recomputation

In the previous section, it is shown that at each turn of the loop of the table recomputation, it is possible to extract a value depending on the mask. As a consequence it is possible to use all of these values to perform a multivariate attack. In this subsection we give the formal formula of this new attack. Let us define the leakages of the table recomputation. The leakage of the masked random index in the loop is given by: $\mathsf{HW}[\Phi(\omega) \oplus M] + N_\omega^{(1)}$. The leakage of the random index is given by: $\mathsf{HW}[\Phi(\omega)] + N_\omega^{(2)}$.

Depending on the knowledge about the model, the leakage could be centered by the "true" expectation or by the estimation of this expectation. We assume this expectation is a known value given by: $\mathbb{E}\left[\mathsf{HW}[\Phi(\omega) \oplus m] + N_\omega^1\right] = \mathbb{E}\left[\mathsf{HW}[\Phi(\omega)] + N_\omega^2\right] = \frac{n}{2}$. Then let us denote by:

$$X_\omega^{(1)} = \mathsf{HW}[\Phi(\omega) \oplus M] + N_\omega^{(1)} - \frac{n}{2}, \tag{6}$$

$$X_\omega^{(2)} = \mathsf{HW}[\Phi(\omega)] + N_\omega^{(2)} - \frac{n}{2}. \tag{7}$$

Let us denote the leakage of the masked AddRoundKey:

$$X^\star = \mathsf{HW}[T \oplus M \oplus k^\star] + N - \frac{n}{2}. \tag{8}$$

To use all the leakages of the table recomputation an original combination function could be defined.

Definition 2. *The combination function exploiting the leakage of the table recomputation C_{tr} is given by:*

$$C_{tr}: \qquad \mathbb{R}^{2^{n+1}} \times \mathbb{R} \qquad \longrightarrow \qquad \qquad \mathbb{R}$$
$$\left(\left(X_\omega^{(1)}, X_\omega^{(2)}\right)_\omega, X^\star\right) \longmapsto \left(-2 \times \frac{1}{2^n} \sum_{\omega=0}^{2^n-1} X_\omega^{(1)} \times X_\omega^{(2)}\right) \times X^\star.$$

Following the Fig. 1 it can be noticed that C_{tr} is in fact the combination of two sub-combination functions. Indeed first the leakages of the table recomputation are combined, the results of this combination is the following value:

$$X_{tr} = -2 \times \frac{1}{2^n} \sum_{\omega=0}^{2^n-1} X_\omega^{(1)} \times X_\omega^{(2)}. \tag{9}$$

Then this value is combined with $X^\star$.

Based on the combination function C_{tr}, a multivariate attack can be built.

Definition 3. *The MultiVariate Attack exploiting the leakage of the table recomputation is given by the function:*

$$MVA_{tr}: \quad \mathbb{R}^{2^{n+1}} \times \mathbb{R} \times \mathbb{R} \longrightarrow \mathbb{F}_2^n$$
$$\left(\left(X_\omega^{(1)}, X_\omega^{(2)}\right)_\omega, X^\star, Y\right) \longmapsto \underset{K \in \mathbb{F}_2^n}{\mathrm{argmax}}\, \rho\left[C_{tr}\left(\left(X_\omega^{(1)}, X_\omega^{(2)}\right)_\omega, X^\star\right), Y\right],$$

where $Y = \mathbb{E}\left[\left(\mathsf{HW}[T \oplus M \oplus K] - \frac{n}{2}\right) \cdot \left(\mathsf{HW}[M] - \frac{n}{2}\right) | T, K\right]$ *and* ρ *the Pearson coefficient.*

Proposition 1. *MVA_{tr} is sound.*

Remark 1. *The attack presented in Definition 3 is a $2^{n+1}+1$ multivariate third order attack.*

Let us denote the leakage of the mask by:

$$X^{(3)} = \mathsf{HW}[M] + N^{(3)} - \frac{n}{2}. \tag{10}$$

In the rest of the paper we denote by 2O-CPA the CPA using the centered product as combination function.

$$\text{2O-CPA}: \quad \mathbb{R} \times \mathbb{R} \times \mathbb{R} \longrightarrow \mathbb{F}_2^n$$
$$\left(X^{(3)}, X^\star, Y\right) \longmapsto \underset{K \in \mathbb{F}_2^n}{\mathrm{argmax}}\, \rho\left[X^{(3)} \times X^\star, Y\right].$$

Using the Definitions 2, 3 and Eq. 9, it can be noticed that the only difference between the MVA_{tr} and the 2O-CPA is the use of X_{tr} instead of $X^{(3)}$. X_{tr} will act as the leakage of the mask. Let us call X_{tr} the *second order leakage*.

Remark 2. *The informative part of the second order leakage is the same as the informative part of the leakage mask i.e.*

$$\mathbb{E}\left[X_{tr}|M = m\right] = \mathbb{E}\left[X^{(3)}|M = m\right].$$

Proof. Straightforward application of the results of [20]   □

4.3 Leakage Analysis

By using the formula of the theoretical success rate we show that as the same operations are targeted by the MVA_{tr} and the 2O-CPA then it is equivalent to compare the SNR and compare the SR of the attacks. Based on this fact we can theoretically establish the conditions in which the MVA_{tr} outperforms the 2O-CPA. This conditions are given in Theorem 2.

Recently A.A Ding et al. [10, Sect. 3.4] give the following formula to establish the Success Rate (SR) of second-order attacks:

$$\text{SR} = \Phi_{N_k-1}\left(\frac{\sqrt{b}\delta_0\delta_1}{4}K^{-1/2}\kappa\right).$$

In this formula:

- δ_0 denotes the SNR of the first share and δ_1 denotes the SNR of the second one;
- Φ_{N_k-1} denotes the cumulative distribution function of $(N_k - 1)$-dimensional standard Gaussian distribution; as underlined by the authors in [10], if the noise distribution is not multi-variate Gaussian, then Φ_{N_k} is to be understood as its cumulative distribution function.
- N_k denotes the number of key candidates.
- K denotes the confusion matrix and κ the confusion coefficient.
- b denotes the number of traces.

This formula allows to establish the link between the SNR and SR of second order attacks against Boolean masking schemes.

Let us apply the A.A Ding et al. formula in the case of our two attacks:

$$\text{SR}_{\text{2O CPA}} = \Phi_{2^n-1}\left(\sqrt{b}\frac{\text{SNR}\left[X^{(3)}, M\right]\text{SNR}\left[X^\star, (T, M)\right]}{4}K^{-1/2}\kappa\right),$$

$$\text{SR}_{\text{MVA}_{tr}} = \Phi_{2^n-1}\left(\sqrt{b}\frac{\text{SNR}\left[X_{tr}, M\right]\text{SNR}\left[X^\star, (T, M)\right]}{4}K^{-1/2}\kappa\right).$$

We target the same operation for the share that leaks the secret key ($X^\star$). Moreover by Remark 2 the informative parts of the leakages depending on the mask (X_{tr} and $X^{(3)}$) is the same in the two leakages. As a consequence the K and κ are the same in the two attacks.

It can be noticed that the only difference in the formulas of the success rate is the use of $\text{SNR}\left[X_{tr}, M\right]$ instead of $\text{SNR}\left[X^{(3)}, M\right]$. Then it is equivalent to compare these values and compare the SR of the attacks.

Theorem 2. *The SNR of the "second-order leakage" is greater than the SNR of the leakage of the mask if and only if*

$$\sigma^2 \leqslant 2^{n-2} - \frac{n}{2},$$

where σ denotes the standard deviation of the Gaussian noise.

As a consequence MVA_{tr} will be better than 2O-CPA in this interval

Theorem 2 gives us the cases where exploiting the second-order leakage will give better results than exploiting the classical leakage of the mask. For example if $n = 8$ (the case of AES) the second-order leakage is better until $\sigma^2 \leqslant 60$.

Figure 2 shows when the SNR of X_{tr} is greater than the SNR of X^3. In order to have a better representation of this interval $1/\text{SNR}$ is also plotted in Fig. 2a.

It is easy to observe that the largest difference in Fig. 2a occurs at $\frac{1}{2}\left(2^{n-2} - \frac{n}{2}\right)$, i.e., in the middle of the *useful interval of variance*.

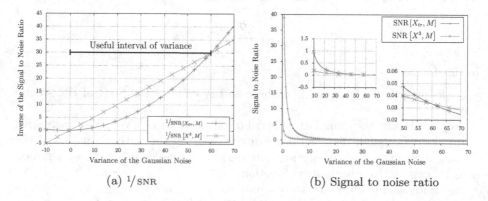

(a) $1/\text{SNR}$ (b) Signal to noise ratio

Fig. 2. Comparison between the variance of the noise for the classical leakage and the second-order and the impact of these noises on the SNR.

4.4   Simulation Results

In order to validate empirically the results of the Sect. 4, we test the method presented on simulated data. The target is a first order protected AES with table recomputation. To simulate the leakages we assume that each value leaks its Hamming weight with a Gaussian noise of standard deviation σ. The 512 leakages of the table recomputation are those given in Subsect. 4.2.

1000 attacks are realized to compute the success rate of each experiment. In this part, the comparisons are done on the number of traces needed to reach 80 % of success.

It can be seen in Fig. 3a and b that the difference between the two attacks is null for $\sigma = 0$ and $\sigma = 8$. It confirms the bound of the interval shown in Fig. 2. This also confirms that comparing the SNR is equivalent to comparing the SR.

It can be seen in Fig. 3 that in presence of noise the MVA_{tr} outperforms the 2O-CPA. The highest difference between the MVA_{tr} and 2O-CPA is reached when $\sigma = 3$. In this case, the MVA_{tr} needs 2500 traces to mount the attack while the 2O-CPA needs 7500 traces. This represents a gain of 200 %. The gain decreases to 122 % when $\sigma = 4$ Fig. 3d.

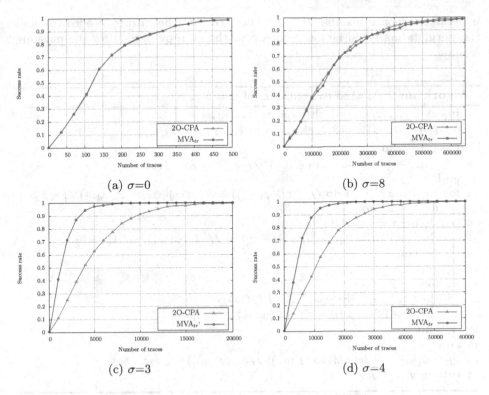

(a) $\sigma=0$

(b) $\sigma=8$

(c) $\sigma=3$

(d) $\sigma-4$

Fig. 3. Comparison between 2O-CPA and MVA$_{tr}$.

5   An Example on High-Order Countermeasure

The result of the previous section could be extended to any masking scheme based on table recomputation. In particular the MVA$_{tr}$ could be extended to High-Order masking schemes.

5.1   Coron Masking Scheme Attack and Countermeasure

The use of table recomputation could be extended to High-Order masking schemes. An approach has been proposed by Schramm and Paar [22]. However this masking scheme can be defeated by a third order attack [8]. To avoid this vulnerability Coron recently presented [7] a new method based on table recomputation. This method provides a high-order masking (see Algorithm 2). The core idea of this method is to mask each output of the S-Box by different mask and refresh the set of masks between each shift of the table. HV attacks are still a threat against such schemes. Indeed iteratively an attacker will recover each input mask x_i. Afterwards he will be able to perform a first order attack on the AddRoundKey to recover the key. To prevent attacks based on the exploitation of the leakages of the input masks an approach based on the randomization of the index of the loop is possible. It can be noticed that the entropy needed to build the permutation could be low compare to the entropy needed for the masking scheme.

Algorithm 2. Masked computation of $y = S(x)$

---

    input : $x_1, \ldots, x_d$, such that $x = x_1 \oplus \ldots \oplus x_d$
    output: $y_1, \ldots, y_d$, such that $y = y_1 \oplus \ldots \oplus y_d = S(x)$

1 **for** $\omega \in \mathbb{F}_2^n$ **do**
2 | $T(\omega) \leftarrow (S(\omega), 0, \ldots, 0) \in (\mathbb{F}_2^n)^d$ // $\oplus(T(\omega)) = S(u)$
3 **end**
4 **for** $i = 1$ to $i = d - 1$ **do** // $\oplus(T(\varphi(\omega))) = S(\varphi(\omega) \oplus x_1, \ldots, \oplus x_{d-1}) \forall \omega \in \mathbb{F}_2^n$
5 | **for** $\omega \in \mathbb{F}_2^n$ **do**
6 | | **for** $j = 1$ **to** d **do**
7 | | | $T'(\varphi(\omega))[j] \leftarrow T(\varphi(\omega) \oplus x_i)[j]$ // $T'(\varphi(\omega)) \leftarrow T(\varphi(\omega) \oplus x_i)$
8 | | **end**
9 | **end**
10 | **for** $\omega \in \mathbb{F}_2^n$ **do**
11 | | $T(\varphi(\omega)) \leftarrow \mathsf{RefreshMasks}(T(\varphi(\omega)))$
        | | // $\oplus(T(\varphi(\omega))) = S(\varphi(\omega) \oplus x_1, \ldots, \oplus x_i)$
12 | **end**
13 **end**
14 $(y_1, \ldots, y_d) \leftarrow \mathsf{RefreshMasks}(T(x_n))$ // $\oplus(T(x_d)) = S(x)$
15 **return** $y_1, \ldots, y_n$

5.2 Attack on the Countermeasure

Similarly to the definitions in Subsect. 4.2 let us define the leakages of the table recomputation of the masking scheme of Coron where the order of the masking is $d - 1$: $X^{(1)}_{(\omega,i,j)} = \mathsf{HW}[\Phi_i(\omega) \oplus M_i] + N^{(1)}_{(\omega,i,j)} - \frac{n}{2}$ and $X^{(2)}_{(\omega,i,j)} = \mathsf{HW}[\Phi_i(\omega)] + N^{(2)}_{(\omega,i,j)} - \frac{n}{2}$. where $i \in [\![1, d-1]\!]$ will index the $d - 1$ masks. The d-th share is the masked sensitive value. And $j \in [\![1, d]\!]$ denotes the index of the loop from lines 6 to lines 9 of the Algorithm 2.

The leakage of the masks is given by $X^{(3)}_i = \mathsf{HW}[M_i] + N^{(3)}_i - \frac{n}{2}$

And let us denote by: $X^\star = \mathsf{HW}[\bigoplus_{i=0}^{d-1}(M_i) \oplus k^\star \oplus T] + N - \frac{n}{2}$ the leakages of the masked value.

Definition 4. *The combination function exploiting the leakage of the table recomputation C_{tr} is given by:*

$$C_{cs}^d : \qquad \mathbb{R}^{d \times (d-1) \times 2^{n+1}} \times \mathbb{R} \qquad \rightarrow \qquad\qquad \mathbb{R}$$

$$\left(\left(X^{(1)}_{(\omega,i,j)}, X^{(2)}_{(\omega,i,j)} \right)_{\substack{\omega \in \mathbb{F}_{2^n} \\ i \in [\![1,d-1]\!] \\ j \in [\![1,d]\!]}}, X^\star \right) \mapsto \prod_{i=1}^{d-1} \left(\frac{-2}{d 2^n} \sum_{\substack{\omega \in \mathbb{F}_{2^n} \\ j \in [\![1,d]\!]}} X^{(1)}_{(\omega,i,j)} \times X^{(2)}_{(\omega,i,j)} \right) \times X^\star.$$

Similarly to Subsection 4.3 we could define:

$$X_{CS_i}(d) = \frac{-2}{d2^n} \sum_{\substack{\omega \in \mathbb{F}_{2^n} \\ j \in [\![1,d]\!]}} X^{(1)}_{(\omega,i,j)} \times X^{(2)}_{(\omega,i,j)}.$$

This value is the combination of all the leaking values of the table recomputation depending of one share. Based on the combination function a multivariate attack can be built.

Definition 5. *The MultiVariate Attack exploiting the leakage of the table recomputation of the $d-1$ order Coron masking Scheme is given by:*

$$MVA^d_{cs}: \qquad \mathbb{R}^{d \times (d-1) \times 2^{n+1}} \times \mathbb{R} \times \mathbb{R} \qquad \longrightarrow \qquad \mathbb{F}^n_2$$

$$\left(\left(X^{(1)}_{(\omega,i,j)}, X^{(2)}_{(\omega,i,j)} \right)_{\substack{\omega \in \mathbb{F}_{2^n} \\ i \in [\![1,d-1]\!] \\ j \in [\![1,d]\!]}}, X^\star, Y \right) \mapsto \underset{K \in \mathbb{F}^n_2}{\mathrm{argmax}}\, \rho \left[\prod_{i=1}^{d-1} \left(X_{CS_i}(d) \right) \times X^\star, Y \right],$$

where $Y = \mathsf{HW}[T \oplus K] - \frac{n}{2}$

Proposition 3. *MVA_{cs} is sound.*

Remark 3. *The attack presented in Definition 3 is a $d \times (d-1) \times 2^{n+1} + 1$ multivariate $2 \times (d-1) + 1$ order attack.*

HOCPA can be built by combining the d shares using the centered product combination function. In the rest of this article we denote such attacks by "classical" dO-CPA.

$$d\text{O-CPA}: \qquad \mathbb{R}^{d-1} \times \mathbb{R} \times \mathbb{R} \qquad \longrightarrow \qquad \mathbb{F}^n_2$$

$$\left(\left(X^{(3)}_i \right)_{i \in [\![1,d-1]\!]}, X^\star, Y \right) \longmapsto \underset{K \in \mathbb{F}^n_2}{\mathrm{argmax}}\, \rho \left[X^\star \times \prod_{i=1}^{d-1} X^{(3)}_i, Y \right].$$

5.3   Leakage Analysis

The difference between the two attacks is the use of $X_{CS_i}(d)$ instead of $X^{(3)}_i$ as the leakage of the $d-1$ shares which do not leak the secret key. A.A Ding et al. also provides a formula to compute the SR of HOCPA [10, Sect. 3.4].

Similarly to Sect. 4 the only differences in the formula are the SNR of the shares which do not leak the key. Then by comparing the SNR $[X_{CS_i}(d), M_i]$ and SNR $\left[X^{(3)}_i, M_i \right]$ we compare the success rate of the attacks. It can be noticed that in our model the SNR does not depend on i.

Theorem 4. *The SNR of the "second-order leakage" is greater than the SNR of the leakage of the mask if and only if*

$$\sigma^2 \leqslant d \times 2^{n-2} - \frac{n}{2}, \qquad (11)$$

where σ denotes the standard deviation of the Gaussian noise.

As a consequence MVA_{tr} will be better than 2O-CPA when the noise is in this interval. We can immediately deduce that the size of the Useful Interval of Variance increases linearly with the order of the masking scheme.

Figure 4a and b show the impact of the order d of the attack on the interval of noise where the MVA_{CS}^d outperfoms dO-CPA (let us called this interval the Useful Interval of Variance). We can see that the size of these intervals increases with the order. For example for $d = 3$ the useful interval of variance is $[0, 124]$. It is almost impossible to perform a second order attack with a noise variance of 124.

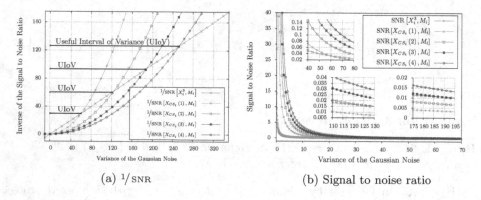

(a) $1/\text{SNR}$ \qquad\qquad (b) Signal to noise ratio

Fig. 4. Comparison between the signal to noise ratio of X_i^3 and signal to noise ratio of $X_{CS}\,(d-1)$ (where d is the order of the attack)

5.4   Simulation Results on Coron Masking Scheme

In order to validate the theoretical results of the Subsect. 5.3 the MVA_{CS} was tested on simulated data and compared to dO-CPA. The simulations have been done with the Hamming weight model and Gaussian noise such as the leakages defined in Subsect. 5.2. We test these attacks against a second and a third order masking scheme.

To compute the success rate the attacks are redone 500 times for the second order masking and 100 times for the third order masking.

In Fig. 5a it can be seen that MVA_{cs}^3 reaches 80 % of success rate for less the 20000 traces while the 3O-CPA does not reach 30 % for 100000. In Fig. 5b it can be seen that MVA_{cs}^4 reaches 80 % of success rate for less than 200000 traces while the 4O-CPA does not reach 5 %.

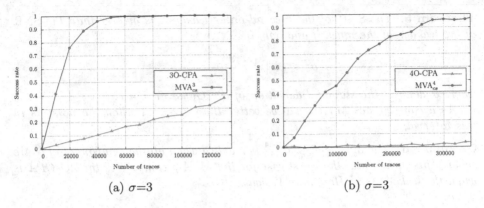

Fig. 5. Comparison between the 4O-CPA and the MVA_{cs}^4

6   A Note on Affine Model

In Sect. 4 the leakage function was expected to be the Hamming weight. Let us now study the impact of the leakage function on the MVA_{tr}. We suppose that the leakage function is affine.

6.1   Properties of the affine model

A leakage function is said affine if this function is a weighted sum of the bit of the leaking value. As a consequence the leakage function could be rewritten as $\Psi_\alpha(V) = \alpha \cdot V$, where V is the leaking value, α the weight of the leakage of each bit and $\cdot$ the inner product.

Assumption 1. *In order to compare the results in case of an affine model and the Hamming weight model let us assume that the variance is the same in the two cases i.e. $Var[\mathcal{L}(\alpha, V)] = Var[\mathrm{HW}[V]]$ this is equivalent to $\|\alpha\|_2^2 = n$.*

Let us also assume that all the values manipulated during the algorithm leak in the same way i.e. the weight vector α of the sum is the same for all the variables V of the algorithm.

Let us redefine the leakage of the table recomputation the (centered) leakage of the random index: $X_\omega^{(1)} = \alpha \cdot (\Phi(\omega) \oplus M) + N_\omega^{(1)} - \frac{1}{2}(\alpha \cdot \mathbf{1})$, the (centered) leakage of the mask random index: $X_\omega^{(2)} = \alpha \cdot (\Phi(\omega)) + N_\omega^{(2)} - \frac{1}{2}(\alpha \cdot \mathbf{1})$. And the (centered) leakage of the mask: $X^{(3)} = \alpha \cdot M - \frac{1}{2}(\alpha \cdot \mathbf{1})$. And let $X^\star$ be the leakage of a sensitive value depending on the key.

6.2   Theoretical Analysis

Similarly to the Subsection 4.3 let us study the impact of the affine model on the success of the MVA_{tr} compared to the 2O-CPA.

As motivated in Sect. 4.1, we can modify the MVA_{tr} in order to target the last round S-Box input: $X^\star = \alpha \cdot \left(\mathrm{Sbox}^{-1}[T \oplus k^\star] \oplus M\right) + N - \frac{1}{2}(\alpha \cdot \mathbf{1})$.

Theorem 5. *The* SNR *of the "second-order leakage" is greater than the* SNR *of the leakage of the mask if and only if*

$$\sigma^2 \leqslant \|\alpha\|_4^{\,4} \times \frac{2^{n-2}}{n} - \frac{n}{2},$$

where σ denotes the standard deviation of the Gaussian noise.

As a consequence MVA$_{tr}$ will be better than 2O-CPA when the noise is in this interval.

Corollary 6. *The* $\min_{\|\alpha\|_2^2=n} \|\alpha\|_4^{\,4}$ *is reached when all the component of α are equal. This means that the worst case for the MVA$_{tr}$ compare to the 2O-CPA is when the leakage is in Hamming Weight.*

6.3 Simulation Results

In order to validate the results of the theoretical study of the previous section some simulations have been done.

The target considered is the input of the S-Box of the last round; as a consequence we consider $X^{\star} = \alpha \cdot \left(\text{Sbox}^{-1}[T \oplus k^{\star}] \oplus M\right) + N - \frac{1}{2}\left(\alpha \cdot \mathbf{1}\right)$.

The mask M and the plain text T are randomly drawn from $\mathbb{F}_2^8$. The noises are drawn from a Gaussian distribution with different variance σ^2. The results of the attacks are expressed using the Success rate. To compute the success rates the experiments have been redone 1000 times. For each experiment the secret key $k^{\star}$ are randomly drawn over $\mathbb{F}_2^8$. To compare the efficiency of the two attacks we compare the number of traces needed to reach 80 % of success.

For the first experiment let us choice α such as $\alpha_i = \sqrt{\left(1 + (-1)^{i \bmod 2} \times \varepsilon\right)}$

with $\varepsilon = 0,9$. In this case $\|\alpha\|_4^{\,4} = 14.480$ and following the result of the Theorem 5, the MVA$_{tr}$ should outperform the classical success rate in the interval: $[0, 111]$. It can be seen in Fig. 6a and b that in such case when $\sigma^2 = 0$ or when $\sigma^2 = 111$ the MVA$_{tr}$ and the 2O-CPA need the same number of traces to reach 80 % of success. This confirms first of all the soundness of our model and also that in case of affine model when the target is proceeded in a non linear part of the cryptographic algorithm, the main difference between the two attacks is the SNR. When the standard deviation of the Gaussian noise $\sigma = 3$ the 2O-CPA needs around 3800 traces to reach 80 % of success whereas the MVA$_{tr}$ needs around 1000 traces (Fig. 6c). This represents a gain of 280 %. Compared to the gain observed in case of the Hamming weight model this confirm that the MVA$_{tr}$ performs better compare to the 2O-CPA in case of an affine model. It can be seen in Fig. 6d, when the $\sigma = 4$, the number of traces needed to reach 80 % of success is around 2500 for the MVA$_{tr}$ and around 10000 for the 2O-CPA; this represents a gain of 300 %.

7 Practical Validation

This section presents the results of the multivariate attack exploiting the table recomputation stage on true traces. The traces are electromagnetic leakages of

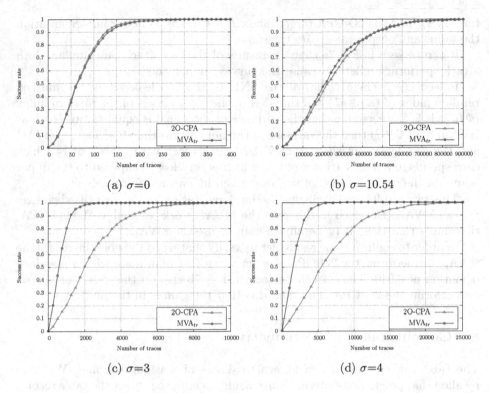

(a) $\sigma=0$ (b) $\sigma=10.54$

(c) $\sigma=3$ (d) $\sigma=4$

Fig. 6. Comparison between 2O-CPA and MVA$_{tr}$ for $\varepsilon = 0.9$.

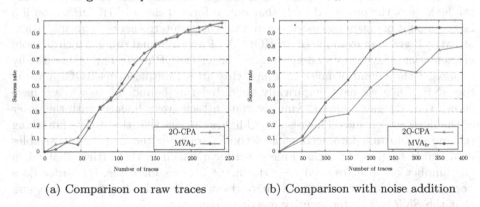

(a) Comparison on raw traces   (b) Comparison with noise addition

Fig. 7. Comparison of the SR of the MVA$_{tr}$ and the 2O-CPA

the execution of an AES with table recomputation executed on an ATMega163 8-bit smartcard which is known to be leaky. To build our experiments 13000 traces have been acquired.

Let us first study the results of the attack. They are expressed using the success rate. The leakage function as been recovered using a linear regression. Both the MVA_{tr} and the 2O-CPA target: $Sbox[T \oplus k^\star] \oplus M$ as in our implementation the input and output masks are the same.

It can be seen in Fig. 7a that the results of the two attacks are similar. Both attacks perform similarly because the curves are not noisy.

Indeed the average values of the SNR of the 256 leakages of the masked random index $(\Phi(\omega) \oplus M)$ and the SNR of the 256 leakages of the random index $(\Phi(\omega))$ is 5. If we assume that the variance of the signal is equal to two (such as HW on 8 bit CPU) then the variance of the noise is less than 0.5. The mask (M) and the key-dependent share $Sbox[T \oplus k^\star] \oplus M)$ leak with a SNR of 14 which corresponds to a noise variance of 0.1, which is very low (compared to the upper bound of the useful interval of variance given in Theorem 2, namely 60).

This two results are specific to the implementation and a clear disadvantage for the MVA_{tr}. But even in this case the MVA_{tr} works as well as the 2O-CPA, this shows that there is (generally) a gain to use the MVA_{tr}.

In order to confirm these results let us verify that when the noise increases the MVA_{tr} outperforms the 2O-CPA. Let us add a Gaussian noise with a standard deviation of 0.040. Then it can be seen in Fig. 7b that in this case the MVA_{tr} outperforms the 2O-CPA. This confirms that the gain is in the SNR.

8   Conclusions and Perspectives

The table recomputation is a known weakness of masking schemes. We have recalled that practical countermeasures could be built to protect the table recomputation. In this article, we have presented a new multivariate attack exploiting the leakage of the protected table that outperformed classical HODPA even if a large amount of entropy is used to generate the countermeasure. This multivariate attack gives an example of an HOSCA of non-minimal order which is more efficient than the corresponding minimal order HODPA. We have theoretically expressed the bound of noise in which this attack outperforms HOCPA using the SNR. Then we have empirically validated this bound. Moreover, we have shown that the gain to use the multivariate attack grows linearly with the order of the masking schemes. This result highlights the fact that the study of masking scheme should take into account as second parameter the number of variables exploitable by theses attacks. Indeed we have shown in this article that when the number of variables used to perform the attacks increases, the *order* does not alone provide a criterion to evaluate the security of the countermeasure, and that the *SNR* is a better security metric to consider.

In future works we will investigate how to protect table recomputation against such attacks and investigate the cost of such countermeasures, evaluate the threat of such attacks on high-order masking schemes implemented on real component. We will also investigate how multivariate attacks could be applied on other masking schemes and protection techniques. And then, we will quantify the impact of these attacks.

References

1. Akkar, M.-L., Giraud, C.: An implementation of DES and AES, secure against some attacks. In: Koç, Ç.K., Naccache, D., Paar, C. (eds.) CHES 2001. LNCS, vol. 2162, pp. 309–318. Springer, Heidelberg (2001)
2. Blömer, J., Guajardo, J., Krummel, V.: Provably secure masking of AES. In: Handschuh, H., Hasan, M.A. (eds.) SAC 2004. LNCS, vol. 3357, pp. 69–83. Springer, Heidelberg (2004)
3. Brier, E., Clavier, C., Olivier, F.: Correlation power analysis with a leakage model. In: Joye, M., Quisquater, J.-J. (eds.) CHES 2004. LNCS, vol. 3156, pp. 16–29. Springer, Heidelberg (2004)
4. Bruneau, N., Guilley, S., Heuser, A., Rioul, O.: Masks will fall off. In: Sarkar, P., Iwata, T. (eds.) ASIACRYPT 2014, Part II. LNCS, vol. 8874, pp. 344–365. Springer, Heidelberg (2014)
5. Chari, S., Jutla, C.S., Rao, J.R., Rohatgi, P.: Towards sound approaches to counteract power-analysis attacks. In: Wiener, M. (ed.) CRYPTO 1999. LNCS, vol. 1666, p. 398. Springer, Heidelberg (1999)
6. Clavier, C., Feix, B., Gagnerot, G., Roussellet, M., Verneuil, V.: Improved collision-correlation power analysis on first order protected AES. In: Preneel, B., Takagi, T. (eds.) CHES 2011. LNCS, vol. 6917, pp. 49–62. Springer, Heidelberg (2011)
7. Coron, J.-S.: Higher order masking of look-up tables. In: Nguyen, P.Q., Oswald, E. (eds.) EUROCRYPT 2014. LNCS, vol. 8441, pp. 441–458. Springer, Heidelberg (2014)
8. Coron, J.-S., Prouff, E., Rivain, M.: Side channel cryptanalysis of a higher order masking scheme. In: Paillier, P., Verbauwhede, I. (eds.) CHES 2007. LNCS, vol. 4727, pp. 28–44. Springer, Heidelberg (2007)
9. DeTrano, A., Guilley, S., Guo, X., Karimi, N., Karri, R.: Exploiting small leakages in masks to turn a second-order attack into a first-order attack. In: Proceedings of the Fourth Workshop on Hardware and Architectural Support for Security and Privacy, HASP 2015, pp. 7:1–7:5. ACM, New York (2015)
10. Ding, A.A., Zhang, L., Fei, Y., Luo, P.: A statistical model for higher order DPA on masked devices. In: Batina, L., Robshaw, M. (eds.) CHES 2014. LNCS, vol. 8731, pp. 147–169. Springer, Heidelberg (2014)
11. Fei, Y., Luo, Q., Ding, A.A.: A statistical model for DPA with novel algorithmic confusion analysis. In: Prouff, E., Schaumont, P. (eds.) CHES 2012. LNCS, vol. 7428, pp. 233–250. Springer, Heidelberg (2012)
12. Goubin, L., Patarin, J.: DES and differential power analysis the "Duplication" method. In: Koç, Ç.K., Paar, C. (eds.) CHES 1999. LNCS, vol. 1717, pp. 158–172. Springer, Heidelberg (1999)
13. Kocher, P.C., Jaffe, J., Jun, B.: Differential power analysis. In: Wiener, M. (ed.) CRYPTO 1999. LNCS, vol. 1666, pp. 388–397. Springer, Heidelberg (1999)
14. Maghrebi, H., Prouff, E., Guilley, S., Danger, J.-L.: A first-order leak-free masking countermeasure. Cryptology ePrint Archive, Report 2012/028 (2012). http://dblp.uni-trier.de/rec/bibtex/conf/ctrsa/MaghrebiPGD12
15. Messerges, T.S.: Securing the AES finalists against power analysis attacks. In: Schneier, B. (ed.) FSE 2000. LNCS, vol. 1978, pp. 150–164. Springer, Heidelberg (2000)
16. Messerges, T.S.: Using second-order power analysis to attack DPA resistant software. In: Paar, C., Koç, Ç.K. (eds.) CHES 2000. LNCS, vol. 1965, pp. 238–251. Springer, Heidelberg (2000)

17. Oswald, E., Mangard, S.: Template attacks on masking—resistance is futile. In: Abe, M. (ed.) CT-RSA 2007. LNCS, vol. 4377, pp. 243–256. Springer, Heidelberg (2006)

18. Pan, J., den Hartog, J.I., Lu, J.: You cannot hide behind the mask: power analysis on a provably secure s-box implementation. In: Youm, H.Y., Yung, M. (eds.) WISA 2009. LNCS, vol. 5932, pp. 178–192. Springer, Heidelberg (2009)

19. Prouff, E., Rivain, M.: A generic method for secure sbox implementation. In: Kim, S., Yung, M., Lee, H.-W. (eds.) WISA 2007. LNCS, vol. 4867, pp. 227–244. Springer, Heidelberg (2008)

20. Prouff, E., Rivain, M., Bevan, R.: Statistical analysis of second order differential power analysis. IEEE Trans. Comput. 58(6), 799–811 (2009)

21. Rivain, M., Prouff, E.: Provably secure higher-order masking of AES. In: Mangard, S., Standaert, F.-X. (eds.) CHES 2010. LNCS, vol. 6225, pp. 413–427. Springer, Heidelberg (2010)

22. Schramm, K., Paar, C.: Higher order masking of the AES. In: Pointcheval, D. (ed.) CT-RSA 2006. LNCS, vol. 3860, pp. 208–225. Springer, Heidelberg (2006)

23. Standaert, F.-X., Veyrat-Charvillon, N., Oswald, E., Gierlichs, B., Medwed, M., Kasper, M., Mangard, S.: The world is not enough: another look on second-order DPA. In: Abe, M. (ed.) ASIACRYPT 2010. LNCS, vol. 6477, pp. 112–129. Springer, Heidelberg (2010)

24. Tunstall, M., Whitnall, C., Oswald, E.: Masking tables - an underestimated security risk. IACR Cryptology ePrint Archive 2013: 735 (2013). http://dblp.uni-trier.de/rec/bibtex/conf/fse/TunstallWO13

25. Waddle, J., Wagner, D.: Towards efficient second-order power analysis. In: Joye, M., Quisquater, J.-J. (eds.) CHES 2004. LNCS, vol. 3156, pp. 1–15. Springer, Heidelberg (2004)

Leakage Assessment Methodology

A Clear Roadmap for Side-Channel Evaluations

Tobias Schneider[(✉)] and Amir Moradi

Horst Görtz Institute for IT-Security, Ruhr-Universität Bochum, Bochum, Germany
{tobias.schneider-a7a,amir.moradi}@rub.de

Abstract. Evoked by the increasing need to integrate side-channel countermeasures into security-enabled commercial devices, evaluation labs are seeking a standard approach that enables a fast, reliable and robust evaluation of the side-channel vulnerability of the given products. To this end, standardization bodies such as NIST intend to establish a leakage assessment methodology fulfilling these demands. One of such proposals is the Welch's t-test, which is being put forward by Cryptography Research Inc., and is able to relax the dependency between the evaluations and the device's underlying architecture. In this work, we deeply study the theoretical background of the test's different flavors, and present a roadmap which can be followed by the evaluation labs to efficiently and correctly conduct the tests. More precisely, we express a stable, robust and efficient way to perform the tests at higher orders. Further, we extend the test to multivariate settings, and provide details on how to efficiently and rapidly carry out such a multivariate higher-order test. Including a suggested methodology to collect the traces for these tests, we point out practical case studies where different types of t-tests can exhibit the leakage of supposedly secure designs.

1 Introduction

The threat of side-channel analysis attacks is well known by the industry sector. Hence, the necessity to integrate corresponding countermeasures into the commercial products has become inevitable. Regardless of the type and soundness of the employed countermeasures, the security evaluation of the prototypes with respect to the effectiveness of the underlying countermeasure in practice is becoming one of the major concerns of the producers and evaluation labs. For example, the power of side-channel analysis as devastating attacks motivated the NIST to hold the "Non-Invasive Attack Testing Workshop" in 2011 to establish a testing methodology capable of robustly assessing the physical vulnerability of cryptographic devices.

With respect to common criteria evaluations – defined and used by governing bodies like ANSSI and BSI – the evaluation labs need to *practically* examine the feasibility of the state-of-the-art attacks conducted on the device under test (DUT). The examples include but not restricted to the classical differential power analysis (DPA) [12], correlation power analysis (CPA) [4], and mutual

© International Association for Cryptologic Research 2015
T. Güneysu and H. Handschuh (Eds.): CHES 2015, LNCS 9293, pp. 495–513, 2015.
DOI: 10.1007/978-3-662-48324-4_25

information analysis (MIA) [8]. To cover the most possible cases a large range of intermediate values as well as hypothetical (power) models should be examined to assess the possibility of the key recovery. This methodology is becoming more challenging as the number and types of known side-channel attacks are steadily increasing. Trivially, this time-consuming procedure cannot be comprehensive even if a large number of intermediate values and models in addition to several know attacks are examined. In fact, the selection of the hypothetical model is not simple and strongly depends on the expertise of the evaluation labs' experts. If the models were poorly chosen and as a result none of the key-recovery attacks succeeded, the evaluation lab would issue a favorable evaluation report even though the DUT might be vulnerable to an attack with a more advanced and complex model. This strongly motivates the need for an evaluation procedure which avoids being dependent on attack(s), intermediate value(s), and hypothetical model(s).

On one hand, two information-theoretic tests [5,6] are known which evaluate the leakage distributions either in a continuous or discrete form. These approaches are based on the mutual information and need to estimate the probability distribution of the leakages. This adds other parameter(s) to the test with respect to the type of the employed density estimation technique, e.g., kernel or histogram and their corresponding parameters. Moreover, they cannot yet focus on a certain statistical order of the leakages. This becomes problematic when e.g., the first-order security of a masking countermeasure is expected to be assessed. On the other hand, two leakage assessment methodologies (*specific* and *non-specific t*-tests) based on the Student's *t*-distribution have been proposed (at the aforementioned workshop [9]) with the goal to detect any type of leakage at a certain order. A comparative study of these three test vectors is presented in [14], where the performance of specific *t*-tests (only at the first order) is compared to that of other mutual information-based tests.

In general, the *non-specific t*-test examines the leakage of the DUT without performing an actual attack, and is in addition independent of its underlying architecture. The test gives a level of confidence to conclude that the DUT has an exploitable leakage. It indeed provides no information about the easiness/hardness of an attack which can exploit the leakage, nor about an appropriate intermediate value and the hypothetical model. However, it can easily and rapidly report that the DUT fails to provide the desired security level, e.g., due to a mistake in the design engineering or a flaw in the countermeasure [2].

Our Contribution. The Welch's *t*-test has been used in a couple of research works [2,3,13,16,20,21,23,26] to investigate the efficiency of the proposed countermeasures, but without extensively expressing the challenges of the test procedure. This document aims at putting light on a path for e.g., evaluation labs, on how to examine the leakage of the DUT at any order with minimal effort and without any dependency to a hypothetical model. Our goal in this work is to cover the following points:

- We try to explain the underlying statistical concept of such a test by a (hopefully) more understandable terminology.
- In the seminal paper by Goodwill et al. [9] it has been shown how to conduct the test at the first order, i.e., how to investigate the first-order leakage of the DUT. The authors also shortly stated that the traces can be preprocessed to run the same test at higher orders. Here we point out the issues one may face to run such a test at higher orders, and provide appropriate solutions accordingly. As a motivating point we should refer to [14], where the t-test is supposed to be able to be performed at only the first order.
- More importantly, we extend the test to cover multivariate leakages and express the necessary formulations in detail allowing us to efficiently conduct t-tests at any order and any variate.
- In order to evaluate the countermeasures (mainly those based on masking at high orders) several million traces might be required (e.g., see [3,13]). Hence we express the procedures which allow conducting the tests by means of multi-core CPUs in a parallelized way.
- We give details of how to design appropriate frameworks to host the DUT for such tests, including both software and hardware platforms. Particularly we consider a microcontroller as well as an FPGA (SASEBO) for this purpose.
- Depending on the underlying application and platform, the speed of the measurement is a bottleneck which hinders the collection of several million measurements. Due to this reason, the evaluation labs are usually restricted (commonly by common criteria) to measure not more than one million traces from any DUT. We also demonstrate a procedure to accelerate the measurement process allowing the collection of e.g., millions of traces per hour.

2   Statistical Background

A fundamental question in many different scientific fields is whether two sets of data are significantly different from each other. The most common approach to answer such a question is Welch's t-test in which the test statistic follows a Student's t distribution. The aim of a t-test is to provide a quantitative value as a probability that the mean μ of two sets are different. In other words, a t-test gives a probability to examine the validity of the *null hypothesis* as the samples in both sets were drawn from the same population, i.e., the two sets are not distinguishable.

Hence let $\mathcal{Q}_0$ and $\mathcal{Q}_1$ indicate two sets which are under the test. Let also μ_0 (resp. μ_1) and $s_0{}^2$ (resp. $s_1{}^2$) stand for the sample mean and sample variance of the set $\mathcal{Q}_0$ (resp. $\mathcal{Q}_1$), and n_0 and n_1 the cardinality of each set. The t-test statistic and the degree of freedom v are computed as

$$t = \frac{\mu_0 - \mu_1}{\sqrt{\frac{s_0{}^2}{n_0} + \frac{s_1{}^2}{n_1}}}, \qquad v = \frac{\left(\frac{s_0{}^2}{n_0} + \frac{s_1{}^2}{n_1}\right)^2}{\frac{\left(\frac{s_0{}^2}{n_0}\right)^2}{n_0 - 1} + \frac{\left(\frac{s_1{}^2}{n_1}\right)^2}{n_1 - 1}}. \qquad (1)$$

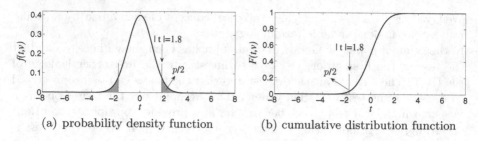

(a) probability density function　　　(b) cumulative distribution function

Fig. 1. Student's t distribution functions and two-tailed Welch's t-test (examples for $v = 10,000$)

In cases, where $s_0 \approx s_1$ and $n_0 \approx n_1$, the degree of freedom can be estimated by $v \approx n_0 + n_1 = n$. As the final step, we estimate the probability to accept the null hypothesis by means of Student's t distribution density function. In other words, based on the degree of freedom v the Student's t distribution function is drawn

$$f(t, v) = \frac{\Gamma(\frac{v+1}{2})}{\sqrt{\pi v}\, \Gamma(\frac{v}{2})} \left(1 + \frac{t^2}{v}\right)^{-\frac{v+1}{2}},$$

where $\Gamma(.)$ denotes the gamma function. Based on the two-tailed Welch's t-test the desired probability is calculated as

$$p = 2 \int_{|t|}^{\infty} f(t, v)\, dt.$$

Figure 1(a) represents a graphical view of such a test.

As an alternative, we can make use of the corresponding cumulative distribution function

$$F(t, v) = \frac{1}{2} + t\Gamma\left(\frac{v+1}{2}\right) \frac{{}_2F_1\left(\frac{1}{2}, \frac{v+1}{2}; \frac{3}{2}; -\frac{x^2}{v}\right)}{\sqrt{\pi v}\, \Gamma\left(\frac{v}{2}\right)},$$

with ${}_2F_1(.,.;.;.)$ the hypergeometric function. Hence the result of the t-test can be estimated as

$$p = 2\, F(-|t|, v).$$

For a graphical view see Fig. 1(b). Note that such a function is available amongst the MATLAB embedded functions as $\mathtt{tcdf}(\cdot, \cdot)$ and for R as $\mathtt{qt}(\cdot, \cdot)$.

Hence, small p values (alternatively big t values) give evidence to reject the null hypothesis and conclude that the sets were drawn from different populations. For the sake of simplicity, usually a threshold $|t| > 4.5$ is defined to reject the null hypothesis without considering the degree of freedom and the aforementioned cumulative distribution function. This intuition is based on the fact that $p = 2\, F(-4.5, v > 1000) < 0.00001$ which leads to a confidence of > 0.99999 to reject the null hypothesis.

3   Methodology

Suppose that in a side-channel evaluation process, with respect to n queries with associated data (e.g., plaintext or ciphertext) $D_{i \in \{1,\dots,n\}}$, n side-channel measurements (so-called traces) are collected while the device under test operates with a secret key that is kept constant. Let us denote each trace by $T_{i \in \{1,\dots,n\}}$ containing m sample points $\{t_i^{(1)}, \dots, t_i^{(m)}\}$.

As a straightforward evaluation process, the traces are categorized into two sets $\mathcal{Q}_0$ and $\mathcal{Q}_1$ and the test is conducted at each sample point $\{1, \dots, m\}$ separately. In other words, the test is performed in a *univariate* fashion. At this step such a categorization is done by means of an intermediate value corresponding to the associated data D. Since the underlying process is an evaluation procedure, the secret key is known and all the intermediate values can be computed. Based on the concept of the classical DPA [12], a bit of an intermediate value (e.g., an Sbox output bit at the first cipher round) is selected to be used in the categorization.

$$\mathcal{Q}_0 = \{T_i \,|\, \text{target bit}(D_i) = 0\}, \qquad \mathcal{Q}_1 = \{T_i \,|\, \text{target bit}(D_i) = 1\}.$$

If the corresponding t-test reports that with a high confidence the two trace groups (at certain sample points) are distinguishable from each other, it is concluded that the corresponding DPA attack is – most likely – able to recover the secret key.

Such a test (so-called *specific* t-test) is not restricted to only single-bit scenarios. For instance, an 8-bit intermediate value (e.g., an Sbox output byte) can be used to categorize the traces as

$$\mathcal{Q}_0 = \{T_i \,|\, \text{target byte}(D_i) = \mathrm{x}\}, \qquad \mathcal{Q}_1 = \{T_i \,|\, \text{target byte}(D_i) \neq \mathrm{x}\}.$$

In this case, a particular value for x should be selected prior to the test. Therefore, in case of an 8-bit target intermediate value 256 specific t-tests can be performed. It should be noted that in such tests, n_0 and n_1 (as the cardinality of $\mathcal{Q}_0$ and $\mathcal{Q}_1$) would be significantly different if the associated data D were drawn randomly. Hence, the accuracy of the estimated (sample) means (μ_0, μ_1) as well as variances ($s_0{}^2$, $s_1{}^2$) would not be the same. However, this should not – in general – cause any issue as the two-tailed Welch's t-test covers such a case.

Therefore, the evaluation can be performed by many different intermediate values. For example, in case of an AES-128 encryption engine by considering the AddRoundKey, SubBytes, ShiftRows, and MixColumns outputs, 4×128 bit-wise tests and $4 \times 16 \times 256$ byte-wise tests (only at the first cipher round) can be conducted. This already excludes the XOR result between the intermediate values, which depending on the underlying architecture of the DUT (e.g., a serialized architecture) may lead to potential leaking sources. Therefore, such tests suffer from the same weakness as state-of-the-art attacks since both require to examine many intermediate values and models, which prevents a comprehensive evaluation.

To cope with this imperfection a *non-specific* t-test can be performed, which avoids being dependent on any intermediate value or a model. In such a test the associated data should follow a certain procedure during the trace collection. More precisely a fixed associated data D is preselected, and the DUT is fed by D or by a random source in a non-deterministic and randomly-interleaved fashion. As a more clear explanation suppose that before each measurement a coin is flipped, and accordingly D or a fresh-randomly selected data is given to the DUT. The corresponding t-test is performed by categorizing the traces based on the associated data (D or random). Hence such a test is also called *fixed vs. random t-test*.

The randomly-interleaved procedure is unavoidable; otherwise the test may issue a false-positive result on the vulnerability of the DUT. It is mainly due to the fact that the internal state of the DUT at the start of each query should be also non-deterministic. As an example, if the traces with associated data D are collected consecutively, the DUT internal state is always the same prior to each measurement with D. As another example, if the traces with random associated data and D are collected one after each other (e.g., D_i being random for even i and D for odd i), the DUT internal state is always the same prior to each measurement with random associated data.

In order to explain the concept behind the non-specific t-test, assume a specific t-test based on a single-bit intermediate variable w of the underlying process of the DUT and the corresponding sample point j where the leakage associated to w is measured. Further, let us denote the estimated means of the leakage traces at sample point j by $\mu_{w=0}$ and $\mu_{w=1}$, i.e., those applied in the specific t-test. If these two means are **largely enough** different from each other, each of them is also distinguishable from the overall mean μ ($\approx \frac{\mu_{w=0} + \mu_{w=1}}{2}$ supposing $n_0 \approx n_1$).

From another perspective, consider two non-specific t-tests with the fixed associated data $D_{w=0}$ and $D_{w=1}$, where $D_{w=0}$ leads to the intermediate value $w = 0$ (respectively for $D_{w=1}$). Also, suppose that in each of these two tests $\mathcal{Q}_0$ corresponds to the traces with the fixed associated data and $\mathcal{Q}_1$ to those with random. Hence, in the non-specific test with $D_{w=0}$, the estimated mean μ_0 at sample point j is close to $\mu_{w=0}$ (respectively to $\mu_{w=1}$ in the test with $D_{w=1}$). But in both tests the estimated mean μ_1 (of $\mathcal{Q}_1$) is close to μ (defined above). Therefore, in both tests the statistic ($t^{non-spec.}$) is smaller than that of the specific test ($t^{spec.}$) since $\mu_{w=0} < \mu < \mu_{w=1}$ (or respectively $\mu_{w=1} < \mu < \mu_{w=0}$). However, even supposing $n_0 \approx n_1$ it **cannot** be concluded that

$$|t^{non-spec.}| = |t^{spec.}|/2$$

since the estimated overall variance at sample point j (which is that of $\mathcal{Q}_1$ in both non-specific tests) is

$$s_1{}^2 = \frac{(s_{w=0})^2 + (s_{w=1})^2}{2} + \left(\frac{\mu_{w=0} - \mu_{w=1}}{2}\right)^2 \neq (s_{w=0/1})^2,$$

assuming $n_0 \approx n_1$.

As a result if a non-specific t-test reports a detectable leakage, the specific one results in the same conclusion but with a higher confidence. Although any intermediate value (either bit-wise or at larger scales) as well as the combination between different intermediate values are covered by the non-specific t-test, the negative result (i.e., no detectable leakage) cannot be concluded from a single non-specific test due to its dependency to the selected fixed associated data D. In other words, it may happen that a non-specific t-test by a certain D reports no exploitable leakage, but the same test using another D leads to the opposite conclusion. Hence, it is recommended to repeat a non-specific test with a couple of different D to avoid a false-positive conclusion on resistance of the DUT.

The non-specific t-test can also be performed by a set of particular associated data $\mathcal{D}$ instead of a unique D. The associated data in $\mathcal{D}$ are selected in such a way that all of them lead to a certain intermediate value. For example, a set of plaintexts which cause half of the cipher state at a particular cipher round to be constant. In this case $\mathcal{Q}_0$ refers to the traces with associated data – randomly – selected from $\mathcal{D}$ (respectively $\mathcal{Q}_1$ to the traces with random associated data). Such a non-specific t-test is also known as the *semi-fixed vs. random* test [7], and is particularly useful where the test with a unique D leads to a false-positive result on the vulnerability of the DUT. We express the use cases of each test in more details in Sect. 6.

Order of the Test. Recalling the definition of first-order resistance, the estimated means of leakages associated to the intermediate values of the DUT should not be distinguishable from each other (i.e., the concept behind the Welch's t-test). Otherwise, if such an intermediate value is sensitive and predictable knowing the associated data D (e.g., the output of an Sbox at the first cipher round) a corresponding first-order DPA/CPA attack is expected to be feasible. It can also be extended to the higher orders by following the definition of univariate higher-order attacks [17]. To do so (as also stated in [9]) the collected traces need to be preprocessed. For example, for a second-order evaluation each trace – at each sample point independently – should be mean-free squared prior to the t-test. Here we formalize this process slightly differently as follows.

Let us first denote the dth-order raw statistical moment of a random variable X by $M_d = \mathsf{E}(X^d)$, with $\mu = M_1$ the mean and $\mathsf{E}(.)$ the expectation operator. We also denote the dth-order $(d > 1)$ central moment by $CM_d = \mathsf{E}\left((X - \mu)^d\right)$, with $s^2 = CM_2$ the variance. Finally, the dth-order $(d > 2)$ standardized moment is denoted by $SM_d = \mathsf{E}\left(\left(\frac{X-\mu}{s}\right)^d\right)$, with SM_3 the skewness and SM_4 the kurtosis.

In a first-order univariate t-test, for each set ($\mathcal{Q}_0$ or $\mathcal{Q}_1$) the mean (M_1) is estimated. For a second-order univariate test the mean of the mean-free squared traces $Y = (X - \mu)^2$ is actually the variance (CM_2) of the original traces. Respectively, in a third and higher $(d > 2)$ order test the standardized moment SM_d is the estimated mean of the preprocessed traces. Therefore, the higher-order tests can be conducted by employing the corresponding estimated (central or standardized) moments instead of the means. The remaining point is how to estimate the variance of the preprocessed traces for higher-order tests. We deal with this issue in Sect. 4.2 and explain the corresponding details.

As stated, all the above given expressions are with respect to univariate evaluations, where the traces at each sample point are independently processed. For a bivariate (respectively multivariate) higher-order test different sample points of each trace should be first combined prior to the t-test, e.g., by centered product at the second order. A more formal definition of these cases is given in Sect. 5.

4 Efficient Computation

As stated in the previous section, the first order t-test requires the estimation of two parameters (sample mean μ and sample variance s^2) for each set $\mathcal{Q}_0$ and $\mathcal{Q}_1$. This can lead to problems concerning the efficiency of the computations and the accuracy of the estimations. In the following we address most of these problems and propose a reasonable solution for each of them. For simplicity we omit to mention the sets $\mathcal{Q}_0$ and $\mathcal{Q}_1$ (and the corresponding indices for the means and variances). All the following expressions are based on focusing on one of these sets, which should be repeated on the other set to complete the required computations of a t-test. Unless otherwise stated, we focus on a univariate scenario. Hence, the given expressions should be repeated at each sample point separately.

Using the basic definitions given in Sect. 3, it is possible to compute the first raw and second central moments (M_1 and CM_2) for a first order t-test. However, the resulting algorithm is inefficient as it requires to process the whole trace pool (a single point) twice to estimate CM_2 since it requires M_1 during the computation.

An alternative would be to use the displacement law to derive CM_2 from the first two raw moments as

$$CM_2 = \mathsf{E}(X^2) - \mathsf{E}(X)^2 = M_2 - M_1{}^2. \tag{2}$$

whereas it results in a one-pass algorithm, it is still not the optimal choice as it may be numerically unstable [10]. During the computation of the raw moments the intermediate values tend to become very large which can lead to a loss in accuracy. Further, M_2 and $M_1{}^2$ can be large values, and the result of $M_2 - M_1{}^2$ can also lead to a significant accuracy loss due to the limited fraction significand of floating point formats (e.g., IEEE 754).

In the following we present a way to compute the two required parameters for the t-test at any order in one pass and with proper accuracy. This is achieved by using an incremental algorithm to update the *central sums* from which the needed parameters are derived.

4.1 Incremental One-Pass Computation of All Moments

The basic idea of an incremental algorithm is to update the intermediate results for each new trace added to the trace pool. This has the advantage that the computation can be run in parallel to the measurements. In other words, it is not necessary to collect all the traces, estimate the mean and then estimate the variance. Since the evaluation can be stopped as soon as the t-value surpasses the threshold, this helps to reduce the evaluation time even further. Finding such an algorithm for the raw moments is trivial. In the following we recall the algorithm of [18] to compute all central moments iteratively, and further show how to derive the standardized moments accordingly.

Suppose that $M_{1,\mathcal{Q}}$ denotes the first raw moment (sample mean) of the given set $\mathcal{Q}$. With y as a new trace to the set, the first raw moment of the enlarged set $\mathcal{Q}' = \mathcal{Q} \cup \{y\}$ can be updated as

$$M_{1,\mathcal{Q}'} = M_{1,\mathcal{Q}} + \frac{\Delta}{n},$$

where $\Delta = y - M_{1,\mathcal{Q}}$, and n the cardinality of $\mathcal{Q}'$. Note that $\mathcal{Q}$ and $M_{1,\mathcal{Q}}$ are initialized with $\emptyset$ and respectively zero.

This method can be extended to compute the central moments at any arbitrary order $d > 1$. We first introduce the term central sum as

$$CS_d = \sum_i (x_i - \mu)^d, \qquad \text{where } CM_d = \frac{CS_d}{n}.$$

Following the same definitions, the formula to update CS_d can be written as [18]

$$CS_{d,\mathcal{Q}'} = CS_{d,\mathcal{Q}} + \sum_{k=1}^{d-2} \binom{d}{k} CS_{d-k,\mathcal{Q}} \left(\frac{-\Delta}{n}\right)^k + \left(\frac{n-1}{n}\Delta\right)^d \left[1 - \left(\frac{-1}{n-1}\right)^{d-1}\right],$$
(3)

where Δ is still the same as defined above. It is noteworthy that the calculation of $CS_{d,\mathcal{Q}'}$ requires $CS_{i,\mathcal{Q}}$ for $1 < i \leq d$ as well as the estimated mean $M_{1,\mathcal{Q}}$.

Based on these formulas the first raw and all central moments can be computed efficiently in one pass. Furthermore, since the intermediate results of the central sums are mean free, they do not become significantly large that helps preventing the numerical instabilities. The standardized moments are indeed the central moments which are normalized by the variance. Hence they can be easily derived from the central moments as

$$SM_d = \frac{1}{n} \sum_i \left(\frac{x_i - \mu}{s}\right)^d = \frac{CM_d}{(\sqrt{CM_2})^d}.$$
(4)

Therefore, the first parameter of the t-test (mean of the preprocessed data) at any order can be efficiently and precisely estimated. Below we express how to derive the second parameter for such tests at any order.

4.2 Variance of Preprocessed Traces

A t-test at higher orders operates on preprocessed traces. In particular it requires to estimate the variance of the preprocessed traces. Such a variance does in general not directly correspond to a central or standardized moment of the original traces. Below we present how to derive such a variance at any order from the central and standardized moments.

Equation (2) shows how to obtain the variance given only the first two raw moments. We extend this approach to derive the variance of the preprocessed traces. In case of the second order, the traces are mean-free squared, i.e., $Y = (X - \mu)^2$. The variance of Y is estimated as

$$
\begin{aligned}
s_Y{}^2 &= \frac{1}{n} \sum \left((x - \mu)^2 - \frac{1}{n} \sum (x - \mu)^2 \right)^2 = \frac{1}{n} \sum \left((x - \mu)^2 - CM_2 \right)^2 \\
&= \frac{1}{n} \sum (x - \mu)^4 - \frac{2}{n} CM_2 \sum (x - \mu)^2 + CM_2{}^2 \\
&= CM_4 - CM_2{}^2.
\end{aligned}
\tag{5}
$$

Therefore, the sample variance of the mean-free squared traces (required for a second-order t-test) can be efficiently derived from the central moments CM_4 and CM_2. Note that the values processed by the above equations (CM_4 and CM_2) are already centered hence avoiding the instability issue addressed in Sect. 4. For the cases at the third order, the traces are additionally standardized, i.e., $Z = \left(\frac{X - \mu}{s} \right)^3$. The variance of Z can be written as

$$
\begin{aligned}
s_Z{}^2 &= \frac{1}{n} \sum \left((\frac{x - \mu}{s})^3 - \frac{1}{n} \sum (\frac{x - \mu}{s})^3 \right)^2 = \frac{1}{n} \sum \left((\frac{x - \mu}{s})^3 - SM_3 \right)^2 \\
&= \frac{1}{n} \sum (\frac{x - \mu}{s})^6 - \frac{2}{n} SM_3 \sum (\frac{x - \mu}{s})^3 + SM_3{}^2 \\
&= SM_6 - SM_3{}^2 = \frac{CM_6 - CM_3{}^2}{CM_2{}^3}.
\end{aligned}
\tag{6}
$$

Since the tests at third and higher orders use standardized traces, it is possible to generalize Eq. (6) for the variance of the preprocessed traces at any order $d > 2$ as

$$
SM_{2d} - SM_d{}^2 = \frac{CM_{2d} - CM_d{}^2}{CM_2{}^d}.
\tag{7}
$$

Therefore, a t-test at order d requires to estimate the central moments up to order $2d$. With the above given formulas it is now possible to extend the t-test to any arbitrary order as we can estimate the corresponding required first and second parameters efficiently. In addition, most of the numerical problems are eliminated in this approach. The required formulas for all parameters of the tests up to the fifth order are provided in the extended version of this article [22]. We also included the formulas when the first and second parameters of the tests (up to the fifth order) are derived from raw moments.

In order to give an overview on the accuracy of different ways to compute the parameters for the t-tests, we ran an experiment with 100 million simulated traces with $\sim \mathcal{N}(100, 25)$, which fits to a practical case where the traces (obtained from an oscilloscope) are signed 8-bit integers. We computed the second parameter for t-tests using (i) three-pass algorithm, (ii) the raw moments, and (iii) our proposed method. Note that in the three-pass algorithm first the mean μ is estimated. Then, having μ the traces are processed again to estimate all required central and standardized moments, and finally having all moments the traces are preprocessed (with respect to the desired order) and the variances (of the preprocessed traces) are estimated. The corresponding results are shown in Table 1. In terms of accuracy, our method matches the three-pass algorithm. The raw moments approach suffers from severe numerical instabilities, especially at higher orders where the variance of the preprocessed traces becomes negative.

Table 1. Comparison of the accuracy of different methods to compute the second parameter of the t-tests, 100 million simulated traces $\sim \mathcal{N}(100, 25)$

	1st order	2nd order	3rd order	4th order	5th order
Three pass	25.08399	1258.18874	15.00039	96.08342	947.25523
Raw moments	25.08399	1258.14132	14.49282	-1160.83799	-1939218.83401
Our method	25.08399	1258.18874	15.00039	96.08342	947.25523

4.3 Parallel Computation

Depending on the data complexity of the measurements, it is sometimes favorable to parallelize the computation in order to reduce the time complexity. To this end, a straightforward approach is to utilize a multi-core architecture (a CPU cluster) which computes the necessary central sums for multiple sample points in parallel. This can be achieved easily as the computations on different sample points are completely independent of each other. Consequently, there is no communication overhead between the threads. This approach is beneficial in most measurement scenarios and enables an extremely fast evaluation depending on the number of available CPU cores as well as the number of sample points in each trace. As an example, we are able to calculate all the necessary parameters of five non-specific t-tests (at first to fifth orders) on $100,000,000$ traces (each with $3,000$ sample points) in 9 hours using two Intel Xeon X5670 CPUs @ 2.93 GHz, i.e., 24 hyper-threading cores.

A different approach can be preferred if the number of points of interest is very low. In this scenario, suppose that the trace collection is already finished and the t-tests are expected to be performed on a small number of sample points of a large number of traces. The aforementioned approach for parallel computing might not be the most efficient way as the degree of parallelization is bounded by the number of sample points. Instead, it is possible to increase the degree by splitting up the computation of the central sums for each sample point. For this, the set of traces of one sample point $\mathcal{Q}$ is partitioned into c subsets $\mathcal{Q}^{*i}$, $i \in \{1, \ldots, c\}$, and the necessary central sums $CS_{d,\mathcal{Q}^{*i}}$ are computed for each subset in parallel using the equations introduced in Sect. 4.1. Afterward all $CS_{d,\mathcal{Q}^{*i}}$ are combined using the following exemplary equation for $c = 2$ [18]:

$$CS_{d,\mathcal{Q}} = CS_{d,\mathcal{Q}^{*1}} + CS_{d,\mathcal{Q}^{*2}} + \sum_{k=1}^{d-2} \binom{d}{k} \left[\left(-\frac{n^{*2}}{n} \right)^k CS_{d-k,\mathcal{Q}^{*1}} \right.$$

$$\left. + \left(\frac{n^{*1}}{n} \right)^k CS_{d-k,\mathcal{Q}^{*2}} \right] \Delta_{2,1}{}^k + \left(\frac{n^{*1} n^{*2}}{n} \Delta_{2,1} \right)^d \left[\frac{1}{(n^{*2})^{d-1}} - \left(\frac{-1}{n^{*1}} \right)^{d-1} \right],$$

with $\mathcal{Q} = \mathcal{Q}^{*1} \cup \mathcal{Q}^{*2}$, $n^{*i} = |\mathcal{Q}^{*i}|$, $n = n^{*1} + n^{*2}$, and $\Delta_{2,1} = M_{1,\mathcal{Q}^{*2}} - M_{1,\mathcal{Q}^{*1}}$. Further, the mean of $\mathcal{Q}$ can be trivially obtained as

$$M_{1,\mathcal{Q}} = \frac{n^{*1} M_{1,\mathcal{Q}^{*1}} + n^{*2} M_{1,\mathcal{Q}^{*2}}}{n}.$$

5 Multivariate

The equations presented in Sect. 4 only consider univariate settings. This is typically the case for hardware designs in which the shares are processed in parallel, and the sum of the leakages appear at a sample point. For software implementations this is usually not the case as the computations are sequential and split up over multiple clock cycles.

In this scenario the samples of multiple points in time are first combined using a combination function, and an attack is conducted on the combination's result. If the combination function (e.g., sum or product) does not require the mean, the extension of the equations to the multivariate case is trivial. It is enough to combine each set of samples separately and compute the mean and variance of the result iteratively as shown in the prior section.

However, this approach does not apply to the optimum combination function, i.e., the centered product [19,24]. Given d sample point indices $\mathcal{J} = \{j_1, ..., j_d\}$ as points of interest and a set of sample vectors $\mathcal{Q} = \{ \boldsymbol{V}_{i \in \{1,...,n\}} \}$ with $\boldsymbol{V}_i = \left(t_i^{(j)} \mid j \in \mathcal{J} \right)$, the centered product of the i-th trace is defined as

$$\prod_{j \in \mathcal{J}} \left(t_i^{(j)} - \mu_{\mathcal{Q}}^{(j)} \right), \tag{8}$$

where $\mu_{\mathcal{Q}}^{(j)}$ denotes the mean at sample point j over set $\mathcal{Q}$. The inclusion of the means is the reason why it is not easily possible to extend the equations from Sect. 4 to compute this value iteratively.

There is an iterative algorithm to compute the covariance similar to the aforementioned algorithms. This corresponds to the first parameter in a bivariate second-order scenario, i.e., $d = 2$. The covariance $\frac{C_{2,\mathcal{Q}'}}{n}$ is computed as shown in [18] with

$$C_{2,\mathcal{Q}'} = C_{2,\mathcal{Q}} + \frac{n-1}{n} \left(y^{(1)} - \mu_{\mathcal{Q}}^{(1)} \right) \left(y^{(2)} - \mu_{\mathcal{Q}}^{(2)} \right) \tag{9}$$

for $Q' = Q \cup \{(y^{(1)}, y^{(2)})\}$, $|Q'| = n$, and an exemplary index set $\mathcal{J} = \{1, 2\}$. Still, even with this formula it is not possible to compute the required second parameter for the t-test. In the following, we present an extension of this approach to d sample points and show how this can be used to compute both parameters for a dth-order d-variate t-test.

First, we define the sum of the centered products which is required to compute the first parameter. For d sample points and a set of sample vectors Q, we denote the sum as

$$C_{d,Q,\mathcal{J}} = \sum_{V \in Q} \prod_{j \in \mathcal{J}} \left(t^{(j)} - \mu_Q^{(j)} \right). \tag{10}$$

In addition, we define the k-th order power set of $\mathcal{J}$ as

$$\mathcal{P}_k = \{\mathcal{S} \mid \mathcal{S} \in \mathbb{P}(\mathcal{J}), |\mathcal{S}| = k\}, \tag{11}$$

where $\mathbb{P}(\mathcal{J})$ refers to the power set of the indices of the points of interest $\mathcal{J}$. Using these definitions we derive the following theorem.

Theorem 1. *Let $\mathcal{J}$ be a given set of indices (of d points of interest) and V the given sample vector with $V = (y^{(1)}, ..., y^{(d)})$. The sum of the centered products $C_{d,Q',\mathcal{J}}$ of the extended set $Q' = Q \cup V$ with $\Delta^{(i \in \mathcal{J})} = y^{(j)} - \mu_Q^{(j)}$ and $|Q'| = n > 0$ can be computed as:*

$$C_{d,Q',\mathcal{J}} = C_{d,Q,\mathcal{J}} + \left(\sum_{k=2}^{d-1} \sum_{\mathcal{S} \in \mathcal{P}_k} C_{k,Q,\mathcal{S}} \prod_{j \in \mathcal{J} \setminus \mathcal{S}} \left(\frac{\Delta^{(j)}}{-n} \right) \right)$$

$$+ \left(\frac{(-1)^d(n-1) + (n-1)^d}{n^d} \prod_{j \in \mathcal{J}} \Delta^{(j)} \right). \tag{12}$$

The proof of Theorem 1 is given in the extended version of this article [22]. Equation (12) can be also used to derive the second parameter of the t-tests. To this end, let us first recall the definition of the second parameter in the dth-order d-variate case:

$$s^2 = \frac{1}{n} \sum_{V \in Q} \left(\prod_{j \in \mathcal{J}} \left(t^{(j)} - \mu_Q^{(j)} \right) - \frac{C_{d,Q,\mathcal{J}}}{n} \right)^2$$

$$= \frac{1}{n} \left(\sum_{V \in Q} \prod_{j \in \mathcal{J}} \left(t^{(j)} - \mu_Q^{(j)} \right)^2 \right) - \left(\frac{C_{d,Q,\mathcal{J}}}{n} \right)^2. \tag{13}$$

The first term of the above equation can be written as

$$\frac{1}{n} \sum_{V \in Q} \prod_{j \in \mathcal{J}} \left(t^{(j)} - \mu_Q^{(j)} \right)^2 = \frac{1}{n} \sum_{V \in Q} \left(\prod_{j \in \mathcal{J}} \left(t^{(j)} - \mu_Q^{(j)} \right) \prod_{j \in \mathcal{J}} \left(t^{(j)} - \mu_Q^{(j)} \right) \right)$$

$$= \frac{C_{2d,Q,\mathcal{J}'}}{n}. \tag{14}$$

Hence, the iterative algorithm (Eq. (12)) can be performed with multiset $\mathcal{J}' = \{j_1, ..., j_d, j_1, ..., j_d\}$ to derive the first term of Eq. (13). It is noteworthy that at the first glance Eq. (13) looks like Eq. (2), for which we addressed low accuracy issues. However, data which are processed by Eq. (13) are already centered, that avoids the sums $C_{d,\mathcal{Q},\mathcal{J}}$ being very large values. Therefore, the accuracy issues which have been pointed out in Sect. 4 are evaded.

By combining the results of this section with that of Sect. 4, it is now possible to perform a t-test with any variate and at any order efficiently and with sufficient accuracy. As an example, we give all the formulas required by a second-order bivariate ($d = 2$) t-test in the extended version of this article [22].

6   Case Studies

Security evaluations consist of the two phases *measurement* and *analysis*. All challenges regarding the second part, which in our scenario refers to the computation of the t-test statistics, have been discussed in detail in the previous sections. However, this alone does not ensure a correct evaluation as malpractice in the measurement phase can lead to faulty results in the analysis. Below, we first describe the pitfalls that can occur during the measurement phase and provide solutions to ensure the correctness of evaluations. After that, two case studies are discussed that exemplary show the applications of our proposed evaluation framework.

6.1   Framework

If the DUT is equipped with countermeasures, the evaluation might require the collection of many (millions of) traces and, thus, the measurement rate (i.e., the number of collected traces per a certain period of time) can become a major hurdle. Following the technique suggested in [7,11] we explain how the measurement phase can be significantly accelerated. The general scenario (cf. Fig. 2) is based on the assumption that the employed acquisition device (e.g., oscilloscope) includes a feature usually called *sequence mode* or *rapid block mode*. In such a mode – depending on the length of each trace as well as the size of the sampling memory of the oscilloscope – the acquisition device can record multiple traces. This is beneficial since the biggest bottleneck in the measurement phase is the low speed of the communication between e.g., the PC and the DUT (usually realized by UART). In the scenario shown in Fig. 2 it is supposed that **Target** is the DUT, and **Control** a microcontroller (or an FPGA) which communicates with the DUT as well as with the PC. The terms **Target** and **Control** correspond to the two FPGAs of e.g., a SAKURA (SASEBO) platform [1], but in some frameworks these two parties are merged, e.g., a microcontroller-based platform. Further, the PC is already included in modern oscilloscopes.

Profiting from the sequence mode the communication between the PC and the DUT can be minimized in such a way that the PC sends only a single request to collect multiple N traces. The measurement rate depends on the size of the

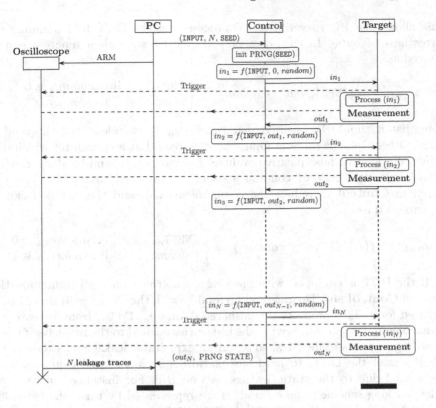

Fig. 2. An optimized measurement process

oscilloscope's sampling memory, the length of each trace as well as the frequency of operation of the DUT. As an example, by means of an oscilloscope with 64 MByte sampling memory (per channel) we are able to measure $N = 10,000$ traces per request when each trace consists of 5,000 sample points. This results in being able to collect 100 million traces (for either a specific or non-specific t-test) in 12 hours. We should point out that the given scenario is not specific to t-test evaluations. It can also be used to speed up the measurement process in case of an evaluation by state-of-the-art attacks when the key is known.

To assure the correctness of the measurements, the PC should be able to follow and verify the processes performed by both **Control** and the DUT. Our suggestion is to employ a random number generator which can be seeded by the PC[1]. This allows the PC to check the consistency of out_N as well as the PRNG state. With respect to Fig. 2, $f(.,.,.)$ is defined based on the desired evaluation scheme. For a specific t-test (or any evaluation method where no control over e.g., plaintexts is necessary) our suggestion is:

$$in_{i+1} = f(\text{INPUT}, out_i, random) = out_i \oplus random.$$

---

[1] For example an AES encryption engine in counter mode.

This allows the PC to verify all N processes of the DUT by examining the correctness of out_N. In case of a non-specific t-test, such a function can be realized as

$$in_{i+1} = f(\text{INPUT}, out_i, random) = \begin{cases} \text{INPUT} & \text{if } random_{bit} \text{ is } 0 \\ random & \text{if } random_{bit} \text{ is } 1 \end{cases}.$$

Note that it should be ensured that $random_{bit}$ is excluded from the random input. Otherwise, the random inputs become biased at a certain bit which may potentially lead to false-positive evaluation results. If a semi-fixed vs. random t-test is conducted, INPUT contains a set of certain fixed inputs (which can be stored in **Control** to reduce the communications), and the function can be implemented as

$$in_{i+1} = f(\text{INPUT}, out_i, random) = \begin{cases} \text{INPUT}_{random} & \text{if } random_{bit} \text{ is } 0 \\ random & \text{if } random_{bit} \text{ is } 1 \end{cases}.$$

If the DUT is equipped with masking countermeasures, all communication between **Control** and **Target** (and preferably with the PC as well) should be in a shared form. This prevents the unshared data, e.g., INPUT, from appearing in **Control** and **Target**. Otherwise, the leakage associated to the input itself would cause, e.g., a non-specific t-test to report an exploitable leakage regardless of the robustness of the DUT. In hardware platforms such a shared communication is essential due to the static leakage as well [15]. For instance, in a second-order masking scheme (where variables are represented by three shares) INPUT should be a 3-share value $(\text{INPUT}^1, \text{INPUT}^2, \text{INPUT}^3)$, and respectively $in_{i+1} = (in_{i+1}^1, in_{i+1}^2, in_{i+1}^3)$. In such a case, a non-specific t-test (including semi-fixed vs. random) should be handled as

$$\begin{aligned} in_{i+1} &= f(\text{INPUT}, out_i, random) \\ &= \begin{cases} (\text{INPUT}^1 \oplus r^1, \text{INPUT}^2 \oplus r^2, \text{INPUT}^3 \oplus r^1 \oplus r^2) & \text{if } random_{bit} \text{ is } 0 \\ (r^1, r^2, r^3) & \text{if } random_{bit} \text{ is } 1 \end{cases}, \end{aligned}$$

with r^1 as a short notation of $random^1$. In other words, the fixed input should be freshly remasked before being sent to the DUT. Consequently, the last output $(out_N^1, out_N^2, out_N^3)$ is also sent in a shared form to the PC.

In general we suggest to apply the tests with the following settings:

- non-specific t-test (fixed vs. random): with shared communication between the parties, if the DUT is equipped with masking.
- non-specific t-test (semi-fixed vs. random): without shared communication, if the DUT is equipped with hiding techniques.
- specific t-tests: with the goal of identifying a suitable intermediate value for a key-recovery attack, if the DUT is not equipped with any countermeasures or failed in former non-specific tests. In this case, a shared communication is preferable if the DUT is equipped with masking.

We also provided two practical case studies, one based on an Atmel microcontroller platform (the DPA contest v4.2 [25]) and the other one by means of an FPGA-based platform (SAKURA-G [1]), which are given in details in the extended version of this article [22].

7   Conclusions

Security evaluations using Welch's t-test have become popular in recent years. In this paper we have extended the theoretical foundations and guidelines regarding the leakage assessment introduced in [9]. In particular we have given more detailed instructions how the test can be applied in a higher-order setting. In this context, problems that can occur during the computation of this test vector have been highlighted. We have proposed solutions to perform the t-test efficiently and accurately at any order and any variate. In addition, we have discussed and given guidelines for an optimized measurement setup which allows high measurement rate and avoids faulty evaluations. As a future work, the presented robust incremental approach can be extended to correlation-based evaluation schemes.

Acknowledgment. The research in this work was supported in part by the DFG Research Training Group GRK 1817/1.

References

1. Side-channel AttacK user reference architecture. http://satoh.cs.uec.ac.jp/SAKURA/index.html
2. Balasch, J., Gierlichs, B., Grosso, V., Reparaz, O., Standaert, F.-X.: On the cost of lazy engineering for masked software implementations. In: Joye, M., Moradi, A. (eds.) CARDIS 2014. LNCS, vol. 8968, pp. 64 81. Springer, Heidelberg (2015)
3. Bilgin, B., Gierlichs, B., Nikova, S., Nikov, V., Rijmen, V.: Higher-order threshold implementations. In: Sarkar, P., Iwata, T. (eds.) ASIACRYPT 2014, Part II. LNCS, vol. 8874, pp. 326–343. Springer, Heidelberg (2014)
4. Brier, E., Clavier, C., Olivier, F.: Correlation power analysis with a leakage model. In: Joye, M., Quisquater, J.-J. (eds.) CHES 2004. LNCS, vol. 3156, pp. 16–29. Springer, Heidelberg (2004)
5. Chatzikokolakis, K., Chothia, T., Guha, A.: Statistical measurement of information leakage. In: Esparza, J., Majumdar, R. (eds.) TACAS 2010. LNCS, vol. 6015, pp. 390–404. Springer, Heidelberg (2010)
6. Chothia, T., Guha, A.: A statistical test for information leaks using continuous mutual information. In: IEEE Computer Security Foundations Symposium - CSF 2011, pp. 177–190, IEEE Computer Society (2011)
7. Cooper, J., Demulder, E., Goodwill, G., Jaffe, J., Kenworthy, G., Rohatgi, P.: Test vector leakage assessment (TVLA) methodology in practice. In: International Cryptographic Module Conference (2013). http://icmc-2013.org/wp/wp-content/uploads/2013/09/goodwillkenworthtestvector.pdf
8. Gierlichs, B., Batina, L., Tuyls, P., Preneel, B.: Mutual information analysis. In: Oswald, E., Rohatgi, P. (eds.) CHES 2008. LNCS, vol. 5154, pp. 426–442. Springer, Heidelberg (2008)

9. Goodwill, G., Jun, B., Jaffe, J., Rohatgi, P.: A testing methodology for side channel resistance validation. In: NIST Non-Invasive Attack Testing Workshop (2011). http://csrc.nist.gov/news_events/non-invasive-attack-testing-workshop/papers/08_Goodwill.pdf

10. Higham, N.J.: Accuracy and Stability of Numerical Algorithms, 2nd edn. SIAM, Philadelphia (2002)

11. Kizhvatov, I., Witteman, M.: Academic vs. industrial perspective on SCA, and an industrial innovation. Short talk at COSADE (2013)

12. Kocher, P.C., Jaffe, J., Jun, B.: Differential power analysis. In: Wiener, M. (ed.) CRYPTO 1999. LNCS, vol. 1666, pp. 388–397. Springer, Heidelberg (1999)

13. Leiserson, A.J., Marson, M.E., Wachs, M.A.: Gate-level masking under a path-based leakage metric. In: Batina, L., Robshaw, M. (eds.) CHES 2014. LNCS, vol. 8731, pp. 580–597. springer, Heidelberg (2014)

14. Mather, L., Oswald, E., Bandenburg, J., Wójcik, M.: Does my device leak information? An *a priori* statistical power analysis of leakage detection tests. In: Sako, K., Sarkar, P. (eds.) ASIACRYPT 2013, Part I. LNCS, vol. 8269, pp. 486–505. Springer, Heidelberg (2013)

15. Moradi, A.: Side-channel leakage through static power. In: Batina, L., Robshaw, M. (eds.) CHES 2014. LNCS, vol. 8731, pp. 562–579. Springer, Heidelberg (2014)

16. Moradi, A., Hinterwälder, G.: Side-channel security analysis of ultra-low-power FRAM-based MCUs. In: Mangard, S., Poschmann, A.Y. (eds.) COSADE 2015. LNCS, vol. 9064, pp. 239–254. Springer, Heidelberg (2015)

17. Moradi, A., Mischke, O.: How far should theory be from practice? In: Prouff, E., Schaumont, P. (eds.) CHES 2012. LNCS, vol. 7428, pp. 92–106. Springer, Heidelberg (2012)

18. Pébay, P.: Formulas for robust, one-pass parallel computation of covariances and arbitrary-order statistical moments. Sandia Report SAND2008-6212, Sandia National Laboratories (2008)

19. Prouff, E., Rivain, M., Bevan, R.: Statistical analysis of second order differential power analysis. IEEE Trans. Comput. 58(6), 799–811 (2009)

20. Sasdrich, P., Mischke, O., Moradi, A., Güneysu, T.: Side-channel protection by randomizing look-up tables on reconfigurable hardware. In: Mangard, S., Poschmann, A.Y. (eds.) COSADE 2015. LNCS, vol. 9064, pp. 95–107. Springer, Heidelberg (2015)

21. Sasdrich, P., Moradi, A., Mischke, O., Güneysu, T.: Achieving side-channel protection with dynamic logic reconfiguration on modern FPGAs. In: Symposium on Hardware-Oriented Security and Trust - HOST 2015, pp. 130–136, IEEE (2015)

22. Schneider, T., Moradi, A.: Leakage assessment methodology - a clear roadmap for side-channel evaluations. In: Güneysu, T., Handschuh, H. (eds.) CHES 2015. LNCS, vol. 9293, pp. xx–yy, Cryptology ePrint Archive, Report 2015/207. Springer, Heidelberg (2015). http://eprint.iacr.org/

23. Schneider, T., Moradi, A., Güneysu, T.: Arithmetic addition over Boolean masking - towards first- and second-order resistance in hardware. In: Malkin, T., Kolesnikov, V., Lewko, A.B., Polychronakis, M. (eds) Applied Cryptography and Network Security - ACNS 2015. LNCS, vol. 9092, pp. 517–536. Springer, Heidelberg (2015)

24. Standaert, F.-X., Veyrat-Charvillon, N., Oswald, E., Gierlichs, B., Medwed, M., Kasper, M., Mangard, S.: The world is not enough: another look on second-order DPA. In: Abe, M. (ed.) ASIACRYPT 2010. LNCS, vol. 6477, pp. 112–129. Springer, Heidelberg (2010)

25. TELECOM ParisTech. DPA Contest (4th edition) (2013–2015). http://www.DPAcontest.org/v4/

26. Wild, A., Moradi, A., Güneysu, T.: Evaluating the duplication of dual-rail precharge logics on FPGAs. In: Mangard, S., Poschmann, A.Y. (eds.) COSADE 2015. LNCS, vol. 9064, pp. 81–94. Springer, Heidelberg (2015)

Physically Unclonable Functions and Hardware Trojans

Secure Key Generation from Biased PUFs

Roel Maes[1]([⊠]), Vincent van der Leest[1], Erik van der Sluis[1],
and Frans Willems[2]

[1] Intrinsic-ID, Eindhoven, The Netherlands
{roel.maes,vincent.van.der.leest,erik.van.der.sluis}@intrinsic-id.com
[2] T.U. Eindhoven, Eindhoven, The Netherlands
f.m.j.willems@tue.nl

Abstract. PUF-based key generators have been widely considered as a root-of-trust in digital systems. They typically require an error-correcting mechanism (e.g. based on the code-offset method) for dealing with bit errors between the enrollment and reconstruction of keys. When the used PUF does *not* have full entropy, entropy leakage between the helper data and the device-unique key material can occur. If the entropy level of the PUF becomes too low, the PUF-derived key can be attacked through the publicly available helper data. In this work we provide several solutions for preventing this entropy leakage for PUFs suffering from i.i.d. *biased bits*. The methods proposed in this work pose no limit on the amount of bias that can be tolerated, which solves an important open problem for PUF-based key generation. Additionally, the solutions are all evaluated based on reliability, efficiency, leakage and reusability showing that depending on requirements for the key generator different solutions are preferable.

1 Introduction

A Physically Unclonable Function (PUF) implemented on an integrated circuit (IC) can be used as a hardware root-of-trust for a digital system, e.g. to generate and store the system's private master keys. These PUF-based key generators provide a secure and efficient alternative for protected non-volatile memories (e.g. Flash, EEPROM, antifuses, etc.). For such applications, a high-quality PUF is needed which is both unpredictable as well as reliable, i.e. PUF responses are random per instantiation but repeatable with limited noise over time and under all circumstances. To achieve this, both entropy extraction (for unpredictability) and error-correction coding (for reliability) are required in key generators. A secure key derivation function is used for entropy extraction to derive a cryptographic key from a random seed. For error-correction, a commonly used technique is the code-offset method that stores helper data during an enrollment phase, which is later used to correct bit errors that occur in the PUF response when reconstructing the key. This helper data should not provide any information about the key, because it is generally stored and/or transferred publicly.

It has recently been pointed out [9] that if a PUF does *not* have full entropy, information about the secret key material is leaked by the helper data. If this

© International Association for Cryptologic Research 2015
T. Güneysu and H. Handschuh (Eds.): CHES 2015, LNCS 9293, pp. 517–534, 2015.
DOI: 10.1007/978-3-662-48324-4_26

entropy leakage becomes too large, the derived key will not have full entropy; this poses a serious threat to the security of the key generator. The main focus of this work is the development of (pre-)processing methods that prevent this leakage in case of biased PUFs. Using innovative approaches, the overhead of these algorithms on PUF size is minimized, while guaranteeing reliability of the system.

Related Work. PUF-based key generators based on error-correcting codes were firstly introduced in [13] for Arbiter PUFs and later on in [5] for SRAM PUFs, both using a configuration based on linear block codes. Efficiency optimizations were proposed based on code concatentation [1] and soft-decision decoding [10,17]. Later key generators based on ring oscillator PUFs were presented in [18,22]. Potential security issues can arise with these key generators when their input (i.e. the PUF response) does not have full entropy, see e.g. [6], which was recently emphasized strongly in [9].

Contributions. The primary contribution of this work is the introduction of a number of solutions that prevent entropy leakage between helper data and the secret of a PUF-based key generator, in case of i.i.d. but biased PUF response bits. The presented solutions are all scalable in that they can handle an arbitrary amount of PUF response bias, given that the available PUF response is large enough to provide a sufficient input bits. This solves an important open problem with existing PUF-based key generators, which was even hypothesized to be unsolvable in [9]. The introduced methods are all proven to be secure and are compared based on their reliability, efficiency, leakage and reusability. This comparison shows that depending on requirements for the key generator, different solutions are preferable. Additionally, this work provides a new model for entropy leakage due to PUF bias as well as a model for the relation between PUF bias and the bit error rate of the corresponding PUF. The first model is an improvement over existing models, e.g. as used in [9], while the second model is a new concept which is an extension on the models from [14].

2   PUF-based Key Generation and Bias

2.1   General Construction

Figure 1 shows a generic PUF-based key generator using the code-offset method from [4], with which many earlier proposed implementations (e.g. [1,5,10,17]) conceptually comply. Encode() and Decode() are the encoding and corresponding decoding function of an error-correcting code. In this work it is considered that the error-correcting code is a binary linear block code. KDF() is a key derivation function for generating a strong key from a random source with possibly reduced entropy. This can be a strong extractor [4] (for information-theoretic security), or a cryptographically secure key derivation function, see e.g. [11,12]. KDF() could also be applied on the PUF response X instead of on the random seed S. However, for analysis in this work, both variants are equivalent (see [16]). Key generators have the following two key properties:

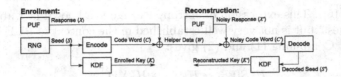

Fig. 1. PUF-based key generator based on the code-offset method.

1. *Reliability:* if the occurence of (bit) errors between X and X' is limited, then with high probability K' will be equal to K.
2. *Security:* if X is sufficiently unpredictable, then K is secure even to a party which observes W.

Reliability is accomplished by use of an error-correcting code able to cope with typically occuring amounts of bit errors. In a construction like Fig. 1 this results in a disclosure of information by W on X, since W is assumed to be public. However, the security property guarantees that *if there is sufficient entropy in* X, there will be enough left after this disclosure to derive a secure key. The security of the key is hence conditioned on the entropy of X. This aspect is the main subject of this work, where we will make this condition explicit and study its implications.

2.2 Entropy Leakage

Given that KDF() is a secure key derivation function, the security of the derived key K depends on the unpredictability of the input of KDF(). In a construction as in Fig. 1, the input of KDF() is a seed S which is randomly generated during the one-time enrollment, and reconstructed from W and a noisy PUF response X' during later reconstructions. Since W is considered public, S needs to be sufficiently unpredictable even when conditioned on W. In terms of entropy,[1] this is expressed as follows:

$$H(S|W) = H(S) - I(S;W), \tag{1}$$

or the conditional entropy of S given W is the original entropy of S reduced with the *entropy leakage* of S by W, which is expressed by the mutual information between S and W.[2] For the remainder of this work it is assumed that S is a fully random bit string of length k, i.e. $H(S) = |S| = k$. For a key generator design as in Fig. 1, deploying a linear block code with generator matrix $\mathbf{G}$ (where all rows of $\mathbf{G}$ are independent) and parity-check matrix $\mathbf{H}$, the entropy leakage is:

$$I(S; X \oplus S\mathbf{G}) = k - H(X) + H(X\mathbf{H}^\top), \tag{2}$$

---

[1] In this work, unpredictability of random variables is expressed by Shannon entropy, as is done in many earlier work on this subject, e.g. [7]. Note that Shannon entropy serves as a lower bound for average guesswork [19]. For a stronger (less practical) provable security notion, the more pessimistic min-entropy measure should be used.

[2] Note that $H(X|W) = H(S|W)$, see [16]. This shows the equivalence in security (in terms of entropy) for a key generated from S or X.

(proof, see [16]). This expression of entropy leakage is a known fact about code-offset schemes,[3] but is not very well-established in the context of PUF-based key generators.[4] Combining (1) and (2) gives:

$$H(S|W) = H(X) - H(X\mathbf{H}^\top). \tag{3}$$

The remaining entropy of S after observing W is hence equal to the entropy of the PUF response X reduced with the entropy of the *syndrome* of X under the used linear error-correcting block code.

If X has full entropy then the entropy leakage as given by (2) becomes zero and $H(S|W) = k$. Hence, in that case S remains fully random and can be used as a secure input for key derivation. However, if X does *not* have full entropy, the entropy leakage might no longer be zero and S might not be completely unpredictable after observation of W. In the following, we study the effect of reduced entropy of X on the security of S, and in particular what occurs when X suffers from *bias*.

2.3   Entropy Leakage Due to PUF Bias

The most common cause of reduced entropy of X is the presence of *global bias* on the bits of X, i.e. globally '0'-bits occur consistently more often than '1'-bits or vice-versa. We say that an n-bit PUF response X is p-biased ($0 \le p \le 1$) if the a-priori expected number of '1'-bits in X is $p \cdot n$, or p is the a-priori probability of a random bit of a PUF response evaluating to '1'. An unbiased PUF has $p = 50\%$, but from experiments it is clear for most PUFs p deviates slightly from 50%, or even significantly (see e.g. [7,8,13]).

We now investigate entropy leakage on S when X has reduced entropy caused *only* by global bias. In that case $H(X) = nh(p)$ with $h()$ the binary entropy function. From (2) and (3) it is evident that the quantity $H(X\mathbf{H}^\top)$ plays a central role in the entropy leakage. In any case, it holds that $H(X\mathbf{H}^\top) \le |X\mathbf{H}^\top| = (n - k)$, which results in the lower bound:

$$H(S|W) \ge k - n(1 - h(p)). \tag{4}$$

This is a known practical bound for constructing a secure PUF-based key generator (see e.g. [15]), but it needs to be stressed that this is a *lower bound* and hence any conclusions based on it could be overly pessimistic.[5]

We present two methods for calculating the entropy leakage exactly in the case of global bias for codes with certain properties:

---

[3] E.g., a variant thereof appeared before in an early version of [21].

[4] This has led to some confusion and occasional misinterpretations, i.e. under- or overestimations of the leakage. A discussion on this is e.g. found in [3].

[5] Note that in particular for a too high bias this entropy bound even becomes negative, making it absolutely clear that this is a pessimistic lower bound.

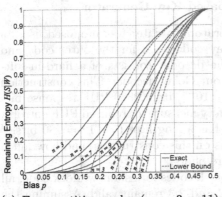

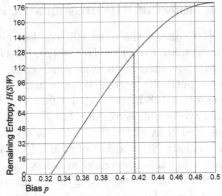

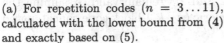

(a) For repetition codes ($n = 3 \ldots 11$), calculated with the lower bound from (4) and exactly based on (5).

(b) For the key generator from [10], calculated with the lower bound formula following from plugging (6) into (3).

Fig. 2. $H(S|W)$ in case of a p-biased PUF response.

- For codes with a simple structure, a closed expression for $H(X\mathbf{H}^\top)$ can be derived. In particular for repetition codes it holds that:[6]

$$H(X\mathbf{H_{rep}}^\top) = -\sum_{t=0}^{n-1} \binom{n-1}{t} f(t; n, p) \log_2 f(t; n, p) \tag{5}$$

with $f(t; n, p) = p^t(1-p)^{n-t} + p^{n-t}(1-p)^t$.
- For non-trivial but relatively short codes (e.g. $n < 32$), the distribution of $X\mathbf{H}^\top$ can be determined exhaustively from the known distribution of X. $H(X\mathbf{H}^\top)$ then follows from the distribution of $X\mathbf{H}^\top$.

Figure 2(a) shows $H(S|W)$ for repetition codes with a p-biased PUF.[7] Both the lower bound (4) and the exact calculation (5) are shown. It is clear that for $p \not\approx 50\,\%$, the lower bound is not tight and significantly underestimates the remaining entropy; e.g. for $n = 5$ the lower bound reaches zero for $p = 24\,\%$, while exact calculation shows that about 0.35 bit of entropy is actually still left. The lower bound is hence rather pessimistic for biases not close to $50\,\%$ and a more exact calculation is preferable. This also partially refutes the so-called *"repetition code pitfall"* as stated in [9] which was solely based on the pessimistic conclusions from (4).

On the other hand, it is clear from Fig. 2(a) that a biased PUF response still severely reduces the remaining entropy of the seed S. This could be problematic, in particular for key generators deploying concatenated codes with a repetition code as the inner code, as shown next.

---

[6] See [16] for the derivation of this formula and similar for min-entropy in [3].
[7] Only $p \leq 0.5$ is shown; entropy-vs-bias graphs are symmetrical around $p = 0.5$.

2.4   Effect of PUF Bias on a PUF-based Key Generator

In [10], one of the most efficient key generators to date[8] was proposed using a concatenation of $r = 15\times$ a $(24, 12)$-Golay code word for the outer code and a $(8, 1)$-repetition code as inner code. The decoder consists of a hard-in-soft-out repetition decoder and a soft-in-hard-out Golay decoder. This construction extracts a 128-bit key with a failure rate $<10^{-6}$, from 2880 PUF response bits with average bit error rate $\leq 15\%$.[9] As a safety measure for reduced PUF entropy, the seed S from which the key is derived has a length of $15 \times 12 = 180$ bits.[10] We will study the effect of global PUF bias on this construction, and how much protection this implemented safety measure offers.

Since the concatenation of two linear block codes forms a new block code, all the entropy leakage results from Sects. 2.2 and 2.3 remain valid. Assuming the bits of X are i.i.d., then it holds for $r\times$ a generic (n_2, k_2)-block code concatenated with a $(n_1, 1)$-repetition code that:

$$H(X\mathbf{H}^\top) \leq r \cdot \left(n_2 \cdot H(X_{1:n_1}\mathbf{H_{rep}}^\top) + H(X_{1:n_2}\mathbf{H_2}^\top) \right), \tag{6}$$

with $X_{1:n_1}$ and $X_{1:n_2}$ vectors of n_1 and n_2 bits from X.[11] This is an upper bound ($\leq$) since the entropy contributions of both right terms in (6) could partially overlap,[12] but the same entropy cannot be leaked twice. We evaluate (6) exactly for the example key generator by calculating the repetition code entropy term using (5), and the Golay code term using the exhaustive method. The result is plugged into (3) and shown in Fig. 2(b).

From Fig. 2(b) it is clear that bias significantly affects the remaining seed entropy for this realistic key generator. For $p < 41.8\%$ ($p > 58.2\%$), the remaining entropy (lower bound) even falls below 128 bits, and the input of the key derivation function has potentially less than 128 bits of entropy. Hence one can no longer claim that the derived 128-bit key has full entropy.[13] Hence, the safety measure of using a 180-bit seed effectively keeps this key generator secure for PUFs with a bias $41.8\% \leq p \leq 58.2\%$.

In case of a seed of only 128 bits, the key's security would be reduced for any PUF with even the slightest bias. On the other hand, in order to cope with even more bias, overhead on the seed length will have to be increased even

---

[8] Efficient in terms of PUF size, while following the design of Fig. 1 and using only a single enrollment measurement per derived key.

[9] The key generator from [10] is based on an SRAM PUF, but in this work we make abstraction of the actual PUF used. Our analysis and solutions apply to all PUF types with i.i.d. response bits suffering from bias.

[10] [10] aims for a seed of 171 bits, but this is rounded up to 180 for practicality. The need for having 171-bit seeds originated in [5], but the reasoning is not fully clear.

[11] Since bits of X are assumed i.i.d., which particular bits from X are considered for the entropy calculation is of no importance.

[12] $X_{1:n_1}\mathbf{H_{rep}}^\top$ and $X_{1:n_2}\mathbf{H_2}^\top$ are not necessarily independent.

[13] Note that this does not directly imply that the key becomes predictable, just that it is potentially less unpredictable than it should be according to its length.

Table 1. Effect of scaling the seed length of the key generator from [10].

Code words r	Seed Length $|S|$	PUF Size $|X|$	Failure Rate	$H(S|W) \geq 128$ for $p \in$
15	180	2880	$4.8 \cdot 10^{-7}$	$50\% \pm 8.2\%$
20	240	3840	$6.4 \cdot 10^{-7}$	$50\% \pm 10.8\%$
25	300	4800	$8.0 \cdot 10^{-7}$	$50\% \pm 12.1\%$
30	360	5760	$9.6 \cdot 10^{-7}$	$50\% \pm 13.0\%$

further. In Table 1 we scaled the seed length (and PUF size and failure rate) with the same code construction but increasing the number of Golay code words r. Unfortunately, the resistance to bias does not scale accordingly. The extra bias this generator can handle by increasing the seed gradually becomes very small. For the used code construction it cannot increase much beyond $50\% \pm 13.0\%$[14]. Also, the cost for achieving this (slightly) increased bias resistance is a *doubling* of the PUF size.

The conclusions about the studied key generator from [10], as summarized by Fig. 2(b) and Table 1, can be generalized to all key generators of the same design. The details differ slightly depending on the used codes, but the tendencies are always the same: global bias on PUFs relatively quickly reduces the remaining seed entropy, and increasing seed length has only a limited effect on the bias resistance and comes at a high cost in PUF size. This restricts the efficient use of key generators like Fig. 1 to PUFs with a limited global bias, roughly in the order $50\% \pm 10\%$. Since many experimentally studied PUF constructions have a global bias within this range, this is not necessarily problematic. However, for other PUFs with larger bias this key generator design cannot be used, and it was hypothesized (e.g. in [9]) that secure key derivation from such PUFs is impossible. In the following we will counter this by presenting a number of solutions that efficiently generate secure keys from PUFs with arbitrarily large global bias. These solutions are generic, so they could be used to deal with other (than global) types of bias with only minor modifications.

3   Debiasing Solutions

3.1   Basic Concept

In Sect. 2.4 we have shown that classic code-offset based key generators can only cope with a limited amount of PUF bias. In order to overcome this, we propose to extend the key generator design with a *debiasing step* prior to generating the code-offset helper data, as shown in Fig. 3. The idea is that the debiased PUF response Y which is actually enrolled is less biased than the original X, and hence the entropy leakage due to bias is reduced, or ideally zero. This seems a rather

---

[14] Note that we cannot increase beyond $r = 31$, without increasing the length of the repetition code, otherwise the failure rate gets too large.

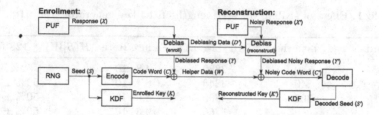

Fig. 3. *Debiasing* PUF-based key generator based on the code-offset method.

straightforward extension of the classic key generator design from Fig. 1, but there are a number of important and non-trivial points to consider when doing this:

Reliability. A debiasing step should not compromise the reliability of the key generator. This requirement excludes many potential debiasing options that blow up the bit error rate of the enrolled bit string. On the other hand, certain debiasing solutions allow for an intelligent combination of debiasing and error-correction, as shown next.

Efficieny. A debiasing step typically compresses or discards part of the PUF response, hence introducing a *debiasing overhead*. It will become clear that basic debiasing methods have a rather high overhead. We propose innovative optimizations specifically tailored for PUF-based key generation which significantly reduce overhead.

Leakage. Debiasing typically also produces side information during enrollment which is required during reconstruction. This *debiasing data D* hence needs to be stored/transfered publicly with the code-offset helper data W, potentially introducing new entropy leakage. For each presented debiasing method, we will prove that the combined entropy leakage of the debiasing data D and helper data W is zero.

Reusability. The classic code-offset scheme from Fig. 1 is *reusable* as shown in [2]. This means that the same PUF can be enrolled many times, each time producing a different key K and helper data W, without leaking more entropy than under just one single enrollment. This property does not necessarily hold when a debiasing step is used. We will investigate the reusability of each proposed debiasing method.

We will now introduce and discuss a number of increasingly more sophisticated debiasing methods and investigate these properties.

3.2 CVN: Classic von Neumann (VN) Debiasing

The classic randomness extractor as proposed by von Neumann [20] considers consecutive pairs of bits. If both bits are equal they are discarded, if they are opposed then the first bit is retained as a debiased bit. It is well known that if the input bits are i.i.d. but globally biased, then the output bits are perfectly random. Figure 4 shows how the *classic von Neumann* (CVN) extractor can be

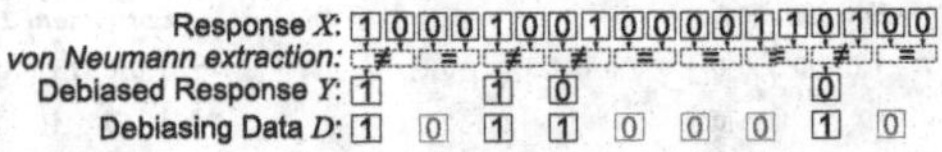

Response X: `1` `0` `0` `0` `1` `0` `0` `1` `0` `0` `0` `0` `1` `1` `0` `1` `0` `0`
von Neumann extraction:
Debiased Response Y: `1`   `1` `0`   `0`
Debiasing Data D: `1`   `0`   `1`   `1`   `0`   `0`   `0`   `1`   `0`

Fig. 4. Debiasing with a classic von Neumann extractor (enrollment only).

used as a debiasing step in a key generator. During enrollment (shown), the output of the CVN extractor becomes the debiased response Y which is used to calculate the code-offset helper data on. Also, for each considered bit pair of X a selection bit is used to show whether (1) or not (0) the first bit of that pair was retained in Y. These selection bits are the *debiasing data* D which is transfered alongside the helper data W. During reconstruction, the retained bits Y' from the noisy PUF reponse X' are selected with the bits in D.

Reliability. A nice feature of debiasing methods like CVN is that they hardly affect the error rate of the PUF response bits, contrary to other methods such as hash functions or XOR-combiners.[15] This is *the* main motivation to use a von Neumann-like extractor as a debiasing step in a PUF-based key generator. Therefore, all following proposed debiasing solutions are variants of this classic von Neumann debiasing.

Efficiency. If X is a p-biased n-bit PUF response, then the number of unbiased bits retained by CVN is binomially distributed with parameters $(\lfloor \frac{n}{2} \rfloor, 2p(1-p))$. The debiasing overhead of CVN is hence very high; even when the input X is already unbiased, CVN will still discard on average $3/4$ of the bits. However, in practical situations this ratio is even lower; to obtain $|Y|$ unbiased bits with a maximum failure rate p_{fail}, n needs to be large enough to meet:

$$F_{\text{bino}}^{-1}\left(p_{\text{fail}}; \lfloor \tfrac{n}{2} \rfloor, 2p(1-p)\right) \geq |Y|. \tag{7}$$

E.g. for $|Y| = 1000$, $p = 50\%$ and $p_{\text{fail}} = 10^{-6}$, this yields $n \geq 4446$, or a debiasing overhead factor of about 4.4. If X is actually biased this even becomes worse; e.g. for $p = 30\%$, $n \geq 5334$ or a factor of 5.3.

Leakage. Due to the properties of CVN, Y will be perfectly random regardless of the bias on X, and hence according to (2) we have $I(S; W) = 0$. However, since CVN debiasing also produces public information D, we need to consider $I(S; (W, D))$ instead. It can be shown that $I(S; (W, D)) = 0$ for CVN (proof, see full version [16]), hence the combination of (W, D) leaks no information on the seed S.

Reusability. A key generator using CVN for debiasing is *not* reusable. An example of the insecurity from enrolling the same PUF more than once is shown in Fig. 5. Here one learns from the helper data $W^{(1)}$ of the first enrollment that the first and fifth bit of $X^{(1)}$ are equal since they are both XOR-ed with the same 2-bit repetition code word. In the second enrollment, $X^{(2)}$ a noisy version of $X^{(1)}$ is enrolled, with differing bits marked in black.

---

[15] Von Neumann extractors have a small effect on bit error rate, shown in Sect. 4.1.

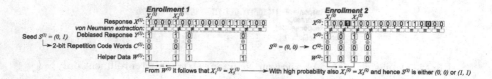

Fig. 5. Insecurity of CVN in case of reuse.

Because of these few differing bits, the first and fifth bit of $X^{(2)}$ are now enrolled in two different code words. However, from the first enrollment one has learned that these two bits are equal. From this knowledge, one can deduce that the two code words in the second enrollment, and their corresponding seed bits, are also equal (with high probability). The 2-bit seed $S^{(2)}$ hence has only two possible values instead of four. In general, one can say that $I\left(S^{(2)};(W^{(1)},D^{(1)},W^{(2)},D^{(2)})\right) > I\left(S;(W,D)\right) = 0$ and hence there is (more) leakage when the PUF is enrolled more than once. The reason for this reuse insecurity is the stochastic nature of the CVN step which is caused by random bit errors in between enrollments. Due to these differing bits, enrolled bits can shift between code words in between enrollments, which causes this particular type of leakage.

Summarizing, by using CVN as a debiasing step in a design like Fig. 3, one can build a PUF-based key generator which leaks no information on the secret seed S even if X is biased. Note that CVN poses no limit on the amount of bias on X that can be tolerated; in theory X can have an arbitrarily high bias, the leakage will always be zero. However, the efficiency restriction as expressed by (7) will pose a limitation in practice, since the PUF size n cannot become arbitrarily large. Nonetheless, this is still a major advancement in PUF-based key generators, since it shows that a secure key can be derived from a PUF with arbitrary bias, whereas the classic design of Fig. 1 was limited to PUFs with a bias in the range $50\% \pm 10\%$ as discussed in Sect. 2.4. The cost paid for this advancement is an increase in the PUF's size (overhead factor > 4) and the loss of the reusability property. In the following we will address these issues, first by proposing overhead optimizations in Sect. 3.3, and next by proposing a debiasing solution which retains the reusability property in Sect. 3.4.

3.3 Pair-Output (2O-VN) and Multi-Pass Tuple-Output VN Debiasing (MP-TO-VN)

The first proposed optimization (shown in Fig. 6(a)) consists of two minor modifications to the CVN debiasing solution of Sect. 3.2:

1. Instead of using only the first bit of each selected pair as in CVN, both bits of a selected pair are retained, hence the name *pair-output von Neumann* or 2O-VN debiasing.
2. The most inner code in the code-offset scheme is an even-length repetition code (e.g. 4 bits in Fig. 6(a)).

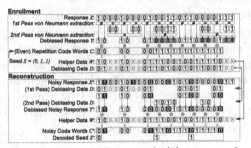

(a) Debiasing with a pair-output von Neumann extractor.

(b) Debiasing with a multi(2)-pass tuple-output von Neumann extractor.

Fig. 6. Key generators with improved efficiency VN debiasing. Extra retained bits are marked in grey. Bit errors during reconstruction are marked in black.

The second modification ensures that each pair retained by the first modification is used within the same repetition code word. This is an important condition for the security of this construction. In Fig. 6(a) the helper data W and the debiasing data D are combined in a single bit string (W, D), where a value 00 signifies that a pair is not retained, whereas a non-zero value (01 or 10) is the code-offset helper data of a retained pair.[16]

Reliability. The reliability analysis of 2O-VN is comparable to CVN and is explained in more detail in Sect. 4.1.

Efficiency. It is clear that the debiasing overhead of 2O-VN is about half that of CVN. The constraint on n now becomes:

$$F_{\text{bino}}^{-1}\left(p_{\text{fail}}; \lfloor \tfrac{n}{2} \rfloor, 2p(1-p)\right) \geq \tfrac{|Y|}{2}. \tag{8}$$

E.g. for $|Y| = 1000$, $p = 50\%$ and $p_{\text{fail}} = 10^{-6}$, this yields $n \geq 2322$, or a debiasing overhead factor of about 2.3, and for $p = 30\%$, $n \geq 2794$ or an overhead factor of 2.8.

Leakage. It can be shown that $I(S; (W, D)) = 0$ still holds for 2O-VN debiasing. This appears counterintuitive since Y is no longer i.i.d. but contains explicit dependencies, i.e. for each pair $(Y_{2i-1}, Y_{2i})_{i>0}$ it holds that $Y_{2i-1} = \overline{Y_{2i}}$ or the parity is odd. However, note that the code-offset helper data of a repetition code anyway discloses the parities of all bit pairs of Y used within the same code word. Hence if a bit pair is used within the same repetition code word, as guaranteed by the 2O-VN modifications, it is no problem that its parity is known since it would have been disclosed anyway. More intuitively, one can see (e.g. in Fig. 6(a)) that the known dependencies in Y do not help an outsider in predicting anything about S from (W, D).

Reusability. 2O-VN debiasing is not reusable for the same reasons as CVN debiasing (see Sect. 3.2).

---

[16] This is just one possible exemplary representation of (W, D).

Extension to Multi-pass Tuple Output (MP-TO-VN). The efficiency of 2O-VN can be further improved by reconsidering the discarded bits in a second pass, shown in Fig. 6(b). Bits are now grouped as quadruplets, and the extractor compares the first half of a quadruplet to the second half. More passes are possible (not shown in Fig. 6(b)) where in general the i-th pass considers tuples of 2^i bits which were not retained by any of the previous passes. Hence the name *multi-pass tuple-output von Neumann* or MP-TO-VN. For (M=2)P-TO-VN, the constraint on n becomes:

$$\sum_{a=0}^{|Y|-1} \sum_{b=0}^{\lfloor \frac{n}{4} \rfloor} f_{\text{bino}}\left(\frac{a-4b}{2}; \lfloor \frac{n}{2} \rfloor, 2p(1-p)\right) \cdot f_{\text{bino}}\left(b; \lfloor \frac{n-(a-4b)}{4} \rfloor, \frac{2p^2(1-p)^2}{(p^2+(1-p)^2)^2}\right) < p_{\text{fail}} \quad (9)$$

E.g. for $|Y| = 1000$, $p = 50\%$ and $p_{\text{fail}} = 10^{-6}$, this yields $n \geq 1538$, or an overhead factor of 1.5, and for $p = 30\%$, $n \geq 2068$ or a factor of 2.1. For more passes similar constraints can be derived and the overhead will reduce even further. However, the extra reduction for each additional pass quickly becomes small and almost negligible for more than three passes.

For MP-TO-VN to be leakage-free, it needs to be ensured that bits which were retained as a 2^i-bit tuple are always used within the bounds of a single repetition code word for calculating the helper data. This could entail that retained tuples need to be reshuffled or that a retained tuple is cropped when a code word bound is reached; e.g. in Fig. 6(b) the final two bits are discarded, they cannot be used for the next code word. Depending on the method used, it could be needed to keep track in which pass a certain bit pair was retained. In Fig. 6(b), this is done by letting D have three possible values for each bit pair, i.e. 'not retained' (00), 'retained in first pass' (01) or 'retained in second pass' (10). The leakage and reusability analysis for MP-TO-VN are the same as for 2O-VN.

3.4 ε-2O-VN: Pair-Output VN Debiasing with Erasures

Now we propose (Fig. 7) a modification of the 2O-VN debiasing solution from Sect. 3.3 which makes the key generator reusable again:

1. During enrollment 2O-VN debiasing is applied, yet bit pairs which are not retained by 2O-VN are not completely discarded but replaced with *erasure symbols* (ϵ), hence the name *pair-output von Neumann debiasing with erasures* or ϵ-2O-VN. The length of Y (i.e. the number of symbols) is hence equal to the length of X.
2. The most inner code is again an even-length repetition code (e.g. 6 bits in Fig. 7). The code-offset helper data between the code words and Y is calculated with the ϵ-XOR operation denoted as $\oplus$, which is defined as the regular XOR ($\oplus$) if both operands are regular bits, but produces an ϵ if one or both of its operands is an ϵ.
3. During reconstruction, the noisy code words will also contain ϵ symbols. These are to be treated as regular bit erasures by the decoder, which hence needs to be able to handle both errors and erasures. Figure 7 uses a concatenated code of an inner 6-bit repetition code and an (exemplary) $(4, 2)$ outer code.

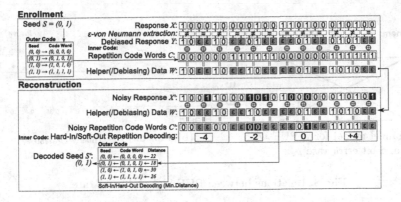

Fig. 7. Debiasing with a pair-output von Neumann extractor with erasures. Bit pairs discarded by 2O-VN are now retained as erasures (ϵ, marked in grey). Bit errors during reconstruction (w.r.t. enrollment) are marked in black.

The repetition code is decoded with a hard-in-soft-out decoder which treats erasures as non-preferential code bits. The outer code is decoded with a soft-in-hard-out decoder (i.e. a trivial minimum-distance list decoder) to retrieve the seed S.

Reliability. It is evident that ϵ-2O-VN debiasing impacts the reliability of a key generator, since the used error-correcting code needs to be able to deal with bit errors caused by noise, as well as with erasures caused by bias. For an n-bit p-biased PUF response X, the probability of having $\frac{\epsilon}{2}$ erasures is binomially distributed with parameters $(\lfloor \frac{n}{2} \rfloor, p^2 + (1-p)^2)$. In Sect. 4.2, it is demonstrated how this affects the reliability/efficiency of a realistic key generator.

Efficiency. ϵ-2O-VN is very efficient in terms of debiasing overhead factor $\frac{|X|}{|Y|}$, since $|X| = |Y|$. However, the cost for ϵ-2O-VN sits in the fact that a more powerful error-correcting code (hence with a smaller code rate) needs to be used to account for the introduced erasures. For ϵ-2O-VN debiasing, reliability and efficiency need to be considered together, as demonstrated in Sect. 4.2.

Leakage. The ϵ-2O-VN debiasing method does not produce any explicit debiasing data D. All required information is contained in W which uses the symbols 0, 1 and ϵ. For leakage, we need to consider $I(S; W)$ again, but now in the new setting of ϵ-2O-VN. It can be shown that *classic* von Neumann debiasing with erasures is leakage-free (proof, see full version [16]). From this, the security of *pair-output* von Neumann debiasing with erasures follows in the same manner as for 2O-VN due to the fact that the most inner code is a repetition code.

Reusability. ϵ-2O-VN debiasing *is* reusable, i.e. $I\left(S^{(i)}; (W^{(1)}, W^{(2)}, \ldots)\right) = I(S; W) = 0$ (proof, see full version [16]). This means that the same PUF can be enrolled an arbitrary number of times without the combination of

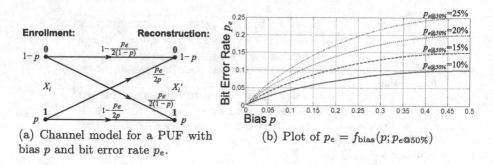

(a) Channel model for a PUF with bias p and bit error rate p_e.

(b) Plot of $p_e = f_{\text{bias}}(p; p_{e@50\%})$

Fig. 8. Relations between PUF bias and error rate.

all produced helper data strings leaking anything about any of the enrolled seeds. A key generator with ϵ-2O-VN debiasing (re)gains this property since the debiasing is no longer stochastic: randomly differing bits between enrollments do no longer affect the selection of bit pairs since all bit pair positions are always retained. Unfortunately, ϵ-2O-VN cannot be extended to multiple passes in the same manner as MP-TO-VN without compromising the reusability property.

4   Objective Comparison of Debiasing Solutions

4.1   Relation Between PUF Bias and Bit Error Rate

Similarly to global bias, we define the *global bit error rate* to be p_e if the a-priori expected number of differing bits between two evaluations X and X' of the same n-bit PUF response is $p_e \cdot n$, or put otherwise p_e is the a-priori probability that $X_i \neq X'_i$ for a random bit i of a PUF.

Firstly, note that a biased PUF will have a different bit error rate for 0 and 1 bits; e.g. for a PUF which is biased towards 0, the probability of a bit error will be higher for a 1-bit than for a 0-bit. Such behavior is typically expressed as a channel model, shown in Fig. 8(a) for our situation. The assumptions are that the bias of X and X' are the same, even with bit errors, and that the *average* bit error rate is equal to p_e. Note that von Neumann-based debiasing methods will (negatively) affect this average bit error rate since the ratio of 0 and 1 bits which are retained will be changed, favoring the lesser occuring but more error-prone kind.

Secondly, one notices that the heavier the bias p of a PUF response, the smaller its bit error rate p_e; e.g. in the extreme case of a $p = 100\%$ biased PUF, the bit error rate p_e will be zero. To objectively compare PUFs with different bias levels, we need to make this relation between biases and error rates explicit; e.g. there is a big difference between a PUF with $p_e = 15\%$ but no bias $p = 50\%$ and another PUF with $p_e = 15\%$ and a heavy bias of $p = 30\%$. For objective comparison, we introduce the *fixed point* $p_{e@50\%}$ which is the (hypothetical) bit

Table 2. Comparison of debiasing solutions for the code-offset key generator from [10]. The *fixed point* bit error rate is set to $p_{e@50\%} = 15\%$. The key generator is failure rate $< 10^{-6}$:

Solution	Reusable?	Bias p	Rescaled Bit Error Rate p_e	Debias Overhead $|X|/|Y|$	Nr. of Golay Code Words r	Repetition Code Length n_{rep}	PUF Size $|X|$	Seed Length $|S|$	Seed Entropy $H(S|(W,D))$	p_{fail} (Enroll)	p_{fail} (Reconstruct)	PUF Size Overhead w.r.t. *
No Debias	Yes	50.0%	15.0%	1.00	11	8	2112	132	132	0	5.61E-7	0.73
No Debias*	Yes	41.8%	14.7%	1.00	15	8	2880	180	128	0	5.00E-7	1.00
No Debias	Yes	40.0%	14.5%	1.00	19	8	3648	228	135	0	2.74E-7	1.27
No Debias	Yes	37.0%	14.2%	1.00	30	8	5760	360	128	0	3.50E-7	2.00
2O-VN	No	40.0%	14.5%	2.31	11	8	4888	132	132	9.14E-7	9.86E-7	1.70
2O-VN	No	35.0%	13.9%	2.45	11	8	5168	132	132	9.42E-7	6.03E-7	1.79
2O-VN	No	30.0%	13.0%	2.66	11	8	5616	132	132	9.63E-7	9.57E-7	1.95
2O-VN	No	25.0%	11.9%	2.99	11	8	6314	132	132	9.90E-7	4.94E-7	2.19
2P-TO-VN	No	40.0%	14.5%	1.58	11	8	3334	132	132	9.98E-7	6.31E-7	1.16
2P-TO-VN	No	35.0%	13.9%	1.73	11	8	3650	132	132	9.44E-7	7.69E-7	1.27
2P-TO-VN	No	30.0%	13.0%	1.96	11	8	4142	132	132	9.53E-7	8.67E-7	1.44
2P-TO-VN	No	25.0%	11.9%	2.32	11	8	4890	132	132	9.92E-7	9.63E-7	1.70
ε-2O-VN	Yes	40.0%	14.5%	1.00	11	20	5280	132	132	0	8.67E-7	1.83
ε-2O-VN	Yes	35.0%	13.9%	1.00	11	22	5808	132	132	0	9.87E-7	2.02
ε-2O-VN	Yes	30.0%	13.0%	1.00	11	26	6864	132	132	0	6.12E-7	2.38
ε-2O-VN	Yes	25.0%	11.9%	1.00	11	28	7392	132	132	0	6.12E-7	2.57

error rate a PUF would have if it would have been unbiased ($p = 50\%$). For a PUF with a given $p_{e@50\%}$, a relation $p_e = f_{\text{bias}}(p; p_{e@50\%})$ can be derived based on the reliability model for PUFs from [14] (see derivation in full version [16]). This function is shown for different values of $p_{e@50\%}$ in Fig. 8(b). This graph should be interpreted as follows: if one wants to objectively compare the efficiency of a key generator for an unbiased PUF, e.g. with $p_e = 15\%$, to a key generator for a biased PUF, e.g. with $p = 30\%$, then the corresponding error rate for the biased PUF should be set to $f_{\text{bias}}(30\%; 15\%) = 13.0\%$.

4.2 Comparison of Debiasing Solutions

The different debiasing solutions proposed in Sect. 3 are evaluated and compared to each other in an objective manner. The evaluation is done for the key generator from [10], which uses a repetition code-Golay code concatenation. The results are shown in Table 2. Three different debiasing solutions are compared amongst each other and against the case when no debiasing is used (see also Table 1)[17]. The row marked with a * is the best proposal from [10] and is used as reference case. To make the comparison objective, the effective bit error rate p_e for each simulation scales with the bias level according to $f_{\text{bias}}(p; p_{e@50\%})$ as shown in Fig. 8(b) with $p_{e@50\%} = 15\%$ corresponding to the error rate assumed in [10] and other works. For realistic simulations, the channel model from Fig. 8(a) is used, so 0-bits and 1-bits have different error probabilities in case of bias.

The three debiasing methods have different properties. 2O-VN and 2P-TO-VN have a non-zero enrollment failure rate; it is possible that insufficient bits are retained after debiasing for successful enrollment. Also, for both of these systems the error-correcting code used does not change depending on the amount of bias (only the size of the PUF changes for maintaining reliability), while for ϵ-2O-VN the repetition length scales with the amount of bias and enrollment is always successful. The PUF size overhead in comparison to * also varies between the mehods. It is clear that the 2P-TO-VN is the most efficient method considering this parameter (only 1.70 times the amount of * is required to deal with the extreme case of 25 % bias), but this method does not allow reuse for enrolling multiple keys. If this property is required ϵ-2O-VN provides a strong alternative, which requires more PUF data (2.57× * at 25 % bias), but provides a combination of properties that was not known to date.

5   Conclusion

This work solves the open problem of secure key generation from *biased* PUFs using code-offset-based constructions. This is accomplished without compromising the secret key's security and for arbitrary bias levels. Existing conventional methods will lead to leakage on the secret key when the PUF is too biased, whereas our proposed debiasing techniques prevent this leakage, while maintaining the high reliability and for some solutions even the reusability of the key generator. This comes at a cost of PUF size overhead, but using innovative approaches we were able to limit this overhead and design a key generator based on the requirements at hand.

Remaining open questions and interesting future research directions include: how to further optimize the efficiency of these debiasing solutions, and how to prevent key leakage for PUFs which suffer from reduced entropy for reasons other than bias, e.g. because of bit correlations.

---

[17] Failure rates differ slightly from the results in Table 1 which were extrapolated from [10]. For objective comparison, the results of Table 2 are based on a new simulations, with the Hackett Golay decoder from [10] implemented in Matlab. The single Golay decoding failure rate $p_{\text{Golay-fail}}$ is estimated as the 95 %-confidence upper bound from the simulations; the actual values for $p_{\text{Golay-fail}}$ are hence likely smaller. The total reconstruction failure rate is computed as $1 - (1 - p_{\text{Golay-fail}})^r$.

References

1. Bösch, C., Guajardo, J., Sadeghi, A.-R., Shokrollahi, J., Tuyls, P.: Efficient helper data key extractor on FPGAs. In: Oswald, E., Rohatgi, P. (eds.) CHES 2008. LNCS, vol. 5154, pp. 181–197. Springer, Heidelberg (2008)
2. Boyen, X.: Reusable cryptographic fuzzy extractors. In: ACM Conference on Computer and Communications Security–CCS 2004, pp. 82–91. ACM Press, New York (2004)
3. Delvaux, J., Gu, D., Schellekens, D., Verbauwhede, I.: Helper data algorithms for PUF-based key generation: overview and analysis. IEEE Trans. Comput. Aided Des. Integr. Circuits Syst. **34**(1), 14 (2014)
4. Dodis, Y., Ostrovsky, R., Reyzin, L., Smith, A.: Fuzzy extractors: how to generate strong keys from biometrics and other noisy data. SIAM J. Comput. **38**(1), 97–139 (2008)
5. Guajardo, J., Kumar, S.S., Schrijen, G.-J., Tuyls, P.: FPGA intrinsic PUFs and their use for IP protection. In: Paillier, P., Verbauwhede, I. (eds.) CHES 2007. LNCS, vol. 4727, pp. 63–80. Springer, Heidelberg (2007)
6. Ignatenko, T., Willems, F.: Information leakage in fuzzy commitment schemes. IEEE Trans. Inf. Forensics Secur. **5**(2), 337–348 (2010)
7. Katzenbeisser, S., Kocabaş, U., Rožić, V., Sadeghi, A.-R., Verbauwhede, I., Wachsmann, C.: PUFs: myth, fact or busted? a security evaluation of physically unclonable functions (PUFs) cast in Silicon. In: Prouff, E., Schaumont, P. (eds.) CHES 2012. LNCS, vol. 7428, pp. 283–301. Springer, Heidelberg (2012)
8. Koeberl, P., Li, J., Maes, R., Rajan, A., Vishik, C., Wójcik, M.: Evaluation of a PUF device authentication scheme on a discrete 0.13um SRAM. In: Chen, L., Yung, M., Zhu, L. (eds.) INTRUST 2011. LNCS, vol. 7222, pp. 271–288. Springer, Heidelberg (2012)
9. Koeberl, P., Li, J., Rajan, A., Wu, W.: Entropy loss in PUF-based key generation schemes: the repetition code pitfall. In: IEEE International Symposium on Hardware-Oriented Security and Trust (HOST), pp. 44–49 (2014)
10. van der Leest, V., Preneel, B., van der Sluis, E.: Soft decision error correction for compact memory-based PUFs using a single enrollment. In: Prouff, E., Schaumont, P. (eds.) CHES 2012. LNCS, vol. 7428, pp. 268–282. Springer, Heidelberg (2012)
11. Lily, C.: NIST Special Publication 800–108: Recommendation for Key Derivation Using Pseudorandom Functions (revised) (2009)
12. Lily, C.: NIST Special Publication 800–56C: Recommendation for Key Derivation through Extraction-then-Expansion (2011)
13. Lim, D., Lee, J., Gassend, B., Suh, G., van Dijk, M., Devadas, S.: Extracting secret keys from integrated circuits. IEEE Trans. Very Large Scale Integr. VLSI Syst. **13**(10), 1200–1205 (2005)
14. Maes, R.: An accurate probabilistic reliability model for silicon PUFs. In: Bertoni, G., Coron, J.-S. (eds.) CHES 2013. LNCS, vol. 8086, pp. 73–89. Springer, Heidelberg (2013)
15. Maes, R.: Physically Unclonable Functions - Constructions, Properties and Applications. Springer, Heidelberg (2013)
16. Maes, R., van der Leest, V., van der Sluis, E., Willems, F.: Secure key generation from biased PUFs. In: Güneysu, T., Handschuh, H. (eds.) CHES 2015. LNCS, vol. 9293, pp. xx–yy, Cryptology ePrint Archive, Report 2015/831, this is the full version of this work (including all appendices). Springer, Heidelberg (2015). http://eprint.iacr.org/

17. Maes, R., Tuyls, P., Verbauwhede, I.: Low-overhead implementation of a soft deci-sion helper data algorithm for SRAM PUFs. In: Clavier, C., Gaj, K. (eds.) CHES 2009. LNCS, vol. 5747, pp. 332–347. Springer, Heidelberg (2009)
18. Maes, R., van Herrewege, A., Verbauwhede, I.: PUFKY: a fully functional PUF-based cryptographic key generator. In: Prouff, E., Schaumont, P. (eds.) CHES 2012. LNCS, vol. 7428, pp. 302–319. Springer, Heidelberg (2012)
19. Massey, J.L.: Guessing and entropy. In: IEEE International Symposium on Infor-mation Theory (ISIT), p. 204 (1994)
20. von Neumann, J.: Various techniques used in connection with random digits. In: Applied Math Series 12. National Bureau of Standards, USA (1951)
21. Skoric, B., de Vreede, N.: The spammed code offset method. Cryptology ePrint Archive, Report 2013/527 (2013). http://eprint.iacr.org/
22. Yu, M.-D.M., M'Raihi, D., Sowell, R., Devadas, S.: Lightweight and secure PUF key storage using limits of machine learning. In: Preneel, B., Takagi, T. (eds.) CHES 2011. LNCS, vol. 6917, pp. 358–373. Springer, Heidelberg (2011)

The Gap Between Promise and Reality: On the Insecurity of XOR Arbiter PUFs

Georg T. Becker[✉]

Horst Görtz Institute for IT-Security, Ruhr Universität Bochum, Bochum, Germany
georg.becker@ruhr-uni-bochum.de

Abstract. In this paper we demonstrate the first real-world cloning attack on a commercial PUF-based RFID tag. The examined commercial PUFs can be attacked by measuring only 4 protocol executions, which takes less than 200 ms. Using a RFID smartcard emulator, it is then possible to impersonate, i.e., "clone" the PUF. While attacking the 4-way PUF used by these tags can be done using traditional machine learning attacks, we show that the tags can still be attacked if they are configured as presumably secure XOR PUFs. We achieved this by using a new reliability-based machine learning attack that uses a divide-and-conquer approach for attacking the XOR PUFs. This new divide-and-conquer approach results in only a linear increase in needed number of challenge and responses for increasing numbers of XORs. This is in stark contrast to the state-of-the-art machine learning attacks on XOR PUFs that are shown to have an exponential increase in challenge and responses.

Hence, it is now possible to attack XOR PUF constructs that were previously believed to be secure against machine learning attacks. Since XOR Arbiter PUFs are one of the most popular and promising electrical strong PUF designs, our reliability-based machine learning attack raises doubts that secure and lightweight electrical strong PUFs can be realized in practice.

Keywords: PUFs · Machine learning · Real-world attacks · XOR PUFs

1 Introduction

Physical Unclonable Functions (PUFs) have gained extensive research attention since they were first proposed in 2001 [21]. PUFs use the inherent manufacturing differences within every physical object to give each physical instance a unique identity. While the first proposal was based on light scattering [21], in the same year the first electrical PUF, the Arbiter PUF, was proposed by Gassend et al. [8]. PUFs have some unique characteristics that make them an interesting research target for lightweight authentication schemes as well as anti-counterfeiting solutions. Furthermore, PUFs have gained a lot of attention as a secure key generation and storage mechanism. One of the key features is their "unclonability", the fact that it should be impossible to build two physical instances of a PUF that have the same characteristics.

© International Association for Cryptologic Research 2015
T. Güneysu and H. Handschuh (Eds.): CHES 2015, LNCS 9293, pp. 535–555, 2015.
DOI: 10.1007/978-3-662-48324-4_27

PUFs are usually divided into two categories: *weak PUFs* and *strong PUFs*. A strong PUF can be queried with an exponential number of challenges to receive an exponential number of responses. They can be used in authentication protocols as well as for key generation and storage. Weak PUFs on the other hand only have a very limited challenge space and can only be used for key generation and storage. In practice, PUFs have two main drawbacks. One drawback is that PUFs are susceptible to environmental conditions and noise and therefore their responses are unreliable. To counter this unreliability, either error correction is needed or some false response bits need to be tolerated by the used PUF protocol. The other major drawback is that existing electrical strong PUFs can be simulated in software and the required parameters for such a software model can be approximated using machine learning techniques. This is particularly true for the Arbiter PUF. Several constructions based on the Arbiter PUF have been proposed such as the XOR PUF [31] and the Feed-Forward PUF [15]. They have have in common that some non-linearity is added to make machine learning attacks more difficult. While it is possible to attack XOR PUFs using machine learning for small numbers of XORs, XOR PUFs are widely assumed to be secure against machine learning attacks if enough XORs are used [12,28,29]. This makes the XOR PUF one of the most promising strong PUF designs.

PUFs have already made the step out of the scientific research labs into commercial products. For example, NXP and Microsemi use PUF-based key storage in some of their products. But PUFs are not only used for secure key storage in commercial products. There are also PUF-based RFID tags available. These extremely lightweight tags are promoted as a secure alternative to memory tags and are proposed as an anti-counterfeit solution for medical drugs and luxury products. They can furthermore be used for access control and payment applications. In this paper we take a closer look at such commercial PUF-based RFID tags. We show that it is possible to perform a machine learning attack on these RFID tags with measurement times below a second. It is then possible to "clone" the RFID tags using an RFID smartcard emulator.

While the examined PUF architecture in these tags is extremely weak and can be attacked in seconds using traditional machine learning attacks, we also show that PUF constructions that are supposedly secure can be attacked. We achieve this by using a new reliability-based machine learning attack. This new attack scales very well with the number of XORs and therefore increasing the number of XORs cannot defeat it.

1.1 Related Work

There has been extensive research on finding different electrical PUFs. Popular weak PUF proposals are for example ring-oscillator PUFs [31], SRAM-PUFs [9], sense-amplifier based PUFs [10,23] or bus-keeper PUFs [30]. Most strong PUF designs are variants of the Arbiter PUF such as the XOR PUF [31], Feed-Forward PUF [15] or the Lightweight PUF [18]. Compared with the number of papers that either propose new PUFs or discuss their performance in terms of reliability and uniqueness, e.g., [14,16,33] relatively little research has focused on machine learning attacks. Most of our knowledge of machine learning attacks on PUFs is based on the 2010 CCS paper by Rührmair *et al.* [29]. In their paper Rührmair *et al.* showed that XOR PUFs, Feed-Forward PUFs and Lightweight PUFs can be attacked using ES and LR-based machine learning algorithms. However, their results showed that the required number of challenge and response pairs (CRPs) to model an XOR PUF grows exponentially with an increase in the number of XORs. Therefore, they concluded that XOR PUFs can withstand these machine learning attacks if enough XORs are used. Their initial analysis was conducted on simulated data but they later verified the results by using measurements taken from an ASIC [26].

Besides the search for PUFs which can withstand machine learning attacks, protocol and system level countermeasures have been proposed to combat machine learning. The first system level countermeasure is the idea of controlled PUFs [7]. In a controlled PUF, the PUF responses are not directly revealed but instead only the hash value of several PUF responses is transmitted. Since PUFs are unreliable, such controlled PUFs also need an error correction mechanism. Other more lightweight proposals are the Reverse Fuzzy Extractor [13] or the the Slender PUF protocol [17,25]. A good overview of different proposals and their security can be found in [6]. Another line of research examines different side-channel attacks on PUFs, e.g., in [3,5,19,24,32]. PUFs have also gained attention as building blocks for cryptographic protocols with formal definitions of strong PUFs [1,4,20]. However, it was pointed out that most existing PUFs do not match the formal PUF models [27].

1.2 Contribution and Organization

The main contribution of the paper can be summarized as follows:

1. We present the first cloning attack on a commercial strong PUF-based RFID tag, demonstrating the gap between the promised and achieved security with strong PUFs in practice. The employed 4-way PUF can be attacked using machine learning with measurement times of less than 200 ms. An RFID smartcard emulator with hardware costs of less than \$25 can then be used to "clone" the PUF.
2. A new reliability-based machine learning attack on XOR PUFs is introduced. Even XOR PUFs with parameters previously considered computationally infeasible to attack using machine learning cannot withstand this new attack. Our results show that the widely believed assumption that the number of required responses for a machine learning attack on XOR PUFs increases exponentially with the number of XORs is wrong. Hence, plain XOR PUFs cannot be used in practice, regardless of the parameters used.

Besides these main results, our analysis of the RFID tags also gives important insight into how many CRPs an attacker can collect in practice. In the security analysis of many designs less than a million challenge and responses are used. In contrast, the measurements of the PUF-based RFID tags show that it is quite realistic that an attacker can collect billions of responses.

The reliability-based machine learning attack introduced in this paper is based on a machine learning algorithm called CMA-ES. This machine learning algorithm together with the Arbiter PUF is introduced in the background section. In Sect. 3, the targeted commercial PUF-based RFID tags are discussed in detail, while in Sect. 4 the cloning attack on these tags is discussed. In Sect. 5 the new reliability-based machine learning attack on XOR PUFs is introduced. Finally, the implications of these attacks are discussed in the last section.

2   Background

The PUF tags that we examine use an n-way PUF, which is a variant of the Arbiter PUF. In this Section we will first introduce the Arbiter PUF and explain how the Arbiter PUF can be modeled in software and then how the needed parameters can be approximated using machine learning.

2.1   Arbiter PUF

The schematic of an Arbiter PUF can be seen in Fig. 1. An Arbiter PUF consists of a top and bottom signal that are fed through k delay stages. Each individual delay stage consists of two 2-bit multiplexers (MUXes) that have identical layouts and that both get the bottom and top signals as inputs. Since the layout of the two paths is identical, one would expect the introduced delay to be identical as well. However, in practice each transistor in the multiplexers has slightly different delay characteristics due to process variations. Hence, the delay introduced by the multiplexers is different for the top and bottom signal. Since each chip has different process variations, these delay differences are unique for every chip. If the challenge bit c_i for stage i is '1', the multiplexers switch the top and bottom signals, if it is '0' the two signals are not switched. This way, the race signal can take different paths: a n-stage Arbiter PUF has 2^n different paths the race signals can take. An arbiter at the end of the PUF determines which of the two signals is faster. The arbiter has an output of '1' if the top signal arrives first and '0' if the bottom signal is the first to arrive.

In order to increase the resistance of Arbiter PUFs against machine learning attacks adding a non-linear element to the PUF design was proposed. One of the most common methods to add non-linearity to a PUF design is the XOR PUF. In an n-XOR PUF, n Arbiter PUFs are placed on the chip. Each of the Arbiter

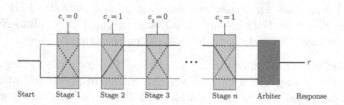

Fig. 1. Schematic of an n-bit Arbiter PUF.

PUFs receives the same challenges and the responses of the n PUFs are XORed to build the final response bits. While the machine learning resistance increases by XORing more PUFs, adding additional PUF instances obviously also increases the area overhead of the design. Furthermore, the XOR PUFs become more unreliable the more PUFs are XORed. This limits the number of XORs that can be used in practice. The response of an n-stage Arbiter PUF is determined by the delay difference between the top and bottom signal. This delay difference is the sum of the delay differences of the individual stages. The delay difference of each stage depends on the corresponding challenge. Hence, there are two delay differences per stage i, the delay differences $\delta_{1,i}$ corresponding to a challenge of '1' and $\delta_{0,i}$ corresponding to a challenge of '0'. The most efficient way to model a k-stage Arbiter PUF is by computing a delay vector $\vec{w} = (w_1, ..., w_{k+1})$ from these stage delay differences as follows:

$$w_1 = \delta_{0,1} - \delta_{1,1}, \tag{1a}$$

$$w_i = \delta_{0,i-1} + \delta_{1,i-1} + \delta_{0,i} - \delta_{1,i} \text{ for } 2 \leq i \leq k, \tag{1b}$$

$$w_{k+1} = \delta_{0,k} + \delta_{1,k} \tag{1c}$$

The delay difference ΔD at the end of the Arbiter is the result of the scalar multiplication of the transposed delay vector $\vec{w}$ with a feature vector $\vec{\Phi}$ that is derived from the challenge c:

$$\Delta D = \vec{w}^T \vec{\Phi} \tag{2a}$$

$$r = \begin{cases} 1, & \text{if } \Delta D < 0. \\ 0, & \text{if } \Delta D > 0. \end{cases} \tag{2b}$$

The feature vector $\vec{\Phi}$ is derived from the challenge vector $\vec{c}$ as follows:

$$\Phi_i = \prod_{l=i}^{k} (-1)^{c_l} \text{ for } 1 \leq i \leq k \tag{3a}$$

$$\Phi_{k+1} = 1 \tag{3b}$$

It was shown in the past how the delay vector $\vec{w}$ can be approximated efficiently using different machine learning techniques.

2.2 Evolution Strategies

Evolution Strategies (ES) are widely used machine learning techniques that are inspired by evolution theory. In evolution, a species can adapt itself to environmental changes by means of natural selection, also called *survival of the fittest*. In every generation, only the fittest specimen survive and reproduce, while the weak specimen die and hence do not reproduce. Since the specimen of the next generation inherit the genes of the fittest specimen of the previous generation, the species continuously improves. In ES-based machine learning attacks on PUFs, the same principle of survival of the fittest is used. As discussed, a PUF instance can be described by its delay vector $\vec{w}$. The goal of a machine learning attack on an Arbiter PUF is to find a delay vector $\vec{w}$ that most precisely resembles the real PUF instance. The main idea of an ES machine learning attack is to generate random PUF instances (i.e., random delay vectors $\vec{w}$) and check which instances are the fittest, i.e., which PUF instances resemble the real PUF model the most. The fittest PUF instances are kept as *parents* for the next *generation* while the other PUF instances are discarded. In the next generation, *children* are generated using the parent's delay vector together with some random *mutations*, i.e., some random modifications of the delay vector. From these child instances the fittest instances are determined again and kept for the next generation as parents. This process is repeated for many generations in which the PUF instances gradually improve and resemble the real PUF behavior more and more.

In order to perform an ES machine learning attack it needs to be possible to describe a PUF instance by a vector $\vec{w}$. Furthermore, a fitness test is needed that, given delay vectors $\vec{w}$, can determine which instances, i.e., which delay vectors, are the fittest. Since Arbiter PUFs can be modeled using the delay vector w, if an ES machine learning attack is feasible depends on whether or not a good fitness test for these PUF models exist. Typically, the used fitness test for an Arbiter PUF is the model accuracy between the measured responses $\vec{r}$ of the physical PUF and the computed responses $\vec{r'}$ of the PUF instance under test. The PUF instances with the highest model accuracies are considered the *fittest*.

There exist many variants of ES machine learning algorithms which mainly differ in how many parents are kept in each generation, how the children are derived from the parents and how the random mutation is controlled. Typically, the mutation is done by adding a random Gaussian variable $N(0, \sigma)$ to each parameter. Different methods have been proposed for controlling the mutation parameter σ. The closer the PUF instances are to the optimal solution, the smaller σ should be. One approach to control σ is to deterministically decrease σ in every generation. In contrast, in self-adaption the mutation parameter adapts itself depending on how the machine learning algorithm is currently performing. For the reliability-based machine learning attack the Covariance Matrix Adaptation (CMA) ES machine learning algorithm with the default parameters suggested in [11] is used. CMA-ES uses recombination, i.e., one child instance depends on several parent instances. It also uses self-adaption, i.e., the mutation strength is not controlled deterministically but adapts itself depending on how the ES algorithm is performing.

3   The PUF-based RFID Tags

We ordered PUF-based RFID tags from an RFID company that — in addition to our main order of plain sticker type tags — provided us with samples in four different formats: smartcard format, sticker format, wristband and anti-metal label. Please note that the RFID company that manufactures the RFID tags is different from the manufacturer of the PUF ICs. A picture of the tags as well as the used RFID reader can be seen in Fig. 2. The sticker-type tags can be used

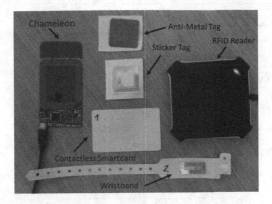

Fig. 2. The RFID smartcard emulator Chameleon and the target PUF-based RFID tags in different formats.

as an anti-counterfeit solution for medical drugs and luxury goods and cost only a few cents when ordered in large quantities. The RFID smartcard format as well as the wristband format can be used for access control, authentication and payment applications. The anti-metal label tags are designed in such a way that they also work when attached to metal and can for example be placed upon a smartphone. The brand names on the sample tags suggest that the smartcard and wristband tags were intended for payment and access control applications while the anti-metal tags featured the brand name of a loyalty program.

In the following the architecture of the tags is described in more detailed. How this architecture has been reverse-engineered is explained in detail in Sect. 4. The main feature of the PUF-based RFID tags is that each tag can be authenticated based on the built-in 4-way Arbiter PUF. The structure of the used 4-way PUF is depicted in Fig. 3. A 64-bit master challenge is sent from the reader to the tag. This master challenge is fed into a 64-bit LFSR that generates subsequent challenges. Each 64-bit challenge is then sent to what we call the *mixer function*. The mixer function generates four subchallenges by shuffling the provided 64-bit challenge similar to a Lightweight PUF. Each of these four subchallenges are fed to the same 64-bit Arbiter PUF. The resulting four response bits are XORed with each other to form a single response bit. Such a PUF, in which a single Arbiter PUF is used and n response bits are XORed, is called an n-way PUF. In the PUF protocol, 256 response bits are generated for each 64-bit master challenge.

Traditionally, the authentication process of an Arbiter PUF is based on a setup stage in which responses for randomly generated challenges are collected and stored in a database. During the authentication step, challenges from this database are selected and sent to the tag. The responses of the tag under test are then compared to the responses stored in the database. If the response matches, the tag is authenticated. However, such a system has some drawbacks. A large database of CRPs needs to be kept for every tag. If the tags are used as an

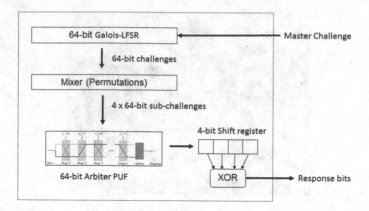

Fig. 3. Internal structure of the PUF tag. A 64-bit Galois LFSR is used to generate challenges from a master challenge. Each challenge is fed into the mixer function which generates four subchallenges by permuting the input challenge. These four subchallenges are successively fed into the 64-stage Arbiter PUF. The four responses of the Arbiter PUF are then XORed to provide a response bit that is sent to the reader.

anti-counterfeit solution, every verifier needs an up-to-date database with the CRPs from all tags. In practice, this requires an internet connection in most scenarios.

For the PUF-based RFID tags a different system that allows offline authentication was chosen. It is based on the idea that Arbiter PUFs can be modeled in software if the internal delay parameters are known. While this usually is an undesired property, it can be helpful to construct PUF protocols that do not need pre-collected CRPs. During a set-up phase, the internal parameters of the 4-way PUF are computed. We are not sure how this is done exactly for the tags under test since this step was already conducted by the manufacturer. One possible solution would be that during the set-up phase the individual PUF responses are directly transmitted without XORing them. With only a few hundred of these response bits it is possible to build an accurate model of the PUF parameters. After a PUF model is built, this phase should be disabled so that only the obfuscated outputs, i.e., the outputs of the 4-way PUF are transmitted.

A verifier that is in possession of these delay parameters does not need a database with stored CRPs to authenticate the tag. Instead, the responses for arbitrary challenges can be computed on-the-fly in software. The distribution of the PUF parameters is realized by storing the parameters on the tag in an encrypted form. A legitimate verifier who has the corresponding key can decrypt the encrypted delay parameters and use these parameters to verify the tag. Note that the encrypted PUF parameters are only stored and not encrypted on the tag. Hence, no encryption function and no secret key is needed on the tag itself. However, this method also has major drawbacks. The verifier needs to be a trusted entity since the security of the system depends on keeping the key secret. This can be problematic and trusted readers need to have the highest standards

Table 1. PUF-based RFID tag protocol

tags	reader/tool
ID, physical PUF, $enc_k(\vec{w})$	ID, k

$$\xleftarrow{\quad auth \quad}$$
$$\xrightarrow{\quad UID, enc_k(\vec{w}) \quad} \text{choose challenge } C$$
$\vec{c} = LFSR(C)$ $\xleftarrow{\quad C \quad}$ $\vec{c} = LFSR(C)$
$\vec{r} \leftarrow PUF(\vec{c})$ $\vec{w} = dec_k(\vec{w})$
$\xrightarrow{\quad \vec{r} \quad}$ $\vec{r'} \leftarrow PUF\_Model(\vec{c}, \vec{w})$
                if $HD(\vec{r}, \vec{r'}) \leq \tau$ accept

of physical attack security. Furthermore, a verifier can make a software clone of a PUF and hence the unclonability is not given any more. Therefore, such a system does not provided one of the key features, that the PUFs are unclonable, anymore.

4 Attacking the PUF Tags

The first step of attacking the PUF tags was to reverse-engineer the used PUF design, which was not known to us in detail. The RFID company provided us with a software tool to test the tags. The authentication protocol used in the software tool is depicted in Table 1. The software tool starts the authentication process by sending a query *auth* to the PUF tag. The PUF tag answers with its UID and the encrypted PUF parameters. Then the tool generates a random master challenge C and sends it to the tag. The tag answers with the corresponding response string $\vec{r}$. The tool decrypts the encrypted PUF delay vector $\vec{w}$ using the secret key k and uses this delay vector to compute the expected response string $\vec{r'}$. If the mismatch between the received response string r and the computed response string r' is below a threshold τ, the PUF tag is authenticated. The tool also supports an "online" verification that works in a similar way. The difference is that the decryption of the PUF parameters and the response computation is performed by a trusted server and not by the software tool. The tags we received were already programmed and contained encrypted PUF parameters with the key from the test tool. The fact that the software tool also computes the PUF responses based on the encrypted PUF parameters made reverse-engineering of the PUF much easier. No hardware reverse-engineering was needed. Instead, the reverse-engineering was performed on the software tool using IDA Pro. Via this reverse-engineering, we were able to derive the structure of the 4-way PUF as already introduced in Fig. 3, including all parameters such as the exact LFSR and the details of the mixer function.

4.1   Machine Learning Attack

To collect the CRPs necessary to attack the 4-way Arbiter PUF, we used a Matlab script to send random challenges to the reader. A single protocol execution, which consisted of sending a 64-bit challenge and receiving a 256-bit response, took roughly 53 ms. However, the response collection can be sped up by not sending a new master challenge between each measurement. Without a new master challenge, the last LFSR state of the previous challenge is used as a new master challenge. Using this trick, the measurement time can be reduced to 43 ms per 256-bit response. Hence, with this setup more than 5,000 response bits can ·be collect in one second and more than 350,000 in one minute. We would like to stress that we see these numbers are of general interest as a reference when accessing the security of PUFs against machine learning. Given a setup like ours, it is quite reasonable that an attacker can collect billions of CRPs.

To attack the PUF tags we tested Logistic Regression (LR) in conjunction with RProp as proposed in [29] as well as a CMA-ES machine learning algorithm. Both algorithms can be used to attack the PUF but the LR algorithm greatly outperforms the CMA-ES algorithm. To evaluate the machine learning attack, a training set was used by the machine learning algorithm to train the PUF parameters and a separate set, the reference set, was used to evaluate the resulting model accuracy. We were able to reliably perform a LR machine learning attack using a training set consisting of data from only 4 protocol executions, i.e., $4 \cdot 256 = 1024$ CRPs with a resulting average model accuracy of 85.8 %. Please note that the achieved model accuracy is very close to the observed average reliability of the PUF tags of 87.5 % and therefore sufficient to impersonate the PUF. All of the 10 different tags we tested could be successfully attacked. The measurement time of 1024 CRPs is only 172 ms and the computation time was in average around 40 seconds on a laptop. When more than 1024 CRPs are used, the computation time actually decreases significantly to a few seconds.

Hence, the 4-way PUF employed on these PUF-based RFID tags does not provide any protection against machine learning attacks and it is trivial for an attacker to recover the PUF parameters needed to model the PUF.

4.2   Cloning a PUF Tag

The machine learning attack from the previous Section provided us, with the PUF parameters that can be used to build a software model of the PUF. The remaining question is how we can actually use these PUF parameters to build a clone of the PUF tags. For this the freely programmable RFID smartcard emulator Chameleon was used. The Chameleon is based on an 8-bit ATXmega32A4U microcontroller clocked at 8 MHz and can be seen on the left side of Fig. 2. It has the size of a standard smartcard, costs less than $25 and is also available in a version powered by a small battery. The Chameleon is an open-source project and details of the Chameleon, the PCB layout and the firmware can be found online at GitHub [22]. One key feature of the Chameleon is that it is possible to set the UID, which cannot be done in most commercial RFID cards and tags.

We implemented the used communication protocol of PUF-based RFID tags on the ATXmega as well as a software model of the 4-way PUF. The computation of the PUF responses is time-critical, as there is a timeout if the computation of the PUF responses takes too long. To speed up the PUF computation we only used 5-bit precision integers for the PUF delay vector $\vec{w}$ since in this case no overflows occur on an 8-bit system. The delay vector has been computed using the machine learning attack described in the previous section.

The implementation was done using C and the computation of a 128-bit response block on the Chameleon took roughly 400,000 clock cycles which results in a computation time of 12.8 ms at a clock frequency of 32 MHz. In our experiments, this was fast enough not to trigger any timeouts. As mentioned, we only used 5-bit delay parameters for each PUF which reduced the model accuracy and resulted in a mismatch of around 20 % between the responses from the Chameleon and the responses computed by the demo tool. The mismatch of around 20 % in average is similar to the mismatch observed between the computed responses of the software tool and legitimate tags. This mismatch is well within the acceptable error rate of the software tool. If 16-bit precision numbers are used, the parameters derived by the machine learning attack actually have a higher model accuracy than the encrypted PUF parameters. We verified this attack using the test tool and the software declared the Chameleon an authentic PUF tag. This proves that cloning attacks on such PUF-based RFID tags can be performed in practice. Interestingly, the biggest challenge for an attacker in practice is actually to find a suitable programmable RFID chip in which the attacker can freely set the UID. However, in absent of freely programmable RFID smartcards, this can be simply solved by building your own RFID smartcard emulator.

5   Reliability-Based Machine Learning Attacks

In the previous section we have seen how to attack commercial PUF tags that are based on a 64-stage 4-way PUF. It is well known that small XOR PUFs can be attacked using machine learning and hence it is not a big surprise that the employed 4-way PUF can be attacked. In this section we therefore take a closer look at more secure architectures. In particular, we introduce a new reliability-based machine learning attack that scales much better with increasing XORs than the machine learning attacks from [29]. In traditional machine learning attacks, the attacker tries to model the PUF-based on the values of the response bits. However, not only the value of the responses contains useful information. The reliability of a response, i.e., how often the PUF evaluates to the same response bit for a given challenge, also holds valuable information. Delvaux *et al.* were the first to point this out [5]. They observed that the delay difference for a specific challenge of an Arbiter PUF is directly proportional to the unreliability of the corresponding response bit if the environmental conditions are kept stable. This is due to the fact that the various sources of noise add an approximately Gaussian delay $D_{noise} = norm(\mu, \sigma)$ to the delay difference ΔD. Hence, when also considering noise, Eq. 2 of the PUF model changes to:

$$\Delta D = \Delta D_{PUF} + D_{noise} = \vec{w}^T \vec{\Phi} + D_{noise} \tag{4a}$$

$$r = \begin{cases} 1, & \text{if } \Delta D_{PUF} + D_{noise} < 0. \\ 0, & \text{if } \Delta D_{PUF} + D_{noise} > 0. \end{cases} \tag{4b}$$

The key observation is that if the delay difference ΔD_{PUF} for a given challenge $\vec{\Phi}$ is very large, it is unlikely that the noise term D_{noise} changes the sign of ΔD. However, if the delay difference ΔD_{PUF} is close to zero, the chance that the response bit changes due to D_{noise} is much higher. Delvaux *et al.* used the exact reliability value of individual response bits to approximate delay differences for this response [5]. With the exact delay difference of individual responses the individual stage delays can be computed by solving a set of linear equations. However, Delvaux *et al.* pointed out that this approach is not as efficient as machine learning algorithms. Furthermore, their method cannot be applied to an XOR PUF, since you need to know the individual response bit for each Arbiter PUF as well as their exact reliability.

Becker *et al.* extended the idea of using unreliability and proposed a fault attack that is based on machine learning [3]. Changing the environmental conditions such as temperature or supply voltage has a similar effect as thermal noise, but is usually larger. The idea of the fault attack on controlled PUFs is to change the supply voltage for specific response bits and observe if the response of the controlled PUF changes. This information is then used in a CMA-ES based machine learning attack. This paper extends the basic idea behind this attack by adding a divide-and-conquer strategy in order to gain the ability to attack XOR PUFs. Furthermore, in this paper no active fault attack by changing the supply voltage is performed. Instead, only the inherent unreliability of the PUF is used. The measurements therefore can be conducted under the same environmental conditions. With this new strategy, we are able to break XOR PUFs that would be computationally infeasible to attack using traditional machine learning algorithms focusing on the output bits.

5.1   CMA-ES Attack Based on Reliability

The main idea of the reliability-based CMA-ES attack is to make repeated measurements for the same challenge so observe which response bits are stable and which response bits sometimes flip. If a response for a given challenge is unstable, it is likely that the corresponding delay difference ΔD_{PUF} is close to zero, i.e., $|\Delta D_{PUF}| < \epsilon$. But if a response bit has a high reliability for a given challenge, it is likely that the delay difference is large, i.e., $|\Delta D_{PUF}| > \epsilon$. We slightly modify the CMA-ES machine learning algorithm by using a fitness function that is based on this observation. The goal of the fitness function is to test which of a given set of PUF models $\vec{w}$ performs best, i.e., which is the fittest. In the first step the same challenge $\vec{\Phi}_i$ is sent to the PUF l times to collect l response bits $r_{i,1}, r_{i,2}, .., r_{i,l}$. Then the reliability h_i is computed for challenge $\vec{\Phi}_i$ using the following formula:

$$h_i = |\frac{l}{2} - \sum_{j=1}^{l} r_{i,j}| \tag{5}$$

To test the fitness of a given PUF model $\vec{w}$ the attacker first computes a hypothetical reliability $\tilde{h}_i$ for all challenges $\vec{\Phi}_i$ by testing if the corresponding absolute delay difference $|\Delta D_i|$ is larger than an error boundary ϵ:

$$\tilde{h}_i = \begin{cases} 1, & \text{if } |\vec{w}^T \vec{\Phi}_i| > \epsilon \\ 0, & \text{if } |\vec{w}^T \vec{\Phi}_i| < \epsilon \end{cases} \tag{6}$$

In the next step the attacker checks how well the hypothetical reliability vector $\tilde{h} = \tilde{h}_1, .., \tilde{h}_n$ matches the measured reliability vector $h = h_1, .., h_n$. This is done by computing the Pearson correlation coefficient between h and $\tilde{h}$. The correlation coefficient shows the linear relationship between the two vectors. It can therefore be used to test how well the hypothetical reliability vector $\tilde{h}$ of a PUF model $\vec{w}$ matches the observed reliabilities h. The higher the correlation coefficient, the *fitter* the PUF model is. The only other modification to the CMA-ES algorithm is that the parameter ϵ is an additional parameter that needs to be approximated by the machine learning algorithm. Hence, $k + 2$ instead of $k + 1$ parameters need to be approximated by the machine learning algorithm for a k-stage Arbiter PUF. Otherwise, the reliability CMA-ES works like a traditional CMA-ES attack: In each generation several PUF models are generated and then evaluated using the fitness test. The best models are kept and are used to generate the PUF models for the next generation. This way the PUF model gradually improves with each generation.

The attack was first tested using CRPs taken from the 4-way PUF of the commercial RFID tags. In a 4-way PUF, four individual response bits are XORed to form the final response bit. Hence, an attacker does not know the reliability for a given PUF response since it is only possible to measure the reliability of the final response bit. Therefore the fitness function needs to be adjusted. In a first step, the reliability values for the four subchallenges of the 4-way PUF are computed and then the reliability values of the four subchallenges are simply added up. Note that the more subchallenges are expected to be unreliable, the more likely it is that the measured response bit is unreliable as well. We performed the reliability-based CMA-ES attack on the 4-way PUF using the reliability information of $l = 5$ measurements. The attack was less efficient than a traditional CMA-ES attack and required around 4,000 CRPs. Nevertheless, the result shows that the reliability CMA-ES attack works in practice. For a larger number of XORs the reliability-based attack outperforms traditional machine learning algorithms significantly. To test this, two consecutive response bits of the 4-way PUF were XORed, effectively turning the 4-way PUF into an 8-way PUF. The number of needed CRPs for a traditional machine learning attack greatly increases when the number of XORs is increased, due to the increased non-linearity of the XORs as well as due to the fact that unreliability also increases. The 8-way PUF could be attacked with 300,000 CRPs using a LR machine learning algorithm. In comparison, the reliability-based CMA-ES attack still only needed 4,000 CRPs.

This result might be surprising at first, since the number of needed CRPs did not increase at all compared to the 4-way PUF. But in the fitness function of a reliability-based machine learning attack on an n-way PUFs, the reliability of each individual response is added and not XORed. Therefore, the number of XORs has only a small impact on the machine learning algorithm. As a matter of fact, we can still attack the PUF with 4,000 CRPs if a 20-way PUF is built by XORing 5 consecutive bits of the 4-way PUF. The reliability of a 20-way PUF is only around 63.1 % and hence not really useable in practice. Still, the reliability-based machine learning attack finds a PUF model with a model accuracy of 61.1 % for the 20-way PUF. The model accuracy of the underlying 4-way PUF is actually still around 87 % for this attack. Hence, unlike for traditional machine learning attacks, increasing the XORs in an n-way PUF does not increase the machine learning resistance.

5.2   Attacking XOR PUFs

The most popular strong PUF design is not the n-way PUF, but the XOR PUF which uses a different Arbiter PUF for each XOR. Every additional XOR also adds additional parameters that need to modeled in addition to the increased non-linearity of the XOR. This leads to an exponential increase in needed CRPs with each additional XOR. It is therefore assumed that if enough stages and XORs are used, XOR PUFs can withstand machine learning attacks [12,28]. However, in the following we show how even XOR PUF instances that are presumably secure can be attacked using the reliability-based machine learning attack.

For an n-XOR, k-stages PUF, $(k + 1) \cdot n$ parameters need to be determined in a machine learning attack. However, in the reliability-based machine learning attack a divide-and-conquer strategy can be used to attack each Arbiter PUF individually. This reduces the parameters that need to be approximated in one machine learning run to only $k + 1$. This is the main reason why the reliability-based machine learning attack significantly outperforms other machine learning attacks on XOR PUFs. The idea behind the divide-and-conquer approach is that the reliability of a response bit depends equally on each of the n employed Arbiter PUFs. Let us assume that for a PUF model $\vec{w}$ and challenge $\vec{\Phi}_i$ of one of the n Arbiter PUFs, the expected reliability is low, i.e., $\tilde{h}_i = 0$. Then the measured reliability h_i should also be low, since a bit flip of one of the response bits that are XORed directly results in a bit flip of the output of an XOR PUF. Hence, in this case the measured reliability h_i matches with the computed reliability $\tilde{h}_i$. If the computed reliability for the challenge $\vec{\Phi}_i$ is high, i.e., $\tilde{h}_i = 1$, and the observed reliability is also high, the computed and observed reliability vectors match each other. However, one of the other $n-1$ remaining Arbiter PUFs might be unreliable for this specific challenge. Hence, we might sometimes observe an unreliable response despite our hypothesis assuming a reliable response. But since we always guess the unreliable case correct, our hypothesis vector $\tilde{h}$ is still correlated with the observed reliability vector h, even if it is not a complete match. The unreliability introduced by the other $n-1$ Arbiter PUFs is therefore nothing else but noise from a machine learning perspective. Since the CMA-ES machine learning algorithm in conjunction with the correlation coefficient as a fitness function is very robust to noise, the CMA-ES algorithm still finds an accurate PUF model for the Arbiter PUF under test. Hence, in this attack we do not target all Arbiter PUFs at once. Instead we model one Arbiter PUF at a time. This is the main reason why our attack scales so well with the number of XORs. Each additional Arbiter PUF only adds additional noise to the computation. Furthermore, the relative increase in noise by adding a single XOR decreases with the number of XORs. Hence, the machine learning attack complexity only increases linear with the number of added XORs.

The only remaining question is how we can target a specif Arbiter PUF from the set of Arbiter PUFs used in the XOR PUF. There are basically two ways to build an XOR PUF. Either the same challenge is applied to all Arbiter PUFs, or each Arbiter PUF gets a different challenge. The classic XOR PUF uses the same challenges for all Arbiter PUFs. But results from [29] suggest that using different challenges for each PUF makes machine learning attacks harder. Let us first consider the case that each of the individual Arbiter PUFs gets their own set of unique challenges. In this case an attacker can target a specific Arbiter PUF based on which challenges the attacker uses in the machine learning attack. Since each Arbiter PUF has a different set of challenges, one Arbiter PUF is attacked after the other. Hence, to attack an n-XOR PUF, n individual reliability-based machine learning attacks are performed. After PUF models for all n PUFs are found, the entire XOR PUF can be modeled by simply XORing the individual responses.

The CMA-ES machine learning algorithm is a non-deterministic algorithm and sometimes does not converge to a near-optimal solution. In this case the algorithm needs to be restarted. Machine learning runs that did not find an accurate PUF model, i.e., that did not converge, have a much smaller fitness value than successful runs. Therefore the correlation coefficient can be used to test if a machine learning run was successful. If it was successful, the next PUF can be targeted, otherwise the machine learning algorithm should be restarted again with the same challenges. To test this we simulated different XOR PUFs by assuming a random Gaussian distribution of the individual stage delay parameters δ of the individual Arbiter PUFs. Assuming a Gaussian distribution is the common approach (e.g. used in [29]) and resembles a best-case scenario from a security perspective. To model the impact of noise a random variable is added to each computed delay difference ΔD_{PUF} with a Gaussian distribution of $norm(0, \sigma_{noise})$. The challenges were generated randomly and all simulations were carried out using matlab. To speed up the computation, a Mex function was written in C for the computationally expensive part of the PUF computations and the attacks were run on a AMD Opteron cluster with 4 nodes and 64 cores each. Each attack only used 16 cores so that in total 16 attacks run simultaneously on the cluster. Now let us consider the case that the same challenge is applied to all Arbiter PUFs, as is done in the classic XOR-Arbiter PUF. In this case an attacker cannot target a specific Arbiter PUF using different challenges since all PUFs get the same challenges. However, the probabilistic nature of

Table 2. Results of a reliability-based CMA-ES on different simulated n-XOR, 128-stage PUFs with a noise level of $\sigma_{noise} = 1$. In the top rows different challenges were used for each Arbiter PUF and in the bottom rows the same challenges were used as done in the classic XOR PUF . The results are the average of 10 independent attacks. "Accuracy single Arbiter" is the maximum and minimum achieved model accuracy of a single Arbiter PUF.

# XORs	Reliability	# CRPs	Accuracy reference set	Accuracy training set	#runs per XOR	Accuracy single Arbiter	Time
1	98.0 %	$20 \cdot 10^3$	99.0	98.3	8.7	98.3 %–99.3 %	0.9 h
4	92.5 %	$150 \cdot 10^3$	97.6 %	94.6 %	4.0	99.0 %–99.6 %	1.8 h
8	86.2 %	$300 \cdot 10^3$	95.3 %	89.0 %	3.4	98.6 %–99.7 %	3.3 h
16	76.0 %	$500 \cdot 10^3$	90.8 %	80.2 %	19.4	98.7 %–99.6 %	30.5 h
32^a	63.7 %	$2000 \cdot 10^3$	83.6 %	68.4 %	9.5	99.1 %–99.6 %	60 h
4	92.5 %	$150 \cdot 10^3$	97.7 %	94.2 %	4.2	99.1 %–99.7 %	1.1 h
8	86.2 %	$300 \cdot 10^3$	95.7 %	89.1 %	7.2	99.1 %–99.7 %	3.4 h
16^b	76.1 %	$500 \cdot 10^3$	90.0 %	80.1 %	30.6	98.7 %–99.6 %	34 h

[a] This row only uses the average from 3 independent attacks and not 10

[b] For the classic 16-XOR PUF a 2-step approach was used in which the first 13 PUFs were attacked using a reliability-based attack and the remaining 3 PUFs were attacked using an traditional CMA-ES. "#runs per XOR" is the average of the 13 PUFs determined by the reliability-based attack.

Table 3. Results of reliability-based CMA-ES attacks on a 8 XOR, 128 stages PUF with different noise values σ_{noise}. Again 10 attacks were performed per entry.

σ_{noise}	Reliability single Arbiter	Reliability XOR PUF	# CRPs	Accuracy reference set	#runs per XOR	Accuracy single Arbiter	Time
0.1	99.8 %	98.4 %	$2500 \cdot 10^3$	96.0 %	6.8	98.9 %–99.7 %	16.7 h
0.25	99.5 %	96.2 %	$1000 \cdot 10^3$	95.5 %	8.1	97.2 %–99.8 %	17.0 h
0.5	99.0 %	92.6 %	$500 \cdot 10^3$	94.7 %	7.5	98.9 %–99.8 %	6.6 h
1	98.0 %	86.2 %	$300 \cdot 10^3$	95.3 %	3.4	98.6 %–99.7 %	3.3 h
2	96.0 %	75.8 %	$200 \cdot 10^3$	94.5 %	1.6	98.8 %–99.6 %	1.2 h
4	92.1 %	62.7 %	$100 \cdot 10^3$	84.6 %	8.5	96.2 %–98.2 %	4.6 h

CMA-ES helps us in this case. The reliability-based machine learning algorithm will converge to one of the Arbiter PUFs of the XOR PUF since the correlation coefficient for a correct PUF model is higher than that for an inaccurate PUF model. If the machine learning algorithm would always converge to the same PUF, the attack would not be very helpful. However, due to the probabilistic nature of CMA-ES, the algorithm converges to different PUFs in different runs, even when called with the same inputs. The idea of the attack is to performed as many independent machine learning runs until all n distinct PUF models are found. Ideally, each of the n Arbiter PUFs should be equally likely to be found by a single run. In practice, some Arbiter PUFs are "easier" and some are "harder" to attack for given challenges and reliability vectors. Hence, the machine learning algorithm converges more often to some PUF instances than others.

In practice, the attacker does not necessarily need to find all of the n PUFs using the reliability-based machine learning attack. If only a few Arbiter PUFs remain, the attacker can find the remaining PUF models using a traditional LR or CMA-ES machine learning attack. When only a few PUFs remain, the chances are high that the machine learning attack converges to a PUF that has already been modeled. Therefore, this two step approach can considerably decreases the attack time for PUFs with many XORs such as a 16-XOR PUF. In general, unsuccessful runs can be aborted early to greatly decrease the computation time of the attack. To determine which runs are likely to be unsuccessful, the global mutation parameter σ in conjunction with the fitness value can be used. Furthermore, the hamming distance between responses from the model under test and the already computed PUF models can be used to detect runs that are converging to a PUF model that has already been found. These runs can also be aborted early to considerably speed up the computation time. The results of the reliability-based machine learning attack are summarized in Table 2. A noise level of $\sigma_{noise} = 1$ was used which resulted in an reliability of 98 % for a 128-stage Arbiter PUF. This is a conservative estimation of the reliability of Arbiter PUFs. For comparison, the observed unreliability of 64-stage Arbiter PUFs in [14] was around 97 % for nominal operation conditions. With this new attack even a 32-XOR PUF could be attacked with only 2 million CRPs, which would be impossible using LR. We also tested the attack for more reliable or less reliable PUFs. The results of this experiment are summarized in Table 3. For very reliable PUFs, more CRPs are needed, but the attack still works. To verify these results using real measurements, we emulated an XOR PUF structure by taking measurements from up to 8 different PUF RFID tags and XORed their corresponding output bits. This effectively turned the 4-way PUF tags into a mixture of an n-way and XOR PUF. In an 8-XOR-4-way PUF, 8 different 4-way PUFs are XORed, which results in a total of 32 XORs for a single response bit. The results of this experiment can be found in Table 4. The 8-XOR-4-way PUF can be successfully attacked using 400,000 CRPs. Hence, our reliability-based machine learning on XOR PUFs also works with real silicon data.

Table 4. Results of a reliability-based CMA-ES on an n-XOR 4-way PUF construction using $l = 5$ repeated measurements from the PUF-based RFID tags in which different challenges were used for each 4-way PUF.

# PUFs	# XORs	# CRPs	Reliability	Accuracy reference set	Accuracy training set	Accuracy 4-way	Time
1	4	$4 \cdot 10^3$	87.5 %	87.1 %	88.6 %	87.1	0.7 m
2	8	$10 \cdot 10^3$	80.0 %	78.5 %	80.3 %	88.0 %	1.6 m
4	16	$40 \cdot 10^3$	69.2 %	67.2 %	69.4 %	87.9 %	1.7 m
8	32	$400 \cdot 10^3$	56.3 %	55.6 %	56.4 %	87.5 %	13.1 m

This shows that the exponential increase in number of required responses for increasing XORs does not hold for the reliability-based machine learning attack. Unlike previously stated, plain XOR PUFs are insecure, regardless of the used parameters.

6 Discussion

In this paper we showed that the security of strong PUFs is still greatly lacking. This is true for both commercially available PUFs as well as strong PUF proposals by the scientific community. A lot of research effort has been focused on finding different PUF architectures. However, we are still far behind to understand the full power of machine learning attacks, in particular if more information than just the plain response bits is used. The newly proposed reliability-based CMA-ES attack is a prime example for this.

Basically, to prevent a reliability-based CMA-ES attack, an attacker should not be able to send the same challenge twice and observe the reliability of the responses. This could be achieved if the challenges are generated by both the tag as well as the verifier. However, this typically means that the verifier needs a software model of the PUF. Proposal for such protocols have already been made, see for example the Slender PUF protocol [25]. However, several key features of PUFs are lost if a software model is needed. For example, the "unclonability" feature is lost since everyone in possession of this software model can create a software clone of the PUF. Furthermore, every entity that authenticates a PUF instance needs to be a trusted entity, since such a software model can be seen as the equivalent of a symmetric key. Such a PUF also violates the "unprotected challenge-response interface" requirement as defined in [28] and hence is not a strong PUF according to formal definitions. Another approach to prevent this attack might be the idea of a controlled PUF [7]. However, recently it was shown that it is possible to perform a reliability-based machine learning attack based on the helper data of error correction codes [2]. Since controlled PUFs rely on error correction code, this attack is directly applicable to controlled PUFs as well. Hence, simply using a controlled PUF does not solve this problem. How to build a strong PUF that resists the reliability-based machine learning attack is therefore an interesting open research problem.

Our attack on the commercial PUF-based RFID tags shows the real-world implications of this research. An attacker only needs to hold an RFID reader or a NFC enabled smartphone within ca. 5 cm of the tags for 200 ms to collect enough CRPs to build an accurate software model. We verified that it is possible to read out the smartcard format PUF tags when they are carried within a wallet in the back-pocket of a jeans. We showed that it is possible to clone the tags using a self-made RFID smartcard emulator from off-the-shelf components for less than $25. This allows an electrical "pickpocketing" attack that can be carried our in real-time. Hence, while a lot of hope was put into strong PUFs as a secure and lightweight authentication solution, it seems that both academia as well as industry are still far away from achieving these goals.

References

1. Armknecht, F., Maes, R., Sadeghi, A., Standaert, F.X., Wachsmann, C.: A formalization of the security features of physical functions. In: IEEE Symposium on Security and Privacy 2011 (SP), pp. 397–412. IEEE (2011)
2. Becker, G.T.: On the pitfalls of using arbiter pufs as building blocks. IEEE Trans. Comput. Aided Des. Integr. Circ. Syst. PP(99), 1 (2015)
3. Becker, G.T., Kumar, R.: Active and passive side-channel attacks on delay based puf designs. IACR Cryptology ePrint Archive 2014, 287 (2014)
4. Brzuska, C., Fischlin, M., Schröder, H., Katzenbeisser, S.: Physically uncloneable functions in the universal composition framework. In: Rogaway, P. (ed.) CRYPTO 2011. LNCS, vol. 6841, pp. 51–70. Springer, Heidelberg (2011)
5. Delvaux, J., Verbauwhede, I.: Side channel modeling attacks on 65nm arbiter pufs exploiting CMOS device noise. In: 6th IEEE International Symposium on Hardware-Oriented Security and Trust (HOST 2013), June 2013
6. Delvaux, J., Gu, D., Schellekens, D., Verbauwhede, I.: Secure lightweight entity authentication with strong PUFs: mission impossible? In: Batina, L., Robshaw, M. (eds.) CHES 2014. LNCS, vol. 8731, pp. 451–475. Springer, Heidelberg (2014)
7. Gassend, B., Clarke, D., Van Dijk, M., Devadas, S.: Controlled physical random functions. In: Proceedings of 18th Annual Computer Security Applications Conference 2002, pp. 149–160 (2002)
8. Gassend, B., Clarke, D., Van Dijk, M., Devadas, S.: Silicon physical random functions. In: Proceedings of the 9th ACM conference on Computer and communications security, pp. 148–160. ACM (2002)
9. Guajardo, J., Kumar, S.S., Schrijen, G.-J., Tuyls, P.: FPGA intrinsic PUFs and their use for IP protection. In: Paillier, P., Verbauwhede, I. (eds.) CHES 2007. LNCS, vol. 4727, pp. 63–80. Springer, Heidelberg (2007)
10. Güneysu, T.: Using data contention in dual-ported memories for security applications. Sign. Proces. Syst. 67(1), 15–29 (2012)
11. Hansen, N.: The CMA evolution strategy: a comparing review. In: Towards a New Evolutionary Computation, Studies in Fuzziness and Soft Computing, vol. 192, pp. 75–102. Springer, Heidelberg (2006)
12. Herder, C., Yu, M.D., Koushanfar, F., Devadas, S.: Physical unclonable functions and applications: a tutorial. Proc. IEEE 102(8), 1126–1141 (2014)
13. Van Herrewege, A., Katzenbeisser, S., Maes, R., Peeters, R., Sadeghi, A.-R., Verbauwhede, I., Wachsmann, C.: Reverse fuzzy extractors: enabling lightweight mutual authentication for PUF-enabled RFIDs. In: Keromytis, A.D. (ed.) FC 2012. LNCS, vol. 7397, pp. 374–389. Springer, Heidelberg (2012)
14. Katzenbeisser, S., Kocabaş, Ü., Rožić, V., Sadeghi, A.-R., Verbauwhede, I., Wachsmann, C.: PUFs: myth, fact or busted? a security evaluation of physically unclonable functions (PUFs) cast in silicon. In: Prouff, E., Schaumont, P. (eds.) CHES 2012. LNCS, vol. 7428, pp. 283–301. Springer, Heidelberg (2012)
15. Lee, J.W., Lim, D., Gassend, B., Suh, G.E., Van Dijk, M., Devadas, S.: A technique to build a secret key in integrated circuits for identification and authentication applications. In: Symposium on VLSI Circuits, 2004. Digest of Technical Papers, 2004. pp. 176–179. IEEE (2004)
16. Maiti, A., Casarona, J., McHale, L., Schaumont, P.: A large scale characterization of ro-puf. In: IEEE International Symposium on Hardware-Oriented Security and Trust (HOST) 2010, pp. 94–99. IEEE (2010)

17. Majzoobi, M., Rostami, M., Koushanfar, F., Wallach, D., Devadas, S.: Slender puf protocol: A lightweight, robust, and secure authentication by substring matching. In: IEEE Symposium on Security and Privacy Workshops (SPW) 2012, pp. 33–44, May 2012

18. Majzoobi, M., Koushanfar, F., Potkonjak, M.: Lightweight secure pufs. In: Proceedings of the 2008 IEEE/ACM International Conference on Computer-Aided Design, pp. 670–673. IEEE Press (2008)

19. Merli, D., Heyszl, J., Heinz, B., Schuster, D., Stumpf, F., Sigl, G.: Localized electromagnetic analysis of ro pufs. In: IEEE International Symposium on Hardware-Oriented Security and Trust (HOST) 2013, pp. 19–24 (2013)

20. Ostrovsky, R., Scafuro, A., Visconti, I., Wadia, A.: Universally composable secure computation with (Malicious) physically uncloneable functions. In: Johansson, T., Nguyen, P.Q. (eds.) EUROCRYPT 2013. LNCS, vol. 7881, pp. 702–718. Springer, Heidelberg (2013)

21. Pappu, R., Recht, B., Taylor, J., Gershenfeld, N.: Physical one-way functions. Science 297(5589), 2026–2030 (2002). http://www.sciencemag.org/content/297/5589/2026.abstract

22. chameleon Project: Chameleon mini, January 2015. https://github.com/emsec/ChameleonMini/wiki

23. Maes, P.T.R., Verbauwhede, I.: Intrinsic PUFs from flip-flops on reconfigurable devices. In: WISSec 2008 (2008)

24. Rührmair, U., Xu, X., Sölter, J., Mahmoud, A., Majzoobi, M., Koushanfar, F., Burleson, W.: Efficient power and timing side channels for physical unclonable functions. In: Batina, L., Robshaw, M. (eds.) CHES 2014. LNCS, vol. 8731, pp. 476–492. Springer, Heidelberg (2014)

25. Rostami, M., Majzoobi, M., Koushanfar, F., Wallach, D., Devadas, S.: Robust and reverse-engineering resilient puf authentication and key-exchange by substring matching. IEEE Trans. Emerg. Top. Comput. **PP**(99), 1 (2014)

26. Rührmair, U., Solter, J., Sehnke, F., Xu, X., Mahmoud, A., Stoyanova, V., Dror, G., Schmidhuber, J., Burleson, W., Devadas, S.: Puf modeling attacks on simulated and silicon data. IEEE Trans. Inf. Forensics Secur. **8**(11), 1876–1891 (2013)

27. Rührmair, U., van Dijk, M.: Pufs in security protocols: attack models and security evaluations. In: IEEE Symposium on Security and Privacy (SP) 2013, pp. 286–300. IEEE (2013)

28. Rührmair, U., Holcomb, D.E.: Pufs at a glance. In: Proceedings of the conference on Design, Automation & Test in Europe, p. 347. European Design and Automation Association (2014)

29. Rührmair, U., Sehnke, F., Sölter, J., Dror, G., Devadas, S., Schmidhuber, J.: Modeling attacks on physical unclonable functions. In: Proceedings of the 17th ACM conference on Computer and communications security. pp. 237–249. CCS 2010, ACM, New York, NY, USA (2010). http://doi.acm.org/10.1145/1866307.1866335

30. Simons, P., van der Sluis, E., van der Leest, V.: Buskeeper PUFs, a promising alternative to D flip-flop PUFs. In: HOST 2012, pp. 7–12. IEEE (2012)

31. Suh, G.E., Devadas, S.: Physical unclonable functions for device authentication and secret key generation. In: Proceedings of the 44th annual Design Automation Conference, pp. 9–14. ACM (2007)

32. Tajik, S., Dietz, E., Frohmann, S., Seifert, J.-P., Nedospasov, D., Helfmeier, C., Boit, C., Dittrich, H.: Physical characterization of arbiter PUFs. In: Batina, L., Robshaw, M. (eds.) CHES 2014. LNCS, vol. 8731, pp. 493–509. Springer, Heidelberg (2014)

33. Yu, M.D., Sowell, R., Singh, A., M'Raihi, D., Devadas, S.: Performance metrics and empirical results of a puf cryptographic key generation asic. In: IEEE International Symposium on Hardware-Oriented Security and Trust (HOST) 2012, pp. 108–115. IEEE (2012)

End-To-End Design of a PUF-Based Privacy Preserving Authentication Protocol

Aydin Aysu[1], Ege Gulcan[1], Daisuke Moriyama[2(✉)],
Patrick Schaumont[1], and Moti Yung[3]

[1] Virginia Tech, Blacksburg, USA
{aydinay,egulcan,schaum}@vt.edu
[2] NICT, Tokyo, Japan
dmoriyam@nict.go.jp
[3] Google Inc. and Columbia University, New York City, USA
motiyung@gmail.com

Abstract. We demonstrate a prototype implementation of a provably secure protocol that supports privacy-preserving mutual authentication between a server and a constrained device. Our proposed protocol is based on a physically unclonable function (PUF) and it is optimized for resource-constrained platforms. The reported results include a full protocol analysis, the design of its building blocks, their integration into a constrained device, and finally its performance evaluation. We show how to obtain efficient implementations for each of the building blocks of the protocol, including a fuzzy extractor with a novel helper-data construction technique, a truly random number generator (TRNG), and a pseudo-random function (PRF). The prototype is implemented on a SASEBO-GII board, using the on-board SRAM as the source of entropy for the PUF and the TRNG. We present three different implementations. The first two execute on a MSP430 soft-core processor and have a security level of 64-bit and 128-bit respectively. The third uses a hardware accelerator and has 128-bit security level. To our best knowledge, this work is the first effort to describe the end-to-end design and evaluation of a privacy-preserving PUF-based authentication protocol.

Keywords: Physically unclonable function · Authentication · Privacy-preserving protocol · Implementation

1 Introduction

Physically Unclonable Functions (PUFs) have been touted as an emerging technology to support authentication of a physical platform. However, the design of PUF-based authentication protocols is complicated, and many pitfalls have been identified with existing protocols [8]. First, many protocols are ad-hoc designs. In the absence of a formal adversary model, one can only hope that no security holes are left. Second, while theoretical security models may provide assurance on the achieved level of security, these models typically lack a consideration of

© International Association for Cryptologic Research 2015
T. Güneysu and H. Handschuh (Eds.): CHES 2015, LNCS 9293, pp. 556–576, 2015.
DOI: 10.1007/978-3-662-48324-4_28

implementation issues. The cryptographic engineering of a PUF-based authentication protocol requires more than a formal proof. Finally, typical PUF-based protocol designs assume ideal PUF behaviors. They make abstraction of complex noise effects that come with real PUF. The actual performance of these protocol designs, and often also their implementation cost, remains unknown.

We believe that these issues can be systematically addressed, by combining a theoretical basis with sound cryptographic engineering [4]. In this paper, we aim to demonstrate this for a PUF-based privacy-friendly authentication protocol.

There are many PUF-based protocols that claim privacy [5,19,21,23,35]. We observed that most of these earlier proposals do not have a formal proof of security and privacy. In our opinion, a formal basis is required to clarify the assumptions of the protocol. For example, a recent analysis by Delvaux *et al.* [8] showed that only one [35] of these privacy-claiming PUF protocols actually provides privacy. Furthermore, none of the earlier proposed PUF-based protocols disclosed an implementation and a performance evaluation. This is required, as well, because the security and privacy properties of a PUF-based protocol are directly derived from the PUF design. These two reasons are the direct motivation for our protocol design, and its evaluation.

A PUF, a central element of our design, returns noisy data and uses a fuzzy extractor (FE) to ensure a reliable operation. The fuzzy extractor associates helper data with every PUF output to enable reconstruction of later noisy PUF outputs. However, the generation of helper data (Gen) and the reconstruction of a PUF output (Rec) are algorithms with asymmetric complexity: helper data generation has lower complexity than PUF output reconstruction. Realizing this property, van Herrewege *et al.* proposed reverse fuzzy extractors, which place the helper data generation within the constrained device [36]. However, the original reverse fuzzy-extractor protocol does not offer privacy. To achieve this objective, we rely on a protocol design by Moriyama *et al.* [28]. Assuming that a PUF is tamper-proof, their design leaves no traceable information within the device. This is achieved by using a different PUF output at every authentication, and thus by changing the device credential after every authentication.

Our proposed protocol starts from this design, and adapts it for a reverse fuzzy-extractor implementation. We maintain the formal basis of the protocol, but we also provide a detailed implementation and evaluation.

We note that there are contextual elements to privacy that are not addressed by our protocol. For example, we cannot offer privacy against an adversary who can physically trace every device in between authentications, or who can use other (non-cryptographic) mechanisms to identify a device [24]. These are context-dependent elements which have to be addressed by the application.

Compared to earlier work, we claim the following innovative features:

Novel Protocol. Our protocol merges privacy with a reverse fuzzy-extraction design, and is therefore suited for implementation on constrained platforms that also need privacy. Our protocol supports mutual (*device-first*) authentication.

End-To-End Design. We demonstrate a complete design trajectory, from provably secure protocol specification towards performance evaluation. We are not aware of any comparable efforts for other protocols. While other authors have suggested possible designs [25,27,36], the actual implementation of such a protocol has, to our knowledge, not yet been demonstrated.

Interleaved Error Correction. We present a novel technique for efficient helper data generation using an interleaved BCH code, as well as its security analysis. Our decoding strategy is computationally simple, and enables the use of a single BCH(63,16,23) primitive while still achieving 10^{-6} overall error rate.

The end-to-end design of a PUF-based protocol covers protocol design, protocol component instantiation, architecture design, and finally evaluation of cost and performance. We build our prototype on top of a SASEBO-GII board, using the resources available on the board to construct the PUF and the protocol engine. We use the 2 Mbit SRAM on the SASEBO-GII board as the source of entropy. We construct the following protocol components: an SRAM PUF, an SRAM TRNG, a pseudorandom function (PRF) design using the SIMON block cipher, and a fuzzy extractor based on an interleaved BCH error corrector and a PRF based strong extractor. We provide a design specification at two security levels, 64-bit and 128-bit.

Next, we implement these protocol components using an MSP430 processor (mapped as a soft-core on the SASEBO-GII board), an SRAM and a non-volatile memory. We also design a hardware accelerator to handle all cryptographic steps of the protocol, including the PRF, message encryption, and PUF output coding. Then, we implement the server-functionality on a PC connected to the SASEBO-GII board, and characterize the performance of the implementation under an actual protocol execution.

The remainder of this paper is organized as follows. Section 2 introduces the privacy preserving authentication protocol, describing its security assumption and important features. Section 3 describes the design of the protocol components: the SRAM PUF, the SRAM TRNG, the PRF, and the fuzzy extractor. Section 4 discusses the prototype implementation of the protocol, covering the system-level (server and device), the device platform, and the accelerator hardware engine. Section 5 presents the results, including implementation complexity and cost. We conclude the paper in Sect. 6.

2   Secure and Private PUF-Based Authentication Protocol

In this section, we describe the protocol notation, the assumed trust model, and the flow of the overall PUF protocol. Due to space limitations, the formal security proof of protocol is not included in this paper and we describe its main features in this paper[1].

2.1   Notation

When A is a set, $y \xleftarrow{\cup} A$ means that y is uniformly selected from A. When A is a deterministic algorithm, $y:=A(x)$ denotes that an output from $A(x)$ with input

---

[1] The detailed security model and security proof will be found in the full version of this paper.

x is assigned to y. When A is a probabilistic machine or an algorithm, $y \xleftarrow{R} A(x)$ denotes that y is randomly selected from A according to its distribution. $HD(x, y)$ denotes the Hamming distance between x and y. $\bar{H}_\infty(x)$ denotes the min-entropy of x. In addition, we use the following notations for cryptographic functions throughout the paper.

(Truly Random Number Generator) TRNG derives a truly random number sequence.

(Physically Unclonable Functions) $f : \mathcal{K} \times \mathcal{D} \rightarrow \mathcal{R}$ which takes as input a physical characteristic $x \in \mathcal{K}$ and message $y \in \mathcal{D}$ and outputs $z \in \mathcal{R}$.

(Symmetric Key Encryption) SKE := (SKE.Enc, SKE.Dec) denotes the symmetric key encryption. SKE.Enc takes as input secret key sk and plaintext m and outputs ciphertext c. SKE.Dec decrypts the ciphertext c using the same secret key sk to generate plaintext m.

(Pseudorandom Function) PRF, PRF$'$: $\mathcal{K}' \times \mathcal{D}' \rightarrow \mathcal{R}'$ takes as input secret key $sk \in \mathcal{K}'$ and message $m \in \mathcal{D}'$ and provides an output which is indistinguishable from random.

(Fuzzy Extractor) FE := (FE.Gen, FE.Rec) denotes a fuzzy extractor. The FE.Gen algorithm takes as input a variable z and outputs randomness r and helper data hd. The FE.Rec algorithm recovers r with input variable z' and hd if $HD(z, z')$ is sufficiently small. If $HD(z, z') \leq d$ and $\bar{H}_\infty(z) \geq h$, the (d, h)-fuzzy extractor provides r which is statistically close to random in $\{0, 1\}^{|r|}$ even if hd is exposed. The fuzzy extractor is usually constructed by combining an error-correction mechanism and a strong extractor.

2.2 Parties and Trust Model

We make assumptions comparable to earlier work in Authentication Protocols for constrained devices [28,35,36]. A trusted server and a set of num deployed devices will authenticate each other where devices require anonymous authentication. Before deployment, the devices are enrolled in a secure environment, using a one-time interface. After deployment, the server remains trusted, but the devices are subject to the actions of a malicious adversary (which is defined further).

Within this hostile environment, the server and the devices will authenticate each other such that the privacy of the devices is preserved against the adversary. The malicious adversary cannot determine the identity of the devices with a probability better than the security bound, and the adversary cannot trace the devices between different authentications.

The malicious adversary can control all communication between the server and (multiple) devices. Moreover, the adversary can obtain the authentication result from both parties and any data stored in the non-volatile memory of the devices. However, the adversary cannot mount implementation attacks against the devices, cannot reverse-engineer the PUF, nor can the adversary obtain any intermediate variables stored in registers or on-device RAM. We do not discount such attacks. For example, PUFs have been broken based on invasive analysis [29], side-channel analysis [9,30,33] and fault injection [10].

However, these attacks do not invalidate the protocol itself, and these attacks can be addressed with countermeasures at the level of the device.

2.3 Secure and Privacy-Preserving Authentication Protocol

We propose a new authentication protocol by combining the privacy-preserving authentication protocol of Moriyama et al. [28] with the reverse fuzzy extractor mechanism of van Herrewege et al. [36].

The reverse fuzzy extractor works as follows [36]. The verifier sends a challenge c to a PUF-enabled device. The device applies the challenge as input to a PUF, and obtains a noisy output z'. The device then computes helper data hd for this noisy output, and returns the helper data hd and a hash of the output z' to the verifier. The verifier, who has previously enrolled the device, knows at least one output z corresponding to the same challenge. The verifier can thus reconstruct z' using the helper data hd and the previous output z. While this protocol moves the computationally expensive reconstruction phase to the verifier, the protocol does not maintain privacy. The device discloses its identity in order to allow the verifier to find a previous PUF output z.

Moriyama et al. proposed a PUF-based protocol that provides provably secure and private authentication [28]. Different from the existing PUF-based protocols, their protocol has a key updating mechanism that changes the shared secret key between the server and the device after each authentication. Furthermore, the secret key is derived from the PUF output. The Moriyama et al. protocol however places the PUF output reconstruction in the device.

The proposed protocol combines these two ideas into a merged protocol, illustrated in Fig. 1. We claim the same formal properties for the proposed protocol as for [28]. It works as follows. Each device is represented as a combination of a secret key sk and a PUF challenge y_1. During secure initialization, the server initializes the secret key sk_1 in the device, and extracts the first PUF response z_1 from the device. The server keeps two copies of this information for each device in the database to support resynchronization. An authentication round proceeds as follows. First, the server sends a nonce to the device. The device extracts a first PUF output to construct an authentication field c and a key r_1. The device then extracts a second PUF output z'_2, which will be used during the next authentication round. The device encrypts this output (into u_1) and computes a MAC over it (into v_1 via PRF). The server will now try to authenticate the device. Initially, the server reconstructs the key r_1 using the reverse fuzzy extraction scheme. The server then performs an exhaustive search over the entire database in order to find a valid index. In case no match is found, the server will perform the same exhaustive search over the set of previous PUF outputs. If any match is found, the server will update its database to the next PUF output, and acknowledge the device. However, if both searches fail, the server will reply a random value. In the final step, the device verifies completion of authentication and updates its key tuple stored in nonvolatile memory in case of acceptance.

The key features of the protocol can be summarized as follows.

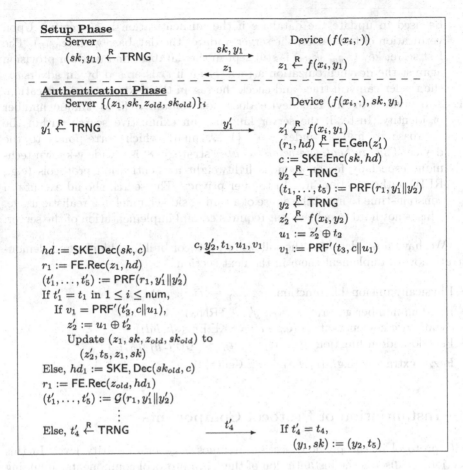

Fig. 1. The proposed PUF-based authentication protocol

Key Derivation via PUF with reverse FE. In the setup phase, the server stores the PUF output z_1 in the database. For each authentication, the device reads the PUF output $z_1' \xleftarrow{R} f(x_i, y_1)$ with physical characteristic x_i and generates helper data as $(r_1, hd) \xleftarrow{R} \text{FE.Gen}(z_1')$. The helper data is encrypted and sent to the server as $c := \text{SKE.Enc}(sk, hd)$. The server decrypts it and executes verification with the shared secret $r_1 := \text{FE.Rec}(z_1, hd)$.

Mutual Authentication and Authenticated Message Transmission. After deriving the shared secret r_1, the device and the server generate a random sequence $(t_1, \ldots, t_5)$. t_1 and t_4 are exchanged between the server and the device, and are used to implement mutual authentication. t_2 is used for XORed encryption of the PUF output, and t_3 is used as a secret key to generate validity check value v_1. v_1 serves as a MAC and prevents any modifications to the message (c, u_1) since the server checks $v_1 = \text{PRF}'(t_3', c\|u_1)$.

Key Update Mechanism. During the authentication, the device reads the PUF output twice, for different challenges. The second PUF output will be used to update the database if the authentication is successful. Upon verification of the device, the server updates the database with (z_2', t_5). The last secret key (z_{old}, sk_{old}) is still kept in the database and used for provision against the desynchronization attack. Even if t_4' is erased by an adversary, the reader can still trace and check the tag in the next protocol invocation.

Exhaustive Search. The device does not contain a fixed unique number of identity. Instead, the server launches an exhaustive search within the database to find an index $i \in \{1, \ldots, \mathsf{num}\}$ which corresponds to the device. This *authenticate-before-identify* strategy [8] is a widely-known technique especially for anonymous lightweight authentication protocols (e.g., RFID authentication in [20]) to offer privacy. The search should execute in constant-time to avoid the abuse of a timing side-channel in a realistic usage. This is not hard to achieve but requires careful implementation of the server.

We have now identified the following protocol building blocks and demonstrate how to implement them in the next section.

- Physically unclonable function (e.g., $z_1' \xleftarrow{\mathsf{R}} f(x_i, y_1)$)
- Random number generator (e.g., $y_2' \xleftarrow{\mathsf{R}} \mathsf{TRNG}$)
- Symmetric key encryption (e.g., $c := \mathsf{SKE.Enc}(sk, hd)$)
- Pseudorandom function (e.g., $(t_1, \ldots, t_5) := \mathcal{G}(r_1, y_1' \| y_2')$)
- Fuzzy extractor (e.g., $(r_1, hd) \xleftarrow{\mathsf{R}} \mathsf{FE.Gen}(z_1')$)

3   Instantiation of Protocol Components

The protocol in the previous section assumes a generic security level. In this section, we discuss the instantiation of the main protocol components, assuming a security level of 128 bits. Our evaluation (Sect. 5) will show results for 64-bit as well as for 128-bit security.

3.1   Architecture Assumptions

Our prototype is implemented on a SASEBO-GII board. Besides the FPGA components, we make use of the on-board 2Mbit static RAM (ISSI IS61LP6432A) and a 16Mbit Flash (ATMEL AT45DB161D). The SRAM is organized as a 64 K memory with a 32-bit output. The Flash memory has an SPI (serial) interface. These component specifications are neither a requirement nor a limitation of our proposed design. Rather, we consider them pragmatic choices based on the available prototyping hardware.

3.2   Design of SRAM PUF

The source of entropy in the design is an SRAM. We choose the SRAM for this role as the SRAM PUF is considered to be one of the most cost-efficient designs among recently proposed PUFs [25, Chapter 4]. It also offers reasonable noise levels. We are not aware of modeling attacks against SRAM PUF [32], and the known physical attacks against it are rather expensive [15,29]. Furthermore, while we acknowledge the diversity of possible PUF designs for FPGA's [1,13,18, 22], the use of an SRAM PUF with simple power-cycling will yield a prototype that is less platform-specific. Our first step is to analyze the min-entropy, and the distribution of the startup values of the SRAM.

Min-Entropy of SRAM. The min-entropy of the SRAM determines how many bytes of SRAM will be needed to construct one PUF output byte. We estimate the min-entropy of the SRAM empirically as follows. We collected the startup values of 90 SRAMs, collected from 90 different SASEBO-GII boards, each measured over 11 power cycles (990×2Mbit).

We then analyzed the Shannon Entropy as well as the min-entropy. Given a source of n symbols with probabilities b_i, the efficiency of the source as measured in Shannon Entropy is computed as $\sum_{i=0}^{n} -b_i \log(b_i)/n \times 100$. At the bit-level, we found an efficiency of 34 to 46%, depending on the board. This means that a bit on the average only holds between 0.34 and 0.46 bit of information, and indicates significant bias. We confirmed that there was bias according to the even and odd positions of the SRAM bytes.

We designed our PUF using the min-entropy, which is a worst-case metric. In this case, the min-entropy rate is computed as $n \times \min\{-b_i \log(b_i)\}_i \times 100$. When we analyzed the SRAM data at the byte level, we found a min-entropy of 5 to 15 %, which appeared to be caused by the abundance of the byte 0xaa at many SRAM locations. We did not investigate the cause of this bias, but we found that its effect can be considerably reduced by XORing adjacent bytes, and operation we will call 2-XOR. In this case the worst-case min-entropy rate becomes 26 %. We designed our PUF based on this value. In other words, we will use about 8 bytes of SRAM data to obtain one byte of entropy. The min-entropy estimate accounts for correlation between bits in a byte, which is more accurate than previous publications that used bit-level min-entropy estimates (e.g., 76 % min-entropy rate in [6]).

Distribution of SRAM Data. A second important factor is the expected noise level for each SRAM, and the expected average Hamming distance between different SRAMs. We analyzed our data set over the different measurements per SRAM. After applying the 2-XOR operation on the data, we found an average Hamming distance between same SRAM outputs of about 6.6 bit per word of 64 bit, which translates to a noise level of 10 %. When the SRAM outputs from different boards are compared, we found an average Hamming distance of 31.9 bit between words at the same address.

3.3   Design of SRAM TRNG

During authentication, the device requires a source of randomness. We reuse the SRAM as a random number generator, in order to minimize the device

Fig. 2. (left) Design of the SRAM-PUF (right) Design of the SRAM-TRNG

implementation cost. To obtain a noisy SRAM output, we XORed SRAM bytes multiple times. For each level of XORing, the noise level of the data is increased. We found that, after 8-fold XORing, the SRAM data passes all experiments in the NIST statistical Test Suite [34]. Hence, to generate a 128-bit random string from the device, we use 1024 bits of raw SRAM data. We can generate as much truly random data as there are available SRAM locations. One iteration of our protocol requires 652 random bits (see Table 1), which are extracted out of 5,216-bit of SRAM data. Of course, the SRAM needs to be power-cycled after each iteration of the protocol.

Practical RAM Organization. Figure 2 shows how the SRAM is used as a PUF and as a TRNG. In order to avoid direct correlation between PUF and TRNG data, we maintain separate address spaces for the PUF and the TRNG. In the prototype implementation, we allocate the first 256 SRAM words (of 32 bit each) for TRNG, while the remaining 65,280 words are used for the PUF. This means that the SRAM holds sufficient space for 2,040 PUF outputs (2,040 authentications). The input challenge to the PUF is therefore a 12-bit value y, which is transformed into a base address for a block of 32 addresses by multiplying it with 32 and adding 0×100.

3.4 Symmetric Key Encryption and PRF

Our protocol requires a PRF and a symmetric-key encryption. We designed a PRF starting from the SIMON block cipher. It has the convenience that both 64-bit and 128-bit key size configurations are supported, and that very efficient implementations of it are known [3]. We select 128-bit block size for 128-bit security. Using SIMON is neither a limitation nor a requirement of the prototype and it can be replaced with a secure symmetric-key cipher algorithm (e.g., AES) which supports the required security level.

Figure 3 shows how a PRF can be created using a block cipher in CBC mode. We assume SIMON does not provide any bias and the ciphertext is indistinguishable from random. An input message $x := (x_0, \ldots, x_n)$ is encrypted with secret key r_1, then expanded into the output sequence $y := (y_0, y_1, \ldots)$ by encrypting a counter value. The insertion of the output length parameter $|y|$ ensures that, even when the input and secret is identical, the PRF produces independent output sequences when the specified output size is different.

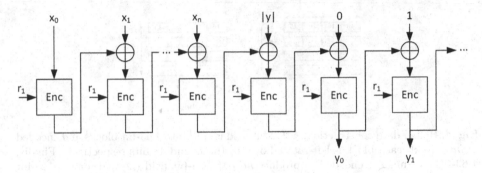

Fig. 3. PRF based on a block cipher in CBC mode. The variable-length message $x_0, .., x_n$ is expanded using a secret r_1 into a message of length $|y|$

3.5 Design of Fuzzy Extractor

In this section, we describe the design of the fuzzy extractor, including the error correction and the strong extractor.

Error Correction. Various techniques for error correction have been proposed in recent years, with mechanisms based on code-offset [11], index-based syndrome coding [37], and pattern matching [31]. We adopt the following code-offset mechanism using a BCH (n_1, k_1, d_1) code [11]. The code allows to correct errors up to $\lfloor (d_1 - 1)/2 \rfloor$-bit within a n_1-bit block. Two procedures, BCH.Gen and BCH.Dec, represent encoding and decoding respectively:

$$\text{Encode}(a): \delta \xleftarrow{R} \text{TRNG} \in \{0,1\}^{k_1}, cw := \text{BCH.Gen}(\delta) \in \{0,1\}^{n_1}, hd := a \oplus cw$$
$$\text{Decode}(a', hd): cw' := a' \oplus hd, cw := \text{BCH.Dec}(cw'), a := cw \oplus hd$$

The PUF output a is XORed with a random codeword cw to construct hd. While hd is not secret, the PUF output a must remain secret. We consider the complexity of finding a. For a single block, this complexity is 2^{k_1}. For a PUF output z_1 mapped into multiple n_1-bit blocks, the complexity is $2^{k_1 \cdot |z_1|/n_1}$. It should be higher than the selected security level of 128 bit.

We use 504 bits of a 512-bit PUF output in 8 blocks of a BCH(63, 16, 23) code, which gives us the desired security level. The BCH(63, 16, 23) code corrects up to 17.5 % noisy bits, which appears to be above the observed SRAM noise level of 10.0 %. However, this is too optimistic. If we assume that a single bit flips with a probability of 10.0 %, then there is a 2.36 % probability that 12 bits or more will flip in a 63-bit block, and thus produce a non-correctable error. This translates to a probability of only $(1 - 0.0236)^8 \times 100 \approx 82.6\,\%$ that 8 blocks of a 504-bit PUF output can be fully corrected. Therefore, we need a better error correction mechanism.

We apply an interleaved coding technique as illustrated in Fig. 4. A 252-bit data field is organized as a matrix with fields of $\{16, 16, 16, 15\}$ bits per row. The encoding of each 63-bit row yields helper data hd_L. Next, each row of the matrix

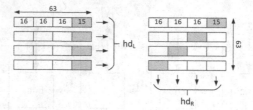

Fig. 4. Helper data construction. A 252-bit field is split into 4 63-bit blocks and encoded as hd_L. Next, each block is left-rotated over 0, 16, 32 and 48 bits respectively. Finally, 4 63-bit columns are encoded to produce hd_R. A 504-bit field (needed for the 128-bit security level) is encoded by applying this construction twice.

is rotated over a multiple of 16-bits, such that 63-bit columns are obtained. The encoding of the columns now yields helper data hd_R. The overall helper data is $hd_L \| hd_R$. To encode a 504-bit field, we apply this construction twice. Compared an earlier interleaved-coding design by Gassend [12], our technique accommodates odd-sized rows and columns.

Error decoding is performed adaptively. We first correct the rows, then decode remaining faulty bits over the columns. Figure 5 plots the probability of a faulty output after the error decoding as a function of the error probability of the PUF output. The residual error rate is $1 - 1.92 \times 10^{-6}$, which is comparable to the acceptable error rate for standard performance levels in [25]. Several authors have proposed techniques to improve the reliability of SRAM PUF with respect to environmental conditions and aging [7, 26]. These techniques, when applied to our design, may allow to reduce the complexity of the error correction code.

The computational complexity to find 252-bit PUF data from the helper data is 2^{64}. The helper data over the rows hd_L and columns hd_R are generated using independent random code-words cw_L and cw_R, respectively. The BCH encoding function expands the randomness of a 16-bit seed into a 63-bit codeword. The method ensures that XOR combinations of hd_L and hd_R do not explicitly leak PUF data, and it employs the working heuristic that these combinations are 'random enough'. We experimentally verified that the 2^{16} possible BCH code words, parsed into $\{16, 16, 16, 15\}$-bit fields, show no collisions within a field. The security level per code word thus is 2^{16}. The entire matrix is covered by four independent code words over the rows, and four independent code words over the columns. An attack of 2^{64} complexity, is to guess four code words and then use the helper data to estimate the PUF output. Since every element of the matrix holds different PUF output bits, the adversary must find at least the code words over *all* the rows, or the code words over the *all* columns. That is a lower bound for this attack strategy, because four codewords over a combination of rows and columns cannot cover the complete matrix, and therefore cannot recover all PUF output bits. As noted above, the dependency $hd_L \oplus cw_L = hd_R \oplus cw_R$, cannot reduce the complexity of the search below 2^{64}, since every single code word has security level 2^{16}, and since the smallest number of code-words required to recover the PUF output data is four.

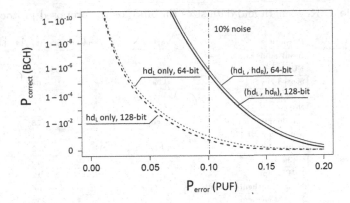

Fig. 5. Probability for a faulty PUF output using the proposed interleaved coding technique.

Strong Extractor. The role of strong extractor is to reduce the non-uniform data (PUF output data) to the required entropy level. We assume the proposed PRF works as a strong extractor. As discussed earlier, the PRF still uses a secret key. The secret key sk' is pre-shared and updated after every successful authentication. The strong extractor is a probabilistic function, and requires a random input rnd. Following Håstad *et al.* [14], we select the size of rnd to be twice the security level. For 128-bit security, $|rnd| = 256$ is sufficient to derive 128-bit randomness with input 128-bit min-entropy data (i.e. 504-bit PUF's output z'_1).

3.6   Relevant Data Sizes and Key Lengths in Protocol

From the above analysis and instantiation, we summarize the length for each variable for 64-bit and 128-bit security in Table 1.

4   Architecture Design

In this section, we describe the architecture design of the implementation. We introduce the overall design, discuss the detailed implementation of the cryptographic accelerator, and finally discuss the prototype evaluation.

4.1   System Design

Figure 6 illustrates the system architecture with the *device* and the *server*. They are emulated with a SASEBO-GII board and a PC respectively. The basis of the device is an MSP430 Microcontroller mapped as a soft-core into the Crypto FPGA of the SASEBO-GII board. The design integrates an SRAM, a non-volatile memory, a UART, and optionally a hardware accelerator. The MSP430 core has its own program memory and data memory; the SRAM is used solely as a source of entropy. The power source to the device is controlled as part of the testing environment.

Table 1. Key length and data sizes (in bits) for the proposed protocol

Category	Purpose	Variables	64-bit security	128-bit security
Setup phase	Input address	y_1	12	12
	PUF's output	z_1	252	504
	Stored key	sk, sk'	64	128
Authentication phase	PUF's output	z_1', z_2'	252	504
	Nonce	y_1', y_2'	64	128
	Randomness for FE	δ, rnd	128	256
	Secret key for PRF	r_1	64	128
	Helper data	hd (includes rnd)	632	1,264
	Ciphertext	c	640	1,280
	PUF's input	y_2	12	12
	Mutual authentication	t_1, t_4	64	128
	XORed element	t_2	252	504
	Secret key for PRF' and MAC	t_3, s_1	64	128
	Updated stored key	t_5	128	256
Communication	First message (from server)	y_1'	64	128
	Second message (from device)	(c, y_2', t_1, u_1, s_1)	1,084	2,168
	Third message (from server)	t_4'	64	128
Memory	Persistent State (NVM)	(sk, sk', y_1)	140	268
	SRAM area for PUF		504	1,008
	SRAM area for RNG		2,656	5,216

The server manages a database with secret keys and PUF responses. For each device authenticated through this server, the database stores two pairs of keys and PUF responses, one for the current authentication (z_1, sk), and one from the previous authentication (z_{old}, sk_{old}). The communication between the device and the server is implemented through a serial connection.

The 16-bit MSP430 microcontroller is configured with 8 KByte of data memory and 16 KByte of program memory. We will discuss the detailed memory requirements of the protocol in Sect. 5. We implement two different versions of this design. In the first version, the protocol is mapped fully in C and executed on the MSP430. In the second version, the major computational bottlenecks, including Fuzzy Extractor Generation (FE.Gen), PRF computation (PRF and PRF') and Encryption (SKE.Enc) are executed in the hardware engine. In this configuration, the MSP430 is used as a data multiplexer between the UART, the SRAM, the non-volatile memory and the hardware engine.

Protocol Mapping and Execution. The protocol includes a single setup phase, followed by one or more authentication phases. Before the execution of each phase, we power-cycle the device to re-initialize the SRAM PUF. This gives us a real SRAM PUF noise profile. Table 2 shows a detailed description of the protocol authentication phase on the architecture of Fig. 6. The operations are shown for the software-only implementation (Ver. 1) as well as for the hardware-engine enabled implementation (Ver. 2). Table 2 demonstrates the principal data flows in the architecture. For example, "SPIROM.Read → MSP430.DM" means that data is copied from the SPI-ROM to the MSP430 data memory.

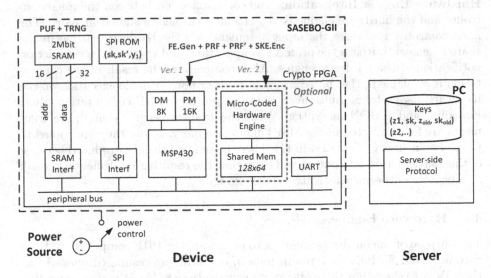

Fig. 6. System architecture of the device and server

Table 2. Principal data flows during execution of the authentication protocol on the device. Dataflow notation $A.a \rightarrow B.b$ indicates that data from A (port/method a) is forwarded to B (port/method b)

Seq	Authentication step	MSP430	MSP430 + HW engine
		Fig. 6 Ver. 1	Fig. 6 Ver. 2
1	Receive y_1'	UART.Receive → MSP430.DM	UART.Receive → MSP430.DM
2	Read sk, sk', y_1	SPIROM.Read → MSP430.DM	SPIROM.Read → MSP430.DM
3	$z_1' \xleftarrow{R} f(x_i, y_1)$	SRAM.PUF → MSP430.DM	SRAM.PUF → MSP430.DM
4	$(r_1, hd_1) \xleftarrow{R} \mathsf{FE.Gen}(z_1')$	MS430.run(PRF)	
		MS430.run(BCH.Enc)	
5	$m_2 \xleftarrow{R} \mathsf{TRNG}$	SRAM.TRNG → MSP430.DM	SRAM.TRNG → MSP430.DM
	$y_2 \xleftarrow{R} \mathsf{TRNG}$		
6	$(t_1, \ldots, t_5) := \mathsf{PRF}(r_1, y_1' \| y_2')$	MS430.run(PRF)	
7	$c := \mathsf{SKE.Enc}(sk, hd_1)$	MS430.run(Enc)	
8	$z_2' \xleftarrow{R} f(x_i, y_2)$	SRAM.PUF → MSP430.DM	SRAM.PUF → MSP430.DM
9	$u_1 := z_2' \oplus t_2$	MSP430.run(xor)	
10	$v_1 := \mathsf{PRF'}(t_3, c \| u_1)$	MS430.run(PRF)	
11	*HW Execution step*		MSP430.DM → HW.SharedMem
			HW.run
			HW.SharedMem → MS430.DM
12	Send c, m_2, t_1, u_1, v_1	MSP430.DM → UART.Send	MSP430.DM → UART.Send
13	Receive t_4'	UART.Receive → MSP430.DM	UART.Receive → MSP430.DM
14	Write y_2, t_5	MSP430.DM → SPIROM.Write	MSP430.DM→ SPIROM.Write

Hardware Engine Integration. The communication between the microcontroller and the hardware engine is implemented through a shared-memory. The microcontroller initializes the input arguments for the hardware engine in the shared memory, initiates the protocol computation, and waits until a completion notification of the hardware engine. After completion, the result of the computation is available in the shared memory. Furthermore, a single execution on the hardware engine takes multiple steps in the protocol: PRF computation, BCH Encoding, and SIMON encryption. When the hardware engine is used, the arguments are first collected in the MSP430 data memory, before they are copied to the shared memory (Table 2 step 11). There is some overhead introduced because of this particular design, but we will show that the resulting implementation still significantly outperforms a software-only design.

4.2 Hardware Engine

The purpose of the hardware engine is to accelerate the PRF computation, BCH encoding, and SIMON encryption. Indeed, our profiling results (discussed further, Table 5) show that these operations constitute to 88 % of the total execution time. The protocol can be realized with a small and fixed microprogram so we applied a micro-coded design methodology. Moreover, since it is efficient to use a RAM to store the protocol variables, the very same memory can also store the micro-coded instructions. Although this design is prototyped on FPGAs, it can also target dedicated hardware. By changing the microprogram, we can extend this architecture to other protocols as well.

Figure 7 shows the block diagram of the hardware engine. It uses the round-serial version of SIMON 128/128 for the PRF and encryption operations, and an LFSR-based implementation of the BCH encoding for the error correction part of the FE.Gen. Therefore, it takes 68 clock cycles to encrypt one 128-bit block and 16 clock cycles to encode one 16-bit block.

The shared memory between the MSP430 and the micro-coded hardware engine is a single memory element which has a word size of 72-bits. The least

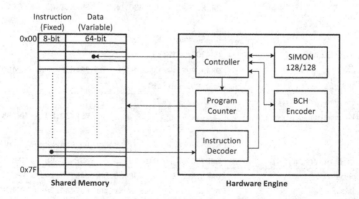

Fig. 7. Block diagram of the hardware engine

significant 64-bits of each word store the data, while the most significant 8-bits store the micro-coded instruction. Since these instructions are fixed at design time, this section of the memory is treated as a ROM. After the hardware engine reads a word from the memory, it decodes the micro-coded instruction. Then based on the decoded value, the controller selects which operation to run with the associated data and updates the value of the program counter.

5 Evaluation

In this section, we first discuss the device implementation cost, and then evaluate the system performance of our protocol. We implemented three different device configurations, including the 64-bit and 128-bit security level of the software-only implementation (Fig. 6 Ver. 1), as well as the 128-bit security level of the hardware-engine enabled implementation (Fig. 6 Ver. 2).

5.1 Implementation Cost

Table 3 shows the memory footprint required for each version, including the size of the MSP430 object code, and the data-memory requirements. We used the GNU gcc version 4.6.3 to compile C for the MSP430 at optimization level 2. As our main objective was to demonstrate the implementation of the complete protocol, we did not use low-level programming techniques. However, the data indicates that the protocol already fits into a small microcontroller. When the hardware engine is enabled, the tasks of the MSP430 reduce to interfacing the SRAM, NVM and UART. We envisage that it is feasible to completely remove

Table 3. MSP430 Memory footprint. Data area includes global and local variables (stack, bss and data).

Category		64-bit MSP430	128-bit MSP430	128-bit HW engine + MSP430	Unit
Text	HW abstraction	1,022	1,022	1,398	bytes
	Communications	496	644	628	bytes
	SIMON PRF	1,604	2,440	0	bytes
	BCH encoding	1,214	1,214	0	bytes
	PUF + Fuzzy Extr	562	646	590	bytes
	TRNG	396	456	396	bytes
	Protocol	1,568	1,682	1,908	bytes
Overall text		6,862	8,104	4,920	bytes
Data	Variables	424	656	656	bytes
	Constants	197	197	73	bytes
Overall data		621	853	729	bytes

Table 4. Hardware utilization (Xilinx XC5VLX30-1FFG324 system clock 1.846 MHz)

Module	LUT	Registers	Block RAM
MSP430 Core	2084	684	
MSP430 Program mem			4
MSP430 Data mem			2
SRAM Interface	54	30	
SPI ROM interface	45	30	
UART	139	106	
HW engine	1221	441	
HW Shared mem			2
Overall	3543	1275	8

the MSP430 microcontroller by having the hardware engine directly access these peripherals.

Table 4 lists the hardware requirements for the baseline design, which is shared among all versions of the protocol. The hardware engine is about half as big as the MSP430 core.

5.2 Performance

Table 5 lists the performance of our design, measured in system clock cycles. We implemented this design at a System Clock of 1.846 Mhz to reflect the constrained platform for the device. The hardware engine can drastically reduce the cycle count of the implementation. The cycle count shown for the hardware engine includes the overhead of preparing data; the actual compute time is only 4,486 cycles.

Table 5. Implementation performance in system clock cycles.

Protocol step	Implementation target	64-bit Fig. 6 Ver. 1	128-bit Fig. 6 Ver. 1	128-bit w. HW engine Fig. 6 Ver. 2
Read sk, sk', y_1	Read ROM (SPI)	31,356	61,646	61,646
$y_2' \xleftarrow{R}$ TRNG, $y_2 \xleftarrow{R}$ TRNG	SRAM TRNG	11,552	23,341	22,981
$z_1' \xleftarrow{R} f(x_i, y_1)$, $z_2' \xleftarrow{R} f(x_i, y_2)$	SRAM PUF	4,384	9,082	8,741
$(r_1, hd) \xleftarrow{R}$ FE.Gen(z_1')	BCH Encoder	268,820	485,094	18,597
	Strong extractor	28,691	205,080	
$(t_1, \ldots, t_5) := $ PRF$(r_1, y_1' \| y_2')$	PRF	44,355	299,724	
$c := $ SKE.Enc(sk, hd)	Encryption	39,583	252,829	
$v_1 := $ PRF$'(t_3, c \| u_1)$	PRF'	57,601	394,126	
Overall		486,343	1,730,922	111,965
Write y_2, t_5	Write ROM (SPI)	76,290	128,829	128,849

Table 6. Comparison with previous work

Reference	PUFKY [25]	Slender [27]	Reverse-FE [36]	This work
Operation	Key generation	Protocol	Protocol	Protocol
Privacy	No	No	No	Yes
Security flaws	No	Major [8]	Minor [8]	No
Implemented parties	N/A	Device	Device	Device, Server
Communication interface	Yes: Bus	No	No	Yes: Bus, UART
Flexibility	Low	Low	Low	High
Reconfiguration method	Redesign hardware	Redesign hardware	Redesign hardware	Modify software, Update microcode
Demonstrator	FPGA	FPGA	FPGA	FPGA + PC
Security-level	128-bits	128-bits	128-bits	64,128-bits
Execution time (clock cycles)	55,310	-	-	18,597
Logic Cost (w/o PUF)	210 Slices	144 LUT, 274 Register	658 LUT, 496 Register	1221 LUT, 441 Register
PUF-type	Strong-PUF	Strong-PUF	-	Weak-PUF
PUF-instance	RO-PUF	XOR-Arbiter	-	SRAM
Hardware platform	XC6SLX45	XC5VLX110T	XC5VLX50	XC5VLX30

5.3 Related Work

The comparison of this design to related works is not obvious because previous publications did not implement an end-to-end demonstrator. Table 6 presents a comparison of related realizations. We emphasize our design has many advantages (such as flexibility, formal properties, full implementation) that cannot be expressed as a single quantity.

5.4 Benchmark Analysis

We analyzed our protocol with respect to a recently published benchmark for PUF based protocols [8]. Our protocol is implemented using a weak PUF. The protocol requires $n + 1$ challenge-response pairs for n authentications. The total number of PUF responses depends on the anonymity needs of the application.

The protocol supports server authenticity, device authenticity, device privacy, and leakage resilience. It can use d-enrollments for a perfect privacy use-case and (∞)-enrollments without token anonymity. The system is noise-robust and modelling-robust. Mutual authentication provides both server and user authenticity. Moreover, since the protocol does not have an internal synchronization, it is not susceptible to DoS attacks. Our protocol enables token privacy and the security proof confirms leakage resilience.

6   Conclusion

We demonstrated the challenging path from the world of protocol theory to concrete software/hardware realization for the case of a privacy preserving authentication protocol. We observe that bringing all components of a protocol together in a single embodiment is a vital and important step to check its feasibility. Furthermore, the formal basis of the protocol is crucial to prevent *cutting corners* in the implementation.

Even though we claim this work is the first demonstration of a PUF-based protocol with a formal basis, there is always room for improvement. First, the current implementation can be optimized at the architectural level, for throughput, area, or power [2]. Second, new components and algorithms, such as novel PUF architectures [17] or novel coding techniques [16], may enable us to revisit steps within the protocol itself.

Acknowledgements. The project was supported in part by the National Science Foundation Grant 1314598 and 1115839. Part of the work of Moti Yung was done when visiting the Simons Institute for Theory of Computing, U.C. Berkeley. The authors thank the reviewers for their comments and discussions with Mandel Yu.

References

1. Anderson, J.H.: A PUF design for secure FPGA-based embedded systems. In: ASP-DAC 2010, pp. 1–6, IEEE (2010)
2. Aysu, A., Gulcan, E., Schaumont, P.: SIMON says: break area records of block ciphers on FPGAs. Embed. Syst. Lett. **6**(2), 37–40 (2014)
3. Beaulieu, R., Shors, D., Smith, J., Treatman-Clark, S., Weeks, B., Wingers, L.: The SIMON and SPECK families of lightweight block ciphers. IACR Crypt. ePrint Arch. **2013**, 404 (2013)
4. Bernstein, D.J.: Error-prone cryptographic designs. In: Real World Cryptography Workshop, January 2015. http://cr.yp.to/talks/2015.01.07/slides-djb-20150107-a4.pdf
5. Bolotnyy, L., Robins, G.: Physically unclonable function-based security and privacy in RFID systems. In: PerCom 2007, pp. 211–220, IEEE (2007)
6. Claes, M., van der Leest, V., Braeken, A.: Comparison of SRAM and FF PUF in 65 nm technology. In: Laud, P. (ed.) NordSec 2011. LNCS, vol. 7161, pp. 47–64. Springer, Heidelberg (2012)
7. Cortez, M., Hamdioui, S., van der Leest, V., Maes, R., Schrijen, G.J.: Adapting voltage ramp-up time for temperature noise reduction on memory-based PUFs. In: HOST 2013, pp. 35–40, IEEE (2013)
8. Delvaux, J., Gu, D., Peeters, R., Verbauwhede, I.: A survey on lightweight entity authentication with strong PUFs. IACR Cryptology ePrint Archive 2014, 977 (2014). http://eprint.iacr.org/2014/977

9. Delvaux, J., Verbauwhede, I.: Side channel modeling attacks on 65nm arbiter PUFs exploiting CMOS device noise. In: HOST 2013, pp. 137–142, IEEE (2013)
10. Delvaux, J., Verbauwhede, I.: Fault injection modeling attacks on 65 nm arbiter and RO sum PUFs via environmental changes. IEEE Trans. Circ. Syst. **61–I**(6), 1701–1713 (2014)
11. Dodis, Y., Ostrovsky, R., Reyzin, L., Smith, A.: Fuzzy extractors: how to generate strong keys from biometrics and other noisy data. SIAM J. Comput. **38**(1), 97–139 (2008)
12. Gassend, B.: Physical random fuctions. Master's thesis, Massachusetts Institute of Technology (2003)
13. Güneysu, T.: Using data contention in dual-ported memories for security applications. Sig. Proc. Syst. **67**(1), 15–29 (2012)
14. Håstad, J., Impagliazzo, R., Levin, L.A., Luby, M.: A pseudorandom generator from any one-way function. SIAM J. Comput. **28**(4), 1364–1396 (1999)
15. Helfmeier, C., Boit, C., Nedospasov, D., Seifert, J.: Cloning physically unclonable functions. In: HOST 2013, pp. 1–6, IEEE (2013)
16. Herder, C., Ren, L., van Dijk, M., Yu, M.M., Devadas, S.: Trapdoor computational fuzzy extractors. IACR Cryptology ePrint Archive 2014, 938 (2014). http://eprint. iacr.org/2014/938
17. Holcomb, D.E., Fu, K.: Bitline PUF: building native challenge-response PUF capability into any SRAM. In: Batina, L., Robshaw, M. (eds.) CHES 2014. LNCS, vol. 8731, pp. 510–526. Springer, Heidelberg (2014)
18. Hori, Y., Kang, H., Katashita, T., Satoh, A., Kawamura, S., Kobara, K.: Evaluation of physical unclonable functions for 28-nm process field-programmable gate arrays. JIP **22**(2), 344–356 (2014)
19. Jin, Y., Xin, W., Sun, H., Chen, Z.: PUF-based RFID authentication protocol against secret key leakage. In: Sheng, Q.Z., Wang, G., Jensen, C.S., Xu, G. (eds.) APWeb 2012. LNCS, vol. 7235, pp. 318–329. Springer, Heidelberg (2012)
20. Juels, A., Weis, S.A.: Defining strong privacy for RFID. ACM Trans. Inf. Syst. Secur. **13**(1), 7 (2009)
21. Jung, S.W., Jung, S.: HRP: a HMAC-based RFID mutual authentication protocol using PUF. In: ICOIN 2013, pp. 578–582, IEEE (2013)
22. Krishna, A.R., Narasimhan, S., Wang, X., Bhunia, S.: MECCA: a robust low-overhead PUF using embedded memory array. In: Preneel, B., Takagi, T. (eds.) CHES 2011. LNCS, vol. 6917, pp. 407–420. Springer, Heidelberg (2011)
23. Kulseng, L., Yu, Z., Wei, Y., Guan, Y.: Lightweight mutual authentication and ownership transfer for RFID systems. In: 2010 Proceedings IEEE INFOCOM, pp. 251–255, IEEE (2010)
24. Lee, M.Z., Dunn, A.M., Katz, J., Waters, B., Witchel, E.: Anon-pass: practical anonymous subscriptions. IEEE Secur. Priv. **12**(3), 20–27 (2014)
25. Maes, R.: Physically Unclonable Functions - Constructions Properties and Applications. Springer, Heidelberg (2013)
26. Maes, R., van der Leest, V.: Countering the effects of silicon aging on SRAM PUFs. In: HOST 2014, pp. 148–153, IEEE (2014)
27. Majzoobi, M., Rostami, M., Koushanfar, F., Wallach, D.S., Devadas, S.: Slender PUF protocol: a lightweight, robust, and secure authentication by substring matching. In: IEEE Security & Privacy, pp. 33–44, IEEE (2012)
28. Moriyama, D., Matsuo, S., Yung, M.: PUF-based RFID authentication secure and private under complete memory leakage. IACR Cryptology ePrint Archive 2013, 712 (2013). http://eprint.iacr.org/2013/712

29. Nedospasov, D., Seifert, J., Helfmeier, C., Boit, C.: Invasive PUF analysis. In: Fischer, W., Schmidt, J. (eds.) FDTC 2013, pp. 30–38. IEEE, Los Alamitos (2013)
30. Oren, Y., Sadeghi, A.-R., Wachsmann, C.: On the effectiveness of the remanence decay side-channel to clone memory-based PUFs. In: Bertoni, G., Coron, J.-S. (eds.) CHES 2013. LNCS, vol. 8086, pp. 107–125. Springer, Heidelberg (2013)
31. Paral, Z.S., Devadas, S.: Reliable and efficient PUF-based key generation using pattern matching. In: HOST 2011, pp. 128–133, IEEE (2011)
32. Rührmair, U., Sölter, J., Sehnke, F., Xu, X., Mahmoud, A., Stoyanova, V., Dror, G., Schmidhuber, J., Burleson, W., Devadas, S.: PUF modeling attacks on simulated and silicon data. IEEE Trans. Inf. Forensics Secur. 8(11), 1876–1891 (2013)
33. Rührmair, U., Xu, X., Sölter, J., Mahmoud, A., Majzoobi, M., Koushanfar, F., Burleson, W.: Efficient power and timing side channels for physical unclonable functions. In: Batina, L., Robshaw, M. (eds.) CHES 2014. LNCS, vol. 8731, pp. 476–492. Springer, Heidelberg (2014)
34. Rukhin, A., Soto, J., Nechvatal, J., Smid, M., Barker, E., Leigh, S., Levenson, M., Vangel, M., Banks, D., Heckert, A., Dray, J., Vo, S.: A statistical test suite for the validation of random number generators and pseudo random number generators for cryptographic applications. Special Publication 800–22 Revision 1a, April 2010
35. Sadeghi, A.R., Visconti, I., Wachsmann, C.: Enhancing RFID security and privacy by physically unclonable functions. In: Sadeghi, A.-R., Naccache, D. (eds.) Towards Hardware-Intrinsic Security, pp. 281–305. Springer, Heidelberg (2010)
36. Van Herrewege, A., Katzenbeisser, S., Maes, R., Peeters, R., Sadeghi, A.-R., Verbauwhede, I., Wachsmann, C.: Reverse fuzzy extractors: enabling lightweight mutual authentication for PUF-enabled RFIDs. In: Keromytis, A.D. (ed.) FC 2012. LNCS, vol. 7397, pp. 374–389. Springer, Heidelberg (2012)
37. Yu, M.D., M'Raïhi, D., Devadas, S., Verbauwhede, I.: Security and reliability properties of syndrome coding techniques used in PUF key generation. In: 38th GOMACTech Conference, pp. 1–4 (2013)

Improved Test Pattern Generation for Hardware Trojan Detection Using Genetic Algorithm and Boolean Satisfiability

Sayandeep Saha[1]([⊠]), Rajat Subhra Chakraborty[1],
Srinivasa Shashank Nuthakki[2], Anshul[1],
and Debdeep Mukhopadhyay[1]

[1] Department of Computer Science and Engineering,
Indian Institute of Technology Kharagpur, Kharagpur 721302, India
{sahasayandeep91,rschakraborty,debdeep}@cse.iitkgp.ernet.in
[2] Department of Electronics and Electrical Communication Engineering,
Indian Institute of Technology Kharagpur, Kharagpur 721302, India

Abstract. Test generation for *Hardware Trojan Horses* (HTH) detection is extremely challenging, as Trojans are designed to be triggered by very rare logic conditions at internal nodes of the circuit. In this paper, we propose a *Genetic Algorithm* (GA) based Automatic Test Pattern Generation (ATPG) technique, enhanced by automated solution to an associated *Boolean Satisfiability* problem. The main insight is that given a specific internal trigger condition, it is not possible to attack an arbitrary node (payload) of the circuit, as the effect of the induced logic malfunction by the HTH might not get propagated to the output. Based on this observation, a fault simulation based framework has been proposed, which enumerates the feasible payload nodes for a specific triggering condition. Subsequently, a compact set of test vectors is selected based on their ability to detect the logic malfunction at the feasible payload nodes, thus increasing their effectiveness. Test vectors generated by the proposed scheme were found to achieve higher detection coverage over large population of HTH in ISCAS benchmark circuits, compared to a previously proposed logic testing based Trojan detection technique.

1 Introduction

Modern electronic design and manufacturing practices make a design vulnerable to malicious modifications. Malicious circuitry embedded as a result of such modifications, commonly referred to as *Hardware Trojan Horses* (HTHs), have been demonstrated to be potent threats [6]. The stealthy nature of HTHs help them to evade conventional post-manufacturing testing. Once deployed in-field, HTHs get activated under certain rare conditions (depending on internal or external stimulus), and can potentially cause disastrous functional failure or leakage of secret information.

Recent research on HTHs mainly focuses on the modelling and detection of HTHs [4,13,16,17,19,21]. A vast majority of the detection mechanisms proposed

T. Güneysu and H. Handschuh (Eds.): CHES 2015, LNCS 9293, pp. 577–596, 2015.
DOI: 10.1007/978-3-662-48324-4_29

till date utilizes the anomaly in the side-channel signatures (e.g. delay, transient and leakage power) in the presence of HTH in the circuit [2,11,19]. However, side-channel approaches are susceptible to experimental and process variation noise. Thus, detection of small Trojans, especially combinatorial ones, becomes challenging through these approaches. Another approach is to employ design modification techniques to either prevent Trojan insertion or to make inserted Trojans more easily detectable [3,17,20].

An adversary may use very rare internal logic conditions to trigger a HTH, so that it remains well hidden during testing. Usually, it is assumed that the attacker will generate the trigger signal form a combination of internal nets of the circuit whose transition probability is very low. She may try to activate them simultaneously to their rare values thus achieving an extremely low triggering probability. Based on this assumption, several Trojan detection techniques have been proposed till date [5,17] which try to activate the Trojans either fully or partially by triggering the rare nodes, thus creating anomaly at the output logic values, or in some side channel signals viz. transient power. In [17,21] the authors proposed a design-for-testability (DFT) technique which inserts dummy scan flip-flops to make the transition probability of low transition nets higher in a special "authentication mode". However, it was found that careful attackers can evade this scheme easily [18]. Another powerful DFT technique is obfuscating or encrypting the design by inserting some extra gates in it [3,7], so that the actual functionality of the circuit is hidden, consequently making it difficult for an adversary to estimate the actual transition probabilities at the internal nodes. However, such "logic encryption" schemes have been recently broken [14].

Observing the vulnerability of DFT techniques against intelligent attackers, in [5] a test pattern generation scheme called *MERO* was proposed. *MERO* uses the philosophy of N-detect test to activate individually a set of nodes in a circuit to their less-probable values whose transition probabilities are below a specific threshold (termed *rareness threshold* and usually denoted by θ).

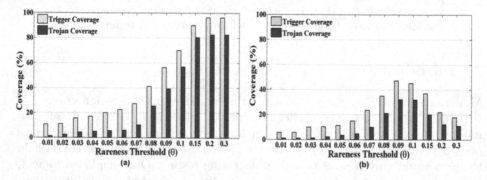

Fig. 1. Motivational example: variation of trigger and Trojan coverage with rareness threshold (θ) by the *MERO* [5] technique for c7552 (a) on sets of Trojans considered as in [5]; (b) on a set of rarely triggered Trojans (effective triggering probability below 10^{-6}).

The test generation is continued until each of the nodes gets activated to their rare values at least N-times. It was shown through simple theoretical analysis and experimental results that if N is sufficiently large, then a Trojan whose trigger condition is composed jointly of rare values at these rare nodes, is highly likely to be activated by the application of this test set.

Although *MERO* proposes a relatively simple heuristic for test generation it is found to have the following shortcomings:

1. When tested on a set of "hard-to-trigger" Trojans (with *triggering probability* in the range of 10^{-6} or less), the test vector set generated by *MERO* was found to have poor coverage both over triggering combinations and Trojans. Figure 1(b) presents the variation of trigger and Trojan coverage with the *rareness threshold* (θ) value for the ISCAS–85 circuit c7552, where the Trojan trigger probability is the *effective* Trojan triggering probability considering all the nodes together, unlike in [5], which considered trigger probability at individual nodes (see Fig. 1(a)). It was found that best coverage was achieved for θ in the range $0.08 - 0.12$, and this trend was consistent for all the benchmark circuits considered. However, the best achievable coverage was still below 50%, for even circuits of moderate size like c7552.
2. Although individual activation of each individual rare nodes at least N-times increases the activation probability of rare node combinations on average, there is always a finite probability that combinations with extremely low activation probability will not be triggered for a given value of N. As a result, even for small ISCAS–85 circuits like c432, the *MERO* test generation method misses some rare node patterns even after several independent runs. This fact can be utilized by an intelligent adversary.
3. *MERO* explores a relatively small numbers of test vectors, as the heuristic perturbs only a single bit at a time of an obtained test vector to generate new test vectors.
4. Another problem with the *MERO* algorithm is that, **while generating the test vectors, it only considers the activation of the triggering conditions, and ignores whether the triggered Trojan actually caused any logic malfunction at the primary output of the circuit under test.**

1.1 Main Idea and Our Contribution

Motivated by the above mentioned shortcomings of [5], in this paper we propose an improved ATPG scheme to detect small combinational and sequential HTHs, which are otherwise often difficult to detect by side channel analysis, or can bypass design modification based detection schemes. We note that **for higher effectiveness, a test generation algorithm for Trojan detection must simultaneously consider trigger coverage and Trojan coverage.** Firstly, we introduce a combined *Genetic Algorithm* (GA) and Boolean satisfiability (SAT) based approach for test pattern generation. GA has been used in the past for fault simulation based test generation [15]. GA is attractive for getting reasonably good test coverage over the fault list very quickly, because of the inherent parallelism of GA which enables relatively rapid exploration of a search space. However, it does not guarantee the detection of all possible faults, specially for those which are hard to detect. On the other hand, SAT based test generation has been found to be remarkably useful for hard-to-detect faults. However, it targets the faults one by one, and thus incurs higher execution time for easy-to-detect faults which typically represent the majority of faults [8]. It has another interesting feature that it can declare whether a fault is untestable or not.

In case of HTH, the number of candidate trigger combinations has an exponential dependence on the number of rare nodes considered. Even if we limit the number of Trojan inputs to four (because of VLSI design and side–channel information leakage considerations), the count is quite large. Thus, we have a large candidate trigger list and it is not possible to handle each fault in that list sequentially. However, many of these trigger conditions are not actually satisfiable, and thus cannot constitute a feasible trigger. Hence, we combine the "best of both worlds" for GA and SAT based test generation. The rationale is that most of the easy-to-excite trigger conditions, as well as a significant number of hard-to-excite trigger conditions will be detected by the GA within reasonable execution time. The remaining unresolved trigger patterns are input to the SAT tool; if any of these trigger conditions is feasible, then SAT returns the corresponding test vector. Otherwise, the pattern will be declared unsolvable by the SAT tool itself. As we show later, this combined strategy is found to perform significantly better than *MERO*. In the second phase of the scheme, we refine the test set generated by GA and SAT, by judging its effectiveness from the perspective of potency of the triggered Trojans. For each feasible trigger combination found in the previous step, we find most of the possible payloads using a fault simulator. For this, **we model the effect of each Trojan instance (defined by a combination of a feasible trigger condition and the payload node) as a stuck-at fault, and test whether the fault can be propagated to the output by the same test vector which triggered the Trojan. This step helps to find out a compact test set which remarkably improves the Trojan coverage.** To sum up, the following are the main contributions of this paper:

1. An improved ATPG heuristic for small combinational and sequential HTH detection is presented which utilizes two well known computational tools, GA and SAT. The proposed heuristic is able to detect HTH instances triggered by extremely rare internal node conditions, while having acceptable execution time. Previous work has reported that partial activation of the Trojan with accompanying high sensitivity side channel analysis is quite effective in detecting large HTHs [17], but not so effective for ultra-small Trojans. Hence, our work fills an important gap in the current research.
2. The tuning of the test vector set considering the possible payloads for each trigger combination makes the test set more compact, and increases its effectiveness of exploring the Trojan space.

3. The relative efficacy of the proposed scheme with respect to the scheme proposed in [5] has been demonstrated through experimental results on a subset of ISCAS–85 and ISCAS–89 circuits.
4. Since the triggering condition, corresponding triggering test vectors, as well as the possible payload information for each of the feasible triggers are generated during the execution, a valuable Trojan database for each circuit is created, which may be utilized for diagnosis purposes too. This database is enhanced for multiple runs of the algorithm, because of the inherent randomized nature of the GA which enables newer portions of the Trojan design space to be explored.

The rest of the paper is organized as follows. Section 2 presents a brief introduction to GA and SAT, as relevant in the context of ATPG for Trojan detection. The complete ATPG scheme is described in Sect. 3. Experimental results are presented and analyzed in Sect. 4, along with discussions on the possible application of the proposed scheme for Trojan diagnosis and side channel analysis based Trojan detection. The paper is concluded in Sect. 5, with directions of future work.

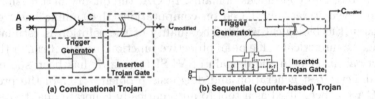

Fig. 2. Example of (a) combinational and (b) sequential (counter-like) Trojan. The combinational Trojan is triggered by the simultaneous occurrence of logic–1 at two internal nodes. The sequential (counter-like) Trojan is triggered by 2^k positive $(0 \to 1)$ transitions at the input of the flip-flops.

2   GA and SAT in the Context of ATPG for Trojan Detection

2.1   Hardware Trojan Models

We consider simple combinational and sequential HTHs, where a HTH instance is triggered by the simultaneous occurrence of rare logic values at one or more internal nodes of the circuit. We find the rare nodes $(\mathcal{R})$ of the circuit with a probabilistic analysis. Details of this analysis can be found in [17,21]. Once activated, the Trojan flips the logic value at an internal *payload* node. Figure 2 shows the type of Trojans considered by us.

Notice that it is usually infeasible to enumerate all HTHs in a given circuit. Hence, we are forced to restrict ourselves to analysis results obtained from a randomly selected subset of Trojans. The cardinality of the set of Trojans selected depends on the size of the circuit being analyzed. Since we are interested only in small Trojans, a random sample S of up to four rare node combinations is considered. Let us denote the set of rare nodes as $\mathcal{R}$, with $|\mathcal{R}| = r$ for a specific rareness threshold (θ). The set of all possible rare node combinations is then the *power set* of $\mathcal{R}$, denoted by $2^{\mathcal{R}}$). Thus, the population of Trojans under consideration is the set $\mathcal{K}$, where $\mathcal{K} \subseteq 2^{\mathcal{R}}$ and $|\mathcal{K}|$ is $\binom{r}{1} + \binom{r}{2} + \binom{r}{3} + \binom{r}{4}$. Thus, $S \subseteq \mathcal{K}$.

We intentionally chose $\theta = 0.1$ for our experiments, which is lower than the value considered in [5] $(\theta = 0.2)$. The choice is based on the observed coverage trends of our experiments on "hard-to-trigger" Trojans in Sect. 1, where it was observed that the coverage is maximized for θ values in the range $0.08 - 0.12$ for most ISCAS benchmark circuits.

2.2   Genetic Algorithm (GA) for ATPG

Genetic algorithm (GA) is an well known bio-inspired, stochastic, evolutionary search algorithm based upon the principles of natural selection [10]. GA has been widely used in diverse fields to tackle difficult non-convex optimization problems, both in discrete and continuous domains. In GA, the quality of a feasible solution is improved iteratively, based on computations that mimic basic genetic operations in the biological world. The quality of the solution is estimated by evaluating the numerical value of an objective function, usually termed the "fitness function" in GA. In the domain of VLSI testing, it has been successfully used for difficult test generation and diagnosis problems [15]. In the proposed scheme, GA has been used as a tool to automatically generate quality test patterns for Trojan triggering. During test generation using GA, two points were emphasized:

- an effort to generate test vectors that would activate the most number of sampled trigger combinations, and,
- an effort to generate test vectors for hard-to-trigger combinations.

However, as mentioned in the previous section, the major effort for GA was dedicated to meet the first objective.

To meet both of the goals, we used a special data structure as well as a proper fitness function. The data structure is a hash table which contains the triggering combinations and their corresponding activating test vectors. Let S denote the sampled set of trigger conditions being considered. Each entry in the hash table $(\mathcal{D})$ is a tuple $(s, \{t_i\})$, where $s \in S$ is a trigger combination from the sampled set (S) and $\{t_i\}$ is the set of distinct test vectors activating the trigger combination s. Note that, a single test vector t_i may trigger multiple trigger combinations and thus can be present multiple times in the data structure for different trigger combinations (s). The data structure is keyed with trigger combination s. Initially, $\mathcal{D}$ is empty; during the GA run, $\mathcal{D}$ is updated dynamically, whenever new triggering combinations from S are found to be satisfied. The fitness function is expressed as:

$$f(t) = R_{count}(t) + w * I(t) \tag{1}$$

where $f(t)$ is the fitness value of a test vector t; $R_{count}(t)$ counts the number of rare nodes triggered by the test vector t; w (> 1) is a constant scaling factor, and $I(t)$ is a function which returns the *relative improvement* of the database $\mathcal{D}$ due to the test vector t. The term *"relative improvement of the database"* ($I(t)$) can be explained as follows. Let us interpret the data structure $\mathcal{D}$ as a histogram where the bins are defined by unique trigger combinations $s \in \mathcal{S}$, and each bin contains its corresponding activating test vectors $\{t_i\}$. Before each update of the database, we calculate the number of test patterns in each bin which is to be updated. The *relative improvement* is defined as:

$$I(t) = \frac{n_2(s) - n_1(s)}{n_2(s)} \tag{2}$$

where: $n_1(s)$ is the number of test patterns in bin s before update, and $n_2(s)$ is the number of test patterns in bin s after update.

Note that for each test pattern t that enters the database D, the numerator will be either 0 or 1 for an arbitrary trigger combination s. However, the denominator will have larger values with the minimum value being 1. Thus, for any bin s, when it gets its 1st test vector, the above mentioned ratio achieves the maximum value 1, whereas when a bin gets its nth test vector, the fraction is $\frac{1}{n}$. The value gradually decreases as the number of test vectors in s increases. This implies that **as a newer test vector is generated, its contribution is considered more important if it has been able to trigger an yet unactivated trigger condition s, than if it activates a trigger condition that has already been activated by other test vector(s)**. Note that, for bins s having zero test vectors before and after update (i.e. trigger conditions which could not be activated at the first try), we assign a very small value 10^{-7} for numerical consistency. The scaling factor w is proportional to the relative importance of the relative improvement term; in our implementation, w was set to have the value 10.

The rationale behind the two terms in the fitness function is as follows. The first term in the fitness function prefers test patterns that simultaneously activate as many trigger nodes as possible, thus recording test vectors each of which can potentially cover many trigger combinations. The inclusion of the second term has two effects. Firstly, the selection pressure of GA is set towards hard-to-activate patterns by giving higher fitness value to those test patterns that are capable of hard–to–trigger conditions. Secondly, it also helps the GA to explore the sampled trigger combination space evenly. To illustrate this, let us consider the following example.

Suppose, we have five rare nodes r_1, r_2, r_3, r_4, r_5. We represent the activation of these five nodes by a binary vector $\mathbf{r}$ of length five, where $r_i = 1$ denotes that the ith rare node has been activated to its rare value and $r_i = 0$ otherwise. Thus, a pattern 11110 implies the scenario where the first four rare nodes have been simultaneously activated. Now, the test vector t, which generates this rare node triggering pattern also triggers the patterns 10000, 01000, 00100, 00010, 11000, ..., 11100, i.e. any subset of the triggered rare nodes. Mathematically, **if there are in total r rare nodes and r' rare nodes are simultaneously triggered in a pattern $(r' < r)$ by a test vector t, then the $2^{r'}$ subsets of the triggered rare nodes are also triggered by the same test vector. Hence, maximizing r' increases the coverage over the trigger combination sample set.**

The test generation problem is modelled as a maximization problem, and solved using a variation of GA termed *Binary Genetic Algorithm* (BGA) [10]. Each individual in the population is a bit pattern called a "chromosome", which represents an individual test vector. Two operations generate new individuals by operating on these chromosomes: *crossover* and *mutation*. *Crossover* refers to the exchange of parts of two chromosomes to generate new chromosomes, while *mutation* refers to the random (probabilistic) flipping of bits of the chromosomes to give rise to new behaviour. Figure 3 shows examples of two–point crossover and mutation in BGA. We used a two–point crossover and binary mutation, with a crossover probability of 0.9 and mutation probability of 0.05, respectively. The collection of individuals at every iteration is termed a *population*. A population size of 200 was used for combinatorial circuits and 500 for sequential circuits. Two terminating conditions were used: (i) when the total number of distinct test vectors in the database crosses a certain threshold value $\#T$, or (ii) if 1000 generations had been reached. The initialization of the population is done by test vectors satisfying some rare node combinations from the sample set. These rare node combinations are randomly selected and the test vectors were found using SAT tools (details are given in the following subsection). Algorithm 1, shows the complete test generation scheme using GA. Notice that the initial test vector population is generated by solving a small number of triggering conditions using SAT.

Among the sampled trigger instances, many might not be satisfiable, as we do not have any prior information about them. Moreover, although GA traverses the given trigger combination sample space reasonably rapidly, it cannot guarantee to be able to generate test vectors that would activate all the hard-to-trigger patterns. Thus, even after the GA test generation step, we were

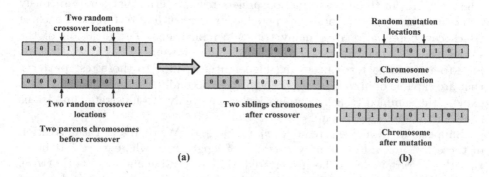

Fig. 3. Example of two–point crossover and mutation in Binary Genetic Algorithm.

Algorithm 1. *TESTGEN_GA*

/* Generate Triggering Test Vectors Using Genetic Algorithm */

Input: Circuit Netlist, Set of rare nodes ($\mathcal{R}$), Set of sampled trigger combinations ($\mathcal{S}$), G_{max}, T_{max}, crossover probability, mutation probability, (empty) trigger database ($\mathcal{D}$)

Output: Data structure ($\mathcal{D}$) filled with triggering test vectors, set of unsatisfied trigger combinations ($\mathcal{S}' \subset \mathcal{S}$)

1: Fill $\mathcal{D}$ with tuples (s, ϕ), $\forall s \in \mathcal{S}$
2: Select a random subset $\mathcal{S}_{init} \subset \mathcal{S}$, such that $|\mathcal{S}_{init}| = k * |\mathcal{S}|$
   /* k is 0.025 for combinatorial and 0.055 for sequential circuits */
3: Solve all trigger combinations $s \in \mathcal{S}_{init}$ using SAT tool and generate corresponding set of test vectors (T_{init})
4: Update $\mathcal{D}$ with tuples (s, t). where $s \in \mathcal{S}_{init}$ and $t \in T_{init}$
5: **set** *vectcount* $\leftarrow |T_{init}|$
6: **set** *gencount* $\leftarrow 0$
7: **set** $\mathcal{S}' \leftarrow \phi$
8: Initialize the population of GA (P) with T_{init}.
9: **repeat**
10:   **for all** $t \in P$ **do**
11:     Simulate the circuit with test vector t and find the corresponding rare node activation pattern (**r**).
12:     Search $\mathcal{D}$ for all triggering patterns covered by **r**.
13:     Compute the fitness using Eq. 1
14:     Update $\mathcal{D}$ with all tuples (s, t), where s is a triggering pattern covered by **r**.
15:     **set** *vectcount* $\leftarrow$ *vectcount* $+ 1$
16:   **end for**
17:   Perform Crossover on P
18:   Perform Mutation on P
19:   Update P with the best individuals
20:   **set** *gencount* $\leftarrow$ *gencount* $+ 1$
21: **until** (*gencount* $\leq G_{max}$ || *vectcount* $\leq T_{max}$)
22: **for all** $(s, \{t_i\}) \in \mathcal{D}$ **do**
23:   **if** ($\{t_i\} = \phi$) **then**
24:     Include s in $\mathcal{S}'$
25:   **end if**
26: **end for**

---

left with some trigger combinations among which some are not satisfiable and others are extremely hard to detect. However, as the number of such remaining combinations are quite less (typically 5–10 % of the selected samples) we can apply SAT tools to solve them. We nest describe the application of SAT in our ATPG scheme.

2.3   SAT for Hard–to–Activate Trigger Conditions

Boolean Satisfiability (SAT) tools are being used to solve ATPG problems since the last decade [8]. They are found to be robust, often succeeding to find test patterns in large and pathological ATPG problems, where traditional ATPG algorithms have been found wanting. Unlike classical ATPG algorithms, SAT

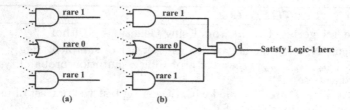

Fig. 4. Illustration: formulation of a SAT instance which activates 3 rare nodes simultaneously.

Algorithm 2. TESTGEN_SAT

/* Solve the triggering patterns which remain unsolved by GA ($\mathcal{S}'$) using SAT tool */

Input: Set of triggering patterns unsolved by GA ($\mathcal{S}'$), Data structure $\mathcal{D}$
Output: Updated $\mathcal{D}$ with triggering patterns generated by SAT tool
1: **for all** $s \in \mathcal{S}'$ **do**
2:     Input the triggering combination to SAT tool.
3:     **if** (SAT(s) = SOLVED) **then**
4:         Retrieve corresponding test vector t.
5:         Update $\mathcal{D}$ with tuple (s, t)
6:         $\mathcal{S}_{sat} \leftarrow \{s\}$
7:     **else**
8:         $\mathcal{S}_{unsat} \leftarrow \{s\}$
9:     **end if**
10: **end for**

---

solver based schemes do not work on the circuit representation (e.g. netlist of logic gates) directly. Instead, they formulate the test pattern generation problem as one or more SAT problems. A n-variable Boolean formula $f(x_1, x_2, \ldots, x_n)$ in *Conjunctive Normal Form* (CNF) is said to be *satisfiable* if there exists a value assignment for the n variables, such that $f = 1$. If no such assignment exists, f is said to be *unsatisfiable*. Boolean satisfiability is an NP-Complete problem. Sophisticated heuristics are used to solve SAT problems, and powerful SAT solver software tools have become available in recent times (many of them are free). The ATPG problem instance is first converted into a CNF and then input to a SAT solver. If the solver returns a satisfiable assignment within a specified time the problem instance is considered to be satisfiable and unsatisfiable, otherwise.

As mentioned previously, we apply the SAT tool only for those trigger combinations for which GA fails to generate any test vector. Let us denote the set of such trigger combinations as $\mathcal{S}' \subseteq \mathcal{S}$. We consider each trigger combination $s \in \mathcal{S}'$, and input it to the SAT tool. This SAT problem formulation is illustrated by an example in Fig. 4. Let us consider the three rare nodes shown in Fig. 4(a) with their rare values. To create a satisfiability formula which simultaneously activates these three nodes to their rare value, we construct the circuit shown in Fig. 4(b). The SAT instance is thus formed which tries to achieve a value 1 at wire(node) d.

After completion of this step, most trigger combinations in the set $\mathcal{S}'$ will be found to be satisfiable by the SAT tool, which will also return the corresponding test vectors. However, some of the trigger combinations will still remain unsolved, which would be lebelled as unsatisfiable. Thus the set $\mathcal{S}'$ is partitioned into two disjoint subsets $\mathcal{S}_{sat}$ and $\mathcal{S}_{unsat}$. The first subset is accepted and the data structure $\mathcal{D}$ is updated with the patterns in this subset, whereas the second subset is discarded. This part of the flow has been summarized in Algorithm 2.

The basic ATPG mechanism now in place, we next describe the refinement of the scheme to take the impact of the payload into consideration, and also achieve test compaction in the process.

3 Improving the Proposed Scheme: Payload Aware Test Set Selection and Test Compaction

3.1 Payload Aware Test Vector Selection

Finding out proper trigger-payload pairs to enumerate feasible HTH instances a is non-trivial computational problem. In combinational circuits, one necessary condition for a node to be a payload is that its topological rank must be higher than the topologically highest node of the trigger combination, otherwise there is a possibility of forming a "combinational loop"; however, this is not a sufficient condition. In general, a successful Trojan triggering event provides no guarantee regarding its propagation to the primary output to cause functional failure of the circuit. As an example, let us consider the circuit of Fig. 5(a). The Trojan is triggered by an input vector 1111. Figures 5(b) and 5(c) show two potential payload positions. It can be easily seen that independent of the applied test vector at in circuit input, for position-1 the Trojan effect gets masked and cannot be detected. On the other hand, the Trojan effect at position-2 can be detected.

It is important to identify, for each trigger combination, the constrained primary input values. For this, we consider each Trigger combination and their corresponding set of trigger test vectors at a time. To be precise, we consider the entries $(s, \{t_i\})$ from the database $\mathcal{D}$, one at a time. Let us denote the set of test vectors corresponding to a specific s as $\{t_i^s\}$. Next, for each test vector $t \in \{t_i^s\}$, we find out which of the primary inputs, if any, remains static at a specific value (either logic–0 or logic–1). These input positions are the positions needed to be constrained to trigger the triggering combination. We fill the rest

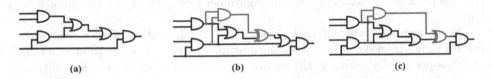

(a)   (b)   (c)

Fig. 5. Impact of Trojan payload selection: (a) golden circuit; (b) payload-1 which has no effect on output; (c) payload-2 which has effect on the output.

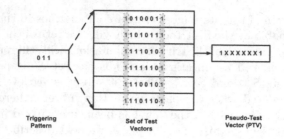

Fig. 6. PTV generation example: (a) triggering pattern; (b) corresponding set of test vectors; (c) generated PTV.

Algorithm 3. *SELECT_TEST_VECT*

/* Select Payload Aware test vectors */
Input: Data structure $\mathcal{D}$, circuit netlist
Output: Final test set (T_{final})
1: set $T_{final} \leftarrow \phi$
2: **for all** $(s, \{t_i\}) \in \mathcal{D}$ **do**
3:    Retrieve the test vector set $\{t_i\}$
4:    Compute the corresponding PTV
5:    **do** 3-value logic simulation and create the initial fault list $\mathcal{F}_s$
6:    **if** $|\{t_i^s\}| > 5$ **then**
7:       set $Test\_set \leftarrow \{t_i^s\}$
8:    **else**
9:       Generate extra test vectors $\{t_{ext}^s\}$ by randomly filling the X positions of the PTV
10:      Simulate the circuit with $\{t_{ext}^s\}$ and keep vectors satisfying s
11:      set $Test\_set \leftarrow \{t_i^s\} \cup \{t_{ext}^s\}$
12:   **end if**
13:   **do** fault simulation using HOPE with inputs $\mathcal{F}_s$ and $Test\_set$
14:   Retrieve $\mathcal{F}_{detected}^s \subseteq \mathcal{F}_s$ and $Test\_set_{detected} \subseteq Test\_set$
15:   Keep the subset $Test\_set_{comp}$ of $Test\_set_{detected}$, which completely covers $\mathcal{F}_{detected}^s$.
16:   set $T_{final} \leftarrow Test\_set_{comp}$
17: **end for**
18: **return** T_{final}

---

of the input positions with don't-care (X) values, thus creating a single test-vector containing 0, 1 and X values. We call such 3-valued vectors *Pseudo Test Vector* (PTV). Figure 6 illustrates the process of PTV generation with a simple example, where the leftmost and the rightmost positions of the vectors are at logic-1.

At the next step, we perform a three-value logic simulation of the circuit with the PTV and note down values obtained at all the internal wires (nodes) which are at topologically higher positions from the nodes in the trigger combination.

Then for each of these nodes we consider a stuck-at fault according to the following rule:

1. If the value at that node is 1, we consider a stuck-at-zero fault there.
2. If the value at that node is 0, we consider a stuck-at-one fault there.
3. If the value at that node is X, we consider a both stuck-at-one and stuck-at-zero fault at that location.

At the next step, this fault list ($\mathcal{F}_s$) and the set of test vectors considered ($\{t_i^s\}$) is input to a fault simulator. We used the HOPE [12] fault simulator in diagnostic mode for this purpose. The output will be the set of faults that are detected ($\mathcal{F}_{detected}^s \subseteq \mathcal{F}_s$) as well as the corresponding test vectors which detect them. The detected faults constitutes the list of potential payload positions for the trigger combination. Thus, after detecting the feasible payloads, we greedily select a subset of the test vector set $\mathcal{T}_s \subseteq \{t_i^s\}$ which achieves complete coverage for the entire fault list. The test vectors belonging to the rest of $\{t_i^s\}$, i.e. $\{t_i^s\} - \mathcal{T}_s$, can be discarded to be redundant. Although a greedy selection, we found that this step reduces the overall test set size significantly. Further test compaction can be achieved, at the cost of additional computational overhead, using specialized test compaction schemes (Fig. 7).

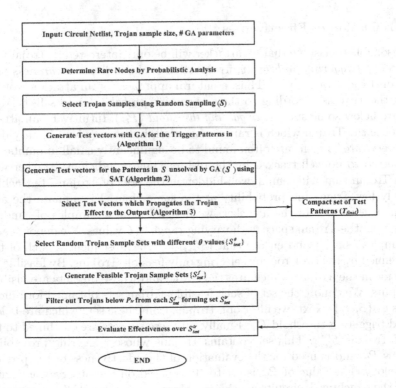

Fig. 7. The complete test generation and evaluation flow.

One important point worth noting is that, it is not guaranteed by the proposed test generation scheme that all possible test vectors which trigger a particular trigger combination will get generated. As the fault list $(\mathcal{F}_s)$ is calculated only based on the test vectors in $\{t_i^s\}$, it might not cover all possible payloads for a trigger combination s. However, for each test vector $t \in \{t_i^s\}$, it is guaranteed that all feasible payloads will be enumerated. Further, it can be deterministically decided if a test vector $t \in \{t_i^s\}$ will have any payload or not. In fact, for most of the trigger combinations, we got test vectors which are either redundant, or doesn't have any payload. It is also observed that the number of test vectors for some hard-to-activate trigger combinations are really low (typically 1 to 5 vectors). For these cases, the fault coverage may be poor and many payloads for the trigger combination remains unexplored. To resolve this issue, we add some extra test vectors derived by filling the don't care bits (if any) of the PTV. This is only done for those trigger combinations for which the number of triggering vectors are less than five. These newly generated vectors are needed to be checked by simulation so that they successfully trigger the corresponding triggering combination, before their inclusion to the test set $\{t_i^s\}$. This step is found to improve the test coverage. The compacted test vector selection scheme is described in Algorithm 3. At the end of this step, we obtain a compact set of test vectors with high trigger and Trojan coverage.

3.2   Evaluation of Effectiveness

It is reasonable to assume that an attacker will be only interested in Trojans with low *effective triggering probability*, irrespective of the individual *rareness values* of the constituent rare nodes. Thus, a natural approach for an attacker would be to rank the Trojans according to their *triggering probability* and select Trojans which are below some specific *triggering threshold* (P_{tr}). Intuitively, an attacker may choose the Trojan which is rarest among all, but it may lead to easy detection as very rare Trojans are often found to be significantly small in number and are expected to be well tracked by the tester. Thus, a judicious attacker would select a Trojan that will remain well-hidden in the pool of Trojans, but achieves extremely low Triggering probability at the same time. To simulate the above mentioned behaviour of the attacker, we first select new samples of candidate Trojans from the Trojan space with varying range of θ values. We denote each of such samples as $\mathcal{S}_{test}^\theta$ and ensure that $|\mathcal{S}_{test}^\theta| = |\mathcal{S}|$. Subsequently, each of these sets is refined by the SAT tool by selecting only feasible Trojans. By feasible Trojans we mean the Trojans which are triggerable and whose impacts are visible at the outputs. We denote the set of such feasible Trojan sets obtained for different θ values as $\{\mathcal{S}_{test}^f\}$. Next, we filter out Trojans from these sets which are below a specified triggering threshold P_{tr}. Finally, all these subsets are combined to form a set of Trojans $\mathcal{S}_{test}^{tr}$. This set contains Trojans whose triggering probabilities are below P_{tr} and is used for the evaluation of the effectiveness of the proposed methodology. The value of P_{tr} is set to 10^{-6} based on the observation that for most of the benchmark circuits considered, there are roughly 30% Trojans which have triggering probabilities below 10^{-6}. Also, below the range $(10^{-7} - 10^{-8})$

the number of Trojans are extremely low, which may leave the attacker only with a few options.

4 Experimental Results and Discussion

4.1 Experimental Setup

The test generation scheme, including the GA and the evaluation framework, were implemented using C++. We used the *zchaff* SAT solver [9] and *HOPE* fault simulator [12]. We restricted ourselves to a random sample of $100,000$ trigger combinations [5], each having up to four rare nodes as trigger nodes. We also implemented the *MERO* methodology side by side for comparison. We evaluated the effectiveness of the proposed scheme on a subset of ISCAS-85 and ISCAS-89 benchmark circuits, with all ISCAS-89 sequential circuits converted to full scan mode. The implementation was performed and executed on a Linux workstation with a 3 GHz processor and 8 GB of main memory.

4.2 Test Set Evaluation Results

Table 1 presents a comparison of the testset lengths generated by the proposed scheme, with that generated by *MERO*. It also demonstrates the impact of Algo-3, by comparing the test vector count before Algo-3 (TC_{GASAT}) and after Algo-3 (TC_f). As would be evident, for similar number of test patterns the proposed scheme achieves significantly better trigger as well as Trojan coverage than *MERO*. The gate count of the circuits and the time required to generate the corresponding testsets is also presented to exhibit the scalability of the ATPG heuristic.

Table 1. Comparison of the proposed scheme with *MERO* with respect to testset length.

Ckt.	Gates	Testset (before Algo.-3)	Testset (after Algo.-3)	Testset (MERO)	Runtime (sec.)
c880	451	6674	5340	6284	9798.84
c2670	776	10,420	8895	9340	11299.74
c3540	1134	17,284	16,278	15,900	15720.19
c5315	1743	17,022	14,536	15,850	15877.53
c7552	2126	17,400	15,989	16,358	16203.02
s15850	9772	37,384	37,052	36,992	17822.67
s35932	16065	7849	7078	7343	14273.09
s38417	22179	53,700	50,235	52,735	19635.22

Table 2. Trigger and Trojan coverage at various stages of the proposed scheme. at $\theta = 0.1$ for random sample of Trojans upto 4 rare node triggers (Sample size is $100,000$ for combinational circuits and $10,000$ for sequential circuits).

Ckt.	GA only		GA + SAT		GA + SAT + Algo. 3	
	Trig. Cov.	Troj. Cov.	Trig. Cov.	Troj. Cov.	Trig. Cov.	Troj. Cov.
c880	92.12	83.59	96.19	85.70	96.19	85.70
c2670	81.63	69.27	87.31	75.17	87.15	75.82
c3540	80.58	57.21	82.79	59.07	81.55	60.00
c5315	83.79	64.45	85.11	65.04	85.91	71.13
c7552	73.73	64.05	78.16	68.95	77.94	69.88
s15850	64.91	51.95	70.36	57.30	68.18	57.30
s35932	81.15	71.77	81.90	73.52	81.79	73.52
s38417	55.03	29.33	61.76	36.50	56.95	38.10

Table 2 presents the improvement in trigger and Trojan coverage at the end of each individual step of the proposed scheme, to establish the importance of each individual step. From the table, it is evident that the first two steps consistently increase the trigger and Trojan coverage. However, after the application of payload aware test set selection (Algo-3), the trigger coverage slightly decreases for some circuits, whereas the Trojan coverage slightly increases. The decrement in trigger coverage is explained by the fact that some of the trigger combinations do not have any corresponding payload – as a result of which they are removed. In contrary, the addition of some "extra test vectors" by Algo-3 helps to improve the Trojan coverage.

Table 3 presents the trigger and Trojan coverage for eight benchmark circuits, compared $MERO$ test patterns with $N = 1000$ and $\theta = 0.1$. In order to make a fair comparison, we first count the number of distinct test vectors generated by $MERO$ (TC_{MERO}) with the above mentioned setup, and then set GA to run until the number of distinct test vectors in the database becomes higher than TC_{MERO}. We denote the number of distinct test vectors after GA run as TC_{GA}. Note that, the SAT step is performed after the GA run, and thus the total number of test vectors after the SAT step (TC_{GASAT}) is slightly higher than TC_{MERO}. The test vector count further reduces after the Algo-3 is run. We denote the final test vector count as TC_f.

To further illustrate the effectiveness of the proposed scheme, in Fig. 8 we compare the trigger and Trojan coverage obtained from $MERO$ with that of the proposed scheme, by varying the rareness threshold (θ) for the c7552 benchmark circuit. It is observed that the proposed scheme outperforms $MERO$ to a significant extent. Further, it is interesting to note that both $MERO$ and the proposed scheme achieve the best coverage at $\theta = 0.09$. The coverage gradually decreases towards both higher and lower values of θ. The reason is that for higher θ

Table 3. Comparison of trigger and Trojan Coverage among *MERO* patterns and patterns generated with the proposed scheme with $\theta = 0.1$; $N = 1000$ (for *MERO*) and for trigger combinations containing up to four rare nodes.

Ckt.	*MERO*		Proposed Scheme	
	Trigger Coverage	Trojan Coverage	Trigger Coverage	Trojan Coverage
c880	75.92	69.96	96.19	85.70
c2670	62.66	49.51	87.15	75.82
c3540	55.02	23.95	81.55	60.00
c5315	43.50	39.01	85.91	71.13
c7552	45.07	31.90	77.94	69.88
s15850	36.00	18.91	68.18	57.30
s35932	62.49	34.65	81.79	73.52
s38417	21.07	14.41	56.95	38.10

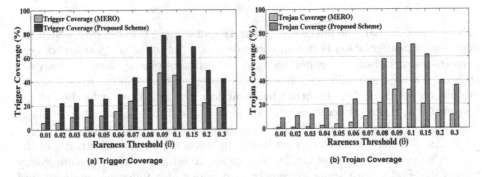

Fig. 8. Comparison of trigger and Trojan coverage of the proposed scheme with *MERO*, with varying triggering threshold (θ).

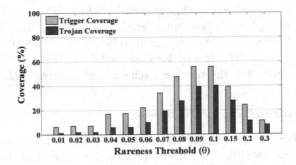

Fig. 9. Trigger and Trojan coverage of the proposed scheme on a set of special Trojans, which combine some easily triggerable nodes with some extremely rare nodes.

Table 4. Coverage comparison between *MERO* and the proposed Scheme for sequential Trojans. The sequential Trojan model considered is same as [5].

Ckt.	Trig. Cov. for Proposed Scheme		Trig. Cov. for *MERO*	
	Trojan State Count		Trojan State Count	
	2	4	2	4
s15850	64.91	45.55	31.70	26.00
s35932	78.97	70.38	58.84	49.59
s38417	48.00	42.17	16.11	8.01
Ckt.	Troj. Cov. for Proposed Scheme		Trig. Cov. for *MERO*	
	Trojan State Count		Trojan State Count	
	2	4	2	4
s15850	46.01	32.59	13.59	8.95
s35932	65.22	59.29	25.07	15.11
s38417	30.52	19.92	9.06	2.58

values (e.g. 0.2, 0.3), the initial candidate Trojan sample set ($\mathcal{S}$), over which the heuristic implementation is tuned, contains a large number of "easy-to-trigger" combinations. Hence, the generated test set remains biased towards "easy-to-trigger" Trojans and fails to achieve good coverage over the "hard-to-trigger" evaluation set used. On the other hand, at low θ values the cardinality of the test vector set created becomes very small as the number of potent Trojans at this range of θ is few, and they are sparsely dispersed in the candidate Trojan set $\mathcal{S}$. As a result, this small test set hardly achieves significant coverage over the Trojan space. The coverage for Trojans constructed by combining some easily triggerable nodes with some extremely rare nodes also follows a similar trend (shown in Fig. 9). It can be thus remarked that the tester should choose a θ value, so that the initial set $\mathcal{S}$ contains a good proportion of Trojans with low triggering probability, while also covering most of the moderately rare nodes.

Finally, we test our scheme with sequential Trojans. The counter based Trojan model as described in [5] was considered. We consider Trojans up to four states, as larger Trojans have been reported to be easily detectable by side channel analysis techniques [17]. It can be observed form Table 4 that as for the combinational circuits, the the proposed scheme outperforms *MERO*.

4.3   Application to Trojan Diagnosis

Diagnosis of a Trojan once it gets detected is important for system-level reliability enhancement. In [19], the authors proposed a gate-level-characterization (GLC) based Trojan diagnosis method. The scheme proposed in this paper can be leveraged for a test diagnosis methodology. The data structure $\mathcal{D}$ can be extended to a complete Trojan database, which will contain four-tuples (s, V, P, O), where s is a trigger combination, V is the set of corresponding triggering test vectors, P is the set of possible payloads, and O is the set of faulty outputs corresponding to the test patterns in V, due to the activation of some Trojan instance. Based on this information, one can design diagnosis schemes using simple *cause-effect-analysis*, or other more sophisticated techniques. The complete description of a diagnosis scheme is however out of the scope of this paper.

4.4   Application to Side Channel Analysis Based Trojan Detection

Most recent side-channel analysis techniques target the preferential activation of a specific region of the circuit, keeping the other regions dormant [1,19], since side channel analysis is more effective if the Trojan is activated, at least partially [17]. Hence, the proposed technique, with its dual emphasis on test pattern generation directed towards triggering of Trojans, as well as propagation of the Trojan effect to the primary output, can be a valuable component of a side channel analysis based Trojan detection methodology.

5   Conclusions

Detection of ultra small Hardware Trojans has traditionally proved challenging by both logic testing and side channel analysis. We have developed an ATPG scheme for detection of HTHs dependent on rare input triggering conditions, based on the dual strengths of Genetic Algorithm and Boolean Satisfiability. The technique achieves good test coverage and compaction and also outperforms a previously proposed ATPG heuristic for detecting HTHs for benchmark circuits. Future research would be directed towards developing comprehensive Trojan diagnosis methodologies based on the database created by the current technique.

Acknowledgments. The authors would like to thank the anonymous reviewers and Dr. Georg T. Becker of Ruhr-Universität Bochum for their valuable suggestions regarding this work. The authors also wish to thank Indian Institute of Technology, Kharagpur for providing partial funding support through the project named "Next Generation Secured Internet of Things" (NGI).

References

1. Banga, M., Hsiao, M.: A region based approach for the identification of hardware Trojans. In: Proceedings of International Symposium on HOST, pp. 40–47 (2008)
2. Banga, M., Chandrasekar, M., Fang, L., Hsiao, M.S.: Guided test generation for isolation and detection of embedded Trojans in ICs. In: Proceedings of the 18th ACM Great Lakes Symposium on VLSI, pp. 363–366. ACM (2008)
3. Chakraborty, R.S., Bhunia, S.: Security against hardware Trojan through a novel application of design obfuscation. In: Proceedings of the 2009 International Conference on Computer-Aided Design, pp. 113–116. ACM (2009)

4. Chakraborty, R.S., Narasimhan, S., Bhunia, S.: Hardware Trojan: Threats and emerging solutions. In: Proceedings of IEEE International Workshop on HLDVT, pp. 166–171. IEEE (2009)
5. Chakraborty, R.S., Wolff, F., Paul, S., Papachristou, C., Bhunia, S.: *MERO*: a statistical approach for hardware trojan detection. In: Clavier, C., Gaj, K. (eds.) CHES 2009. LNCS, vol. 5747, pp. 396–410. Springer, Heidelberg (2009)
6. DARPA: TRUST in Integrated Circuits (TIC) (2007). http://www.darpa.mil/MTO/solicitations/baa07-24
7. Dupuis, S., Ba, P.S., Di Natale, G., Flottes, M.L., Rouzeyre, B.: A novel hardware logic encryption technique for thwarting illegal overproduction and Hardware Trojans. In: 2014 IEEE 20th International On-Line Testing Symposium (IOLTS), pp. 49–54. IEEE (2014)
8. Eggersglüß, S., Drechsler, R.: High Quality Test Pattern Generation and Boolean Satisfiability. Springer, US (2012)
9. Fu, Z., Marhajan, Y., Malik, S.: Zchaff sat solver (2004). http://www.princeton.edu/chaff
10. Goldberg, D.E.: Genetic algorithms. Pearson Education, Boston (2006)
11. Jin, Y., Makris, Y.: Hardware Trojan detection using path delay fingerprint. In: IEEE International Workshop on Hardware-Oriented Security and Trust, 2008, HOST 2008, pp. 51–57. IEEE (2008)
12. Lee, H.K., Ha, D.S.: HOPE: an efficient parallel fault simulator for synchronous sequential circuits. IEEE Trans. Comput. Aided Des. Integr. Circ. Syst. **15**(9), 1048–1058 (1996)
13. Mingfu, X., Aiqun, H., Guyue, L.: Detecting hardware trojan through heuristic partition and activity driven test pattern generation. In: Communications Security Conference (CSC), pp. 1–6. IET (2014)
14. Rajendran, J., Pino, Y., Sinanoglu, O., Karri, R.: Security analysis of logic obfuscation. In: Proceedings of the 49th Annual Design Automation Conference, pp. 83–89. ACM (2012)
15. Rudnick, E.M., Patel, J.H., Greenstein, G.S., Niermann, T.M.: A genetic algorithm framework for test generation. IEEE Trans. Comput. Aided Des. Integr. Circ. Syst. **16**(9), 1034–1044 (1997)
16. Salmani, H., Tehranipoor, M., Plusquellic, J.: A layout-aware approach for improving localized switching to detect hardware Trojans in integrated circuits. In: 2010 IEEE International Workshop on Information Forensics and Security (WIFS), pp. 1–6. IEEE, December 2010
17. Salmani, H., Tehranipoor, M., Plusquellic, J.: A novel technique for improving hardware Trojan detection and reducing Trojan activation time. IEEE Trans. Very Large Scale Integr. (VLSI) Syst. **20**(1), 112–125 (2012)
18. Shekarian, S.M.H., Zamani, M.S., Alami, S.: Neutralizing a design-for-hardware-trust technique. In: 2013 17th CSI International Symposium on Computer Architecture and Digital Systems (CADS), pp. 73–78. IEEE (2013)
19. Wei, S., Potkonjak, M.: Scalable hardware Trojan diagnosis. IEEE Trans. Very Large Scale Integr. (VLSI) Syst. **20**(6), 1049–1057 (2012)
20. Zhang, X., Tehranipoor, M.: RON: An on-chip ring oscillator network for hardware Trojan detection. In: Design, Automation and Test in Europe Conference and Exhibition (DATE), pp. 1–6. IEEE (2011)
21. Zhou, B., Zhang, W., Thambipillai, S., Teo, J.: A low cost acceleration method for hardware Trojan detection based on fan-out cone analysis. In: Proceedings of the 2014 International Conference on Hardware/Software Codesign and System Synthesis, p. 28. ACM (2014)

Side-Channel Attacks in Practice

DPA, Bitslicing and Masking at 1 GHz

Josep Balasch[✉], Benedikt Gierlichs, Oscar Reparaz,
and Ingrid Verbauwhede

Department of Electrical Engineering-ESAT/COSIC and iMinds, KU Leuven,
Kasteelpark Arenberg 10, 3001 Leuven-Heverlee, Belgium
{Josep.Balasch,Benedikt.Gierlichs,Oscar.Reparaz,
Ingrid.Verbauwhede}@esat.kuleuven.be

Abstract. We present DPA attacks on an ARM Cortex-A8 processor
running at 1 GHz. This high-end processor is typically found in portable
devices such as phones and tablets. In our case, the processor sits in a
single board computer and runs a full-fledged Linux operating system.
The targeted AES implementation is bitsliced and runs in constant time
and constant flow. We show that, despite the complex hardware and
software, high clock frequencies and practical measurement issues, the
implementation can be broken with DPA starting from a few thousand
measurements of the electromagnetic emanation of a decoupling capacitor near the processor. To harden the bitsliced implementation against
DPA attacks, we mask it using principles of hardware gate-level masking.
We evaluate the security of our masked implementation against first-
order and second-order attacks. Our experiments show that successful
attacks require roughly two orders of magnitude more measurements.

Keywords: Side-channel analysis · DPA · ARM Cortex-A8 · Bitslicing ·
Gate-level masking

1 Introduction

Side-channel attacks allow to extract secrets, such as cryptographic keys or pass-
words, from embedded devices with relatively low effort. Kocher reported in his
seminal paper [23] extracting cryptographic keys from the observation of the
execution time taken by an implementation of Diffie-Hellman, RSA or DSS.
A common characteristic of side-channel attacks is that they target concrete
implementations, and thus they are oblivious to the intrinsic mathematical security of the algorithm. They can be readily applied to implementations of algorithms that are resistant to traditional mathematical attacks.

Apart from timing, many other side-channels have been discussed in the
literature. Most notably, the instantaneous power consumption is a powerful
side-channel for embedded devices [24], and efficient exploitation mechanisms,
such as Differential Power Analysis (DPA), are known. DPA requires access to
the target device to collect a number of instantaneous power consumption traces

© International Association for Cryptologic Research 2015
T. Güneysu and H. Handschuh (Eds.): CHES 2015, LNCS 9293, pp. 599–619, 2015.
DOI: 10.1007/978-3-662-48324-4_30

while the device is running the cryptographic implementation. The key can be derived from the statistical analysis of the power consumption traces.

A popular variant of power analysis attacks are Electromagnetic Analysis (EMA) attacks [17,38]. EMA attacks measure the electromagnetic emanations from the device and subsequently apply similar statistical techniques as DPA. An advantage is that electromagnetic measurements do not require to establish electrical contact, thus EMA can be less invasive than conventional power analysis.

Side-channel attacks on small embedded devices, such as microcontrollers and cryptographic co-processors, are nowadays a well-understood threat and a fruitful field of academic research. However, there are only a few studies of side-channel attacks on more powerful general-purpose systems. This is highly relevant to the gradual paradigm shift towards moving the cryptographic operation to the main processor, as proposed in mobile payments and host card emulation.

In this paper we investigate the DPA susceptibility of block-cipher implementations on high-end embedded devices. As an illustrative test case, we focus on the Advanced Encryption Standard [2] (AES) and an ARM Cortex-A8 processor. This processor core is found in portable consumer electronic devices, such as phones (Apple iPhone4, Samsung Galaxy S, Google Nexus S), tablets, set-top boxes, multimedia entertainment systems (Apple TV, Apple iPod Touch 4th gen), home networking or storage appliances and printers.

The Cortex-A8 is a powerful and complex processor that features significant differences with typical targets of side-channel attacks. It is a 32-bit processor with a 13-stage pipeline, dynamic branch prediction, L1 and L2 cache memories, a rich ARMv7 instruction set and a separate SIMD execution pipeline and register file (NEON). It can run at up to 1 GHz clock frequency. At the software level, there is normally a full multi-tasking operating system with shared resources, different competing processes and interrupts. It is not clear if DPA can be successfully applied to such target devices. One goal of our work is to fill this gap.

1.1   Related Work

AES on High-End Embedded Devices. An efficient option for AES software implementations on high-end processors is the *T-table* approach due to Daemen and Rijmen [14]. Its core idea is to merge three of the four AES transformations (SubBytes, ShiftRows and MixColumns) into four lookup tables. At the cost of storing 4 kbytes, this method allows to compute an AES-128 encryption using only 160 table lookups and 44 XOR operations. Since the four lookup tables are rotations of each other, it is possible to reduce the memory requirements to 1 kbyte by storing a single table. For architectures with inline barrel shifter such as ARM, this characteristic can be used without performance loss [33].

While efficient, implementations based on lookup tables are a target for side-channel attacks on processors with cache memories. Exploiting cache-related timing variabilities was already mentioned by Kocher [23], and further elaborated on by Kelsey *et al.* [21] and Page [36]. In recent years, several practical attacks against the T-table AES implementation of OpenSSL have been published, see for instance the works of Bernstein [6], Bonneau and Mironov [9] and Osvik *et al.* [34]. The root of the problem stems from the difficulty to load array entries into the CPU registers without this depending on the index pointer. As suggested by Bernstein *et al.* [7], a secure library should systematically avoid loads from addresses that depend on secret data. While one could always resort to *computing* the AES S-Box to achieve constant execution time, the performance penalties of straightforward implementations would be considerable.

It is in this context that bitsliced implementations rise as an attractive alternative for AES in software. Originally proposed by Biham [8] to improve the performance of DES in software, the idea behind bitslicing consists in describing a cryptographic algorithm as a sequence of Boolean operations which can be implemented with only bitwise instructions. Since there are no table lookups, bitsliced implementations are inherently resilient to cache timing attacks. The first bitsliced software implementation of the AES for x64 processors is due to Matsui [27]. An alternative implementation for 64-bit platforms is presented by Könighofer [25]. The advent of Single Instruction Multiple Data (SIMD) extensions on Intel Core2 processors has enabled a more efficient usage of the 128-bit XMM registers. Matsui and Nakajima [28] were first to take advantage of this and proposed a high-speed bitsliced implementation of the AES at 9.2 cycles/byte, albeit conditioned to input data blocks of 2 kbytes. More recently, Käsper and Schwabe [20] proposed the fastest implementations of AES-CTR and AES-GCM up to date, running at 7.59 cycles/byte and 10.68 cycles/byte, respectively.

Side-Channel Attacks on High-End Embedded Devices. With the notable exception of cache timing attacks, the susceptibility of high-end embedded processors to side-channel attacks has received only little attention in the literature, particularly when compared to the attention that has been given to less complex platforms. Gebotys *et al.* [18] showed how to attack Java implementations of AES and ECC running on a PDA equipped with a "mid-range" 32-bit ARM7TDMI at 40 MHz. The authors performed a differential EMA attack in the frequency domain in order to deal with the issue of trace misalignment. A follow-up work by Aboulkassimi *et al.* [3] similarly used differential EMA to attack AES implementations. The target device was a mobile phone with a 32-bit processor running at 370 MHz. Kenworthy and Rohatgi [22] applied Simple Power Analysis (SPA) and leakage detection techniques to show the susceptibility of several implementations to EMA. Although no processor frequency is specified, the acquisition bandwidth of the setup used was limited to 60 MHz. Finally, Nakano *et al.* [31] performed SPA attacks on ECC and RSA implementations running on an Android Smartphone clocked at 832 MHz.

Masking Countermeasures. A popular and well-studied countermeasure to thwart power analysis attacks is masking [12,19]. Contrary to other approaches, masking is a provable sound countermeasure and widely employed in practice.

In its simplest form, masking consists of splitting every key-dependent intermediate s that appears throughout the computation into two shares (s_1, s_2) such that $s_1 \star s_2 = s$. The group operation $\star$ is typically XOR. The splitting is such that each share s_i is statistically independent of the intermediate s. This condition should be preserved throughout the entire masked computation, and implies that knowledge of any individual s_i does not reveal any information about the intermediate s, and thus about the key.

Masking can be applied at different abstraction levels: from the algorithmic level (public key cryptography algorithms [13,30] as well as symmetric key algorithms such as DES [19] or AES [4]) to the gate level [42]. Algorithm-level masking can result in more compact implementations. However, this masking method is not a general approach as it is tied to a specific algorithm. On the other hand, gate-level masking performs the splitting at the bit level and provides the implementer with a set of secure logic gates to compute on. It it thus a versatile method to securely implement any given circuit.

1.2   Contributions

Our first contribution is to investigate the feasibility of DPA attacks on modern gigahertz embedded processors. Our experimental platform is a Sitara ARM Cortex-A8 32-bit RISC processor mounted on a Beaglebone Black (BBB) platform and running a complete Ångström Linux distribution. Our test application is a bitsliced implementation of AES-128 encryption immune to cache timing attacks. Our experiments show that the most difficult part of an attack is of practical nature (measurement point, triggering, alignment) and that basic DPA attacks succeed with a few thousand measurements. For the sake of reproducibility, we describe all steps carried out in our analysis in detail.

Our second contribution is to apply gate-level hardware masking to protect our implementation. We show that it is not difficult to equip an unprotected bitsliced implementation with masking. In addition we fully implement a masked AES on the same platform and test its resistance to first-order and secondorder attacks. Our experiments show that breaking our masked implementation requires roughly two orders of magnitude more measurements than breaking the unprotected implementation.

2   A Bitsliced AES Implementation

Our test application is a bitsliced implementation of the AES based on the construction of Könighofer [25]. We adapted it for our 32-bit processor. Note that this is a poor decision if one aims for performance, i.e. bitsliced implementations pay off in software contexts only if the target processor contains large (and possibly many) registers. Nevertheless, our aim is neither to propose nor to achieve high-throughput implementations, but rather analyze bitsliced implementations from the DPA-security standpoint. In fact, and as will become clear later, our insights also apply for larger wordsize architectures such as e.g. NEON.

Hardware Description of AES. In the following we focus on AES-128 encryption. The first step towards a bitsliced description consists in describing all cipher transformations (AddRoundKey, SubBytes, ShiftRows and MixColumns) as a fixed sequence of Boolean operations. The goal is to employ only bitwise operations i.e. an equivalent gate representation in hardware contexts. The main difficulty of this process consists in finding an efficient way to compute the non-linear part of the AES S-Box.

There exist many hardware flavours of AES depending on whether they aim for throughput, area, low-power, etc. For bitsliced contexts, we are interested in *compact* implementations. Most successful designs in this direction compute the inverse in $GF(2^8)$ using subfield arithmetic, as originally suggested by Rijmen [39]. This is the case of the works due to Rudra *et al.* [40], Wolkerstorfer *et al.* [44] and Satoh *et al.* [41], the latter building also on the tower-field representation of Paar [35]. As in [25], we employ the AES S-Box representation by Canright [11] illustrated in Fig. 1.

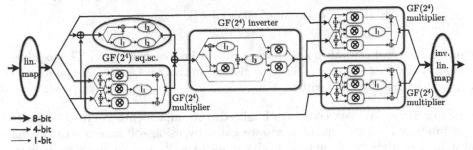

Fig. 1. AES S-Box representation due to Canright [11].

Bitsliced Format. In the standard AES representation a 128-bit input message block A is described as a 4×4 byte matrix. This is illustrated in the upper left hand side of Fig. 2. Each byte is addressed as A_i. The cipher transformations are commonly defined at byte level in order to operate on the matrix representation of the state, e.g. either at element level (AddRoundKey and SubBytes), at row level (ShiftRows) or at column level (MixColumns). This representation is however inadequate for bitsliced implementations, as all steps are defined at bit level. Therefore, one needs to find a different representation of the cipher state. The most straightforward option consists in arranging the state as a vector of 128 elements, each corresponding to a bit. This choice is however unsuitable in practice, as the state cannot be fully kept in registers and memory accesses easily become a major bottleneck.

An alternative bitsliced representation uses a more compact state of 8 elements [20,25,27], each containing a particular bit of the 16 state bytes A_i. Let us denote the bitsliced state elements by $\mathcal{R}_i$. Going to the bitsliced domain requires to split the bytes A_i and store the bits, from LSB to MSB, to the corresponding registers, $\mathcal{R}_1$ to $\mathcal{R}_8$. Note that one input message block A fills only 16 bits in each $\mathcal{R}_i$. Therefore several input messages can be processed in parallel, e.g. by

Normal Byte Ordering   **Bitsliced Ordering**

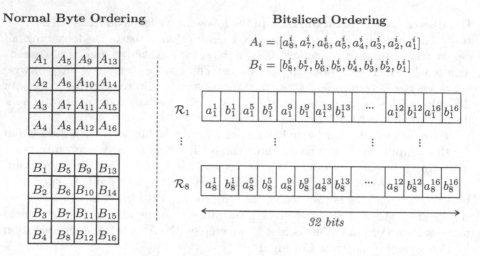

Fig. 2. Layout of bitsliced AES registers.

storing bits from several input message blocks into each register. This is illustrated in Fig. 2 for the case of 32-bit registers. In this case, a second plaintext B is processed concurrently with A.

Coding Style. We have coded our bitsliced AES implementation in C language and mimicked the concept of hardware gates by using software macros for all atomic operations. This approach allows us to write our program as a fixed sequence of calls to five main macros: bitwise operations (XOR, AND and NOT), data transfers (MOV) and left rotates (ROTL):

```
#define XOR(c,a,b)    c = a ^ b;
#define AND(c,a,b)    c = a &b;
#define NOT(c,a)      c = ~ a;
#define MOV(c,a)      c = a;
#define ROTL(c,a,l)   c = (a << l) | (a >> (32 - l));
```

The main benefit of this approach is that protecting the implementation with gate-level masking requires only rewriting the macros. This point will be elaborated on in Sect. 4.

3   Developing an Attack

The BBB is a complex single board computer. The main component is a high-performance TI AM3358 Sitara System on Chip (SoC) based on the ARM Cortex-A8 core. To give an idea of the complexity, we point out that the main processor can be clocked up to 1 GHz and that the SoC features a DDR3 memory controller, a 3D graphics engine, a vast array of peripheral support (incl. USB, ethernet) and two 32-bit sub-processors (technically, programmable real-time units) for time-critical tasks, among others.

3.1   Strategies for Side-Channel Measurements

From all the components of the single board computer, we are mostly interested in the side-channel leakage of the ARM processor. An obvious way to access it would be to measure the SoC's power consumption. However, performing a power measurement on a BGA package is not straightforward, as the pins are covered by the package and not easily accessible.

A second strategy might be to measure the power consumption of the entire single board computer. At least, doing the actual measurement should not be difficult as the entire board is powered by a single 5 V supply (via USB or a dedicated connector, e.g. if more than 500 mA is needed). But we expect the global power consumption to be very noisy (many active components on the board). Furthermore, there is a dedicated power management IC and numerous decoupling capacitors between the power supply and the SoC. The high operating frequencies of the processor require capacitor banks that can deal with low, medium and high frequencies.

The third approach is the one we actually followed. We opted for a "contactless power measurement". To clarify, others have used the same technique and called it "electromagnetic measurement". We do use an electromagnetic pen probe but we do not aim at measuring emanations from the ARM processor. Rather, we measure the EM field around different components on the board that are somehow involved in the current loop to the ARM core. In general, voltage regulators and decoupling capacitors [15,32] are promising candidates. In our case, the dedicated power management IC is quite complex and physically located far away from the ARM core. For these reasons, we do not think that it would provide a useful signal. Therefore the decoupling capacitors are the best candidates. In general, the closer the capacitor is to the processor, the better signal it can provide. In summary, we use an electromagnetic probe to measure a signal that is correlated with the chip's power consumption. We therefore think of the technique as a contact-less power measurement.

3.2   Experimental Setup

Our experimental setup comprises:

- A stock BBB platform running a complete Linux Ångström distribution. We did not modify the software or the hardware and operate the board in its factory configuration. The Linux distribution is based on Debian 7 with kernel version 3.8.13-bone47 (root@imx6q-wandboard-2gb-0). This is a preemptive multitasking operating system with plenty of simultaneously running processes. We did not switch off any running service. The command ps aux reports 102 processes running on the system. Among others, we found running the Xorg graphical server (with the onboard HDMI driver output activated), the apache2 webserver (including the nodejs server-side javascript runtime environment, to our surprise) and the sshd server (with an open session running throughout all experiments for monitoring purposes). We power the board via the USB connection from the measurement PC. We did not make any effort to supply the board with a particularly clean voltage. The board is connected to the measurement PC via ethernet-over-USB. We did not disable the blinking blue leds that indicate activity.

– A Langer magnetic near field probe, model RF-B. The reported frequency bandwidth is from 30 MHz to 3 GHz [16].
– A wideband 30 dB low-noise amplifier from Langer, model PA 303. The reported frequency bandwidth goes from DC to 3 GHz.
– A Tektronix DPO70404C 8-bit oscilloscope with an analog bandwidth of 4 GHz. Most of the time we sampled at 6 GS/s to make full use of our setup's bandwidth (Nyquist rate).

We use the Linux command `cpufreq-set -f 1000 MHz` to bring the system into a high-performance state. In this state the board cannot enter low-power mode and the processor core is permanently clocked at 1 GHz, which is well within the bandwidth of our measurement setup. Figure 3 shows a photo of our experimental setup (left) and a representation of our EM probe and the field orientation it is able to register (right).

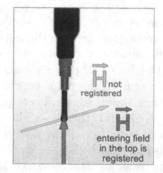

Fig. 3. Photo of our setup (left) and EM antenna schematic [16] (right).

3.3 Approach

Our first step is to find a suitable measurement position for the EM antenna. The EM antenna tip is small enough (we measured a diameter of 2 mm) to allow us to get in between components and to measure individual components' EM field without picking up too many signals from neighboring components. For the purpose of locating an appropiate position for the EM antenna, we wrote a short C program that exercises memory accesses and ran it on the BBB in a loop. The program executes 1000 NOPs, then repeatedly fills a buffer in memory with the value 0x00000000 and then with the value 0xffffffff 1000 times, followed by again 1000 NOPs. We manually move the antenna over the PCB surface and slowly from component to component. We carefully monitor the sampled signal on the oscilloscope for a pattern that looks correlated to the execution of our

C code. We begin doing this by trial and error, and we focus on the capacitors in the SoC's power supply as explained above. Note that this is a tedious task because we need to get not only the probe's tip in the right *location* but we also need to get the probe in the right *orientation* (see Fig. 3 right). As the search was very time consuming we had a look at the BBB PCB schematics [1]. We identified a bank of capacitors in the SoC's VDD core supply. They should be good candidates for measurement points as their EM fields should contain a lot of useful signal about the processor core's activity. Next we locate these decoupling capacitors on the PCB and manually scan them with the EM probe one by one.

We did not find a useful signal around these capacitors (that does not mean there is no useful signal) and reverted to trial and error testing of other decoupling capacitors in the SoC's supply network. Eventually we found a good signal near C66 (see Appendix A in the full version of this paper [5]), a 0.1 μF multilayer ceramic capacitor in a 3.3 V supply rail. We used this probe position and orientation for all measurements and did not further explore the board for other useful signals.

Now that we found a suitable measurement point, the next step is to deal with the timing and triggering. We run our bitsliced implementation of AES 128 encryption from Sect. 2 on the BBB. We can send the inputs from the measurement PC and read back the outputs as well. Recall that we keep an SSH connection open between the measurement PC and the BBB for this purpose and for monitoring. After some trial and error work we find a good pattern (related to I/O) to trigger the oscilloscope on. Figure 4 shows the plot of an overview measurement. Note that we need to substantially lower the sampling rate for some of these long measurements. The execution of our C program causes the dense pattern in the middle of the plot. The isolated peaks left and right of the dense pattern are caused by other processes.

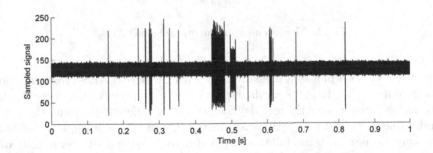

Fig. 4. Overview measurement of our unprotected AES.

Figure 5 shows the plot of a more focused measurement. We see patterns caused by the reception of 34 bytes (two plaintext blocks of 16 bytes each and two control words) followed by patterns caused by the AES encryption in the

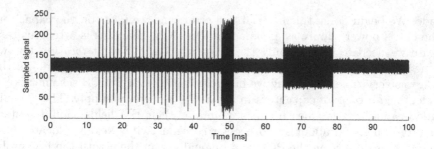

Fig. 5. Overview measurement of our unprotected AES.

middle of the figure. We do not know what causes the "block" pattern on the figure's right hand side.

Figure 6 shows a zoom on the patterns caused by the AES operation. It is tempting to let the human eye search for patterns of the ten AES rounds, but in fact the AES makes only a small part of this measurement (as marked by the dotted red rectangle in the figure). We are not sure what the other processing is. We know that some of it is the conversion of plaintexts to the bitsliced format, and from bitsliced format to ciphertexts.

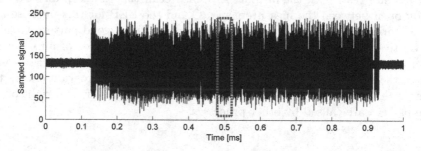

Fig. 6. Measurement of our unprotected AES.

Figure 7 shows a plot of a measurement with the actual AES-128 encryption in the middle of the plot. One would expect to see a sequence of nine very similar patterns (the first nine AES rounds) followed by a different pattern (the tenth round without `MixColumns`). However, in this figure we see a sequence of only eight very similar patterns followed by a different pattern. It seems that our measurement is missing one normal round. Our experiments confirm that what we recognize corresponds to rounds two to ten. The execution of the first AES round leads to a pattern that is more scattered over time, but it fills up the instruction cache so that the next rounds are executed much faster which leads to a more dense and clear pattern.

When we execute several encryptions in a batch, the second and all following encryptions typically run from cache and show clear patterns also for the first

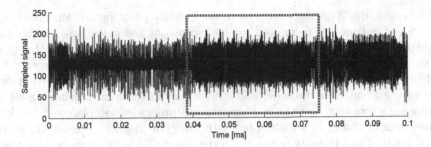

Fig. 7. One of the first measurements of our unprotected AES.

round that we can use for alignment. Figure 8 shows the single-sided amplitude spectrum of a measurement. The spectrum shows a clear and sharp peak at 1 GHz.

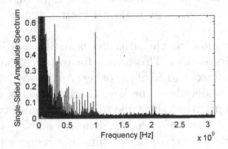

Fig. 8. Single-sided amplitude spectrum of a measurement.

Even though we found a seemingly stable trigger, the measurements of the AES encryption are actually heavily desynchronized. Recall that we are working with a high-end ARM processor on a complex SoC and that our C program is only one of more than 100 running processes (and we do not run it with elevated priority!). Therefore, filtering out mis-triggered measurements and carefully aligning the remaining measurements is crucial. In fact, we spend about seven times more time on the post-processing than on the measurement.

3.4 Attack

We aim to break our unprotected implementation with a first-order correlation DPA attack [10] against the first round. The next step is to try to find a pattern in the traces that is related to the (S-box computation in the) first round, and to align all useful traces on that pattern. Finally we try to attack the implementation with 10 000 aligned measurements.

We need to think about a power model because the implementation is bit-sliced. A typical byte-oriented implementation uses an S-box table in memory and processes the AES state byte by byte. The key point here is that all 8 bits of an S-box output are computed (or looked-up) at the same time. Hence one can expect all bits of the S-box output to leak at the same time and this gives rise to the commonly used "Hamming weight of the S-box output" power model. This is different for our bitsliced implementation. The eight S-box output bits are computed one after the other and stored in eight different registers. So if we assume for a moment that the implementation processes one plaintext block at a time, each of the eight registers holds 16 bits. For instance register $\mathcal{R}_1$ stores the 16 LSBs of the 16 state bytes. With the usual divide and conquer approach we aim to recover the key byte by byte. If we make a guess about one key byte we can predict one S-box output but the eight bits are spread over eightregisters that are not processed at the same time. For a normal univariate attack we can therefore exploit only one bit effectively. The other 15 bits in the same register are algorithmic noise. If we want to exploit more bits in the same register we need to guess more key bytes, which quickly becomes computationally expensive. Alternatively we can think to attack each of the eight bits of one S-box output separately and then perform some majority voting, but we did not investigate this approach.

Now in our implementation the situation is similar but it actually processes two plaintext blocks in parallel. This means for instance that register $\mathcal{R}_1$ stores 32 LSBs, 16 of one plaintext and 16 of the other. As the key is fixed both plaintext blocks get encrypted under the same key. Making a guess on one key byte we can attack both encryptions at the same time and predict two bits in a register (2 out of 32 instead of 1 out of 16 in the example above). Our power model is hence the Hamming weight (HW) of two bits in a register that are affected by the same sub-key. We stress that this observation has an *important consequence*: processing more plaintext blocks in parallel does not make an attack harder if the adversary is aware of the bitsliced implementation. In fact, the ratio of predicted bits and processed bits, and hence the ratio of signal to algorithmic noise, is constant.

Figure 9 shows an exemplary result of a 2-bit attack against one key byte. The plot on the left hand side shows the correlation traces for all key hypotheses obtained using 10 000 measurements. The trace for the correct key hypothesis is plotted in black. The plot shows that the correct key hypothesis leads to a distinguishable and clear correlation peak. The plot on the right hand side shows the highest and lowest correlation value for each key hypothesis (from the overall time frame) over the number of measurements. In addition we also plot the 99.99 % confidence interval for sample correlation equal to zero (dashed lines). The plot shows that only few thousand measurements are required for the correct key (black line) to stand out and hence for the attack to succeed.

Attacks targeting the same (other) key byte(s) using the leakage of other (the same) register(s) give very similar results. Surprisingly full key recovery is hence possible using only a few thousand measurements!

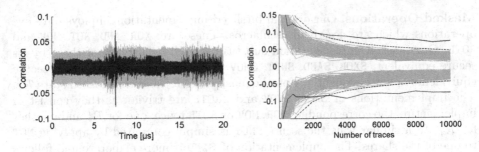

Fig. 9. Result of attack against unprotected implementation.

4 Masking a Bitsliced AES Implementation

Since a bitsliced software implementation mimics a hardware circuit, gate-level masking appears as a very attractive candidate to protect our AES implementation. Applying gate-level masking to an already existing implementation can actually be done in a pretty straightforward manner. It only requires to protect the design's elementary Boolean functionalities, while the original sequence of operations remains unmodified. A direct consequence of this is that any optimization performed in the unprotected implementation, e.g. to improve the design's throughput, is automatically inherited by the protected implementation.

Generally, linear functions such as the XOR gate, are trivial to mask by just computing on each share independently. The challenging part of gate-level masking is to provide a construction for non-linear gates. One of the first works tackling this problem is due to Trichina [43]. Trichina gives a secure AND gate that takes two shares of each input bit a, b and produces two output shares of $c = a \cdot b$. The secure AND gate consumes one fresh random bit r. If the input bit a (resp. b) is shared into a_1 and a_2 (resp. b_1 and b_2), the two output shares c_1, c_2 of the Trichina gate are defined as

$$c_1 = r \tag{1}$$
$$c_2 = (((a_1 b_1 \oplus r) \oplus a_1 b_2) \oplus a_2 b_1) \oplus a_2 b_2. \tag{2}$$

It is easy to verify that this AND gate description is correct, namely, that the output shares XOR to $a \cdot b$. The description is also secure against first-order attacks: each variable occurring during the execution is independent of any unshared value a, b or c. Note however that the order of partial computations of c_2 is relevant for the security of the gate.

Masked Bitsliced Format. Applying first-order Boolean masking requires to split any sensitive intermediate variable s into two shares such that $s = s_1 \oplus s_2$. For our implementation, this implies that each of the eight original state registers $\mathcal{R}_i$ becomes a pair $(\mathcal{R}_i^1, \mathcal{R}_i^2)$ such that $\mathcal{R}_i = \mathcal{R}_i^1 \oplus \mathcal{R}_i^2$. We denote $\mathcal{R}_i^1$ as mask state and $\mathcal{R}_i^2$ as masked state. The plaintext in bitsliced format is shared in this way at the beginning of the execution.

Masked Operations. Our original bitsliced implementation employs only five operations which are described as macros. These are: XOR, AND, NOT, MOV and ROTL. Our masked implementation substitutes each occurrence of these by its secure equivalent: SXOR, SAND, SNOT, SMOV and SROTL, respectively. The secure equivalents operate sequentially on the mask state $\mathcal{R}_i^1$ and the masked state $\mathcal{R}_i^2$. The implementations of SXOR, SMOV and SROTL are trivial, as they consist of implementing the corresponding XOR, MOV or ROTL twice: one for $\mathcal{R}_i^1$ and another for $\mathcal{R}_i^2$. In a similar way, the secure SNOT is simply computed by applying NOT to one of the shares. The implementation of SAND is more elaborate and follows closely the lines of the Trichina gate. A circuit representation of the gate is shown in the left part of Fig. 10, while its macro representation is given in the right part of Fig. 10.

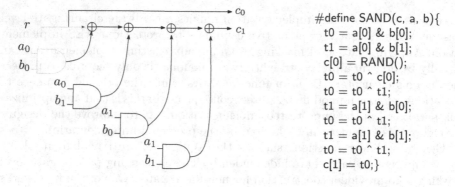

Fig. 10. Left: Trichina construction for the masked AND gate. Right: pseudocode for the SAND operation following the Trichina AND construction.

In contrast to the original bitsliced macros, each variable in the macro is now an array of 2 elements: mask state and masked state. Each of the two input arrays (a, b) is thus composed of two registers (a[0],a[1]) and (b[0],b[1]), respectively. Two temporal registers (t0 and t1) are additionally used to preserve the correctness of the macro in case one of the source registers is also the destination, e.g. to prevent errors when the macro is called as SAND(a,a,b). The result is placed in the output array c composed of registers c[0] and c[1].

Randomness Generation. The two operations that require randomness in the masked bitsliced implementation are the initial plaintext sharing and each SAND operation. We use the kernel's /dev/urandom cryptographic RNG to obtain the required randomness. We do not read a single byte each time a random byte is needed, instead, we read a chunk of randomness and place it in an internal buffer at the beginning of each encryption. Then, during the actual encryption the randomness is simply taken from this internal buffer. We implemented this mechanism to minimally interrupt the execution of the encryption and get clean measurements.

We note that masking typically does not need cryptographically strong random numbers for the masks. Although we used a cryptographically strong source of randomness for the masks, a lighter RNG can be used if needed, e.g. for performance reasons. When we later report that the RNG is switched off, we fill the internal buffer from /dev/zero instead of from /dev/urandom.

Performance. We have compiled our implementations directly in the BBB using the compiler version available in the Ångström Linux distribution, i.e. gcc version 4.6.3. No special flags have been used. The throughput loss of the protected implementation is roughly a factor 5 compared to the unprotected implementation. Further, the RAM usage increases by 32 bytes because of doubling the register state size. Our internal buffer for storing random numbers holds 2048 bytes. The only macro in our implementation that consumes randomness is SAND, which is used 37 times during the calculation of SubBytes. Taking into account that 32 bytes are required to mask the input plaintexts, this gives $32 + 10 \times (37 \times 4) = 1512$ random bytes per AES execution, or equivalently, 756 bytes per plaintext block.

5   Evaluation of Masked Implementation

In this section we evaluate the DPA resistance of our bitsliced and first-order masked AES implementation.

5.1   Attack When RNG is Off

We first attack the implementation with the RNG switched off. In this case the implementation is effectively unprotected and we aim to break it with the same first-order attack as before: we guess one key byte and use the HW of the two affected bits in a register as power model. Since the code is different, the shape of the measurements is different as well, and we need to work through trial and error again to find a good pattern for trace alignment. And this is where the fact that the implementation is effectively unprotected helps. We should be able to break it easily, and we can use the attack result to judge and improve the discarding of mis-triggered measurements and the alignment step until we are satisfied. As a side note we also mention that we need to take longer measurements because in particular the S-box computation takes more time.

Figure 11 shows the result of an exemplary attack against one key byte. The plot on the left hand side shows that using 10 000 measurements the correct key hypothesis leads to a clear correlation peak. The plot on the right hand side confirms that, if the RNG is switched off, our masked implementation is as insecure as the unprotected implementation and can be broken with a few thousand measurements. Also in this case attacks targeting other key bytes and using the leakage of other registers give similar results. Full key extraction with a first-order attack is possible with a few thousand measurements.

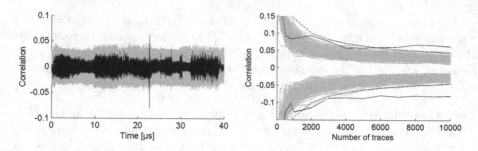

Fig. 11. Result of attack against masked implementation with RNG off.

5.2 Attack When RNG is On

Now we switch on the RNG and evaluate how much protection our masked implementation provides. Having performed the attacks with the RNG switched off has two important advantages. First, we can keep all settings for triggering, for discarding mis-triggered measurements, and for alignment because the executed code is exactly the same and the general shape of the measurements does not change. And second, we know exactly when the S-box computations are performed and we can therefore narrow down the time window to analyze (including some margin).

It is well known that implementing masking securely in software is very difficult, and we do not expect our first attempt to mask a bitsliced implementation to provide a high level of resistance to attacks. Nevertheless, to ensure that we have enough measurements at hand to break our implementation we acquired 2 000 000 measurements. We stress that trace acquisition is rather quick, but in contrast to most academic works we have to deal with the computationally intensive and hence slow post-processing (discarding mis-triggered measurements and alignment). After post-processing we are left with about 1.2 million aligned measurements.

We applied the same 2-bit first-order DPA attack as before in various settings, targeting different key bytes and registers. The results differ a lot depending on the specific setting. To give an idea of the range, we provide two results in Fig. 12. They target different key bytes and registers but both plots on the left hand side are computed using 1.2 million measurements. While in the upper plots the attack clearly succeeds and requires about 600 000 measurements, the attack in the lower plots fails even if using 1.2 million traces. Nevertheless, we confirmed that, using alternative combinations of target key byte and register, full key extraction with first-order DPA and using 1.2 million measurements is possible.

Considering the well known difficulties with masking in software and the surprisingly easy attacks against the unprotected implementation, we expected attacks against our masked implementation to succeed with much less traces. Our results are therefore promising and good news for the idea to combine bitsliced software and gate-level masking. Recall that our implementations are

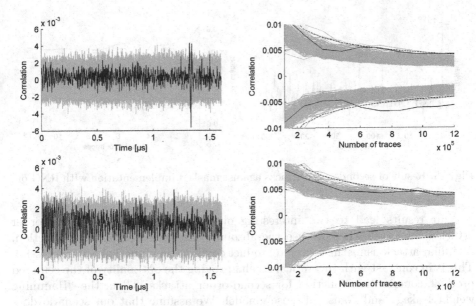

Fig. 12. Results of first-order attacks against masked implementation with RNG on.

coded in C, processed by a compiler and we have little control over the code that is eventually executed. Also, we stress that this is our first attempt to mask the implementation. The fact that the result of each individual Boolean operation is registered in a bitsliced implementation probably helps. Glitches that are an issue for masked *hardware* implementations [26] are no threat here.

We also performed a few exemplary univariate and bivariate second-order attacks. Concretely, we processed the measurements to combine each pair of time samples using the absolute difference combination function [29] or the centered product combination function [37]. This combination step yields a combinatorial blow-up in the number of time sample pairs to be analyzed jointly and makes these attacks very computationally expensive.

We then applied the same 2-bit attack to the combined measurements. Figure 13 depicts the results of an exemplary attack using the absolute difference combination function. The plot on the left hand side shows the maximum absolute value of the correlation coefficient for each key byte hypothesis across *all pairs* of time samples when using 1.2 million measurements. The correct value (indicated by a dashed vertical line) clearly stands out. For the plot on the right hand side we restrict the analysis to the single pair of time samples for which the correct key guess gives maximal correlation. The plot shows that the attack can be successful starting from around 400 000 measurements if the adversary already knows which pair of time samples to analyze. In other words, a more realistic attack will very likely require more measurements to succeed. An analysis over all pairs of time samples is, however, computationally expensive.

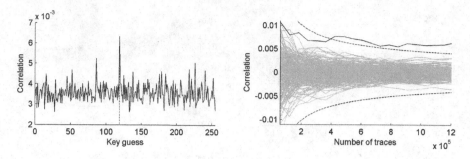

Fig. 13. Result of second-order attacks against masked implementation with RNG on.

Our results lead to two interesting observations. First, the second-order attack only works when we use the absolute difference combination function. A similar attack using the centered product combination function is unsuccessful. This is in contrast with theoretical results proving the optimality of the centered product combination function for second-order attacks [37] in the "Hamming weight leakage and Gaussian noise" model. We assume that our scenario does not meet this model and that the absolute difference combination function has a wider scope. And second, the number of measurements required for a successful first-order attack is not substantially lower than the number of measurements needed for our "idealized" second-order attack. This indicates that our masking is effective (albeit its implementation is not perfect).

6   Conclusion

The threat of side-channel attacks to the security of microcontrollers and cryptographic co-processors appears to be well understood by both industry and academia. Yet the same cannot be said for high-end embedded processors as used in phones and tablets. In this situation one may naturally wonder whether such complex, high-performance devices operating in the GHz range and executing multitasking operating systems are at all vulnerable to DPA. In this work we answer this question positively. By means of experiments we show that DPA attacks against constant-time bitsliced implementations of the AES running on a 1 GHz ARM Cortex-A8 processor are not only possible, but in fact rather easy to mount. The most challenging parts of an attack are triggering and trace alignment. Finally, we mask our implementation inspired by gate-level masking and evaluate its resistance against first-order and second-order DPA attacks. Our results indicate that the implementation is more secure than we anticipated and therefore highlight the potential of combining bitsliced software implementations and gate-level masking.

Acknowledgements. We would like to thank the CHES 2015 reviewers for their valuable feedback. This work has been supported in part by the Research Council of KU Leuven (GOA/11/007), by the Flemish Government FWO G.0550.12N and by the

Hercules foundation (AKUL/11/19). Oscar Reparaz is funded by a PhD fellowship of the Fund for Scientific Research - Flanders (FWO). Benedikt Gierlichs is a Postdoctoral Fellow of the Fund for Scientific Research - Flanders (FWO).

References

1. BBB PCB schematics. http://elinux.org/Beagleboard:BeagleBoneBlack#Board_Revisions_and_Changes
2. Specification for the Advanced Encryption Standard (AES). Federal Information Processing Standards (FIPS) Publication 197 (2001)
3. Aboulkassimi, D., Agoyan, M., Freund, L., Fournier, J., Robisson, B., Tria, A.: ElectroMagnetic analysis (EMA) of software AES on Java mobile phones. In: Information Forensics and Security - WIFS 2011, pp. 1–6. IEEE (2011)
4. Akkar, M.-L., Giraud, C.: An Implementation of DES and AES, Secure against Some Attacks. In: Koç, Ç.K., Naccache, D., Paar, C. (eds.) CHES 2001. LNCS, vol. 2162, pp. 309–318. Springer, Heidelberg (2001)
5. Balasch, J., Gierlichs, B., Reparaz, O., Verbauwhede, I.: DPA, Bitslicing and Masking at 1 GHz. Cryptology ePrint Archive, Report 2015/727 (2015). http://eprint.iacr.org/
6. Bernstein, D.J.: Cache-timing attacks on AES (2005). http://cr.yp.to/antiforgery/cachetiming-20050414.pdf
7. Bernstein, D.J., Lange, T., Schwabe, P.: The security impact of a new cryptographic library. In: Hevia, A., Neven, G. (eds.) LatinCrypt 2012. LNCS, vol. 7533, pp. 159–176. Springer, Heidelberg (2012)
8. Biham, E.: A fast new DES implementation in software. In: Biham, E. (ed.) FSE 1997. LNCS, vol. 1267, pp. 260–272. Springer, Heidelberg (1997)
9. Bonneau, J., Mironov, I.: Cache-collision timing attacks against AES. In: Goubin, L., Matsui, M. (eds.) CHES 2006. LNCS, vol. 4249, pp. 201–215. Springer, Heidelberg (2006)
10. Brier, E., Clavier, C., Olivier, F.: Correlation power analysis with a leakage model. In: Joye, M., Quisquater, J.-J. (eds.) CHES 2004. LNCS, vol. 3156, pp. 16–29. Springer, Heidelberg (2004)
11. Canright, D.: A very compact S-box for AES. In: Rao, J.R., Sunar, B. (eds.) CHES 2005. LNCS, vol. 3659, pp. 441–455. Springer, Heidelberg (2005)
12. Chari, S., Jutla, C.S., Rao, J.R., Rohatgi, P.: Towards sound approaches to counteract power-analysis attacks. In: Wiener, M. (ed.) CRYPTO 1999. LNCS, vol. 1666, pp. 398–412. Springer, Heidelberg (1999)
13. Coron, J.-S.: Resistance against differential power analysis for elliptic curve cryptosystems. In: Koç, Ç.K., Paar, C. (eds.) CHES 1999. LNCS, vol. 1717, pp. 292–302. Springer, Heidelberg (1999)
14. Daemen, J., Rijmen, V.: The Design of Rijndael: AES - The Advanced Encryption Standard. Information Security and Cryptography. Springer, Heidelberg (2002)
15. Danis, A.U., Ors, B.: Differential power analysis attack considering decoupling capacitance effect. In: Circuit Theory and Design - ECCTD 2009, pp. 359–362 (2009). doi:10.1109/ECCTD.2009.5274996
16. Langer EMV. Probe specification. http://www.langer-emv.com
17. Gandolfi, K., Mourtel, C., Olivier, F.: Electromagnetic analysis: concrete results. In: Koç, Ç.K., Naccache, D., Paar, C. (eds.) CHES 2001. LNCS, vol. 2162, pp. 251–261. Springer, Heidelberg (2001)

18. Gebotys, C.H., Ho, S., Tiu, C.C.: EM analysis of Rijndael and ECC on a wireless Java-based PDA. In: Rao, J.R., Sunar, B. (eds.) CHES 2005. LNCS, vol. 3659, pp. 250–264. Springer, Heidelberg (2005)

19. Goubin, L., Patarin, J.: DES and differential power analysis. In: Koç, Ç.K., Paar, C. (eds.) CHES 1999. LNCS, vol. 1717, pp. 158–172. Springer, Heidelberg (1999)

20. Käsper, E., Schwabe, P.: Faster and timing-attack resistant AES-GCM. In: Clavier, C., Gaj, K. (eds.) CHES 2009. LNCS, vol. 5747, pp. 1–17. Springer, Heidelberg (2009)

21. Kelsey, J., Schneier, B., Wagner, D., Hall, C.: Side channel cryptanalysis of product ciphers. J. Comput. Securi. 8(2/3), 141–158 (2000)

22. Kenworthy, G., Rohatgi, P.: Mobile Device Security: The case for side-channel resistance (2012). http://www.cryptography.com/technology/dpa/dpa-research.html

23. Kocher, P.C.: Timing attacks on implementations of Diffie-Hellman, RSA, DSS, and other systems. In: Koblitz, N. (ed.) CRYPTO 1996. LNCS, vol. 1109, pp. 104–113. Springer, Heidelberg (1996)

24. Kocher, P.C., Jaffe, J., Jun, B.: Differential power analysis. In: Wiener, M. (ed.) CRYPTO 1999. LNCS, vol. 1666, pp. 388–397. Springer, Heidelberg (1999)

25. Könighofer, R.: A fast and cache-timing resistant implementation of the AES. In: Malkin, T. (ed.) CT-RSA 2008. LNCS, vol. 4964, pp. 187–202. Springer, Heidelberg (2008)

26. Mangard, S., Popp, T., Gammel, B.M.: Side-channel leakage of masked CMOS gates. In: Menezes, A. (ed.) CT-RSA 2005. LNCS, vol. 3376, pp. 351–365. Springer, Heidelberg (2005)

27. Matsui, M.: How far can we go on the x64 processors? In: Robshaw, M. (ed.) FSE 2006. LNCS, vol. 4047, pp. 341–358. Springer, Heidelberg (2006)

28. Matsui, M., Nakajima, J.: On the power of bitslice implementation on Intel Core2 processor. In: Paillier, P., Verbauwhede, I. (eds.) CHES 2007. LNCS, vol. 4727, pp. 121–134. Springer, Heidelberg (2007)

29. Messerges, T.S.: Using second-order power analysis to attack DPA resistant software. In: Paar, C., Koç, Ç.K. (eds.) CHES 2000. LNCS, vol. 1965, p. 238. Springer, Heidelberg (2000)

30. Messerges, T.S., Dabbish, E.A., Sloan, R.H.: Power analysis attacks of modular exponentiation in smartcards. In: Koç, Ç.K., Paar, C. (eds.) CHES 1999. LNCS, vol. 1717, pp. 144–157. Springer, Heidelberg (1999)

31. Nakano, Y., Souissi, Y., Nguyen, R., Sauvage, L., Danger, J.-L., Guilley, S., Kiyomoto, S., Miyake, Y.: A pre-processing composition for secret key recovery on Android smartphone. In: Naccache, D., Sauveron, D. (eds.) WISTP 2014. LNCS, vol. 8501, pp. 76–91. Springer, Heidelberg (2014)

32. O'Flynn, C., Chen, Z.: A case study of side-channel analysis using decoupling capacitor power measurement with the OpenADC. In: Garcia-Alfaro, J., Cuppens, F., Cuppens-Boulahia, N., Miri, A., Tawbi, N. (eds.) FPS 2012. LNCS, vol. 7743, pp. 341–356. Springer, Heidelberg (2013)

33. Osvik, D.A., Bos, J.W., Stefan, D., Canright, D.: Fast software AES encryption. In: Hong, S., Iwata, T. (eds.) FSE 2010. LNCS, vol. 6147, pp. 75–93. Springer, Heidelberg (2010)

34. Osvik, D.A., Shamir, A., Tromer, E.: Cache attacks and countermeasures: the case of AES. In: Pointcheval, D. (ed.) CT-RSA 2006. LNCS, vol. 3860, pp. 1–20. Springer, Heidelberg (2006)

35. Paar, C.: Efficient VLSI architectures for bit-parallel computation in Galois fields. PhD thesis, University of Essen (1994)

36. Page, D.: Theoretical Use of Cache Memory as a Cryptanalytic Side-Channel. Cryptology ePrint Archive, Report 2002/169 (2002). http://eprint.iacr.org/
37. Prouff, E., Rivain, M., Bevan, R.: Statistical analysis of second order differential power analysis. IEEE Trans. Comput. **58**(6), 799–811 (2009)
38. Quisquater, J.-J., Samyde, D.: ElectroMagnetic Analysis (EMA): measures and counter-measures for smart cards. In: Attali, S., Jensen, T. (eds.) E-smart 2001. LNCS, vol. 2140, pp. 200–210. Springer, Heidelberg (2001)
39. Rijmen, V.: Efficient implementation of the Rijndael S-box (2001)
40. Rudra, A., Dubey, P.K., Jutla, C.S., Kumar, V., Rao, J.R., Rohatgi, P.: Efficient Rijndael encryption implementation with composite field arithmetic. In: Koç, Ç.K., Naccache, D., Paar, C. (eds.) CHES 2001. LNCS, vol. 2162, pp. 171–184. Springer, Heidelberg (2001)
41. Satoh, A., Morioka, S., Takano, K., Munetoh, S.: A Compact Rijndael hardware architecture with S-box optimization. In: Boyd, C. (ed.) ASIACRYPT 2001. LNCS, vol. 2248, pp. 239–254. Springer, Heidelberg (2001)
42. Messerges, T.S., Dabbish, E.A., Puhl, L.: Method and apparatus for preventing information leakage attacks on a microelectronic assembly. US Patent 6,295,606, 25 September 2001
43. Trichina, E.: Combinational Logic Design for AES SubByte Transformation on Masked Data. Cryptology ePrint Archive, Report 2003/236 (2003). http://eprint.iacr.org/
44. Wolkerstorfer, J., Oswald, E., Lamberger, M.: An ASIC implementation of the AES SBoxes. In: Preneel, B. (ed.) CT-RSA 2002. LNCS, vol. 2271, pp. 67–78. Springer, Heidelberg (2002)

SoC It to EM: ElectroMagnetic Side-Channel Attacks on a Complex System-on-Chip

J. Longo[1]([✉]), E. De Mulder[2], D. Page[1], and M. Tunstall[2]

[1] Department of Computer Science, University of Bristol,
Merchant Venturers Building, Woodland Road, Bristol BS8 1UB, UK
{jake.longo,daniel.page}@bristol.ac.uk
[2] Rambus Cryptography Research Division, 425 Market Street, 11th Floor,
San Francisco, CA 94105, USA
{elke.demulder,michael.tunstall}@cryptography.com

Abstract. Increased complexity in modern embedded systems has presented various important challenges with regard to side-channel attacks. In particular, it is common to deploy SoC-based target devices with high clock frequencies in security-critical scenarios; understanding how such features align with techniques more often deployed against simpler devices is vital from both destructive (i.e., attack) and constructive (i.e., evaluation and/or countermeasure) perspectives. In this paper, we investigate electromagnetic-based leakage from three different means of executing cryptographic workloads (including the general purpose ARM core, an on-chip co-processor, and the NEON core) on the AM335x SoC. Our conclusion is that addressing challenges of the type above *is* feasible, and that key recovery attacks can be conducted with modest resources.

Keywords: Side-Channel · ElectroMagnetic · System on Chip · ARM · NEON

1 Introduction

A significant proportion of academic literature on side-channel attacks *already* targets real-world devices: even a very limited list of examples, such as those against KeeLoq keyless entry systems [20,27], Xilinx FPGA bit-stream encryption [34], or Atmel CryptoMemory [5] authentication, provides compelling evidence of their potency. However, and although clear counter-examples are identifiable, such devices may often be characterised as electronically and/or architecturally simple (the cryptographic aspects at least). From one perspective, this is a non-issue: use-cases such as contact-based and contactless payment cards, and trends such as Internet of Things (IoT) suggest devices of this type will abound for some time to come; the simplicity of a target in no way implies that developing and mounting attacks is simple nor without more general value. However, from a different perspective, it may seem unsatisfactory since it contrasts sharply with trends in commodity micro-electronics. In particular, more

© International Association for Cryptologic Research 2015
T. Güneysu and H. Handschuh (Eds.): CHES 2015, LNCS 9293, pp. 620–640, 2015.
DOI: 10.1007/978-3-662-48324-4_31

complex devices with richer functionality are now routinely deployed in contexts where side-channel attacks are a threat. For example, smart-phones now house multi-core, System-on-Chip (SoC) components with multi-gigahertz clock frequencies as standard, and, modulo constraints such as energy efficiency, market forces will drive increased use of similar components over time.

Within this context, use of ElectroMagnetic (EM) side-channel leakage is particularly attractive. Rohatgi [38] offers a comprehensive overview of both the physical phenomenon itself plus seminal results such as [3,21,37], neither of which we expand on unless specifically relevant. Versus power analysis [28], the non-contact, spatially flexible nature of an EM-based alternative means it a) represents a less invasive means of taking acquisitions, b) avoids issues such as on-chip voltage regulation and, most importantly, c) permits targeting of specific regions of (or components on) an SoC that otherwise offer composite leakage.

Our goal in this paper is to demonstrate that by carefully translating and refining existing techniques, EM-based side-channel attacks are viable against modern, complex targets. The challenges of evaluation and countermeasure instrumentation already motivate such work, but are arguably magnified by other constructive applications of side-channels (e.g., protection of intellectual property [7] and Trojan hardware detection [19]) relevant to SoCs: *all* benefit from better, *open* (noting this topic seems to represent an active but largely undocumented focus of various security services [40]) understanding of the associated leakage characteristics. We explore a single exemplar target device, namely the Texas Instruments (TI) AM335x SoC on a BeagleBone Black development board, with respect to three options for execution of cryptographic workloads. Following the relevant background material in Sect. 2, our contribution is, concretely, the EM-based analysis of

1. AES executed by an OpenSSL server on the ARM core (Sect. 3),
2. the proprietary AES co-processor (Sect. 4), and
3. the NEON[1] core, including bit-sliced AES (Sect. 5).

A central conclusion is that, while some effort is required to characterise the leakage, attack complexity does not *necessarily* scale in line with perceived device complexity. For example, in the first case above we are able to acquire and exploit leakage at *much* lower frequencies than suggested by the 1 GHz system clock; this implies attack cost may also be lower than expected, and hence relying on device complexity (resp. obscurity) to provide security is dubious at best.

2   Background

2.1   An Overview of the BeagleBone Platform

BeagleBone Black is a single-board computer built around a AM335x "Sitara" SoC. Constituent components can be grouped logically into four sub-systems

---

[1] Note that by targeting NEON, we specifically aim to add detail to the premise introduced during the CHES 2014 rump session talk of Bernstein and Lange: see http://cr.yp.to/talks/2014.09.25-2/slides-dan+tanja-20140925-2-4x3.pdf.

per [25, Figure 1-1]; the sub-systems are able to communicate via a dedicated Network-on-Chip (NoC), or interconnect. The following section focus on the Micro-Processor Unit (MPU) and the cryptographic co-processor. Although the latter lacks public documentation of the internal design (bar device driver source code[2] that interfaces with it), the former warrants further analysis: we refer to the extensive literature[3] for in-depth coverage.

The central point to take away from such analysis is the high degree of architectural complexity evident, even ignoring the number of components. For example, the MPU alone has a total of 3 clock and 4 power domains. Such features make the SoC an extremely challenging target with respect to Signal-to-Noise Ratio (SNR), and underlines the advantages offered by EM-based leakage.

2.2   Experimental Environment

Acquisition and measurement equipment. To allow reproducibility, the equipment used throughout this paper is listed below:

- Tektronix DPO7104 1GHz oscilloscope,
- Signatec PX14400 400 MS/s digitiser,
- Langer PA303 pre-amplifier plus various (e.g., low-pass) hardware filters,
- Langer RF-3 mini near-field probe set,
- Langer ICS105 IC scanner (or XY-table),
- Matlab 2014b (with signal processing toolbox).

The configuration was therefore very standard: the target device was mounted on the XY-table to allow micro-positioning of the probe(s), which supplied an amplified, filtered signal to either the digitiser (Sects. 3 and 5) or oscilloscope (Sect. 4, to cope with a higher sampling rate). This limits our remit strictly to close-range acquisitions, rather than at a distance, e.g., per [43].

Software stack. We used a standard BeagleBone Black distribution of Debian "Wheezey" on the target device (Linux kernel version 3.13.3). The device was booted from on-board embedded MultiMediaCard (eMMC) storage as is; no standard system processes were disabled. On top of this platform we use OpenSSL 1.0.1*j*, with the `cryptodev` extension[4] enabled when appropriate.

2.3   Leakage Detection and Exploitation Strategy

Notation. For some set or sequence x of length n, we let $x[j]$ denote the j-th element of x such that $0 \leq j < n$; x_i then denotes the i-th such object within a larger collection, with the subscript omitted where irrelevant. We use $\mathcal{H}(x)$ and

---

[2] http://github.com/torvalds/linux/blob/master/drivers/crypto/omap-aes.c.
[3] http://www.arm.com/files/pdf/A8_Paper.pdf.
[4] http://cryptodev-linux.org/.

$\mathcal{D}(x, y)$ to denote the Hamming weight and distance, respectively, of some x and y. As such,

$$r_i = \mathsf{DUT}_k^f(x_i) \leadsto \lambda_i$$

models some i-th execution of an operation f on the target device DUT, involving a security critical datum k (e.g., key material), accepting input x_i and yielding an output r_i and an EM-based trace of leakage λ_i (a sequence of samples). Depending on the context, the target operation ranges from single instructions to entire algorithms (e.g., AES), and, from the attacker perspective, r_i and/or x_i may be known or unknown and controlled or uncontrolled.

λ is essentially a function of the target device (or leakage model), the operation f and input x_i, *plus* the probe type and location (and any other parameters of the experimental environment). With this in mind, mounting a concrete attack demands an attacker a) determines when and where (in time and/or frequency domains) λ contains useful, exploitable leakage, and b) selects a probe configuration to maximise said leakage (i.e., maximise the SNR).

Leakage detection. While several strategies, e.g., [11,12,23], have been proposed to address the former challenge above, throughout this paper we use Welch's t-test. More specifically, we use the Test Vector Leakage Assessment (TVLA) methodology of Goodwill et al. [23]. Although there are several variants (fixed-versus-random and semi-fixed-versus-random for instance), the basic idea involves constructing two sets of test vectors V_0 and V_1: the former contains a single (semi-)fixed vector, whereas the latter contains (a large number of) vectors chosen uniformly at random.

For each i-th invocation of the target device, the input is selected by first randomly selecting a test vector type, i.e., a $b \xleftarrow{\$} \{0,1\}$, then a test vector from the appropriate set, i.e., an $x_i \xleftarrow{\$} V_b$; the resulting trace of leakage, λ_i, is added to a set Λ_b based on the test vector type. Then, we compute the t-statistic trace as

$$t = \frac{\bar{\Lambda}_0 - \bar{\Lambda}_1}{\sqrt{\frac{\sigma_0^2}{|\Lambda_0|} + \frac{\sigma_1^2}{|\Lambda_1|}}}$$

where $|\Lambda_b|$, $\bar{\Lambda}_b$ and σ_b^2 respectively denote the sample size, sample mean and sample variance of set Λ_b. The idea is that given a threshold τ (say $\tau = 4.5$ per [23, Section 3]), if we find $|t[j]| > \tau$ then we claim significant leakage is detected at the j-th sample: at that point there is a statistically observable difference between fixed and random test vectors, so there may be data-dependent and thus potentially exploitable information present. Each following section uses this approach: section-specific detail is included where appropriate, with a comprehensive overview deferred to the full version of this paper [29, Appendix A].

3   Software-Based AES

In the literature, it is common to target embedded devices (e.g., a microcontroller) executing a program on "bare-metal", i.e., directly on the hardware.

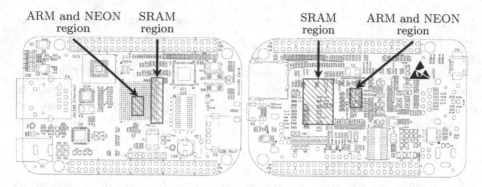

Fig. 1. BeagleBone Black schematic (source: http://github.com/CircuitCo/ BeagleBone-Black/blob/rev_a5c/BBB_PCB.zip) from front-side (left) and back-side (right), annotated with probe locations for leakage from the SRAM (red) and ARM and NEON cores (blue) (Color figure online).

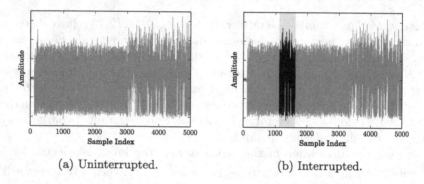

(a) Uninterrupted.   (b) Interrupted.

Fig. 2. Impact of interrupts on the acquisition process in Sect. 3: whereas the uninterrupted case (left) yields a "clean" trace, the interrupted case (right) is corrupted (during the annotated period).

Although reasonable for some scenarios, a growing number of targets will execute an Operating System (OS) kernel; this is even true of many smart-cards (cf. JavaCard or MULTOS). Perhaps due to the perceived increase in complexity, related attacks are less common than the bare-metal case: selected examples include Uno et al. [42] and Genkin et al. [22] who mount non-differential EM-based attacks on RSA (plus ElGamal in the latter case only) executing under Android (on ARM) and Windows XP (on x86), Aboulkassimi et al. [1,2] who mount differential EM-based attacks on AES executing under Java ME (on ARM), and Pellegrini et al. [35] who mount voltage depletion fault attacks on RSA executing under Linux (on SPARC).

In this section we consider a systems-oriented scenario of the latter type. Specifically, we imagine the target is a communications device (e.g., a

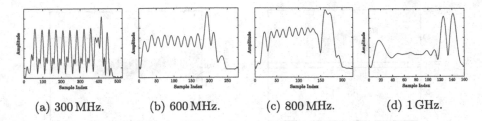

(a) 300 MHz.   (b) 600 MHz.   (c) 800 MHz.   (d) 1 GHz.

Fig. 3. Impact of clock scaling on the acquisition process in Sect. 3: each trace represents execution of AES under one of the four available clock frequencies.

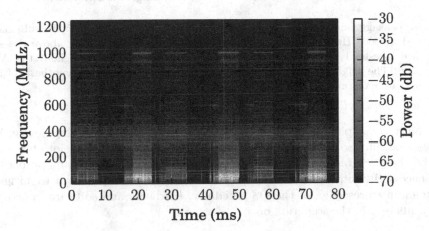

Fig. 4. Spectrogram plot of frequency band 0 to 1.25 GHz at our attack location, with the profiling device cycling through three kernels: a total of three iterations (left-to-right) of the memory intensive, spin-lock and computational (i.e., AES) kernels is illustrated. Note (a) the indicative frequency response of AES, and (b) the relatively narrow, low frequency range required to capture this response.

smart-phone) engaged in a TLS-based session with some server. As such, the attacker can observe computation of

$$c_i = \mathsf{DUT}_k^{\text{AES-128-CBC}}(m_i) \rightsquigarrow \lambda_i.$$

That is, AES-128 encryption, in CBC mode, of some unknown plaintext m_i under k to yield a known ciphertext c_i (since it is communicated across the network). Concretely, each encryption operation is performed by OpenSSL in software via the default T-tables-based [14, Section 4.2] implementation.

3.1 Experimental Outline

Before considering an attack strategy to exploit λ and recover k, a host of experimental challenges need to be addressed: the first relates to acquisition of λ. In common with analysis of other unknown/as yet unprofiled target devices, we

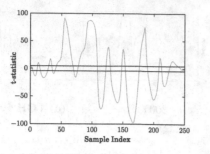
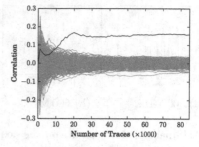

(a) Fixed-versus-random test.   (b) Single-bit correlation.

Fig. 5. Leakage analysis results for a free-running target using 85000 sub-traces matched at 600MHz. The leakage detection test (left) shows leakage above the significance threshold $\tau = 4.5$ (marked in black on the Y-axis) throughout the AES execution. The single-bit analysis (right) tracks the correct key bit hypothesis of the first byte over the number of sub-traces used.

rely on initial exploration based on full control of a replica profiling device. We stress that our use of the profiling device is simply to give insight into the associated signal characteristics: although it is well known that such an approach is not necessarily sufficient for building templates [13], we simply use it to mitigate systemic features (e.g., of the OS scheduler, hardware and software interrupts etc.) inherent in the scenario above.

Probe location. An initial, manual scan of the SoC surface was conducted in several stages to identify leakage related to the execution of three kernels: a set of memory intensive operations, a spin-lock, and a set of computationally intensive operations (namely AES encryption, as performed by OpenSSL). By periodically cycling through the kernels and monitoring the frequency response (illustrated by Fig. 4), two distinct regions of interest were identified (shown in Fig. 1). We attribute one region (straddling the SoC edge and SRAM bus) to the memory intensive kernel, and hence memory access. Given that the memory bus is specific to this development kit, that no effort appears to have been made to secure it, and that a complete operational datasheet is available[5], we did not feel it warranted further investigation even though it will likely yield exploitable leakage. The second region is located centrally on the AM335x surface, over a cluster of capacitors on the back-side of the board (specifically, around C94 and C46). Motivated by a) the magnitude of the frequency response observed during the AES execution, but also b) the long-term trend toward stacked fabrication processes (and associated decrease in SNR), we fixed the probe location over this support circuitry.

Acquisition tuning. The leakage from the selected region was identifiable using relatively low frequencies alone, i.e., below 100 MHz. We expect this, to some

---

[5] http://www.micron.com/parts/dram/ddr3-sdram/mt41k256m16ha-125.

degree, since a) AES throughout is clearly lower than the system clock frequency (one round is requires more than one instruction), and b) the on-chip discrete components coupled with the capacitor behave as a low-pass filter. As such, we applied a band-pass filter to the amplified signal centred on 45 MHz with a bandwidth of 24 MHz. This is interesting in so far as it allows use of less capable, and hence less expensive acquisition equipment. That is, rather than use a high-specification oscilloscope, we were able to use a lower-specification digitiser.

Bulk, or multi-block acquisitions. Our next step was to replace the artificial kernels with a "free-running" uninstrumented OpenSSL client instance: no artificial (e.g., hardware, via a GPIO pin) triggers are inserted. A coarse, soft trigger is attractive, but strictly to limit acquisitions to a target session (i.e., one k) rather than to provide alignment per se: each trace λ_i acquired therefore relates to l invocations of AES rather than 1, i.e., each c_i is now a $(16 \cdot l)$-byte or l-block ciphertext, as generated by the TLS record layer. Such a soft trigger is easily realised via traffic analysis, and is additionally beneficial since it permits c_i to be known (i.e., sniffed) rather than controlled (i.e., injected) by the attacker.

Although we argue that this choice is more realistic than the alternative, it has both positive and negative effects. On one hand, bulk acquisition significantly reduces the wall-clock time required [6, Section 3] and allows the effect of data and instruction caches to be largely ignored (since all but the first few AES invocations will occur with a warm cache). On the other, we must address various challenges relating to systematic noise that occurs over the longer time period (and which for "one-shot" devices such as smart-cards, are normally irrelevant).

Interrupt detection and synchronisation. The OS may preempt a user process if it does not voluntarily yield, or if the kernel needs to service an interrupt: use of bulk acquisition necessitates we account for these interrupts, because they will be observed more frequently during the computation of longer ciphertexts.

Figure 2 demonstrates that an uninterrupted versus interrupted trace can be identified visually. We *automate* similar identification using the trace alignment scores (i.e., a measure of the least squares [31, page 208]). To do so, we manually identify and select a single uninterrupted trace for use as a template. We then perform coarse alignment of all traces and record their score (versus the template): if the score is above an experimentally determined threshold, the trace is assumed to have been interrupted. For interrupted traces, we then have two choices: discard them, or "clean" them by pruning the interrupted region. We found the low sample rate used means interrupt pruning is highly error prone (it is not always clear at which exact point the interrupt has ended and the OpenSSL process has resumed); such errors desynchronise the trace (i.e., the sub-trace for a given AES invocation) from the associated ciphertexts. Although discarding traces imposes a penalty on the total number of traces required, we opted for this approach.

Clock scaling. Finally, the OS may attempt to scale (or throttle) the clock frequency to optimise power consumption. We observed cases where this occurred, although found the device would typically stabilise at 600 MHz once the OpenSSL process becomes active. AES execution under each clock configuration is shown in Fig. 3, with the difference between cases clearly highlighting the resulting misalignment.

By sampling well above the Nyquist rate, it may be possible to *infer* the clock rate by examining the response at specific frequencies (i.e., at 300 MHz, 600 MHz, 800 MHz and 1 GHz); such an approach may also facilitate interrupt pruning (per the above). However, use of a low sampling rate, while advantageous in other respects, rules this approach out. Instead, we simply created a template of AES execution at each clock frequency: any trivial comparison between each template and target trace reveals the clock frequency used, and yields a usable subset of traces whose clock frequency is uniform.

3.2 Analysis and Discussion

Summarising the section above, to mount a concrete attack we performed an acquisition phase as follows:

1. Bulk acquire $n = 1000$ traces, each including $l = 256$ encryption operations (meaning 4 kB of traffic per trace, and ~ 4 MB in total).
2. Deal with systemic noise by filtering for interrupts and clock scaling; in our experience, this means discarding $\sim 20\%$.
3. From each remaining trace, extract a fragment or sub-trace for each encryption operation; match these with the associated ciphertexts.
4. Realign each sub-trace, and discard any corrupted or low-quality cases; in our experience, this means discarding a further $\sim 5\%$.

This process yields a set of $s < n \cdot l$ remaining (sub-)traces, and for such n and l took ~ 6 min. Based on this set, we then attempted to exploit the leakage. To do so, we mounted a single-bit correlation-based attack targeting the T-table (or S-box) look-up in the final AES round. Figure 5b illustrates, without loss of generality, an example for the first byte of k: it shows growth of the correlation coefficient as the number of (sub-)traces increases. Note the correct (highlighted) hypothesis is clearly distinguished using around 20,000 (sub-)traces, meaning we *could* have bulk acquired as few as 100 traces (~ 400 kB) and still have been successful. In reality, fine-tuning n before the acquisition phase is difficult since the attacker cannot control l (and indeed this may change from one trace to another). However, using an adaptive choice of n such that s is large enough, the attack still succeeds.

We benchmarked this attack against a traditional alternative where an artificial hardware trigger (which simultaneously aligns traces, and avoids the issue of interrupts) and fixed clock frequency were used. We found key recovery was possible with only 3,000 (sub-)traces, ~ 7 times fewer than our free-running scenario. We posit the gap between the two *can* be incrementally reduced, since it essentially represents pre-processing inefficiency, deferring this to future work.

4   Hardware-Based AES

In this section, we shift focus to hardware-based execution of AES using the cryptographic co-processor. As in Sect. 3, the attacker can still observe the computation of

$$c_i = \mathsf{DUT}_k^{\text{AES-128-CBC}}(m_i) \rightsquigarrow \lambda_i$$

as invoked via OpenSSL. However, the underlying encryption operations are performed using a hardware-based AES implementation. We suggest this is likely to reflect use-cases such as Full Disk Encryption (FDE) given the potential to marshal operations via DMA. In such a use-case, the attacker can access c_i since this will represent (a block of) ciphertext stored on, and readable from, the disk in question.

4.1   Experimental Outline

As noted in Sect. 2.1, there is scant documentation for the AM335x cryptographic co-processor: our only insight into the internal design stems from device drivers that support interaction with it. Since the drivers do not expose any system calls for use by user processes, such interaction is realised concretely by enabling the OpenSSL `cryptodev` extension: each encryption operation invoked is processed, by OpenSSL, via the associated `cryptodev` kernel module and ultimately performed by the co-processor.

Black-box architectural analysis. Treating the co-processor as a black-box, we use the functionality offered (i.e., ECB, CBC and CTR modes, with 128-, 192- and 256-bit key sizes) and the extensive literature on similar hardware designs to infer the (probable) internal design. Specifically, the registers exposed (e.g., for the IV) and requirement to reinitialise the key register per invocation (so the key schedule is likely recomputed for each encryption) suggest an iterative design: a single (combinatorial) core is likely used by surrounding control logic in multiple steps to realise each mode. The default driver behaviour capitalises on hardware DMA support, via the scatter-gather mechanism, to operate autonomously from the ARM core.

Signal hunting. During any exploration phase, it is important to first establish a) an identifiable form and b) a base alignment point for the target signal; doing so maximises the chances of successfully detecting leakage. The two challenges are intrinsically linked, since a well defined form will facilitate alignment. However, the former challenge is perceived as being simple, because the target operation will typically yield a pronounced, identifiable form by virtue of how it is computed and by what. This was true, for instance, in Sect. 3: we were able to easily detect leakage from the ARM core by monitoring the frequency response during execution. In contrast, this is not true for the co-processor: not only is it unclear how AES is computed, we could not identify any periodic leakage signature linked to the AES operation. This is complicated further by virtue of the fact that the co-processor operates (semi-)independently of the ARM core (thus any hardware trigger used will be asynchronous to encryption operations).

Without any visual cues nor a reliable trigger, we were unsuccessful in detecting leakage under fixed-versus-random tests at the probe locations identified in Sect. 3. Further attempts to manually scan the AM335x surface at alternative probe locations did not yield better results. However, we *did* manage to detect the DMA strobes by locating a probe over the memory access region: these are, of course, inherently related to encryption operations and hence (to some degree) yield a (somewhat) synchronous trigger for activity by the co-processor. The difficulty with capitalising on this fact is that *any* memory intensive instruction sequence can cause false positives, rendering the trigger less reliable.

To combat this issue, we instead rely on saturating the DMA engine with *other* work: this forces the driver into a non-DMA fall-back mode, which issues interrupts for any memory management. These interrupts are used as a trigger for AES operations on the co-processor. While less ideal than the free-running scenario in Sect. 3, we argue this *is* incrementally better than a GPIO-based hardware trigger. Specifically, it requires an attacker controlled process be co-resident on the target device (cf. "spy process" in access-driven cache attacks such as [36]) rather than invasive alteration of the target process.

Testing strategy. With the trigger mechanism active, we placed several probes at various locations on the AM335x surface and repeated the same fixed-versus-random tests as above (using all available channels on the oscilloscope, sampling at a rate of 2.5 GS/s). Their repeated failure led us to abandon generic fixed-versus-random tests, and instead focus on more specifically tailored leakage detection test vectors. A test plan was developed to target several leakage models, using semi-fixed-versus-random [6, Section 5] test vectors. The only strategy to yield detectable leakage (which we focus on subsequently as a result) was Hamming distance; the associated test vectors force a small Hamming distance between round input and output. Figure 6 shows an averaged trace and the resulting t-test result (over 10000 traces); note that the t-statistic far exceeds our significance threshold of $\tau = 4.5$.

Signal processing and detrending. Although the leakage detection step was successful, it gave us little insight into the signal characteristics. As a first step, we carried out an automated scan of the AM335x surface, performing semi-fixed-versus-random tests (over 400 traces) at increments of 1 mm in each dimension; the location yielding the highest t-statistic will likely maximise our chances of success during key recovery.

Having optimised the probe location, we applied wavelet analysis [15] in an attempt to increase the SNR. There are already results [10,16] demonstrating wavelet transforms effective for filtering (denoising) and decomposition analysis in the context of side-channel attack. In general, denoising involves applying a soft-threshold [17,18] on the details components at each filter level before resynthesising the (clean) signal. However, a high-magnitude, semi-correlated interference signal overlaid the low-magnitude signal of interest. Both signals separately

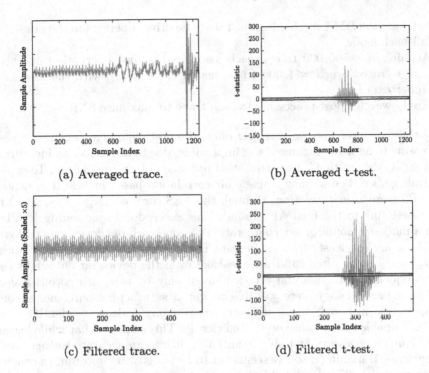

(a) Averaged trace.

(b) Averaged t-test.

(c) Filtered trace.

(d) Filtered t-test.

Fig. 6. Leakage detection test results for the AES co-processor running with a saturated DMA. The two columns relate to an averaged trace (left) and the related t-test result (right). The rows are indicative of raw unprocessed traces (top) and traces post-processed via the wavelet analysis (bottom).

had low-noise but the interference reduced the SNR of the signal of interest. As the interference contained overlapping frequencies with the signal of interest, a wavelet based detrending scheme, as used in [39], provided an effective and efficient approach for separation. After trying various wavelets, ones with a lower number of vanishing moments provided better results, indicating the need for a fast response to sudden changes in the interference [15,41]. The detrending technique follows a simple algorithm, inspired by the wavelet shrinkage techniques as described in [10,16]. First, perform the DWT [30] with the Haar wavelet. The low ratio of the sampling rate over frequency content of the signal required only a single level computed. Then, set all of the resulting approximation coefficients to zero before performing an inverse DWT on the detail coefficients. The resulting signal (shown in Fig. 6) with the interference extracted, yields a stronger result from the leakage detection test.

4.2   Analysis and Discussion

Summarising the section above, to mount a concrete attack we performed an acquisition phase as follows:

1. Saturate the DMA mechanism such that the driver operates in the non-DMA fall-back mode.
2. Acquire $n = 500,000$ traces, each associated with 1 encryption operation and averaged over $l = 1,000$ trials; match these traces with the associated ciphertexts.
3. Apply wavelet post-processing to each trace to maximise SNR.

Note that our interrupt-based trigger offers the best alignment achievable; post-processing to improve alignment was impossible, due to the lack of an identifiable form for AES operations. The acquisition process took around 3 days. To exploit the leakage, we then applied a single-bit correlation-based attack: if s_i denotes the AES state after i iterations through the AES core, we target $\mathcal{D}(s_{i-1}, s_i)$ for $i = 10$ relating to the final AES round. This succeeded in recovering k (albeit with a modest amount of key enumeration to cope with one lower-ranked byte).

There are (at least) three important conclusions to draw from the above. First, the effort required to identify leakage from the device far outweighs that of subsequent acquisition and attack phases: only by using a rigorous leakage detection methodology were we able to get a satisfactory outcome. Second, a gap exists: although Fig. 6 indicates that strong leakage *is* identified, our attack is unable to capitalise on this efficiently. This suggests that while leakage detection is a necessary first step, translating it into an accurate leakage model (in our case, Hamming distance seems not to be so) is also important in concrete attack scenarios. Third, while black-box analysis gave some insight into the co-processor architecture, this did not extend to the internal implementation. In particular, the initial failure of our testing strategy suggests either a) the trigger mechanism is not accurate enough to align traces correctly, hence decimating the SNR, and/or b) the co-processor is, in some way, protected against side-channel attacks. *If* the latter is true, it remains unclear *which* countermeasure is implemented: in contrast with Heinz et al. [24], for example, there is no structure in the signal that suggests time-based hiding, but equally attempted higher-order attacks on possible masking strategies were unsuccessful. Either way, *if* a countermeasure is implemented, then we conclude it only seems effective in increasing attack cost rather than preventing an attack.

5   NEON

NEON is a general-purpose SIMD extension to Cortex A-series ARM cores, harnessed, for example, by Bernstein and Schwabe [8] to both accelerate cryptographic workloads and deliver constant execution time. In terms of the ISA, each vector instruction $\odot^w$ processes vector operands with $l = \frac{n}{w}$ elements (or sub-words), each w-bits in size; $n \in \{64, 128\}$ is determined by the instruction type (more specifically, whether the operands are double- or quad-words). For the simplest case of a pure vector operation, we can therefore say

$$\boldsymbol{r} = \boldsymbol{x} \odot^w \boldsymbol{y} \mapsto \langle r^w[0] = x^w[0] \odot^w y^w[0], \dots, r^w[l-1] = x^w[l-1] \odot^w y^w[l-1]\rangle$$

where $t^w[j] = t[j \cdot w, \ldots, (j+1) \cdot w - 1]$ is the j-th w-bit (scalar) sub-word of vector t, and $\odot^w$ is the operation $\odot$ for such sub-words. The ISA naturally captures standard logical (e.g., $\odot^{1=} = \oplus$ with $w = 1$) and arithmetic (e.g., $\odot = +$ with $w = 8$, $w = 16$ or $w = 32$) operations, plus various more specialist extensions. Note that although the semantics of quad-word NEON instructions suggest they process 128-bit operands, the pipeline will in fact issue two 64-bit micro-operations.

5.1 Instruction-Level Characterisation

In this section we study leakage from (a subset of) NEON instructions by focusing on observation of

$$r_i = \mathsf{DUT}^{\odot^w}(x_i, y_i) \rightsquigarrow \lambda_i$$

for a range of $\odot^w$ but, without loss of generality, on $w \in \{8, 32\}$ bit sub-words within double-word, i.e., $n = 64$ bit, operands. Given that the NEON pipeline is tightly coupled to the ARM pipeline, we reason the two will be physically close on the AM335x surface; as such, we retain the same experimental configuration (e.g., same probe location) as Sect. 3. However, our specific remit means we compromise by using a strictly controlled profiling device: a hardware trigger is used throughout to support instruction-level (i.e., cycle-accurate) alignment and hence a lower bound on success rate.

Leakage detection. We performed an initial exploration focused on a limited, indicative set of NEON instructions: the aim was to gather general intuition about their leakage characteristics. As such, we considered various potential sources of leakage. Consider, for example, execution of a vector XOR instruction (e.g., `veor.u32 d0,d1,d2`): one could potentially observe leakage related to operand reads (i.e., from `d1` and/or `d2`), computation of the operation, or result write-back (i.e., to `d0`).

In summary, the results show that a) clear operation-dependent SPA leakage is evident, allowing, for example, construction of per-instruction templates, and b) data-dependent leakage is evident, but from result write-back only: we could identify no leakage relating to operand reads. The latter fact, i.e., the statistically observable difference between write-back of random versus fixed results, confirms that the leakage point relates to said step (not reading operands from memory).

Hamming weight leakage. Having identified a set of leakage points, our next goal was to analyse and exploit their structure. More specifically, we attempted to align the characterisation with standard attacks by tracking the Hamming weight of results written-back against associated leakage. This is achieved by amending the fixed-versus-random methodology, so semi-fixed test vectors are selected (for a given Hamming weight).

The results of this analysis, plus their utility, are discussed in the following section. We stress that, throughout, the Hamming weight of the entire n-bit result is considered: our results show that focusing on an individual w-bit sub-word *is* feasible, but with the expected increase the number of traces. That is, if one considers leakage with regards to a single w-bit sub-word then the other $l - 1$ sub-words can be considered noise (thus overcome by acquiring more traces).

Arithmetic and logical operations. Figure 7 illustrates leakage from two specific NEON instructions pertinent to cryptography. The (vector) XOR case is indicative of most instructions, in the sense that clear separation between distinct Hamming weights is evident. In contrast, the vector polynomial multiplication is something of a special case. The separation between distinct Hamming weights is still evident, and potentially relevant to cryptographic use-cases (e.g., [9]). However, unlike the other instructions there is some "cross over" with regard to the Hamming weight and signal that we cannot currently explain.

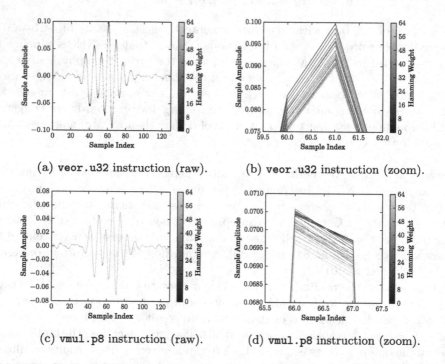

(a) `veor.u32` instruction (raw).   (b) `veor.u32` instruction (zoom).

(c) `vmul.p8` instruction (raw).   (d) `vmul.p8` instruction (zoom).

Fig. 7. Illustration of Hamming weight leakage for a (limited) set of NEON arithmetic and logical instructions (where $w = 32$).

Comparison operations. Figure 8 illustrates leakage from a NEON vector comparison instruction. In contrast to a scalar comparison on the ARM core (which produces a 1-bit result in the CPSR status register), a NEON vector comparison sets (or clears) all w bits in each sub-word to signal true or false (i.e., forms a mask). Without loss of generality, we focus on equality comparison:

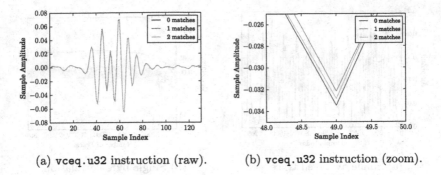

(a) `vceq.u32` instruction (raw).   (b) `vceq.u32` instruction (zoom).

Fig. 8. Illustration of Hamming weight leakage for NEON comparison instructions (where $w = 32$).

$$r^w[j] = \begin{cases} 2^w - 1 & \text{if } x^w[j] = y^w[j], \\ 0 & \text{otherwise.} \end{cases}$$

This can be used to support branch-free, constant-time implementations: the resulting mask is used to control conditional execution of subsequent operations in each sub-word, replacing conditional *control*-flow by conditional *data*-flow.

Our results demonstrate two important facts. First, analysis of leakage from a vector comparison reveals the (total) number of sub-word results that were true (or false); this is as expected, given the maximal and minimal Hamming weight of the outputs (i.e., masks) produced in each case. Second, as demonstrated by Fig. 10, it is possible to target a *specific* sub-word, and hence ascertain whether it has the value $2^w - 1$ or 0. Doing so means considering each sub-word independently, treating the remaining sub-words as noise (cf. single-bit DPA).

5.2 A Concrete Attack on AES

The charactisation above clearly suggests Hamming weight leakage can be leveraged in concrete attacks. As justification, we consider a scenario where the attacker can observe computation of

$$m_i = \text{DUT}_k^{\text{AES-128-CBC}}(c_i) \rightsquigarrow \lambda_i$$

but alter how AES itself is realised (compared with Sect. 3 and Sect. 4): we instead target the NEON-based bit-sliced implementation in OpenSSL (which stems from work by Käsper and Schwabe [26], and was enabled via the preprocessor flag -DBSAES_ASM).

This particular implementation is triggered if c_i is sufficiently large (namely 128 bytes, falling-back to an alternative implementation otherwise). Although we note the techniques in Sect. 3 remain broadly applicable, for clarity we retain the same experimental environment as Sect. 5.1 (e.g., with a hardware trigger). The

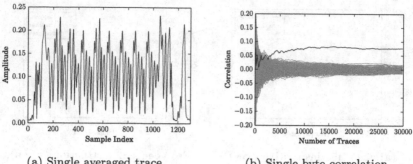

(a) Single averaged trace.   (b) Single byte correlation.

Fig. 9. Illustration of decryption (for a 128-byte ciphertext) using the NEON-based bit-sliced implementation of AES in OpenSSL; the corresponding correlation coefficient evolution suggests the attack succeeds with $\sim 5,000$ traces.

attack then proceeds in a fairly straightforward manner: we simply use key (byte, due to the representation of data used by the implementation) hypotheses based on Hamming weight of the intermediate state after the first round `InvSubBytes` operation in a standard, correlation-based approach. The attack succeeds with $\sim 5,000$ traces, requiring $5000 \cdot 128 = 625$ kB of ciphertext as illustrated in Fig. 9.

5.3   A Theoretical Attack on NORX

Perhaps more so than other operations, the relevance of leakage from a vector comparison needs motivation. As such, consider NORX [4], an AEAD-based CAESAR candsidate whose reference implementation[6] harnesses NEON. The NORX32-6-1 parametrisation (i.e., for 32-bit word size, 6 rounds, parallelism degree 1, and 128-bit tag size) verifies tags as follows

```
/* Verify tag */ A = vceqq_u32(A, LOADU(c + 0)); return 0xFFFFFFFF
== (vgetq_lane_u32(A, 0) & vgetq_lane_u32(A, 1) &
                    vgetq_lane_u32(A, 2) & vgetq_lane_u32(A, 3)) ? 0 : -1;
```

noting the state `A` (representing the computed tag) is compared with the received tag using vector comparison on 32-bit sub-words.

On one hand this *is* attractive since a) it is likely more efficient than four sequential 32-bit comparisons, and b) it is constant-time, unlike an alternative such as use of `memcmp`. On the other hand, consider a (purely hypothetical) scenario where an attacker has access to a decryption oracle, i.e., execution of

$$\mathsf{DUT}_k^{\mathrm{NORX32\text{-}6\text{-}1}}(c_i) \rightsquigarrow \lambda_i$$

for chosen c_i can be observed. The resulting leakage can be used to enable tag forgery: the attacker is able to determine the total number of matching sub-words

---

[6] See http://github.com/norx/NORX. We stress our analysis should in no way be inferred as criticism of NORX within the context of CAESAR.

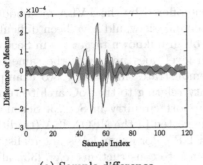
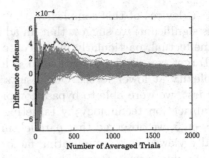

(a) Sample difference.   (b) Difference over averaged trials.

Fig. 10. Illustration of a single-word attack on `vceq.u32`: the black hypothesis for $r^w[j] = 2^w - 1$ (i.e., where the comparison is true, without loss of generality for $j = 0$) is clearly distinguished after averaging over 1000 trials.

Table 1. Summary of results.

Section	Operation	Implementation	Hardware	Trigger	Acquisitions	Data
3	Decryption	T-tables	ARM core	GPIO-based	3,000	46 kB
3	Encryption	T-tables	ARM core	Network-based	100	400 kB
4	Encryption	Hardware	Co-processor	DMA-based	500,000	7 GB
5	Decryption	Bit-sliced	NEON core	GPIO-based	5,000	625 kB

for a candidate tag, so requires $O(2^{32})$ queries (albeit with a constant factor that hides the cost of dealing with noise etc. in acquisitions) to brute-force search for a tag matching ciphertext of their choice. Whether or not such an approach is feasible in practice clearly depends on the context, but equally clear is the gap between this and the supposed (theoretical) security level.

6 Conclusions

In this paper we present concrete, EM-based analysis of the AM335x SoC and software executing on it. Although hard to compare directly, a summary of our results targeting CBC-based AES is shown in Table 1. Beyond this, however, we draw several more general conclusions:

1. Despite suggestions to the contrary [32], higher clock frequency does not *imply* a requirement for a high sampling rate: instruction- or cycle-level resolution *may* yield better results, but we still observed exploitable leakage at much lower frequencies (mirroring observations such as in [22]). This fact refutes any suggestion that the impact of EM-based attacks (against targets of this complexity) is lessened by cost: for example, in Sect. 3a (post-characterisation, i.e., excluding the XY-table) attack can be mounted using $\sim \$1,800$ of equipment (including a suitable low-end oscilloscope in place of the digitiser, and hand-made 30 AWG coil, 15-turn probe).

2. For devices of this complexity, the value offered by the TVLA methodology is significant: we suggest that an ad hoc analysis would have been difficult or ineffectual, particularly in the context of an unknown target (as in Sect. 4).
3. Target complexity suggested at a high level does *not* imply the same complexity at lower levels. Our results demonstrate this fact in two examples. First, we were able to bypass complexity relating to the SoC architecture or fabrication technology by targeting support circuitry in Sect. 3. Second, in Sect. 5, we observed that parallelism suggested in the NEON ISA (traditionally viewed as a complicating factor in DPA, for example) is not realised in the micro-architecture: This is of relevance to constructions (e.g., [33], albeit studied in the context of hardware) that *rely* on parallelism somehow.
4. Although the drive for efficient, constant-time implementation using NEON is clearly important, it seems prudent to proactively consider when/how such an approach can enable other forms of leakage. For example, Sect. 5 demonstrates that vector comparison, while advantageous in the sense of having a fixed latency, will still leak information about sub-word (in)equality.
5. Software such as OpenSSL is now becoming commonplace in (embedded) scenarios in which it might traditionally have been deemed too heavy-weight. As a result, alongside the challenging goal of securing such software against network-based attacks, it is starting to seem of long-term importance that countermeasures for hardware side-channels are also proactively considered.

Acknowledgements. Jake Longo has been supported in part by a studentship under the EPSRC Doctoral Training Partnership (DTP) scheme. The authors would like to thank Pankaj Rohatgi for general discussion, and Sami Saab for specific help with signal processing/analysis. We also thank both Billy Brumley and Markku Saarinen for their insight on NEON-based implementation, Martijn Stam for discussion about AEAD, and the NORX team, all of who help improved Sect. 5.

References

1. Aboulkassimi, D., Agoyan, M., Freund, L., Fournier, J.J.A., Robisson, B., Tria, A.: ElectroMagnetic Analysis (EMA) of software AES on Java mobile phones. In: Information Forensics and Security (WIFS), pp. 1–6 (2011)
2. Aboulkassimi, D., Fournier, J.J.A., Freund, L., Robisson, B., Tria, A.: EMA as a physical method for extracting secret data from mobile phones. IJCSA **2**(1), 16–25 (2013)
3. Agrawal, D., Archambeault, B., Rao, J.R., Rohatgi, P.: The EM side-channel(s). In: Kaliski, B.S., koç, Ç.K., Paar, C. (eds.) CHES. LNCS, pp. 29–45. Springer, Heidelberg (2003)
4. Aumasson, J.-P., Jovanovic, P., Neves, S.: NORX. CAESAR submission specification, version 1.1, (2014). http://norx.io/data/norx.pdf
5. Balasch, J., Gierlichs, B., Verdult, R., Batina, L., Verbauwhede, Ingrid: Power analysis of atmel cryptomemory – recovering keys from secure EEPROMs. In: Dunkelman, O. (ed.) CT-RSA 2012. LNCS, vol. 7178, pp. 19–34. Springer, Heidelberg (2012)

6. Becker, G.T., Cooper, J., DeMulder, E., Goodwill, G., Jaffe, J., Kenworthy, G., Kouzminov, T., Leiserson, A., Marson, M., Rohatgi, P., Saab, S.: Test vector leakage assessment (TVLA) methodology in practice. In: ICMC (2013)
7. Becker, G.T., Kasper, M., Moradi, A., Paar, C.: Side-channel based watermarks for IP protection. In: COSADE, pp. 47–50 (2010)
8. Bernstein, D.J., Schwabe, P.: NEON crypto. In: Prouff, E., Schaumont, P. (eds.) CHES 2012. LNCS, vol. 7428, pp. 320–339. Springer, Heidelberg (2012)
9. Câmara, D., Gouvêa, C.P.L., López, J., Dahab, R.: Fast software polynomial multiplication on ARM processors using the NEON engine. In: Cuzzocrea, A., Kittl, C., Simos, D.E., Weippl, E., Xu, Lida (eds.) CD-ARES Workshops 2013. LNCS, vol. 8128, pp. 137–154. Springer, Heidelberg (2013)
10. Charvet, X., Pelletier, H.: Improving the DPA attack using wavelet transform. In: NIST Physical Security Testing Workshop (2005)
11. Chothia, T., Guha, A.: A statistical test for information leaks using continuous mutual information. In: CSF, pp. 177–190 (2011)
12. Choudary, O., Kuhn, M.G.: Efficient template attacks. In: Francillon, A., Rohatgi, P. (eds.) CARDIS 2013. LNCS, vol. 8419, pp. 253–270. Springer, Heidelberg (2014)
13. Choudary, O., Kuhn, M.G.: Template attacks on different devices. In: Prouff, E. (ed.) COSADE 2014. LNCS, vol. 8622, pp. 179–198. Springer, Heidelberg (2014)
14. Daemen, J., Rijmen, V.: The Design of Rijndael. Springer, Heidelberg (2002). doi:10.1007/978-3-662-04722-4
15. Daubechies, I.: Ten Lectures on Wavelets. In: CBMS-NSF Regional Conference Series in Applied Mathematics. Society for Industrial and Applied Mathematics (1992)
16. Debande, N., Souissi, Y., Aabid, M.A.E., Guilley, S., Danger, J.: Wavelet transform based pre-processing for side channel analysis. In: MICROW, pp. 32–38 (2012)
17. Donoho, D.L.: De-noising by soft-thresholding. IEEE Trans. Inf. Theory 41(3), 613–627 (1995)
18. Donoho, D.L., Johnstone, I.M.: Ideal spatial adaptation by wavelet shrinkage. Biometrika 81(3), 425–455 (1994)
19. Du, D., Narasimhan, S., Chakraborty, R.S., Bhunia, S.: Self-referencing: a scalable side-channel approach for hardware trojan detection. In: Mangard, S., Standaert, F.-X. (eds.) CHES 2010. LNCS, vol. 6225, pp. 173–187. Springer, Heidelberg (2010)
20. Eisenbarth, T., Kasper, T., Moradi, A., Paar, C., Salmasizadeh, M., Shalmani, M.T.M.: On the power of power analysis in the real world: a complete break of the KEELOQ code hopping scheme. In: Wagner, D. (ed.) CRYPTO 2008. LNCS, vol. 5157, pp. 203–220. Springer, Heidelberg (2008)
21. Gandolfi, K., Mourtel, C., Olivier, F.: Electromagnetic analysis: concrete results. In: Koç, C.K., Naccache, D., Paar, C. (eds.) CHES 2001. LNCS, vol. 2162, p. 251. Springer, Heidelberg (2001)
22. Genkin, D., Pachmanov, L., Pipman, I., Tromer, E.: Stealing keys from PCs by radio: cheap electromagnetic attacks on windowed exponentiation. Cryptology ePrint Archive, Report 2015/170 (2015). http://eprint.iacr.org/
23. Goodwill, G., Jun, B., Jaffe, J., Rohatgi, P.: A testing methodology for side-channel resistance validation. In: NIST Non-Invasive Attack Testing Workshop (2011)
24. Heinz, B., Heyszl, J., Stumpf, F.: Side-channel analysis of a high-throughput AES peripheral with countermeasures. In: ISIC, pp. 25–29 (2014)
25. Texas Instruments. AM335x Sitara processor datasheet. Technical Report SPRS717G, TI (2014). http://www.ti.com/lit/ds/symlink/am3358.pdf

26. Käsper, E., Schwabe, P.: Faster and timing-attack resistant AES-GCM. In: Clavier, C., Gaj, K. (eds.) CHES 2009. LNCS, vol. 5747, pp. 1–17. Springer, Heidelberg (2009)

27. Kasper, M., Kasper, T., Moradi, A., Paar, C.: Breaking KEELOQ in a flash: on extracting keys at lightning speed. In: Preneel, B. (ed.) AFRICACRYPT 2009. LNCS, vol. 5580, pp. 403–420. Springer, Heidelberg (2009)

28. Kocher, P.C., Jaffe, J., Jun, B.: Differential power analysis. In: Wiener, M. (ed.) CRYPTO 1999. LNCS, vol. 1666, p. 388. Springer, Heidelberg (1999)

29. Longo, J., De Mulder, E., Page, D., Tunstall, M.: SoC it to EM: electromagnetic side-channel attacks on a complex system-on-chip. Cryptology ePrint Archive, (2015). http://eprint.iacr.org/

30. Mallat, S.G.: A theory for multiresolution signal decomposition : the wavelet representation. IEEE Trans. Pattern Anal. Mach. Intell. **11**(7), 674–693 (1989)

31. Mangard, S., Oswald, E., Popp, T.: Power analysis attacks: Revealing the secrets of smart cards. Springer, US (2008)

32. Mateos, E., Gebotys, C.H.: Side channel analysis using Giant Magneto-Resistive (GMR) sensors. In: COSADE, pp. 42–49 (2011)

33. Medwed, M., Standaert, F.-X., Joux, A.: Towards super-exponential side-channel security with efficient leakage-resilient PRFs. In: Prouff, E., Schaumont, P. (eds.) CHES 2012. LNCS, vol. 7428, pp. 193–212. Springer, Heidelberg (2012)

34. Moradi, A., Barenghi, A., Kasper, T., Paar, C.: On the vulnerability of FPGA bitstream encryption against power analysis attacks: extracting keys from Xilinx Virtex-II FPGAs. In: CCS, pp. 111–124 (2011)

35. Pellegrini, A., Bertacco, V., Austin, T.: Fault-based attack of RSA authentication. In: DATE, pp. 855–860 (2010)

36. Percival, C.: Cache missing for fun and profit (2005). http://www.daemonology. net/papers/htt.pdf

37. Quisquater, J.-J., Samyde, D.: ElectroMagnetic Analysis (EMA): measures and counter-measures for smart cards. In: Attali, S., Jensen, T. (eds.) E-smart 2001. LNCS, vol. 2140, p. 200. Springer, Heidelberg (2001)

38. Rohatgi, P.: Electromagnetic attacks and countermeasures. In:Cryptographic Engineering, pp. 407–430. Springer, US (2009)

39. Saab, S., Leiserson, A., Tunstall, M.: Efficient key extraction from the primary side of a switched-mode power supply. In: Cryptology ePrint Archive, Report 2015/512 (2015). http://eprint.iacr.org/

40. Scahill, J., Begley, J.: iSpy: The CIA campaign to steal Apple's secrets. The Intercept (2015). http://firstlook.org/theintercept/2015/03/10/ispy-cia-cam paign-steal-apples-secrets/

41. Strang, G., Fix, G.J.: An Analysis of the Finite Element Method. Automatic Computation, Prentice-Hall, Englewood Cliffs (1973)

42. Uno, H., Endo, S., Hayashi, Y., Homma, N., Aoki, T.: Chosen-message electromagnetic analysis against cryptographic software on embedded OS. In: EMC (2014)

43. Zajic, A., Prvulovic, M.: Experimental demonstration of electromagnetic information leakage from modern processor-memory systems. IEEE Trans. Electromagn. Compat. **56**(4), 885–893 (2014)

Finding the AES Bits in the Haystack: Reverse Engineering and SCA Using Voltage Contrast

Christian Kison[1,2]($\boxtimes$), Jürgen Frinken[2], and Christof Paar[1]

[1] Horst Görtz Institute for IT Security, Ruhr University Bochum, Bochum, Germany
[2] Bundeskriminalamt, Kriminaltechnisches Institut, Wiesbaden, Germany
Christian.Kison@rub.de

Abstract. In this paper, we demonstrate how the Scanning Electron Microscope (SEM) becomes a powerful tool for Side Channel Analysis (SCA) and Hardware Reverse Engineering. We locate the AES hardware circuit of a XMEGA microprocessor with Capacitive-Coupled Voltage Contrast (CCVC) images and use them in a powerful Voltage Contrast Side Channel Analysis (VCSCA). This enables an attacker to locate AES bit-wires in the top metal-layer and thus, to recover valuable netlist information. An attacker gets a valuable entry-point to look for weaknesses or Intellectual Property (IP) in the AES circuit. Additionally we show the great potential of the VCSCA in a non-invasive Side Channel Analysis for Reverse Engineering (SCARE) approach. Finally, we recover the full key of the AES hardware-engine in a practical template-based VCSCA and a no-plaintext, no-ciphertext and no-key Simple Side Channel Analysis (SSCA). We show that future VCSCA attacks present a big hardware security-risk that IC vendors need to consider.

Keywords: Side channel analysis · SCA · hw reverse engineering · Voltage contrast · AES · Full key recovery · Scare

1 Introduction

A crucial part in hardware reverse engineering is to know the location of their Region of Interest (ROI) prior to their delayering process. Without this knowledge, the literal search for the needle in the haystack can become a major obstacle for the reverser. ROIs are usually security-sensitive elements, e.g., fuse bytes, cryptographic algorithms or proprietary parts of an Integrated Circuit (IC) [14,24]. We may have luck if vendors "mark" sensitive areas with a shield or we already know the basic structure from a similar IC within the same vendor family. However, this is an exception especially in today's multi-million gate ICs. Identifying crucial elements is often extremely difficult.

The classical approach is a stepwise delayering down to the silicon substrate while taking images from each layer. After assembling and overlaying the different layers, a hardware reverse engineer can begin to interpret the logical cells to find his ROI. Even with semi-automated tools that help to recognize standard cells of a library and wirings, we need to attend and review the process

© International Association for Cryptologic Research 2015
T. Güneysu and H. Handschuh (Eds.): CHES 2015, LNCS 9293, pp. 641–660, 2015.
DOI: 10.1007/978-3-662-48324-4_32

of millions of gates to get a flawless netlist from the chip structure: There is not feedback mechanism that alerts of the reverser about mistakes and even the slightest mistake in the image acquisition might lead to faulty connections and a complete different circuit behavior. To make things worse, it is difficult to completely planarize the die with low to medium prized equipment, resulting in bad layer images and therefore worse recognition rates with the current chip-area-to-layer-thickness ratio.

Pinpointing the delayering process to a ROI reduces the costs and processing time when the user can focus on keeping the structure of the ROI still recognizable, neglecting the rest of the chip. Another reason is to achieve better signal-to-noise-ratio with located EM-traces or make other (fault-)attacks possible [18,19]. Sometimes this might even enable more advanced analysis like inter-gate side channel leakages as discussed in [27].

2   Related Work

In order to find the hot spot or ROI,multiple more practical approaches emerged, often in combination with a Side Channel (SC). The EM near-field cartography, thermal analysis and optical photon emission are the three most noteworthy examples [3,9,12,16,18,19,23]. All techniques are semi-invasive attacks [25]. They depackage the IC to strengthen existing side channels like EM emanation (to make pinpointed small loop measurements possible) and to gain access to additional SC s like photon emission and heat distribution. The mentioned semi-invasive techniques are possible from the top- and backside of the chip, whereby the backside approach usually needs additional equipment for milling and thinning the silicon bulk [12].

To be precise enough for locating the smallest activity areas, spatial located EM emanation cartography takes several hours. It finds multiple high Signal-To-Noise-Ratio (SNR) spots along the power distribution, as the radiation is directly related to the power consumption. Furthermore EM emanation often results in better SNR from the frontside, as the probe can be moved closer to the emanation source [16,18,19]. Nevertheless this approach allows to find a ROI within µm range. Thus, we can skip most parts of the chip and concentrate on the ROI. The drawback for EM near-field cartography is the long measurement time to scan the whole die surface and may show multiple hot spots.

In the case of the photon emission, the price of the equipment maps directly onto the measuring time and quality: An IR-range sensitive camera with good Quantum Efficiency (QE) and low dark-current costs several 10k€. Transistors have a probability to emit a photon during a state transition which passes through the thinned silicon backside. A first mandatory preparation is the thinning of the silicon bulk on the backside. The basic idea is to capture the emitted photons and visualize them in a highly spatial resolute setup. This becomes a major obstacle for modern CMOS processes, due to the diffraction limit of IR light. Additional preparation steps after the thinning, like a Numerical Aperture Increasing Lens (NAIL), might become necessary [28]. This extends the preparation time and bears the risk of breaking the chip. After a camera-dependent image integration time, we can find the activity of individual transistors during the loop execution of one code fragment [23]. By increasing the supply voltage during the interesting clock cycles, the authors enhance the IR photon emission probability to highlight corresponding areas. Using this technique the authors of [22] successfully extracted an AES key by observing the memory access pattern of the subbytes routine. Meanwhile [12] pinpoints a Picosecond Imaging Circuit Analysis (PICA) attack on single transistors to find xor values. Finding the respective hot spots and transistors is done with an optical long time image integration like in [22,23]. Once a ROI has been determined, PICA can be used to see transistor switches in high-frequency ICs.

Surface Liquid Crystal (LC) is a wide spread analysis method based on the thermal radiation for failure analysis in the industry. It is well established and can be exploited for ROI localisation from the attacker's point of view. LCs allow spatial resolutions of $4\,\mu m$ and better [3]. For modern CMOS processes this approach has equal spatial limitations, due to the IR light diffraction limit. Therefore new approaches like the Fluorescent Microthermal Imaging (FMI) emerged which try to fluoresce light with shorter wavelength [3]. Furthermore did the authors of [11] try to extend the thermal hot spot detection to the IC backside. Depending on the camera, are thermal and photon emission failure analysis methods qualified to find the ROIs. Both approaches are usually done over multiple program executions to heat-up or gather enough emitted photons in a normal working chip. These failure analysis methods face big challenges and difficulties with the upcoming CMOS sizes and decreasing power supply voltages. The modern CMOS size is below the diffraction limit of IR light and the decreasing power supply voltage drops the probability of photons being emitted and reduce the produced heat due to smaller currents.

This paper uses the Scanning Electron Microscope (SEM) as advanced inspection tool. Access to a suitable SEM should not be problematic as bigger institutes and universities with mid-class laboratories usually own one, due to their distribution in many academic fields. Companies and private persons can find second hand SEMs for under 10k€ or rent it on a hourly basis. A well-funded hardware reverse engineer usually has access to a SEM for taking layer images. Once the setup is built and the Device Under Test (DUT) is vulnerable to our approach, we are able identify the ROI faster as the EM cartography and have less sample preparation compared to the photon emission analysis. Furthermore do we not need to run the chip multiple times and have better spatial resolution than thermal analysis methods.

Our contribution in this paper is the following:

1. We demonstrate an approach to pinpoint the AES location of the XMEGA microprocessor with Voltage Contrast (VC) analysis comparable to related work.
2. We exploit the VC as a SC and perform a full key-recovery in a template-attack and a Simple Side Channel Analysis (SSCA).
3. Using the VC images reveals additional information of the AES circuit useful for a reverse engineer. Furthermore are we showing the potential of VC SC

in a Side Channel Analysis for Reverse Engineering (SCARE) approach to find additional circuit netlist information.

4. The results show a possibility to counter hardware-obfuscation and hardware protection and to verify parts of an extracted netlist.

The rest of this paper is structured as follows: Sect. 3 describes the different Voltage Contrast (VC) analysis methods and their physical understanding. Section 4 locates the AES circuit with the common Dynamic Voltage Contrast (DVC) analysis. Section 5 is the main contribution that gives a Proof-of-Concept (PoC) for the Voltage Contrast Side Channel Attack (VCSCA). The DUT is a widespread Atmel XMEGA microcontroller. We show a template-attack and a Simple Side Channel Analysis (SSCA) approach to recover the full AES key. Section 6 concludes this work.

3   Voltage Contrast

The SEM has become a powerful diagnostic tool during the last 60 years, used in many applications for IC inspection and failure analysis. When an electron beam-gun fires (primary) electrons on a scanning surface, secondary electrons are hit out of a solid specimen. These emitted secondary electrons have usually low energy (0–50 eV), which makes them easily detectable by using a positive electrical-field metal-plate as a detector. Out of the SEM images are the secondary electron images the most widely used, due to their ease of production and similarity to light microscope with improved depth of field [6].

During VC failure analysis, the natural negative charge of the electrons is used to view different voltage potentials, with the help of their electrical field and their direct influence to secondary electrons. Note that VC also works with positive ions in a Focused Ion Beam (FIB), since only the difference in charge is important. Using VC with positive ions from a FIB achieves better results[1] and the voltage interpretation of brightness and darkness is reversed compared to the SEM VC [5–7]. VC analysis needs the chip to be depackaged to gain access to the die surface.

VC analysis can be classified into two categories, which are on the one hand the static VC methods, including Passive Voltage Contrast (PVC) and Active Voltage Contrast (AVC) and on the other hand the Dynamic Voltage Contrast (DVC).

3.1   Static Voltage Contrast

The static VC is performed on chips with removed passivation layer or even partly delayered chips. Static VC is split in the two sub-techniques PVC and AVC. The PVC does not connect the DUT to any signals or voltages and thereby shows the charging up of floating gates and capacitances. It is often used to find

---

[1] With individually optimized parameters.

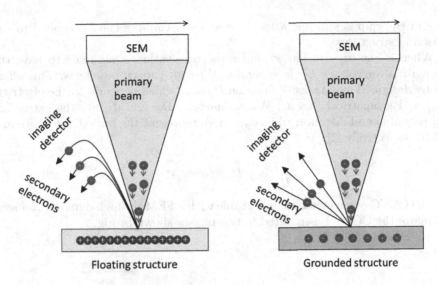

Fig. 1. Passive Voltage Contrast

shorts and imperfectly connected wires and structures during chip manufacturing. The DUT does not have to be functional anymore, allowing to take VC images of intermediate layers. Note that is possible to create floating structures by removing metal layers or by wire cutting with a FIB [17]. To pinpoint shorts and badly connected wires, the structures are split and analyzed separately by applying a voltage in the AVC.

Figure 1 shows the PVC. Isolated structures are charging up, due to second electrons being hit out of the structure. In the immediate consequence the majority of produced secondary electrons are prevented to reach the detector by the inverted electrical field. These structures appear dark in the image. Grounded structures do not appear bright, because of the high yield [17].

AVC differs from PVC as it applies voltages in some structures to force them look dark or bright in flawless structures. Is the outcome not as expected, a short or open connection can be assumed. Knowing the detailed place-and-route of the netlist and structures is very helpful, but not mandatory. The authors of [26] use the PVC to detect stealthy dopant-level circuits (trojans).

3.2 Dynamic Voltage Contrast

DVC is performed during dynamic rather than static operation of the DUT. In the scope of an IC or microcontroller (μC), the device is running normally, while performing the voltage contrast. If the device is still under a the passivation layer, Capacitive Coupled Voltage Contrast (CCVC) can be applied. CCVC exploits the property that the voltage potentials of the top metal-wires are electrically coupled with the covering dielectric passivation of the die, forming a capacitor. Therefore, CCVC is performed while the passivation layer is still covering the die and the chip is still operational, or at least voltages can be applied to top wires and structures.

When a line or wire buried under the passivation is assumed to have the voltage U_p, an voltage U_S is generated through capacitive effects. This effect can be described as a transfer function U_S/U_p, which depends on the electrical (U_E) and geometrical (d_e, d_p, W) parameters. U_E and d_E are the extraction grid potential and distance, while d_p and W represent the buried line depth and width, respectively [2]:

$$\frac{U_S}{U_p} = f(U_E, d_E, d_p, W) \tag{1}$$

The CCVC phenomena is made visible with a SEM through dynamic changes. Therefore the CCVC is separated in two phases shown in Fig. 2.

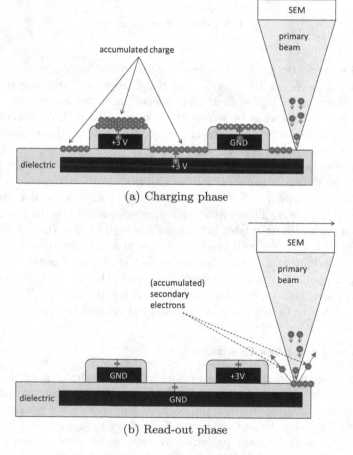

(a) Charging phase

(b) Read-out phase

Fig. 2. Capacitive Coupled Voltage Contrast

The first phase charges up the ICs surface with the electron-beam with location-depending accumulated charges (due to U_S), coupled to the underlaying electrical potentials (U_p). In the second phase, the accumulated electrons are hit out as secondary electrons. Compared to the normal structures, are these more detected electrons, brightening the structure. The electrical potential of the top layers can be data-dependent. Please not that this is not always the case as modern CMOS processes route the VCC or GND signal through the top metal layer. The data dependency leaks further information in a SC that are meant to be kept secret. This has already been seen as a theoretical threat in [8]. We show a practical attack and utilise the CCVC as a SC, not considered in the SC community so far[2].

Furthermore we emphasize that the authors of [20,21] show a possibility for backside CCVC or E-beam probing (EBP). This imposes a big threat for IC vendors and designs, if backside CCVC is scalable to big areas like the shown frontside approach. Backside CCVC has the potential to become one of the most threatening SCs, as there is almost no IC backside protections in todays IC structures. In this work we show a PoC for the frontside CCVC that can be extended to the backside in future work. Therefore we refer to frontside CCVC throughout the rest of this paper, if not stated otherwise.

Note that the DUT needs to be depackaged and we require the passivation layer, which classifies the CCVC as a common semi-invasive approach. If the attacker is able to remove the passivation with the DUT still operational, other DVC s are possible as well. Therefore we will stick to the term of DVC throughout this paper, rather than CCVC. Figure 2 shows the electrical properties of the CCVC, separated in charging phase in Fig. 2(a) and read-out phase in Fig. 2(b).

We described in Sect. 3.1 the possibility to distinguish between high and low voltages on the surface from the brightness in the SEM image. With carefully selected SEM parameters, we can see dynamic changes during the clock transition for a short time. By optimizing the parameters, we were even able to observe changes in the second metal layer[3], easily distinguishable as 90° rotated wires.

As the CCVC is built from two phases and especially the first phase needs some time to charge the surface, the clock speed of the DUT has to be very slow. With an external clock, this can be done in a trivial manner. In more complex scenarios, clock stretching [7], invasive mechanical probing or even EM based attacks on ring oscillators [4] could be feasible. By reducing the size of the ROI in the SEM a clock speed of some Hz to some kHz might be possible, as only this small region is charged and read-out. Other DVC techniques solve this problem by introducing a pulse gate in stroboscopic SEMs [29]. Academic publications show scans within GHz clock speed range [30], while commercial EBP products can be found with similar capabilities [20].

---

[2] To the best of our knowledge.

[3] Layers from top to bottom.

4   Voltage Contrast Analysis

In this section we describe a DVC analysis for successfully locating the AES circuit of our DUT. The DUT is a decapsulated XMEGA32A4U, an 8-bit μC with a dedicated AES hardware unit. The AES-128 core needs 376 clock cycles to en- or decrypt blocks of 16 bytes, with the option to xor the result once more for different AES modes [1].

The user can read the last round key from the key register. After each block encryption, the key has to be set again. The AES hardware is driven by the peripheral clock, which can be fully controlled externally or can be set to a multiple of the internal generated CPU clock.

Locating the AES Circuit. As a first test, we tried to identify the AES circuit by looping the AES encryption with unknown data at 2 MHz, while performing a DVC in the SEM. The CPU is in sleep mode during the encryption. The electron beam accelerating voltage is set to 1 keV and the beam scanning time is set to repeat as fast as possible. We achieved best results with a Through the Lens Detector (TLD). Figure 3 shows the result of the DVC.

 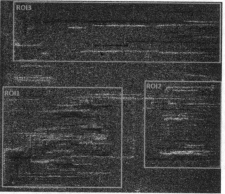

(a) AES area

(b) Zoomed-in AES area with labeled regions. Image is saturated for improved visualisation.

Fig. 3. AES located with DVC

A high activity in the bottom right corner indicates a repetitive computation, assumed to be the AES circuit. To verify our assumption we run a normal CPU program without using the AES core and observed the ROI. As it did not show any activity during the verification run, we concluded that the ROI is indeed the AES.

As shown in Fig. 3 we were already able to identify the AES circuit by simply running the algorithm and observing the top metal layer using the SEM. We note that this step is considerably simpler and faster compared to other approaches such as EM cartography, thermal imaging or photon emission discussed in Sect. 2. Also the EM trace acquisition is often non-trivial. Subsequently, a reverser can focus his attacks to the ROI.

5   Voltage Contrast Side Channel Analysis (VCSCA)

This section is the main contribution of this paper. We describe a Side Channel Analysis (SCA) with the DVC explained in Sect. 3.2. We use the VC as a side channel and perform a SCA to retrieve additional information of the AES circuit positions. Additionally, we recover the full AES key in 2 SCAs explained in Sects. 5.4 and 5.5. However, the attack has a significant potential as a general-purpose tool for extracting data and performing hardware reverse engineering against unknown circuits. This tool has a big potential, even for modern CMOS processes, if we include backside CCVC shown in [20,21].

Before explaining the VCSCA in more detail, we want to point out, that we performed an optional EM-based collision-attack in advance. This additional SCA was done to synchronize the retrieved byte-order and timing information with ROI1-3 in Fig. 3b. This allowed us to identify ROI1 as the addroundkey subroutine. During this section this information became obsolete, as the DUT is vulnerable to the more powerful introduced VCSCA. Nevertheless the combination with another SCA is a general-purpose approach to further reduce the ROI, even if the VCSCA is not applicable. We describe the setup and attack of the VCSCA in more detail during this section.

5.1   Obtaining Voltage Contrast Traces

A simple AES encryption program for the XMEGA has been written. It receives a 16 byte key and plaintext over USART and encrypts a AES-128 data block. Just before the AES is starting, the clock is set to react to an external pin and the main CPU is configured to enter sleep-mode.

In Sect. 3.2 we explained that the accumulated charges from the charging-phase disappear quickly after the clock transition. Therefore we have to time a single picture very accurately. To circumvent this problem, we decided to start recording a movie using the SEM software and cover multiple clock cycles in one recording. During the VCSCA the clock has been set to 3 Hz. The SEM parameter are the same as described in Sect. 4. The final setup can be seen in Fig. 4.

Figure 4 shows the setup of the VCSCA. This rather complex setup is needed as the DVC needs to be synchronized with the external clock. The dynamic changes appear only for a brief moment, which led us to start recording a movie. For synchronizing the DUT clock with the recording, an $\mu C(3)$ is set up to simulate a keyboard to start the recording of videotraces within the SEM - control Software (2). The clock is set to 3 Hz as this is the optimized speed to see each DVC change on the surface, without overlapping charging effects from the clock cycle before. This can be seen in Fig. 5. About every 4-5th frame in the

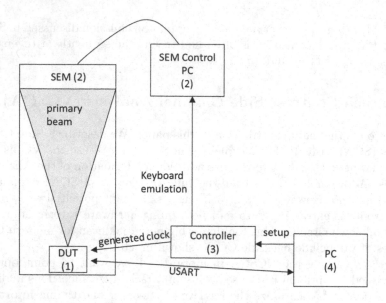

Fig. 4. The setup for the VCSCA

recorded video is a "clockframe". They have visible DVC changes and minimal charges from the previous clock cycle. The PC (4) is used to generate, send and validate the plaintext, key and received ciphertext. 300 videotraces with 200 frames each were acquired for the VCSCA. Each frame has the image resolution of 1024 × 885 pixels. Plaintext and keys are chosen randomly, but are known.

5.2 Locating AES Bit Wires in a VCSCA

In this section we determine the Pearson correlation coefficient between all pixels and the emulated internal AES bit values. The AES is emulated in software with known key and plaintext. Therefore we know every intermediate value, but concentrate on the first AES round. The correlation is done on every pixel in every frame extracted from the (video-)traces. Overall this makes 1024×885×300 values for each frame and hypothesis to calculate the Pearson correlation from.

Note that we are using the absolute bitvalue (Hamming weight) of single bits and know the key, plaintext and respective processing order from an optional SCA collision Attack. This reduces the computation time significantly, as we know in which frames (clock cycles) the bytes are processed. The CPU overhead for calculating the hypothesis can be neglected. This step can further be optimized to work on some smaller regions and selective pixels if necessary. Please note that we do not try to optimize our trace number or calculation time. Other possible correlation-based approaches could lead to better results, but are not the focus of this paper. The result of the differential VCSCA can be seen in the correlation image in Fig. 6.

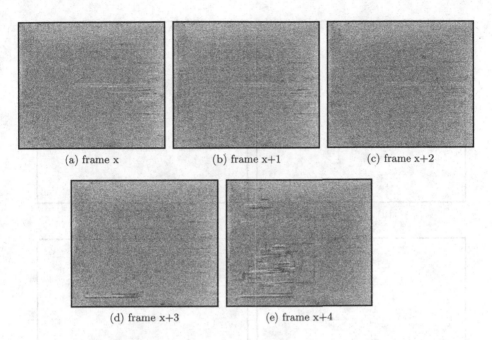

(a) frame x   (b) frame x+1   (c) frame x+2

(d) frame x+3   (e) frame x+4

Fig. 5. Consecutive frames within one trace. A clock transition takes place, while the SEM scans the last third of frame $x + 3$. The previous clock effect fades out (a)–(d). The colors are inverted for improved visualisation.

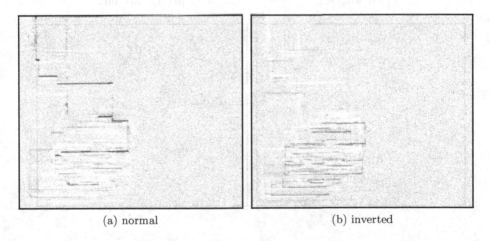

(a) normal   (b) inverted

Fig. 6. Results of the correlation based VCSCA of the 8th addroundkey-bit in clock cycle 42. The colors are inverted for improved visualisation.

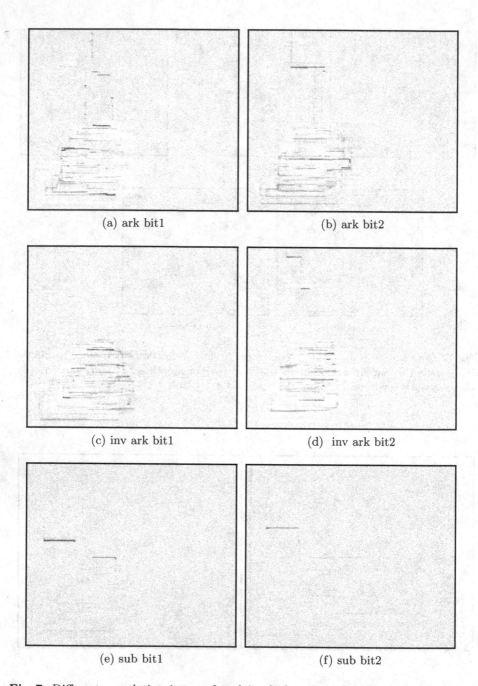

(a) ark bit1   (b) ark bit2

(c) inv ark bit1   (d) inv ark bit2

(e) sub bit1   (f) sub bit2

Fig. 7. Different correlation images found in clock cycle 42; addroundkey, inverted addroundkey and subbytes. The colors are inverted for improved visualisation.

Figure 7 shows the correlation images of further bits after different AES subroutines (`addroundkey` and `subbytes`). Each have different peak-locations, showing the position of the processed bits. Images labeled with "inverted" invert the sign of the pearson correlation. Each image cuts negative correlations to 0. With this we get two different images for each bit processed that show logical inverted signals and their locations as well. The corresponding hypothesis and respective clock cycles are listed in the subcaption. A high correlation for `addroundkey`, `subbytes` and the plaintext was found in resp. 16 consecutive clock cycles. Interestingly did we find the plaintext bits on the very same spots as the `addroundkey`, indicating a common load/store unit or bus structure within the AES.

These information immediately allow an attacker to retrieve unknown keys in a template based VCSCA approach. This attack is done in Sect. 5.4 to recover the full AES key.

Before we introduce a template based key extraction we would like to emphasize the fact that the correlation images provides valuable information for a reverse engineer or sophisticated attacker. We know the location and meaning of selected wires in the highest metal layers. This reveals the location of AES calculations on gate-level when the wires are tracked into the polysilicon layer. The attacker is able to interpret neighboring and connected signals immediately. This might reveal further weaknesses or even whole Intellectual Property (IP) cores.

Furthermore it is also possible to apply other approaches easily, as the locations of the AES bits in top metal-layers are known. Mechanical probing or fault attacks are two examples to retrieve or alter intermediate AES bits. Figure 8 shows cropped images of the 2 top metal layers from the XMEGA microcontroller scanned with a SEM, overlayed with the extrapolated correlation image of `addroundkey` bit 2. The correlation image is 50 % transparent to visualize the manual mapping process.

In Fig. 8 we demonstrate that we are capable of identifying the tracked wires of bit 2 in the first two metal-layers. Continuing this, we would be able to pinpoint the location of the origin in the polysilicon and the next "processing steps" after the `addroundkey` subroutine. Nevertheless this is out of the scope for this paper. It is noteworthy that the two marked wires from the top layer are connected in the second layer. This is a good indication that we hit the right wires from our results.

5.3   Extracting Additional Netlist Information

So far we analyzed bits within the AES circuit that are supposed to be part of the AES calculation. We did not look into the possibilities of how the `subbytes` routine or other subroutines are built. Therefore we provide a Side Channel Analysis for Reverse Engineering (SCARE) like approach in this section.

We applied every $2 \rightarrow 1$ function from the 8 `addroundkey`-bits possible and used the result as a new hypothesis. Each possible $2 \rightarrow 1$ function is given in Table 1 from [13]. The results of the 2bit-function hypotheses revealed additional circuit operations not known so far. For example did we find a correlation of a

(a) Top metal layer

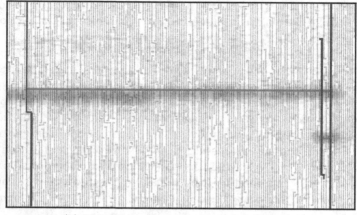

(b) Metal layer beneath the top metal layer

Fig. 8. Marked wire of bit 2 of addroundkey in the two top layers. The black "cloud" is the extrapolated correlation image in this ROI. The colors are inverted for improved visualisation (Color figure online).

xor between Bit 3 and Bit 4 of the addroundkey bits. This allows us to build basic netlist operations and we are able to verify an extracted netlist (by usual means) with these findings or counter hardware obfuscation techniques like the one introduced in [15]. Some hardware protection might even play in our hands by routing sensitive wires through multiple layers, including the top metal [10].

Following this approach we might be able to reverse engineer whole subroutines, without invasive methods. This is not in the scope of this paper and can be done in future work. This small PoC shows the great potential for the VC side channel in SCARE like approaches.

In the following sections we use the VC in more common SCAs, to recover the AES key with our current setup. We execute a template-attack and independently another SSCA on a single trace in a no-plaintext, no-ciphertext and no-key attack. In both cases we retrieve the AES key successfully.

5.4 Template Attack with VCSCA

The setup for the key-recovering template attack is the same as described in Sect. 5.1, with the difference of choosing a constant (assumed unknown) key

Table 1. $2 \rightarrow 1$ functions

Index of f	f(B,A)				Boolean equation	Name
	$f(1,1)$	$f(1,0)$	$f(0,1)$	$f(0,0)$		
0	0	0	0	0	0	Zero
1	0	0	0	1	$\overline{B+A}$	NOR2
2	0	0	1	0	$\overline{B} \cdot A$	AND2B
3	0	0	1	1	$\overline{B}$	NOTB
4	0	1	0	0	$B \cdot \overline{A}$	AND2A
5	0	1	0	1	$\overline{A}$	NOTA
6	0	1	1	0	$B \oplus A$	XOR2
7	0	1	1	1	$\overline{B \cdot A}$	NAND2
8	1	0	0	0	$B \cdot A$	AND2
9	1	0	0	1	$\overline{B \oplus A}$	XNOR2
10	1	0	1	0	A	A
11	1	0	1	1	$\overline{B} + A$	OR2B
12	1	1	0	0	B	B
13	1	1	0	1	$B + \overline{A}$	OR2A
14	1	1	1	0	$B + A$	OR2
15	1	1	1	1	1	One

for all the traces. 250 Traces are acquired and random plaintexts are AES-128 encrypted by the DUT.

The "templates" are the correlation images generated in Sect. 5.2. The idea is to correlate the frames that process a specific byte and correlate the resulting addroundkey bit with a single key bit hypothesis. The resulting correlation image is either the "normal" or the "inverted" correlation image e.g. of bit 8 shown in Fig. 6.

To explain the process, we give a short example with the 8th bit of byte 16 of the i-th trace ($p_{i\_16\_8}$). As we know the that the 16th byte is processed in the 42th frame of each trace, we extract this frame from every trace. Let us assume that our hypothesis of the 8th keybit of byte 16 is "1". We correlate each pixel of these frames with the addroundkey hypothesis which is calculated ($p_{i\_16\_8}$ xor hypothesis). This results in a correlation image that is either close to Fig. 6a or Fig. 6b. If the assumption is correct, we will get a correlating image close to Fig. 6a. Otherwise the hypothesis is wrong and the 8th bit is "0". Repeating this process, every keybit can be recovered. Taking 250 traces is an estimated value to make sure that the attack succeeds, as we need to extract the right clockframes of the DVC video and to get a good average over noisy images. We verified that the attack is feasible with less traces.

5.5   Simple VCSCA

Realizing that the XMEGA reuses the same circuit for every byte sequentially, the bit locations are the same for every round and byte within the AES. Therefore we aim to find plain or key bytes directly being loaded or processed during the AES setup. Interestingly did we find the plaintext being loaded 13 clock cycles before the addroundkey function on the same bit locations as the addroundkey bit. This indicates a common load/store unit or a bus architecture. During this section we assume not knowing the key once more. Knowing that the plaintext is being processed right before the addroundkey allows an attacker a no-plaintext, no-ciphertext **and** no-key SSCA against the XMEGA AES engine. The aim of this section is therefore a PoC of the simple VCSCA with a single trace and 1 byte.

Section 5.2 already revealed the location and timing of individual addroundkey bits being processed. These bits have a key dependence through the xor with the plaintext, which can be read-out 13 clock cycles before. Therefore, this attack first recovers the plaintext bit and secondly reads-out the processed addroundkey bit in a SSCA. The recovered bits are xored to get the corresponding keybit as we only target the first round. This is repeated for 8 bits within byte 16 in a single trace. Figure 9 shows the wire positions for 2 bits that we used for recognition. The wire positions are chosen from multiple options, as they are reliable measured by the DVC and are easy recognisable.

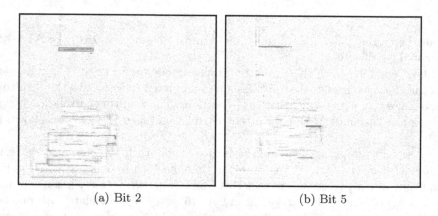

(a) Bit 2   (b) Bit 5

Fig. 9. Correlation Image of keybits within clock cycle 48. The colors are inverted for improved visualisation (Color figure online).

In Fig. 10 we demonstrate the simple VCSCA based on Bit 5. The other bits can be done in a similar manner.

A direct xor of both values, reveals the 5th keybit of byte 16. The keybit correctness was verified for every bit in Byte 16. We discovered that is not easy to find a trace that shows all bits recognizable at once, as the DVC images depend on the previous top-metal layer voltage and the exact beam position during the

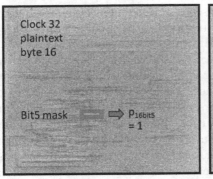
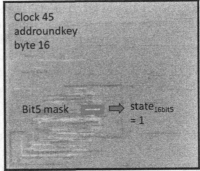

(a) Clock 32 plaintext   (b) Clock 45 addroundkey

Fig. 10. Extracted states of byte 16 bit 5 within one trace. The colors are inverted for improved visualisation (Color figure online).

clock transition. We verified that is possible to acquire at least one key-byte with one single trace. We did not look for further keybits, since the recognition was done manually. If we would want to automate this process, more traces should be used in order to work on mean images.

6 Conclusion

In this paper we revise an approach to pinpoint the ROI for ICs with VC images. This reduces the complexity of hardware reverse engineers by gaining a-priori knowledge of the location of security-relevant ROIs and allows to perform EM-based SCA with better signal-to-noise ratio. Furthermore this enables more advanced SCAs like inter-gate leakages discussed in [27] and reduces the exhaustive search for fault attacks.

The shown approach is at least as fast and easy to comparable approaches like EM cartography, thermal imaging and photon emission. The only required tool is a SEM, well distributed in universities and institutes due to its application in many academic fields. A SEM can be bought second hand for under 10k€. Specialized commercial EBPs for high speed measurements are also available.

We use the VC as a side channel that exploits the capacitive coupling effect of top metal layers through the covering passivation. We are able to see voltage alterations of the ICs surface in a SEM, revealing secret information through top metal-wire voltage changes. A PoC with a XMEGA microcontroller to locate and identify top metal layers holding intermediate AES bits is given. Any sophisticated attacker can track the wires to the polysilicon layer, revealing data flip-flops and memory structures of the AES. Furthermore we use the VC in multiple SCA approaches to recover the full AES key.

For the VCSCA template-attack, less then 100 traces are enough to reveal the key, while the simple VCSCA is performed in a no-plaintext, no-ciphertext and no-key attack scenario. Additionally we show a SCARE approach to recover further netlist information, that can be used to reverse engineer hardware circuits in a non-invasive way. The gained information can be used to partly verify an extracted netlist or to counter simple hardware obfuscation techniques.

Additionally is the backside CCVC or EBP shown in [20,21], a high hardware security threat, if the backside thinning is applicable to big areas and is used in a SCA. IC vendors and designers need to implement front- and backside hardware protection. Especially routing sensitive information into higher metal layers can easily be avoided by the routing software and should be done for multiple reasons: Firstly an attacker can probe the wires easily by mechanical means. Secondly it results in more power and EM emanation leakage, because of the higher capacitances of longer and thicker wires. The device will be vulnerable to a power or EM-based SCA and last but not least is the device vulnerable to the frontside VCSCA approach, shown in this paper.

Acknowledgement. The authors would like to thank Michael Gilberg from the Bundeskriminalamt for his valuable experience and technical help with the FIB and SEM. Furthermore we would like to thank the anonymous reviewers at CHES 2015 for their valuable comments and additional references.

References

1. Atmel. Atmel AVR XMEGA AU Manual, April 2013
2. Barille, R.: Analytical formulation of the capacitive coupling voltage contrast of a buried line. Electron. Lett. **29**(20), 1756–1758 (1993)
3. Barton, D.L., Tangyunyong, P.: Thermal defect detection techniques. In: The EDFAS Desk Reference Committee (ed.) Microelectronics Failure Analysis: Desk Reference, p. 378. ASM International, Materials Park (2004)
4. Bayon, P., Bossuet, L., Aubert, A., Fischer, V., Poucheret, F., Robisson, B., Maurine, P.: Contactless electromagnetic active attack on ring oscillator based true random number generator. In: Schindler, W., Huss, S.A. (eds.) COSADE 2012. LNCS, vol. 7275, pp. 151–166. Springer, Heidelberg (2012)
5. Benzel, J.D.: Bugs in black and white: imaging IC logic levels with voltage contrast. Hewlett Packard J. **46**(00000), 102–106 (1995)
6. Bertsche, K.J., Charles, Jr., H.K.: The practical implementation of voltage contrast as a diagnostic tool. In: 20th Annual Reliability Physics Symposium, 1982, pp. 167–178, March 1982
7. Bindell, J., McGinn, J.: Voltage contrast SEM observations with microprocessor controlled device timing. In: 18th Annual Reliability Physics Symposium, 1980, pp. 55–58, April 1980
8. Boit, C., Helfmeier, C., Kerst, U.: Security risks posed by modern IC debug and diagnosis tools. In: 2013 Workshop on Fault Diagnosis and Tolerance in Cryptography (FDTC), pp. 3–11. IEEE (2013)
9. Breitenstein, O., Schmidt, C., Karg, D.: Thermal failure analysis by IR lock-in thermography. In: The EDFAS Desk Reference Committee (ed.) Microelectronics Failure Analysis: Desk Reference, 5th edn. ASM International, Materials Park (2004)

10. Briais, S., Caron, S., Cioranesco, J.-M., Danger, J.-L., Guilley, S., Jourdan, J.-H., Milchior, A., Naccache, D., Porteboeuf, T.: 3D hardware canaries. In: Prouff, E., Schaumont, P. (eds.) CHES 2012. LNCS, vol. 7428, pp. 1–22. Springer, Heidelberg (2012)

11. Crépel, O., Beaudoin, F., de Morais, L.D., Haller, G., Goupil, C., Desplats, R., Lewis, D.: Backside hot spot detection using liquid crystal microscopy. Microelectron. Reliab. 42(9–11), 1741–1746 (2002)

12. Ferrigno, J., Hlavac, M.: When AES blinks: introducing optical side channel. Inf. Secur. IET 2(3), 94–98 (2008)

13. Guilley, S., Sauvage, L., Micolod, J., Réal, D., Valette, F.: Defeating any secret cryptography with SCARE attacks. In: Abdalla, M., Barreto, P.S.L.M. (eds.) LATINCRYPT 2010. LNCS, vol. 6212, pp. 273–293. Springer, Heidelberg (2010)

14. Kammerstetter, M., Muellner, M., Burian, D., Platzer, C., Kastner, W.: Breaking integrated circuit device security through test mode silicon reverse engineering. In: Proceedings of the 2014 ACM SIGSAC Conference on Computer and Communications Security, CCS 2014, pp. 549–557. ACM, New York (2014)

15. Rajendran, J., Sam, M., Sinanoglu, O., Karri, R.: Security analysis of integrated circuit camouflaging. In: Proceedings of the 2013 ACM SIGSAC Conference on Computer and Communications Security, CCS 2013, pp. 709–720. ACM, New York (2013)

16. Real, D., Valette, F., Drissi, M.: Enhancing correlation electromagnetic attack using planar near-field cartography. In: Design, Automation Test in Europe Conference Exhibition, 2009, DATE 2009, pp. 628–633, April 2009

17. Rosenkranz, R.: Failure localization with active and passive voltage contrast in FIB and SEM. J. Mater. Sci.: Mater. Electron. 22(10), 1523–1535 (2011)

18. Sauvage, L., Guilley, S., Danger, J.-L., Homma, N., Hayashi, Y.: Practical results of EM cartography on a FPGA-based RSA hardware implementation. In: 2011 IEEE International Symposium on Electromagnetic Compatibility (EMC), pp. 768–772, August 2011

19. Sauvage, L., Guilley, S., Mathieu, Y.: Electromagnetic radiations of FPGAs: high spatial resolution cartography and attack on a cryptographic module. ACM Trans. Reconfigurable Technol. Syst. 2(1), 4:1–4:24 (2009)

20. Schlangen, R., Leihkauf, R., Kerst, U., Boit, C., Jain, R., Malik, T., Wilsher, K., Lundquist, T., Kruger, B.: Backside e-beam probing on nano scale devices. In: 2007 IEEE International Test Conference (2007)

21. Schlangen, R., Leihkauf, R., Kerst, U., Boit, C., Kruger, B.: Functional IC analysis through chip backside with nano scale resolution-E-beam probing in FIB trenches to STI level. In: 14th International Symposium on the Physical and Failure Analysis of Integrated Circuits, 2007, IPFA 2007. IEEE (2007)

22. Schlösser, A., Nedospasov, D., Krämer, J., Orlic, S., Seifert, J.-P.: Simple photonic emission analysis of AES. In: Prouff, E., Schaumont, P. (eds.) CHES 2012. LNCS, vol. 7428, pp. 41–57. Springer, Heidelberg (2012)

23. Skorobogatov, S.: Using optical emission analysis for estimating contribution to power analysis. In: 2009 Workshop on Fault Diagnosis and Tolerance in Cryptography (FDTC), pp. 111–119, September 2009

24. Skorobogatov, S., Woods, C.: Breakthrough silicon scanning discovers backdoor in military chip. In: Prouff, E., Schaumont, P. (eds.) CHES 2012. LNCS, vol. 7428, pp. 23–40. Springer, Heidelberg (2012)

25. Skorobogatov, S.P.: Semi-invasive attacks - a new approach to hardware security analysis (2005)

26. Sugawara, T., Suzuki, D., Fujii, R., Tawa, S., Hori, R., Shiozaki, M., Fujino, T.: Reversing stealthy dopant-level circuits. In: Batina, L., Robshaw, M. (eds.) CHES 2014. LNCS, vol. 8731, pp. 112–126. Springer, Heidelberg (2014)
27. Sugawara, T., Suzuki, D., Saeki, M., Shiozaki, M., Fujino, T.: On measurable side-channel leaks inside ASIC design primitives. In: Bertoni, G., Coron, J.-S. (eds.) CHES 2013. LNCS, vol. 8086, pp. 159–178. Springer, Berlin Heidelberg (2013)
28. Tian, L.: Simple, novel and low cost numerical aperture increasing lens system for high resolution infrared image in backside failure analysis. In: 2014 IEEE 21st International Symposium on the Physical and Failure Analysis of Integrated Circuits (IPFA) (2014)
29. Ura, K., Fujioka, H., Hosokawa, T.: Stroboscopic scanning electron microscope to observe two-dimensional and dynamic potential distribution of semiconductor devices. In: 1977 International Electron Devices Meeting, vol. 23, pp. 502–505 (1977)
30. Ura, K., Fujioka, H., Hosokawa, T.: Picosecond pulse stroboscopic scanning electron microscope. J. Electron Microsc. **27**(4), 247–252 (1978)

Lattice-Based Implementations

Efficient Ring-LWE Encryption
on 8-Bit AVR Processors

Zhe Liu[1]([⊠]), Hwajeong Seo[2], Sujoy Sinha Roy[3], Johann Großschädl[1],
Howon Kim[2], and Ingrid Verbauwhede[3]

[1] University of Luxembourg, 6, rue Richard Coudenhove-Kalergi,
1359 Luxembourg, Luxembourg
{zhe.liu,johann.groszschaedl}@uni.lu
[2] Pusan National University, San-30, Jangjeon-Dong,
Geumjeong-Gu, Busan 609-735, Korea
{hwajeong,howonkim}@pusan.ac.kr
[3] Katholieke Universiteit Leuven, Kasteelpark Arenberg 10,
3001 Leuven-Heverlee, Belgium
{sujoy.sinharoy,ingrid.verbauwhede}@esat.kuleuven.be

Abstract. Public-key cryptography based on the "ring-variant" of the
Learning with Errors (ring-LWE) problem is both efficient and believed
to remain secure in a post-quantum world. In this paper, we introduce
a carefully-optimized implementation of a ring-LWE encryption scheme
for 8-bit AVR processors like the ATxmega128. Our research contributions include several optimizations for the Number Theoretic Transform
(NTT) used for polynomial multiplication. More concretely, we describe
the Move-and-Add (MA) and the Shift-Add-Multiply-Subtract-Subtract
(SAMS2) technique to speed up the performance-critical multiplication
and modular reduction of coefficients, respectively. We take advantage
of incompletely-reduced intermediate results to minimize the total number of reduction operations and use a special coefficient-storage method
to decrease the RAM footprint of NTT multiplications. In addition, we
propose a byte-wise scanning strategy to improve the performance of a
discrete Gaussian sampler based on the Knuth-Yao random walk algorithm. For medium-term security, our ring-LWE implementation needs
590 k, 672 k, and 276 k clock cycles for key-generation, encryption, and
decryption, respectively. On the other hand, for long-term security, the
execution time of key-generation, encryption, and decryption amount to
2.2 M, 2.6 M, and 686 k cycles, respectively. These results set new speed
records for ring-LWE encryption on an 8-bit processor and outperform
related RSA and ECC implementations by an order of magnitude.

Keywords: Ring learning with errors (Ring-LWE) · Public-key encryption · Number-theoretic transform · Discrete Gaussian sampling

1 Introduction

The vast majority of today's widely-used public-key cryptosystems is based on
integer factorization and discrete logarithm problems, which are believed to be

© International Association for Cryptologic Research 2015
T. Güneysu and H. Handschuh (Eds.): CHES 2015, LNCS 9293, pp. 663–682, 2015.
DOI: 10.1007/978-3-662-48324-4_33

intractable with current computing technology. However, these hard problems can be solved by using Shor's algorithm [31] (or a variant of it) on a quantum computer. Lattice-based cryptography is often considered a premier candidate for realizing post-quantum cryptosystems [27]. Its security relies on worst-case computational assumptions in lattices that will remain hard even for quantum computers. In the recent past, a large body of research has been devoted to the efficient implementation of lattice-based cryptosystems, whereby resource-constrained environments received particular attention (see e.g. [5,9,21]). This is much owed to the fact that the Internet is currently in the midst of a transition from a network connecting commodity computers (i.e. PCs and notebooks) to a network of smart objects ("things"). Even today, there are significantly more non-traditional computing devices connected to the Internet than conventional computers [13]. Among the smart devices that are populating the Internet are various kinds of sensors, actuators, meters, consumer electronics, medical monitors, household appliances, vehicles, and even items of clothing. Many of these devices are very restricted in terms of computing power, memory capacity, and energy supply. For example, a typical wireless sensor node, like the widely-used MICAz mote, features an 8-bit AVR ATmega processor clocked at 8 MHz and a few kB of RAM. However, in order to enable such devices to communicate in a secure way, they need to be capable of executing public-key cryptography as otherwise end-to-end authentication and end-to-end key exchange would not be possible. Implementing public-key algorithms on an 8-bit processor poses quite a challenge, not only for RSA and ECC, but also post-quantum techniques like lattice-based cryptography. This raises the question of how well the "cryptosystems of the future" are suited for the "Internet of the future," i.e. the so-called "Internet of Things (IoT)," and one aspect of this question is the performance of lattice-based cryptosystems on 8-bit platforms such as AVR [2].

The introduction of the Learning With Errors (LWE) problem [27] and its ring variant (i.e. ring-LWE) [20] opened up a way to build efficient lattice-based public-key cryptosystems. The first practical evaluations of LWE and ring-LWE encryption were presented by Göttert et al. at CHES 2012 [14]. According to their results, the ring-LWE encryption scheme is at least four times faster and requires less memory than the encryption scheme based on the standard LWE problem. A large variety of subsequent hardware and software implementations of ring-LWE-based public-key encryption or digital signature schemes improved performance and memory footprint [5,6,9,21,25]. Oder et al. [21] introduced an efficient implementation of Bimodal Lattice Signature Schemes (BLISS) on a 32-bit ARM Cortex-M4F processor; the most optimized variant of their software needs 6 M cycles for signing, 1 M cycles for verification, and 368 M cycles for key generation, respectively, at a medium-term security level. Recently, de Clercq et al. [9] described a ring-LWE encryption scheme on exactly the same ARM platform and reported an execution time of 121 k cycles per encryption and 43.3 k cycles per decryption for medium-term security, which increases to 261 k cycles (encryption) and roughly 96.5 k cycles (decryption) when long-term security is desired. The first implementation of a lattice-based cryptosystem on an 8-bit processor was published by Boorghany et al. in 2014 [5,6]. They evaluated four lattice-based authentication protocols on both an 8-bit AVR and a 32-bit ARM processor. On the 8-bit platform (i.e. AVR), their implementation of the Fast Fourier Transform (FFT) needs 755 k and 2.2 M cycles for medium and long-term security, respectively. Thanks to the efficiency of the polynomial multiplication and the Gaussian sampler function, their LWE-based encryption scheme achieves an execution time of 2.8 M cycles for key generation, 3 M cycles for encryption, as well as 1.4 M cycles for decryption, all at a medium-term security level. Very recently, Pöppelmann et al. [25] compared implementations of ring-LWE encryption and the Bimodal Lattice Signature Scheme (BLISS) on an 8-bit ATxmega128 processor. For medium-term security, they reported 1.3 M cycles for ring-LWE encryption and 381 k cycles for decryption, respectively.

1.1   Research Contributions

This paper continues the line of research on the efficient implementation of the ring-LWE encryption scheme on 8-bit AVR processors. Our core contributions are several optimizations to reduce the execution time and RAM requirements of ring-LWE encryption, decryption, and key generation. More specifically, the contributions of this paper can be summarized as follows.

1. The efficiency of coefficient modular multiplication is crucial for high-speed NTT operations. We present the Move-and-Add (MA) method to perform the coefficient multiplication and the Shift-Add-Multiply-Subtract-Subtract (SAMS2) technique to accelerate the reduction operation. The former aims at reducing the number of add instructions by rescheduling the order of the byte multiplications, whereas the latter replaces expensive MUL instructions by cheaper shifts and additions.
2. In the NTT computations, the vast majority of execution time is spent on performing modular reduction since it is the most frequent operation in the innermost loop. We exploit the idea of incomplete modular arithmetic (see e.g. [32]), which means we allow (i.e. tolerate) incompletely reduced intermediate results for the coefficients and perform the reduction operation in a "lazy" fashion. Our experimental results show that this approach decreases the overall number of modular reductions by 6 % on average.
3. The intermediate coefficients during the computation of an NTT require a considerable amount of RAM. We use a special coefficient-storage method that enables us to make full use of the allocated space. For example, when the coefficients are 13 bits long, we keep 16 coefficients in 26 bytes, and save in this way up to 19 % RAM compared to the straightforward approach.
4. To increase efficiency of our discrete Gaussian sampler based on the Knuth-Yao random walk algorithm [16], we propose a byte-scanning technique to minimize execution time.

On basis of these optimizations, we present a total of four implementations of a ring-LWE encryption scheme for the 8-bit AVR platform (e.g. AT(x)mega microcontrollers); two at the medium-term security level and two for long-term security. For each of these two security levels, we developed both a High-Speed (HS) and a Memory-Efficient (ME) variant. For medium-term security, the HS implementation requires roughly 590 k, 672 k, and 276 k clock cycles to perform a key-generation, encryption, and decryption, respectively. Alternatively, at the long-term security level, the speed-optimized key-generation, encryption, and decryption take 2.2 M, 2.6 M, and 686 k clock cycles, respectively. Both our HS and ME implementation significantly improve the speed records for ring-LWE encryption on an 8-bit AVR processor. Furthermore, it should be noted that all optimizations described in this paper can also be used to speed up LWE-based signature schemes (e.g. [23]) on the AVR platform.

1.2   Paper Outline

The rest of this paper is organized as follows. In the next section, we recap the concepts of ring-LWE encryption schemes, including the NTT and Knuth-Yao sampler. In Sect. 3, we focus on certain optimization techniques for NTT on 8-bit AVR processors. In particular, we present several optimizations to reduce the execution time and memory consumption of NTT. In Sect. 4, we propose optimizations for the Knuth-Yao sampler. Then, in Sect. 5, we summarize all implementation results we obtained and compare them with some state-of-the-art implementations of public-key cryptosystems, in particular LWE, RSA, and ECC, on the same platform. Finally, we draw conclusions in Sect. 6.

2   Background

2.1   The Ring-LWE Encryption Scheme

The encryption schemes used in this paper are based on the ring version of the Learning With Errors (i.e. ring-LWE) problem. The more general form of this problem, i.e. the LWE problem, is parameterized by a dimension $n \geq 1$, a modulus q, and an error distribution. This error distribution is generally taken as a discrete Gaussian distribution $\mathcal{X}_\sigma$ with standard deviation σ and mean 0 so as to achieve the best entropy/standard deviation ratio [10]. In the literature, the LWE problem is, in general, defined as follows: Two polynomials $\mathbf{a}$ and $\mathbf{s}$ are chosen uniformly from $\mathbb{Z}_q^n$. The first polynomial is a global polynomial, whereas the second polynomial must be kept as a secret. The LWE distribution $A_{s,\mathcal{X}}$ is defined over $\mathbb{Z}_q^n \times \mathbb{Z}_q$ and comprises the elements $(\mathbf{a}, t)$ where $t = \langle \mathbf{a}, \mathbf{s} \rangle + e \bmod q \in \mathbb{Z}_q$ for some error polynomial e sampled from the error distribution $\mathcal{X}_\sigma$. In the *search* version of the LWE problem, an attacker is provided with a polynomial number of $(\mathbf{a}, t)$ pairs sampled from $A_{s,\mathcal{X}}$ and his task is to try to find the secret polynomial $\mathbf{s}$. Similarly, in the *decision* version of the LWE problem, the attacker attempts to distinguish between a polynomial number of samples from $A_{s,\mathcal{X}}$ and the same number of samples from $\mathbb{Z}_q^n \times \mathbb{Z}_q$.

In 2010, Lyubashevsky et al. [20] proposed an encryption scheme based on a more practical algebraic variant of the LWE problem defined over polynomial rings $R_q = \mathbb{Z}_q[\mathbf{x}]/\langle f \rangle$ with an irreducible polynomial $f(x)$ and a modulus q. As the name suggests, in the the ring-LWE problem, the elements a, s, and t are polynomials in the ring R_q. Lyubashevsky et al.'s ring-LWE encryption scheme was later optimized by Roy et al. [28] with the aim of reducing the cost of the polynomial arithmetic. In their scheme, the polynomial arithmetic carried out during a decryption operation requires only one Number Theoretic Transform (NTT) operation. Besides this computational optimization, Roy et al.'s scheme performs sampling from the discrete Gaussian distribution using a Knuth-Yao sampler. In the remainder of this section, we will first describe the major steps of Roy et al.'s version of the encryption scheme and thereafter we will recap the mathematical concepts of the NTT and the Knuth-Yao sampling.

2.2   Key Generation, Encryption, and Decryption

In the following, we describe the steps used in the encryption scheme proposed by Roy et al. [28]. We denote the NTT of a polynomial a by $\tilde{a}$.

- Key generation stage **Gen($\tilde{a}$)**: Two error polynomials $r_1, r_2 \in R_q$ are sampled from the discrete Gaussian distribution $\mathcal{X}_\sigma$ by applying the Knuth-Yao sampler twice:

$$\tilde{r_1} = \text{NTT}(r_1), \ \tilde{r_2} = \text{NTT}(r_2)$$

and then an operation $\tilde{p} = \tilde{r_1} - \tilde{a} \cdot \tilde{r_2} \in R_q$ is performed. The public key is the polynomial pair $(\tilde{a}, \tilde{p})$ and the private key is the polynomial $\tilde{r_2}$.
- Encryption stage **Enc($\tilde{a}$, $\tilde{p}$, M)**: The input message $M \in \{0,1\}^n$ is a binary vector of n bits. This message is first encoded into a polynomial in the ring R_q by multiplying the bits of the message M by $q/2$. Thereafter, three error polynomials $e_1, e_2, e_3 \in R_q$ are sampled from $\mathcal{X}_\sigma$. The ciphertext can be obtained as a set of two polynomials $(\tilde{C}_1, \tilde{C}_2)$:

$$(\tilde{C}_1, \tilde{C}_2) = (\tilde{a} \cdot \tilde{e}_1 + \tilde{e}_2, \tilde{p} \cdot \tilde{e}_1 + \text{NTT}(e_3 + M'))$$

- Decryption stage **Dec($\tilde{C}_1$, $\tilde{C}_2$, $\tilde{r_2}$)**: One inverse NTT has to be performed to recover M':

$$M' = \text{INTT}(\tilde{r_2} \cdot \tilde{C}_1 + \tilde{C}_2)$$

and then a decoder is used to recover the original message M from M'.

2.3   Number Theoretic Transform

Our implementation adopts the Number Theoretic Transform (NTT) [7] to perform the required polynomial multiplications. An NTT can be seen as a variant of the Fast Fourier Transform (FFT) that operates in a finite ring $\mathbb{Z}_q$. Instead of using complex roots of unity, an NTT evaluates a polynomial multiplication $a(x) = \sum_{i=0}^{n-1} a_i x^i \in \mathbb{Z}_q$ in the n-th roots of unity ω_n^i for $i = 0, \ldots, n-1$, where

---

Algorithm 1. Iterative Number Theoretic Transform

Input: Polynomial $a(x) \in \mathbb{Z}_q[x]$ of degree $n-1$, primitive n-th root of unity $\omega \in \mathbb{Z}_q$
Output: Polynomial $a(x) = \mathrm{NTT}(a) \in \mathbb{Z}_q[x]$
1: $a \leftarrow \mathrm{BitReverse}(a)$
2: **for** i from 2 by $2i$ to n **do**
3:      $\omega_i \leftarrow \omega_n^{n/i}, \; \omega \leftarrow 1$
4:      **for** j from 0 by 1 to $i/2 - 1$ **do**
5:          **for** k from 0 by i to $n-1$ **do**
6:              $U \leftarrow a[k+j]$
7:              $V \leftarrow \omega \cdot a[k+j+i/2]$
8:              $a[k+j] \leftarrow U + V$
9:              $a[k+j+i/2] \leftarrow U - V$
10:          **end for**
11:          $\omega \leftarrow \omega \cdot \omega_i$
12:      **end for**
13: **end for**
14: **return** a

ω_n denotes a primitive n-th root of unity. Algorithm 1 shows the iterative form of the NTT algorithm, which is taken from Cormen et al. [7].

As can be seen from Algorithm 1, an iterative NTT consists of three nested loops. The outermost loop (i-loop, lines 2 to 13) starts with $i = 2$ and increases i by doubling it in each iteration. When $i = n$, the loop terminates, and so the overall number of iterations is only $\log_2(n)$. In each iteration, the value of the so-called twiddle factor ω_i is computed via an exponentiation $\omega_i = \omega_n^{n/i}$, while the value of ω is initialized with 1. Compared to the i-loop, the j-loop (i.e. lines 4 to 12) executes more iterations, whereby the actual number of iterations can be seen as a sum of a geometric progression for 2^i with i starting from 0 and having a maximum value of $\log_2(n-1)$. Thus, the j-loop is iterated $n-1$ times and, in each iteration, the twiddle factor ω is updated by performing a coefficient modular multiplication (line 11). Apparently, the innermost loop (i.e. the k-loop, lines 5 to 10) consumes the majority of the total execution time of the NTT algorithm since it is iterated roughly $\frac{n}{2} \cdot \log_2(n)$ times. In each iteration of the innermost loop, the two coefficients $a[i+j]$ and $a[i+j+i/2]$ are loaded from memory into registers, and then $a[i+j+i/2]$ is multiplied by the twiddle factor ω. Thereafter, the values of $a[k+j]$ and $a[k+j+i/2]$ are updated and stored in memory.

2.4 Gaussian Sampler

The ring-LWE cryptosystem needs samples from a discrete Gaussian distribution to provide the error polynomials during the key generation and encryption operations. There are several approaches for sampling from a discrete Gaussian distribution, among which we chose the algorithm of Knuth and Yao [16]. This algorithm stores the probabilities of the sample points and performs a random walk by following a binary tree, known as the Discrete Distribution Generating

---

Algorithm 2. Low-level implementation of Knuth-Yao sampling [29]

Input: Probability matrix P_{mat}, random number r, modulus q
Output: Sample value s

1:   $d \leftarrow 0$
2:   **for** col from 0 by 1 to $MAXCOL$ **do**
3:      $d \leftarrow 2d + (r\&1)$
4:      $r \leftarrow r \gg 1$
5:      **for** row from $MAXROW$ by -1 to 0 **do**
6:        $d \leftarrow d - P_{mat}[row][col]$
7:        **if** $d = -1$ **then**
8:          **if** $(r\&1) = 1$ **then**
9:            **return** $q - row$
10:        **else**
11:            **return** row
12:        **end if**
13:        **end if**
14:      **end for**
15: **end for**
16: **return** 0

(DDG) tree [12,16,29]. Such a DDG tree efficiently counts the visited non-zero nodes to find the sample based on probability.

A low-level implementation of the Knuth-Yao random walk along the DDG tree was described by Roy et al. [29] and is shown in Algorithm 2. The random walk reads the probability bits of the sample points from a matrix, called the probability matrix P_{mat}. The i-th row of P_{mat} is the probability of the sample point $|i|$. The algorithm uses two loops with counters col and row to read the bits from the columns and rows of P_{mat}, respectively. The two loop boundaries $MAXCOL$ and $MAXROW$ represent the overall number of columns and rows of P_{mat}. Before starting the random walk, a counter d has to be initialized to zero. Whenever a new column of P_{mat} is to be read, the counter d is updated using a random bit r. During the random walk, the visited column of P_{mat} is scanned bit-by-bit, and each non-zero bit in the column decrements the value of d. When d becomes negative for the first time, the random walk stops and the value of the row counter is taken as the magnitude of the sample. Now, another random bit is generated to determine the sign of the sample. We refer to [29] for a more-detailed description. Faster versions of the Knuth-Yao random walk algorithm using small lookup tables were presented in [9,28].

2.5 Parameter Selection

Our implementation of ring-LWE encryption adopts the parameter set (n, q, σ) with $(256, 7681, 11.31/\sqrt{2\pi})$ and $(512, 12289, 12.18/\sqrt{2\pi})$ to match the common 128 and 256-bit security levels, respectively. The discrete Gaussian sampler is limited to 12σ to have a high-precision statistical difference from the theoretical distribution, which is less than 2^{-90}. These parameter sets were also used by most of the previous hardware (e.g. [14,28]) and software implementations (e.g. [5,6,9]), which facilitates a comparison with these works.

3 Optimization Techniques for NTT Computation

3.1 Look-Up Table for Twiddle Factors

In each iteration of the j-loop of Algorithm 1, a new twiddle factor ω is computed through a modular multiplication (line 11). The total number of times a new ω is obtained in an NTT operation amounts to $n-1$. A straightforward computation of ω on-the-fly involves two memory accesses (to load ω and ω_i) and a modular multiplication. Hence, in an NTT computation, a considerable portion of the execution time is spent with calculating the twiddle factors. On the other hand, storing all intermediate twiddle factors ω and ω_i in memory is also problematic due to the fact that a standard 8-bit AVR processor features only a few kB of RAM.

Both the computation of the (n/i)-th power of ω_n in the i-loop (line 3) and the modular multiplication $\omega \cdot \omega_i$ in the j-loop (line 11) can be considered as fixed costs. Based on this observation, our solution is to store all the twiddle factors ω in ROM (resp. flash), very similar to the approach used in [24] for a hardware implementation. More concretely, we pre-compute the twiddle factors "off-line" and store them in a look-up table in ROM or flash so that we need to transfer only the twiddle factor that is required for the current iteration of the j-loop from ROM to RAM. In this way, only two bytes in RAM are needed.

3.2 Algorithmic Optimizations

The parameter sets of our ring-LWE encryption scheme given in the previous section use a modulus q that is prime and satisfies $q \equiv 1 \bmod 2n$ [28]. In such a setting, a polynomial multiplication can be carried out efficiently with only n-point NTTs (resp. INTT) due to special technique known as negative wrapped convolution, which has used before in a number of hardware implementations [23,28]. We remark that, for a more generic implementation, such restrictions on the parameter set may not be applicable. Our choice to use such restricted parameter sets is mainly driven by the fact that our target platform, an 8-bit AVR processor, is severely limited in resources, and performing $2n$-point NTTs (resp. a $2n$-point INTT) during a polynomial multiplication would increase the execution time and RAM requirements. Besides the application of the negative wrapped convolution, we adopt some other optimization techniques that were firstly proposed for hardware designs, but are suitable to improve the execution time of a software implementation too. These optimizations include the interchanging of the j and k-loops in the NTT algorithm [3], and the merging of the scaling operation by n^{-1} with the chain of multiplications performed during the post-processing operation in the inverse NTT [28].

3.3   Fast Coefficient Multiplication

During an NTT computation, $\frac{n}{2} \cdot \log_2(n)$ coefficient multiplications are carried out in the nested loops. Therefore, an efficient implementation of the coefficient multiplication operation is essential to achieve fast execution time. Due to the parameter sets we use, the coefficients are 13 or 14 bits long, and, thus, can be stored in two 8-bit registers. Inspired by the hybrid method for multi-precision multiplication [15], we propose a "Move-and-Add" (MA) technique to perform the coefficient multiplications. The MA multiplication technique, illustrated in Fig. 1, aims at minimizing the total number of adc instructions. First, the two coefficients a and b are loaded from RAM and stored in two registers. We then multiply the lower byte of a (i.e. a_L) by the lower byte of b (i.e. b_L) and move the product to two result registers $r0$ and $r1$ with help of the movw instruction [2]. Next, we form the product $a_H \cdot b_H$ and move the result to registers $r2$ and $r3$. Thereafter, we multiply byte a_H by byte b_L, add the resulting 16-bit product $a_L \cdot b_H$ to the register pair $r1, r2$, and propagate a potential carry from the last addition to $r3$. Finally, we perform the byte multiplication of a_L by b_H in the same way as before, i.e. the product is added to the registers $r1, r2$ and the carry bit is propagated into $r3$. In summary, the execution of our MA method for fast coefficient multiplication involves four mul, two movw, and a total of six add or adc instructions.

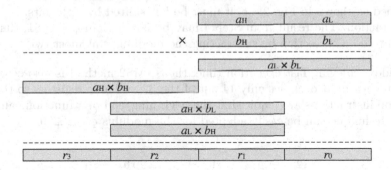

Fig. 1. The Move-and-Add (MA) coefficient multiplication

3.4   Fast Reduction of Coefficient-Products

In an NTT computation, the majority of execution time is spent on performing modular reduction of coefficient products since this operation is costly and has to be carried out in the innermost k-loop. Thus, an efficient reduction operation is a perquisite for a high-speed implementation of the NTT algorithm.

We propose a special Shift-Add-Multiply-Subtract-Subtract (SAMS2) technique to perform the reduction operation modulo $q = 7681$ and $q = 12289$. The main idea is as follows. Let z be a product of two coefficients, i.e. $z = a \cdot b$. To obtain $z \bmod q$, we estimate the quotient $t = z/q$, and then subtract $t \cdot q$ from

z, i.e. we compute $z - t \cdot q$. This result may not be fully reduced, which means it can be necessary to do a correction, i.e. to do a few final subtractions. Since $2^{13} \equiv 2^9 - 1 \bmod 7681$, it is not difficult to see that t can be approximated via $(z \gg 13) + (z \gg 17) + (z \gg 21)$. Consequently, the modular reduction involves four different basic operations, namely, Shifting $\rightarrow$ Addition $\rightarrow$ Multiplication $\rightarrow$ Subtraction $\rightarrow$ Subtraction (SAMS2). As illustrated in Fig. 2, we keep the product z in the four 8-bit registers $r3$, $r2$, $r1$, and $r0$, all of which are marked by different colors. A fully colored register means that all its bits are occupied (e.g. $r0$–$r2$), whereas white squares indicate that the corresponding bits of the register are empty (e.g. $r3$). The reduction modulo 7681 is done as follows:

1. Shifting: We first shift the three bytes in the registers $(r3, r2, r1)$ one bit to the right and store the result in the registers $(s1, s0, sx)$, whereby only the former two are shown in Fig. 2. Then, we right-shift $(s1, s0, sx)$ by four bits and write the result (which consists of only two bytes) to the two registers $(t1, t0)$. The content of register $u0$ is the same as that of $t1$.
2. Addition: We compute the sum of $(s1, s0)$, $(t1, t0)$, and $u0$. Apparently, this sum is always less than 16 bits long and can be stored in two registers.
3. Multiplication: Now, we multiply the sum from Step 2 by the constant 0x1e (i.e. the upper byte of 7681), which is a (16×8)-bit multiplication.
4. Subtraction: In this step, we subtract both the sum obtained in Step 2 and the product computed in Step 3 from z. The product from Step 3 has to be aligned as shown in Fig. 2, i.e. it must be left-shifted by eight bits.
5. Subtraction. The result from Step 4 may be larger than $q = 7681$; thus, we need to do a correction by subtracting the modulus q at most twice.

Besides achieving fast execution time, the SAMS2 method is also economic in register usage; it occupies only 14 out of the 32 available registers so that no push/pop instructions are required at the beginning/end of a function call. The SAMS2 technique can be easily adapted for the modulus $q = 12289$.

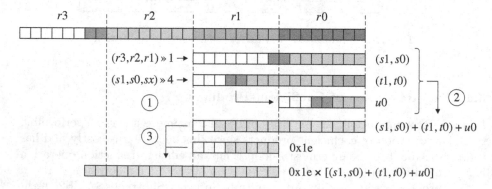

Fig. 2. The first three steps of the SAMS2 method for reduction modulo 7681. ①: shifting; ②: addition; ③: multiplication (Color figure online)

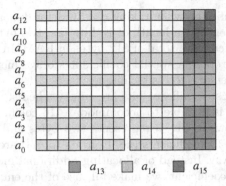

Fig. 3. Refined coefficient storage method to reduce the RAM footprint for $q = 7681$. Each row consists of two bytes, whereby each square represents a single bit (Color figure online).

3.5 Minimizing the Number of Reduction Operations

Apart from the coefficient multiplications, addition and subtraction operations are also executed in the innermost NTT loop. In general, a coefficient addition $r = a + b \bmod q$ is carried out via a "conventional" integer addition of the two operands, followed by a conditional subtraction of the modulus q if the sum is not smaller than q to get a final result in the range of $[0, q-1]$. A subtraction of coefficients can be performed in a similar fashion.

Inspired by the concept of "incomplete" modular arithmetic, as explained in e.g. [32], our implementation does not make an exact comparison between the sum $s = a + b$ and q, but rather compares s with 2^m where $m = \lceil \log_2(q) \rceil$, the bit-length of q. Taking $q = 7681$ as an example, the incomplete addition works as follows. We first perform a normal coefficient addition and then compare the higher byte of s with 2^5. If this byte is greater than or equal to 2^5 (which also means $r \geq 2^{13}$), then a subtraction of q needs to be performed. However, if the operands a and b are incompletely reduced (i.e. in the range $[0, 2^{13} - 1]$), up to two subtractions of q may be necessary [17]. Our implementation accepts two operands that are at most 13 bits long, but not necessarily smaller than q, and returns a result r for which the same holds. In the last iteration of the outermost loop of the NTT (i.e. when $i = 256$ in our case), a final correction process is performed to bring the result back into the range $[0, q-1]$. This incomplete reduction technique can be used for coefficient addition, subtraction, as well as multiplication. Our practical results show that this approach allows one to save roughly 6% of the reduction operations, thereby speeding up the NTT.

3.6 Reducing the RAM Consumption

The NTT computation requires to store the coefficients of intermediate results in RAM, which is a precious resource on our target platform. This can pose a problem since the number of coefficients is very large and each coefficient needs two bytes. More specifically, when taking $q = 7681$ for dimension $n = 256$ as an example, each coefficient has a length of 13 bits (i.e. two bytes) and, hence, the intermediate result occupies a total of 512 bytes in RAM. In order to reduce the RAM footprint, we propose a special coefficient storage method (illustrated in Fig. 3) and refined memory-access technique.

Since the three most significant bits are empty when storing a 13-bit coefficient in two bytes, it is possible to accommodate 16 coefficients in 26 bytes in RAM. Each of the rows in Fig. 3 represents two bytes and each square marks a single bit. The first 13 coefficients (i.e. from a_0 to a_{12}) are stored in the rows in a straightforward way. Instead of allocating additional memory space for the 14th, 15th, and 16th coefficient, we make full use of the empty bits in the rows to store them. More precisely, we divide the 14th coefficient (i.e. a_{13} in Fig. 3) into two parts; the first part contains the lower 12 bits of a_{13} and gets placed in the empty space of the rows a_0, a_1, a_2, and a_3, while the second part, i.e. the most significant bit of a_{13}, is stored in the 14th bit of the 13th row. We do the same with the coefficients a_{14} and a_{15}, which are marked by different colors in Fig. 3. Due to this special storage method, the loading of the coefficients from RAM to registers needs some "post processing." The coefficients a_0 to a_{12} can be obtained via an AND operation with 0x1fff, while a_{13}, a_{14}, and a_{15} require to perform several loads and then an "assembling" of the bits to get the actual coefficient. Thanks to this coefficient-storage method, we are able to reduce the RAM requirements by 18.75 % for $q = 7681$. A similar approach can be applied to the modulus $q = 12289$.

4   Optimization of the Knuth-Yao Sampler

The Knuth-Yao algorithm [16] requires a probability matrix P_{mat} that contains the probabilities of sampling a random number at a discrete position from the Gaussian distribution. Our Knuth-Yao implementation for AVR mainly adopts the optimizations in [9]; in addition, we propose a byte-wise scanning method to further reduce the execution time.

Probability Matrix with Low Memory Footprint. To ensure a precision of 2^{-90} for dimension $n = 256$, the Knuth-Yao algorithm is suggested to have a probability matrix P_{mat} of 55 rows and 109 columns [9]. On our AVR processor, we stored each 55-bit column in seven words, where each word is 8 bits long. In this case, only one bit is wasted per column and the probability matrix just occupies 6,104 bytes in total[1].

Byte-Wise Scanning. The bit-scanning operation as specified in Algorithm 2 (line 6) requires to check each bit and decreases the distance (d) whenever the

---

[1] The ROM footprint of the probability matrix can be further reduced to 4352 bytes by eliminating consecutive zero bits. In order to make a balance between execution time and ROM consumption, we decided to use the original variant in our work.

Algorithm 3. Knuth-Yao sampling with byte-wise scanning

Input: Probability matrix P_{mat}, random number r, modulus q
Output: Sample value s

1: $index \leftarrow r\&255$
2: $r \leftarrow r \gg 8$
3: $s \leftarrow LUT1[index]$
4: **if** $MSB(s) = 0$ **then**
5:   **if** $(r\&1) = 1$ **then**
6:    **return** $q - s$
7:   **else**
8:    **return** s
9:   **end if**
10: **end if**
11: $d \leftarrow s\&7$
12: **for** col **from** 8 **by** 1 **to** $MAXCOL$ **do**
13:   $d \leftarrow 2d + (r\&1)$
14:   $r \leftarrow r \gg 1$
15:   **for** row **from** $MAXROW$ **by** -8 **to** 0 **do**
16:    **if** $(P_{mat}[row][col] \| P_{mat}[row-1][col] \| \ldots \| P_{mat}[row-7][col]) > 0$ **then**
17:     $sum = \sum_{i=row}^{row-7}(P_{mat}[i][col])$
18:     $d \leftarrow d - sum$
19:     **if** $d < 0$ **then**
20:      **if** $d = -1$ **then**
21:       **for** j **from** $row - 7$ **by** 1 **to** row **do**
22:        **if** $P_{mat}[j][col] = 1$ **then**
23:         **if** $(r\&1) = 1$ **then**
24:          **return** $q - j$
25:         **else**
26:          **return** j
27:         **end if**
28:        **end if**
29:       **end for**
30:      **else**
31:       **for** j **from** $row - 7$ **by** 1 **to** row **do**
32:        $d \leftarrow d + P_{mat}[j][col]$
33:        **if** $d = -1$ **then**
34:         **if** $(r\&1) = 1$ **then**
35:          **return** $q - j$
36:         **else**
37:          **return** j
38:         **end if**
39:        **end if**
40:       **end for**
41:      **end if**
42:     **end if**
43:    **end if**
44:   **end for**
45: **end for**
46: **return** 0

---

bit is set. Instead of doing this scanning operation at the bit level, we perform it in a byte-wise fashion. As indicated in Algorithm 3 (lines 17 to 18), the byte-wise method only requires eight additions, one subtraction and one conditional branch statement, which means it saves seven branches at the (slight) expense of one subtraction.

Efficient Skipping of All-Zero Bytes. Another issue related to the probability matrix is the occurrence of all-zero bytes. In order to efficiently skip the scanning operations for such bytes, we compare the eight concatenated bits in line 16 of Algorithm 3 with 0. Since these eight bits fit into one byte, a simple byte-comparison allows us to determine whether the bits are 0 or not. In this way, we can save a number of scanning operations and, thereby, speed up the whole sampling process.

Look-Up Table in DDG Tree. We applied the Look-Up Table (LUT)-based approach proposed in [9] to our byte-wise scanning implementation (shown in line 1 to 10 of Algorithm 3). At first, we do the sampling with an 8-bit random number as index to the LUT in the first eight levels for a Gaussian distribution with $\sigma = 11.31/\sqrt{2\pi}$. If the most significant bit of the look-up result is cleared then the algorithm completed the look-up operation successfully. Otherwise, the most significant bit of the look-up result is set, which means a look-up failure has occurred and we proceed with the next level of the sampling. Similarly, a second LUT is used for level 9 to 13 in the same Gaussian distribution.

4.1 Pseudo-Random Number Generation Using AES Accelerator

Our implementation adopts the PRNG algorithm suggested in [26], which runs the AES block cipher in counter mode, i.e. it encrypts successive values of an incrementing counter. The Atmel ATxmega128A1 microcontroller features an AES crypto-accelerator that allows one to perform encryptions with reasonable computational overhead (375 clock cycles) and small memory footprint for the AES trigger program. This is a significant improvement compared to software implementations of the AES, which require (at least) 1993 cycles per block and occupy some 2 kB program memory on an ATmega128 [22]. Another attractive feature of the ATxmega's built-in AES crypto-accelerator is that it can operate independently of the processor, which allows one to "hide" the latencies due to AES encryption [30]. We exploit this feature in our Knuth-Yao sampler implementation, i.e. we trigger the next AES operation immediately after getting the result of the current one and then proceed with other tasks. Unfortunately, the AES accelerator of the ATxmega128A1 can only support 128-bit keys, which is not sufficient for long-term security. Therefore, we decided to use the software AES from the AVR Crypto Lib [8] for the long-term security level; it requires 3521 clock cycles to encrypt a block under a 256-bit key.

5 Performance Evaluation and Comparison

5.1 Experimental Platform

Our prototyping platform is an Atmel Xplained evaluation board that contains an ATxmega128A1 processor. This processor can be clocked with a maximum frequency of 32 MHz and features 128 kB flashable program memory as well as 8 kB SRAM. It is popular 8-bit processor with an AES crypto-accelerator and can be used in a wide range of applications. Our ring-LWE software is written in a mix of ANSI C and Assembly language. More precisely, while most functions of our ring-LWE encryption scheme are written in ANSI C, we implemented all modular arithmetic operations for the NTT in Assembly language to reduce the execution time. We compiled our software with Atmel Studio 6.2 and applied the speed optimization option O3. In order to obtain accurate timings, we ran each operation at least 1000 times and calculated the average cycle count.

5.2 Experimental Results

Table 1 specifies the execution time of the main components (i.e. the NTT, the Knuth-Yao sampler, key-generation, encryption, and decryption) of our ring-LWE encryption schemes for both medium-term and long-term security. As was mentioned earlier in this paper, we implemented two versions of the arithmetic operations for each security level, one that is optimized for speed and a second aiming at low memory footprint (i.e. memory efficiency). The two high-speed (HS) implementations make full use of the optimization techniques described in Sect. 3 (except Subsect. 3.6) and Sect. 4, whereby all data is kept in RAM. On the other hand, the memory-efficient (ME) implementations use the optimized coefficient storage method and memory access scheme from Subsect. 3.6 for all basic operations and store the pre-computed look-up tables in flash ROM.

Table 1. Execution time (in clock cycles) of the major components of our ring-LWE encryption scheme

Implementation	NTT	KY	Key-Gen	Enc	Dec
HS-256	193,731	26,763	589,900	671,628	275,646
ME-256	322,288	39,027	1,310,616	1,532,823	673,489
HS-512	441,572	255,218	2,165,239	2,617,459	686,367
ME-512	917,866	300,780	3,738,052	4,270,671	1,444,786

As shown in Table 1, the NTT operation requires only 194 k clock cycles in the case of the HS-256 implementation, but the execution time increases quite sharply to 442 k cycles for the HS-512 variant. The Knuth-Yao sampler for the HS-256 implementation takes an average of about 27 k cycles, while more than 255 k clock cycles are needed for HS-512. The former increase can be explained by the fact that the number of coefficients for HS-512 is doubled compared to HS-256 and the modular reduction operation for $q = 12889$ is more costly than for $q = 7681$. On the other hand, the pseudo-random number generation at the medium-term security level can take advantage of the AES accelerator, whereas for long-term security, the required 256-bit AES operations need to be carried out in software. It is also interesting to compare the execution time of the HS and ME variants at the same security level. Taking HS-256 as an example, the key generation, encryption, and decryption need about 590 k, 672 k, and 276 k cycles, respectively, which is more than twice as fast as the memory-optimized variant ME-256. Apparently, this is primarily because of the more costly access to the coefficients, which slows down all basic operations. More specifically, the coefficient addition, subtraction, as well as multiplication up to the NTT, the Knuth-Yao sampler and each component consume more execution time to load the coefficients from memory and write them back to memory.

Table 2. RAM and ROM requirements (in bytes) of key generation, encryption, and decryption

Implementation	Key-Gen	Enc	Dec	Total
HS-256: RAM/ROM	1,585/8,884	2,609/8,812	1,585/6,026	2,609/13,604
ME-256: RAM/ROM	1,297/9,260	2,129/8,536	1,297/6,016	2,129/13,756
HS-512: RAM/ROM	3,121/12,074	6,193/13,486	3,121/8,512	6,193/18,894
ME-512: RAM/ROM	2,737/12,106	4,529/12,166	2,737/8,614	4,529/18,010

Table 2 shows the RAM and ROM requirements of key-generation, encryption, and decryption. In the case of HS-256, the full ring-LWE implementation requires some 2.6 kB RAM and 13.6 kB ROM, while the ME-256 variant needs roughly 2.1 kB RAM and 13.7 kB ROM. Due to the special coefficient-storage method described in Subsect. 3.6, the memory-optimized implementations save roughly 19 % (for medium-term security) and 21 % (long-term security) in RAM requirements while consuming approximately the same amount of ROM as the HS implementations.

5.3   Comparison with Related Work

Table 3 compares software implementations of lattice-based cryptosystems on several different processors. For the 8-bit AVR platform, the implementations in [5,6,25] and our software use the same parameter sets as mentioned before in Subsect. 2.5. Compared to the recent work in [25], our HS-256 version requires only 672 k and 276 k cycles for encryption and decryption, which is roughly 2.0 and 1.4 times faster, respectively. This progress is mainly due to a combination of algorithmic optimizations and the proposed low-level techniques to speed up the NTT multiplication and the Gaussian sampling operation.

Table 3. Performance comparison of software implementations of lattice-based cryptosystems on different processors

Implementation	NTT/FFT	Sampling	Key-Gen	Enc	Dec
Implementations on high-performance processors, e.g. Core 2 Duo:					
Göttert [14] (256)	n/a	n/a	9,300,000	4,560,000	1,710,000
Göttert [14] (512)	n/a	n/a	13,590,000	9,180,000	3,540,000
Implementations on 32-bit ARM processors, e.g. Cortex-M4F:					
de Clercq [9] (256)	31,583	7,296	117,009	121,166	43,324
de Clercq [9] (512)	71,090	14,592	252,002	261,939	96,520
Oder [21] (512)	122,619	935,936	n/a	n/a	n/a
Implementations on 8-bit AVR processors, e.g. ATxmega64, ATxmega128:					
Boorghany [6] (256)	1,216,000	n/a	n/a	5,024,000	2,464,000
Boorghany [5] (256)	754,668	n/a	2,770,592	3,042,675	1,368,969
Pöppelmann [25] (256)	334,646	n/a	n/a	1,314,977	381,254
This work (HS-256)	193,731	26,763	589,900	671,628	275,646
Boorghany [5] (512)	2,207,787	617,600	n/a	n/a	n/a
Pöppelmann [25] (512)	855,595	n/a	n/a	3,279,142	1,019,350
This work (HS-512)	441,572	255,218	2,165,239	2,617,459	686,367

Table 4 compares the results of our ring-LWE encryption scheme with some classical public-key encryption algorithms, in particular recent RSA and ECC implementations for the 8-bit AVR platform. The to-date fastest RSA software for an AVR microcontroller was reported in [18]; it achieves an execution time of approximately 76.6 M clock cycles for decryption at the 80-bit security level (i.e. 1024-bit modulus)[2]. For comparison, our HS-256 implementation requires only 276 k cycles for decryption, which is more than 278 times faster despite a much higher (i.e. 128-bit) security level. There exist quite a few ECC software implementations for 8-bit AVR processors. Recently, Düll et al. [11] managed to achieve an execution time of 13.9 M clock cycles (HS version) and 14,1 M cycles (ME version) for a variable-base scalar multiplication on Curve25519 [4]. The widely-used Elliptic Curve Integrated Encryption Scheme (ECIES) is based on scalar multiplications; the encryption involves two scalar multiplications (one with a fixed base point and the other with a random point), while a decryption operation requires a scalar multiplication with a random point. The HS version of our ring-LWE encryption scheme beats any of the ECC implementations in [1,11,19] by at least one order of magnitude. Our results also show that ring-LWE encryption is superior to traditional public-key schemes when high speed on resource-constrained devices is desired.

---

[2] To the best of our knowledge, no RSA implementation providing 128-bit security on an 8-bit processors exists. Thus, we use the 80-bit security level for comparison.

Table 4. Comparison of Ring-LWE encryption schemes with RSA and ECC on 8-bit AVR processors (RAM and ROM in bytes, Enc and Dec in clock cycles)

Implementation	Scheme	RAM	ROM	Enc	Dec
Gura et al. [15]	RSA-1024	n/a	n/a	3,440,000	87,920,000
Liu et al. [18]	RSA-1024	n/a	n/a	n/a	75,680,000
Düll et al. [11] (ME)	ECC-255	510	9,912	28,293,688	14,146,844
Düll et al. [11] (HS)	ECC-255	494	17,710	27,800,794	13,900,397
Liu et al. [19]	ECC-256	556	14,700	30,539,566	21,118,778
Aranha et al. [1]	ECC-233	3,700	38,600	11,796,480	5,898,240
This work (HS)	LWE-256	2,609	13,604	671,628	275,646
This work (ME)	LWE-256	2,129	13,756	1,532,823	673,489

6 Conclusions

This paper presented several optimizations to efficiently implement a ring-LWE encryption scheme on the 8-bit AVR platform. In particular, we proposed three optimizations to accelerate the execution time and a special coefficient-storage technique along with a refined access strategy to reduce the RAM requirements of NTT-based polynomial multiplication. A combination of these optimizations yields a very efficient NTT computation, which is twice as fast as the previous best implementation in the literature. We also reported the results we obtained for a performance-oriented and a memory-efficient implementation at both the medium-term and long-term security level, respectively. In all four settings, the results we achieved set new speed records for a ring-LWE encryption scheme on an 8-bit AVR processor. Finally, a comparison of our work with RSA and ECC implementations confirms that ring-LWE encryption schemes are a good choice for high-speed public-key cryptography on resource-constrained devices.

Acknowledgments. The authors thank Frederik Vercauteren and Ruan de Clercq from KU Leuven for fruitful discussions and useful suggestions that helped to improve the work described in this paper.

Zhe Liu is supported by the Fonds National de la Recherche (FNR) Luxembourg under AFR grant No. 1359142. Hwajeong Seo is supported by Institute for Information & Communications Technology Promotion (IITP) grant funded by Korea government (MSIP) [No. 10043907, Development of high-performance IoT device and an open platform with intelligent software]. Sujoy Sinha Roy is supported by an Erasmus Mundus Ph.D. scholarship. This work is supported by the Research Council KU Leuven: TENSE GOA/11/007, by iMinds, by the Flemish Government, FWO G.0550.12N, G.00130.13N, FWO G.0876.14N, and by the Hercules Foundation AKUL/11/19.

References

1. Aranha, D.F., Dahab, R., López, J.C., Oliveira, L.B.: Efficient implementation of elliptic curve cryptography in wireless sensors. Adv. Math. Commun. 4(2), 169–187 (2010)
2. Atmel Corporation. 8-bit AVR® Instruction Set. User Guide, July 2010. http://www.atmel.com/dyn/resources/prod_documents/doc0856.pdf
3. Aysu, A., Patterson, C., Schaumont, P.: Low-cost and area-efficient FPGA implementations of lattice-based cryptography. In: HOST, pp. 81–86. IEEE (2013)
4. Bernstein, D.J.: Curve25519: new Diffie-Hellman speed records. In: Yung, M., Dodis, Y., Kiayias, A., Malkin, T. (eds.) PKC 2006. LNCS, vol. 3958, pp. 207–228. Springer, Heidelberg (2006)
5. Boorghany, A., Bayat-Sarmadi, S., Jalili, R.: On constrained implementation of lattice-based cryptographic primitives and schemes on smart cards. Cryptology ePrint Archive, Report 2014/514 (2014). http://eprint.iacr.org/2014/514.pdf
6. Boorghany, A., Jalili, R.: Implementation and comparison of lattice-based identification protocols on smart cards and microcontrollers. Cryptology ePrint Archive, Report 2014/078 (2014). http://eprint.iacr.org/2014/078.pdf
7. Cormen, T.H., Leiserson, C.E., Rivest, R.L.: Introduction to Algorithms. MIT Press and McGraw-Hill, New York (1990)
8. Das Labor. AVR Crypto Lib (2012). http://avrcryptolib.das-labor.org/trac
9. de Clercq, R., Roy, S.S., Vercauteren, F., Verbauwhede, I.: Efficient software implementation of ring-LWE encryption. In: 18th Design, Automation and Test in Europe Conference and Exhibition-DATE (2015)
10. Ducas, L.: Lattice based signatures: attacks, analysis and optimization. Ph.D. thesis, ENS Paris and Université Paris Diderot, France (2013)
11. Düll, M., Haase, B., Hinterwälder, G., Hutter, M., Paar, C., Sánchez, A.H., Schwabe, P.: High-speed Curve25519 on 8-bit, 16-bit, and 32-bit microcontrollers. Cryptology ePrint Archive, Report 2015/343 (2015). http://eprint.iacr.org/2015/343.pdf
12. Dwarakanath, N.C., Galbraith, S.D.: Sampling from discrete Gaussians for lattice-based cryptography on a constrained device. Appl. Algebra Eng. Commun. Comput. 25, 159–180 (2014)
13. Evans, D.: The Internet of things: how the next evolution of the Internet is changing everything. Cisco IBSG white paper, April 2011. http://www.cisco.com/web/about/ac79/docs/innov/IoT_IBSG_0411FINAL.pdf
14. Göttert, N., Feller, T., Schneider, M., Buchmann, J., Huss, S.: On the design of hardware building blocks for modern lattice-based encryption schemes. In: Prouff, E., Schaumont, P. (eds.) CHES 2012. LNCS, vol. 7428, pp. 512–529. Springer, Heidelberg (2012)
15. Gura, N., Patel, A., Wander, A., Eberle, H., Shantz, S.C.: Comparing elliptic curve cryptography and RSA on 8-bit CPUs. In: Joye, M., Quisquater, J.-J. (eds.) CHES 2004. LNCS, vol. 3156, pp. 119–132. Springer, Heidelberg (2004)
16. Knuth, D.E., Yao, A.C.: The complexity of nonuniform random number generation. In: Traub, J.F. (ed.) Algorithms and Complexity: New Directions and Recent Results, pp. 357–428. Academic Press, New York (1976)
17. Liu, Z., Großschädl, J.: New speed records for montgomery modular multiplication on 8-bit AVR microcontrollers. In: Pointcheval, D., Vergnaud, D. (eds.) AFRICACRYPT. LNCS, vol. 8469, pp. 215–234. Springer, Heidelberg (2014)

18. Liu, Z., Großschädl, J., Kizhvatov, I.: Efficient and side-channel resistant RSA implementation for 8-bit AVR microcontrollers. In: Proceedings of the 1st International Workshop on the Security of the Internet of Things (SECIOT 2010) (2010)

19. Liu, Z., Wenger, E., Großschädl, J.: MoTE-ECC: energy-scalable elliptic curve cryptography for wireless sensor networks. In: Boureanu, I., Owesarski, P., Vaudenay, S. (eds.) ACNS 2014. LNCS, vol. 8479, pp. 361–379. Springer, Heidelberg (2014)

20. Lyubashevsky, V., Peikert, C., Regev, O.: On ideal lattices and learning with errors over rings. In: Gilbert, H. (ed.) EUROCRYPT 2010. LNCS, vol. 6110, pp. 1–23. Springer, Heidelberg (2010)

21. Oder, T., Pöppelmann, T., Güneysu, T.: Beyond ECDSA and RSA: lattice-based digital signatures on constrained devices. In: 51st Annual Design Automation Conference-DAC (2014)

22. Osvik, D.A., Bos, J.W., Stefan, D., Canright, D.: Fast software AES encryption. In: Hong, S., Iwata, T. (eds.) FSE 2010. LNCS, vol. 6147, pp. 75–93. Springer, Heidelberg (2010)

23. Pöppelmann, T., Ducas, L., Güneysu, T.: Enhanced lattice-based signatures on reconfigurable hardware. In: Batina, L., Robshaw, M. (eds.) CHES 2014. LNCS, vol. 8731, pp. 353–370. Springer, Heidelberg (2014)

24. Pöppelmann, T., Güneysu, T.: Towards efficient arithmetic for lattice-based cryptography on reconfigurable hardware. In: Hevia, A., Neven, G. (eds.) LatinCrypt 2012. LNCS, vol. 7533, pp. 139–158. Springer, Heidelberg (2012)

25. Pöppelmann, T., Oder, T., Güneysu, T.: Speed Records for Ideal Lattice-Based Cryptography on AVR. http://eprint.iacr.org/2015/382.pdf

26. Prescott, T.: Random number generation using AES. Technical report, Atmel Inc. (2011). http://www.atmel.com/ja/jp/Images/article_random_number.pdf

27. Regev, O.: On lattices, learning with errors, random linear codes, and cryptography. In: Proceedings of the Thirty-Seventh Annual ACM Symposium on Theory of Computing, STOC 2005, pp. 84–93. ACM, New York (2005)

28. Roy, S.S., Vercauteren, F., Mentens, N., Chen, D.D., Verbauwhede, I.: Compact ring-LWE cryptoprocessor. In: Batina, L., Robshaw, M. (eds.) CHES 2014. LNCS, vol. 8731, pp. 371–391. Springer, Heidelberg (2014)

29. Roy, S.S., Vercauteren, F., Verbauwhede, I.: High precision discrete Gaussian sampling on FPGAs. In: Lange, T., Lauter, K., Lisoněk, P. (eds.) SAC 2013. LNCS, vol. 8282, pp. 383–401. Springer, Heidelberg (2014)

30. Seo, H., Kim, J., Choi, J., Park, T., Liu, Z., Kim, H.: Small private key MQPKS on an embedded microprocessor. Sensors 14(3), 5441–5458 (2014)

31. Shor, P.: Algorithms for quantum computation: discrete logarithms and factoring. In: 1994 Proceedings of the 35th Annual Symposium on Foundations of Computer Science, pp. 124–134, November 1994

32. Yanık, T., Savaş, E., Koç, Ç.K.: Incomplete reduction in modular arithmetic. IEE Proc. - Comput. Digit. Tech. 149(2), 46–52 (2002)

A Masked Ring-LWE Implementation

Oscar Reparaz$^{(\boxtimes)}$, Sujoy Sinha Roy,
Frederik Vercauteren, and Ingrid Verbauwhede

Department of Electrical Engineering-ESAT/COSIC and iMinds,
KU Leuven, Kasteelpark Arenberg 10, 3001 Leuven-Heverlee, Belgium
{oscar.reparaz,sujoy.sinharoy,frederik.vercauteren,
ingrid.verbauwhede}@esat.kuleuven.be

Abstract. Lattice-based cryptography has been proposed as a postquantum public-key cryptosystem. In this paper, we present a masked ring-LWE decryption implementation resistant to first-order side-channel attacks. Our solution has the peculiarity that the entire computation is performed in the masked domain. This is achieved thanks to a new, bespoke masked decoder implementation. The output of the ring-LWE decryption are Boolean shares suitable for derivation of a symmetric key. We have implemented a hardware architecture of the masked ring-LWE processor on a Virtex-II FPGA, and have performed side channel analysis to confirm the soundness of our approach. The area of the protected architecture is around 2000 LUTs, a 20 % increase with respect to the unprotected architecture. The protected implementation takes 7478 cycles to compute, which is only a factor ×2.6 larger than the unprotected implementation.

1 Introduction

Once the quantum computer is built, Shor's algorithm will make most current cryptographic algorithms obsolete. In particular, public-key cryptosystems that rely on number-theoretic hardness assumptions such as integer factorization (RSA) or discrete logarithms, either in $\mathbb{Z}_p^*$ (Diffie-Hellman) or in elliptic curves over finite fields, will be insecure. On the bright side, there is an entire branch of postquantum cryptography that is believed to resist mathematical attacks running on quantum computers.

There are three main branches of postquantum cryptosystems: based on codes, on multivariate quadratic equations or on lattices [1]. Lattice-based cryptographic constructions, founded on the *learning with errors* (LWE) problem [21] and its ring variant known as ring-LWE problem [15], have become a versatile tool for designing asymmetric encryption schemes [15], digital signatures [8] and homomorphic encryption schemes [3,9]. Several hardware and software implementations of such schemes have appeared in the literature. So far, the reported implementations have focused mainly on efficient implementation strategies, and very little research work has appeared in the area of side channel security of the lattice-based schemes.

© International Association for Cryptologic Research 2015
T. Güneysu and H. Handschuh (Eds.): CHES 2015, LNCS 9293, pp. 683–702, 2015.
DOI: 10.1007/978-3-662-48324-4_34

It comes as no surprise that implementations of postquantum algorithms are vulnerable to side-channel attacks. Side-channel attacks, as introduced by Kocher [13], exploit timing, power consumption or the electromagnetic emanation from a device executing a cryptographic implementation to extract secrets, such as cryptographic keys. A particularly powerful side-channel technique is Differential Power Analysis (DPA), introduced by Kocher et al. [14]. In a typical DPA attack, the adversary measures the instantaneous power consumption of a device, places hypotheses on subkeys and applies statistical tests to confirm or reject the hypotheses. DPA attacks can be surprisingly easy to mount even with low-end equipment, and hence it is important to protect against them.

There are plenty of countermeasures against DPA. Most notably, masking [6,12] is both a provably sound and popular in industry. Masking effectively randomizes the computation of the cryptographic algorithm by splitting each intermediate into several shares, in such a way that each share is independent from any secret. This property is preserved through the entire computation. Thus, observing any single intermediate (for example, by a side-channel, be it known or unknown) reveals nothing about the secret. However, there are not many masking schemes specifically designed for postquantum cryptography. In [4] Brenner et al. present a masked FPGA implementation of the postquantum pseudo-random function SPRING.

In the rest of the paper, we focus on protecting the ring-LWE decryption operation against side-channel attacks with masking. The decryption algorithm is considerably exposed to DPA attacks since it repeatedly uses long-term private keys. In contrast, the encryption or key-generation procedures use ephemeral secrets only [24].

Our contribution. In this paper we present a very compact masked implementation of the ring-LWE decryption function. The masking countermeasure adds very limited overhead compared to other previous approaches, thanks to a bespoke probabilistic masked decoder designed specifically for our implementation. We implemented the design on a Virtex-II FPGA and tested the side-channel security with practical experiments that demonstrate the validity of our approach.

Organization. The paper is structured as follows: we provide a brief mathematical background of the ring-LWE encryption scheme in Sect. 2 and describe a high-level overview of the proposed masked ring-LWE decryption in Sect. 3. In the next section we construct the masked decoder and in Sect. 5 we show the experimental results. We analyze the error rates of the decryption operation in Sect. 6 and apply error correcting codes. We dedicate Sect. 7 for the side channel evaluation.

2   Preliminaries

Notation. The Latin letters r, c_i indicate polynomials. When we want to explicitly access a coefficient of the polynomial we write $r[i]$. Multiplication of polynomials is written as $r * c_1$. Coefficient-wise multiplication is denoted as $r \cdot c_1$. The letter m denotes a string of bits, and q is an integer. Letters with prime x' or double prime x'' represent shares of variable x. Depending on the context, these shares are split either arithmetically $x = x' + x''$ (mod q) or Boolean $x = x' + x''$ (mod 2). A polynomial r is shared into (r', r'') by additively sharing each of its coefficients $r[i]$ such that $r = r' + r''$.

Ring-LWE. For completeness, we give in this section a description of the three major algorithms of the ring-LWE public-key cryptosystem [15]: key-generation, encryption and decryption.

The ring-LWE encryption scheme works with polynomials in a ring $R_q = \mathbb{Z}_q[\mathbf{x}]/(f(x))$, where $f(x)$ is an irreducible polynomial of degree n. During the key generation, encryption and decryption operations, polynomial arithmetic such as polynomial addition, subtraction and multiplication are performed. In addition, the key-generation and encryption operations require sampling of error polynomials from an error distribution (typically a discrete Gaussian.)

The ring-LWE encryption scheme is described in this way:

- In the key generation phase, two error polynomials r_1 and r_2 are sampled from the discrete Gaussian distribution. The secret key is the polynomial r_2 and the public key is the polynomial $p = r_1 - g * r_2$. After key generation, there is no use of the polynomial r_1. The polynomial g is globally known.
- In the encryption operation of a binary message vector m of length n, the message is first lifted to a ring element $\bar{m} \in R_q$ by multiplying the message bits by $q/2$. The ciphertext is computed as a pair of polynomials (c_1, c_2) where $c_1 = g * e_1 + e_2$ and $c_2 = p * e_1 + e_3 + \bar{m} \in R_q$. The encryption operation requires generation of three error polynomials e_1, e_2 and e_3.
- The decryption operation uses the private key r_2 to compute the message as $m = \text{th}(c_1 * r_2 + c_2)$. The decoding function th is a simple threshold decoder that is applied coefficient-wise and is defined as

$$\text{th}(x) = \begin{cases} 0 & \text{if } x \in (0, q/4) \cup (3q/4, q) \\ 1 & \text{if } x \in (q/4, 3q/4) \end{cases} \tag{1}$$

Efficiency improvements. To achieve an efficient implementation of the encryption scheme, the irreducible polynomial $f(x)$ is taken as $x^n + 1$ where n is a power of two, and the modulus q is chosen as a prime number satisfying $q \equiv 1$ mod $2n$ [18,25]. In this setting, polynomial multiplications can be efficiently performed in $O(n \log n)$ time using the Number Theoretic Transform (NTT).

Following [25], we keep the ciphertext polynomials c_1 and c_2 in the NTT domain to reduce the computation cost of the decryption operation. The decryption operation thus computes the decrypted message as

$$m = \text{th}\big(\text{INTT}(\tilde{c}_1 \cdot \tilde{r}_2 + \tilde{c}_2)\big). \tag{2}$$

Here the symbol $\tilde{r}$ represents the NTT of a polynomial r, and INTT($\cdot$) represents the inverse NTT operation. The multiplication of $\tilde{c}_1 \cdot \tilde{r}_2$ is thus performed coefficient-wise (as well as the addition $\tilde{c}_1 \cdot \tilde{r}_2 + \tilde{c}_2$.) For convenience, we drop the tildes in the rest of the paper and work with c_1, c_2 and r_2 in the NTT domain. We furthermore refer to $\tilde{r}_2$ simply as r. (We recall that the INTT is a linear transformation applied to the n coefficients of $a = r \cdot c_1 + c_2$.) The decoding function th applies a threshold function to each coefficient of a as defined in Eq. 1 to output n recovered message bits.

3 High-Level Overview

In this section, we give a high-level view of the masked ring-LWE implementation. The most natural way to split the computation of the decryption as Eq. 2 is to split the secret polynomial r additively into two shares r' and r'' such that $r[i] = r'[i] + r''[i]$ (mod q) for all i. The n coefficients of r' are chosen uniformly at random in $\mathbb{Z}_q$ in each execution of the decryption.

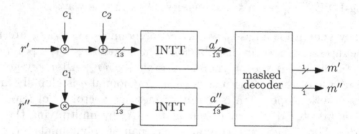

Fig. 1. General data flow of the masked ring-LWE decryption. r' and r'' are the arithmetic shares of the private key r; c_1 and c_2 are the input unmasked ciphertext; m' and m'' are the Boolean shares of the recovered plaintext.

The bulk of the computation from Eq. 2 is amenable to this splitting, since by linearity of the multiplication and INTT operation, we have that $\text{INTT}(r \cdot c_2 + c_1) = \text{INTT}(r' \cdot c_2 + c_1) + \text{INTT}(r'' \cdot c_2)$. Thus, we can split almost the entire computation from Eq. 2 into two branches, as drawn in Fig. 1. The first branch computes on r' to determine the polynomial

$$a' = \text{INTT}(r' \cdot c_2 + c_1) \tag{3}$$

and the second branch operates on r'' to determine

$$a'' = \text{INTT}(r'' \cdot c_2). \tag{4}$$

The advantage of such a high-level masking is that the operations of Eqs. 3 and 4 can be performed on an arithmetic processor without any particular protection against DPA. (This is because any intermediate appearing in either branch is independent of the secret r. This situation is very similar to, for example, base point blinding in elliptic curve scalar multiplication.) We can reuse an existing ring-LWE processor for these operations, and leverage the numerous optimizations carried out for this block [18,25].

The final threshold th($\cdot$) operation of Eq. 2 is obviously non-linear in the base field $\mathbb{F}_q$, and hence cannot be independently applied to each branch (Eqs. 3 and 4). There are generic approaches to mask arbitrary functions. For instance, in [4] an approach based on masked tables was used. However, these generic approaches are usually quite expensive in terms of area or randomness. In the following Sect. 4, we pursue another direction. We design a bespoke masked decoder that results in a very compact implementation.

4   Masked Decoder

In this section we describe a very compact, probabilistic masked decoder. In the sequel, a denotes a single coefficient and (a', a'') its shares such that $a' + a'' = a$ (mod q). The decoder computes the function th(a) from the shares (a', a''). We also drop the symbol (mod q) when obvious.

First crack. The key idea of the efficient masked decoder is that we do not need to know the exact values of the shares a' and a'' of a coefficient a in order to compute th(a). For example, if $0 < a' < q/4$ and $q/4 < a'' < q/2$ then $a = a' + a''$ is bounded by $q/4 < a < 3q/4$, and thus th(a) = 1. That is, we learnt th(a) from only a few most significant bits from a' and a''. We can use this idea to substantially simplify the complexity of the masked th function.

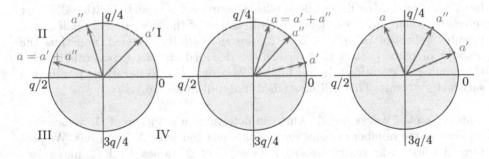

Fig. 2. Idea for the masked decoder. Elements in $\mathbb{Z}_q$ are shown in a circle. Adding two elements translates into adding their respective angles. Left: case $0 < a' < q/4$, $q/4 < a'' < q/2$, and therefore th(a) = 1. Center and right: case $0 < a' < q/4$, $0 < a'' < q/4$, which does not allow to infer th(a).

4.1   Rules

Figure 2, left, illustrates the situation from the last paragraph. In this case, $0 < a' < q/4$ and $q/4 < a'' < q/2$ so obviously a can range only from $q/4$ to $3q/4$, and hence th(a) = 1. Analogously to this rule, we can formulate 3 other rules:

- If $q/2 < a' < 3q/4$ and $3q/4 < a'' < q$ then $q/4 < a < 3q/4$ and thus th$(a) = 1$.
- If $q/4 < a' < q/2$ and $q/2 < a'' < 3q/4$ then a belongs to $(0, q/4) \cup (3q/4, q)$ and thus th$(a) = 0$ (quadrants I and IV, left half of the circle).
- If $3q/4 < a' < q$ and $0 < a'' < q/4$ then a belongs to $(0, q/4) \cup (3q/4, q)$ and thus th$(a) = 0$.

There are 4 other rules that result from interchanging a' with a'' in the above expressions. (This follows straight from the symmetry of the additive splitting.) Essentially, with the only information of the *quadrant* of each share a' and a'' we can, in half of the cases, deduce the output of th(a). (For the explanation simplicity, we obviated what happens in the boundaries of the quadrant intervals. Similar conclusions hold when including them.)

What if no rule is hit? In roughly half of the cases, we can apply one of the 8 rules previously described to deduce the value of th(a). However, in the other half of the cases, none of the rules applies. A representative case of this event is shown in Fig. 2, center and right. In both cases, $0 < a' < q/4$ and $0 < a'' < q/4$. This situation is not covered by any of the 8 rules previously described. We see that in the center sub figure th$(a) = 0$ while in the right sub figure th$(a) = 1$, so in this case the quadrants of each share a' and a'' do not allow us to infer th(a).

The solution in this case is to refresh the splitting (a', a''), that is, update $a' \leftarrow a' + \Delta_1$ and $a'' \leftarrow a'' - \Delta_1$ for certain Δ_1. (This refreshing naturally preserves the unshared value $a = a' + a''$.) After the refreshing, the 8 rules can be checked again. If still no rule applies, the process is repeated with a different refreshing value Δ_i. Note that in each iteration of the step, roughly half of the possible values of $(a', a'') \in \mathbb{Z}_q \times \mathbb{Z}_q$ are successfully decoded, and thus the amount of pairs (a', a'') that do not get decoded shrinks exponentially with the number of iterations. In our implementation, $N = 16$ iterations produces a satisfactory result. This will be studied in detail in Sect. 6.1.

Optimal cooked values for Δ_i. One can determine a sequence of Δ_i values that maximizes the number of pairs successfully decoded after N iterations. We performed a first-order search for such a sequence of Δ_i values. Each Δ_i maximizes the number of successfully decoded pairs after $i - 1$ iterations. See the extended version of this paper[1] for exemplary values of Δ_i.

Architecture. The hardware architecture for the masked decoder follows from the previous working principle description. Our implementation is shown in Fig. 3. From left to right, we see the first refreshing step by the constants Δ_i. The constants Δ_i vary from iteration to iteration. After the refreshing step, the quadrant function is applied to each share a', a''. This quadrant function outputs x if a belongs to the x-th quadrant, and thus the output consists of 2 bits. These blocks

---

[1] http://www.reparaz.net/oscar/ches2015-lwe/.

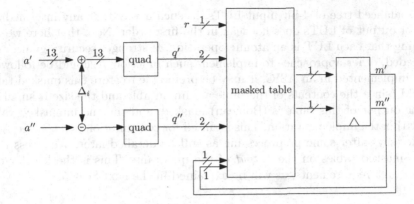

Fig. 3. The masked decoder.

are essentially 13-bit comparators, and thus relatively inexpensive in logic.[2] The subsequent rule checking on (q', q'') is performed by a masked table lookup that is described in the following section. The whole process is repeated $N = 16$ iterations, and this number of iterations stays fixed even if the decoding is successful after the few first iterations.

4.2 Masked Table Lookup

The final step in the masked decoder is a masked table lookup. This table implements the rules described in Sect. 4.1, and essentially maps the output of each quadrant q'_i and q''_i (2 bits each) after the i-the iteration ($i \in [1, N]$) to a (Boolean) masked output bit value (m'_i, m''_i). In our specific implementation, we have other inputs: the result of the decoding from the previous iteration (m'_{i-1}, m''_{i-1}) and an extra randomness bit r (fresh at each of the N iterations for each of the n coefficients).

This is a well-studied problem that arises in other situations (for instance, when masking the sbox lookup in a typical block cipher) and there are plenty of approaches here to implement such masked table lookup. We opted for the approach of masked tables as in [26]. We set $m'_i \leftarrow r$ and we compute $m''_i \leftarrow f(r, q'_i, q''_i, m'_{i-1}, m''_{i-1})$. The function f essentially bypasses the previous decoded value when no rule applies to q'_i, q''_i by setting the output m''_i to $r + m'_{i-1} + m''_{i-1}$ (refreshing the content of the output registers). If a rule applies to q'_i, q''_i, it sets the output m''_i accordingly. By doing this, we can register always the output of this table and no control logic to enable such output register is needed (it is implicitly integrated into this masked table.) This is the reason why the table sees also the previous decoded value m'_{i-1} and m''_{i-1}.

The usual precautions are applied when implementing f. For our target FPGA platform, we carefully split the 7-bit input to 1-bit output function f

---

[2] Note that in the special case that q is a prime close to a power of two the construction of the quadrant block can be further simplified.

into a balanced tree of 4-bit input LUTs, in such a way that any intermediate input or output of LUTs does not leak in the first order. Note that here we are assuming that each LUT is an atomic operation. If stronger security guarantees are needed, other approaches to implement such function f should be followed. When implemented in an ASIC, it may be preferable to store this masked table in ROM (since the contents of the table are immutable and the size is small.)

The output of this table is (Boolean) masked, and thus no unmasked value lives within the implementation. This is suited for consumption of a masked AES module (say) after some preprocessing as will be detailed later. We stress that we use masked tables on the *output* of the quadrants. This is the key for our reduced area requirements, as will be explained in the next Sect. 5.

5   Implementation Results

We implemented the fully masked ring-LWE decryption system with the parameter set $(n, q, s) = (256, 7681, 11.32)$ first introduced in [11], corresponding to a medium-term security level. The target platform is a Xilinx Virtex-II xc2vp7 FPGA. The HDL files were synthesized within Xilinx ISE v8.2 with optimization settings set to balanced and KEEP HIERARCHY flag when appropriate to prevent optimization of security-critical components. We base our arithmetic processor on the design from [25].

5.1 Area

In our case, a single arithmetic coprocessor performs serially the computations of Eq. 3 and then that of Eq. 4. This incurs in a very slight area overhead (only the control microcode is slightly modified, plus the masked decoder), at the obvious cost of an increased execution time. In comparison to the unprotected version, our protected decryption scheme consumes more memory as now we store two shares r' and r'' of the secret polynomial r, and the two output polynomials a' and a'' from the two INTT operations.

In Table 1, we can see that the proposed masking of the ring-LWE architecture incurs an additional area overhead of only 301 LUTs and 129 FFs in comparison to the unprotected version. This additional area cost is mostly due to a pair of masked decoders. Due to its low area overhead, we chose to keep two masked decoders in parallel, decoding two coefficients simultaneously. (This nicely fits with the memory organization of the arithmetic coprocessor, since it fits two 13-bit coefficients in each memory word.) Thus, we use two addition and subtraction circuits for the refreshing with Δ_i (accounting for 160 LUTs) and two masked tables (90 LUTs in total.)

We note that we could straightforward reduce the additional area cost by reusing the 13-bit addition and subtraction circuits present in the arithmetic coprocessor. Since during a decoding operation, the arithmetic coprocessor remains idle, reusing of the addition and subtraction circuits do not cause any increase in the cycle count. For simplicity, we did not implement this approach.

Table 1. Performance and Comparison on Xilinx Virtex-II xc2vp7 FPGA. Note that these results are not directly comparable with [25], since the latter were obtained from a more advanced Virtex-6 FPGA, which has 6-bit input LUTs and superior routing mechanisms in comparison to our target FPGA.

Implementation algorithm	LUTs/FFs/DSPs	Freq MHz	Cycles/Time (μs) decryption
Unprotected RLWE	1713/830/1	120	2.8 k/23.5
Protected RLWE	2014/959/1	100	7.5 k/75.2

5.2   Cycle Count

The cycle count for our approach is decomposed in the computation of Eqs. 3 and 4 and the masked decoder. Equation 3 takes 2840 cycles (one unprotected ring-LWE decryption), Eq. 4 takes 2590 cycles, slightly less than Eq. 3 since there is no addition present in the second branch.

The two-way parallel masked decoder takes $\frac{1}{2} \times n \times N + \epsilon$ cycles to decode all the coefficients into message bits. In our case with $n = 256$, $N = 16$ the masked decoder takes 2048 cycles. Thus in total, a masked decryption operation requires 7478 cycles. The arithmetic coprocessor and the masked decoder run in constant time and constant flow.

5.3   Comparison with an Elliptic-Curve Cryptosystem

We compare our protected decryption scheme with the unprotected high-speed elliptic curve scalar multiplier architecture proposed by Rebeiro et al. in [20]. The architecture for the field $GF(2^{233})$ consumes 23 147 LUTs and computes an unprotected scalar multiplication in 12.5 μs on a more advanced Virtex-4 FPGA. Thus the scalar multiplier has an area × time product of approximately 289 337. Our protected ring-LWE decryption (for a similar security) achieves an area × time product of approximately 151 452 on a Virtex-2 FPGA; thus achieving at least 1.9 times better figure of merit.

5.4   Trade-offs

The previous figures are subject to trade-offs. If smaller latency is desired instead of a compact implementation, two coprocessors can perform the two computations of Eqs. 3 and 4 in parallel. Trade-offs also apply to the masked decoder, and the parallelization could be extended easily to reduce latency in this stage. Since the BRAMs present in the Xilinx FPGAs support reading of multiple consecutive words, we could keep more pairs of masked decoders in parallel and reduce the number of cycles. Another alternative is to keep the masked decoder in pipeline with the polynomial arithmetic block. Such type of setting is suitable for systems where many decryption operations are performed in a chain. While the masked decoder works on the coefficients of a previous computation, the polynomial arithmetic unit processes new ciphertexts. Since the masked decoder is faster than the polynomial arithmetic unit, the cycle count of the masked decoder is not an overhead in such type of setting. But of course, in this situation we could not reuse the arithmetic circuitry of the arithmetic coprocessor for the refreshing operation of the masked decoder.

5.5 Maximum Frequency

We note that the arithmetic coprocessor is a very optimized unit with a complex pipeline organization. We thus insert two pipeline stages in the masked decoder to match the maximum frequency of the whole system to that of the arithmetic coprocessor. In this way, the design can run up to almost 100 MHz. The critical path is inside the arithmetic multiplier.

6   Discussion

6.1 Error Rates

Cryptosystems based on ring-LWE are inherently probabilistic. This means that there is a non-zero probability that the recovered plaintext after ring-LWE decryption is not exactly the plaintext before encryption. In our case, due to the probabilistic nature of our masked decoder approach, there is a second source of noise. Since the number of iterations of the masked decoder is finite, there are some pair values (a', a'') that will not get decoded within the fixed finite number of iterations. In this section, we first explain the error rate of the probabilistic decoding in isolation, and then we switch to the global system error rate and point out strategies to mitigate it.

Errors due to the probabilistic decoding. In this section, we assume that the plaintext bit is 1 and the unmasked input a to the masked decoder is in $(q/4, 3q/4)$. The additional error due to the probabilistic masked decoder is the probability p_e that (a', a'') does not get successfully decoded. Let us write $p_s = 1 - p_e$.

This probability p_s is influenced by two distributions. We have that

$$p_s = \sum \Pr[\text{successful decode}|a] \cdot \Pr[a] \tag{5}$$

where the sum is taken over $a \in (q/4, 3q/4)$. On the one hand, $\Pr[\text{successful decode}|a]$ is the probability that the decoder successfully decodes a. On the other, $\Pr[a]$ is the probability with which a takes various values in $(q/4, 3q/4)$.

The distribution of the decoder success probability $\Pr[\text{successful decode}|a]$ as a function of the unshared input value a to the decoder can be easily computed by averaging over all possible pairs (a', a'') such that $a' + a'' = a$. Since for any given value of a, its shares a' or a'' are (individually) equiprobable, we compute $\Pr[\text{successful decode}|a]$ as $\Pr[\text{successful decode}|a] = \frac{1}{q} \sum_{a'+a''=a} \Pr[\text{successful decode of } (a', a'')]$.

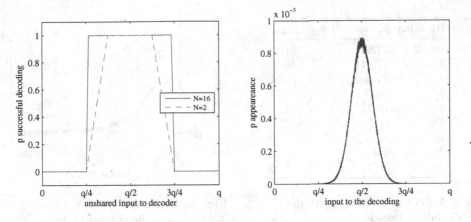

Fig. 4. Left: empirical success distribution for the masked decoder. Right: Distribution of a when plaintext is 1.

The distribution $\Pr[\text{successful decode}|a]$ is shown in Fig. 4, left. We see that the decoder performs best when $a \approx q/2$, in which case all possible inputs get decoded correctly. Only when the input value a approaches $q/4$ or $3q/4$, the performance degrades. When using a larger number of iterations $N = 16$ this effect is less pronounced when compared to $N = 2$ iterations, as Fig. 4 shows.

On the other hand, it is easy to see that not all unshared inputs a to the decoder are equally likely. By the construction of the ring-LWE decryption function, the unshared input to the decoder a is either centered around $q/2$ (resp. 0) when the message bit is 1 (resp. 0). This distribution $\Pr[a]$ is plotted in Fig. 4, right.

These two observations combined produce a nice interaction between the *prior* distribution $\Pr[a]$ of a (given by the ring-LWE decryption) and the success distribution of the masked decoder $\Pr[\text{successful decode}|a]$ as in Eq. 5. Namely, values of a that are difficult to decode (those with low $\Pr[\text{successful decode}|a]$) are quite unlikely to appear as input to the masked decoder (their $\Pr[a]$ is also low). This positive interaction keeps the global error rate of the system quite low. This is precisely quantified in the next paragraph.

Global error rate and number of iterations. We performed simulations to estimate the global error rate and determine the required number of iterations N in our design. Over 10^6 bits, the average error per bit using a deterministic decoder was $p_{\text{baseline}} = 3.634375 \times 10^{-5}$. This is a baseline error intrinsic to the ring-LWE construction. When we plug in the probabilistic decoder, the global, end-to-end, error rate per bit p_g increases. (We have $p_g = p_{\text{baseline}} + p_e$.) In Fig. 5, we can find the global error rate for different values of the number of iterations N of the decoding. At $N = 3$, for instance, the error rate is $p_g = 1.7844 \times 10^{-3}$, which is ≈ 49 times larger than p_{baseline}. As already hinted, the error rate quickly decreases with N (roughly exponentially, as can be see in Fig. 6). In our design, we set $N = 16$ (we iterate 16 times per coefficient) as a balanced tradeoff between

Iterations	p_g [$\times 10^{-5}$]	p_g/p_{baseline}
$N = 2$	332.24	91.41
3	178.44	49.09
4	25.36	6.97
5	20.77	5.71
6	16.22	4.46
8	6.97	1.91
16	4.32	1.19
24	4.06	1.11
30	3.87	1.06

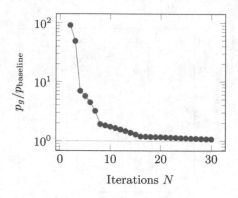

Fig. 5. Global error rates with the probabilistic decoder.

Fig. 6. Evolution of the ratio p_g/p_{baseline} as the number of iterations N grows.

cycle count and error rate. The impact of the masked probabilistic decoder on the global error rate is quite low, adding less than 20 % to the intrinsic error rate when compared to a deterministic decoder, as it can be see in Fig. 5.

6.2 Comparison with Other Decoding Strategies

We are only aware of a similar masked decoder, the one presented in [4]. There the authors resort to a generic masking method, namely masked tables, to perform the decoding. Translating the ideas of [4] in our context, we would need two tables of 2^{13} bits (one of them random). For a smaller group $\mathbb{Z}_d$ with $d = 257$ the authors report an utilization of 1331 slices on a Virtex 6 FPGA. While the results in slices are not directly comparable with ours, we point out that the size of the masked table following the approach of [4] grows linearly in the group size q, while for our solution the size of the masked table stays constant (independent of q), and the quadrant blocks grow only logarithmically in q. The cycle count, however, is larger in our solution. The critical observation of our masked decoder is that we can *compress* the input coefficient shares a' and a'' to a mere two bit per share (the output of each quadrant) and then perform the decoding based on the information of the two quadrants (4 bits.)

6.3 Post-Processing

Albeit the computation from Eq. (2) is commonly referred as the "ring-LWE decryption", the decryption process should include a post-processing on the recovered message m. This post-processing consists of error correction and padding verification.

Linear codes with masking. One approach to deal with the probabilistic nature of the ring-LWE decryption system is to use forward error correcting codes (FEC).

The message prior to encryption is encoded using a FEC and the resulting composite is ring-LWE encrypted. The output of the ring-LWE decryption should be corrected for errors, preferably in the masked domain. For syndrome decoding of linear codes, this can easily be done by masking the syndrome table.

Padding schemes. As presented, the ring-LWE system is malleable. CCA security can be achieved with a padding mechanism. The Fujisaki-Okamoto [10] padding scheme is known to work with ring-LWE [17]. This padding scheme makes use of standard symmetric cryptographic constructions whose masked implementations are well studied. We point out that key-encapsulation mechanisms may result in a more compact and simpler implementation.

6.4 Extension to Higher-Order Security

We point out that the approach laid out in Sect. 3 scales quite well with the security order. To achieve security at level $d+1$, one would need to split the computation of Eq. 2 into d branches analogously to Eq. 3. The masked decoder can follow the same principles with the appropriate modifications. The complexity of this decoder obviously grows. Generic approaches to perform this computation have been discussed in [2, 7, 22].

7 Evaluation

For the purposes of a side-channel evaluation, we implemented the full design on a SASEBO G board. The design was clocked at 18.75 MHz and the power consumption was sampled at 500 MS/s. This platform is very low noise.

We provide a very advantageous setting for the adversary: we assume that the evaluator knows the details about the implementation (for example, pipeline stages). In addition, we assume that while guessing a subkey, the adversary knows the rest of the key. These assumptions allow to comfortably place predictions on intermediates arbitrarily deep into the computation. While this may represent a very powerful attacker and somewhat unrealistic, the algebraic structure of such cryptosystem may help the attacker to predict deep intermediates with relatively low effort. We refer the reader to the extended version of this paper for an attack on half-masked ring-LWE decryption that uses these ideas. This stresses the necessity of masking the decoding function entirely.

The evaluation methodology to test if the masking is sound is as follows. We first proceed with first-order key-recovery attacks when the randomness source (PRNG) is switched off. We demonstrate that in that situation the attacks are successful, indicating that the setup and procedure is sound. Then we switch on the PRNG and repeat the attacks. If the masking is sound, the first-order attacks shall not succeed. In addition, we perform second-order attacks to confirm that the previous first-order analyses were carried out with enough traces.

We test 4 different points which covers all the relevant parts of the computation. The targets are the first 13-bit coefficient of $r' \cdot c_1 + c_2$, the first 13-bit

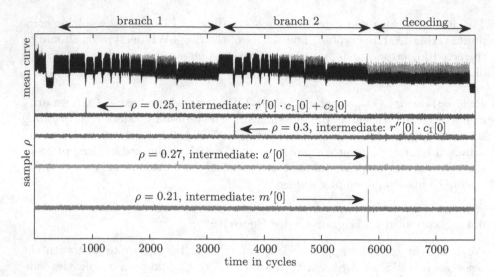

Fig. 7. PRNG off. On top, black, one power consumption trace. The different computational stages can be distinguished: first branch, second branch and decoding. Next, in blue, the correlation trace for the value $r'[0] \cdot c_1[0] + c_2[0]$. The correlation achieves a maximum value of $\rho = 0.25$. Below, in red, correlation for $r'' \cdot c_1$ (max $\rho \approx 0.3$); in green: correlation for the input of the masked decoder $a'[0]$. At the bottom: correlation with one message bit $m'[0]$ (Color figure online).

coefficient of $r'' \cdot c_1$, the first input coefficient to the shared decoder and the first output bit. We modeled the power consumption of a register as the Hamming distance between two consecutive values held in the register, and used Pearson's correlation coefficient to compare predictions with measurements [5].

7.1 PRNG Off

We first begin the experiments when the PRNG is off. That is, the sharing of r into r' and r'' on each execution is deterministic. This would not happen in practice, as an active PRNG would randomize the representation of r in each execution. In our setting, this would mean that the masking is switched off.

In Fig. 7 we draw the result of correlating against the 4 intermediates with 10 000 traces. On top, we draw a mean trace for orientation. The correlation values are, from top to bottom, 0.25, 0.3, 0.27 and 0.21, respectively. This means that the attacks are successful, and confirms the soundness of our setting. In Fig. 8 we can see the evolution of the correlation coefficient as the number of traces increases for the first two intermediates. We can see that starting from hundred traces the attack is successful. Similar behavior was observed for other intermediates.

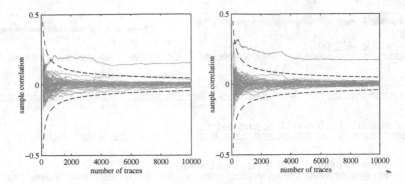

Fig. 8. PRNG off. Evolution of the correlation coefficient as the number of traces increases for the intermediates $r'[0] \cdot c_1[0] + c_2[0]$ (left) and $r''[0] \cdot c_1[0]$ (right). Correct subkey guess in red, all other guesses in green. A 99.99 % confidence interval for $\rho = 0$ is plotted in black discontinuous line. We can see that starting from hundred measurements the attacks are successful (Color figure online).

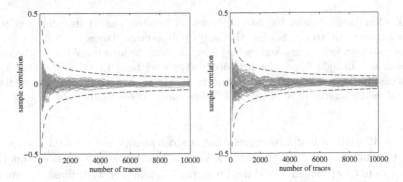

Fig. 9. Analogous to Fig. 8, but with PRNG on. The correct subkey is no longer identifiable. This is expected and means that the masking is effective.

7.2 PRNG On

In Fig. 9 we draw the result of the previous analysis when the masks are switched on. This corresponds to the situation that an adversary would face in reality. We can see that the correct key guess is no longer distinguishable, even when using 10 000 traces. We repeated the same experiments for other intermediates and other intermediate positions with identical results.

7.3 Second-Order Attacks

To confirm that we used enough traces in our previous analyses, we perform here second-order attacks on the masked implementation with the PRNG on. We will focus on the masked decoder. In Fig. 10 we draw on top a mean curve in the region of 7 400 to 7 700 cycles, corresponding to the end of the masked decoding. We target one output bit of the decoding: $m[254]$.

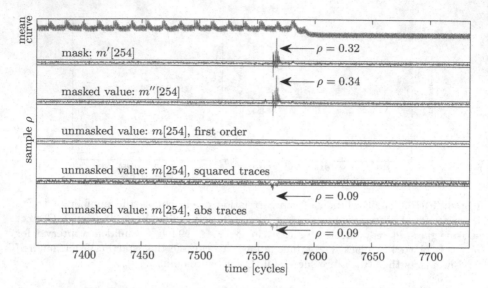

Fig. 10. Correlation traces for intermediates within the shared decoder. On top, a power measurement trace showing the last 15 decodings. Below, correlation traces. The first two (masks and masked values) assume that the adversary knows the masks. The third one, in light blue, is a first-order attack without knowing the attack, and is unsuccessful. In contrast, the second-order attack against the same intermediate is successful, as the traces in magenta and yellow show (Color figure online).

In Fig. 10 we first begin by correlating against masks and masked values. This is a test scenario, since for this attack we need to know the masks, something that would not happen in a real deployment. Correlation with masks or masked value yield high correlation as expected ($\rho = 0.32$ and $\rho = 0.34$, respectively). In contrast, when correlating against the unshared value (in light blue), the correlation coefficient does not traverse the confidence interval for $\rho = 0$. This indicates that the masking is effective. We can repeat the same attack against centered and squared traces [6,19]. This is effectively a second-order attack, and is expected to work. It is shown in magenta in Fig. 10, and we can see that the attack succeeds. Using the centered absolute value to pre-process traces also works as expected, as shown in yellow.

In Fig. 11 we can see the evolution as a function of the number of traces. We can see that starting from ≈ 2000 measurements this second-order attack is successful. This confirms that the first-order attacks of Sect. 7.2 were carried out with enough traces, since a second-order attack is already successful starting from ≈ 2000 measurements.

We remark that the relatively low number of traces required for the second-order attack is due to the very friendly scenario for the evaluator. The platform is low noise and no other countermeasure except than masking was implemented. In practice, masking needs a source of noise to be effective, and consequently the

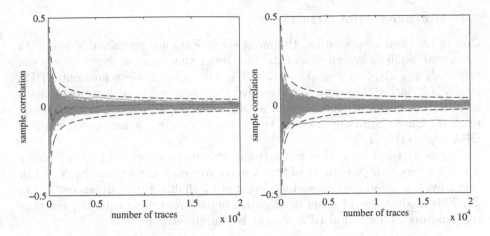

Fig. 11. Left: correlation as the number of traces increases for the first-order attack (PRNG on), around clock cycle 7560. Right: correlation for the second-order attack with masks on. The attack begins to be successful with 2 000 measurements.

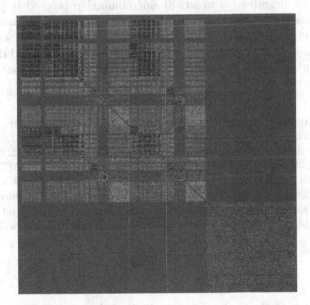

Fig. 12. Crosscorrelation trace. The x and y axes represent time, flowing from the upper left hand side corner to the lower right. The entire figure spans 7500 cycles (as Fig. 7). It is possible to distinguish the two branch computations (including its components) and the decoding. Colors enhanced to improve contrast (Color figure online).

higher-order attacks would be harder to mount, requiring more traces [6] and more computation [23].

7.4   Horizontal DPA Attacks

During the decoder operation, the input coefficients are refreshed $N - 1 = 15$ times with publicly known offsets Δ_i. The device thus handles consecutively the values a', $a' + \Delta_1$, ..., $a' + \Delta_1 + \ldots + \Delta_{15}$. This may enable a horizontal DPA attack [16] during the operation: the adversary may collect a single trace, split it into 16 chunks and then perform a DPA on these 16 chunks to recover the mask a'. Once the masks from all traces are discovered, a first-order, vertical DPA applies (Fig. 12).

There are two factors that mitigate this threat. First, we note the adversary is given a very limited number of traces to recover each mask (namely, $N = 16$). Secondly, this attack can be easily prevented by shuffling the public coefficients Δ_i. This randomizes the order of execution of each refreshing with Δ_i, and thus the exposure to horizontal DPA attacks is minimized.

8   Conclusion

In this paper we described a practical side-channel protected implementation of the lattice-based ring-LWE asymmetric decryption. Our solution is based on the sound principles of masking and incurs in a manageable overhead (in cycles and area). A key component of our solution is a bespoke masked decoder. Our implementation performs the entire ring-LWE decryption computation in the masked domain.

Acknowledgements. The authors would like to thank the CHES 2015 reviewers for their valuable comments. This work has been supported in part by the European Commission through the ICT programme under contracts H2020-ICT-645622 PQCRYPTO, H2020-ICT-644209 HEAT and FP7-ICT-2013-10-SEP-210076296 PRACTICE; by the Research Council KU Leuven TENSE (GOA/11/007); by the Flemish Government FWO G.0550.12N, G.00130.13N and G.0876.14N; and by the Hercules Foundation AKUL/11/19. Oscar Reparaz is funded by a PhD fellowship of the Fund for Scientific Research - Flanders (FWO). Sujoy Sinha Roy was supported by Erasmus Mundus PhD Scholarship.

References

1. Bernstein, D.J., Buchmann, J., Dahmen, E.: Post Quantum Cryptography, 1st edn. Springer, Heidelberg (2008)
2. Bilgin, B., Gierlichs, B., Nikova, S., Nikov, V., Rijmen, V.: Higher-order threshold implementations. In: Sarkar, P., Iwata, T. (eds.) ASIACRYPT 2014, Part II. LNCS, vol. 8874, pp. 326–343. Springer, Heidelberg (2014)
3. Bos, J.W., Lauter, K., Loftus, J., Naehrig, M.: Improved security for a ring-based fully homomorphic encryption scheme. In: Stam, M. (ed.) IMACC 2013. LNCS, vol. 8308, pp. 45–64. Springer, Heidelberg (2013)
4. Brenner, H., Gaspar, L., Leurent, G., Rosen, A., Standaert, F.-X.: FPGA implementations of SPRING. In: Batina, L., Robshaw, M. (eds.) CHES 2014. LNCS, vol. 8731, pp. 414–432. Springer, Heidelberg (2014)

5. Brier, E., Clavier, C., Olivier, F.: Correlation power analysis with a leakage model. In: Joye, M., Quisquater, J.-J. (eds.) CHES 2004. LNCS, vol. 3156, pp. 16–29. Springer, Heidelberg (2004)
6. Chari, S., Jutla, C.S., Rao, J.R., Rohatgi, P.: Towards sound approaches to counteract power-analysis attacks. In: Wiener, M. (ed.) CRYPTO 1999. LNCS, vol. 1666, pp. 398–412. Springer, Heidelberg (1999)
7. Coron, J.-S.: Higher order masking of look-up tables. In: Nguyen, P.Q., Oswald, E. (eds.) EUROCRYPT 2014. LNCS, vol. 8441, pp. 441–458. Springer, Heidelberg (2014)
8. Ducas, L., Durmus, A., Lepoint, T., Lyubashevsky, V.: Lattice signatures and bimodal gaussians. In: Canetti, R., Garay, J.A. (eds.) CRYPTO 2013, Part I. LNCS, vol. 8042, pp. 40–56. Springer, Heidelberg (2013)
9. Fan, J., Vercauteren, F.: Somewhat practical fully homomorphic encryption. Cryptology ePrint Archive, Report 2012/144 (2012). http://eprint.iacr.org/
10. Fujisaki, E., Okamoto, T.: Secure integration of asymmetric and symmetric encryption schemes. J. Cryptol. $26(1)$, 80–101 (2013)
11. Göttert, N., Feller, T., Schneider, M., Buchmann, J., Huss, S.: On the design of hardware building blocks for modern lattice-based encryption schemes. In: Prouff, E., Schaumont, P. (eds.) CHES 2012. LNCS, vol. 7428, pp. 512–529. Springer, Heidelberg (2012)
12. Goubin, L., Patarin, J.: DES and differential power analysis the "Duplication" method. In: Koç, Ç.K., Paar, C. (eds.) CHES 1999. LNCS, vol. 1717, pp. 158–172. Springer, Heidelberg (1999)
13. Kocher, P.C.: Timing attacks on implementations of Diffie-hellman, RSA, DSS, and other systems. In: Koblitz, N. (ed.) CRYPTO 1996. LNCS, vol. 1109, pp. 104–113. Springer, Heidelberg (1996)
14. Kocher, P.C., Jaffe, J., Jun, B.: Differential power analysis. In: Wiener, M. (ed.) CRYPTO 1999. LNCS, vol. 1666, pp. 388–397. Springer, Heidelberg (1999)
15. Lyubashevsky, V., Peikert, C., Regev, O.: On ideal lattices and learning with errors over rings. In: Gilbert, H. (ed.) EUROCRYPT 2010. LNCS, vol. 6110, pp. 1–23. Springer, Heidelberg (2010). Full Version available at Cryptology ePrint Archive, Report 2012/230
16. Pan, J., den Hartog, J.I., Lu, J.: You cannot hide behind the mask: power analysis on a provably secure s-box implementation. In: Youm, H.Y., Yung, M. (eds.) WISA 2009. LNCS, vol. 5932, pp. 178–192. Springer, Heidelberg (2009)
17. Peikert, C.: Lattice cryptography for the internet. In: Mosca, M. (ed.) PQCrypto 2014. LNCS, vol. 8772, pp. 197–219. Springer, Heidelberg (2014)
18. Pöppelmann, T., Güneysu, T.: Towards practical lattice-based public-key encryption on reconfigurable hardware. In: Lange, T., Lauter, K., Lisoněk, P. (eds.) SAC 2013. LNCS, vol. 8282, pp. 68–85. Springer, Heidelberg (2014)
19. Prouff, E., Rivain, M., Bevan, R.: Statistical analysis of second order differential power analysis. IEEE Trans. Comput. $58(6)$, 799–811 (2009)
20. Rebeiro, C., Roy, S.S., Mukhopadhyay, D.: Pushing the limits of high-speed $GF(2^m)$ elliptic curve scalar multiplication on FPGAs. In: Prouff, E., Schaumont, P. (eds.) CHES 2012. LNCS, vol. 7428, pp. 494–511. Springer, Heidelberg (2012)
21. Regev, O.: On lattices, learning with errors, random linear codes, and cryptography. In: Proceedings of the Thirty-Seventh Annual ACM Symposium on Theory of Computing, STOC 2005, pp. 84–93. ACM, New York (2005)
22. Reparaz, O., Bilgin, B., Nikova, S., Gierlichs, B., Verbauwhede, I.: Consolidating masking schemes. In: CRYPTO 2015. LNCS, vol. 9215, pp. 764–783. Springer, Heidelberg (2015)

23. Reparaz, O., Gierlichs, B., Verbauwhede, I.: Selecting time samples for multivariate DPA attacks. In: Prouff, E., Schaumont, P. (eds.) CHES 2012. LNCS, vol. 7428, pp. 155–174. Springer, Heidelberg (2012)
24. Sinha Roy, S., Reparaz, O., Vercauteren, F., Verbauwhede, I.: Compact and side channel secure discrete gaussian sampling. IACR Cryptology ePrint Archive, 2014:591 (2014)
25. Roy, S.S., Vercauteren, F., Mentens, N., Chen, D.D., Verbauwhede, I.: Compact ring-LWE cryptoprocessor. In: Batina, L., Robshaw, M. (eds.) CHES 2014. LNCS, vol. 8731, pp. 371–391. Springer, Heidelberg (2014)
26. Trichina, E.V.: Table lookup operation on masked data (2013). US Patent 8,422,668

Author Index

Printed in the United States
By Bookmasters

Printed in the United States
By Bookmasters